Key to the Group Accounts

Each group of related species is introduced by a summary of the characteristics of the group. These accounts show all species in a family (or subfamily or order) for comparison. Look here to see the range of variation in the group, as well as fundamental similarities and differences among genera.

Indicates a new group is beginning.

Common name of the family or group.

Latin name of the family (or the families) described in the account.

This paragraph highlights the general characteristics of the group and gives the numbers of species and genera that are covered in the book. Typical habits and behaviors (including nesting, foraging, etc.) are described.

All species in the group, except the very rare, are pictured on this page. They are grouped by genus and all are shown to scale. In most cases the relatively drab female or immature plumages are shown, as these present the greatest identification problems.

Mimids

Family: Mimidae

11 species in 4 genera. These medium-size, long-tailed songbirds are generally solitary. They forage mainly on the ground, using their long, sturdy bills to toss leaves and sticks, raking the dirt in search of food. Most species frequently run on the ground with their tails raised; they will often run to escape danger rather than flying. Flight is generally low and rapid. Nest is a bulky stick cup in a bush. Adults are shown.

Genus *Mimus*

NORTHERN MOCKINGBIRD

BAHAMA MOCKINGBIRD

Genus *Dumetella*

GRAY CATBIRD

Genus *Oreoscoptes*

SAGE THRASHER

Genus *Toxostoma*

BROWN THRASHER Eastern

LONG-BILLED THRASHER

Key to the Range Maps

The range maps show the complete distribution of each species. Bear in mind that within the mapped range, each species occurs only in appropriate habitat and at variable density (common to scarce).

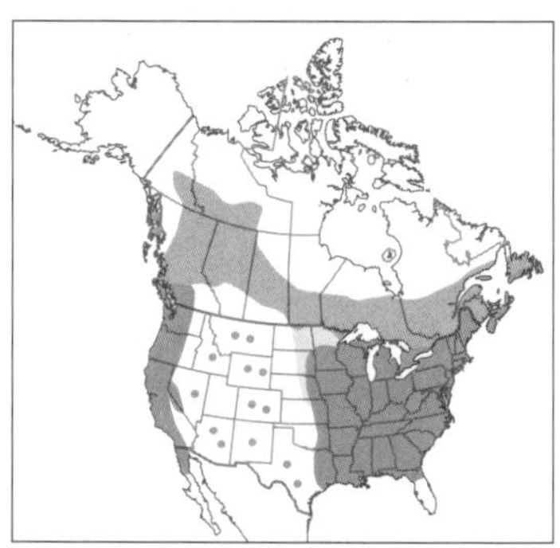

Winter Shows the normal winter distribution of the species. Many species are somewhat nomadic in winter, occupying only parts of the mapped range at any given time.

Summer For virtually all species this is the breeding range and is more consistently and uniformly occupied than the winter range.

Year-round Indicates that the species can be found all year in this area, even though winter and summer populations may involve different individual birds. Only a few species are truly resident.

Migration Main migration routes are shown, as well as areas of regular dispersal and post-breeding wandering. Note that migration also passes through the summer and winter ranges.

Rare Green dots represent locations of rare occurrence (may be a single record or up to a few records a year). These dots are included to show broad patterns of occurrence, not necessarily precise details of rare records.

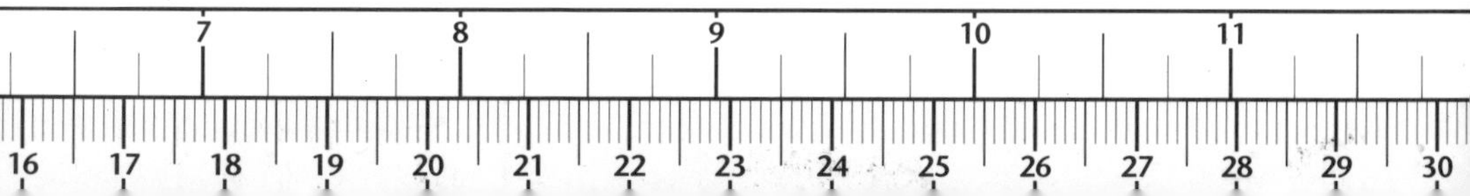
7
8
9
10
11
16
17
18
19
20
21
22
23
24
25
26
27
28
29
30

NATIONAL AUDUBON SOCIETY

The SIBLEY *Guide to Birds*

A Chanticleer Press Edition

NATIONAL AUDUBON SOCIETY

The SIBLEY *Guide to Birds*

Written and Illustrated by

DAVID ALLEN SIBLEY

To Martin and Barbara

Good Birding!

David Sibley

May 2001

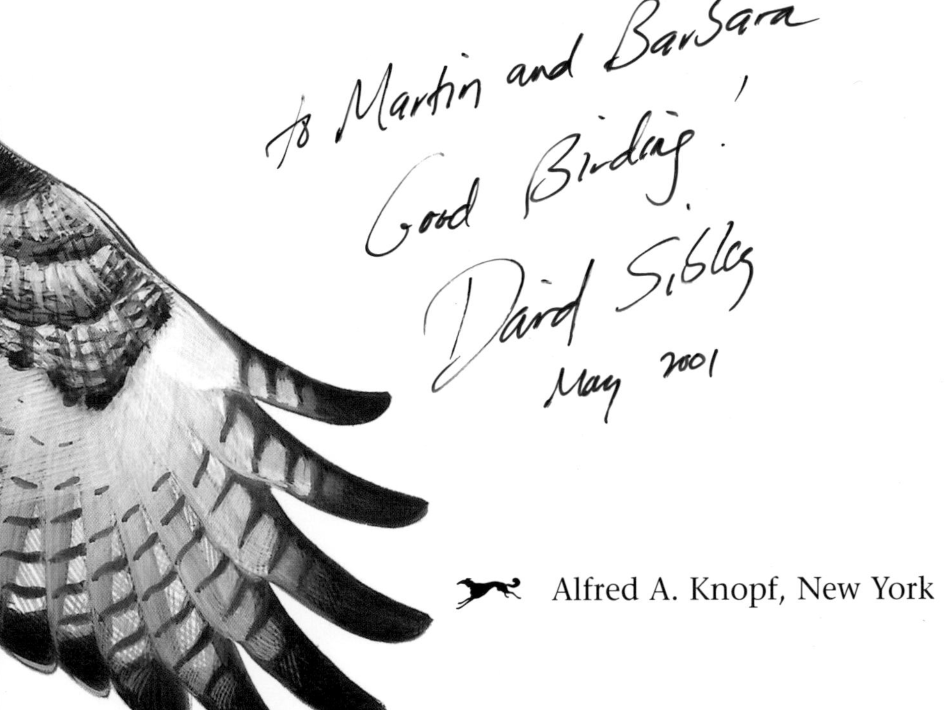

Alfred A. Knopf, New York

For Joan, Evan, and Joel

This is a Borzoi Book.
Published by Alfred A. Knopf, Inc.

 Published in the United States by Alfred A. Knopf, Inc., New York, and simultaneously in Canada by Random House of Canada Limited, Toronto. Distributed by Random House, Inc., New York.

www.randomhouse.com

Knopf, Borzoi Books, and the colophon are registered trademarks of Random House, Inc.

Prepared and produced by Chanticleer Press, Inc., New York.

Printed and bound by Dai Nippon Printing Co., Ltd., Hong Kong.

First Edition
Published October 2000
Second Printing, December 2000

Library of Congress Cataloging-in-Publication Data

Sibley, David Allen, 1961-
National Audubon Society The Sibley Guide to Birds / written and illustrated by David Allen Sibley. — 1st ed.
p. cm.
ISBN 0-679-45122-6
1. Birds—North America—Identification. I. Title.
QL681.S497 2000
598'.097—dc21 00-041239

Contents

PREFACE

In the narrow view, this book is the product of about five years of work, but the larger volume of work was done before that. In the broader view, the project goes back to the 1970s, when I first started playing with the idea of producing a field guide. As I traveled around the continent during the 1980s—studying, sketching, and watching birds—ideas began to form about just how my field guide would be different.

I wanted a book that would show every plumage and every subspecies, at rest and in flight. A book that would give details on the plumages and habits of each species, describe songs and calls, and show the complete distribution of each species, all on the same page and all in a format that would allow easy comparisons between species.

For more than five years (1988–1993) I worked sporadically on a field guide, and even though I was unhappy with the layout and ultimately repainted all of the work from that period, the time was well spent researching the birds, refining my painting technique, and working out some of the inevitable compromises of the book (no single book could accommodate everything I wanted to include). The ideas that finally crystallized into this book came to me during a trip to Europe in the fall of 1993, and by July 1994 I had started painting the final draft.

From then on it was five years of desk work. People often ask how I was able to keep at it for so long. Well, I would hesitate to do it again, but the work has been immensely satisfying. The rewards have been in the process more than in the product, as I studied each species and compiled my notes and sketches into a concise presentation. This was merely the finish work after twenty years of watching.

I kept on bird-watching for those two decades for all the reasons that anyone watches birds. Birds are beautiful, in spectacular as well as subtle ways; their colors, shapes, actions, and sounds are among the most aesthetically pleasing in nature. Then there is the adventure of seeking out scarce species in remote wilderness or in specialized habitats close to home; the wonder of seeing thousands of birds pass by on migration; the excitement of finding a stray from some far corner of the globe. The predictable and the unpredictable events in birding make every day unique.

On top of everything else is the intellectual challenge of identifying birds, which offers rewards at every level and draws on so many disciplines. For the neophyte there is the challenge of making sense of the birds in the garden; for the expert there are complex identification problems and distributional patterns to be unraveled. Making a contribution to the field requires nothing more than careful observation. I still learn new things every time I go birding, and I am certain that the opportunities for learning will never end.

David Sibley
March 2000
Concord, MA

Acknowledgments

I should begin by thanking everyone who has ever taken the time to talk with me about birds, and especially everyone who has published anything about bird identification. Their ideas, in one form or another, have been incorporated into this book. I wish it were possible to name more of them, as this book represents the combined work of many hundreds of people. Below, I name only the people who were directly consulted on this project, but the contributions of all the others are no less significant.

I have been fortunate to have lived at Point Reyes, California, and Cape May, New Jersey, and to have worked for WINGS, Inc., making friends and sharing ideas with many of the best birders in North America. Thanks to all.

For answering queries, reviewing drafts, and providing photos, reprints, and other material assistance, thanks to Per Alstrom, John Arvin, Richard C. Banks, Bob Behrstock, Chris Benesh, Craig Benkman, Louis Bevier, Bryan Bland, Tony Bledsoe, Rick Bowers, Eric Breden, Ned Brinkley, Rick Cech, Patrick Comins, Richard Crossley, Mike Danzenbaker, Jon Dunn, Pete Dunne, Barny Dunning, Vince Elia, Chris Elphick, Ted Eubanks, Shawneen Finnegan, Kimball Garrett, Frank Gill, Bob Hamlin, Keith Hansen, Paul Holt, Steve N. G. Howell, Alvaro Jaramillo, Kevin Karlson, Kenn Kaufman, Greg Lasley, Sheila Lego, Paul Lehman, Tony Leukering, Ian Lewington, Jerry Liguori, Bruce Mactavish, Bob Maurer, Killian Mullarney, Marleen Murgitroyde, Frank Nicolletti, Michael O'Brien, Brian Patteson, Ron Pittaway, Noble Proctor, Peter Pyle, Gary Rosenberg, Margaret Rubega, Will Russell, Ray Schwartz, Debra Love Shearwater, Mitchell Smith, P. William Smith, Rich Stallcup, Clay and Pat Sutton, Thede Tobish, Joe, Sandy, Catherine, and Michelle Usewicz, John Vanderpoel, Dave Ward, Paige Warren, Sophie Webb, Sheri Williamson, Tom Wood, Gail Diane Yovanovich, and John Cameron Yrizarry.

Staff at the following institutions provided logistical support and/or access to collections: California Academy of Sciences, San Francisco; VIREO and the Academy of Natural Sciences, Philadelphia; American Museum of Natural History, New York; United States National Museum, Washington, D.C.; Peabody Museum, Yale University, New Haven, Connecticut; University of California, Berkeley and Irvine; North Carolina State Museum, Raleigh; Louisiana State University, Baton Rouge; Cornell University, Ithaca, New York; Library of Natural Sounds, Cornell University Laboratory of Ornithology; University of Alaska, Fairbanks; New Jersey Audubon Society's Cape May Bird Observatory; Point Reyes Bird Observatory, Stinson Beach, California; Manomet Bird Observatory, Manomet, Massachusetts; University of Georgia, Athens; Savannah River Ecology Laboratory, Aiken, South Carolina; and University of Arizona, Tucson.

My family has supported my desire to draw birds since preschool days; the love and support of my parents, Fred and Peggy Sibley, has carried me through all these years, and the practical benefits of having an ornithologist father cannot be overstated.

I thank my agent, Russell Galen, for smoothing the way.

Thanks to the editing and design team at Chanticleer Press (Amy K. Hughes, George Scott, Lisa R. Lester, Drew Stevens, Anthony Liptak, Melissa Martin, Vincent Mejia, and Bernadette Vibar) and Thumb Print (Areta Buk, James Waller, and Jeffrey Edelstein) for their careful and expert handling of what must have seemed like an endless task.

I thank John Cameron Yrizarry for reviewing all the original artwork (sometimes more carefully than I did myself) and for offering many helpful suggestions.

Thanks to Vince Elia and Shawneen Finnegan for help in preparing the range maps, to Paul Lehman for reviewing all the maps, and to Gary Antonetti and Ortelius Design for creating the final maps.

Thanks to technical reviewers Will Russell, Kimball Garrett, Jon Dunn, Steve N. G. Howell, Chris Elphick, and Frank Gill. Will Russell provided generous support and advice at all stages of this project, from indulging my wanderings in the early years to the careful reading of the entire manuscript.

I must single out the influence of the late Ray Schwartz, whose companionship and support through the formative years of this project were a constant source of strength.

Last, I thank my wife, Joan Walsh, and my sons, Evan and Joel, who really made me believe that I could do this—and then managed to put up with the lifestyle that developed as a result. It's done!

Introduction

This book covers the identification of 810 species (plus 350 regional forms) found in the continent of North America north of Mexico, including the United States and Canada and all adjacent islands, but excluding Hawaii, Bermuda, and Greenland. Offshore waters are included to a distance of 200 miles (320 km) or halfway to the nearest land that is not part of the North American region, whichever is closer. These boundaries conform to the American Birding Association's established definition of the North American region.

I have included species and identifiable populations that occur regularly within this area, including most rare but regular visitors. *Rare but regular visitors* included in this book are defined loosely as those species recorded 10 or more times in the last 25 years, but some arbitrary decisions were made to include less frequently recorded species or to exclude a few that are seen more frequently. Some species that occur regularly only in western Alaska, and nowhere else in North America, are excluded. Established introduced species such as the Rock Dove and Chukar are included, as are frequently seen exotic species. Escaped exotic species include many waterfowl, upland game birds, parrots, mynas, and finches; some of these have established small feral populations.

Classification of Birds

Birds, like all other living things, are classified by scientists in a system of groups and subgroups, each with a unique scientific name. Birds make up the class Aves. The class is subdivided into orders, each order into families, each family into genera, each genus into species, and many species into subspecies. The Red-tailed Hawk is classified as class Aves, order Falconiformes, family Accipitridae, genus *Buteo,* species *jamaicensis.* There are several subspecies, including the western *calurus* subspecies (full name *Buteo jamaicensis calurus*).

The taxonomy of families, genera, and species as well as all common and scientific names used in this book follow the seventh edition (1998) of the American Ornithologists' Union (AOU) *Check-list of North American Birds,* and the 42nd supplement (2000) to the *Check-list.* Only the sequence of species has been altered to allow better comparisons for identification.

I have intentionally avoided using scientific names for subspecies, as these can be more confusing than helpful to the nonspecialist. Instead, recognizable subspecies populations are named by the geographic region in which they breed (and sometimes by established English names). These regional populations as defined here may include one or several named subspecies. Most subspecies variation is determined by climate and follows a few simple rules; thus the boundaries between regional populations are surprisingly consistent (shown on the map below). For more details on the distribution, identification, and nomenclature of subspecies, refer to the AOU's 1957 *Check-list* (fifth edition) and Peter Pyle's *Identification Guide to North American Birds* (Slate Creek Press, Bolinas, CA, 1997).

Among ornithologists there is an ongoing debate about the definition of a species, and related debate over the status of certain species. Rumors of splitting (one species into more) and lumping (two or more species into one) are constantly circulating among birders, who are concerned almost entirely with species. The check-list committee of the AOU makes final decisions in such matters, but even its decisions reflect prevailing opinion (albeit based on published and carefully considered scientific research), and the list will always be a work in progress.

In this book I have tried to illustrate all distinctive regional populations, emphasizing variation rather than the species unit, on the premise that any distinguishable population is noteworthy, whether classified as a species or not. Many of these regional populations are not safely identified outside their known range, or are identifiable with only a low level of confidence; further study will increase those levels in many cases, and some populations will undoubtedly be elevated to full species status.

Learning to Identify Birds

If you are reading this book, you presumably have an interest in learning how to identify birds. A few suggestions for getting started are outlined below, but all build on the same theme: to become an expert birder, you must study birds. Sketching and taking notes in the field are exercises that will force you to look more closely, reinforce your memory, and greatly increase the rate at which you learn. The joy of small discoveries is part of the great appeal of birding, and patient study is always rewarded.

The first rule is simple: *Look at the bird.* Don't fumble with a book, because by the time you find the right picture the bird will most likely be gone. Start by looking at the bird's bill and facial markings. Watch what the bird does, watch it fly away, and only then try to find it in your book.

Practice seeing details. Much of the skill involved in identifying birds is being able to sort out the details of the bird's appearance at a distance. To build an understanding of how plumage patterns work, practice with the Bird Topography diagrams below. Study details at close range whenever possible.

Recognize patterns. There is order in the universe, and birds are no exception. All the minutiae of variation (appearance, behavior, occurrence, etc.) fit into predictable patterns, and as you gain experience these patterns coalesce into a framework of knowledge.

Use multiple field marks when trying to identify a bird. Birds are variable, and there are exceptions to every rule. Don't be discouraged by this, but do look for several different field marks on any bird. If one doesn't match up, the bird may require more study. Experience will allow you to judge the reliability of different characteristics.

Study shapes. Experienced birders use shape as an important clue for identifying broad groups, such as genera, as well as individual species. Paying attention to shape

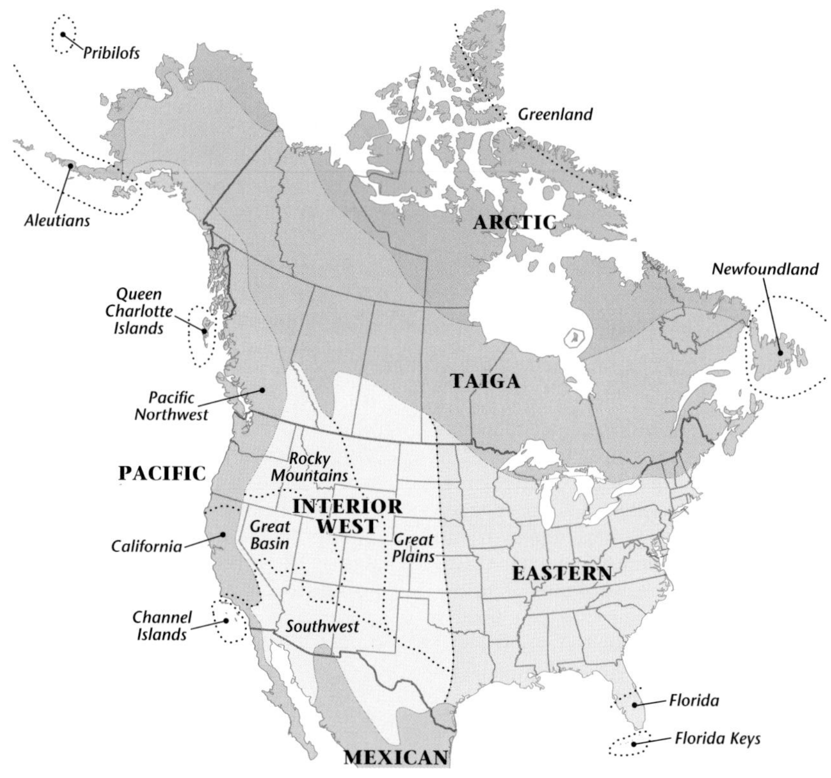
Pribilofs
Greenland
Aleutians
ARCTIC
Newfoundland
Queen Charlotte Islands
TAIGA
Pacific Northwest
PACIFIC
Rocky Mountains
INTERIOR WEST
Great Basin
California
Great Plains
EASTERN
Channel Islands
Southwest
Florida
Florida Keys
MEXICAN

North America, showing regions used to define subspecies populations. Main regions are shown in color, while dotted lines outline subregions. The Pacific and Interior West regions together form the Western region. These regions offer a rough guide to subspecies distribution, but the distribution of each population differs somewhat from the regions outlined. Note that populations living in more humid climates (especially the Pacific Northwest) tend to be darker than those in arid regions (especially the Southwest).

may also reveal differences in posture, actions, and even plumage.

Study habits. Although behavior is never absolutely reliable for identification, habits provide strong supporting clues. Birds spend virtually all their active moments searching for food, so almost all their actions and habitat choices relate to food.

Beware of misjudging size. Size is very difficult to judge at a distance, and for the beginner, size is nearly useless for identification except when making direct comparisons. Experienced observers do find size a helpful indicator, but only in familiar surroundings or with reference points that allow an accurate judgment of distance.

Meet other birders. Your best source of information on local birds and birding will be other birders. In many areas, nature centers, sanctuaries, local Audubon Society chapters, and bird clubs offer regular field trips and meetings, and these can be extremely useful sources of information and camaraderie. The American Birding Association (2812 W. Colorado Ave., Colorado Springs, CO 80904), which publishes the bimonthly magazine *Birding,* is a national organization serving avid birders. The ABA's sales department stocks regional bird guides for virtually every state and for many local areas.

Variation in Appearance

You should not expect any bird seen in the field to match exactly the picture of its species in this field guide. Every bird is an individual, and each species is variable (and no field guide's pictures are absolutely accurate). Variation occurs in every aspect of a bird's appearance, behavior, and voice, and only experience can teach you to recognize the normal range of variation within a species.

Many characteristics are presented in this book as *average differences.* It is important to understand this concept. Average differences are noticeable in a series of individuals but can be contradicted (sometimes dramatically so) by single individuals. One good example involves the bill length of Semipalmated and Western Sandpipers. On average, Western Sandpipers are longer-billed than Semipalmated, but there is some overlap, so while very long-billed and very short-billed birds can be safely identified, a large number of individuals have ambiguous bill length. Likewise, among the large gulls, most species show average differences in shape and size—for example, Iceland Gulls average smaller and shorter-billed than Herring Gulls, but some Herring Gulls are quite small and short-billed, and some Icelands are large and long-billed. This extensive overlap makes it unwise to attempt an identification based solely on silhouette.

The overall impression you receive from the combination of subtle differences is often referred to as *gestalt* or *jizz* (from G.I.S.—"general impression and shape"). It is a useful concept to understand—that the sum of several vague average differences can together make for a fairly reliable identification—but it is a "soft" characteristic and should not be overemphasized. Observers should beware of using jizz as a substitute for careful study and thought.

Most variation in birds' appearance can be accounted for by the age and sex of individual birds and the subspecies to which they belong. Typical examples showing the range of these variations are illustrated in this book. Within this basic range, however, there are many other variations that observers should be aware of.

Geographic Variation and Subspecies

Many regional variations within species are illustrated in this book. These cover the spectrum from distinctive populations that may eventually be considered full species themselves to subtle and inconsistent variations that are evident only upon careful comparison. Much of the variation in subspecies populations is gradual, or *clinal,* across a species' range. Such clinal variation makes it impossible to divide a species into well-defined subspecies populations, even though the birds at the ends of the clines may be strikingly different in appearance. For example, the white spotting on the wing coverts of Downy and Hairy woodpeckers is most extensive in the east, and least extensive in the Pacific Northwest. The extremes are easily recognized, and large regions are occupied by birds of relatively uniform appearance; but between each of these regions there is a broad area of clinal change. Within the transitional areas many intermediate birds occur that cannot be assigned to any specific population.

Polymorphism

Some species, particularly some herons, geese, hawks, and jaegers, occur in a variety of plumage colors that have no relation to age or sex. Typically, color morphs are not evenly distributed throughout the range of a species but are found mainly or exclusively in certain populations.

Wear and Fading

From the moment they grow, a bird's feathers are constantly subjected to the combined effects of abrasion and bleaching. Given how much wear and tear feathers sustain, it is remarkable that many species keep most of their body feathers for a full year, and some for even longer.

With practice it is possible to recognize worn plumage even when the species is unknown. Several important effects of plumage wear on a bird's appearance can be considered and may aid in identification:

- —Worn plumage looks frayed, ragged, and colorless; paler than fresh plumage.
- —Light-colored feathers wear more quickly than dark, because melanin (dark pigment) actually strengthens the feather.
- —The delicate cinnamon wash seen on many juvenile shorebirds, terns, and hawks fades to white within weeks.
- —Juvenal feathers are particularly weak and wear faster and fade more than adult feathers under the same conditions. The most faded and worn gulls are 1st summer birds, which still retain some juvenal plumage.

Changes in Posture and Head Shape

Shape is a very important clue for identification. In most species, all individuals have the same general shape regardless of age, sex, or season. But while certain aspects of shape are consistent, others are extremely variable. Shapes of bills and feet exhibit little variation, and primary projection and spacing, tail shape, and tail length are all relatively constant features of plumage. Body and head shape, however, depend largely on the position of the overlying feathers and can change dramatically as a bird ruffles or smooths its feathers.

Light and Atmospheric Conditions

Light—its variation at different times of day and under different atmospheric conditions—can play tricks on the birder. Colors and contrasts appear to change, and even the size and proportions of a bird may seem to alter as it passes from a back-lit silhouette to a well-lit portrait. Strong light washes out colors. Birds in fog appear larger than normal; birds flying at twilight appear smaller.

Cosmetic Coloration and Staining

Certain gulls and terns show a variable pinkish blush on body feathers, apparently related to diet. Geese and cranes (and other waterbirds in some situations) often become stained with iron, which gives their feathers a rusty or orange color. Occasional birds are seen with chemical stains—most often waterbirds with dark brown or blackish oil stains on their undersides.

In some research studies, birds are trapped and dyed (usually yellow-orange) or otherwise marked so that large-scale movement patterns can be monitored. These markers are usually brightly colored and very conspicuous and should rarely cause any identification problems.

Aberrant Plumages

From time to time you may encounter birds that are truly aberrant. Though rare, a few plumage conditions appear with some regularity:

- —In *albinism* and *partial albinism* all or some feathers are pure white. Partial albinism often follows feather groups, so that white spectacles or an entirely white head might appear. Certain species, including Red-tailed Hawk, Willet, gulls, American Robin, blackbirds, and grackles, seem more prone to albinism than others.

Examples of abnormally colored Willets. Left: A bird with leucistic (or dilute) plumage, whitish overall, with faint pattern. Right: The much scarcer melanistic/partial albino, mainly sooty with scattered white feathers.

—In *leucism* (also referred to as *dilute plumage*) normal patterns are visible, but all plumage is paler than normal, usually pale, creamy brown.

—*Melanism* is caused by an excess of dark (brown or black) pigment. It is less frequent than albinism and leucism and may occur in combination with partial albinism.

Other color aberrations, involving an excess or absence of particular pigments, are very rare.

Bill Deformities

Birds' bills are constantly growing—like human fingernails—but they are subjected to constant wear, which maintains them at their proper length. An injury or slight deformity can result in abnormal growth or an unusually long or twisted bill.

Hybrids

Hybrids are the offspring of parents of two different species. The offspring of parents of two different subspecies (of the same species) are known as *intergrades* rather than hybrids (e.g., Yellow-rumped Warbler).

Hybrids occur frequently between certain closely related species and are often overlooked by birders. The most regularly seen crosses are illustrated in this book, but many other crosses are nearly as frequent, and a great number of other hybrids have been recorded. The groups most prone to hybridization are geese, ducks, grouse, gulls, and hummingbirds.

It is important to point out that hybrids are extremely variable—even siblings within a single brood of hybrids can look quite different from one another—and the illustrations included in this book only begin to cover the subject. Most hybrid birds are fertile, and mate with one of their parent species or with another hybrid to produce *backcrosses,* which can then go on to produce more backcrosses, etc., leading to a complete spectrum of variation between the two pure parental types (e.g., Western and Glaucous-winged Gulls).

Hybrids can show unexpected characteristics not present on either parent, and it is often impossible to determine whether an individual bird is in fact a hybrid or to say with certainty which species are the parents. The standard terminology applied to all such cases is *apparent hybrid.*

Learning Songs and Calls

It is sometimes said that expert birders make 90 percent of their identifications by ear. In forests, where birds are difficult to see, this is probably true. It is also said that no aspect of birding is more frustrating for the beginner and more difficult to master than voice identification. As with so many other skills, there is no substitute for personal experience. The first step is simply to pay attention to bird voices. Learning bird songs can be compared to learning a foreign language: the keys are repetition and (for rapid learning) total immersion.

Written voice descriptions such as those included in this book can be helpful for pointing out differences between similar songs and calls or for bringing to mind songs and calls already heard, but words at best provide a very feeble sound impression. A great deal of the variation in songs and calls cannot be put into words, and no one should expect to learn bird songs by reading about them. Listening to recordings is much more useful (especially in conjunction with reading descriptions). Nothing, however, can replace actual field experience: hearing a song, tracking down the singer, and watching it sing. The best way to remember these experiences is to keep notes: listen to the song, try to imitate it, and describe it in your own words.

Songs—as opposed to calls—are the most distinctive vocalizations of most species, since birds sing to establish territories and to create and maintain pair bonds.

Calls are generally shorter and simpler than songs, and each species has a variety of different calls used for different communication purposes. The most frequent calls, heard year-round, are referred to as the *contact call* and the *flight call* (even though so-called flight calls are often given by perching birds). These sounds can be very useful for identification, but only for a birder with sharp ears and a good deal of experience.

The most important characteristics to listen for in bird vocalizations are *pitch* (high or low, rising or falling), *quality* (harsh, clear, liquid, buzzy, etc.), and *rhythm* (fast, slow, choppy, singsong, etc.). The length of a song, the length of time between songs, and whether subsequent songs are the same or different can also be useful in identifying species.

With experience you will begin to recognize the basic qualities of birds' voices—for example a thrushlike or other quality. This kind of broad determination can be a very helpful first step toward identification.

Finding Rare Birds

Most birders who find rare birds are looking for rare birds. This is not to say that one can find a rarity simply by looking for it, but the observer who is prepared will find rare species far more often than the observer who is not. An intimate knowledge of the common species is essential (an equivalent knowledge of the rare species always helps, of course). The expert will keep an open mind, so that a mere flash of color, a slightly different shape, or just an impression of "something not quite right" may focus attention and lead to the detection of a rare bird. Knowing patterns of occurrence also improves your chances, as rare species tend to occur in specific habitats and at certain seasons.

While rarity-hunting is one of the most exciting aspects of bird-watching, it does carry a measure of responsibility. You must be prepared to defend your identification, and to this end it is worthwhile to take extensive notes and attempt to photograph or tape-record a bird you think may be a rarity. Use extra care when identifying rare birds, considering alternatives such as aberrant plumages of common species. Contact other birders as soon as possible so that they have an opportunity to see the bird. Don't be afraid to propose an identification or to question the identifications of others; everyone makes mistakes (even the experts). Do be cautious, be honest with yourself and others, and when mistakes are made try to learn from them.

Ethics

As more and more people take up bird-watching, the behavior of every individual birder becomes more important. In all situations you must first consider the welfare of the birds. Avoid making a disturbance, especially at roosting and nesting sites. Tread lightly and encourage others to do the same. Be respectful and helpful to others, especially to nonbirders (who may not appreciate someone trampling lawns or blocking traffic just to see a bird).

Extinct Species

Sadly, the following North American species and subspecies are all presumed extinct. The year and location of the last confirmed record in the wild is given.

Labrador Duck *(Camptorhynchus labradorius).* 1878 in New York.

Heath Hen *(Tympanuchus cupido cupido).* 1931 in Massachusetts.

Eskimo Curlew *(Numenius borealis).* 1962 in Texas; 1963 in Barbados.

Great Auk *(Pinguinus impennis).* 1830s off Newfoundland; 1844 off Iceland.

Passenger Pigeon *(Ectopistes migratorius).* 1900 in Ohio.

Carolina Parakeet *(Conuropsis carolinensis).* 1905 in Missouri.

Ivory-billed Woodpecker *(Campephilus principalis).* Mid-1950s in Louisiana; 1987 in Cuba.

Bachman's Warbler *(Vermivora bachmanii).* 1962 in South Carolina.

Dusky Seaside Sparrow *(Ammodramus maritimus nigrescens).* 1980 in Florida.

The greatest threat facing North American birds today, as in the past, is habitat destruction; coastal dunes, freshwater wetlands, and grasslands are in the greatest danger. To learn more—and to help—contact any of the local, national, or international conservation organizations, including the following:

National Audubon Society
700 Broadway
New York, NY 10003-9562
(212) 979-3000
www.audubon.org

The Nature Conservancy
4245 N. Fairfax Drive
Arlington, VA 22203-1606
(703) 841-5300
www.tnc.org

Bird Topography

Birders deal with feathers. The actual flesh and bones of a bird's body are barely visible, and the varied shapes and colors of birds are almost entirely created by the feathers. Even though the colors and shapes of individual feathers are so variable, the arrangement of feathers on a bird's body is similar across all species.

Birds' bodies are not uniformly covered with feathers. The feathers grow in discrete groups (within several tracts), leaving other parts of the body bare. Knowing the basic feather groups and how the feathers in each group are arranged may be the most important tools a birder can possess when trying to identify a bird by its appearance. Even on a uniformly black species, such as a crow, one can identify all the basic feather groups described below. Studying a common bird—a House Sparrow, a gull, even a pet parakeet—is one way to familiarize yourself with feather groups.

Within each group, feathers grow in orderly rows, overlapping like shingles on a roof. The shape and arrangement of all feathers is perfectly coordinated to cover the bird's entire body with a streamlined and waterproof insulating jacket.

Plumage patterns almost invariably follow the contours of feather groups, and most markings can be described by reference to the relatively simple framework that feather groups provide. Learning the basis of common markings (e.g., wing-bars, eye-ring, etc.) will greatly enhance your understanding of birds' appearance.

One of the most frequent patterns seen on feathers is a simple dark streak along the shaft of each feather. Such streaks on the breast and flank feathers line up to form the long rows of streaked feathers characteristic of many songbirds. Differences among species are entirely the result of differences in the color and shape of feather markings, not of any difference in the shape or arrangement of feathers.

Parts of a Passerine

This figure shows the basic parts of a passerine, or songbird.

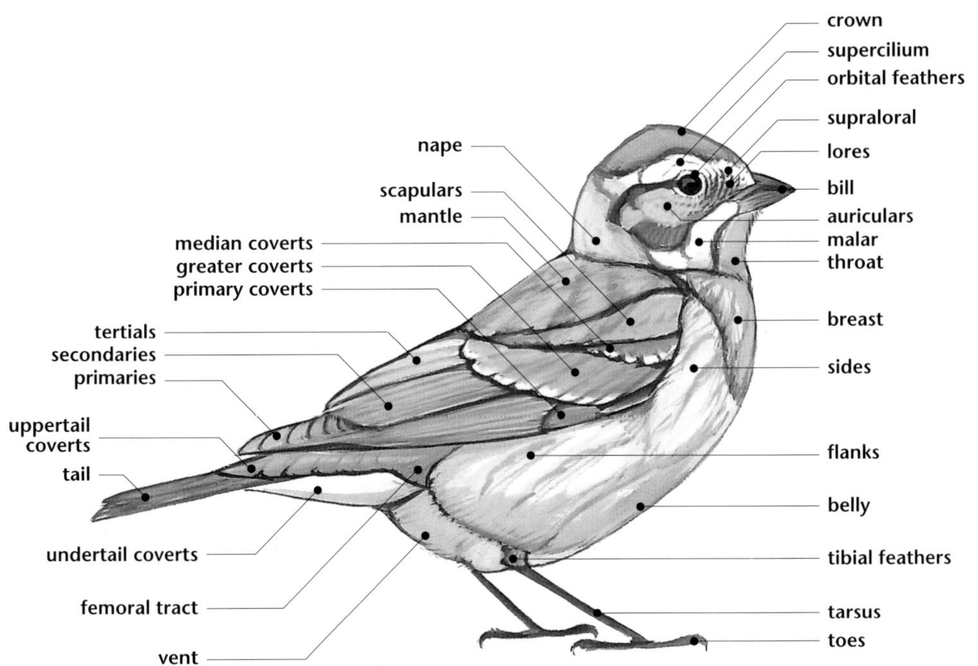
crown
supercilium
orbital feathers
supraloral
lores
bill
auriculars
malar
throat
breast
sides
flanks
belly
tibial feathers
tarsus
toes
nape
scapulars
mantle
median coverts
greater coverts
primary coverts
tertials
secondaries
primaries
uppertail coverts
tail
undertail coverts
femoral tract
vent

HEAD FEATHERS

Detailed topography of head feather groups, showing complexity of head feathering on a typical passerine. Top: A schematic diagram of the groups. Bottom: The actual markings on White-throated Sparrow.

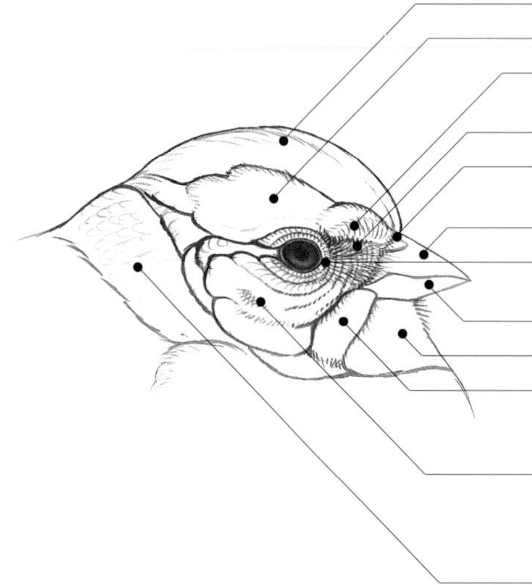

Crown Covers top of head.

Supercilium Side of head above eye.

Supraloral or fore-supercilium Front end of supercilium, just above lores.

Lores Tiny feathers between eye and bill.

Nasal tuft or nasal bristles Well developed in some families.

Upper mandible Upper half of bill.

Orbital feathers Several rows of tiny feathers encircling eye.

Lower mandible Lower half of bill.

Throat Spans underside of lower jaw.

Malar Feathers along side of lower jaw. Sometimes called *submoustachial stripe,* when "malar" is used for dark lateral throat-stripe.

Auriculars or cheeks Complex set of feathers that channels sound into ear. Feathers at rear border of auriculars are short, sturdy, and densely colored. Feathers over ear opening are lacy and unpatterned.

Nape Back of neck. Area just behind auriculars may be referred to as *sides of neck.*

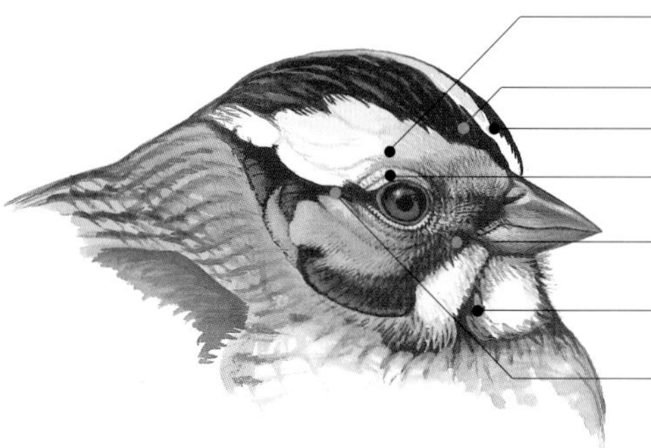

Supercilium or eyebrow Variable on other species, not necessarily following outline of this feather group.

Lateral crown-stripe

Median crown-stripe

Eye-arcs or broken eye-ring Pale orbital feathers. *Eye-ring* and *spectacles* also include orbital feathers.

Mustache stripe or moustachial stripe Follows lower border of auriculars.

Lateral throat-stripe Often referred to as *malar stripe;* does not include any malar feathers.

Eye-line or eyestripe Variable marking following upper border of auriculars.

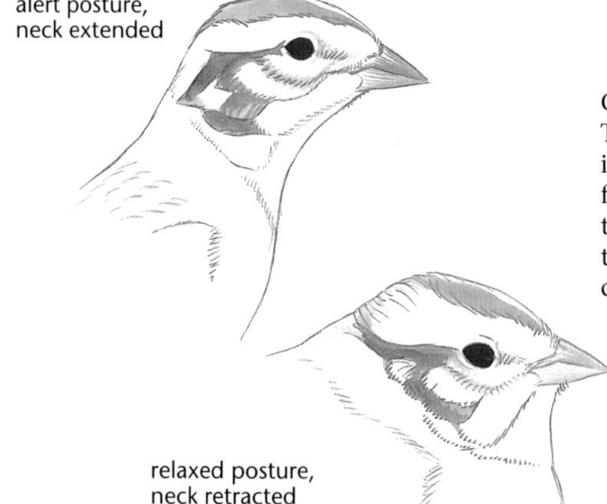
alert posture,
neck extended
relaxed posture,
neck retracted

Changes in posture create changes in pattern. These illustrations show the head of a sparrow in alert and relaxed postures. Note how the feather groups on the front of the head maintain their shape, while the feather groups on the neck and back of the head expand and contract dramatically to maintain coverage.

Body Feathers

Top: Basic passerine body feathers, from front. Center: Basic passerine body feathers, from behind, with feathers fluffed.

nape
scapulars
median coverts
greater coverts
secondaries
primaries
tail

Malar Feathers along side of lower jaw.

Throat Spans underside of lower jaw.

Breast Feathers continuous across front of body. Actually attached to neck; entire group expands and contracts markedly as neck is raised and lowered.

Sides Overlapping bend of wing.

Flanks Long feathers along side of body.

Belly Actually unfeathered; covered by long feathers growing inward from flanks.

Tibial feathering Tiny feathers covering upper leg; barely visible.

Vent Several small groups of feathers between belly and undertail coverts.

Undertail coverts Overlap base of tail, below.

malar
throat
breast
sides
flanks
vent

Nape Back of neck.

Mantle Center of back, often patterned as streaks. A pair of contrasting pale stripes on the mantle on some species are called *braces.*

Scapulars Overlap base of wing, above. Mantle and scapulars are together referred to as the *back.*

Rump Rump feathers lie under the folded wings; arbitrarily divided into *upper rump* and *lower rump.* The contrasting rump-patch of many species involves uppertail coverts as well as rump feathers.

Femoral tract Sides of rump; mostly hidden by longest flank feathers.

Uppertail coverts Overlap base of tail, above.

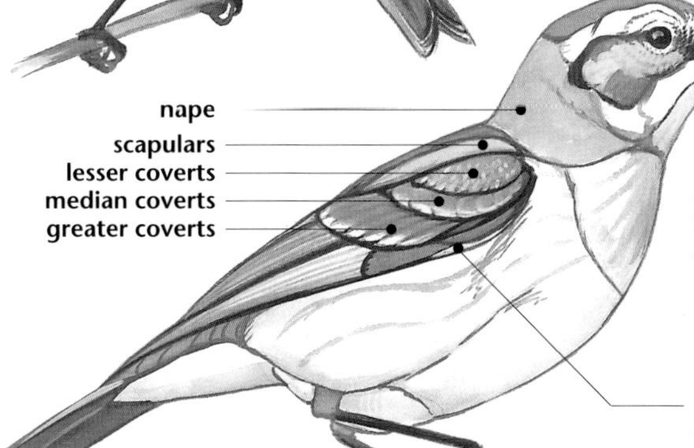
nape
scapulars
lesser coverts
median coverts
greater coverts

Passerine in alert, sleeked posture. In this pose, with the wings held out from the body, the usually concealed lesser coverts and marginal coverts are easily seen.

Marginal coverts Tiny feathers at bend of wing covering bony leading edge of "hand."

Wing Feathers

Top: Right wing of a passerine, closed but held loosely. Note how the feathers stack up, with the innermost tertial on top and the outermost primary on the bottom. With the wing folded against the body, only the outer edges of the remiges are visible. Secondaries and primaries are numbered from center of wing (same order in which most species molt).

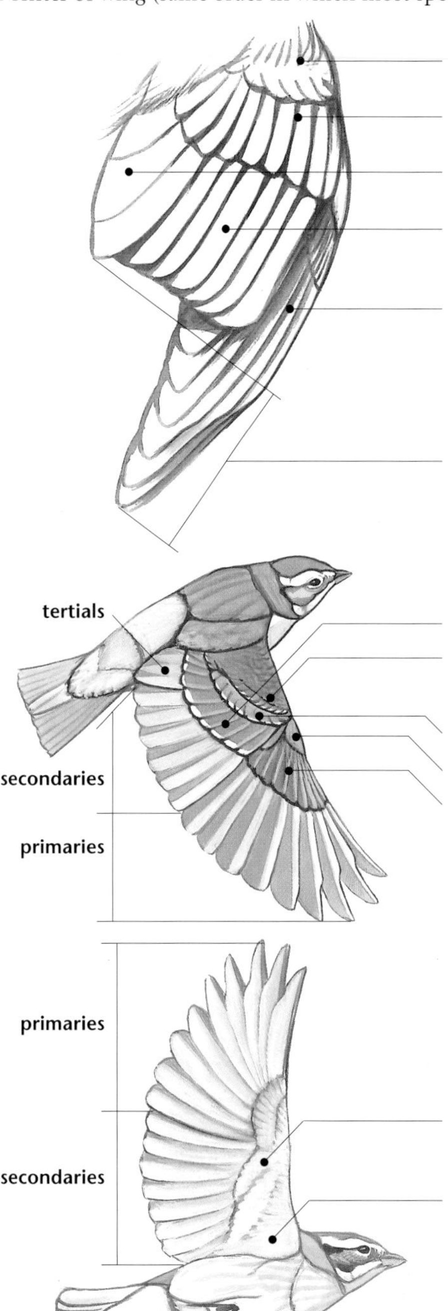
tertials
secondaries
primaries
primaries
secondaries
tail

Median secondary coverts Overlap bases of greater coverts. Pale tips form *upper wing-bar.*

Greater secondary coverts Overlap bases of secondaries. Pale tips form *lower wing-bar.*

Tertials Three innermost secondaries. On folded wing these broad feathers rest on top of other secondaries.

Secondaries Six on most songbirds (plus three tertials); long flight feathers growing from "forearm" bones.

Primaries Nine or ten long flight feathers growing from "hand" bones and forming lower border of folded wing.

Remiges Primaries, secondaries, and tertials together. Remiges and tail feathers *(rectrices)* are collectively called *flight feathers.*

Primary projection Projection of primary tips beyond tertial tips. Length of primaries relative to tail is also a useful measure in identifying many species.

Passerine in flight, from above. Note that outer webs of flight feathers are visible.

Greater secondary coverts

Lesser secondary coverts Overlap bases of median coverts. Rarely visible on passerines; usually concealed by scapulars and sides when wing is folded.

Median secondary coverts

Alula Three feathers on the "thumb."

Greater primary coverts Overlap bases of primaries.

Passerine in flight, from below. Note that inner webs of flight feathers are visible.

Underwing coverts The "wing linings." Rows of feathers corresponding to upperwing coverts, but less easily distinguished.

Axillaries The "armpit." Overlap base of wing, below.

Tail or rectrices Simply a fan that can be spread open or folded closed.

PARTS OF A SHOREBIRD

Top: Small shorebird, relaxed. This typical shorebird differs significantly from passerines in wing structure and in its two distinguishable groups of scapulars, which are much more prominent than the scapulars on passerines. The scapulars hang loosely when relaxed, covering most of the wing. (They are often pulled up when active, exposing the wing coverts.) The secondaries and primaries are nearly or entirely concealed when the wings are folded. Note the many rows of lesser coverts (bottom illustration). The pale V on the back of many shorebirds is formed by pale edges on the mantle and upper scapular feather groups.

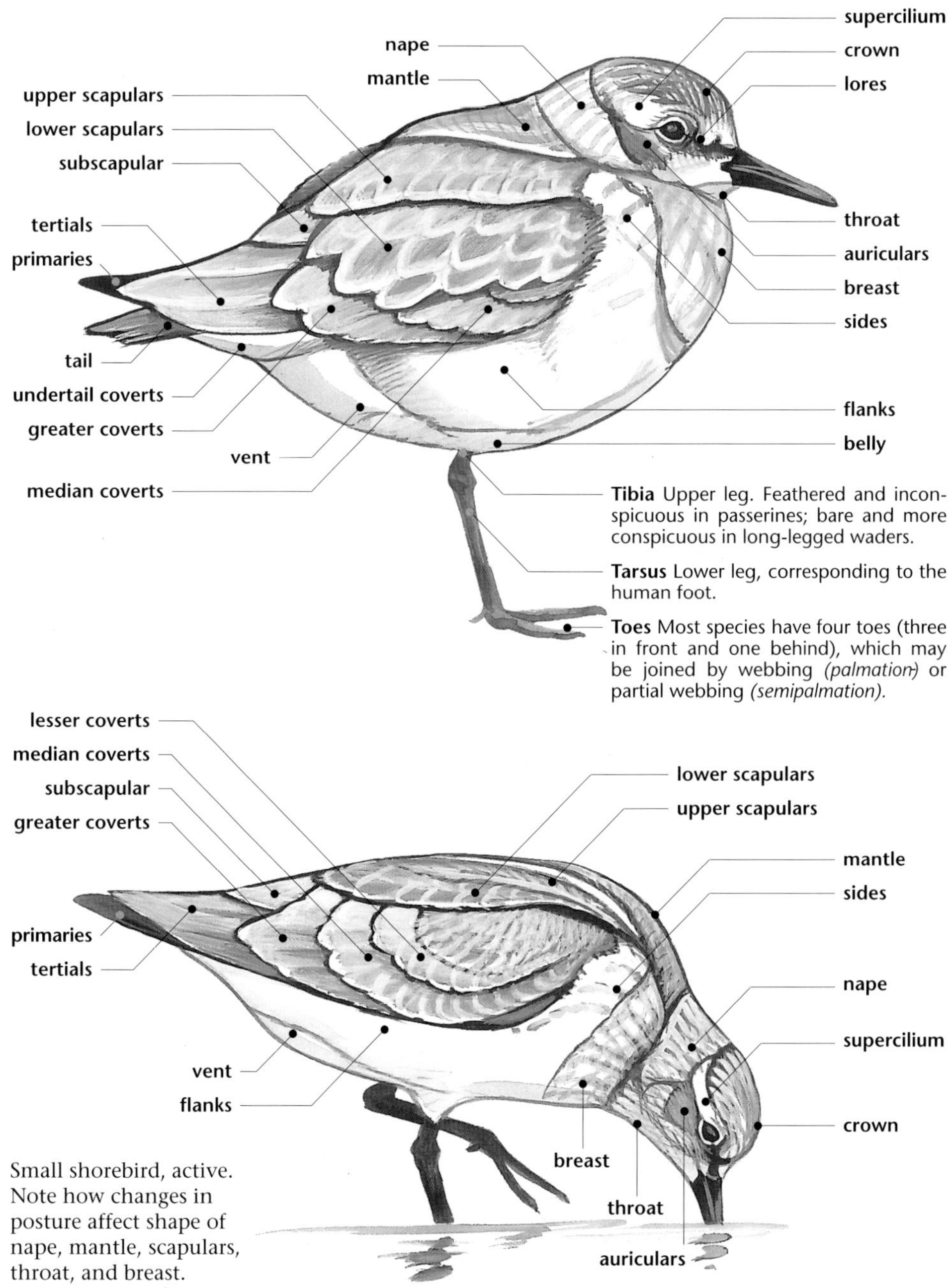
supercilium
crown
lores
nape
mantle
upper scapulars
lower scapulars
subscapular
tertials
primaries
throat
auriculars
breast
sides
tail
undertail coverts
greater coverts
vent
median coverts
flanks
belly
Tibia Upper leg. Feathered and inconspicuous in passerines; bare and more conspicuous in long-legged waders.
Tarsus Lower leg, corresponding to the human foot.
Toes Most species have four toes (three in front and one behind), which may be joined by webbing *(palmation)* or partial webbing *(semipalmation).*
lesser coverts
median coverts
subscapular
greater coverts
lower scapulars
upper scapulars
mantle
sides
primaries
tertials
nape
supercilium
vent
flanks
crown
breast
throat
auriculars

Small shorebird, active. Note how changes in posture affect shape of nape, mantle, scapulars, throat, and breast.

Parts of a Duck

Duck, swimming. Note that waterbirds such as ducks and shorebirds are more or less uniformly covered with feathers to create seamless waterproofing. It may be difficult to distinguish the feather groups on any part of a bird that is normally in contact with water.

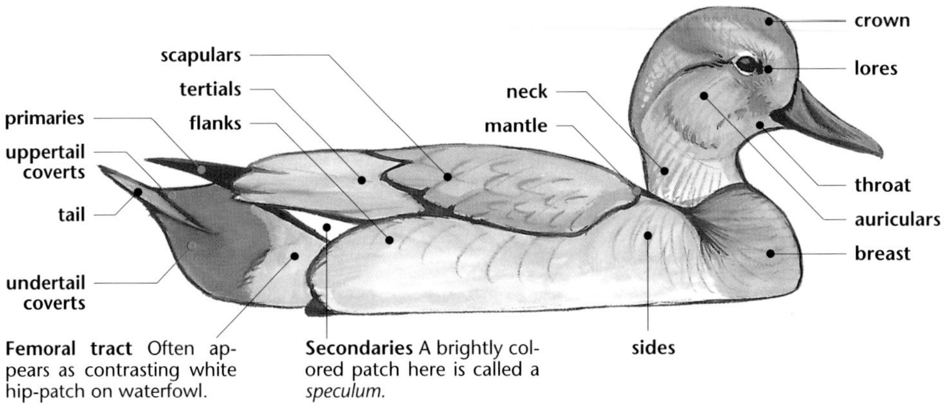
crown
lores
scapulars
tertials
neck
primaries
flanks
mantle
uppertail
coverts
throat
tail
auriculars
breast
undertail
coverts
Femoral tract Often appears as contrasting white hip-patch on waterfowl.
Secondaries A brightly colored patch here is called a *speculum.*
sides

Parts of a Gull

Large gull, standing. All feather groups are essentially the same as on a shorebird.

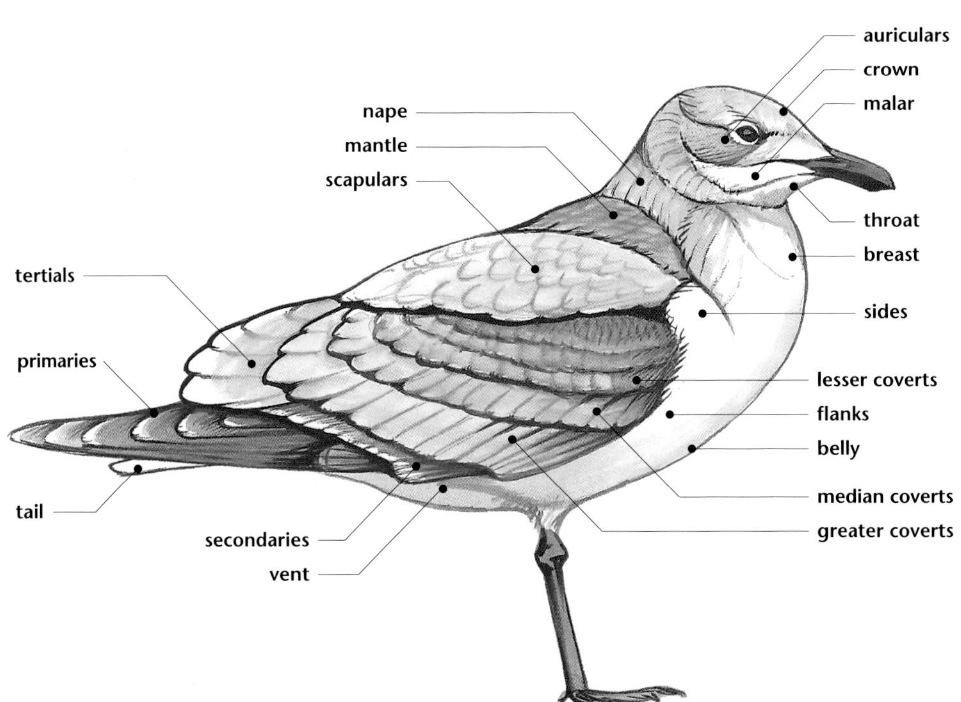
auriculars
crown
malar
nape
mantle
scapulars
throat
breast
tertials
sides
primaries
lesser coverts
flanks
belly
tail
median coverts
greater coverts
secondaries
vent

PARTS OF A GULL

Gull in flight, showing feathers typical of most long-winged species. Left: From below. Right: From above. The pale *wingstripe* seen on many shorebirds is formed by pale bases of secondaries and/or primaries (often combined with white tips on greater coverts). *Windows* are translucent patches on flight feathers, visible on a flying bird, where lightly pigmented areas allow light to pass through. A *carpal-bar* is a contrastingly colored band on the upperwing, extending along a diagonal line from tertials to carpal joint, or "wrist" (not always the entire distance). A dark carpal bar forms part of the M pattern seen on many species. Interestingly, this bar crosses all the rows of wing coverts and does not follow the contours of any single feather-tract.

primaries
underwing coverts
axillaries
secondaries
tail
undertail coverts
vent
flanks
belly
sides
breast

primaries
secondaries
primary coverts
alula
greater coverts
median coverts
lesser coverts
scapulars
mantle
nape
tail
uppertail coverts
rump

BARE PARTS

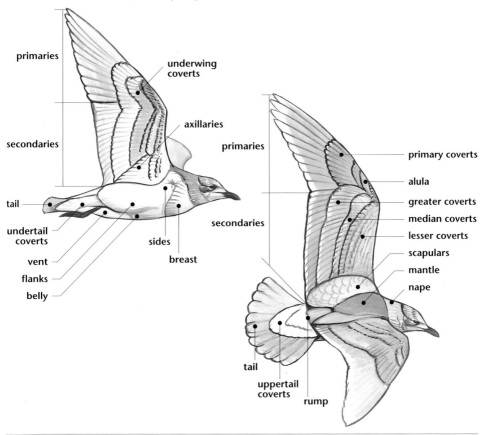

Head of large gull, showing bare parts that are important in gull identification.

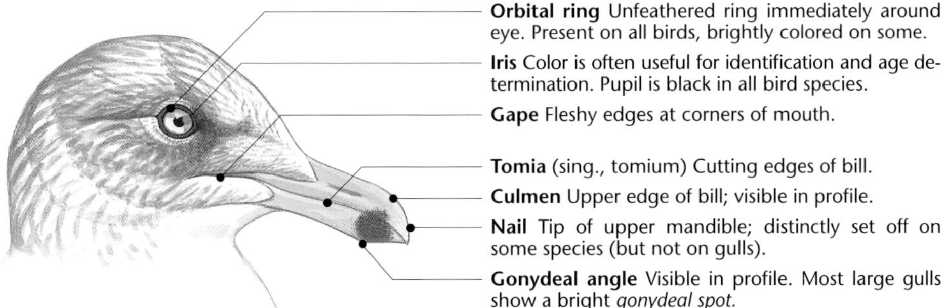
Orbital ring Unfeathered ring immediately around eye. Present on all birds, brightly colored on some.
Iris Color is often useful for identification and age determination. Pupil is black in all bird species.
Gape Fleshy edges at corners of mouth.
Tomia (sing., tomium) Cutting edges of bill.
Culmen Upper edge of bill; visible in profile.
Nail Tip of upper mandible; distinctly set off on some species (but not on gulls).
Gonydeal angle Visible in profile. Most large gulls show a bright *gonydeal spot.*

Molt and Plumage

For birds, molting is the process of dropping old feathers and growing new ones in their place, and most birds molt at least once a year. Observers can nearly always identify a bird without reference to molt, but a basic understanding of molt can be helpful for determining the age of a bird, for assessing plumage variation, and for identification.

The process of growing an entirely new set of feathers is so demanding that it cannot coincide with other activities such as nesting or migrating. Each species (or subspecies) has evolved a schedule that allows it to molt at a time when food is readily available and other demands are not too high. In general, long-distance migrants molt after fall migration, other species molt before; this schedule differs among some closely related species (e.g., peeps, nighthawks, swallows, etc.).

Age terminology can be confusing, as several different systems are used by birders. In this book, age of immature birds is described using the *life-year system,* which calculates age in the same way that we figure our own ages. *1st year* applies to a bird during its first year of life, from fledgling through the 1st winter and 1st summer, ending around its first "birthday," as it begins the molt to 2nd year plumage. Most passerines molt into adult plumage at one year of age, but many nonpasserines have distinguishable 2nd, 3rd, and even 4th year plumages before reaching adulthood.

Seasonal plumages of adults are described in this book as *breeding* and *nonbreeding.* A few species have a third plumage either before or after breeding, called a *supplemental plumage.*

It is important to realize that the labels used in this book describe the bird's appearance and do not always have a connection to molt. For example, a 1st summer appearance or adult breeding appearance (e.g., Snow Bunting) may simply result from the alteration of feathers grown in a previous molt, and not from any new molt.

Alternative terminologies include the *calendar-year system,* which describes immature birds as 1st calendar year (or hatching year) until December 31, 2nd calendar year until the next December 31, etc.

Ornithologists who study molt use a third set of terms, the *Humphrey-Parkes system,* which is purposely devoid of references to calendars and breeding cycles. Plumages are described based on the molt by which they are acquired. Although initially somewhat difficult to understand, this terminology is essential for any in-depth study of molt. For further details consult Pyle's *Identification Guide* (see page 9, above).

MOLT CYCLE OF TYPICAL PASSERINE

In this hypothetical example, changing colors indicate newly molted feathers. Note that flight feathers are retained for a full year, while body feathers may be molted two or three times a year. The dates and feather replacements shown are examples only. There is tremendous variation among species in the timing and extent of each molt, but virtually all species have a complete molt each year after breeding.

Labels compare three alternate terminologies. Listed first is the life-year (LY) system, the terminology used in this book, second is the calendar-year (CY) system, third is the Humphrey-Parkes (HP) system.

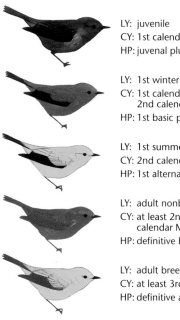

LY: juvenile
CY: 1st calendar Jul–Aug
HP: juvenal plumage

LY: 1st winter
CY: 1st calendar Aug to 2nd calendar Mar
HP: 1st basic plumage

LY: 1st summer
CY: 2nd calendar Apr–Jul
HP: 1st alternate plumage

LY: adult nonbreeding
CY: at least 2nd calendar Aug to 3rd calendar Mar
HP: definitive basic plumage

LY: adult breeding
CY: at least 3rd calendar Apr–Jul
HP: definitive alternate plumage

Loons
Family: Gaviidae

5 species in 1 genus. Loons are medium to large fish-eating birds that capture prey by diving and pursuing underwater. Loons are longer-bodied than ducks, with legs set far back on their bodies, and have straight, daggerlike bills. All nest on banks of ponds or lakes and winter on open water. Bill shape is not fully developed until end of 1st year; all species may hold their bills angled above the horizontal. Immature and nonbreeding plumages are similar in all species, and identification requires careful attention to the exact pattern of head and neck. 1st year birds (except Red-throated) have pale-tipped scapulars that are rounder (less square) than on adults. All species retain winterlike plumage through 1st summer, Common and Yellow-billed through 2nd summer. Compare grebes, cormorants, ducks (especially mergansers), and alcids. Nonbreeding adults are shown.

Genus *Gavia*

RED-THROATED LOON
PACIFIC LOON
ARCTIC LOON

COMMON LOON
YELLOW-BILLED LOON

migrate in loose groups or singly, never in organized flocks; often fly high above water or land; wingbeats strong, steady

slide on belly when landing
unable to walk on land

Red-throated Loon
Gavia stellata

L 25" WS 36" WT 3.1 lb (1,400 g) ♂>♀

Our smallest and most slender loon; distinguished from grebes by longer body and relatively short neck.

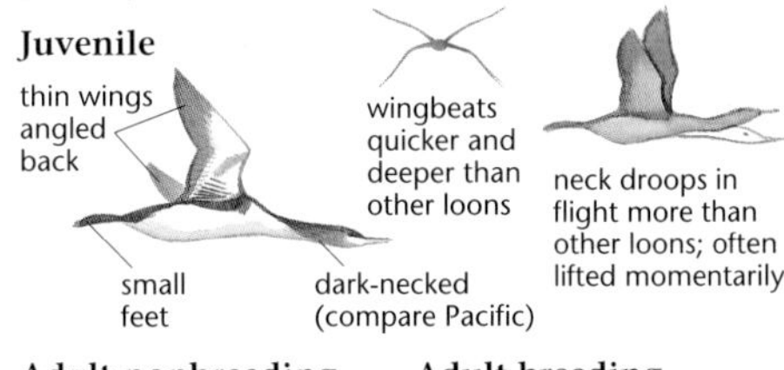

Juvenile
thin wings angled back
wingbeats quicker and deeper than other loons
neck droops in flight more than other loons; often lifted momentarily
small feet
dark-necked (compare Pacific)

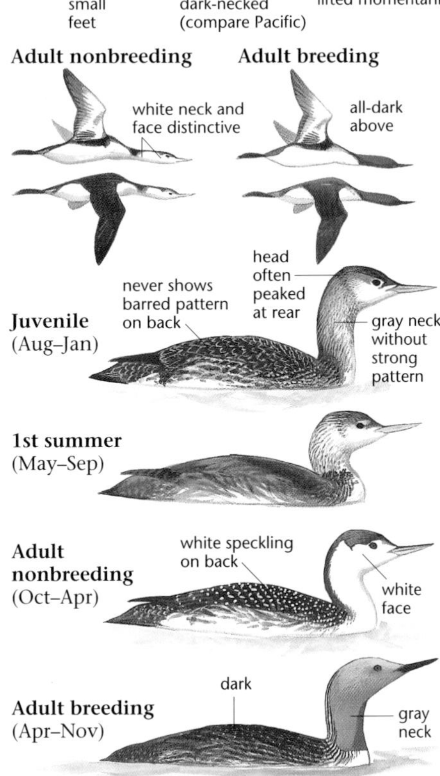

Adult nonbreeding
Adult breeding
white neck and face distinctive
all-dark above
Juvenile (Aug–Jan)
never shows barred pattern on back
head often peaked at rear
gray neck without strong pattern
1st summer (May–Sep)
Adult nonbreeding (Oct–Apr)
white speckling on back
white face
Adult breeding (Apr–Nov)
dark
gray neck

Voice: Drawn-out, gull-like wailing or shrieking *aarOOoa, aarOOoa . . .* ; less rhythmic than Red-necked Grebe. Adult flying over nesting territories gives short, nasal quacks *bek, bek, bek . . .* , sometimes building to cackling *kark kark kark karkarak karkarak*.

Loons

These two medium-size loons are very similar and until recently were considered a single species, Arctic Loon. Both are found on open ocean and bays, preferring deep water.

Pacific Loon

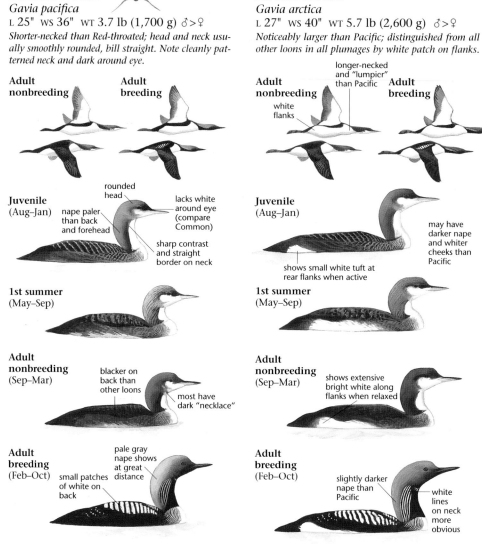

Gavia pacifica

L 25" WS 36" WT 3.7 lb (1,700 g) ♂>♀

Shorter-necked than Red-throated; head and neck usually smoothly rounded, bill straight. Note cleanly patterned neck and dark around eye.

Adult nonbreeding

Adult breeding

Juvenile (Aug–Jan)

rounded head

nape paler than back and forehead

lacks white around eye (compare Common)

sharp contrast and straight border on neck

1st summer (May–Sep)

Adult nonbreeding (Sep–Mar)

blacker on back than other loons

most have dark "necklace"

Adult breeding (Feb–Oct)

pale gray nape shows at great distance

small patches of white on back

Voice: Calls mainly on breeding grounds, giving plaintive, yodeling *o-lo-lee.* Long call a mournful but rather high and strident *ooaLEE-kow, ooaLEE-kow, ooaLEE-kow.* Also a ravenlike *kowk* and other growls and croaks.

Arctic Loon

Gavia arctica

L 27" WS 40" WT 5.7 lb (2,600 g) ♂>♀

Noticeably larger than Pacific; distinguished from all other loons in all plumages by white patch on flanks.

Adult nonbreeding

white flanks

longer-necked and "lumpier" than Pacific

Adult breeding

Juvenile (Aug–Jan)

may have darker nape and whiter cheeks than Pacific

shows small white tuft at rear flanks when active

1st summer (May–Sep)

Adult nonbreeding (Sep–Mar)

shows extensive bright white along flanks when relaxed

Adult breeding (Feb–Oct)

slightly darker nape than Pacific

white lines on neck more obvious

Voice: Calls mainly on breeding grounds; calls similar to Pacific but deeper. Long call a slurred *owiiil-ka owiiil-ka owiiil-ka;* lower-pitched, less strident, simpler than Pacific. Also a ravenlike *kraaw* and a muffled *aahaa* like Canada Goose.

Extent of white on flanks of Arctic Loon varies depending on bird's posture: shows less white when active, more white when relaxed and floating high on water. Other species may roll over to expose white belly, often when preening. Injured or oiled birds may persistently lean to one side.

Large Loons

These two species are very similar to one another; they can be distinguished from all other loons by their very large size; thick, boldly patterned necks; heavy bills; and relatively large feet.

Common Loon

Gavia immer

L 32" WS 46" WT 9 lb (4,100 g) ♂>♀

Heavy and gooselike in flight; thick-necked and thick-billed. Feet appear large.

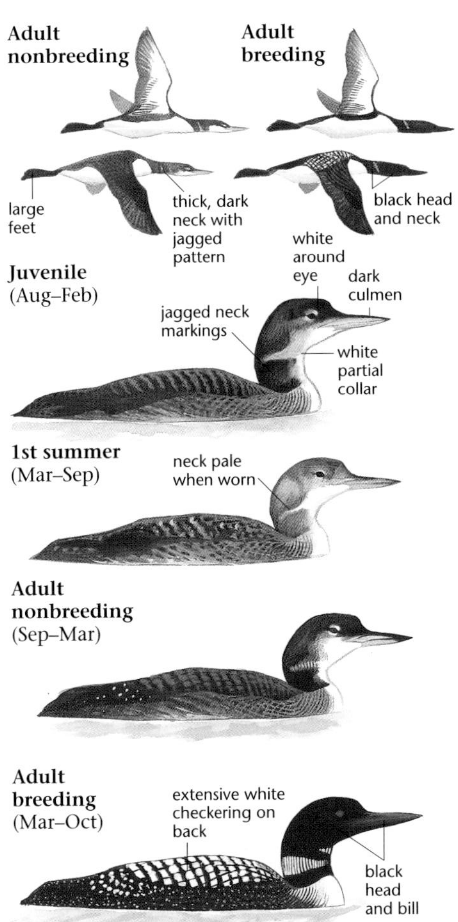

Adult nonbreeding
Adult breeding
large feet
thick, dark neck with jagged pattern
black head and neck
white around eye
Juvenile (Aug–Feb)
dark culmen
jagged neck markings
white partial collar
1st summer (Mar–Sep)
neck pale when worn
Adult nonbreeding (Sep–Mar)
Adult breeding (Mar–Oct)
extensive white checkering on back
black head and bill

Voice: Low, melancholy yodeling or wailing cries. Tremolo of five to ten notes on even pitch *hahahahahaha* heard year-round, often in flight; sometimes a short *kuk* or *gek* in flight. In summer an undulating *whe-ooo quee* and rising wail *hoooo-lii.*

Yellow-billed Loon

Gavia adamsii

L 35" WS 49" WT 11.8 lb (5,400 g) ♂>♀

Obviously larger and heavier than Common; relatively thick-necked and long-billed; bill angled up; appears small-eyed. Peak of back at mid-body.

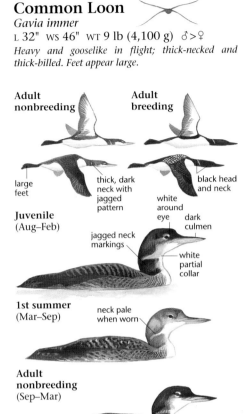

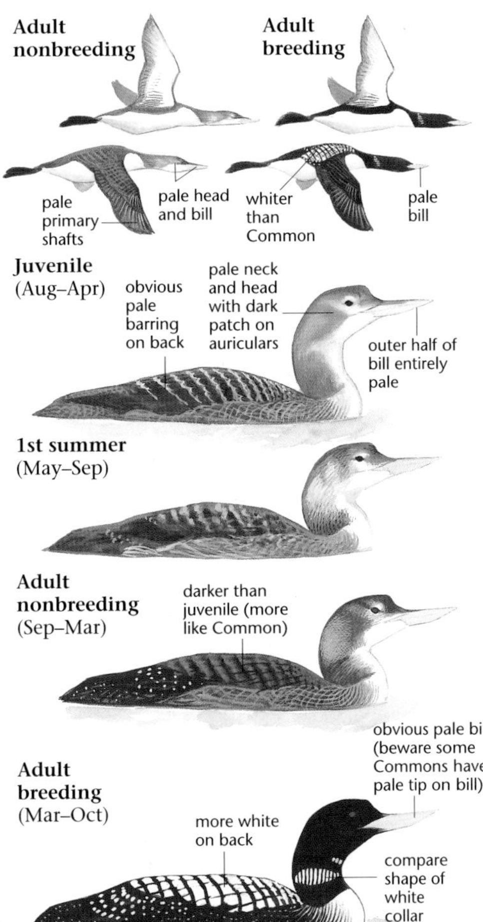

Adult nonbreeding
Adult breeding
pale primary shafts
pale head and bill
whiter than Common
pale bill
Juvenile (Aug–Apr)
obvious pale barring on back
pale neck and head with dark patch on auriculars
outer half of bill entirely pale
1st summer (May–Sep)
Adult nonbreeding (Sep–Mar)
darker than juvenile (more like Common)
obvious pale bill (beware some Commons have pale tip on bill)
Adult breeding (Mar–Oct)
more white on back
compare shape of white collar

Voice: Voice like Common but lower-pitched, harsher, delivered more slowly.

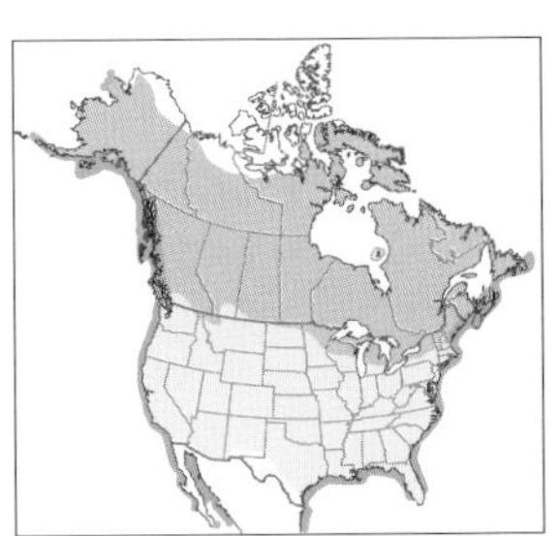

Most are easily identified, but some individuals of these two species can be very similar (hybrids have been recorded, but rarely). Bill shape and color are the most reliable clues at close range: Yellow-billed is longer-billed with nearly straight culmen, the culmen pale on the outer half.

Grebes

Family: Podicipedidae

7 species in 4 genera. Superficially similar to loons, grebes are smaller, with lobed toes and longer necks. Their small and insignificant tail feathers are invisible among fluffy tail coverts. Grebes fly less often and less strongly than loons. They forage by diving for small aquatic animals. All build floating nest on marshy ponds and winter on open water. Compare loons, cormorants, ducks (especially mergansers), and alcids. Nonbreeding adults are shown.

Genus *Podiceps*

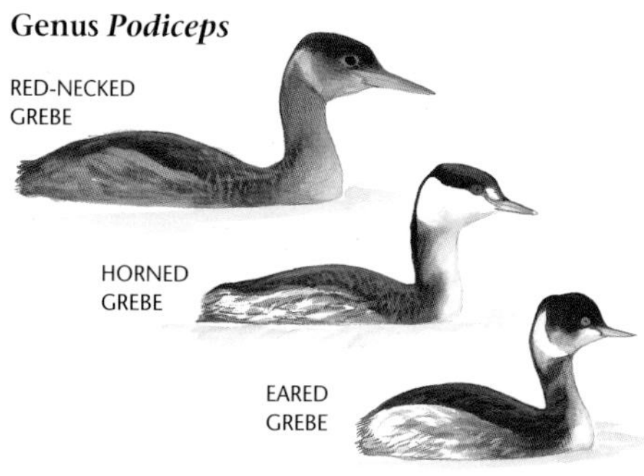
RED-NECKED GREBE
HORNED GREBE
EARED GREBE

Small Pond Grebes Genus *Podilymbus*

Genus *Tachybaptus*

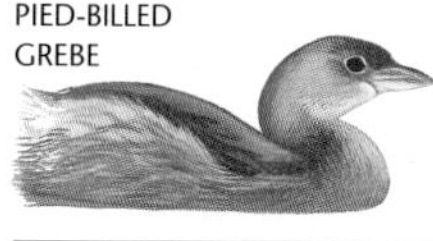
PIED-BILLED GREBE

LEAST GREBE

Genus *Aechmophorus*

WESTERN GREBE
CLARK'S GREBE

grebes sleep with bill pointed forward, nestled in side of neck
grebes walk with difficulty (Western and Clark's incapable of walking)
young grebes ride on parents' backs

Red-necked Grebe

Podiceps grisegena

L 18" WS 24" WT 2.2 lb (1,000 g)

Fairly large and stocky; long, heavy bill, thick neck, triangular head. Winters mainly on deep, open water.

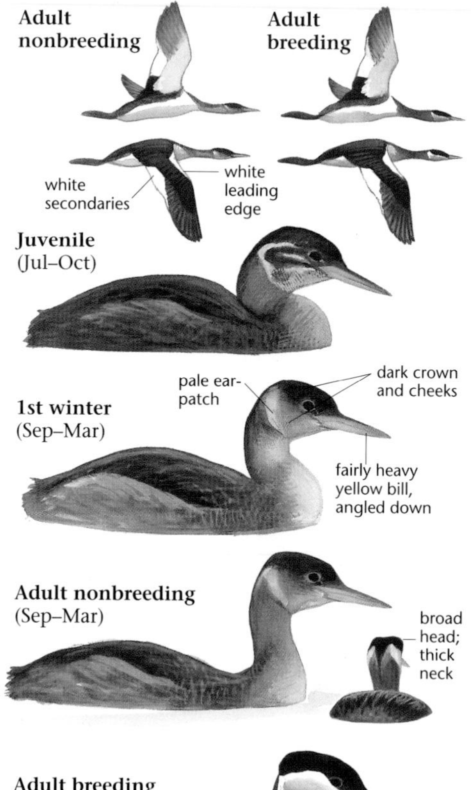
Adult nonbreeding
Adult breeding
white secondaries
white leading edge
Juvenile (Jul–Oct)
1st winter (Sep–Mar)
pale ear-patch
dark crown and cheeks
fairly heavy yellow bill, angled down
Adult nonbreeding (Sep–Mar)
broad head; thick neck
Adult breeding (Feb–Aug)

Voice: Song a loud series, beginning with nasal, gull-like quality, then braying chatter with quavering end. Male calls higher-pitched than female. Also a loud, nasal quacking series *ga-ga-ga-ga. . . .* Low, grunting notes sometimes heard in winter.

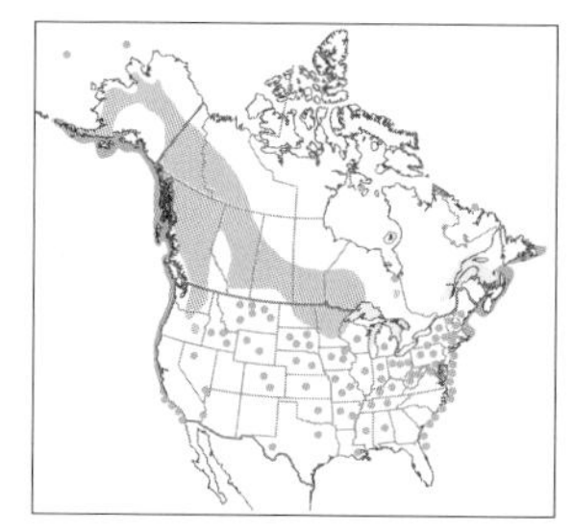

GREBES: SMALL *PODICEPS*

These two species share small size and short, pointed bills. Eared is more likely to be found inland on shallow, fresh water and in huge numbers on saline lakes in the west.

Horned Grebe

Podiceps auritus

L 14" WS 18" WT 1 lb (450 g)

Slightly larger and much heavier than Eared, with thicker neck; relatively larger, flat-topped head; and straight bill.

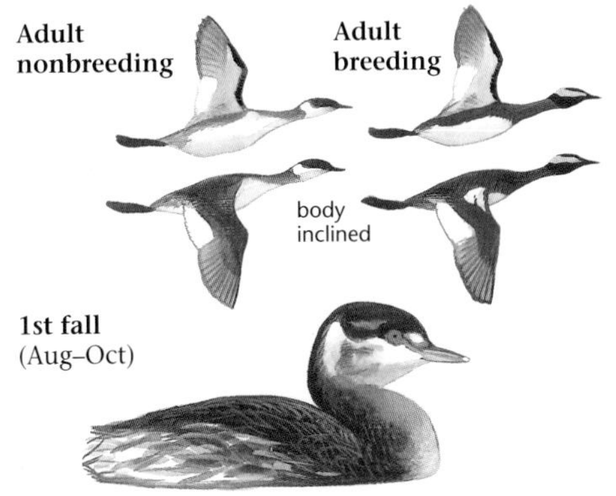

Adult nonbreeding
Adult breeding
body inclined
1st fall (Aug–Oct)

Adult nonbreeding (Sep–Mar)
peak behind eye
Adult nonbreeding (Sep–Mar)
whitish tip on bill
all-white
usually white neck

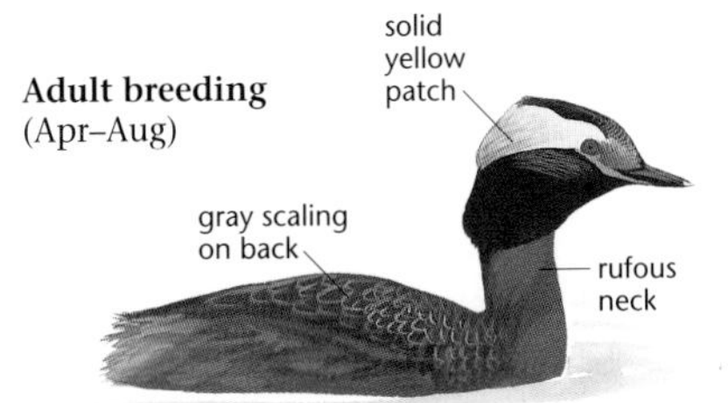

Adult breeding (Apr–Aug)
solid yellow patch
gray scaling on back
rufous neck

Voice: Song trilling, usually in duet, with rising and falling pulses of sound: squeaky, giggling, nasal. Drier chatter in alarm. Common call in summer a whining, nasal *way-urrr* or *ja-orrrr* descending, ending in throaty rattle, repeated. High, thin notes sometimes heard in winter.

Eared Grebe

Podiceps nigricollis

L 13" WS 16" WT 11 oz (300 g)

Small and thin-necked, with slender and upturned bill; relatively small head with peak over eye. Often fluffs rear feathers, creating "high-stern" shape.

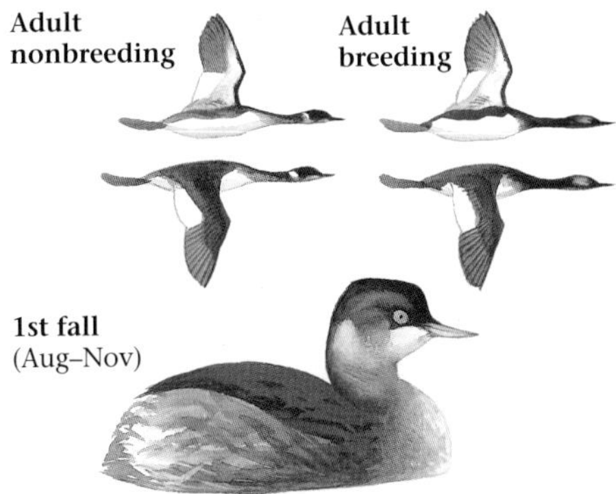

Adult nonbreeding
Adult breeding
1st fall (Aug–Nov)

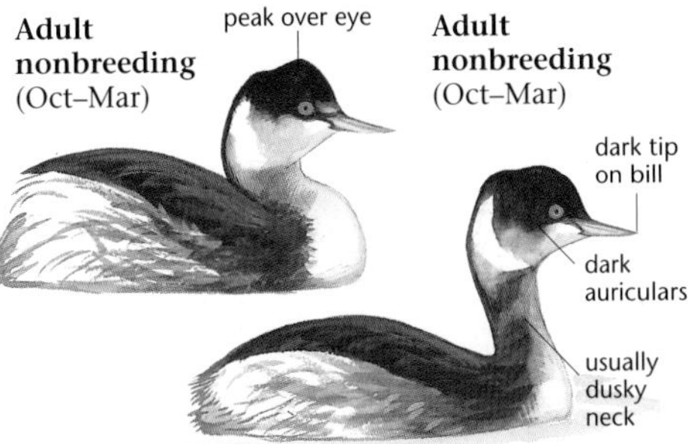

Adult nonbreeding (Oct–Mar)
peak over eye
Adult nonbreeding (Oct–Mar)
dark tip on bill
dark auriculars
usually dusky neck

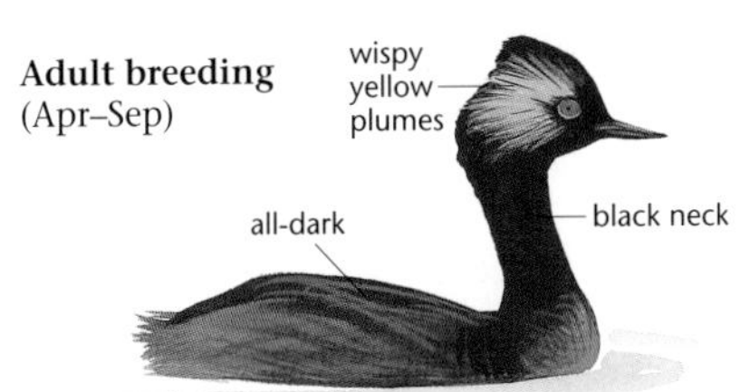

Adult breeding (Apr–Sep)
wispy yellow plumes
all-dark
black neck

Voice: Generally quieter and less harsh than Horned. Song a high, rising, squeaky whistle *ooEEK* or *ooEEKa* repeated; reminiscent of Sora but shorter, weaker. Other calls on breeding grounds mainly shrill, chittering series usually ending in upslur *hik*.

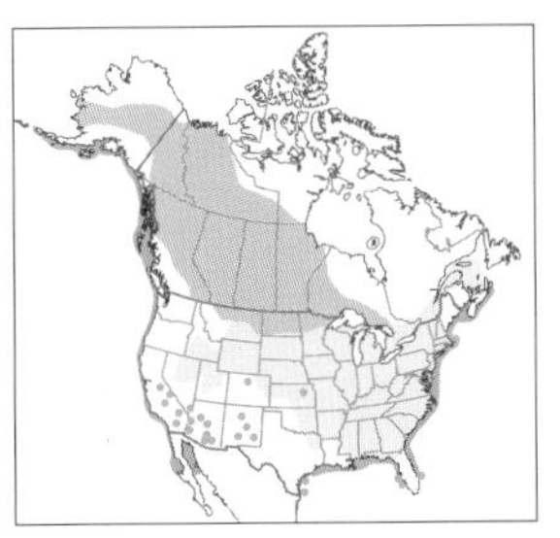

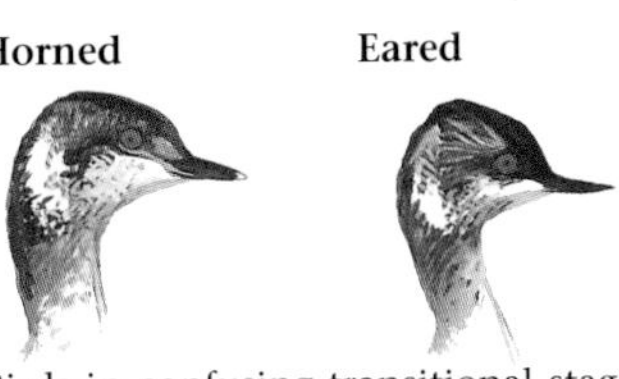

Horned
Eared

Birds in confusing transitional stage during molt to breeding plumage (Mar–Apr).

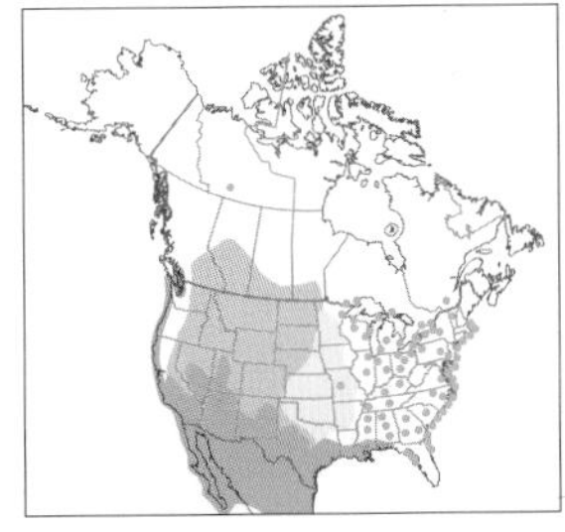

Small Pond Grebes

These two species, similar in habits, are more vocal and more secretive than other grebes; they are usually found on sheltered ponds near vegetation. Both have drab plumage year-round.

Pied-billed Grebe

Podilymbus podiceps

L 13" WS 16" WT 1 lb (450 g) ♂>♀

Generally appears tawny-brown. Stockier overall than Horned, with distinctive thick bill.

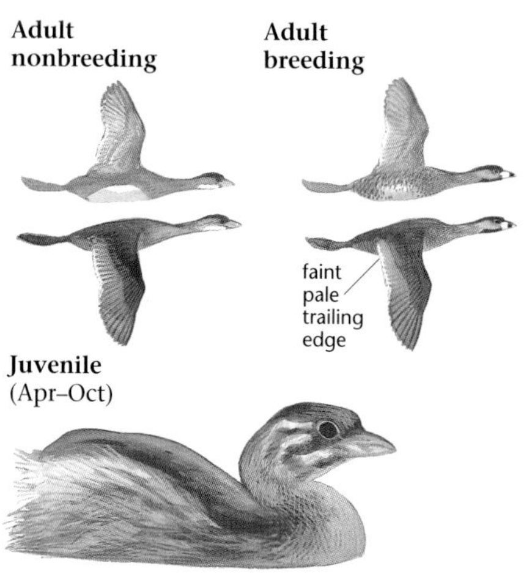

Adult nonbreeding
Adult breeding
faint pale trailing edge
Juvenile (Apr–Oct)

Adult nonbreeding (Sep–Mar)
dark eye
thick bill
reddish

Adult breeding (Feb–Sep)
whitish bill with black band

Voice: Song of male far-carrying, vibrant, throaty barks *ge ge gadum gadum gadum gaum gaom gwaaaaaow gwaaaaaaow gaom*. Female gives low grunting notes. In aggression a drawn-out, nasal chatter slightly descending and fading away (compare Least).

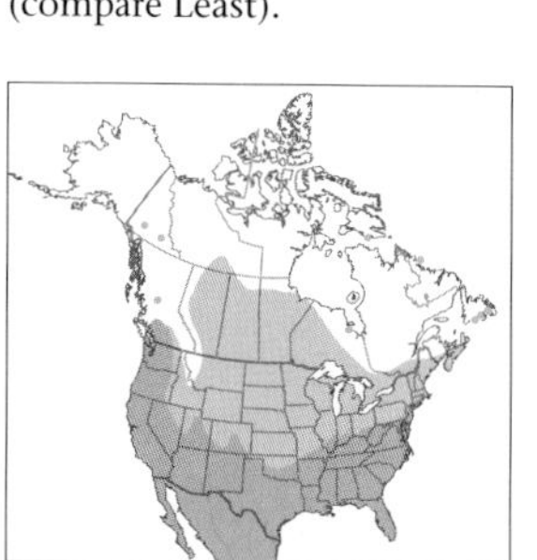

Least Grebe

Tachybaptus dominicus

L 9.5" WS 11" WT 4 oz (115 g)

By far our smallest grebe; always dark grayish with yellow eyes, thin neck, and thin, straight bill.

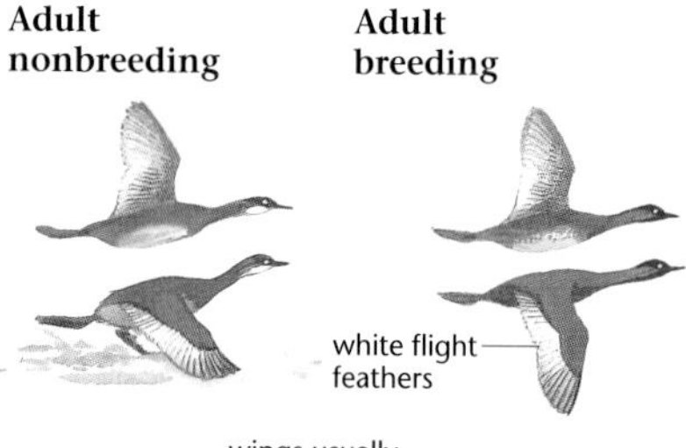

Adult nonbreeding
Adult breeding
white flight feathers

Juvenile (Jun–Oct)

wings usually raised high, showing fluffy tail coverts

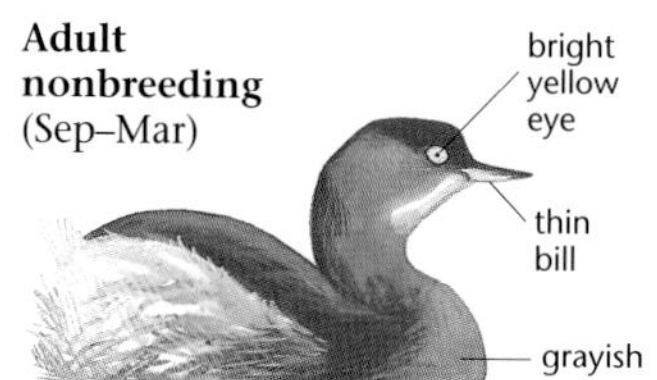

Adult nonbreeding (Sep–Mar)
bright yellow eye
thin bill
grayish

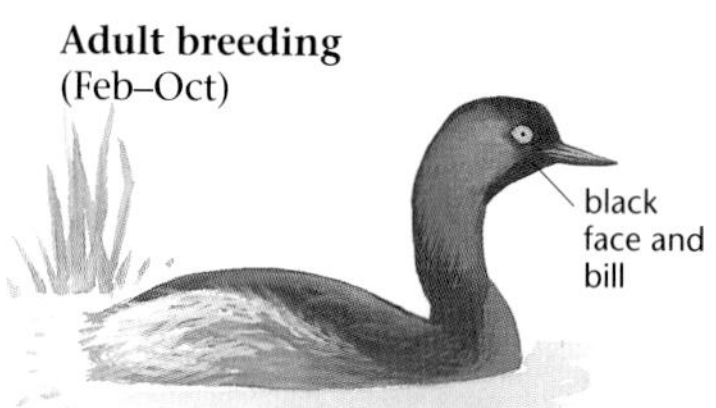

Adult breeding (Feb–Oct)
black face and bill

Voice: Loud, ringing, nasal *beep* or *teeen* and nasal, whining *verr*. Rapid, nasal, buzzy chatter descending *vvvvvvvvvvvv* analogous to Pied-billed call but higher-pitched, much more rapid and buzzing. No sound analogous to song of Pied-billed.

GREBES: GENUS *AECHMOPHORUS*

These large, long-necked grebes were recently considered a single species, Western Grebe. Their ranges overlap broadly; Western is much more numerous than Clark's to the north and east.

Western Grebe

Aechmophorus occidentalis

L 25" WS 24" WT 3.3 lb (1,500 g)

Large and very slender with long neck and long, thin bill. Clean dark gray and white plumage.

Adult

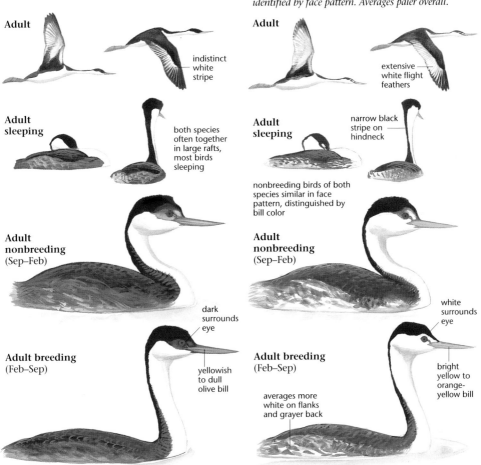

indistinct white stripe

Adult sleeping

both species often together in large rafts, most birds sleeping

Adult nonbreeding (Sep–Feb)

dark surrounds eye

Adult breeding (Feb–Sep)

yellowish to dull olive bill

Clark's Grebe

Aechmophorus clarkii

L 25" WS 24" WT 3.1 lb (1,400 g)

Structurally identical to Western but averages a little smaller. Best distinguished by bill color; most can be identified by face pattern. Averages paler overall.

Adult

extensive white flight feathers

Adult sleeping

narrow black stripe on hindneck

nonbreeding birds of both species similar in face pattern, distinguished by bill color

Adult nonbreeding (Sep–Feb)

white surrounds eye

Adult breeding (Feb–Sep)

bright yellow to orange-yellow bill

averages more white on flanks and grayer back

Voice: Both species give high, creaking, far-carrying calls. Most common year-round call a two-part *kreed-kreet* by Western and a simpler *kreeeed* or *kreee-eed* by Clark's. Courting female gives long series of begging notes: Western gives *krDEE krDEE . . .* ; Clark's may give higher, scratchier *kweea kweea . . .* or *weeweewee-wee. . . .* Various other calls on breeding grounds include a high, thin whistle.

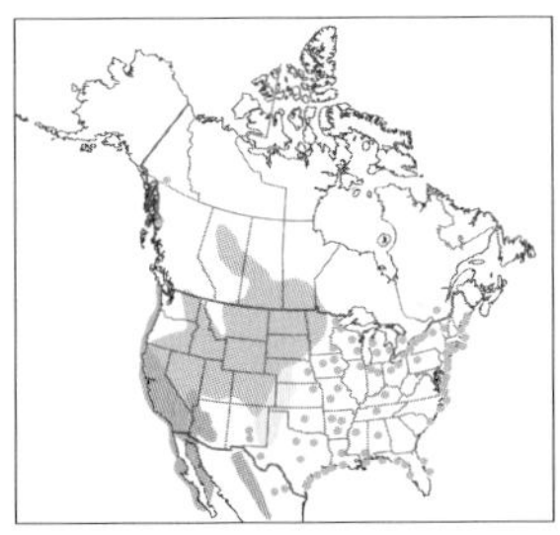

Intermediate birds, seen regularly, especially during winter, are unidentifiable. Some may be hybrids.

Albatrosses, Petrels, and Shearwaters

Families: Diomedeidae, Procellariidae

20 species in 5 genera; all in family Procellariidae, except albatrosses in Diomedeidae. These medium to large, long-winged seabirds come to land only when nesting. All fly with stiff wingbeats and long, arcing glides. They feed on small animals and carrion found at the water's surface; some species make shallow dives to capture submerged prey. All are characterized by tubular nostrils (also on storm-petrels). Most can be found in large numbers where prey is concentrated, resting on the water in tight flocks. All nest on islands; most are visitors to North America, nesting elsewhere. Compare Northern Gannet, boobies, jaegers, gulls, and terns. Adults are shown.

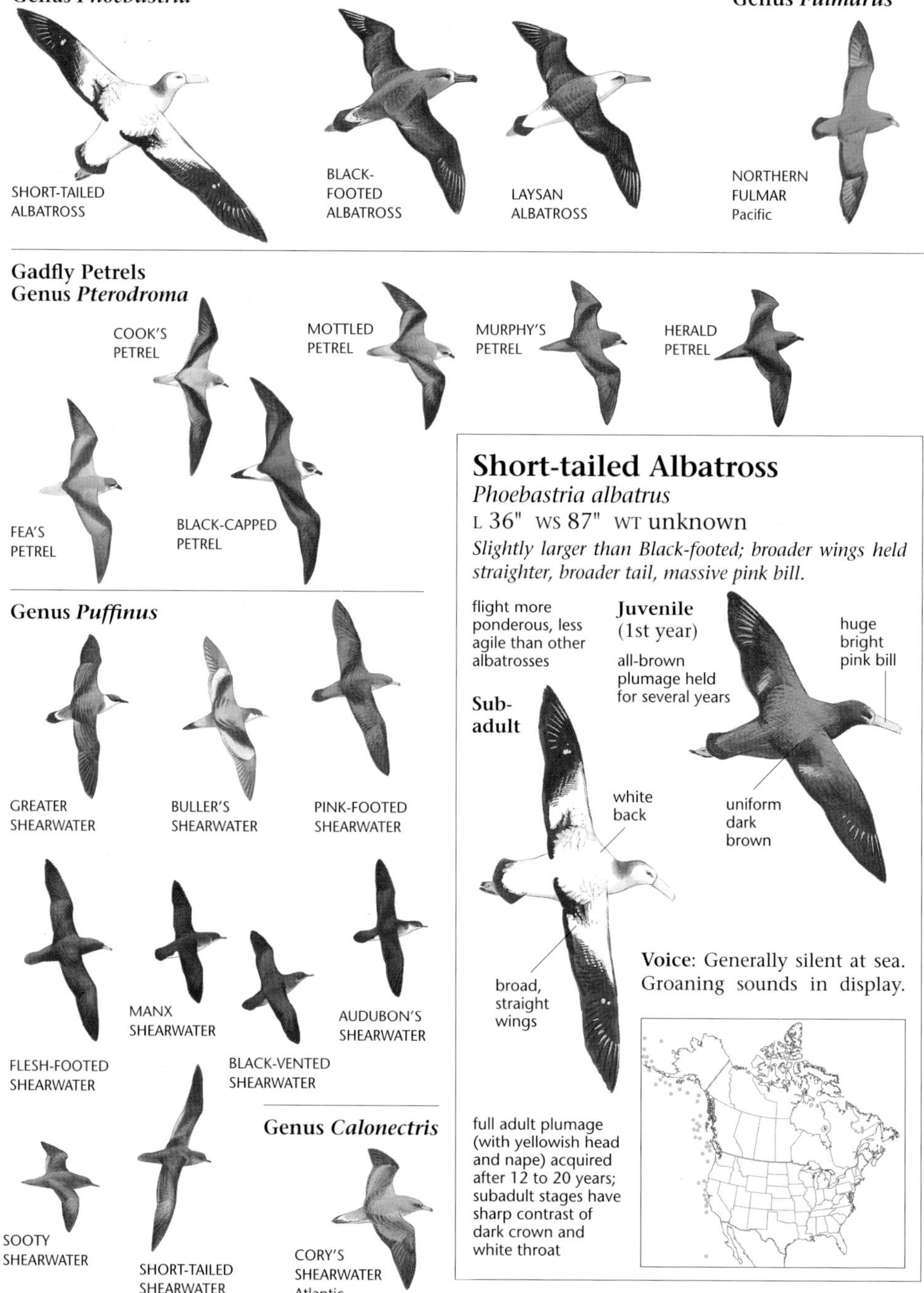

Genus *Phoebastria*
SHORT-TAILED ALBATROSS
BLACK-FOOTED ALBATROSS
LAYSAN ALBATROSS
Genus *Fulmarus*
NORTHERN FULMAR Pacific
Gadfly Petrels Genus *Pterodroma*
COOK'S PETREL
MOTTLED PETREL
MURPHY'S PETREL
HERALD PETREL
FEA'S PETREL
BLACK-CAPPED PETREL
Genus *Puffinus*
GREATER SHEARWATER
BULLER'S SHEARWATER
PINK-FOOTED SHEARWATER
FLESH-FOOTED SHEARWATER
MANX SHEARWATER
BLACK-VENTED SHEARWATER
AUDUBON'S SHEARWATER
SOOTY SHEARWATER
SHORT-TAILED SHEARWATER
Genus *Calonectris*
CORY'S SHEARWATER Atlantic

Short-tailed Albatross

Phoebastria albatrus

L 36" WS 87" WT unknown

Slightly larger than Black-footed; broader wings held straighter, broader tail, massive pink bill.

flight more ponderous, less agile than other albatrosses
Juvenile (1st year)
all-brown plumage held for several years
huge bright pink bill
Sub-adult
white back
uniform dark brown
broad, straight wings
full adult plumage (with yellowish head and nape) acquired after 12 to 20 years; subadult stages have sharp contrast of dark crown and white throat

Voice: Generally silent at sea. Groaning sounds in display.

Albatrosses

Albatrosses are distinguished from all other seabirds by their large size, large bills, and long, slender wings. Their flight is ponderous and steady, with slow turns and endless gliding on stiff wings.

Laysan Albatross

Phoebastria immutabilis

L 32" WS 78" WT 6.6 lb (3,000 g) ♂>♀

Slightly smaller and slimmer than Black-footed; gull-like plumage, but note dark eye-smudge and dark tail.

Juvenile (1st year)

Adult

underwing pattern varies from dark to pale; not age-related

white head and body

pale bill

dark upper rump

dark tail

dark eye-smudge

swimming albatrosses have distinctive hump

Adult

pinkish bill

Voice: Voice quieter, higher, and less harsh and nasal than Black-footed; otherwise similar. Courtship dance at nest site more elaborate and with slower tempo than Black-footed.

Black-footed Albatross

Phoebastria nigripes

L 32" WS 84" WT 7 lb (3,200 g) ♂>♀

Huge and long-winged, but at times looks rather stocky in flight.

Juvenile (1st year)

Adult

uniform brown

pale

dark bill

white tail coverts

Light adult

rare; can be confused with other albatross species or with rare Black-footed × Laysan hybrids

dusky pink

dark collar

pale gray-brown

pale face

gray-brown overall

Adult

Voice: Noisy in groups at sea: groaning or squealing noises, also bill-snapping. Courtship display at nest site involves melancholy groaning and bill-snapping in a simple dance.

Black-footed Albatross

Typical silhouettes in flight.

Northern Fulmar

Two populations are distinguished from shearwaters and gulls by their overall shape and proportions and stout, pale bills. Their plumage varies from pale gray (like gulls) to dark brownish-gray.

Northern Fulmar

Fulmarus glacialis

L 18" WS 42" WT 1.3 lb (600 g) ♂>♀

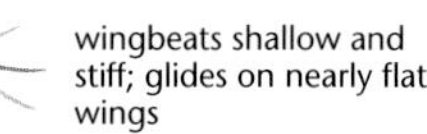

wingbeats shallow and stiff; glides on nearly flat wings

Stocky and thick-necked, with rather short, rounded wings; short, thick, pale bill; and short, rounded tail. All have pale patch on inner primaries, dark eye-smudge. Upperwing lacks M pattern of shearwaters and petrels.

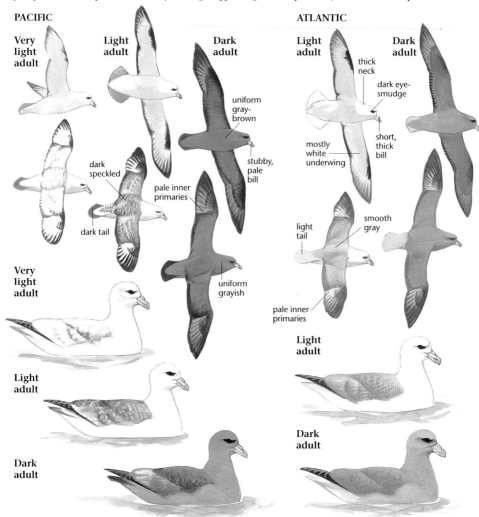

PACIFIC

Very light adult

Light adult

Dark adult

uniform gray-brown

stubby, pale bill

dark speckled

pale inner primaries

dark tail

uniform grayish

Very light adult

Light adult

Dark adult

ATLANTIC

Light adult

Dark adult

thick neck

dark eye-smudge

short, thick bill

mostly white underwing

smooth gray

light tail

pale inner primaries

Light adult

Dark adult

Voice: Feeding flock at sea rather noisy: a hoarse, throaty cackling and grunting. At nest site loud cackling of variable pattern *AARK aaw* or *aak aak aak*. . . . Pacific apparently similar to Atlantic.

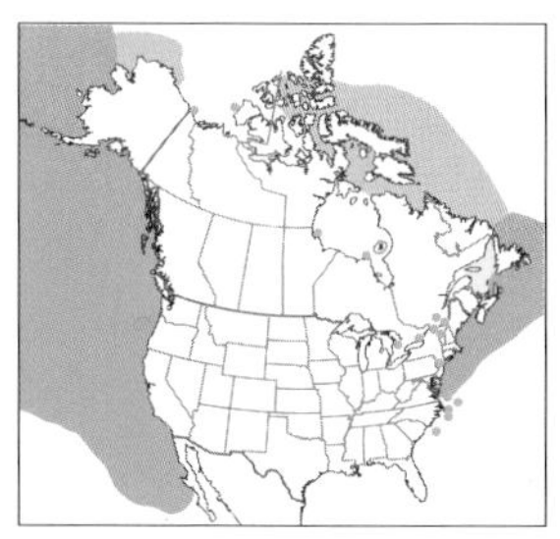

Pacific birds are similar to Atlantic in shape and habits but average a little thinner-billed. Best distinguished by tail color: always contrastingly dark on Pacific but pale gray (like the rump) on Atlantic. Pacific also has lighter and darker extremes than Atlantic, and the upperparts are usually more mottled. Percentage of dark and light morph birds varies between colonies, dark generally most numerous in Aleutian and Labrador breeders.

Pacific Gadfly Petrels

These two species, like most gadfly petrels, are scarce and irregular visitors found in very small numbers over deep water. Identification is based on underwing pattern, head pattern, and size.

Mottled Petrel

Pterodroma inexpectata

L 14" WS 32" WT 11 oz (320 g)

Heavy-bodied and stout-billed; very powerful and fast flier. Dark gray belly contrasting with white vent and underwing is distinctive, as is bold black bar on underwing.

Adult

dark gray belly contrasts with white vent and underwing

strong black bar

gray belly can be paler or mottled

dark gray back with fairly strong M pattern

pale gray uppertail coverts

M pattern on the upperwing of this and other species is dependent on lighting; conspicuous at certain angles, invisible at others

Adult

gray flanks

stout bill

Voice: Generally silent at sea.

Cook's Petrel

Pterodroma cookii

L 13" WS 30" WT 7 oz (190 g)

Distinctly small and lightweight with relatively long, thin bill; flight rapid and erratic with quick turns and jerky movements. Mostly white underwing unlike other Pterodroma *petrels.*

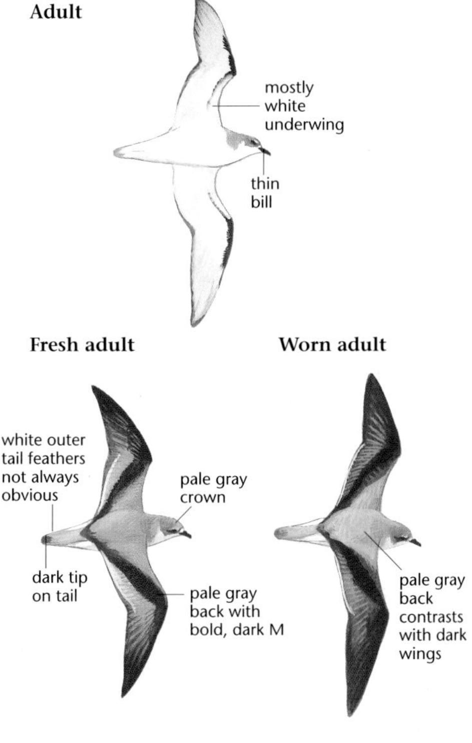
Adult
mostly white underwing
thin bill
Fresh adult
Worn adult
white outer tail feathers not always obvious
pale gray crown
dark tip on tail
pale gray back with bold, dark M
pale gray back contrasts with dark wings

Adult
gray crown
white flanks
thin bill

Voice: Generally silent at sea.

Note that several other *Pterodroma* species have been recorded rarely off our Pacific coast, including Stejneger's Petrel *(P. longirostris),* which is very similar to Cook's. Identification requires careful study of size and bill shape and patterns of underwing, head, rump, and tail.

Gadfly Petrels

These two dark species can be confused with shearwaters or jaegers, but note their short black bills and underwing pattern. Murphy's is found over deep water, Herald over warm Gulf Stream water.

Murphy's Petrel

Pterodroma ultima

L 15" WS 35" WT 13 oz (360 g)

Slender and fast-flying, like Sooty Shearwater; note overall grayish cast with faint M pattern above, pale chin, and pale flash at base of primaries.

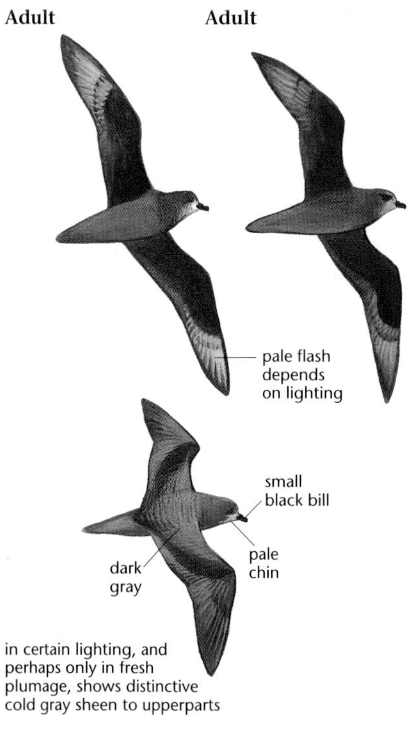

Adult
Adult
pale flash depends on lighting
small black bill
pale chin
dark gray
in certain lighting, and perhaps only in fresh plumage, shows distinctive cold gray sheen to upperparts

Adult

Voice: Generally silent at sea.

Herald Petrel

Pterodroma arminjoniana

L 15" WS 35" WT 12 oz (330 g)

More slender and longer-winged than other Pterodroma *petrels. Distinguished from jaegers by flight actions and structure.*

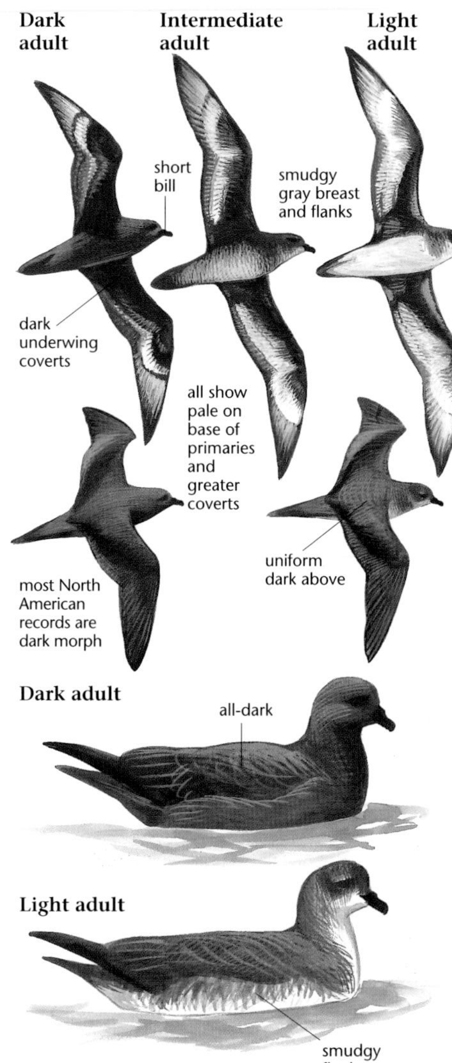

Dark adult
Intermediate adult
Light adult
short bill
smudgy gray breast and flanks
dark underwing coverts
all show pale on base of primaries and greater coverts
uniform dark above
most North American records are dark morph
Dark adult
all-dark
Light adult
smudgy flanks

Voice: Generally silent at sea.

Both of these species resemble Sooty Shearwater. At a distance note high, arcing flight, more angled wings, longer tail, shorter head, dark underwing coverts, and pale remiges; closer views reveal short black bill and rounded head.

Atlantic Gadfly Petrels

These two strong and dynamic fliers, found in warm Gulf Stream water, are always white-bellied. Rare individuals are similar in underwing pattern but are always distinguishable by tail color.

Fea's Petrel

Pterodroma feae

L 15" WS 34" WT unknown

Shape like Black-capped but smaller; dark underwing, pale gray rump and tail, and gray nape distinctive.

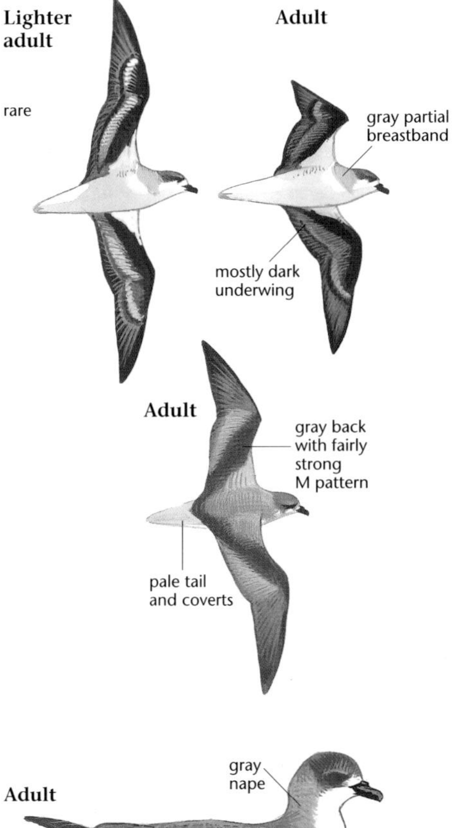
Lighter adult
rare
Adult
gray partial breastband
mostly dark underwing
Adult
gray back with fairly strong M pattern
pale tail and coverts
Adult
gray nape

Black-capped Petrel

Pterodroma hasitata

L 16" WS 37" WT unknown

Like shearwaters but with relatively longer, pointier wings; short, thick bill; and long, pointed tail. Striking white uppertail coverts and black bar on underwing distinctive.

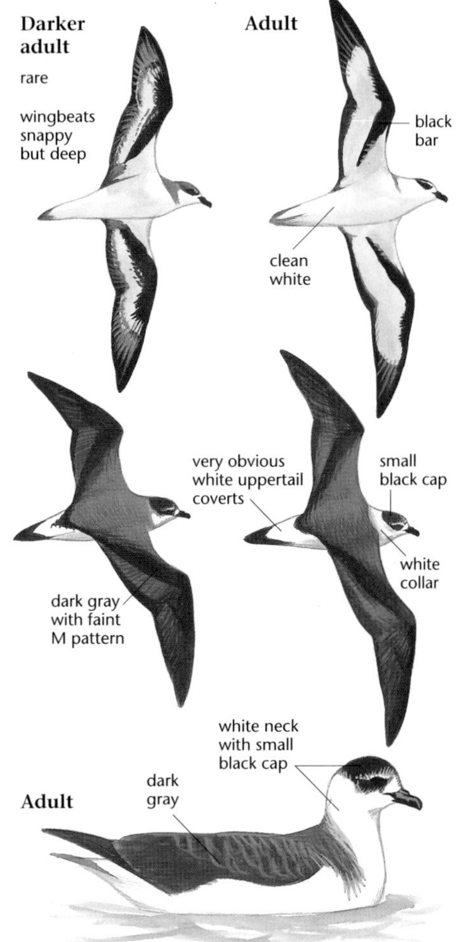
Darker adult
rare
wingbeats snappy but deep
Adult
black bar
clean white
very obvious white uppertail coverts
small black cap
white collar
dark gray with faint M pattern
white neck with small black cap
dark gray
Adult

Voice: Generally silent at sea.

Voice: Generally silent at sea.

Darker Black-capped Petrels can be confused with the very similar Bermuda Petrel *(P. cahow)* recorded several times off North Carolina. Bermuda Petrel is smaller with grayer uppertail coverts.

Our largest Atlantic shearwaters, these two species are quite different in overall shape and flight style. Habitat overlaps broadly, but Cory's generally prefers warm water, Greater cold.

Cory's Shearwater

Calonectris diomedea

L 18" WS 44" WT 1.8 lb (800 g) ♂>♀

Large and heavy; broad and blunt-tipped wings held hunched and bowed down. Yellow bill, dusky head, pale back, and clean white underparts distinctive.

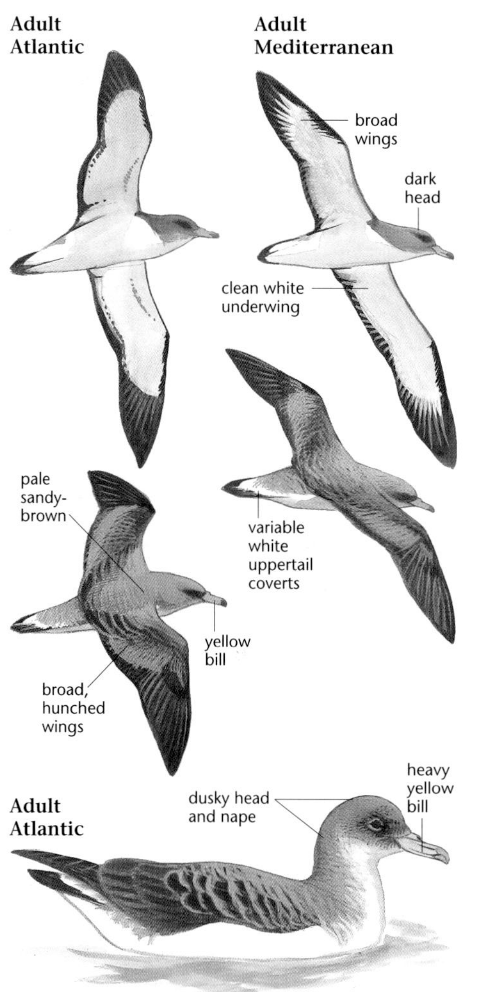
Adult Atlantic
Adult Mediterranean
broad wings
dark head
clean white underwing
pale sandy-brown
variable white uppertail coverts
yellow bill
broad, hunched wings
Adult Atlantic
dusky head and nape
heavy yellow bill

Voice: Generally silent at sea. Occasionally a raucous, descending bleating similar to Greater.

Greater Shearwater

Puffinus gravis

L 18" WS 42" WT 1.8 lb (840 g)

Heavy but sleek with straight, narrow, pointed wings. Neat, dark cap and dark markings on underwings distinctive.

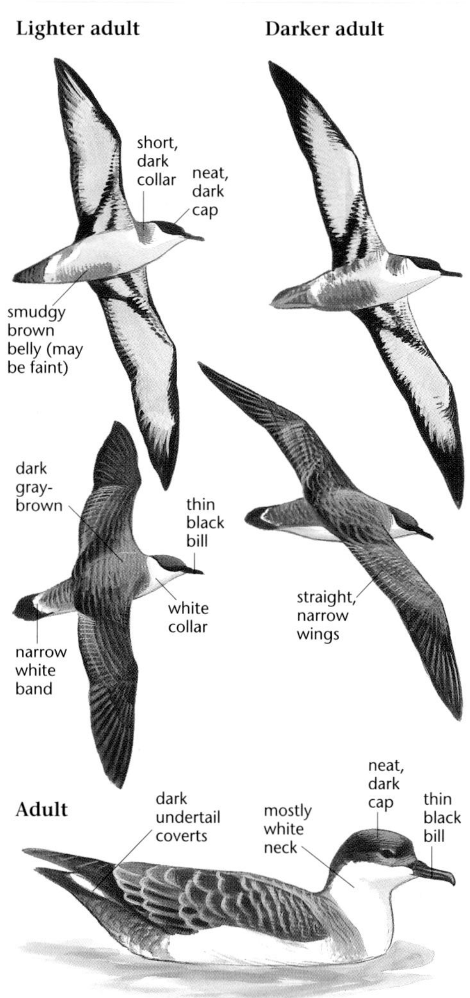
Lighter adult
Darker adult
short, dark collar
neat, dark cap
smudgy brown belly (may be faint)
dark gray-brown
thin black bill
white collar
narrow white band
straight, narrow wings
Adult
dark undertail coverts
mostly white neck
neat, dark cap
thin black bill

Voice: Generally silent at sea. Vocal in feeding groups, often bleating *waaan* like a lamb.

Two populations of Cory's Shearwater both disperse to North America and are sometimes considered separate species but may be indistinguishable in the field. Mediterranean breeders average smaller and smaller-billed than Atlantic. They may also have more white on the inner webs of the primaries and average paler brown on the back.

Pacific Shearwaters

These two species are the only large white-bellied shearwaters off our Pacific coast, although Pink-footed resembles the much smaller Black-vented. Buller's is present only Aug–Nov.

Buller's Shearwater

Puffinus bulleri

L 16" WS 40" WT 13 oz (370 g)

Slender and buoyant, with long tail but rather broad-based wings; graceful soaring flight and slow, easy wingbeats. Striking plumage with clean white underparts and neatly patterned upperside.

Adult

entirely clean white with narrow, dark border

gray bill

Adult

neat, dark cap and nape

Adult

striking pattern of blackish and pale gray

Adult

gray

white flanks

neat head pattern

Voice: Generally silent at sea.

Pink-footed Shearwater

Puffinus creatopus

L 19" WS 43" WT 1.6 lb (720 g)

Stocky and rather broad-winged, with heavy, labored wingbeats. Dusky head, smudgy markings on underparts, pale belly.

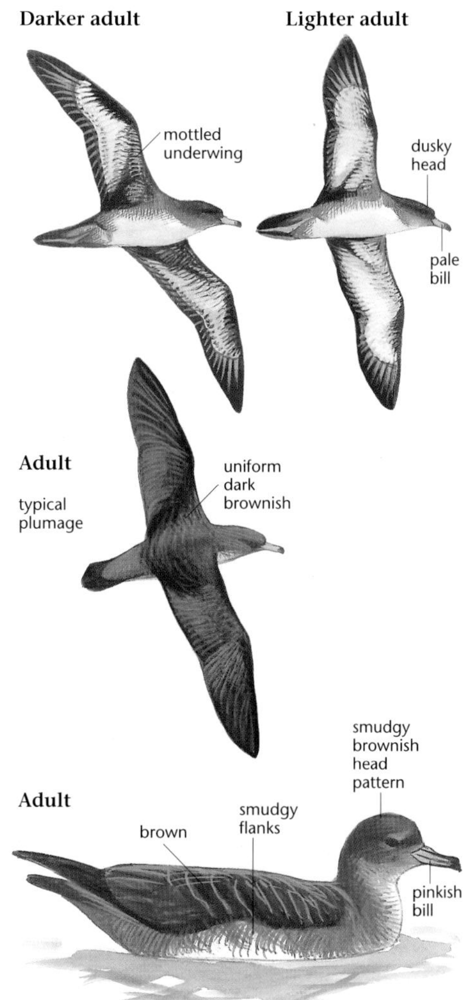
Darker adult
mottled underwing
Lighter adult
dusky head
pale bill
Adult
typical plumage
uniform dark brownish
Adult
brown
smudgy flanks
smudgy brownish head pattern
pinkish bill

Voice: Generally silent at sea. Vocal in feeding groups, giving a nasal, descending whinny.

Some shearwaters and gadfly petrels undergo rapid molt of wing feathers May–Jul, in which missing feathers produce striking white bars on coverts, white patches in primaries, and odd wing shapes.

Flesh-footed Shearwater, a scarce visitor nearly always seen singly, is closely related to Pink-footed. Black-vented, related to Manx, is found on warm water, usually close to land.

Flesh-footed Shearwater

Puffinus carneipes

L 17" WS 40" WT 1.4 lb (620 g)

Structure like Pink-footed; distinctly broader-winged than Sooty, with slower and more labored wingbeats.

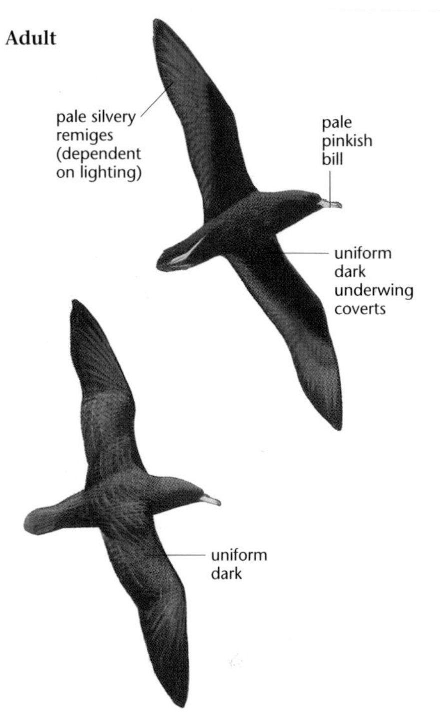
Adult
pale silvery remiges (dependent on lighting)
pale pinkish bill
uniform dark underwing coverts
uniform dark

Adult

Voice: Generally silent at sea. Sometimes utters high-pitched bark.

Black-vented Shearwater

Puffinus opisthomelas

L 14" WS 34" WT 9 oz (270 g)

Our smallest Pacific shearwater; relatively short-winged, with quick, choppy wingbeats. Plumage close to Pink-footed. Note dark bill.

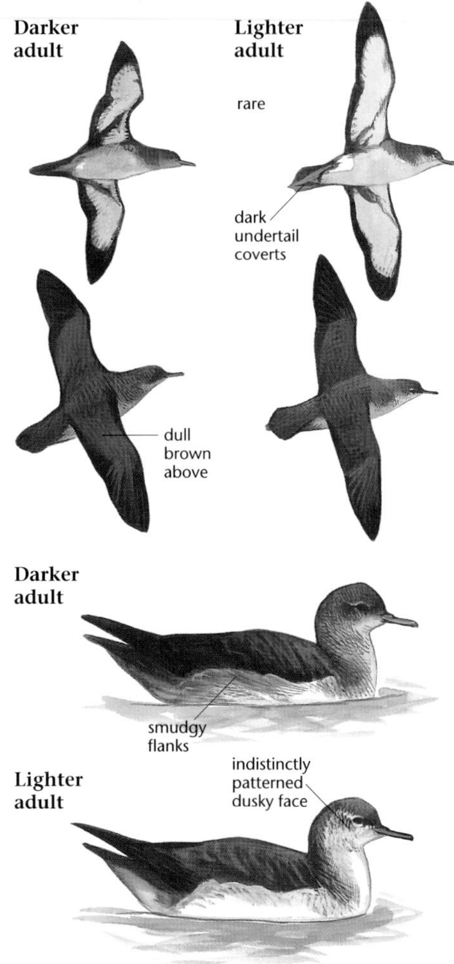
Darker adult
Lighter adult
rare
dark undertail coverts
dull brown above
Darker adult
smudgy flanks
Lighter adult
indistinctly patterned dusky face

Voice: Generally silent at sea. Voice at nest site undescribed.

Foot color is not an important field mark for Flesh-footed Shearwater, as Sooty and Short-tailed can also show pale flesh-colored feet. Furthermore, all shearwaters (and many other species) often fold the legs up beneath the flank feathers while flying, concealing the feet entirely.

Small Atlantic Shearwaters

Closely related to Black-vented, these two small, contrastingly colored species differ in shape and plumage details. In addition, Manx prefers cold water, Audubon's warm.

Manx Shearwater

Puffinus puffinus

L 13.5" WS 33" WT 1 lb (450 g)

Small, but proportions closer to large shearwaters than to Audubon's. Note dark auriculars with pale crescent behind, white undertail coverts.

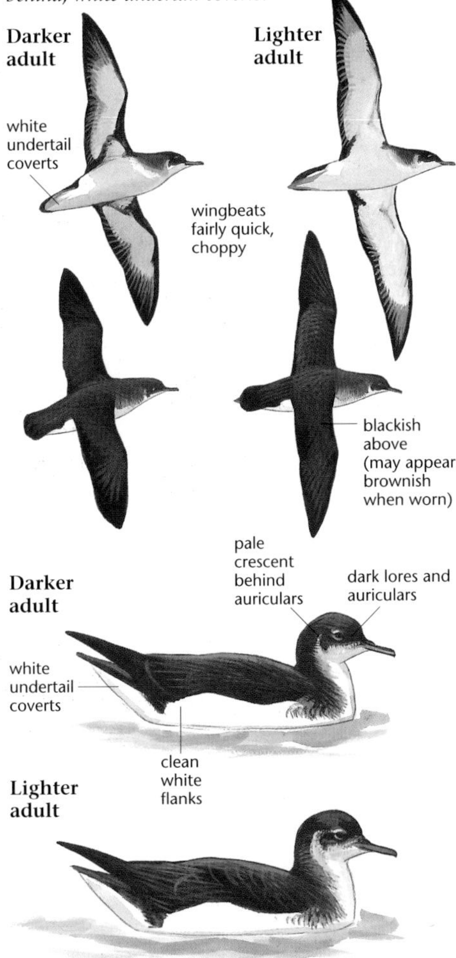

Darker adult
Lighter adult
white undertail coverts
wingbeats fairly quick, choppy
blackish above (may appear brownish when worn)
Darker adult
pale crescent behind auriculars
dark lores and auriculars
white undertail coverts
clean white flanks
Lighter adult

Voice: Generally silent at sea. At nest site at night a cackling then crooning series *cack cack cack carrr ho.* From ground a squalling sound rising to a crescendo of crowing when excited.

Audubon's Shearwater

Puffinus lherminieri

L 12" WS 27" WT 6 oz (180 g)

Our smallest shearwater; relatively short-winged and long-tailed. Flight and plumage may recall large alcids; white markings around eye; partly dark undertail coverts.

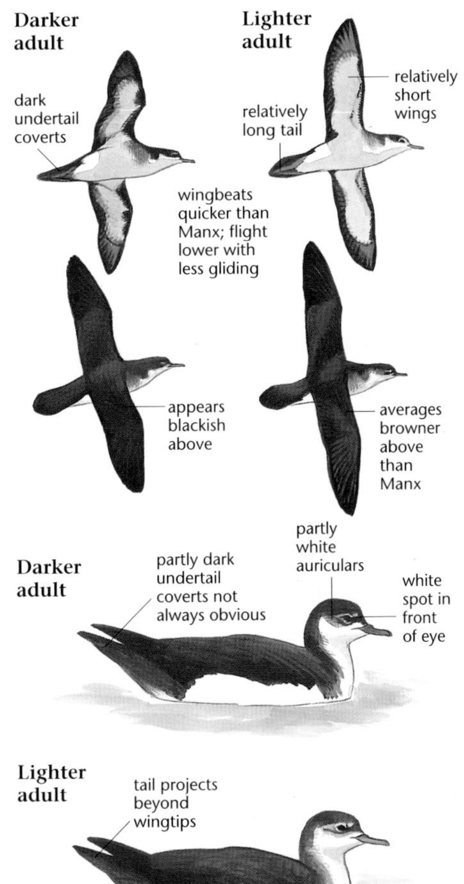

Darker adult
Lighter adult
dark undertail coverts
relatively long tail
relatively short wings
wingbeats quicker than Manx; flight lower with less gliding
appears blackish above
averages browner above than Manx
Darker adult
partly dark undertail coverts not always obvious
partly white auriculars
white spot in front of eye
Lighter adult
tail projects beyond wingtips

Voice: Generally silent at sea. Sometimes gives a high, nasal whining.

Separation of the small shearwaters can be difficult; at close range check face pattern. Manx and Black-vented have similar shape, and rare lighter Black-vented individuals may appear similar to Manx. Audubon's has different shape and flight actions and can be distinguished at a distance with experience.

Dark Shearwaters

In the Pacific these two very similar species are the most numerous shearwaters, sometimes occurring in flocks of millions and often visible from land. Short-tailed is scarce south of Alaska.

Short-tailed Shearwater

Puffinus tenuirostris

L 16" WS 38" WT 1.2 lb (550 g)

Distinctly smaller-billed and rounder-headed than Sooty. Averages smaller with narrower and more angled wings; these and most plumage differences subtle and overlapping.

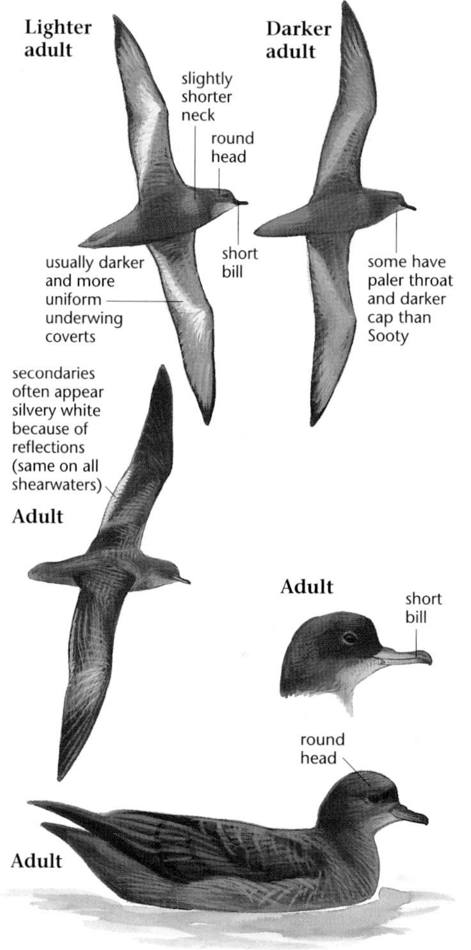

Lighter adult
slightly shorter neck
round head
short bill
usually darker and more uniform underwing coverts
Darker adult
some have paler throat and darker cap than Sooty
secondaries often appear silvery white because of reflections (same on all shearwaters)
Adult
Adult
short bill
round head
Adult

Voice: Generally silent at sea. Calls at nest higher, more screeching than Sooty.

Sooty Shearwater

Puffinus griseus

L 17" WS 40" WT 1.7 lb (780 g)

Slender and narrow-winged with deep, slicing wingbeats. Dark body and silvery underwing coverts distinctive.

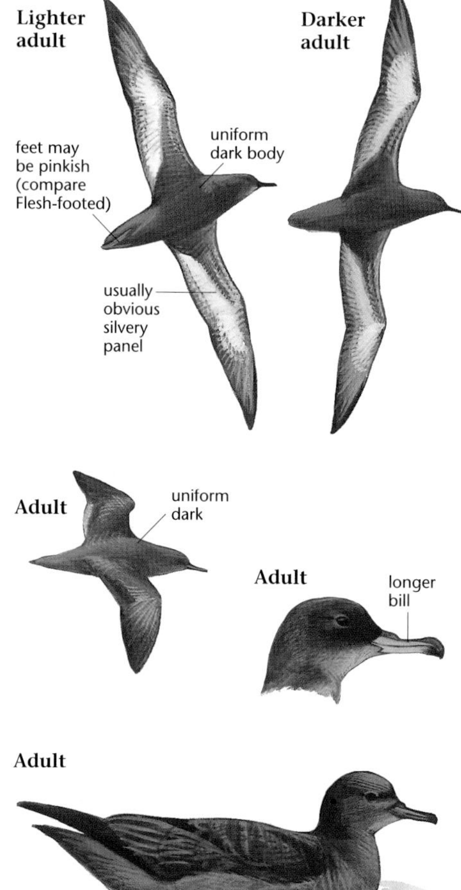

Lighter adult
Darker adult
feet may be pinkish (compare Flesh-footed)
uniform dark body
usually obvious silvery panel
Adult
uniform dark
Adult
longer bill
Adult

Voice: Generally silent at sea. In feeding group occasionally gives raucous cry: a relatively high, nasal *aaaa.*

Underwing color of these species differs on average. Sooty flashes brighter and more contrasting patches on the underwing coverts, while Short-tailed is duller brownish and more uniform. In practice this difference is overlapping and very light-dependent.

Storm-Petrels
Family: Hydrobatidae

8 species in 3 genera. These small oceanic birds come to land only at night when nesting. There are two main groups: Southern Hemisphere breeders have relatively short "arms" and long legs; Northern have longer "arms" (more angled wings) and shorter legs. All forage on minute prey captured by picking at the water's surface, usually while flying. Flight actions of storm-petrels depend on many factors such as wind conditions and the motivation of the bird. Watch for differences between foraging and traveling flight of each species as well as the less often seen escape flight (as when alarmed by an approaching boat). In judging tail shape, note that the outer tail feathers of all species flex upward in flight, creating the illusion of a notched tail when viewed from most angles. Also note that the toes of long-legged species can look like the fork of a tail. Compare shearwaters, swallows, and nighthawks. Adults are shown.

Southern Hemisphere
Genus *Pelagodroma* **Genus *Oceanites***

WHITE-FACED STORM-PETREL

WILSON'S STORM-PETREL

Northern Hemisphere Genus *Oceanodroma*

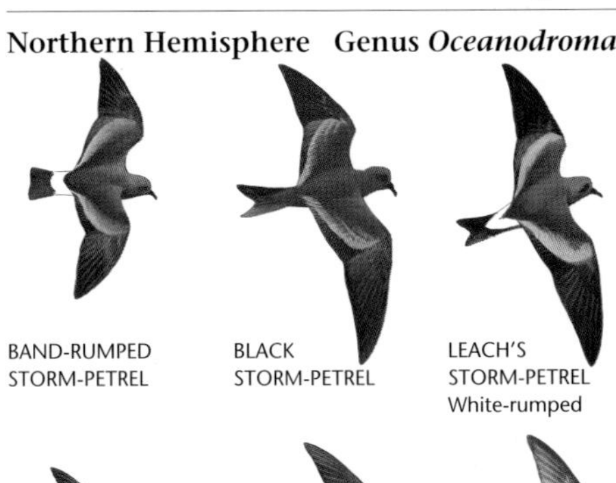

BAND-RUMPED STORM-PETREL

BLACK STORM-PETREL

LEACH'S STORM-PETREL White-rumped

LEAST STORM-PETREL

ASHY STORM-PETREL

FORK-TAILED STORM-PETREL

Wilson's Storm-Petrel molting adult
Typical of adult May–Jul in the northern Atlantic. Watch for differences in molt timing among species and age classes (e.g., 1st year Wilson's and adult Leach's molt Nov–Apr in Southern Hemisphere).

White-faced Storm-Petrel
Pelagodroma marina
L 7.5" WS 19" WT 1.6 oz (46 g)
Short-winged and round-tailed, with very long legs. Normal flight stiff-winged like Spotted Sandpiper.

Adult

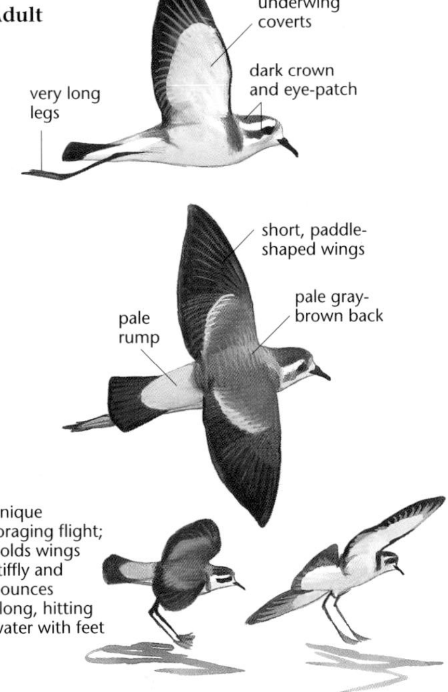
white underwing coverts
dark crown and eye-patch
very long legs
short, paddle-shaped wings
pale gray-brown back
pale rump
unique foraging flight; holds wings stiffly and bounces along, hitting water with feet

Adult

distinctive head pattern (compare phalaropes)

Voice: Generally silent at sea.

White-rumped Storm-Petrels

Though similar in plumage, these two species differ in size and especially in wing and tail shape and leg length. Band-rumped is scarce and prefers warm water; Wilson's is widespread.

Wilson's Storm-Petrel

Oceanites oceanicus

L 7.25" WS 18" WT 1.2 oz (34 g)

Short inner wing creates relatively straight-edged triangular wing shape. Tail square; legs very long with feet projecting beyond tip of tail.

Adult

faint pale center of underwing

toes project beyond tail tip

extensive white on undertail coverts

very dark blackish overall

wingbeats shallow and stiff; flight swallowlike

glides with wings slightly pressed down

Fresh adult

square tail often appears notched

narrow whitish tips on greater coverts

Worn adult

larger white patch than Band-rumped

obvious pale greater coverts

Adult

obvious white patch

Voice: Generally silent at sea. At close range a peeping or chattering sound may occasionally be heard from feeding groups.

Band-rumped Storm-Petrel

Oceanodroma castro

L 9" WS 19" WT 1.5 oz (42 g)

Larger and longer-winged than Wilson's; broader-winged and shorter-tailed than Leach's. Note white on undertail coverts, dark upperwing.

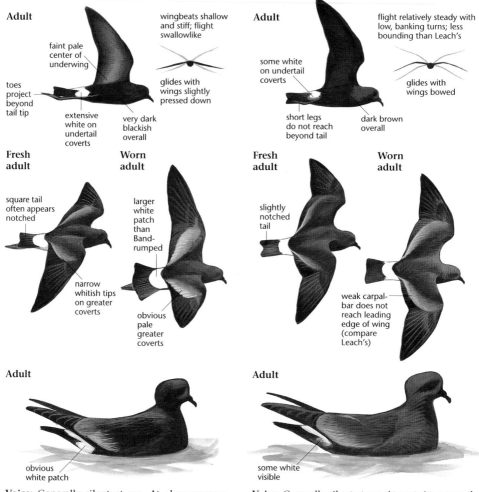

Adult

some white on undertail coverts

short legs do not reach beyond tail

dark brown overall

flight relatively steady with low, banking turns; less bounding than Leach's

glides with wings bowed

Fresh adult

slightly notched tail

Worn adult

weak carpal-bar does not reach leading edge of wing (compare Leach's)

Adult

some white visible

Voice: Generally silent at sea. At nest site a squeak like a finger across a wet pane of glass, followed by low purring.

Wilson's Storm-Petrel

All species perform "foot-pattering" action while feeding, longer-legged Wilson's more frequently than others.

LEACH'S STORM-PETREL
Both white- and dark-rumped forms are distinguished from other species by wing and tail shape, details of upperwing, and rump pattern. They are usually found singly over warm or cold waters.

Leach's Storm-Petrel

Oceanodroma leucorhoa

L 8" WS 20" WT 1.4 oz (40 g)

Slender and very long-winged; wings pointed, angled, and swept back; long, notched tail. Note bold, pale carpal bar, dark undertail coverts.

DARK-RUMPED

Adult

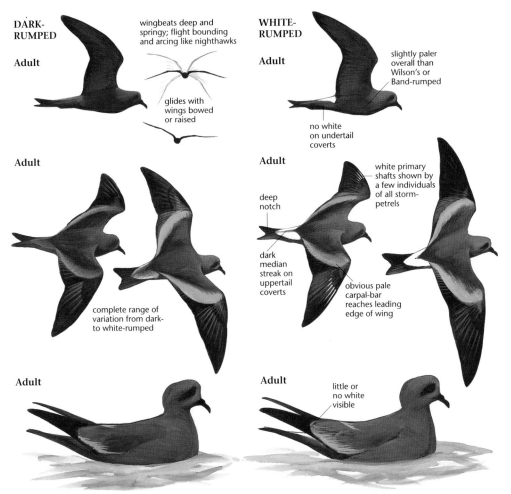

wingbeats deep and springy; flight bounding and arcing like nighthawks

glides with wings bowed or raised

WHITE-RUMPED

Adult

slightly paler overall than Wilson's or Band-rumped

no white on undertail coverts

Adult

complete range of variation from dark- to white-rumped

Adult

deep notch

dark median streak on uppertail coverts

white primary shafts shown by a few individuals of all storm-petrels

obvious pale carpal-bar reaches leading edge of wing

Adult

Adult

little or no white visible

Voice: Generally silent at sea. At nest site a musical purring three to four seconds long, rising slightly in pitch and interspersed with inhaled *whee.* In flight over colony a chuckling chatter *pwa putaDEEPto-ditado.* Winter breeding population of Guadalupe Island (not proven to occur in North America) has slightly different vocalizations.

All Atlantic and northern Pacific birds are white-rumped; the percentage of dark-rumped individuals increases abruptly off southern California. Birds breeding in southern California average smaller with rounder wingtips, and shorter "arms" than northern birds, but these differences are very subtle. Southern California breeding birds are 80 to 90 percent white-rumped, but those breeding just south of Mexican border are 90 to 100 percent dark-rumped. Dark-rumped birds tend to forage over shallow, warm water close to shore, white-rumped over deeper, cooler water far offshore. Two other (more distinctive) populations breed on Guadalupe Island off Mexico and could wander to California waters. More study is needed.

Dark-rumped Storm-Petrels

These two lanky, all-dark species can be difficult to identify. Both are normally found in small numbers far offshore but gather in large numbers in Monterey Bay, California, Aug–Oct.

Ashy Storm-Petrel

Oceanodroma homochroa

L 8" WS 18" WT 1.3 oz (37 g)

Smaller than Black, but relatively longer-tailed; paler and grayer overall than Black.

Adult

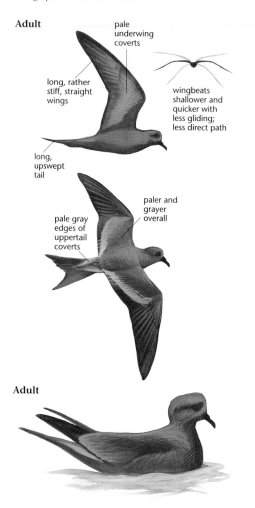

pale underwing coverts

long, rather stiff, straight wings

wingbeats shallower and quicker with less gliding; less direct path

long, upswept tail

paler and grayer overall

pale gray edges of uppertail coverts

Adult

Voice: Generally silent at sea. At nest site a purring like Leach's, rising and falling with inhaled gasp. In flight over colony a harsh, squeaky chuckling.

Black Storm-Petrel

Oceanodroma melania

L 9" WS 22" WT 2.1 oz (59 g)

Our largest storm-petrel. Large and lanky with long wings and tail.

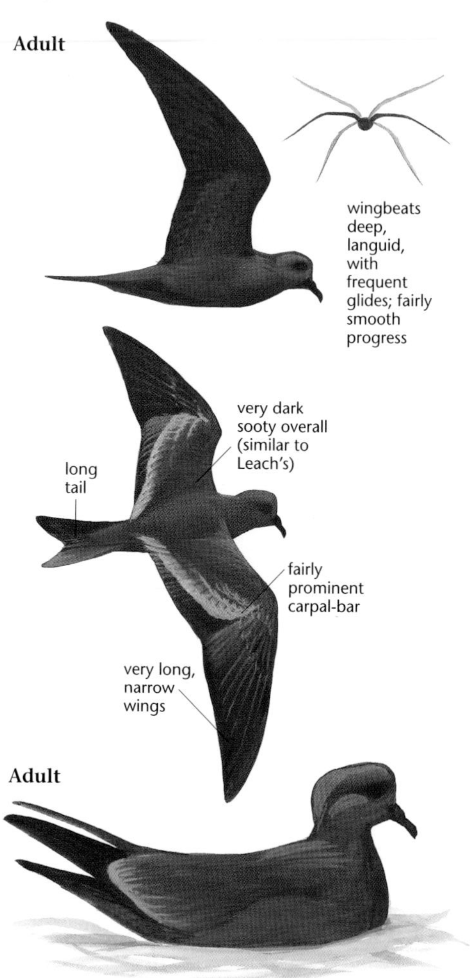

Adult
wingbeats deep, languid, with frequent glides; fairly smooth progress
very dark sooty overall (similar to Leach's)
long tail
fairly prominent carpal-bar
very long, narrow wings
Adult

Voice: Generally silent at sea. At nest site a purring or rattling 10 to 12 seconds long. In flight over colony a loud, screechy chattering *pukaree puck-puckaroo.*

Four species of all-dark storm-petrels occur off California: Ashy, Black, Least, and some Leach's. Identification requires experience, but differences in tail length, wingbeats, and overall color should allow quick separation of even distant birds.

Least and Fork-tailed Storm-Petrels

The tiny and all-dark Least Storm-Petrel disperses irregularly north to warm offshore waters mainly Aug–Oct. The distinctively colored Fork-tailed is found over cold water.

Least Storm-Petrel

Oceanodroma microsoma

L 5.75" WS 15" WT 0.74 oz (21 g)

Our smallest storm-petrel. Tiny with very short, wedge-shaped tail and long, thin wings.

Adult

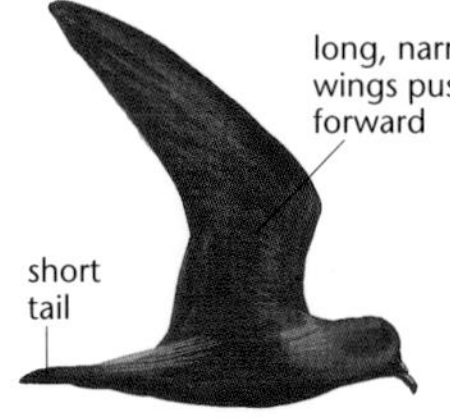
long, narrow
wings pushed
forward
wingbeats deep
like Black but
quicker, snappier
(with less gliding);
flight erratic,
batlike
short
tail

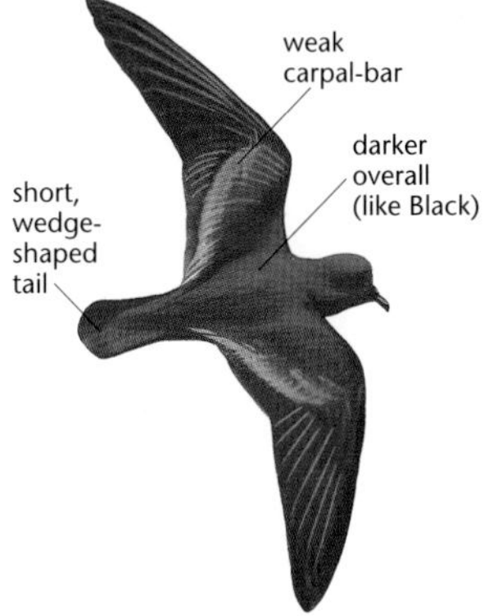
weak
carpal-bar
darker
overall
(like Black)
short,
wedge-
shaped
tail

Adult

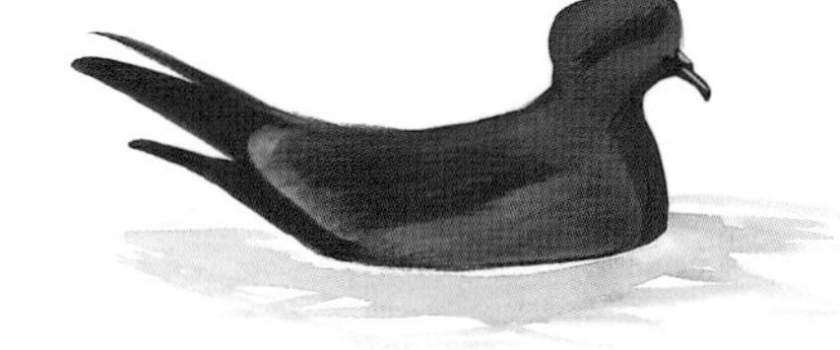

Voice: Generally silent at sea. At nest site a soft, rapid purring call, three to four seconds long with occasional inhaled notes. In flight over colony a harsh, accelerating chatter like Black but weaker.

Fork-tailed Storm-Petrel

Oceanodroma furcata

L 8.5" WS 19" WT 1.9 oz (54 g)

Rather stocky and broad-winged with distinctive gray plumage (compare Red Phalarope).

Adult

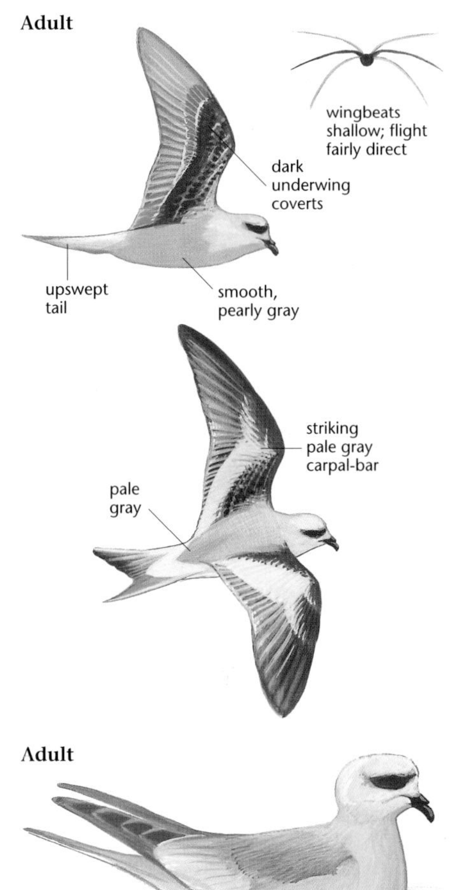
wingbeats
shallow; flight
fairly direct
dark
underwing
coverts
upswept
tail
smooth,
pearly gray
striking
pale gray
carpal-bar
pale
gray
Adult

Voice: Generally silent at sea. At nest site a soft twittering or high, complaining, rasping notes *skveeeee skwe skwe*.

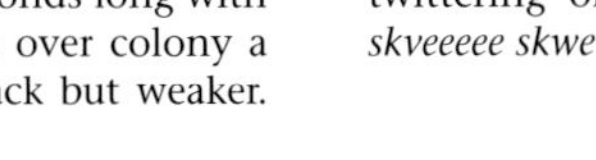

Beware that albinism and leucism (pale but not white plumage) are occasionally shown by storm-petrels, and these aberrant birds are easily confused with the paler species (Fork-tailed and White-faced).

PELECANIFORMES

Families: Anhingidae, Fregatidae, Pelecanidae, Phaethontidae, Phalacrocoracidae, Sulidae

17 species in 7 genera (including cormorants and Anhinga, shown on page 50); pelicans in family Pelecanidae, Magnificent Frigatebird in Fregatidae, tropicbirds in Phaethontidae, Northern Gannet and boobies in Sulidae, cormorants in Phalacrocoracidae, Anhinga in Anhingidae. All are fish-eating waterbirds with four toes joined by webbing, but beyond that there are few similarities. Juveniles are shown.

Genus *Pelecanus*

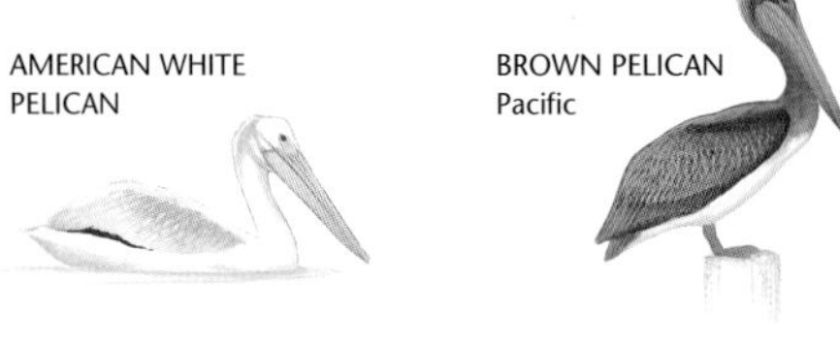
AMERICAN WHITE PELICAN
BROWN PELICAN
Pacific

Genus *Fregata*

MAGNIFICENT FRIGATEBIRD

Genus *Phaethon*

RED-BILLED TROPICBIRD
WHITE-TAILED TROPICBIRD

Genus *Sula*

Genus *Morus*

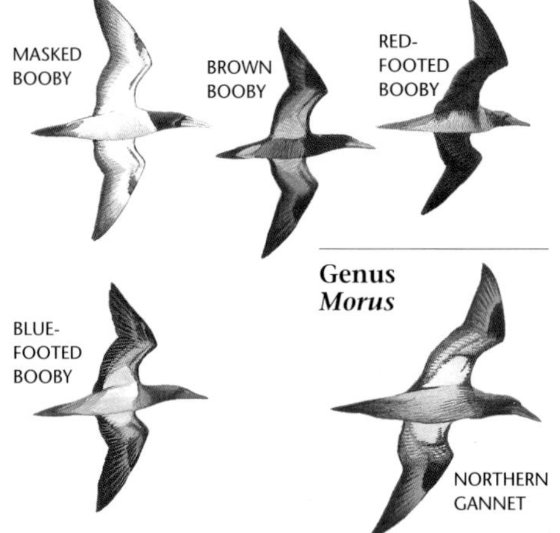
MASKED BOOBY
BROWN BOOBY
RED-FOOTED BOOBY
BLUE-FOOTED BOOBY
NORTHERN GANNET

American White Pelican

Pelecanus erythrorhynchos

L 62" WS 108" WT 16.4 lb (7,500 g) ♂>♀

Immense, always white with black flight feathers and pinkish or yellow-orange bill.

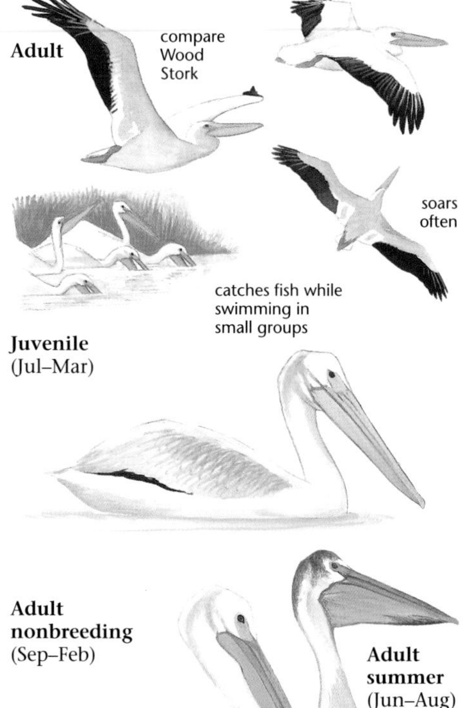
Adult
compare
Wood
Stork
soars
often
catches fish while
swimming in
small groups

Juvenile
(Jul–Mar)

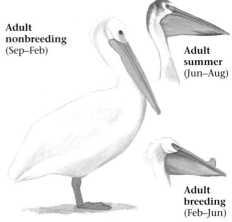

Adult nonbreeding
(Sep–Feb)

Adult summer
(Jun–Aug)

Adult breeding
(Feb–Jun)

Voice: Generally silent away from breeding grounds. At nest utters quiet, low grunting or croaking sounds. Young give whining grunt or weak, sneezy bark.

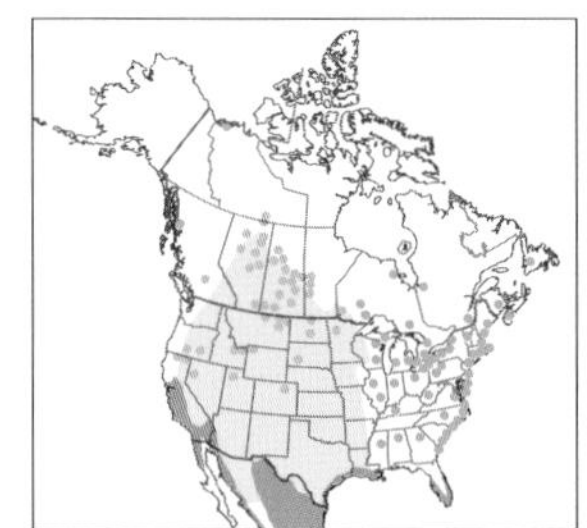

BROWN PELICAN

Large and well known, pelicans are unmistakable. Brown Pelican is found along ocean shores and bays, White on lakes and shallow lagoons. The two species differ dramatically in foraging methods.

Brown Pelican

Pelecanus occidentalis

L 51" WS 79" WT 8.2 lb (3,740 g) ♂>♀

Smaller and more slender than White Pelican and more agile in flight, but still a very large and ponderous bird with trademark pelican bill.

Juvenile

2nd year

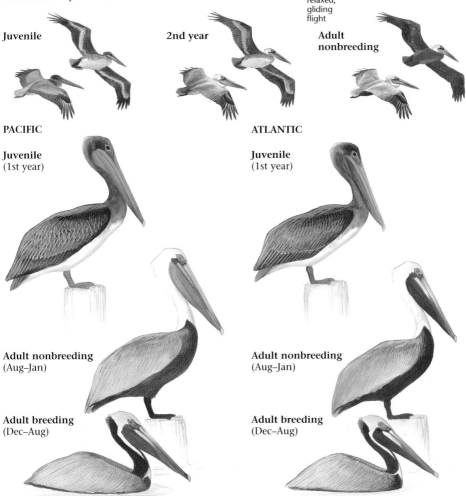

relaxed, gliding flight

Adult nonbreeding

PACIFIC

Juvenile
(1st year)

Adult nonbreeding
(Aug–Jan)

Adult breeding
(Dec–Aug)

ATLANTIC

Juvenile
(1st year)

Adult nonbreeding
(Aug–Jan)

Adult breeding
(Dec–Aug)

Voice: Generally silent after fledging. Young in nest give groaning or screeching calls.

Atlantic birds average smaller than Pacific, with darker gray or brown pouch (olive to red on Pacific), and breeding adults have slightly paler brown hindneck. Reliability of these characteristics is unknown. Interior records of this species at least as far west as Colorado and Wyoming are apparently of Atlantic birds.

hunts fish with spectacular twisting plunge-dives from the air

Magnificent Frigatebird

A distinctive aerial pirate, with the longest wings relative to weight of any bird, this species endlessly soars high over the water, never landing on its surface.

Magnificent Frigatebird

Fregata magnificens

L 40" WS 90" WT 3.3 lb (1,500 g) ♀>♂

Strikingly long, pointed black wings look sharp-edged and angular.

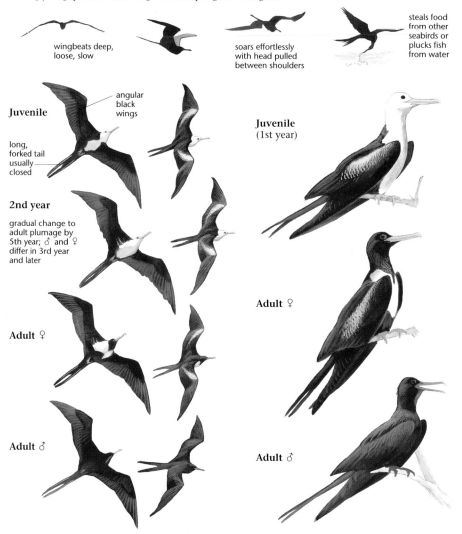

wingbeats deep, loose, slow

soars effortlessly with head pulled between shoulders

steals food from other seabirds or plucks fish from water

Juvenile

angular black wings

long, forked tail usually closed

2nd year

gradual change to adult plumage by 5th year; ♂ and ♀ differ in 3rd year and later

Adult ♀

Adult ♂

Juvenile (1st year)

Adult ♀

Adult ♂

Voice: Generally silent away from colony. Displaying male gives rapid bill-clattering and resonant, knocking sounds; female and young give high, wheezy sounds. Short, wheezy or grating calls in interactions: *wik wik wikikik,* etc.

Adult ♂ Displaying at nest site.

Tropicbirds

These two species of oceanic birds, found far offshore over warm water, are often seen resting on the water. Their flight is high and steady, and they plunge into the water to catch fish.

Red-billed Tropicbird

Phaethon aethereus

L 18" (adult to 36") WS 44" WT 1.6 lb (750 g)

Larger and larger-billed than White-tailed; black primary coverts always distinctive but can be difficult to ascertain.

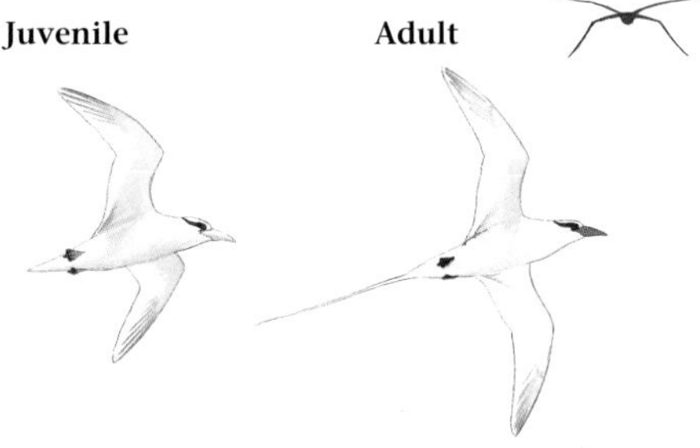

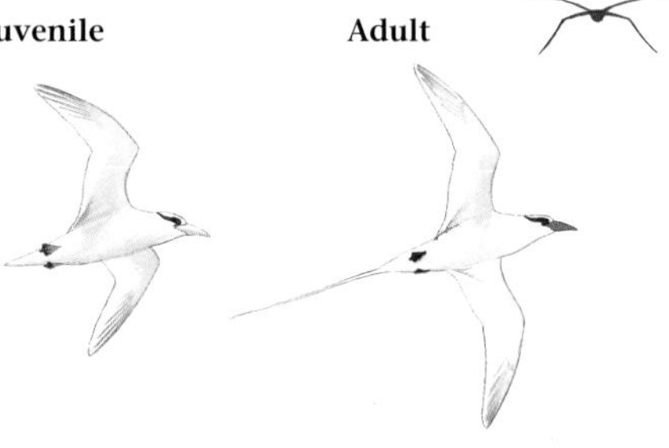
Juvenile
Adult

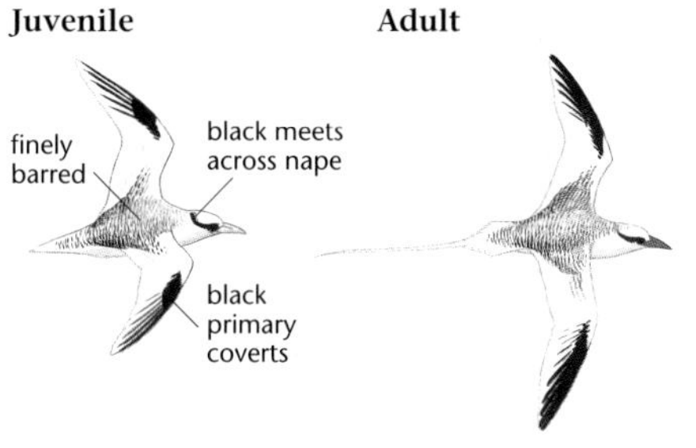
Juvenile
Adult
finely barred
black meets across nape
black primary coverts

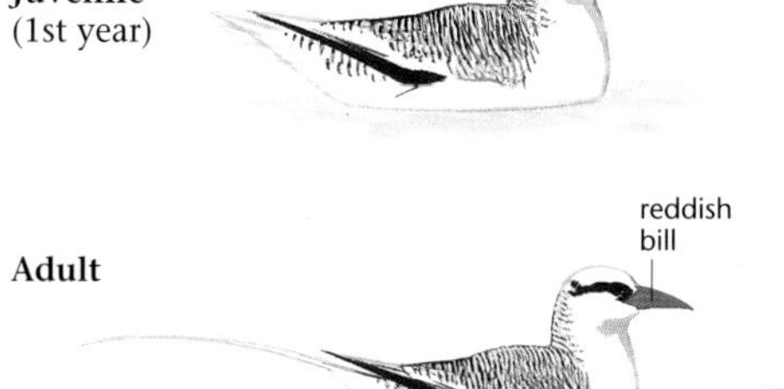
Juvenile (1st year)
Adult
reddish bill

Voice: Generally silent at sea. Sometimes gives shrill grating or rattling notes. In display, shrill, harsh screams, recalling Common Tern in quality.

White-tailed Tropicbird

Phaethon lepturus

L 15" (adult to 29") WS 37" WT 11 oz (300 g)

Smaller and more buoyant than Red-billed, with smaller bill; wingbeats quicker and more flicking. Note short, dark eye-line.

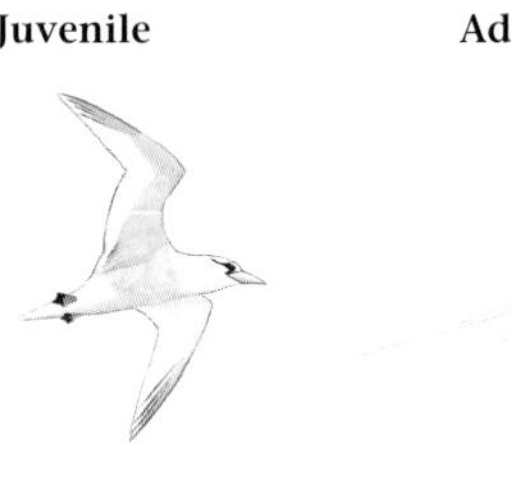
Juvenile

Adult

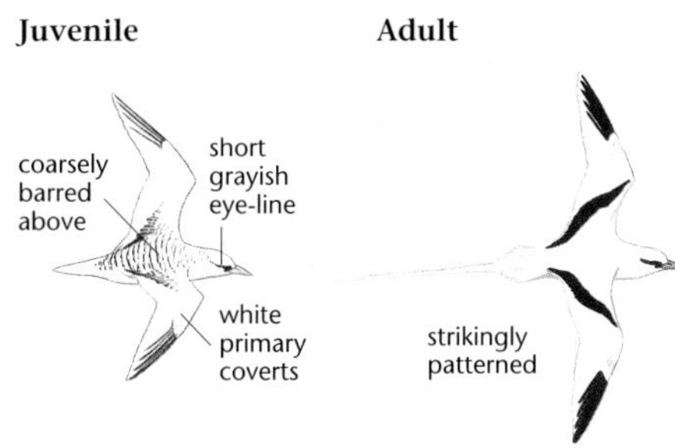
Juvenile
Adult
coarsely barred above
short grayish eye-line
white primary coverts
strikingly patterned

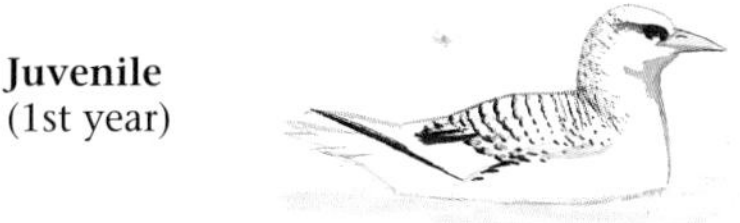
Juvenile (1st year)

Adult
yellowish bill
floats high on water with tail streamers raised

Voice: Generally silent at sea. Voice harsh, squeaky, and ternlike.

Royal Terns (and other terns) are often mistaken for tropicbirds. Tropicbirds have more direct, less buoyant flight with shallower, quicker, stiffer wingbeats, clean white secondaries, dark tertials, and front-heavy proportions. Note that Red-tailed Tropicbird (*P. rubricauda*) is a rare visitor to waters far off California.

True Cormorants

Great Cormorant is closely related to Double-crested and Neotropic but is found mainly on salt water, especially along rocky shores, and occasionally on fresh water.

Cormorants and Anhinga

Identification is usually easy given good views. Useful clues are color and pattern of throat and bill, proportions of bill, neck, and tail, and habits. True cormorants usually fly high, often over land, with slower wingbeats and necks kinked, unlike Pacific cormorants (also called shags). Anhinga is unique. Juveniles are shown.

True Cormorants **Genus *Phalacrocorax***

broad head

GREAT CORMORANT

DOUBLE-CRESTED CORMORANT

NEOTROPIC CORMORANT

Pacific Cormorants **Genus *Phalacrocorax***

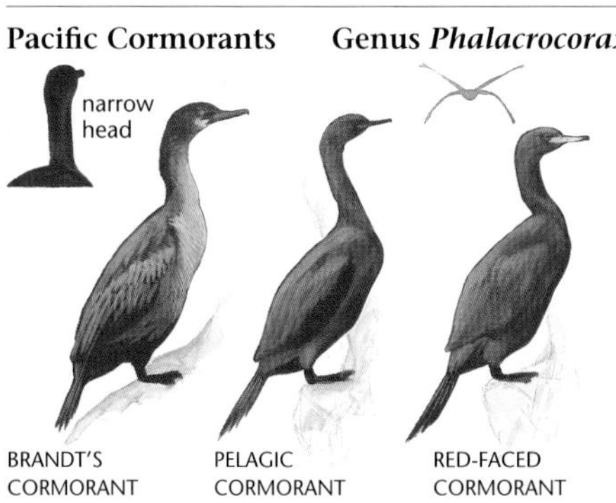
narrow head
BRANDT'S CORMORANT
PELAGIC CORMORANT
RED-FACED CORMORANT

Genus *Anhinga*

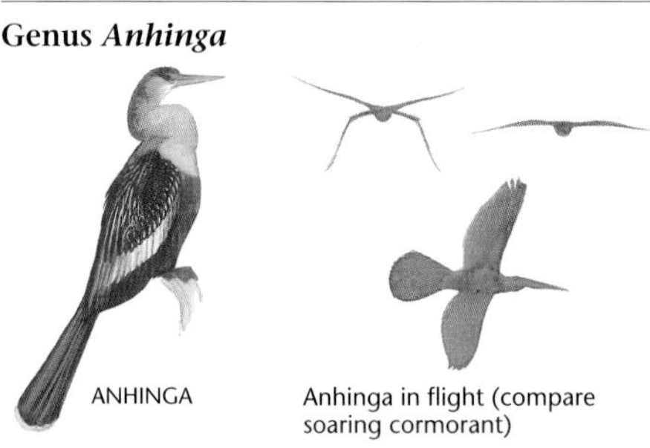
ANHINGA
Anhinga in flight (compare soaring cormorant)

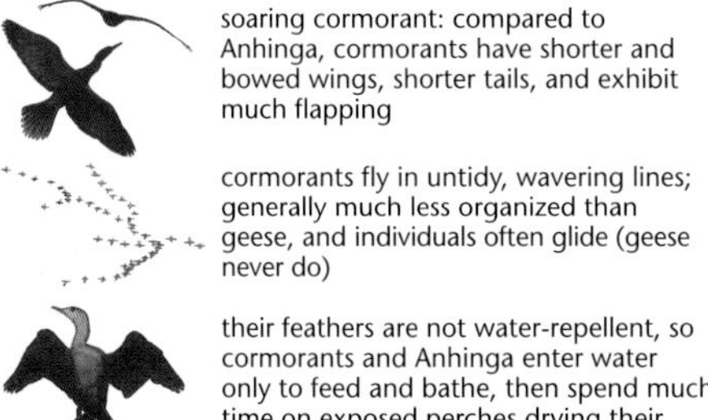
soaring cormorant: compared to Anhinga, cormorants have shorter and bowed wings, shorter tails, and exhibit much flapping
cormorants fly in untidy, wavering lines; generally much less organized than geese, and individuals often glide (geese never do)
their feathers are not water-repellent, so cormorants and Anhinga enter water only to feed and bathe, then spend much time on exposed perches drying their plumage with wings spread

Great Cormorant

Phalacrocorax carbo

L 36" WS 63" WT 7.2 lb (3,300 g)

Our largest cormorant. Best distinguished from Double-crested by plumage marks, although larger size and heavier bill are often evident.

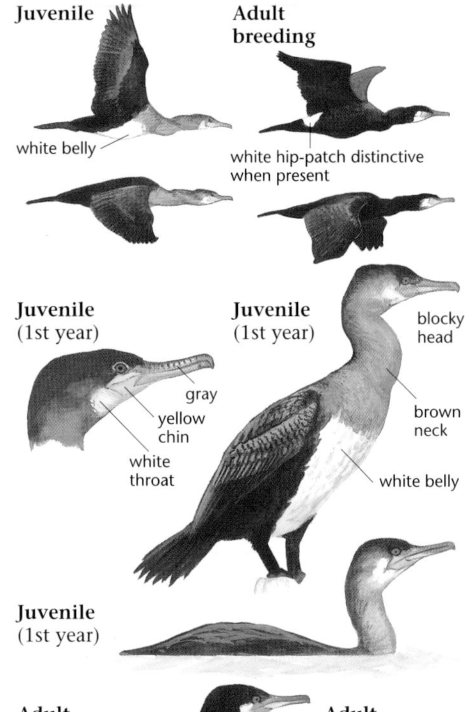
Juvenile
Adult breeding
white belly
white hip-patch distinctive when present
Juvenile (1st year)
Juvenile (1st year)
gray
yellow chin
white throat
blocky head
brown neck
white belly
Juvenile (1st year)

Adult nonbreeding (Jun–Jan)

Adult breeding (Jan–May)

white throat

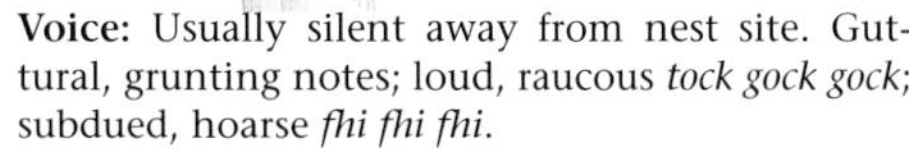

Voice: Usually silent away from nest site. Guttural, grunting notes; loud, raucous *tock gock gock;* subdued, hoarse *fhi fhi fhi.*

These two species are found on any open water from ponds to ocean, often in flocks. No other cormorants are commonly found on fresh water. Flocks fly high and form lines or V shapes like geese.

Double-crested Cormorant

Phalacrocorax auritus

L 33" WS 52" WT 3.7 lb (1,700 g) ♂>♀

Larger and shorter-tailed than Neotropic; distinguished from Brandt's by orange chin, longer tail, and more buoyant flight, usually higher and often over land. Flies with neck kinked.

Juvenile
Adult
variation in color of juveniles
Juvenile (1st year)
orange lores
orange
rounded border of bare skin
Juvenile (1st year)
usually pale breast
dark belly

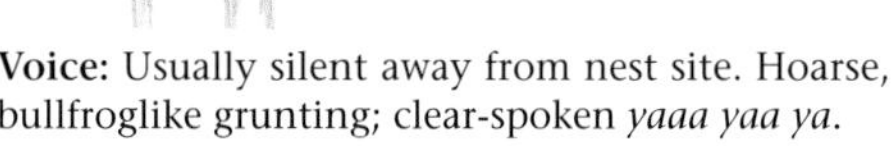
Juvenile (1st year)

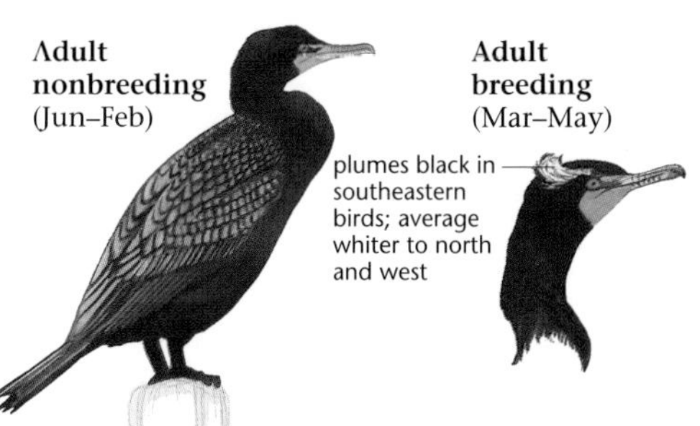
Adult nonbreeding (Jun–Feb)
Adult breeding (Mar–May)
plumes black in southeastern birds; average whiter to north and west

Voice: Usually silent away from nest site. Hoarse, bullfroglike grunting; clear-spoken *yaaa yaa ya.*

Neotropic Cormorant

Phalacrocorax brasilianus

L 25" WS 40" WT 2.6 lb (1,200 g) ♂>♀

Smaller and thinner than Double-crested with relatively longer tail, shorter wings, shorter bill. In flight neck about as long as tail (noticeably longer than other cormorants' tails).

Juvenile
Adult
long tail (as long as neck)
small head, short bill
Juvenile (1st year)
Juvenile (1st year)
dark lores
gray
pointed border
long tail
usually dark brown breast
Juvenile (1st year)

Adult nonbreeding (Jun–Mar)
Adult breeding (Apr–May)
white V

Voice: Usually silent away from nest site. Low, short, froglike grunts and baritone croaking.

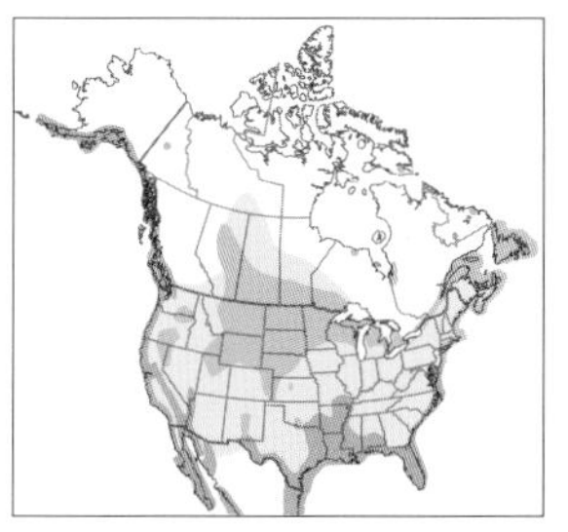

Juvenile plumage is variable in cormorants. Great Cormorant is distinctive with clean white belly (although some juveniles reportedly have all-black plumage). Double-crested varies from nearly white-breasted (especially when worn in spring) to dark brownish-black. Neotropic averages darker but varies from blackish to pale brown.

Pacific Cormorants (Shags)

These two species are found exclusively along rocky ocean shores. They roost and nest on narrow cliff ledges and forage close to rocks. Both are usually solitary or in very small groups.

Red-faced Cormorant

Phalacrocorax urile

L 29" WS 46" WT 4.6 lb (2,100 g)

Stockier than Pelagic; usually thicker-billed but some overlap; averages thicker- and shorter-necked.

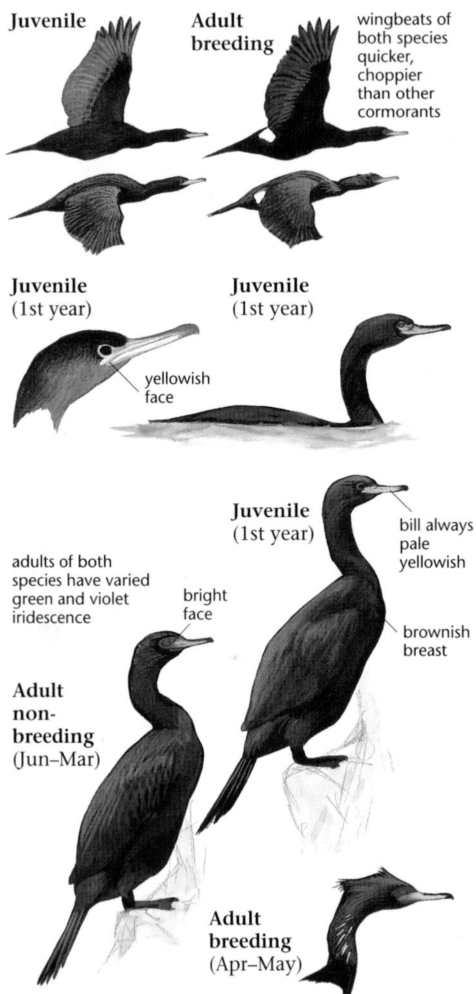

Juvenile
Adult breeding
wingbeats of both species quicker, choppier than other cormorants
Juvenile (1st year)
yellowish face
Juvenile (1st year)
Juvenile (1st year)
bill always pale yellowish
brownish breast
adults of both species have varied green and violet iridescence
bright face
Adult non-breeding (Jun–Mar)
Adult breeding (Apr–May)

Voice: Usually silent away from nest site. Low, droning, guttural croak.

Pelagic Cormorant

Phalacrocorax pelagicus

L 28" WS 39" WT 3.9 lb (1,800 g) N > S

Our smallest and thinnest cormorant with long, incredibly slender "broomstick" neck and very thin bill.

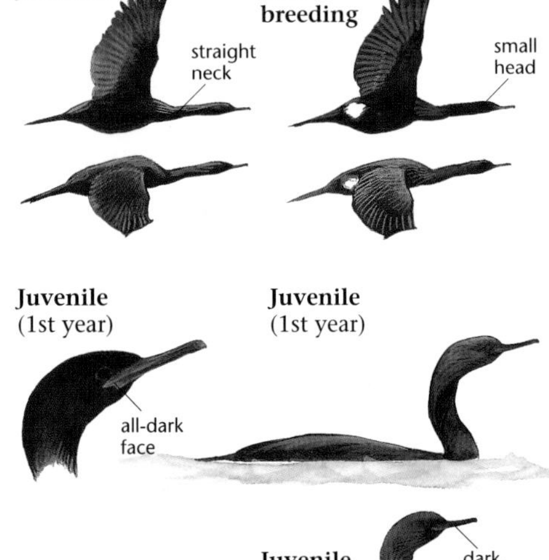

Juvenile
straight neck
Adult breeding
small head
Juvenile (1st year)
all-dark face
Juvenile (1st year)

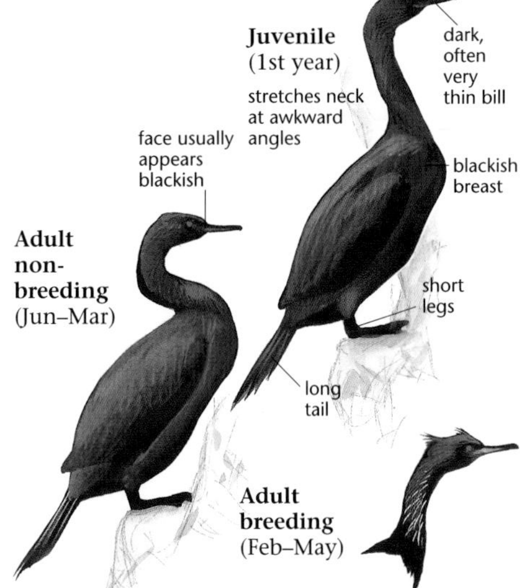

Juvenile (1st year)
stretches neck at awkward angles
dark, often very thin bill
face usually appears blackish
blackish breast
Adult non-breeding (Jun–Mar)
short legs
long tail
Adult breeding (Feb–May)

Voice: Usually silent away from nest site. Varied low grunts, painful groaning, also hissing.

Pelagic Cormorant showing variation in bill size: Bering Sea population averages larger with thicker bill, but large individuals occur throughout range.

The gregarious, marine Brandt's Cormorant roosts and nests in large groups on rocks and forages on open ocean. Anhinga, found in swamps and wooded ponds, differs fundamentally from cormorants.

Brandt's Cormorant

Phalacrocorax penicillatus

L 34" WS 48" WT 4.6 lb (2,100 g)

Larger than Pelagic with relatively short tail, round head, more graceful neck, and more upright stance. Also more gregarious, often feeding and flying in flocks.

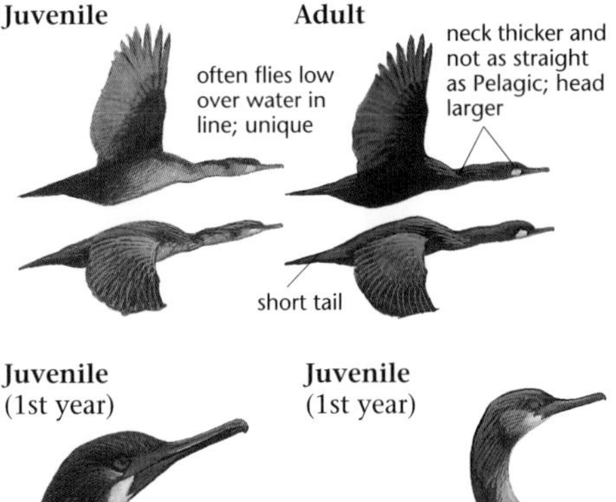
Juvenile
Adult
often flies low over water in line; unique
neck thicker and not as straight as Pelagic; head larger
short tail

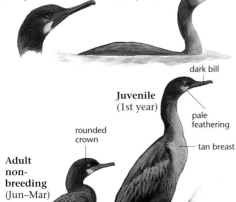

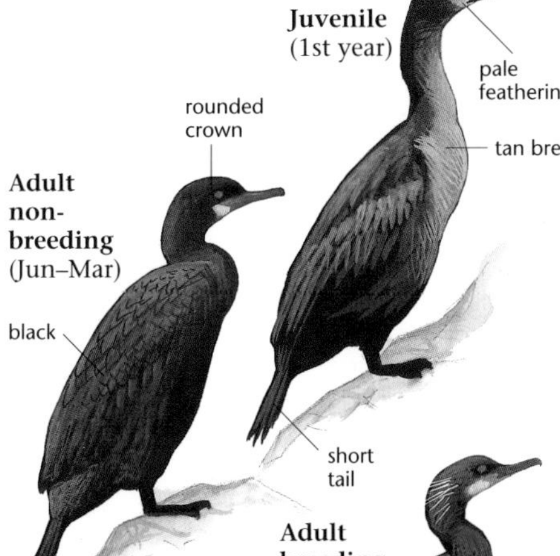
Juvenile (1st year)
Juvenile (1st year)
dark bill
Juvenile (1st year)
pale feathering
rounded crown
tan breast
Adult non-breeding (Jun–Mar)
black
short tail

Adult breeding (Apr–Jun)

Voice: Usually silent away from nest site. Hoarse guttural croak or growl given in aggression.

Anhinga

Anhinga anhinga

L 35" WS 45" WT 2.7 lb (1,250 g)

Unique, with heronlike neck and bill; long, fan-shaped tail; and long, pointed wings. Swims with only head exposed.

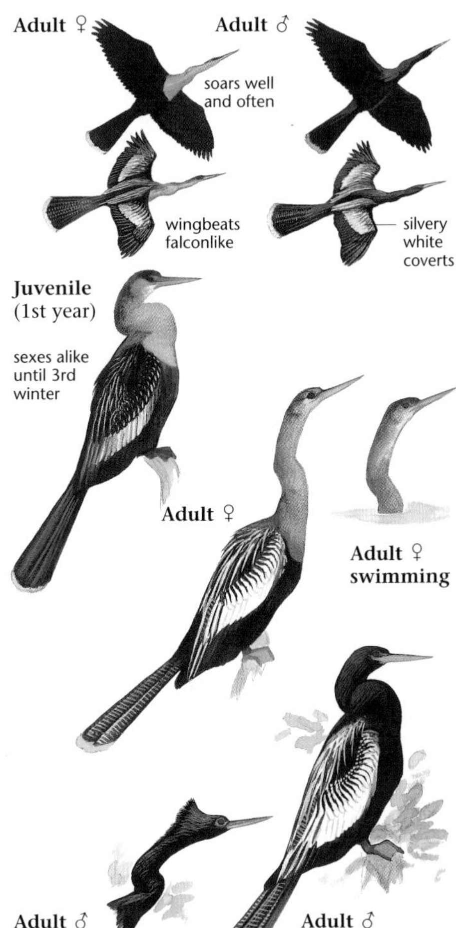
Adult ♀
Adult ♂
soars well and often
wingbeats falconlike
silvery white coverts
Juvenile (1st year)
sexes alike until 3rd winter
Adult ♀
Adult ♀ swimming
Adult ♂ breeding (Feb–Jun)
Adult ♂ nonbreeding

Voice: Quite vocal when perched. A descending series of mechanical croaks, almost clicking: *krr kr krr kr kr krrrr krr;* also low, nasal, froglike grunts.

Northern Gannet

This species is found over open ocean often close to shore and in loose groups. Like boobies, it often rests on water but unlike them virtually never rests on land away from nest site.

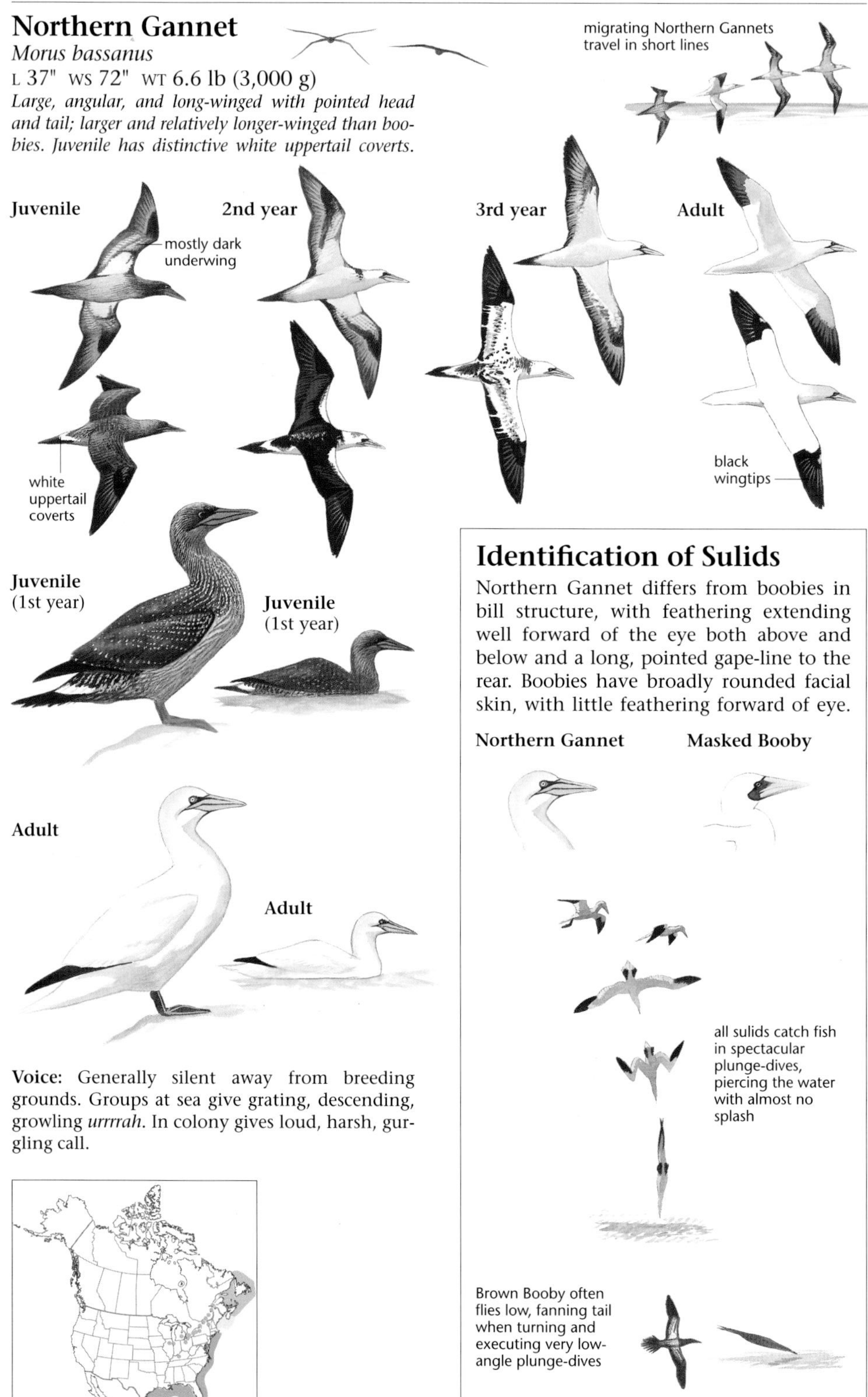

migrating Northern Gannets travel in short lines
Juvenile
2nd year
3rd year
Adult
mostly dark underwing
white uppertail coverts
black wingtips
Juvenile (1st year)
Juvenile (1st year)
Adult
Adult
Northern Gannet
Masked Booby
all sulids catch fish in spectacular plunge-dives, piercing the water with almost no splash
Brown Booby often flies low, fanning tail when turning and executing very low-angle plunge-dives

Northern Gannet

Morus bassanus

L 37" WS 72" WT 6.6 lb (3,000 g)

Large, angular, and long-winged with pointed head and tail; larger and relatively longer-winged than boobies. Juvenile has distinctive white uppertail coverts.

Voice: Generally silent away from breeding grounds. Groups at sea give grating, descending, growling *urrrrah.* In colony gives loud, harsh, gurgling call.

Identification of Sulids

Northern Gannet differs from boobies in bill structure, with feathering extending well forward of the eye both above and below and a long, pointed gape-line to the rear. Boobies have broadly rounded facial skin, with little feathering forward of eye.

Boobies

These two warm-water species are usually found far offshore. Brown Booby often perches on trees or navigational towers; Masked Booby usually perches on the ground.

Masked Booby

Sula dactylatra

L 32" WS 62" WT 3.3 lb (1,550 g) ♀>♂

Slightly smaller than Northern Gannet; larger and relatively shorter-tailed than other boobies. All-dark remiges and greater coverts with mostly white underwing distinctive in all plumages.

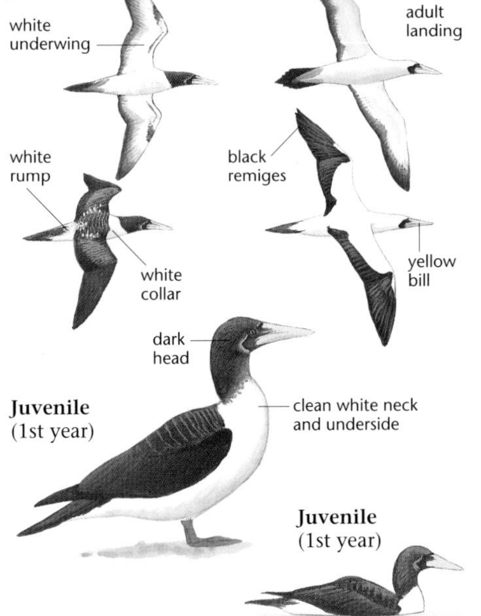

Juvenile
white underwing
Adult
adult landing
white rump
black remiges
white collar
yellow bill
dark head
Juvenile (1st year)
clean white neck and underside

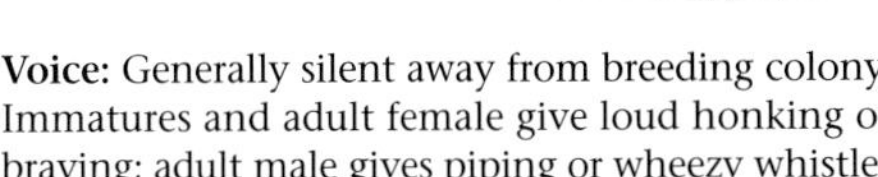

Juvenile (1st year)
Adult
black coverts
Adult

Voice: Generally silent away from breeding colony. Immatures and adult female give loud honking or braying; adult male gives piping or wheezy whistle.

Brown Booby

Sula leucogaster

L 30" WS 57" WT 2.4 lb (1,100 g) ♀>♂

Smaller than Northern Gannet and Masked Booby, with relatively short wings and long tail; size and shape differences surprisingly difficult to judge.

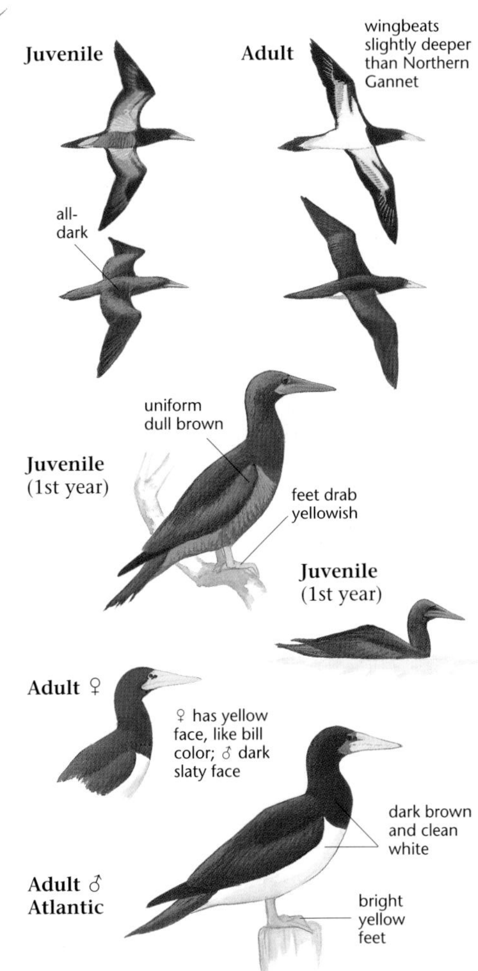

Juvenile
Adult
wingbeats slightly deeper than Northern Gannet
all-dark
uniform dull brown
Juvenile (1st year)
feet drab yellowish
Juvenile (1st year)
Adult ♀
♀ has yellow face, like bill color; ♂ dark slaty face
dark brown and clean white
Adult ♂ Atlantic
bright yellow feet

Voice: Generally silent away from breeding colony. Immatures and adult female give strident honking and grunting; male gives quieter, high, whistled *schweee;* in aggression a nasal croaking *gaan gaan.*

Pacific Brown Booby adult ♂

Adult males of eastern Pacific population have very pale, frosty gray head.

Boobies (continued)

These species are normally found on warm offshore waters, although many records of Blue-footed come from interior lakes. Red-footed usually perches in trees, Blue-footed on rocks.

Blue-footed Booby

Sula nebouxii

L 32" WS 62" WT 3.4 lb (1,550 g) ♀>♂

Shape like Brown Booby but slightly larger and lankier; note underwing pattern, pale tail, gray bill.

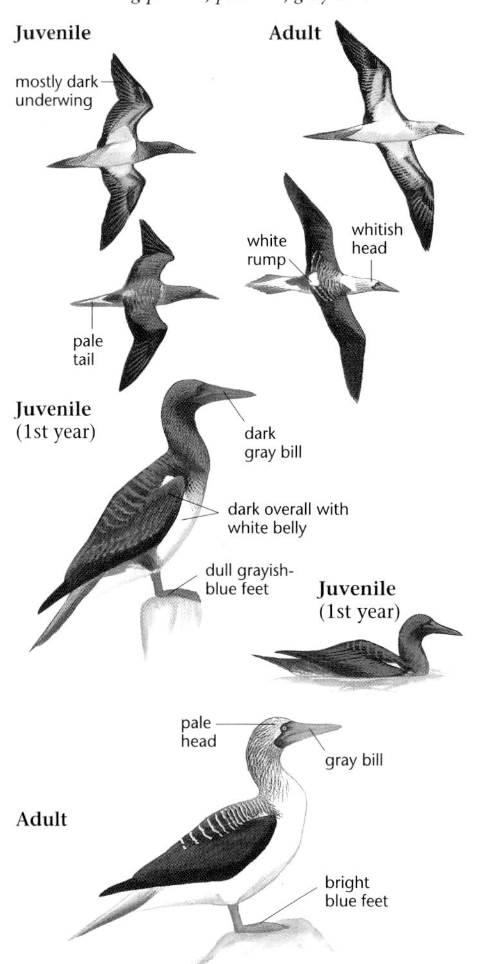
Juvenile
Adult
mostly dark underwing
white rump
whitish head
pale tail
Juvenile (1st year)
dark gray bill
dark overall with white belly
dull grayish-blue feet
Juvenile (1st year)
pale head
gray bill
Adult
bright blue feet

Voice: Generally silent away from breeding colony. Juvenile and adult female give resonant trumpeting or honking; adult male gives weak, plaintive whistles; both calls slightly deeper than Brown Booby.

Red-footed Booby

Sula sula

L 28" WS 60" WT 2.2 lb (1,000 g) ♀>♂

Our smallest booby, relatively short-necked and long-tailed with slender bill, rounded head.

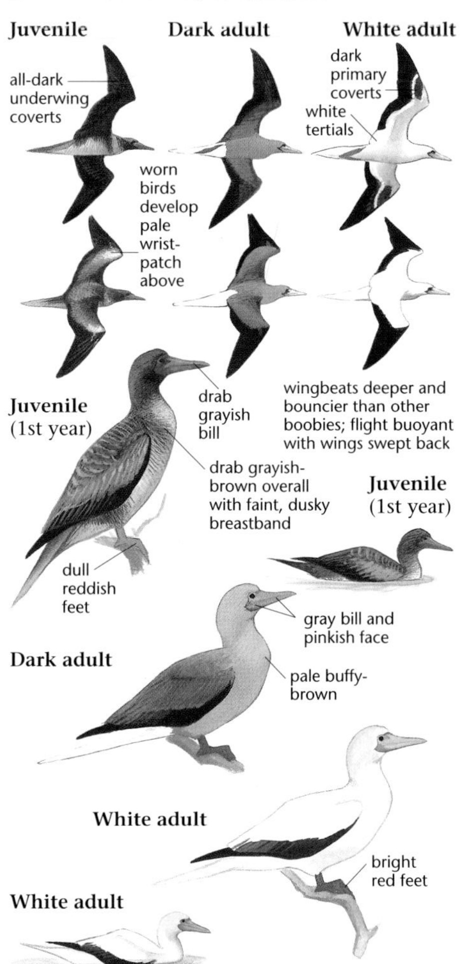
Juvenile
Dark adult
White adult
all-dark underwing coverts
dark primary coverts
white tertials
worn birds develop pale wrist-patch above
Juvenile (1st year)
drab grayish bill
wingbeats deeper and bouncier than other boobies; flight buoyant with wings swept back
drab grayish-brown overall with faint, dusky breastband
Juvenile (1st year)
dull reddish feet
gray bill and pinkish face
Dark adult
pale buffy-brown
White adult
bright red feet
White adult

Voice: Generally silent away from breeding colony. Both sexes give guttural screeching or rattling squawks.

Adult Red-footed Boobies are polymorphic (but all juveniles are dark). Caribbean birds are illustrated; eastern Pacific adults are all dark-tailed with white or dark body.

Wading Birds

Families: Ardeidae, Ciconiidae, Phoenicopteridae, Threskiornithidae

20 species in 13 genera; bitterns, herons, and egrets in family Ardeidae, ibises and Roseate Spoonbill in Threskiornithidae, Wood Stork in Ciconiidae, Greater Flamingo in Phoenicopteridae. All are long-legged waders. Bitterns, herons, and egrets have long necks and long, pointed bills used to spear fish or other prey. Ibises have curved bills used to probe in mud. Roseate Spoonbill, Wood Stork, and Greater Flamingo have specialized bill shapes and correspondingly specialized foraging methods. Compare cranes. Adults are shown.

Genus *Egretta*
REDDISH EGRET White
LITTLE EGRET
SNOWY EGRET
TRICOLORED HERON
LITTLE BLUE HERON
Genus *Ardea*
GREAT BLUE HERON
GREAT EGRET
Genus *Botaurus*
AMERICAN BITTERN
Genus *Ixobrychus*
LEAST BITTERN
Genus *Bubulcus*
CATTLE EGRET
Genus *Butorides*
GREEN HERON
Genus *Mycteria*
WOOD STORK
Genus *Nycticorax*
BLACK-CROWNED NIGHT-HERON
Genus *Nyctanassa*
YELLOW-CROWNED NIGHT-HERON
Genus *Plegadis*
WHITE-FACED IBIS
GLOSSY IBIS
Genus *Phoenicopterus*
GREATER FLAMINGO American
Genus *Eudocimus*
WHITE IBIS
Genus *Ajaia*
ROSEATE SPOONBILL

Bitterns

These secretive, cryptically colored marsh birds are unique among herons in being more easily heard than seen. They move slowly through dense marsh grass (compare night-herons and Green Heron).

American Bittern

Botaurus lentiginosus

L 28" WS 42" WT 1.5 lb (700 g)

Large and heavy-bodied with relatively long neck tapering to pointed bill. Distinguished from night-herons by longer bill, tapered neck, habits, and plumage.

Adult

flight usually low and direct

hunchbacked, long-headed

dark flight feathers contrast with pale coverts

relatively pointed wings (compare night-herons)

Juvenile (Jul–Sep)

dark malar

smudgy brown

bold stripes

Adult

agonizingly slow gait

Voice: Song a deep, gulping, pounding *BLOONK-Adoonk* repeated. When flushed a rapid, throaty *kok kok kok*. In flight a loud, hoarse, nasal *squark* intermediate between night-herons and Mallard.

Least Bittern

Ixobrychus exilis

L 13" WS 17" WT 2.8 oz (80 g)

Our smallest heron; relatively long-necked but usually seen crouched in reeds. Distinctive bright, buffy color.

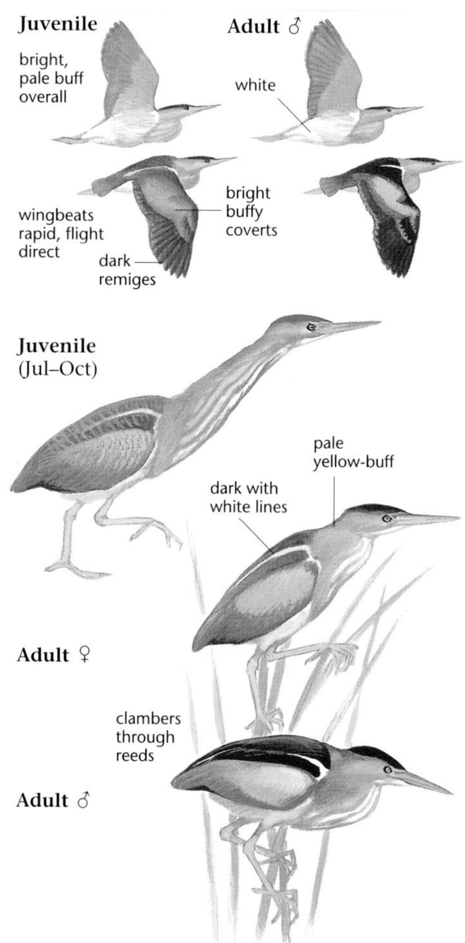
Juvenile
bright, pale buff overall
Adult ♂
white
wingbeats rapid, flight direct
bright buffy coverts
dark remiges
Juvenile (Jul–Oct)
pale yellow-buff
dark with white lines
Adult ♀
clambers through reeds
Adult ♂

Voice: Song a low, cooing *poopoopoo* descending, like Black-billed Cuckoo but lower-pitched with wooden, not whistled, quality. Common call (year-round) loud, harsh, quacking, rail-like *rick-rick-rick-rick*. In flight short, flat *kuk* or *gik*.

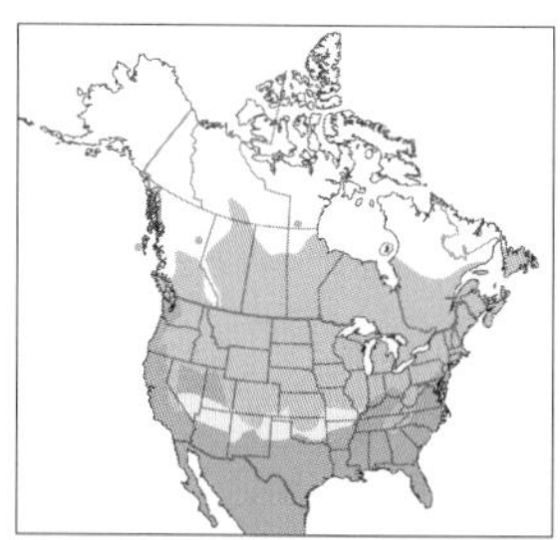

Least Bittern dark morph (Cory's Least Bittern) adult ♂
Rare, unrecorded since 1928.

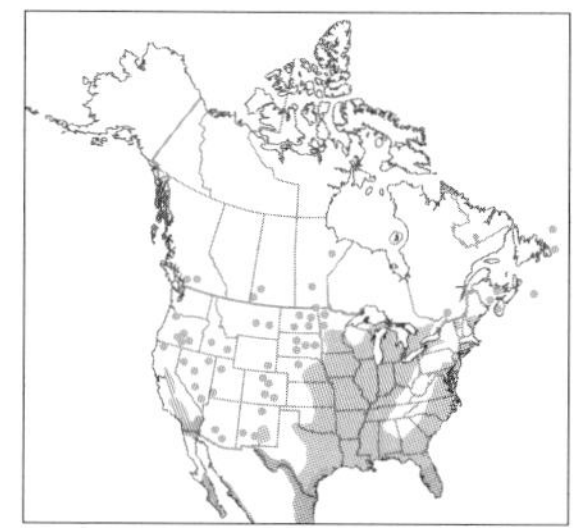

Little Egret

This rare but perhaps increasing visitor is the Eurasian counterpart of Snowy Egret. It forages in shallow water, often with Snowy; the two species are always difficult to distinguish.

Identification of White Herons

The seven species of white herons (Little Egret, Great Blue Heron, Great Egret, Snowy Egret, Reddish Egret, Little Blue Heron, and Cattle Egret) can be confusing to identify, and some individuals can be extremely difficult to separate even with close views. This is particularly true of recently fledged (Jul–Oct) Snowy Egret, Little Blue Heron, and Little Egret juveniles.

Aging can be an important first step in identification. Characteristics of very young juveniles include: fluffy down retained on rounded head, short bill, clumsy actions, and uniformly fresh feathers lacking all plumes. At close range a pattern of neatly arranged, short, rounded feathers may be seen on the neck and scapulars. Adults in fall show signs of molt and often show old, worn, and stained plumes.

Foraging postures and actions provide one of the best clues for identification of white herons. Great Blue Heron and Great Egret are stately and slow-moving. Snowy Egret may be active or crouch quietly but generally holds its neck tightly coiled before striking. Little Blue Heron, in contrast, walks slowly with neck outstretched and bill pointed down, striking downward somewhat awkwardly. Reddish Egret is very active and animated, dancing and spinning as it chases fish. Cattle Egret forages in upland fields, walking slowly with exaggerated strutting actions. Note, however, that any species may alter its habits somewhat to take advantage of abundant food.

Some juvenile Snowy Egrets have dark grayish lores at fledging (Jul–Sep), changing within days or weeks to dull greenish. These very young birds may be indistinguishable from Little Egret; check for signs of very young age. Little Egret has, on average, a longer and less tapered bill, feathering extending farther forward on chin and forehead (longer face), and more black on legs, but none of these characteristics are definitive.

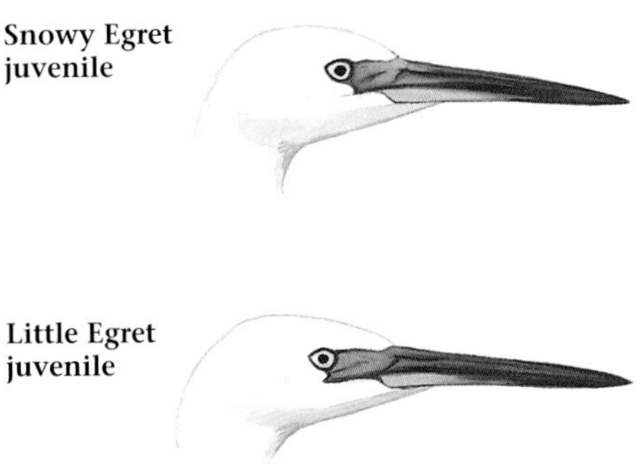

Snowy Egret juvenile
Little Egret juvenile

Little Egret

Egretta garzetta

L 25" WS 42" WT 15 oz (420 g)

Slightly more slender overall than Snowy. Note dark lores, mostly black legs, and stringy breast plumes. Certain foraging poses are more reminiscent of Great Egret than of Snowy.

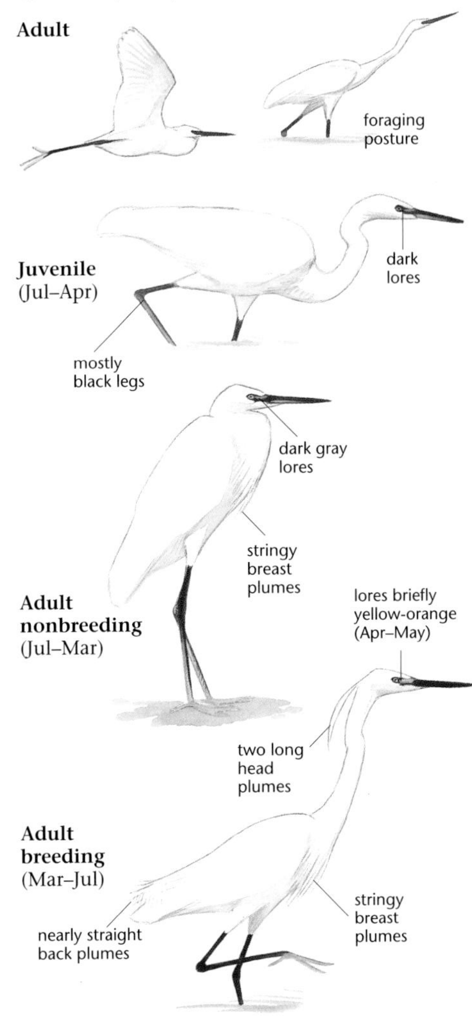

Adult
foraging posture
Juvenile (Jul–Apr)
dark lores
mostly black legs
dark gray lores
stringy breast plumes
Adult nonbreeding (Jul–Mar)
lores briefly yellow-orange (Apr–May)
two long head plumes
Adult breeding (Mar–Jul)
nearly straight back plumes
stringy breast plumes

Voice: Presumably similar to Snowy Egret.

Great Blue Heron

Our largest and heaviest heron is one of the most vocal, calling frequently in flight. Generally solitary and nocturnal, it hunts fish and other animals while wading slowly in quiet waters.

Great Blue Heron

Ardea herodias

L 46" WS 72" WT 5.3 lb (2,400 g) ♂>♀

Large, sturdy; heavy bill. White morph resembles Great Egret, but note greater size and bulk, overall off-white color, heavy bill with straight culmen, paler legs.

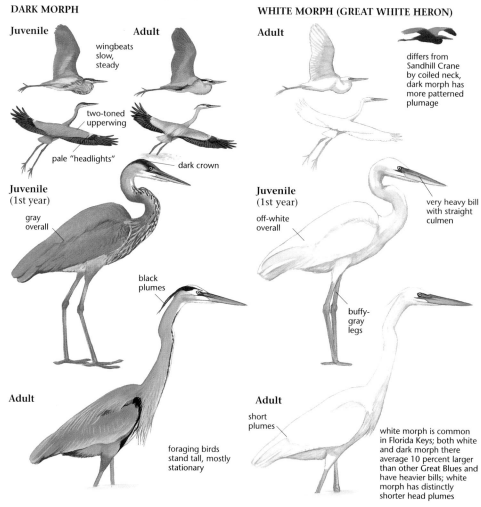

DARK MORPH

Juvenile

Adult

wingbeats slow, steady

two-toned upperwing

pale "headlights"

dark crown

Juvenile (1st year)

gray overall

black plumes

Adult

foraging birds stand tall, mostly stationary

WHITE MORPH (GREAT WHITE HERON)

Adult

differs from Sandhill Crane by coiled neck, dark morph has more patterned plumage

Juvenile (1st year)

off-white overall

very heavy bill with straight culmen

buffy-gray legs

Adult

short plumes

white morph is common in Florida Keys; both white and dark morph there average 10 percent larger than other Great Blues and have heavier bills; white morph has distinctly shorter head plumes

Voice: Voices of all forms similar. Flight call a very deep, hoarse, trumpeting *fraaahnk* or *braak*. In aggression a slow series *fraank fraank fraank taaaaw taaaaw;* last notes lower, croaking.

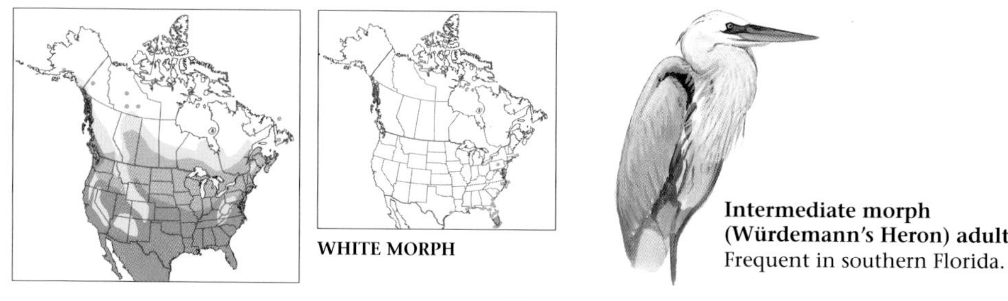
WHITE MORPH

Intermediate morph (Würdemann's Heron) adult
Frequent in southern Florida.

White Egrets

These widespread species, always white, often gather in loose flocks (especially Snowy) and feed mainly on fish captured in open water. Note their structure, bill and leg color, size, and feeding actions.

Great Egret

Ardea alba

L 39" WS 51" WT 1.9 lb (870 g) ♂>♀

Tall, extremely slender, and long-necked.

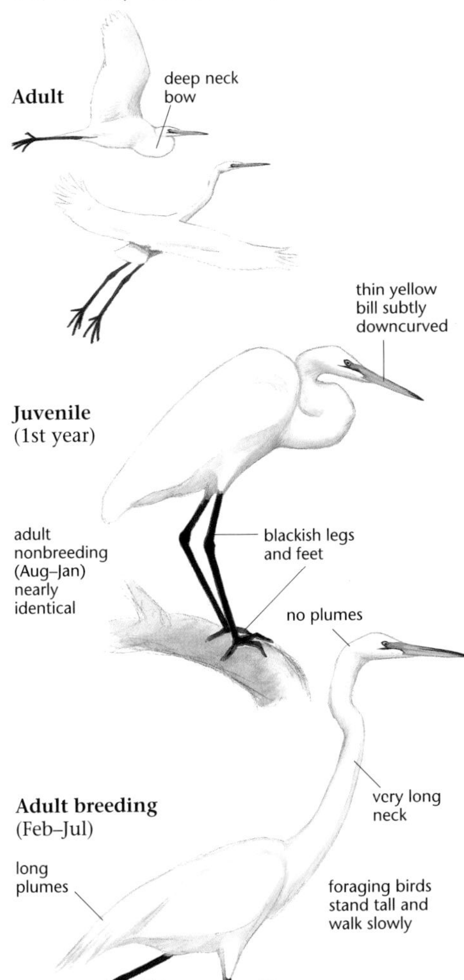

Adult
deep neck bow
thin yellow bill subtly downcurved
Juvenile (1st year)
adult nonbreeding (Aug–Jan) nearly identical
blackish legs and feet
no plumes
very long neck
Adult breeding (Feb–Jul)
long plumes
foraging birds stand tall and walk slowly

Voice: Very deep, low, gravelly *kroow,* grating unmusical *karrrr,* and other low croaks; fading at end; lower and coarser than Great Blue Heron without trumpeting quality.

Snowy Egret

Egretta thula

L 24" WS 41" WT 13 oz (360 g)

Small and slender; yellow feet contrasting with dark legs distinctive.

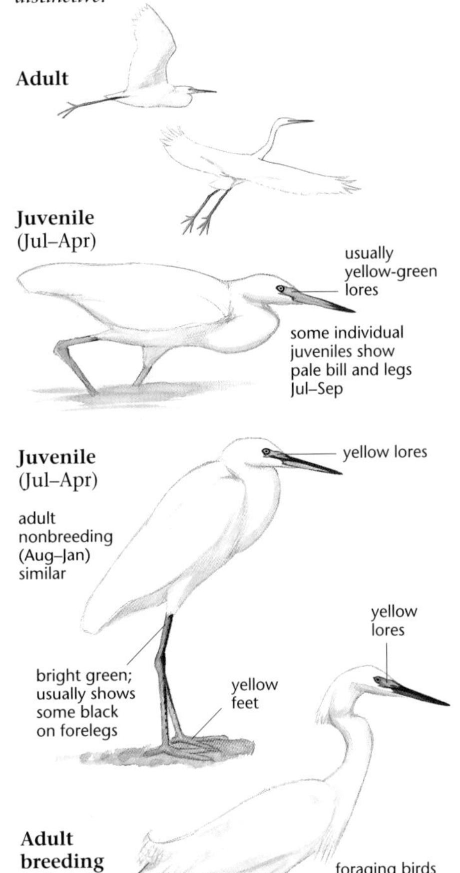

Adult
Juvenile (Jul–Apr)
usually yellow-green lores
some individual juveniles show pale bill and legs Jul–Sep
Juvenile (Jul–Apr)
yellow lores
adult nonbreeding (Aug–Jan) similar
yellow lores
bright green; usually shows some black on forelegs
yellow feet
Adult breeding (Feb–Jul)
lacy plumes
foraging birds may be stationary and crouching or active and erect

Voice: Hoarse, rasping *raarr* or nasal *hraaa* very similar to Little Blue Heron; higher and more nasal than Great Egret. In flight occasionally a hoarse cough *charf.*

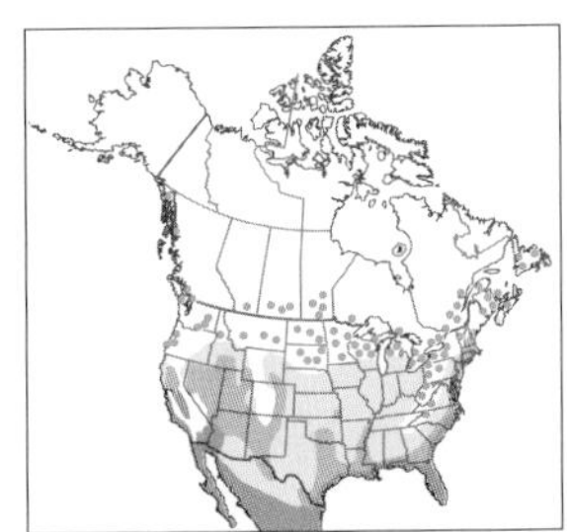

Reddish Egret

This relatively large and slender species is usually found singly in expanses of shallow salt water, where it is very active, chasing fish on foot, running, jumping, and spinning.

Reddish Egret

Egretta rufescens

L 30" WS 46" WT 1 lb (450 g)

Slender, relatively long-necked and long-legged; bill fairly heavy and straight. Note shaggy, stringy plumes, distinctive foraging actions.

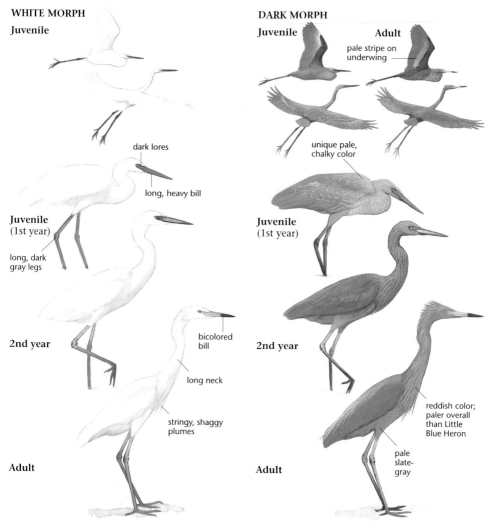

WHITE MORPH

Juvenile

dark lores

long, heavy bill

Juvenile (1st year)

long, dark gray legs

2nd year

bicolored bill

long neck

stringy, shaggy plumes

Adult

DARK MORPH

Juvenile

Adult

pale stripe on underwing

unique pale, chalky color

Juvenile (1st year)

2nd year

reddish color; paler overall than Little Blue Heron

pale slate-gray

Adult

Voice: Calls relatively infrequent, soft groan and short grunt, not rasping; similar to Tricolored Heron but lower-pitched.

Two morphs with few intermediates. In Gulf of Mexico, white morph birds represent 2 to 7 percent of the total. Pacific population is all-dark.

Distinctive animated actions of foraging Reddish Egrets.

Little Blue Heron is unique in having all-white plumage through the 1st year (very similar to Snowy Egret) and all-dark thereafter. Both species, usually solitary, catch fish in shallow water.

Tricolored Heron

Egretta tricolor

L 26" WS 36" WT 13 oz (380 g)

Extremely long-necked and long-billed; very active. Note bicolored underparts.

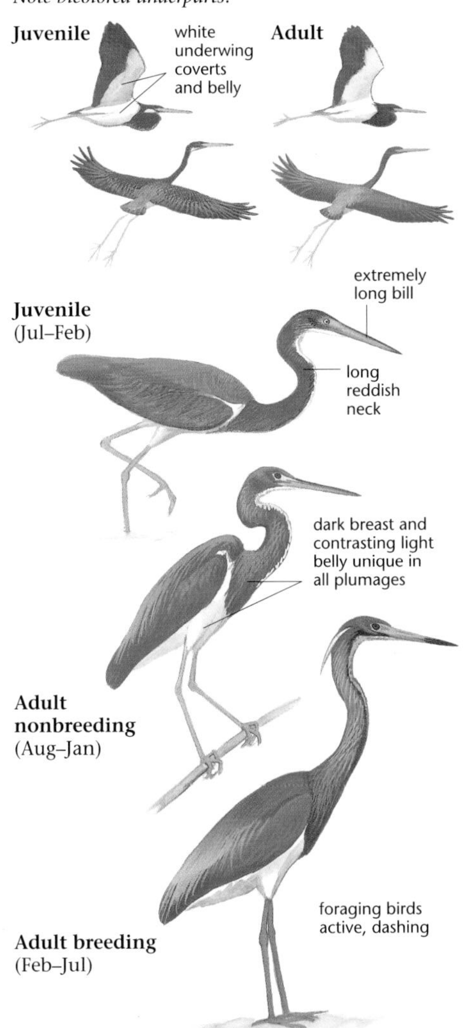
Juvenile
white underwing coverts and belly
Adult
extremely long bill
Juvenile (Jul–Feb)
long reddish neck
dark breast and contrasting light belly unique in all plumages
Adult nonbreeding (Aug–Jan)
foraging birds active, dashing
Adult breeding (Feb–Jul)

Voice: Soft, nasal moaning; usually lacking scratchy or rasping quality of most other herons and egrets. Similar to ibises.

Little Blue Heron

Egretta caerulea

L 24" WS 40" WT 12 oz (340 g)

Slightly stockier, thicker-necked, thicker-legged, and thicker-billed than Snowy Egret. Often selects fresh water with more emergent vegetation than other species.

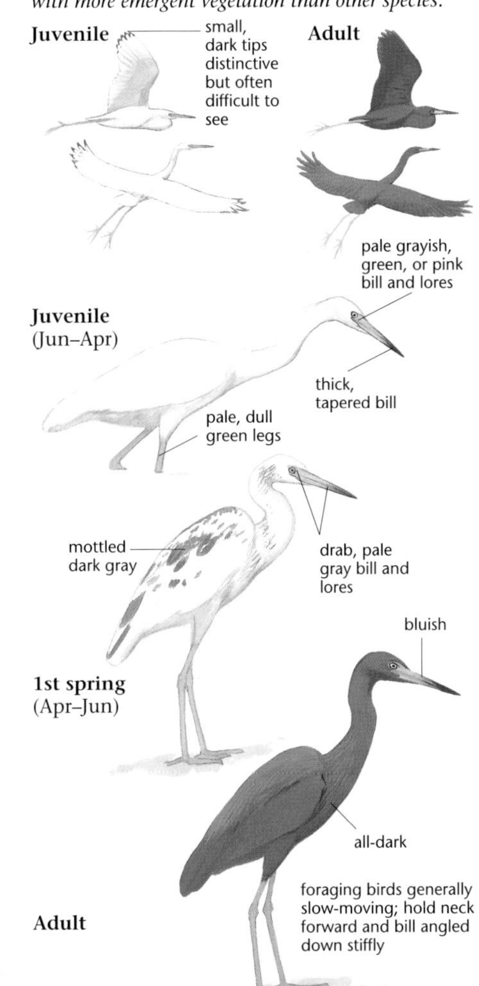
Juvenile
small, dark tips distinctive but often difficult to see
Adult
pale grayish, green, or pink bill and lores
Juvenile (Jun–Apr)
thick, tapered bill
pale, dull green legs
mottled dark gray
drab, pale gray bill and lores
1st spring (Apr–Jun)
bluish
all-dark
foraging birds generally slow-moving; hold neck forward and bill angled down stiffly
Adult

Voice: Various hoarse squawks, fairly high *raaaaa raaa . . .* (compare Snowy Egret); sometimes with trumpeting or squealing quality *geeep*.

Little Blue Heron juvenile

Snowy Egret juvenile

Some individuals show extreme similarity Jul–Oct.

Cattle Egret is found in small flocks in upland habitats, often near livestock, where it feeds mainly on insects. The solitary, secretive Green Heron captures fish along wooded streams and ponds.

Cattle Egret

Bubulcus ibis

L 20" WS 36" WT 12 oz (340 g)

Shorter-necked and shorter-billed than other white egrets.

Adult nonbreeding

wingbeats deeper than other egrets

Adult breeding

stocky

Juvenile (Jul–Oct)

black bill and legs recall Snowy and Reddish Egrets, but shape and habits distinctive

short, dark legs

short yellow bill

stocky neck

black legs

Adult nonbreeding (Aug–Feb)

foraging birds walk slowly with exaggerated head-bobbing, usually following livestock or tractors; never in water

pale orange patches

Adult breeding (Mar–Jul)

Voice: Short croaks or quacks on breeding grounds; generally silent elsewhere. Most common year-round call a subdued, nasal quack *brek* or *rick rak;* occasionally a short, soft moan.

Green Heron

Butorides virescens

wingbeats deep, snappy

L 18" WS 26" WT 7 oz (210 g)

Small and stocky with relatively long, straight bill. Note dark color (compare night-herons, bitterns).

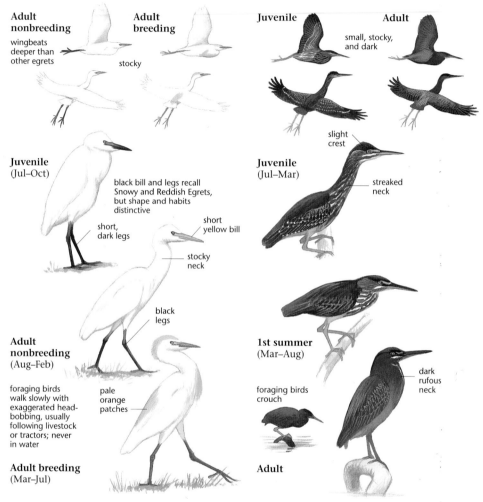

Juvenile

Adult

small, stocky, and dark

slight crest

Juvenile (Jul–Mar)

streaked neck

1st summer (Mar–Aug)

foraging birds crouch

dark rufous neck

Adult

Voice: Common call in flight an explosive, sharp, swallowed *SKEEW* or *skeow*. When nervous an irregular series of low, knocking notes *kuk kuk kuk kuk. . . .*

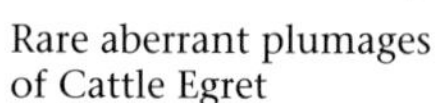

Rare aberrant plumages of Cattle Egret

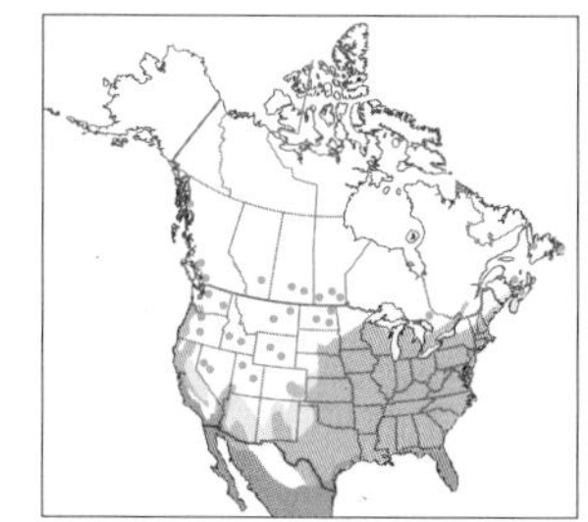

Night-Herons

These two species of stocky, nocturnal herons roost during the day in trees or marshes. At night they forage in shallow ponds and marshes; Black-crowned eats mainly fish, Yellow-crowned mainly crabs.

Black-crowned Night-Heron

Nycticorax nycticorax

L 25" WS 44" WT 1.9 lb (870 g)

Very stocky, large-headed, and short-necked.

Juvenile
Adult
only part of foot projects beyond tail
very stocky, chunky
Juvenile (Jul–Jan)
heavy but sharply pointed, extensively yellowish bill
broad, blurry streaks
large white spots on wing coverts
1st summer (Feb–Aug)
foraging birds crouch
Adult

Voice: Common call in flight a flat, barking *quok* or *quark*. Other calls of similar quality given in nesting colony.

Yellow-crowned Night-Heron

Nyctanassa violacea

L 24" WS 42" WT 1.5 lb (690 g)

Stout-billed but rather slender and long-necked; more strictly nocturnal than Black-crowned.

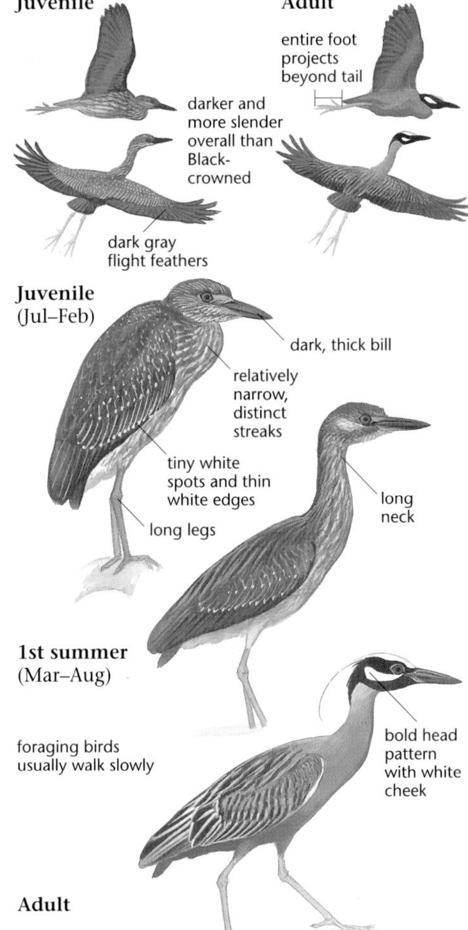

Juvenile
Adult
entire foot projects beyond tail
darker and more slender overall than Black-crowned
dark gray flight feathers
Juvenile (Jul–Feb)
dark, thick bill
relatively narrow, distinct streaks
tiny white spots and thin white edges
long legs
long neck
1st summer (Mar–Aug)
foraging birds usually walk slowly
bold head pattern with white cheek
Adult

Voice: Common call in flight a high, squawking bark *kowk* or *kaow* similar to Black-crowned but higher, more crowlike; approaching Green Heron but deeper and less sharp.

Typical sleeping posture of Black-crowned, with bill tucked into breast feathers.

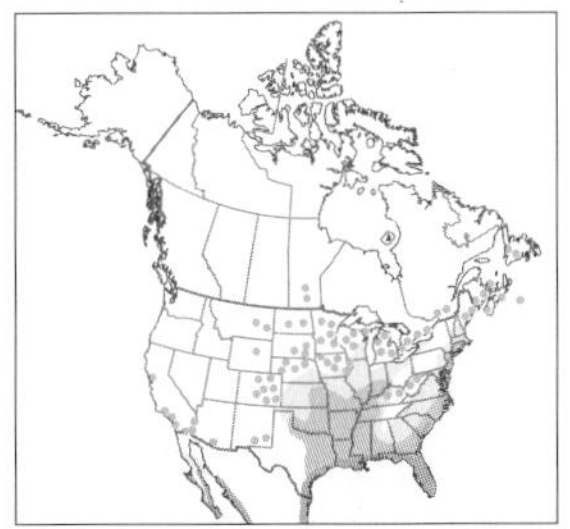

IBISES

All ibises forage in groups by walking slowly with heads down, probing mud with their long, curved bills. They fly in lines with necks extended and rather weak, shallow wingbeats.

White Ibis

Eudocimus albus

L 25" WS 38" WT 2 lb (900 g) ♂>♀

Larger and heavier than other ibises with thicker bill, broader wings.

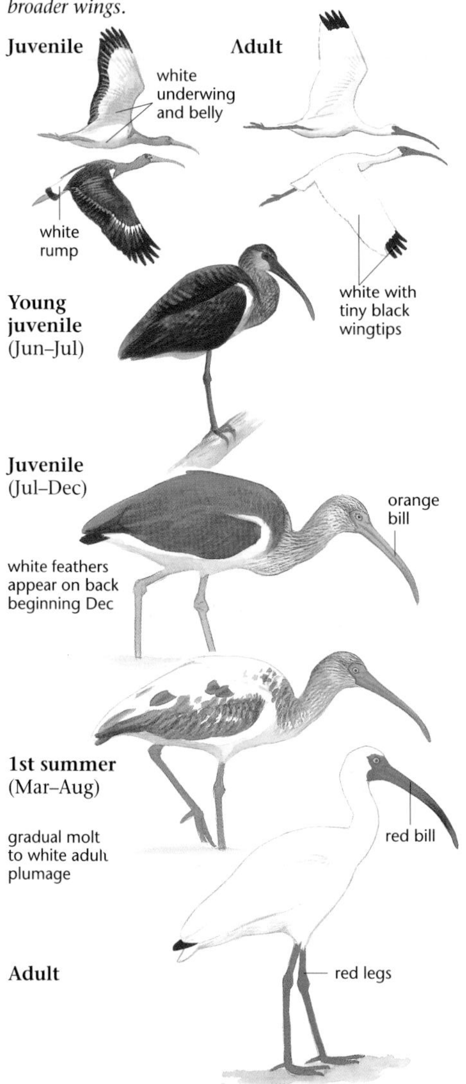

Juvenile
Adult
white underwing and belly
white rump
white with tiny black wingtips
Young juvenile (Jun–Jul)
Juvenile (Jul–Dec)
orange bill
white feathers appear on back beginning Dec
1st summer (Mar–Aug)
gradual molt to white adult plumage
red bill
Adult
red legs

Voice: In flight a harsh, nasal *urnk urnk urnk* lower than other ibises. Scarlet identical to white.

Scarlet Ibis

Eudocimus ruber

L 25" WS 38" WT 2 lb (900 g) ♂>♀

Identical to White Ibis except in color. Occasionally seen in southern Florida (introduced and/or escaped).

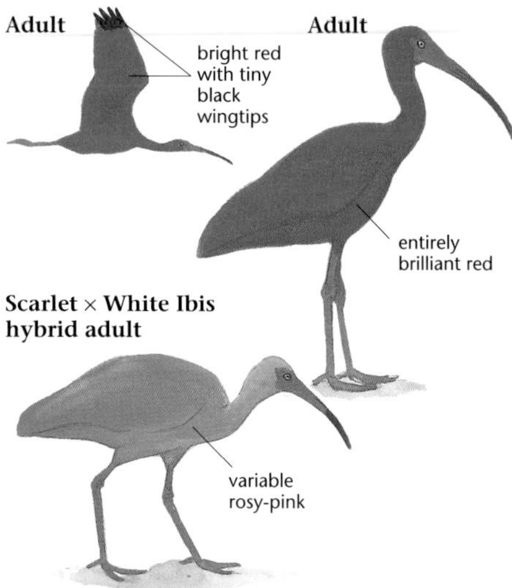

Adult
Adult
bright red with tiny black wingtips
entirely brilliant red
Scarlet × White Ibis hybrid adult
variable rosy-pink

Identification of Dark Ibises

Variation in face pattern of breeding adults is shown here; note that the face pattern of White-faced can nearly duplicate Glossy, but most are easily separated by face color and eye color. The intermediate individual shown below is infrequent and may represent a hybrid; some are not safely identified.

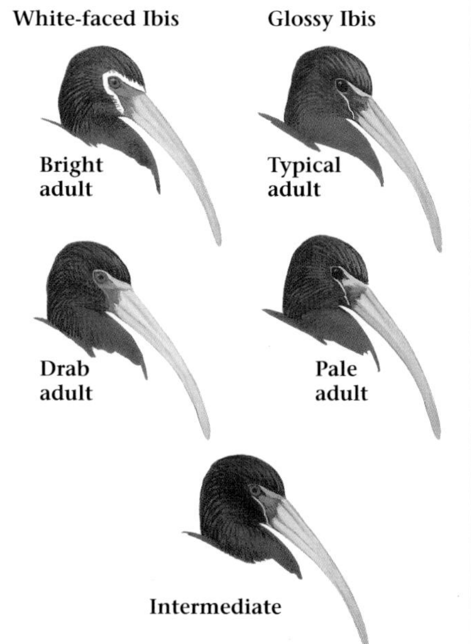

White-faced Ibis
Glossy Ibis
Bright adult
Typical adult
Drab adult
Pale adult
Intermediate

Dark Ibises

These two species are distinctive as a pair but are nearly identical at all ages. Their habits are similar to White Ibis, but the species rarely mix. They nest and roost in trees with other wading birds.

White-faced Ibis

Plegadis chihi

L 23" WS 36" WT 1.3 lb (610 g) ♂>♀

Identical to Glossy in shape but averages slightly larger; averages paler overall, but reliably distinguished only by eye and face color.

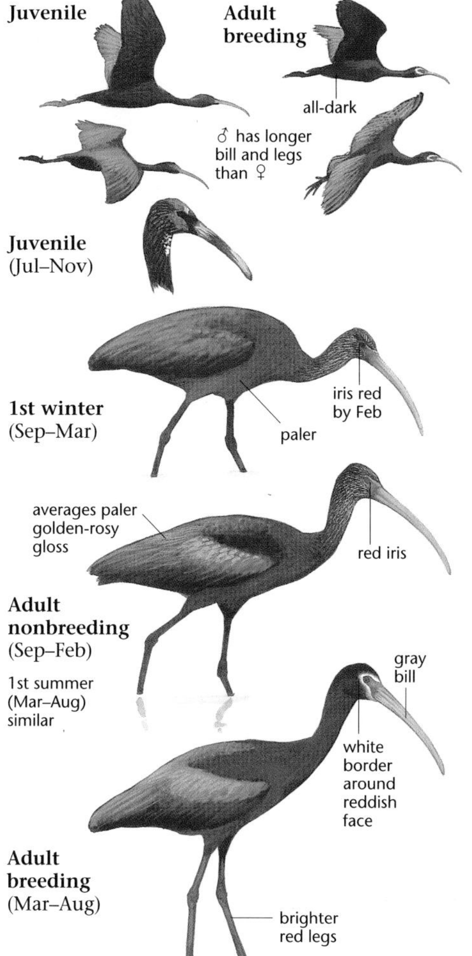
Juvenile
Adult breeding
all-dark
♂ has longer bill and legs than ♀
Juvenile (Jul–Nov)
1st winter (Sep–Mar)
iris red by Feb
paler
averages paler golden-rosy gloss
red iris
Adult nonbreeding (Sep–Feb)
1st summer (Mar–Aug) similar
gray bill
white border around reddish face
Adult breeding (Mar–Aug)
brighter red legs

Glossy Ibis

Plegadis falcinellus

L 23" WS 36" WT 1.2 lb (550 g) ♂>♀

Smaller and thinner than White; plumage always entirely dark. Adults distinguished from White-faced by eye color. Subadults more difficult to identify, but subtle differences in color of body and bill may allow separation at close range.

both species identical in flight; flocks flying in lines can be confused with cormorants but are more spindly, lighter, with less steady flight

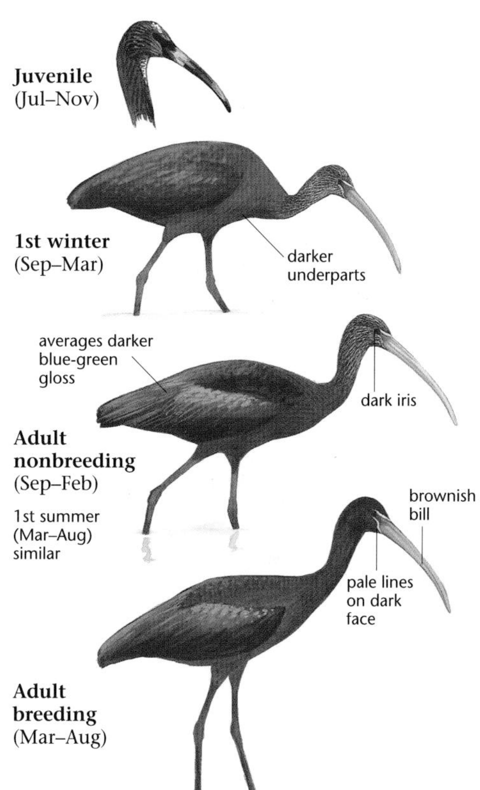
Juvenile (Jul–Nov)
1st winter (Sep–Mar)
darker underparts
averages darker blue-green gloss
dark iris
Adult nonbreeding (Sep–Feb)
1st summer (Mar–Aug) similar
brownish bill
pale lines on dark face
Adult breeding (Mar–Aug)

Voice: Voices of White-faced and Glossy apparently identical: when flushed a nasal, moaning *urnn urnn urnn* or a rapid series of nasal quacks *waa waa waa waa. . . .* Birds in feeding flock give soft, nasal, often doubled grunt *wehp-ehp.*

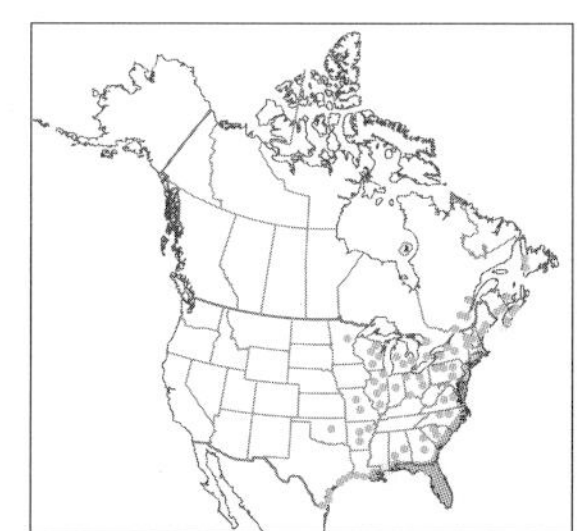

Roseate Spoonbill and Wood Stork

Both these distinctive large waders forage in shallow water by specialized methods. Roseate Spoonbill is related to ibises; Wood Stork, with many distinctive habits, is in a separate family.

Roseate Spoonbill

Ajaia ajaja

L 32" WS 50" WT 3.3 lb (1,500 g)

Spatulate bill and, as a result, distinctive foraging actions. Larger than ibises; color unique.

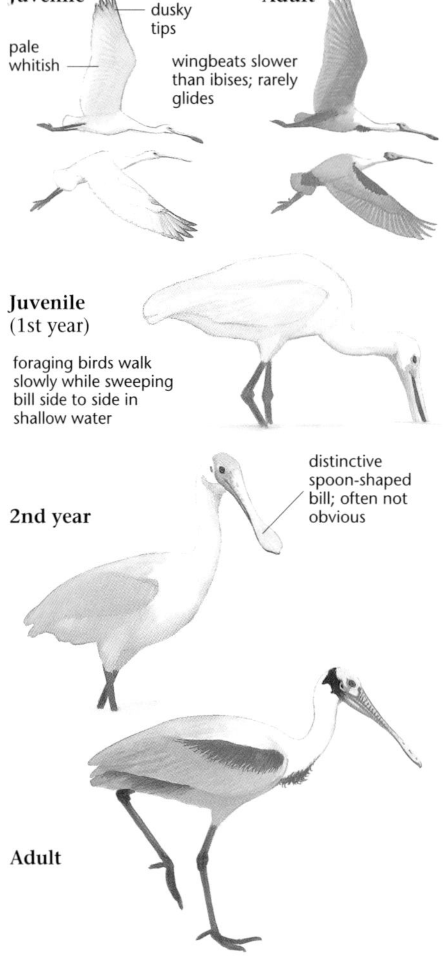
Juvenile
dusky tips
pale whitish
Adult
wingbeats slower than ibises; rarely glides
Juvenile (1st year)
foraging birds walk slowly while sweeping bill side to side in shallow water
distinctive spoon-shaped bill; often not obvious
2nd year
Adult

Voice: Low, ibislike grunting *huh-huh-huh-huh* without change in pitch or volume. Also a fairly rapid, dry, rasping *rrek-ek-ek-ek-ek-ek,* much lower, rougher, faster than ibises.

Wood Stork

Mycteria americana

L 40" WS 61" WT 5.3 lb (2,400 g) ♂>♀

Large, slow-moving, and heavy-billed.

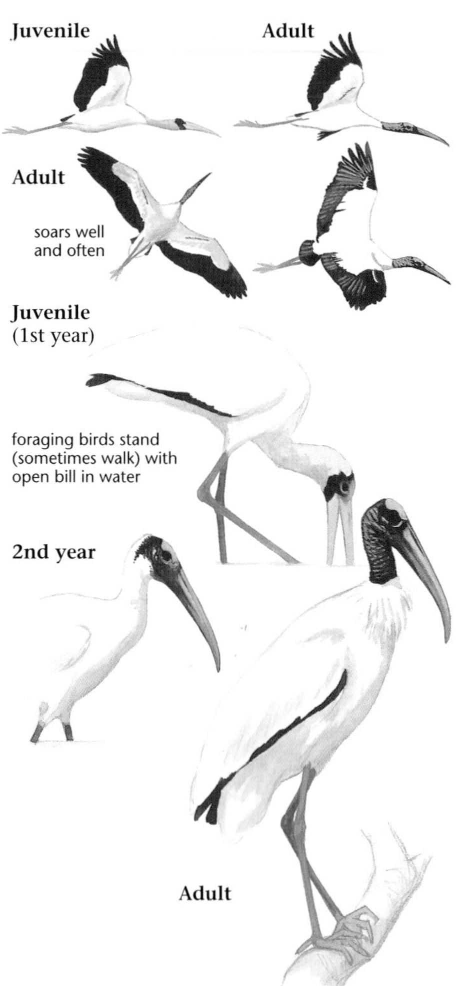
Juvenile
Adult
Adult
soars well and often
Juvenile (1st year)
foraging birds stand (sometimes walk) with open bill in water
2nd year
Adult

Voice: Usually silent after 1st year except for hissing and bill-clattering in nest displays. Young bird occasionally gives nasal, barking *nyah nyah nyah.*

Wood Stork and American White Pelican share white body with black remiges; both also regularly soar. They are usually easily distinguished by legs and bill; note also that pelicans often fly in lines or V formations and that soaring flocks of pelicans turn in unison, while storks form an uncoordinated "kettle" of soaring birds.

Flamingos

These extremely tall, slender birds are found on broad expanses of shallow water. American Greater occurs naturally in North America; the others have been recorded as escapes from captivity.

Greater Flamingo

Phoenicopterus ruber

AMERICAN
Phoenicopterus ruber ruber
L 46" WS 60" WT 5.6 lb (2,550 g) ♂>♀
Taller and more slender than Roseate Spoonbill and other waders; foraging motions different.

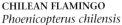

Juvenile
Adult
flight seems slow; wingbeats steady
runs when taking off and landing
Juvenile (Aug–Nov)
Subadult (all year)
transition to adult plumage gradual over 3 to 4 years
pale bill with pink and black tip
uniform pink
foraging birds walk in shallow water with heads down, swinging bills rhythmically side to side
dull pink legs; brightest on joints
Adult

Voice: In flight honk like barnyard geese but deeper. Flock gives low, conversational gabble while feeding. Courting pair gives *eep eep cak cak eep eep cak cak. . .* ; higher *eep* notes by female, lower *cak* notes by male.

EURASIAN
Phoenicopterus ruber roseus
L 46" WS 60" WT 6.3 lb (2,900 g) ♂>♀
Bill pink with small black tip; legs brighter pink; plumage mostly whitish.

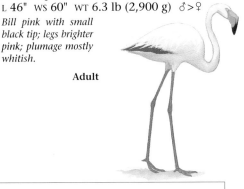

Adult

CHILEAN FLAMINGO
Phoenicopterus chilensis
L 44" WS 57"
WT 5 lb (2,300 g) ♂>♀
Bill whitish with extensive black on tip; legs relatively short and grayish with contrasting pink joints; plumage whitish with faint pink tinge.

Adult

LESSER FLAMINGO
Phoeniconaias minor
L 37" WS 48"
WT 4.2 lb (1,900 g) ♂>♀
Averages smaller overall with shorter bill; bill much darker; legs bright red; plumage strongly washed pink.

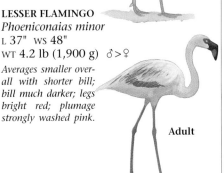

Adult

Typical adults are shown, but note that captive adults given improper diet may lose pink color. Immatures of all species are whitish, gradually acquiring pink adult color. Two other species—Andean *(Phoenicoparrus andinus)* and Puna *(Phoenicoparrus jamesi)*—are very rare in captivity; both have dark bills and black surrounding their eyes.

SWANS, GEESE, AND DUCKS

Family: Anatidae

SWANS AND GEESE 11 species in 4 genera. Generally larger than ducks, swans and geese are long-necked and feed by tipping up or grazing. Usually found in flocks, they call loudly in flight. Adults are shown.

Genus *Cygnus*

MUTE SWAN

TUNDRA SWAN
American (Whistling)

TRUMPETER SWAN

Genus *Branta*

CANADA GOOSE
Common

BRANT
Black

BARNACLE GOOSE

Genus *Anser*

GREATER WHITE-FRONTED GOOSE
Tundra

Genus *Chen*

EMPEROR GOOSE

SNOW GOOSE
Lesser

ROSS'S GOOSE

DABBLING DUCKS 16 species in 4 genera. Dabbling ducks rarely dive; they feed mainly by dabbling their bills in water or by tipping forward. All take off directly, without running. Adult females are shown.

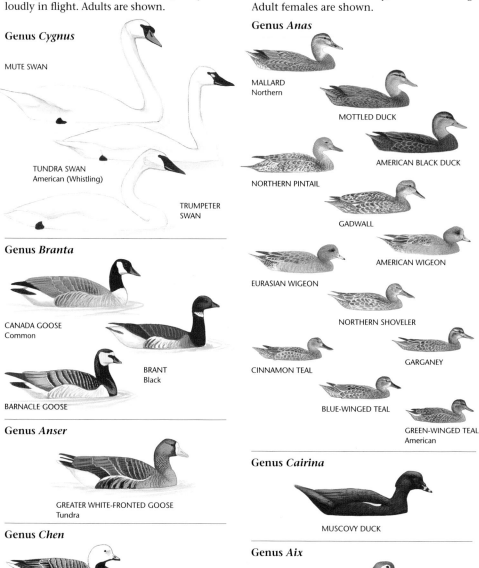

Genus *Anas*

MALLARD
Northern

MOTTLED DUCK

AMERICAN BLACK DUCK

NORTHERN PINTAIL

GADWALL

AMERICAN WIGEON

EURASIAN WIGEON

NORTHERN SHOVELER

GARGANEY

CINNAMON TEAL

BLUE-WINGED TEAL

GREEN-WINGED TEAL
American

Genus *Cairina*

MUSCOVY DUCK

Genus *Aix*

WOOD DUCK

Genus *Dendrocygna*

FULVOUS WHISTLING-DUCK

BLACK-BELLIED WHISTLING-DUCK

DIVING DUCKS 23 species in 11 genera. A more diverse group than dabblers, diving ducks frequent deeper water and normally dive underwater for food, but beware that dabblers are capable of diving, and divers will dabble in shallow water (some species often do so). Diving ducks are generally relatively heavier-bodied with smaller wing areas (higher wing-loading) than dabblers, so they fly faster with quicker wingbeats and usually run along surface of water before becoming airborne. Other ducklike swimming birds include loons, grebes, cormorants, American Coot, Common Moorhen, and alcids. Adult females are shown.

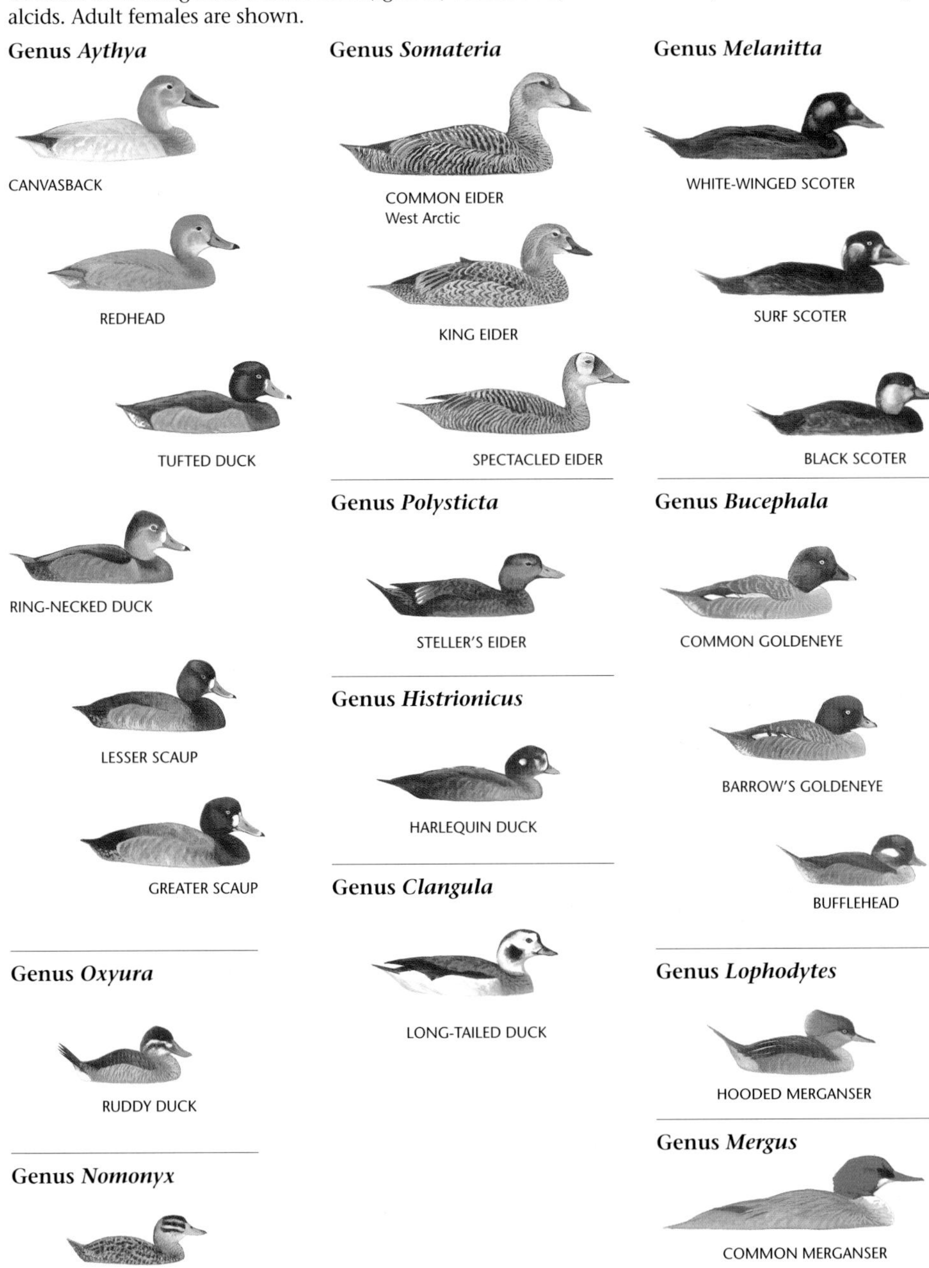

Genus *Aythya*
CANVASBACK
REDHEAD
TUFTED DUCK
RING-NECKED DUCK
LESSER SCAUP
GREATER SCAUP
Genus *Oxyura*
RUDDY DUCK
Genus *Nomonyx*
MASKED DUCK
Genus *Somateria*
COMMON EIDER
West Arctic
KING EIDER
SPECTACLED EIDER
Genus *Polysticta*
STELLER'S EIDER
Genus *Histrionicus*
HARLEQUIN DUCK
Genus *Clangula*
LONG-TAILED DUCK
Genus *Melanitta*
WHITE-WINGED SCOTER
SURF SCOTER
BLACK SCOTER
Genus *Bucephala*
COMMON GOLDENEYE
BARROW'S GOLDENEYE
BUFFLEHEAD
Genus *Lophodytes*
HOODED MERGANSER
Genus *Mergus*
COMMON MERGANSER
RED-BREASTED MERGANSER

Swans

Mute Swan, introduced from Europe, is found in ponds and bays, usually near people. Trumpeter is often seen with Tundra Swan but usually prefers more wooded ponds and rivers.

Mute Swan

Cygnus olor

L 60" WS 75" WT 22 lb (10 kg) ♂>♀

Longer-tailed than other swans and relatively heavy; gently curved neck and pale bill with dark base distinctive.

Dark juvenile
Adult
long, pointed tail
White juvenile (Jun–Sep)
common, outnumbers dark
Dark juvenile (Jun–Sep)
common
1st fall (Aug–Nov)
mostly white by Nov
orange bill unique
Adult

Voice: Not mute; gives a variety of calls. In aggression an explosive, exhaling *kheorrrr* with rumbling end; sometimes a clear, bugling *kloorrr* reminiscent of Tundra Swan, also hissing and snorting. Immature gives higher gurgling note. Wings produce loud, resonant, throbbing hum in flight, unlike other swans.

Trumpeter Swan

Cygnus buccinator

L 60" WS 80" WT 23 lb (10.5 kg) ♂>♀

Our largest swan; larger overall with longer neck and bill than Tundra. Overlaps little in size; identification best based on voice and bill shape. 1st year retains gray-brown upperparts through June.

Juvenile
Adult
White juvenile (Aug–Dec)
rare, recorded in Wyoming
bill always black at base
Dark juvenile (Aug–Dec)
1st summer (Oct–Jul)
gray-brown
back tends to be more evenly rounded than Tundra
Adult
long, straight bill

Voice: Less vocal and voice much lower-pitched than Tundra Swan. Gentle nasal honking, slightly hoarse *hurp* or *hur di di,* like the honk of a European taxi; lower-pitched and less urgent than Canada Goose. Immature gives higher-pitched toy-trumpet-like calls, changing to hoarse version of adult calls during 1st winter.

Mute Swan adult in distinctive aggressive posture

Tundra, our smallest and most numerous swan, nests on tundra ponds. Other seasons it is found on marshes, rivers, and shallow ponds, often in large flocks and grazing like geese on open fields.

Tundra Swan

Cygnus columbianus

L 52" WS 66" WT 14.4 lb (6,600 g) ♂>♀

Our smallest swan; relatively short-necked and gooselike.

AMERICAN (WHISTLING)

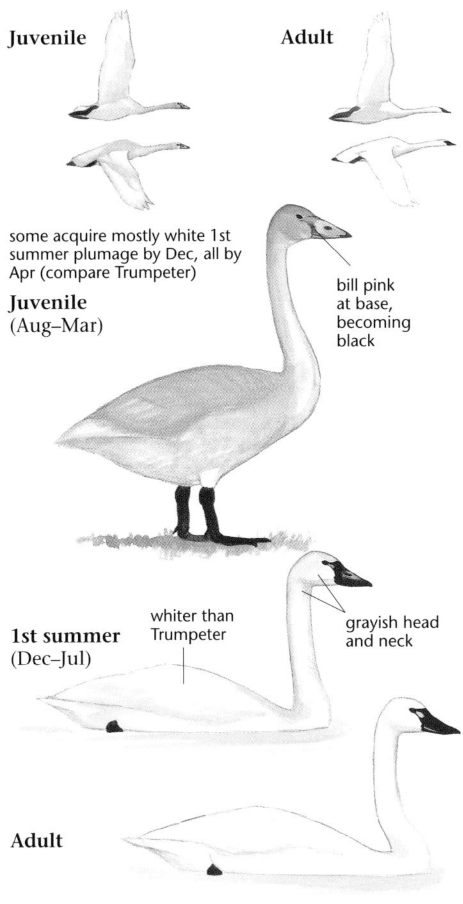
Juvenile
Adult
some acquire mostly white 1st summer plumage by Dec, all by Apr (compare Trumpeter)
Juvenile
(Aug–Mar)
bill pink at base, becoming black
1st summer
(Dec–Jul)
whiter than Trumpeter
grayish head and neck
Adult

Voice: A melancholy, clear, singing *klooo* or *kwooo* with hooting or barking quality. Distant flock sounds like baying hounds, rather gooselike; resting flock gives gentle, musical murmuring. Immature calls wheezier, becoming adultlike by 2nd year.

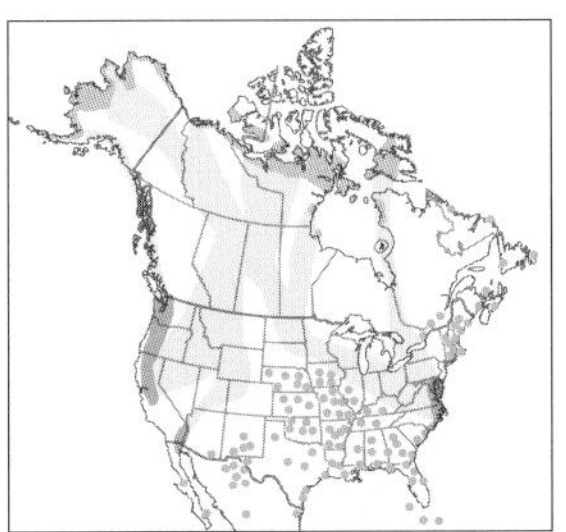

Identification of Swans

Trumpeter Swan is best distinguished from Tundra by its longer bill with straighter base (lacking sharp curve at gape).

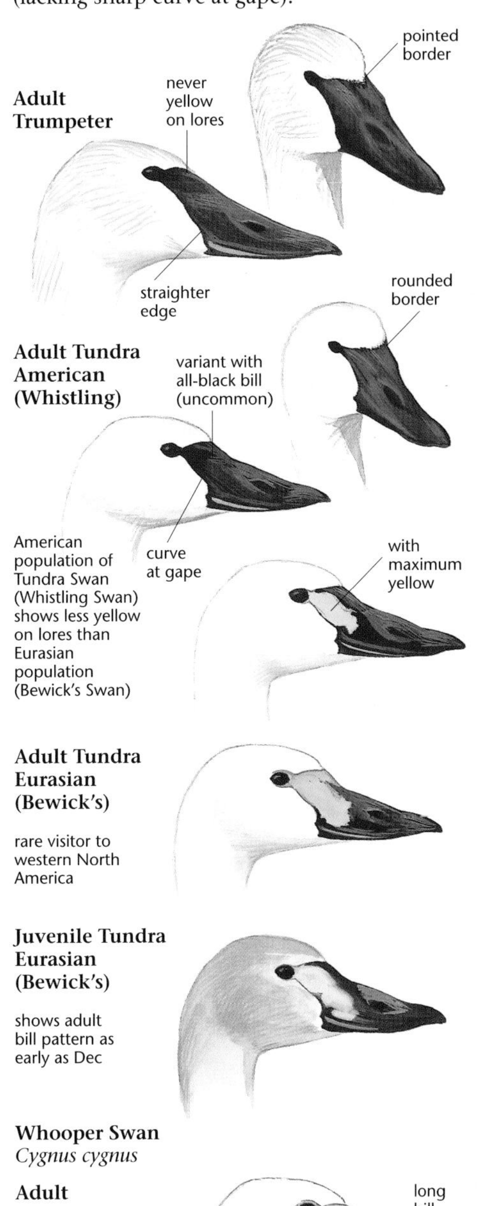
Adult Trumpeter
never yellow on lores
pointed border
straighter edge
Adult Tundra American (Whistling)
rounded border
variant with all-black bill (uncommon)
American population of Tundra Swan (Whistling Swan) shows less yellow on lores than Eurasian population (Bewick's Swan)
curve at gape
with maximum yellow
Adult Tundra Eurasian (Bewick's)
rare visitor to western North America
Juvenile Tundra Eurasian (Bewick's)
shows adult bill pattern as early as Dec

Whooper Swan
Cygnus cygnus

Adult

rare visitor to western North America (escapes are occasionally seen elsewhere); larger than Tundra

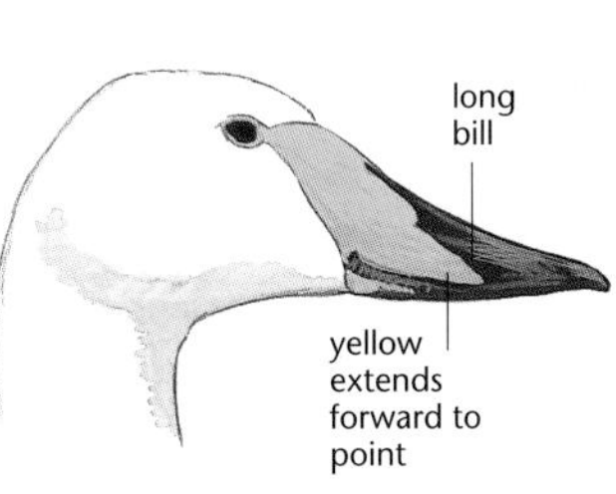
long bill
yellow extends forward to point

Geese

Canada, our most widespread goose and one of our most familiar birds, is found on ponds, marshes, and farmland. Barnacle is a closely related but rare visitor; many records refer to escapes.

Barnacle Goose

Branta leucopsis

L 27" WS 50" WT 3.7 lb (1,700 g) ♂>♀

Small with relatively long wings and very short bill. Note black breast and bicolored underwing.

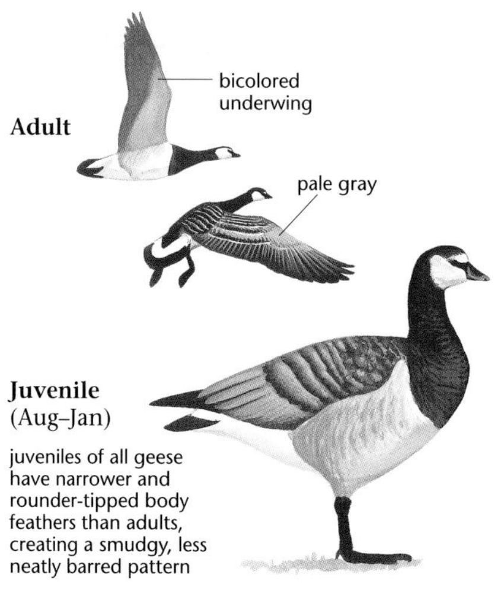
Adult
bicolored underwing
pale gray
Juvenile
(Aug–Jan)
juveniles of all geese have narrower and rounder-tipped body feathers than adults, creating a smudgy, less neatly barred pattern

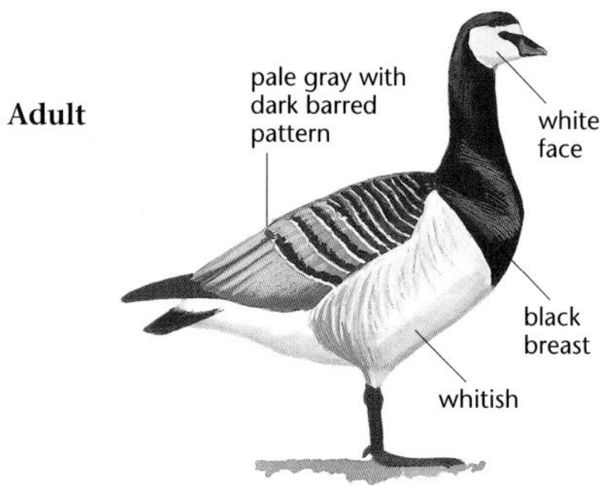
Adult
pale gray with dark barred pattern
white face
black breast
whitish

Adult

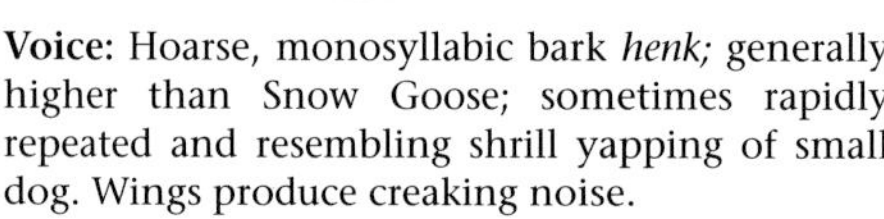

Voice: Hoarse, monosyllabic bark *henk;* generally higher than Snow Goose; sometimes rapidly repeated and resembling shrill yapping of small dog. Wings produce creaking noise.

Canada Goose

Branta canadensis

L 25–45" WS 43–60"

WT 3.5–9.8 lb (1,600–4,500 g) ♂>♀

This variable species includes our largest and nearly our smallest geese. All have black necks, brownish breasts, and white cheeks.

COMMON
Adult
Juvenile
(Aug–Jan)

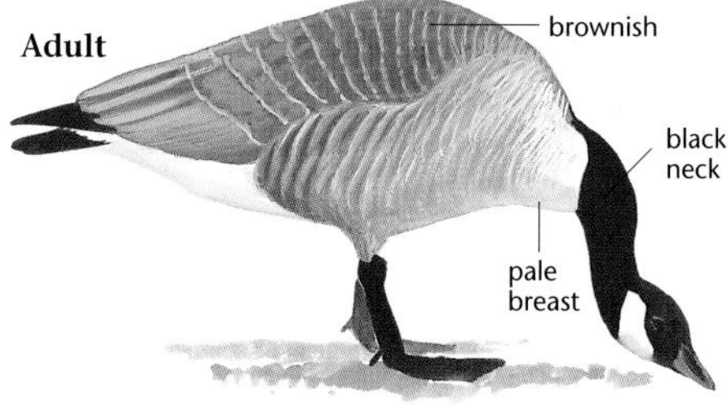
Adult
brownish
black neck
pale breast

Adult

Voice: Familiar call a loud, resonant, and musical honk *h-ronk* and *h-lenk;* flock chorus gentle, slow-paced, mellow; no harsh or sharp notes. Other soft, grunting calls.

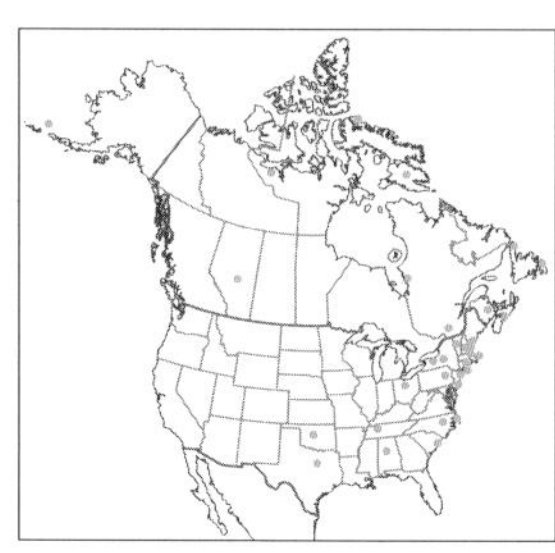

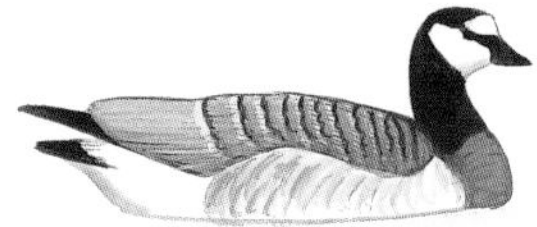

Barnacle × Canada Goose hybrid adult

Snow × Canada Goose hybrids are also seen occasionally.

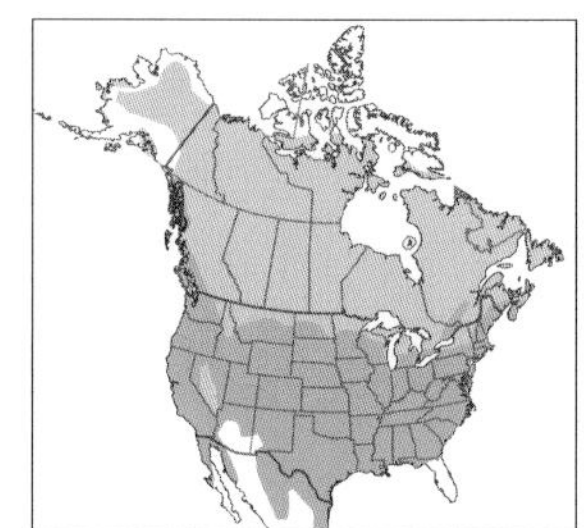

Geese: Subspecies of Canada Goose

Canada Geese are extremely variable in size, with at least six recognizable populations, all with similar habits. All populations are variable; many intermediate birds cannot be identified.

Canada Goose

Branta canadensis

Smaller birds are relatively small-billed and short-necked. Pacific breeders are darker than all others, and northern breeders are smaller than southern. Adults are shown.

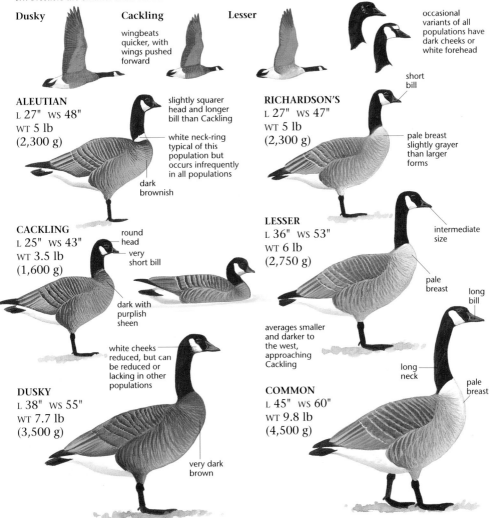

Dusky

Cackling

wingbeats quicker, with wings pushed forward

Lesser

occasional variants of all populations have dark cheeks or white forehead

ALEUTIAN
L 27" WS 48"
WT 5 lb
(2,300 g)

slightly squarer head and longer bill than Cackling

white neck-ring typical of this population but occurs infrequently in all populations

dark brownish

RICHARDSON'S
L 27" WS 47"
WT 5 lb
(2,300 g)

short bill

pale breast slightly grayer than larger forms

CACKLING
L 25" WS 43"
WT 3.5 lb
(1,600 g)

round head

very short bill

dark with purplish sheen

LESSER
L 36" WS 53"
WT 6 lb
(2,750 g)

intermediate size

pale breast

averages smaller and darker to the west, approaching Cackling

DUSKY
L 38" WS 55"
WT 7.7 lb
(3,500 g)

white cheeks reduced, but can be reduced or lacking in other populations

very dark brown

COMMON
L 45" WS 60"
WT 9.8 lb
(4,500 g)

long bill

long neck

pale breast

Voice: Voice very similar in most populations; averages higher-pitched in smaller birds, but even Richardson's sounds quite similar to Common. Cackling, however, gives distinctly high-pitched, squeaking *yeek* or *uriik*.

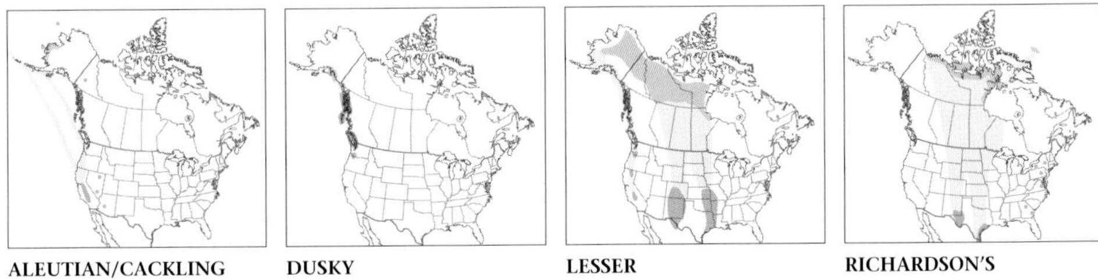

ALEUTIAN/CACKLING — DUSKY — LESSER — RICHARDSON'S

Brant, which is almost exclusively coastal, is found in flocks on shallow bays and marshes. Its flight is usually low and fast, with swept-back wings.

Brant

Branta bernicla

L 25" WS 42" WT 3.1 lb (1,400 g) ♂>♀

flock adopts more irregular shapes than other geese

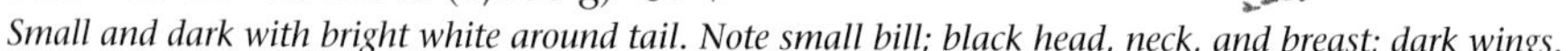

Small and dark with bright white around tail. Note small bill; black head, neck, and breast; dark wings.

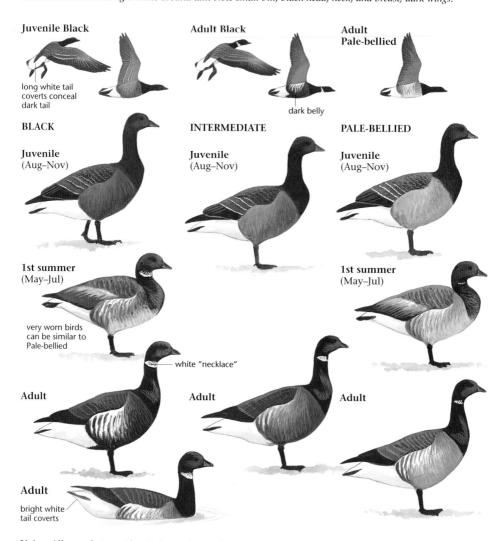

Juvenile Black

long white tail coverts conceal dark tail

Adult Black

dark belly

Adult Pale-bellied

BLACK

Juvenile (Aug–Nov)

1st summer (May–Jul)

very worn birds can be similar to Pale-bellied

white "necklace"

Adult

Adult

bright white tail coverts

INTERMEDIATE

Juvenile (Aug–Nov)

Adult

PALE-BELLIED

Juvenile (Aug–Nov)

1st summer (May–Jul)

Adult

Voice: All populations identical; a soft, gargling *rrot* or *cronk* and a hard *cut-cut* in flight. Flock chorus a constant, low, murmuring, gargling sound with little variation.

Three populations are distinguished by plumage, with little range overlap in winter, but intergrade freely where breeding ranges meet. Black nests in western part of breeding range and winters on Pacific coast of California and Mexico; Intermediate nests on Melville Island and winters in Puget Sound; Pale-bellied nests in eastern part of breeding range and winters on our Atlantic coast and Ireland. All forms are rare visitors inland and on opposite coast. Black is darkest overall, with little contrast between breast and belly and white "necklace" continuous across foreneck. Black × Pale-bellied intergrades are apparently identical to the stable Intermediate population of Melville Island.

Geese (continued)

This species, found on marshes and fields, nests on marshy ponds in the tundra or taiga, depending on subspecies. Beware confusion with the superficially similar domestic Graylag Goose.

Greater White-fronted Goose

Anser albifrons

L 28" WS 53" WT 4.8 lb (2,200 g) ♂>♀

Slender and agile, with long, narrow wings; note bright orange legs, white tip on tail, gray upperwing.

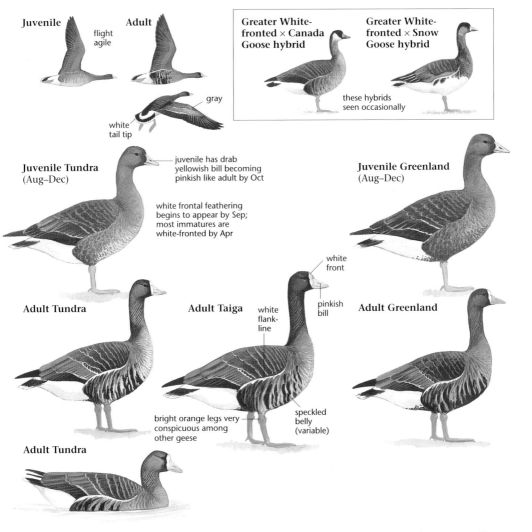

Juvenile **Adult**

flight agile

gray

white tail tip

Greater White-fronted × Canada Goose hybrid

Greater White-fronted × Snow Goose hybrid

these hybrids seen occasionally

Juvenile Tundra (Aug–Dec)

juvenile has drab yellowish bill becoming pinkish like adult by Oct

white frontal feathering begins to appear by Sep; most immatures are white-fronted by Apr

Juvenile Greenland (Aug–Dec)

white front

pinkish bill

Adult Tundra

Adult Taiga

white flank-line

Adult Greenland

bright orange legs very conspicuous among other geese

speckled belly (variable)

Adult Tundra

Voice: Common honk a distinctive quick, high-pitched laughing or yelping of two or three rising syllables *ho-leeleek* or *kilik*. Flock noise higher, clearer, with more rapid syllables than other geese; feeding flock gives low, buzzing chorus.

Three populations are distinguished, but differences are rather slight and many birds are intermediate. Tundra breeders are smallest and palest. Taiga breeders, especially Tule Goose (nesting in south-central Alaska, wintering in northern California), are 10 percent larger, 15 percent longer-billed, darker brown, often showing yellow orbital ring, and average less black on belly and more white on face than Tundra. Greenland breeders (wintering in Ireland, rare on our Atlantic coast) are medium-size, darkest overall with slaty cast, and have long orange bill (more pinkish on others), narrow pale edges on back feathers, and more black on belly.

Geese (continued)

Emperor Goose is found mainly on sheltered coastal lagoons. Ross's is very similar to Snow Goose and is often found with that species, although it forms separate flocks in its main winter range.

Emperor Goose

Chen canagica

L 26" WS 47" WT 6.1 lb (2,800 g)

Small and stocky; very round-bodied with short neck, small bill, broad wings.

Juvenile **Adult**

uniform gray

unique dark tail coverts with white tail

Juvenile (Aug–Nov)

white tail

dark coverts

yellow legs

Adult

small pinkish bill

silvery gray overall with white head and tail

orange legs

Adult

Voice: High-pitched, rapid, triple- or double-note tinny honk *kla-ha* like Snow Goose; also high, clear, trumpeting *tedidi.* Low grunting from ground.

Ross's Goose

Chen rossii

L 23" WS 45" WT 2.7 lb (1,250 g)

Smaller than Snow Goose, with tiny bill; best distinguished by bill shape.

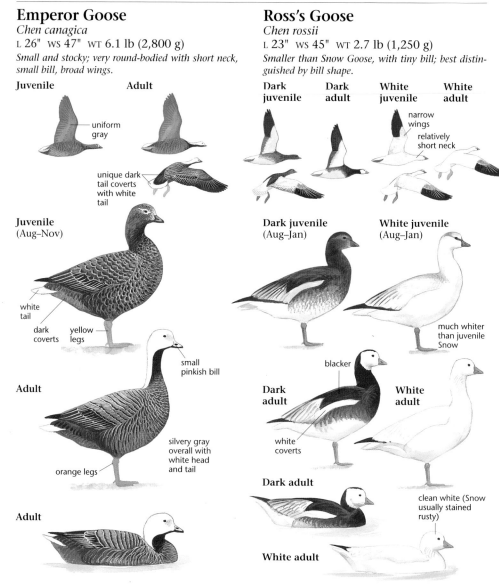

Dark juvenile **Dark adult** **White juvenile** **White adult**

narrow wings

relatively short neck

Dark juvenile (Aug–Jan)

White juvenile (Aug–Jan)

much whiter than juvenile Snow

blacker

Dark adult

white coverts

White adult

Dark adult

clean white (Snow usually stained rusty)

White adult

Voice: Generally quiet, less vocal than Snow Goose; calls a squealing *keek-keek* and a grunting low *kowk;* higher-pitched and more rapid than Snow.

Dark morph of Ross's is rare; many dark birds may be Ross's × Snow Goose hybrids. Differs from dark Snow Goose in blacker scapulars and neck, whiter coverts and tertials, and all-dark neck with restricted white face. The combination of dark neck and white belly is not shown by Snow Goose.

This species nests colonially on Arctic tundra; it winters on marshes and open fields. The dark morph, which has increased in occurrence, was formerly considered a separate species, Blue Goose.

Snow Goose

Chen caerulescens

LESSER L 28" WS 53" WT 5.3 lb (2,420 g) ♂>♀

GREATER L 31" WS 56" WT 7.4 lb (3,400 g) ♂>♀

Rather stocky, short-necked, and large-headed. Dark morph has bicolored underwing.

LESSER

Dark juvenile

Dark adult

White juvenile

White adult

Dark juvenile (Aug–Jan)

variable; dark gray-brown overall

White juvenile (Aug–Jan)

variable; always dingy gray on upperside, darker than juvenile Ross's

Dark adult

White adult

Dark adult

White adult

GEESE HEAD AND BILL SHAPES

Ross's Goose
small with rounded head and stubby bill; little or no "grin patch"; border at base of bill straight and vertical; bluish on base of bill; dark morph rare

Ross's × Lesser Snow Goose hybrid
intermediate in size and bill structure

Lesser Snow Goose
larger than Ross's with more wedge-shaped head; obvious black "grin patch"; strongly curved border at base of bill; dark morph common in east, scarce in west

Greater Snow Goose
averages 20 percent longer-billed than Lesser; looks longer-faced with head even more strongly wedge-shaped; dark morph rare

Voice: Common call a harsh, monosyllabic, descending *whouk* or higher *heenk;* harsher and more raucous than other geese, recalling Great Blue Heron. Flock chorus slow-paced with single honks on varied pitches; whole pitch range greater than other geese. Also lower, grunting *hu-hu-hur* from foraging birds. Voice of Greater Snow Goose slightly lower-pitched and more resonant than Lesser.

GREATER

A complete range of intermediate birds occurs between white and dark morph.

Whistling-Ducks

These oddly gooselike ducks are found in flocks, grazing in open fields or tipping up in shallow ponds. They call constantly in flight, when their broad, rounded wings and long legs are apparent.

Black-bellied Whistling-Duck

Dendrocygna autumnalis

L 21" WS 30" WT 1.8 lb (830 g)

Striking white upperwing and dark body.

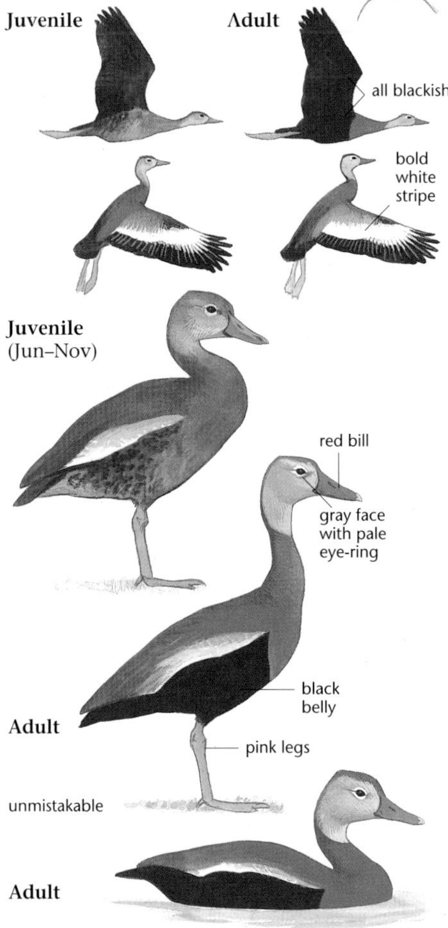

Juvenile
Adult
all blackish
bold white stripe
Juvenile (Jun–Nov)
red bill
gray face with pale eye-ring
black belly
Adult
pink legs
unmistakable
Adult

Voice: Wheezy but sharp whistle, softer and more musical than Fulvous and typically five or six syllables *pit pit pit WEEE do deew.* Also high, weak *yip* singly or in series when flushed.

Fulvous Whistling-Duck

Dendrocygna bicolor

L 19" WS 26" WT 1.5 lb (670 g)

Slightly smaller with thinner wings and shorter neck and legs than Black-bellied.

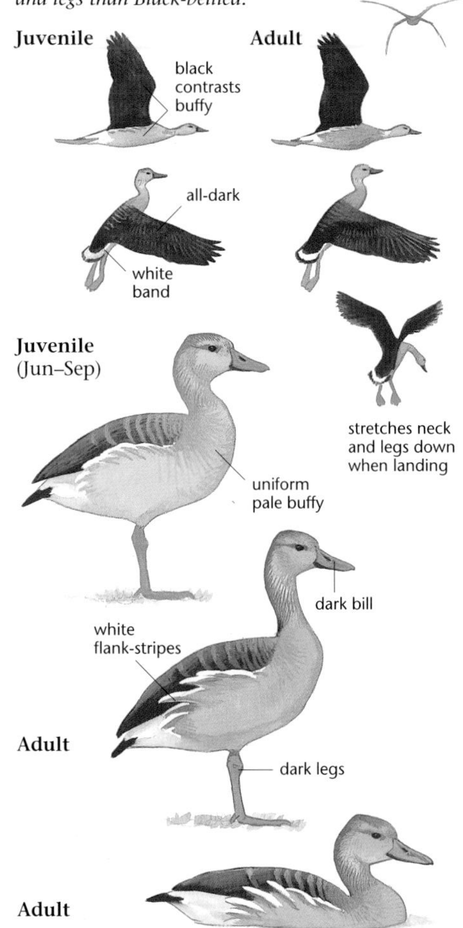

Juvenile
Adult
black contrasts buffy
all-dark
white band
stretches neck and legs down when landing
Juvenile (Jun–Sep)
uniform pale buffy
dark bill
white flank-stripes
Adult
dark legs
Adult

Voice: A thin, squeaky whistle *pi-piTEEEEW* or *pitheeew.* Also a soft, conversational *cup-cup-cup.* Male calls distinctly higher-pitched than female.

Downy young Black-bellied is similar to Fulvous (compare Masked Duck).

Perching Ducks

Both these species are short-legged and long-tailed, and both prefer sheltered water with trees—rivers, ponds, wooded swamps—but they share few other similarities.

Muscovy Duck

Cairina moschata

♂ L 31" WS 48" WT 6.6 lb (3,000 g)
♀ L 25" WS 38" WT 3.3 lb (1,500 g)

Large (especially male), heavy, broad-tailed, and broad-winged. Cormorant-like in flight.

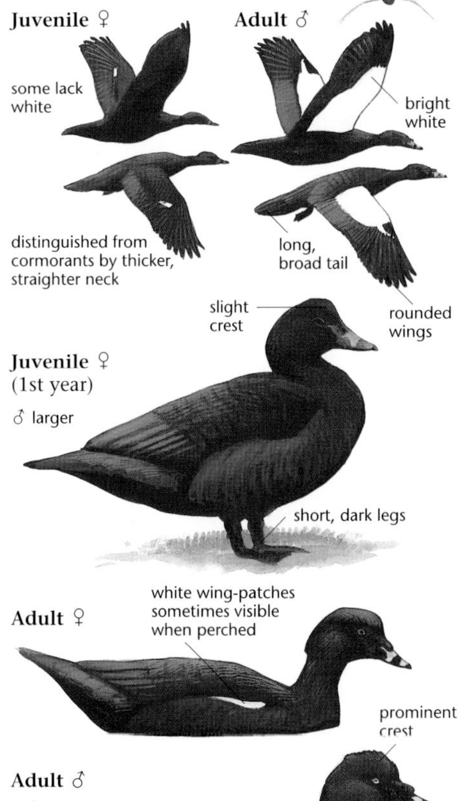
Juvenile ♀
Adult ♂
some lack white
bright white
distinguished from cormorants by thicker, straighter neck
long, broad tail
rounded wings
slight crest
Juvenile ♀ (1st year)
♂ larger
short, dark legs
Adult ♀
white wing-patches sometimes visible when perched
prominent crest
Adult ♂
warty face

Voice: Rarely heard. Female gives a soft quack. Male gives rhythmic puffs in display, also hisses.

Wood Duck

Aix sponsa

L 18.5" WS 30" WT 1.3 lb (600 g) ♂>♀

Small-billed and long-tailed, with bushy mane. White eye-patch of female and white "bridle" of male distinctive.

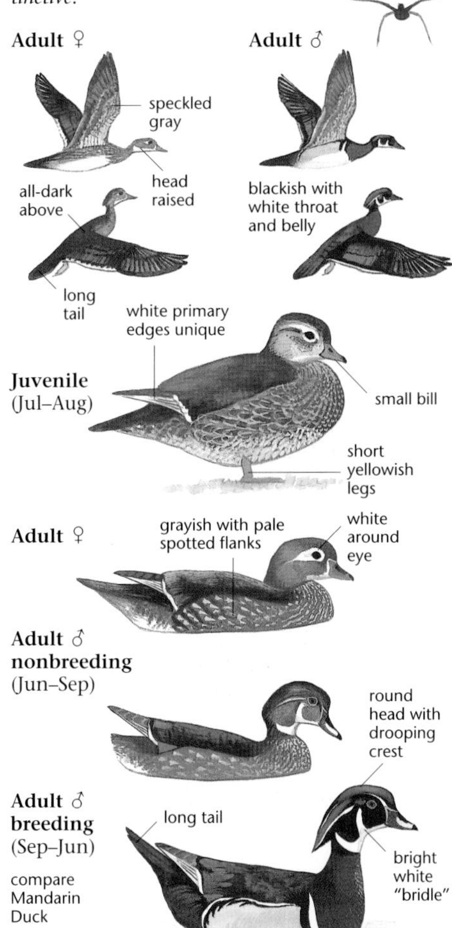
Adult ♀
Adult ♂
speckled gray
head raised
all-dark above
long tail
blackish with white throat and belly
white primary edges unique
Juvenile (Jul–Aug)
small bill
short yellowish legs
Adult ♀
grayish with pale spotted flanks
white around eye
Adult ♂ nonbreeding (Jun–Sep)
round head with drooping crest
Adult ♂ breeding (Sep–Jun)
long tail
compare Mandarin Duck
bright white "bridle"

Voice: Mainly thin, squeaky whistles. Female a penetrating squeal *ooEEK ooEEK . . .* ; also a raucous quack, rarely heard. Male a thin, high, drawn-out *jeweeep* or *sweeoooo, kip kip kip*. Male wing whistle similar to Mallard.

The domestic Muscovy has established feral populations in Florida, Texas, and elsewhere. These birds are usually heavier than the wild Muscovy and show patches of white on head and body and redder face; some are entirely white with red face (see Domestic Waterfowl).

Ducks: Mallard Group

Our largest dabbling duck, the familiar Mallard is found in any wet habitat from city parks to tundra ponds. The Mexican population, formerly a separate species, is found in marshy ponds.

Mallard

Anas platyrhynchos

L 23" WS 35" WT 2.4 lb (1,100 g) ♂>♀

Large and heavy, with broader wings and slower wingbeats than other dabbling ducks. Note female's long orange and black bill, dark eye-line, orange legs, and upperwing pattern.

NORTHERN

Adult ♀

Adult ♂

wingbeats slower, shallower than other ducks

whitish tail

bold white bars

Juvenile (Jul–Sep)

whitish

pale belly

orange bill with dark center

Adult ♀

Adult ♂ nonbreeding (Jun–Sep)

Adult ♂ breeding (Oct–May)

dark head

pale body

MEXICAN

Adult ♀

averages 10 percent smaller than Northern; darker overall, lacking bright male plumage

Adult ♂

narrow white bars

Juvenile (Jul–Sep)

dark, rich brown overall

distinguished from Mottled Duck by darker crown and eye-line; white border in front of speculum; slightly more grayish-streaked face; most show intergradation with Northern

dark tail and undertail coverts

Adult ♀

dark crown

finely streaked neck

olive-drab to orange bill

Adult ♂

yellow bill

Voice: Female gives familiar, loud quacking calls; also deep, reedy laughing; similar calls by other dabblers are shorter, harsher, often higher. Also single loud quacks in a variety of situations (e.g., when flushed a series of single rising quacks *brehk, brehk . . .*). Male gives a similar short, rasping *quehp*. Displaying male gives short whistle *piu* similar to teals but weaker. Wings whistle faintly in flight.

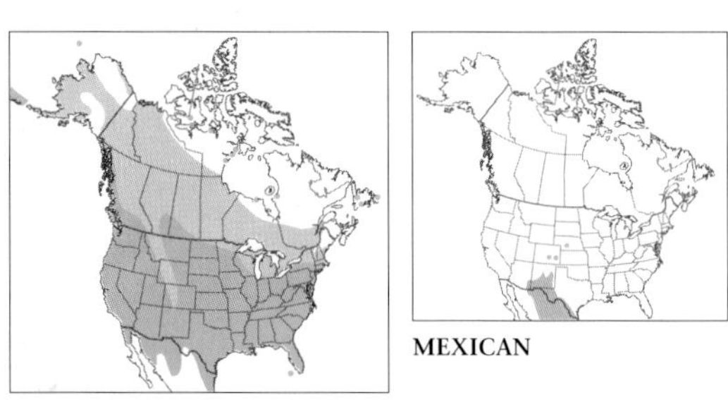
MEXICAN

Mexican × Northern Mallard intergrade adult ♂ breeding
Virtually no pure Mexican Mallards occur in North America.

Ducks: Mallard Group (continued)

These two very dark species are closely related to the Mallard and are sometimes considered conspecific. They can be found in any pond or marsh habitat but are especially fond of saltmarshes.

Mottled Duck

Anas fulvigula

L 22" WS 30" WT 2.2 lb (1,000 g) ♂>♀

Averages slightly smaller and thinner-necked than Mallard; always darker than Mallard, paler and buffier than American Black Duck.

Adult ♀

Adult ♂

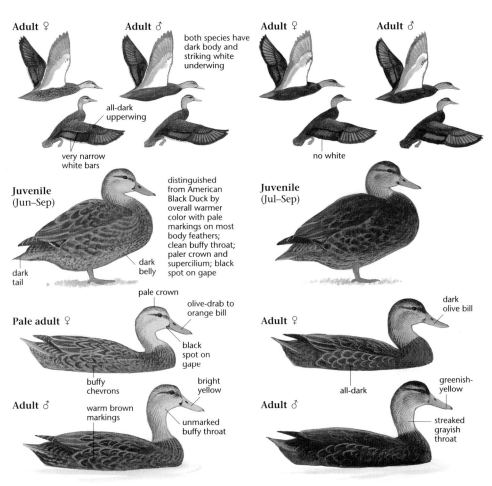

both species have dark body and striking white underwing

all-dark upperwing

very narrow white bars

Juvenile (Jun–Sep)

distinguished from American Black Duck by overall warmer color with pale markings on most body feathers; clean buffy throat; paler crown and supercilium; black spot on gape

dark belly

dark tail

Pale adult ♀

pale crown

olive-drab to orange bill

black spot on gape

buffy chevrons

Adult ♂

bright yellow

warm brown markings

unmarked buffy throat

Voice: Voice like Mallard, but female quack may be a little weaker and softer on average.

American Black Duck

Anas rubripes

L 23" WS 35" WT 2.6 lb (1,200 g) ♂>♀

Structure like Mallard but much darker with cold grayish tones; body feathers essentially all-dark with thin, pale fringes.

Adult ♀

Adult ♂

no white

Juvenile (Jul–Sep)

Adult ♀

dark olive bill

all-dark

Adult ♂

greenish-yellow

streaked grayish throat

Voice: Voice like Mallard, but female quack averages slightly lower-pitched.

American Black Duck × Mallard hybrid adult ♂ breeding

Seen regularly. Mottled Duck × Mallard is rarely recorded.

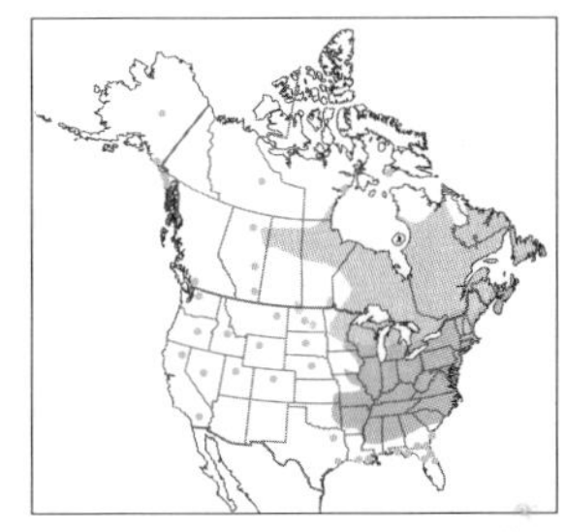

Gadwall and Northern Pintail

These fairly large dabbling ducks are found in shallow ponds and marshes. Pintail is abundant in the west and flies in line formation; Gadwall flight is direct in smaller, compact flocks.

Gadwall

Anas strepera

L 20" WS 33" WT 2 lb (910 g) ♂>♀

Stocky and Mallard-like in shape, with round head and thin bill. Floats high on water, picking food like wigeons.

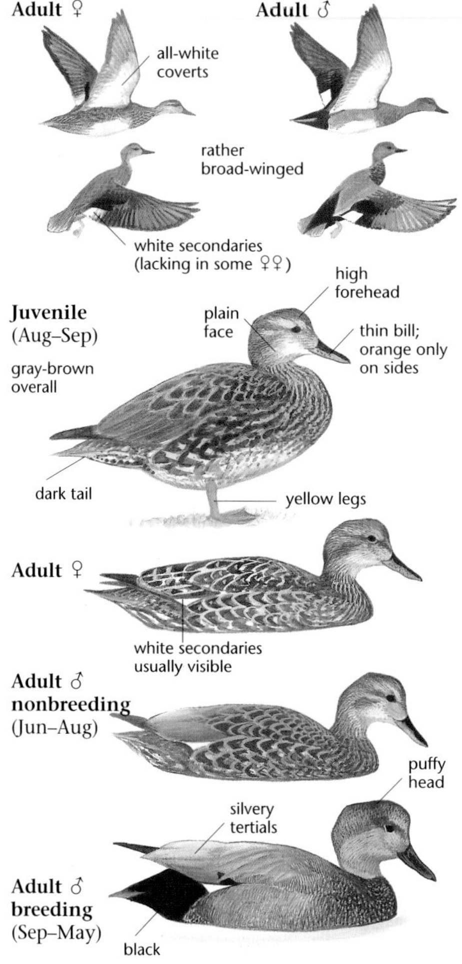

Adult ♀
Adult ♂
all-white coverts
rather broad-winged
white secondaries (lacking in some ♀♀)
Juvenile (Aug–Sep)
gray-brown overall
plain face
high forehead
thin bill; orange only on sides
dark tail
yellow legs
Adult ♀
white secondaries usually visible
Adult ♂ nonbreeding (Jun–Aug)
puffy head
silvery tertials
Adult ♂ breeding (Sep–May)
black

Voice: Female quack similar to Mallard but coarser, more nasal. Male in courtship gives low, nasal burp *mepp;* often combined with quiet, high squeak *tiMEPP.*

Northern Pintail

Anas acuta

L 21" (♂ to 25") WS 34" WT 1.8 lb (800 g) ♂>♀

Slender and elegant, the "greyhound of ducks," with long, narrow wings and long neck and tail.

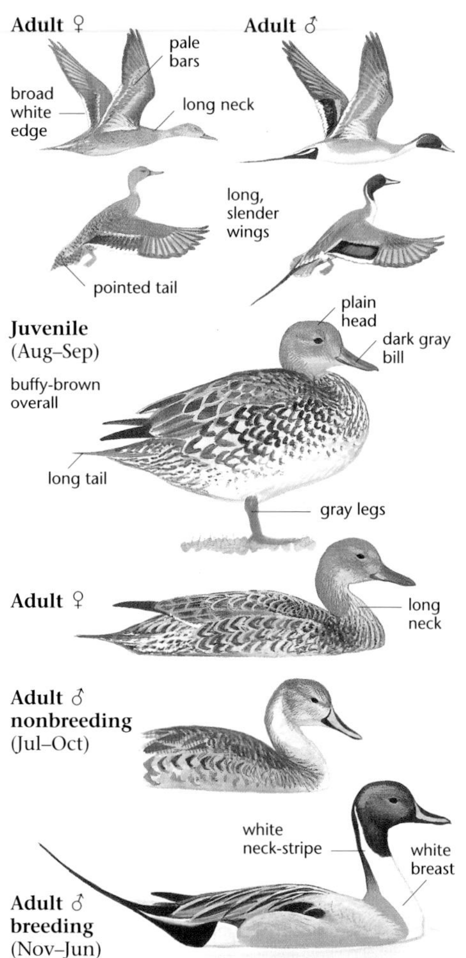

Adult ♀
Adult ♂
pale bars
broad white edge
long neck
long, slender wings
pointed tail
Juvenile (Aug–Sep)
buffy-brown overall
plain head
dark gray bill
long tail
gray legs
Adult ♀
long neck
Adult ♂ nonbreeding (Jul–Oct)
white neck-stripe
white breast
Adult ♂ breeding (Nov–Jun)

Voice: Female quack quieter, hoarser than Mallard. Courting male gives high, wiry, drawn-out *zoeeeeeaa* and short, mellow whistle *toop* or *prudud;* lower-pitched and more melodious than Green-winged Teal, often doubled.

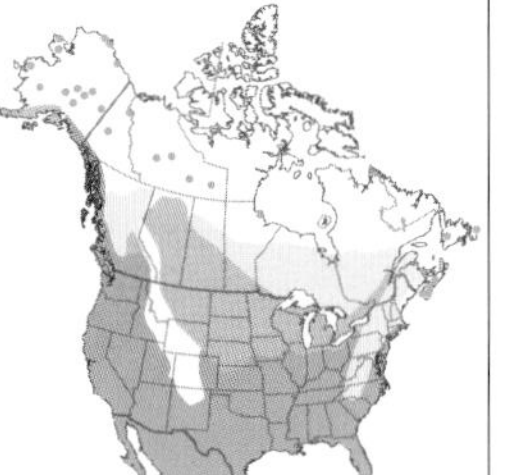

Most species of ducks hybridize with others. Some of the combinations seen occasionally are Mallard × Northern Pintail, Gadwall × American Wigeon, Northern Shoveler × Blue-winged Teal. Many other combinations have been recorded rarely, as have aberrant plumages not caused by hybridization.

Wigeons

These two species are very closely related. They pick food from the surface of shallow ponds and marshes or graze gooselike in open fields. Their flight is agile, in compact groups or uneven lines.

American Wigeon

Anas americana

L 20" WS 32" WT 1.6 lb (720 g) ♂>♀

Short bluish bill, rounded head, rather long, pointed tail. Note dark eye-patch, white on upperwing.

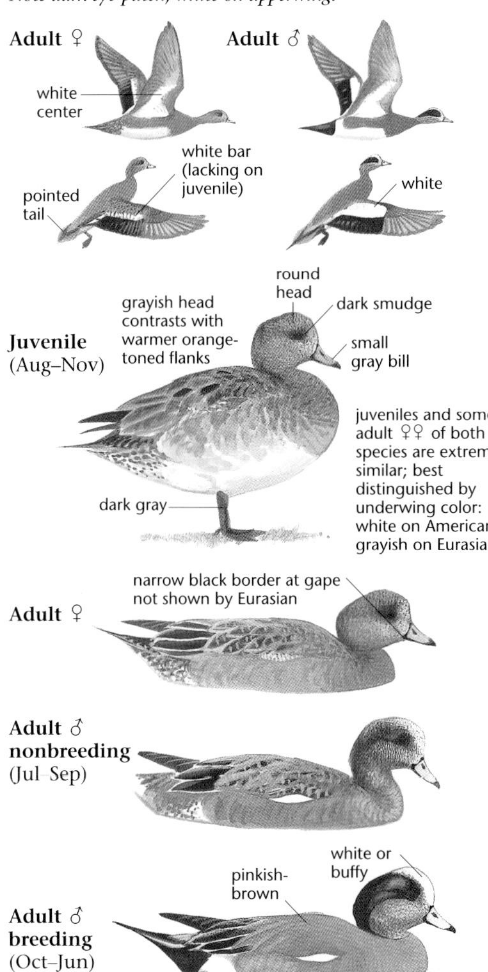

Adult ♀
Adult ♂
white center
white bar (lacking on juvenile)
pointed tail
white
round head
grayish head contrasts with warmer orange-toned flanks
dark smudge
small gray bill
Juvenile (Aug–Nov)
juveniles and some adult ♀♀ of both species are extremely similar; best distinguished by underwing color: white on American, grayish on Eurasian
dark gray
narrow black border at gape not shown by Eurasian
Adult ♀
Adult ♂ nonbreeding (Jul–Sep)
white or buffy
pinkish-brown
Adult ♂ breeding (Oct–Jun)

Voice: Female quack low, harsh, growling *rred* or *warr warr warr* similar to *Aythya* ducks. Male a distinctive airy whistle of two or three syllables *wi-WIW-weew* or *Wiwhew.*

Eurasian Wigeon

Anas penelope

L 20" WS 32" WT 1.5 lb (690 g) ♂>♀

Nearly identical to American. Female usually warmer brown on head; best distinguished by underwing color.

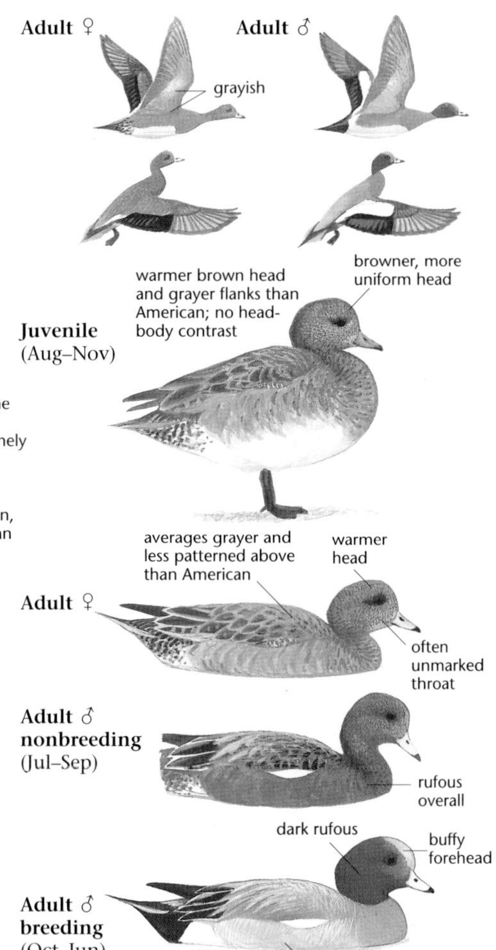

Adult ♀
Adult ♂
grayish
warmer brown head and grayer flanks than American; no head-body contrast
browner, more uniform head
Juvenile (Aug–Nov)
averages grayer and less patterned above than American
warmer head
Adult ♀
often unmarked throat
Adult ♂ nonbreeding (Jul–Sep)
rufous overall
dark rufous
buffy forehead
Adult ♂ breeding (Oct–Jun)
pale gray

Voice: Female quack may be even harsher than American. Male whistle distinctive, similar to American but higher, stronger, more vibrant descending single note *hwEEEEEEr.*

American × Eurasian Wigeon hybrid adults ♂ breeding
Variable.

Blue-winged Ducks

These species (and Cinnamon and Blue-winged Teals), found in shallow marshy ponds, rarely tip up but filter mud with their bills. All fly low in compact bunches, weaving like shorebirds.

Northern Shoveler

Anas clypeata

L 19" WS 30" WT 1.3 lb (610 g) ♂>♀

Medium-size, slender, with strikingly long spatulate bill. Feeds by skimming water with bill.

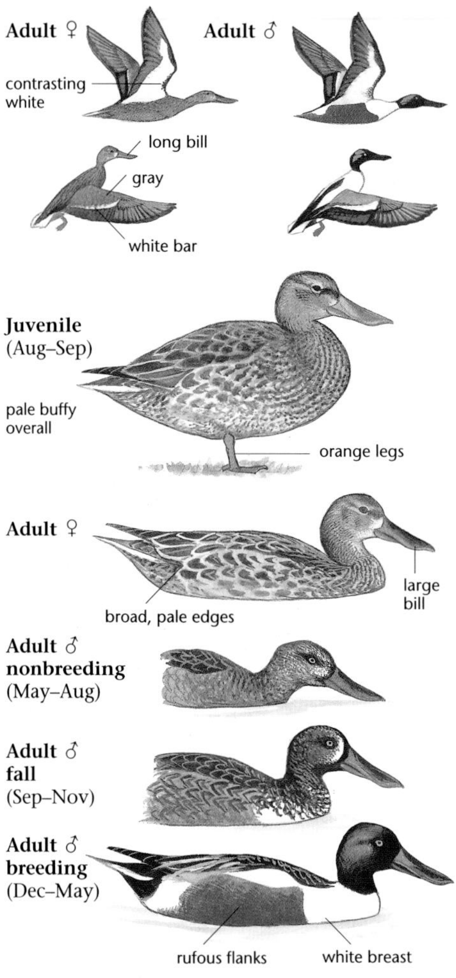
Adult ♀
Adult ♂
contrasting white
long bill
gray
white bar
Juvenile (Aug–Sep)
pale buffy overall
orange legs
Adult ♀
large bill
broad, pale edges
Adult ♂ nonbreeding (May–Aug)
Adult ♂ fall (Sep–Nov)
Adult ♂ breeding (Dec–May)
rufous flanks
white breast

Voice: Female quack deep and hoarse *kwarsh* and short *gack gack ga ga ga.* Male in courtship gives nasal, unmusical *thuk-thUK* and in fall a loud, nasal *paay.* Male's wings produce rattling sound on takeoff.

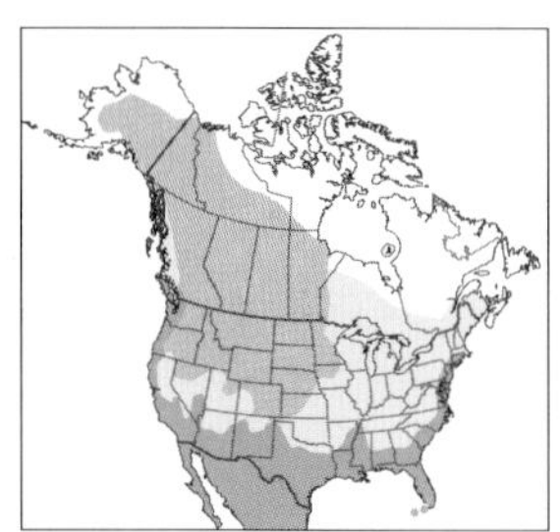

Garganey

Anas querquedula

L 15.5" WS 24" WT 13 oz (375 g) ♂>♀

Small; relatively square-headed, thick-necked, and heavy-billed. Note dark cheek-line, pale gray upperwing.

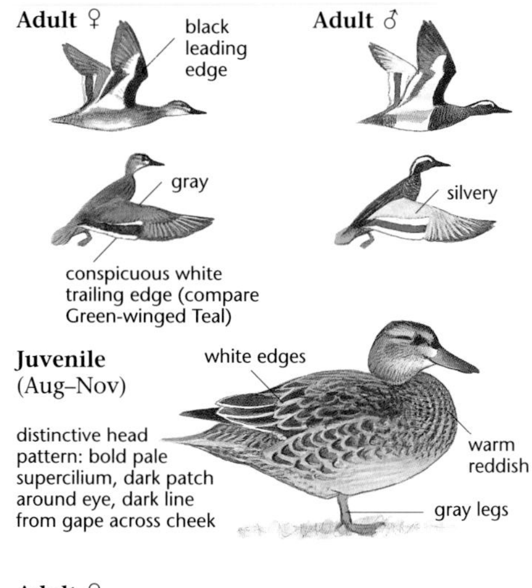
Adult ♀
black leading edge
Adult ♂
gray
silvery
conspicuous white trailing edge (compare Green-winged Teal)
Juvenile (Aug–Nov)
white edges
distinctive head pattern: bold pale supercilium, dark patch around eye, dark line from gape across cheek
warm reddish
gray legs

Adult ♀ nonbreeding (Jun–Feb)

Adult ♂ nonbreeding (Jun–Feb)

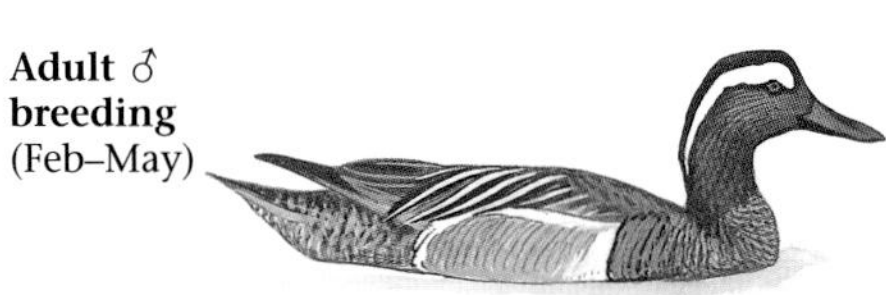
Adult ♂ breeding (Feb–May)

Voice: Female gives a feeble, shrill croak like Green-winged Teal; some calls like Blue-winged Teal or Northern Shoveler. Male in display gives a drawn-out, dry clicking like winding of a fishing reel, similar to Cinnamon Teal.

These two species are very similar; adult males are distinctive but other plumages are nearly identical. They are found in shallow water with emergent vegetation and filter mud with their bills.

Cinnamon Teal

Anas cyanoptera

L 16" WS 22" WT 14 oz (400 g) ♂>♀

Averages slightly larger, longer- and heavier-billed, thicker-necked, and shorter-winged than Blue-winged but differences subtle.

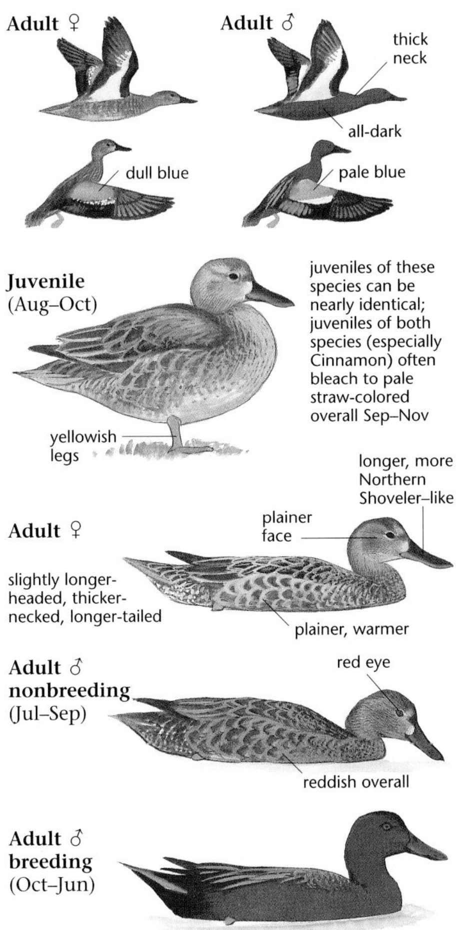
Adult ♀
Adult ♂
thick neck
all-dark
dull blue
pale blue
Juvenile (Aug–Oct)
juveniles of these species can be nearly identical; juveniles of both species (especially Cinnamon) often bleach to pale straw-colored overall Sep–Nov
yellowish legs
longer, more Northern Shoveler–like
plainer face
Adult ♀
slightly longer-headed, thicker-necked, longer-tailed
plainer, warmer
red eye
Adult ♂ nonbreeding (Jul–Sep)
reddish overall
Adult ♂ breeding (Oct–Jun)

Voice: Female quack like Blue-winged. Male in display gives a dry, chattering or rattling *gredek gredek . . .* ; vaguely reminiscent of Northern Shoveler, unlike the whistle of Blue-winged.

Blue-winged Teal

Anas discors

L 15.5" WS 23" WT 13 oz (380 g) ♂>♀

Small, rather long-bodied, and long-billed.

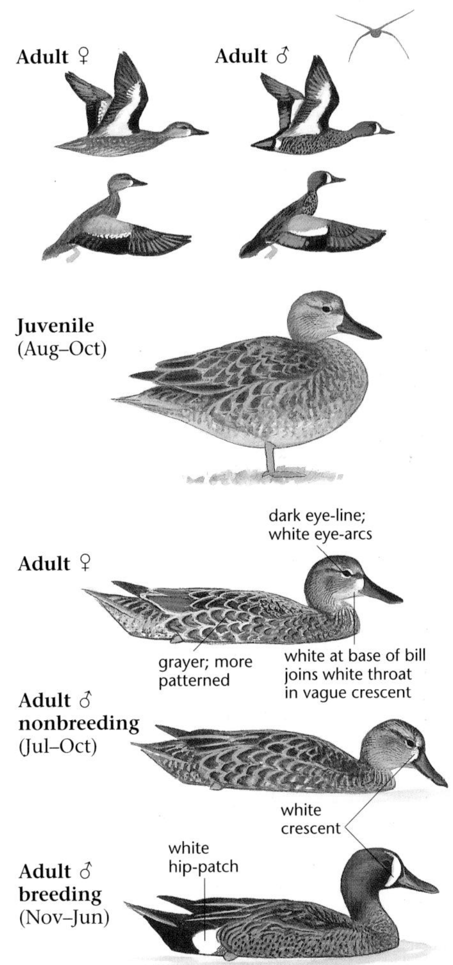
Adult ♀
Adult ♂
Juvenile (Aug–Oct)
dark eye-line; white eye-arcs
Adult ♀
grayer; more patterned
white at base of bill joins white throat in vague crescent
Adult ♂ nonbreeding (Jul–Oct)
white crescent
white hip-patch
Adult ♂ breeding (Nov–Jun)

Voice: Female quack coarse, high, less nasal than Green-winged; higher than Northern Shoveler. Courting male gives a rather thin, high whistle *pwis* or *peeew;* sometimes a nasal *paay* like Northern Shoveler.

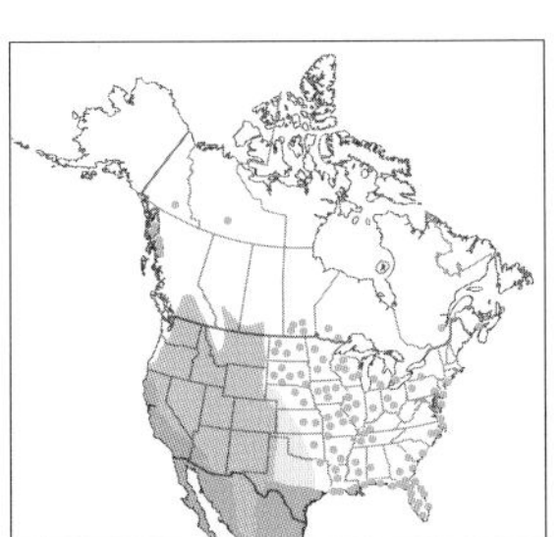

Blue-winged × Cinnamon Teal hybrid adult ♂ breeding
Seen occasionally.

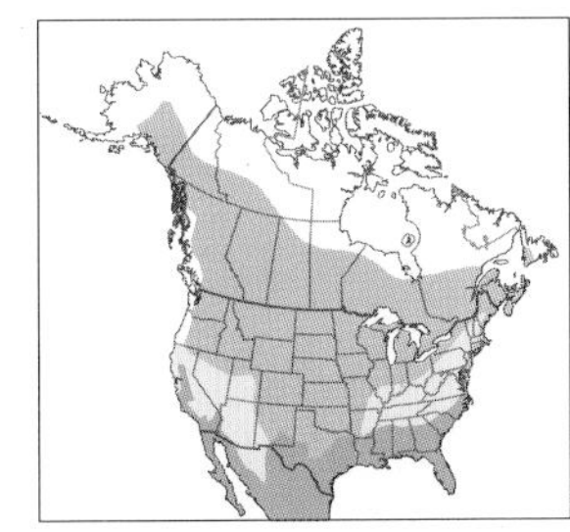

Green-winged Teal

This small, compact species is active and agile. Found in tight flocks on shallow, marshy or muddy ponds, it feeds mainly by dabbling its bill at the surface of water or mud.

Green-winged Teal

Anas crecca

L 14" WS 23" WT 12 oz (350 g) ♂>♀

Our smallest dabbling duck; smaller and more compact than other teals. Note round head, narrow bill, short body. Always shows clean buffy streak on undertail coverts.

AMERICAN

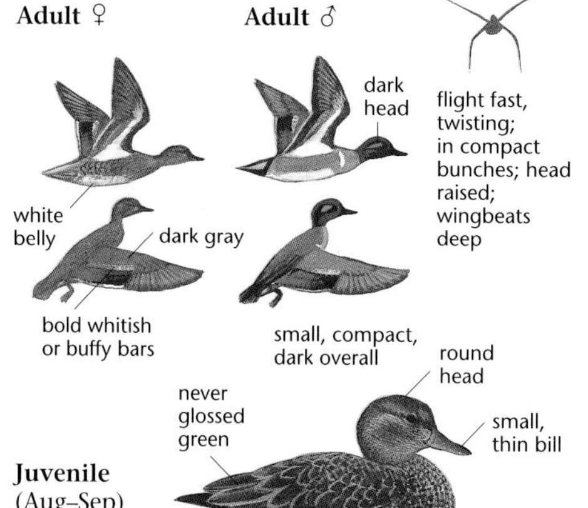

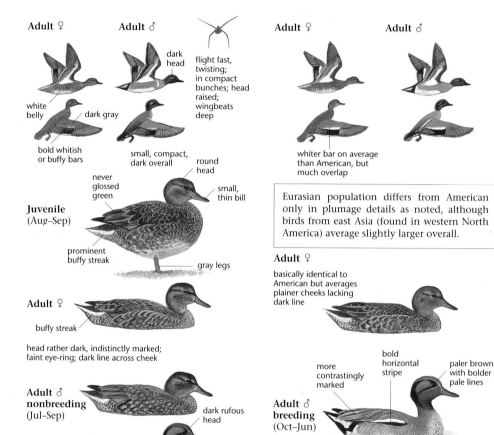

Adult ♀
Adult ♂
dark head
flight fast, twisting; in compact bunches; head raised; wingbeats deep
white belly
dark gray
bold whitish or buffy bars
small, compact, dark overall
round head
never glossed green
small, thin bill
Juvenile (Aug–Sep)
prominent buffy streak
gray legs

Adult ♀
buffy streak

head rather dark, indistinctly marked; faint eye-ring; dark line across cheek

Adult ♂ nonbreeding (Jul–Sep)

dark rufous head

Adult ♂ breeding (Oct–Jun)

white bar

EURASIAN (COMMON TEAL)

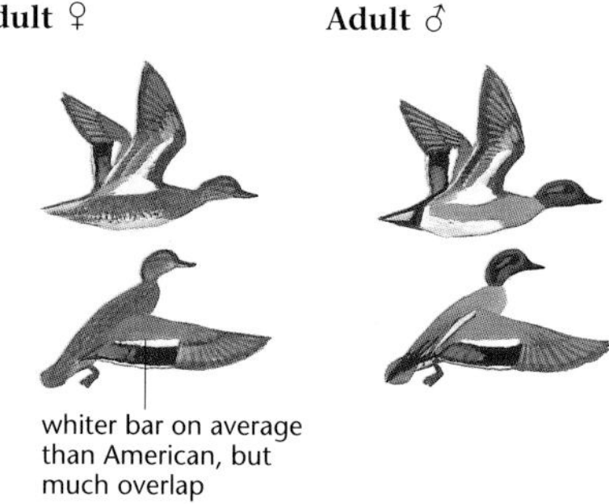

Adult ♀
Adult ♂
whiter bar on average than American, but much overlap

Eurasian population differs from American only in plumage details as noted, although birds from east Asia (found in western North America) average slightly larger overall.

Adult ♀

basically identical to American but averages plainer cheeks lacking dark line

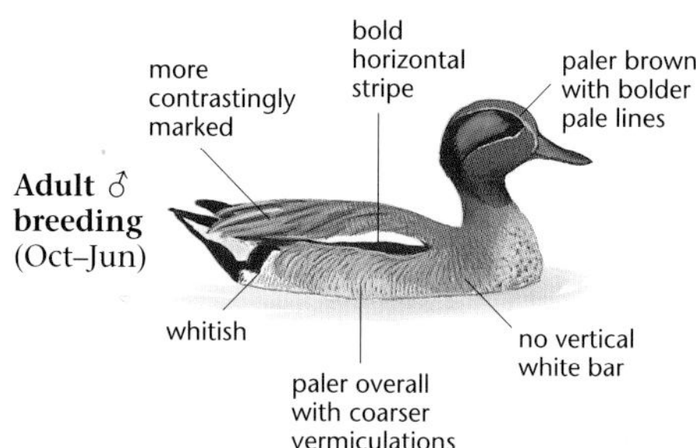

bold horizontal stripe
more contrastingly marked
paler brown with bolder pale lines
Adult ♂ breeding (Oct–Jun)
whitish
no vertical white bar
paler overall with coarser vermiculations

Voice: Female voice shriller, feebler than other ducks: high, nasal, scratchy *SKEEE we we we;* quality like snipes. Courting male gives a shrill, ringing whistle *kreed* or *krick* like Spring Peeper, sometimes in series of short phrases *te tiu ti,* etc.; males in fall give hoarser whistle.

EURASIAN

American × Eurasian intergrade adult ♂ breeding

Combines white bar on breast and white stripe on scapulars.

Domestic Waterfowl

The common domestic forms below are found on farm ponds and in city parks. Interbreeding produces a bewildering variety of plumages and sizes; some bear little resemblance to the parent species.

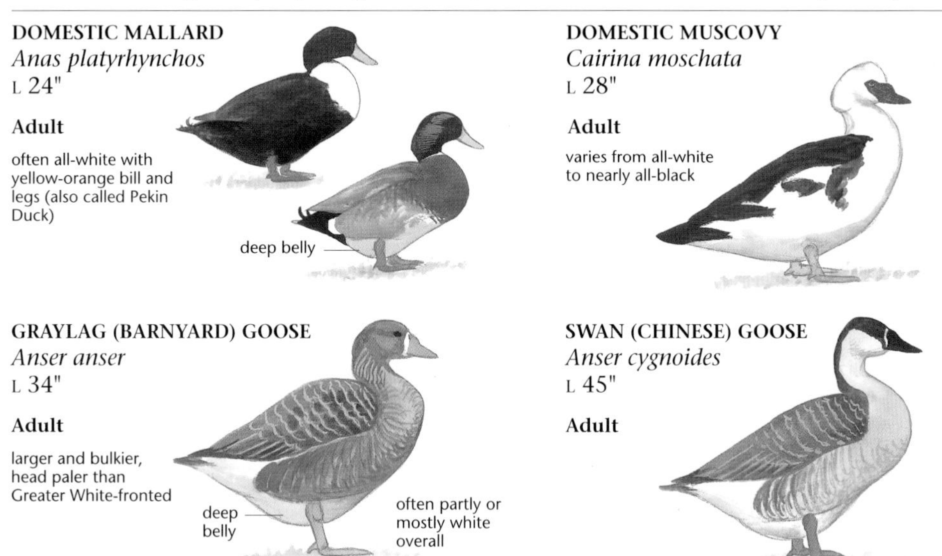

DOMESTIC MALLARD
Anas platyrhynchos
L 24"

Adult

often all-white with yellow-orange bill and legs (also called Pekin Duck)

deep belly

DOMESTIC MUSCOVY
Cairina moschata
L 28"

Adult

varies from all-white to nearly all-black

GRAYLAG (BARNYARD) GOOSE
Anser anser
L 34"

Adult

larger and bulkier, head paler than Greater White-fronted

deep belly

often partly or mostly white overall

SWAN (CHINESE) GOOSE
Anser cygnoides
L 45"

Adult

Exotic Waterfowl

Exotic species frequently escape from zoos and private collections; virtually any of the world's waterfowl species can occasionally be seen free-flying in North America. (Illustrations below are not to scale.)

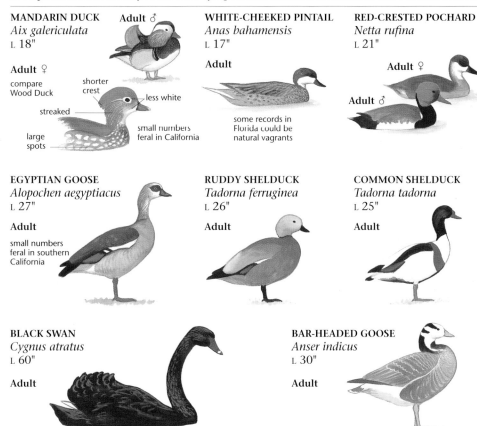

MANDARIN DUCK
Aix galericulata
L 18"

Adult ♂

Adult ♀

compare Wood Duck

shorter crest

less white

streaked

large spots

small numbers feral in California

WHITE-CHEEKED PINTAIL
Anas bahamensis
L 17"

Adult

some records in Florida could be natural vagrants

RED-CRESTED POCHARD
Netta rufina
L 21"

Adult ♀

Adult ♂

EGYPTIAN GOOSE
Alopochen aegyptiacus
L 27"

Adult

small numbers feral in southern California

RUDDY SHELDUCK
Tadorna ferruginea
L 26"

Adult

COMMON SHELDUCK
Tadorna tadorna
L 25"

Adult

BLACK SWAN
Cygnus atratus
L 60"

Adult

BAR-HEADED GOOSE
Anser indicus
L 30"

Adult

DUCKS: GENUS *AYTHYA*

These two species differ dramatically in head shape. Both nest on marshy lakes and ponds and winter in large flocks on sheltered bays and lakes, often mixed with each other and with scaup.

Canvasback

Aythya valisineria

L 21" WS 29" WT 2.7 lb (1,220 g) ♂>♀

Unique head shape with long black bill and flat forehead. Note female's overall pale color.

Adult ♀
long, straight neck
Adult ♂
flight fast and direct
extensive white
extensive white
little contrast
smooth slope; long, pointed bill
Juvenile (Aug–Oct)
long, stout neck
black
Adult ♀ breeding (Oct–Apr)
pale gray-brown
Adult ♂ nonbreeding (Jul–Sep)
black
white body
Adult ♂ breeding (Oct–Jun)
white tertials
limited black

Voice: Female gives a low, rough, growling *grrrt grrrt . . .* like other *Aythya* ducks; also a repeated *kuck.* Male in display gives eerie hooting *go-hWOOO-o-o-o* with weird, squeaky overtones.

Redhead

Aythya americana

L 19" WS 29" WT 2.3 lb (1,050 g) ♂>♀

Overall round; high, rounded back; puffy, round head. Note female's overall brown color.

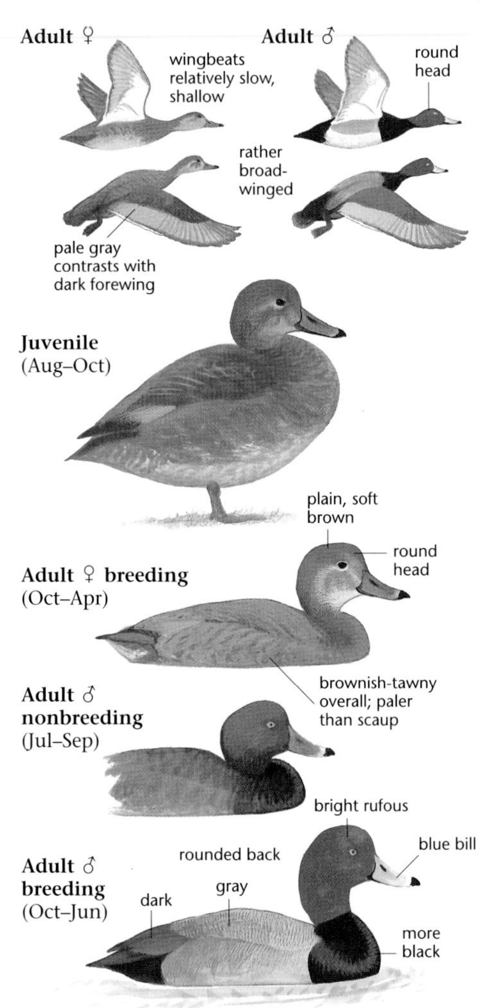

Adult ♀
wingbeats relatively slow, shallow
Adult ♂
round head
rather broad-winged
pale gray contrasts with dark forewing
Juvenile (Aug–Oct)
plain, soft brown
round head
Adult ♀ breeding (Oct–Apr)
brownish-tawny overall; paler than scaup
Adult ♂ nonbreeding (Jul–Sep)
bright rufous
rounded back
blue bill
Adult ♂ breeding (Oct–Jun)
dark
gray
more black

Voice: Female gives a rather soft, low, nasal *grehp* or harsher *squak.* Courting male gives distinctive and far-carrying catlike, nasal *waow.*

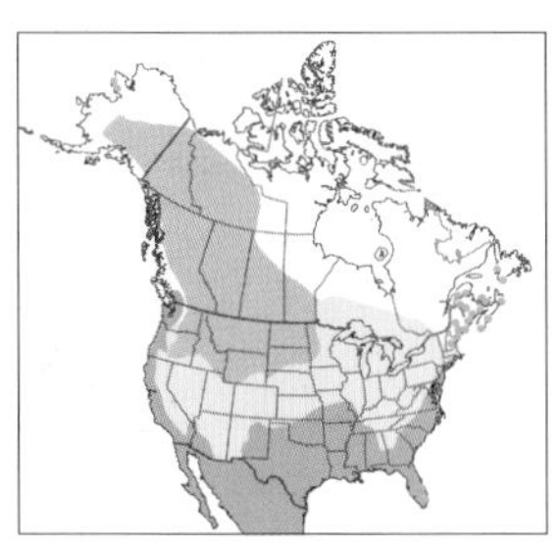

The six species in the genus *Aythya* all hybridize occasionally. Tufted Duck × Scaup is shown opposite; other combinations include Ring-necked Duck × Scaup and Canvasback × Redhead. Only male hybrids are readily identified; many are probably overlooked.

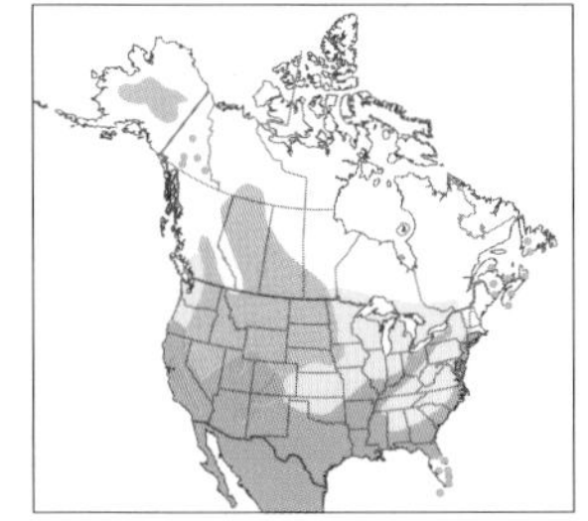

These two dark-backed species are similar to other *Aythya* ducks. Tufted is found on sheltered ponds and bays, usually with Lesser Scaup; Ring-necked prefers smaller, often wooded ponds.

Tufted Duck

Aythya fuligula

L 17" WS 26" WT 1.6 lb (740 g) ♂>♀

Round head with distinctive tuft; uniform dark back; extensive white wingstripe.

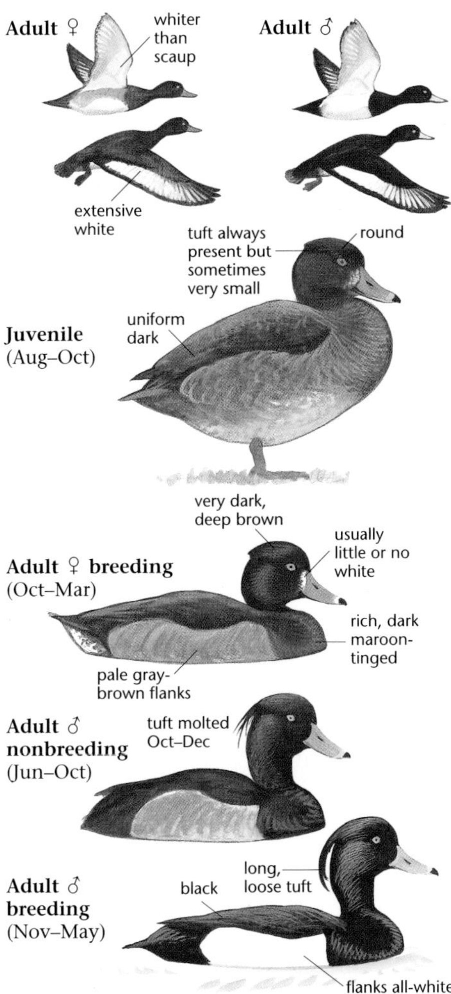

Adult ♀
whiter than scaup
Adult ♂
extensive white
tuft always present but sometimes very small
round
uniform dark
Juvenile
(Aug–Oct)
very dark, deep brown
usually little or no white
Adult ♀ breeding
(Oct–Mar)
rich, dark maroon-tinged
pale gray-brown flanks
Adult ♂ nonbreeding
(Jun–Oct)
tuft molted Oct–Dec
Adult ♂ breeding
(Nov–May)
black
long, loose tuft
flanks all-white

Voice: Female gives a soft, growling *kerrb.* Courting male produces a rapid, whistled giggle *WHA-wa-whew;* also a hoarse *wheeoo* and high peeping during display.

Ring-necked Duck

Aythya collaris

L 17" WS 25" WT 1.5 lb (700 g) ♂>♀

Compact; distinctive peaked head, dark back, pale "spur" on breast sides. Rises easily from water; flight more erratic and twisting than other Aythya *ducks.*

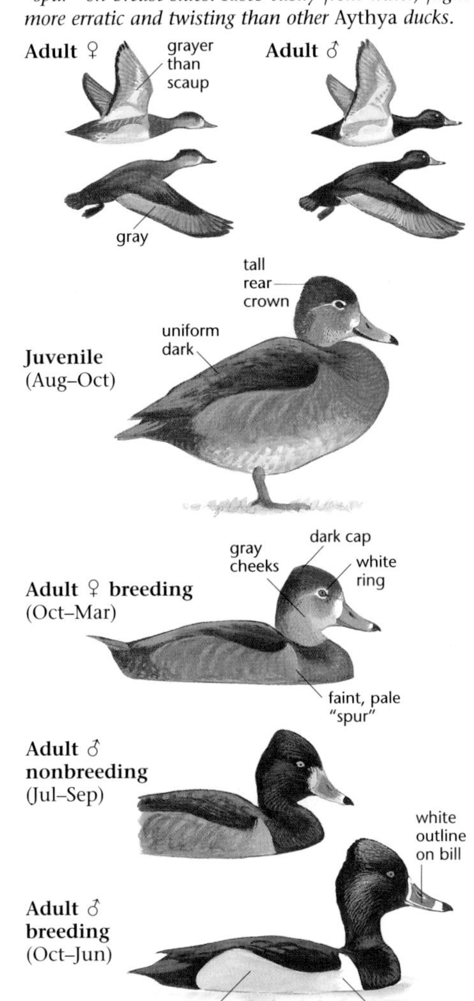

Adult ♀
grayer than scaup
Adult ♂
gray
tall rear crown
uniform dark
Juvenile
(Aug–Oct)
gray cheeks
dark cap
white ring
Adult ♀ breeding
(Oct–Mar)
faint, pale "spur"
Adult ♂ nonbreeding
(Jul–Sep)
white outline on bill
Adult ♂ breeding
(Oct–Jun)
gray
white "spur"

Voice: Female gives a purring or rough growl *kerp kerp. . . .* Male usually silent; during display gives a low-pitched, hissing whistle like a person blowing through a tube.

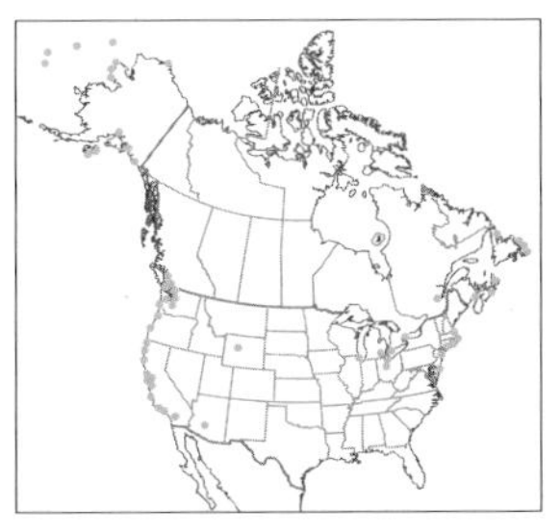

Tufted Duck × Scaup hybrid adult ♂ breeding
Seen occasionally.

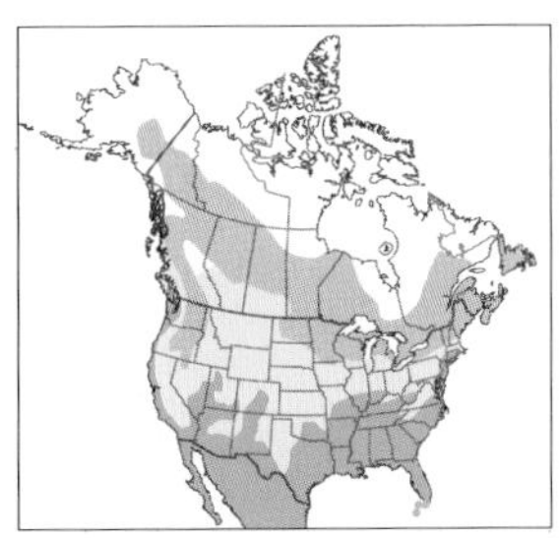

The two scaup are very similar in all plumages. In winter Lesser prefers fresh water and smaller ponds, and Greater prefers more open salt water, but there is complete overlap in habitat choice.

Greater Scaup

Aythya marila

L 18" WS 28" WT 2.3 lb (1,050 g) ♂>♀

Larger than Lesser with more rounded head, longer white wingstripe.

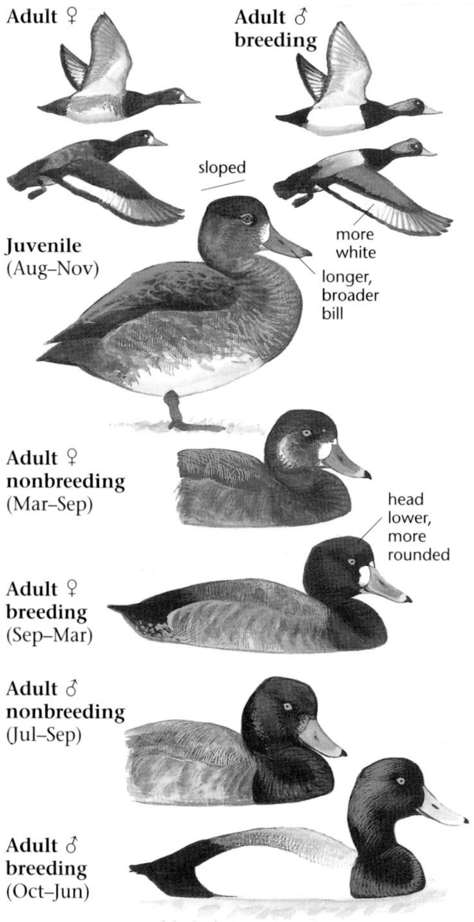
Adult ♀
Adult ♂ breeding
sloped
more white
Juvenile (Aug–Nov)
longer, broader bill
Adult ♀ nonbreeding (Mar–Sep)
head lower, more rounded
Adult ♀ breeding (Sep–Mar)
Adult ♂ nonbreeding (Jul–Sep)
Adult ♂ breeding (Oct–Jun)

Voice: Female gives very rough, hoarse *karr karr* . . . ; more rasping than other *Aythya* ducks; also softer, muffled *garrp garrp*. . . . Male in display often silent; sometimes produces a soft, hollow, bubbling hoot *blup BIDIVooo*.

Lesser Scaup

Aythya affinis

L 16.5" WS 25" WT 1.8 lb (830 g) ♂>♀

Smaller than Greater with thinner and straighter bill, thinner neck, smaller head with taller crown and more obvious, more vertical corner at rear crown.

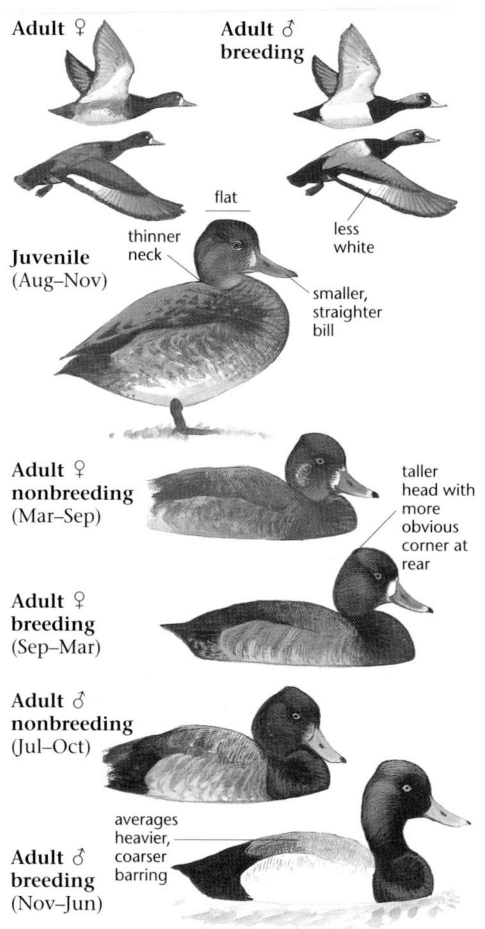
Adult ♀
Adult ♂ breeding
flat
less white
thinner neck
Juvenile (Aug–Nov)
smaller, straighter bill
Adult ♀ nonbreeding (Mar–Sep)
taller head with more obvious corner at rear
Adult ♀ breeding (Sep–Mar)
Adult ♂ nonbreeding (Jul–Oct)
averages heavier, coarser barring
Adult ♂ breeding (Nov–Jun)

Voice: Female gives rough, grating *garf garf* . . . ; possibly slightly higher and thinner than Greater. Male in display produces a husky whistled phrase higher-pitched and less hollow than Greater so that the effect is more peeping than bubbling; also a quiet whistle *pilt*.

The oft-discussed head color differences in scaup are essentially useless in the field. Both species can show bright green or purple gloss, depending on the bird's behavior and the observer's viewing angle.

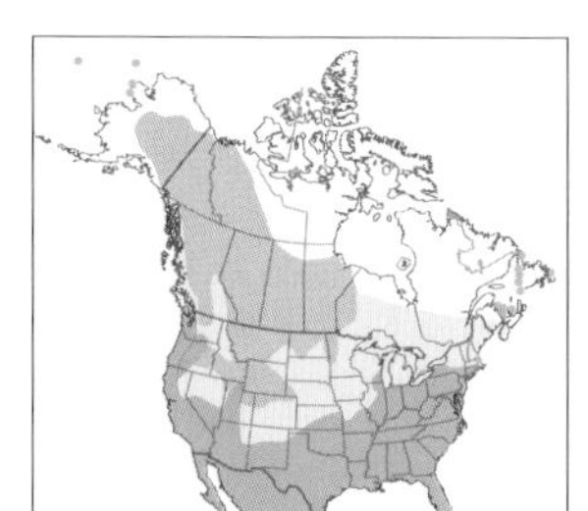

Identification of Scaup

The head shape of both species of scaup varies depending on activity, from active diving (top) to relaxed (bottom). Differences between the species are most apparent when relaxed and largely disappear when birds are active. (Watch for similar changes in the head shape of other ducks, e.g., goldeneyes.) Note the more rounded nape contour and the peak of the head farther forward on Greater.

Greater Scaup **Lesser Scaup**

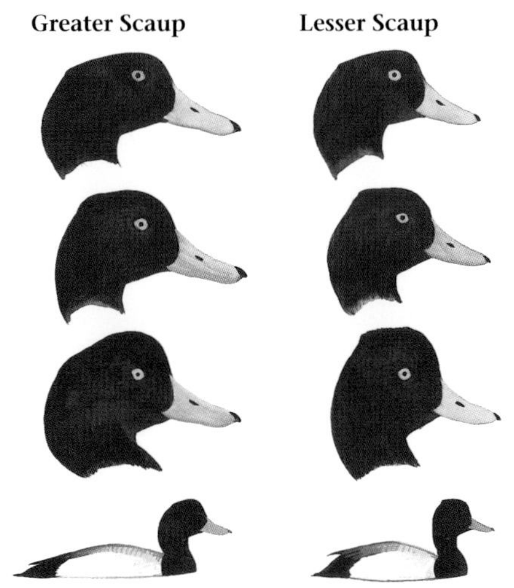

Lesser has a taller and narrower head (most evident when relaxed), with narrower, more straight-sided bill. Black nail at tip of bill averages smaller on Lesser, but there is much overlap.

Greater Scaup **Lesser Scaup**

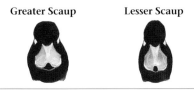

Differences in head shape are easily seen on sleeping birds in fully relaxed state. Scaup are often more easily identified when sleeping than when awake.

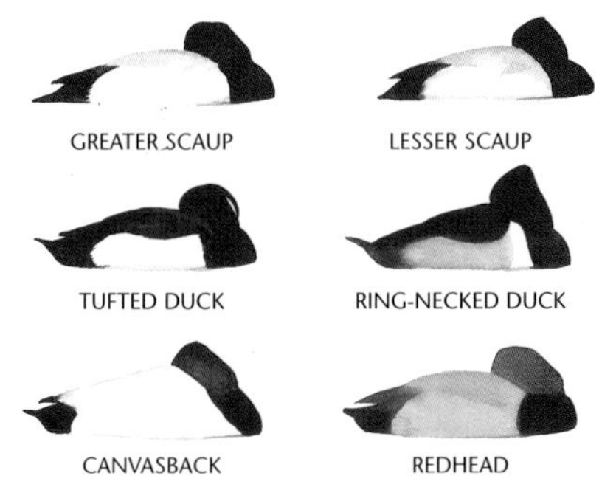
GREATER SCAUP
LESSER SCAUP
TUFTED DUCK
RING-NECKED DUCK
CANVASBACK
REDHEAD

Identification of Eiders

The exact shape and structure of the bill can be an important identification clue on eiders. Note especially the pattern of feathering around the base of the bill. The four populations of Common Eider shown here differ only on average, with many intermediate individuals. Females are shown; the bill shapes of adult male Common and King Eiders are quite different.

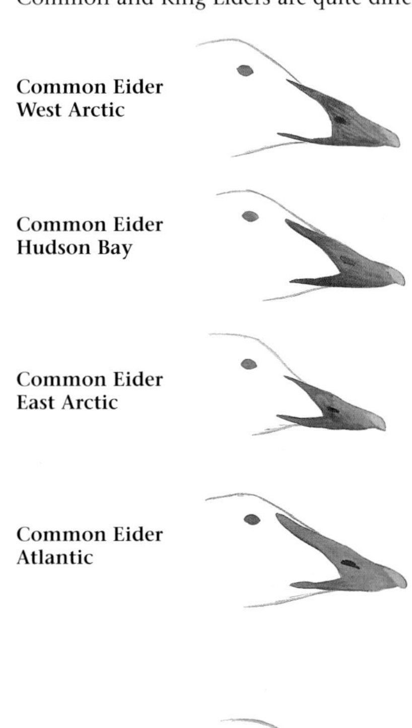
Common Eider West Arctic
Common Eider Hudson Bay
Common Eider East Arctic
Common Eider Atlantic

King Eider

Spectacled Eider

All eiders take two years to acquire adult male plumage, with a long and variable transition from the all-dark juvenile plumage to the white and black adult male plumage. Some individuals acquire a fairly striking pied face pattern, as shown.

Common Eider
1st spring ♂
(about Jun)

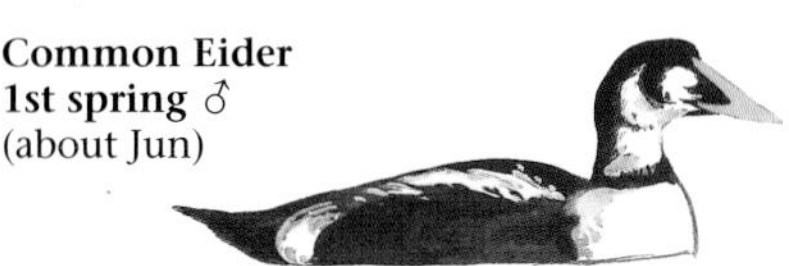

EIDERS: GENUS *SOMATERIA*

Somateria eiders nest on tundra ponds and rocky shores but in other seasons are found on open ocean. Males are strikingly patterned; females are best identified by head and bill shape.

Common Eider

Somateria mollissima

L 24" WS 38" WT 4.7 lb (2,150 g) ♂>♀

Our largest sea duck; large, wedge-shaped head with long bill, broad wings, heavy body.

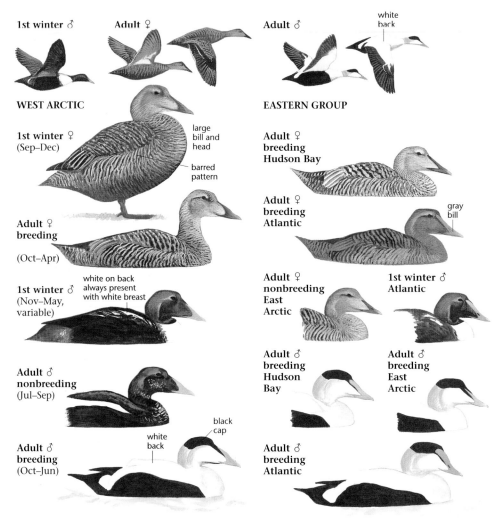

1st winter ♂

Adult ♀

Adult ♂

white back

WEST ARCTIC

1st winter ♀ (Sep–Dec)

large bill and head

barred pattern

Adult ♀ breeding (Oct–Apr)

1st winter ♂ (Nov–May, variable)

white on back always present with white breast

Adult ♂ nonbreeding (Jul–Sep)

Adult ♂ breeding (Oct–Jun)

white back

black cap

EASTERN GROUP

Adult ♀ breeding Hudson Bay

Adult ♀ breeding Atlantic

gray bill

Adult ♀ nonbreeding East Arctic

1st winter ♂ Atlantic

Adult ♂ breeding Hudson Bay

Adult ♂ breeding East Arctic

Adult ♂ breeding Atlantic

Voice: Female gives hoarse, guttural croaking or groaning sounds, from single *grog* to rapid clucking series *kokokokok*. Courting male gives a very low, hollow, ghostly moan *oh-OOOOooo*.

Populations vary in bill shape and overall color of females. West Arctic birds are most distinctive: largest with narrow, pointed bill lobes and broad, rounded point of feathering on lores (all others have loral feathering tapered to a point); female averages plain brownish. Hudson Bay birds have broad bill lobes; female averages pale silvery gray. East Arctic have short, narrow, pointed bill lobes; female averages grayer in color. Atlantic have long, broad bill lobes with rounded tip; female averages dark rufous. All females average grayer in summer and browner in winter, and color varies considerably within populations. Identification at this level is often impossible.

Eiders: Genus *Somateria* (continued)

Both these species are closely related to Common Eider. Some join flocks of other species, but in general eiders do not mix freely. They fly in long lines, bunched at the front, low over water.

King Eider

Somateria spectabilis

L 22" WS 35" WT 3.7 lb (1,670 g) ♂>♀

Slightly smaller than Common; oblong head and relatively small bill. Dark bill contrasts with pale feathering.

1st winter ♂ **Adult ♀** **Adult ♂**

black

1st winter ♀ (Sep–Dec)

small head and bill

short-lobed, dark bill and upturned gape create "grinning" expression

scaly pattern

Adult ♀ breeding (Nov–Apr)

nonbreeding averages buffier, paler

pale line more prominent than on Common

thick neck

1st winter ♂ (Nov–Apr, variable)

no white on back

orange bill

Adult ♂ nonbreeding (Jul–Nov)

Adult ♂ breeding (Dec–Jun)

Voice: Female gives low, wooden *gogogogogo . . .*; deeper than Common Eider. Courting male gives a low, hollow, quavering moan in crescendoing series *broo broooo brOOOOO broo.*

Spectacled Eider

Somateria fischeri

L 21" WS 33" WT 3.4 lb (1,570 g) ♂>♀

Smallest of the genus; unique pale "goggles" and dark forehead. Short bill extensively feathered at base.

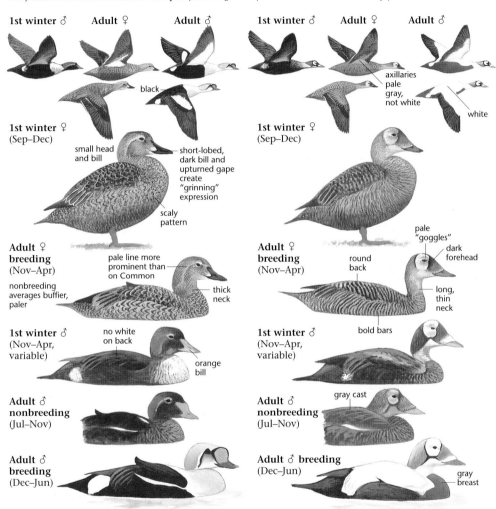

1st winter ♂ **Adult ♀** **Adult ♂**

axillaries pale gray, not white

white

1st winter ♀ (Sep–Dec)

pale "goggles"

dark forehead

Adult ♀ breeding (Nov–Apr)

round back

long, thin neck

bold bars

1st winter ♂ (Nov–Apr, variable)

gray cast

Adult ♂ nonbreeding (Jul–Nov)

Adult ♂ breeding (Dec–Jun)

gray breast

Voice: Generally silent. Female gives *gogogo . . .* like other eiders; croaking and clucking sounds at nest. Male in display gives faint *ho-HOO;* weaker than similar call of Common Eider.

Overall color can be useful for separation of female King and Common Eiders. King Eider is consistently grayish to buffy-brown throughout its range (averaging grayer in summer). West and East Arctic Common Eiders average slightly darker and duller brown than King; Hudson Bay birds paler and grayer; Atlantic birds darker and more rufous.

Distinctive Sea Ducks

Eiderlike in plumage but with unique shape and habits, Steller's Eider is found mainly in sheltered lagoons and bays. The small and agile Harlequin Duck favors extremely turbulent water.

Steller's Eider

Polysticta stelleri

L 17" WS 27" WT 1.9 lb (860 g) ♂>♀

Smaller than other eiders with square head, "normal" bill structure, longer tail.

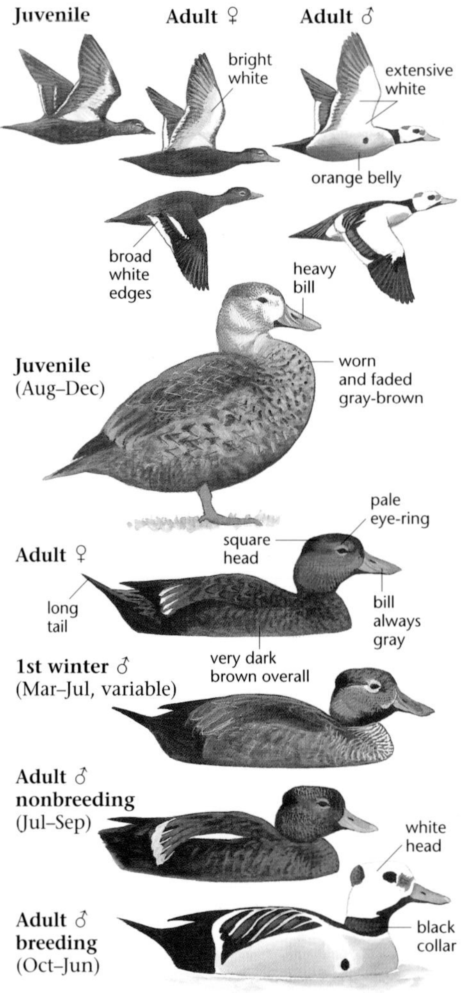

Juvenile
Adult ♀
Adult ♂
bright white
extensive white
orange belly
broad white edges
heavy bill
Juvenile (Aug–Dec)
worn and faded gray-brown
pale eye-ring
square head
Adult ♀
long tail
bill always gray
very dark brown overall
1st winter ♂ (Mar–Jul, variable)
Adult ♂ nonbreeding (Jul–Sep)
white head
Adult ♂ breeding (Oct–Jun)
black collar

Voice: Generally quiet. Female gives rapid, guttural calls and loud *cooay* in winter flocks; lacks *gog* call of *Somateria* eiders. Male essentially silent. Wings produce whistle in flight, louder than goldeneyes.

Harlequin Duck

Histrionicus histrionicus

L 16.5" WS 26" WT 1.3 lb (600 g) ♂>♀

Small with small bill, thick neck, long tail; female resembles Surf Scoter but size and bill shape obvious.

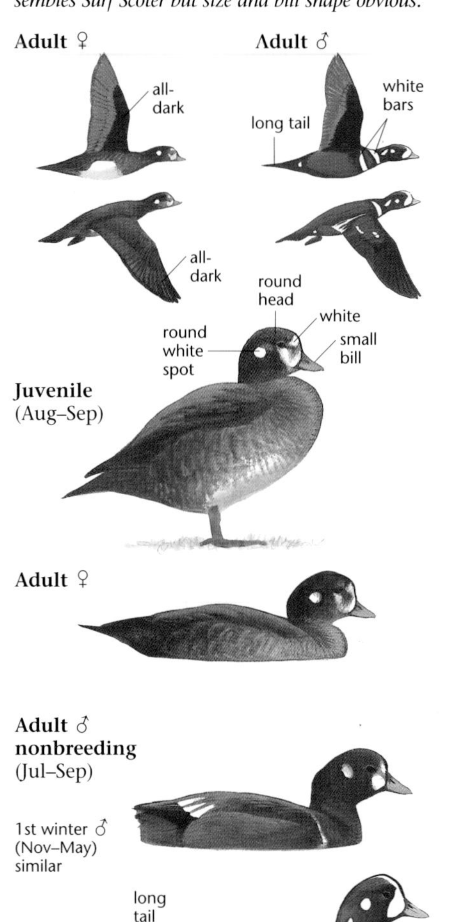

Adult ♀
Adult ♂
all-dark
white bars
long tail
all-dark
round head
white
round white spot
small bill
Juvenile (Aug–Sep)
Adult ♀
Adult ♂ nonbreeding (Jul–Sep)
1st winter ♂ (Nov–May) similar
long tail
Adult ♂ breeding (Oct–Jun)
precise pattern

Voice: Female gives an agitated, nasal *ekekekekek . . .* ; also smooth quacking. Male gives a high, squeaky whistle *tiiv,* sometimes rapidly repeated; reminiscent of Spotted Sandpiper alarm note.

This distinctive, heavy-bodied sea duck has a small bill and is very vocal. It nests on shallow tundra ponds and winters in small groups on shallow, open ocean over sandy bottom.

Long-tailed Duck

Clangula hyemalis

L 16.5" (adult ♂ to 21") WS 28"
WT 1.6 lb (740 g) ♂>♀

Round body; short, pointed, dark wings distinctive in all plumages. Formerly known as Oldsquaw.

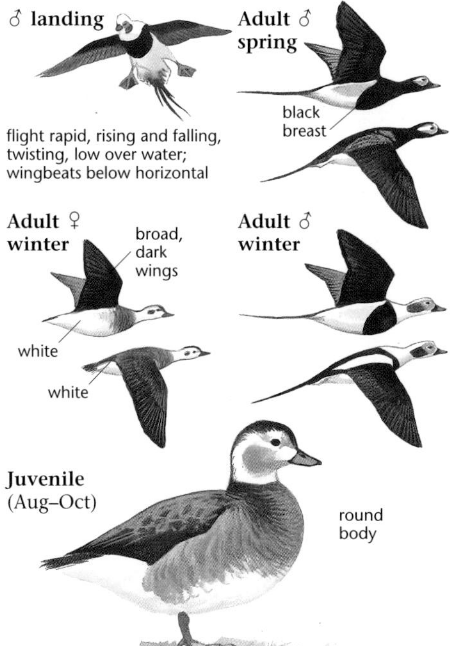
♂ landing
flight rapid, rising and falling, twisting, low over water; wingbeats below horizontal
Adult ♂ spring
black breast
Adult ♀ winter
broad, dark wings
white
white
Adult ♂ winter
Juvenile (Aug–Oct)
round body

DIVING MOTIONS

Diving motions of birds can be useful for identification at great distance.

Most diving ducks (and other diving birds) use only their feet for underwater propulsion and dive with wings closed tightly against the body.

Some ducks use their wings and feet for propulsion underwater and dive with a noticeable wing flick: Long-tailed Duck, Harlequin Duck, scoters (except Black), and eiders.

Alcids use only their wings for propulsion underwater and dive by simply tipping their bodies forward with their wings open and feet up and held loosely.

Adult ♀ spring (May–Jun)
small bill
always white
white face
Adult ♀ winter (Nov–Apr)

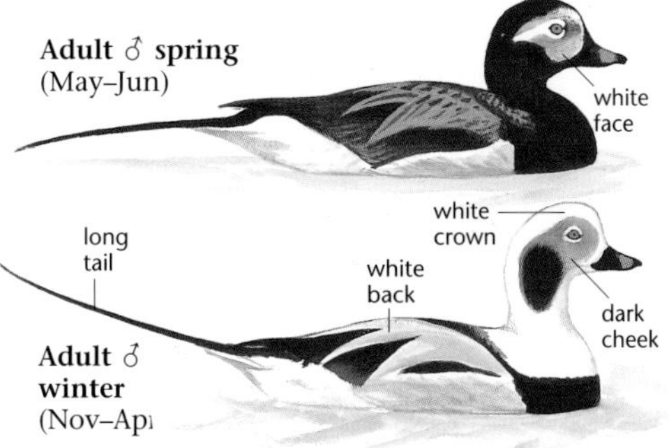
Adult ♂ spring (May–Jun)
white face
long tail
white crown
white back
dark cheek
Adult ♂ winter (Nov–Apı

Voice: Very vocal Feb–Jun. Female calls vary: soft grunting/quacking *urk urk* or *kak kak kak kak*. Male gives a melodious yodeling with clear, baying quality *upup OW OweLEP*.

Most ducks undergo two molts each year: a molt in early summer to nonbreeding or "eclipse" plumage, followed by a molt in fall back to bright breeding plumage. Long-tailed Duck begins molt earlier in spring and has a more complex schedule of interrupted and partial molts, such that an individual bird molts almost continuously Apr–Oct, undergoing a series of four different plumages (only two are illustrated above).

These two dark-winged species differ from each other in head and bill shape and head pattern. They are often found in mixed flocks, and large numbers migrate along both coasts.

Surf Scoter

Melanitta perspicillata

L 20" WS 30" WT 2.1 lb (950 g) ♂>♀

Square head and deep-based triangular bill most obvious on adult male; wings a little more pointed and body thinner than Black.

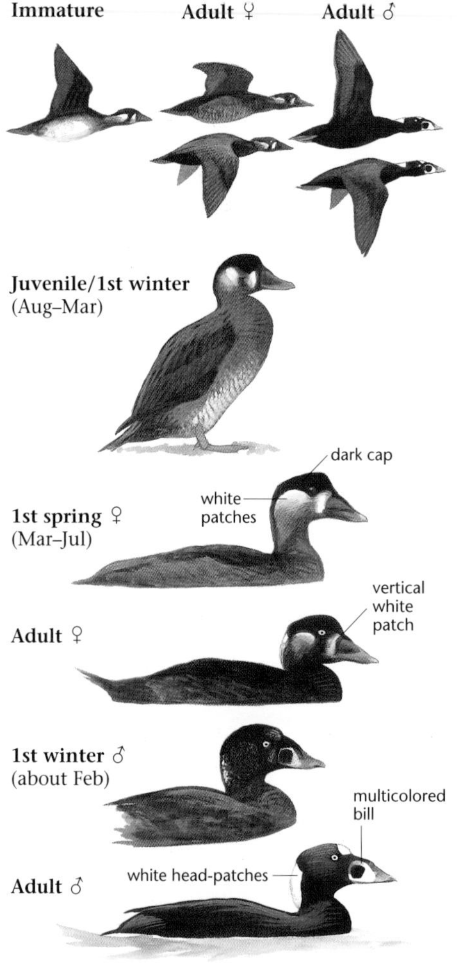
Immature
Adult ♀
Adult ♂
Juvenile/1st winter
(Aug–Mar)
dark cap
white patches
1st spring ♀
(Mar–Jul)
vertical white patch
Adult ♀
1st winter ♂
(about Feb)
multicolored bill
white head-patches
Adult ♂

Voice: Usually silent. Female gives a croaking *krrrraak krrraak*. Male produces a low, clear whistle or liquid, gurgling *puk puk*. Adult male's wings produce a low, hollow, whistling.

Black Scoter

Melanitta nigra

L 19" WS 28" WT 2.1 lb (950 g) ♂>♀

Slightly smaller and stockier than Surf, with round head and small bill.

Immature
Adult ♀
Adult ♂
Juvenile/1st winter
(Aug–Mar)
1st spring ♀
(Mar–Jul)
dark cap
thin bill
clean pale cheeks
Adult ♀
1st winter ♂
(about Feb)
yellow knob
all-black
Adult ♂

Voice: Most vocal scoter. Female calls low, hoarse, growling *kraaaa*. Male gives slurred, mellow, piping *peeeew* and plaintive whistle *cree*. Adult male's wings produce quiet, shrill whistling.

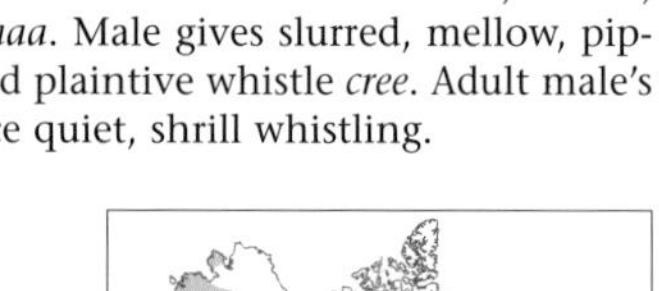

Black Scoter throws head downward when exercising wings, a distinctive motion.

Scoters (continued)

The three scoters are often found together in mixed flocks, but White-winged seems to prefer more sandy shores (less rocky). All nest on freshwater ponds and lakes.

White-winged Scoter

Melanitta fusca

L 21" WS 34" WT 3.7 lb (1,670 g) ♂>♀

Our largest scoter; sloping forehead and white secondaries distinctive.

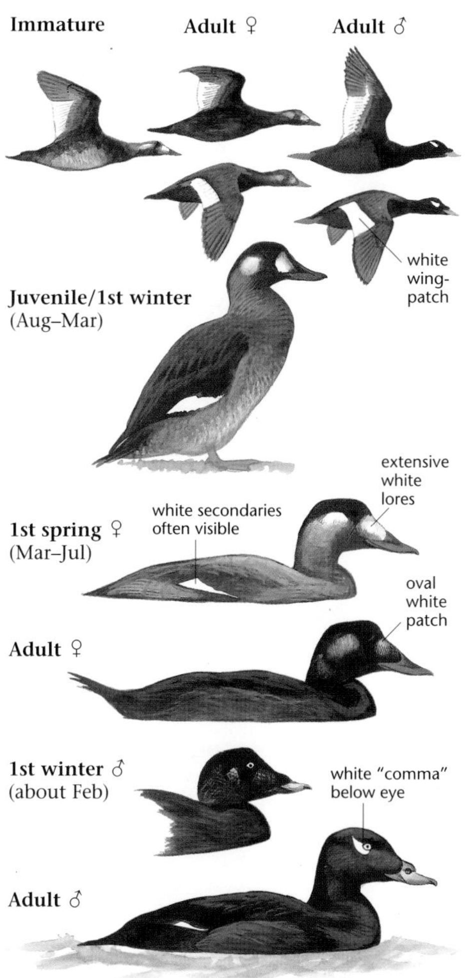
Immature
Adult ♀
Adult ♂
white wing-patch
Juvenile/1st winter (Aug–Mar)
extensive white lores
white secondaries often visible
1st spring ♀ (Mar–Jul)
oval white patch
Adult ♀
1st winter ♂ (about Feb)
white "comma" below eye
Adult ♂

Voice: Usually silent; calls brief, crude. Female and male give harsh, guttural croak/quack. Male in display gives thin whistle *wher-er.* Male's wings produce quiet, whistling sound in certain flight displays.

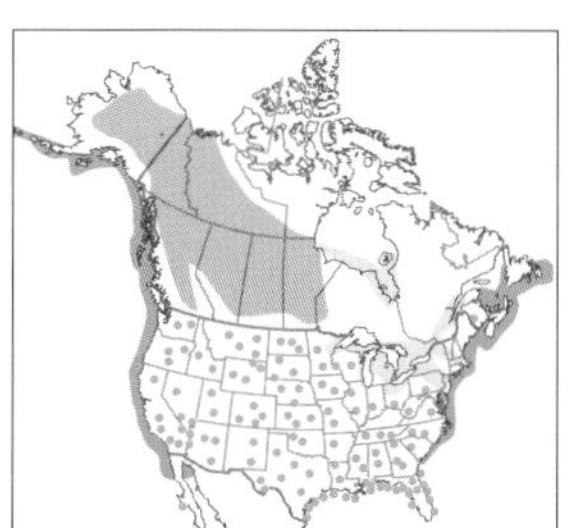

Identification of Scoters

Note the dramatic differences in patterns of feathering around the base of the bill, with no overlap between species. Differences in bill shape are most pronounced in adult males and least in juvenile females, but differences in feathering do not vary. The forward extension of feathering on White-winged is often pale or whitish, while the same area on Surf and Black is always unfeathered and dark.

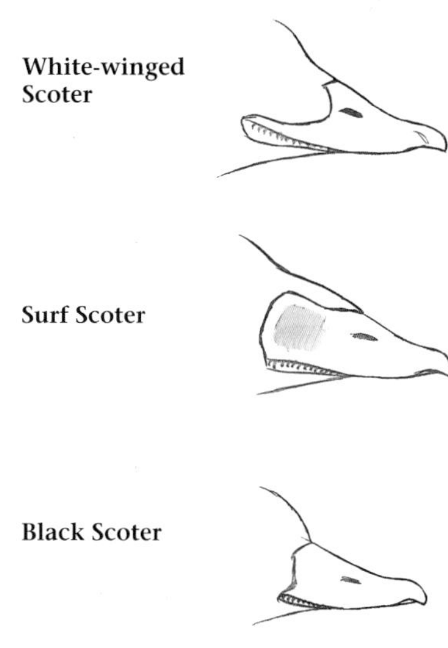
White-winged Scoter
Surf Scoter
Black Scoter

Identification of Goldeneyes

Note that Barrow's has a steeper forehead, shorter and relatively deeper bill, and the nail on the tip of the bill is relatively larger and slightly raised. This all contributes to the impression of a shorter and more stubby bill than Common. These differences may not be apparent in very young birds, and intermediate shapes are found on adult birds, but most individuals show noticeably different bill shapes.

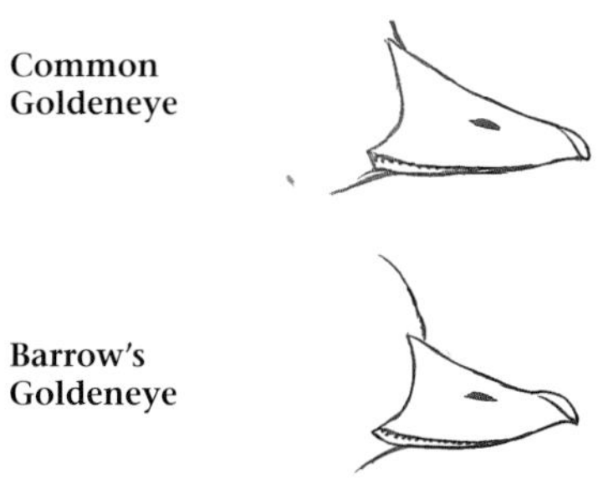
Common Goldeneye
Barrow's Goldeneye

GOLDENEYES

These two closely related species nest in tree cavities near ponds and lakes and winter in small flocks on bays, lakes, rivers. Similar in all plumages and best distinguished by bill and head shape.

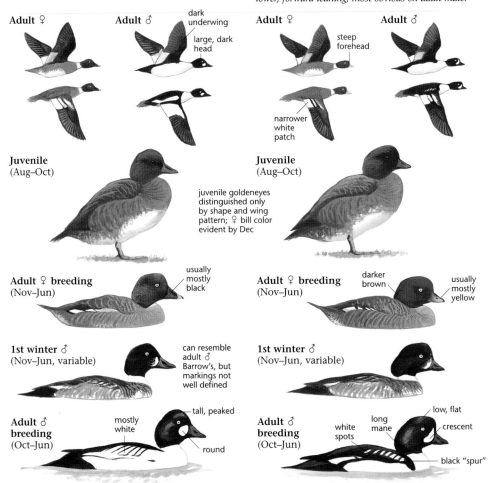

Common Goldeneye

Bucephala clangula

L 18.5" WS 26" WT 1.9 lb (850 g) ♂>♀

Stocky; rather large-headed like Barrow's. Flies in small bunches with deep wingbeats.

Adult ♀

Adult ♂

dark underwing

large, dark head

Juvenile
(Aug–Oct)

juvenile goldeneyes distinguished only by shape and wing pattern; ♀ bill color evident by Dec

Adult ♀ breeding
(Nov–Jun)

usually mostly black

1st winter ♂
(Nov–Jun, variable)

can resemble adult ♂ Barrow's, but markings not well defined

Adult ♂ breeding
(Oct–Jun)

mostly white

tall, peaked

round

Voice: Female gives low, grating *arr arr . . .* like *Aythya* ducks, often in flight. Male in display gives rasping, buzzy whistle *jip JEEEEV* and low, hollow rattle. Wings produce low, metallic whistle in flight; loudest in adult male, female nearly silent.

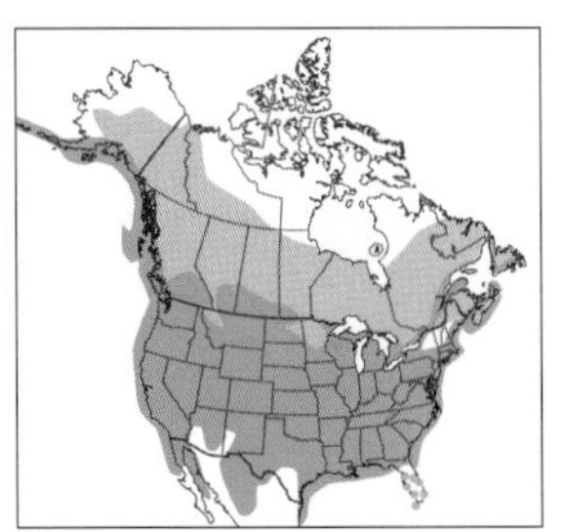

Barrow's Goldeneye

Bucephala islandica

L 18" WS 28" WT 2.1 lb (950 g) ♂>♀

Slightly larger than Common. Bill shorter, deeper with higher nail. Forehead steeper, mane longer; head appears lower, forward-leaning; most obvious on adult male.

Adult ♀

steep forehead

narrower white patch

Adult ♂

Juvenile
(Aug–Oct)

Adult ♀ breeding
(Nov–Jun)

darker brown

usually mostly yellow

1st winter ♂
(Nov–Jun, variable)

Adult ♂ breeding
(Oct–Jun)

white spots

long mane

low, flat

crescent

black "spur"

Voice: Female call like Common but possibly a little higher-pitched. Male in display gives weak, grunting *kaKAA,* unlike Common. Wings produce low whistle in flight; possibly quieter and less metallic than Common.

Common × Barrow's Goldeneye hybrid adult ♂ breeding
Intermediate shape and pattern with maroon head gloss.

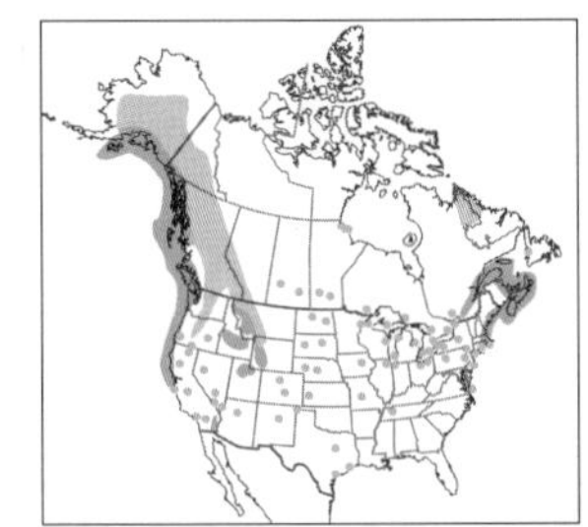

Bufflehead and Hooded Merganser

Bufflehead is similar to goldeneyes but smaller; Hooded Merganser is distinctive. Both nest in tree cavities and winter in small flocks on lakes and bays; Hooded prefers smaller, often wooded ponds.

Bufflehead

Bucephala albeola

L 13.5" WS 21" WT 13 oz (380 g) ♂>♀

Our smallest duck; tiny, compact, and short-billed with relatively large head.

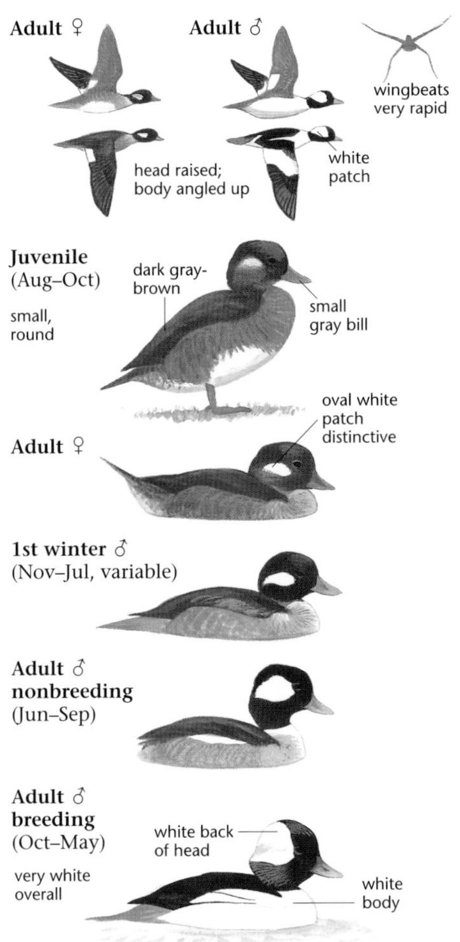

Adult ♀
Adult ♂
wingbeats very rapid
head raised; body angled up
white patch
Juvenile (Aug–Oct)
dark gray-brown
small, round
small gray bill
oval white patch distinctive
Adult ♀
1st winter ♂ (Nov–Jul, variable)
Adult ♂ nonbreeding (Jun–Sep)
Adult ♂ breeding (Oct–May)
white back of head
very white overall
white body

Voice: Usually silent. Female gives a low, hollow *prrk prrk* . . . similar to goldeneyes but weaker, softer. Male produces a squealing or growling call.

Hooded Merganser

Lophodytes cucullatus

L 18" WS 24" WT 1.4 lb (620 g) ♂>♀

Our smallest merganser; long-bodied and long-tailed with unique "hammerhead" crest.

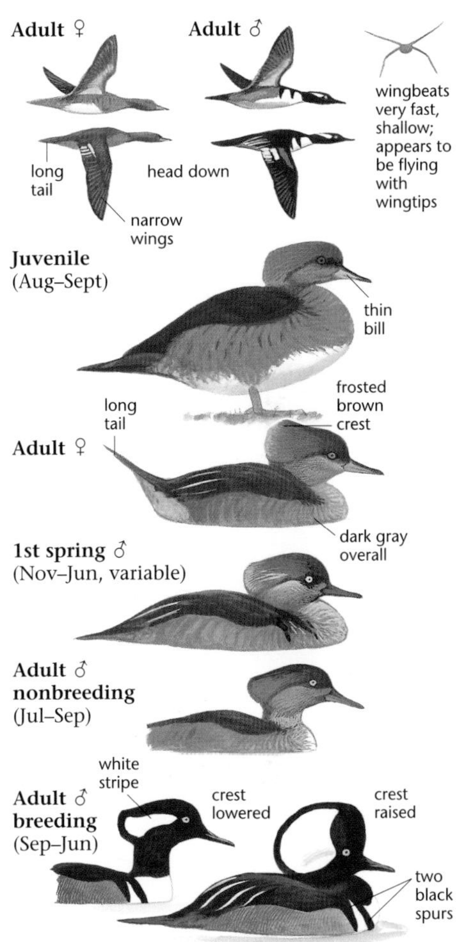

Adult ♀
Adult ♂
wingbeats very fast, shallow; appears to be flying with wingtips
long tail
head down
narrow wings
Juvenile (Aug–Sept)
thin bill
frosted brown crest
long tail
Adult ♀
dark gray overall
1st spring ♂ (Nov–Jun, variable)
Adult ♂ nonbreeding (Jul–Sep)
white stripe
Adult ♂ breeding (Sep–Jun)
crest lowered
crest raised
two black spurs

Voice: Female gives a soft croak *wrrep;* sometimes *ca ca ca ca ca* . . . in flight. Male in display gives a low, purring croak, descending and slowing *pah-hwaaaaaa.* Wings produce high, cricketlike trill in flight; loudest in adult male.

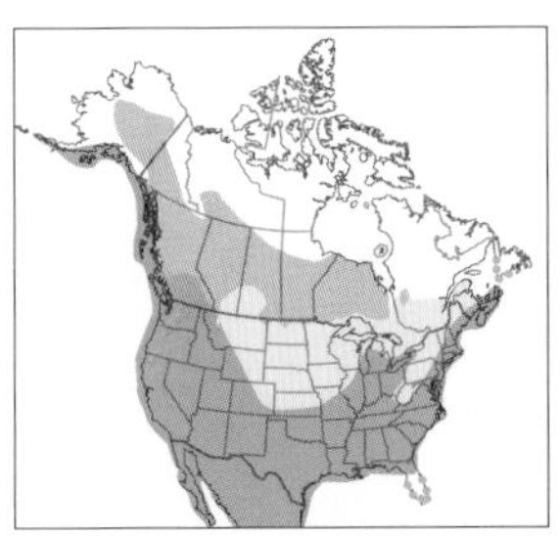

There are numerous records of apparent Hooded Merganser × Common Goldeneye (and some apparent Hooded Merganser × Bufflehead) hybrids. Size and bill shape are intermediate; males show all-dark head with reduced crest.

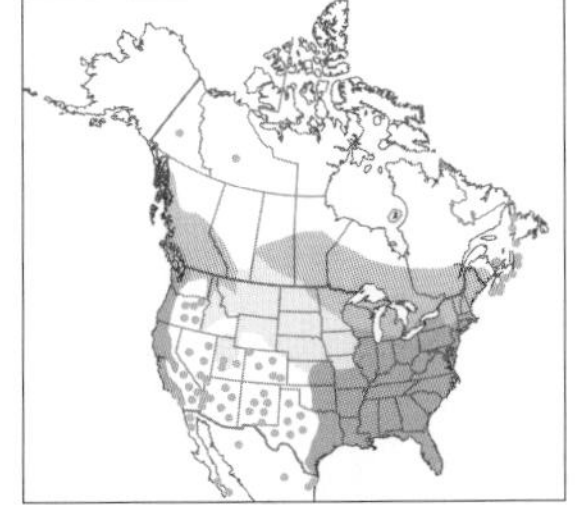

Large Mergansers

These two saw-bills are long-bodied and ride low in the water. Both are found on open water: Common prefers deep, clear lakes and rivers; Red-breasted prefers shallow, sheltered salt water.

Common Merganser

Mergus merganser

L 25" WS 34" WT 3.4 lb (1,530 g) ♂>♀

Distinctly larger and heavier than Red-breasted; shorter crest creates smoother head shape. Bill relatively deep-based, tapered.

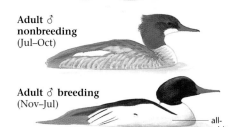

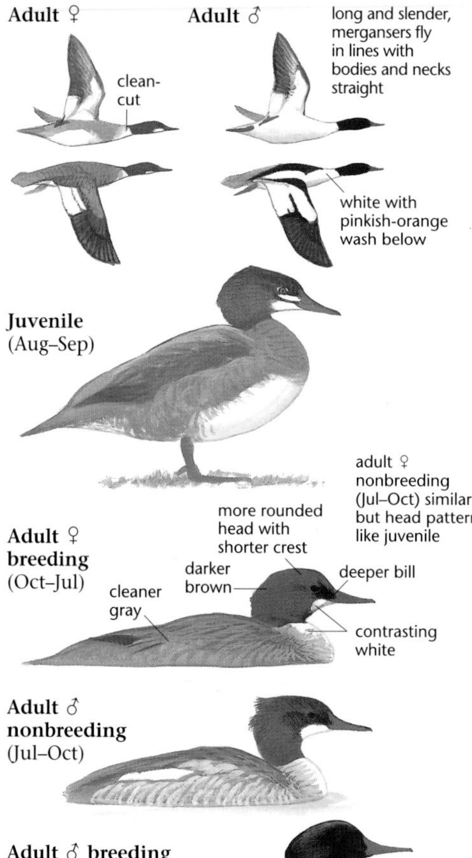

Adult ♀
Adult ♂
clean-cut
long and slender, mergansers fly in lines with bodies and necks straight
white with pinkish-orange wash below
Juvenile (Aug–Sep)
adult ♀ nonbreeding (Jul–Oct) similar but head pattern like juvenile
more rounded head with shorter crest
Adult ♀ breeding (Oct–Jul)
darker brown
deeper bill
cleaner gray
contrasting white
Adult ♂ nonbreeding (Jul–Oct)
Adult ♂ breeding (Nov–Jul)
all-white

Voice: Female call a deep, harsh, croaking *kar-r-r* in flight, sometimes accelerating to cackling *kokokokok*. Male also gives hoarse croaking notes; in display faint twanging or bell-like single notes.

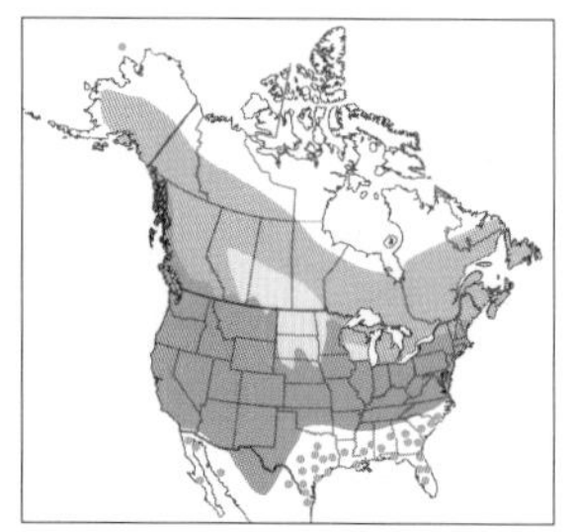

Red-breasted Merganser

Mergus serrator

L 23" WS 30" WT 2.3 lb (1,060 g) ♂>♀

Smaller and more spindly than Common with ragged crest. Compare loons, cormorants.

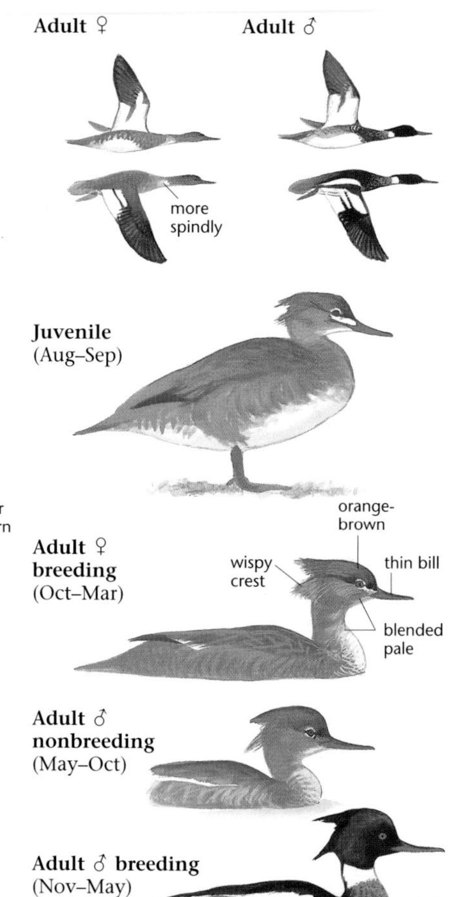

Adult ♀
Adult ♂
more spindly
Juvenile (Aug–Sep)
orange-brown
Adult ♀ breeding (Oct–Mar)
wispy crest
thin bill
blended pale
Adult ♂ nonbreeding (May–Oct)
Adult ♂ breeding (Nov–May)
dark

Voice: Female gives *prek prek . . .* in flight, similar to Common Merganser but slightly higher-pitched. Male mostly silent; in display a purring or scraping *ja-aah* and wheezy, metallic *yeow.*

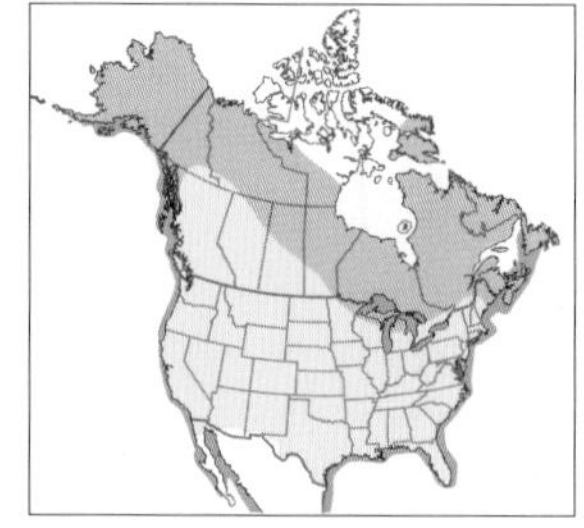

Stifftails

These small ducks both have long, spiky tails. Ruddy is found on open ponds and bays, often in tight flocks. The secretive Masked is found in marshy ponds and seldom ventures far from cover.

Masked Duck

Nomonyx dominicus

L 13.5" WS 17" WT 13 oz (380 g) ♂>♀

Smaller than Ruddy with relatively shorter bill, flatter crown. Note striped face and barred back of female.

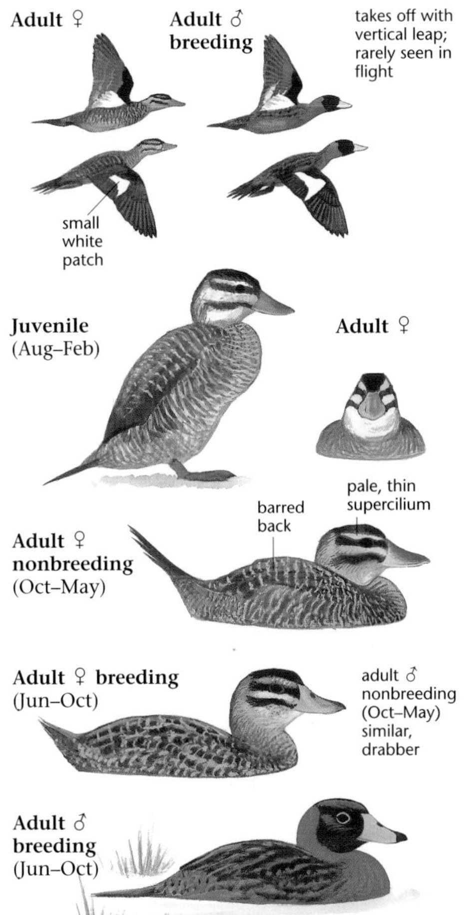

Adult ♀
Adult ♂ breeding
takes off with vertical leap; rarely seen in flight
small white patch
Juvenile (Aug–Feb)
Adult ♀
barred back
pale, thin supercilium
Adult ♀ nonbreeding (Oct–May)
Adult ♀ breeding (Jun–Oct)
adult ♂ nonbreeding (Oct–May) similar, drabber
Adult ♂ breeding (Jun–Oct)

Voice: Generally silent. Female gives a short hissing noise. Male in display gives a long series *kirri kirroo kirri kirroo kirroo kirroo kirrrr;* also quiet, throaty, puffing sounds *oo-oo-oo*, apparently nonvocal; also a short, low bark *bek*.

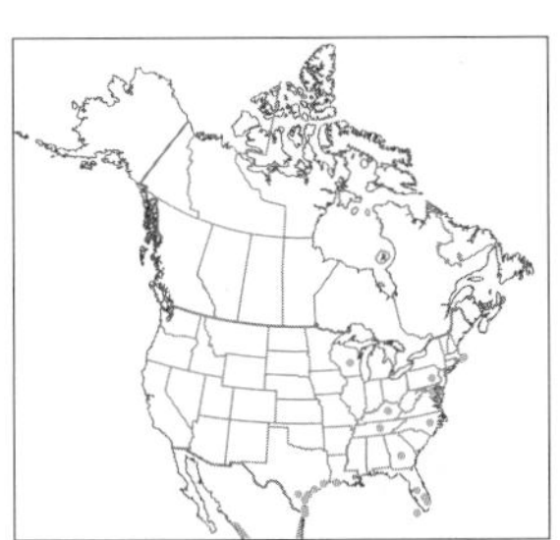

Ruddy Duck

Oxyura jamaicensis

L 15" WS 18.5" WT 1.2 lb (560 g) ♂>♀

Small and compact with large head and long tail. Note dark cap and pale cheeks.

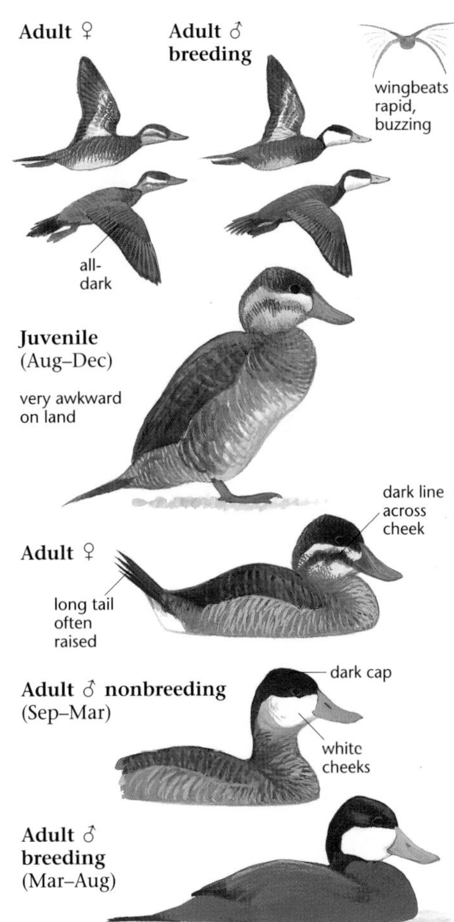

Adult ♀
Adult ♂ breeding
wingbeats rapid, buzzing
all-dark
Juvenile (Aug–Dec)
very awkward on land
dark line across cheek
Adult ♀
long tail often raised
Adult ♂ nonbreeding (Sep–Mar)
dark cap
white cheeks
Adult ♂ breeding (Mar–Aug)

Voice: Female gives a low, nasal *raanh;* also a high, sharp squeak and falsetto *queer*. Male essentially silent except during display: muffled popping series *jif jif jif jif ji ji ji ji jijijijijijwirrrrr;* also series of staccato pops produced by feet running on surface of water.

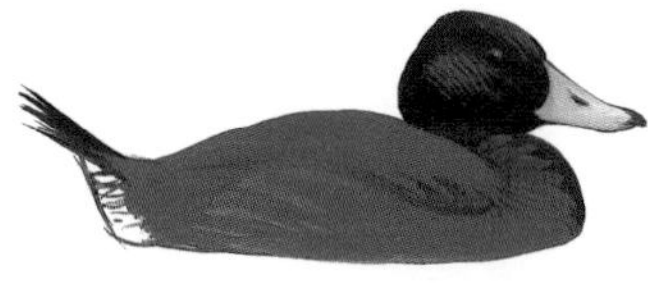

Rare dark Ruddy Duck adult ♂ has mostly or entirely black head.

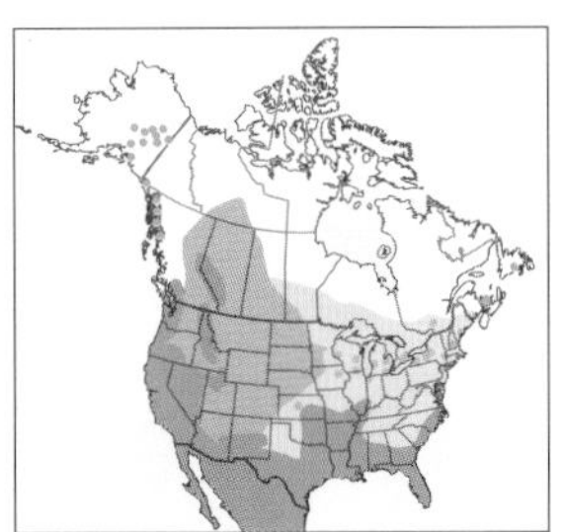

Diurnal Raptors

Families: Accipitridae, Cathartidae, Falconidae

34 species in 19 genera; all in family Accipitridae, except New World vultures in Cathartidae and true falcons and Crested Caracara in Falconidae. The varieties of wing shapes and body proportions are related to hunting style and preferred prey. Species with similar shapes tend to have similar habitats. Most raptors are very aerial and soar for long distances in search of food. Soaring raptors can be confused with unrelated soaring species: pelicans, Magnificent Frigatebird, Anhinga, Wood Stork, cranes, gulls, swallows, and ravens. Compare owls. Juveniles are shown (except vultures).

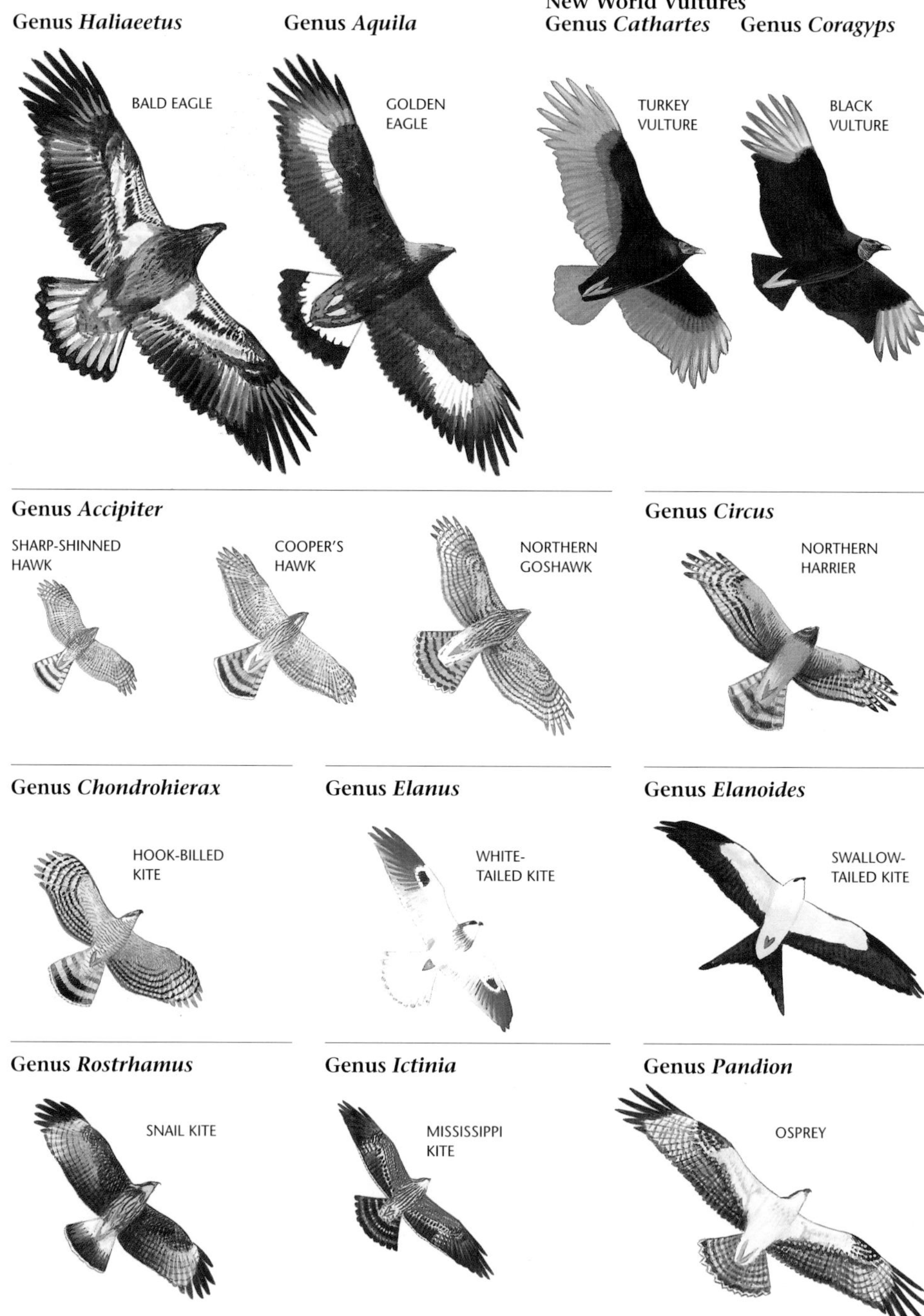

Genus *Haliaeetus*
BALD EAGLE
Genus *Aquila*
GOLDEN EAGLE
New World Vultures
Genus *Cathartes*
TURKEY VULTURE
Genus *Coragyps*
BLACK VULTURE
Genus *Accipiter*
SHARP-SHINNED HAWK
COOPER'S HAWK
NORTHERN GOSHAWK
Genus *Circus*
NORTHERN HARRIER
Genus *Chondrohierax*
HOOK-BILLED KITE
Genus *Elanus*
WHITE-TAILED KITE
Genus *Elanoides*
SWALLOW-TAILED KITE
Genus *Rostrhamus*
SNAIL KITE
Genus *Ictinia*
MISSISSIPPI KITE
Genus *Pandion*
OSPREY

Buteo-like Hawks

Genus *Buteogallus*

COMMON BLACK-HAWK

Genus *Parabuteo*

HARRIS'S HAWK

Genus *Asturina*

GRAY HAWK

Genus *Buteo*

RED-SHOULDERED HAWK
Eastern

BROAD-WINGED HAWK

SHORT-TAILED HAWK

ZONE-TAILED HAWK

SWAINSON'S HAWK

WHITE-TAILED HAWK

RED-TAILED HAWK
Western

ROUGH-LEGGED HAWK

FERRUGINOUS HAWK

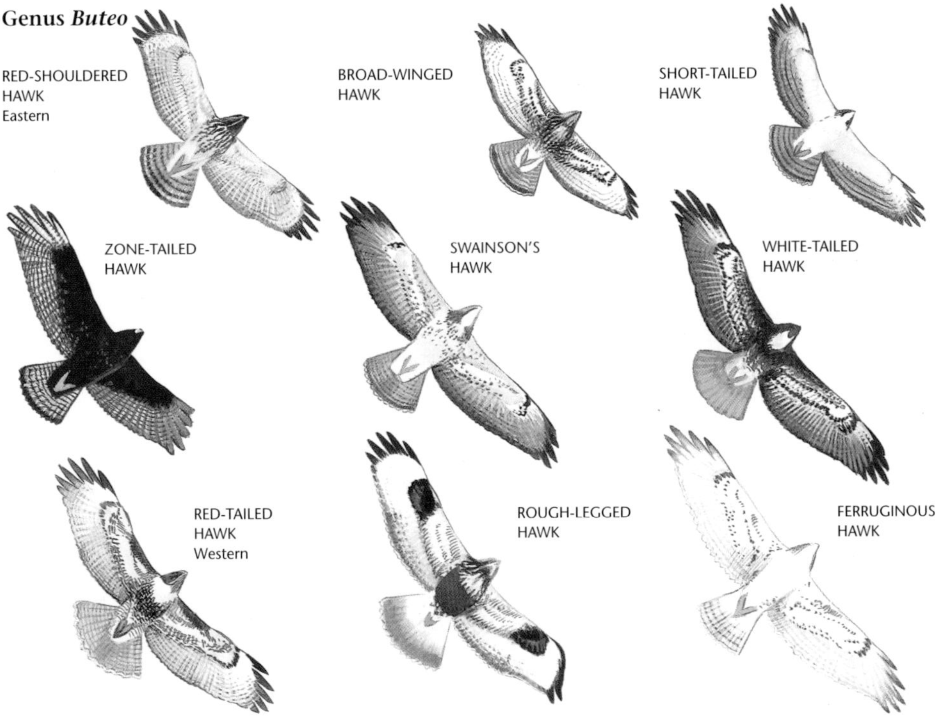

True Falcons
Genus *Falco*

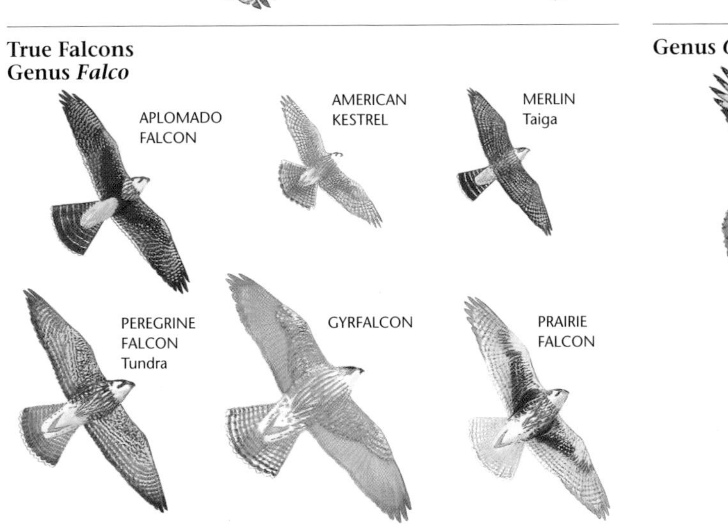
APLOMADO FALCON
AMERICAN KESTREL
MERLIN
Taiga
PEREGRINE FALCON
Tundra
GYRFALCON
PRAIRIE FALCON

Genus *Caracara*

NORTHERN CARACARA

California Condor is one of our largest and rarest birds. Rescued from extinction by intensive human efforts, it is now found in several locations where captive-bred birds have been released.

California Condor

Gymnogyps californianus

L 46" WS 109" WT 23 lb (10.5 kg)

Our largest raptor, larger than eagles; broad wings with long, "fingered" primaries.

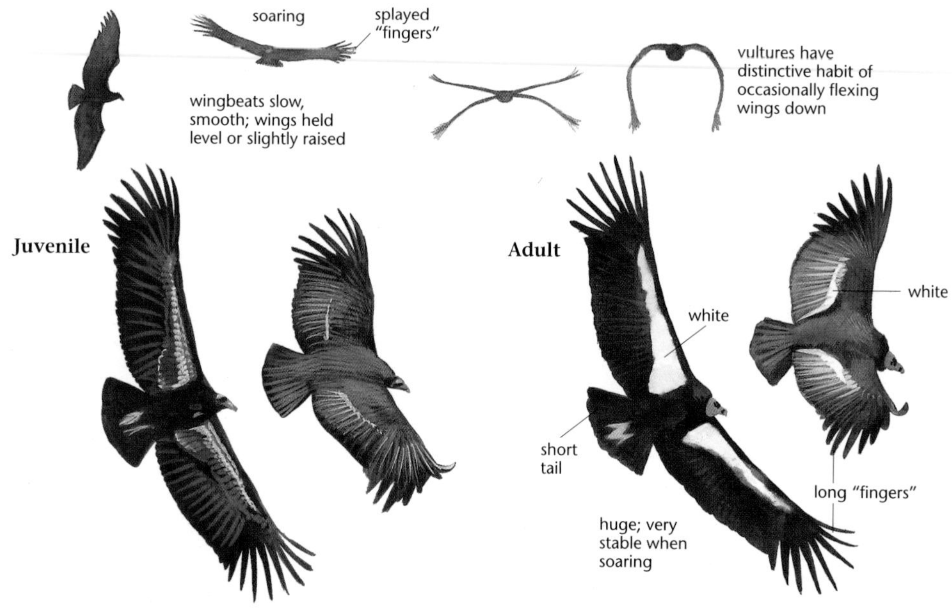
soaring
splayed "fingers"
wingbeats slow, smooth; wings held level or slightly raised
vultures have distinctive habit of occasionally flexing wings down
Juvenile
Adult
white
white
short tail
long "fingers"
huge; very stable when soaring

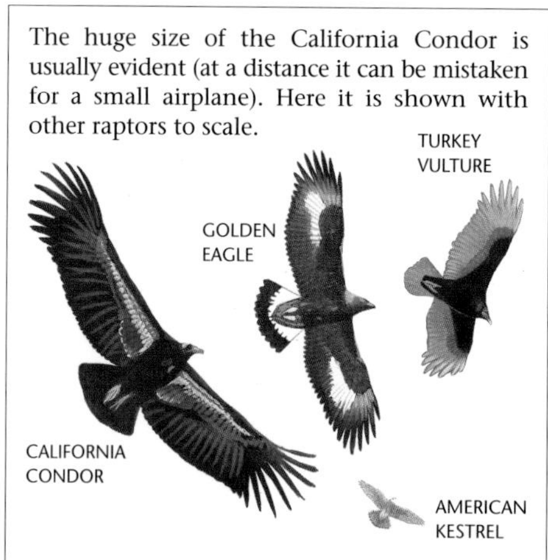
The huge size of the California Condor is usually evident (at a distance it can be mistaken for a small airplane). Here it is shown with other raptors to scale.
TURKEY VULTURE
GOLDEN EAGLE
CALIFORNIA CONDOR
AMERICAN KESTREL

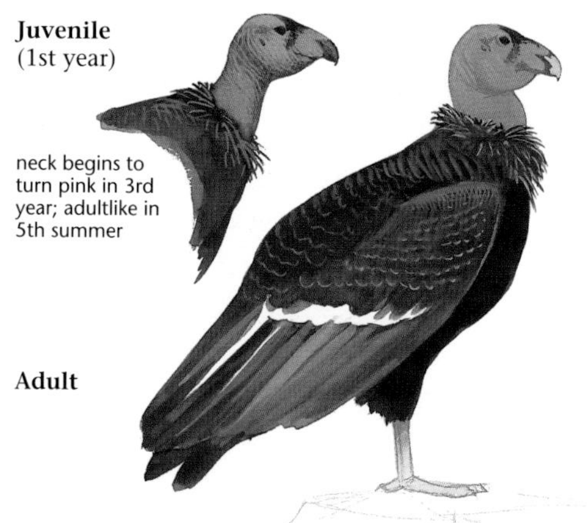
Juvenile (1st year)
neck begins to turn pink in 3rd year; adultlike in 5th summer
Adult

Voice: Usually silent; limited to hissing and grunting. Wings produce loud swishing noise.

Recent research suggests that New World vultures are more closely related to storks than to hawks and eagles; some authorities even merge vultures and storks into a single family. In this book, vultures are retained in their traditional position alongside hawks and eagles because of the strong (even if only superficial) resemblance between the groups.

These two species of carrion-feeders are often seen soaring or roosting in groups. They are easily distinguished from each other by shape and wingbeats. Turkey Vulture finds food by smell.

Turkey Vulture

Cathartes aura

L 26" WS 67" WT 4 lb (1,830 g)

Soars with pronounced dihedral; small head and two-toned underwing distinctive.

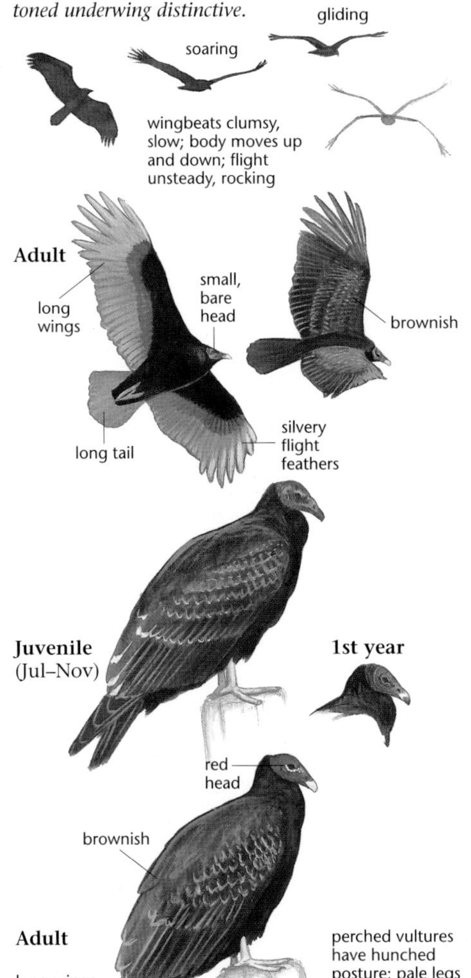
gliding
soaring
wingbeats clumsy, slow; body moves up and down; flight unsteady, rocking
Adult
long wings
small, bare head
brownish
long tail
silvery flight feathers
Juvenile (Jul–Nov)
1st year
red head
brownish
Adult
long wings and tail
perched vultures have hunched posture; pale legs visible

Voice: Usually silent; limited to soft hissing, clucking, and whining.

Black Vulture

Coragyps atratus

L 25" WS 59" WT 4.4 lb (2,000 g)

Soars with slight dihedral; note short tail and quick, choppy wingbeats.

soaring
wings nearly flat
gliding
wingbeats snappy, quick

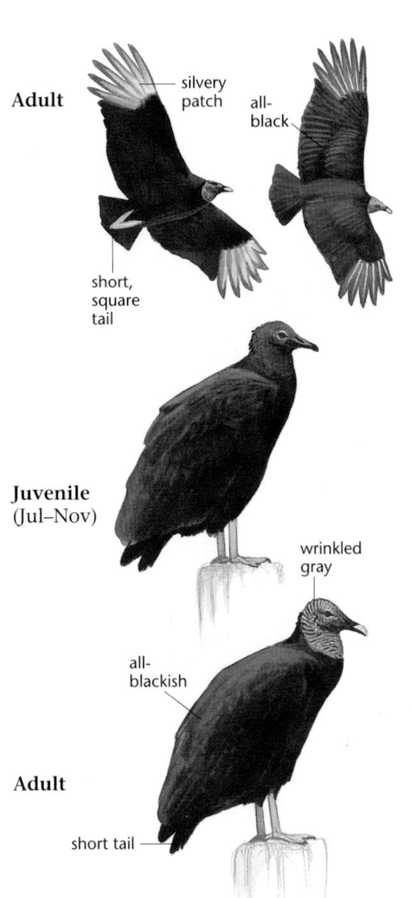
Adult
silvery patch
all-black
short, square tail
Juvenile (Jul–Nov)
wrinkled gray
all-blackish
Adult
short tail

Voice: Usually silent; limited to soft hissing and barking.

All vultures often spread their wings when roosting.

Slender and buoyant with an owl-like facial disc, Northern Harrier is usually seen coursing low over fields or marshes; it captures small birds and mammals with a sudden pounce.

Northern Harrier

Circus cyaneus

L 18" WS 43" WT 15 oz (420 g) ♀>♂

Slender with long wings and tail; wings raised in dihedral.

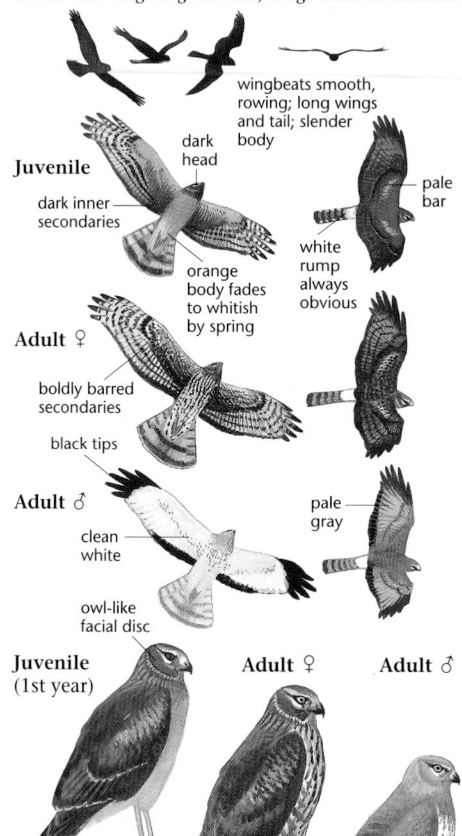

wingbeats smooth, rowing; long wings and tail; slender body
Juvenile
dark head
dark inner secondaries
orange body fades to whitish by spring
pale bar
white rump always obvious
Adult ♀
boldly barred secondaries
black tips
Adult ♂
clean white
pale gray
owl-like facial disc
Juvenile (1st year)
Adult ♀
Adult ♂
often perches on low post or on ground

Voice: Two call types. Piercing, insistent whistle *eeeya* or high, very thin *sseeeew* given mainly by female and young. Dry clucking or barking series *chef chef chef . . .* to rapid staccato *kekekekeke . . .* given mainly by male.

Harrier Flight Shapes

Like other raptors, harriers present a wide array of different shapes, depending on their mode of flight. Northern Harrier can be particularly confusing in this respect since most observers are accustomed to seeing it low over fields or marshes; its unexpected appearance high overhead baffles many observers. Five different shapes here show the range of variation between soaring and gliding flight.

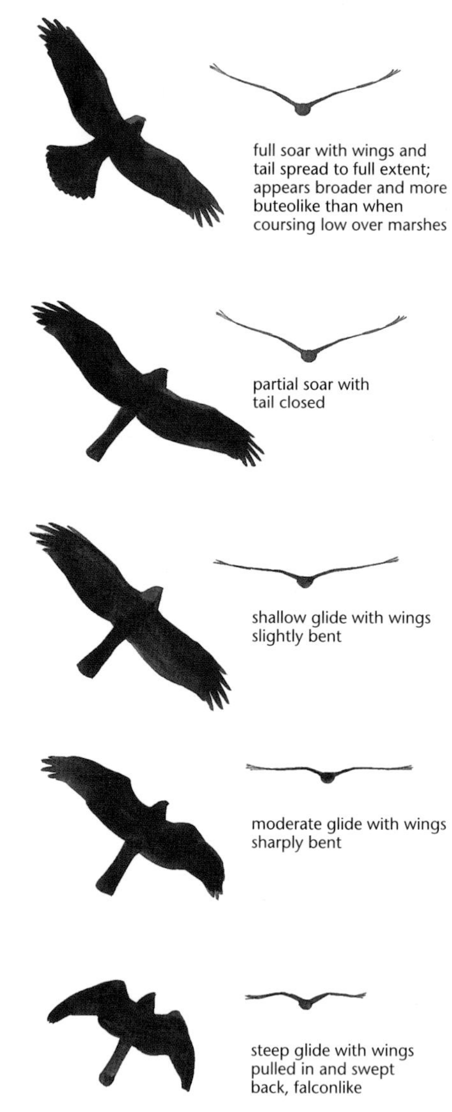

full soar with wings and tail spread to full extent; appears broader and more buteolike than when coursing low over marshes
partial soar with tail closed
shallow glide with wings slightly bent
moderate glide with wings sharply bent
steep glide with wings pulled in and swept back, falconlike

The distinctive Hook-billed Kite is found in dense, brushy woods, where it feeds on tree snails it acquires by clambering parrotlike through trees. It is usually seen in family groups year-round.

Raptor Hunting Techniques

Hunting techniques of raptors are extremely varied, and all species are opportunistic to some extent, taking advantage of easily captured prey by whatever method possible. Nevertheless, the actions of a foraging bird can provide some general clues to identification. Some highly specialized species feed exclusively on one type of prey by one method (e.g., Hook-billed Kite, Snail Kite, Osprey); otherwise there are few absolute rules. Experience in one's local area is most important. Often an observation that a bird is acting "weird" provides the first clue of a different species, but these impressions should always be backed up by other characteristics. Common hunting techniques include:

Perching: just sitting and waiting

Hovering: holding position over the ground with quick, shallow wingbeats

Kiting: holding position over the ground simply by hanging in the wind

Pursuing: level, flapping flight

Coursing: low, patrolling flight over grassy or weedy areas

Stooping: spectacular dive from high altitude

Flycatching: grabbing flying insects in midair with feet

Mississippi Kite
flycatching

Species that feed on big prey items eat a large amount of food at once. Excess is stored in the crop and can be seen as a bulge on the throat in flight. A raptor with a full crop can be mistaken for a very large-headed bird.

Cooper's Hawk
full crop

Hook-billed Kite

Chondrohierax uncinatus

L 18" WS 36" WT 10 oz (280 g)

Strikingly broad, paddle-shaped wings; flight shape most like Harris's Hawk and Red-shouldered Hawk.

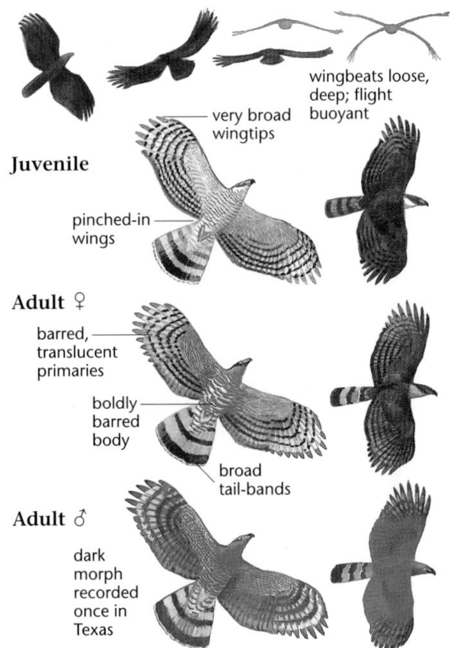
wingbeats loose, deep; flight buoyant
very broad wingtips
Juvenile
pinched-in wings
Adult ♀
barred, translucent primaries
boldly barred body
broad tail-bands
Adult ♂
dark morph recorded once in Texas

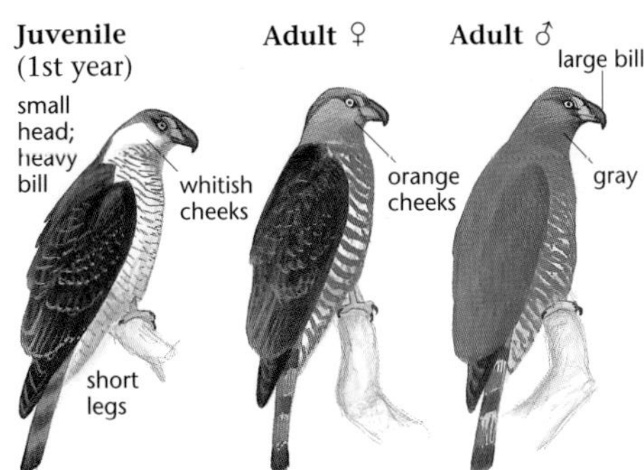
Juvenile (1st year)
small head; heavy bill
whitish cheeks
short legs
Adult ♀
orange cheeks
Adult ♂
large bill
gray

Voice: A clucking or rattling chatter *kekekekeke-kekekekeke;* highest in middle, quality like Northern Flicker but more rapid; also a soft, conversational *huey.* Juvenile call similar to adult.

These two species are distinctive. Snail Kite feeds on water snails it plucks from marsh grass in flight. White-tailed Kite hunts rodents in open areas by hovering and dropping to the ground.

Snail Kite

Rostrhamus sociabilis

L 17" WS 42" WT 15 oz (420 g)

Broad-winged and short-tailed; slow, floating flight.

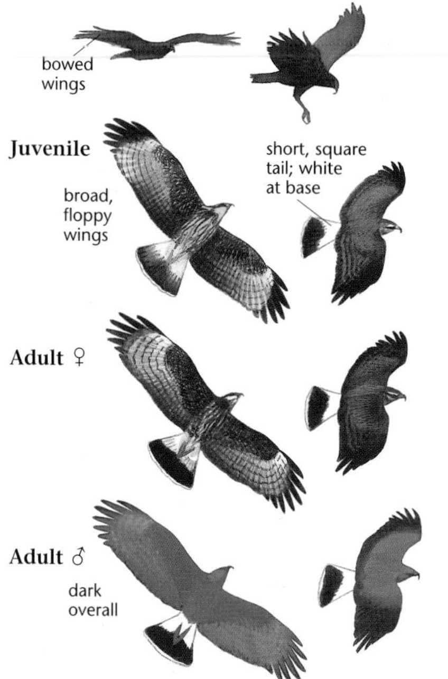
bowed
wings
Juvenile
broad,
floppy
wings
short, square
tail; white
at base
Adult ♀
Adult ♂
dark
overall

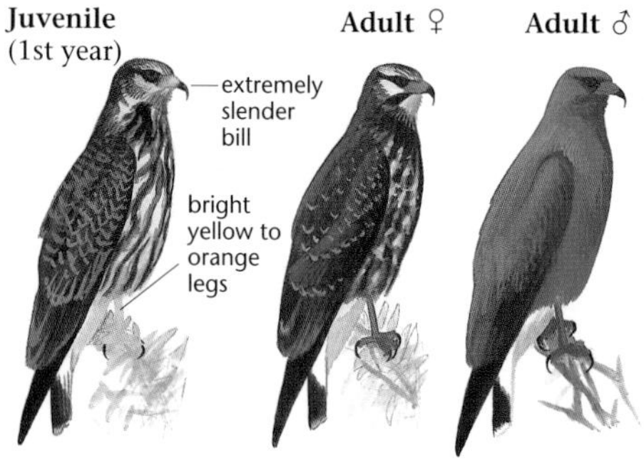
Juvenile
(1st year)
Adult ♀
Adult ♂
extremely
slender
bill
bright
yellow to
orange
legs

Voice: Usually silent. Gives a harsh, cackling *ka-ka-ka-ka-ka* . . . or grating *krrkrr* . . . ; harsh *ker-wuck* repeated. Juvenile gives a harsh, coarse scream.

White-tailed Kite

Elanus leucurus

L 15" WS 39" WT 12 oz (340 g)

Ternlike plumage; pointed wings usually held in dihedral.

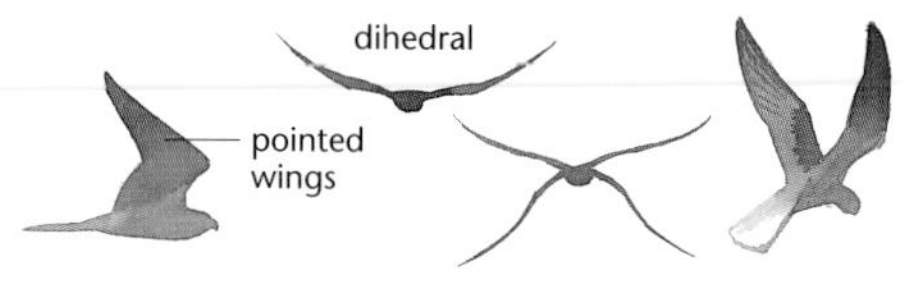
dihedral
pointed
wings

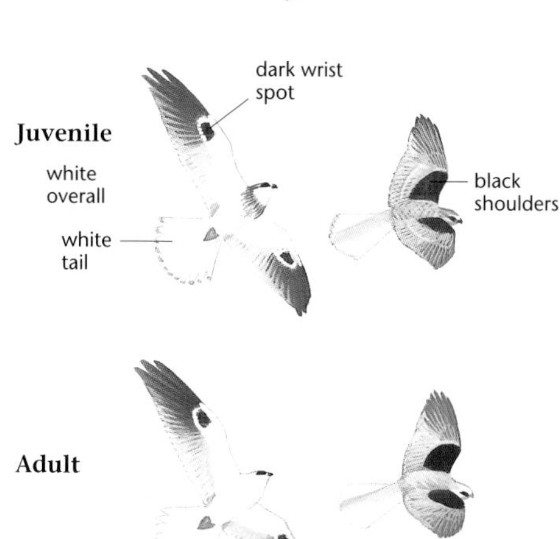
Juvenile
dark wrist
spot
white
overall
white
tail
black
shoulders

Adult
Juvenile
(1st year)
Adult
pale gray
with black
shoulders
buffy wash
fades within
weeks

Voice: Varied: mellow whistle/yelp *eerk, eerk* . . . ; high, thin, rising whistle followed by low, dry, harsh notes *sweeekrrkrr*. In aggression a low, grating *karrrrr*. Juvenile gives an Osprey-like whistle *teewp*.

Kites (continued)

These two highly aerial species have long, pointed wings and very buoyant flight. Both capture and eat insects in midair; Swallow-tailed also plucks prey from treetops. Both are found over edges of woods.

Mississippi Kite

Ictinia mississippiensis

L 14" WS 31" WT 10 oz (280 g)

Falconlike shape but more buoyant flight; wings broadest at wrist; short outermost primary distinctive.

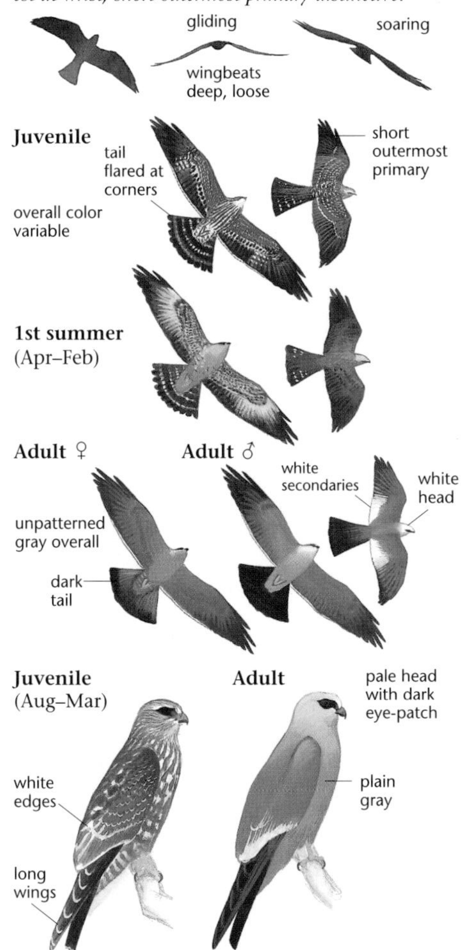

gliding
soaring
wingbeats deep, loose
Juvenile
tail flared at corners
overall color variable
short outermost primary
1st summer (Apr–Feb)
Adult ♀
Adult ♂
unpatterned gray overall
dark tail
white secondaries
white head
Juvenile (Aug–Mar)
Adult
pale head with dark eye-patch
white edges
long wings
plain gray

Voice: A high, thin whistle *pe-teew* or *pee-teeeer,* similar to Broad-winged Hawk but descending; sometimes a more excited *pee-tititi.* Juvenile call similar to adult.

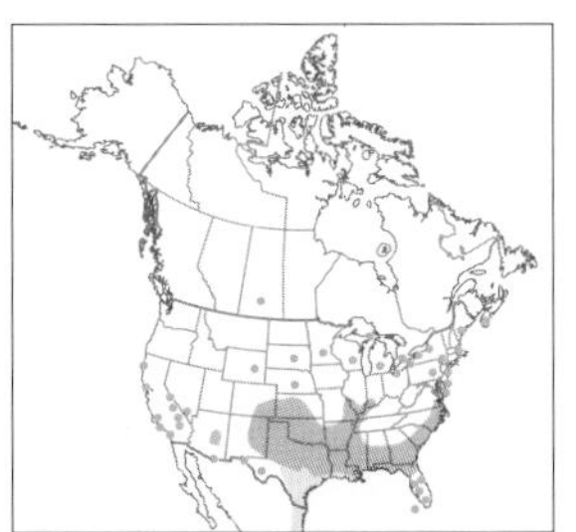

Swallow-tailed Kite

Elanoides forficatus

L 22" WS 51" WT 15 oz (420 g)

Unmistakable; incredibly graceful, flowing flight. Plucks lizards and insects from treetops.

gliding
soaring
Juvenile
striking black and white plumage
long, forked tail
long wings
Adult
Juvenile (Jul–Feb)
Adult
buffy wash fades in weeks

Voice: Short, weak, high whistles *hu-kli-kli-kli;* high, clear, rising *eeep* or *eeeip* repeated. Juvenile call similar to adult.

Hawks: Genus *Accipiter*

Sharp-shinned and Cooper's are very similar to Northern Goshawk in shape, habits, and plumage; long-tailed and short-winged, all are agile in pursuing small birds through trees and bushes.

Sharp-shinned Hawk

Accipiter striatus

L 11" WS 23" WT 5 oz (140 g) ♀>♂

Our smallest accipiter; relatively small-headed, small-billed, and broad-winged.

gliding
wingbeats quick and flicking
Juvenile
wings pushed forward
dark brown
small head
coarsely streaked and barred
narrow white tip
Adult
shorter, square tail
Juvenile (1st year)
Adult ♀
Adult ♂
coarse brown streaks
legs thinner than Cooper's

Voice: Adult at nest gives a series of short, sharp notes *kiw kiw kiw* . . . ; sometimes a high, thin *keeeeeep*. Juvenile gives a clear, light chip *tewp* in fall; juvenile begging call a high-pitched *eee*.

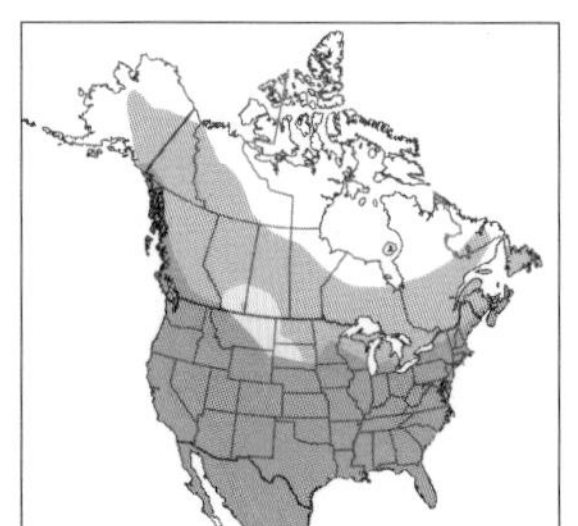

Cooper's Hawk

Accipiter cooperii

L 16.5" WS 31" WT 1 lb (450 g) ♀>♂ E >W

Medium-size accipiter with relatively large head, long tail; holds wings straight when soaring.

soaring
gliding
wingbeats stiff and choppy
Juvenile
wings straight
pale buffy tips
large head
white with fine streaks
broad white tip
Adult
longer, rounded tail

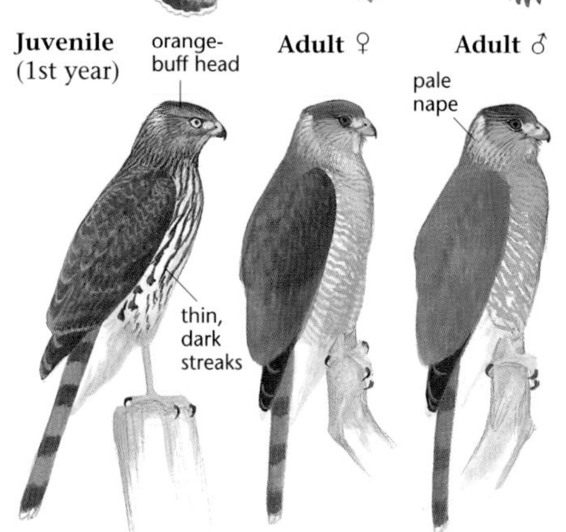
Juvenile (1st year)
orange-buff head
Adult ♀
Adult ♂
pale nape
thin, dark streaks

Voice: Adult at nest gives a series of flat, nasal, barking notes *pek pek* . . . ; also long *keeee* (male) or *whaaaaa* (female); male also gives a single *kik*. Juvenile begs with repeated squeaky whistle *kleeer* (sometimes low and nasal, like sapsuckers' call). Juvenile also gives high, rapid *kih kih kih*.

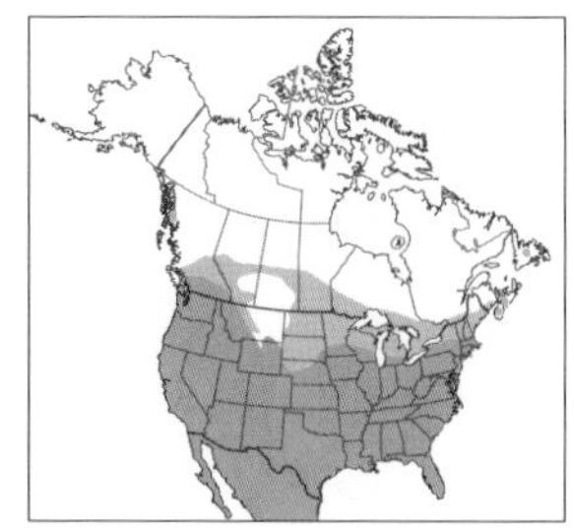

This species, our largest accipiter, is at times confused with buteos. It is found in and at the edges of mixed or coniferous forests, hunting medium-size birds in ambush attacks through dense cover.

Northern Goshawk

Accipiter gentilis

L 21" WS 41" WT 2.1 lb (950 g) ♀>♂

Large, relatively stocky with broad body; short, broad tail; long, fairly pointed wings.

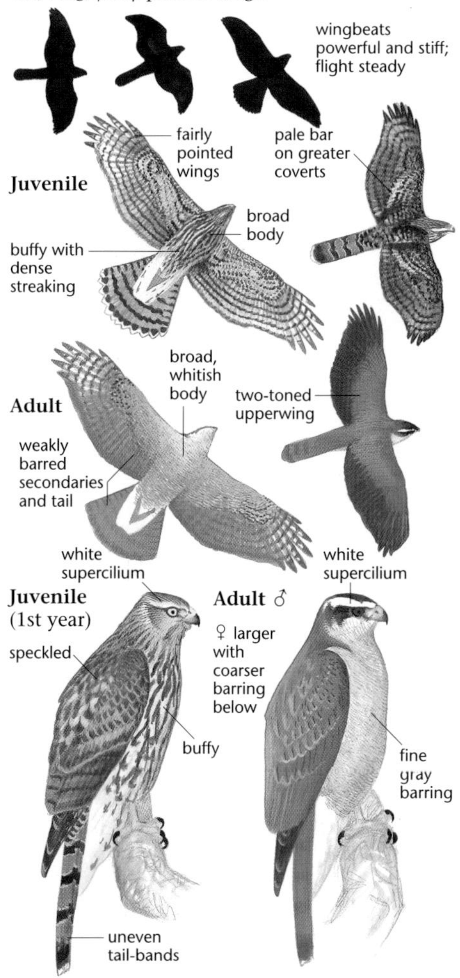
wingbeats powerful and stiff; flight steady
fairly pointed wings
pale bar on greater coverts
Juvenile
broad body
buffy with dense streaking
broad, whitish body
two-toned upperwing
Adult
weakly barred secondaries and tail
white supercilium
white supercilium
Juvenile (1st year)
Adult ♂
♀ larger with coarser barring below
speckled
buffy
fine gray barring
uneven tail-bands

Voice: Adult at nest gives a loud cackling *kye kye kye . . .* ; wilder-sounding, slower, and higher-pitched than Cooper's. Display call of adult a wailing, gull-like *KREE-ah* repeated regularly. Male gives wooden *guck* near nest. Juvenile begging call a plaintive scream *kree-ah.*

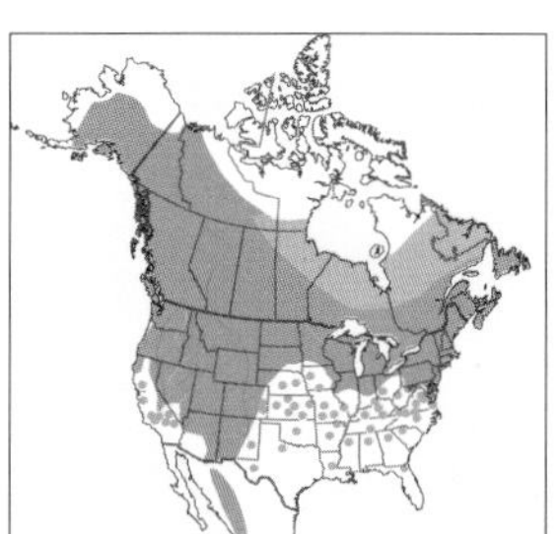

Identification of Accipiters

All three accipiters are relatively short-winged and long-tailed; although some buteos have similar proportions, it is normally easy to classify a bird as an accipiter. Distinguishing one accipiter species from another, however, can be very difficult. Overall plumage is of little use; only the adult Northern Goshawk is distinctive. Identification depends on careful study of plumage details and proportions; wingbeats are one of the most useful clues for experienced observers. Sightings of accipiters are often very distant or very brief, and many birds must go unidentified.

- On flying birds look at shape, wingbeats, and overall color and pattern of underparts.
- On perched birds study color and pattern of head, nape, and underparts and leg thickness.
- Size is useful, but as male of all species averages much smaller than female, this variation within each species can obscure the size differences between species. Adults average heavier, stockier, shorter-winged and -tailed than juveniles.

Northern Goshawk is the largest and bulkiest accipiter (often mistaken for a buteo in flight). Adults appear whitish below with boldly patterned head. Juveniles are washed buffy overall with thick, spotty streaks below and bold white supercilium. Upperside is paler overall and more patterned than other accipiters, with unique spotted pattern and obvious pale bar on greater coverts.

Cooper's and Sharp-shinned Hawks are nearly identical in all plumages. Cooper's is the lankiest accipiter, with large head, long neck and tail, and relatively narrow, straight-edged wings. Sharp-shinned is small-headed with relatively long, broad wings that are hunched, pushed forward, and slightly more fingered at the tips. Cooper's wingbeats are stiffer and shallower, while Sharp-shinned's are deeper, with more flicking "wrist action." This characteristic can be useful in identifying very distant birds.

In all plumages Cooper's tail tip is more rounded, with feathers of graduated lengths and rounded corners; Sharp-shinned's is more square-tipped with sharper corners, but this should be used only as a supporting characteristic. In fall Cooper's has a broader, more obvious white tail tip (often worn off by spring).

Bill size and leg thickness (relatively larger on Cooper's) can be useful on perched birds but are difficult to see. Although habits and habitat overlap entirely, Cooper's often perches on fence posts or poles, as well as tree branches, while Sharp-shinned almost always perches on tree branches.

Identification of Buteos

Identification of buteos is complicated by extensive variation in plumage and shape within each species. Also troubling is the fact that most buteos are seen only in flight at a distance. A good understanding of flight characteristics and some experience is necessary to identify these birds.

For flying birds, concentrate on wing shape, the pattern of the underside of the flight feathers and underwing coverts, and tail pattern. In all species female averages larger than male, and juvenile averages narrower wings and longer tail than adult. A small, slender juvenile male and a large, bulky adult female can be mistaken for two different species based on shape alone. Wing shape appearance is strongly influenced by the wing postures of different species. Be sure to study the flying bird from different angles, as very distinctive shapes might appear momentarily as the bird turns in flight. Wingbeats vary depending on weather, motivation of the bird, and even the age and sex of the bird (adults with their broader wings tend to have stiffer wingbeats than juveniles of the same species).

All species have a distinct juvenal plumage worn throughout the 1st year. Some species have a recognizable 2nd year plumage as well. Six species are polymorphic, with dark, light, and intermediate morphs shown by all ages.

It is usually possible to age buteos (and other hawks) by feather characteristics, even without knowing the species, and correct aging can simplify identification. Juveniles have narrower and more pointed flight feathers; the trailing edge of the wing and tip of the spread tail have a saw-tooth edge, unlike the smoother edge of an adult's wing. In addition, the markings on flight feathers of juveniles tend to be paler, less distinct, and more translucent than on adults; juveniles in fall and winter look clean and neat, with all flight feathers the same age, while adults usually show a mixture of old and new feathers. Since the juvenal remiges are shorter and more pointed than adults, and tail feathers longer and more pointed, 2nd year buteos can often be identified by the presence of both juvenal and adult feathers on a single bird. Any buteo showing signs of molt (active or not) is at least ten months old.

Identifying perched buteos can be challenging, since the important clues of wing shape and markings are not visible. Concentrate on structural details, such as bill size and wingtip, tail, and leg length. In most areas, Red-tailed Hawk is the most frequently seen roadside buteo. Familiarity with the blocky shape, speckled white scapular V, streaked belly-band, and off-white breast (light morphs) of this species will simplify the identification of many perched birds.

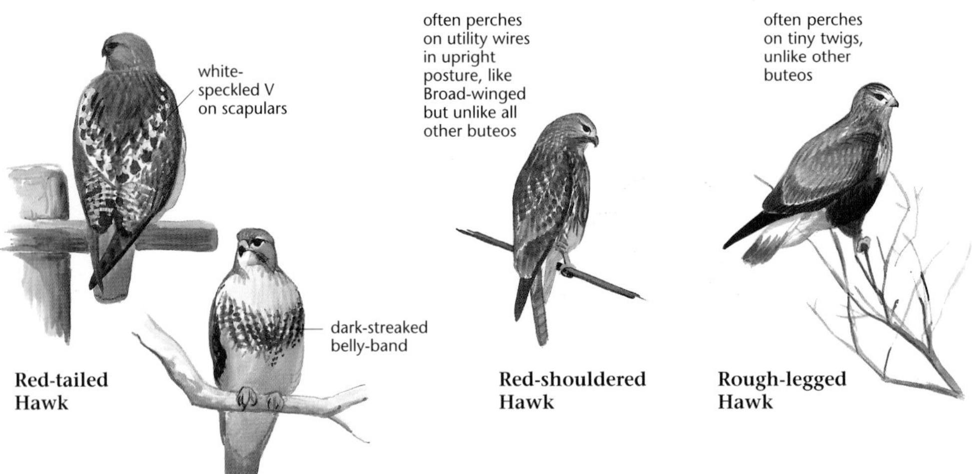
white-speckled V on scapulars
dark-streaked belly-band
often perches on utility wires in upright posture, like Broad-winged but unlike all other buteos
often perches on tiny twigs, unlike other buteos

Red-tailed Hawk

Red-shouldered Hawk

Rough-legged Hawk

These two species belong to separate genera. Common Black-Hawk hunts amphibians from perches along streams. Harris's Hawk, usually in pairs or trios, hunts birds and mammals in brush.

Common Black-Hawk

Buteogallus anthracinus

L 21" WS 46" WT 2.1 lb (950 g)

Long legs and extremely broad wings.

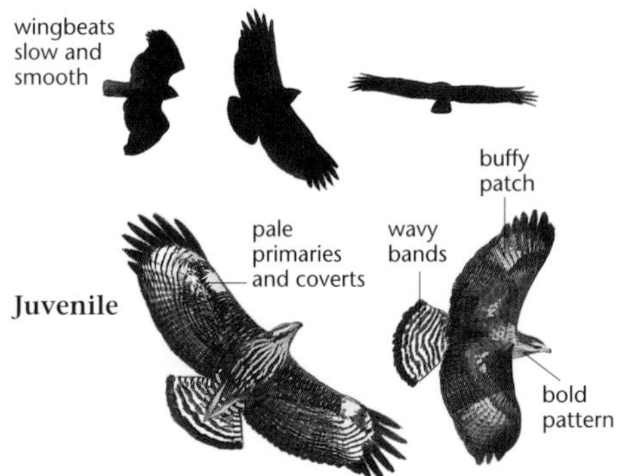
wingbeats slow and smooth
buffy patch
pale primaries and coverts
wavy bands
Juvenile
bold pattern

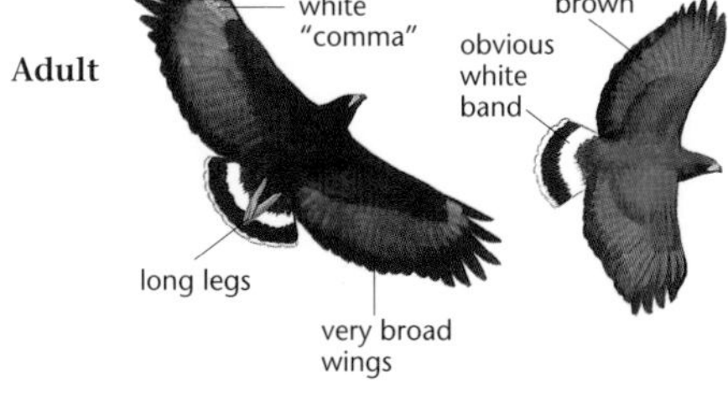
tinged brown
white "comma"
obvious white band
Adult
long legs
very broad wings

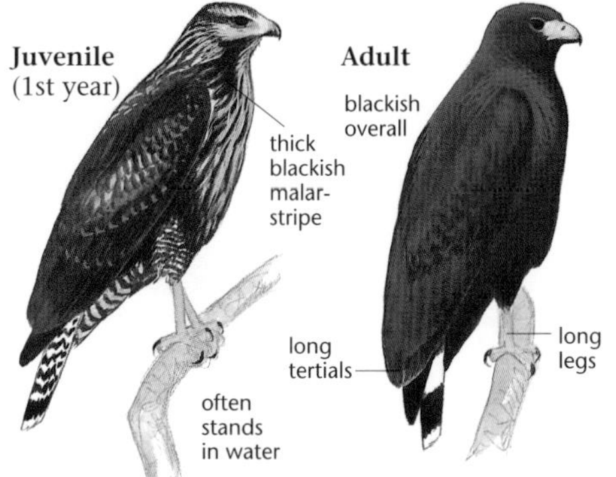
Juvenile (1st year)
Adult
blackish overall
thick blackish malar-stripe
long tertials
long legs
often stands in water

Voice: Adult gives a series of high, sharp whistles/screams *kle KLEE KLEE klee kle kle kle kle kle,* increasing abruptly then trailing off in intensity. Juvenile gives rapid, high whistles.

Common Black-Hawk can be difficult to distinguish from Zone-tailed Hawk when perched. Note yellow lores, long tertials.

Harris's Hawk

Parabuteo unicinctus

L 20" WS 42" WT 2 lb (900 g) ♀>♂

Accipiter-like proportions but broader-winged, stockier.

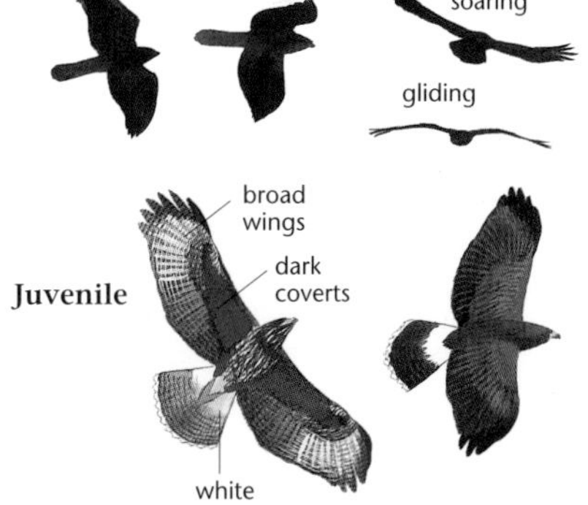
soaring
gliding
broad wings
dark coverts
Juvenile
white

white uppertail coverts and tail tip
Adult
rufous shoulders
all-dark wings

Juvenile (1st year)
Adult
dark brown
short wings
long legs
erect posture
long tail

Voice: Very raucous, harsh *raaaak* lasting up to three seconds; from nest a low, grating, toneless *keh keh keh keh keh keh keh keh.* Juvenile gives slow, squealing *skeeei skeeei . . .* or *kweeeurr.*

Gray Hawk hunts small prey in riparian woods and edges. Zone-tailed, found in wooded canyons and riparian woods, hunts birds and small mammals from high in the air.

Gray Hawk

Asturina nitida

L 17" WS 34" WT 1.2 lb (540 g) ♀>♂

Rather small and accipiter-like; relatively long-tailed.

wingbeats quick and choppy
soaring

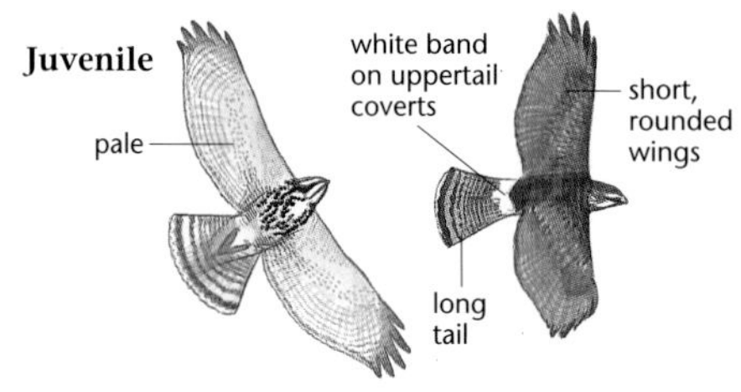

Juvenile
pale
white band on uppertail coverts
short, rounded wings
long tail

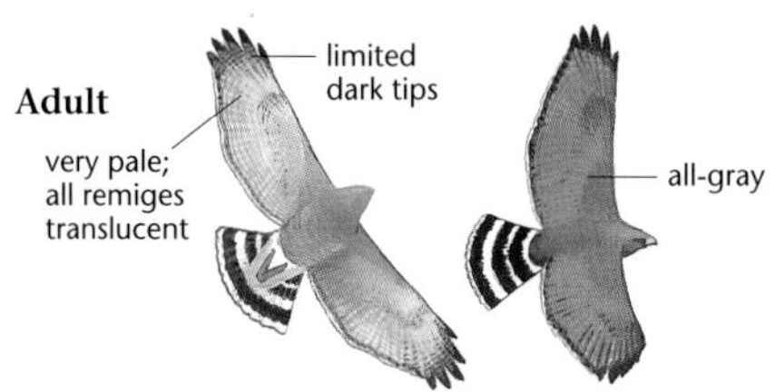

Adult
limited dark tips
very pale; all remiges translucent
all-gray

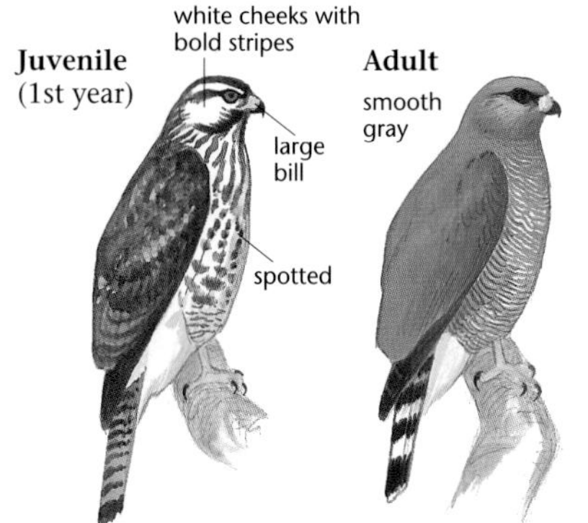

Juvenile (1st year)
white cheeks with bold stripes
large bill
spotted
Adult
smooth gray

Voice: Display call a series of long, plaintive whistles *hoooooweeo hoooooweeo* . . . or higher *pidiweeeeeeerh pidiweeeeeeerh*. . . . Juvenile call a high, squeaky *KEE-errrrrrrrrr;* adult gives similar scream when alarmed.

Zone-tailed Hawk

Buteo albonotatus

L 20" WS 51" WT 1.8 lb (810 g) ♀>♂

Overall incredibly similar to Turkey Vulture, with which it often soars; distinguished only by details.

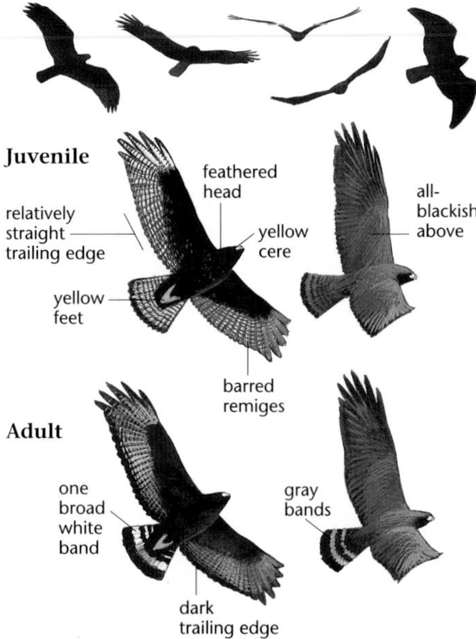

Juvenile
feathered head
relatively straight trailing edge
yellow cere
yellow feet
barred remiges
all-blackish above

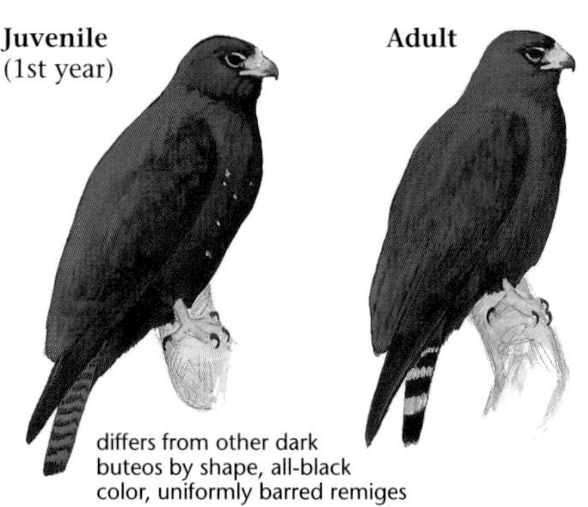

Adult
one broad white band
gray bands
dark trailing edge

Juvenile (1st year)
Adult
differs from other dark buteos by shape, all-black color, uniformly barred remiges

Voice: High scream *koweeeeeur* clearer and lower than Red-tailed; nearly level but variable. Juvenile call a high, clear, nasal *tleeeeer;* also high, squealing series *hwee hwee hwee hwEEEeeeer*.

Buteos (continued)

This small forest buteo, usually found near water, hunts mainly mammals and some reptiles and amphibians from perches. California birds differ significantly from the two eastern types.

Red-shouldered Hawk

Buteo lineatus

L 17" WS 40" WT 1.4 lb (630 g) ♀>♂

Rather compact, stocky, and accipiter-like with relatively short, broad wings; all show translucent pale crescent across wingtips.

wingbeats choppy, quick (especially California)

soars with wings slightly bowed

glides with wings bowed

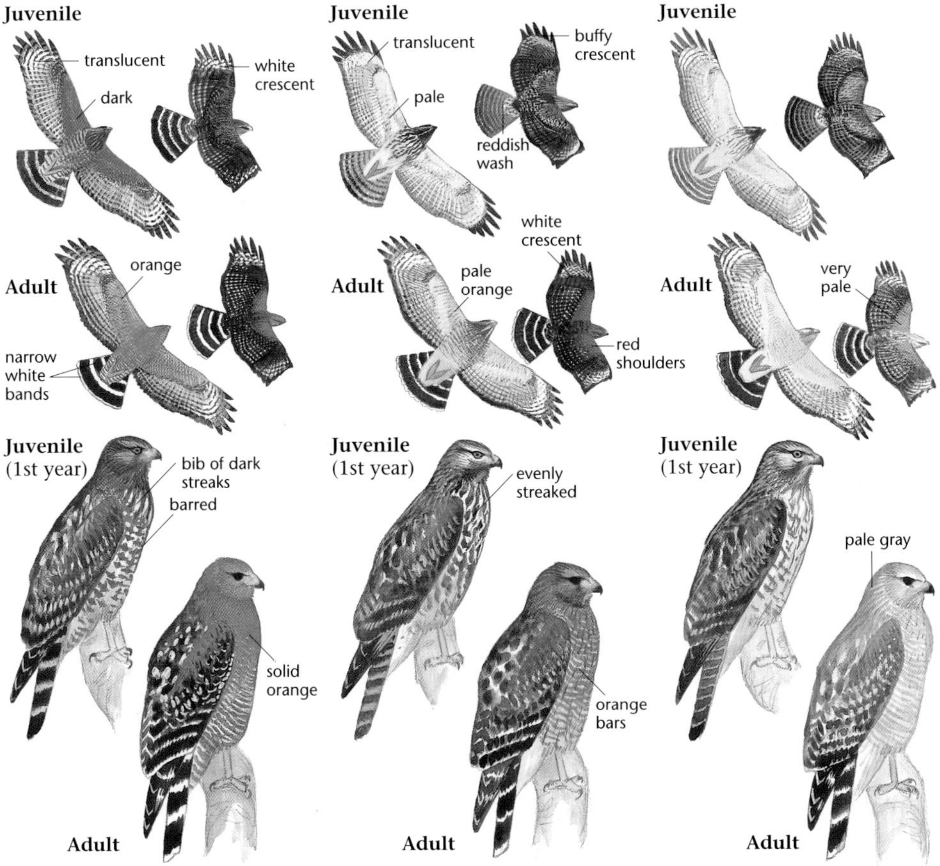

CALIFORNIA

Juvenile

translucent

dark

white crescent

Adult

orange

narrow white bands

Juvenile (1st year)

bib of dark streaks

barred

solid orange

Adult

EASTERN

Juvenile

translucent

pale

buffy crescent

reddish wash

Adult

white crescent

pale orange

red shoulders

Juvenile (1st year)

evenly streaked

orange bars

Adult

FLORIDA

Juvenile

Adult

very pale

Juvenile (1st year)

pale gray

Adult

Voice: Very vocal, with distinctive, far-carrying calls. Adult territorial call a high, clear, squealing *keeyuur keeyuur . . .* repeated steadily; often imitated by Blue Jay and Steller's Jay. Also a single or slowly repeated high, sharp *kilt*. Juvenile similar to adult. Calls of California may be a bit shorter, higher, and sharper than Eastern and Florida but very similar.

All eastern birds are similar, although southern Florida adult is much paler. California adult is more richly colored with solid orange breast lacking dark streaks, tibia feathers darker orange than belly, and fewer and broader white tail-bands. Juvenile is more like adult than eastern juveniles, with black and white wings and tail and dark rufous underwing coverts.

This rather retiring forest buteo hunts small prey from a perch within woods. It occurs in two morphs with no intermediates; the dark morph is rare. Migrants gather in large flocks along favored routes.

Broad-winged Hawk

Buteo platypterus

L 15" WS 34" WT 14 oz (390 g) ♀>♂

Our smallest buteo; wings fairly pointed with smooth contours, lacking bulging secondaries or long primaries of other buteos; tail relatively short.

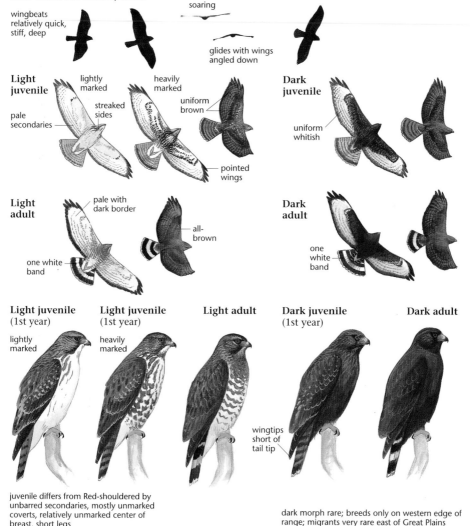

wingbeats relatively quick, stiff, deep

soaring

glides with wings angled down

Light juvenile

lightly marked

heavily marked

streaked sides

pale secondaries

uniform brown

pointed wings

Dark juvenile

uniform whitish

Light adult

pale with dark border

all-brown

one white band

Dark adult

one white band

Light juvenile (1st year) lightly marked

Light juvenile (1st year) heavily marked

Light adult

Dark juvenile (1st year)

Dark adult

wingtips short of tail tip

juvenile differs from Red-shouldered by unbarred secondaries, mostly unmarked coverts, relatively unmarked center of breast, short legs

dark morph rare; breeds only on western edge of range; migrants very rare east of Great Plains

Voice: A piercing, thin, high whistle *teeteeeeee* on one pitch; male higher than female but no other significant call known. Juvenile similar to adult. Compare Mississippi Kite.

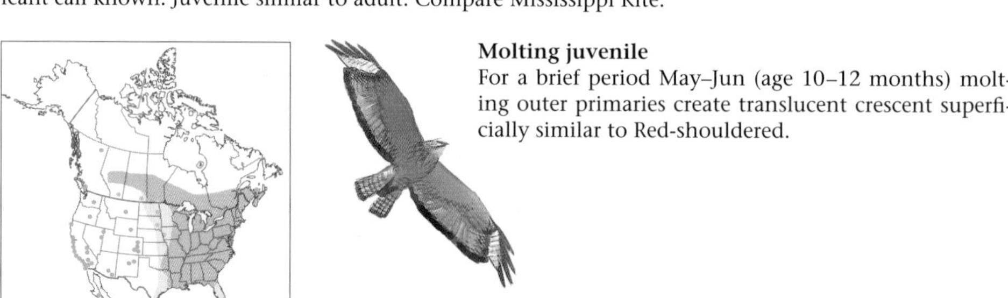

Molting juvenile

For a brief period May–Jun (age 10–12 months) molting outer primaries create translucent crescent superficially similar to Red-shouldered.

This retiring forest buteo perches invisibly within the forest canopy. It hunts mainly small birds, kiting high above woods. Of the two morphs (no intermediates), dark predominates.

Short-tailed Hawk

Buteo brachyurus

L 16" WS 37" WT 15 oz (420 g) ♀>♂

Superficially similar to Broad-winged, but wings longer and less pointed; dark secondaries distinctive.

wingbeats relatively shallow and slow

often seen kiting high overhead with wingtips upswept

Light juvenile

primaries long, but wings less pointed than Broad-winged

dark secondaries

all-white

white oval

Dark juvenile

Light adult

whitish patch

dark secondaries

Dark adult

weakly patterned tail

Light juvenile (1st year)

clean whitish

Light adult

Dark juvenile (1st year)

wingtips reach tail tip

Dark adult

Florida population up to 80 percent dark morph

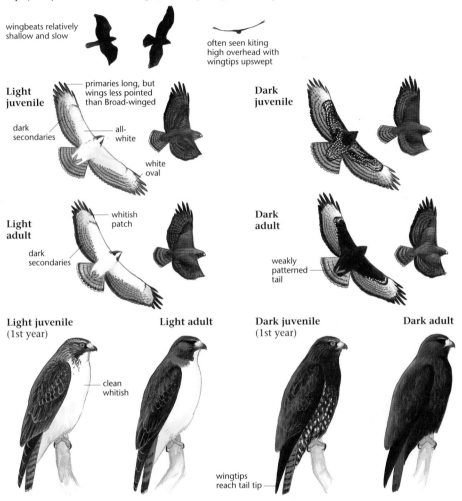

Voice: High, clear *keeeea* long and drawn-out, sometimes quavering; also high *keee* or *kleee,* often in slow series; nearly as high as Broad-winged but with harsher, less thin quality. Juvenile similar to adult.

Wings actually broader than Broad-winged, with longer primaries often swept back to point or curving up. Longer secondaries create a bulge on trailing edge of wing more like Red-tailed, rather than the smoother lines of Broad-winged. Wing coloration suggests Swainson's Hawk, but note wing shape and the more extensive white on outer primaries.

This slender prairie buteo hunts small mammals and insects in grassland—kiting, coursing, perched, or walking. Migrants gather in large flocks along favored routes. Light morph is most common.

Swainson's Hawk

Buteo swainsoni

L 19" WS 51" WT 1.9 lb (855 g) ♀>♂

Our most slender buteo; relatively long tail, long and fairly pointed wings; note dark remiges.

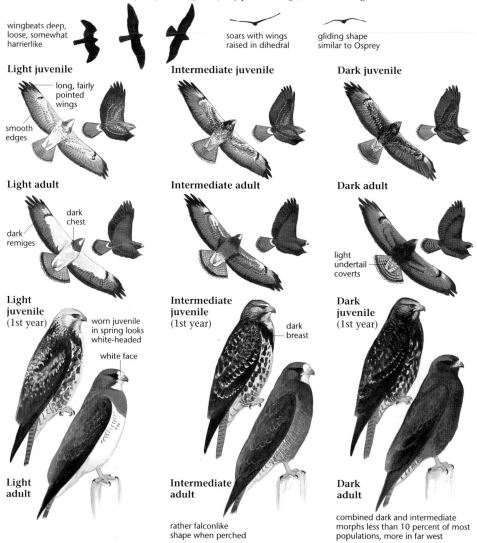

wingbeats deep, loose, somewhat harrierlike

soars with wings raised in dihedral

gliding shape similar to Osprey

Light juvenile

long, fairly pointed wings

smooth edges

Intermediate juvenile

Dark juvenile

Light adult

dark chest

dark remiges

Intermediate adult

Dark adult

light undertail coverts

Light juvenile (1st year)

worn juvenile in spring looks white-headed

white face

Light adult

Intermediate juvenile (1st year)

dark breast

Intermediate adult

rather falconlike shape when perched

Dark juvenile (1st year)

Dark adult

combined dark and intermediate morphs less than 10 percent of most populations, more in far west

Voice: Long, high scream like Red-tailed but higher, clearer, weaker; may be short *cheeeeew* or long, drawn-out *kweeaaaaaah;* sometimes a series of whistled notes *pi tip, pi tip. . . .* Juvenile gives soft, plaintive whistle or mew.

2nd year Swainson's has body plumage similar to juvenile. These birds (age over one year) are distinguished from juveniles (age under one year) during late summer/fall by a mixture of fresh and worn (retained juvenile) remiges. Age of other 2nd year buteos can also be determined by the same molt characteristics, even though their body plumage is essentially like adults. White-tailed Hawk is the only buteo with an easily recognizable 2nd year plumage.

Buteos (continued)

This species of the Texas coastal savanna hunts small mammals and birds, usually while hovering or kiting high in the air. Juvenile shows much darker plumage than adult.

White-tailed Hawk

Buteo albicaudatus

L 20" WS 51" WT 2.3 lb (1,035 g) ♀>♂

Distinctive; rather stocky, but with long, fairly pointed wings.

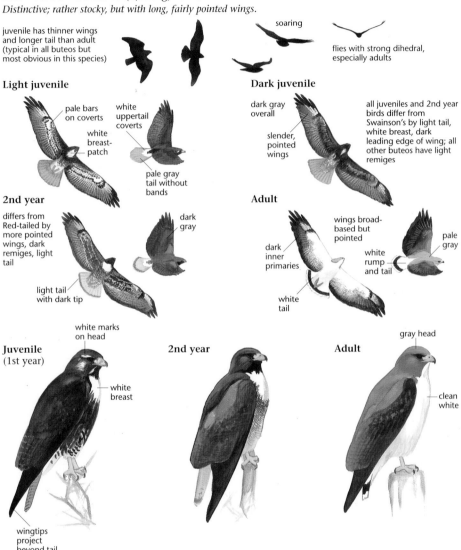

juvenile has thinner wings and longer tail than adult (typical in all buteos but most obvious in this species)

soaring

flies with strong dihedral, especially adults

Light juvenile

pale bars on coverts

white breast-patch

white uppertail coverts

pale gray tail without bands

Dark juvenile

dark gray overall

slender, pointed wings

all juveniles and 2nd year birds differ from Swainson's by light tail, white breast, dark leading edge of wing; all other buteos have light remiges

2nd year

differs from Red-tailed by more pointed wings, dark remiges, light tail

dark gray

light tail with dark tip

Adult

wings broad-based but pointed

dark inner primaries

white tail

pale gray

white rump and tail

Juvenile (1st year)

white marks on head

white breast

wingtips project beyond tail

2nd year

Adult

gray head

clean white

Voice: Rather high, laughing *reeeEEE ke-HAK ke-HAK keHAK* (female call differently accented); also a high, harsh *kareeeev,* sneezy *tseef.* Juvenile (through 1st winter) begs with high, mewing squeal *meeeii.*

Swainson's, Broad-winged, and White-tailed Hawks have four notched primaries ("fingers"). All other buteos have five. These feathers can often be counted in close views of soaring birds and create the impression of more pointed wings on these three species.

The buteo to which all others are compared, this large, conspicuous hawk often perches along roadsides. It hunts mainly mammals from a perch or by kiting.

Red-tailed Hawk

Buteo jamaicensis

L 19" WS 49" WT 2.4 lb (1,080 g) ♀>♂

Stocky, broad-winged, with bulging secondaries. Adult has distinctive red tail; juvenile has distinctive pale primaries and coverts (upperside). Western populations vary from dark to light morph.

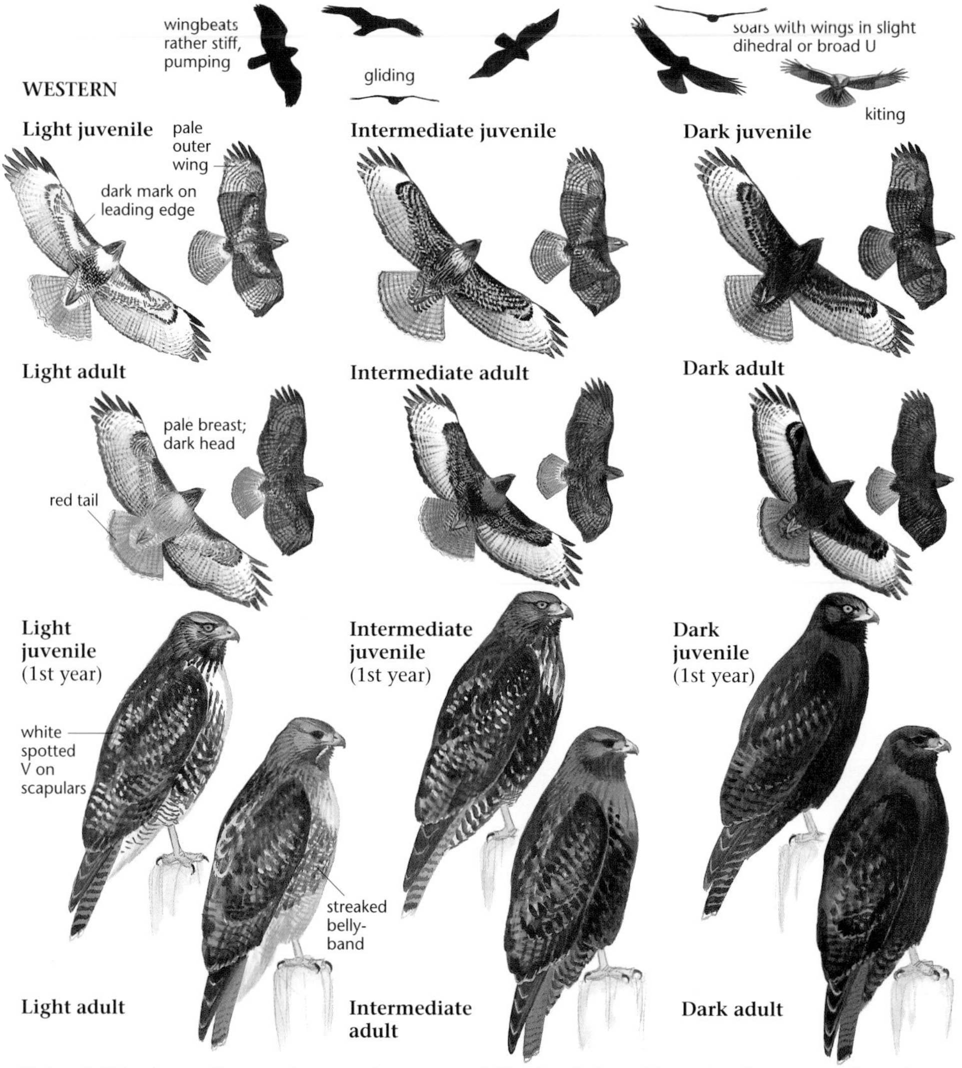

wingbeats rather stiff, pumping

gliding

soars with wings in slight dihedral or broad U

kiting

WESTERN

Light juvenile

pale outer wing

dark mark on leading edge

Intermediate juvenile

Dark juvenile

Light adult

pale breast; dark head

red tail

Intermediate adult

Dark adult

Light juvenile (1st year)

white spotted V on scapulars

Intermediate juvenile (1st year)

Dark juvenile (1st year)

streaked belly-band

Light adult

Intermediate adult

Dark adult

Voice: A distant-sounding, rasping, scraping scream, falling in pitch and intensity *cheeeeeeewv;* also a shorter scream that may be repeated in series. Juvenile begs with measured, insistent whistles *pweee, pweee. . . .*

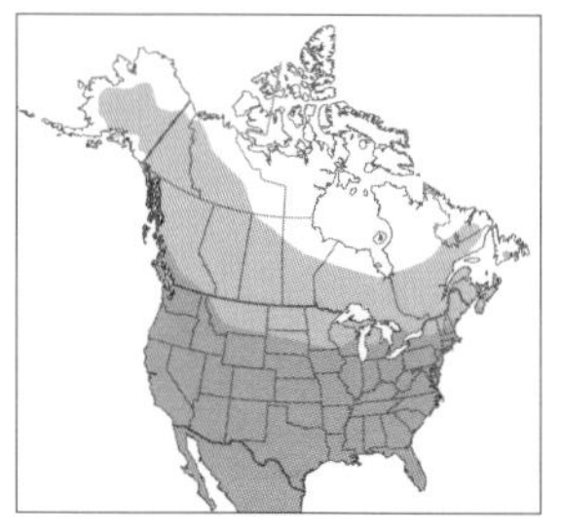

Pale outer upperwing of juvenile shows from below as a translucent square on the inner primaries. Patterns of wing translucence vary between species and, with experience, can be useful for identification.

Western population is the most variable population of Red-tailed Hawk, with complete range from light to dark plumage. Note rufous wash on underparts, finely barred tail, dark throat (but see Eastern). Dark and intermediate morphs account for 10 to 20 percent of Western population with scattered records east to Atlantic states.

Red-tailed Hawk shows much geographic variation, all relatively minor except for the distinctive Harlan's. All subspecies are similar in shape and habits; most are similar in plumage.

Red-tailed Hawk

Buteo jamaicensis

SOUTHWESTERN

Proportions like Western; belly faintly streaked or clean, tail often pale.

Juvenile Adult

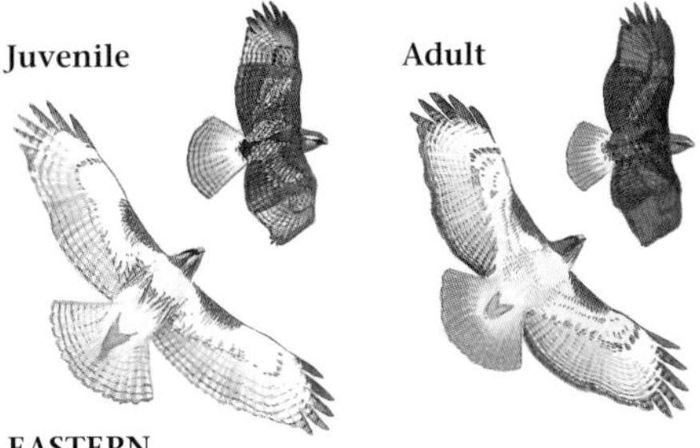

EASTERN

Slightly shorter-winged than Western; white throat, well-defined belly-band and whitish breast. Populations in Florida and eastern Canada show characteristics of Western.

Juvenile Adult

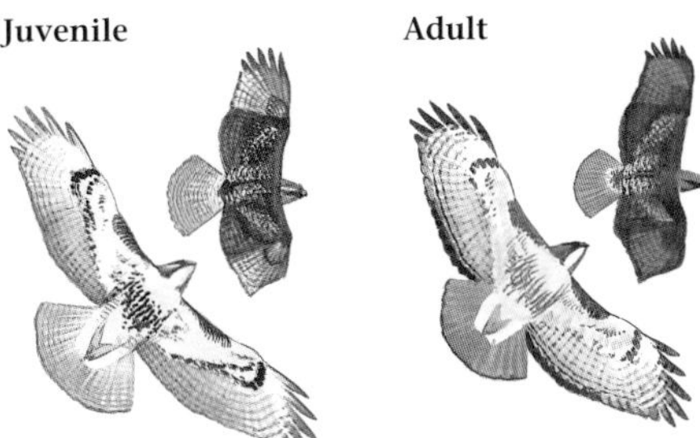

KRIDER'S

This scarce, pale Prairie variant is always outnumbered by normal light-morph birds. Underparts white with faint or no belly-band, tail whitish, much white on upperparts, often white-headed. Compare Ferruginous Hawk.

Juvenile Adult

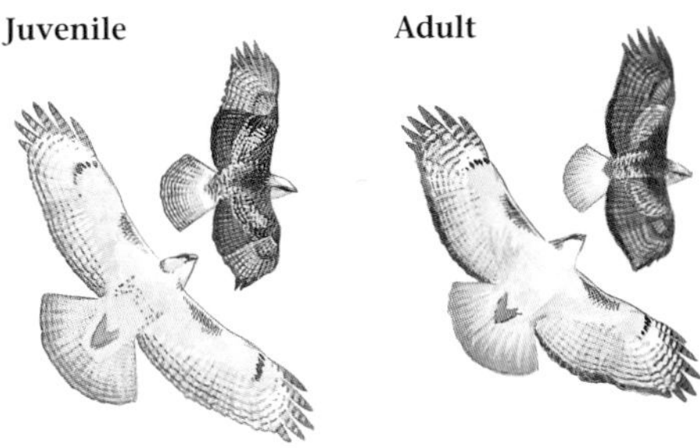

The subspecies shown above are typical of their respective regions but blend with adjacent subspecies where ranges meet. Large areas (e.g., much of western Canada) are occupied by intergrades. Albino Red-tailed is rare but regular throughout entire species range.

HARLAN'S

Plumage blackish and white, lacking brown tones. Intergrades with Western Red-tailed where ranges overlap.

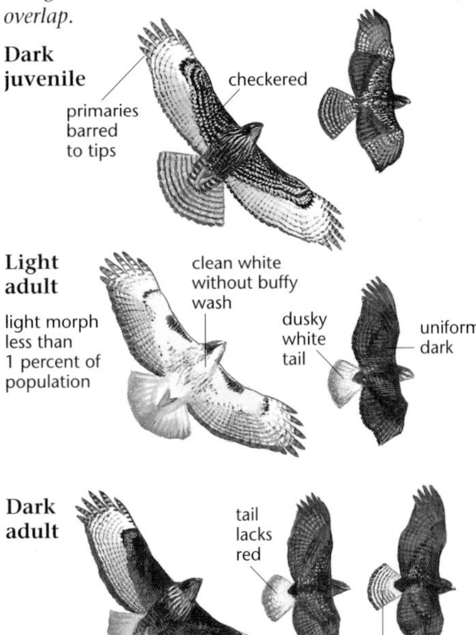
Dark juvenile
primaries barred to tips
checkered
Light adult
light morph less than 1 percent of population
clean white without buffy wash
dusky white tail
uniform dark

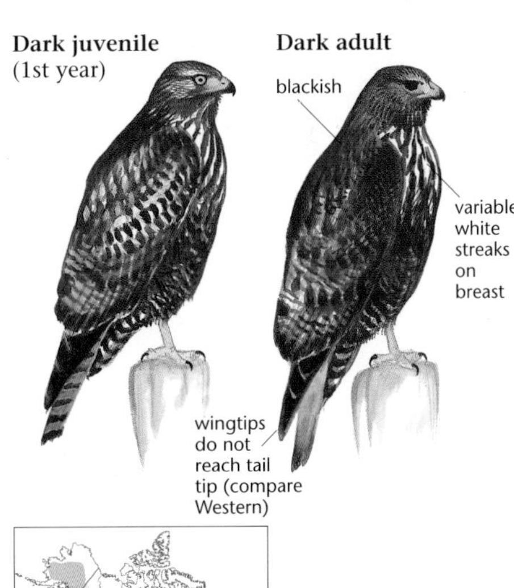
Dark adult
tail lacks red
banded tail infrequent
Dark juvenile (1st year)
Dark adult
blackish
variable white streaks on breast
wingtips do not reach tail tip (compare Western)

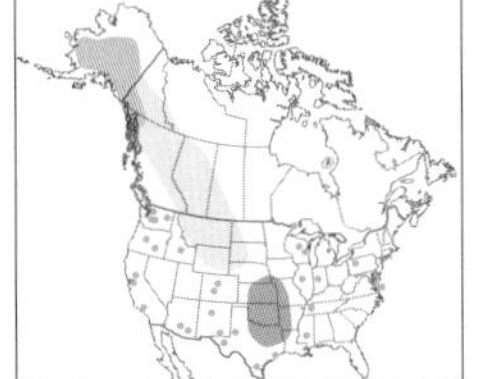

HARLAN'S

This buteo of arid grasslands hunts small mammals from a perch or by kiting; it often perches on poles or the ground. Two morphs occur with no intermediates; the dark is less frequent.

Ferruginous Hawk

Buteo regalis

L 23" WS 56" WT 3.5 lb (1,600 g) ♀>♂

Large and heavy, with long, fairly pointed wings and large bill; all show light patch on upper primaries.

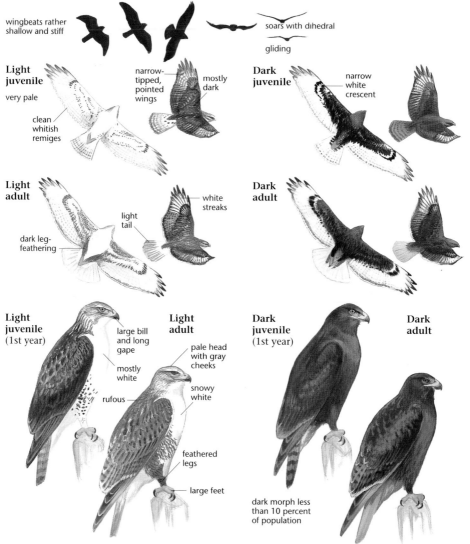

wingbeats rather shallow and stiff

soars with dihedral

gliding

Light juvenile

very pale

clean whitish remiges

narrow-tipped, pointed wings

mostly dark

Dark juvenile

narrow white crescent

Light adult

dark leg-feathering

light tail

white streaks

Dark adult

Light juvenile (1st year)

large bill and long gape

mostly white

rufous

Light adult

pale head with gray cheeks

snowy white

feathered legs

large feet

Dark juvenile (1st year)

Dark adult

dark morph less than 10 percent of population

Voice: A melancholy whistle *k-hiiiiiiiw* or *geeer;* lower-pitched and less harsh than other buteos. Juvenile gives high scream.

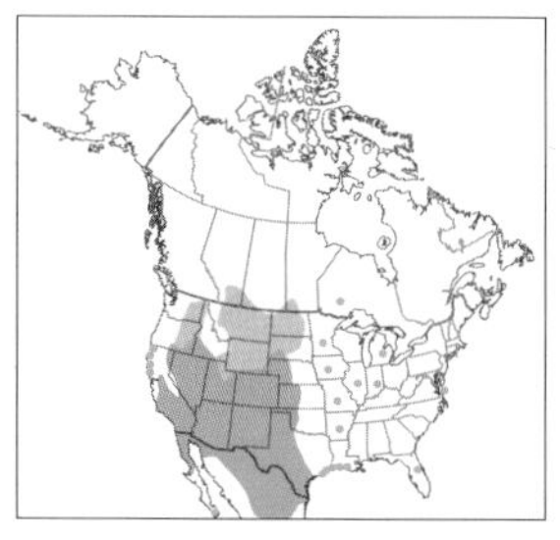

On average our largest buteo, this species has a broad head and distinctively tapered and narrow-tipped wings. Very clean white underside of remiges with tiny, dark tips is not matched by any other buteo. White inner webs of primaries and sometimes secondaries also show on upperside of spread wing. Only juvenile Rough-legged has a similar upperwing pattern.

BUTEOS (CONTINUED)

This large, lanky buteo of wide-open marshes, fields, or tundra hunts small rodents from the air, hovering easily. Two morphs occur with few intermediates; light outnumbers dark.

Rough-legged Hawk

Buteo lagopus

L 21" WS 53" WT 2.2 lb (990 g) ♀>♂

Relatively long-winged with small bill and feet.

gliding

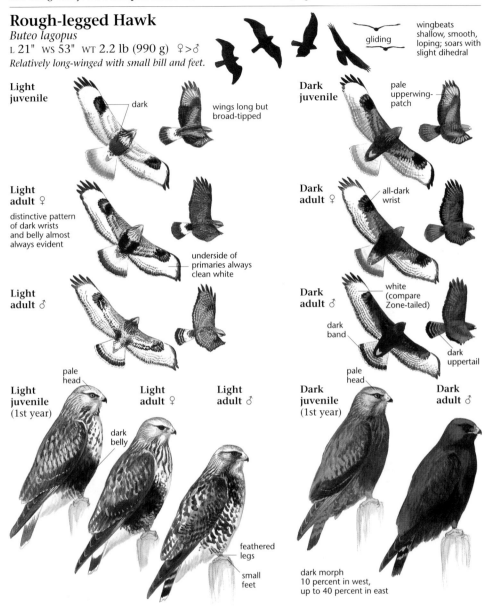

wingbeats shallow, smooth, loping; soars with slight dihedral

Light juvenile

dark

wings long but broad-tipped

Dark juvenile

pale upperwing-patch

Light adult ♀

distinctive pattern of dark wrists and belly almost always evident

underside of primaries always clean white

Dark adult ♀

all-dark wrist

Light adult ♂

Dark adult ♂

white (compare Zone-tailed)

dark band

dark uppertail

Light juvenile (1st year)

pale head

dark belly

Light adult ♀

Light adult ♂

feathered legs

small feet

Dark juvenile (1st year)

pale head

Dark adult ♂

dark morph 10 percent in west, up to 40 percent in east

Voice: A simple, high squeal *keert* or *keeeeeer,* less rasping than Red-tailed. Juvenile begs with thin, rising *skwee, skwee. . . .*

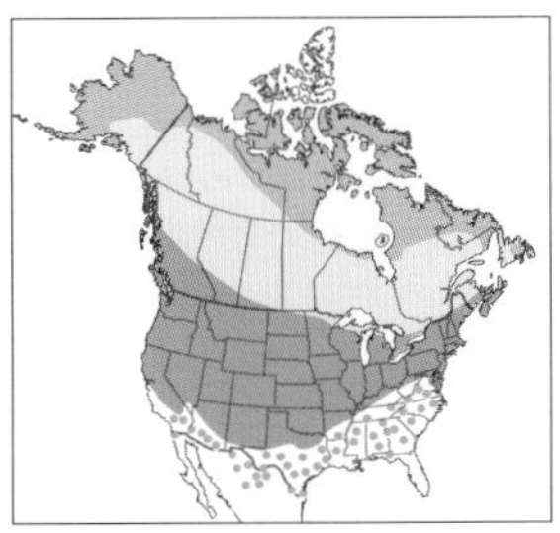

Fluffy plumage, small bill, and small feet are all adaptations to Arctic life, giving this species a distinctive appearance. In flight the long, rounded wings, smooth wingbeats, and very pale underside of remiges are distinctive. This species has the most different male and female plumages of all our buteos; the sex of most adults can be determined readily by plumage patterns, but intermediates occur and variation is complex.

Golden Eagle

This majestic species is closely related to buteos but much larger with longer wings. Found in mountainous areas, it hunts mammals and birds mainly from the air, often in spectacular stoops.

Golden Eagle

Aquila chrysaetos

L 30" WS 79" WT 10 lb (4,575 g) ♀>♂

Very large and dark; "broad-handed." Head relatively small; golden nape shown in all plumages.

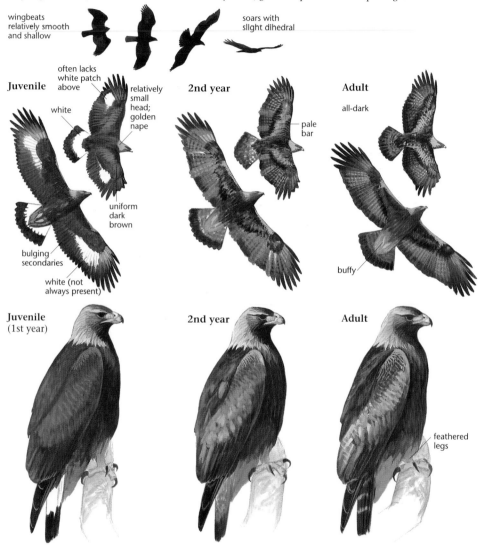

wingbeats relatively smooth and shallow

soars with sllght dlhedral

Juvenile

often lacks white patch above

white

relatively small head; golden nape

uniform dark brown

bulging secondaries

white (not always present)

2nd year

pale bar

Adult

all-dark

buffy

Juvenile (1st year)

2nd year

Adult

feathered legs

Voice: Rather weak, high yelping. Adult gives two-syllable *kee-yep* or *chiup* in slow, measured series. Juvenile begs with piercing, insistent *ssseeeeeee-chk* or chittering *kikikikikikiki-yelp*.

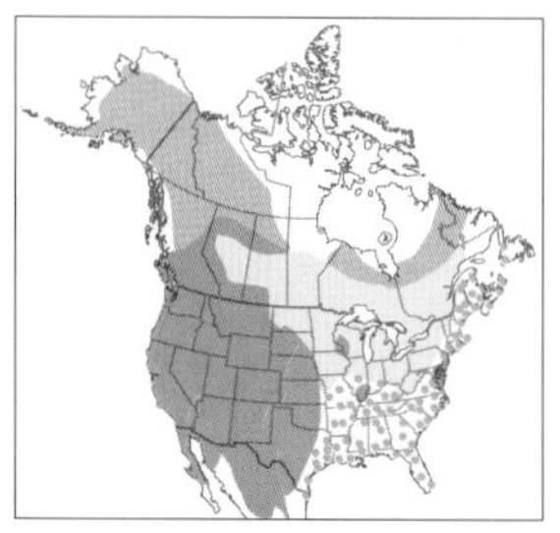

Golden Eagle could be mistaken for Turkey Vulture and even some dark buteos, but note much larger size, relatively long wings, steady flight. Separation from Bald Eagle is usually easy, based on wing and tail pattern, but occasional Golden Eagles have white markings on the underwing coverts. Check other plumage marks, shape, and proportions.

BALD EAGLE
This species is not closely related to Golden Eagle. Usually found near water (in large numbers where prey is abundant), it feeds mainly on fish (often scavenged) and waterfowl captured in pursuit.

Bald Eagle

Haliaeetus leucocephalus

L 31" WS 80" WT 9.5 lb (4,325 g) ♀>♂

Less buteolike than Golden Eagle. Relatively large head and bill; broad, straight-edged wings with relatively narrow "hands."

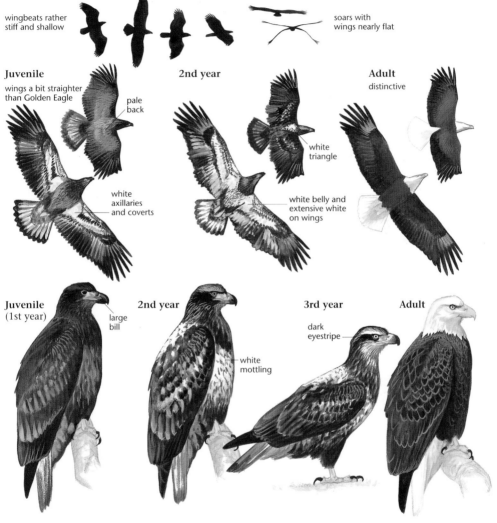

wingbeats rather stiff and shallow

soars with wings nearly flat

Juvenile
wings a bit straighter than Golden Eagle

pale back

white axillaries and coverts

2nd year

white triangle

white belly and extensive white on wings

Adult
distinctive

Juvenile (1st year)

large bill

2nd year

white mottling

3rd year

dark eyestripe

Adult

Voice: Call rather weak, flat, chirping whistles, stuttering, variable. Immature calls generally harsher, more shrill than adult until three to four years old.

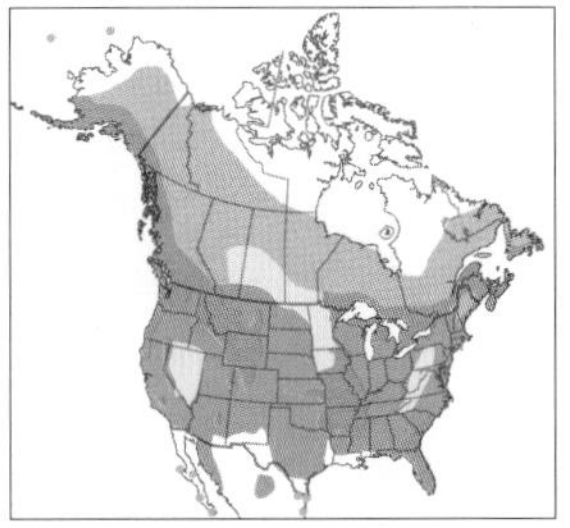

Southern breeders smaller, average 10 percent shorter-winged and 20 percent shorter-tailed than northern breeders; differences are broadly clinal. Southern juveniles fledge in Mar; northern juveniles are not independent until Aug. Southern juveniles wander north to Canada May–Sep and can sometimes be distinguished from the northern by date and relatively worn plumage.

Juveniles of both Bald and Golden Eagles have broader wings and longer tails than adults. 2nd year birds retain longer juvenile feathers among shorter new ones.

Osprey

This unique species, sometimes placed in its own family, feeds on fish it captures by hovering, then plunging feet-first into water. Flying birds are more often confused with gulls than with hawks.

Osprey

Pandion haliaetus

L 23" WS 63" WT 3.5 lb (1,600 g)

Long, narrow wings always angled and bowed down; gull-like. Shape and underwing pattern distinctive.

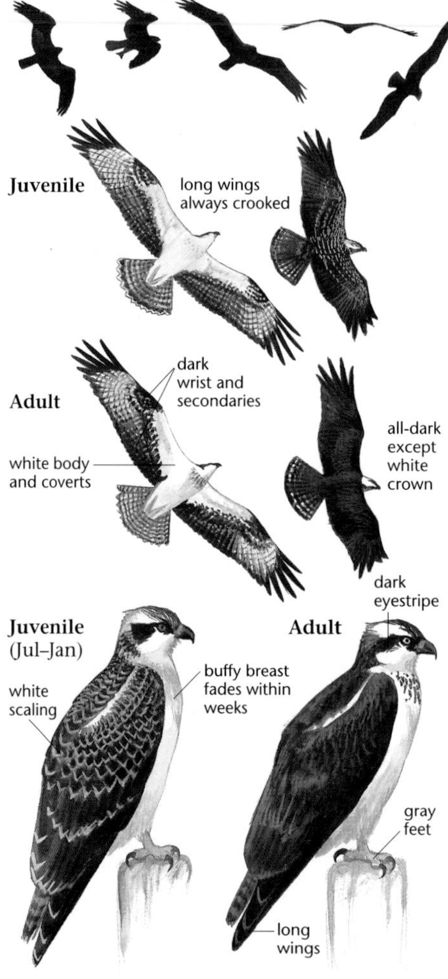
Juvenile
long wings
always crooked
Adult
dark
wrist and
secondaries
white body
and coverts
all-dark
except
white
crown
dark
eyestripe
Juvenile
(Jul–Jan)
Adult
white
scaling
buffy breast
fades within
weeks
gray
feet
long
wings

Voice: Quite vocal; all calls short, shrill whistles *tewp, tewp, tewp, teelee, teelee, tewp;* commonly single loud, shrill, slightly slurred whistle *teeeeaa.* Juvenile similar to adult.

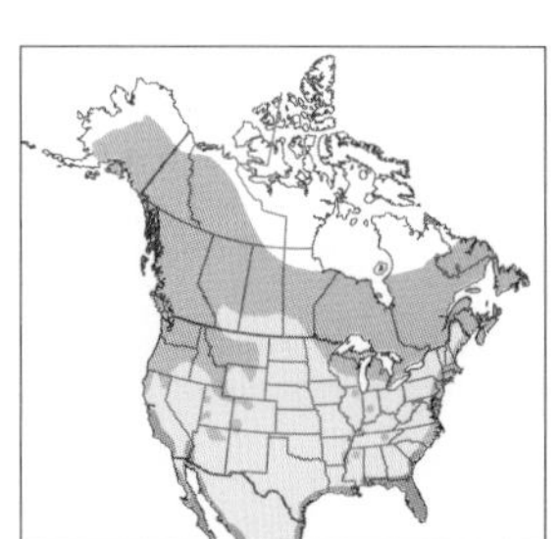

Identification of Falcons

The family Falconidae is represented in North America by two subfamilies: Caracara and true falcons. Northern Caracara has a long neck and legs and long, rounded wings; its flight and shape are unlike any other raptor. True falcons are characterized by long, pointed wings, round heads, and fast flight.

Nesting habits vary: Northern Caracara builds an open nest of sticks, while the true falcons make do with whatever they find; American Kestrel uses cavities such as old woodpecker holes; Aplomado Falcon and Merlin use abandoned nests in trees or bushes; the three large falcon species usually nest on cliff ledges.

Falcons are generally easily distinguished from other raptors. They are more frequently confused with nonraptors:

- Jaegers flying low over the water have the purposeful flight and dark, pointed wings typical of falcons; they are more slender, however, with relatively longer wings and different plumage patterns.
- Gulls (especially soaring) have a falconlike shape but are more slender and much less powerful.
- Pigeons can be deceptively falconlike, as they have fast and powerful flight, but their wingbeats are more erratic, without steady pumping, and they differ in shape and plumage.
- Swallows (especially Purple Martin) are very similar in shape to Merlin and can easily be mistaken despite the difference in size. A few moments studying flight actions should eliminate any confusion.

Parasitic
Jaeger
California
Gull

Rock
Dove
Purple
Martin

Northern Caracara, found in open savanna or desert, feeds mainly on carrion it locates by patrolling at low altitude. Aplomado Falcon, found in a yucca/grassland habitat, hunts small birds and insects.

Northern Caracara

Caracara cheriway

L 23" WS 49" WT 2.2 lb (990 g)

Distinctive shape, long neck and legs; dark with white ends.

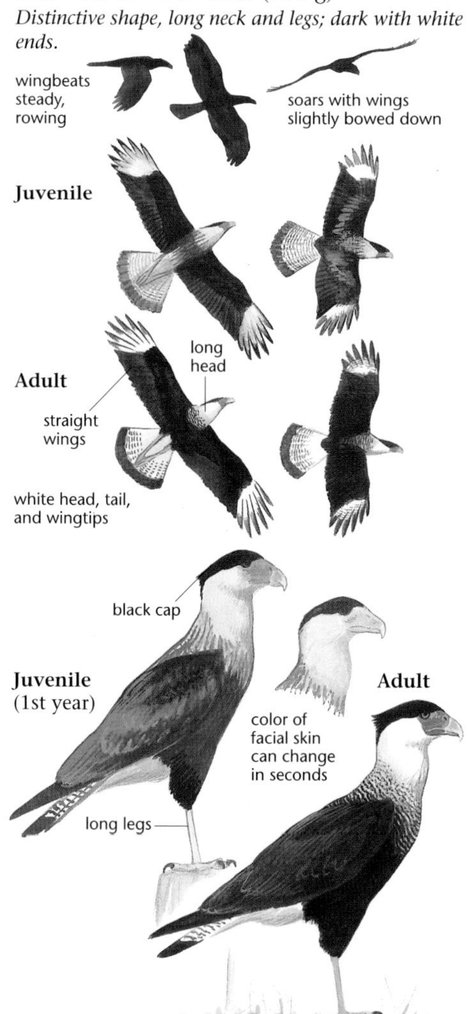
wingbeats steady, rowing
soars with wings slightly bowed down
Juvenile
long head
Adult
straight wings
white head, tail, and wingtips
black cap
Juvenile (1st year)
Adult
color of facial skin can change in seconds
long legs

Voice: Usually silent; low, toneless, croaking *grrrrk* or more complex call of several syllables. Juvenile begs with hoarse or wheezy scream.

Aplomado Falcon

Falco femoralis

L 16" WS 35" WT 12 oz (335 g) ♀>♂

Very long-tailed and long-winged; strikingly patterned.

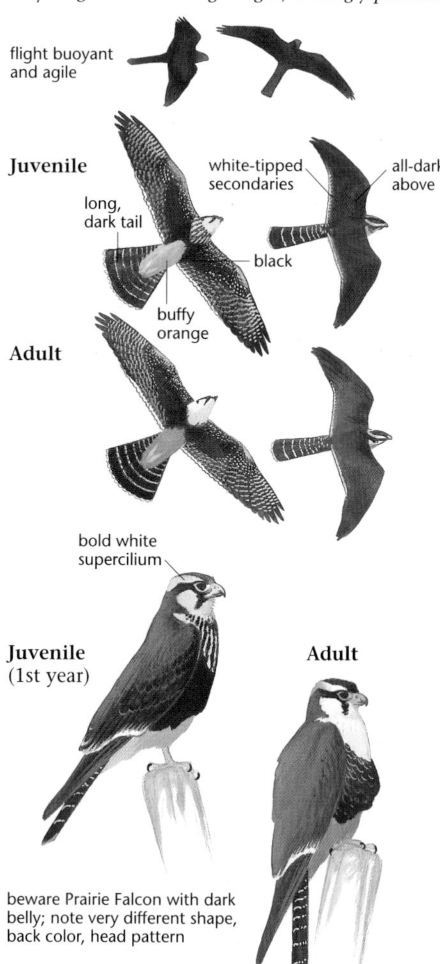
flight buoyant and agile
Juvenile
white-tipped secondaries
all-dark above
long, dark tail
black
buffy orange
Adult
bold white supercilium
Juvenile (1st year)
Adult
beware Prairie Falcon with dark belly; note very different shape, back color, head pattern

Voice: Alarm a harsh series *kek kek kek . . .* faster and higher than Prairie or Peregrine; also a sharp *chip;* female gives plaintive wailing. Juvenile begs with high-pitched chittering.

Aplomado Falcon formerly (pre-1910) nested in desert grasslands from Arizona to Texas, but few have been recorded since. It is now being reintroduced in southern Texas. Northern Caracara was formerly known as Crested Caracara.

This small, very fast falcon is found in wide-open space and open woods; it captures birds and insects in midair by a level sprint, finishing with abrupt turns. Three populations differ in overall color.

Merlin

Falco columbarius

L 10" WS 24" WT 6.5 oz (190 g) ♀>♂

Small, compact, powerful, and very aggressive; wings short and pointed, always angular; most appear dark.

flight faster and stronger than American Kestrel

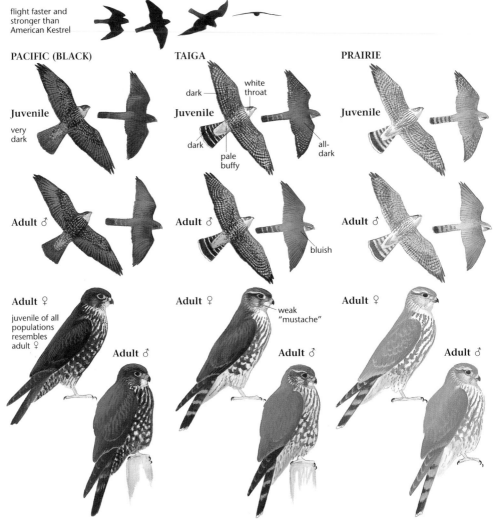

PACIFIC (BLACK)

Juvenile

very dark

Adult ♂

Adult ♀

juvenile of all populations resembles adult ♀

Adult ♂

TAIGA

Juvenile

dark

white throat

dark

pale buffy

all-dark

Adult ♂

bluish

Adult ♀

weak "mustache"

Adult ♂

PRAIRIE

Juvenile

Adult ♂

Adult ♀

Adult ♂

Voice: Alarm call rapid, accelerating series of strident notes, rising then falling, with quality like Killdeer but harsher *twi twitwitwitititititititit;* female lower, slower, harsher than male; also single hard *peek* reminiscent of Black-headed Grosbeak. Juvenile call similar to adult.

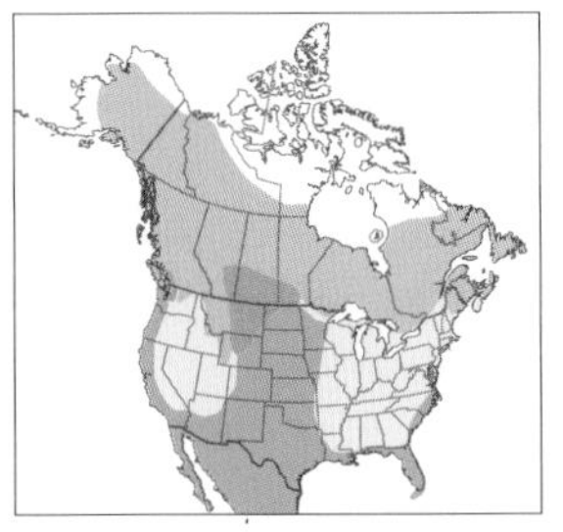

Three different populations differ in overall color, reflected in the prominence of the dark "mustache," width of dark tail-bands, extent of flank and underwing covert markings, and back color. Typical individuals are readily identified, but intermediates occur where ranges meet. Occasional Taiga birds from the east apparently resemble Black. Taiga population is widespread, wintering along both coasts. Prairie birds winter from Canada to Mexico, occasionally west to California. Black population winters along Pacific coast south to California, rarely east to New Mexico.

FALCONS (CONTINUED)

American Kestrel is often seen hovering or perched on wires in open areas, hunting insects and small mammals. Prairie Falcon is found in arid open country; it hunts birds and small mammals.

American Kestrel

Falco sparverius

L 9" WS 22" WT 4.1 oz (117 g) ♀>♂

Our smallest and most delicate falcon; long-winged and long-tailed. Wingtips blunt when spread, often swept back.

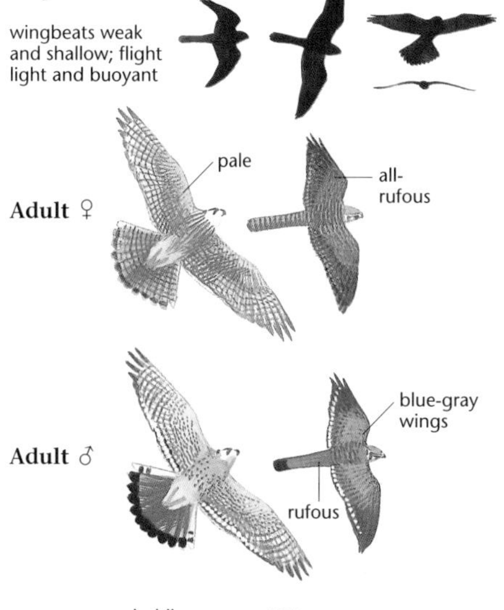

wingbeats weak and shallow; flight light and buoyant
Adult ♀
pale
all-rufous
Adult ♂
blue-gray wings
rufous

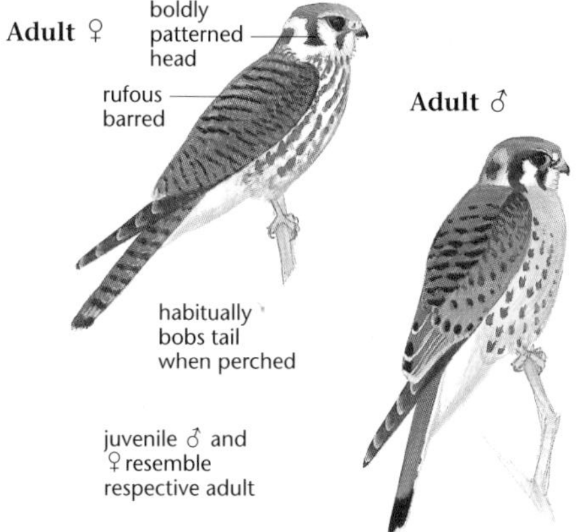

Adult ♀
boldly patterned head
rufous barred
Adult ♂
habitually bobs tail when perched
juvenile ♂ and ♀ resemble respective adult

Voice: Common call a shrill, clear screaming *kli kli kli kli kli kli kli kli* or *killy killy killy*, higher and weaker than other raptors. Juvenile call similar to adult.

Prairie Falcon

Falco mexicanus

L 16" WS 40" WT 1.6 lb (720 g) ♀>♂

Size and shape similar to Peregrine Falcon: wingtips less pointed, tail longer, paler brown above with diagnostic dark axillaries.

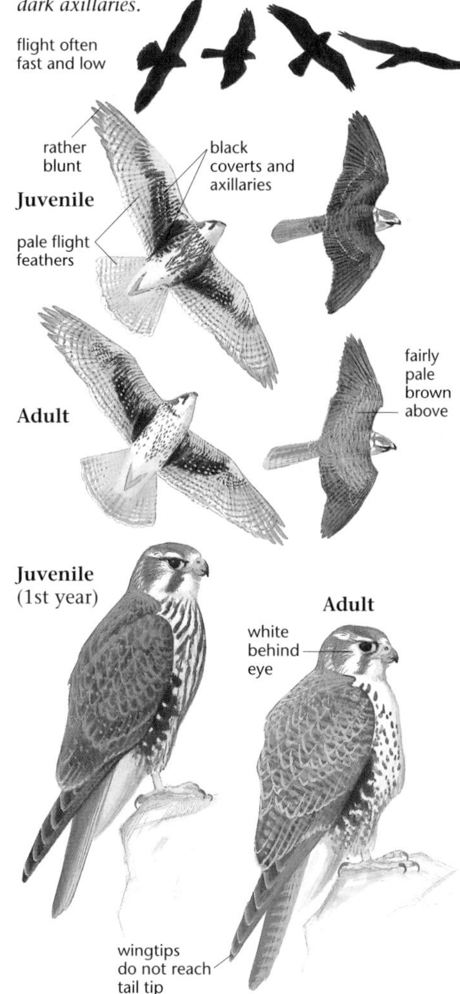

flight often fast and low
rather blunt
black coverts and axillaries
Juvenile
pale flight feathers
fairly pale brown above
Adult
Juvenile (1st year)
Adult
white behind eye
wingtips do not reach tail tip

Voice: Generally similar to Peregrine. Alarm an angry, harsh *ree-kree-kree-kree . . .* similar to Peregrine but higher; also a high, rising scream *keeeee* repeated.

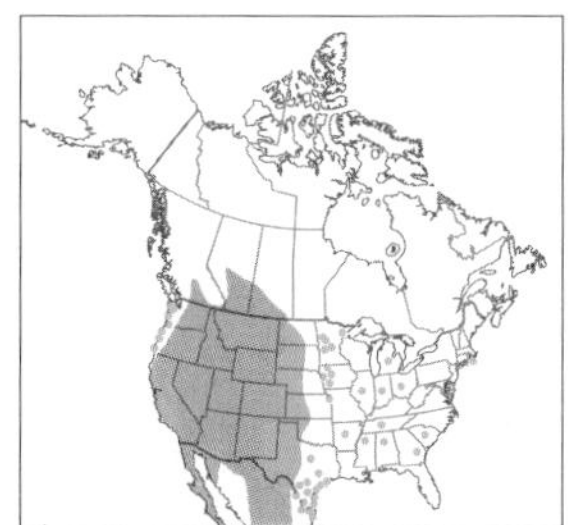

Falcons (continued)

Our largest falcon, this powerful, deceptively fast species is found on Arctic tundra or similar habitat. It hunts birds mainly in level chase. Most are gray, but white and dark morphs occur.

Gyrfalcon

Falco rusticolus

L 22" WS 47" WT 3.1 lb (1,400 g) ♀>♂

Stocky, broad body; broad wings with blunt tips, relatively long-tailed.

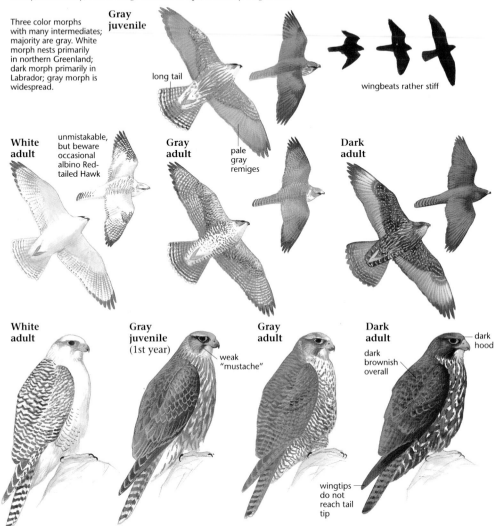

Three color morphs with many intermediates; majority are gray. White morph nests primarily in northern Greenland; dark morph primarily in Labrador; gray morph is widespread.

Gray juvenile

long tail

wingbeats rather stiff

White adult

unmistakable, but beware occasional albino Red-tailed Hawk

Gray adult

pale gray remiges

Dark adult

White adult

Gray juvenile (1st year)

weak "mustache"

Gray adult

Dark adult

dark hood

dark brownish overall

wingtips do not reach tail tip

Voice: Alarm a hoarse, nasal *KYHa KYHa KYHa* . . . ; a deep, hoarse *kwah kwah kwah* . . . lower, gruffer, with more trumpeting quality than Peregrine. Juvenile begs with wailing call and gives hoarse series like adult.

Gyrfalcon's blunt wingtips suggest Northern Goshawk or even buteos; note face pattern, more uniform plumage. Northern Goshawk is usually found in the woods, whereas Gyrfalcon stays in the open. Gyrfalcon is distinguished from Peregrine by broader, blunter wings, weaker "mustache," longer tail, more uniform plumage, and underwing coverts darker than remiges.

Falcons (continued)

This sleek, powerful falcon has long been considered the embodiment of speed and power. Found in open areas, it hunts mainly medium-size birds from high above in spectacular stoops.

Peregrine Falcon

Falco peregrinus

L 16" WS 41" WT 1.6 lb (720 g) ♀>♂

Relatively large and stocky, with pointed wings and short tail; note dark "mustache" and uniformly patterned underwing.

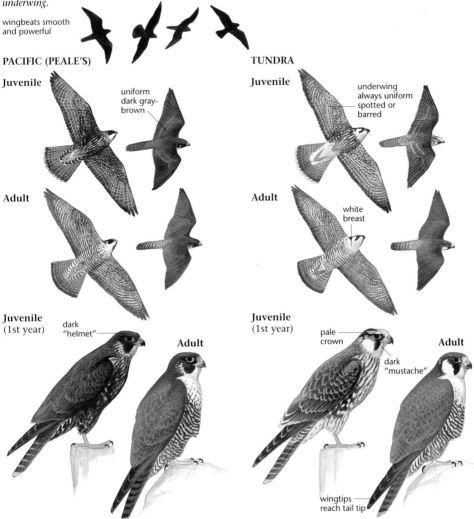

wingbeats smooth and powerful

PACIFIC (PEALE'S)

Juvenile

uniform dark gray-brown

Adult

Juvenile (1st year)

dark "helmet"

Adult

TUNDRA

Juvenile

underwing always uniform spotted or barred

Adult

white breast

Juvenile (1st year)

pale crown

dark "mustache"

Adult

wingtips reach tail tip

Voice: Alarm a slow, scolding *rehk rehk rehk . . .* ; harsh, raucous, each note rising. In aggression a hard, mechanical *wiSHEP koCHE koCHE koCHEcheche*. Peale's calls possibly lower, more throaty, less mechanical than Interior West population (see below). Juvenile call similar to adult.

Tundra breeding population is widespread in migration and winter. The Interior West population (not shown) is similar to Peale's but with unmarked, pale breast and cheeks. Peale's is mainly resident coastally from Washington to Alaska. Recent reintroductions in many areas involve captive-bred form similar to Peale's, and Peale's-like birds are now found across North America.

Upland Game Birds

Families: Cracidae, Odontophoridae, Phasianidae

22 species in 15 genera; all in family Phasianidae, except quail and Northern Bobwhite in Odontophoridae and Plain Chachalaca in Cracidae. All are chickenlike ground-dwelling birds that forage quietly on plant matter and some insects; they are usually quite secretive and often found in small flocks called coveys. Their explosive takeoff with stiff beats of rounded wings is characteristic. Note that in all species, downy young develop functional flight feathers when only a week old and about a third the size of adults; beware mistaking these birds for smaller species. Compare rails, American Coot, and doves. Adult females are shown.

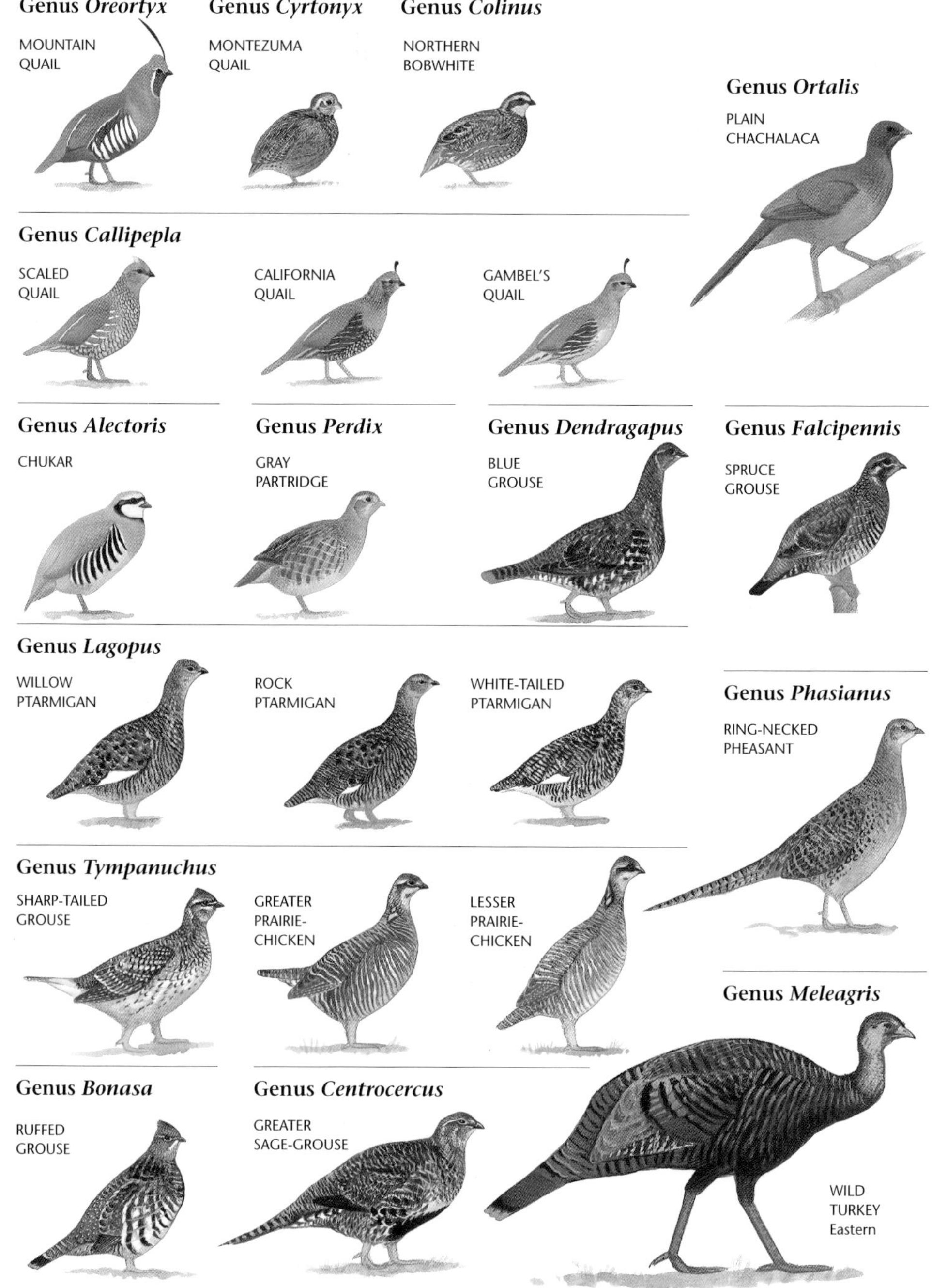

Genus *Oreortyx*
MOUNTAIN QUAIL
Genus *Cyrtonyx*
MONTEZUMA QUAIL
Genus *Colinus*
NORTHERN BOBWHITE
Genus *Ortalis*
PLAIN CHACHALACA
Genus *Callipepla*
SCALED QUAIL
CALIFORNIA QUAIL
GAMBEL'S QUAIL
Genus *Alectoris*
CHUKAR
Genus *Perdix*
GRAY PARTRIDGE
Genus *Dendragapus*
BLUE GROUSE
Genus *Falcipennis*
SPRUCE GROUSE
Genus *Lagopus*
WILLOW PTARMIGAN
ROCK PTARMIGAN
WHITE-TAILED PTARMIGAN
Genus *Phasianus*
RING-NECKED PHEASANT
Genus *Tympanuchus*
SHARP-TAILED GROUSE
GREATER PRAIRIE-CHICKEN
LESSER PRAIRIE-CHICKEN
Genus *Meleagris*
Genus *Bonasa*
RUFFED GROUSE
Genus *Centrocercus*
GREATER SAGE-GROUSE
WILD TURKEY Eastern

Exotic Game Birds

Many species of upland game birds have been released in North America. Most releases have been organized by hunting groups and have failed to establish feral populations.

RED-LEGGED PARTRIDGE
Alectoris rufa
L 14" ♂>♀
No established populations, but frequently released.
Voice: Rapid series of hard clucking notes similar to Chukar.

Adult

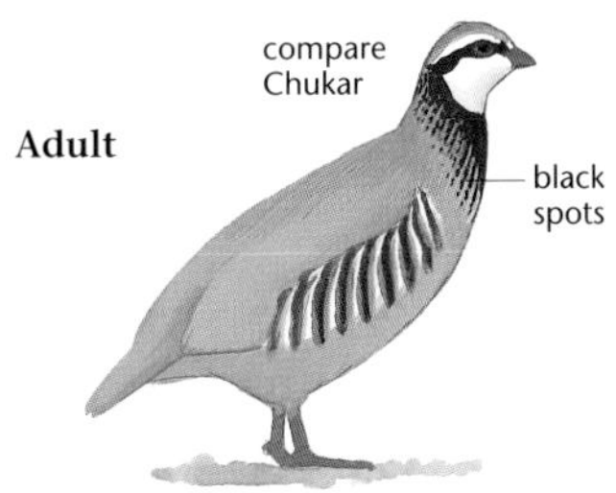
compare
Chukar
black
spots

BLACK FRANCOLIN
Francolinus francolinus
L 14" ♂>♀
Small populations in Louisiana and Florida, apparently no longer persisting.
Voice: Male gives harsh, rhythmic series *kok, KEEK kee-kee-ka ke-KEEK.*

Adult ♀ **Adult ♂**

HELMETED GUINEAFOWL
Numida meleagris
L 23"
Common in zoos and farmyards; a feral population may exist in southern Florida.
Voice: Raucous notes in rhythmic series.

Adult

HIMALAYAN SNOWCOCK
Tetraogallus himalayensis
L 28"
A small population is established in the Ruby Mountains of Nevada.
Voice: A curlewlike whistle in display; low clucking and shrill cackles.

Adult

mostly white
primaries
conspicuous
in flight

COMMON PEAFOWL
Pavo cristatus
L 40" (adult ♂ to 90")
Common in zoos; small feral populations exist in southern California.
Voice: Male gives very loud, wailing cries.

Adult ♀

Adult ♂

Plain Chachalaca and Montezuma Quail

The noisy Plain Chachalaca is found in small groups in dense, brushy woods, often climbing in trees. Montezuma Quail is usually found in pairs, hiding in dense grass among scattered oak trees.

Plain Chachalaca

Ortalis vetula

L 22" WS 26" WT 1.2 lb (550 g) ♂>♀

Noisy but otherwise inconspicuous. Fairly large; long-necked with long, rounded tail; drab color.

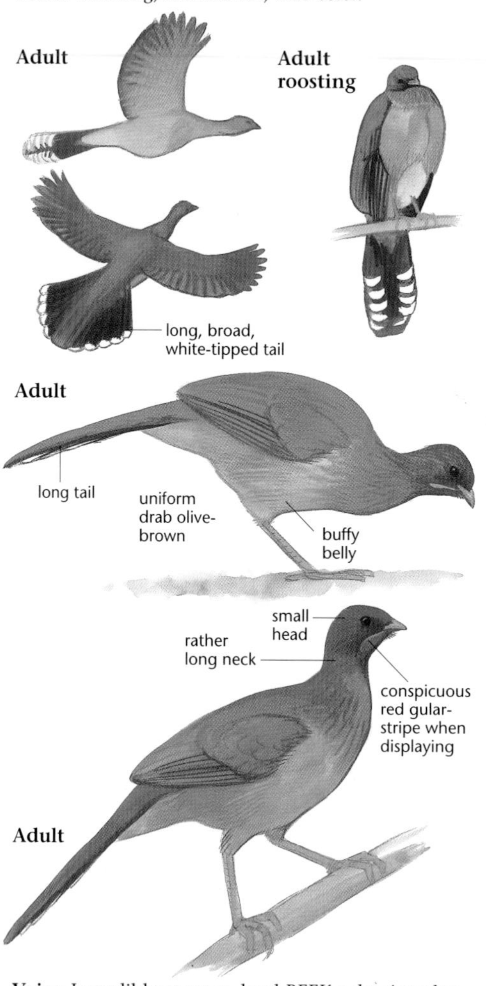

Adult
Adult roosting
long, broad, white-tipped tail
Adult
long tail
uniform drab olive-brown
buffy belly
small head
rather long neck
conspicuous red gular-stripe when displaying
Adult

Voice: Incredibly raucous, loud *REEK a der* given by many birds in synchronized chorus. Lead bird low-pitched *gra da da* joined by others giving squeakier, higher-pitched *gree de de*. A muffled, toneless *krrrr* given when nervous, leading into raucous clattering *KLOK aTOK aTOK aTOK* as birds take flight.

Montezuma Quail

Cyrtonyx montezumae

L 8.75" WS 15" WT 6 oz (180 g) ♂>♀

Round body with very short tail and round head; note clownish face pattern, intricately patterned body.

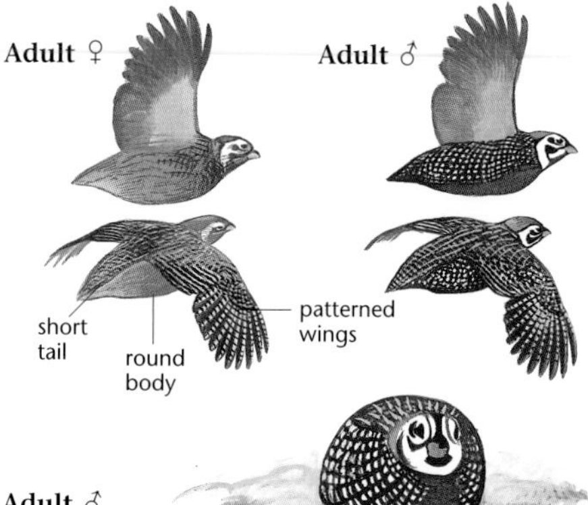

Adult ♀
Adult ♂
short tail
round body
patterned wings

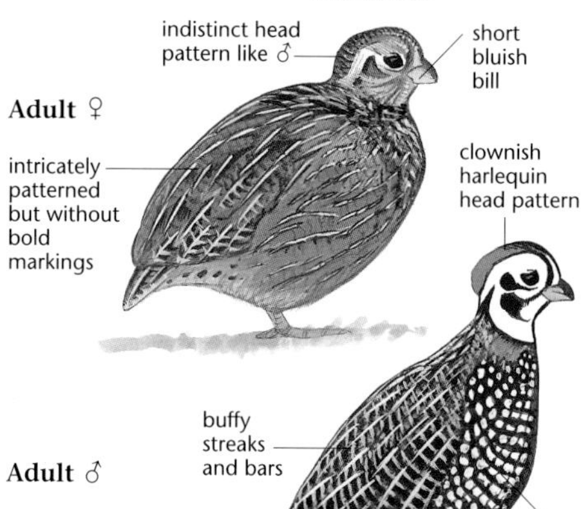

Adult ♂ crouching
dark center of underside
indistinct head pattern like ♂
short bluish bill
Adult ♀
intricately patterned but without bold markings
clownish harlequin head pattern
buffy streaks and bars
Adult ♂
white dots

Voice: Male song an eerie, melancholy, vibrant, descending whistle *vwirrrrr;* also gives piping *querp* or louder *querp-quueeep*. Other calls include low *wep wep . . .* and soft, low *pwew;* assembly call a low, whistled series of six to nine notes descending in pitch. Flush with loud, popping wing noise.

Northern Bobwhite is the only quail over most of its range. Secretive, it is more often heard than seen and is found in brushy woods and fields in coveys of up to 20 birds.

Northern Bobwhite

Colinus virginianus

L 9.75" WS 13" WT 6 oz (170 g)

Small and round-bodied, with short tail and neck; reddish and gray plumage distinctive. Unmistakable in most areas, often the only quail-size bird, but beware small juveniles of larger species such as pheasants.

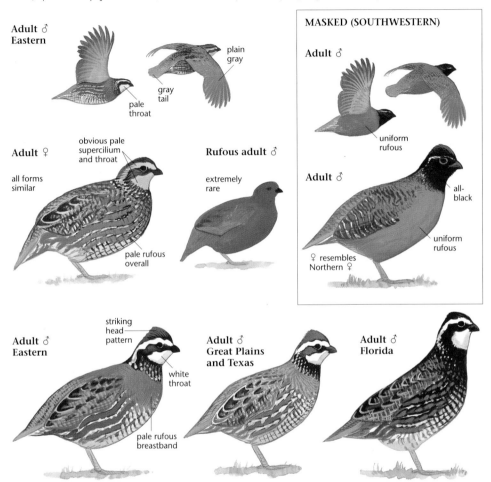

Adult ♂ Eastern

pale throat

gray tail

plain gray

Adult ♀

all forms similar

obvious pale supercilium and throat

pale rufous overall

Rufous adult ♂

extremely rare

MASKED (SOUTHWESTERN)

Adult ♂

uniform rufous

Adult ♂

all-black

uniform rufous

♀ resembles Northern ♀

Adult ♂ Eastern

striking head pattern

white throat

pale rufous breastband

Adult ♂ Great Plains and Texas

Adult ♂ Florida

Voice: Male song a strong, clear whistle *pup WAAAYK* or *bob WHITE* (often imitated by starlings, mockingbirds, etc.); also a loud, harsh *quaysh* or *quEEEak*. Covey calls include *hoy, hoypoo,* and *koilee;* contact calls a soft *took* and *pitoo*. Ground predators elicit soft, musical *tirree,* changing to *ick-ick-ick* or *toil-ick-ick-ick;* avian predators elicit throaty *errrk*. Male in southern Texas gives harsher *bob WHIISH* than northern birds.

Regional variation in male plumage is considerable but nearly all clinal, with many intermediates; smaller and darker to the southeast, paler and grayer to the west. Females are less variable. The disjunct Masked population is found in grasslands of southeastern Arizona. Male is strikingly colored, but female is virtually identical to Northern female. Voice is apparently identical.

Quail (continued)

These two species are very closely related but have little range overlap. Both are found in dense, brushy cover, often in large groups, most often seen walking across open areas.

California Quail

Callipepla californica

L 10" WS 14" WT 6 oz (180 g)

Rather slender and long-tailed for a quail; distinguished from Gambel's by darker overall color, nape pattern, belly pattern, and other plumage details.

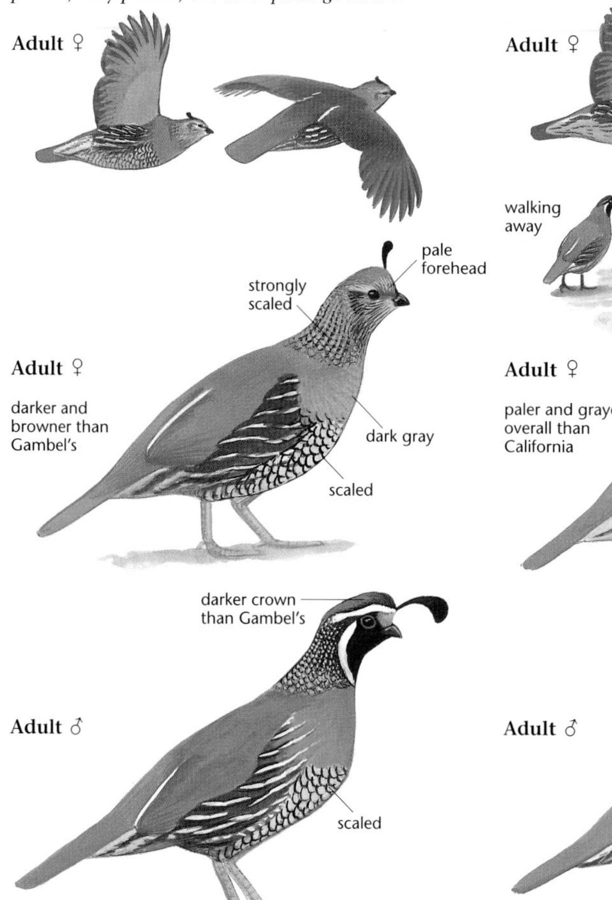

Adult ♀
pale forehead
strongly scaled
Adult ♀
darker and browner than Gambel's
dark gray
scaled
darker crown than Gambel's
Adult ♂
scaled

Voice: Male song a repeated, nasal *put way doo* similar to Gambel's, but final note longer and descending, individually variable. Other calls include relaxed *waaaaw* or *waay;* rapid spitting *spwik wik wiw;* sharp, metallic alarm *pit-pit;* soft clucking *ut, ut. . . .*

Gambel's Quail

Callipepla gambelii

L 10" WS 14" WT 6 oz (180 g)

Very similar overall to California; longer-tailed than Scaled, with very different plumage.

Adult ♀
uniform grayish
rather long, gray tail
walking away
weakly patterned
Adult ♀
paler and grayer overall than California
pale with fine streaks
unmarked creamy
dark forehead
Adult ♂
unmarked
dark patch

Voice: Male song a repeated, nasal *pup waay pop* or *pup waay pop pop* with short, clipped final note. Other calls include a descending or moaning *where* or *uweeea;* high, sharp *spik* notes; hoarse, trumpeting *krrt;* soft clucking notes. Some quite distinct from California.

California and Gambel's hybridize in the few areas where their ranges overlap.

Scaled Quail, found in small coveys in arid, brushy grasslands, is related to California and Gambel's Quails, despite different appearance. Mountain is distinctive and found in montane chaparral.

Scaled Quail

Callipepla squamata

L 10" WS 14" WT 6 oz (180 g)

Stockier and shorter-tailed than Gambel's, with short white tuft rather than black plume on head.

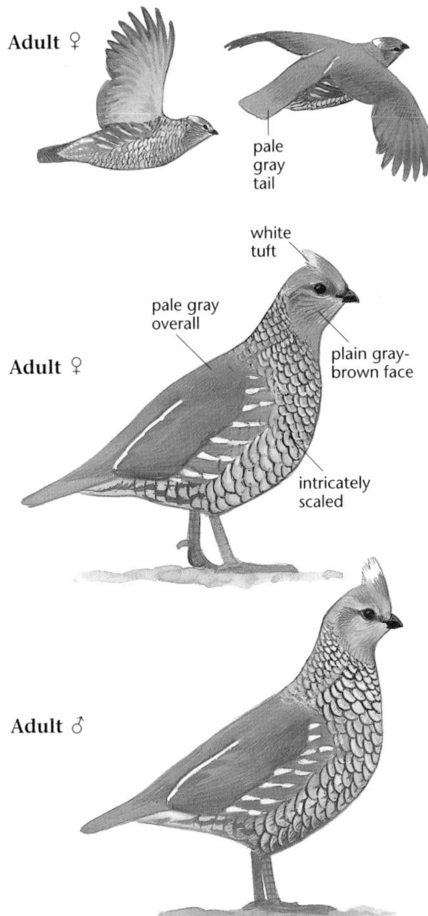
Adult ♀
pale gray tail
white tuft
pale gray overall
plain gray-brown face
Adult ♀
intricately scaled
Adult ♂

Voice: Male song a high, raucous outburst *QUEESH* or *BEISH*; also slow, rhythmic, coarse clucking *kek kut, kek kut . . .* or *kek kyurr, kek kyurr. . . .* Other calls include high, sharp chip or trill of sharp notes reminiscent of passerines.

Mountain Quail

Oreortyx pictus

L 11" WS 16" WT 8 oz (220 g)

Larger and shorter-tailed than California, with numerous plumage differences, including bold white bars on flanks.

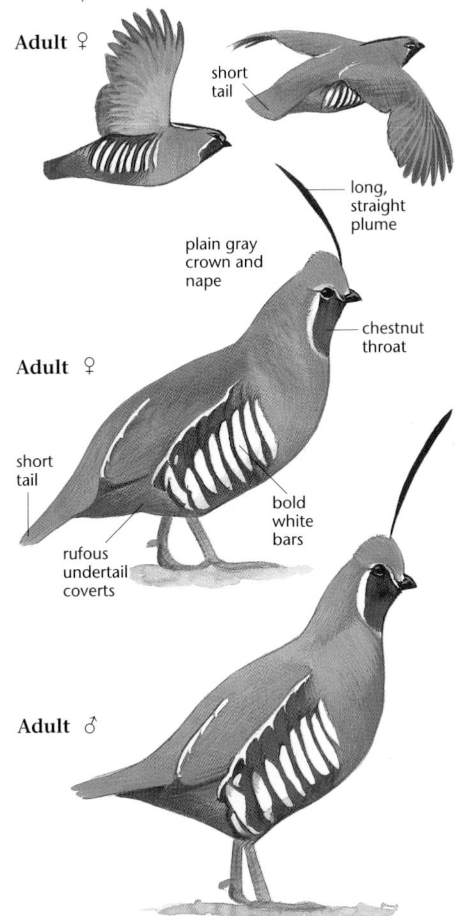
Adult ♀
short tail
long, straight plume
plain gray crown and nape
chestnut throat
Adult ♀
short tail
bold white bars
rufous undertail coverts
Adult ♂

Voice: Male song loud, raucous, two-syllable *QUEark*, like Scaled Quail but lower, descending (and no range overlap). Loud *cle-cle-cle* or *kow kow kow* series reunites covey. Other soft clucking and trilled notes given by both sexes.

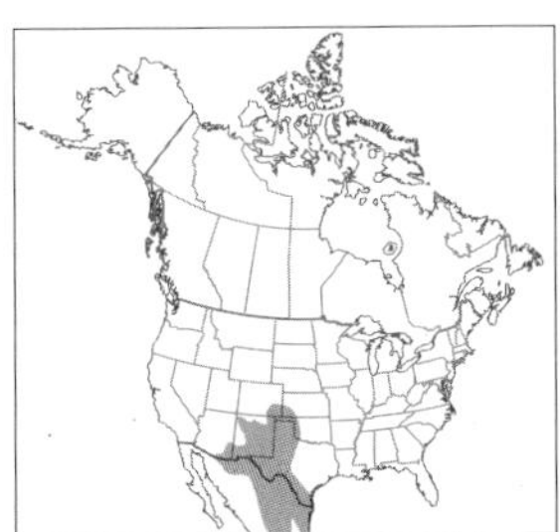

Scaled × Gambel's Quail hybrid adult ♂ Recorded rarely where ranges overlap.

Partridges

These two Eurasian species have been introduced widely in North America. Both are usually seen in small groups: Chukar in rocky desert canyons, Gray Partridge in flat agricultural land.

Chukar

Alectoris chukar

L 14" WS 20" WT 1.3 lb (590 g) ♂>♀

Larger than quail, short-tailed; pale but strikingly patterned, with red bill and legs.

Adult

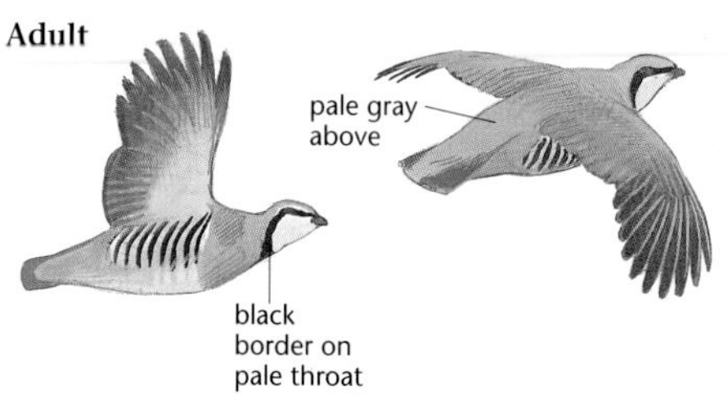
pale gray above
black border on pale throat

Adult ♀

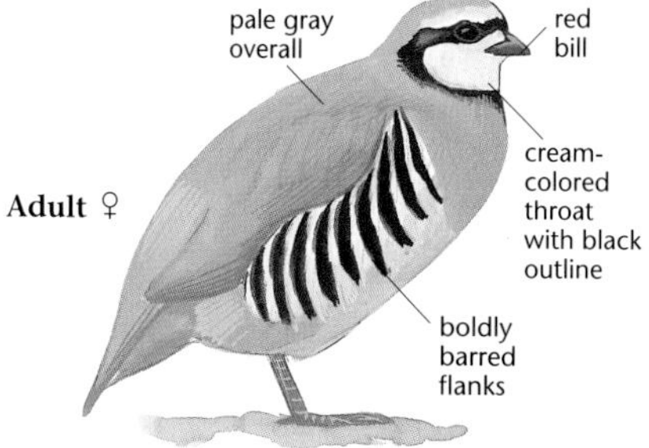
pale gray overall
red bill
cream-colored throat with black outline
boldly barred flanks

Adult ♂

Voice: A series of nasal, clipped clucks *kakakaka-kakakachukAR chuKAR chuKAR.* In flight quiet clucking sounds and loud, harsh note followed by softer notes *PITCH-oo-whidoo.*

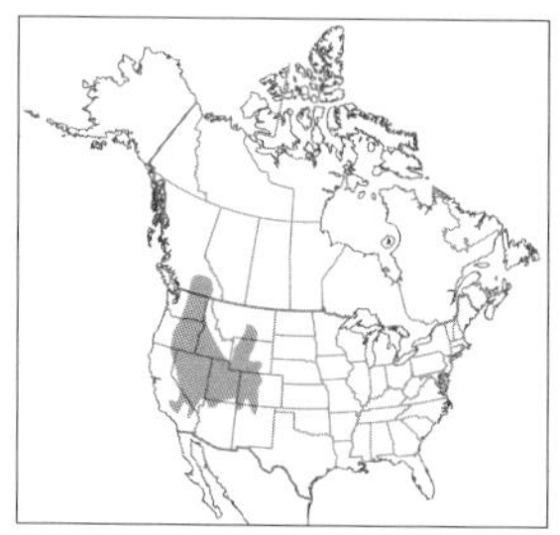

Chukars are released regularly in all states for hunting and other purposes, so are frequently seen outside of the mapped range. Compare Red-legged Partridge, which is also released in many areas.

Gray Partridge

Perdix perdix

L 12.5" WS 19" WT 14 oz (390 g)

Size and shape like Chukar; larger than quail, but smaller than grouse.

Adult ♂

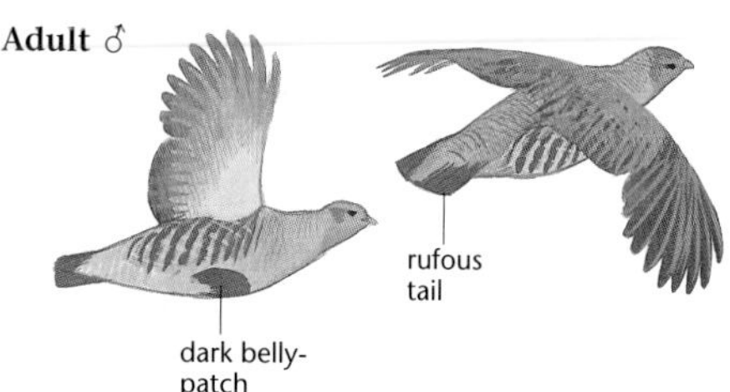
rufous tail
dark belly-patch

Adult ♀

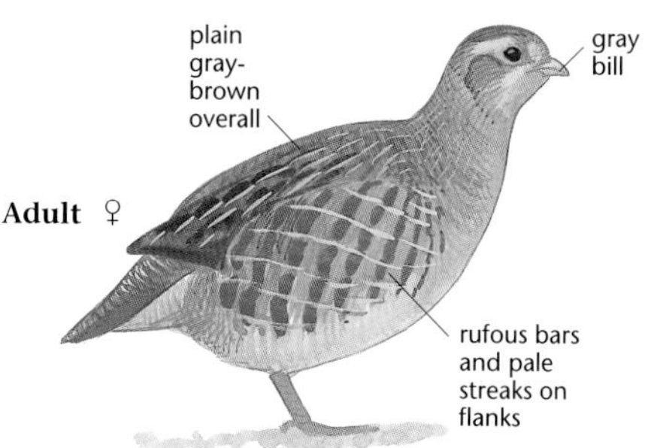
plain gray-brown overall
gray bill
rufous bars and pale streaks on flanks

Adult ♂

distinctive habit of flicking tail open to show orange-rufous outer feathers

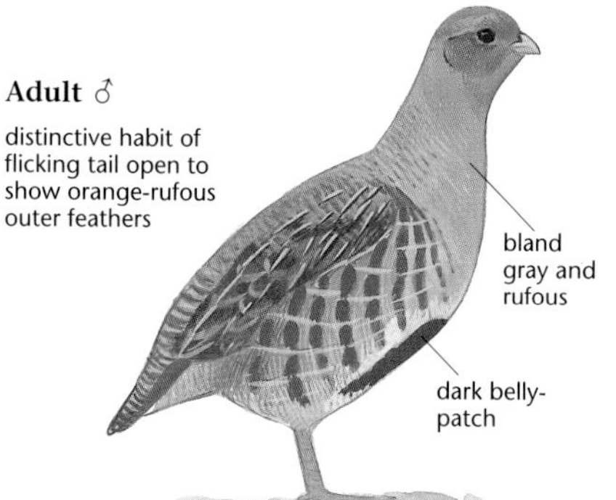
bland gray and rufous
dark belly-patch

Voice: Male gives repeated scratchy *Kishrrr* or *kshEEErik;* quality reminiscent of guineafowl. Both sexes give *keeeah* and clucking notes. Covey flushes with wing noise and loud, high *keep, keep . . .* in cackling chorus.

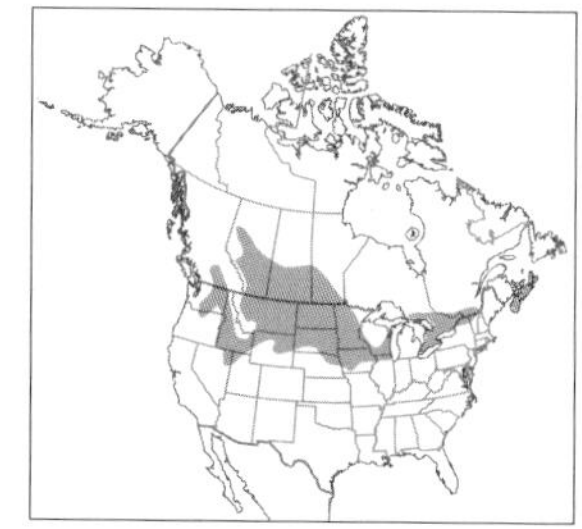

PHEASANTS

Widely introduced from Eurasia, pheasants occur in open fields and along brushy, weedy hedgerows and forest edges. Many North American populations are maintained by continued introduction.

Ring-necked Pheasant

Phasianus colchicus

L 21" (adult ♂ to 35") WS 31" WT 2.5 lb (1,150 g) ♂>♀

A medium-size to large game bird with long, pointed tail in all plumages. Male strikingly colored and very long-tailed; female brownish and uniformly patterned.

Adult ♀

long, pointed tail

drab buffy-brown overall

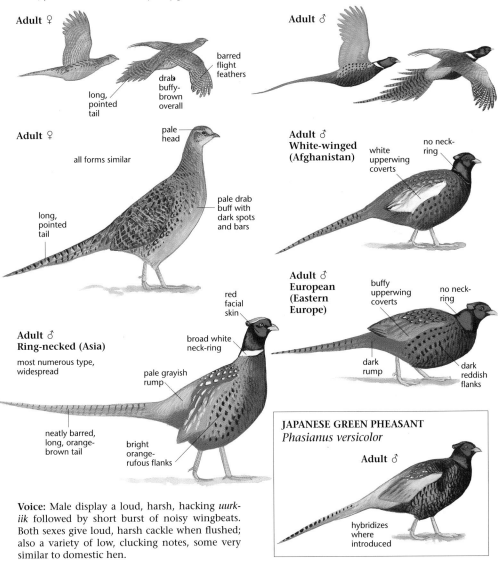

barred flight feathers

Adult ♂

Adult ♀

all forms similar

pale head

pale drab buff with dark spots and bars

long, pointed tail

Adult ♂ White-winged (Afghanistan)

white upperwing coverts

no neck-ring

Adult ♂ European (Eastern Europe)

buffy upperwing coverts

no neck-ring

dark rump

dark reddish flanks

Adult ♂ Ring-necked (Asia)

most numerous type, widespread

red facial skin

broad white neck-ring

pale grayish rump

neatly barred, long, orange-brown tail

bright orange-rufous flanks

Voice: Male display a loud, harsh, hacking *uurk-iik* followed by short burst of noisy wingbeats. Both sexes give loud, harsh cackle when flushed; also a variety of low, clucking notes, some very similar to domestic hen.

JAPANESE GREEN PHEASANT

Phasianus versicolor

Adult ♂

hybridizes where introduced

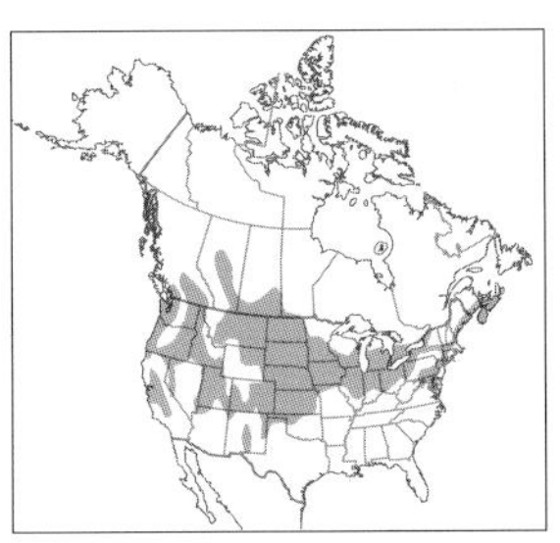

The North American population is an amalgam of many different subspecies. Typical examples are shown, but many intermediates occur. New varieties are continually being bred and released for sport hunting. White-winged birds are established in parts of the west. European birds and intergrades with Ring-necked are found in scattered locations. Japanese Green Pheasant, often considered a separate species, has been introduced locally in Virginia and Delaware. Females of all forms are similar, although female Japanese Green averages more densely spotted with black on the breast.

GROUSE

Found singly in dense spruce woods with mossy ground, this species is noted for its tameness, often feeding on berries or spruce needles without concern just a few feet from observers.

Spruce Grouse

Falcipennis canadensis

L 16" WS 22" WT 1 lb (460 g) ♂>♀

Medium-size, stocky, short-necked, and short-tailed. Male distinctively patterned; on female note overall color and barred pattern.

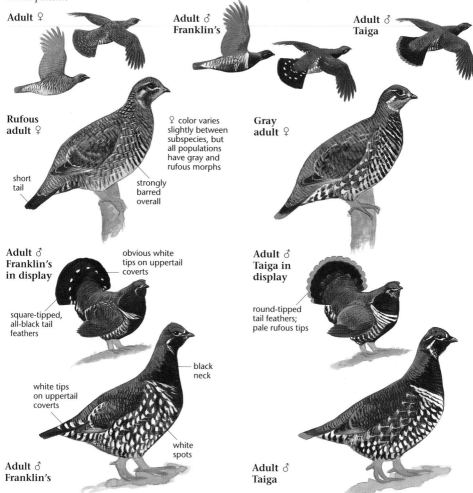

Adult ♀

Adult ♂ Franklin's

Adult ♂ Taiga

Rufous adult ♀

♀ color varies slightly between subspecies, but all populations have gray and rufous morphs

short tail

strongly barred overall

Gray adult ♀

Adult ♂ Franklin's in display

obvious white tips on uppertail coverts

square-tipped, all-black tail feathers

Adult ♂ Taiga in display

round-tipped tail feathers; pale rufous tips

black neck

white tips on uppertail coverts

white spots

Adult ♂ Franklin's

Adult ♂ Taiga

Voice: Male in display gives extremely low hoot or series of hoots. Both sexes give guttural notes and clucks. Display of male differs between populations: Taiga display involves gliding from 10 to 20 feet up in tree, turning body vertically and hovering to ground; Franklin's display involves gliding 50 to 100 yards from perch and producing two loud wing claps (like gunshots) before settling on ground.

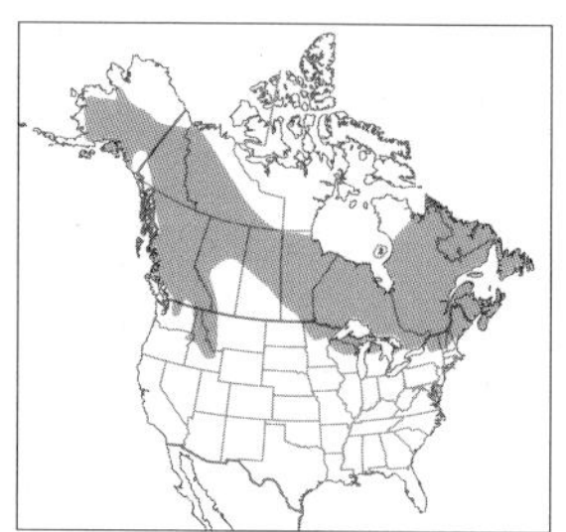

Two populations are distinctive in plumage and display, but with intergrades found in a broad area where ranges meet. Franklin's is found south of a line from southernmost Alaska to central Alberta. Male Franklin's (compared to Taiga) has obvious white tips on tertials and uppertail coverts, larger white tips on flank feathers, less white on head and breast, and square-tipped tail feathers that are black to their tips. Differences in display are described above. Females in both populations vary from gray to rufous; tail pattern is variable but differs on average between populations (pale rufous tips on Taiga).

Grouse (continued)

This large grouse is found singly in mature pine or fir forests, generally in open woods or clearings. It is larger and more wary than Spruce Grouse.

Blue Grouse

Dendragapus obscurus

L 20" WS 26" WT 2.3 lb (1,050 g) ♂>♀

One of our largest grouse; relatively long-necked and long-tailed. All plumages fairly uniform grayish or gray-brown without strong plumage contrasts.

Adult ♀

Adult ♂ Interior

dark tail

Adult ♀

all populations similar, variable

gray-brown and speckled overall

PACIFIC (SOOTY)

Darker adult ♂ in display

narrow, light gray tips

Paler adult ♂ in display

dark gray

Adult ♂

INTERIOR (DUSKY)

Darker adult ♂ in display

dark gray tips

Paler adult ♂ in display

Adult ♂

Voice: Male in display gives single low hoot; advertising call a series of very low, pulsing hoots *whoof whoof whoof whoof whoof whoof,* rising then falling slightly (compare Great Gray Owl). Both sexes give a low *gr gr gr gr* and soft clucking or barking sounds. Male hooting series differs between populations: usually six syllables, higher-pitched, and audible at a quarter mile in Pacific; usually five syllables, lower-pitched, and audible at only 50 yards in Interior.

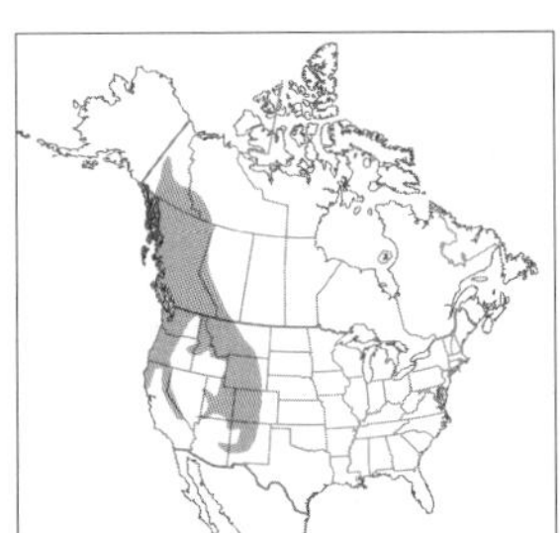

Two populations intergrade broadly where ranges meet. Both are darker in the north, paler in the south. Male Pacific averages darker overall; tail is slightly rounded or wedge-shaped (vs. square) and tail feathers are round-tipped (vs. square) with narrow, light gray tips (but note that 1st year males of both populations have narrower, rounded tail feathers); also usually has 18 tail feathers (vs. 20). In display Pacific male shows warty, bright yellow air sacs on neck with less extensive white-feathered border; Interior has fleshy purple air sacs with smoother surface and broader white border. Differences in display are described above.

Grouse (continued): Ptarmigan

Ptarmigan have feathered feet and other adaptations for Arctic life. They are found on tundra: White-tailed in barren, rocky areas; Willow usually in low, dense vegetation at treeline.

White-tailed Ptarmigan

Lagopus leucurus

L 12.5" WS 22" WT 13 oz (360 g) ♂>♀

Our smallest ptarmigan, with small bill. White tail distinctive but difficult to confirm (black feathers of other species often concealed).

Adult nonbreeding

white tail

Adult ♀ breeding

white tail

Adult late summer (Jul–Oct)

grayish

Adult nonbreeding (Oct–Apr)

Adult ♀ breeding (May–Jul)

fairly cold yellowish speckled

Adult ♂ breeding (Apr–Jul)

speckled black on white

Voice: Male in display gives rapid clucking *pik pik pik pik piKEEA* and low, hoarse *pwirrr* while alternating fast and slow strutting; no flight display. Both sexes give clucking notes.

Willow Ptarmigan

Lagopus lagopus

L 15" WS 24" WT 1.2 lb (550 g) ♂>♀

Our largest ptarmigan, with distinctively thick bill. Rich rufous head and neck of breeding male distinctive.

Adult nonbreeding

Adult ♀ breeding

Adult nonbreeding (Oct–Apr)

stout bill

Adult ♂ courtship plumage (Apr–Jun)

Adult ♀ breeding (May–Jul)

warm brown

Adult ♂ breeding (May–Jul)

solid rufous head and neck

Voice: Male in display gives comical, nasal barking calls in series *goBEK goBEK goBEK, poDAYdo poDAYdo . . .* and a smoothly accelerating laugh. Female gives barking *dyow;* both sexes give clucking notes.

Identification of ptarmigan in plumages other than adult male breeding can be very difficult. Check bill size, overall color, and habitat.

GROUSE (CONTINUED): PTARMIGAN

Closely related to White-tailed and Willow, this species is found on barren, rocky tundra (except Aleutian populations). All ptarmigan are found singly in summer and in small flocks in winter.

Rock Ptarmigan

Lagopus mutus

L 14" WS 23" WT 15 oz (420 g) ♂>♀

Slightly smaller than Willow and larger than White-tailed, with relatively thin bill. Courting male still has mostly white winter plumage; never as rufous-colored as male Willow.

Juvenile

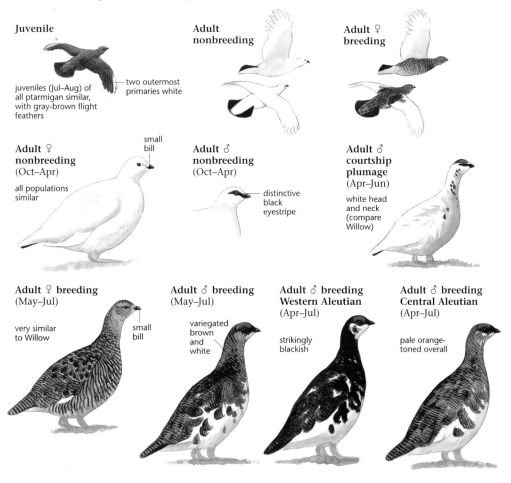

juveniles (Jul–Aug) of all ptarmigan similar, with gray-brown flight feathers

two outermost primaries white

Adult nonbreeding

Adult ♀ breeding

Adult ♀ nonbreeding (Oct–Apr)

all populations similar

small bill

Adult ♂ nonbreeding (Oct–Apr)

distinctive black eyestripe

Adult ♂ courtship plumage (Apr–Jun)

white head and neck (compare Willow)

Adult ♀ breeding (May–Jul)

very similar to Willow

small bill

Adult ♂ breeding (May–Jul)

variegated brown and white

Adult ♂ breeding Western Aleutian (Apr–Jul)

strikingly blackish

Adult ♂ breeding Central Aleutian (Apr–Jul)

pale orange-toned overall

Voice: Male in display gives guttural, croaking rattle followed by quiet hiss *krrrr-Karrrrr, wsshhh* very unlike Willow. Displays mainly on ground: sliding on breast, rolling, leaping. Flight display ending with croaking call may be more common in Aleutian populations. Both sexes give clucking notes.

Aleutian populations average larger with heavier bill than continental birds. They are found in grassy lowlands rather than rocky tundra, with possibly different courtship habits. Note striking differences in male breeding plumage.

All ptarmigan have three molts each year: in autumn a complete molt to all-white nonbreeding plumage; in spring a partial molt to strongly patterned breeding plumage; and another partial molt to more cryptically patterned late-summer plumage. Timing and extent of molts are influenced by climate: in warmer climates molts occur earlier in spring and later in fall.

The distinctive Ruffed Grouse is found singly in mixed woods. Sharp-tailed is closely related to prairie-chickens and is found in open prairie with patches of trees or in aspen parkland.

Ruffed Grouse

Bonasa umbellus

L 17" WS 22" WT 1.3 lb (580 g) ♂>♀

Slender with relatively long, rounded tail; long neck; slightly crested head.

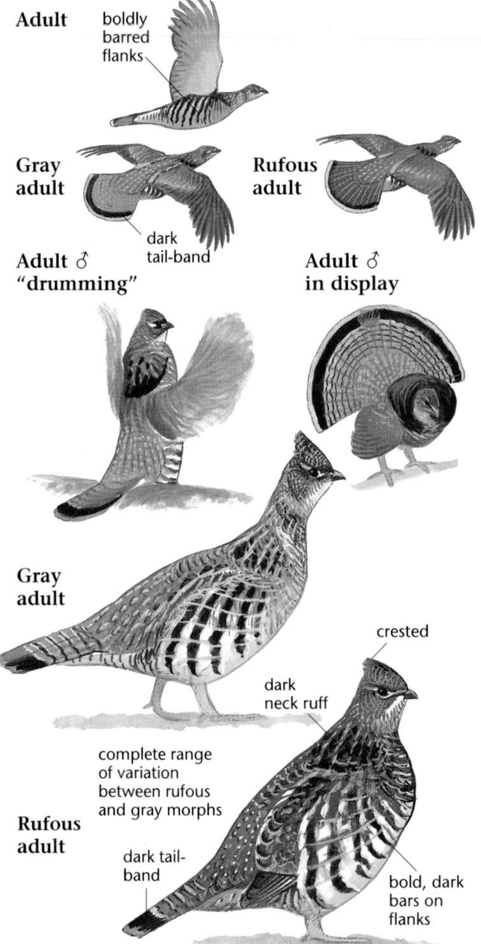

Adult
boldly barred flanks
Gray adult
Rufous adult
dark tail-band
Adult ♂ "drumming"
Adult ♂ in display
Gray adult
crested
dark neck ruff
complete range of variation between rufous and gray morphs
Rufous adult
dark tail-band
bold, dark bars on flanks

Voice: Male display is a series of accelerating, muffled thumps, produced by beating wings rapidly while standing, that sound like a distant motor starting (this low-pitched "drumming" is often felt rather than heard). Both sexes give clucking notes and higher squeal when alarmed.

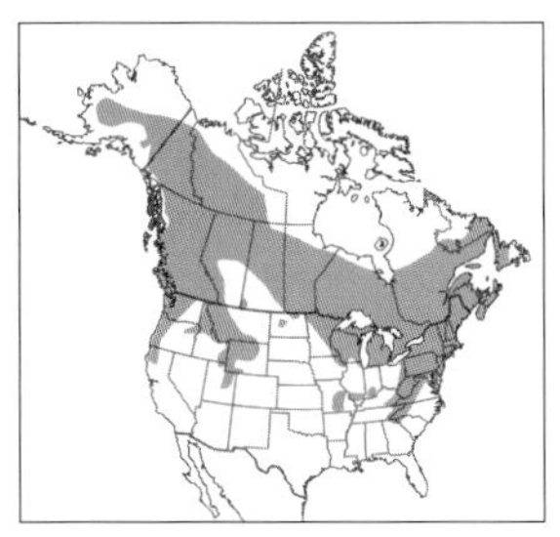

Sharp-tailed Grouse

Tympanuchus phasianellus

L 17" WS 25" WT 1.9 lb (880 g) ♂>♀

Similar in size and shape to prairie-chickens but with light-colored, sharply pointed tail.

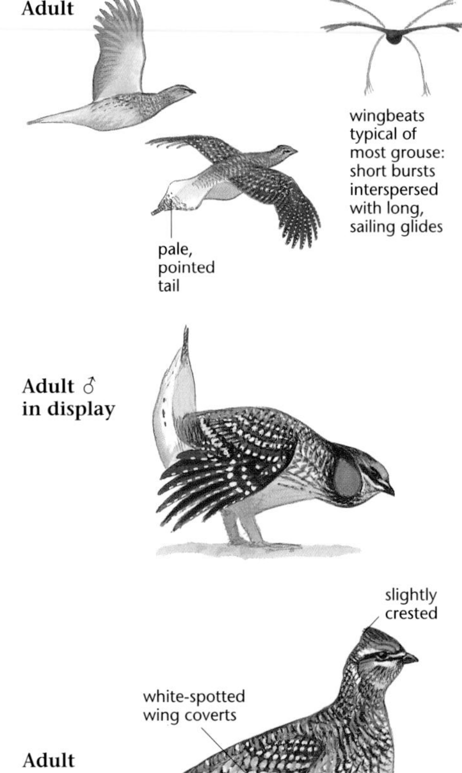

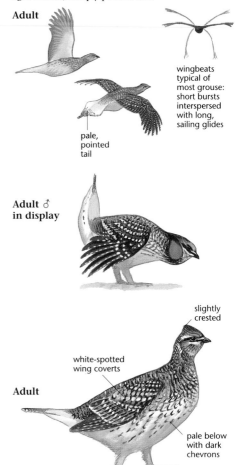

Adult
wingbeats typical of most grouse: short bursts interspersed with long, sailing glides
pale, pointed tail
Adult ♂ in display
slightly crested
white-spotted wing coverts
Adult
pale below with dark chevrons

Voice: Male display includes weird, unearthly hoots *yooowm, gyowdowdyom, gloooowm . . .* ; higher-pitched, more varied than prairie-chickens; hoots are interspersed with quacking *wek* and soft, dry chatter produced by stamping feet on ground. Both sexes give clucking notes.

Sharp-tailed Grouse occasionally hybridizes with Greater Prairie-Chicken where ranges overlap. Prairie-chickens, Sharp-tailed Grouse, and sage-grouse each gather at communal display grounds called leks.

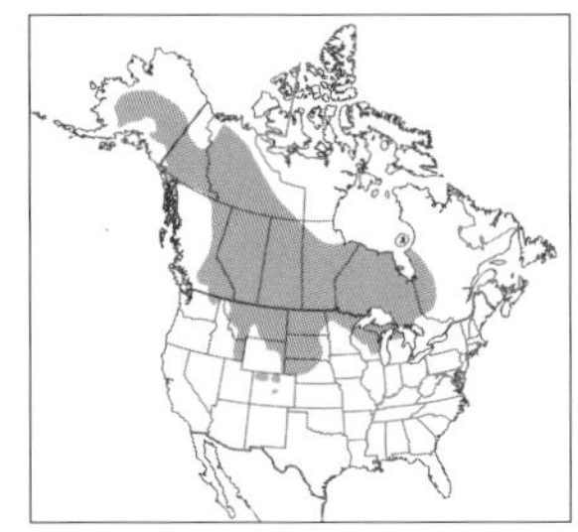

These species are very closely related, but their ranges and habitats do not overlap. Both are found in small groups in native prairie habitats: Lesser in arid prairie, Greater in wetter areas.

Lesser Prairie-Chicken

Tympanuchus pallidicinctus

L 16" WS 25" WT 1.6 lb (750 g) ♂>♀

Stocky, oval shape; small head; short, rounded tail. Note uniformly barred plumage, dark eyestripe.

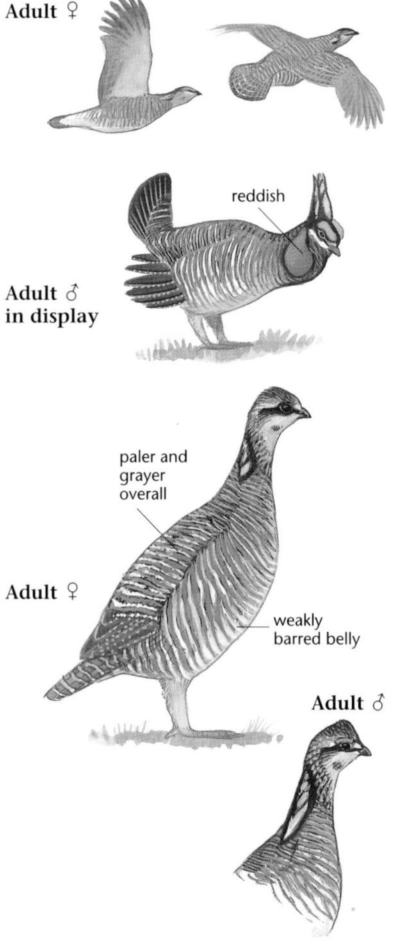
Adult ♀
reddish
Adult ♂
in display
paler and
grayer
overall
Adult ♀
weakly
barred belly
Adult ♂

Voice: All calls higher-pitched and shorter than Greater. Male display a bubbling, hooting *wamp wamp wodum wodum* and wild clucking in descending series; also a sharp *pike* in presence of female. Both sexes give clucking notes.

Greater Prairie-Chicken

Tympanuchus cupido

L 17" WS 28" WT 2 lb (900 g) ♂>♀

Virtually identical to Lesser in appearance but slightly darker and browner; most populations average larger.

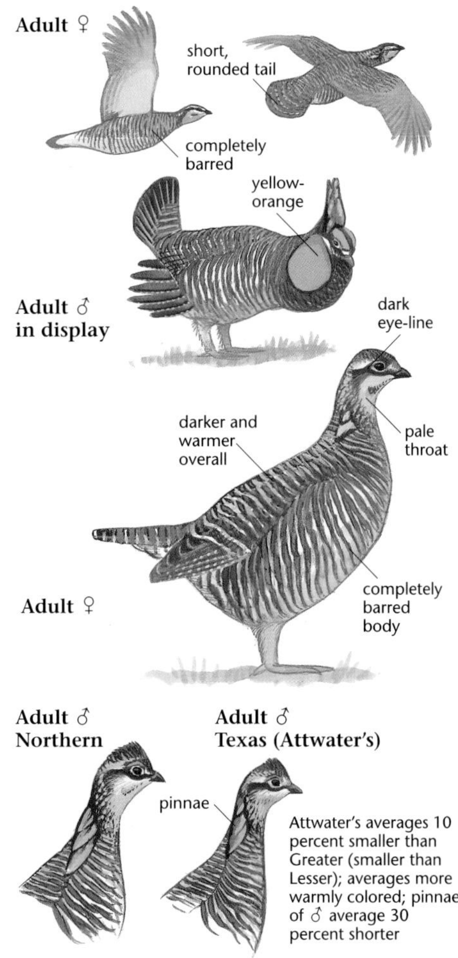
Adult ♀
short,
rounded tail
completely
barred
yellow-
orange
Adult ♂
in display
dark
eye-line
darker and
warmer
overall
pale
throat
completely
barred
body
Adult ♀
Adult ♂
Northern
Adult ♂
Texas (Attwater's)
pinnae
Attwater's averages 10 percent smaller than Greater (smaller than Lesser); averages more warmly colored; pinnae of ♂ average 30 percent shorter

Voice: Male display includes long, low, hooting moan *oooa-hoooooom* about two seconds long (like air blown across the top of a bottle); also high, wild clucking sounds, *hoaa* notes, foot stamping, and a *pwoik* in presence of female. Both sexes give clucking notes.

Display pattern differs between these species. During display male Greater fans tail several times at beginning and end; Lesser fans tail only at beginning of display sequence.

These two similar species are heavy, with long, spiky, pointed tails. Both are found almost exclusively in dry sagebrush plains, usually in small groups. Formerly considered a single species: Sage Grouse.

Gunnison Sage-Grouse

Centrocercus minimus

♂ L 22" WS 30" WT 4.6 lb (2,100 g)
♀ L 18" WS 26" WT 2.4 lb (1,100 g)

Similar to Greater but smaller, with different display and paler tail; no range overlap.

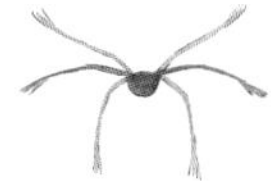

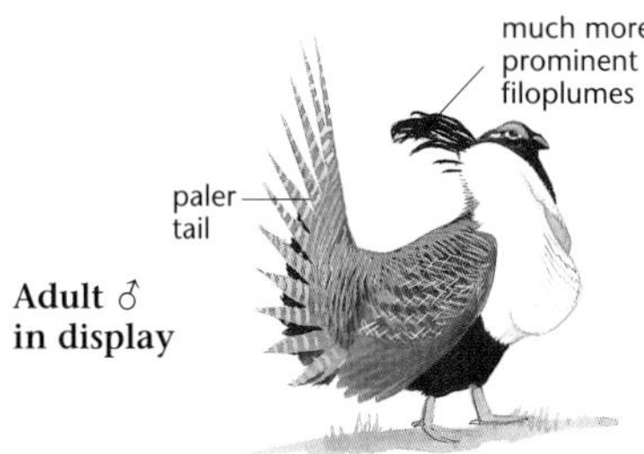
much more prominent filoplumes
paler tail
Adult ♂ in display

Greater Sage-Grouse

Centrocercus urophasianus

♂ L 28" WS 38" WT 6.3 lb (2,900 g)
♀ L 22" WS 33" WT 3.3 lb (1,500 g)

Large, heavy; small-headed and long-tailed. Note black belly and clean white underwing coverts.

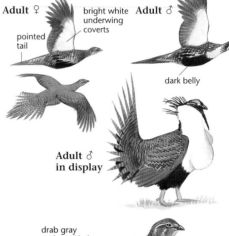

Adult ♀
bright white underwing coverts
pointed tail
Adult ♂
dark belly
Adult ♂ in display

Adult ♀
tail paler than uppertail coverts; light bars as broad as dark bars
Adult ♂
drab gray and speckled overall
Adult ♀
black belly
pointed tail
black throat
Adult ♂
white breast

Voice: Display of Greater male includes two swishing sounds as wings brush against body, then two weird hooting, popping sounds *oo-WIdoo-WIdoo-wup*. Display of Gunnison male very different, with nine lower-pitched hooting or popping sounds; three faint wing-swish sounds in middle of display (very little wing movement); the whole display low-pitched and monotonic. Gunnison also constantly raises thicker filoplumes above head, and its display often ends with a tail-shaking motion (with the tail still raised) absent in Greater. All give gutteral clucking and cackling notes.

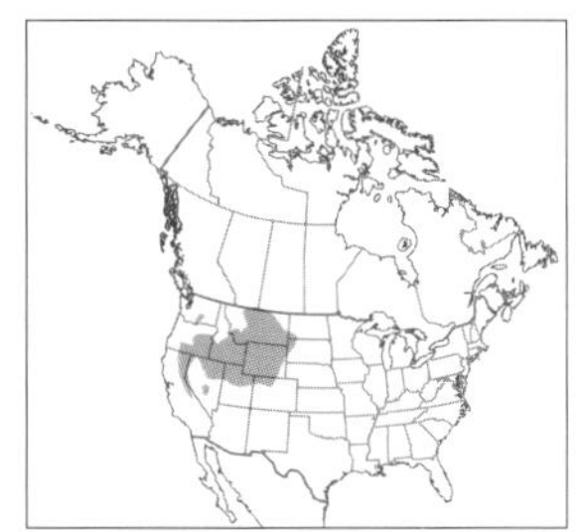

Wild Turkey

One of our largest birds, Wild Turkey is found in flocks in open woods with fields or clearings, usually in oak or beech woods. It is often seen strolling across open ground in flocks of up to 60.

Wild Turkey

Meleagris gallopavo

♂ L 46" WS 64" WT 16.2 lb (7,400 g)

♀ L 37" WS 50" WT 9.2 lb (4,200 g)

Very large and dark, with heavy, dark body incongruously joined to thin neck, small head, and long legs.

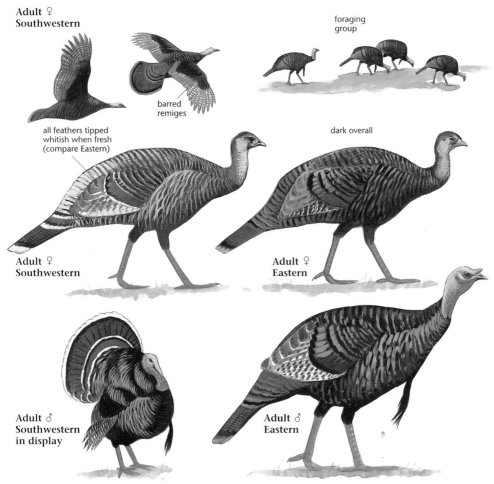

Adult ♀ Southwestern

foraging group

barred remiges

all feathers tipped whitish when fresh (compare Eastern)

dark overall

Adult ♀ Southwestern

Adult ♀ Eastern

Adult ♂ Southwestern in display

Adult ♂ Eastern

Voice: Male in display gives familiar descending gobble. Female gives loud, sharp *tuk* and slightly longer, whining *yike, yike* . . . repeated in slow series. Both sexes give a variety of other soft clucks and rolling calls.

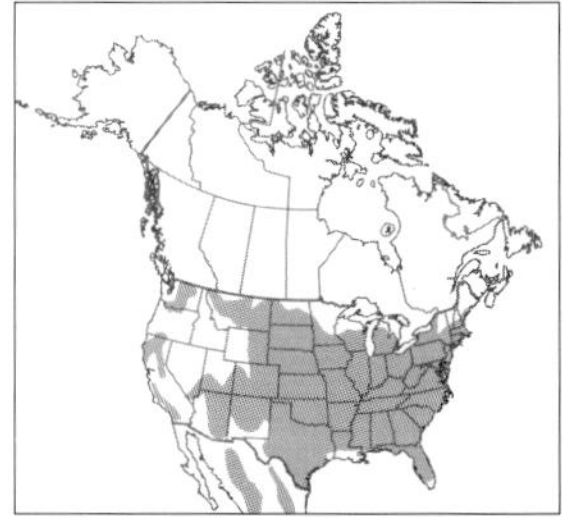

Southwestern populations have tail and uppertail coverts tipped pale buffy or whitish, creating a strikingly different appearance than the darker, rufous-tipped Eastern birds, but the change is broadly clinal. Domestic turkeys, often escaped or released, average heavier than Wild Turkey and have white-tipped tail feathers similar to Southwestern birds. Furthermore, birds of mixed ancestry have been widely introduced, and the species is now found farther north and much farther west than ever before.

GRUIFORMES

Families: Aramidae, Gruidae, Rallidae

12 species in 9 genera; all in family Rallidae, except cranes in Gruidae and Limpkin in Aramidae. All inhabit marshy wetlands, where they feed on plants and small animals, although the foraging habits of genera differ greatly. Cranes are conspicuous, foraging in flocks and flying in gooselike formations; compare herons and geese. Limpkin is solitary and secretive; compare herons. Rails are very secretive, while Purple Gallinule, American Coot, and Common Moorhen are more ducklike; compare ducks and shorebirds. Adults are shown.

Genus *Grus*

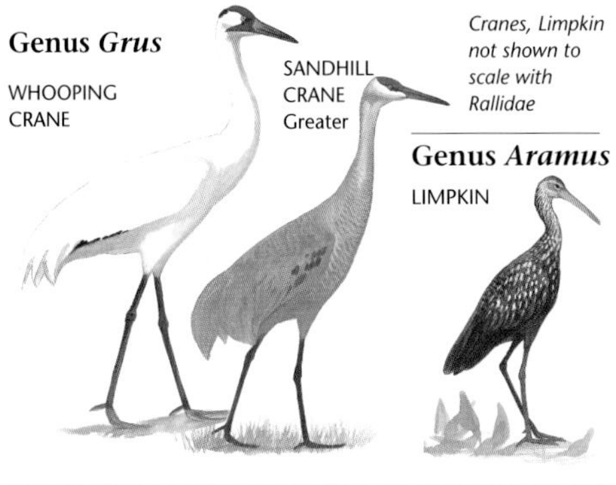
WHOOPING CRANE
SANDHILL CRANE Greater
Cranes, Limpkin not shown to scale with Rallidae
Genus Aramus
LIMPKIN

Genus *Rallus*

CLAPPER RAIL California
VIRGINIA RAIL
KING RAIL

Genus *Coturnicops*

YELLOW RAIL

Genus *Laterallus*

BLACK RAIL

Genus *Gallinula*

COMMON MOORHEN

Genus *Porzana*

SORA

Genus *Fulica*

AMERICAN COOT

Genus *Porphyrula*

PURPLE GALLINULE

Purple Gallinule

Porphyrula martinica

L 13" WS 22" WT 8 oz (235 g) ♂>♀

Relatively long-winged and especially long-legged; usually walks on floating vegetation or climbs through brush rather than swimming.

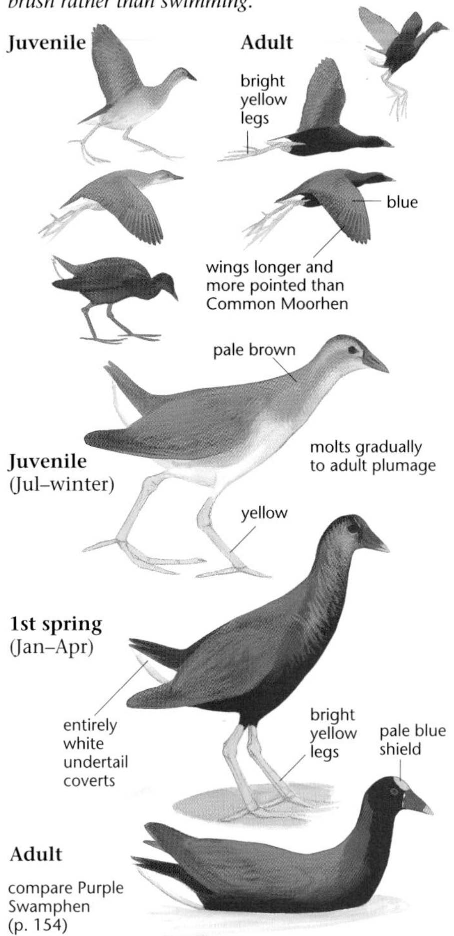
Juvenile
Adult
bright yellow legs
blue
wings longer and more pointed than Common Moorhen
pale brown
Juvenile (Jul–winter)
molts gradually to adult plumage
yellow
1st spring (Jan–Apr)
entirely white undertail coverts
bright yellow legs
pale blue shield
Adult
compare Purple Swamphen (p. 154)

Voice: Varied, but never whining notes. Long rhythmic series distinctive: rather slow, nasal, honking *pep pep pep pePAA pePAA* . . . or *to to to terp to terp to to terp*. . . . Also a deep grunting series similar to King Rail and a variety of sharp, single notes: low *pep;* short, high *kit;* and high, sharp *kidk*.

Common Moorhen and American Coot

These two superficially ducklike species have conical bills. Generally solitary, Common Moorhen walks or swims, gleaning small animals from plants. The gregarious American Coot dives for aquatic plants.

Common Moorhen

Gallinula chloropus

L 14" WS 21" WT 11 oz (315 g) ♂>♀

Smaller and more slender than American Coot; actions more delicate.

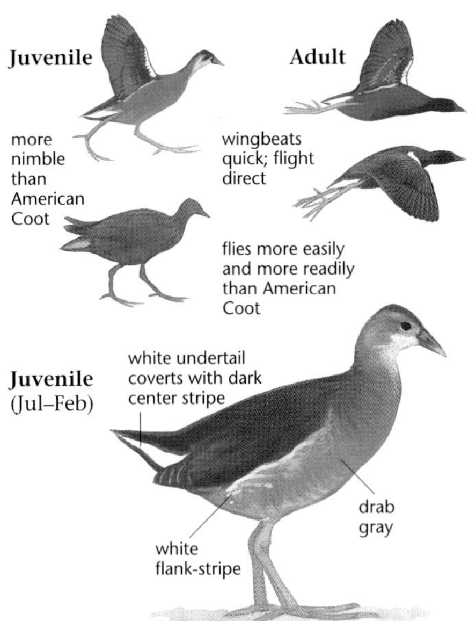
Juvenile
Adult
more nimble than American Coot
wingbeats quick; flight direct
flies more easily and more readily than American Coot
Juvenile (Jul–Feb)
white undertail coverts with dark center stripe
drab gray
white flank-stripe

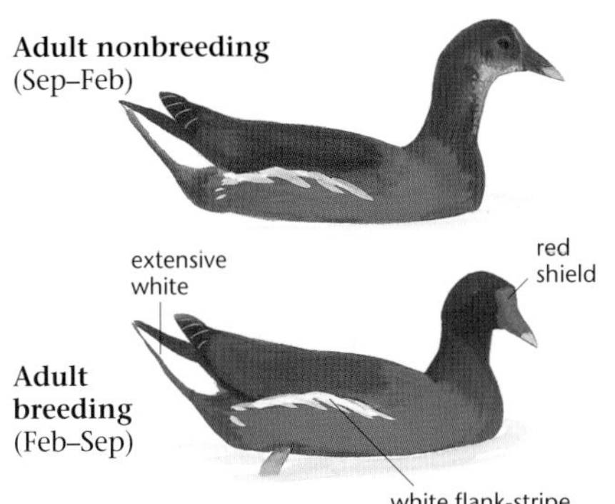
Adult nonbreeding (Sep–Feb)
extensive white
red shield
Adult breeding (Feb–Sep)
white flank-stripe

Voice: Varied; a slowing series of clucks ending with distinctive long, whining notes *pep pep pep pehr pehr peehr peeehr pehr*. Quality varies from low and nasal to higher and creaking. Other whining, creaking notes; also varied short clucks from low, heavy *kulp* to high, sharp *keek*.

American Coot

Fulica americana

L 15.5" WS 24" WT 1.4 lb (650 g) ♂>♀

Stocky, with relatively thick neck and stout bill. Floats like a cork.

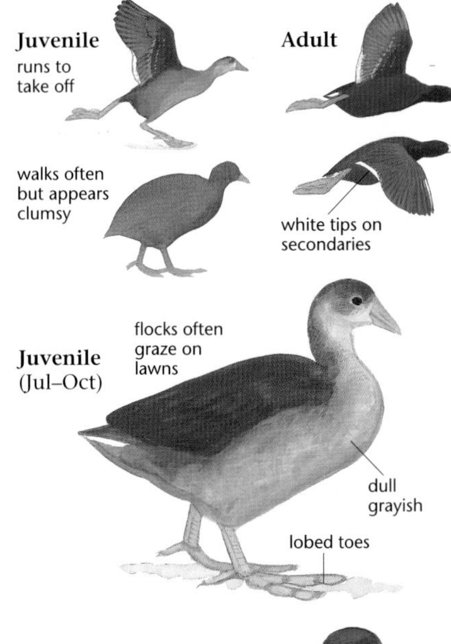
Juvenile
runs to take off
Adult
walks often but appears clumsy
white tips on secondaries
Juvenile (Jul–Oct)
flocks often graze on lawns
dull grayish
lobed toes

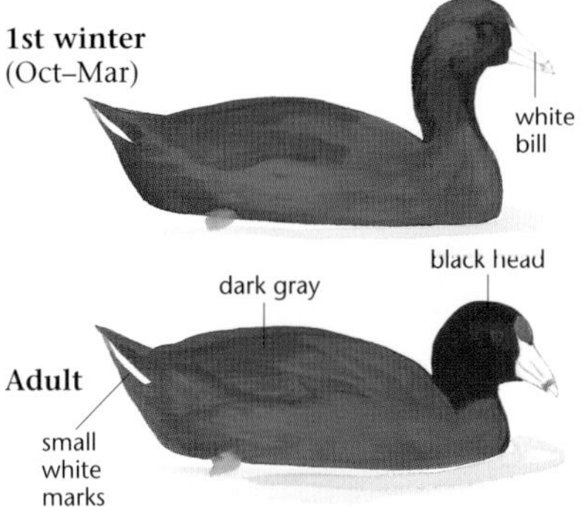
1st winter (Oct–Mar)
white bill
black head
dark gray
Adult
small white marks

Voice: A variety of short, clucking notes: most with hollow, trumpeting quality and coarse, rattling undertone; usually lower than Common Moorhen. Most commonly a short single note *krrp* or *prik*, often strung together in long series *priKI priKI*. . . . Voice of female low and nasal, male high and clear.

American Coot variant adult ♂

Swollen white frontal shield is shown by occasional males throughout range (more often in the south); similar to Caribbean Coot *(F. caribaea)*, which is unrecorded in North America.

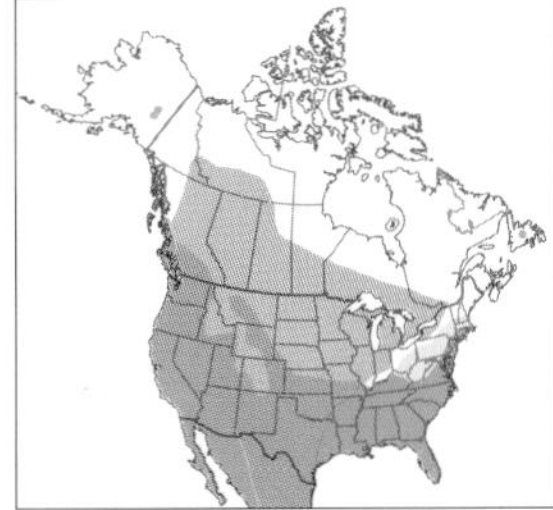

Large Rails

This species and King Rail are very closely related and sometimes considered conspecific. Both are large, long-billed, long-necked rails found in grassy marshes; they differ in plumage and voice.

Clapper Rail

Rallus longirostris

L 14.5" WS 19" WT 10 oz (290 g) ♂>♀

Large, long-billed, and long-necked; much larger and less richly colored than Virginia Rail. Eastern birds slightly smaller and drabber than King Rail.

CALIFORNIA

Adult

Juvenile (Jul–Sep)

Adult

heavy-billed

orange cheeks

GULF COAST

Adult

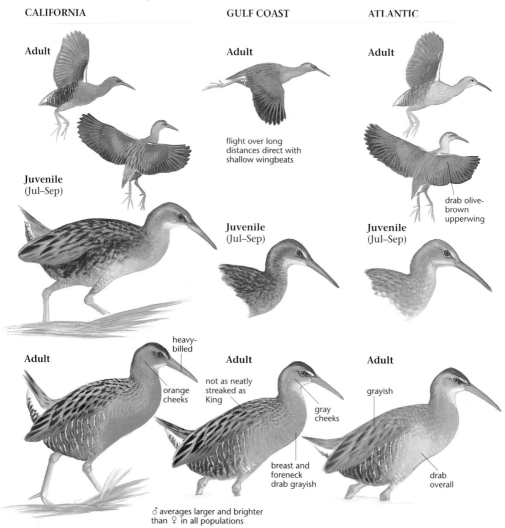

flight over long distances direct with shallow wingbeats

Juvenile (Jul–Sep)

Adult

not as neatly streaked as King

gray cheeks

breast and foreneck drab grayish

ATLANTIC

Adult

drab olive-brown upperwing

Juvenile (Jul–Sep)

Adult

grayish

drab overall

♂ averages larger and brighter than ♀ in all populations

Voice: Atlantic and Gulf Coast birds give clappering series (4–5 notes/sec); grunting series (4–7 notes/sec). California gives clappering series (5–6 notes/sec); grunting call undescribed, may be rare. See King Rail.

Subspecies differ in plumage color and subtly in size and proportions. California birds, sometimes considered a subspecies of King Rail, are relatively large and brightly colored like King, with orange cheeks unlike other Clappers. Atlantic coast birds are smaller and much drabber, without blackish or rufous markings. Gulf Coast birds are similar to Atlantic but more richly colored. King Rail hybridizes with Clapper Rail on Atlantic coast; these hybrids appear very similar to Gulf Coast Clapper Rails. King presumably also hybridizes with Clapper Rail along Gulf Coast, but such hybrids would be almost impossible to detect given the similarity of male Clapper and female King.

This species is found in freshwater marshes with grassy or reedy vegetation. It is usually segregated from Clapper Rail by salinity, overlapping only narrowly in brackish marshes.

King Rail

Rallus elegans

L 15" WS 20" WT 13 oz (360 g) ♂>♀

Averages slightly larger than eastern Clapper Rails, but identification must be based on plumage details, especially contrast of streaking on upperparts.

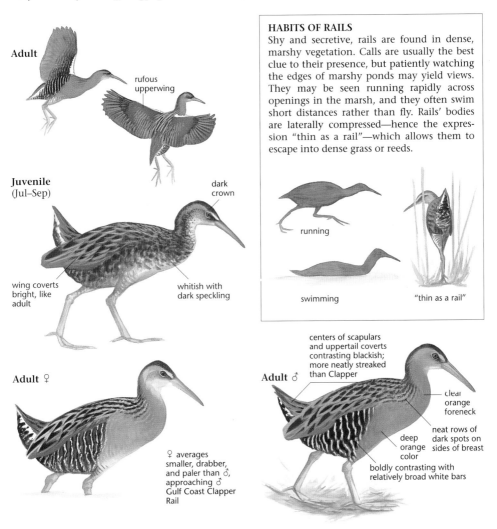

Adult

rufous upperwing

Juvenile (Jul–Sep)

dark crown

wing coverts bright, like adult

whitish with dark speckling

HABITS OF RAILS

Shy and secretive, rails are found in dense, marshy vegetation. Calls are usually the best clue to their presence, but patiently watching the edges of marshy ponds may yield views. They may be seen running rapidly across openings in the marsh, and they often swim short distances rather than fly. Rails' bodies are laterally compressed—hence the expression "thin as a rail"—which allows them to escape into dense grass or reeds.

running

swimming

"thin as a rail"

Adult ♀

♀ averages smaller, drabber, and paler than ♂, approaching ♂ Gulf Coast Clapper Rail

Adult ♂

centers of scapulars and uppertail coverts contrasting blackish; more neatly streaked than Clapper

clear orange foreneck

neat rows of dark spots on sides of breast

deep orange color

boldly contrasting with relatively broad white bars

Voice: Clappering series and grunting series (usually 2 notes/sec). All calls average deeper and more resonant than Clapper, but quality overlaps extensively; slower tempo is more reliable for identification.

King and Clapper Rail share basic vocal repertoire. Clappering call a series of unmusical *kek* notes, slower at beginning and end; the tempo of the fastest portion is useful for species identification. Grunting series is of steady tempo but falling pitch. Individuals may give faster or slower calls depending on mood, but such departures are usually brief. Long, consistent bouts of typical calls can be reliably identified. Males of both species give single hard *ket* notes repeated monotonously (about 2 notes/sec). Females of both species give dry, clattering *ket ket karrrrr*. Other calls include rapid, high *kek* notes and a raucous squawk like a startled chicken.

Small Rails

These two species are found in marsh habitats (usually freshwater). Both species, especially Sora, can be quite bold, sometimes walking or feeding in full view.

Virginia Rail

Rallus limicola

L 9.5" WS 13" WT 3 oz (85 g) ♂>♀

Rounded wings and long bill. Like a miniature King Rail but easily distinguished by size.

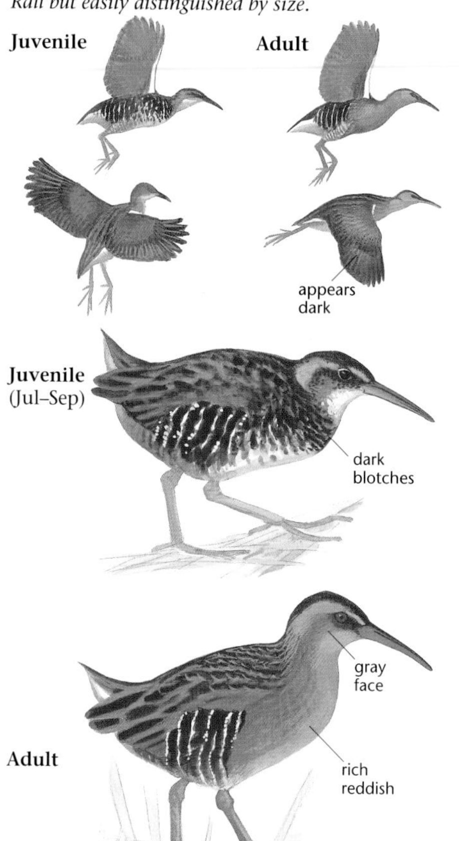

Juvenile
Adult
appears dark
Juvenile (Jul–Sep)
dark blotches
gray face
Adult
rich reddish

Voice: Wheezy, piglike grunting series *wep wep wep wepwepwepwepwepwepppprrr* descending and usually accelerating; higher-pitched than Clapper Rail. Female gives sharp, metallic notes followed by rich churring *chi chi chi chi treerrr.* Male gives a hard, mechanical *gik gik gik gidik gidik gidik gidik;* also squealing or clattering, hard *skew, kweek* or *kikik ik-ik* in dispute or in alarm; most calls harsher or more nasal than Sora.

Sora

Porzana carolina

L 8.75" WS 14" WT 2.6 oz (75 g) ♂>♀

Relatively long wings and tail, short bill.

Juvenile
Adult
long wings
pale trailing edge
Juvenile (Jul–Nov)
dull buffy
white-speckled
Adult nonbreeding (Aug–Feb)
Adult breeding (Mar–Aug)

Voice: A long, high, squealing whinny, descending and slowing at end *ko-WEEeee-e-e-e-e-e, ee, ee* given by both sexes; high, clear, sharp, whistled *kooEE.* In alarm a surprisingly loud, sharp *keek* and a variety of other notes; some fairly mellow, some with plaintive quality *(keeeoo).* Also a sharp, staccato *kiu* like Virginia Rail, but other calls usually clearer, more whistled.

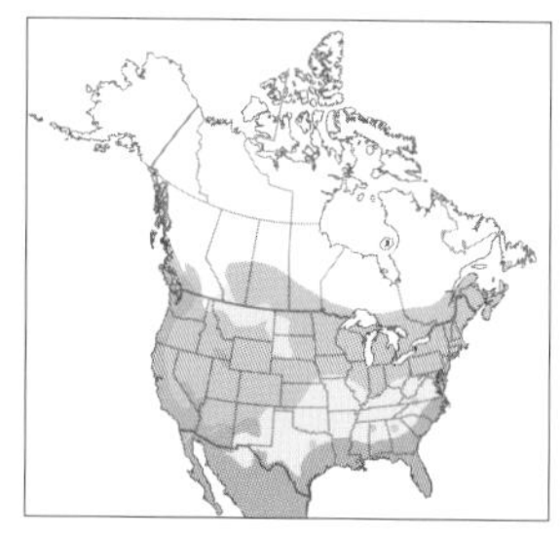

PURPLE SWAMPHEN

Porphyrio porphyrio

L 16" WS 35"

WT 1.5 lb (700 g)

Introduced locally in Florida.

Adult

Juvenile

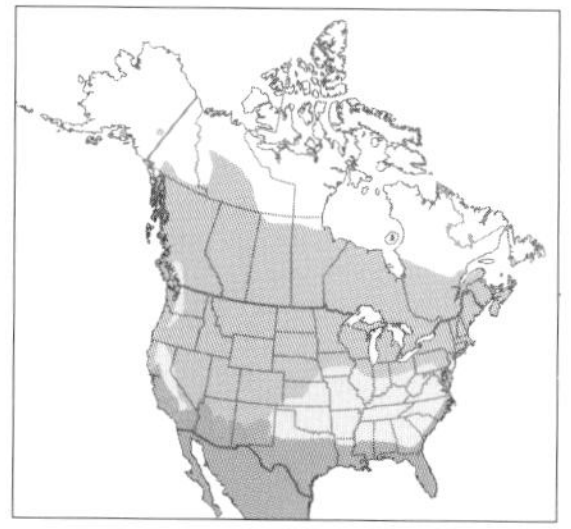

SMALL RAILS (CONTINUED)
These two tiny, extremely secretive species are as hard to see as mice; very difficult to flush, they never willingly give good views of themselves. They are found in damp areas with dense grass.

Yellow Rail

Coturnicops noveboracensis

L 7.25" WS 11" WT 1.8 oz (50 g)

Small, short-tailed, and short-billed; buffy back stripes and white secondaries distinctive.

Adult

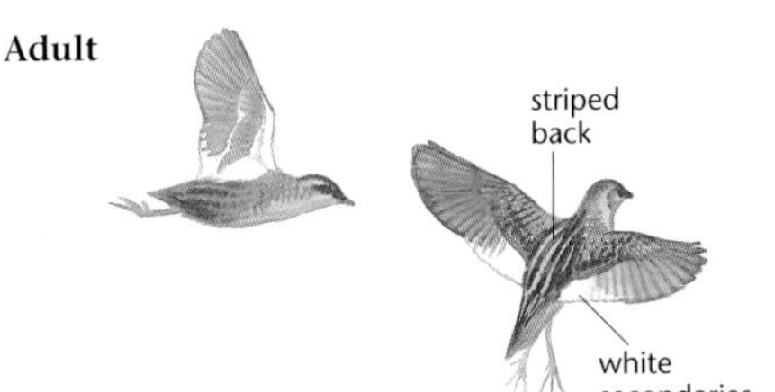
striped back
white secondaries

Juvenile (Aug–Feb)

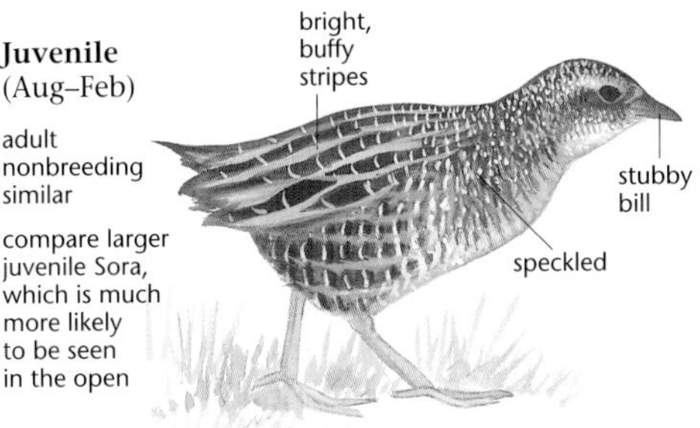
adult nonbreeding similar
compare larger juvenile Sora, which is much more likely to be seen in the open
bright, buffy stripes
stubby bill
speckled

Adult breeding (Mar–Aug)

yellow-buff

Voice: Territorial song of male (given at night) a mechanical clicking sound (easily imitated by tapping two pebbles together) usually in distinctive rhythm *tic-tic tictictic, tic-tic tictictic . . .* ; clicking sound nearly duplicated by Cricket Frog but rhythm unique to Yellow Rail. Other calls include descending cackle of about ten notes, with three to four notes that sound like distant knocking on door; quiet croaking; also soft wheezing or clucking notes.

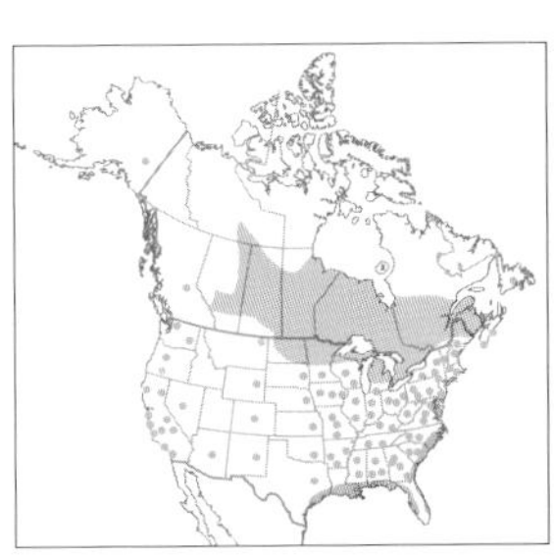

Black Rail

Laterallus jamaicensis

L 6" WS 9" WT 1.1 oz (30 g)

Tiny and dark; distinctive.

Adult

all-dark

Juvenile (Aug–Feb)

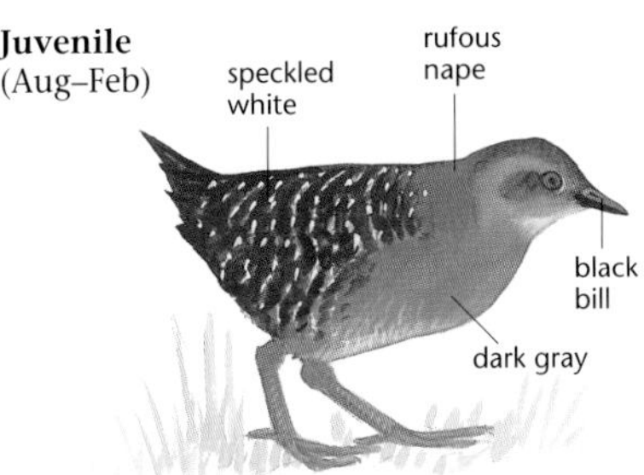
speckled white
rufous nape
black bill
dark gray

Adult ♂

Voice: Territorial call of male (given mainly at night) a rich, nasal *keekeedrrr* or *deedeedunk;* typically two high notes followed immediately by one lower solid note, but number of notes variable; when agitated a growling *krr-krr-krr.* Female (rarely) gives a quick, low, cooing *croocroocroo* of two or three notes similar to Least Bittern. Adult also gives soft, nasal barking *churt* or scolding notes *ink-ink-ink-ink.*

Virginia Rail
Sora

Downy young of all rails are black and similar in size to adult Black Rail.

Limpkin and Whooping Crane

The inconspicuous Limpkin is found in wooded and brushy swamps, where it feeds on shellfish. Whooping Crane is found in marshy habitats, traveling in family groups year-round.

Limpkin

Aramus guarauna

L 26" WS 40" WT 2.4 lb (1,100 g)

Tall with relatively long and heavy bill; broad-winged. Brown plumage with white streaks unique.

Adult
wingbeats floppy with quick, flicking upstroke
dark brown with white spots
Juvenile (1st year)
Adult
slow, strolling gait

Voice: Loud, anguished, wild-sounding scream/wail, clear with some rattling overtones, higher-pitched than cranes; *kwEEEeeer* or *klAAAar* with quieter wooden clicking *t-t-t-t-t-tklAAAaar.* Unmistakable.

Whooping Crane

Grus americana

L 52" WS 87" WT 15 lb (6,850 g)

Our tallest bird; distinctly larger than Sandhill. Always essentially white plumage with black primaries.

Juvenile
Adult
red crown
red malar
Juvenile (1st year)
brown fades away during 1st winter

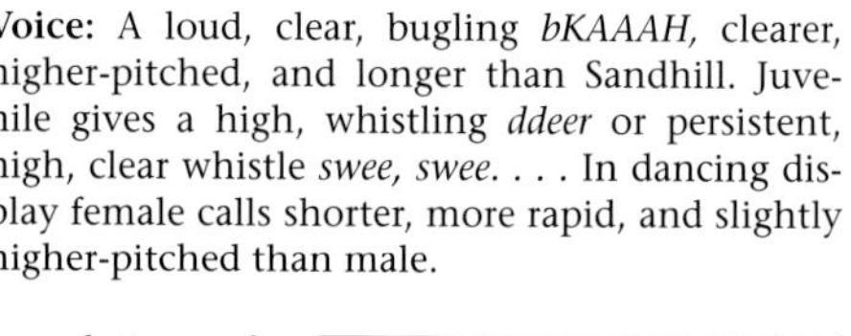

all-white
Adult

Voice: A loud, clear, bugling *bKAAAH,* clearer, higher-pitched, and longer than Sandhill. Juvenile gives a high, whistling *ddeer* or persistent, high, clear whistle *swee, swee. . . .* In dancing display female calls shorter, more rapid, and slightly higher-pitched than male.

The total world's population of Whooping Crane numbers about 200 individuals, most of which migrate between Canada and Texas. Experimental introduced populations in Idaho, New Mexico, and Florida account for only a few individuals.

Gregarious, noisy, and conspicuous, Sandhill Crane is found in open fields or meadows, often in large flocks. Cranes differ from herons in many characteristics of posture and behavior.

Sandhill Crane

Grus canadensis

GREATER L 46" WS 77" WT 10.6 lb (4,850 g) ♂>♀

LESSER L 41" WS 73" WT 7.3 lb (3,350 g) ♂>♀

Always smaller than Whooping Crane but similar in proportions; entirely gray plumage distinctive.

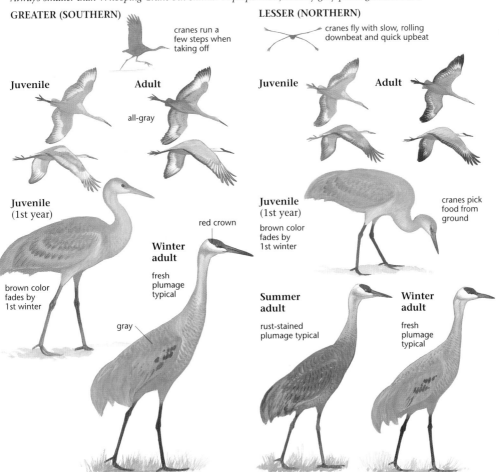

GREATER (SOUTHERN)

cranes run a few steps when taking off

Juvenile

Adult

all-gray

Juvenile (1st year)

brown color fades by 1st winter

red crown

Winter adult

fresh plumage typical

gray

LESSER (NORTHERN)

cranes fly with slow, rolling downbeat and quick upbeat

Juvenile

Adult

Juvenile (1st year)

brown color fades by 1st winter

cranes pick food from ground

Summer adult

rust-stained plumage typical

Winter adult

fresh plumage typical

Voice: A loud, resonant, wooden rattle *hkkkkkk* or *hkarrrr,* variable; a rolling bugle, typically a long, slightly descending roll, but some variation. Juvenile until at least Apr (age ten months) gives high, squeaky or trilled *tweer.* Dancing display of adults accompanied by complex duet, female giving more rapid, higher-pitched calls than male. Greater adult call deeper, slower, and more resonant than Lesser; Greater juvenile gives lower and more husky *chwerrr.*

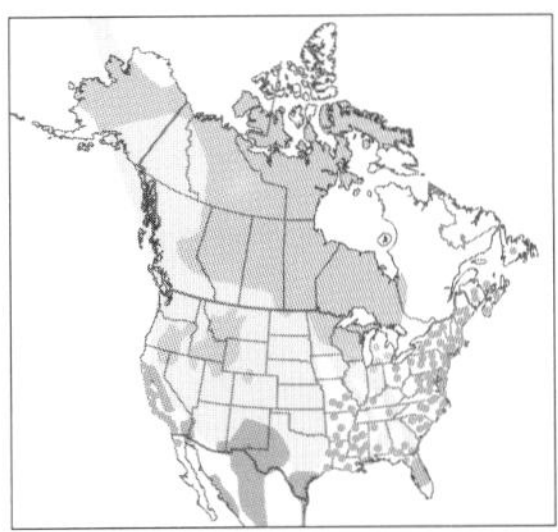

Lesser breeds in far north; it is small, short-billed, and short-legged, with relatively long wings. Greater breeds from central Canada southward; it is larger and up to 50 percent longer-billed than Lesser, with little overlap, and is relatively short-winged. Greater also has paler primaries with whitish shafts. Extremes are easily identified, but much of central Canada is occupied by an intermediate population. Most of the intermediate birds winter midcontinent, and in those areas many individuals are difficult to assign to subspecies.

Shorebirds

Families: Charadriidae, Haematopodidae, Jacanidae, Recurvirostridae, Scolopacidae

62 species in 23 genera; all in family Scolopacidae, except plovers in Charadriidae, oystercatchers in Haematopodidae, American Avocet and Black-necked Stilt in Recurvirostridae, and rare Northern Jacana in Jacanidae. All are small to medium-size with relatively thin bills and long legs; they frequent open shoreline habitats, where they forage on small aquatic insects, worms, and other animals by picking or probing. Habitat choice and foraging motions often provide identification clues. Bill shape and body proportions are important for identification. Nonbreeding adults are shown.

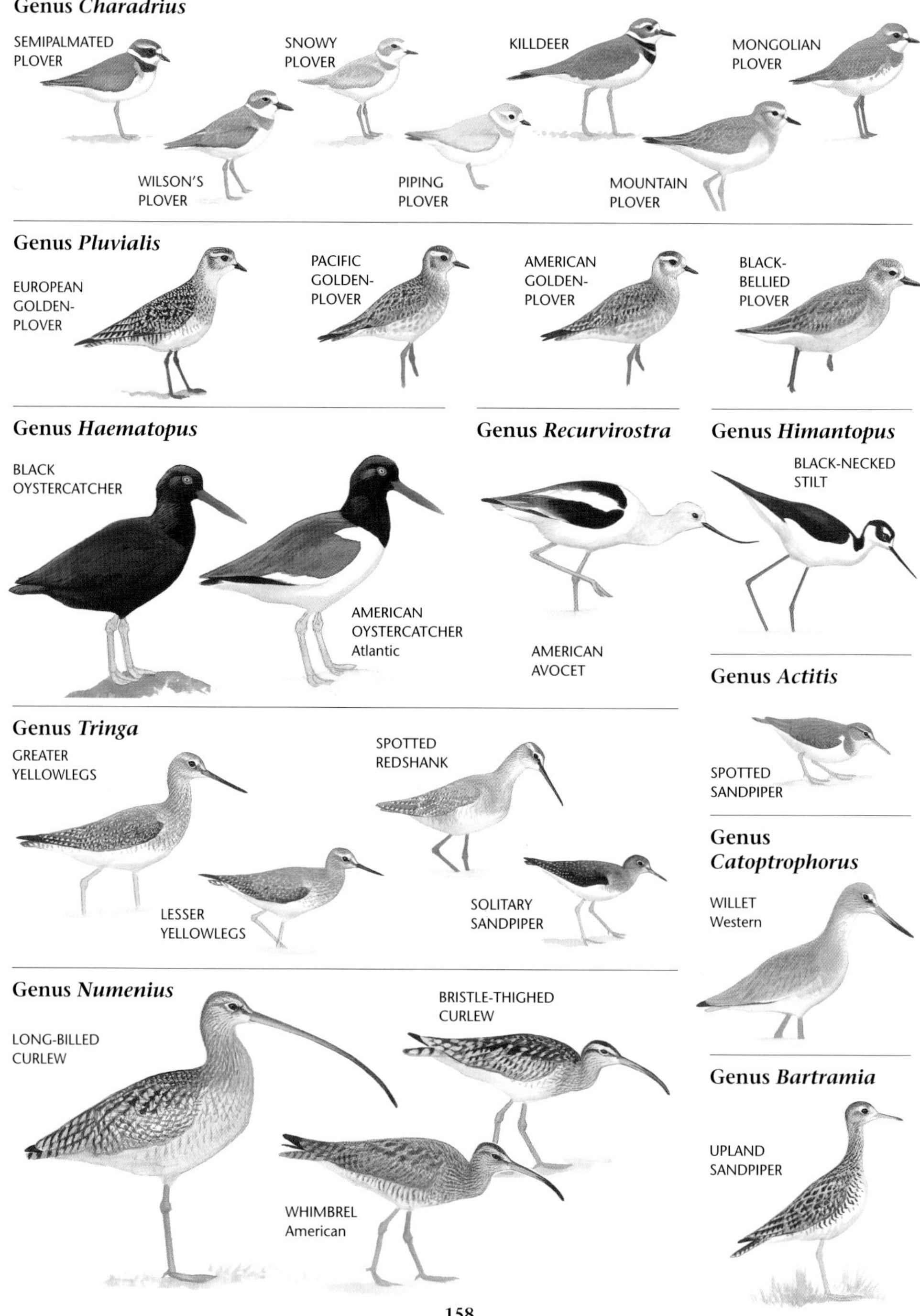

Genus *Charadrius*
SEMIPALMATED PLOVER
SNOWY PLOVER
KILLDEER
MONGOLIAN PLOVER
WILSON'S PLOVER
PIPING PLOVER
MOUNTAIN PLOVER
Genus *Pluvialis*
EUROPEAN GOLDEN-PLOVER
PACIFIC GOLDEN-PLOVER
AMERICAN GOLDEN-PLOVER
BLACK-BELLIED PLOVER
Genus *Haematopus*
BLACK OYSTERCATCHER
AMERICAN OYSTERCATCHER
Atlantic
Genus *Recurvirostra*
AMERICAN AVOCET
Genus *Himantopus*
BLACK-NECKED STILT
Genus *Actitis*
SPOTTED SANDPIPER
Genus *Tringa*
GREATER YELLOWLEGS
SPOTTED REDSHANK
LESSER YELLOWLEGS
SOLITARY SANDPIPER
Genus *Catoptrophorus*
WILLET
Western
Genus *Numenius*
LONG-BILLED CURLEW
BRISTLE-THIGHED CURLEW
WHIMBREL
American
Genus *Bartramia*
UPLAND SANDPIPER

Genus *Limosa*

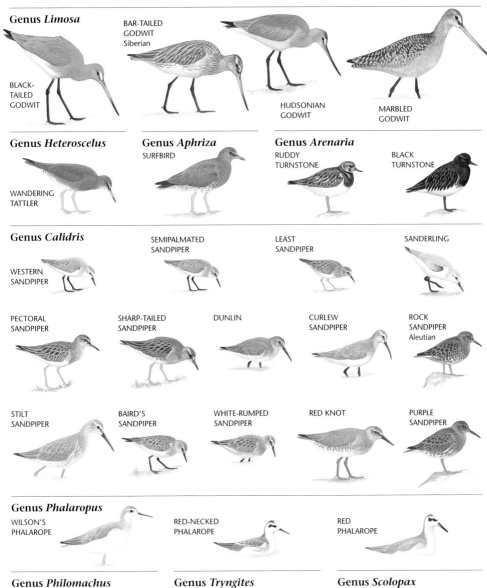

BLACK-TAILED GODWIT

BAR-TAILED GODWIT Siberian

HUDSONIAN GODWIT

MARBLED GODWIT

Genus *Heteroscelus*

WANDERING TATTLER

Genus *Aphriza*

SURFBIRD

Genus *Arenaria*

RUDDY TURNSTONE

BLACK TURNSTONE

Genus *Calidris*

WESTERN SANDPIPER

SEMIPALMATED SANDPIPER

LEAST SANDPIPER

SANDERLING

PECTORAL SANDPIPER

SHARP-TAILED SANDPIPER

DUNLIN

CURLEW SANDPIPER

ROCK SANDPIPER Aleutian

STILT SANDPIPER

BAIRD'S SANDPIPER

WHITE-RUMPED SANDPIPER

RED KNOT

PURPLE SANDPIPER

Genus *Phalaropus*

WILSON'S PHALAROPE

RED-NECKED PHALAROPE

RED PHALAROPE

Genus *Philomachus*

RUFF

Genus *Tryngites*

BUFF-BREASTED SANDPIPER

Genus *Scolopax*

AMERICAN WOODCOCK

Genus *Limnodromus*

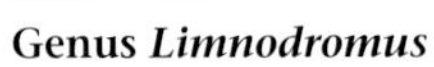

SHORT-BILLED DOWITCHER

LONG-BILLED DOWITCHER

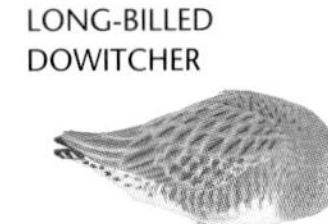

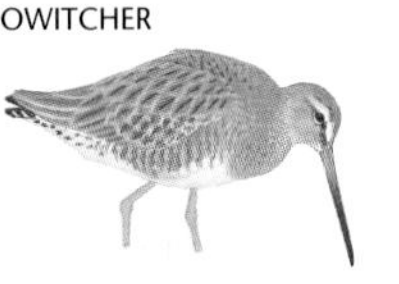

Genus *Gallinago*

COMMON SNIPE American

Northern Jacana, although superficially gallinule-like, is more closely related to shorebirds. It is found on ponds with emergent vegetation; Northern Lapwing is found on open fields and mudflats.

Northern Jacana

Jacana spinosa

L 9.5" WS 20" WT 3.3 oz (95 g) ♀>♂

Slender and dainty; uses its incredibly long toes to walk across floating vegetation.

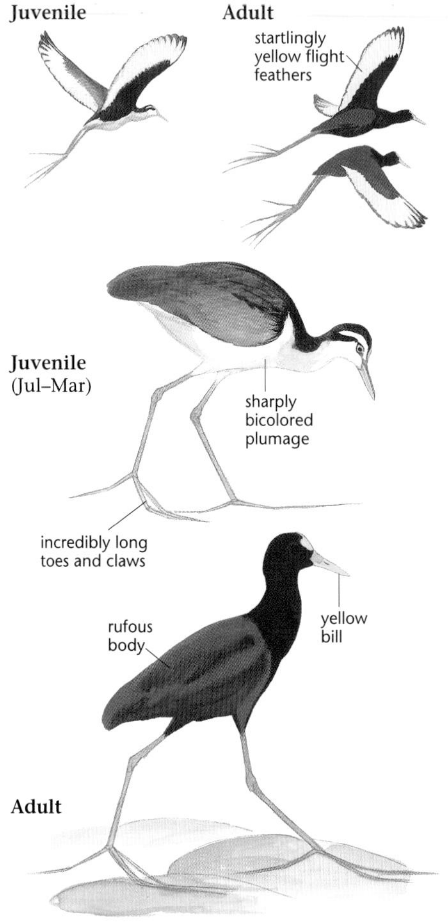
Juvenile
Adult
startlingly yellow flight feathers
Juvenile (Jul–Mar)
sharply bicolored plumage
incredibly long toes and claws
rufous body
yellow bill
Adult

Voice: High, harsh squawking (usually in flight) *scraa scraa scraa . . . ;* usually with sharp *keek* notes interspersed.

Northern Lapwing

Vanellus vanellus

L 12.5" WS 33" WT 7 oz (210 g)

A large, stocky plover with strikingly broad, rounded wings and pigeonlike flight. Black breast and pale head distinctive.

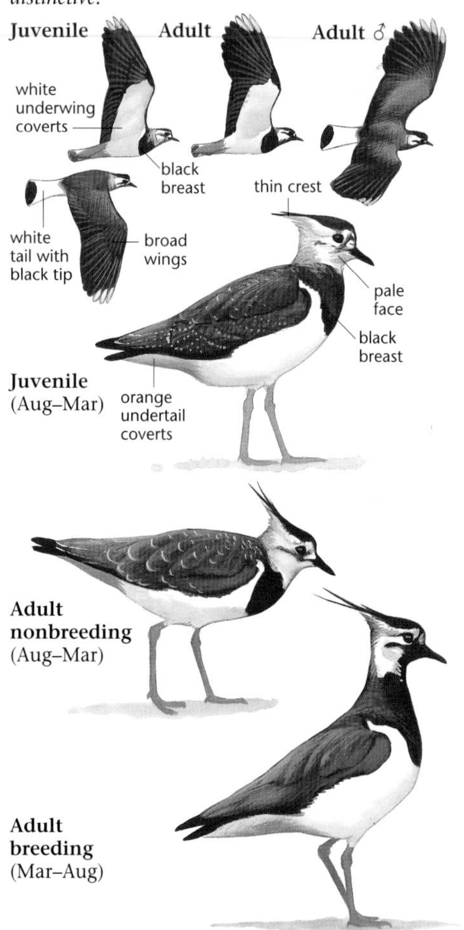
Juvenile
Adult
Adult ♂
white underwing coverts
black breast
thin crest
white tail with black tip
broad wings
pale face
black breast
Juvenile (Aug–Mar)
orange undertail coverts
Adult nonbreeding (Aug–Mar)
Adult breeding (Mar–Aug)

Voice: High, thin whistles with quality of kitten mewing *chee* or *peewi,* and short, sharp *peet.* Song given in roller-coaster flight *airr willucho weep weep weep ee yo weep.*

Common Ringed Plover is virtually identical to Semipalmated Plover in appearance and habits. It is often impossible to distinguish in the field; only the voice is diagnostic.

Common Ringed Plover

Charadrius hiaticula

L 7.5" WS 20" WT 2.1 oz (60 g)

Averages larger than Semipalmated, with longer, less tapered bill; longer wings; white wingstripe broader, more obvious in flight. Difference in toe webbing (semipalmation) impossible to see in the field. All characteristics subtle; voice overrides all others for identification.

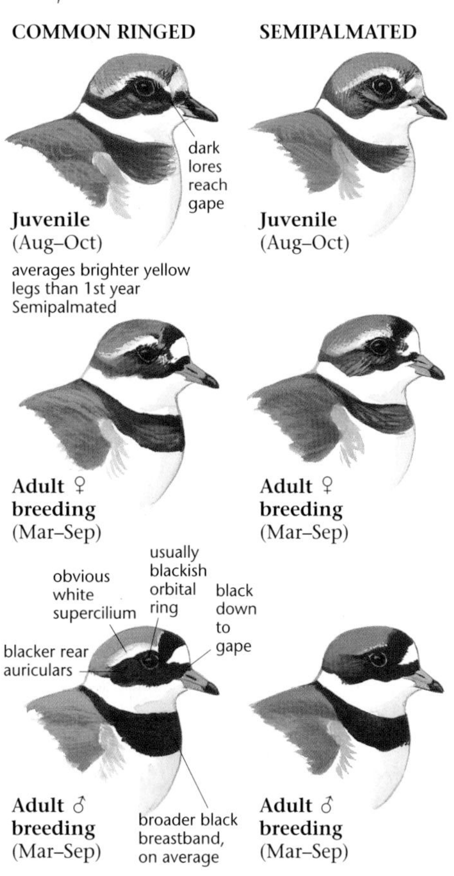
COMMON RINGED
SEMIPALMATED
dark lores reach gape
Juvenile (Aug–Oct)
averages brighter yellow legs than 1st year Semipalmated
Juvenile (Aug–Oct)
Adult ♀ breeding (Mar–Sep)
Adult ♀ breeding (Mar–Sep)
usually blackish orbital ring
obvious white supercilium
black down to gape
blacker rear auriculars
Adult ♂ breeding (Mar–Sep)
broader black breastband, on average
Adult ♂ breeding (Mar–Sep)

Voice: Common call a soft *tooe* or *toolip;* lower and more wooden than Semipalmated (quality more like Piping) with emphasis on first rather than second syllable. Threat call a rapid, low, mellow *towidi towidi towidi* . . . reminiscent of Lesser Yellowlegs. Display song *TOO-widee-TOO-widee*. . . .

Rare Shorebirds

Shorebirds are well known for long-distance vagrancy. This book covers the species of shorebirds that have occurred at least five times in North America outside of western Alaska. The following eight species occur in western Alaska (especially Saint Lawrence Island, the Pribilof Islands, and the western Aleutians); most have been recorded several times farther south and east in North America.

Wood Sandpiper (*Tringa glareola* L 8" WS 21" WT 2.3 oz, 65 g) Superficially resembles Lesser Yellowlegs but about the size of Solitary Sandpiper. Note whitish tail, pale supercilium, dark cap, and yellow-green legs. Call a sharp *chif-chif.*

Common Greenshank (*Tringa nebularia* L 14" WS 28" WT 6 oz, 170 g) Very similar to Greater Yellowlegs but legs greenish and rump entirely white, creating dowitcher-like white stripe up back. Call similar to yellowlegs.

Terek Sandpiper (*Xenus cinereus* L 9" WS 22" WT 2.8 oz, 80 g) Very distinctive and active. Shape somewhat similar to Spotted Sandpiper but slightly larger; pale grayish above, with a long, upturned bill. Call a series of clear whistles reminiscent of Wandering Tattler.

Common Sandpiper (*Actitis hypoleucos* L 8" WS 16" WT 1.6 oz, 46 g) Very similar to Spotted Sandpiper but slightly longer-tailed, lacking spots in breeding plumage; bill and leg colors average duller at all seasons. Flight call sharper than Spotted.

Gray-tailed Tattler (*Heteroscelus brevipes* L 10" WS 25" WT 1.6 oz, 46 g) Very similar to Wandering Tattler but paler overall, with a preference for wet flats rather than rocks. Call a clear, slurred whistle like Pacific Golden-Plover.

Great Knot (*Calidris tenuirostris* L 11" WS 26" WT 6 oz, 170 g) Similar to Red Knot but larger, relatively longer-billed, and white uppertail coverts contrast with darker tail. Breeding plumage of adult resembles breeding plumage of Surfbird. Generally silent.

Long-toed Stint (*Calidris subminuta* L 6.25" WS 13.5" WT 0.74 oz, 21 g) Variation within very similar Least Sandpiper renders identification extremely difficult: slightly larger and relatively longer-toed, straighter bill with pale base of lower mandible, details of face pattern differ. Flight call averages lower-pitched.

Temminck's Stint (*Calidris temminckii* L 6.25" WS 13" WT 0.77 oz, 22 g) Most closely resembles Least Sandpiper, with gray-brown breast, thin bill, yellowish legs; distinctively long-tailed with white outer tail feathers. Rattling flight call.

Large Plovers

These sturdy plovers have long, narrow wings; adults are black-bellied in breeding plumage. All are found on open ground (tundra, mudflats, pastures) and have evocative, whistled flight calls.

Black-bellied Plover

Pluvialis squatarola

L 11.5" WS 29" WT 8 oz (240 g)

Our largest plover, with relatively large head and large, heavy bill; white tail and black axillaries distinctive.

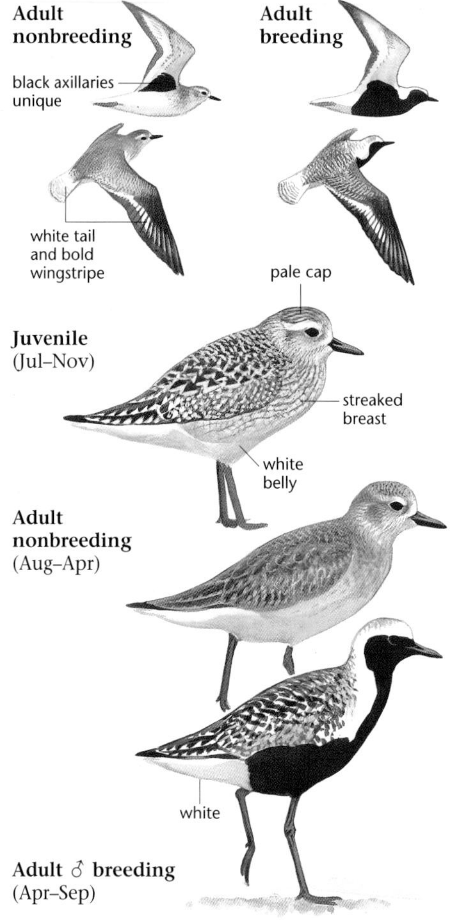

Adult nonbreeding
black axillaries unique
Adult breeding
white tail and bold wingstripe
pale cap
Juvenile (Jul–Nov)
streaked breast
white belly
Adult nonbreeding (Aug–Apr)
white
Adult ♂ breeding (Apr–Sep)

Voice: Flight call distinctive: high, clear whistles; melancholy and gently slurred *PLEEooee* or *peeooEEE;* variations with first or last syllable highest. Flight display song a melodious, ringing *kudiloo* or *trillii* repeated.

European Golden-Plover

Pluvialis apricaria

L 10.5" WS 26" WT 7 oz (210 g)

Similar to other golden-plovers but distinctly shorter-winged, stockier, and relatively large-headed and short-billed. Best distinguished by white underwing.

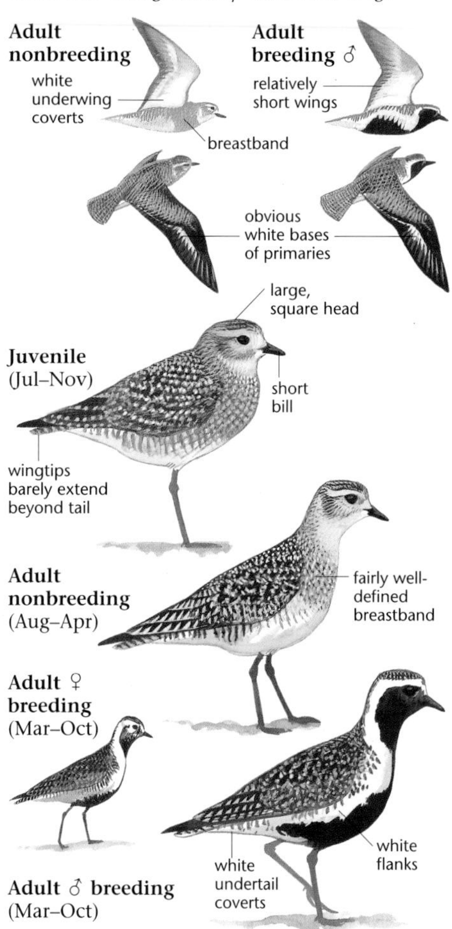

Adult nonbreeding
white underwing coverts
breastband
Adult breeding ♂
relatively short wings
obvious white bases of primaries
large, square head
Juvenile (Jul–Nov)
short bill
wingtips barely extend beyond tail
Adult nonbreeding (Aug–Apr)
fairly well-defined breastband
Adult ♀ breeding (Mar–Oct)
white undertail coverts
white flanks
Adult ♂ breeding (Mar–Oct)

Voice: Flight calls generally lower and simpler than American or Pacific: a plaintive, liquid *tlui;* soft, piping *wheep wheep;* and short, single notes *teep*. Flight song *perPEEoo* repeated.

Some juvenile Black-bellied Plovers in fresh plumage have strong yellow wash above, matching golden-plovers; average differences in intensity of yellow should be used only as a supporting characteristic. Yellow color in all species fades as feathers wear.

Formerly a single species (Lesser Golden-Plover), these plovers prefer pastures to mudflats (unlike Black-bellied). Pacific nests on wetter lowland tundra, American on drier slopes.

Pacific Golden-Plover

Pluvialis fulva

L 10.25" WS 24" WT 4.6 oz (130 g)

Similar to American, but averages slightly shorter wings, longer bill and legs. Averages more boldly spangled yellow above but some overlap.

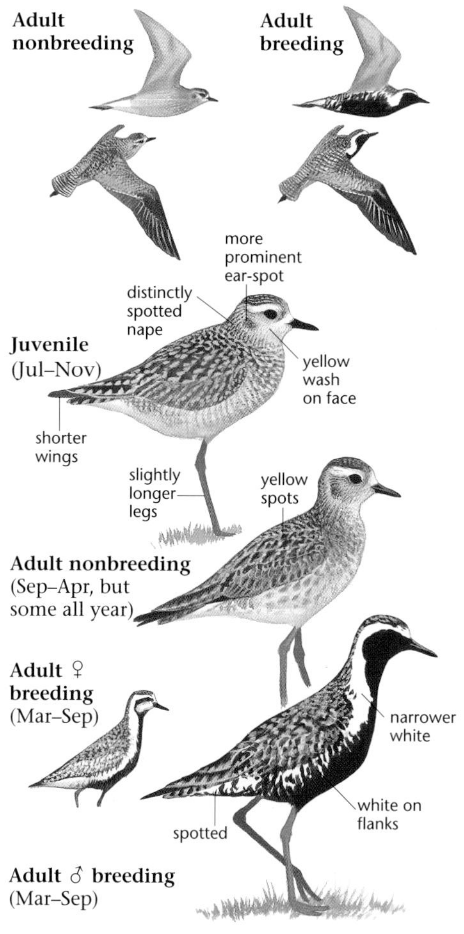
Adult nonbreeding
Adult breeding
more prominent ear-spot
distinctly spotted nape
Juvenile (Jul–Nov)
yellow wash on face
shorter wings
slightly longer legs
yellow spots
Adult nonbreeding (Sep–Apr, but some all year)
Adult ♀ breeding (Mar–Sep)
narrower white
white on flanks
spotted
Adult ♂ breeding (Mar–Sep)

Voice: Flight call a rising *quit, koWIT,* or *kowidl;* lower, simpler than American; sharply accented on rising second syllable like Semipalmated Plover. Flight song relatively slow, slurred whistles with long pauses between phrases *tuee tooEEEE; tuee tooEEEE. . . .*

American Golden-Plover

Pluvialis dominica

L 10.5" WS 26" WT 5 oz (145 g)

Distinguished from Black-bellied by smaller size, smaller head and bill, dark rump and wings, gray underwing.

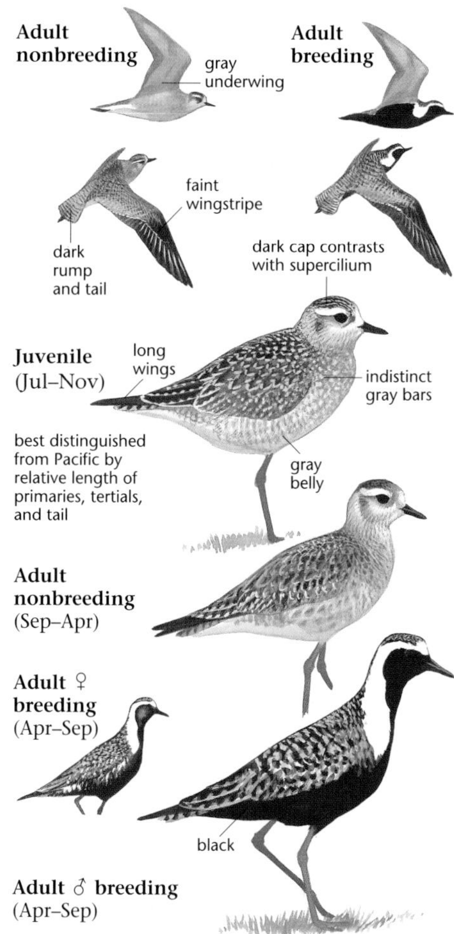
Adult nonbreeding
gray underwing
Adult breeding
faint wingstripe
dark rump and tail
dark cap contrasts with supercilium
Juvenile (Jul–Nov)
long wings
indistinct gray bars
best distinguished from Pacific by relative length of primaries, tertials, and tail
gray belly
Adult nonbreeding (Sep–Apr)
Adult ♀ breeding (Apr–Sep)
black
Adult ♂ breeding (Apr–Sep)

Voice: Flight call a sad-sounding, urgent *queedle;* higher than Black-bellied with little pitch change. Varies from high, sharp *quit* to *koweeawi* but always with vibrant, urgent tone. Flight song endlessly repeated *koweedl* or *tlueek* notes or a repeated *wit wit weee wit wit weee. . . .*

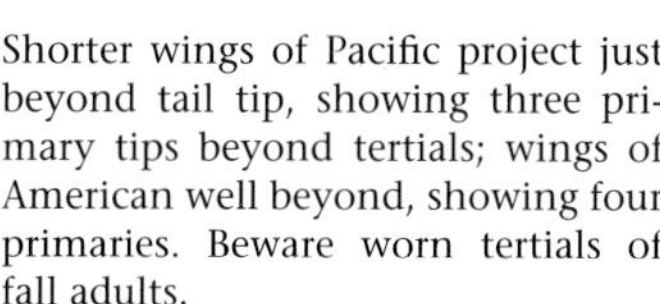
American
Pacific

Shorter wings of Pacific project just beyond tail tip, showing three primary tips beyond tertials; wings of American well beyond, showing four primaries. Beware worn tertials of fall adults.

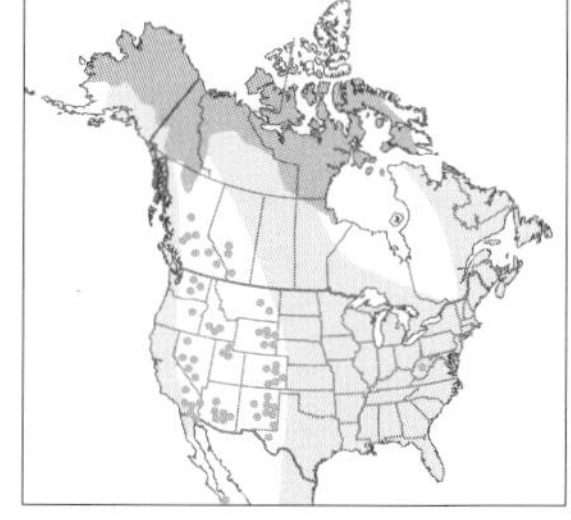

Small Belted Plovers

These two species are closely related, with whistled flight calls and stubby orange bills. Piping is found on sandy beaches, often well above the water line, Semipalmated on mudflats or beaches.

Piping Plover

Charadrius melodus

L 7.25" WS 19" WT 1.9 oz (55 g)

Stockier than other small plovers; pale upperparts and plain face distinctive.

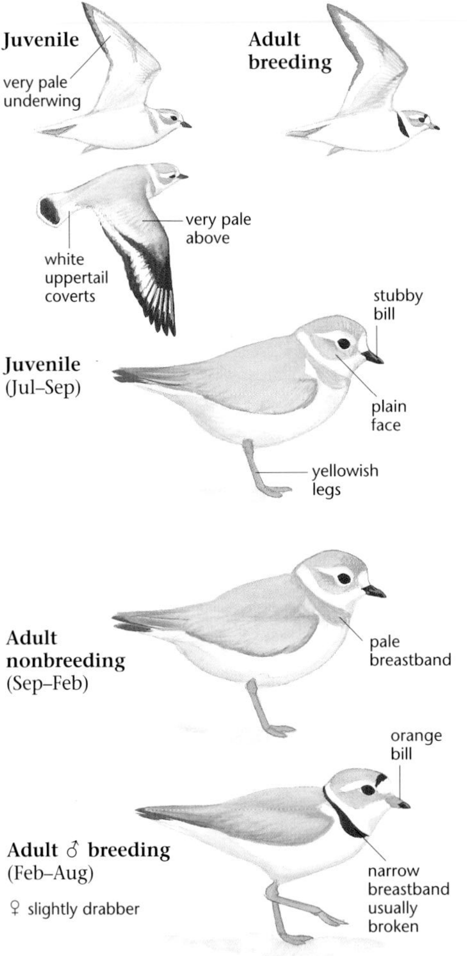

Juvenile
very pale underwing
Adult breeding
white uppertail coverts
very pale above
stubby bill
Juvenile (Jul–Sep)
plain face
yellowish legs
Adult nonbreeding (Sep–Feb)
pale breastband
orange bill
Adult ♂ breeding (Feb–Aug)
♀ slightly drabber
narrow breastband usually broken

Voice: Clear, mellow whistles *peep, peeto,* or *peep-lo;* low-pitched and gentle. When agitated endless series of low, soft whistles *pehp, pehp, pehp, pehp. . . .* Display song a steadily repeated, whistled *pooeep pooeep . . .* and variations.

Semipalmated Plover

Charadrius semipalmatus

L 7.25" WS 19" WT 1.6 oz (45 g)

Relatively long-winged and large-headed; dark brown back and yellow-orange legs distinctive (compare Common Ringed Plover).

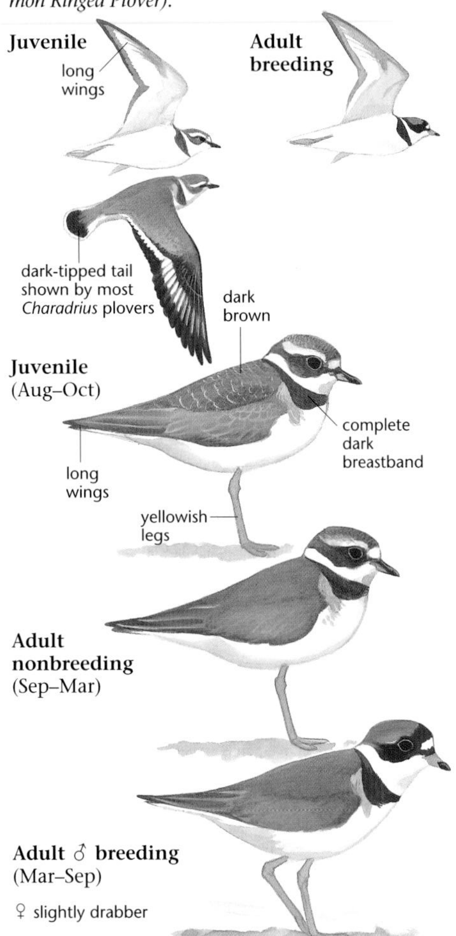

Juvenile
long wings
Adult breeding
dark-tipped tail shown by most Charadrius plovers
dark brown
Juvenile (Aug–Oct)
complete dark breastband
long wings
yellowish legs
Adult nonbreeding (Sep–Mar)
Adult ♂ breeding (Mar–Sep)
♀ slightly drabber

Voice: Flight call a short, husky whistle *chuWEE* or *kweet* and variations. In aggression a low, husky *kwiip.* Threat call a rapid, descending series *wyeep wyeep yeep yip yipyiyiyiyiyi.* Flight song a repeated husky whistled *too-ee, too-ee . . .* and various other calls.

Semipalmated Plover

Size and shape of breastband changes with posture.

These closely related species have pointed black bills, relatively long legs and bills, and short wings. They are found on sandy beaches, barren salt pans, or dry mudflats, rarely on wet mudflats.

Snowy Plover

Charadrius alexandrinus

L 6.25" WS 17" WT 1.4 oz (40 g)

Relatively long legs and short wings; appears front-heavy when standing.

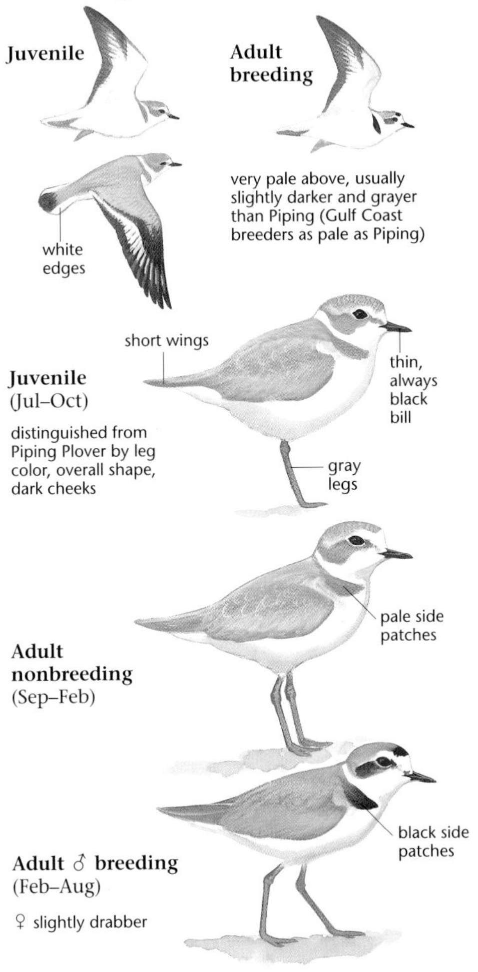
Juvenile
Adult breeding
very pale above, usually slightly darker and grayer than Piping (Gulf Coast breeders as pale as Piping)
white edges
short wings
Juvenile (Jul–Oct)
thin, always black bill
distinguished from Piping Plover by leg color, overall shape, dark cheeks
gray legs
pale side patches
Adult nonbreeding (Sep–Feb)
black side patches
Adult ♂ breeding (Feb–Aug)
♀ slightly drabber

Voice: Flight call *koorWIJ;* more nasal, husky, and complex than the whistle of Semipalmated; also rather hard *quip* or slightly rough *krip* or *quirr.* Display song (from ground) a repeated whistled *tuEEoo.*

Wilson's Plover

Charadrius wilsonia

L 7.75" WS 19" WT 2.1 oz (60 g)

Larger than other belted plovers; disproportionately long, heavy bill distinctive.

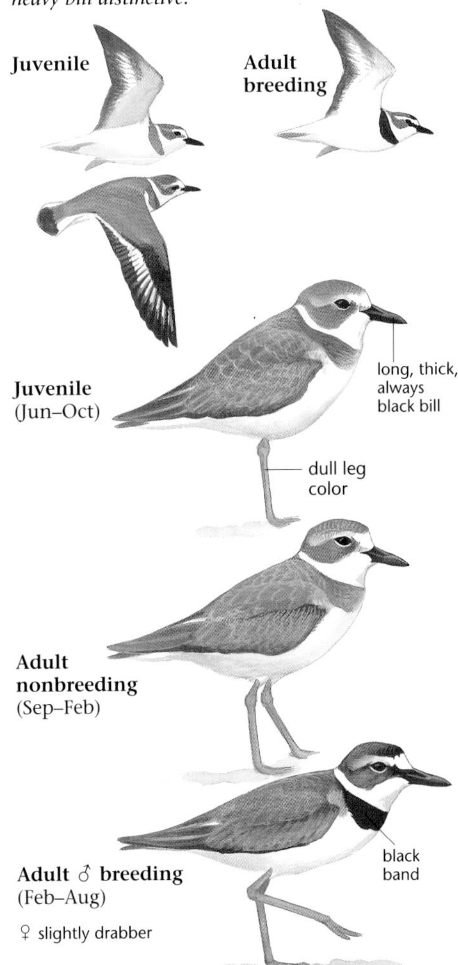
Juvenile
Adult breeding
long, thick, always black bill
Juvenile (Jun–Oct)
dull leg color
Adult nonbreeding (Sep–Feb)
black band
Adult ♂ breeding (Feb–Aug)
♀ slightly drabber

Voice: Flight call loud, sharp, high, and liquid *quit* or *queet.* When flushed a high, hard *dik* or *kid;* also a higher, squeakier *keest.* Grating or rattling, rasping notes in flight display and when agitated *jrrrrid jrrrrrid. . . .*

Wilson's Plover alert posture

Rare Plovers

These two species are rare visitors from Asia. Mongolian is related to and often seen with Semipalmated. Eurasian Dotterel prefers barren upland habitats (rocky tundra, dunes, pastures).

Mongolian Plover

Charadrius mongolus

L 7.5" WS 22" WT 2.5 oz (70 g)

Slightly larger, longer-legged, and longer-billed than Semipalmated; lack of white collar distinctive in all plumages.

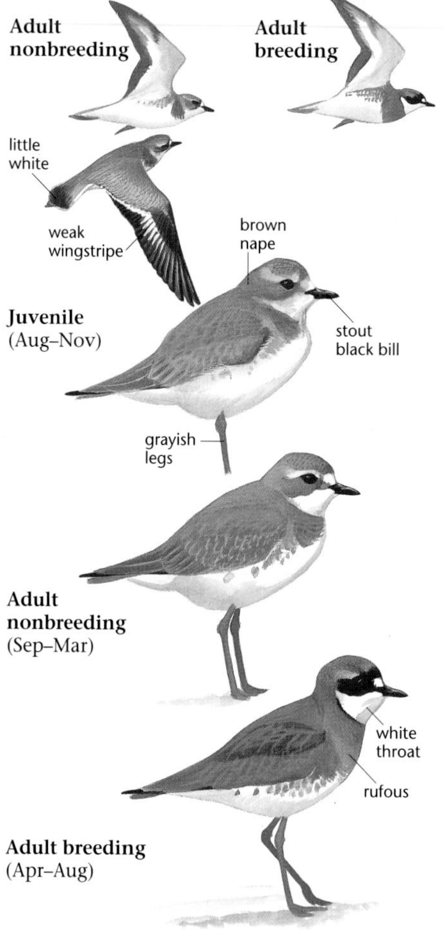

Adult nonbreeding
Adult breeding
little white
weak wingstripe
brown nape
Juvenile (Aug–Nov)
stout black bill
grayish legs
Adult nonbreeding (Sep–Mar)
white throat
rufous
Adult breeding (Apr–Aug)

Voice: Flight call a short, hard rattle *drrit* or *ddddd* slightly rising; reminiscent of longspurs or turnstones.

Eurasian Dotterel

Charadrius morinellus

L 8.25" WS 23" WT 3.9 oz (110 g) ♀>♂

Typical plover shape and actions; small bill; long, pale supercilium always obvious.

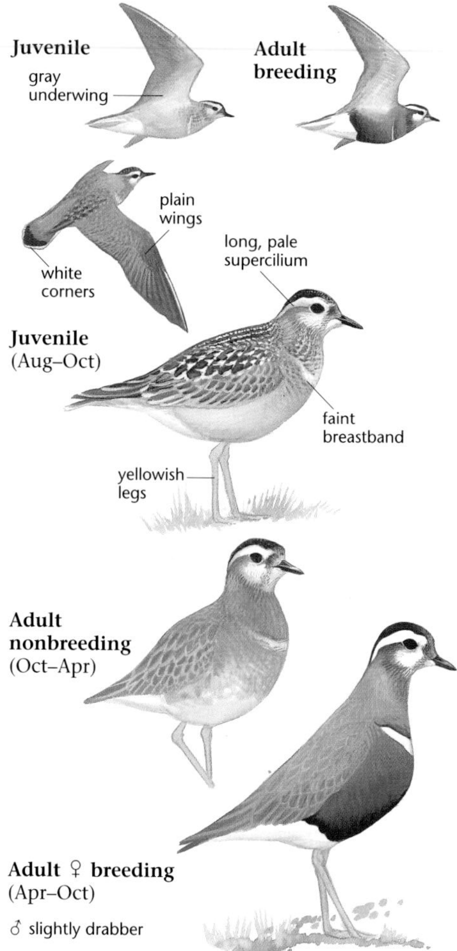

Juvenile
gray underwing
Adult breeding
plain wings
white corners
long, pale supercilium
Juvenile (Aug–Oct)
faint breastband
yellowish legs
Adult nonbreeding (Oct–Apr)
Adult ♀ breeding (Apr–Oct)
♂ slightly drabber

Voice: Most common call a Dunlin-like *keerrr* when taking off; also a soft *put put* or other soft or grating notes. Flight song a high, rapidly repeated *pwit pwit pwit. . . .*

Upland Plovers

These two species are found in upland habitats often far from water, especially Mountain Plover, seen on dry, barren fields. Killdeer is widespread on farmland, ballfields, and the like.

Mountain Plover

Charadrius montanus

L 9" WS 23" WT 3.7 oz (105 g) ♀>♂

Longer-legged and shorter-tailed than Killdeer; distinctively plain in all plumages.

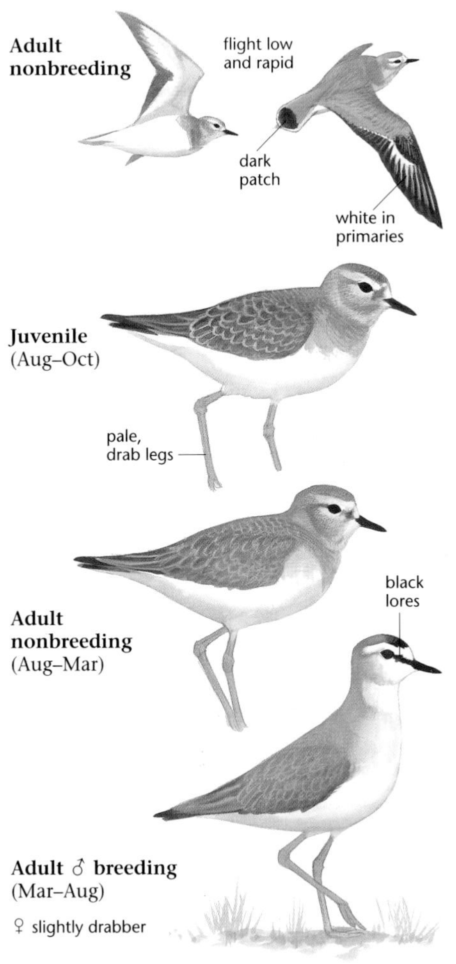
Adult nonbreeding
flight low and rapid
dark patch
white in primaries
Juvenile (Aug–Oct)
pale, drab legs
Adult nonbreeding (Aug–Mar)
black lores
Adult ♂ breeding (Mar–Aug)
♀ slightly drabber

Voice: Flight call a coarse *grrrt;* lower single note *dirp* like Western Meadowlark; also a coarse, grating *ji ji ji ji ji.* In courtship a low, soft moan very similar to distant cow mooing. Flight song a rapidly repeated, wild, harsh whistle *we we we we we. . . .*

Killdeer

Charadrius vociferus

L 10.5" WS 24" WT 3.3 oz (95 g) ♀>♂

Lanky, with slender wings and very long tail; orange rump and double breastband distinctive.

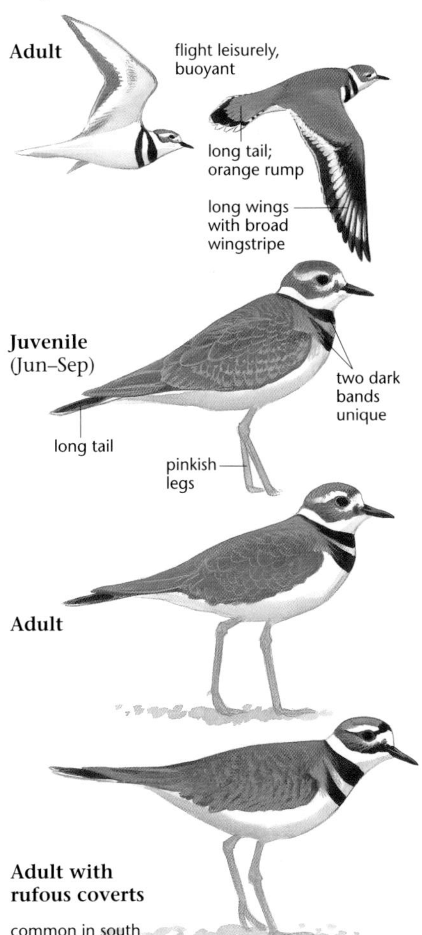
Adult
flight leisurely, buoyant
long tail; orange rump
long wings with broad wingstripe
Juvenile (Jun–Sep)
two dark bands unique
long tail
pinkish legs
Adult
Adult with rufous coverts
common in south

Voice: Calls high, strident piping, often drawn-out *deee, deeeyee, tyeeeeeee deew deew, Tewddew* (or "kill deer"). When agitated a strident, clear *teeeee di di* repeated; high, rapid trill *tttttttttt* when very nervous. Display song a rapid, high, rolling *dideeerr dideeerr . . .* with high, thin quality like other calls.

Downy young Killdeer has single breastband, like small plovers.

Oystercatchers

These two closely related species have distinctive stocky shapes, heavy red bills, and piping calls. Exclusively coastal, Black is found on rocks, American on beaches and shellbars.

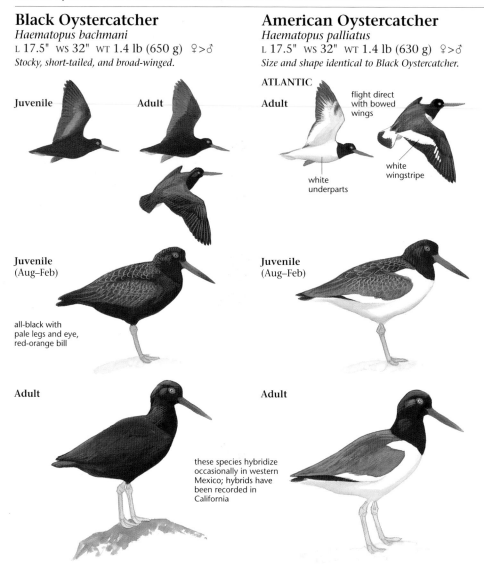

Black Oystercatcher

Haematopus bachmani

L 17.5" WS 32" WT 1.4 lb (650 g) ♀>♂

Stocky, short-tailed, and broad-winged.

Juvenile

Adult

Juvenile
(Aug–Feb)

all-black with
pale legs and eye,
red-orange bill

Adult

these species hybridize occasionally in western Mexico; hybrids have been recorded in California

American Oystercatcher

Haematopus palliatus

L 17.5" WS 32" WT 1.4 lb (630 g) ♀>♂

Size and shape identical to Black Oystercatcher.

ATLANTIC

Adult

flight direct
with bowed
wings

white
underparts

white
wingstripe

Juvenile
(Aug–Feb)

Adult

Voice: Voices of Black and American apparently identical: loud whistled yelps or high, clear, piping whistles *queep, weeyo,* etc. In display a long accelerating series *queep queep quee deedeedeedeedeedededededdddddrrr* rising and then descending. Alarm a clear *kleep, kleep, klidik-klideeew;* falcon alarm a rapid *whidididew.*

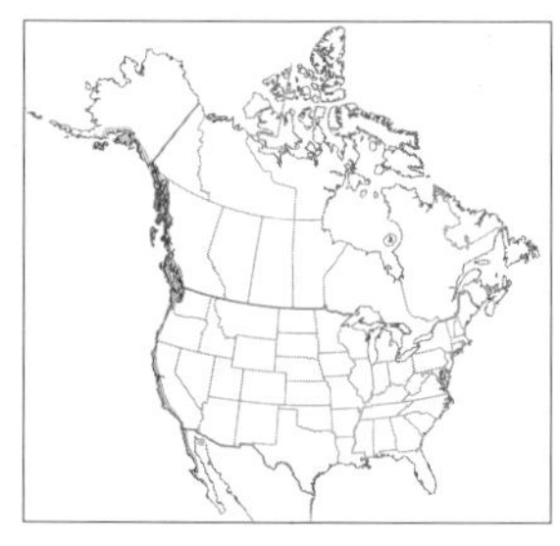

American Oystercatcher adult Pacific

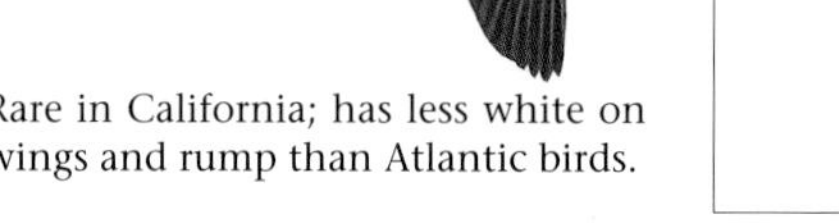

Rare in California; has less white on wings and rump than Atlantic birds.

AMERICAN AVOCET AND BLACK-NECKED STILT

These two striking species are found in shallow, marshy or muddy ponds. American Avocet feeds by sweeping its bill side-to-side through mud or water; Black-necked Stilt feeds by picking.

American Avocet

Recurvirostra americana

L 18" WS 31" WT 11 oz (315 g)

Elegant yet sturdy, with very thin, upcurved bill; broad black and white stripes on back distinctive.

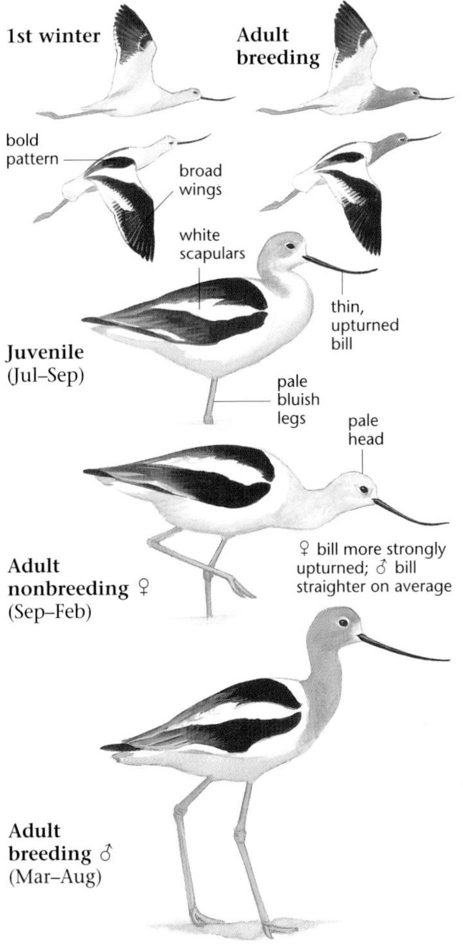
1st winter
Adult breeding
bold pattern
broad wings
white scapulars
thin, upturned bill
Juvenile (Jul–Sep)
pale bluish legs
pale head
♀ bill more strongly upturned; ♂ bill straighter on average
Adult nonbreeding ♀ (Sep–Feb)
Adult breeding ♂ (Mar–Aug)

Voice: Less vocal than Black-necked Stilt. Mainly single note calls ranging from high, sharp *kweep* to lower *pwik* or sharp *pleek;* all higher than similar calls of Black-necked Stilt. Some calls reminiscent of yellowlegs.

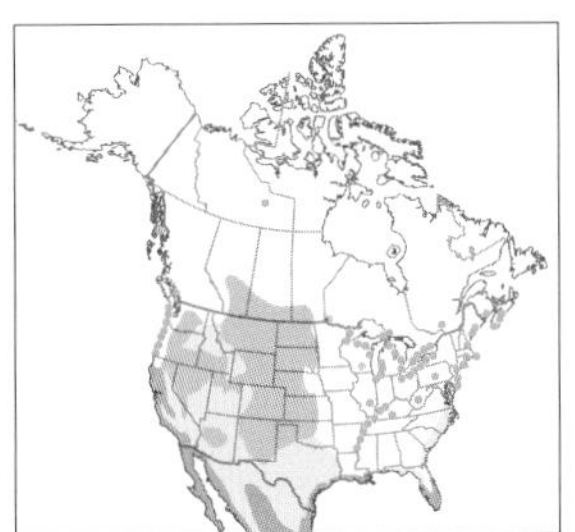

Black-necked Stilt

Himantopus mexicanus

L 14" WS 29" WT 6 oz (160 g)

Extraordinarily tall and slender; unique black and white plumage and long red legs.

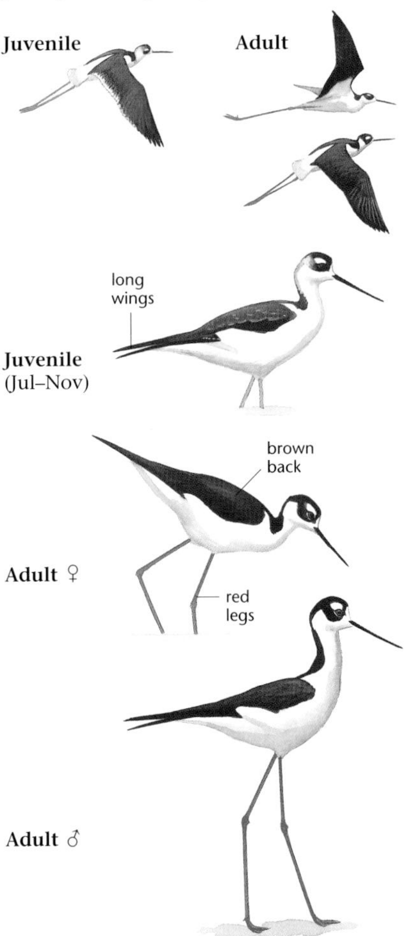
Juvenile
Adult
long wings
Juvenile (Jul–Nov)
brown back
Adult ♀
red legs
Adult ♂

Voice: Common call a loud, sharp *taawh* or *pleek* often repeated incessantly; ranges from short *kik kik* . . . to complaining *keef keef* . . . and harsher *wreek wreek* . . . ; lower and louder than American Avocet. Juvenile often gives a high, sharp *peek* or *pidi* similar to Long-billed Dowitcher.

Long-legged Waders: Genus *Tringa*

These two slender, elegant waders are found in a variety of shallow-water habitats. They forage actively, even running after small fish, and bob the head and body emphatically when alarmed.

Greater Yellowlegs

Tringa melanoleuca

L 14" WS 28" WT 6 oz (160 g)

Like Lesser Yellowlegs: tall and active, thin neck, long yellow legs. Distinguished by structure and voice.

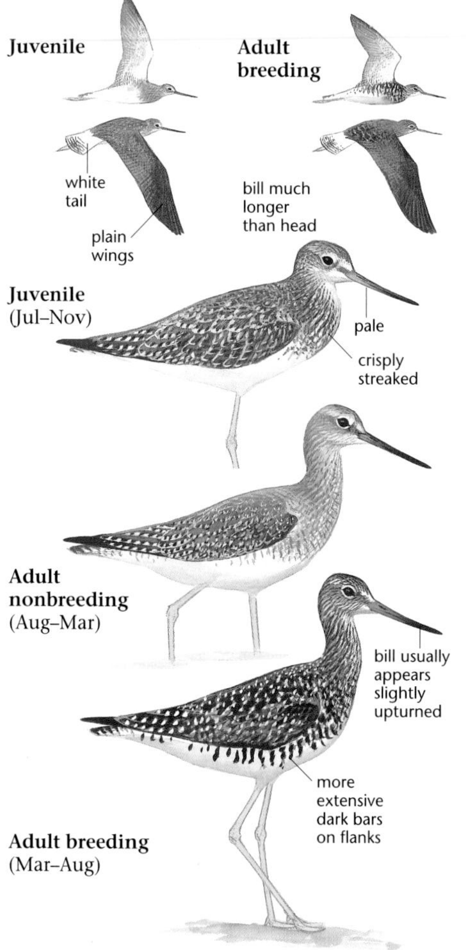

Juvenile
Adult breeding
white tail
plain wings
bill much longer than head
Juvenile (Jul–Nov)
pale
crisply streaked
Adult nonbreeding (Aug–Mar)
bill usually appears slightly upturned
more extensive dark bars on flanks
Adult breeding (Mar–Aug)

Voice: Flight call a loud ringing *deew deew deew;* typically three or four notes; higher than Lesser with strident overtones. In agitation an endlessly repeated single note *tew, tew. . . .* Feeding bird gives soft, single notes. Display song a melodious, rolling *kleewee kleewee. . . .*

Lesser Yellowlegs

Tringa flavipes

L 10.5" WS 24" WT 2.8 oz (80 g)

Smaller with shorter bill but relatively longer legs and wings; appears more elongated and delicate.

Juvenile
Adult breeding
bill just longer than head
Juvenile (Jul–Nov)
grayer, less distinctly marked
Adult nonbreeding (Oct–Mar)
yellowlegs feed actively, picking and jabbing at prey; often run through water
Adult breeding (Apr–Sep)

Voice: Flight call of short whistles *tip* or *too-too* typically flatter and softer than Greater; usually only one or two notes. In agitation a repeated *tiw, tiw. . . .* Alarm a rising, trilled *kleet.* Threat a low, rolling trill. Display song a rapid, rolling *towidyawid, towidyawid . . .*; lower-pitched than flight call.

Greater Yellowlegs adult

Greater Yellowlegs with molting primaries is a common sight Aug–Sep. Lesser molts later, after migration.

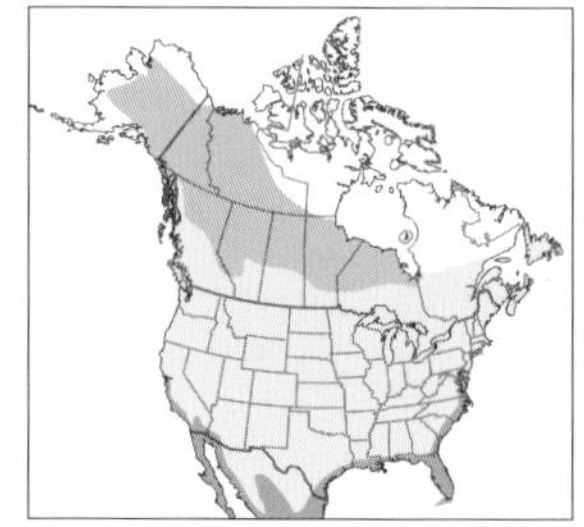

Related to yellowlegs, these species are subtly distinctive. Spotted Redshank, a rare visitor, is usually found with yellowlegs, Solitary Sandpiper in muddy, vegetation-enclosed ponds and creeks.

Spotted Redshank

Tringa erythropus

L 12.5" WS 25" WT 6 oz (165 g)

Size intermediate between the two yellowlegs, but relatively short-winged and long-billed. Note entirely white rump.

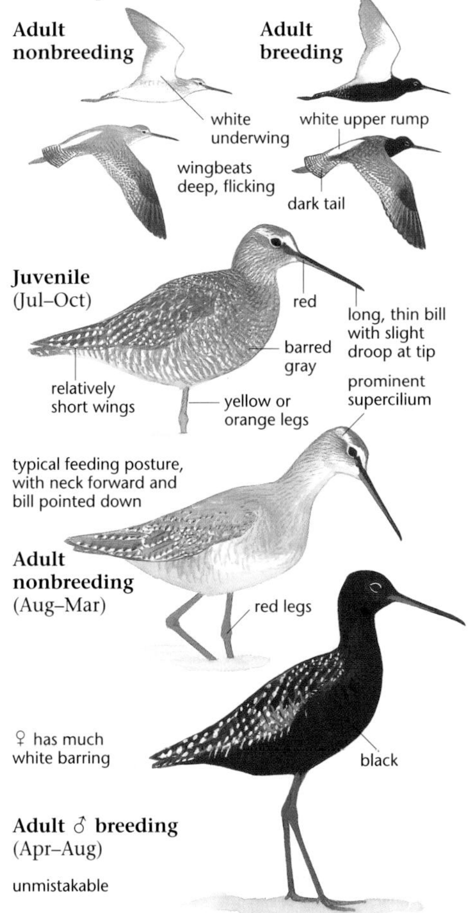
Adult nonbreeding
Adult breeding
white underwing
white upper rump
wingbeats deep, flicking
dark tail
Juvenile (Jul–Oct)
red
long, thin bill with slight droop at tip
barred gray
relatively short wings
yellow or orange legs
prominent supercilium
typical feeding posture, with neck forward and bill pointed down
Adult nonbreeding (Aug–Mar)
red legs
♀ has much white barring
black
Adult ♂ breeding (Apr–Aug)
unmistakable

Voice: Flight call a husky *chuwit* or *kawit;* very similar to Semipalmated Plover but harder, stronger, deeper. On rising sometimes gives a chuckling *chu, chu* or loud, slightly husky *kweep kip kip.* Display song varied; includes shrill, grinding *krr-WEEa* phrases and short bouts of sharp notes.

Yellowlegs can rarely have bright orange legs; beware of confusing such birds with Spotted Redshank.

Solitary Sandpiper

Tringa solitaria

L 8.5" WS 22" WT 1.8 oz (50 g)

Smaller than yellowlegs; shorter-legged and shorter-necked like Spotted Redshank. Relatively dark plumage with small white dots distinctive.

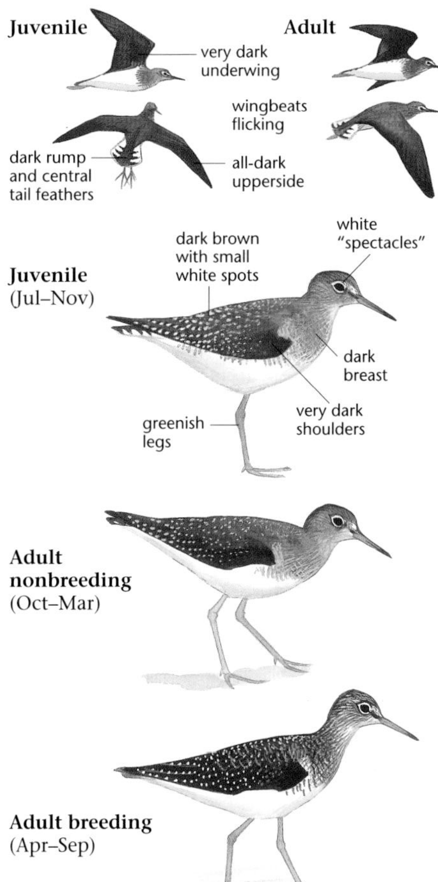
Juvenile
Adult
very dark underwing
wingbeats flicking
dark rump and central tail feathers
all-dark upperside
dark brown with small white spots
white "spectacles"
Juvenile (Jul–Nov)
dark breast
very dark shoulders
greenish legs
Adult nonbreeding (Oct–Mar)
Adult breeding (Apr–Sep)

Voice: Flight call a clear, high, rising whistle *peet-WEET* or *peet weet weet;* higher and more urgent than Spotted Sandpiper. Alarm from ground a very hard, sharp *plik.* Display song a series of short phrases reminiscent of flight call but more complex, with startling, bell-like quality.

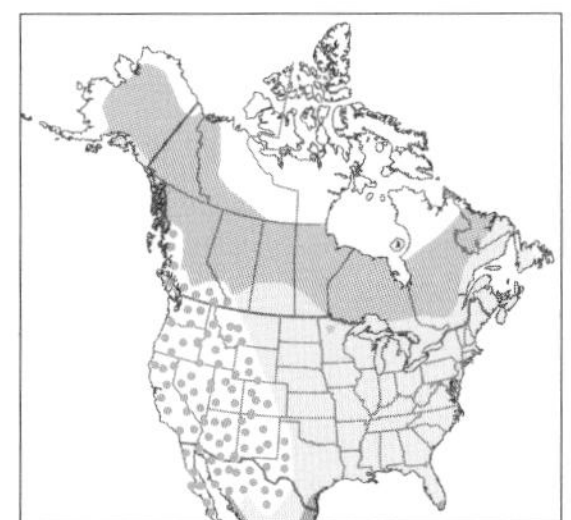

Willet

This species is a large, rather heavyset wader with a striking wing pattern revealed in flight. Found in many habitats—from marshes to rocky shores—it is often seen singly on beaches.

Willet

Catoptrophorus semipalmatus

L 15" WS 26" WT 8 oz (215 g)

Stockier than yellowlegs, with relatively large head and thick bill; broad, rounded wings.

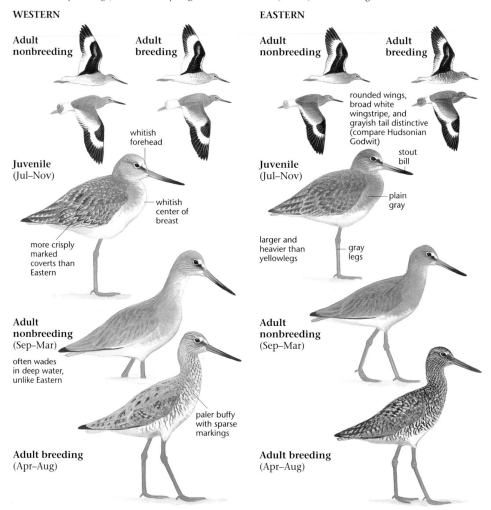

WESTERN

Adult nonbreeding

Adult breeding

whitish forehead

Juvenile (Jul–Nov)

whitish center of breast

more crisply marked coverts than Eastern

Adult nonbreeding (Sep–Mar)

often wades in deep water, unlike Eastern

paler buffy with sparse markings

Adult breeding (Apr–Aug)

EASTERN

Adult nonbreeding

Adult breeding

rounded wings, broad white wingstripe, and grayish tail distinctive (compare Hudsonian Godwit)

stout bill

Juvenile (Jul–Nov)

plain gray

larger and heavier than yellowlegs

gray legs

Adult nonbreeding (Sep–Mar)

Adult breeding (Apr–Aug)

Voice: Flight call a clear, loud, ringing *kyaah yah* or *kleee lii* or simply a descending *haaaa.* When flushed *kleeliilii* and variations; in alarm a monotonously repeated *wik, wik* . . . or more intense *kliK, kliK.* . . . Territorial song a rolling, clear chant *pilly WILL WILLET* repeated steadily. Voices of subspecies similar but all calls of Western birds average lower-pitched than Eastern. Western call on flushing a more raucous rolled *krrri lii liit;* territorial song of Western birds lower-pitched and longer with relatively long *will* note.

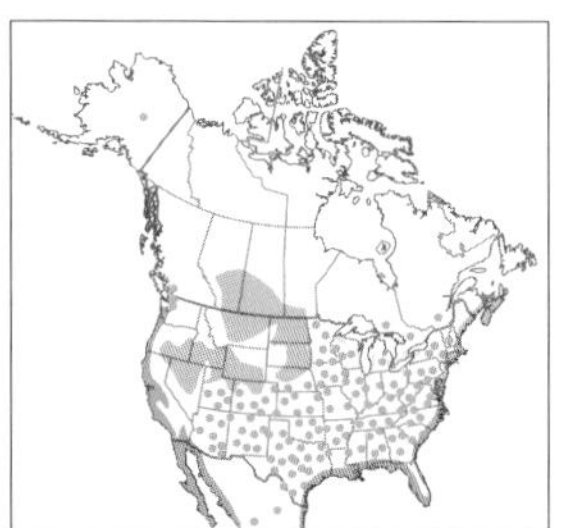

Eastern birds strictly coastal all year; Western breeds inland and migrates to both coasts, but rare north of New Jersey. Western birds are 10 percent larger with 15 percent longer bill and legs and little overlap; bill is relatively slender and often slightly upturned; wingtips may project slightly farther beyond tail tip. Western's more godwitlike feeding habits are related to its structure. It is paler overall and its white wingstripe averages broader; other plumage characteristics noted above.

Distinctive Sandpipers

These two species are distinctive. Spotted is found singly at water's edge, often on the steep banks of ponds or creeks. Upland, related to curlews but smaller, is found in dry, open grassland.

Spotted Sandpiper

Actitis macularia

L 7.5" WS 15" WT 1.4 oz (40 g)

Oddly short-necked and long-tailed for a sandpiper, with an exaggerated bobbing motion.

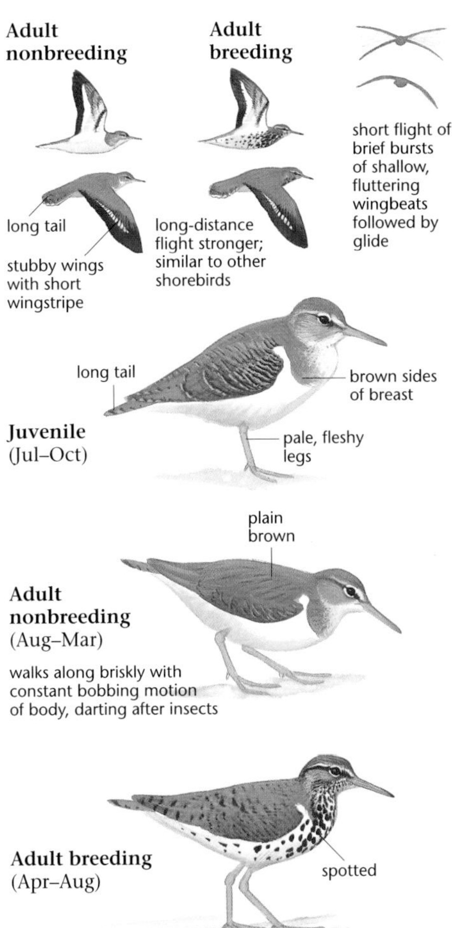

Adult nonbreeding
Adult breeding
short flight of brief bursts of shallow, fluttering wingbeats followed by glide
long tail
stubby wings with short wingstripe
long-distance flight stronger; similar to other shorebirds
long tail
brown sides of breast
Juvenile (Jul–Oct)
pale, fleshy legs
plain brown
Adult nonbreeding (Aug–Mar)
walks along briskly with constant bobbing motion of body, darting after insects
Adult breeding (Apr–Aug)
spotted

Voice: Flight call a high, clear, whistled *twii twii* or a descending series *peet weet weet*; lazier and lower-pitched than Solitary; often a single note *peet* or repeated whistle *pweet, pweet. . . .* Display song a rolling, clear, whistled *tototowee, tototowee. . . .*

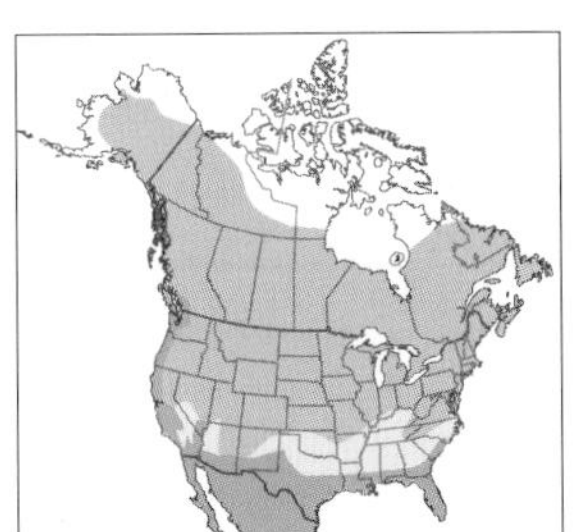

Upland Sandpiper

Bartramia longicauda

L 12" WS 26" WT 6 oz (170 g) ♀>♂

Habits, voice, and structure similar to curlews; long tail, short bill, and thin neck distinctive. Often perches on fence posts on breeding grounds.

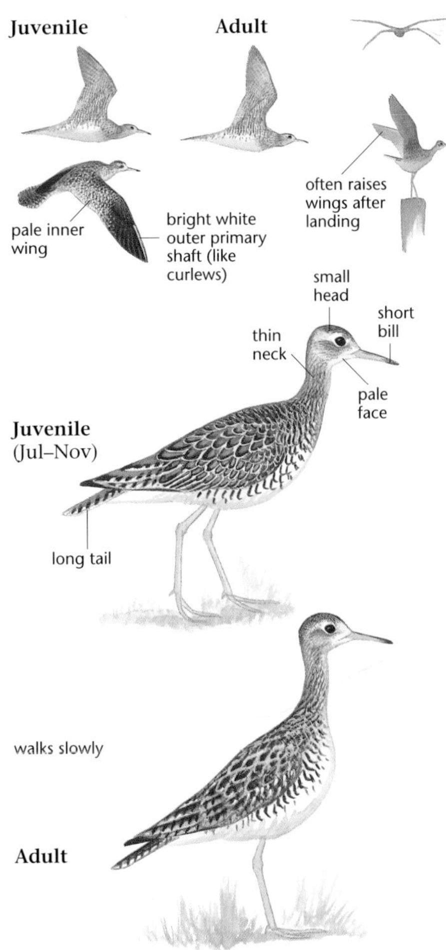

Juvenile
Adult
pale inner wing
bright white outer primary shaft (like curlews)
often raises wings after landing
small head
short bill
thin neck
pale face
Juvenile (Jul–Nov)
long tail
walks slowly
Adult

Voice: Flight call a low, strong, liquid *qui-di-di-du;* last note lower and weaker; distinctively loud and clear. Alarm a nasal, growling *grrgrrgrrgrrgrr.* Flight song a weird, unearthly, bubbling whistle, slowly rising then falling *bububuLEE-hLEEyooooooo.*

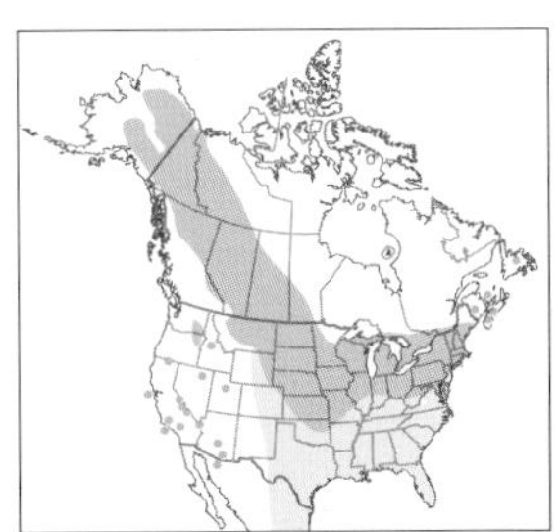

Curlews

This primarily coastal species is found on marshes, beaches, and rocky shores, often in flocks, but it forages singly. It feeds more by picking, less by probing, than Long-billed Curlew and godwits.

Whimbrel

Numenius phaeopus

L 17.5" WS 32" WT 14 oz (390 g) ♀>♂

Sturdy and sleek with pointed wings. Longer-bodied and shorter-billed than Long-billed Curlew; similar to Marbled Godwit. American population grayish-brown overall.

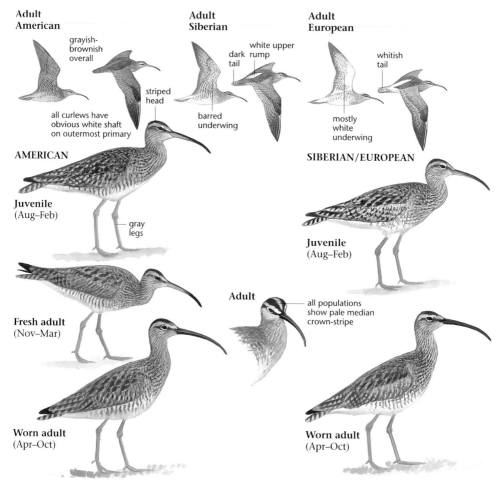

Adult American

grayish-brownish overall

striped head

all curlews have obvious white shaft on outermost primary

Adult Siberian

dark tail

white upper rump

barred underwing

Adult European

whitish tail

mostly white underwing

AMERICAN

Juvenile (Aug–Feb)

gray legs

Fresh adult (Nov–Mar)

Worn adult (Apr–Oct)

Adult

all populations show pale median crown-stripe

SIBERIAN/EUROPEAN

Juvenile (Aug–Feb)

Worn adult (Apr–Oct)

Voice: Flight call a rapid, forceful, liquid *quiquiquiquiqui* with no change in pitch. Chase call, given in flight, a series of short, varied whistles and trilled notes. Display song a low, clear whistle *oook* repeated, followed by three trills; also a low, vibrato whistle followed by slightly higher trill given frequently on nesting grounds (e.g., when landing). European and Siberian flight call possibly a little weaker and wilder-sounding than American; display flight apparently begins with whistle call during climb (American is silent during climb).

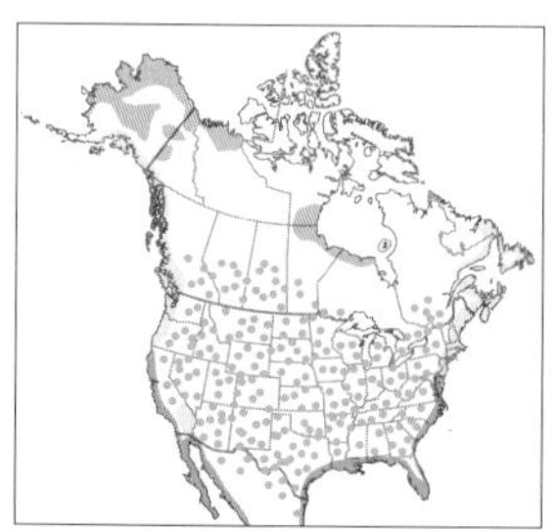

Three populations occur: American throughout; Siberian a rare visitor to Alaska with a few records farther south on Pacific coast; European a very rare visitor to Atlantic coast. They differ only in plumage, especially the whitish ground color of the underparts and rump of European and Siberian birds (vs. buffy-brown of American). Siberian birds are barred dark on underwings and rump, while European birds are cleaner white, but variable. Perched European and Siberian birds may appear grayer overall than American, with more contrastingly pale wing coverts, but there is some overlap.

Bristle-thighed Curlew is similar to Whimbrel but favors drier habitats year-round. Long-billed Curlew, our largest sandpiper, is found on fields and dry prairie as well as mudflats.

Bristle-thighed Curlew

Numenius tahitiensis

L 17" WS 32" WT 1.1 lb (490 g) ♀>♂

Identical to Whimbrel in shape and size; pale rump and voice distinctive.

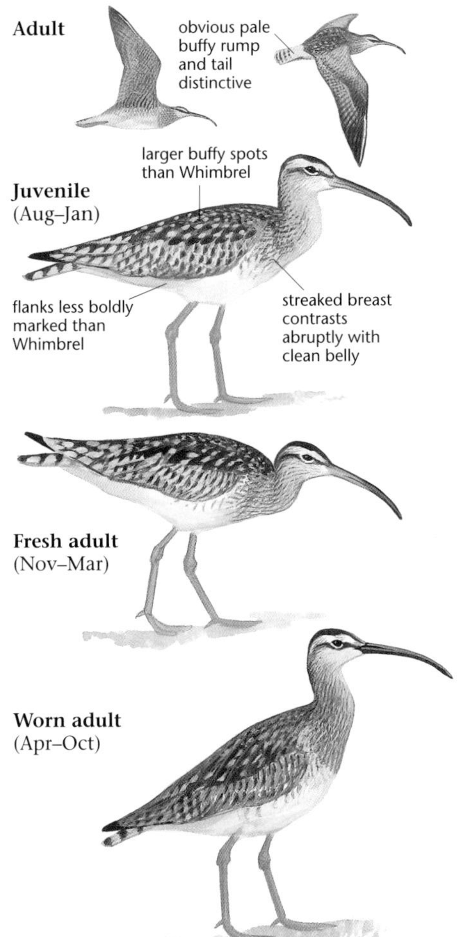
Adult
obvious pale buffy rump and tail distinctive
larger buffy spots than Whimbrel
Juvenile (Aug–Jan)
flanks less boldly marked than Whimbrel
streaked breast contrasts abruptly with clean belly
Fresh adult (Nov–Mar)
Worn adult (Apr–Oct)

Voice: Flight call a clear, insistent whistle of even emphasis *teeoip;* remarkably like human attention whistle; lower than Black-bellied Plover and quite different in character. Display flight soaring; begins with about five *wiiteew* notes, then repeated, complex *pidl WHIDyooooo.*

Long-billed Curlew

Numenius americanus

L 23" WS 35" WT 1.3 lb (590 g) ♀>♂

Distinctively colored; much larger and broader-winged than other curlews. Plumage pattern like Marbled Godwit.

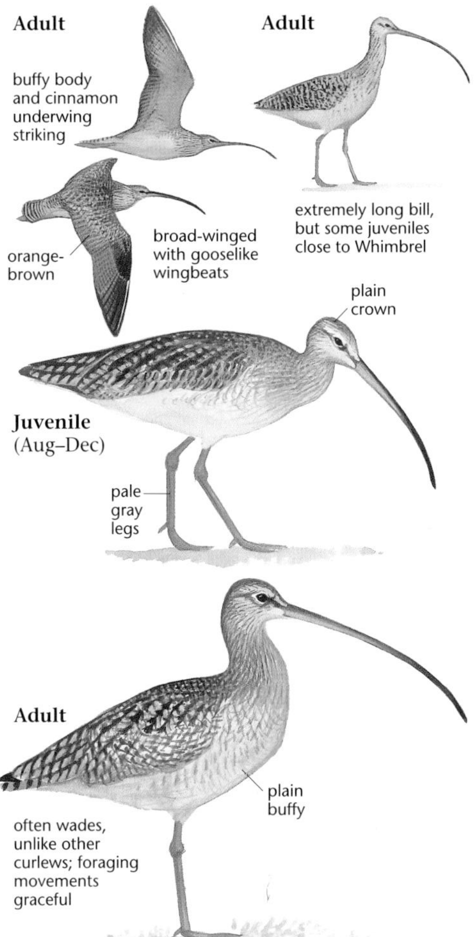
Adult
Adult
buffy body and cinnamon underwing striking
orange-brown
broad-winged with gooselike wingbeats
extremely long bill, but some juveniles close to Whimbrel
plain crown
Juvenile (Aug–Dec)
pale gray legs
Adult
plain buffy
often wades, unlike other curlews; foraging movements graceful

Voice: Flight calls clear whistles, most commonly a short, rising *coooLI* with sharp rise at end. Also *kwid wid wid wid,* a loud, whistled *wrrreeep,* and variations. Song of low, rich, whistled notes building to long, slurred whistle *pr pr pr pr pr prrreeeep prrrreeeeeerrr.*

At a distance, when bill shape and size are not apparent, Long-billed Curlew (and sometimes Whimbrel) can be confused with Marbled Godwit. Curlews have pale gray legs and forage with more graceful movements than godwits.

Godwits

The four godwits are all large, with long, upcurved bills. Bar-tailed, strictly coastal, is found on beaches and mudflats; Black-tailed prefers a marshy habitat, often freshwater.

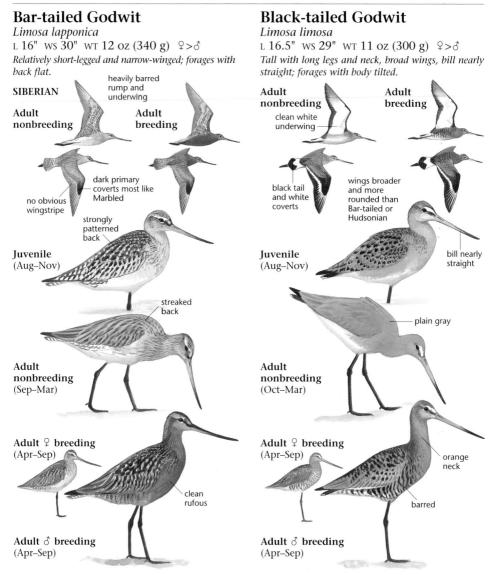

Bar-tailed Godwit

Limosa lapponica

L 16" WS 30" WT 12 oz (340 g) ♀>♂

Relatively short-legged and narrow-winged; forages with back flat.

SIBERIAN

heavily barred rump and underwing

Adult nonbreeding

Adult breeding

no obvious wingstripe

dark primary coverts most like Marbled

strongly patterned back

Juvenile (Aug–Nov)

streaked back

Adult nonbreeding (Sep–Mar)

Adult ♀ breeding (Apr–Sep)

clean rufous

Adult ♂ breeding (Apr–Sep)

Voice: Calls creaking, nasal. Flight call *kee kee kaa* or *kooy kooy kooy* very similar to Hudsonian but slightly lower-pitched and with more even pitch. Display song more melodic and varied in rhythm and pitch than other godwits.

Black-tailed Godwit

Limosa limosa

L 16.5" WS 29" WT 11 oz (300 g) ♀>♂

Tall with long legs and neck, broad wings, bill nearly straight; forages with body tilted.

Adult nonbreeding

clean white underwing

Adult breeding

black tail and white coverts

wings broader and more rounded than Bar-tailed or Hudsonian

Juvenile (Aug–Nov)

bill nearly straight

plain gray

Adult nonbreeding (Oct–Mar)

Adult ♀ breeding (Apr–Sep)

orange neck

barred

Adult ♂ breeding (Apr–Sep)

Voice: Calls rather strident, nasal, mewing; most commonly *weeka weeka weeka;* variety of other short notes includes soft *kaa* with mewing quality and sharper *kip*. Display song of repeated two- or three-syllable phrases.

European Bar-tailed Godwit

A rare visitor to the Atlantic coast; similar to Siberian but with clean white upper rump and underwing.

GODWITS (CONTINUED)

Both of these species nest near grassy marshes. At other seasons they are found on beaches, mudflats, and shallow pools, walking and probing the mud with their long bills, often in flocks.

Hudsonian Godwit

Limosa haemastica

L 15.5" WS 29" WT 11 oz (300 g) ♀>♂

Our smallest godwit, not much larger than Greater Yellowlegs; black underwing coverts unique.

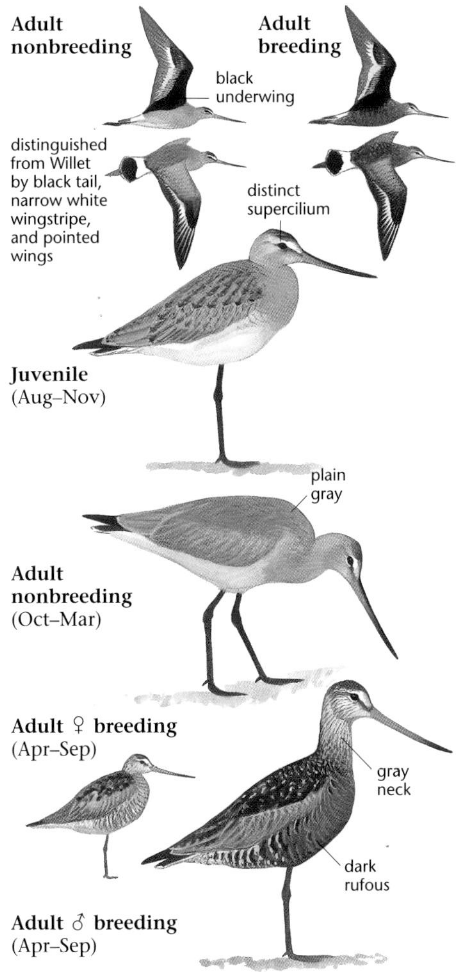

Adult nonbreeding
Adult breeding
black underwing
distinguished from Willet by black tail, narrow white wingstripe, and pointed wings
distinct supercilium
Juvenile (Aug–Nov)
plain gray
Adult nonbreeding (Oct–Mar)
Adult ♀ breeding (Apr–Sep)
gray neck
dark rufous
Adult ♂ breeding (Apr–Sep)

Voice: Flight call high falsetto *kwidWID* or *kweh-weh* and variations, each syllable rising; higher-pitched than other godwits; also high *week* or *kwee* like Black-necked Stilt but softer. Display song a repeated three-syllable phrase.

Marbled Godwit

Limosa fedoa

L 18" WS 30" WT 13 oz (370 g) ♀>♂

Larger and broader-winged than Hudsonian, with very different plumage (compare Long-billed Curlew).

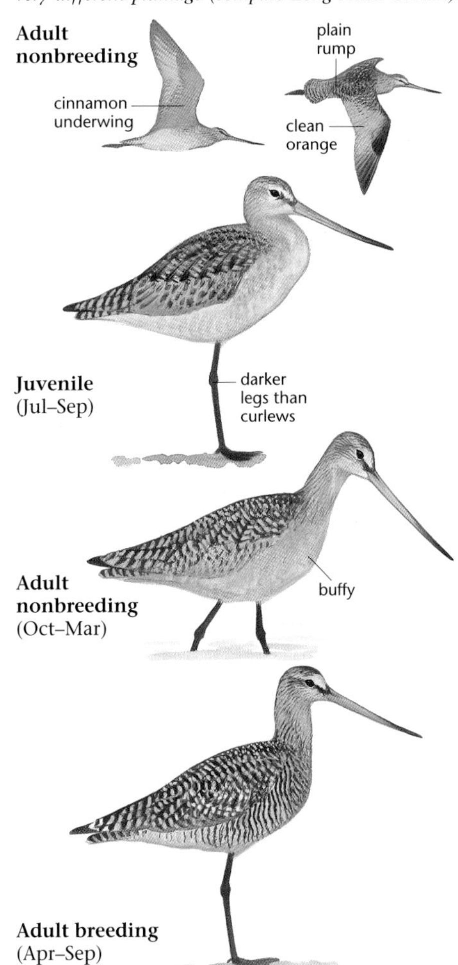

Adult nonbreeding
plain rump
cinnamon underwing
clean orange
Juvenile (Jul–Sep)
darker legs than curlews
buffy
Adult nonbreeding (Oct–Mar)
Adult breeding (Apr–Sep)

Voice: In flight tentative, hoarse, trumpeting *kweh* or *kaaWEK* like Laughing Gull; lower-pitched than other godwits. Rolling series with nasal quality *kowEto kowEto* . . . and soft *ked ked* . . . combined into long, alternating series in territorial chase.

Females of all godwits and curlews are longer-billed than males, with little overlap; females are only slightly larger in other measurements.

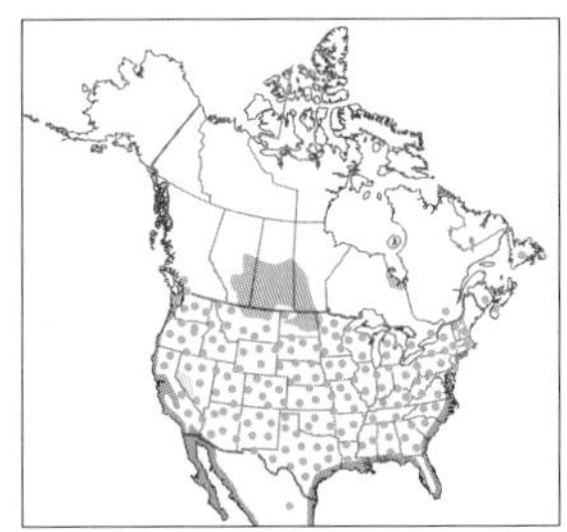

Turnstones

These closely related species are found mainly on rocky shores, Ruddy also on beaches (sometimes mudflats). Both use their short, upturned bills to flip over rocks and debris in search of food.

Ruddy Turnstone

Arenaria interpres

L 9.5" WS 21" WT 3.9 oz (110 g) ♀>♂

Both turnstones are short-legged with short, pointed bills; orange legs and calico pattern distinctive.

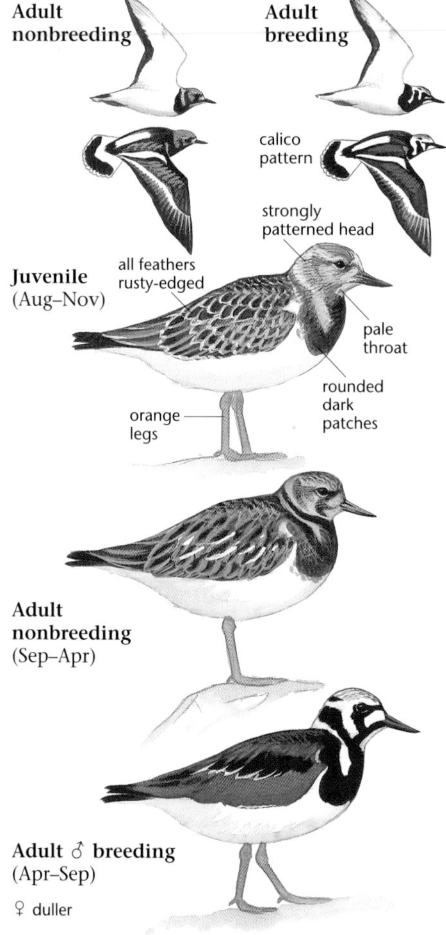
Adult nonbreeding
Adult breeding
calico pattern
strongly patterned head
all feathers rusty-edged
Juvenile (Aug–Nov)
pale throat
rounded dark patches
orange legs
Adult nonbreeding (Sep–Apr)
Adult ♂ breeding (Apr–Sep)
♀ duller

Voice: Flight call a relatively low, mellow, bouncing rattle; more nasal, harder than Short-billed Dowitcher. Also a single, sharp *klew* or hard, nasal *gaerrt.* Threat a long, low rattle *k-k-k-k-k-k-k-k.* Flight song a long, rolling rattle.

Black Turnstone

Arenaria melanocephala

L 9.25" WS 21" WT 4.2 oz (120 g) ♀>♂

Slightly bulkier than Ruddy; darker with darker legs and higher-pitched calls.

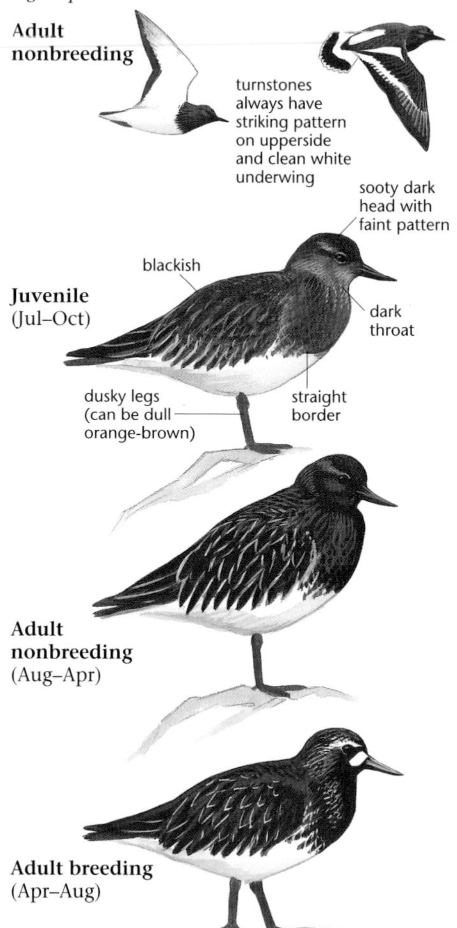
Adult nonbreeding
turnstones always have striking pattern on upperside and clean white underwing
sooty dark head with faint pattern
blackish
Juvenile (Jul–Oct)
dark throat
dusky legs (can be dull orange-brown)
straight border
Adult nonbreeding (Aug–Apr)
Adult breeding (Apr–Aug)

Voice: Flight call a shrill, high chatter *keerrt* similar to high call of Belted Kingfisher; higher and more clicking than Ruddy. Threat a long, low rattle with slight pitch changes *krkrkrkrkrkrkr . . .* ; also clear, nasal *WEEpa WEEpa WEEpa. . . .* Song a long trill or rattle, changing pitch a few times.

Wandering Tattler and Surfbird

These two distinctive species winter along rocky coasts, Wandering Tattler singly and Surfbird in flocks. Wandering Tattler nests along mountain streams, Surfbird on rocky alpine ridges.

Wandering Tattler

Heteroscelus incanus

L 11" WS 26" WT 3.9 oz (110 g)

Short-legged, long-winged, and fairly long-billed; uniform gray plumage and bobbing movements distinctive.

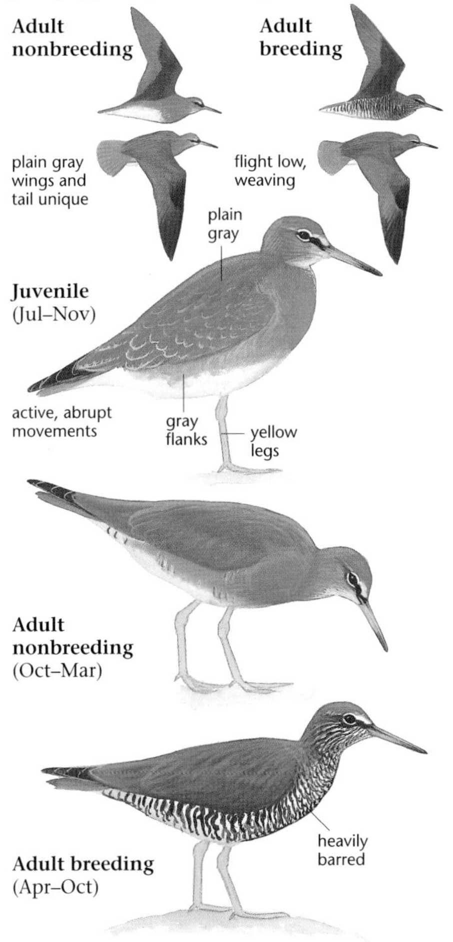

Adult nonbreeding
Adult breeding
plain gray wings and tail unique
flight low, weaving
plain gray
Juvenile (Jul–Nov)
active, abrupt movements
gray flanks
yellow legs
Adult nonbreeding (Oct–Mar)
heavily barred
Adult breeding (Apr–Oct)

Voice: Flight call a high, clear piping on one pitch, a rapid, almost unbroken trill *lidididi*; also a sharp, high *klee-ik*. Flight song a ringing, whistled *deedle-deedle-deedle-dee*.

Surfbird

Aphriza virgata

L 10" WS 26" WT 7 oz (190 g) ♀>♂

Stocky and stout-billed with short legs and striking tail pattern; larger than other "rock-pipers."

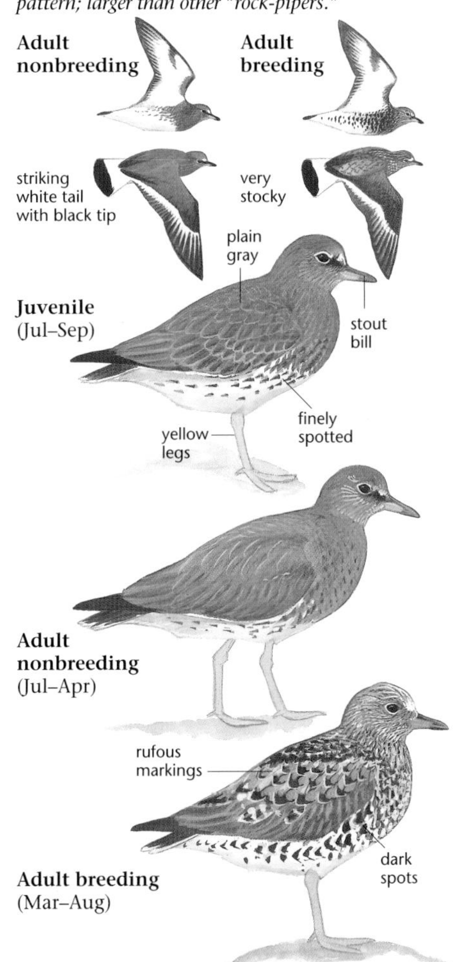

Adult nonbreeding
Adult breeding
striking white tail with black tip
very stocky
plain gray
Juvenile (Jul–Sep)
stout bill
finely spotted
yellow legs
Adult nonbreeding (Jul–Apr)
rufous markings
dark spots
Adult breeding (Mar–Aug)

Voice: Generally quiet. Flight call a soft *iif iif iff. . . .* Feeding flock gives constant chatter of high, nasal squeaks. Flight song nasal, buzzy notes in series *kwii kwii kwii kwirr kwirr kwirr kwirr skrii skrii skrii kikrrri kikrrri kikrrri kikrrri;* similar phrases given in other situations (e.g., alarm).

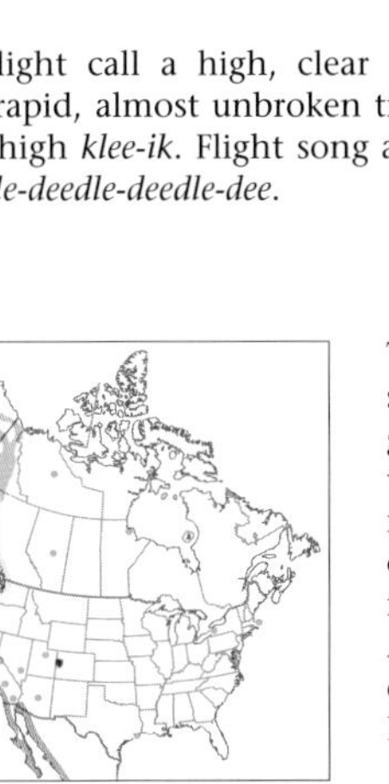

These two species, along with turnstones and Rock Sandpiper, form a group of species often found together on rocky Pacific shores and referred to as "rock-pipers." All feed on invertebrates gleaned from rocks in the intertidal zone. On the Atlantic coast the same niche is occupied by Ruddy Turnstone and Purple Sandpiper.

Rock Sandpiper

This species is very closely related to Purple Sandpiper. Both are chubby, hardy sandpipers found in small flocks gleaning food from coastal rocks, often with other "rock-pipers."

Rock Sandpiper

Calidris ptilocnemis

L 9" WS 17" WT 2.5 oz (70 g) ♀>♂

Short-winged and short-legged with medium-length, drooping bill; Dunlin-like but stockier.

PRIBILOF

Adult nonbreeding

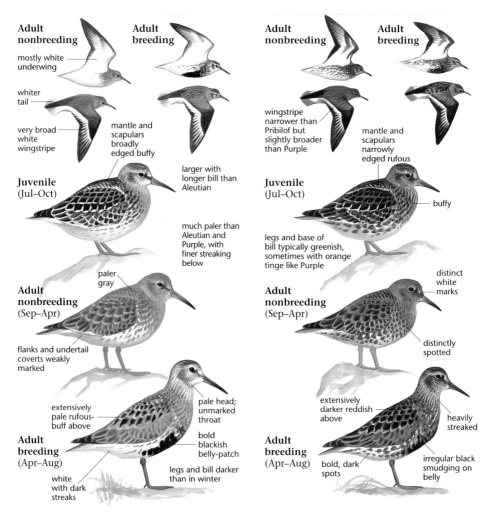

mostly white underwing

whiter tail

very broad white wingstripe

Adult breeding

mantle and scapulars broadly edged buffy

Juvenile (Jul–Oct)

larger with longer bill than Aleutian

much paler than Aleutian and Purple, with finer streaking below

Adult nonbreeding (Sep–Apr)

paler gray

flanks and undertail coverts weakly marked

Adult breeding (Apr–Aug)

extensively pale rufous-buff above

pale head; unmarked throat

bold blackish belly-patch

legs and bill darker than in winter

white with dark streaks

ALEUTIAN

Adult nonbreeding

wingstripe narrower than Pribilof but slightly broader than Purple

Adult breeding

mantle and scapulars narrowly edged rufous

Juvenile (Jul–Oct)

buffy

legs and base of bill typically greenish, sometimes with orange tinge like Purple

Adult nonbreeding (Sep–Apr)

distinct white marks

distinctly spotted

Adult breeding (Apr–Aug)

extensively darker reddish above

heavily streaked

bold, dark spots

irregular black smudging on belly

Voice: Voice not known to differ from Purple Sandpiper, though flight calls may be slightly higher-pitched. Pribilof's flight call a coarse, husky *cherk* sometimes more whistled; flight song of low, growling trills, a series of about ten rising *grreee* notes followed by similar low *grrdee* notes.

Pribilof and Aleutian populations represent extremes of variation. Many intermediates may not be safely identified. Pribilof population winters south to southeastern Alaska and is distinctively large and pale in all plumages. Aleutian birds are resident, small and dark. Birds nesting along Bering Sea coast (not shown) winter south to California; they average slightly larger and paler than Aleutian, and their breeding plumage is patterned more like Pribilof but darker.

This species is virtually identical to Aleutian Rock Sandpiper but does not overlap it in range. It is named for a purple gloss on the back feathers, visible at very close range.

Purple Sandpiper

Calidris maritima

L 9" WS 17" WT 2.5 oz (70 g) ♀>♂

Best distinguished from Aleutian Rock Sandpiper by range; differs subtly in plumage and leg color. Distinguished from Dunlin by chunky shape, dark gray color, and orange legs and bill.

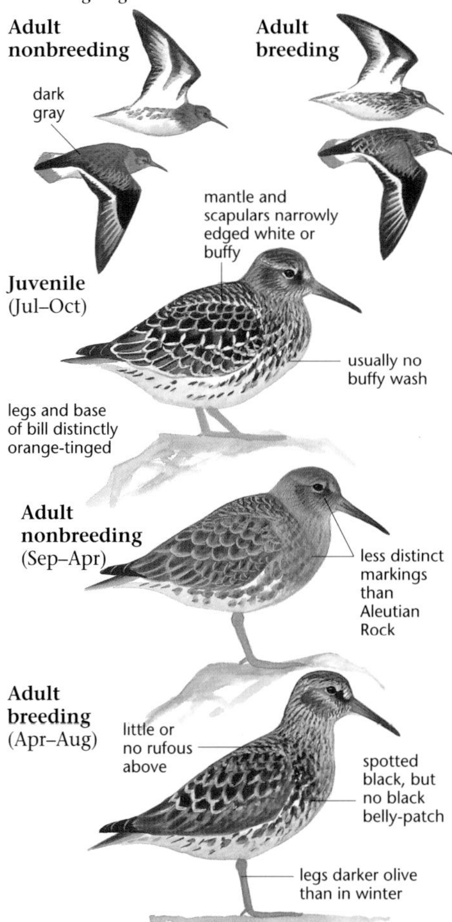
Adult nonbreeding
Adult breeding
dark gray
mantle and scapulars narrowly edged white or buffy
Juvenile (Jul–Oct)
usually no buffy wash
legs and base of bill distinctly orange-tinged
Adult nonbreeding (Sep–Apr)
less distinct markings than Aleutian Rock
Adult breeding (Apr–Aug)
little or no rufous above
spotted black, but no black belly-patch
legs darker olive than in winter

Voice: Flight call a scratchy, low *keesh* or sharper *kwititit-kwit.* Feeding birds give soft, scratchy notes. Chase call a higher-pitched *kif-kif-kif,* not very aggressive. Display song a Dunlin-like wheezing and trilling with several changes in rhythm; also rapid laugh *pupupupupu. . . .*

Aging and Identification of Shorebirds

Shorebirds undergo a series of plumage changes from juvenile to adult. Identification in the fall is often simplified by first correctly aging a bird as juvenile or adult. Fresh juvenal plumage is characterized by uniform feathers, often with bright pale fringes, and scapulars and wing coverts that are shorter and more rounded than the same feathers on adults. Plumage changes of Western Sandpiper are shown.

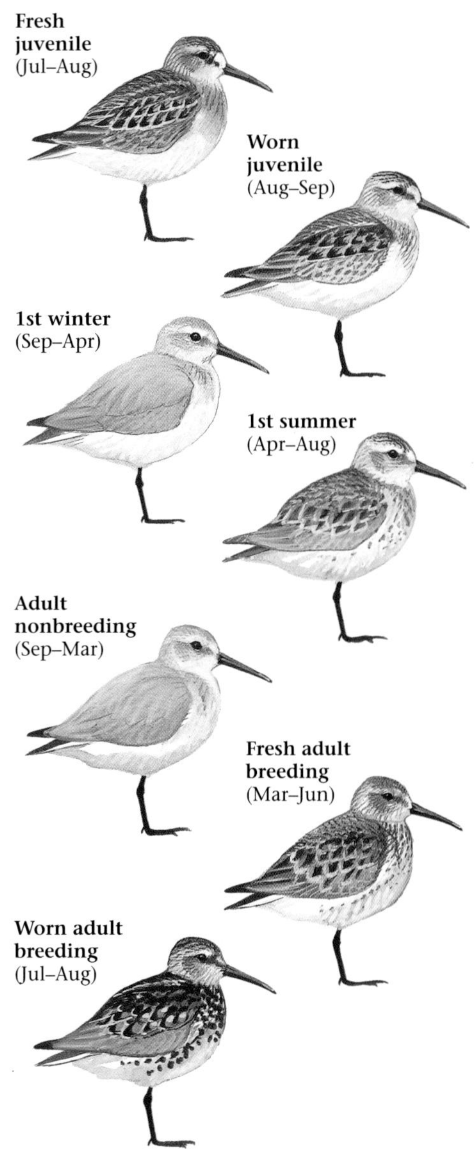
Fresh juvenile (Jul–Aug)
Worn juvenile (Aug–Sep)
1st winter (Sep–Apr)
1st summer (Apr–Aug)
Adult nonbreeding (Sep–Mar)
Fresh adult breeding (Mar–Jun)
Worn adult breeding (Jul–Aug)

These two species are distinctive and short-billed. Red Knot feeds deliberately on beaches and mudflats. Sanderling is the familiar "clockwork toy" bird seen chasing waves on sandy beaches.

Red Knot

Calidris canutus

L 10.5" WS 23" WT 4.7 oz (135 g) ♀>♂

Large, sturdy, short-billed, and long-winged.

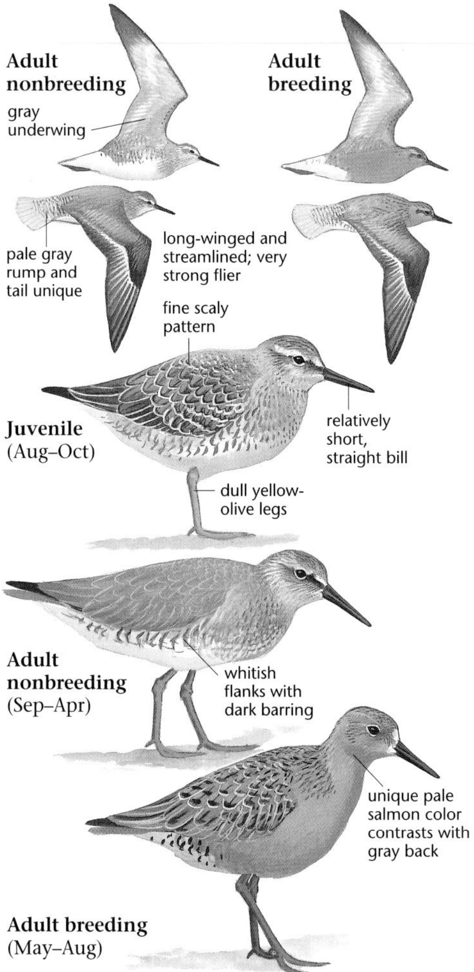
Adult nonbreeding
gray underwing
Adult breeding
pale gray rump and tail unique
long-winged and streamlined; very strong flier
fine scaly pattern
Juvenile (Aug–Oct)
relatively short, straight bill
dull yellow-olive legs
Adult nonbreeding (Sep–Apr)
whitish flanks with dark barring
unique pale salmon color contrasts with gray back
Adult breeding (May–Aug)

Voice: Usually silent; sometimes a low, husky *wett-wet.* Threat call a godwitlike *kowet-kowet.* Display song a low, husky, whistled *kwa-wee, kh-where, kh-where. . . .*

Sanderling

Calidris alba

L 8" WS 17" WT 2.1 oz (60 g) ♀>♂

Larger than peeps, short-billed; smooth running action more persistent and rapid than other sandpipers.

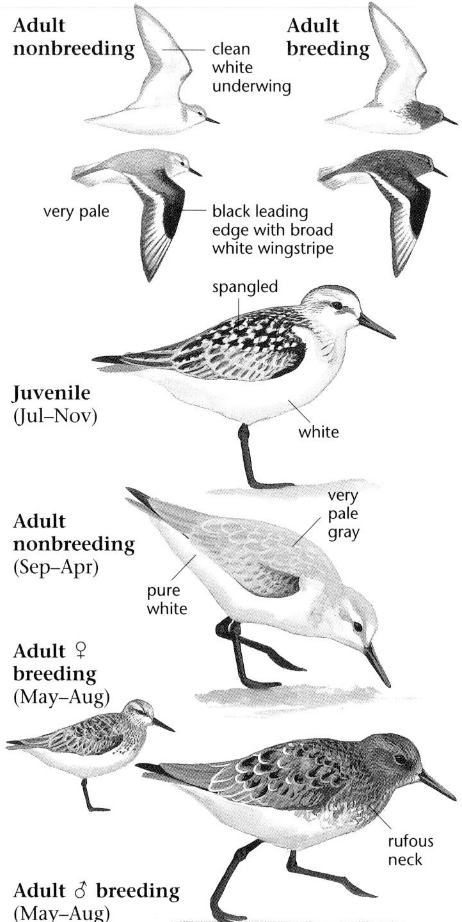
Adult nonbreeding
clean white underwing
Adult breeding
very pale
black leading edge with broad white wingstripe
spangled
Juvenile (Jul–Nov)
white
Adult nonbreeding (Sep–Apr)
very pale gray
pure white
Adult ♀ breeding (May–Aug)
rufous neck
Adult ♂ breeding (May–Aug)

Voice: Common call a short, hard *klit* or *kwit.* Feeding flock gives high, scratchy *tiv* calls. Threat a high, thin, relatively slow *twee twee twee. . . .* Flight song complex: short bursts of churring and trilling with croaking or hissing sounds.

Large *Calidris* Sandpipers (continued): Long-billed

Both of these long-billed species wade in shallow water and probe rapidly. Dunlin is found on beaches and mudflats, often in huge flocks. Curlew Sandpiper prefers freshwater pools.

Dunlin

Calidris alpina

L 8.5" WS 17" WT 2.1 oz (60 g)

Stocky, relatively large-headed, with long drooping bill. Nonbreeding plumage relatively dark brownish-gray, especially on breast.

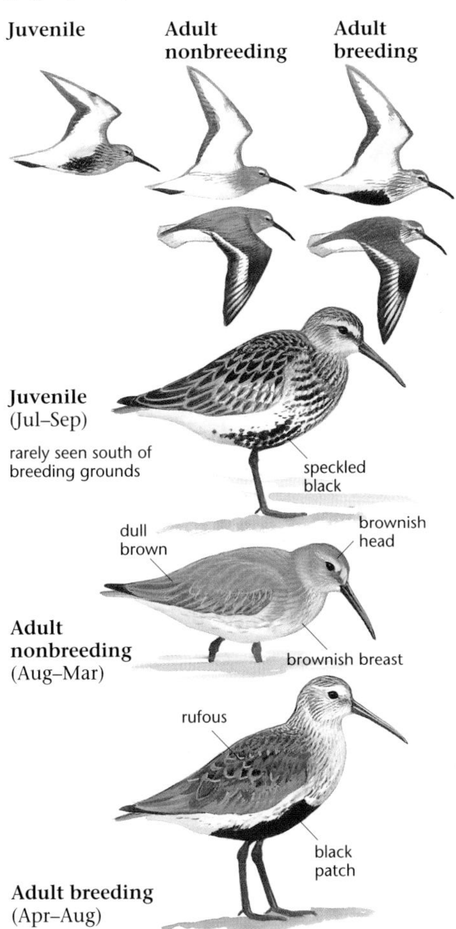

Juvenile
Adult nonbreeding
Adult breeding
Juvenile (Jul–Sep)
rarely seen south of breeding grounds
speckled black
dull brown
brownish head
Adult nonbreeding (Aug–Mar)
brownish breast
rufous
black patch
Adult breeding (Apr–Aug)

Voice: Flight call distinctive, buzzy, rasping *pjeev.* Threat call a low, hoarse *gwrr-drr-drr-drr.* Display song (often heard on migration) a series of rolling, harsh trills *jrrre jrrre jrrrrijijijijijiji jijrrr jrrr jrrr.*

Curlew Sandpiper

Calidris ferruginea

L 8.5" WS 18" WT 2.1 oz (60 g) ♀>♂

More elegant than Dunlin, with longer wings, legs, and neck; bill shape similar. More slender than Stilt Sandpiper, with shorter black legs.

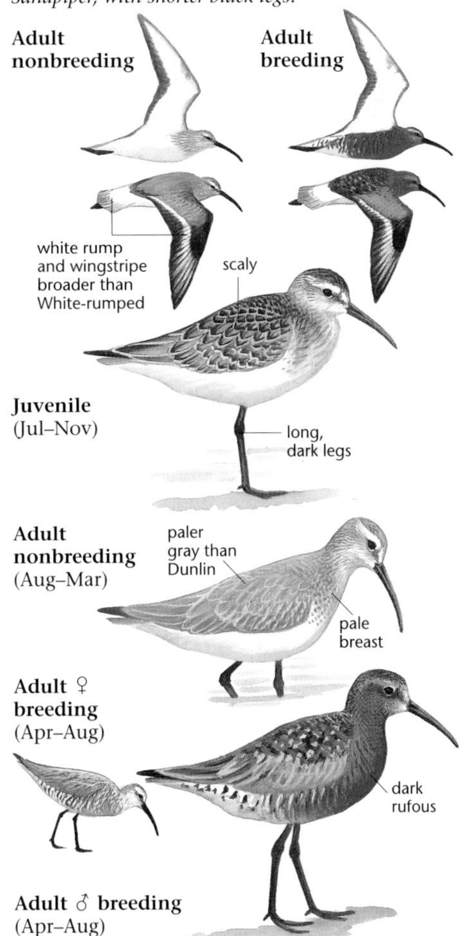

Adult nonbreeding
Adult breeding
white rump and wingstripe broader than White-rumped
scaly
Juvenile (Jul–Nov)
long, dark legs
Adult nonbreeding (Aug–Mar)
paler gray than Dunlin
pale breast
Adult ♀ breeding (Apr–Aug)
dark rufous
Adult ♂ breeding (Apr–Aug)

Voice: Flight call a soft, musical *chirrup;* more liquid than Dunlin, recalls Pectoral Sandpiper. Feeding flock gives constant chorus of low, soft notes. Song complex: chatter followed by harsh two-note phrases ending with several clear, rising *whaaay* notes; fundamentally similar to Stilt Sandpiper.

Dunlin Pacific coast populations are similar to Atlantic but lack fine streaks on rear flanks. Greenland breeding populations (recorded several times on Atlantic coast) are smaller and shorter-billed than American, drabber in breeding plumage, and paler-breasted and grayer in nonbreeding; they molt during or after fall migration.

These two similar species are found on mudflats with short grass or weedy vegetation, not often in water. They are found in small flocks and often crouch among vegetation when alarmed.

Pectoral Sandpiper

Calidris melanotos

L 8.75" WS 18" WT 2.6 oz (73 g) ♂>♀

Resembles a large Least Sandpiper in appearance and habits but longer-winged; contrasting streaked breast distinctive in all plumages.

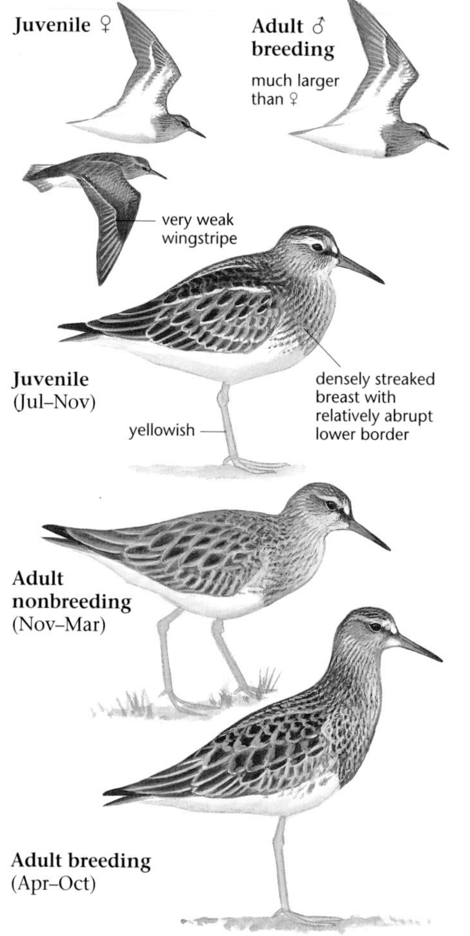

Juvenile ♀
Adult ♂ breeding
much larger than ♀
very weak wingstripe
Juvenile (Jul–Nov)
yellowish
densely streaked breast with relatively abrupt lower border
Adult nonbreeding (Nov–Mar)
Adult breeding (Apr–Oct)

Voice: Flight call a rather low, rich, reedy, harsh trill *drrup* or *jrrff*. Threat a low, soft *goit goit goit*. Display song in low flight a remarkable, rapid, foghornlike hooting *ooah ooah . . .* continuing 10 to 15 seconds; more complex harsh and hooting calls from ground.

Sharp-tailed Sandpiper

Calidris acuminata

L 8.5" WS 18" WT 2.4 oz (68 g) ♂>♀

Rare visitor from Asia; sightings are mostly of juvenile (Aug–Nov). Best distinguished from Pectoral by breast pattern.

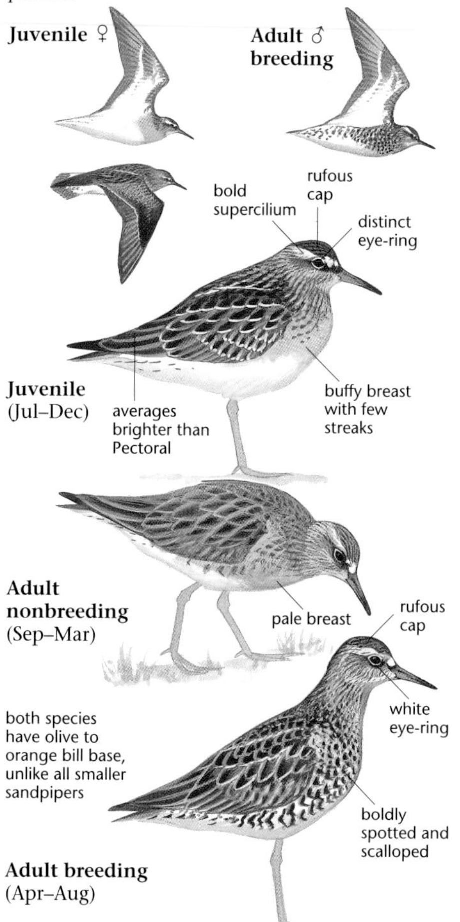

Juvenile ♀
Adult ♂ breeding
bold supercilium
rufous cap
distinct eye-ring
Juvenile (Jul–Dec)
averages brighter than Pectoral
buffy breast with few streaks
Adult nonbreeding (Sep–Mar)
pale breast
rufous cap
white eye-ring
both species have olive to orange bill base, unlike all smaller sandpipers
boldly spotted and scalloped
Adult breeding (Apr–Aug)

Voice: Flight call a soft *weep* or *cheewt;* higher, more musical than Pectoral; also high trills, often in short, twittering sequence. Flight song includes long, rhythmic trill and short, low-pitched hoot.

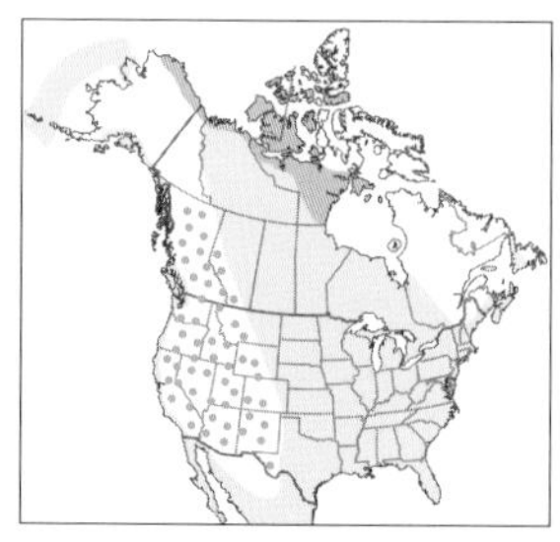

Male of both species is larger than female, especially Pectoral, in which male averages 50 percent heavier and 10 percent longer-winged than female. Other measurements are less dimorphic, so the size difference is much more obvious in flight than on the ground.

These long-winged species can be considered large peeps. White-rumped feeds with peeps, wading in deeper water and probing. Baird's picks food on dry mudflats, often separate from peeps.

White-rumped Sandpiper

Calidris fuscicollis

L 7.5" WS 17" WT 1.5 oz (42 g) ♀>♂

More robust than Baird's; wingtips project beyond tail tip. White rump always distinctive.

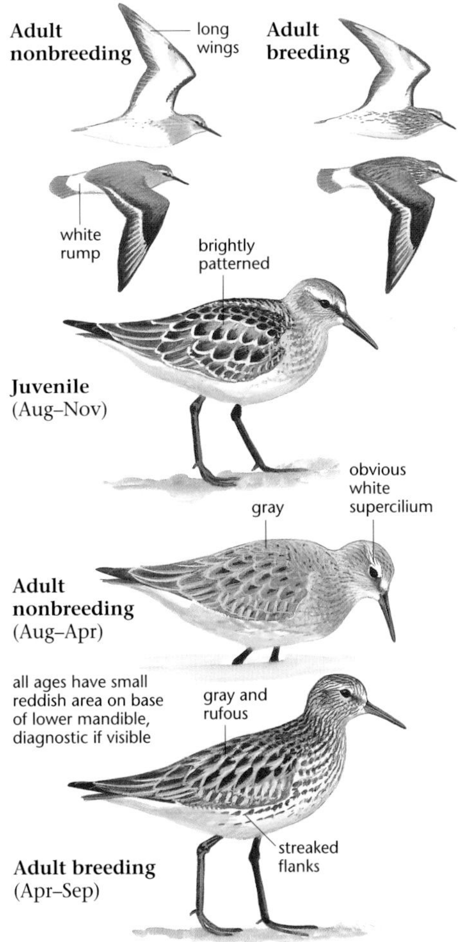
Adult nonbreeding
long wings
Adult breeding
white rump
brightly patterned
Juvenile (Aug–Nov)
obvious white supercilium
gray
Adult nonbreeding (Aug–Apr)
all ages have small reddish area on base of lower mandible, diagnostic if visible
gray and rufous
streaked flanks
Adult breeding (Apr–Sep)

Voice: Flight call distinctive, a very high, thin, mouselike squeak *tzeek* or *tseet.* Threat a very high, insectlike rattle *t-k-k-k-k-k.* Flight song extremely high, mechanical, and insectlike.

Baird's Sandpiper

Calidris bairdii

L 7.5" WS 17" WT 1.3 oz (38 g) ♀>♂

Slender, with wingtips projecting well beyond tail tip; thin, straight bill.

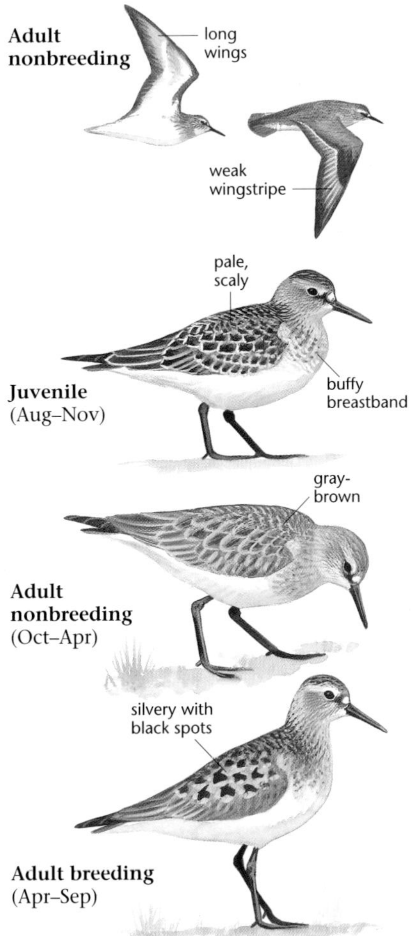
Adult nonbreeding
long wings
weak wingstripe
pale, scaly
Juvenile (Aug–Nov)
buffy breastband
gray-brown
Adult nonbreeding (Oct–Apr)
silvery with black spots
Adult breeding (Apr–Sep)

Voice: Flight call a rough *kreep;* reminiscent of Pectoral Sandpiper but higher-pitched, drier, more distinctly trilled. Flight song a series of buzzy, rising notes and long, level rattling.

Small *Calidris* Sandpipers: Peeps

These two species, similar in all plumages, are found on mudflats and beaches. Western tends to wade in deeper water and probe more methodically than Semipalmated.

Western Sandpiper

Calidris mauri

L 6.5" WS 14" WT 0.91 oz (26 g) ♀>♂

Usually longer-billed than Semipalmated; averages heavier with relatively shorter wings and longer legs, lending a subtly front-heavy appearance.

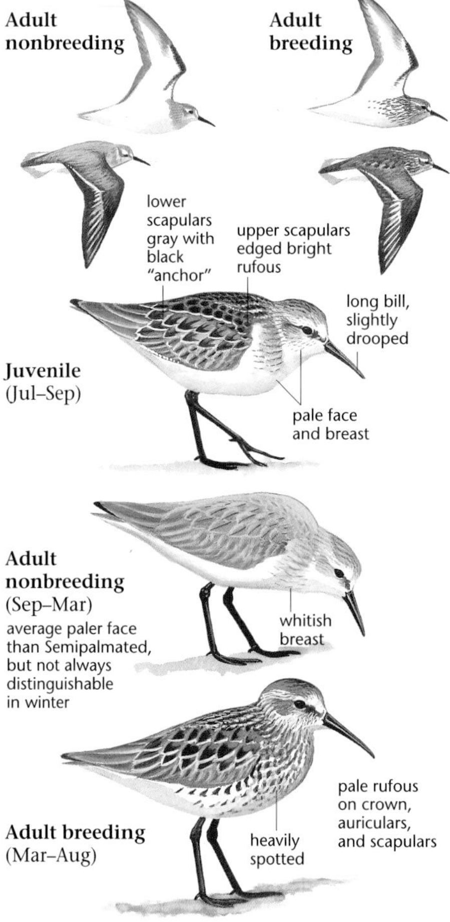
Adult nonbreeding
Adult breeding
lower scapulars gray with black "anchor"
upper scapulars edged bright rufous
long bill, slightly drooped
Juvenile (Jul–Sep)
pale face and breast
Adult nonbreeding (Sep–Mar)
average paler face than Semipalmated, but not always distinguishable in winter
whitish breast
pale rufous on crown, auriculars, and scapulars
Adult breeding (Mar–Aug)
heavily spotted

Voice: Call typically a thin, high, harsh *cheet.* Feeding flock emits a constant twitter of quiet, scratchy notes. In high aggression gives peevish, weak, rising *twee twee twee twee.* Display song scratchy, weak, thin; shorter and simpler than Semipalmated's song, with higher, weaker quality.

Semipalmated Sandpiper

Calidris pusilla

L 6.25" WS 14" WT 0.88 oz (25 g) ♀>♂

Structure similar to Western Sandpiper. Heavier than Least Sandpiper, with longer wings and legs, heavier bill.

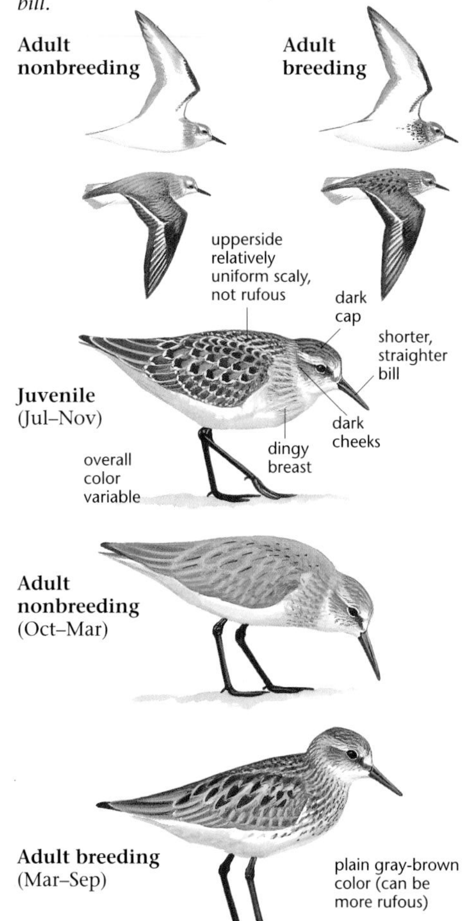
Adult nonbreeding
Adult breeding
upperside relatively uniform scaly, not rufous
dark cap
shorter, straighter bill
Juvenile (Jul–Nov)
dark cheeks
dingy breast
overall color variable
Adult nonbreeding (Oct–Mar)
Adult breeding (Mar–Sep)
plain gray-brown color (can be more rufous)

Voice: Typical flight call a short, husky *chrup* or *chrf;* also gives sharp, thin *cheet* similar to Western. Feeding flock very vocal with rapid, giggling/arguing *twee do do do do.* Display song a continuous rolling trill of varying pitches *grrridi-grrrridi. . . .*

This species, the world's smallest sandpiper, is found on mudflats in or near grassy or weedy vegetation, rarely wading. It is found in smaller flocks and on smaller wetlands than other peeps.

Least Sandpiper

Calidris minutilla

L 6" WS 13" WT 0.7 oz (20 g)

Very small; relatively small-headed with thin, pointed bill. Short legs; crouching posture.

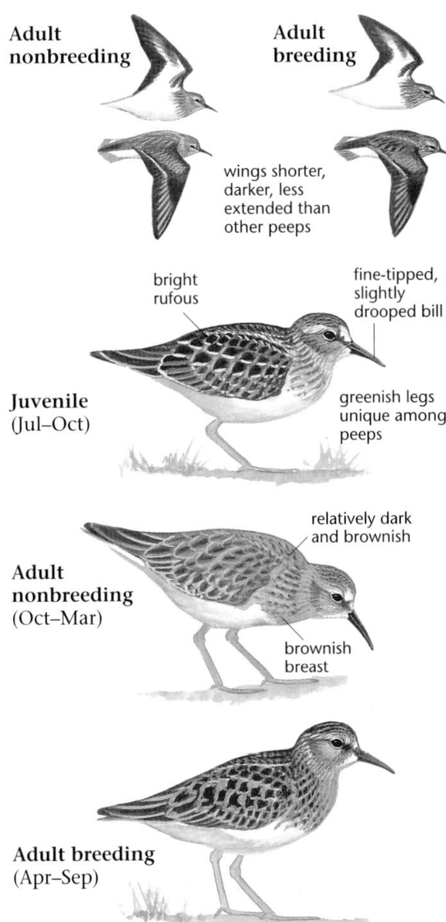
Adult nonbreeding
Adult breeding
wings shorter, darker, less extended than other peeps
bright rufous
fine-tipped, slightly drooped bill
Juvenile (Jul–Oct)
greenish legs unique among peeps
relatively dark and brownish
Adult nonbreeding (Oct–Mar)
brownish breast
Adult breeding (Apr–Sep)

Voice: Typical flight call a high, trilled *prreep;* gentle, rising, and musical. Flock in wheeling flight gives short, weak, high notes in rapid twittering chorus. Threat rapid, giggling, high *didididi.* Display song similar to dowitchers: *b-b-b-trree-trree-trree;* each phrase rising but the series level.

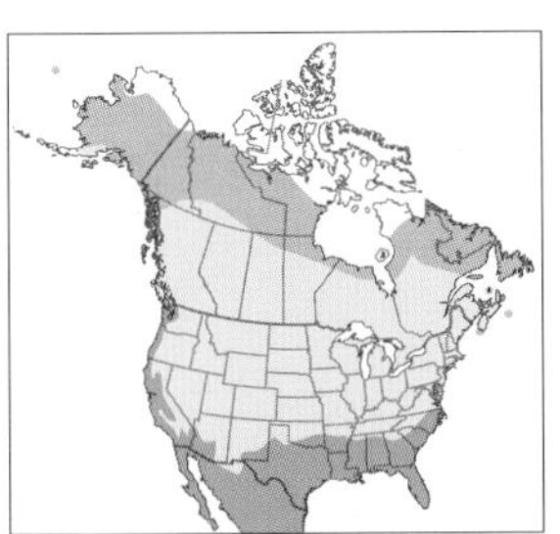

Identification of Peeps

Often occurring in distant mixed flocks, active and variable, Semipalmated, Western, and Least Sandpipers are always challenging to identify. Add to this the frustration of trying to pick out a reported stint or other rarity, and it is no wonder that many birders simply pass them all off as peeps. Experience and careful study of plumage and shape is the surest way to identify peeps.

In the fall, molt provides a very useful clue. Western molts earlier, with many in pale gray nonbreeding plumage by Sep. Semipalmated molts later, retaining some breeding or juvenal plumage into Nov. A flock of uniform gray peeps Sep–Oct are probably Western Sandpipers; a flock of patchy worn birds Sep–Oct are probably Semipalmated.

The darker brownish Least shows little contrast between breeding and nonbreeding plumage and generally appears uniform brownish above. A contrasting salt-and-pepper pattern indicates Western or Semipalmated.

The plumages of juvenile peeps are far more variable than illustrated in this book. Semipalmated is especially variable, with overall color ranging from grayish to golden to rufous-buff. Details of feather pattern and body proportions are more reliable for identification.

Bill length and shape is variable within each species of peep, but differs on average between species. The range of variation in Western and Semipalmated, and the typical bill shape of Least, are shown below. Bill of Western averages longest, with a slight droop and relatively thin tip. Semipalmated averages shorter and straighter than Western but overlaps and tends to be thicker-tipped. Least has a thinner bill overall, with a slight droop and very thin tip.

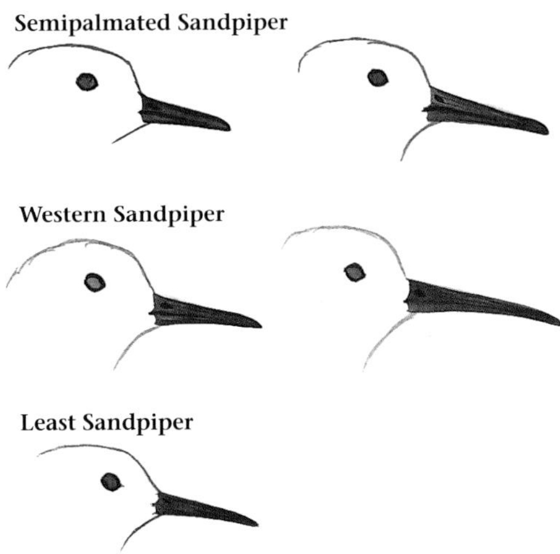
Semipalmated Sandpiper
Western Sandpiper
Least Sandpiper

Small *Calidris* Sandpipers: Peeps (continued)

These two species, rare visitors from Eurasia, are usually seen with other peeps. Only breeding adults are readily identified; identification of other plumages requires very careful study.

Red-necked Stint

Calidris ruficollis

L 6.25" WS 14" WT 0.88 oz (25 g) ♀>♂

Relatively long-winged and short-legged; bill a little thinner than Semipalmated Sandpiper.

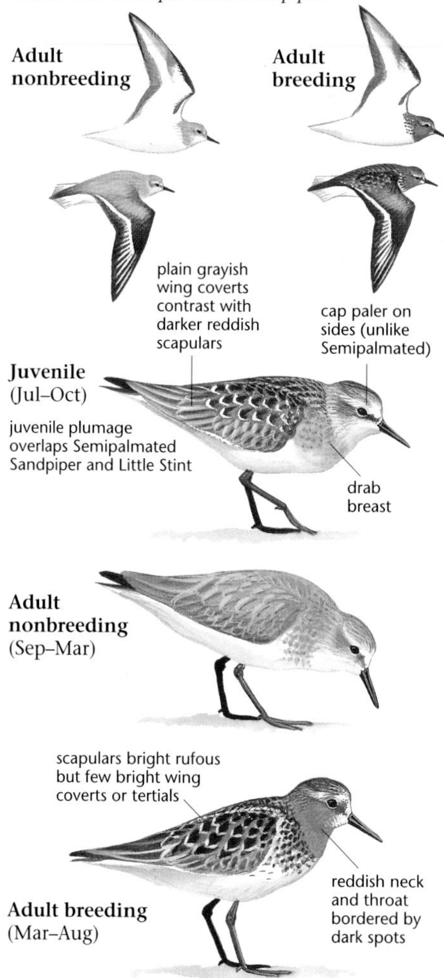

Adult nonbreeding
Adult breeding
plain grayish wing coverts contrast with darker reddish scapulars
cap paler on sides (unlike Semipalmated)
Juvenile (Jul–Oct)
juvenile plumage overlaps Semipalmated Sandpiper and Little Stint
drab breast
Adult nonbreeding (Sep–Mar)
scapulars bright rufous but few bright wing coverts or tertials
Adult breeding (Mar–Aug)
reddish neck and throat bordered by dark spots

Voice: Flight call a high, scraping *quiit* most like Western Sandpiper but huskier; variable and may overlap with other species. Threat unknown. Display song a long, steady repetition of short *yek* notes or low, almost whistled *huee huee huee . . .* series.

Little Stint

Calidris minuta

L 6" WS 14" WT 0.84 oz (24 g) ♀>♂

Relatively short-winged and long-legged with thin bill; small and active with darting movements.

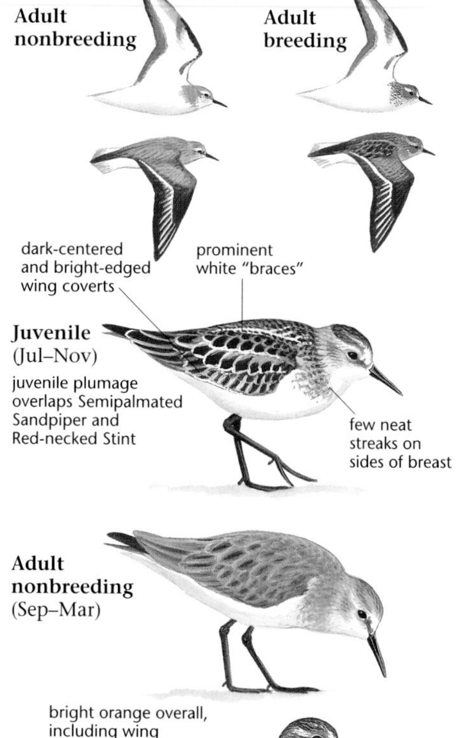

Adult nonbreeding
Adult breeding
dark-centered and bright-edged wing coverts
prominent white "braces"
Juvenile (Jul–Nov)
juvenile plumage overlaps Semipalmated Sandpiper and Red-necked Stint
few neat streaks on sides of breast
Adult nonbreeding (Sep–Mar)
bright orange overall, including wing coverts and tertials
white throat
Adult breeding (Mar–Aug)
breast washed with orange over dark spots

Voice: Flight call a thin, short *tit* or *stit;* other variations similar to Red-necked. Threat a high, weak, level *tee tee tee tee.* Display song includes series of high, thin, squeaky notes *tsee-tsee-tsee . . . ;* recalls distant Arctic Tern courtship.

Stint identification is very challenging, with many pitfalls for the overeager. It is essential to understand variation in these two species as well as the wide variation among common sandpipers. Beware of confusion with breeding-plumaged Sanderling and especially with fresh juvenile sandpipers (e.g., Least) appearing in Jul among worn adults.

Ruff

This rare but regular Eurasian visitor is found in grassy or muddy pools, often with dowitchers or Pectoral Sandpiper, but is taller, more active, and often wading, recalling *Tringa* sandpipers.

Ruff

Philomachus pugnax

L 11" WS 21" WT 5 oz (150 g)

Plumage and size quite variable; male averages 20 percent larger than female. Structure is subtly distinctive: plump body with long legs, relatively small head, and short bill.

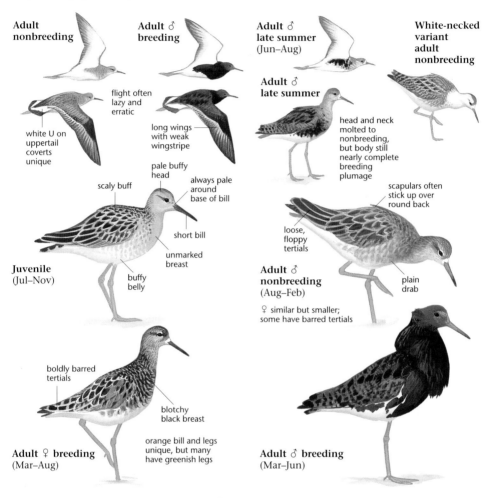

Adult nonbreeding

flight often lazy and erratic

white U on uppertail coverts unique

Adult ♂ breeding

long wings with weak wingstripe

Adult ♂ late summer (Jun–Aug)

Adult ♂ late summer

head and neck molted to nonbreeding, but body still nearly complete breeding plumage

White-necked variant adult nonbreeding

Juvenile (Jul–Nov)

scaly buff

pale buffy head

always pale around base of bill

short bill

unmarked breast

buffy belly

Adult ♂ nonbreeding (Aug–Feb)

scapulars often stick up over round back

loose, floppy tertials

plain drab

♀ similar but smaller; some have barred tertials

Adult ♀ breeding (Mar–Aug)

boldly barred tertials

blotchy black breast

orange bill and legs unique, but many have greenish legs

Adult ♂ breeding (Mar–Jun)

Voice: Essentially silent. Flight call (rarely heard) a muffled croak or low grunt; sometimes a shrill, rising *hoo-ee*.

Adult ♂ breeding in display posture, showing plumage variation.

Stilt Sandpiper and Long-billed Dowitcher

Stilt Sandpiper combines features of dowitchers and *Tringa* sandpipers. It wades in sheltered muddy pools, often with dowitchers. Long-billed Dowitcher is very similar to Short-billed.

Stilt Sandpiper

Calidris himantopus

L 8.5" WS 18" WT 2 oz (58 g) ♀>♂

Smaller than dowitchers, with long legs and shorter, drooping bill; appears large-headed.

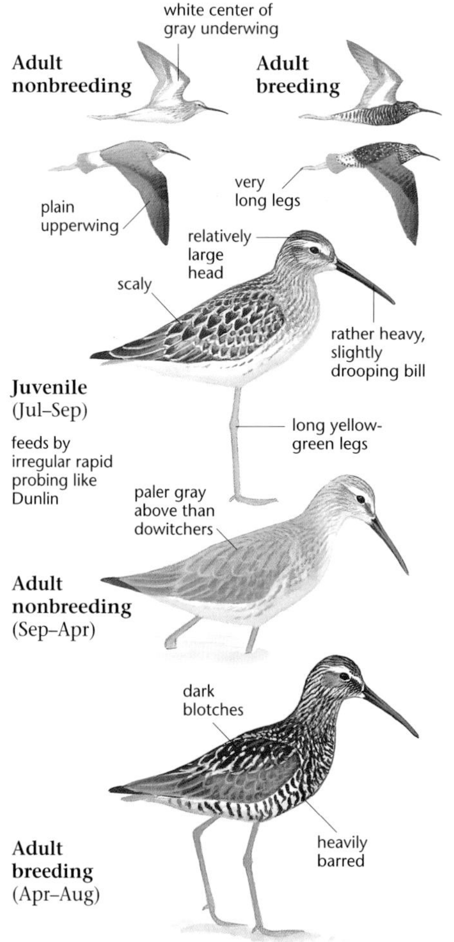

white center of gray underwing
Adult nonbreeding
Adult breeding
plain upperwing
very long legs
relatively large head
scaly
rather heavy, slightly drooping bill
Juvenile (Jul–Sep)
long yellow-green legs
feeds by irregular rapid probing like Dunlin
paler gray above than dowitchers
Adult nonbreeding (Sep–Apr)
dark blotches
heavily barred
Adult breeding (Apr–Aug)

Voice: Flight call a low, soft, muffled, husky *toof* or *jeew,* a quiet background noise among Lesser Yellowlegs; also a sharper, wheezy *keewf* or a clearer, godwitlike *koooWI.* Display song a remarkable series of nasal, dry, buzzy trills (quality like Surfbird).

Long-billed Dowitcher

Limnodromus scolopaceus

L 11.5" WS 19" WT 4 oz (115 g) ♀>♂

Dowitchers are stocky, long-billed, with white upper rump. Compare Short-billed; the two species best distinguished by flight call.

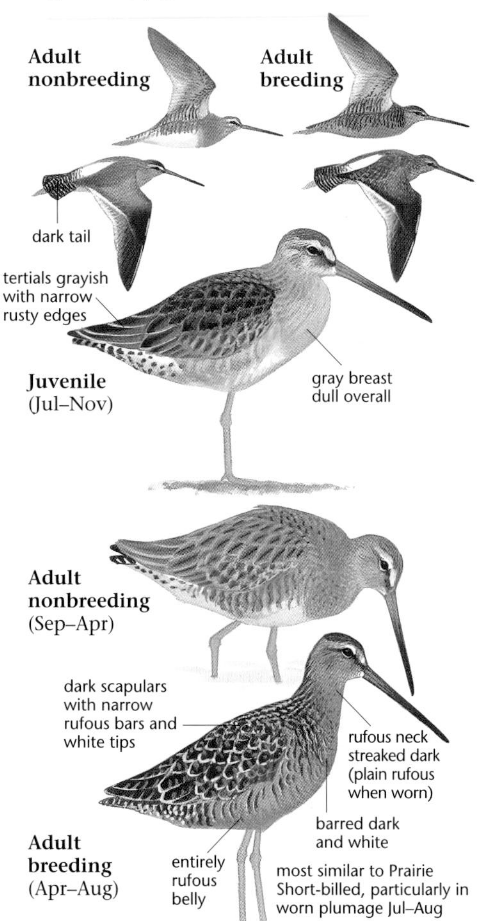

Adult nonbreeding
Adult breeding
dark tail
tertials grayish with narrow rusty edges
Juvenile (Jul–Nov)
gray breast dull overall
Adult nonbreeding (Sep–Apr)
dark scapulars with narrow rufous bars and white tips
rufous neck streaked dark (plain rufous when worn)
barred dark and white
Adult breeding (Apr–Aug)
entirely rufous belly
most similar to Prairie Short-billed, particularly in worn plumage Jul–Aug

Voice: Flight call a high, sharp *keek* or *pweek,* sometimes repeated in accelerating quick, sharp series *kik-kik-kik-kik.* Flock gives constant, soft chatter while feeding (Short-billed flock is quiet). Display song rapid and buzzy; sharper and higher than Short-billed.

When feeding, Stilt Sandpiper's (left) longer legs and shorter bill force it to lean farther forward than dowitchers (right).

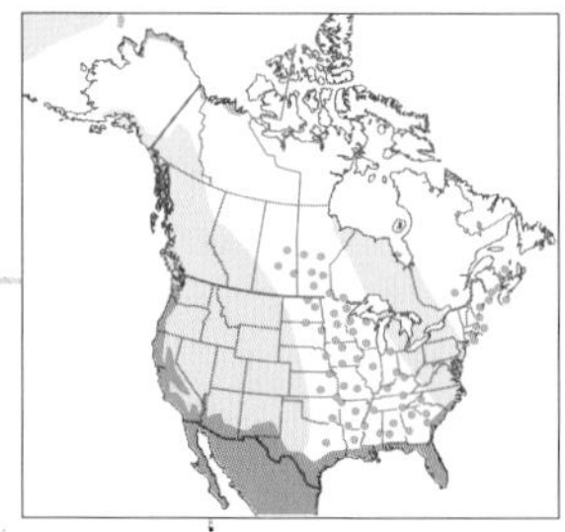

SHORT-BILLED DOWITCHER

The two dowitchers are found in large flocks on mudflats and shallow ponds. Short-billed favors beaches and mudflats, Long-billed grassy freshwater pools, but there is much overlap.

Short-billed Dowitcher

Limnodromus griseus

L 11" WS 19" WT 3.9 oz (110 g) ♀>♂

Very similar to Long-billed and best identified by flight call; averages smaller, slimmer, longer-winged, shorter-legged, and shorter-billed but much overlap; only the longest-billed Long-billed individuals are reliably identified by structure. Breeding adult identified by breast pattern, juvenile by tertial pattern.

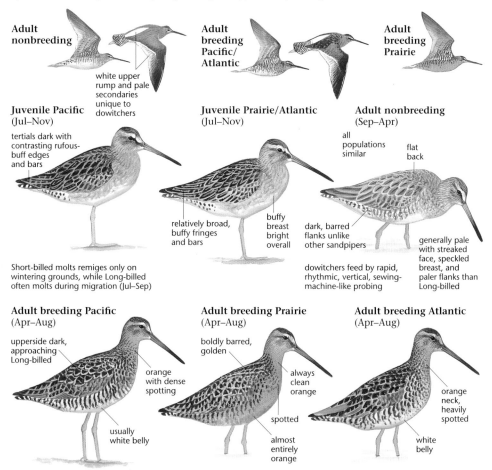

Adult nonbreeding

white upper rump and pale secondaries unique to dowitchers

Adult breeding Pacific/ Atlantic

Adult breeding Prairie

Juvenile Pacific (Jul–Nov)

tertials dark with contrasting rufous-buff edges and bars

Juvenile Prairie/Atlantic (Jul–Nov)

relatively broad, buffy fringes and bars

buffy breast bright overall

Adult nonbreeding (Sep–Apr)

all populations similar

flat back

dark, barred flanks unlike other sandpipers

generally pale with streaked face, speckled breast, and paler flanks than Long-billed

Short-billed molts remiges only on wintering grounds, while Long-billed often molts during migration (Jul–Sep)

dowitchers feed by rapid, rhythmic, vertical, sewing-machine-like probing

Adult breeding Pacific (Apr–Aug)

upperside dark, approaching Long-billed

orange with dense spotting

usually white belly

Adult breeding Prairie (Apr–Aug)

boldly barred, golden

always clean orange

spotted

almost entirely orange

Adult breeding Atlantic (Apr–Aug)

orange neck, heavily spotted

white belly

Voice: All calls lower than Long-billed. Flight call liquid, rapid *kewtutu* or *tlututu,* slightly descending; also harder, level *kitititi;* always faster than Lesser Yellowlegs; cadence recalls Ruddy Turnstone. Feeding flock is normally silent, but occasionally a single *tu* is heard (feeding Long-billed flock gives constant chatter of soft, high notes). Display song similar to Long-billed Dowitcher and Least Sandpiper: *gididi drreee drrooo,* each phrase slightly rising but the series falling (Least Sandpiper series is level).

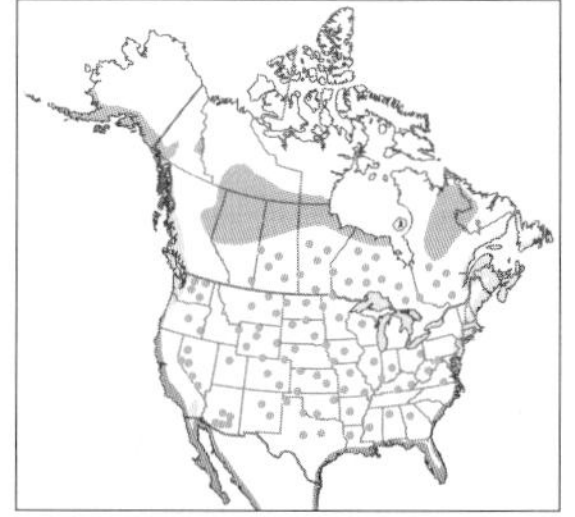

Three populations largely separated by range, but some overlap and some intergrades. In breeding plumage Pacific and Atlantic populations are very similar, with white belly, heavily spotted neck and breast, and narrow reddish fringes on upperparts (Pacific averages darker overall). Prairie population is brighter, with little or no white on belly, limited dark spotting on breast, and broader buff fringes on upperparts. Juvenile Pacific averages darker on the breast, with narrower and darker rufous fringes above than Prairie and Atlantic.

Buff-breasted Sandpiper and American Woodcock

Buff-breasted Sandpiper is found mainly on dry, short-grass habitats. American Woodcock is found in damp, brushy woods; displaying birds choose grassy or brushy fields nearby.

Buff-breasted Sandpiper

Tryngites subruficollis

L 8.25" WS 18" WT 2.2 oz (63 g) ♂>♀

Slender and delicate; very long-winged. Plain upperside and clean buffy breast distinctive; compare Ruff and Pectoral Sandpiper.

Juvenile

Adult

dark rump; plain upperside

pale upper primary coverts

scaly pattern

short bill

plain pale face with obvious dark eye

Juvenile (Aug–Nov)

pale buffy breast with dark spots

yellow legs

Adult nonbreeding (Oct–Mar)

Adult breeding (Apr–Oct)

Voice: Flight call a quiet *greet* similar to Pectoral and Baird's Sandpipers but dry, rattling; also a short *chup* and quiet *tik*. Display includes rapid clicking noises.

American Woodcock

Scolopax minor

L 11" WS 18" WT 7 oz (200 g) ♀>♂

Plump with long bill; large head; broad, rounded wings; short legs. Solitary and secretive with cryptic pattern, unlike any other shorebird.

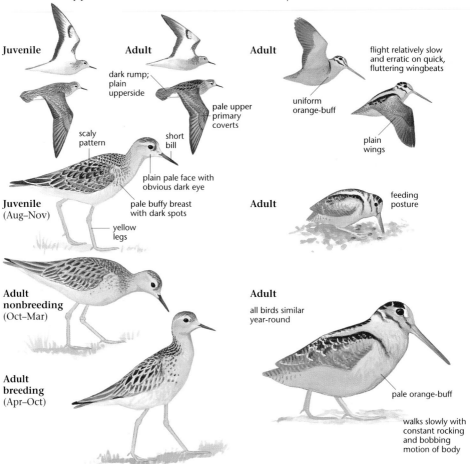

Adult

flight relatively slow and erratic on quick, fluttering wingbeats

uniform orange-buff

plain wings

Adult

feeding posture

Adult

all birds similar year-round

pale orange-buff

walks slowly with constant rocking and bobbing motion of body

Voice: Flight call absent. Wings produce a high twittering on takeoff and when making sharp turns in flight; higher-pitched and clearer than Mourning Dove. Displaying bird on ground gives explosive, very nasal *beent* similar to Common Nighthawk but level, less harsh.

COMMON SNIPE

This cryptically patterned, usually solitary, and somewhat secretive species is found in any damp, muddy habitat where vegetation provides some cover; it is usually seen at edges of shallow ponds.

Common Snipe

Gallinago gallinago

L 10.5" WS 18" WT 3.7 oz (105 g) ♀>♂

Very stocky, short-winged, and short-legged but long-billed. Stockier and less active than dowitchers, with boldly striped back.

AMERICAN

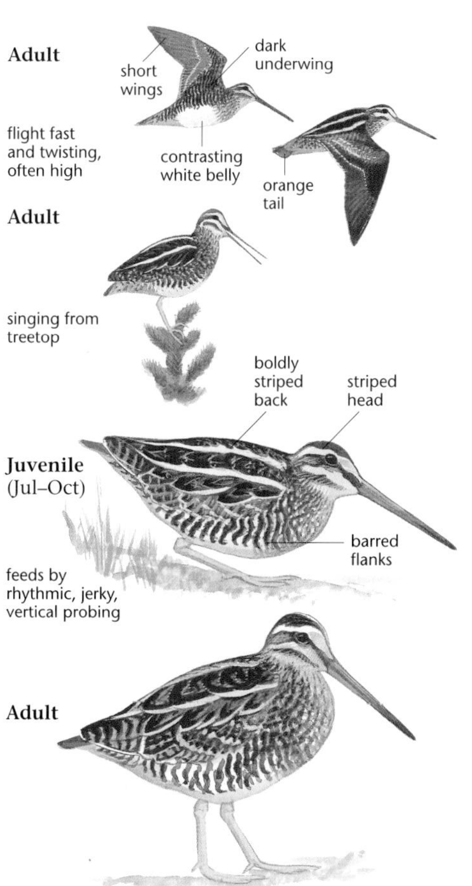

Adult
short wings
dark underwing
flight fast and twisting, often high
contrasting white belly
orange tail
Adult
singing from treetop
boldly striped back
striped head
Juvenile (Jul–Oct)
barred flanks
feeds by rhythmic, jerky, vertical probing
Adult

Voice: Flight call a dry, harsh, scraping *scresh* or *kesh.* Display song from perch a loud *TIKa TIKa TIKa* . . . or *kit kit kit.* . . . In winnowing flight display outer tail feathers produce hollow, low whistle *huhuhuhuhuhuhuhuhuhu* very similar to Boreal Owl's song.

EURASIAN

Very similar to American: differs in wing markings. Also has broader outer tail feathers and usually 14 tail feathers (vs. 16), but these tail features rarely visible in the field.

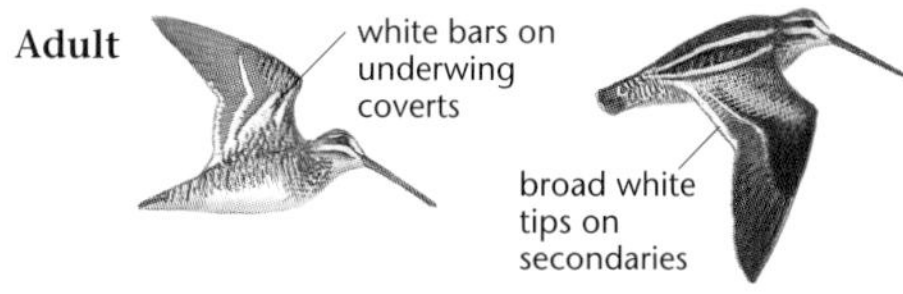

Adult
white bars on underwing coverts
broad white tips on secondaries

Voice: Calls may average slightly higher-pitched than American but similar. Winnowing flight display, by virtue of broader outer tail feathers, is much lower-pitched, a resonant pulsing sound, bearing little resemblance to the hollow whistle of American birds.

AERIAL DISPLAYS OF SNIPE AND WOODCOCK

Common Snipe winnowing flight display

Winnowing flight display of Common Snipe is performed day or night by birds circling high in the air, then suddenly diving down at high speed. The rush of air past the outspread outer tail feathers produces a low, pulsing, whistling sound.

Flight display of American Woodcock is performed at night over open, brushy fields. The movement of air over the narrow outer primaries produces a high twitter. It begins with steady twittering as the bird rises, becoming well-spaced bursts of twittering while bird circles at top of climb. Finally, as the bird plunges toward the ground with sharp changes in direction, a series of louder and more varied chirps results: *tewp tilp tiptooptip.* . . .

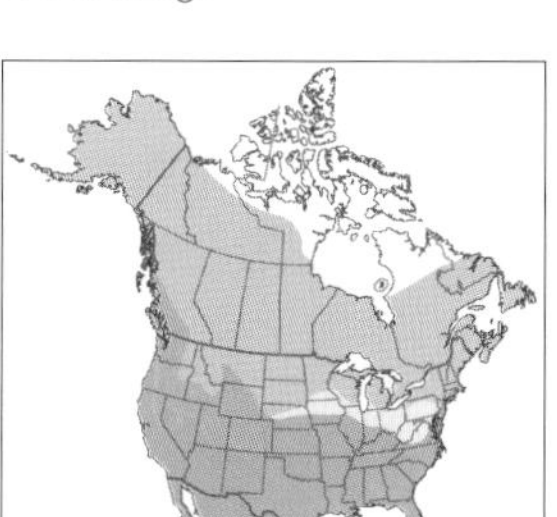

EURASIAN

PHALAROPES

Though closely related to other phalaropes, the distinctive Wilson's Phalarope is superficially more like *Tringa* sandpipers. It is found on shallow, muddy or grassy pools and mudflats, never at sea.

Identification of Phalaropes

The three species in this genus have lobed toes and other distinctive features and at times have been considered a separate family. Females, which are larger and more brightly colored than males, leave after egg-laying, and the males incubate the eggs and raise the young alone.

Phalaropes feed by picking minute food items from the surface of the water. They are very active and nervous, darting and jabbing constantly. They often swim (other sandpipers do so only occasionally) and when swimming often spin rapidly in tight circles to create an upwelling that raises food items to the surface.

Red-necked Phalarope spinning

Stilt Sandpiper and Lesser Yellowlegs are superficially similar to Wilson's Phalarope in nonbreeding plumage but have very different foraging actions. Wilson's Phalarope is very active, with nervous picking actions, often leaning, crouching, and darting; it is also brighter white and pale gray (other species are drabber). Stilt Sandpiper has much more methodical probing actions. Lesser Yellowlegs is often quite active, dashing and jabbing at prey, but is more elegant and graceful and less erratic than Wilson's Phalarope.

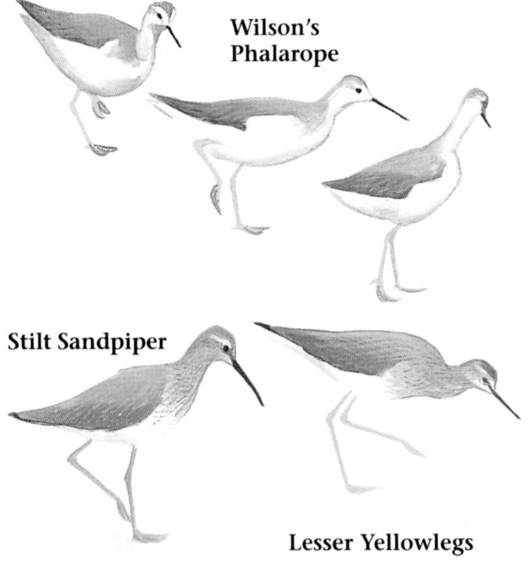
Wilson's Phalarope
Stilt Sandpiper
Lesser Yellowlegs

Wilson's Phalarope

Phalaropus tricolor

L 9.25" WS 17" WT 2.1 oz (60 g) ♀>♂

Overall slender; long-legged, small-headed with thin, needlelike bill. Shape and habits more like Tringa *sandpipers than other phalaropes.*

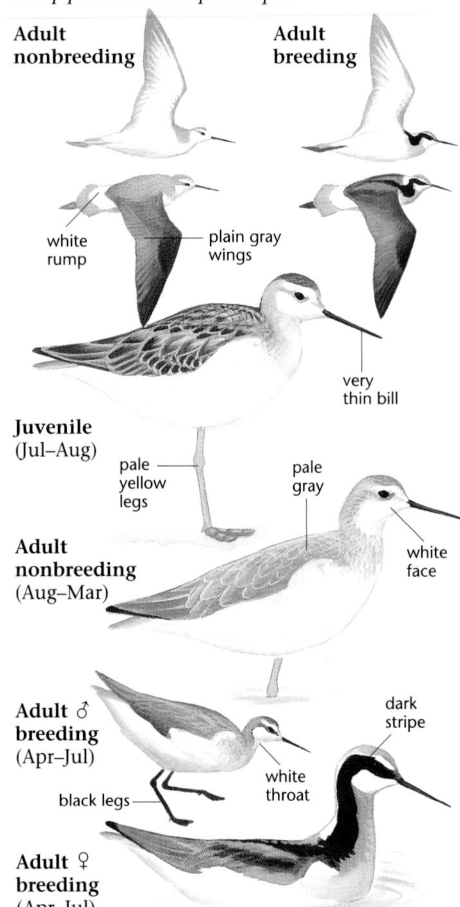
Adult nonbreeding
Adult breeding
white rump
plain gray wings
very thin bill
Juvenile (Jul–Aug)
pale yellow legs
pale gray
white face
Adult nonbreeding (Aug–Mar)
Adult ♂ breeding (Apr–Jul)
dark stripe
white throat
black legs
Adult ♀ breeding (Apr–Jul)

Voice: Flight call a low, muffled, nasal grunting or moaning *wemf, vint,* or *vimp;* soft but distinctive, reminiscent of muffled Black Skimmer.

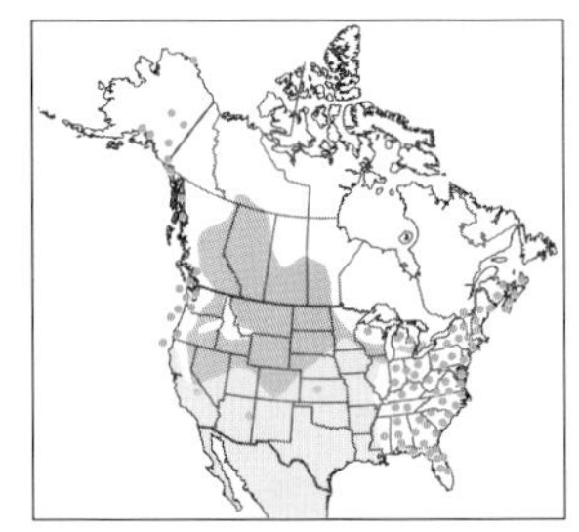

These two species nest on tundra ponds and winter in small flocks along weed lines on open ocean. Red is always rare inland; Red-necked occurs in large numbers on western lakes in the fall.

Red Phalarope

Phalaropus fulicaria

L 8.5" WS 17" WT 1.9 oz (55 g) ♀>♂

Larger, longer-winged, shorter-legged, larger-headed, and much thicker-billed than Red-necked.

Adult nonbreeding
Adult breeding
mostly white underwing
Molting adult
heavy bill, pale at base
Juvenile (Jul–Oct)
relatively short legs
paler gray
Adult nonbreeding (Sep–Apr)
white cheeks
Adult ♂ breeding (Apr–Sep)
Adult ♀ breeding (Apr–Sep)
rufous

Voice: Flight call a distinct, high *piik;* higher and clearer than Red-necked; like flat Long-billed Dowitcher; also a softer *dreet.* On breeding grounds a high, rising *sweeep,* a bit tinny and nasal at start but finishing high and clear; also often a high, rough, buzzy *jeeer* and *pity pity pity pity.*

Red-necked Phalarope

Phalaropus lobatus

L 7.75" WS 15" WT 1.2 oz (35 g) ♀>♂

Small and compact; much thinner-billed than Red. Many plumage features differ.

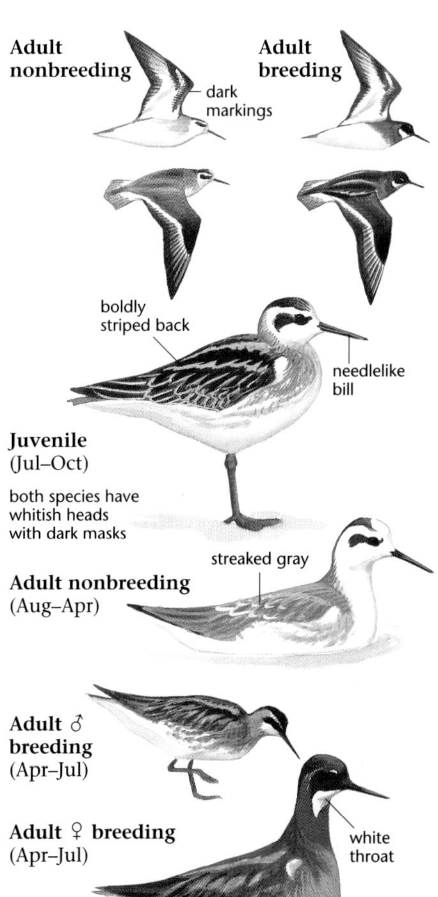
Adult nonbreeding
Adult breeding
dark markings
boldly striped back
needlelike bill
Juvenile (Jul–Oct)
both species have whitish heads with dark masks
streaked gray
Adult nonbreeding (Aug–Apr)
Adult ♂ breeding (Apr–Jul)
Adult ♀ breeding (Apr–Jul)
white throat

Voice: Flight call a short, hard *kett;* sharper, higher, and harder than Sanderling; flatter than Red; at times strongly reminiscent of icterids (e.g., Brewer's Blackbird). Various other buzzy calls given on breeding grounds.

JAEGERS AND SKUAS
Family: Laridae

5 species in 1 genus. Closely related to gulls and in the same family, these species are primarily oceanic, coming to land only when nesting. On nesting grounds they are predatory, feeding on lemmings, small birds, and other animal prey. At other seasons they acquire much of their food by piracy, forcing other seabirds to relinquish fish they have captured. The actions of a jaeger or skua chasing its victim are characteristic, although certain gulls (especially Laughing and Heermann's) engage in the same pirating behavior. Adults are distinctive, but subadult jaegers and skuas can be very difficult to identify, and many birds seen distantly or briefly must be left unidentified. The complex variation of color morphs and ages of all species renders plumage characteristics confusing and subjective, although certain details of pattern and color are fairly reliable. Wing, tail, and bill proportions are always important but should not be relied upon. Identification should be approached cautiously and based on a combination of characteristics. Compare gulls, terns, falcons, shearwaters, and gadfly petrels. Juveniles are shown.

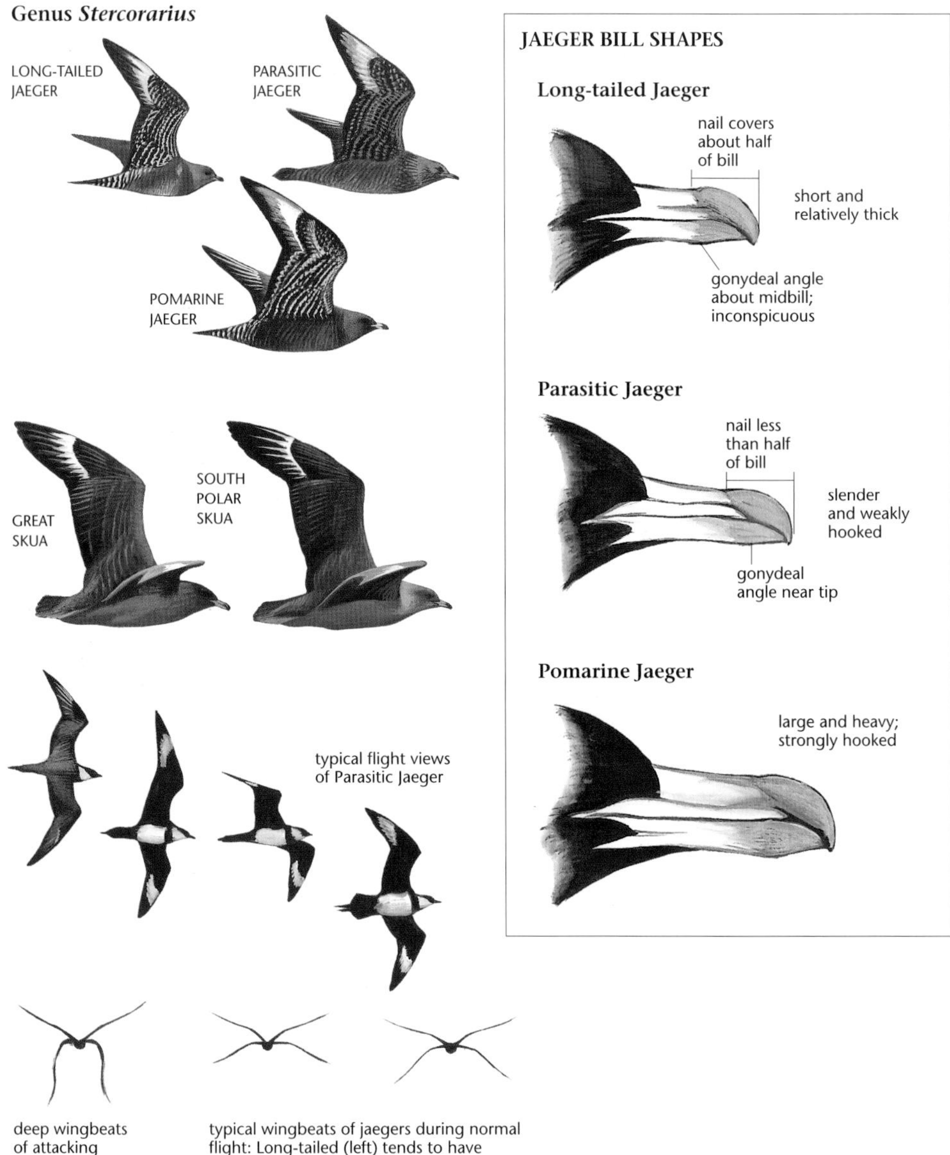

Genus *Stercorarius*
LONG-TAILED JAEGER
PARASITIC JAEGER
POMARINE JAEGER
GREAT SKUA
SOUTH POLAR SKUA
typical flight views of Parasitic Jaeger
deep wingbeats of attacking jaeger
typical wingbeats of jaegers during normal flight: Long-tailed (left) tends to have motion mainly above horizontal; Parasitic and Pomarine (right) more even
JAEGER BILL SHAPES
Long-tailed Jaeger
nail covers about half of bill
short and relatively thick
gonydeal angle about midbill; inconspicuous
Parasitic Jaeger
nail less than half of bill
slender and weakly hooked
gonydeal angle near tip
Pomarine Jaeger
large and heavy; strongly hooked

Jaegers

This smallest and scarcest jaeger is relatively delicate in build. It is less aggressive than other jaegers, occurring mainly far offshore, and its migration tends to follow that of Arctic Tern.

Long-tailed Jaeger

Stercorarius longicaudus

L 15" (adult breeding to 23") WS 43" WT 11 oz (300 g) ♀>♂

Usually appears slender and buoyant with slender belly; narrow wings with narrow "hand"; long-tailed, with the projection of tail behind wings greater than width of wing base; rounded head; short, stout bill. Adult has strikingly long, flowing central tail feathers in breeding season; juvenile usually has blunt-tipped central tail feathers projecting well beyond other tail feathers.

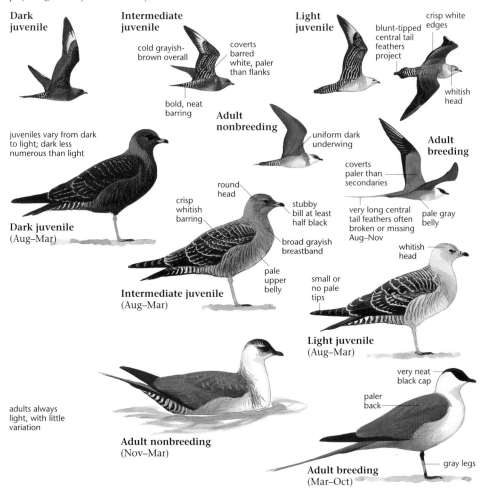

Dark juvenile

Intermediate juvenile

cold grayish-brown overall

coverts barred white, paler than flanks

bold, neat barring

Light juvenile

blunt-tipped central tail feathers project

crisp white edges

whitish head

Adult nonbreeding

uniform dark underwing

Adult breeding

coverts paler than secondaries

very long central tail feathers often broken or missing Aug–Nov

pale gray belly

juveniles vary from dark to light; dark less numerous than light

Dark juvenile
(Aug–Mar)

round head

crisp whitish barring

stubby bill at least half black

broad grayish breastband

pale upper belly

Intermediate juvenile
(Aug–Mar)

whitish head

small or no pale tips

Light juvenile
(Aug–Mar)

adults always light, with little variation

Adult nonbreeding
(Nov–Mar)

very neat black cap

paler back

gray legs

Adult breeding
(Mar–Oct)

Voice: Generally silent away from breeding grounds. All calls higher than other jaegers. Common call a short, trilled *krrip;* also a nasal *kee-ur* like Red-shouldered Hawk, and sharp *kl-dew*. Long call a rattling followed by long, plaintive *feeeeoo* notes.

Structure is important for identification. Normally shows two to three white primary shafts. Adults are fairly distinctive, unique in lacking white wing-patches on underwing. Juveniles are generally grayish-toned, with crisp, pale feather edges. The tail coverts and underwing coverts are very boldly and neatly barred black and white, so that the underwing coverts are paler than the flanks, and the uppertail coverts often appear paler than the rest of the upperside. Some are strikingly pale with whitish head and clean white belly unlike other species. On most juveniles the unpatterned grayish breast and white patch on upper belly is distinctive.

In most coastal locations this is the most frequently seen jaeger, but it is relatively scarce far offshore. It is often seen in prolonged, twisting pursuit of terns or other seabirds.

Parasitic Jaeger

Stercorarius parasiticus

L 16.5" (adult breeding to 20") WS 46" WT 1 lb (470 g) ♀>♂

More slender than Pomarine; a bit bulkier, broader-winged, and shorter-tailed than Long-tailed. Small-headed with peaked crown and slender bill. Central tail feathers pointed, usually projecting little on juvenile.

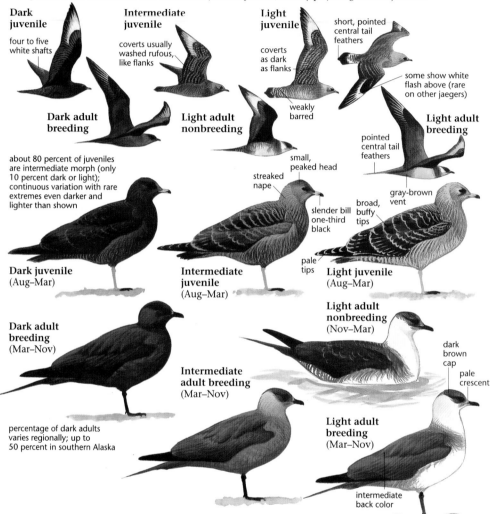

Dark juvenile
four to five white shafts

Intermediate juvenile
coverts usually washed rufous, like flanks

Light juvenile
coverts as dark as flanks

short, pointed central tail feathers

some show white flash above (rare on other jaegers)

weakly barred

Dark adult breeding

Light adult nonbreeding

Light adult breeding
pointed central tail feathers

about 80 percent of juveniles are intermediate morph (only 10 percent dark or light); continuous variation with rare extremes even darker and lighter than shown

small, peaked head

streaked nape

slender bill one-third black

gray-brown vent

broad, buffy tips

pale tips

Dark juvenile (Aug–Mar)

Intermediate juvenile (Aug–Mar)

Light juvenile (Aug–Mar)

Light adult nonbreeding (Nov–Mar)

Dark adult breeding (Mar–Nov)

dark brown cap

pale crescent

Intermediate adult breeding (Mar–Nov)

Light adult breeding (Mar–Nov)

percentage of dark adults varies regionally; up to 50 percent in southern Alaska

intermediate back color

Voice: Generally silent away from breeding grounds. Pitch intermediate between other jaegers. Common call a nasal *KEwet, KEwet . . .* similar to Gull-billed Tern, a little higher than Pomarine Jaeger; also short barking *gek* notes. Long call includes nasal whining or crowing *feee-leerrrr.*

Structure is important for identification. Normally shows three to five white primary shafts. All juveniles except dark morph are distinguished by having warm cinnamon tones to the plumage. The nape is pale cinnamon and distinctly streaked (in close views). The tail coverts and underwing coverts are less boldly and neatly barred than on the other jaegers and are washed with cinnamon so that the underwing coverts are about the same color as the flanks, and the uppertail coverts usually do not contrast strongly with the rest of the upperside. Only pale-headed juveniles show pale uppertail coverts (compare other species).

JAEGERS (CONTINUED)

This stocky and powerful jaeger, found mainly well offshore, chases even the largest shearwaters and gulls. The chases are generally less prolonged and less acrobatic than Parasitic's.

Pomarine Jaeger

Stercorarius pomarinus

L 18.5" (adult breeding to 23") WS 52" WT 1.5 lb (700 g) ♀>♂

Heavy body, broad wings with broad "arm," short tail; large, rounded head with heavy bill. Adult's central tail feathers are long, broad, rounded, and twisted 90 degrees; juvenile has rounded central tail feathers that barely project.

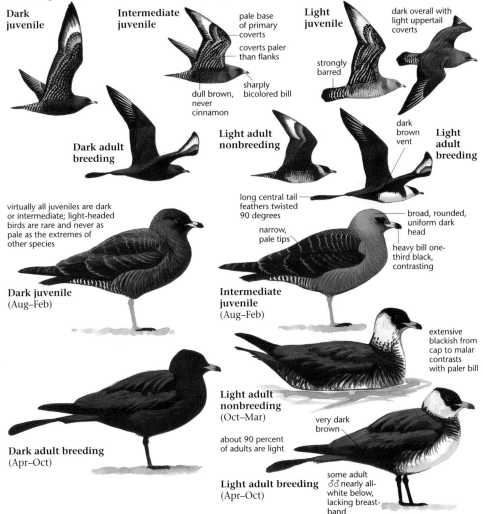

Dark juvenile

Intermediate juvenile

pale base of primary coverts

coverts paler than flanks

sharply bicolored bill

dull brown, never cinnamon

Light juvenile

strongly barred

dark overall with light uppertail coverts

Dark adult breeding

Light adult nonbreeding

dark brown vent

Light adult breeding

long central tail feathers twisted 90 degrees

virtually all juveniles are dark or intermediate; light-headed birds are rare and never as pale as the extremes of other species

Dark juvenile (Aug–Feb)

narrow, pale tips

broad, rounded, uniform dark head

heavy bill one-third black, contrasting

Intermediate juvenile (Aug–Feb)

extensive blackish from cap to malar contrasts with paler bill

Dark adult breeding (Apr–Oct)

Light adult nonbreeding (Oct–Mar)

about 90 percent of adults are light

very dark brown

Light adult breeding (Apr–Oct)

some adult ♂♂ nearly all-white below, lacking breast-band

Voice: Occasionally gives barking calls in winter. On breeding grounds a yelping *vee-veef;* also a short, barking *geck* or complaining and wavering *ehwewewewe.* Long call a series of rising, nasal *weeek* notes, unlike the rising and falling notes of other jaegers.

Structure is important for identification. Normally shows four to six white primary shafts. Whitish bases of underprimary coverts create a small, pale crescent more prominent than on other species. Juveniles are characterized by dull brown color with uniform head and nape. The tail coverts and underwing coverts are boldly and neatly barred and paler than the adjacent feathers, as on Long-tailed. Combination of dark head and light uppertail coverts is typical of Pomarine and is never shown by Parasitic. The large bill is sharply bicolored and contrasts with the dark face, often conspicuous at a distance.

Skuas

This species nests in the Antarctic, visiting North American waters during the southern winter (May–Oct). Most are distinguished from Great Skua by their cold grayish body color.

South Polar Skua

Stercorarius maccormicki

L 21" WS 52" WT 2.5 lb (1,150 g) ♀>♂

Larger and bulkier than Pomarine Jaeger and most gulls, with relatively broader wings and shorter tail. All have blackish underwing coverts, white flash on primaries.

Juvenile

most skuas have obvious white on upperwing, unlike jaegers

all-dark

Juvenile (Apr–Jul)

juveniles of both skuas have neat and uniform scapulars and wing coverts with narrow, pale edges and thin bill with gray base

cold gray-brown overall

Molting adult (May–Jun)

Dark adult

uniform dark above

pale nape

pale crescent

gray-brown

Dark adult

blackish coverts

yellowish nape

Light adult

narrow whitish streaks and edges

pale grayish contrasts with dark upperside

Light adult

pale with blackish underwing coverts

Voice: Generally silent away from breeding grounds. Sometimes gives a weak, nasal, gull-like *haaasi.*

Typical light and dark birds are shown here. There are many intermediates, some even darker or lighter than shown. Most seen in North America are dark. Females average lighter than males.

Both skuas are large and imposing, appearing hunchbacked and broad-winged with striking white patches at the base of the primaries. Great Skua nests on islands in the northeast Atlantic.

Great Skua

Stercorarius skua

L 23" WS 55" WT 3.2 lb (1,450 g) ♀>♂

Averages slightly larger, broader-winged, and larger-billed than South Polar Skua, but these differences not sufficient for identification. With the exception of some juveniles, all have distinct warm tones to plumage.

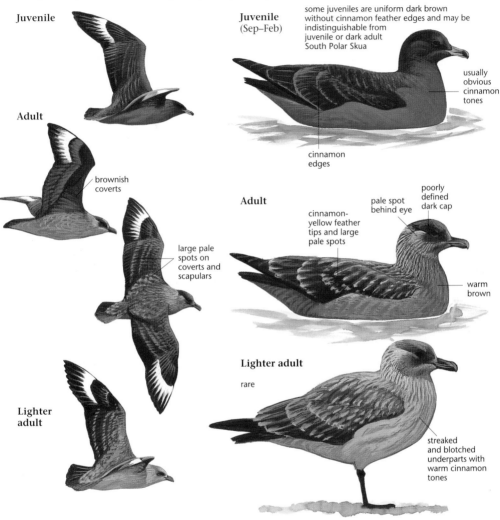

Juvenile

Adult

brownish coverts

large pale spots on coverts and scapulars

Lighter adult

Juvenile (Sep–Feb)

some juveniles are uniform dark brown without cinnamon feather edges and may be indistinguishable from juvenile or dark adult South Polar Skua

usually obvious cinnamon tones

cinnamon edges

Adult

poorly defined dark cap

pale spot behind eye

cinnamon-yellow feather tips and large pale spots

warm brown

Lighter adult

rare

streaked and blotched underparts with warm cinnamon tones

Voice: Generally silent away from breeding grounds. Short call a *hek*. Long call a series of short, nasal *pyeh* notes.

Molt patterns of primaries may provide a clue to identification and age of skuas. Adult South Polar molts primaries very rapidly May–Jul. Juvenile Great molts at about the same time (Apr–Aug) but more slowly, with fewer feathers growing at one time. Adult Great and juvenile South Polar both begin primary molt in Aug, but Great proceeds slowly (Aug–Mar). 2nd year and later molts gradually shift to adult timing over several years.

Gulls, Terns, and Skimmers
Family: Laridae

GULLS 27 species in 5 genera. These generally conspicuous and gregarious species prefer open areas (beaches, lakes, etc.) and are often attracted to dumps, dams, restaurants, and other man-made concentrations of food. Most species belong to the genus *Larus;* all are similar, but within the genus the small hooded species form a distinct group. Large species are omnivorous and all mix freely where food is abundant. Smaller species form large flocks but do not mix as freely with other species. Many species are difficult to identify, and some hybridize frequently. Most nest colonially on the ground, in a sand scrape or a mound they build of seaweed and grasses. Kittiwakes nest on cliff ledges; Bonaparte's Gull builds a stick nest in spruce trees. Nonbreeding adults are shown.

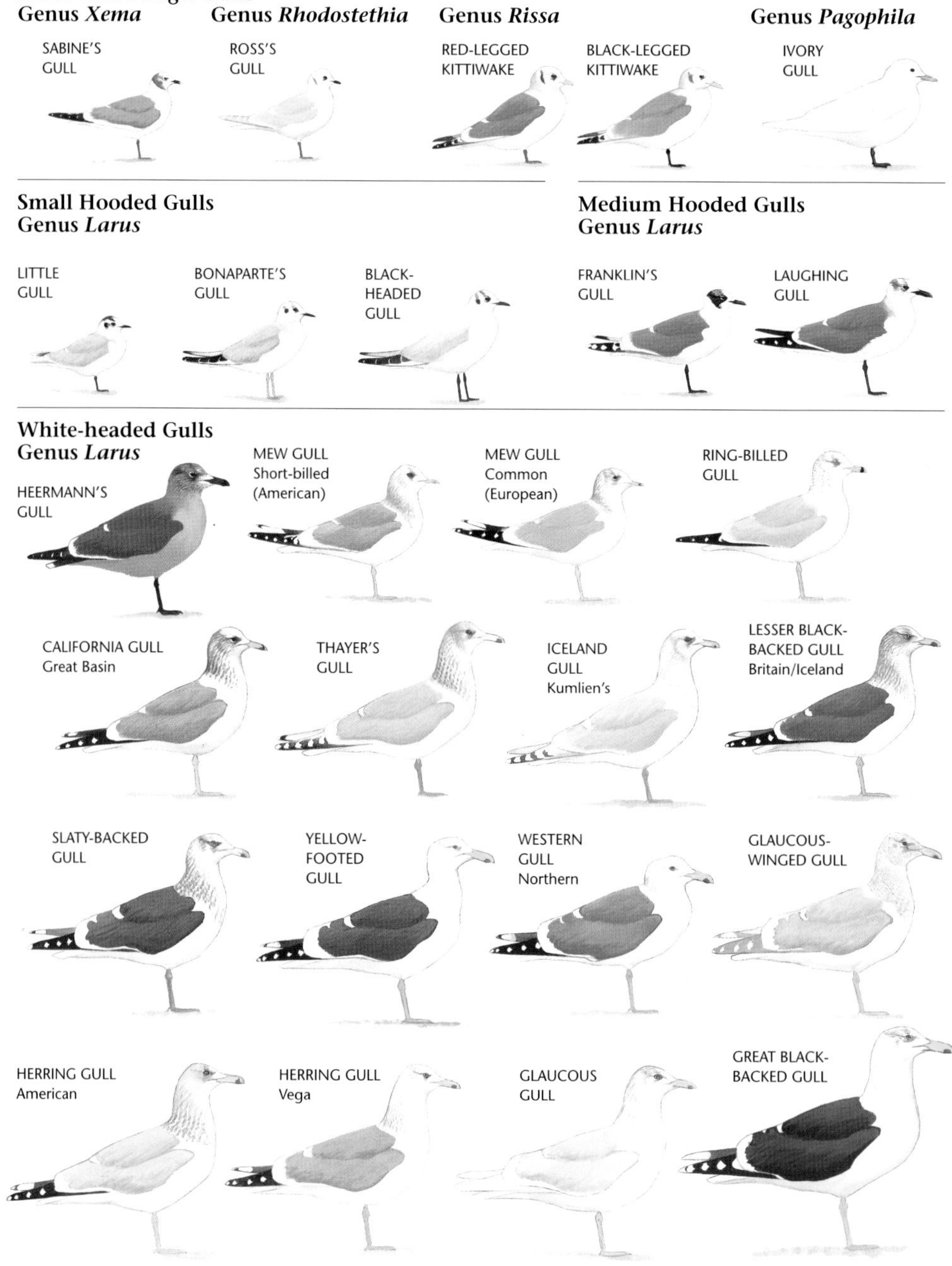

Arctic and Pelagic Gulls
Genus Xema
SABINE'S GULL
Genus Rhodostethia
ROSS'S GULL
Genus Rissa
RED-LEGGED KITTIWAKE
BLACK-LEGGED KITTIWAKE
Genus Pagophila
IVORY GULL
Small Hooded Gulls
Genus Larus
LITTLE GULL
BONAPARTE'S GULL
BLACK-HEADED GULL
Medium Hooded Gulls
Genus Larus
FRANKLIN'S GULL
LAUGHING GULL
White-headed Gulls
Genus Larus
HEERMANN'S GULL
MEW GULL Short-billed (American)
MEW GULL Common (European)
RING-BILLED GULL
CALIFORNIA GULL Great Basin
THAYER'S GULL
ICELAND GULL Kumlien's
LESSER BLACK-BACKED GULL Britain/Iceland
SLATY-BACKED GULL
YELLOW-FOOTED GULL
WESTERN GULL Northern
GLAUCOUS-WINGED GULL
HERRING GULL American
HERRING GULL Vega
GLAUCOUS GULL
GREAT BLACK-BACKED GULL

TERNS AND SKIMMERS 18 species in 4 genera. These species are in the same family as gulls but are generally smaller and more slender, with straight, pointed bills. Most species feed exclusively on small fish, Gull-billed mainly on insects and crabs. The crested and medium-size terns, as well as Roseate and Least, forage mainly by plunge-diving headfirst into water from flight, often from a hovering position; Aleutian and Gull-billed Terns, marsh and tropical terns, and noddies pluck food from the water's surface (Gull-billed and marsh terns also pluck food from mud); Black Skimmer captures fish by skimming the water's surface. Foraging groups may be large and dense where prey is concentrated; all species also roost in large groups on the shoreline. They nest colonially on the ground, most in shallow sand scrapes; marsh terns nest on a floating platform of weeds, and noddies build stick nests in bushes. Nonbreeding adults are shown.

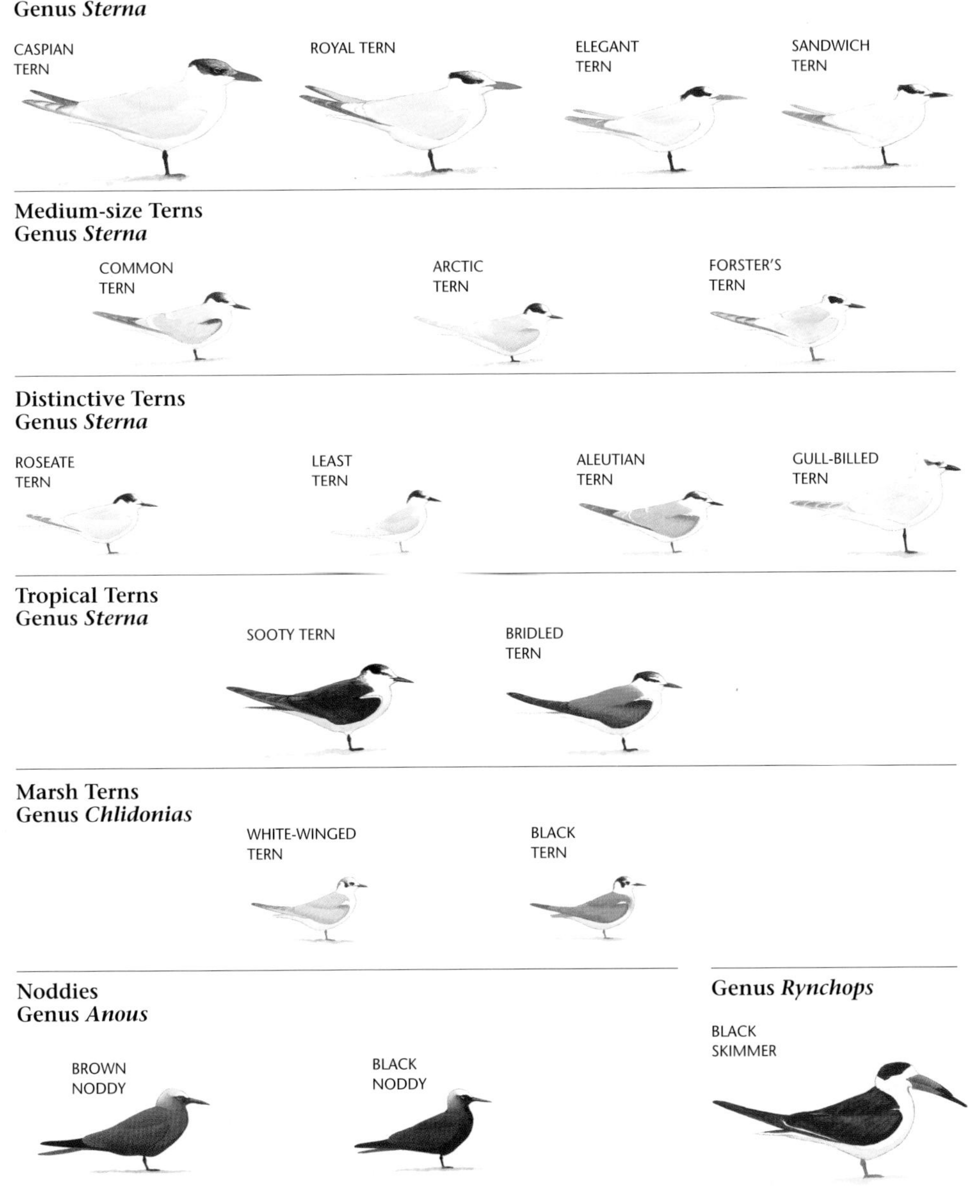

Crested Terns
Genus *Sterna*
CASPIAN TERN
ROYAL TERN
ELEGANT TERN
SANDWICH TERN
Medium-size Terns
Genus *Sterna*
COMMON TERN
ARCTIC TERN
FORSTER'S TERN
Distinctive Terns
Genus *Sterna*
ROSEATE TERN
LEAST TERN
ALEUTIAN TERN
GULL-BILLED TERN
Tropical Terns
Genus *Sterna*
SOOTY TERN
BRIDLED TERN
Marsh Terns
Genus *Chlidonias*
WHITE-WINGED TERN
BLACK TERN
Noddies
Genus *Anous*
BROWN NODDY
BLACK NODDY
Genus *Rynchops*
BLACK SKIMMER

Hybrid Gulls

All large gulls are very closely related; some hybridize frequently. These two hybrid combinations are particularly common and may outnumber their pure parental types in some areas.

GLAUCOUS-WINGED × HERRING GULL

Fairly common from Alaska to California; mainly coastal. Variable in plumage and structure. Head shape may be blocky like Glaucous-winged or slender and angular like Herring. Most are larger, bulkier, and heavier-billed than Thayer's, but some may be indistinguishable from Thayer's.

GLAUCOUS-WINGED × WESTERN GULL

Common coastally from British Columbia to California. Some populations in Washington are mostly hybrids and backcrosses with very few pure birds. Always bulky, broad-winged, and heavy-billed like the parent species.

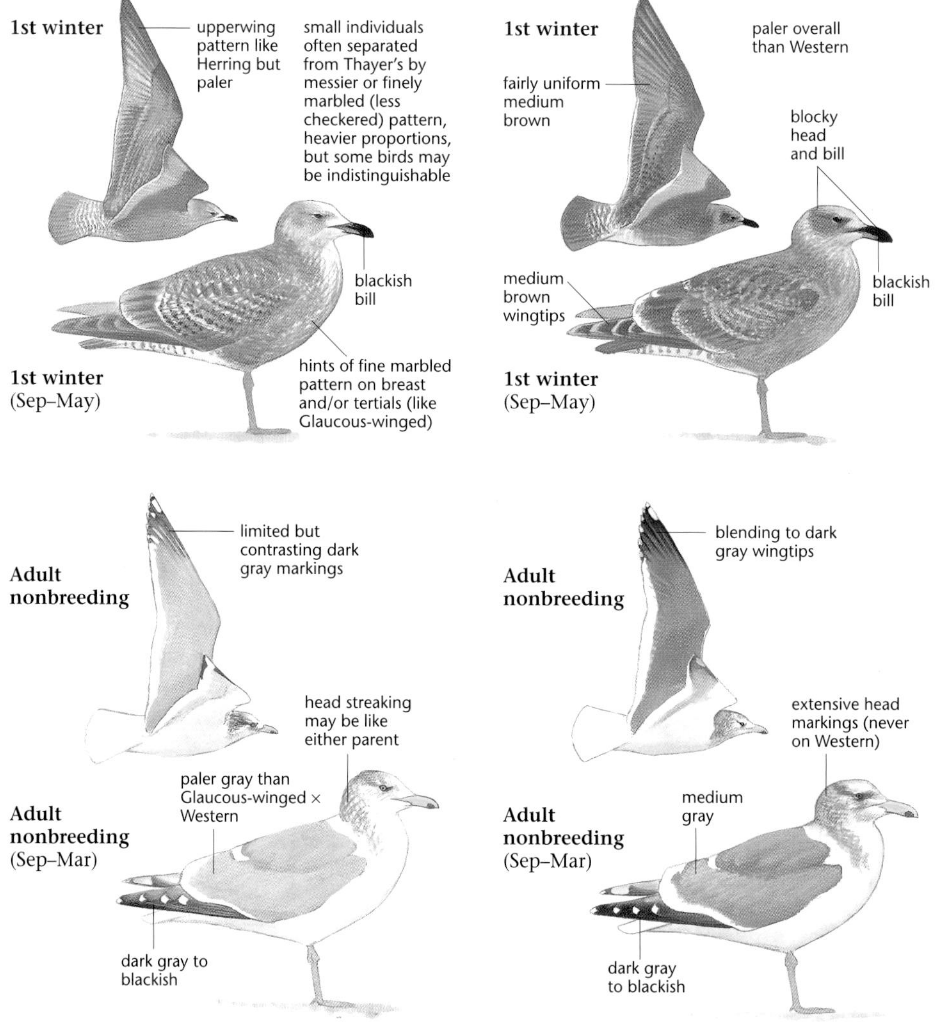

1st winter
upperwing pattern like Herring but paler
small individuals often separated from Thayer's by messier or finely marbled (less checkered) pattern, heavier proportions, but some birds may be indistinguishable
blackish bill
1st winter (Sep–May)
hints of fine marbled pattern on breast and/or tertials (like Glaucous-winged)
1st winter
paler overall than Western
fairly uniform medium brown
blocky head and bill
medium brown wingtips
blackish bill
1st winter (Sep–May)
Adult nonbreeding
limited but contrasting dark gray markings
head streaking may be like either parent
paler gray than Glaucous-winged × Western
Adult nonbreeding (Sep–Mar)
dark gray to blackish
Adult nonbreeding
blending to dark gray wingtips
extensive head markings (never on Western)
medium gray
Adult nonbreeding (Sep–Mar)
dark gray to blackish

Identification of hybrid gulls is difficult and often conjectural. Most hybrids are intermediate between parent species, but individual variation and backcrosses produce a continuum of variation. In cases of frequent hybridization, such as those illustrated on these pages, it is often necessary to use vague titles such as "Herring tending toward Glaucous-winged." Other combinations occur rarely (e.g., Herring × Great Black-backed) or never (Herring × Iceland). Small gulls hybridize much less frequently, but Black-headed Gull occasionally crosses with Laughing and Ring-billed Gulls.

Hybrid Gulls (continued)

These two hybrid combinations occur less frequently than the two opposite and are scarce south of their breeding grounds. Their pale plumage may suggest leucistic individuals of other species.

GLAUCOUS-WINGED × GLAUCOUS GULL

Fairly common locally in western Alaska; less numerous farther south on Pacific coast but probably overlooked. Very difficult to distinguish from pale Glaucous-winged. Always large and large-billed.

1st winter

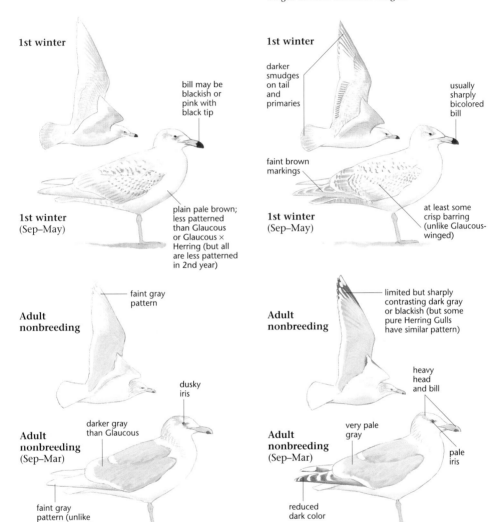

bill may be blackish or pink with black tip

1st winter (Sep–May)

plain pale brown; less patterned than Glaucous or Glaucous × Herring (but all are less patterned in 2nd year)

Adult nonbreeding

faint gray pattern

dusky iris

Adult nonbreeding (Sep–Mar)

darker gray than Glaucous

faint gray pattern (unlike pure Glaucous)

GLAUCOUS × HERRING GULL

Fairly common in some Arctic breeding areas; less numerous farther south wherever Glaucous occurs. Generally Glaucous-like with some intermediate darker plumage characteristics. Never as bulky or broad-winged as most Glaucous-winged.

1st winter

darker smudges on tail and primaries

usually sharply bicolored bill

faint brown markings

1st winter (Sep–May)

at least some crisp barring (unlike Glaucous-winged)

Adult nonbreeding

limited but sharply contrasting dark gray or blackish (but some pure Herring Gulls have similar pattern)

heavy head and bill

Adult nonbreeding (Sep–Mar)

very pale gray

pale iris

reduced dark color

Aberrant plumages such as albinism and leucism (pale but not white plumage) must always be considered when identifying pale gulls. Check bill shape and color and eye color. Leucistic birds may be indistinguishable from Herring × Glaucous or other hybrids and can cause confusion with other pale species, such as Thayer's and Iceland. The presence of unusual plumage contrasts (such as a very pale-winged bird with dark brown tail) is a strong indication of leucism.

Albino Herring Gull
1st year

Rare *Larus* Gulls

These two species are rare but increasingly frequent visitors to North America. Black-tailed is distinctive, but Kelp Gull is difficult to distinguish from Lesser Black-backed and Yellow-footed Gulls.

Black-tailed Gull

Larus crassirostris

L 19" WS 49" WT 1.2 lb (530 g)

Always has white rump and dark tail; long, narrow wings; and long bill. Smaller, more slender, and longer-billed than Lesser Black-backed.

1st winter
2nd winter
Adult nonbreeding
white rump
white-edged black tail
all-black wingtips
smooth, gray-brown breast and neck
white eye-arcs
whitish face
bicolored bill
1st winter (Sep–Mar)
2nd winter (Sep–Mar)
adultlike by 4th winter
Adult nonbreeding (Oct–Mar)
streaked collar
narrow white crescent
Adult breeding (Mar–Sep)
black and red tip

Voice: Nasal, rasping mewing reminiscent of tomcat, higher than Herring Gull.

Kelp Gull

Larus dominicanus

L 24" WS 55" WT 2.3 lb (1,035 g)

Our darkest-mantled gull. Large and stocky with large, square head, heavy bill, and prominent gonydeal angle. Shorter- and broader-winged than Lesser Black-backed.

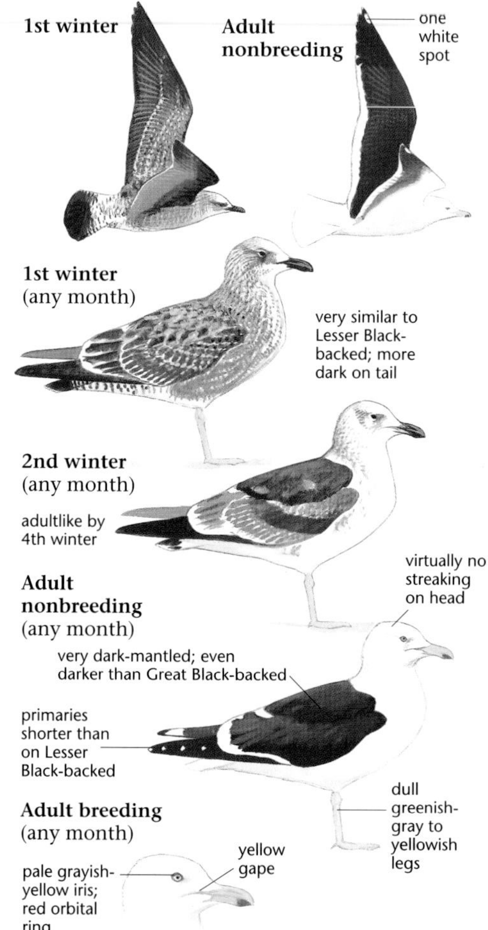

1st winter
Adult nonbreeding
one white spot
1st winter (any month)
very similar to Lesser Black-backed; more dark on tail
2nd winter (any month)
adultlike by 4th winter
Adult nonbreeding (any month)
virtually no streaking on head
very dark-mantled; even darker than Great Black-backed
primaries shorter than on Lesser Black-backed
dull greenish-gray to yellowish legs
Adult breeding (any month)
yellow gape
pale grayish-yellow iris; red orbital ring

Voice: Similar to Herring Gull but hoarser. Call note a two- or three-syllable, staccato, repeated *kwee-ah*. Long call noisier and higher than Yellow-footed, lower than Western.

Far-southern populations of Kelp Gull have molt cycle reversed from Northern Hemisphere gulls; equatorial populations molt in any month; vagrants in North America adapt to northern cycle.

Kelp × Herring hybrids (seen in Louisiana) resemble Yellow-legged or Britain/Iceland Lesser Black-backed but are bulkier, with drab legs.

Yellow-legged and Ivory Gulls

Yellow-legged Gull is a rare visitor, very nearly indistinguishable from Herring and Lesser Black-backed Gulls. Ivory Gull is a distinctive Arctic species found around pack ice.

Yellow-legged Gull

Larus cachinnans

L 25" WS 58" WT 2.5 lb (1,125 g)

Adult differs from Herring Gull in mantle color, wingtip pattern, bare-parts colors, and voice; also averages longer-winged, with large head and heavy, blunt-tipped bill.

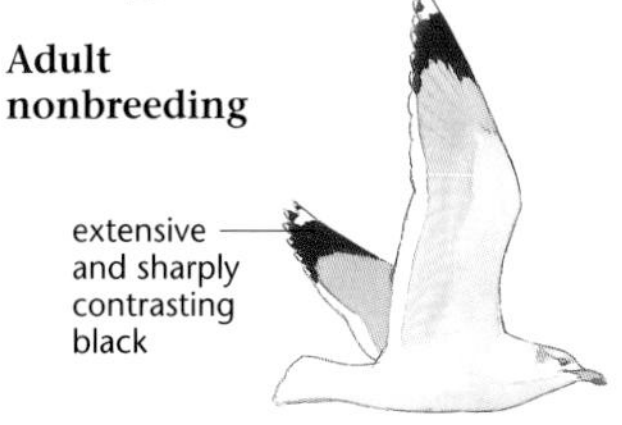

Adult nonbreeding
extensive and sharply contrasting black

Identification of adult is extremely complex, as all characteristics overlap with rare individual Herring Gulls. Positive identification requires careful and extended study and experience with all variations of Herring Gull. Even when all characteristics fit Yellow-legged, the possibility of Herring × Lesser Black-backed hybrids or of very pale-mantled Lesser Black-backed Gulls must be considered. Immatures are similar to Lesser Black-backed and European Herring Gulls; their identification is beyond the scope of this book.

Adult nonbreeding (Aug–Nov)

usually very limited streaking on head

slightly darker gray than Herring

bright yellow

yellow legs

red orbital ring

red gape

Adult breeding (Dec–Jul)

Voice: Calls similar to Lesser Black-backed, deeper and gruffer than Herring. Long call display also similar to Lesser Black-backed, with bill raised beyond vertical.

Yellow-legged Gull long call posture

Ivory Gull

Pagophila eburnea

L 17" WS 37" WT 1.4 lb (630 g) ♂>♀

Fairly small and stocky, with large head; small, straight bill; long, pointed wings; short, sturdy legs.

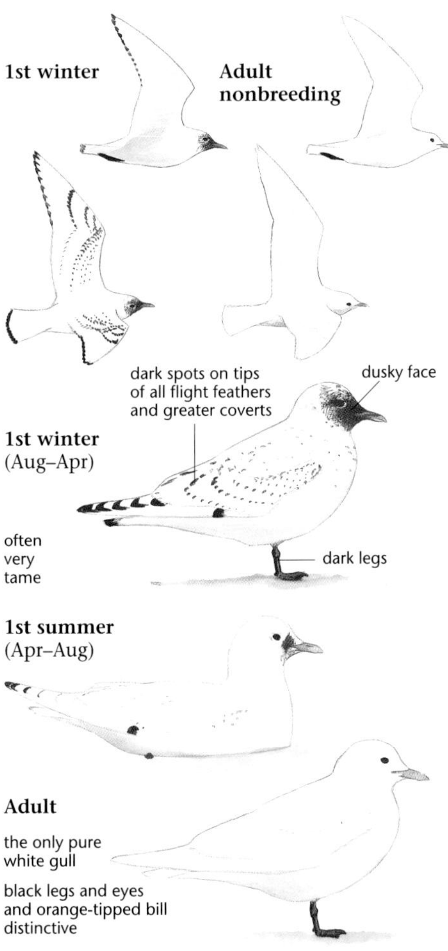

1st winter
Adult nonbreeding
dark spots on tips of all flight feathers and greater coverts
dusky face
1st winter (Aug–Apr)
often very tame
dark legs
1st summer (Apr–Aug)
Adult
the only pure white gull
black legs and eyes and orange-tipped bill distinctive

Voice: Somewhat grating and ternlike: a mewing, high whistle, strongly descending and sometimes slightly trilled *wheeew* or *preeo*.

Little, Bonaparte's, and Black-headed form a group of small, delicate, pale-mantled gulls with dark hoods in breeding plumage. Little is often found with Bonaparte's on open lakes, bays, and ocean.

Identification of Gulls

Gull identification represents one of the most challenging and subjective puzzles in birding and should be approached only with patient and methodical study. A casual or impatient approach will not be rewarded.

Identification problems among the large gulls are compounded by wide variation in virtually every aspect of their appearance.

Males are larger than females, with larger and deeper bills. Juveniles have thinner bills than adults that gradually thicken over several years.

Head shape varies between individuals and also changes with age, weather conditions, and position. Apparent head shape can also be influenced dramatically by facial markings and bill color and size. Although head shape and, more often, "facial expression" is an often-used field mark among gull watchers, few gulls can be identified by silhouette alone.

Variation in plumage falls into three main categories.

— Age variation: The long period of immaturity (up to four years) of large gulls means that some species go through as many as eight different plumage stages, becoming gradually more adultlike.

— Wear and fading: After each molt the feathers gradually change due to abrasion and bleaching until they are finally replaced by the next molt.

— Individual variation: Even when comparing birds of the same age and stage of molt, there is tremendous variation in the color and pattern of the plumage, as well as the colors of bill, legs, and eyes.

Colors of bare parts (legs, bills, eyes) change gradually from drab juvenile colors to brighter adult colors and, on adults, change seasonally from drabber nonbreeding colors to brighter breeding colors. The progress of development of adult colors is variable and does not necessarily follow plumage changes (e.g., an immature with advanced plumage features might be slow to develop mature colors on bare parts).

Bare parts vary just as other characteristics do (e.g., adult Herring Gulls occur with bright yellow legs, red orbital ring, or dark iris). These characteristics should be weighed cautiously and not relied upon for identification.

The shade of gray on the mantle of any large gull is an important identification clue, but assessing mantle color is very difficult under sunny conditions when the orientation of the bird relative to the observer changes the apparent shade of gray. Some individuals become darker when wet. Photographs can be particularly misleading.

Little Gull

Larus minutus

L 11" WS 24" WT 4.2 oz (120 g)

Our smallest gull; wing pattern of adults unique. Rather rounded wingtips; short tail and short, straight bill.

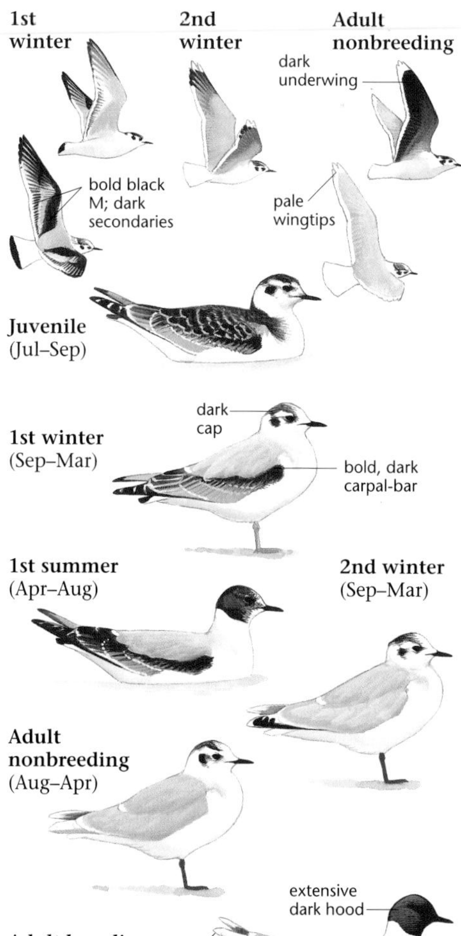
1st
winter
2nd
winter
Adult
nonbreeding
dark
underwing
bold black
M; dark
secondaries
pale
wingtips
Juvenile
(Jul–Sep)
dark
cap
1st winter
(Sep–Mar)
bold, dark
carpal-bar
1st summer
(Apr–Aug)
2nd winter
(Sep–Mar)
Adult
nonbreeding
(Aug–Apr)
extensive
dark hood
Adult breeding
(Apr–Aug)
short, pale
wingtips

Voice: Grating or clear, nasal, most often a short *kek* like Black Tern. In display flight a clear, nasal *teew* and long series *tew tew tikik tikik tikik tikeew tikeew. . . .*

These two small species differ mainly in size, bill color, and wing pattern. Bonaparte's rarely mixes with larger species, but Black-headed often consorts with Laughing and Ring-billed Gulls.

Bonaparte's Gull

Larus philadelphia

L 13.5" WS 33" WT 7 oz (190 g)

Small and ternlike. Bill slender, straight, and pointed; wings rather narrow and straight.

1st winter
Adult nonbreeding
all-white
dark tips
narrow, dark M
Juvenile (Jul–Aug)
1st winter (Sep–Mar)
pink legs
1st summer (Apr–Aug)
dark ear-spot
black bill
Adult nonbreeding (Aug–Apr)
Adult breeding (Apr–Aug)

Voice: Low, wooden, grating or rasping *gerrrr* or *reeek;* ternlike but lower-pitched than most terns. Also clear *kew* notes from flock. Juvenile gives high, somewhat nasal squeal *peeeur.*

Black-headed Gull

Larus ridibundus

L 16" WS 40" WT 9 oz (270 g)

Distinctly larger, longer- and heavier-billed, and broader-winged than Bonaparte's.

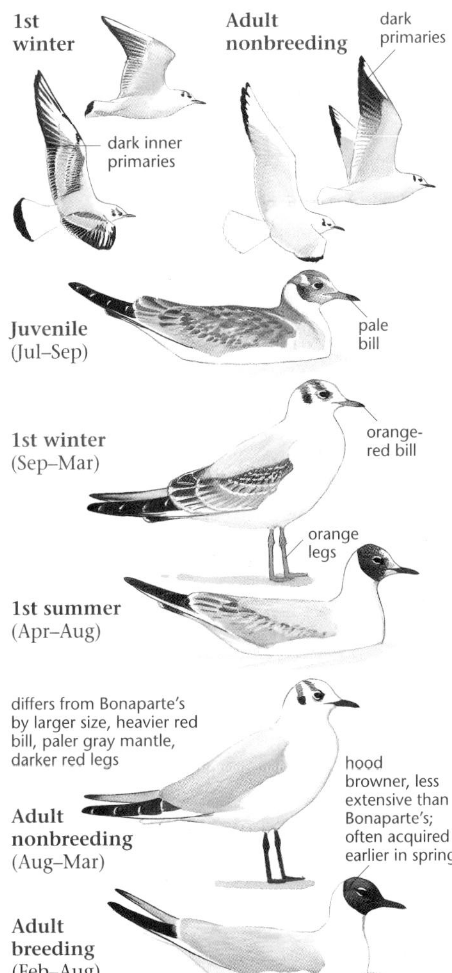
1st winter
Adult nonbreeding
dark primaries
dark inner primaries
Juvenile (Jul–Sep)
pale bill
1st winter (Sep–Mar)
orange-red bill
orange legs
1st summer (Apr–Aug)
differs from Bonaparte's by larger size, heavier red bill, paler gray mantle, darker red legs
hood browner, less extensive than Bonaparte's; often acquired earlier in spring
Adult nonbreeding (Aug–Mar)
Adult breeding (Feb–Aug)

Voice: Harsh grating similar to Bonaparte's but lower, with richer quality like Laughing Gull.

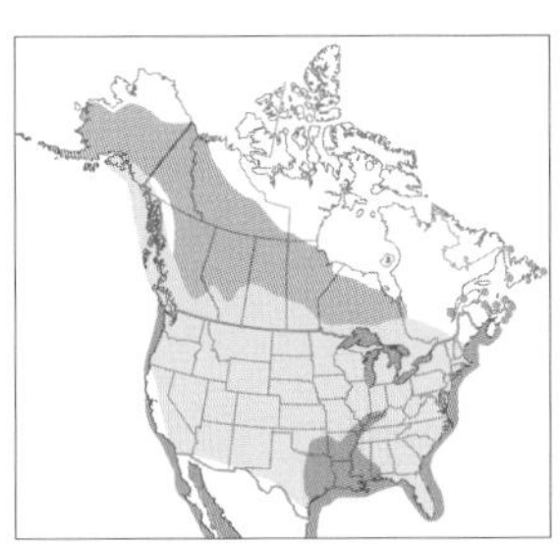

Variation in structure and plumage in these species, as in all other gulls, is dramatic. Careful study of flocks will reveal exceptionally large, small, light, and dark individuals that may cause confusion when seen singly.

Medium Hooded Gulls

This small and relatively dark-mantled gull is closely related to Laughing Gull but differs in structure, wing pattern, and other details. In North America, it is seen mainly inland on ponds and fields.

Franklin's Gull

Larus pipixcan

L 14.5" WS 36" WT 10 oz (280 g) ♂>♀

Smaller and more delicate than Laughing Gull. Bill shorter and less drooped; wings shorter and less pointed; underwing always clean white with limited black tips on primaries; hindneck clean white.

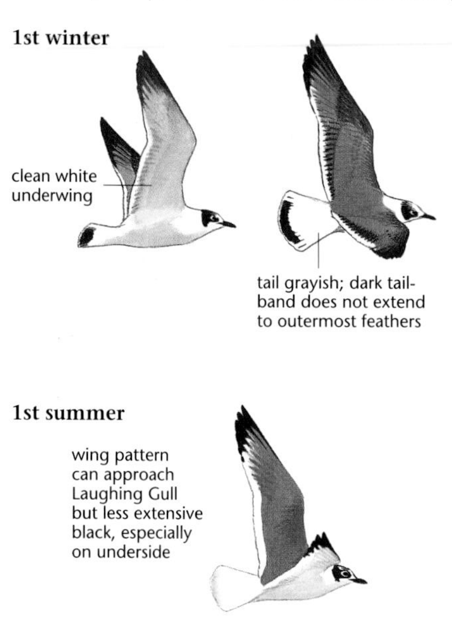
1st winter
clean white underwing
tail grayish; dark tail-band does not extend to outermost feathers

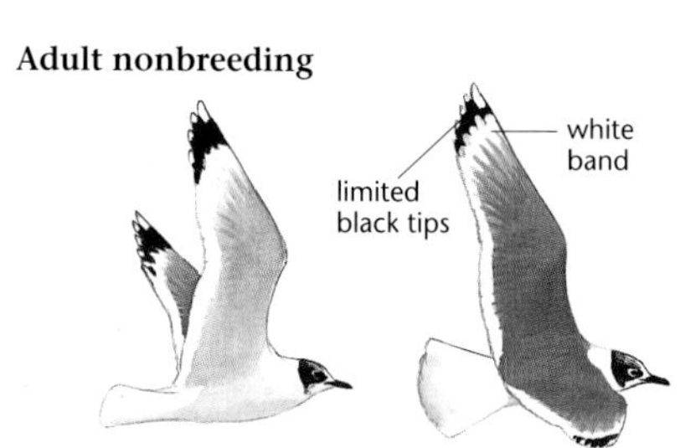
1st summer
wing pattern can approach Laughing Gull but less extensive black, especially on underside

Adult nonbreeding

limited black tips

white band

Juvenile
(Aug–Sep)
dark half-hood neater and more extensive than most Laughing Gulls
hindneck whitish
1st winter
(Sep–Apr)
1st summer
(Apr–Aug)
2nd winter
(Sep–Apr)
probably indistinguishable from adult; may average more black on wingtips
Adult nonbreeding
(Aug–Mar)
extensive hood
small bill
often tinged pink
Adult breeding
(Apr–Aug)
broad white eye-arcs
large white primary tips

Voice: Voice nasal and laughing but hollow-sounding and less penetrating than Laughing Gull. Common call a short, hollow *kowii* or *queel*. Long call descending and accelerating, each note rising; the series with much greater pitch change than Laughing Gull.

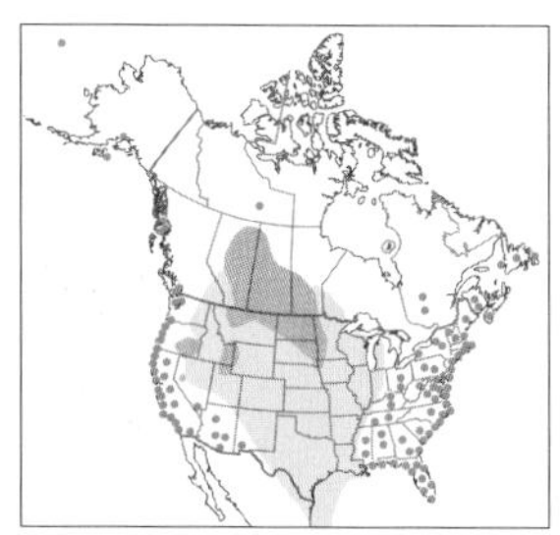

This is the only gull that undergoes two complete molts each year. Thus, the plumage is always fresh (other gulls molt in late summer and appear worn in the following summer); compare 1st summer with same age Laughing Gull.

Found around any open shoreline habitat, this species is a frequent visitor to parking lots and parks. It often chases other waterbirds to steal food, and 1st year birds are often mistaken for jaegers.

Laughing Gull

Larus atricilla

L 16.5" WS 40" WT 11 oz (320 g) ♂>♀

Overall slender; long bill droops at tip. Relatively longer-winged than any other gull; flight graceful with wings swept back and pointed.

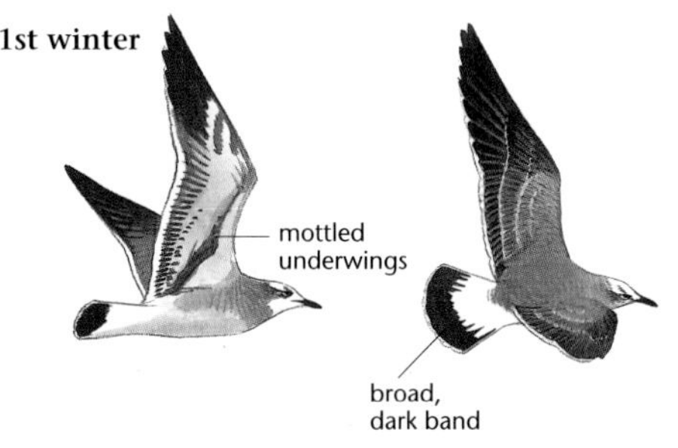
1st winter
mottled underwings
broad, dark band

Juvenile
(Aug–Nov)
dusky brownish
1st winter
(Oct–Mar)
gray-brown hindneck and breast (compare Franklin's)
1st summer
(Mar–Aug)

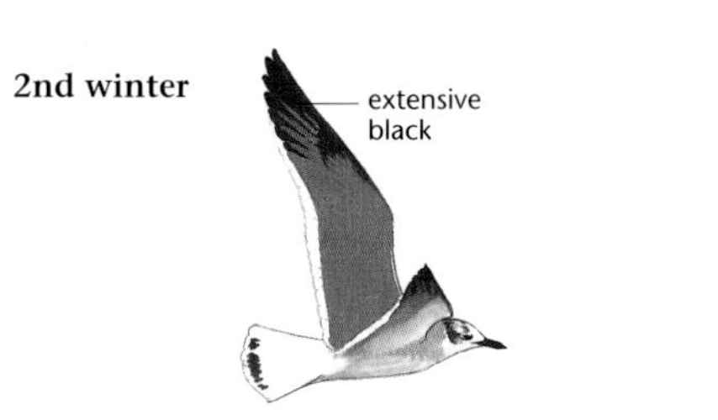
2nd winter
extensive black

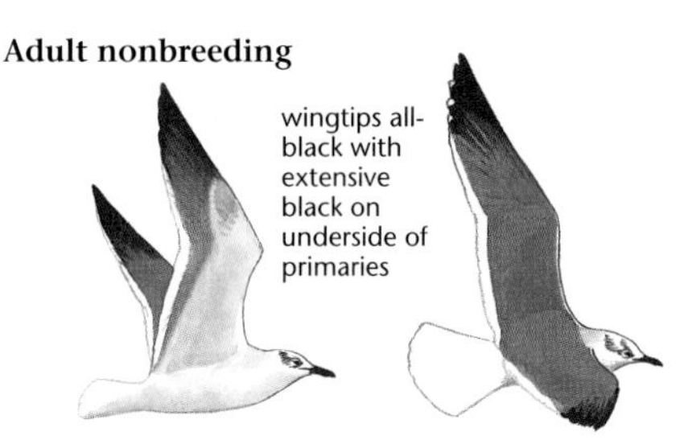
Adult nonbreeding
wingtips all-black with extensive black on underside of primaries

2nd winter
(Sep–Mar)
gray wash on hindneck and sides of breast

Voice: Nasal laughing; common call of adults a two-syllable laugh *kiiwa* or *kahwi*. Long call rapid then slowing.

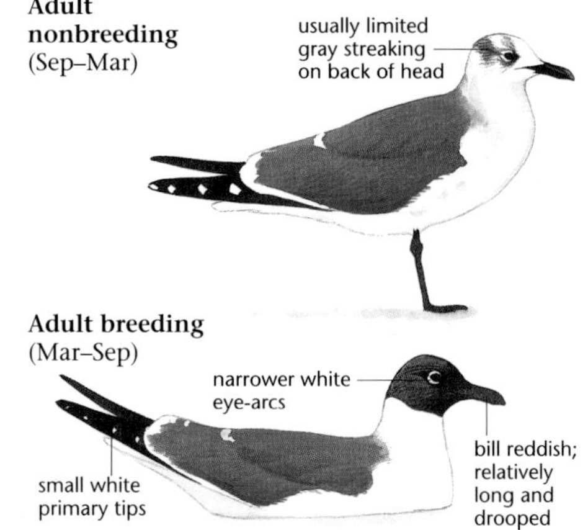
Adult nonbreeding
(Sep–Mar)
usually limited gray streaking on back of head
Adult breeding
(Mar–Sep)
narrower white eye-arcs
small white primary tips
bill reddish; relatively long and drooped at tip

Divided here into American and European populations, our smallest white-headed gull is closely related to Ring-billed but delicate, with a gentle expression.

Mew Gull

Larus canus

L 16" WS 43" WT 15 oz (420 g) ♂>♀

SHORT-BILLED (AMERICAN)

Slightly smaller and more slender than Ring-billed, with shorter and thinner bill, rounder head; eyes appear large. Wings narrower and less pointed than Ring-billed.

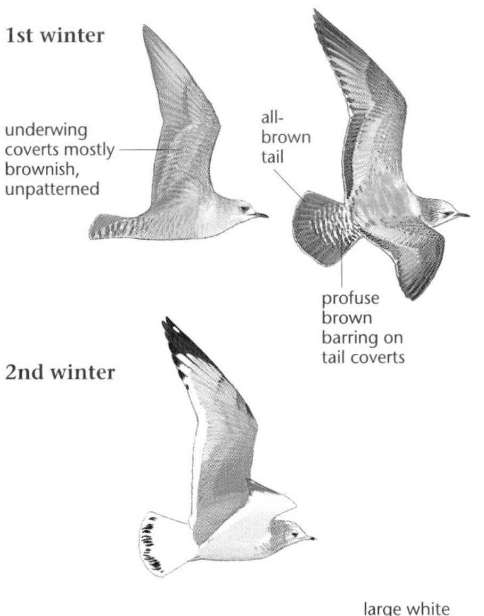
1st winter
underwing coverts mostly brownish, unpatterned
all-brown tail
profuse brown barring on tail coverts
2nd winter

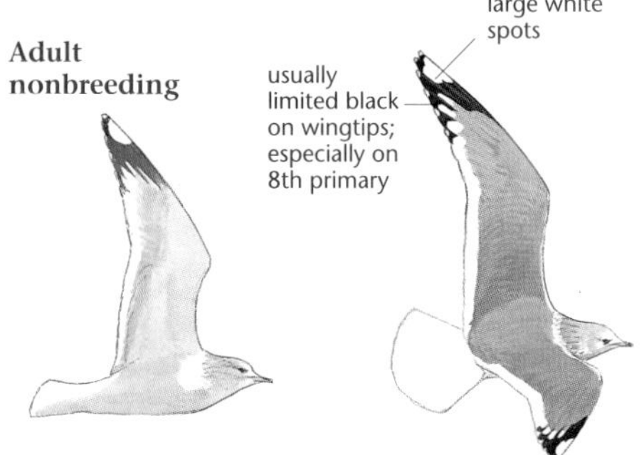
Adult nonbreeding
large white spots
usually limited black on wingtips; especially on 8th primary

Juvenile (Jul–Sep)
1st winter (Oct–Apr)
brownish remiges
small, dull pink bill with dark tip
fairly uniform pale brown; low contrast with smudgy brown on belly
1st summer (Apr–Aug)
often becomes very pale and worn

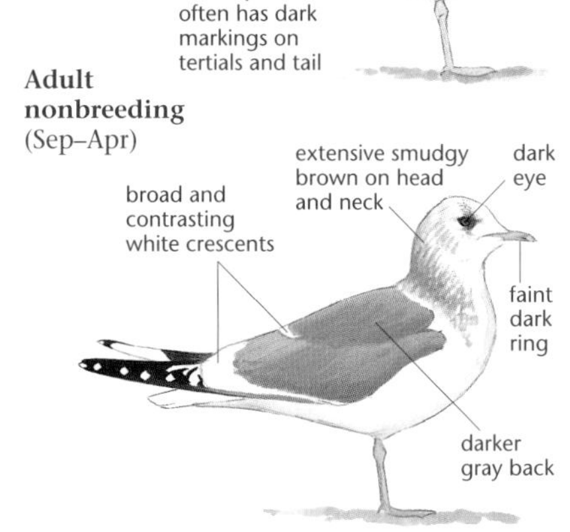
2nd winter (Aug–Apr)
often has dark markings on tertials and tail
Adult nonbreeding (Sep–Apr)
extensive smudgy brown on head and neck
dark eye
broad and contrasting white crescents
faint dark ring
darker gray back

Voice: Voice high and squealing with strident nasal quality, less harsh and more mewing than Ring-billed. Long call falsetto, ending with rapid series of short notes.

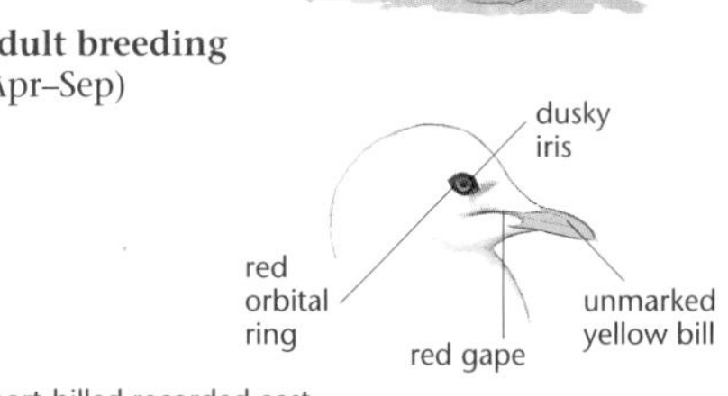
Adult breeding (Apr–Sep)
dusky iris
red orbital ring
red gape
unmarked yellow bill

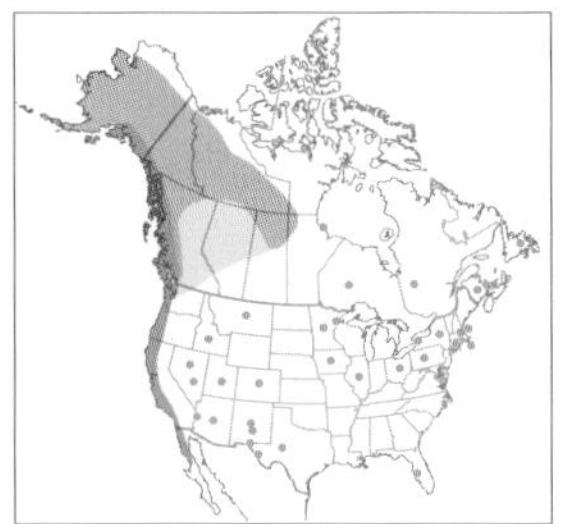

Short-billed recorded east to Atlantic coast

European populations of Mew Gull differ from American birds most obviously in 1st year plumage; they are similar in size, structure, and habits. They are often found with Ring-billed Gulls.

Mew Gull

Larus canus

COMMON (EUROPEAN)

Structure virtually identical to Short-billed; plumage intermediate between Short-billed and Ring-billed.

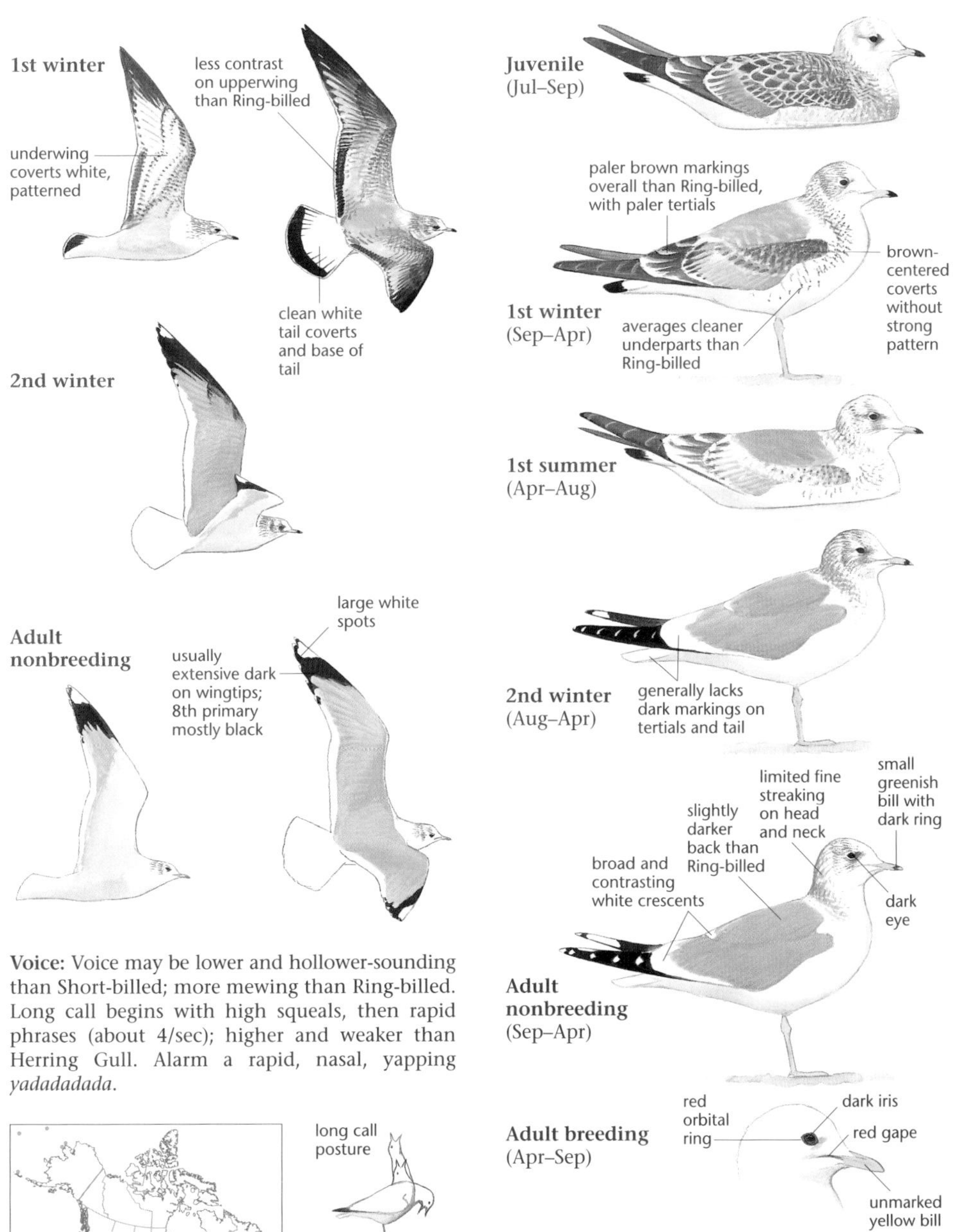

1st winter
less contrast on upperwing than Ring-billed
underwing coverts white, patterned
clean white tail coverts and base of tail
2nd winter
Adult nonbreeding
usually extensive dark on wingtips; 8th primary mostly black
large white spots
Juvenile (Jul–Sep)
paler brown markings overall than Ring-billed, with paler tertials
brown-centered coverts without strong pattern
1st winter (Sep–Apr)
averages cleaner underparts than Ring-billed
1st summer (Apr–Aug)
2nd winter (Aug–Apr)
generally lacks dark markings on tertials and tail
limited fine streaking on head and neck
small greenish bill with dark ring
slightly darker back than Ring-billed
broad and contrasting white crescents
dark eye
Adult nonbreeding (Sep–Apr)

Voice: Voice may be lower and hollower-sounding than Short-billed; more mewing than Ring-billed. Long call begins with high squeals, then rapid phrases (about 4/sec); higher and weaker than Herring Gull. Alarm a rapid, nasal, yapping *yadadadada*.

Adult breeding (Apr–Sep)

red orbital ring

dark iris

red gape

unmarked yellow bill

long call posture

Atlantic coast records are of the European Common population. Records in Alaska are of the Siberian Kamchatka population (not shown): similar to Common but averages larger, with longer bill and more angular head shape; adults are normally pale-eyed. 1st year birds have more heavily marked plumage, tending toward Short-billed.

In most areas this is our most commonly seen gull, found near any water as well as around parking lots, parks, and restaurants continent-wide. Next to Mew Gull, it is our smallest white-headed gull.

Ring-billed Gull

Larus delawarensis

L 17.5" WS 48" WT 1.1 lb (520 g) ♂>♀

Smaller than Herring and California Gulls, with relatively shorter bill, thinner and more pointed wings. Slightly larger and bulkier than Mew Gull.

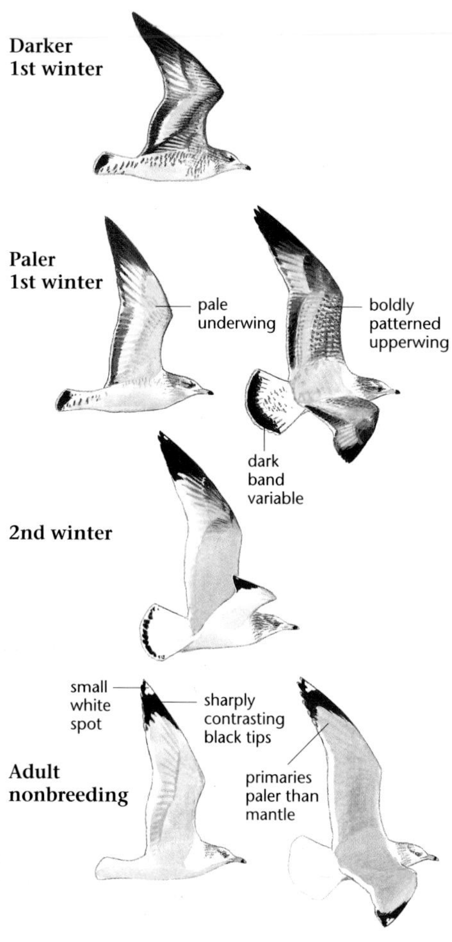
Darker 1st winter
Paler 1st winter
pale underwing
boldly patterned upperwing
dark band variable
2nd winter
small white spot
sharply contrasting black tips
Adult nonbreeding
primaries paler than mantle

Voice: High and rather hoarse with wheezy, scratchy quality; higher than California; higher, harsher, less nasal than Mew. Long call level and rather slow; begins with long, high squeals, then rapid phrases (about 3/sec); ends with long, slurred notes. Also a high *kuleeeeuk* repeated, and *kleeeea* or *k-heeer*. Flight call a high, thin *keeel*.

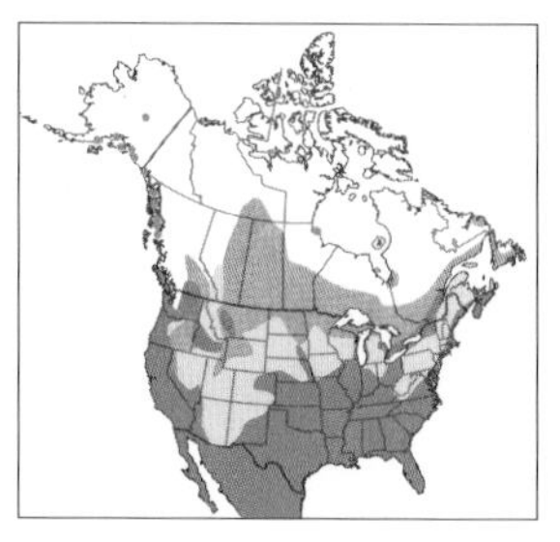

long call posture

Juvenile (Jul–Sep, some to Dec)
1st winter (Sep–Apr)
may resemble 2nd year Herring but smaller; note wing and tail pattern
pink bill with clean-cut black tip
dark bars
sharply contrasting dark centers on coverts
1st summer (Apr–Sep)
2nd winter (Aug–Apr)
Adult nonbreeding (Sep–Apr)
pale mantle like Herring
pale iris
faint white crescents
broad black ring on bill
yellow legs
Adult breeding (Apr–Sep)
pale iris
red orbital ring
broad black ring
red gape

Intermediate in size between Ring-billed and Herring, California is subtly distinctive in structure and plumage. Juvenile is similar to Western and Herring, adult more like Herring and Ring-billed.

California Gull

Larus californicus

L 21" WS 54" WT 1.3 lb (610 g) ♂>♀

Smaller than Herring Gull, with round head, relatively long bill and long wings. Differs from Ring-billed in larger size, longer bill, relatively narrower wings.

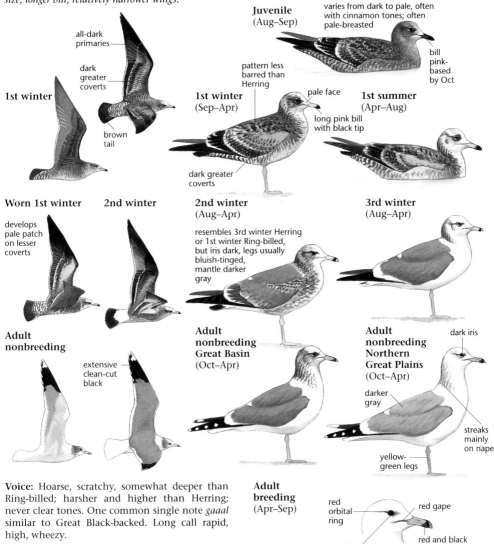

Juvenile (Aug–Sep)

varies from dark to pale, often with cinnamon tones; often pale-breasted

bill pink-based by Oct

1st winter

all-dark primaries

dark greater coverts

brown tail

1st winter (Sep–Apr)

pattern less barred than Herring

pale face

long pink bill with black tip

dark greater coverts

1st summer (Apr–Aug)

Worn 1st winter

develops pale patch on lesser coverts

2nd winter

2nd winter (Aug–Apr)

resembles 3rd winter Herring or 1st winter Ring-billed, but iris dark, legs usually bluish-tinged, mantle darker gray

3rd winter (Aug–Apr)

Adult nonbreeding

extensive clean-cut black

Adult nonbreeding Great Basin (Oct–Apr)

Adult nonbreeding Northern Great Plains (Oct–Apr)

dark iris

darker gray

streaks mainly on nape

yellow-green legs

Voice: Hoarse, scratchy, somewhat deeper than Ring-billed; harsher and higher than Herring; never clear tones. One common single note *gaaal* similar to Great Black-backed. Long call rapid, high, wheezy.

Adult breeding (Apr–Sep)

red orbital ring

red gape

dark iris

red and black marks

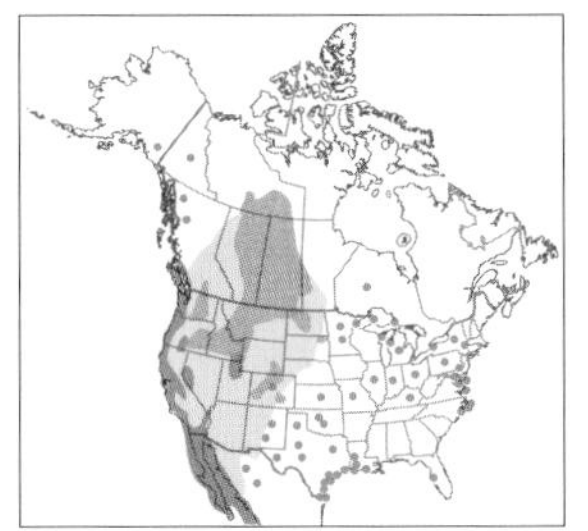

long call posture

Northern Great Plains breeders average larger than Great Basin, and adults average paler-mantled, approaching Herring Gull. These differences are broadly overlapping, however, and only extreme individuals are identifiable.

Our most widespread large gull, Herring Gull is one of our most variable species. Variation in its size, structure, and plumage can create confusion with almost every other large gull species.

Herring Gull

Larus argentatus

L 25" WS 58" WT 2.5 lb (1,150 g) ♂>♀

AMERICAN

Relatively slender compared to other large gulls. Long-billed with peak on rear crown and fairly long, narrow wings. All-brown plumage of 1st year unique in east.

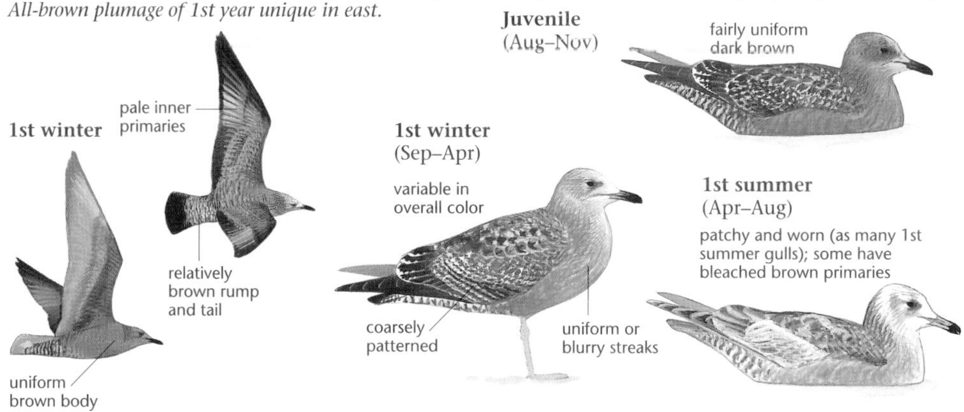
Juvenile
(Aug–Nov)
fairly uniform dark brown
1st winter
pale inner primaries
relatively brown rump and tail
uniform brown body
1st winter
(Sep–Apr)
variable in overall color
coarsely patterned
uniform or blurry streaks
1st summer
(Apr–Aug)
patchy and worn (as many 1st summer gulls); some have bleached brown primaries

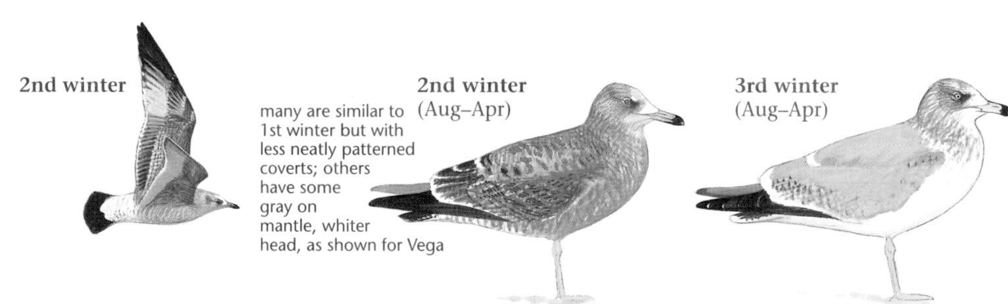
2nd winter
2nd winter
(Aug–Apr)
many are similar to 1st winter but with less neatly patterned coverts; others have some gray on mantle, whiter head, as shown for Vega
3rd winter
(Aug–Apr)

Adult
nonbreeding
limited dark tips, not sharply contrasting
Paler adult
nonbreeding
about 1 percent in east show very limited black in wingtips like Thayer's Gull
Adult
nonbreeding
(Sep–Apr)
usually extensive streaking
pink legs

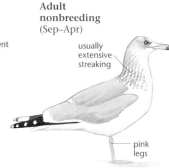

Voice: Clear, flat bugling. Long call higher, clearer, and more two-syllabled than Western; also single notes *klooh, klaaw,* and short, low, hollow *kaaw.* Flight call trumpeting, lower than Ring-billed.

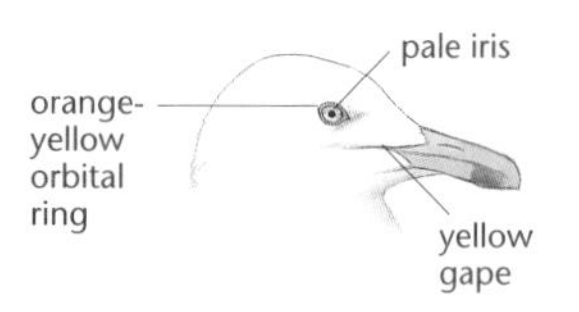
Adult
breeding
(Feb–Sep)
orange-yellow orbital ring
pale iris
yellow gape

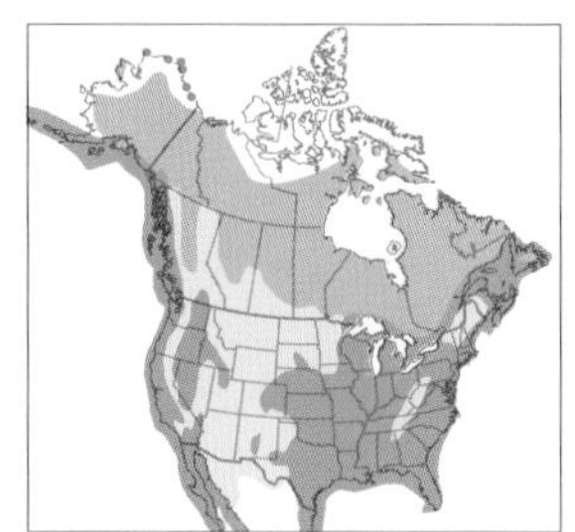

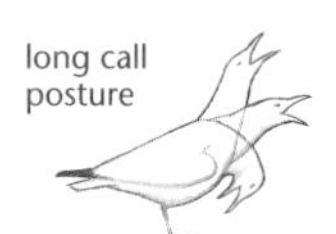
long call posture

1st winter birds are extremely variable; no two are alike. Nevertheless, patterns do exist. A slender, paler, neatly patterned, and pale-headed type (often retaining juvenal plumage through Jan) predominates in the west, while a bulkier, browner, dark-headed type (losing most juvenal plumage by Nov) predominates on the Atlantic coast.

Typical individuals of these Eurasian populations of Herring Gull are fairly distinctive, although variation within North American Herring Gulls makes positive identification nearly impossible.

Herring Gull

Larus argentatus

VEGA (SIBERIAN)

A regular visitor to western Alaska. Averages sleeker and slightly larger than American birds, but much overlap.

1st winter

paler gray inner primaries

broad, dark tail-band

mostly white rump and tail coverts

2nd winter

Adult nonbreeding

white subterminal spots usually obvious

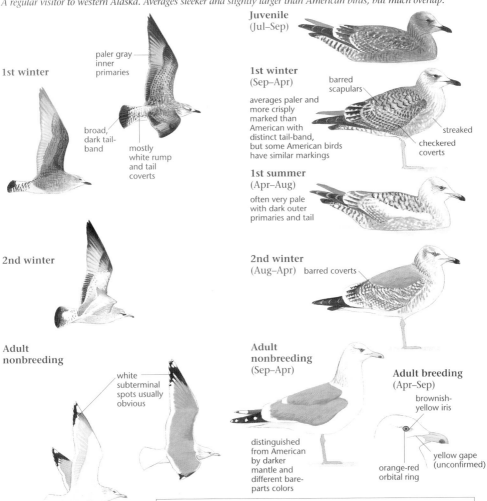

Juvenile (Jul–Sep)

1st winter (Sep–Apr)

averages paler and more crisply marked than American with distinct tail-band, but some American birds have similar markings

barred scapulars

streaked

checkered coverts

1st summer (Apr–Aug)

often very pale with dark outer primaries and tail

2nd winter (Aug–Apr) barred coverts

Adult nonbreeding (Sep–Apr)

distinguished from American by darker mantle and different bare-parts colors

Adult breeding (Apr–Sep)

brownish-yellow iris

yellow gape (unconfirmed)

orange-red orbital ring

Voice: Presumably similar to American Herring. Long call posture like American.

EUROPEAN

A rare visitor to Newfoundland and perhaps farther south on our Atlantic coast. Averages smaller and sleeker (less bulky) than American birds, but much overlap. Adults indistinguishable from American.

Voice: Some short call notes hoarser than American. Long call posture like American.

1st winter
like Vega overall; paler and more crisply marked than American, with even narrower dark tail-band, but all these features matched by some American birds
1st winter
(Sep–May)

White-headed Gulls (continued)

Thayer's is very closely related to Iceland Gull; they are often considered a single species that ranges from the slightly longer, darker Thayer's in the west to the smaller, paler Iceland in the east.

Thayer's Gull

Larus thayeri

L 23" WS 55" WT 2.2 lb (1,000 g) ♂>♀

Structure like Iceland Gull; averages slightly larger and longer-billed, with larger birds overlapping small Herring Gulls, but most indistinguishable from Iceland by structure. (Compare hybrids, especially Glaucous-winged × Herring).

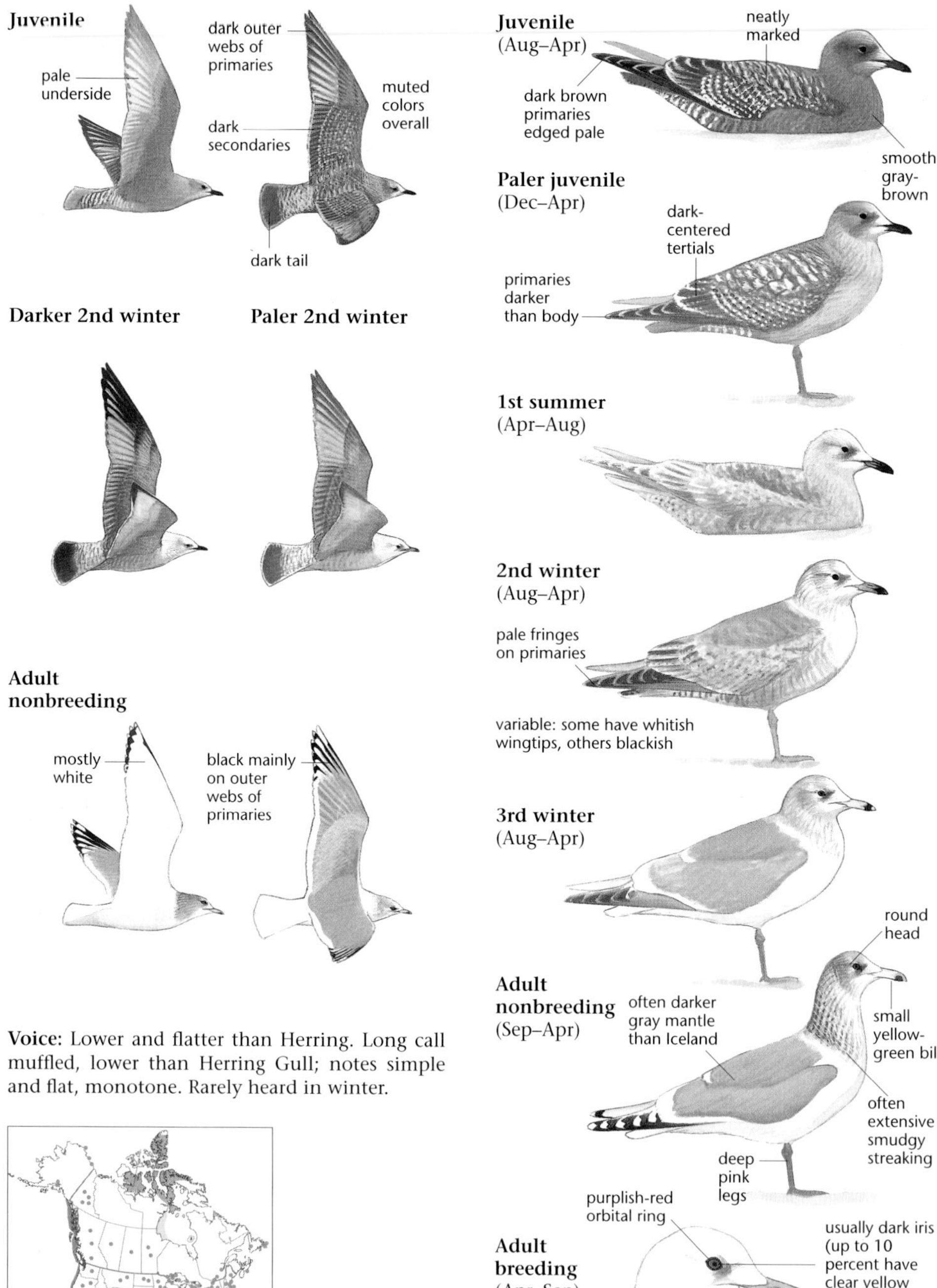

Juvenile
pale underside
dark outer webs of primaries
muted colors overall
dark secondaries
dark tail
Juvenile
(Aug–Apr)
neatly marked
dark brown primaries edged pale
smooth gray-brown
Paler juvenile
(Dec–Apr)
dark-centered tertials
primaries darker than body
Darker 2nd winter
Paler 2nd winter
1st summer
(Apr–Aug)
2nd winter
(Aug–Apr)
pale fringes on primaries
variable: some have whitish wingtips, others blackish
Adult nonbreeding
mostly white
black mainly on outer webs of primaries
3rd winter
(Aug–Apr)
round head
Adult nonbreeding
(Sep–Apr)
often darker gray mantle than Iceland
small yellow-green bill
often extensive smudgy streaking
deep pink legs
purplish-red orbital ring
Adult breeding
(Apr–Sep)
usually dark iris (up to 10 percent have clear yellow iris)
pink gape

Voice: Lower and flatter than Herring. Long call muffled, lower than Herring Gull; notes simple and flat, monotone. Rarely heard in winter.

This small Arctic species is usually subtly distinctive in structure and plumage, but some darker individuals (possibly Iceland × Thayer's hybrids) are indistinguishable from Thayer's Gull.

Iceland Gull

Larus glaucoides

L 22" WS 54" WT 1.8 lb (820 g) ♂>♀

Relatively small with round head and short bill, creating gentle expression. Round body, short bill, short legs, and relatively broad but pointed wings create overall stocky appearance.

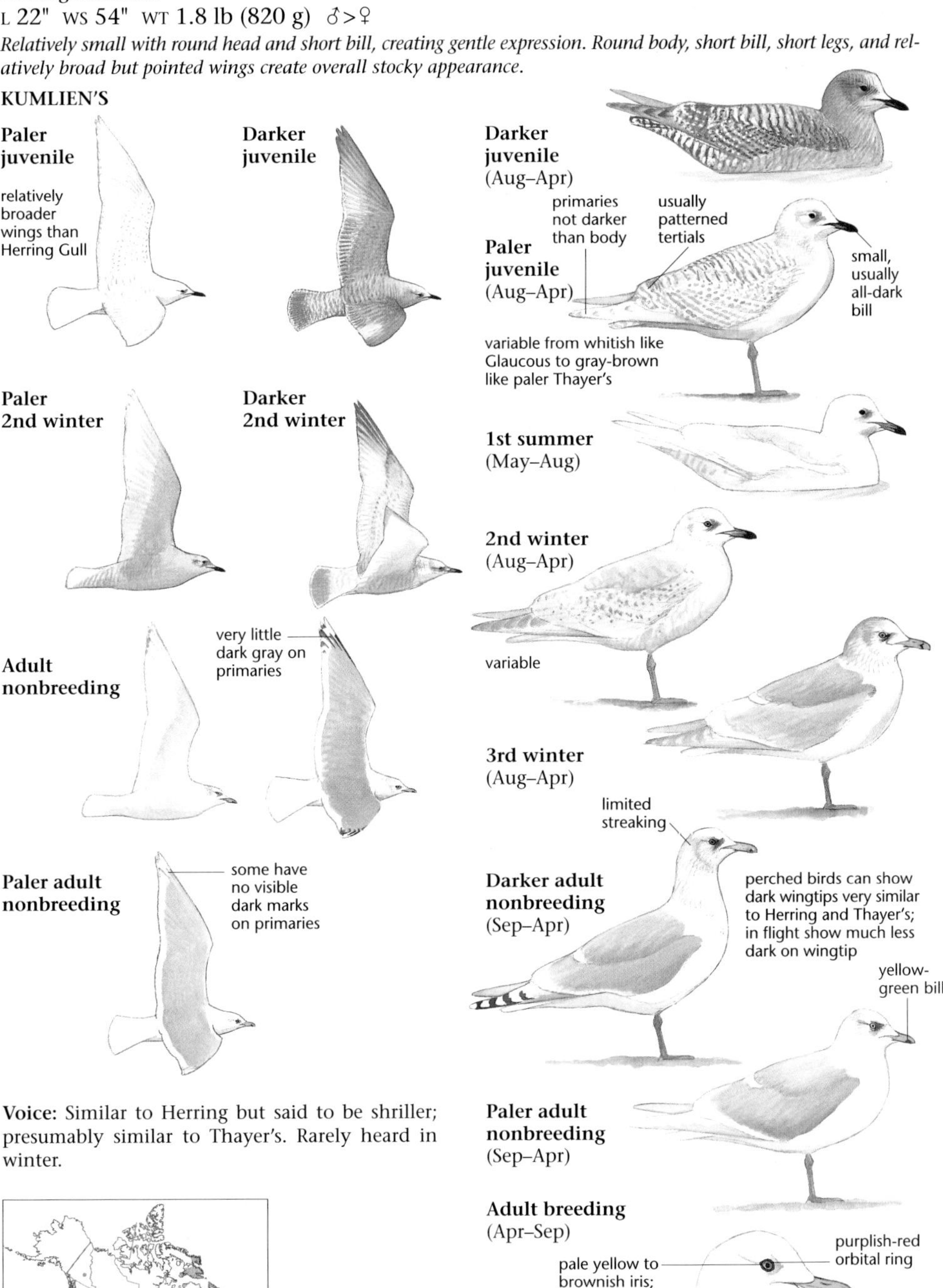
KUMLIEN'S
Paler juvenile
relatively broader wings than Herring Gull
Darker juvenile
Darker juvenile (Aug–Apr)
primaries not darker than body
usually patterned tertials
Paler juvenile (Aug–Apr)
small, usually all-dark bill
variable from whitish like Glaucous to gray-brown like paler Thayer's
Paler 2nd winter
Darker 2nd winter
1st summer (May–Aug)
2nd winter (Aug–Apr)
very little dark gray on primaries
Adult nonbreeding
variable
3rd winter (Aug–Apr)
limited streaking
Paler adult nonbreeding
some have no visible dark marks on primaries
Darker adult nonbreeding (Sep–Apr)
perched birds can show dark wingtips very similar to Herring and Thayer's; in flight show much less dark on wingtip
yellow-green bill
Paler adult nonbreeding (Sep–Apr)
Adult breeding (Apr–Sep)
pale yellow to brownish iris; averages paler than Thayer's
purplish-red orbital ring
pink gape

Voice: Similar to Herring but said to be shriller; presumably similar to Thayer's. Rarely heard in winter.

True Iceland population (not shown) nesting in Greenland may reach our area in small numbers; averages smaller and paler than Kumlien's, but some Kumlien's appear similar and may not be separable.

One of our largest, palest gulls, Glaucous may be confused only with Iceland and Glaucous-winged. This Arctic species hybridizes with Glaucous-winged and Herring.

Glaucous Gull

Larus hyperboreus

L 27" WS 60" WT 3.1 lb (1,400 g) ♂>♀

Large and powerful with very long and straight bill, flat crown, and slight bulge on forehead. Usually larger, longer-billed, and flatter-headed than Iceland, with shorter primary projection.

Juvenile

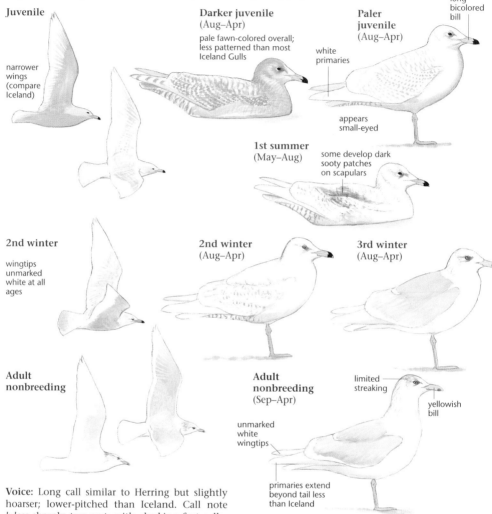

narrower wings (compare Iceland)

Darker juvenile (Aug–Apr)

pale fawn-colored overall; less patterned than most Iceland Gulls

Paler juvenile (Aug–Apr)

long bicolored bill

white primaries

appears small-eyed

1st summer (May–Aug)

some develop dark sooty patches on scapulars

2nd winter

wingtips unmarked white at all ages

2nd winter (Aug–Apr)

3rd winter (Aug–Apr)

Adult nonbreeding

Adult nonbreeding (Sep–Apr)

limited streaking

yellowish bill

unmarked white wingtips

primaries extend beyond tail less than Iceland

Voice: Long call similar to Herring but slightly hoarser; lower-pitched than Iceland. Call note *k-leee* sharply two-part, with clucking first syllable, distinctive; higher and weaker than Herring.

Adult breeding (Mar–Sep)

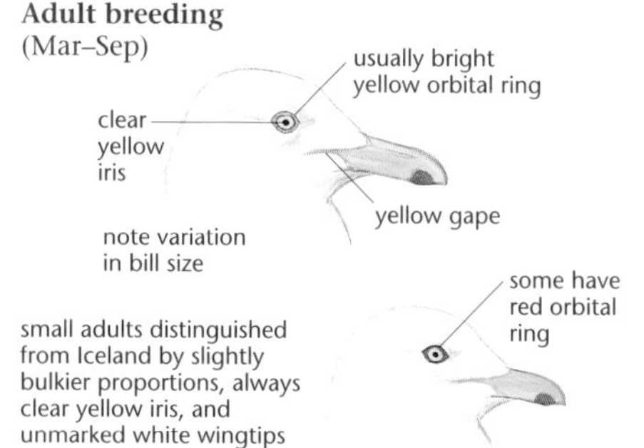
usually bright yellow orbital ring
clear yellow iris
yellow gape
note variation in bill size
some have red orbital ring
small adults distinguished from Iceland by slightly bulkier proportions, always clear yellow iris, and unmarked white wingtips

long call posture

This large and stocky gull is extremely variable in size, proportions, and plumage. The variation is enhanced by hybridization with Herring, Glaucous, and Western Gulls.

Glaucous-winged Gull

Larus glaucescens

L 26" WS 58" WT 2.2 lb (1,000 g) ♂>♀

Most are structurally similar to Western with bulky body and large bill, but extremely variable: some more slender with flat-topped head, matching Herring; some small and small-billed, close to Thayer's. On pure birds the relatively unpatterned and low-contrast plumage distinctive.

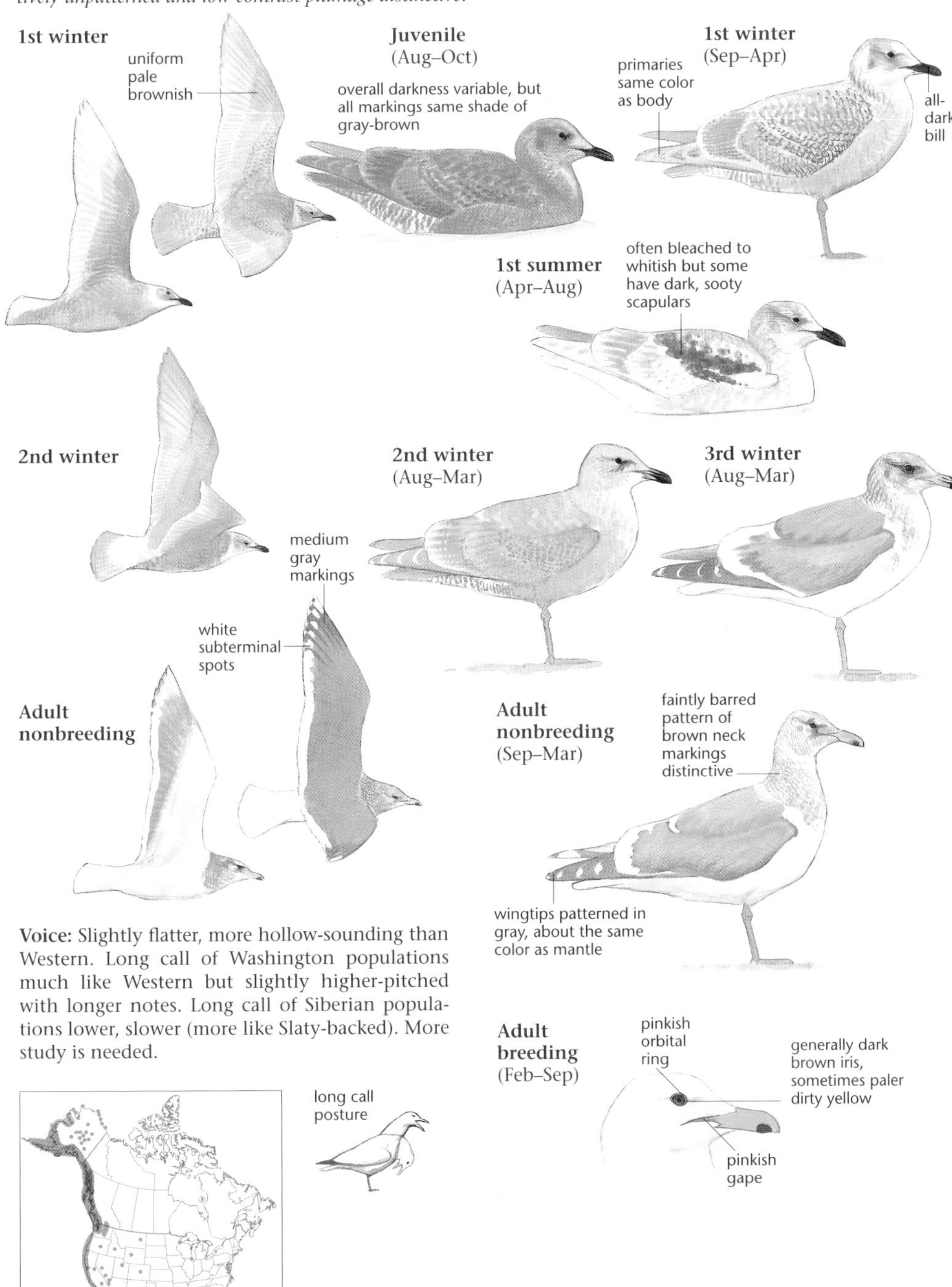
1st winter
uniform pale brownish
Juvenile (Aug–Oct)
overall darkness variable, but all markings same shade of gray-brown
1st winter (Sep–Apr)
primaries same color as body
all-dark bill
1st summer (Apr–Aug)
often bleached to whitish but some have dark, sooty scapulars
2nd winter
2nd winter (Aug–Mar)
3rd winter (Aug–Mar)
medium gray markings
white subterminal spots
Adult nonbreeding
Adult nonbreeding (Sep–Mar)
faintly barred pattern of brown neck markings distinctive
wingtips patterned in gray, about the same color as mantle
Adult breeding (Feb–Sep)
pinkish orbital ring
generally dark brown iris, sometimes paler dirty yellow
pinkish gape
long call posture

Voice: Slightly flatter, more hollow-sounding than Western. Long call of Washington populations much like Western but slightly higher-pitched with longer notes. Long call of Siberian populations lower, slower (more like Slaty-backed). More study is needed.

Most similar to Western Gull and Vega Herring Gull, this species can usually be distinguished by wingtip pattern and mantle color; 1st year birds are very difficult to identify.

Slaty-backed Gull

Larus schistisagus

L 25" WS 58" WT 3 lb (1,350 g) ♂>♀

Rather large and bulky like Western but slightly thinner-billed; stockier and broader-winged than Vega Herring. At all ages, dark color on primaries is mostly on outer webs.

Juvenile (Aug–Nov)
similar to Western and Vega Herring

1st winter

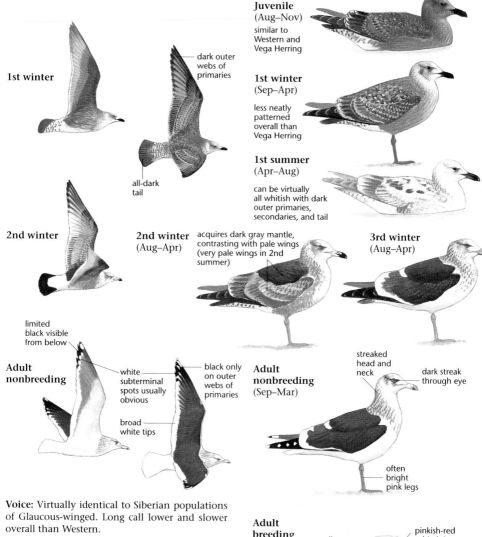

dark outer webs of primaries

all-dark tail

1st winter (Sep–Apr)
less neatly patterned overall than Vega Herring

1st summer (Apr–Aug)
can be virtually all whitish with dark outer primaries, secondaries, and tail

2nd winter

2nd winter (Aug–Apr)
acquires dark gray mantle, contrasting with pale wings (very pale wings in 2nd summer)

3rd winter (Aug–Apr)

limited black visible from below

Adult nonbreeding

white subterminal spots usually obvious

broad white tips

black only on outer webs of primaries

Adult nonbreeding (Sep–Mar)
streaked head and neck
dark streak through eye
often bright pink legs

Voice: Virtually identical to Siberian populations of Glaucous-winged. Long call lower and slower overall than Western.

Adult breeding (Feb–Sep)

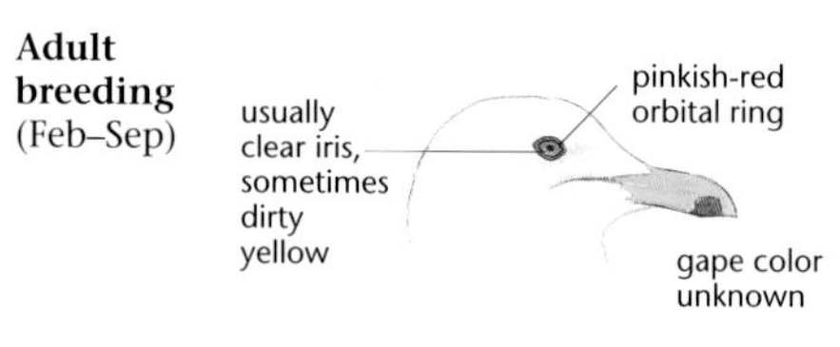
usually clear iris, sometimes dirty yellow
pinkish-red orbital ring
gape color unknown

long call posture

Individuals without white subterminal spots on primaries are distinguished from Western by streaked head (in winter), black only on outer webs of primaries, paler underside of primaries, slightly more slender structure. Hybridizes with Glaucous-winged Gull in Siberia; adult hybrids are paler-mantled but otherwise difficult to distinguish from pure birds.

This large, stocky species is rarely seen away from the Pacific Ocean. Hybridizes extensively with Glaucous-winged Gull along the Washington coast, where hybrids may outnumber pure birds.

Western Gull

Larus occidentalis

L 25" WS 58" WT 2.2 lb (1,000 g) ♂>♀

Very stocky and heavy-billed, the bill slightly drooping and thick-tipped. Peak on head above eye with sloping rear crown. Long secondaries produce broad wings and, when perched, broad tertials and drooping "skirt" along lower edge of folded wing.

Juvenile (Aug–Oct)

uniform dark, sooty brown

1st winter

all-dark tail and paler rump

1st winter (Sep–May)

pale base of lower mandible

1st summer (Apr–Sep)

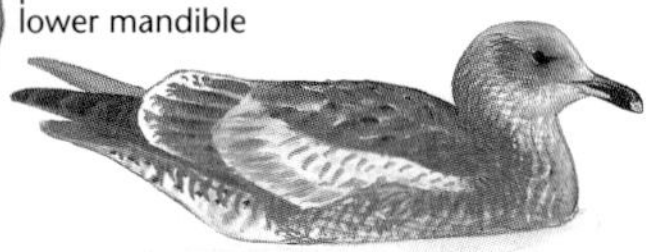

2nd winter

2nd winter (Aug–Mar)

3rd winter (Aug–Mar)

Adult nonbreeding

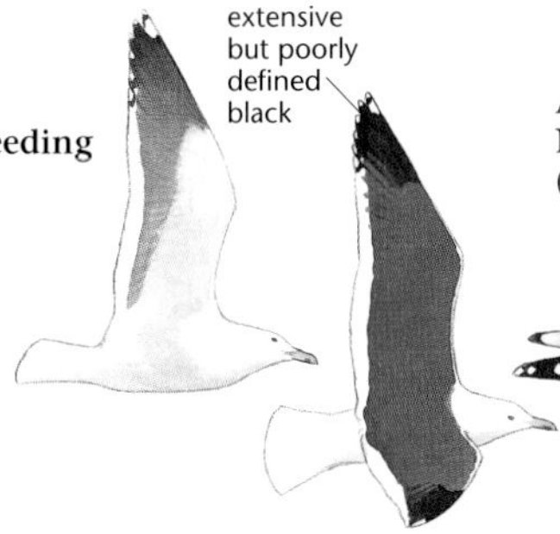

extensive but poorly defined black

Adult nonbreeding Northern (Sep–Mar)

broad tertials and drooping "skirt"

Adult nonbreeding Southern (Sep–Mar)

virtually unstreaked

Voice: Generally similar to Herring but notes a little more clipped, less drawn-out, lower, and less clear. Long call fairly flat, simple, and low. Adult in flight over roost gives deep, gruff *ooowa* or *kwaow* unlike high, clear notes of Herring.

Adult breeding (Feb–Sep)

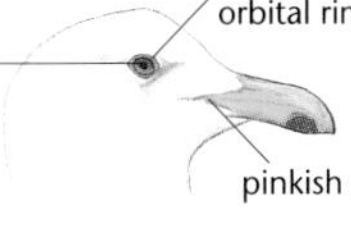

iris varies from dark (mostly Northern) to pale clear yellow (mostly Southern)

orange-yellow orbital ring

pinkish gape

long call posture

Northern birds paler-mantled than Southern with average darker eye, more head-streaking in winter. Variation is clinal, with step in central California.

Closely related to Western and Glaucous-winged but quite distinctive, this large-billed, long-necked species reaches adultlike plumage by its 3rd winter (4th winter for other large gulls).

Yellow-footed Gull

Larus livens

L 27" WS 60" WT 2.8 lb (1,260 g)

Similar to Western Gull but heavier-billed, with strong gonydeal angle, relatively longer neck, and blockier head.

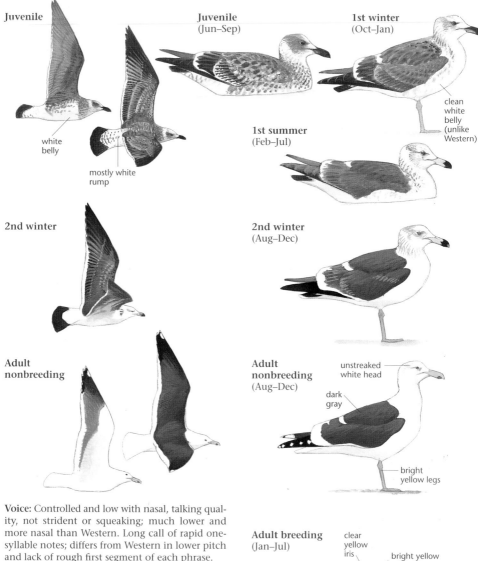

Juvenile

white belly

mostly white rump

Juvenile
(Jun–Sep)

1st winter
(Oct–Jan)

clean white belly (unlike Western)

1st summer
(Feb–Jul)

2nd winter

2nd winter
(Aug–Dec)

Adult nonbreeding

Adult nonbreeding
(Aug–Dec)

unstreaked white head

dark gray

bright yellow legs

Voice: Controlled and low with nasal, talking quality, not strident or squeaking; much lower and more nasal than Western. Long call of rapid one-syllable notes; differs from Western in lower pitch and lack of rough first segment of each phrase.

Adult breeding
(Jan–Jul)

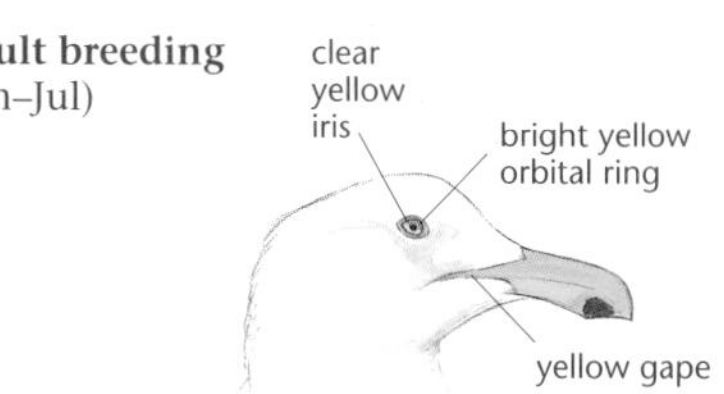
clear yellow iris
bright yellow orbital ring
yellow gape

long call posture

Dark-mantled like Southern Western Gull, but with bright yellow legs; distinguished from Lesser Black-backed by much heavier structure, lack of head-streaking, yellow orbital ring; from Kelp Gull by different head shape, brighter legs, yellow orbital ring, slightly paler back.

This sleek European species has increased dramatically as a visitor to North America. Most are readily identified by slender shape and other details, but larger individuals can be confusing.

Lesser Black-backed Gull

Larus fuscus

L 21" WS 54" WT 1.8 lb (800 g) ♂>♀

Overall very sleek and slender; especially long and narrow wings, recalling Laughing Gull. Small, fairly rounded head with relatively short, thin bill; head and bill structure overlaps broadly with Herring Gull.

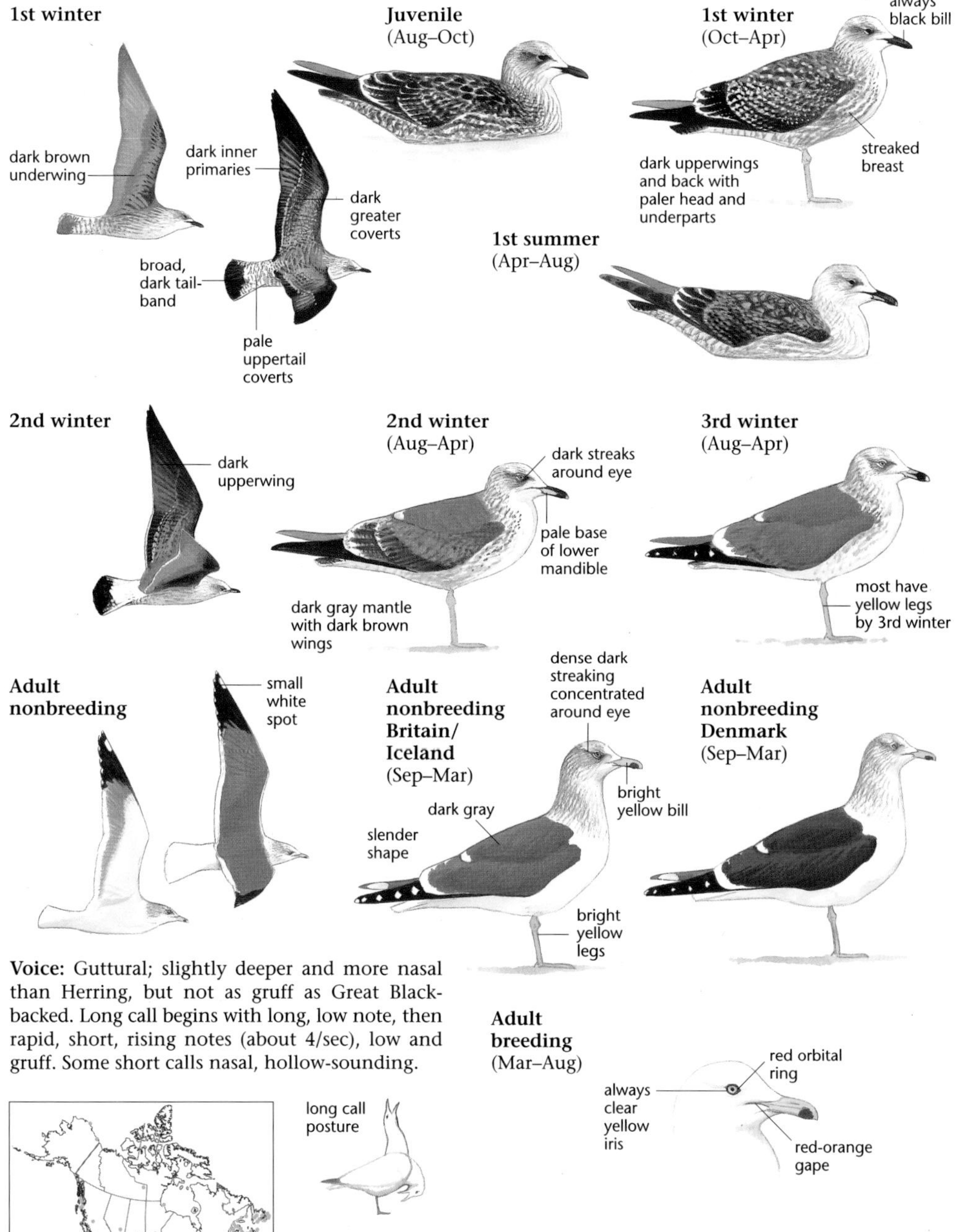

1st winter
dark brown underwing
dark inner primaries
dark greater coverts
broad, dark tail-band
pale uppertail coverts
Juvenile (Aug–Oct)
1st winter (Oct–Apr)
always black bill
streaked breast
dark upperwings and back with paler head and underparts
1st summer (Apr–Aug)
2nd winter
dark upperwing
2nd winter (Aug–Apr)
dark streaks around eye
pale base of lower mandible
dark gray mantle with dark brown wings
3rd winter (Aug–Apr)
most have yellow legs by 3rd winter
Adult nonbreeding
small white spot
Adult nonbreeding Britain/ Iceland (Sep–Mar)
dense dark streaking concentrated around eye
bright yellow bill
dark gray
slender shape
bright yellow legs
Adult nonbreeding Denmark (Sep–Mar)
Adult breeding (Mar–Aug)
red orbital ring
always clear yellow iris
red-orange gape
long call posture

Voice: Guttural; slightly deeper and more nasal than Herring, but not as gruff as Great Black-backed. Long call begins with long, low note, then rapid, short, rising notes (about 4/sec), low and gruff. Some short calls nasal, hollow-sounding.

Nearly all North American records are of the paler-mantled Britain/ Iceland population. A few records apparently refer to the darker Denmark population, which has same mantle color as Great Black-backed and relatively longer wings.

Our largest gull, this North Atlantic species can often be recognized simply by its bulk. Immature has a coarsely checkered pattern above and a pale head; adult has a blackish back.

Great Black-backed Gull

Larus marinus

L 30" WS 65" WT 3.6 lb (1,650 g) ♂>♀

On average our largest gull, but size overlaps with Glaucous, Herring, and others. Long- and broad-winged with lumbering flight; massive head and bill.

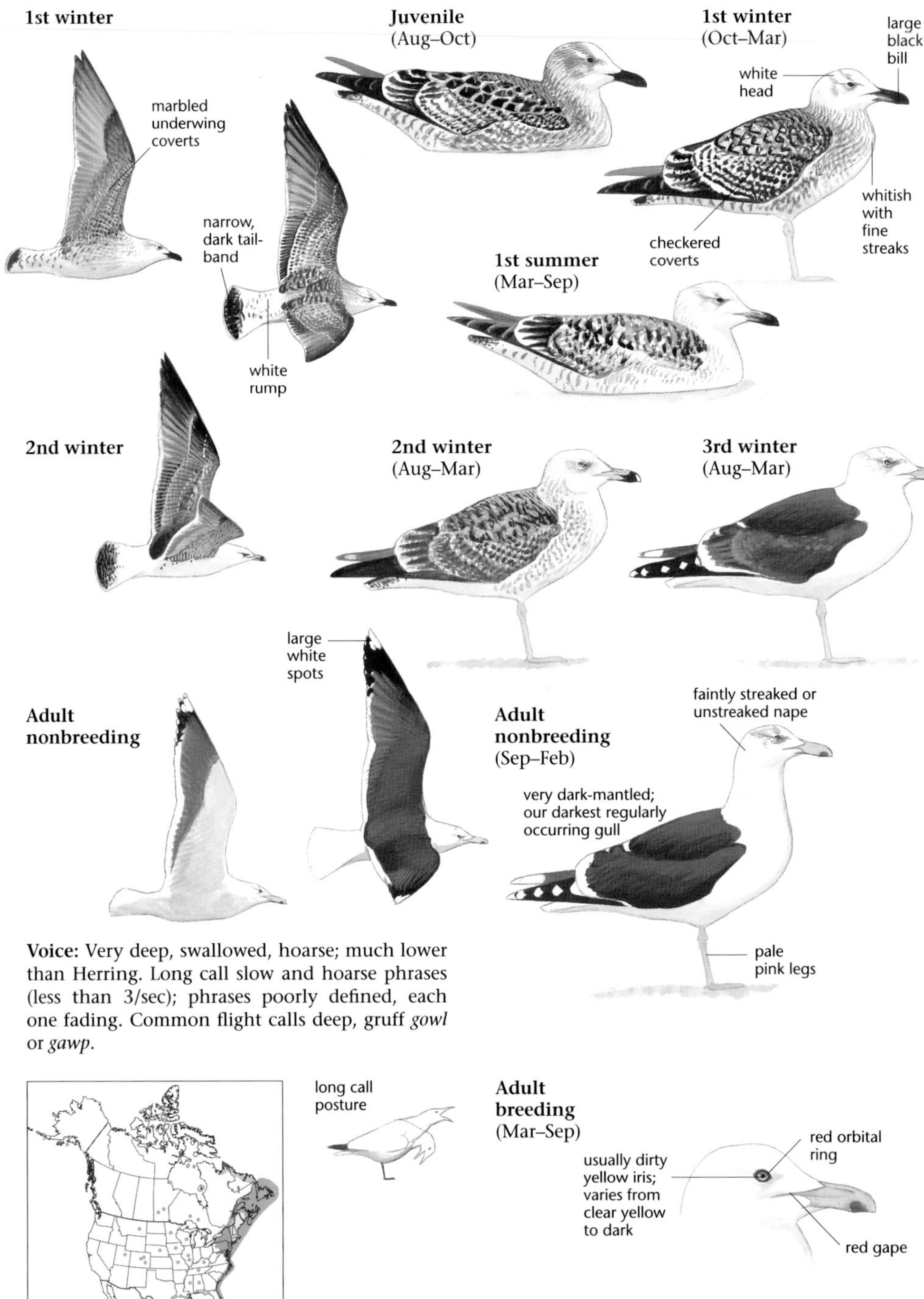
1st winter
marbled underwing coverts
narrow, dark tail-band
white rump
Juvenile (Aug–Oct)
1st winter (Oct–Mar)
large black bill
white head
whitish with fine streaks
checkered coverts
1st summer (Mar–Sep)
2nd winter
2nd winter (Aug–Mar)
3rd winter (Aug–Mar)
large white spots
Adult nonbreeding
Adult nonbreeding (Sep–Feb)
faintly streaked or unstreaked nape
very dark-mantled; our darkest regularly occurring gull
pale pink legs

Voice: Very deep, swallowed, hoarse; much lower than Herring. Long call slow and hoarse phrases (less than 3/sec); phrases poorly defined, each one fading. Common flight calls deep, gruff *gowl* or *gawp*.

long call posture
Adult breeding (Mar–Sep)
usually dirty yellow iris; varies from clear yellow to dark
red orbital ring
red gape

White-headed Gulls (continued)

This unique Pacific species is almost exclusively coastal. With its dark plumage, pointed wings, and habit of chasing other seabirds to steal food, it is often mistaken for a jaeger.

Heermann's Gull

Larus heermanni

L 19" WS 51" WT 1.1 lb (500 g) ♂>♀

A distinctive species: dark and unpatterned. About the size of Ring-billed Gull but stockier, broader-winged, longer-billed; wings broad but pointed.

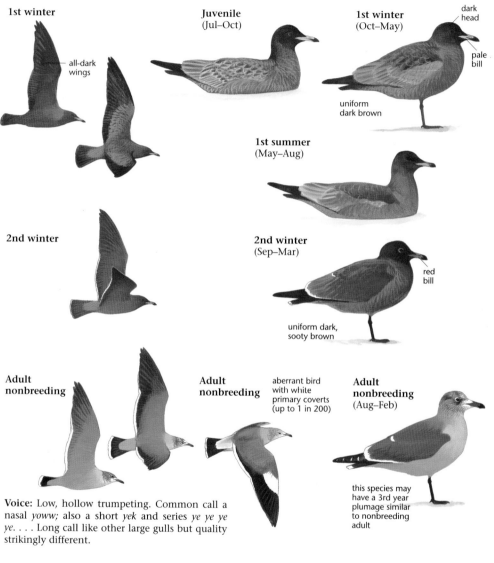

1st winter

all-dark wings

Juvenile
(Jul–Oct)

1st winter
(Oct–May)

dark head

pale bill

uniform dark brown

1st summer
(May–Aug)

2nd winter

2nd winter
(Sep–Mar)

red bill

uniform dark, sooty brown

Adult nonbreeding

Adult nonbreeding

aberrant bird with white primary coverts (up to 1 in 200)

Adult nonbreeding
(Aug–Feb)

this species may have a 3rd year plumage similar to nonbreeding adult

Voice: Low, hollow trumpeting. Common call a nasal *yoww;* also a short *yek* and series *ye ye ye ye. . . .* Long call like other large gulls but quality strikingly different.

Adult breeding
(Dec–Aug)

gray body
and white
head unique

Small Arctic Gulls

These two distinctive small gulls nest on tundra ponds. Ross's winters in the Arctic; vagrants southward are usually found with Bonaparte's Gull. Sabine's is pelagic when not breeding.

Ross's Gull

Rhodostethia rosea

L 13.5" WS 33" WT 6 oz (180 g)

Slightly smaller than Bonaparte's but wings longer and thinner, held more arched and pushed forward. Head distinctly peaked with very short bill. Wedge-shaped tail difficult to see, appears long.

1st winter

bold wing pattern like Black-legged Kittiwake

Adult nonbreeding

broad white trailing edge

gray underwing

Juvenile (Jul–Aug)

1st winter (Sep–Apr)

1st summer (Apr–Aug)

most show strong pink color

Adult nonbreeding (Sep–Apr)

very pale gray above; unmarked wings

Adult breeding (Apr–Aug)

dark collar unique

Voice: High and melodious. Some calls with hollow barking quality like Black-legged Kittiwake; soft, mellow barking *p-dew* or *prrew* and ternlike *kik-kik-kik-kik-kik*. Generally silent in winter.

Sabine's Gull

Xema sabini

L 13.5" WS 33" WT 6 oz (180 g) ♂>♀

Much smaller than kittiwakes. Striking wing pattern and graceful, ternlike flight distinctive. Size like Bonaparte's but wings longer and broad-based, bill shorter.

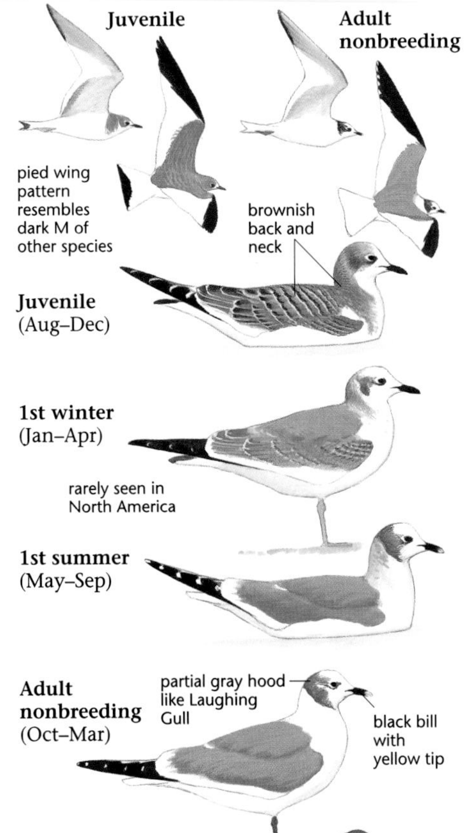
Juvenile
Adult nonbreeding
pied wing pattern resembles dark M of other species
brownish back and neck
Juvenile (Aug–Dec)
1st winter (Jan–Apr)
rarely seen in North America
1st summer (May–Sep)
Adult nonbreeding (Oct–Mar)
partial gray hood like Laughing Gull
black bill with yellow tip
Adult breeding (Apr–Sep)
gray hood with black lower border unique

Voice: Grating, buzzy or trilling ternlike *kyeer, kyeer* . . . or grating *krrr*. Juvenile call a high, clear trill *dededededeer* slightly descending at end.

The pink suffusion shown by most Ross's Gulls is related to diet and can be shown (faintly or intensely) by individuals of other small gull species. It is most consistently shown by Ross's and Franklin's, less often by Laughing and Black-headed, least often by Sabine's, Bonaparte's, and Little.

These two species nest colonially on narrow cliff ledges; away from the nest they are found at sea. Black-legged is often visible from land; Red-legged forages mainly at night over deep water.

Black-legged Kittiwake

Rissa tridactyla

L 17" WS 36" WT 14 oz (400 g) ♂>♀

Slightly smaller than Mew Gull; large-headed, long-winged, with narrow "hand," and short-legged. Flight buoyant and dashing, but wingbeats rather stiff.

Juvenile

Adult nonbreeding

small black tip

pale primaries

bold black M

Juvenile/ 1st winter (Aug–Apr)

black legs

1st summer (Mar–Sep)

Adult nonbreeding (Aug–Mar)

both kittiwakes stand awkwardly with body angled up

Adult breeding (Apr–Sep)

yellow bill

Voice: Hollow, nasal quality like Heermann's Gull. Rhythmic, repeated *kitti-weeeik* . . . given frequently at or near nest site, often in chorus. Generally silent in winter.

Red-legged Kittiwake

Rissa brevirostris

L 15" WS 33" WT 13 oz (380 g) ♂>♀

Slightly smaller than Black-legged, relatively longer- and thinner-winged. Head large and broad, bill very short and thick with distinct curve, red legs shorter.

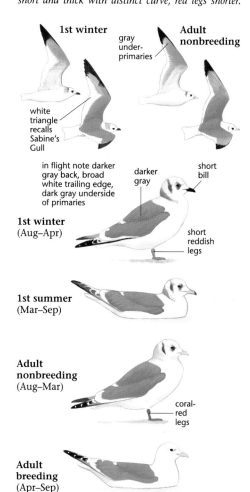

1st winter

gray under-primaries

Adult nonbreeding

white triangle recalls Sabine's Gull

in flight note darker gray back, broad white trailing edge, dark gray underside of primaries

darker gray

short bill

1st winter (Aug–Apr)

short reddish legs

1st summer (Mar–Sep)

Adult nonbreeding (Aug–Mar)

coral-red legs

Adult breeding (Apr–Sep)

Voice: Much higher than Black-legged; a high, falsetto squeal *suWEEEEr* repeated. Generally silent in winter.

As always, beware of basing an identification on a single field mark. Black-legged Kittiwakes with pink, yellow, and even orange-red legs are recorded rarely (mainly 1st year birds) and should not be mistaken for Red-legged Kittiwake. Bill shape, mantle color, and wing pattern are more easily seen field marks.

Large Crested Terns

Our two largest terns are often seen flying steadily 20 to 50 feet above the water patrolling for fish. Caspian is heavy and gull-like; Royal is more closely related to Elegant and Sandwich Terns.

Caspian Tern

Sterna caspia

L 21" WS 50" WT 1.4 lb (660 g) ♂>♀

Heavier, broader-winged, shorter-tailed, and more gull-like than Royal. Neck and bill thicker.

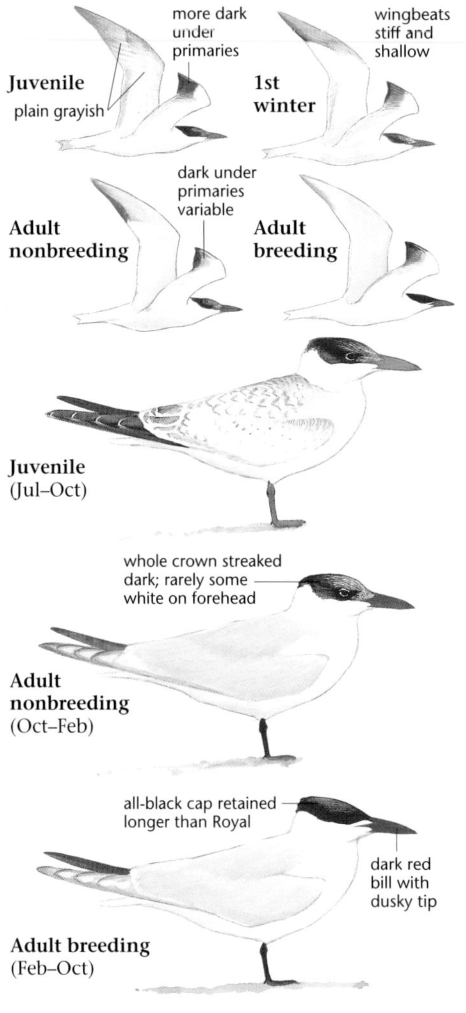

more dark under primaries
wingbeats stiff and shallow
Juvenile
plain grayish
1st winter
dark under primaries variable
Adult nonbreeding
Adult breeding
Juvenile
(Jul–Oct)
whole crown streaked dark; rarely some white on forehead
Adult nonbreeding
(Oct–Feb)
all-black cap retained longer than Royal
dark red bill with dusky tip
Adult breeding
(Feb–Oct)

Voice: Call a deep, very harsh, heronlike scream *aaayayaum*. Juvenile call a high, thin, wheezy whistle *sweeeea* or *fweeeee-er* (heard Jul–Apr).

Royal Tern

Sterna maxima

L 20" WS 41" WT 1 lb (470 g) ♂>♀

Slender and long-winged; bill long and rather heavy. Streamlined and sleek, with powerful, direct flight.

limited dark under primaries

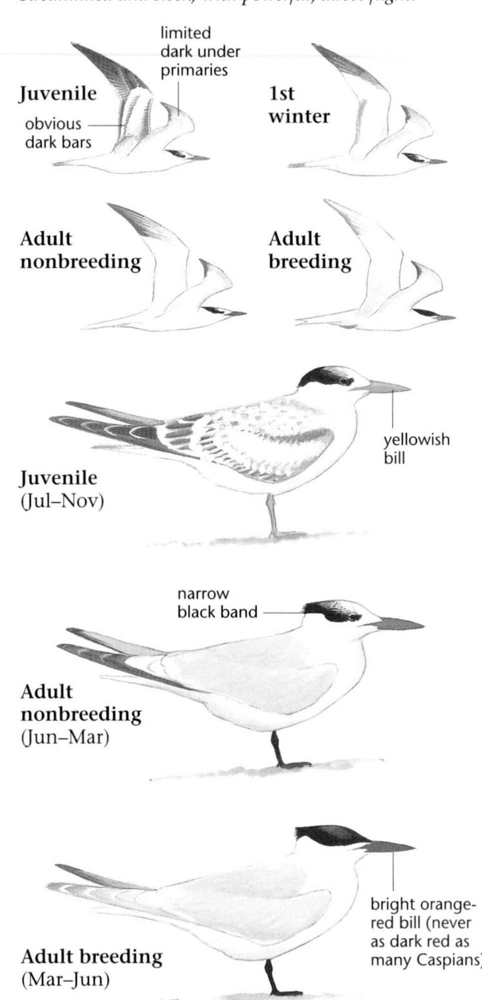

Juvenile
obvious dark bars
1st winter
Adult nonbreeding
Adult breeding
yellowish bill
Juvenile
(Jul–Nov)
narrow black band
Adult nonbreeding
(Jun–Mar)
bright orange-red bill (never as dark red as many Caspians)
Adult breeding
(Mar–Jun)

Voice: Call loud, throaty, rolling *kerrra* or lower *koorrrick;* lower, longer than Sandwich; also soft *youm* or *yeek*. Juvenile begging call two to three piping whistles; also high, ringing *kerreeep*.

Leg color is variable in the crested terns: always black in Sandwich, often yellow in juveniles of the other three species. Only Elegant Tern regularly shows yellow legs as an adult.

Small Crested Terns

Closely related to Royal Tern, these species can be distinguished at a distance from smaller terns by their more powerful flight; long, narrow, angular wings; and longer head and bill.

Elegant Tern

Sterna elegans

L 17" WS 34" WT 9 oz (260 g) ♂>♀

Smaller than Royal, with relatively larger head and shorter tail; appears front-heavy. Best distinguished by relatively longer and thinner bill with distinct down-curve, and by longer, drooping crest.

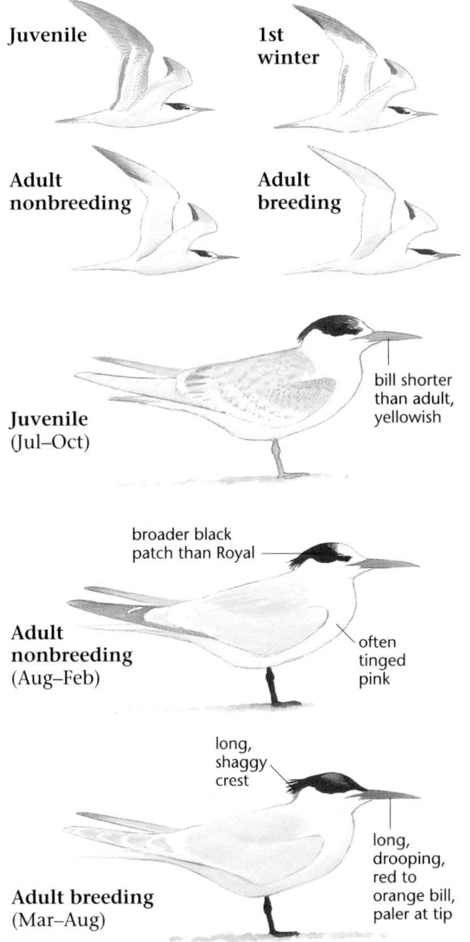

Juvenile
1st winter
Adult nonbreeding
Adult breeding
bill shorter than adult, yellowish
Juvenile (Jul–Oct)
broader black patch than Royal
Adult nonbreeding (Aug–Feb)
often tinged pink
long, shaggy crest
long, drooping, red to orange bill, paler at tip
Adult breeding (Mar–Aug)

Voice: Call a short, low, loud *keerik;* very similar to Sandwich but deeper. Juvenile gives insistent, thin, whistled *sip sip sip . . .* similar to Royal.

Sandwich Tern

Sterna sandvicensis

L 15" WS 34" WT 7 oz (210 g) ♂>♀

Similar to Royal but smaller and a little more slender overall, with thinner black bill.

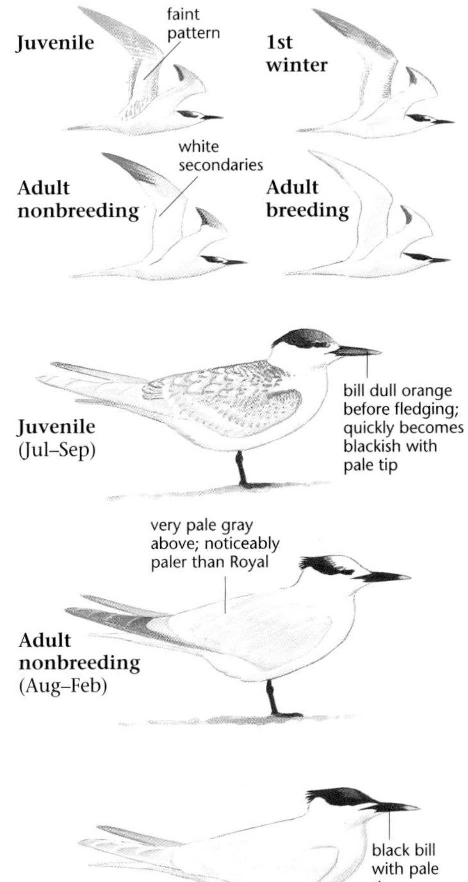

Juvenile
faint pattern
1st winter
white secondaries
Adult nonbreeding
Adult breeding
bill dull orange before fledging; quickly becomes blackish with pale tip
Juvenile (Jul–Sep)
very pale gray above; noticeably paler than Royal
Adult nonbreeding (Aug–Feb)
black bill with pale tip
Adult breeding (Mar–Aug)

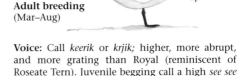

Voice: Call *keerik* or *krjik;* higher, more abrupt, and more grating than Royal (reminiscent of Roseate Tern). Juvenile begging call a high *see see see* like Royal; also a high, ringing *kreep.*

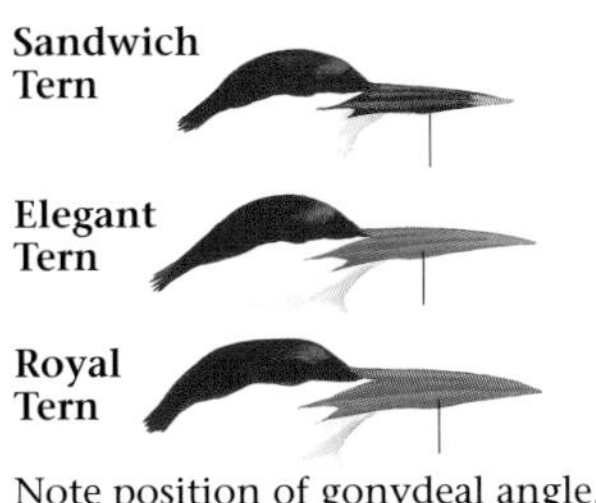

Sandwich Tern
Elegant Tern
Royal Tern

Note position of gonydeal angle.

Medium-size Terns

Common, Arctic, and Forster's Terns form a well-defined group with similar habits, plumage, and voice. Common Tern, the most widespread of the group, is found on lakes, rivers, and oceans.

Common Tern

Sterna hirundo

L 12" WS 30" WT 4.2 oz (120 g)

The "typical" tern; very streamlined with direct but buoyant flight. More slender and buoyant than Forster's, but broader and more powerful than Arctic. Wing pattern is best field mark: dark secondaries and outer primaries frame a translucent triangle on inner primaries.

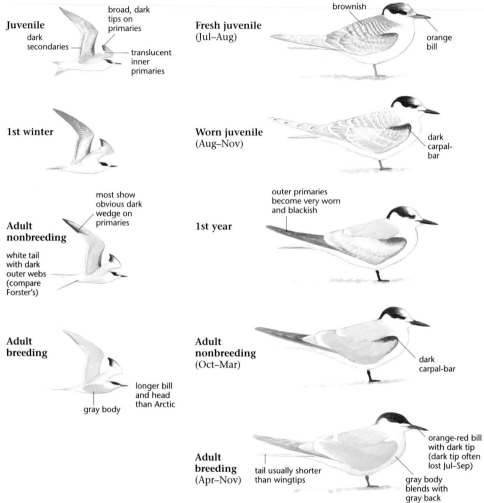

Juvenile
dark secondaries
broad, dark tips on primaries
translucent inner primaries

Fresh juvenile (Jul–Aug)
brownish
orange bill

1st winter

Worn juvenile (Aug–Nov)
dark carpal-bar

Adult nonbreeding
most show obvious dark wedge on primaries
white tail with dark outer webs (compare Forster's)

1st year
outer primaries become very worn and blackish

Adult breeding
longer bill and head than Arctic
gray body

Adult nonbreeding (Oct–Mar)
dark carpal-bar

Adult breeding (Apr–Nov)
tail usually shorter than wingtips
orange-red bill with dark tip (dark tip often lost Jul–Sep)
gray body blends with gray back

Voice: All calls like Arctic and Forster's but richer, more musical, with slurred, two-syllable pattern. Common call a rich, high *keeeyurr* with obvious drop in pitch; a high *kit* or *tyik* and longer, deeper *kiiw*. Adult courtship call a begging *kerri kerri kerri*. . . . Attack call a hacking, dry *k-k-k-k*.

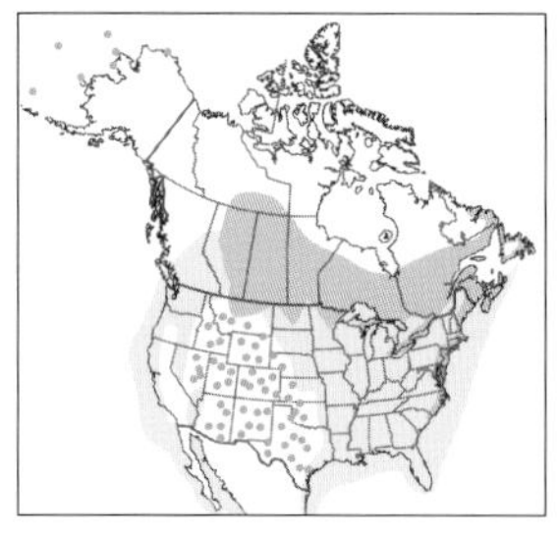

Records in western Alaska are of the Siberian population (not shown), which is identical to American populations except breeding adults have darker gray body plumage (more like Arctic Tern), all-black bill (but a small percentage have red bill base), and dark reddish-brown legs.

This slender, elegant species is very similar to Common Tern. It nests on marshes and shorelines; at other times it is almost exclusively pelagic, rarely seen on land except near nests.

Arctic Tern

Sterna paradisaea

L 12" WS 31" WT 3.9 oz (110 g)

Slightly smaller than Common with much shorter legs; smaller, rounder head; shorter, thinner bill; relatively longer, thinner, and more swept-back wings. Wingbeats deeper and snappier than Common. Wing pattern is best field mark at all ages; note white secondaries and uniform translucent primaries with narrow, dark tips.

Juvenile
white secondaries and tips of greater coverts
translucent primaries with very narrow, dark tips

1st year
primaries dark only on tips

Adult nonbreeding
always uniform gray above

Adult breeding
small head
short bill
long tail
gray body

plunge-dives less often and less vigorously than similar species

Fresh juvenile (Jul–Aug)
generally paler and colder gray than Common
little or no brown
all-black or mostly black bill
dark carpal-bar less obvious

Worn juvenile (Aug–Dec)

1st year
always pale gray primaries
dark on head usually more extensive than on Common
dark carpal-bar becomes more prominent in 1st summer (Apr–Aug)

Adult nonbreeding (Nov–Feb)
rarely seen in North America
uniform pale gray primaries
round head
short bill
dark carpal-bar less obvious than Common

Adult breeding (Mar–Oct)
black cap a little more extensive than Common, nearly reaching gape
small dark red bill
tail usually projects slightly beyond wingtips
very short legs

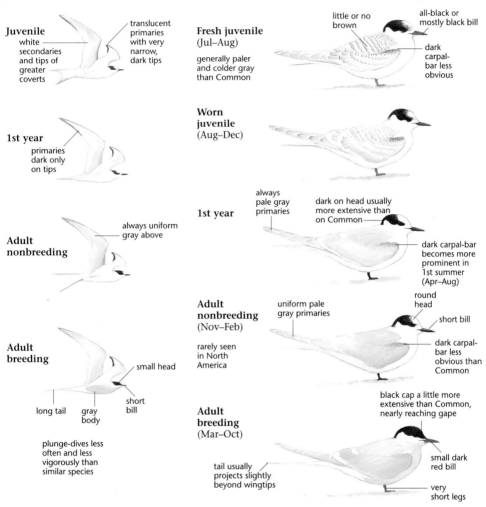

Voice: All calls like Common but higher, squeakier, drier. Common calls rather harsh and buzzy *keeeyurr;* often clipped with sharper pitch change than Common; also *kit* or *keek* notes like Long-billed Dowitcher. Agitated bird gives rhythmic series *titikerri titikerri*. . . . Attack a dry, nasal *raaaz*.

All juvenile terns give high, squeaky renditions of adult calls, gradually acquiring adult voice, but even 1st summer (one-year-old) birds sound higher and squeakier than adults.

Medium-size Terns (continued)

This species is very closely related to Common and Arctic Terns but is larger and bulkier and often found on more sheltered waters—ponds, bays, marshes, and ocean—rarely far offshore.

Forster's Tern

Sterna forsteri

L 13" WS 31" WT 6 oz (160 g)

Slightly larger and bulkier than Common, with broader wings, thicker bill, longer legs; flight less graceful with shallower, stronger wingbeats. Dark eye-patch of nonbreeding birds distinctive. All except very worn 1st year birds have flashing white upper primary coverts.

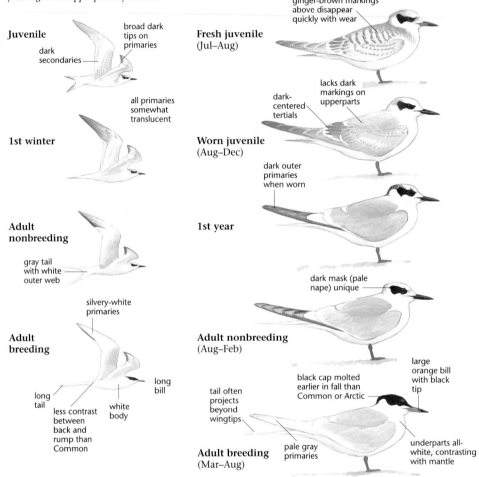

Juvenile
dark secondaries
broad dark tips on primaries

Fresh juvenile (Jul–Aug)
ginger-brown markings above disappear quickly with wear

1st winter
all primaries somewhat translucent

Worn juvenile (Aug–Dec)
dark-centered tertials
lacks dark markings on upperparts

Adult nonbreeding
gray tail with white outer web

1st year
dark outer primaries when worn

Adult nonbreeding (Aug–Feb)
dark mask (pale nape) unique

Adult breeding
silvery-white primaries
long tail
less contrast between back and rump than Common
white body
long bill

Adult breeding (Mar–Aug)
tail often projects beyond wingtips
pale gray primaries
black cap molted earlier in fall than Common or Arctic
large orange bill with black tip
underparts all-white, contrasting with mantle

Voice: All calls similar to Common and Arctic but lower, more wooden and rasping, one syllable. Common call a simple, descending *kerrr;* lower and more wooden-sounding than Common; also *kit* or *kuit.* Adult courtship begging *kerr kerr kerr.* Attack a very low, rasping *zaaaar.*

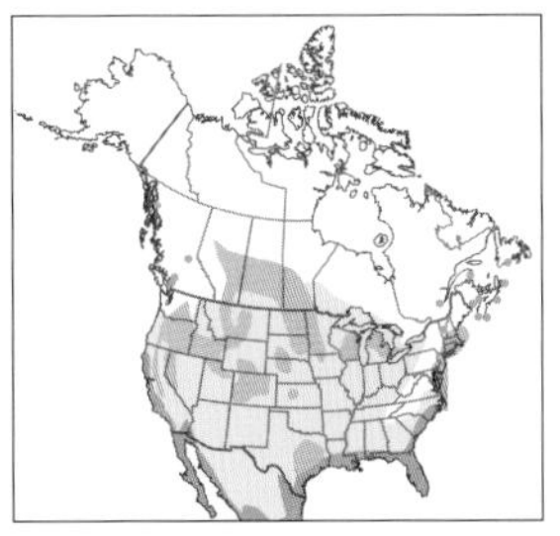

The upperwing patterns of terns illustrated in this book show the typical fresh condition (paler primaries) on adult breeding birds and the typical worn condition (darker primaries) on adult nonbreeding birds. In reality fresh-looking primaries are not strictly related to breeding plumage and can be seen at any time of year. The extent of dark color on the upperside of the primaries is a useful identification clue for some species. Worn 1st year birds of most species develop mostly dark remiges above. The notable exception is Arctic Tern, which always has pale gray and translucent primaries, regardless of age or wear.

Distinctive Terns

These species are often confused with other medium-size terns, but they are fundamentally different in structure and voice. Both are primarily pelagic, coming to land only to nest and roost.

Roseate Tern

Sterna dougallii

L 12.5" WS 29" WT 3.9 oz (110 g)

Structure differs from other medium-size terns: rounded head; long, thin bill; slender, tubular body; and long tail. Wings narrow and relatively short and straight; wingbeats stiff and quick, most like Least.

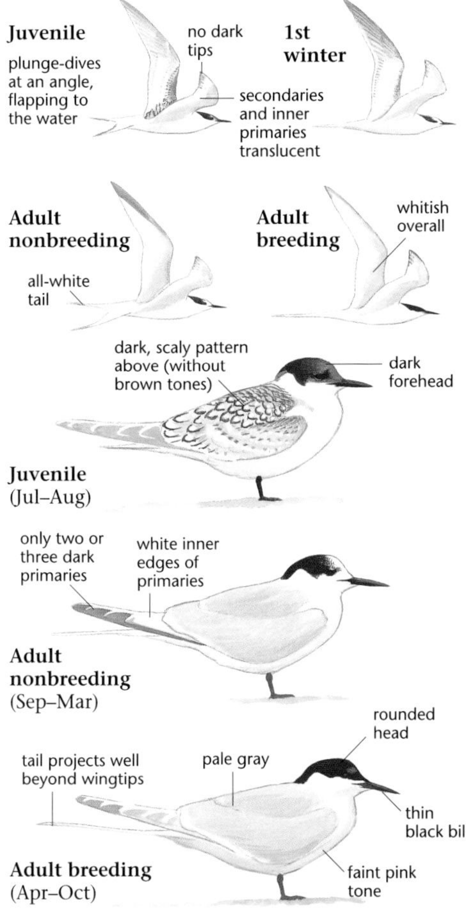

Juvenile
plunge-dives at an angle, flapping to the water
no dark tips
secondaries and inner primaries translucent
1st winter
Adult nonbreeding
all-white tail
Adult breeding
whitish overall
dark, scaly pattern above (without brown tones)
dark forehead
Juvenile (Jul–Aug)
only two or three dark primaries
white inner edges of primaries
Adult nonbreeding (Sep–Mar)
rounded head
tail projects well beyond wingtips
pale gray
thin black bill
faint pink tone
Adult breeding (Apr–Oct)

Voice: Distinctive; abrupt, harsh, two-syllable calls: a rather soft and ploverlike *CHIvik* or *chewVI* or a more insectlike *skivvik*. Alarm a high, clear *keer*. Attack a very harsh, rasping *zhrrraaaaach*. Juvenile gives higher, more trilled *dreewid*.

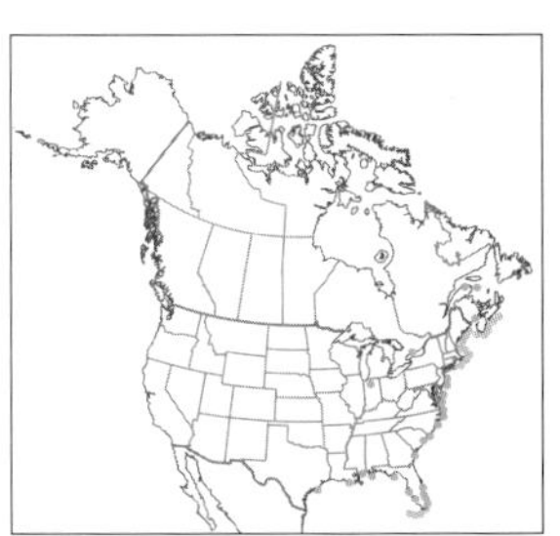

Roseate Tern adult breeding late summer (Jul–Sep)

bill becomes red at base like Common Tern but less extensive and less orange

Aleutian Tern

Sterna aleutica

L 12" WS 29" WT 3.9 oz (110 g)

Similar to Arctic but broader-winged. Short-tailed and very deep-chested; short-necked in flight. Note dark secondaries in all plumages.

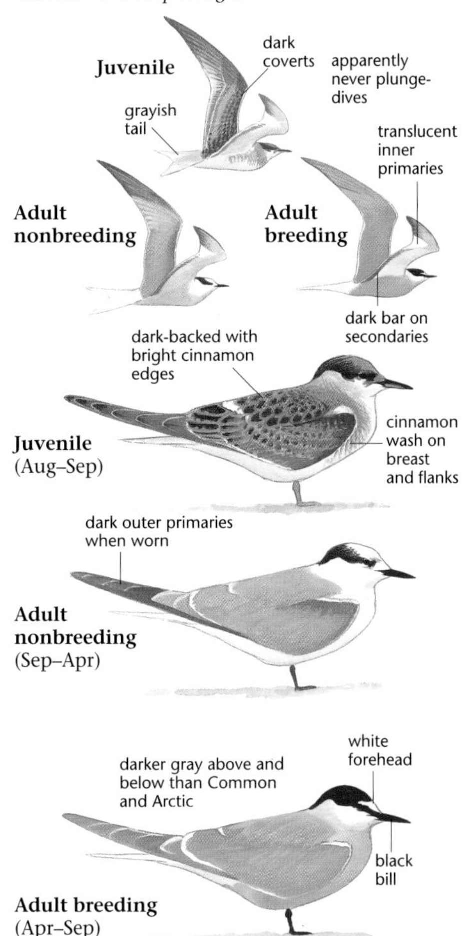

Juvenile
dark coverts
apparently never plunge-dives
grayish tail
translucent inner primaries
Adult nonbreeding
Adult breeding
dark bar on secondaries
dark-backed with bright cinnamon edges
Juvenile (Aug–Sep)
cinnamon wash on breast and flanks
dark outer primaries when worn
Adult nonbreeding (Sep–Apr)
white forehead
darker gray above and below than Common and Arctic
black bill
Adult breeding (Apr–Sep)

Voice: Common call a soft, whistled *whidid* or *whididid* slightly descending; reminiscent of shorebird or even House Sparrow rather than tern. Slightly harsher *whirrr* near nest.

Despite its small size, Least Tern mixes freely with other terns at foraging and roosting sites. Gull-billed keeps to itself, plucking food from mudflats or grassy fields, never plunge-diving.

Least Tern

Sterna antillarum

L 9" WS 20" WT 1.5 oz (42 g)

Our smallest tern. Relatively long, very narrow wings; short tail; long, slightly decurved, tapered bill.

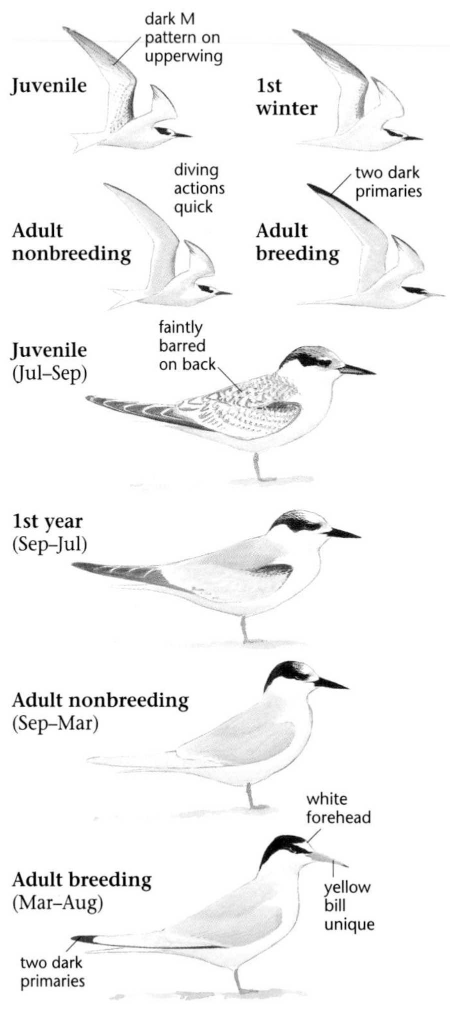
dark M pattern on upperwing
Juvenile
1st winter
diving actions quick
two dark primaries
Adult nonbreeding
Adult breeding
Juvenile (Jul–Sep)
faintly barred on back
1st year (Sep–Jul)
Adult nonbreeding (Sep–Mar)
white forehead
Adult breeding (Mar–Aug)
yellow bill unique
two dark primaries

Voice: Common calls include a rapid, shrill, sharp *piDEEK-adik* or *keDEEK*. Also a weak, nasal *whididi;* high, sharp squeaks *kweek* or *kwik*. Alarm a sharp, rising *zreek*.

Gull-billed Tern

Sterna nilotica

L 14" WS 34" WT 6 oz (170 g)

Slightly larger than Forster's. Long legs; short, thick bill; long wings with very long outer primaries creating graceful curving point.

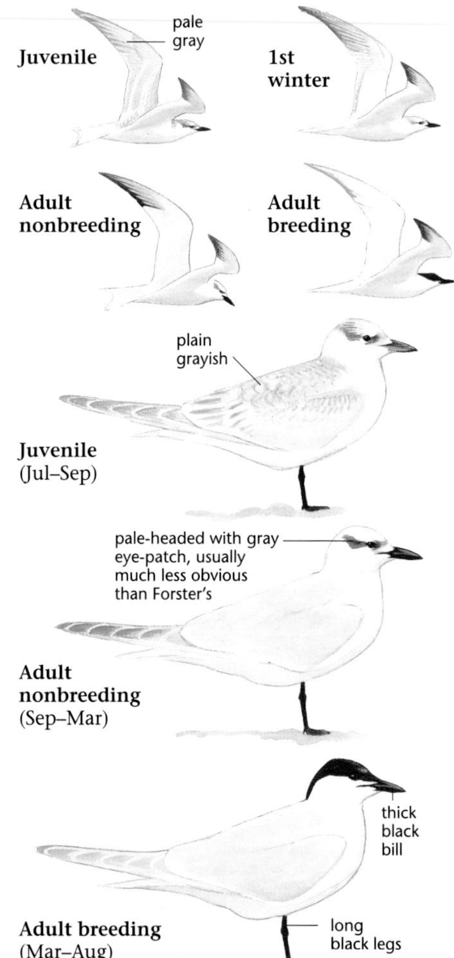
pale gray
Juvenile
1st winter
Adult nonbreeding
Adult breeding
plain grayish
Juvenile (Jul–Sep)
pale-headed with gray eye-patch, usually much less obvious than Forster's
Adult nonbreeding (Sep–Mar)
thick black bill
Adult breeding (Mar–Aug)
long black legs

Voice: Common call a distinctive, nasal yapping *kayWEK;* higher and sharper than Black Skimmer. Alarm a rattling, rasping *aach*. Juvenile begs with high, thin, two-syllable whistle *see-lee*.

Gull-billed Tern molting adult

Gull-billed Tern molts scattered head feathers simultaneously, producing speckled pattern Jul–Aug. Other terns molt front to back, producing white forehead.

Marsh Terns

With buoyant flight, these two broad-winged species swoop to pluck their food from the surface of marshy ponds. They rarely plunge-dive. Migrants are often far offshore over open ocean.

Black Tern

Chlidonias niger

L 9.75" WS 24" WT 2.2 oz (62 g)

Small, broad-winged, small-billed, very short-tailed; always dark grayish above with gray underwing. Wingbeats deep; flight buoyant and erratic with frequent dips to water.

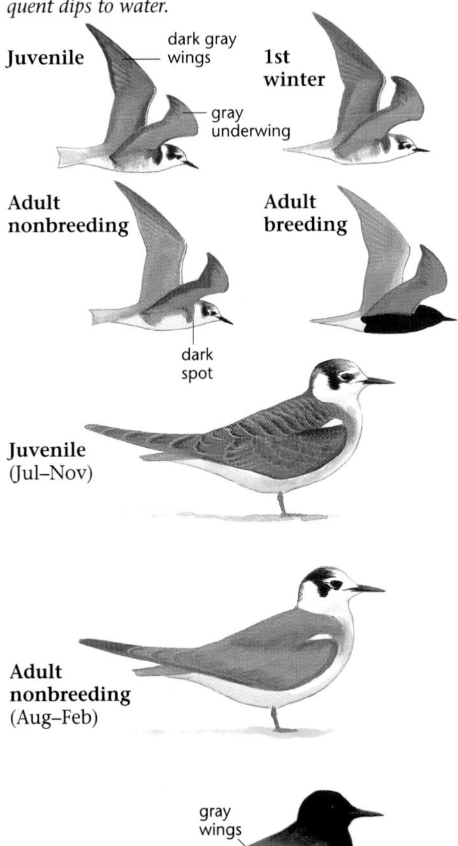

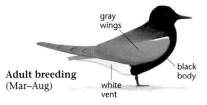

Juvenile
dark gray wings
gray underwing
1st winter
Adult nonbreeding
Adult breeding
dark spot
Juvenile (Jul–Nov)
Adult nonbreeding (Aug–Feb)
gray wings
black body
white vent
Adult breeding (Mar–Aug)

Voice: Call a harsh, sharp, scraping, complaining *keff* or *keef* and higher *kyip;* reminiscent of Black-necked Stilt but higher.

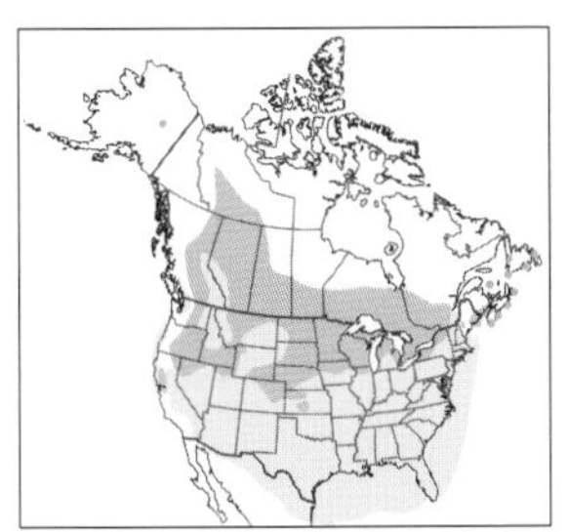

White-winged Tern

Chlidonias leucopterus

L 9.5" WS 23" WT 2.2 oz (63 g)

Overall a little stockier than Black Tern, with straighter, broader wings and shorter bill. Nonbreeding plumage pale, more like Forster's than Black.

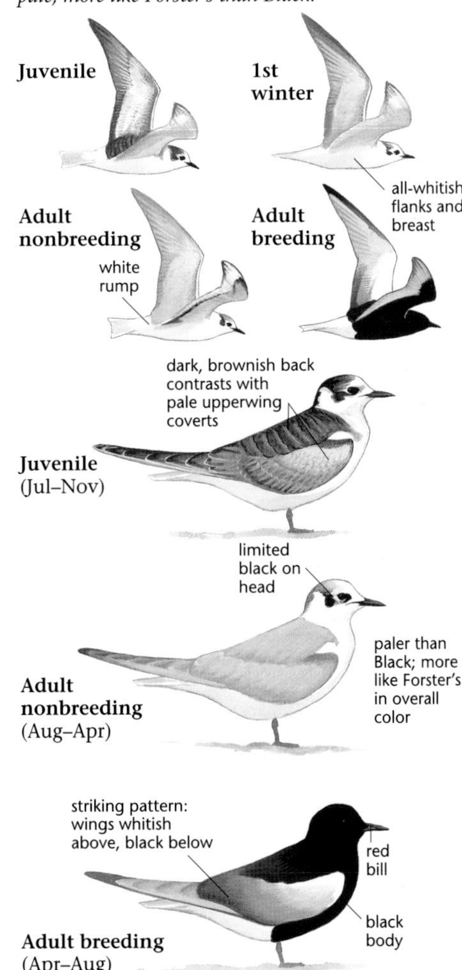

Juvenile
1st winter
all-whitish flanks and breast
Adult nonbreeding
white rump
Adult breeding
dark, brownish back contrasts with pale upperwing coverts
Juvenile (Jul–Nov)
limited black on head
paler than Black; more like Forster's in overall color
Adult nonbreeding (Aug–Apr)
striking pattern: wings whitish above, black below
red bill
black body
Adult breeding (Apr–Aug)

Voice: Calls short *kesch* and *kek;* deeper and harsher than Black Tern.

Tropical Terns

These two species are found over warm water. Bridled is usually found along weed lines, where it habitually perches on floating debris; Sooty virtually never perches except at the nest site.

Bridled Tern

Sterna anaethetus

L 15" WS 30" WT 3.5 oz (100 g)

Size similar to Common Tern but more slender, longer-billed, and longer-legged.

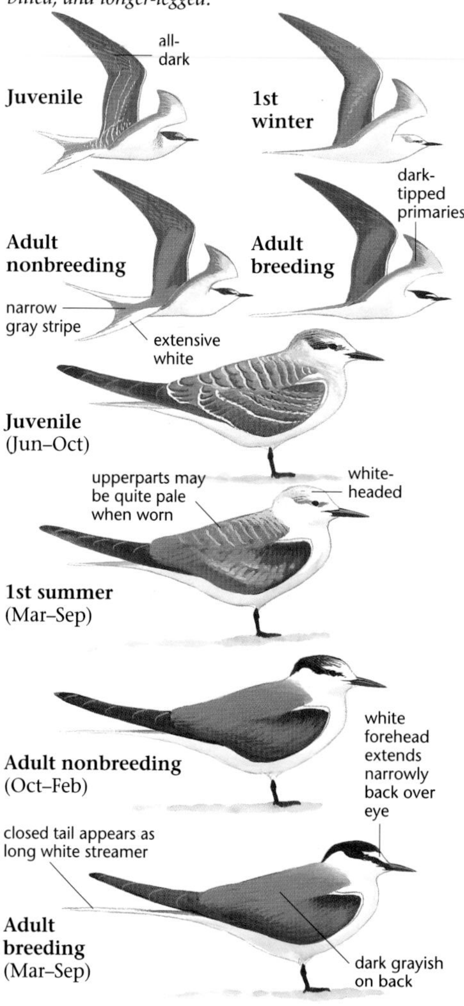

all-dark
Juvenile
1st winter
dark-tipped primaries
Adult nonbreeding
Adult breeding
narrow gray stripe
extensive white
Juvenile (Jun–Oct)
upperparts may be quite pale when worn
white-headed
1st summer (Mar–Sep)
Adult nonbreeding (Oct–Feb)
white forehead extends narrowly back over eye
closed tail appears as long white streamer
Adult breeding (Mar–Sep)
dark grayish on back

Voice: Common call a rather soft, mellow whistle: a rising, nasal *weeeep;* quality like Sooty but higher, softer.

Sooty Tern

Sterna fuscata

L 16" WS 32" WT 6 oz (180 g)

Larger, stockier, and shorter-tailed than Bridled, with broader, stiffer wings and noticeably stronger flight.

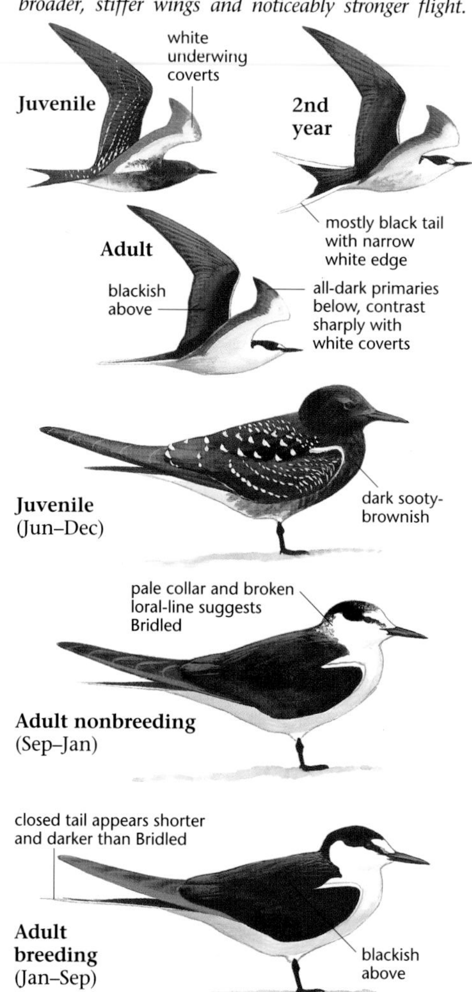

white underwing coverts
Juvenile
2nd year
mostly black tail with narrow white edge
Adult
blackish above
all-dark primaries below, contrast sharply with white coverts
Juvenile (Jun–Dec)
dark sooty-brownish
pale collar and broken loral-line suggests Bridled
Adult nonbreeding (Sep–Jan)
closed tail appears shorter and darker than Bridled
Adult breeding (Jan–Sep)
blackish above

Voice: Calls nasal, laughing *ka weddy weddy* or rapid *ka WEEda WED;* higher than Gull-billed. Threat a nasal, rasping moan *draaaaa*. Juvenile gives high, shrill *wheeer*.

These two species can be difficult to distinguish at sea. Note that Bridled has more buoyant, graceful, and erratic flight, showing off its extensively white tail when banking. Sooty has more powerful, direct flight, and the limited white on its tail is not visible at a distance.

Unlike other terns in many characteristics, noddies are found over warm ocean water, where they feed by swooping or gently dipping to the surface. They nest and roost in trees.

Brown Noddy

Anous stolidus

L 15.5" WS 32" WT 7 oz (200 g)

Distinctive structure: size close to Sooty Tern but wings relatively short and rounded; tail shorter and double-rounded (not forked). Plumage resembles juvenile Sooty Tern but with dark underwing and vent.

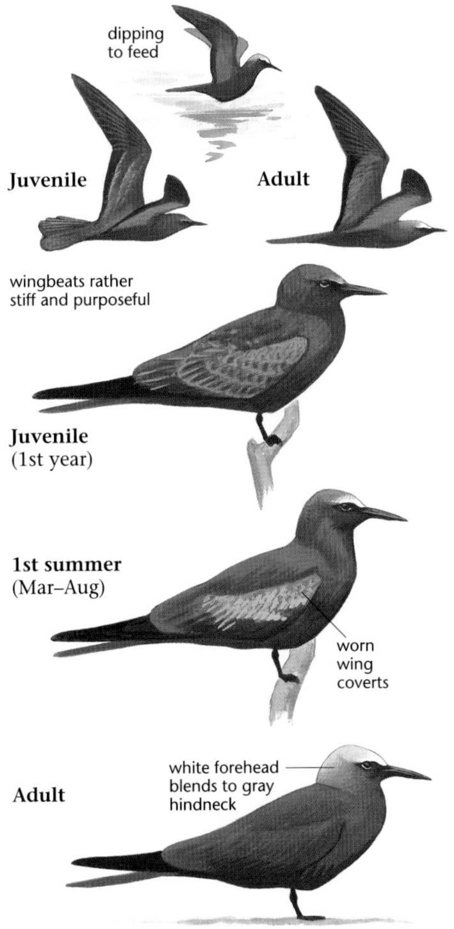
dipping
to feed
Juvenile
Adult
wingbeats rather
stiff and purposeful
Juvenile
(1st year)
1st summer
(Mar–Aug)
worn
wing
coverts
Adult
white forehead
blends to gray
hindneck

Voice: All calls of adults low, grunting, grating, or buzzing; a deep, rattling *garrr* and a rising croak *brraak*. In courtship flight a grating, low *nek nek nek nek nek nekrrr*. 1st year birds give high whistle *tsooeek* and high, clear squawk *kweeer*.

Black Noddy

Anous minutus

L 13.5" WS 30" WT 3.9 oz (110 g)

Similar to Brown Noddy but smaller overall, with longer neck, rounder crown, relatively longer, straight, thin bill; looks smaller-headed. Wings and tail both relatively short; wingtips less pointed.

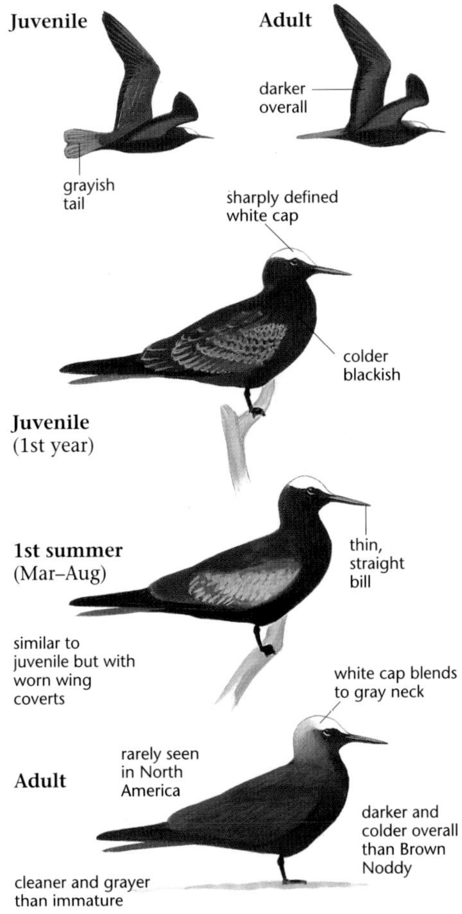
Juvenile
Adult
darker
overall
grayish
tail
sharply defined
white cap
colder
blackish
Juvenile
(1st year)
1st summer
(Mar–Aug)
thin,
straight
bill
similar to
juvenile but with
worn wing
coverts
white cap blends
to gray neck
Adult
rarely seen
in North
America
darker and
colder overall
than Brown
Noddy
cleaner and grayer
than immature

Voice: All calls similar to Brown Noddy but higher and sharper. A low, grating, stuttering *krkrkrkr.* Call of 1st year birds a high, thin, piping *suwee.*

Black Skimmer

Black Skimmer is unmistakable. It forages for small fish mainly at night, flying over shallow water with its lower mandible slicing the surface.

Black Skimmer

Rynchops niger

L 18" WS 44" WT 11 oz (300 g) ♂>♀

Very long-winged and rather broad-winged, with graceful and buoyant flight. Wingbeats mainly above the body; head always held lower than tail. Executes hairpin turns and smooth banks while foraging; flock wheels in unison.

Juvenile
Adult nonbreeding
skimming
Adult breeding
Adult

Juvenile
(Jul–Dec)
1st winter/1st summer
(Dec–Jul)
often rests with head stretched forward on ground

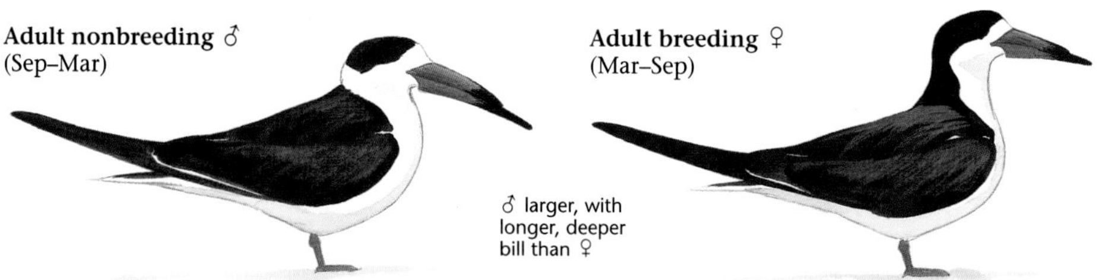
Adult nonbreeding ♂
(Sep–Mar)
Adult breeding ♀
(Mar–Sep)
♂ larger, with longer, deeper bill than ♀

Voice: Call a distinctive, hollow, soft, nasal barking *yep* or *yip*. Alarm a longer *Aaaaw;* quality like Oldsquaw. Juvenile call a higher-pitched *iip*, more squawky than adult.

Alcids
Family: Alcidae

21 species in 10 genera. These oceanic species come to land only to nest. Most nest colonially in crevices or burrows; species choose specific sites. Juveniles of a few species leave the nest before fully grown and complete their development at sea accompanied by one parent. Some species form feeding aggregations where food is abundant but don't strongly flock; certain species are virtually never seen more than two at a time. All use wings to dive underwater (see Long-tailed Duck). Their specialized wing shape makes flight more difficult, and all species have fast, buzzing wingbeats. Specialized bill shapes are related to feeding habits; some have elaborate bill ornamentation in breeding season. Compare loons, grebes, and ducks. Nonbreeding adults are shown.

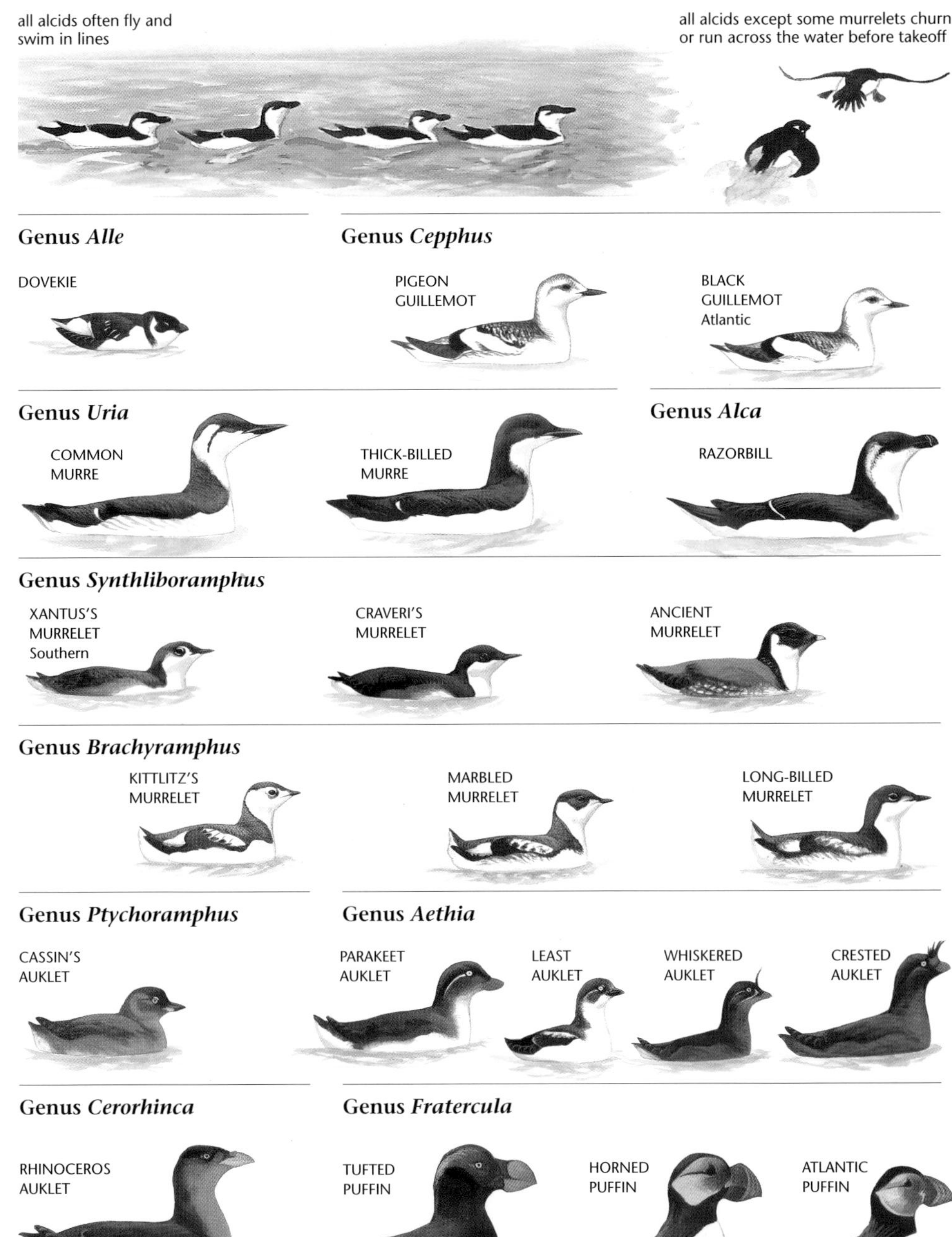

all alcids often fly and swim in lines
all alcids except some murrelets churn or run across the water before takeoff
Genus Alle
DOVEKIE
Genus Cepphus
PIGEON GUILLEMOT
BLACK GUILLEMOT Atlantic
Genus Uria
COMMON MURRE
THICK-BILLED MURRE
Genus Alca
RAZORBILL
Genus Synthliboramphus
XANTUS'S MURRELET Southern
CRAVERI'S MURRELET
ANCIENT MURRELET
Genus Brachyramphus
KITTLITZ'S MURRELET
MARBLED MURRELET
LONG-BILLED MURRELET
Genus Ptychoramphus
CASSIN'S AUKLET
Genus Aethia
PARAKEET AUKLET
LEAST AUKLET
WHISKERED AUKLET
CRESTED AUKLET
Genus Cerorhinca
RHINOCEROS AUKLET
Genus Fratercula
TUFTED PUFFIN
HORNED PUFFIN
ATLANTIC PUFFIN

MURRES: GENUS *URIA*

These large alcids are very similar in all respects. Found singly or in small groups at sea, they nest on open ledges on rocky cliffs, Thick-billed on narrower ledges, seen standing single file.

Common Murre

Uria aalge

L 17.5" WS 26" WT 2.2 lb (990 g)

More slender than other large alcids, with long, straight bill; thinner overall with thinner neck and smaller head than Thick-billed.

1st year

dusky markings

Adult breeding

white behind eye

1st year

white nape

streaked flanks

Adult nonbreeding
(Sep–Mar)

long, straight bill

Adult breeding
(Oct–Aug in California; Mar–Aug in east)

browner

Fledgling
(Jul–Sep)

murre fledglings go to sea with adult when about half-grown (dark individuals shown, some have plumage like 1st year)

Voice: Silent at sea. Call a moaning, nasal *aarrrr;* higher-pitched and more pleasant-sounding than Thick-billed. Juvenile at sea begs with insistent, short, low whistle *pidoo-WHIdoo* while following adult.

Thick-billed Murre

Uria lomvia

L 18" WS 28" WT 2.1 lb (970 g)

Stockier than Common; has shorter bill with decurved culmen, thicker neck, blockier head, and broader wings; more hunched in flight.

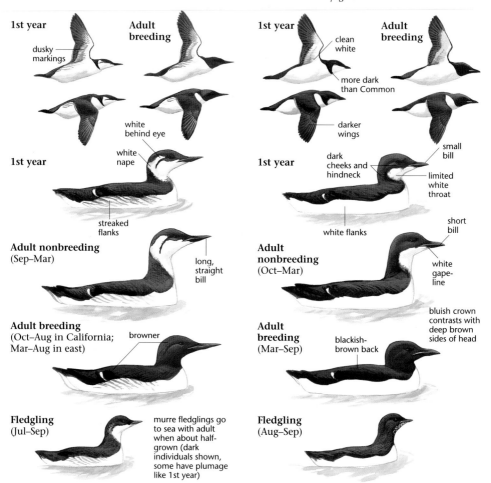

1st year

clean white

more dark than Common

Adult breeding

darker wings

1st year

dark cheeks and hindneck

small bill

limited white throat

white flanks

Adult nonbreeding
(Oct–Mar)

short bill

white gape-line

Adult breeding
(Mar–Sep)

blackish-brown back

bluish crown contrasts with deep brown sides of head

Fledgling
(Aug–Sep)

Voice: Silent at sea. Call a roaring, groaning, angry-sounding *aoorrr*. Juvenile at sea gives whistle call like Common.

Common
Thick-billed

Stance differs slightly: Common more upright and graceful; walks more easily than Thick-billed.

Razorbill

Razorbill is closely related to murres and similar in habits and appearance, but has a deep bill and long tail. It nests in rock crevices, boulder fields, and occasionally rock ledges.

Identification of Murres

Adult bill length of both murres varies regionally: Pacific populations of Common average 8 percent longer-billed than Atlantic, and Pacific Thick-billed averages 20 percent longer-billed than Atlantic. In both species the Pacific birds average about 5 percent larger overall than Atlantic. Note that Common is always longer-billed than Thick-billed: by about 12 percent in Pacific and 25 percent in Atlantic.

Thick-billed Murre 1st winter
bill much smaller than adult; smaller than any Common Murre

Thick-billed Murre adult
culmen decurved and gonydeal angle near midpoint

Common Murre adult
culmen relatively straight and gonydeal angle close to base; note that some show faint, pale gape-line like Thick-billed

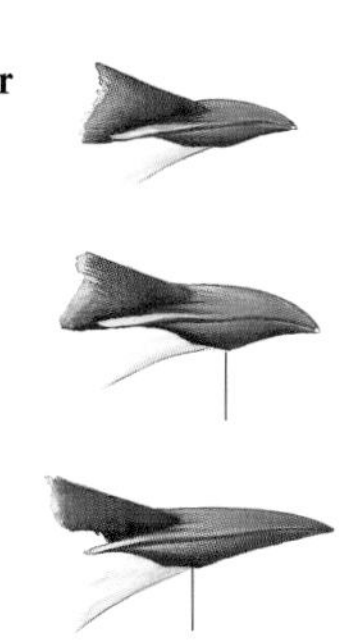

Color of upperparts varies in murres, with Common averaging paler and browner than Thick-billed. This may be useful at times, but Atlantic Common averages darker than Pacific, and 1st year of both species are browner than adult, especially when worn Jan–Jun.

Transitional Common Murre molting between breeding and nonbreeding plumage never acquires the dark hood and white throat of nonbreeding Thick-billed; instead molting of scattered feathers over entire head creates a speckled pattern.

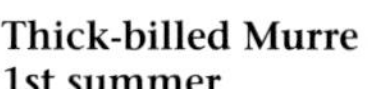

Thick-billed Murre 1st summer

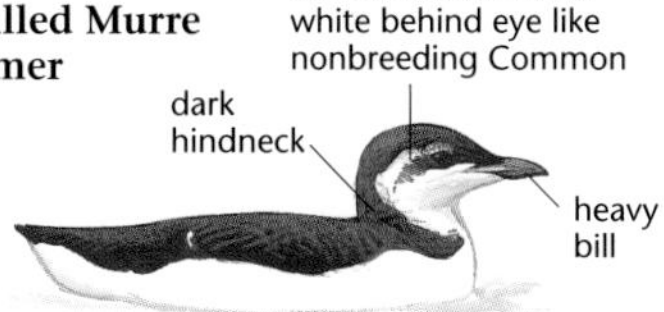
some in Alaska show white behind eye like nonbreeding Common
dark hindneck
heavy bill

Bridled Common Murre adult
10 to 25 percent of Atlantic population; absent in Pacific

Dark Common Murre adult
up to 1 in 1,000 in California, unrecorded elsewhere; extreme dark morph shown (many are intermediate between this and typical)

Razorbill

Alca torda

L 17" WS 26" WT 1.6 lb (720 g)

Deep bill and long, pointed tail distinctive; relatively large-headed and thick-necked, with streamlined body shape in flight, unlike murres. Always black above and clean white below.

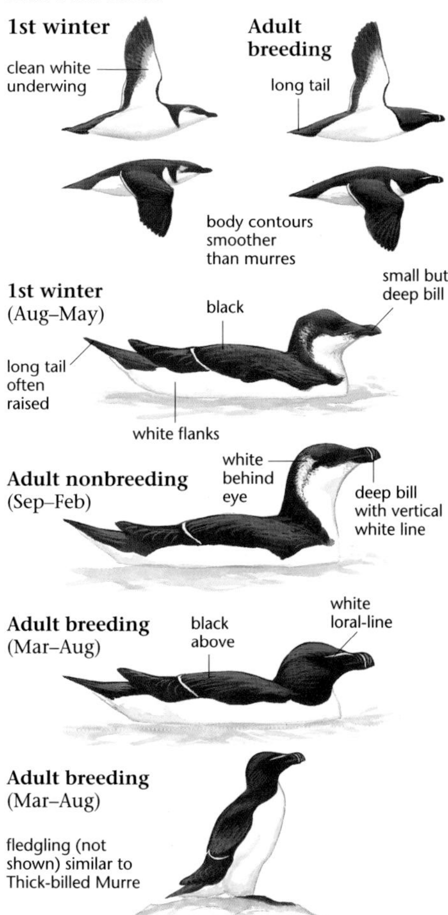
1st winter
clean white underwing
Adult breeding
long tail
body contours smoother than murres
1st winter (Aug–May)
black
small but deep bill
long tail often raised
white flanks
Adult nonbreeding (Sep–Feb)
white behind eye
deep bill with vertical white line
Adult breeding (Mar–Aug)
black above
white loral-line
Adult breeding (Mar–Aug)
fledgling (not shown) similar to Thick-billed Murre

Voice: Silent at sea. Call a grunting *urrr* with dry, rattling quality; more mechanical than murres, with melancholy sound. Juvenile at sea begs with whistled call similar to murres.

Dovekie and Pigeon Guillemot

The distinctive Dovekie is superficially like a diminutive murre; it is found on open ocean except when nesting in rocky crevices. Pigeon Guillemot is very closely related to Black Guillemot.

Dovekie

Alle alle

L 8.25" WS 15" WT 6 oz (160 g)

Small, thick-necked, and large-headed. Short, stout bill; fairly long wings.

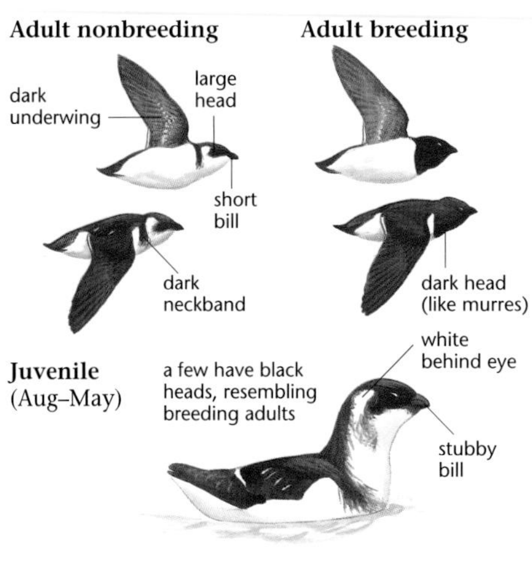

Adult nonbreeding
Adult breeding
dark underwing
large head
short bill
dark neckband
dark head (like murres)

Juvenile (Aug–May)

a few have black heads, resembling breeding adults

white behind eye

stubby bill

Adult nonbreeding (Oct–Mar)

usually swims with head low; looks neckless

Adult breeding (Apr–Sep)

white on sides of breast often appears as a triangle

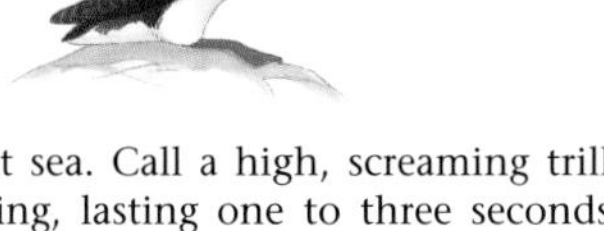

Adult breeding (Apr–Sep)

Voice: Silent at sea. Call a high, screaming trill, rising and falling, lasting one to three seconds. Juvenile at sea gives shrill peeping calls.

Pigeon Guillemot

Cepphus columba

L 13.5" WS 23" WT 1.1 lb (490 g)

Stocky, with round body. Broad, rounded wings; thin, straight bill.

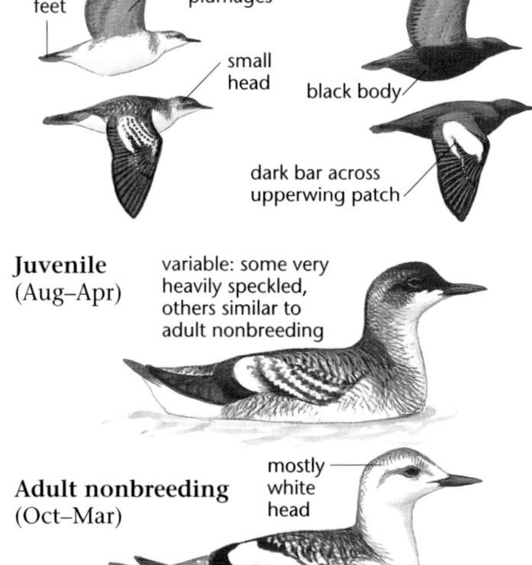

Juvenile
Adult breeding
bright red feet
dull gray underwing in all plumages
small head
black body
dark bar across upperwing patch

Juvenile (Aug–Apr)

variable: some very heavily speckled, others similar to adult nonbreeding

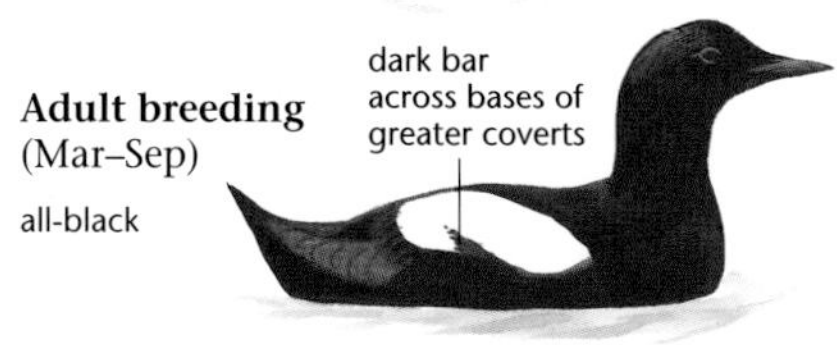

Adult nonbreeding (Oct–Mar)

mostly white head

Adult breeding (Mar–Sep)

all-black

dark bar across bases of greater coverts

Adult breeding (Mar–Sep)

bright red feet

Voice: Similar to Black Guillemot; no differences known.

BLACK GUILLEMOT

The two guillemots are very similar; both are chunky and round-winged. Found close to rocky shores, both nest in rock crevices and are often seen sitting on exposed rocks.

Black Guillemot

Cepphus grylle

L 13" WS 21" WT 15 oz (430 g)

Slightly smaller and smaller-billed than Pigeon Guillemot, with narrower wings; always distinguished by underwing color.

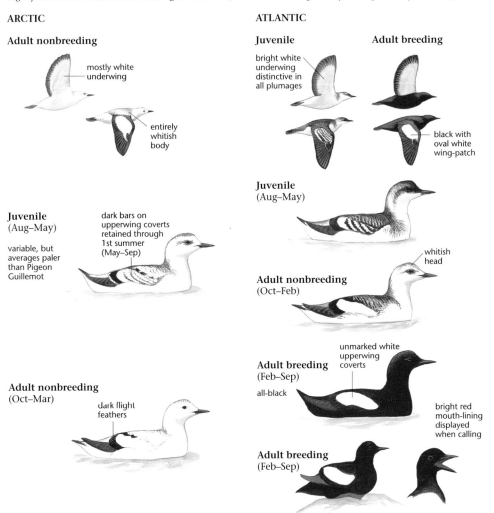

ARCTIC

Adult nonbreeding

mostly white underwing

entirely whitish body

Juvenile
(Aug–May)

variable, but averages paler than Pigeon Guillemot

dark bars on upperwing coverts retained through 1st summer (May–Sep)

Adult nonbreeding
(Oct–Mar)

dark flight feathers

ATLANTIC

Juvenile

bright white underwing distinctive in all plumages

Adult breeding

black with oval white wing-patch

Juvenile
(Aug–May)

Adult nonbreeding
(Oct–Feb)

whitish head

Adult breeding
(Feb–Sep)

unmarked white upperwing coverts

all-black

bright red mouth-lining displayed when calling

Adult breeding
(Feb–Sep)

Voice: Calls frequently near breeding areas: extremely high-pitched, thin, squeaky, or piping whistles; a drawn-out screaming whistle *see-oo* or *swweeeeeer* up to two seconds long. Also short *sit sit sit* . . . notes often leading into series, rising and accelerating then falling at end. Courting group sits on rocks or water and calls while displaying red mouth-lining.

Arctic populations average shorter-billed and paler than Atlantic in all plumages; underwing is more extensively white and many have white bar across upper primary coverts. 1st year Arctic averages paler than Atlantic (especially head, scapulars, rump, and upperwing coverts) and has white-tipped secondaries when fresh. Adult nonbreeding Arctic birds can be nearly all-white with dark flight feathers. There is considerable variation within each population, however, and not all birds can be identified.

MURRELETS: GENUS *SYNTHLIBORAMPHUS*

Found far offshore in warm water, this species nests in crevices and is closely related to Craveri's Murrelet. Both are found in low densities at sea but are often seen in pairs year-round.

Xantus's Murrelet

Synthliboramphus hypoleucus
L 9.75" WS 15" WT 6 oz (170 g)
Relatively slender and thin-billed, with clean black and white pattern.

Synthliboramphus murrelets are able to leap directly into flight without running on water

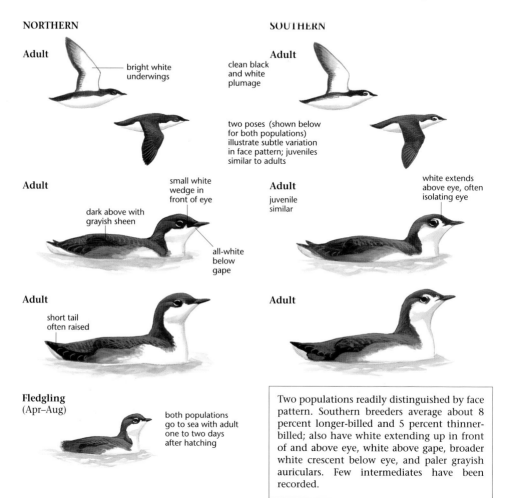

NORTHERN

Adult

bright white underwings

SOUTHERN

Adult

clean black and white plumage

two poses (shown below for both populations) illustrate subtle variation in face pattern; juveniles similar to adults

Adult

small white wedge in front of eye

dark above with grayish sheen

all-white below gape

Adult

juvenile similar

white extends above eye, often isolating eye

Adult

short tail often raised

Adult

Fledgling
(Apr–Aug)

both populations go to sea with adult one to two days after hatching

Two populations readily distinguished by face pattern. Southern breeders average about 8 percent longer-billed and 5 percent thinner-billed; also have white extending up in front of and above eye, white above gape, broader white crescent below eye, and paler grayish auriculars. Few intermediates have been recorded.

Voice: Call of Northern birds a series of three to eight high-pitched peeping notes *seep seep seep seep* unlike Craveri's. Call of Southern birds a rattle similar to Craveri's. Juvenile gives a thin *peer*.

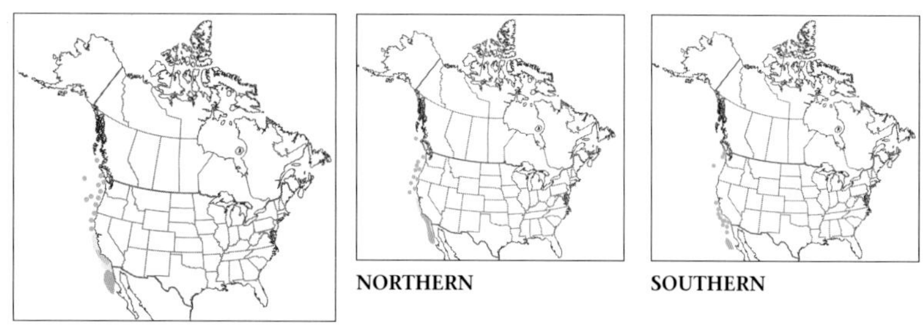

NORTHERN SOUTHERN

Craveri's Murrelet is a warm-water species very closely related to Xantus's. Ancient Murrelet, found at sea in cold water, is often visible from shore; it nests in burrows and crevices.

Craveri's Murrelet

Synthliboramphus craveri

L 9.5" WS 15" WT 5 oz (150 g)

Very similar to Xantus's, slightly smaller; bill about as long as Southern Xantus's but 10 percent thinner than any Xantus's. Best distinguished by underwing color.

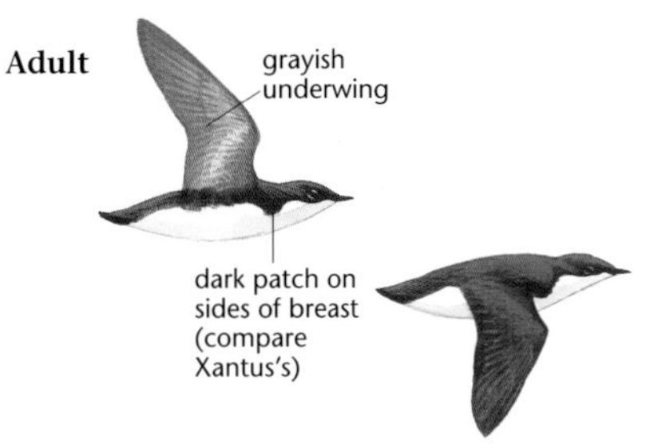
Adult
grayish underwing
dark patch on sides of breast (compare Xantus's)

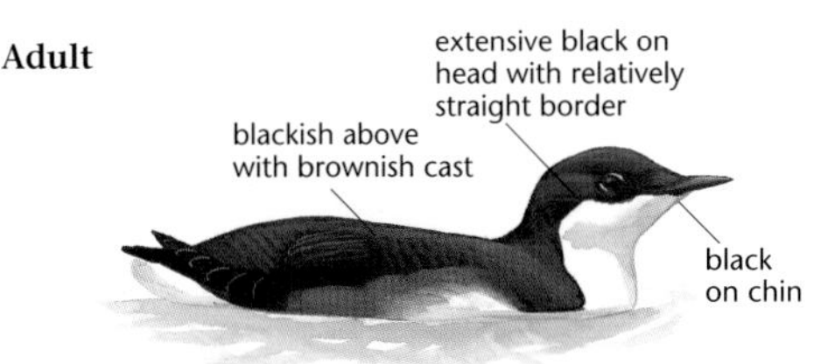
Adult
extensive black on head with relatively straight border
blackish above with brownish cast
black on chin

Adult
slightly longer tail, raised more often than Xantus's

fledgling (not shown) similar to Xantus's; identified by face pattern and accompanying adult

two poses (shown above) illustrate subtle variations in face pattern; juvenile similar to adult

Voice: Poorly known. Adult at sea gives a high, cricket-like rattle or trill *sreeeeer*. Other calls undescribed.

Ancient Murrelet

Synthliboramphus antiquus

L 10" WS 17" WT 7 oz (205 g)

Heavier-bodied and shorter-billed than other murrelets. White patch on sides of neck distinctive at great distance.

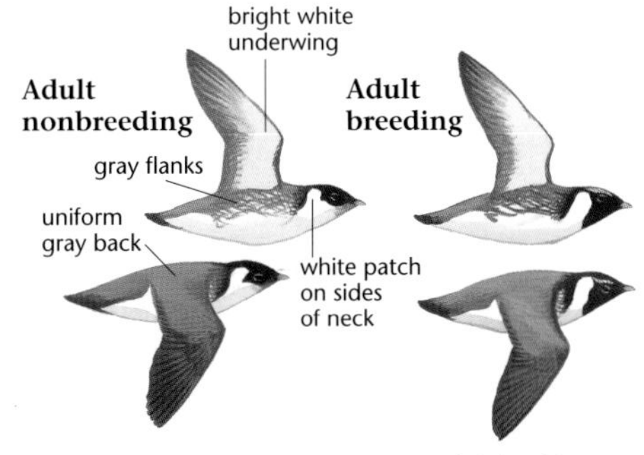
bright white underwing
Adult nonbreeding
Adult breeding
gray flanks
uniform gray back
white patch on sides of neck

Juvenile (Aug–Jan)
uniform gray back
bright white sides of neck very striking
pale bill
scalloped gray on flanks

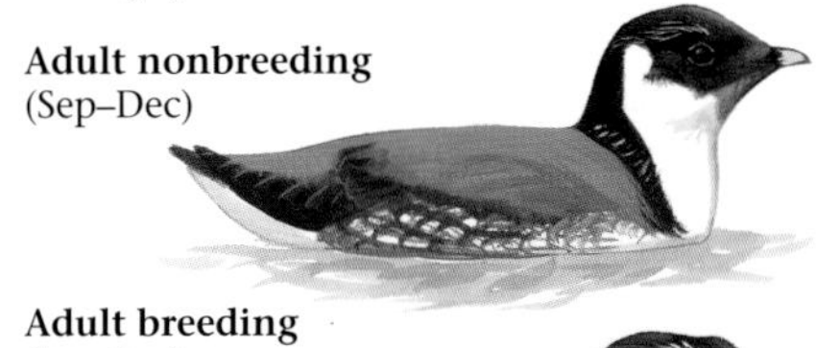
Adult nonbreeding (Sep–Dec)

Adult breeding (Jan–Sep)
black throat

Fledgling (May–Aug)

goes to sea with adult one to two days after hatching

Voice: Adult at sea gives a short, whistled *teep*. Variety of calls at nest site include a short *chirrup* and varied chips, trills, and rasping sounds.

Beware fledgling murres, which go to sea at about age 20 days, when just murrelet-size. These birds can travel long distances from colonies, usually closely accompanied by a parent.

Murrelets: Genus *Brachyramphus*

These two species and Long-billed Murrelet are closely related. Seen on the ocean in pairs or small groups, they nest singly on the ground or (Marbled) on mossy tree branches up to 45 miles inland.

Kittlitz's Murrelet

Brachyramphus brevirostris

L 9.5" WS 17" WT 8 oz (220 g)

Shorter-billed than Marbled; more extensive feathering covers base of bill. White outer tail feathers diagnostic but rarely visible. Pale face contrasts with dark eye.

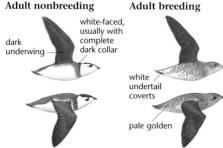

flight of all murrelets low, rapid, with very fast beats of long, pointed wings

Adult nonbreeding

dark underwing

white-faced, usually with complete dark collar

Adult breeding

white undertail coverts

pale golden

Juvenile (Aug–Oct)

Adult nonbreeding (Oct–Mar)

white above eye

white face with narrow dark crown

very short bill

Adult breeding (Apr–Sep)

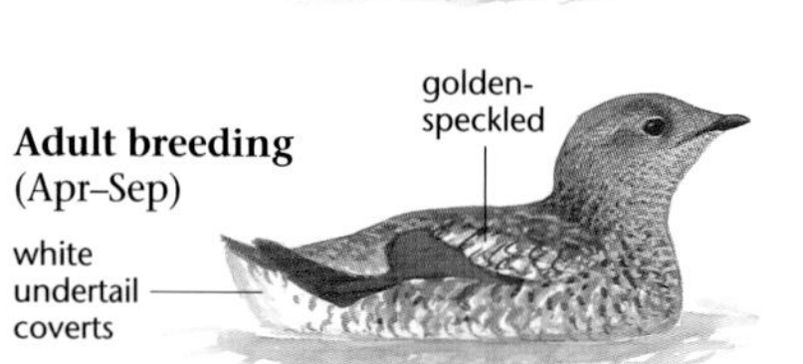
golden-speckled
white undertail coverts

Voice: Less vocal than Marbled. Call a quiet, low groan *urrrhhn,* similar to rarely heard groan call of Marbled. Also a short quack *urgh.*

Marbled Murrelet

Brachyramphus marmoratus

L 9.75" WS 16" WT 8 oz (220 g)

Typical of the genus: slender-billed, with narrow, pointed wings; brownish in breeding plumage; black and white with white scapulars in nonbreeding.

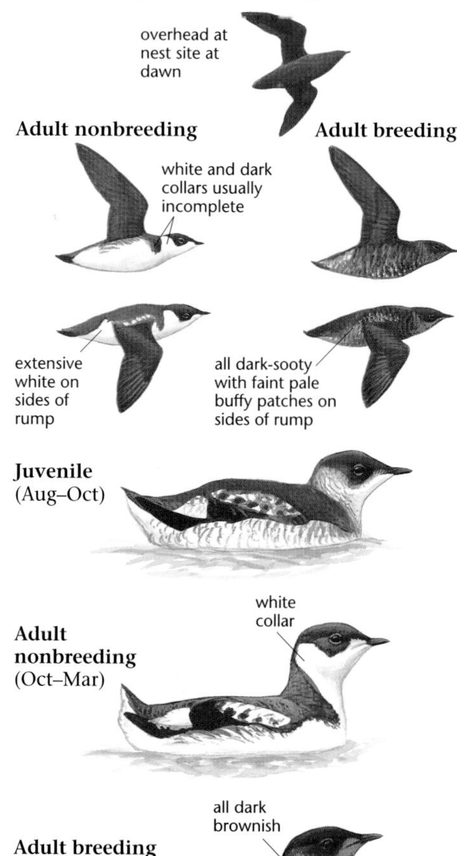
overhead at nest site at dawn
Adult nonbreeding
Adult breeding
white and dark collars usually incomplete
extensive white on sides of rump
all dark-sooty with faint pale buffy patches on sides of rump
Juvenile
(Aug–Oct)
Adult nonbreeding
(Oct–Mar)
white collar
Adult breeding
(Apr–Sep)
all dark brownish

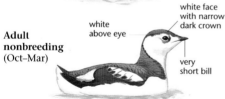

Voice: Quite vocal in flight near nest site as well as at sea. Flight call a squealing, gull-like but high-pitched, slightly descending series *kleeer kleeeer kleeeer. . . .* Also a high, clear *quip.*

Marbled Murrelet

active

relaxed

Overall extent of white changes dramatically when active (diving, wings exposed) or relaxed (wings concealed by white flanks).

Long-billed Murrelet, a rare visitor from Siberia, was formerly considered a subspecies of Marbled Murrelet. The distinctive Cassin's Auklet, seen in large groups at sea, nests in burrows or crevices.

Long-billed Murrelet

Brachyramphus perdix

L 10" WS 17" WT 10 oz (290 g)

Slightly larger and 20 percent longer-billed than Marbled, but difficult to judge. Head and neck pattern distinctive.

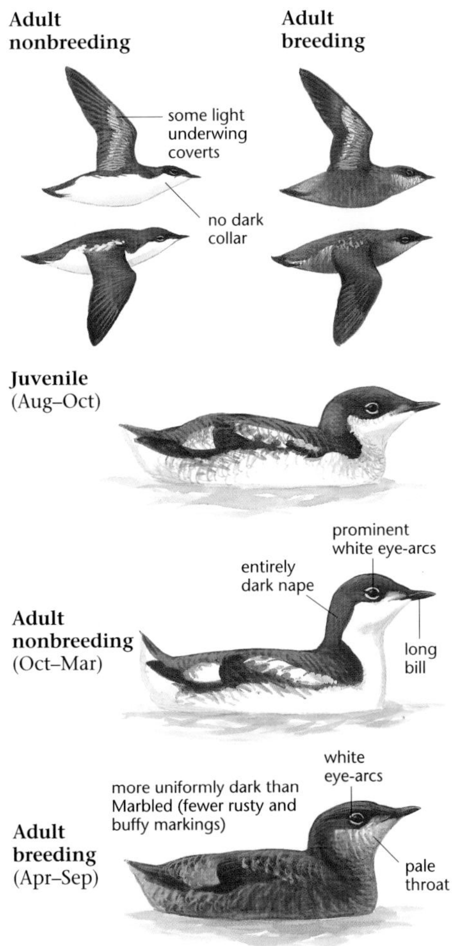
Adult nonbreeding
Adult breeding
some light underwing coverts
no dark collar
Juvenile (Aug–Oct)
prominent white eye-arcs
entirely dark nape
Adult nonbreeding (Oct–Mar)
long bill
white eye-arcs
more uniformly dark than Marbled (fewer rusty and buffy markings)
Adult breeding (Apr–Sep)
pale throat

Voice: Undescribed.

Cassin's Auklet

Ptychoramphus aleuticus

L 9" WS 15" WT 6 oz (185 g)

Small and chunky, with large head and short, triangular bill. Grayish overall; white eye of adult surprisingly conspicuous.

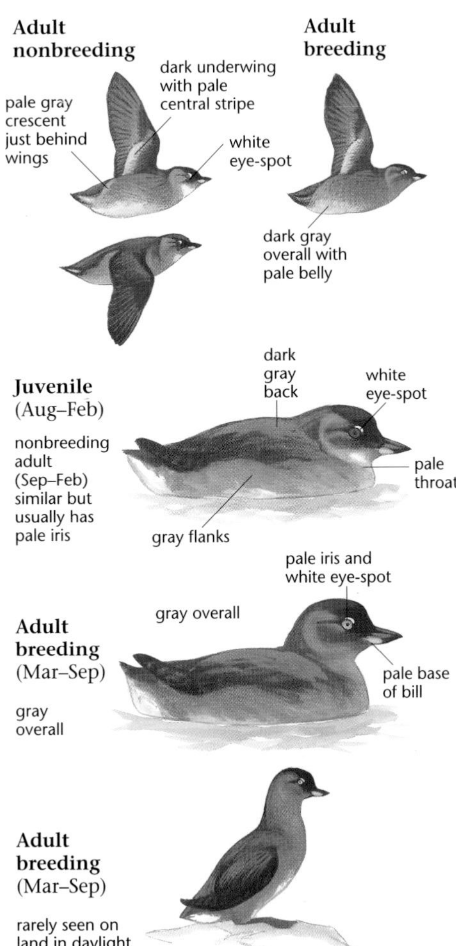
Adult nonbreeding
Adult breeding
dark underwing with pale central stripe
pale gray crescent just behind wings
white eye-spot
dark gray overall with pale belly
Juvenile (Aug–Feb)
dark gray back
white eye-spot
nonbreeding adult (Sep–Feb) similar but usually has pale iris
pale throat
gray flanks
pale iris and white eye-spot
gray overall
Adult breeding (Mar–Sep)
pale base of bill
gray overall
Adult breeding (Mar–Sep)
rarely seen on land in daylight

Voice: Silent at sea. Adults in colony at night give chorus of hoarse, rhythmic calls *RREP-nerreer* with many variations (similar to calls of Parakeet Auklet); also a short, harsh *skreer.*

AUKLETS (CONTINUED)

Both these distinctive species nest in crevices, Least mainly in boulder fields; otherwise they are found at sea. Parakeet Auklet is almost always seen singly, but Least is often found in flocks.

Parakeet Auklet

Aethia psittacula

L 10" WS 18" WT 11 oz (315 g)

Stocky and round-headed, with upturned, nearly circular bill; wings rather broad and rounded.

Juvenile **Adult breeding**

underwing dark with narrow, pale line

head raised

black head

orange bill

uniform blackish upperside

bright white belly

wingbeats slower than other auklets

Juvenile (Aug–Mar)

stubby bill

Adult nonbreeding (Oct–Apr)

single white plume

all-dark

white throat

white flanks

Adult breeding (Apr–Sep)

orange bill

Adult breeding (Apr–Sep)

Voice: Silent at sea. Adults in colony give rhythmic, hoarse calls similar to Cassin's Auklet; also a quavering, descending squeal.

Least Auklet

Aethia pusilla

L 6.25" WS 12" WT 3 oz (85 g)

Our smallest alcid; tiny and compact, with small bill.

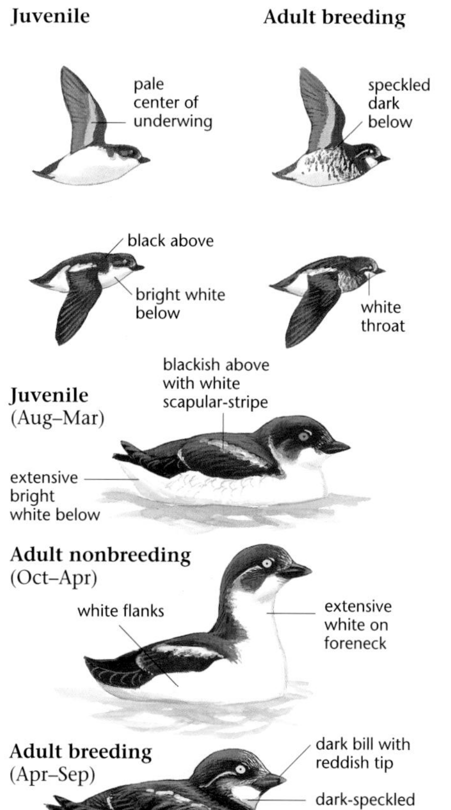

Juvenile
Adult breeding
pale center of underwing
speckled dark below
black above
bright white below
white throat
Juvenile
(Aug–Mar)
blackish above with white scapular-stripe
extensive bright white below
Adult nonbreeding
(Oct–Apr)
white flanks
extensive white on foreneck
Adult breeding
(Apr–Sep)
dark bill with reddish tip
dark-speckled with well-defined white throat
Pale adult breeding
(Apr–Sep)
Dark adult breeding
(Apr–Sep)

Voice: Silent at sea. Adults in colony vocal; varied repertoire not similar to other auklets; mainly a high, grating or churring trill or chatter in pulsing series reminiscent of White-throated Swift.

Dark Auklets

These two small, dark alcids are found in large groups at sea and nest colonially in crevices. Whiskered Auklet forages in powerful tidal rips. Both species have a distinctive citruslike odor.

Whiskered Auklet

Aethia pygmaea

L 7.75" WS 14" WT 4.2 oz (120 g)

Small (close to Least Auklet), with small bill; smaller and more slender than Cassin's Auklet.

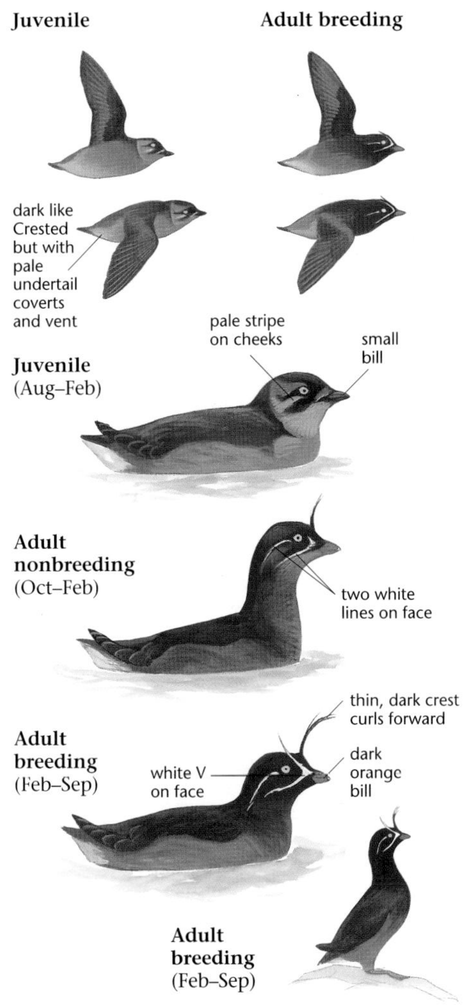

Juvenile
Adult breeding
dark like Crested but with pale undertail coverts and vent
pale stripe on cheeks
small bill
Juvenile (Aug–Feb)
Adult nonbreeding (Oct–Feb)
two white lines on face
thin, dark crest curls forward
Adult breeding (Feb–Sep)
white V on face
dark orange bill
Adult breeding (Feb–Sep)

Voice: Silent at sea. Adults in and near colony give plaintive, high, kittenlike *meew* and rapid series of sharp, two-syllable notes *beedeer beedeer beedeer beedeer bideer bideer bideer bidi bidi bidi bidee.*

Crested Auklet

Aethia cristatella

L 10.5" WS 17" WT 10 oz (285 g)

Heavy-bodied with rather long, thin wings; large head and deep bill.

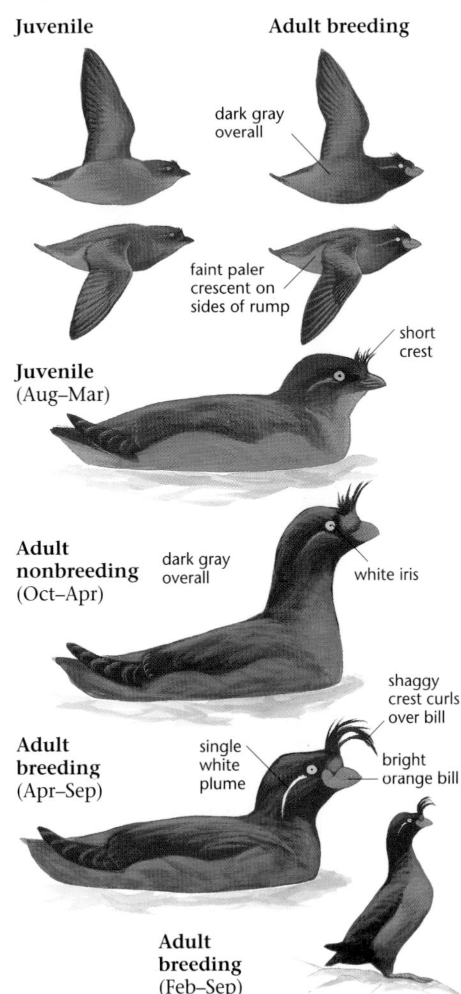

Juvenile
Adult breeding
dark gray overall
faint paler crescent on sides of rump
short crest
Juvenile (Aug–Mar)
Adult nonbreeding (Oct–Apr)
dark gray overall
white iris
shaggy crest curls over bill
Adult breeding (Apr–Sep)
single white plume
bright orange bill
Adult breeding (Feb–Sep)

Voice: Silent at sea. Adults in and near colony give a variety of low barking and hooting calls; a nasal, barking *kyow* like a small dog is frequently heard. Also a short, accelerating series of honking notes.

Rhinoceros Auklet and Tufted Puffin

These two large, dark species are usually found singly at sea and nest in burrows or crevices. Rhinoceros Auklet is related to puffins but thinner, with distinctive bill shape and narrow wings.

Rhinoceros Auklet

Cerorhinca monocerata

L 15" WS 22" WT 1.1 lb (520 g)

Our largest auklet; distinctly smaller than murres. Relatively long-billed with angular head shape.

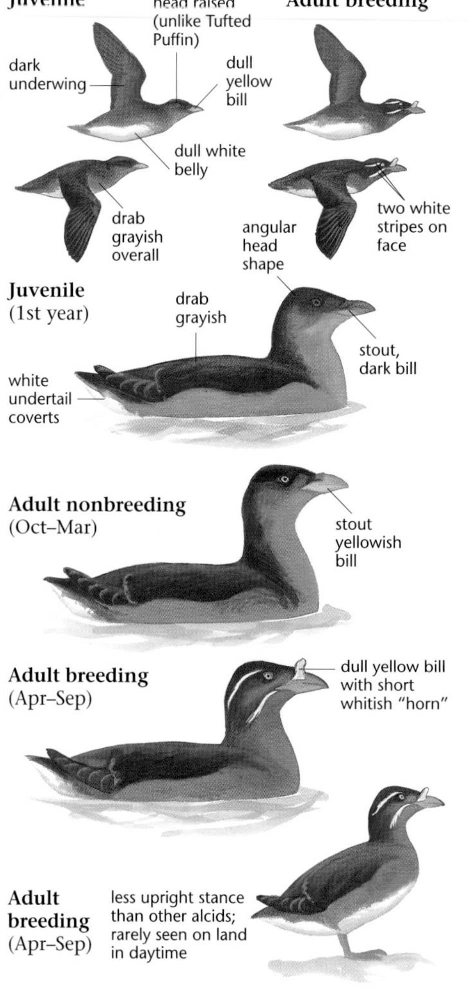
Juvenile
head raised (unlike Tufted Puffin)
Adult breeding
dark underwing
dull yellow bill
dull white belly
drab grayish overall
angular head shape
two white stripes on face
Juvenile (1st year)
drab grayish
stout, dark bill
white undertail coverts
Adult nonbreeding (Oct–Mar)
stout yellowish bill
Adult breeding (Apr–Sep)
dull yellow bill with short whitish "horn"
Adult breeding (Apr–Sep)
less upright stance than other alcids; rarely seen on land in daytime

Voice: Generally silent at sea. Adult near colony at night gives a building and fading series of about ten low, mooing notes; also short barks and single groaning calls.

Tufted Puffin

Fratercula cirrhata

L 15" WS 25" WT 1.7 lb (780 g)

Our largest puffin. Top of head very rounded, dome-shaped; wings rounded with broad "hand."

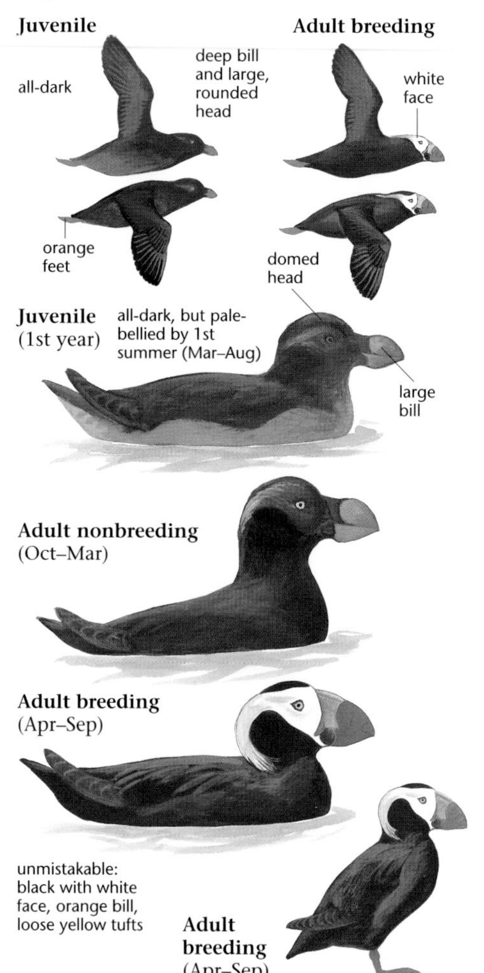
Juvenile
Adult breeding
all-dark
deep bill and large, rounded head
white face
orange feet
domed head
Juvenile (1st year)
all-dark, but pale-bellied by 1st summer (Mar–Aug)
large bill
Adult nonbreeding (Oct–Mar)
Adult breeding (Apr–Sep)
unmistakable: black with white face, orange bill, loose yellow tufts
Adult breeding (Apr–Sep)

Voice: Silent at sea. Adult near colony not very vocal; only a low, rumbling, groaning sound heard.

Alcids fly in lines, often of mixed species, with the slowest birds leading the way. Puffins fly more slowly than murres, so one or more puffins often briefly lead a line of murres.

Horned and Atlantic Puffins

Puffins are unmistakable, with their clownlike faces, very deep bills, and broad wings. All puffins are generally solitary at sea and are rarely seen from land except around nesting burrows.

Horned Puffin

Fratercula corniculata

L 15" WS 23" WT 1.4 lb (620 g)

Larger and longer-tailed than Atlantic Puffin; high culmen ridge slopes down to forehead.

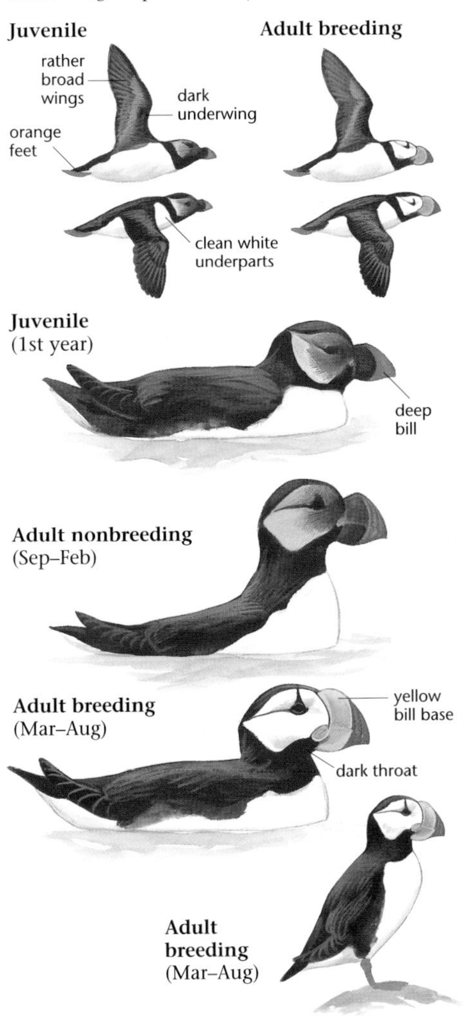

Juvenile
Adult breeding
rather broad wings
dark underwing
orange feet
clean white underparts
Juvenile (1st year)
deep bill
Adult nonbreeding (Sep–Feb)
Adult breeding (Mar–Aug)
yellow bill base
dark throat
Adult breeding (Mar–Aug)

Voice: Silent at sea. Adults in colony give low groaning or growling calls, often in rhythmic pattern unlike the continuous moaning of Atlantic Puffin.

Atlantic Puffin

Fratercula arctica

L 12.5" WS 21" WT 13 oz (380 g)

The smallest puffin, much smaller than murres. Note pale face, dark collar and underwings.

Juvenile
Adult breeding

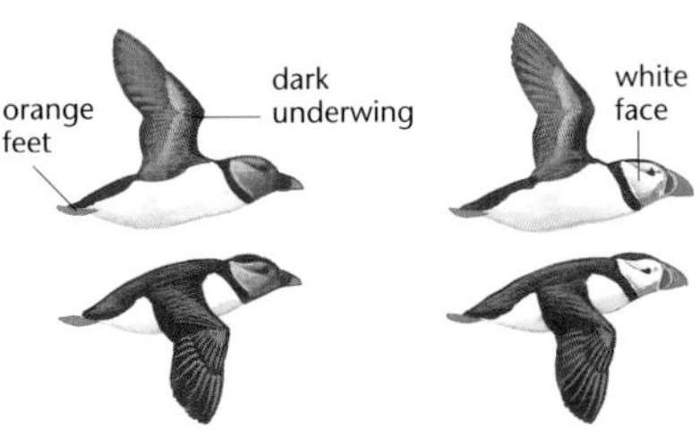

orange feet
dark underwing
white face

Juvenile (1st year)
triangular bill

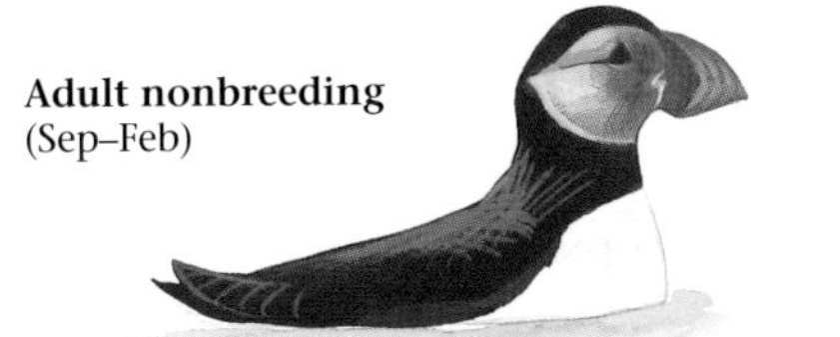

Adult nonbreeding (Sep–Feb)

Adult breeding (Mar–Aug)
dark slaty-blue bill base
gray throat
puffins walk more easily than other alcids
Adult breeding (Mar–Aug)

Voice: Silent at sea. Adults in colony give variations on a low, unmusical moaning or bellowing with slight pitch changes, like the sound of a distant chain saw.

Puffins tend to fly higher than other alcids, up to 30 feet above the water (other alcids usually fly less than 5 feet above surface).

Pigeons and Doves

Family: Columbidae

14 species in 6 genera. Most pick food (seeds and fruit) from ground, walking with mincing steps and bobbing head; wild pigeons forage in treetops. Flight is strong and direct with flicking wingbeats. Doves are usually found in small groups or singly, pigeons often in larger groups. All give low, cooing calls. Nest of all species is a flimsy platform of twigs, placed on a horizontal tree branch. Compare falcons in flight and game birds on the ground. Adults are shown.

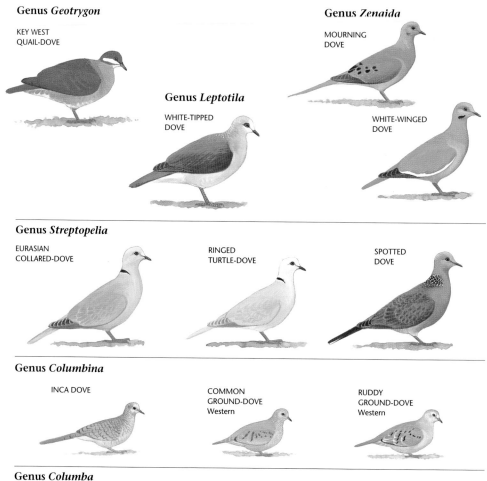

Genus *Geotrygon*

KEY WEST QUAIL-DOVE

Genus *Leptotila*

WHITE-TIPPED DOVE

Genus *Zenaida*

MOURNING DOVE

WHITE-WINGED DOVE

Genus *Streptopelia*

EURASIAN COLLARED-DOVE

RINGED TURTLE-DOVE

SPOTTED DOVE

Genus *Columbina*

INCA DOVE

COMMON GROUND-DOVE Western

RUDDY GROUND-DOVE Western

Genus *Columba*

ROCK DOVE (FERAL PIGEON)
RED-BILLED PIGEON
WHITE-CROWNED PIGEON
BAND-TAILED PIGEON

Doves: Genus *Zenaida*

These two species are closely related but quite different in appearance. Found in brushy, open habitats and suburbs, both are easily identified by tail shape and pattern and by wing pattern.

Mourning Dove

Zenaida macroura

L 12" WS 18" WT 4.2 oz (120 g) ♂>♀

Our most slender dove, with long, pointed tail; fairly narrow, pointed wings held close while flapping.

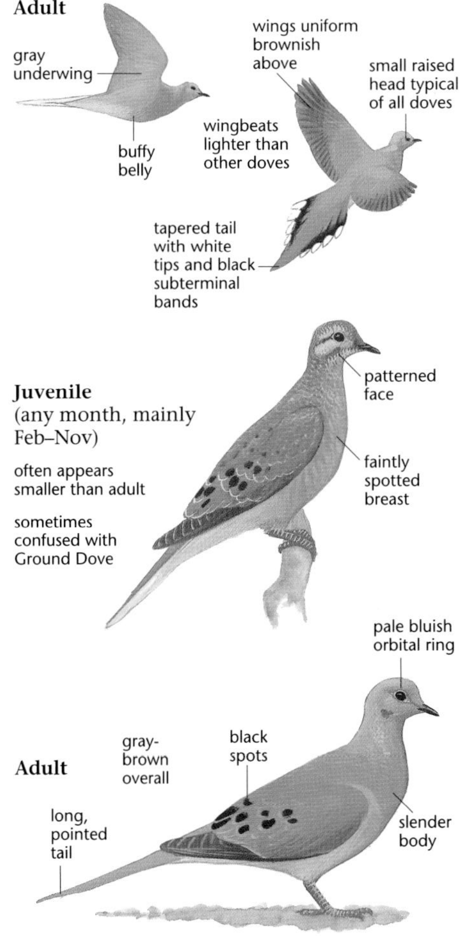

Adult
gray underwing
buffy belly
wings uniform brownish above
small raised head typical of all doves
wingbeats lighter than other doves
tapered tail with white tips and black subterminal bands
Juvenile
(any month, mainly Feb–Nov)
often appears smaller than adult
sometimes confused with Ground Dove
patterned face
faintly spotted breast
pale bluish orbital ring
Adult
gray-brown overall
black spots
long, pointed tail
slender body

Voice: Song a mournful hooting *ooAAH cooo coo coo;* often mistaken for an owl by inexperienced listeners. Much minor individual variation in pattern. Sometimes a strong, single *pooooo.* Wings produce light, airy whistling on takeoff.

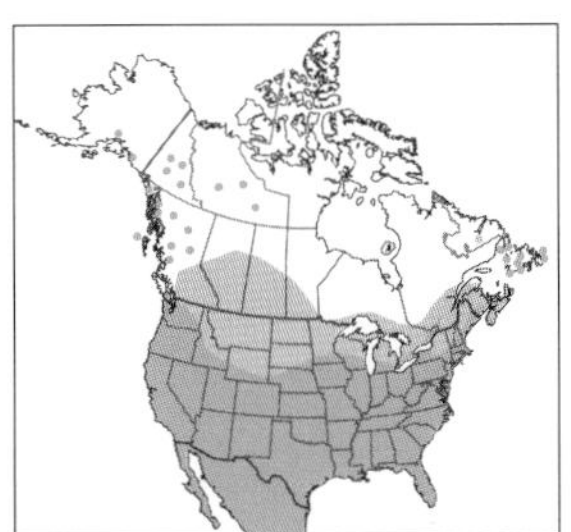

White-winged Dove

Zenaida asiatica

L 11.5" WS 19" WT 5 oz (150 g)

Larger and heavier than Mourning Dove; short, square tail and broad wings.

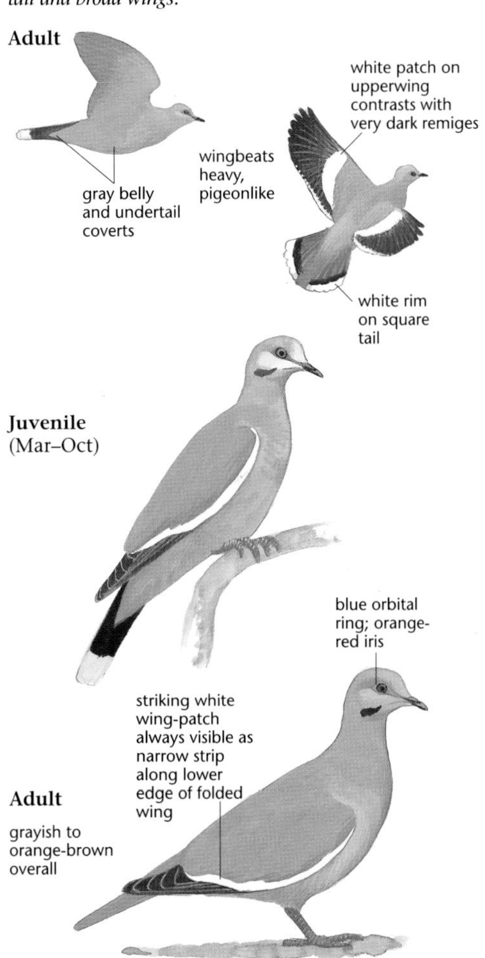

Adult
white patch on upperwing contrasts with very dark remiges
wingbeats heavy, pigeonlike
gray belly and undertail coverts
white rim on square tail
Juvenile
(Mar–Oct)
blue orbital ring; orange-red iris
striking white wing-patch always visible as narrow strip along lower edge of folded wing
Adult
grayish to orange-brown overall

Voice: Song a rhythmic hooting *hhhHEPEP pou pooooo* ("who cooks for you"), reminiscent of Barred or Spotted Owl, and a slow, measured series *pep pair pooa paair pooa paair pooa. . . .* Wings produce weak whistle on takeoff; lower and softer than Mourning Dove.

Collared-Doves

These large but slender doves have long, square to rounded tails. Found in suburbs, often perched on utility poles or rooftops, three species in the genus have been introduced to North America.

Eurasian Collared-Dove

Streptopelia decaocto

L 13" WS 22" WT 7 oz (200 g)

Much larger and heavier than Mourning Dove, with square tail; pale overall.

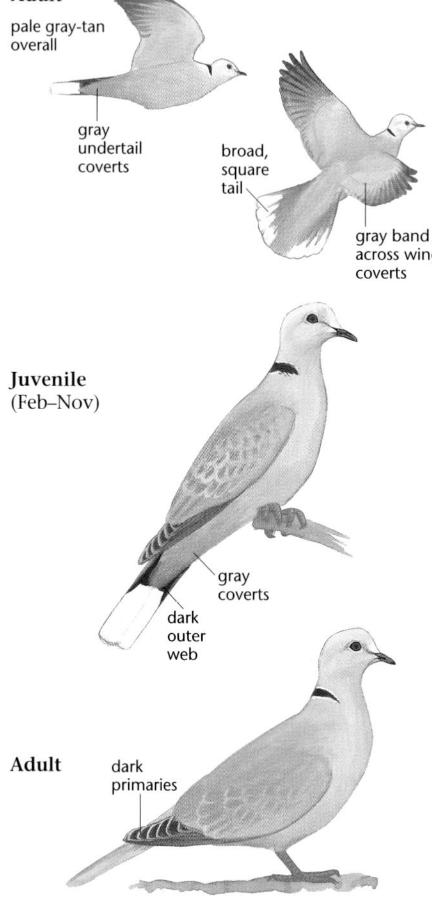

Adult
pale gray-tan overall
gray undertail coverts
broad, square tail
gray band across wing coverts
Juvenile
(Feb–Nov)
gray coverts
dark outer web
Adult
dark primaries

Voice: Song a rhythmic, three-syllable hooting *coo COOO cup* steadily repeated; slightly lower-pitched than Mourning Dove. Display call shorter *COO COO` co;* also a rather harsh, nasal *krreeew* during display flight, reminiscent of Catbird but low and hollow. No wing whistle in flight.

Ringed Turtle-Dove

Streptopelia risoria

L 11" WS 20" WT 6 oz (160 g)

Smaller than Eurasian Collared-Dove but still slightly larger than Mourning Dove. Usually very pale; white undertail coverts diagnostic.

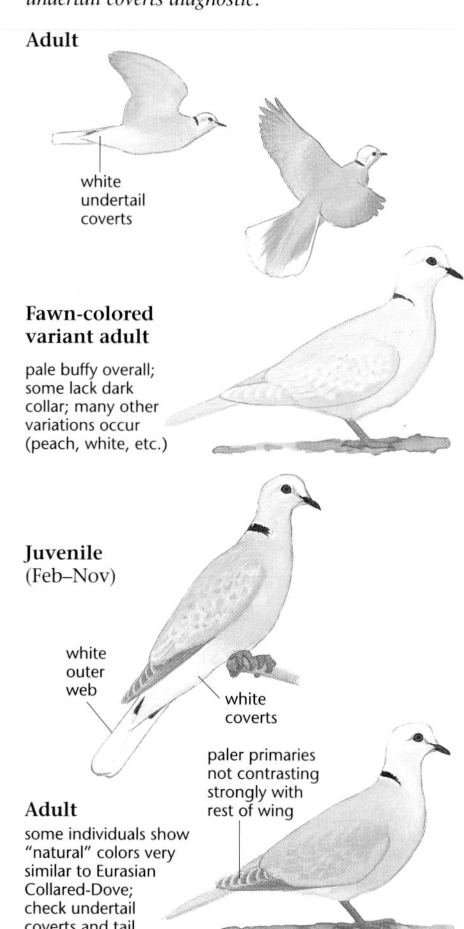

Adult
white undertail coverts
Fawn-colored variant adult
pale buffy overall; some lack dark collar; many other variations occur (peach, white, etc.)
Juvenile
(Feb–Nov)
white outer web
white coverts
paler primaries not contrasting strongly with rest of wing
Adult
some individuals show "natural" colors very similar to Eurasian Collared-Dove; check undertail coverts and tail pattern

Voice: Song a soft, rolling, cooing *cooeh-crrrrooa* not repeated quickly; also a soft, nasal laugh given from perch: a low, hollow *hodo-hoo-hoo-hoo-hoo.*

Eurasian Collared-Dove was introduced from Europe and is rapidly colonizing in North America. Ringed Turtle-Dove is a domestic variety, not a naturally occurring species, and fares poorly in the wild. Small populations may persist in some southern cities, while escapes are seen regularly throughout North America.

Spotted and White-tipped Doves

Spotted Dove, closely related to collared-doves, is found in suburbs. The stocky and secretive White-tipped Dove is found in dense, shady woods, usually walking on the ground.

Spotted Dove

Streptopelia chinensis

L 12" WS 21" WT 6 oz (160 g)

Larger, heavier than Mourning Dove, with long, graduated tail; shape and size similar to Eurasian Collared-Dove but slightly longer-tailed and much darker.

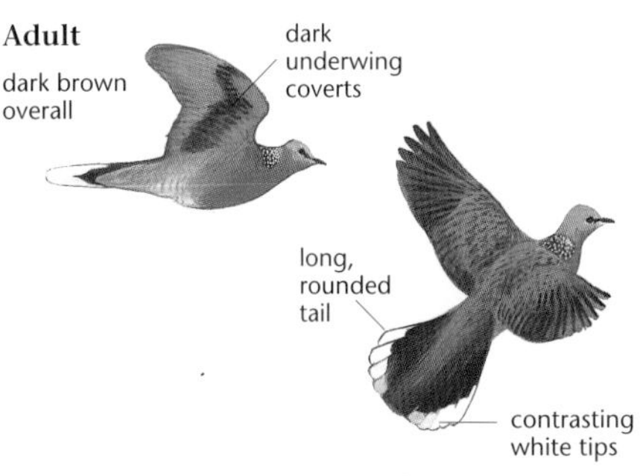
Adult
dark brown overall
dark underwing coverts
long, rounded tail
contrasting white tips

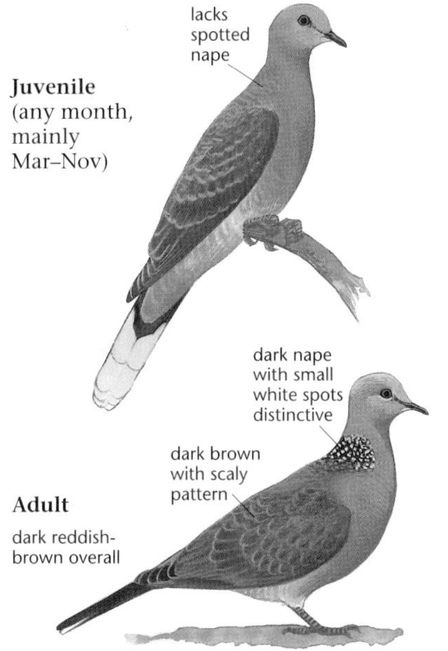
lacks spotted nape
Juvenile (any month, mainly Mar–Nov)

dark nape with small white spots distinctive
dark brown with scaly pattern
Adult
dark reddish-brown overall

Voice: Song a forceful *poo pooorr* or *coo CRRRRRoo cup;* middle note very rough, rolling; final note separate; higher and louder than Mourning Dove. Wings do not whistle in flight.

White-tipped Dove

Leptotila verreauxi

L 11.5" WS 18" WT 5 oz (150 g)

Large, very stocky and rotund, with short tail and short, broad wings.

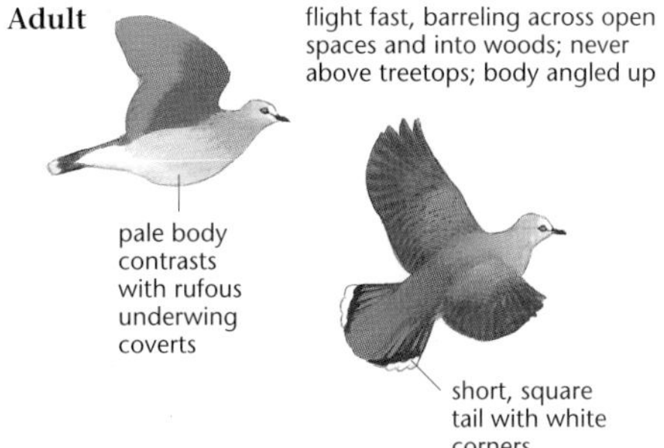
Adult
flight fast, barreling across open spaces and into woods; never above treetops; body angled up
pale body contrasts with rufous underwing coverts
short, square tail with white corners

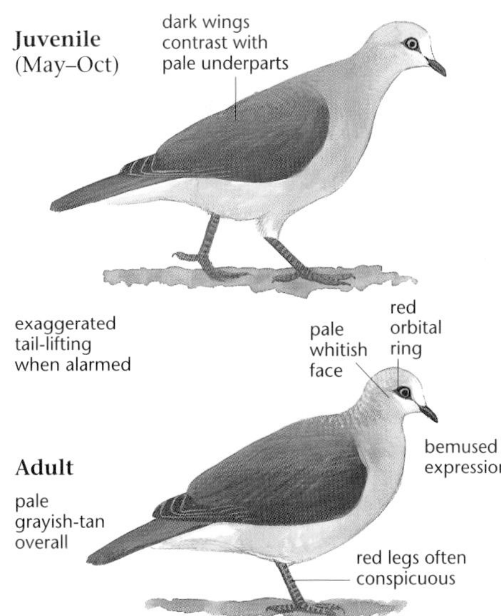
Juvenile (May–Oct)
dark wings contrast with pale underparts

exaggerated tail-lifting when alarmed
pale whitish face
red orbital ring
bemused expression
Adult
pale grayish-tan overall
red legs often conspicuous

Voice: Song a low, hollow moaning or cooing *oh-oohooooooooo,* like the sound made when one blows across the top of a bottle. Wings produce high, thin, sharp whistle (higher than Mourning Dove) on takeoff.

Key West Quail-Dove resembles White-tipped Dove in shape and habits; it is very secretive. Inca Dove, closely related to ground-doves, is found on lawns and gardens, rarely far from buildings.

Key West Quail-Dove

Geotrygon chrysia

L 12" WS 19" WT 6 oz (170 g)

Very rare visitor from West Indies. Very stocky and rotund like White-tipped Dove; looks small-headed.

Adult
reddish-brown

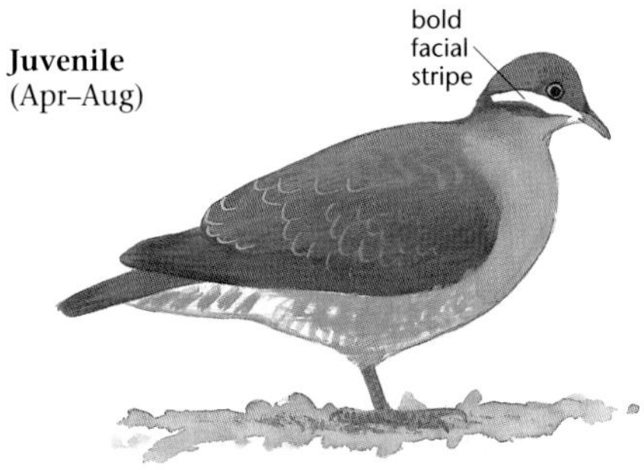
Juvenile
(Apr–Aug)
bold facial stripe

dark rufous-brown back and wings
Adult

Voice: Song a low, moaning *ooooo* slightly descending, or *oooowoo* with second part accented and slightly higher; very similar to White-tipped Dove. Though not loud, call is far-carrying. Calls from low branches (4–6 feet high) within forest.

Inca Dove

Columbina inca

L 8.25" WS 11" WT 1.6 oz (47 g)

Small, slender, and petite, with long, square tail.

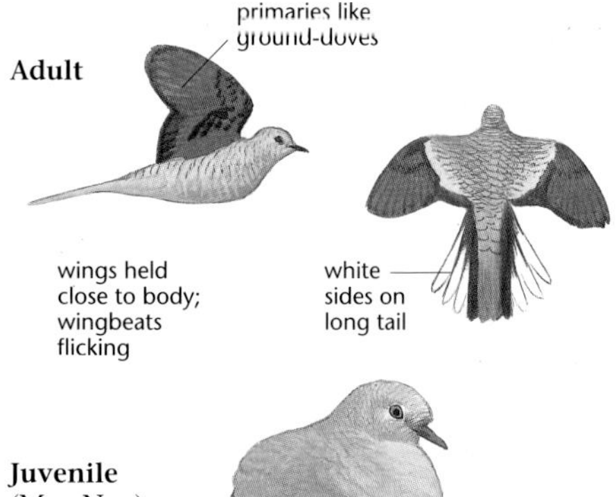
rufous primaries like ground-doves
Adult
wings held close to body; wingbeats flicking
white sides on long tail

Juvenile
(Mar–Nov)
Adult ♀
averages slightly drabber than ♂

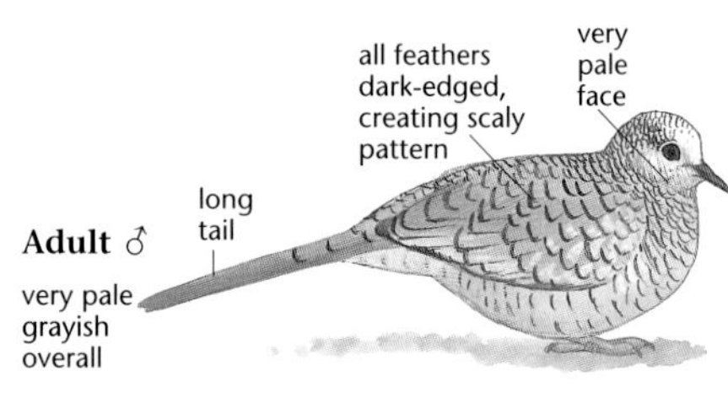
all feathers dark-edged, creating scaly pattern
very pale face
long tail
Adult ♂
very pale grayish overall

Voice: Song a fairly high, forceful cooing *POO-pup* ("no hope") repeated monotonously, less than once per second; also a more intense, hoarse growling *krooor* with soft, burry quality. Wings produce distinctive quiet, dry rattle on takeoff.

Ground-Doves

Our smallest, most compact doves, these similar species are found in dry, brushy areas, foraging on sandy ground (Ruddy prefers wetter habitat like Inca). They are often seen in small groups.

Ruddy Ground-Dove

Columbina talpacoti

L 6.75" WS 11" WT 1.4 oz (40 g)

Similar to Common but slightly larger and longer-tailed; often looks longer-necked. Best distinguished by unpatterned breast and nape, spotted scapulars.

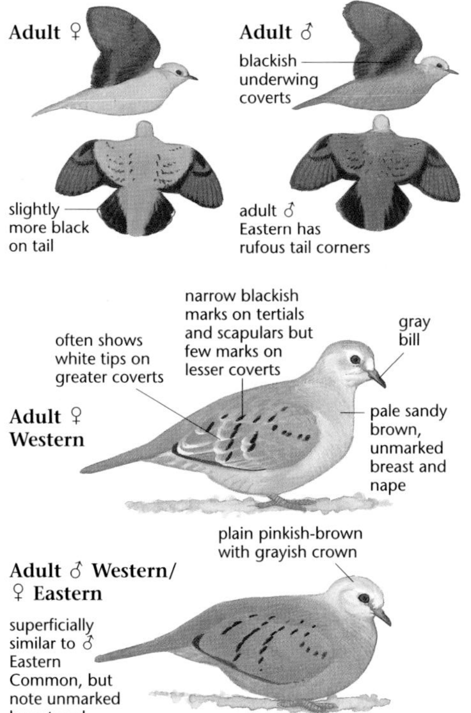
Adult ♀
Adult ♂
blackish underwing coverts
slightly more black on tail
adult ♂ Eastern has rufous tail corners
often shows white tips on greater coverts
narrow blackish marks on tertials and scapulars but few marks on lesser coverts
gray bill
Adult ♀ Western
pale sandy brown, unmarked breast and nape
plain pinkish-brown with grayish crown
Adult ♂ Western/ ♀ Eastern
superficially similar to ♂ Eastern Common, but note unmarked breast and nape, dark bill
striking cinnamon-rufous with blue-gray crown
Adult ♂ Eastern

Voice: Song lower, faster, more complex than Common Ground-Dove: *pidooip* repeated rapidly about twice per second.

Common Ground-Dove

Columbina passerina

L 6.5" WS 10.5" WT 1.1 oz (30 g)

Tiny and stocky with short tail and neck, stubby wings, rufous primaries.

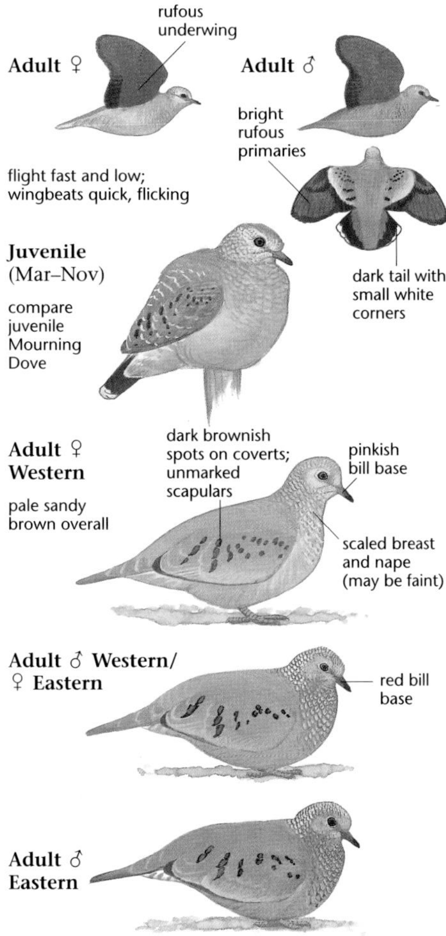
rufous underwing
Adult ♀
Adult ♂
bright rufous primaries
flight fast and low; wingbeats quick, flicking
Juvenile (Mar–Nov)
compare juvenile Mourning Dove
dark tail with small white corners
dark brownish spots on coverts; unmarked scapulars
pinkish bill base
Adult ♀ Western
pale sandy brown overall
scaled breast and nape (may be faint)
Adult ♂ Western/ ♀ Eastern
red bill base
Adult ♂ Eastern

Voice: Song a series of simple, rising coos *hoooip, hoooip, hoooip* . . . repeated slowly about once per second; a little higher and clearer than Mourning Dove. Wings rattle slightly on takeoff; not as clicking as Inca Dove.

Both these species vary geographically: Western birds are paler and grayer, and Eastern richer rufous, such that males of the pale Western populations resemble females of the brighter Eastern. For Common Ground-Dove the division between Eastern and Western occurs in east Texas, for Ruddy Ground-Dove in west Texas.

Pigeons: Genus *Columba*

Rock Dove is the familiar city pigeon, introduced and ubiquitous in North America. Band-tailed Pigeon is found in tall coniferous trees in mountainous areas, usually in flocks.

Rock Dove (Feral Pigeon)

Columba livia

L 12.5" WS 28" WT 9 oz (270 g)

Longer wings and pointier wingtips than other pigeons (more falconlike); stockier, shorter-necked and -tailed.

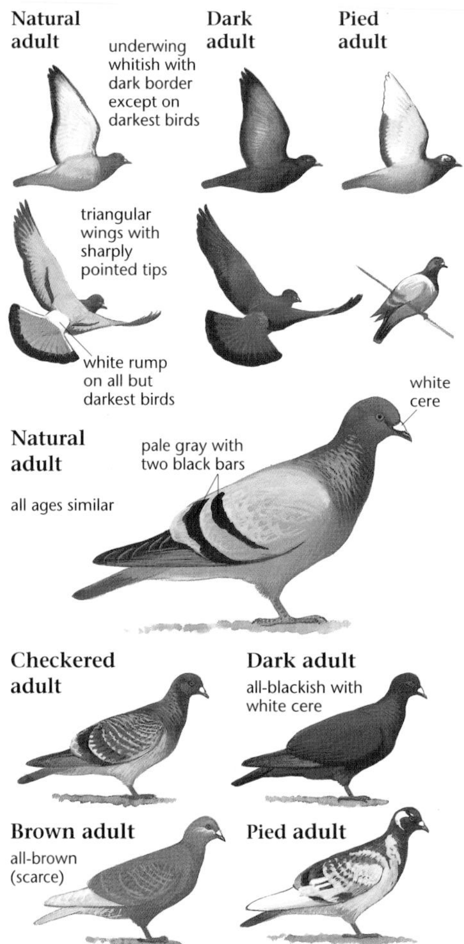

Natural adult
underwing whitish with dark border except on darkest birds
Dark adult
Pied adult
triangular wings with sharply pointed tips
white rump on all but darkest birds
white cere
Natural adult
pale gray with two black bars
all ages similar
Checkered adult
Dark adult
all-blackish with white cere
Brown adult
all-brown (scarce)
Pied adult

Voice: Song a low, muffled, almost humming *bru-u-ooo* or *p-p-p-proo;* also a slow series of low hoots. In display takeoff, wingbeats produce a series of slapping clicks *T-T-T-t-t-t-t-t.* In normal takeoff wings produce soft, humming whistle.

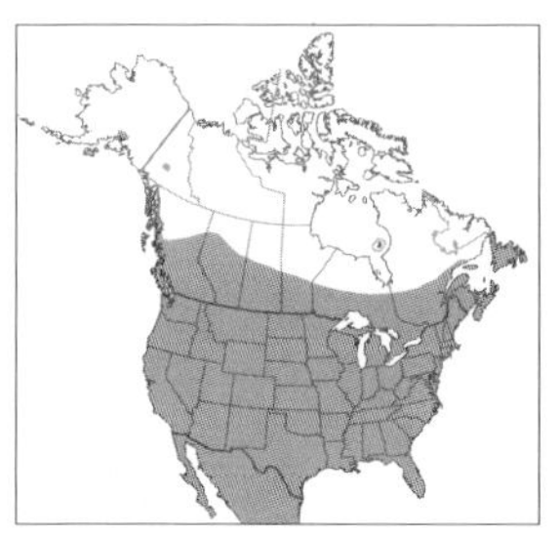

True Rock Doves nest on cliffs in Britain and Europe; their widespread introduction and domestication has created the great variety of plumages we see today. Most can be classified into one of four main plumage types: natural, checkered, dark, or brown. Birds with scattered white feathers (pied) occur frequently in all types; fully white birds are scarce.

Band-tailed Pigeon

Columba fasciata

L 14.5" WS 26" WT 13 oz (360 g) ♂>♀

Large and lanky, with relatively long tail; our largest pigeon.

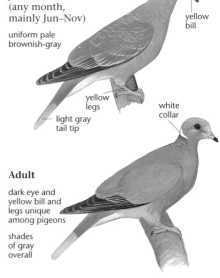

Adult
pale gray bicolored underwing
pointed wings
long tail
pale belly
pale grayish tail
Juvenile
(any month, mainly Jun–Nov)
uniform pale brownish-gray
yellow bill
yellow legs
light gray tail tip
white collar
Adult
dark eye and yellow bill and legs unique among pigeons
shades of gray overall

Voice: Song a deep, somewhat hoarse, repeated, owl-like hooting *hu whoo, hu whoo. . . .* Also a nasal, grating *raaaaaan.* Wings produce loud clapping on takeoff and muffled but far-carrying swoosh in fast descent.

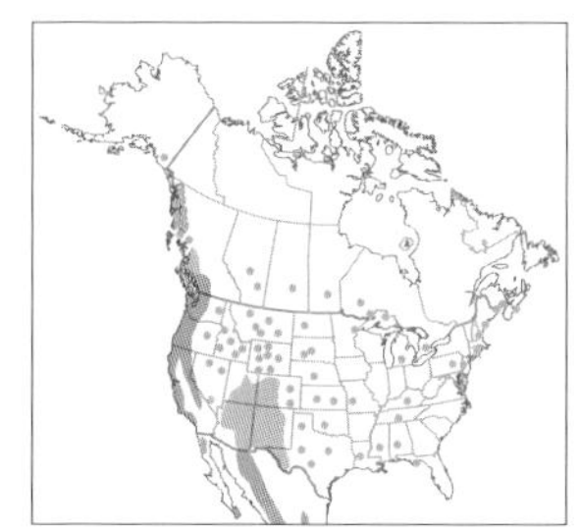

Like Band-tailed Pigeon (but unlike Rock Dove), these two species are wary, staying hidden in treetops and usually flushing without giving clear views.

Red-billed Pigeon

Columba flavirostris

L 14.5" WS 24" WT 11 oz (315 g)

Shape similar to White-crowned but with bulging forehead; longer-necked and rounder-winged than Rock Dove.

Adult

pale gray
underwing

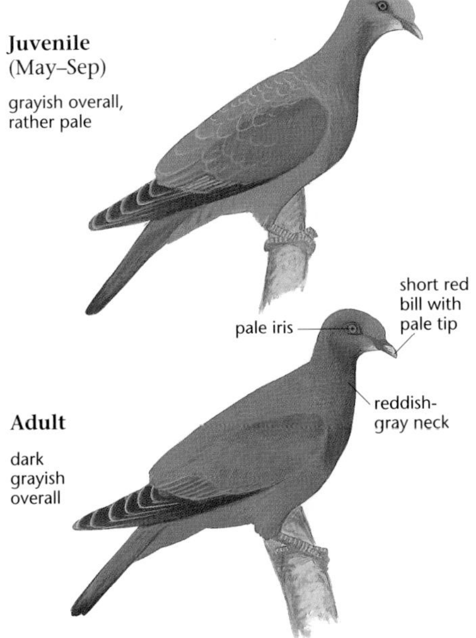
Juvenile
(May–Sep)
grayish overall,
rather pale
pale iris
short red
bill with
pale tip
reddish-
gray neck
Adult
dark
grayish
overall

Voice: Song a hoarse cooing *hup-hupA-hwooooo;* often in long series introduced by single, low, hoarse note *Hhooo; hwooo hwooooo hup hupA hwoooo, hup hupA hwooooo. . . .*

White-crowned Pigeon

Columba leucocephala

L 13.5" WS 24" WT 10 oz (290 g)

Differs from Rock Dove in relatively longer neck and tail, shorter and more rounded wings; tail tip projects much farther beyond wingtips.

Adult

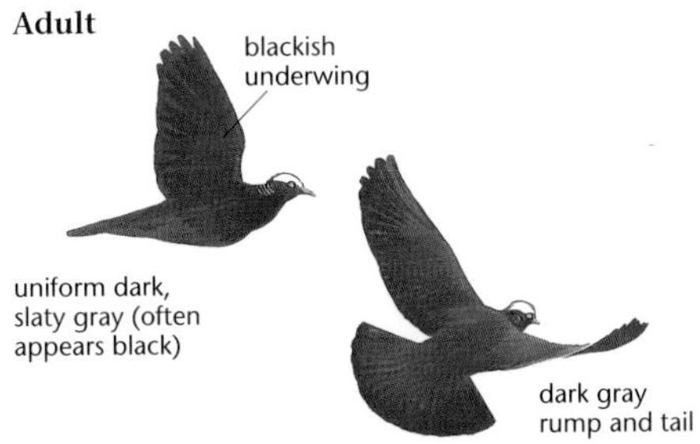
blackish
underwing
uniform dark,
slaty gray (often
appears black)
dark gray
rump and tail

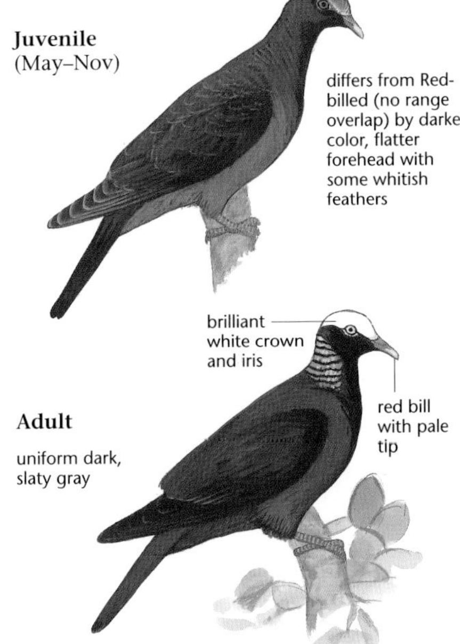
Juvenile
(May–Nov)
differs from Red-
billed (no range
overlap) by darker
color, flatter
forehead with
some whitish
feathers
brilliant
white crown
and iris
red bill
with pale
tip
Adult
uniform dark,
slaty gray

Voice: Song slow, well spaced, fairly high-pitched like Mourning Dove: *woopop wooooo, woopop wooooo. . . .* Rhythmic high, hoarse *hudi-ho-HOOOO* repeated.

Parrots and Their Allies

Family: Psittacidae

27 imported and 1 extirpated native species in 13 genera. There are no longer any native parrots in North America, but the imported species illustrated here are seen regularly. Some have established feral populations, especially in southern cities where exotic plantings create suitable habitat. Many other species can be encountered; more than 65 species have been recorded in Florida alone.

Red-crowned Parrot

Amazona viridigenalis

L 12" WS 25"
WT 11 oz (300 g)

Found in many southern cities; some in southern Texas could be natural vagrants from Mexico.

Voice: Common call a high squeal *weeeoo* followed by harsh, pounding *daak daak daak daak*.

Adult
broad yellow tip on tail
bluish nape
red crown
red forehead
1st year
Adult

Lilac-crowned Parrot

Amazona finschi

L 12.5" WS 24"
WT 11 oz (300g)

Found mainly in Florida and California.

Voice: Similar to Red-crowned.

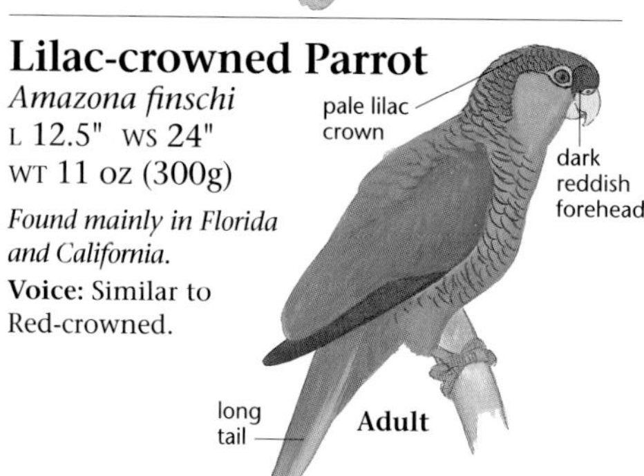

pale lilac crown
dark reddish forehead
long tail
Adult

Yellow-headed Parrot

Amazona oratrix

L 14" WS 28"
WT 1 lb (450 g)

Found mainly in Florida and California.

Voice: Generally mellow and human-voiced *herra* or long, descending *yadadadadada*.

Adult
yellow sides of tail
yellow head
pale bill
little or no yellow on head
Juvenile (any month)
Adult

The four species below are encountered frequently in Florida and/or California. Other *Amazona* species escape occasionally; also beware of hybrids.

RED-LORED PARROT
Amazona autumnalis
L 12.5"

Adult
red forehead with dark bill; some lack yellow on cheeks

BLUE-FRONTED PARROT
Amazona aestiva
L 15"

Adult
yellow face with blue forehead

MEALY PARROT
Amazona farinosa
L 15.5"

Adult
dull green; obvious white orbital ring

ORANGE-WINGED PARROT
Amazona amazonica
L 12.5"

Adult
yellow forehead with blue eye-line

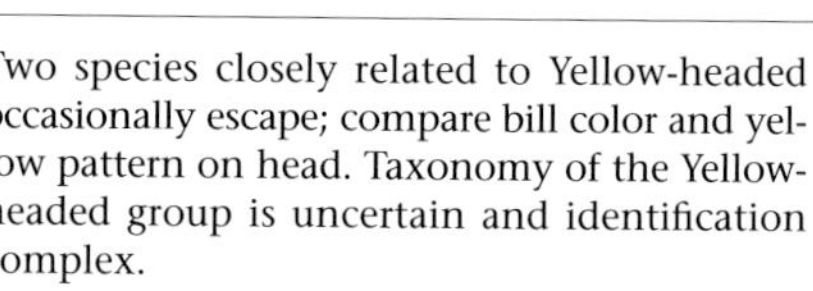

Two species closely related to Yellow-headed occasionally escape; compare bill color and yellow pattern on head. Taxonomy of the Yellow-headed group is uncertain and identification complex.

YELLOW-NAPED PARROT
Amazona auropalliata
L 14"

Adult dark bill; some have yellow on forehead

YELLOW-CROWNED PARROT
Amazona ochrocephala
L 14"

Adult
darkish bill; some have reddish upper mandible

Parrots (continued) and Chestnut-fronted Macaw

Amazona parrots are stocky, broad-winged, and short-tailed. Chestnut-fronted Macaw and Thick-billed Parrot are large-billed and long-tailed, with long, pointed wings.

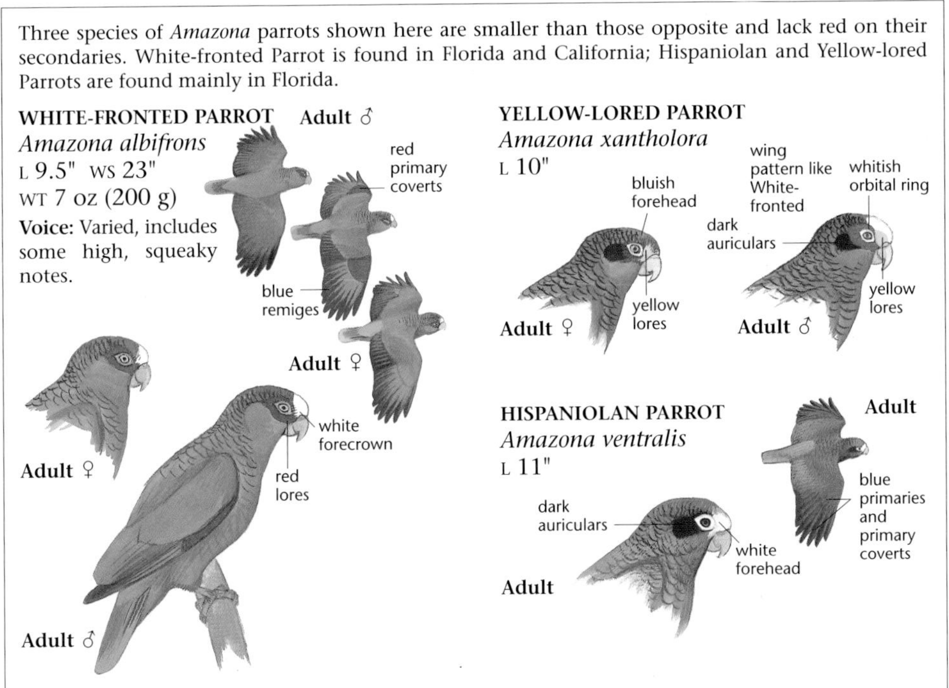

Three species of *Amazona* parrots shown here are smaller than those opposite and lack red on their secondaries. White-fronted Parrot is found in Florida and California; Hispaniolan and Yellow-lored Parrots are found mainly in Florida.
WHITE-FRONTED PARROT
Amazona albifrons
L 9.5" WS 23"
WT 7 oz (200 g)
Voice: Varied, includes some high, squeaky notes.
Adult ♂
red primary coverts
blue remiges
Adult ♀
Adult ♀
white forecrown
red lores
Adult ♂
YELLOW-LORED PARROT
Amazona xantholora
L 10"
bluish forehead
yellow lores
Adult ♀
wing pattern like White-fronted
whitish orbital ring
dark auriculars
yellow lores
Adult ♂
HISPANIOLAN PARROT
Amazona ventralis
L 11"
Adult
blue primaries and primary coverts
dark auriculars
white forehead
Adult

Thick-billed Parrot

Rhynchopsitta pachyrhyncha

L 15" WS 32"
WT 15 oz (440 g)

Native; formerly a rare visitor from Mexico to mountains of Arizona, last recorded in 1938. Reintroduction attempts in 1980s failed.

Voice: All calls talky, clear, not grating; may recall flock of Snow Geese.

Adult
blackish flight feathers
yellow band of greater coverts
longish tail
pointed wings
red forehead reaches behind eye
bright green
black bill
red bend of wing
1st year
Adult

Chestnut-fronted Macaw

Ara severa

L 18" WS 30"
WT 15 oz (430 g)

Found mainly in Florida.

Voice: Very loud, harsh screeching; sometimes like braying donkey.

Adult
chestnut forehead
bare whitish face-patch
massive black bill
all-green underparts
Adult
reddish underwing
blue primaries
long, pointed tail

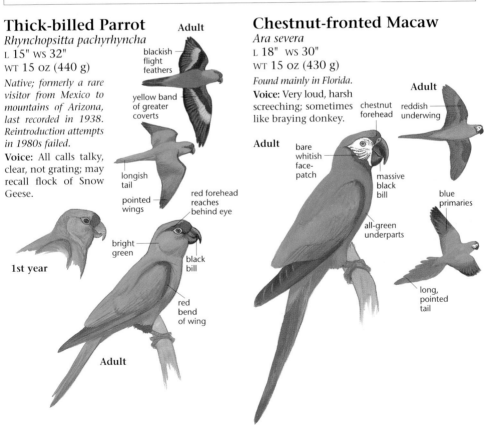

Parakeets: Genus *Aratinga*

The species in this genus (often called conures) are mainly green, with long, pointed tails. Identification is complicated by the existence of several other similar species (not shown here).

Green Parakeet

Aratinga holochlora

L 13" WS 21" WT 8 oz (230 g)

Found in southern Texas, where at least some may be natural vagrants from Mexico.

Voice: A rather high, shrill, raucous chattering.

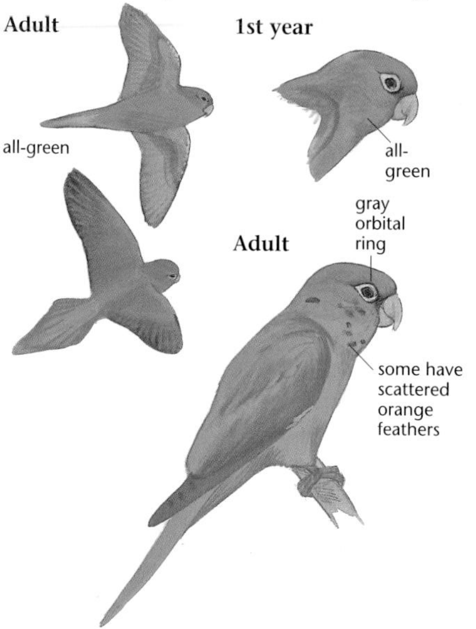
Adult
1st year
all-green
all-green
gray orbital ring
Adult
some have scattered orange feathers

Mitred Parakeet

Aratinga mitrata

L 15" WS 25" WT 7 oz (205 g)

Found mainly in Florida and California.

Voice: A loud, harsh series and rising *kreeep*.

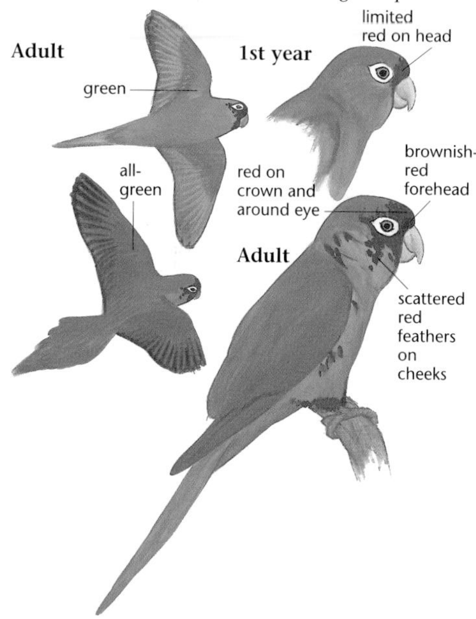
limited red on head
Adult
1st year
green
all-green
red on crown and around eye
brownish-red forehead
Adult
scattered red feathers on cheeks

Red-masked Parakeet

Aratinga erythrogenys

L 13.5" WS 22" WT 6 oz (170 g)

Found mainly in Florida and California.

Voice: Less harsh than Mitred.

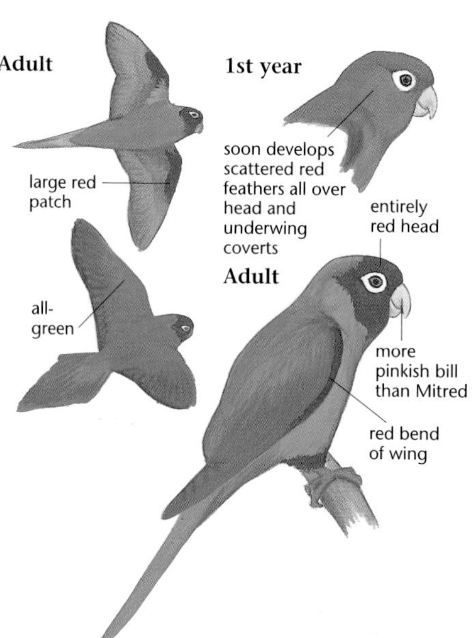
Adult
1st year
large red patch
soon develops scattered red feathers all over head and underwing coverts
entirely red head
Adult
all-green
more pinkish bill than Mitred
red bend of wing

Blue-crowned Parakeet

Aratinga acuticaudata

L 14.5" WS 24" WT 7 oz (200 g)

Found mainly in Florida and California, but capable of surviving farther north as well.

Voice: A relatively low, hoarse, rapidly repeated *reedy reedy reedy*.

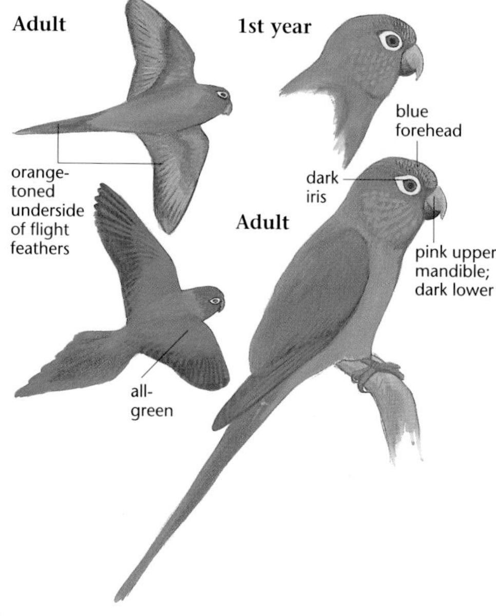
Adult
1st year
blue forehead
orange-toned underside of flight feathers
dark iris
Adult
pink upper mandible; dark lower
all-green

These pointed-tailed parakeets are not as confusingly similar as those shown opposite. *Brotogeris* parakeets are smaller and fly rapidly with wings pulled in close to their bodies.

Dusky-headed Parakeet

Aratinga weddellii

L 11" WS 18" WT 3.9 oz (110 g)

Found mainly in Florida.

Voice: Rather nasal; less grating than similar species.

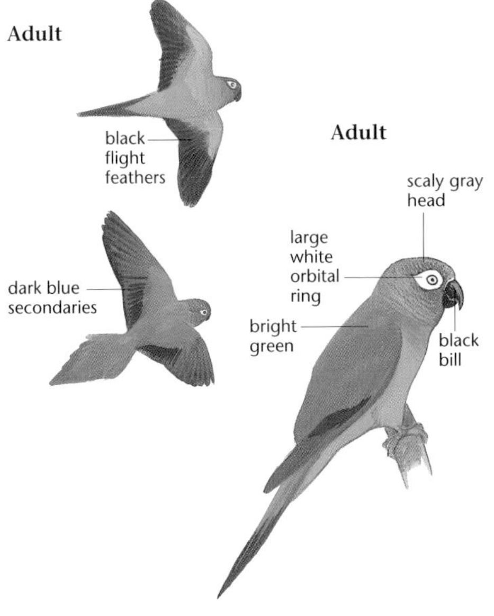
Adult
black flight feathers
dark blue secondaries
Adult
scaly gray head
large white orbital ring
bright green
black bill

Black-hooded Parakeet

Nandayus nenday

L 12" WS 23" WT 4.5 oz (128 g)

Found mainly in Florida and California; small numbers elsewhere.

Voice: Higher than Blue-crowned; a more screeching *graad graad. . . .*

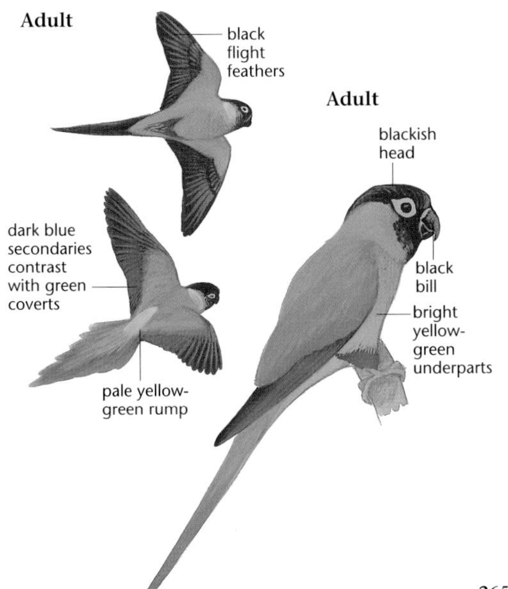
Adult
black flight feathers
dark blue secondaries contrast with green coverts
pale yellow-green rump
Adult
blackish head
black bill
bright yellow-green underparts

Monk Parakeet

Myiopsitta monachus

L 11.5" WS 19" WT 3.5 oz (100 g)

Nesting colonies in Connecticut, New York, Florida, Texas, Illinois, Oregon, and other states.

Voice: A varied, throaty rattling *graaa* and higher, rasping *skveet;* both slightly rising.

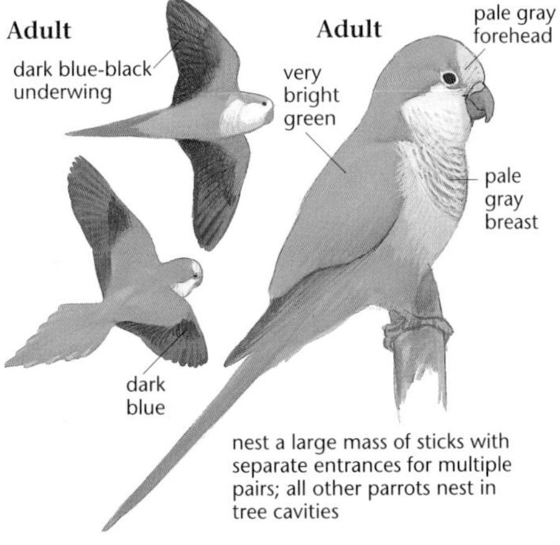
Adult
dark blue-black underwing
dark blue
Adult
pale gray forehead
very bright green
pale gray breast
nest a large mass of sticks with separate entrances for multiple pairs; all other parrots nest in tree cavities

Yellow-chevroned Parakeet

Brotogeris chiriri

L 8.75" WS 15" WT 2.1 oz (60 g)

Found mainly in Florida and California.

Voice: A rather high, scratchy *krere-krere.*

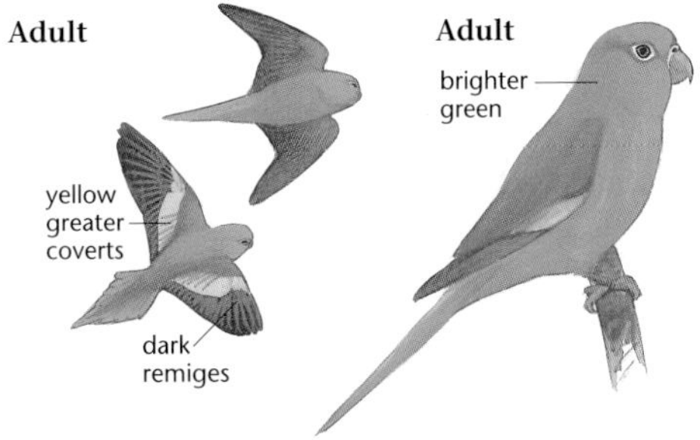
Adult
yellow greater coverts
dark remiges
Adult
brighter green

White-winged Parakeet

Brotogeris versicolurus

L 8.75" WS 15" WT 2.1 oz (60 g)

Found mainly in Florida and California; formerly common but now outnumbered by Yellow-chevroned.

Voice: Similar to Yellow-chevroned but mellower.

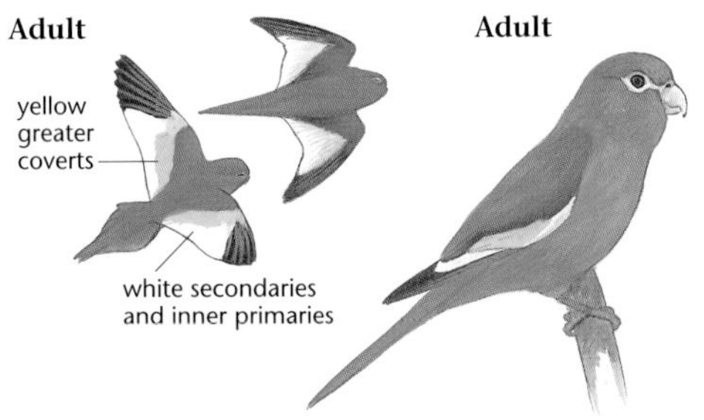
Adult
yellow greater coverts
white secondaries and inner primaries
Adult

Old World Parrots

These species are distinctive. Budgerigar and Rose-ringed Parakeet are locally established; the other species are common in captivity and often escape, but as yet there are no stable feral populations.

Budgerigar

Melopsittacus undulatus

L 7" WS 12" WT 1 oz (29 g)

The most commonly sold parrot. Found in small numbers locally in Florida; frequent escapes nationwide. Domestic varieties range from green (the normal wild form) to blue, yellow, or white.

Voice: High, dry, chattering warbles with squeaky and scratchy quality *chirrup.*

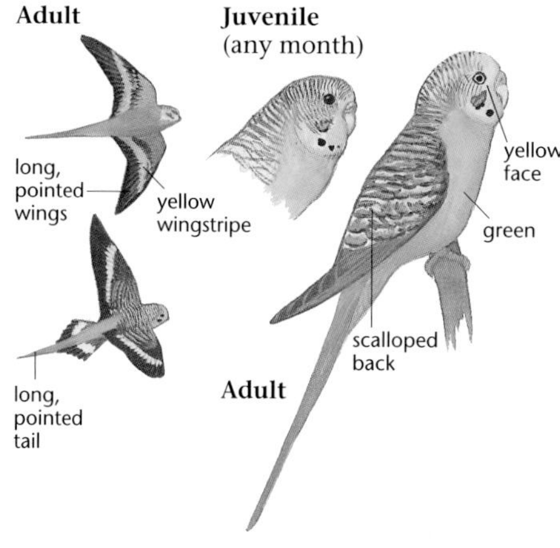
Adult
Juvenile (any month)
long, pointed wings
yellow wingstripe
yellow face
green
scalloped back
long, pointed tail
Adult

Rose-ringed Parakeet

Psittacula krameri

L 16" WS 18.5" WT 4.1 oz (117 g)

Found in Florida and California.

Voice: Includes high, clear squeal *keeew* like Northern Flicker; in series when excited.

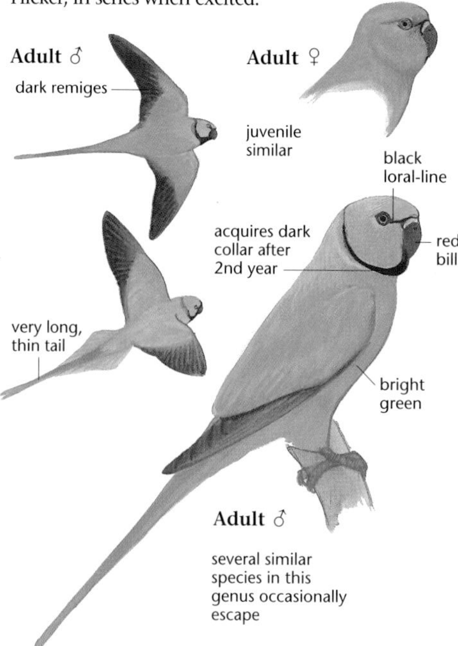
Adult ♂
dark remiges
Adult ♀
juvenile similar
black loral-line
acquires dark collar after 2nd year
red bill
very long, thin tail
bright green
Adult ♂
several similar species in this genus occasionally escape

Sulphur-crested Cockatoo

Cacatua galerita

L 18"

Voice: Extremely loud and harsh, toneless.

yellow crest usually concealed

several other species of white cockatoos may also occur

all-white

broad, rounded wings

short, square tail

Adult

Cockatiel

Nymphicus hollandicus

L 12.5"

Voice: Loud, clear whistles.

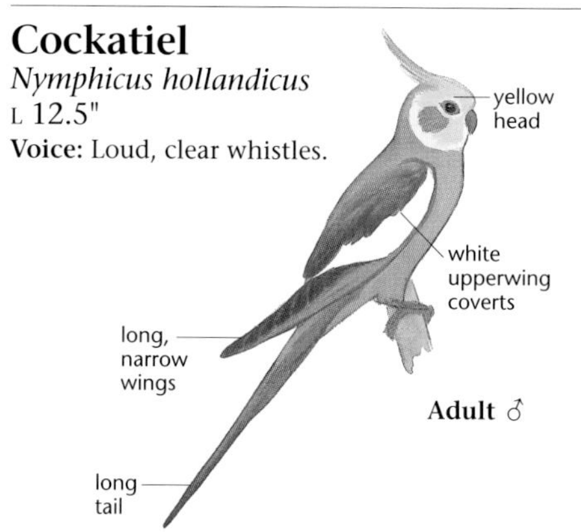
yellow head
white upperwing coverts
long, narrow wings
Adult ♂
long tail

Peach-faced Lovebird

Agapornis roseicollis

L 6.5"

Voice: A short, sharp *skreet.*

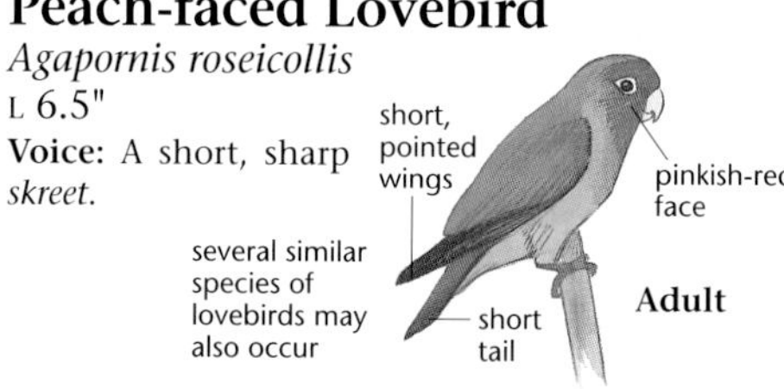
short, pointed wings
pinkish-red face
several similar species of lovebirds may also occur
short tail
Adult

Other species of parrots seen regularly in recent years but not established include Senegal Parrot, Patagonian Conure, Green-cheeked Parakeet, Orange-fronted Parakeet, Orange-chinned Parakeet, Red-shouldered Macaw, and several species of large macaws. Parrots are long-lived, and a single release or series of releases may create a local population that persists for many years without ever reproducing in the wild.

Cuckoos and Their Allies

Family: Cuculidae

6 species in 3 genera. There are three distinctive groups, each with different habits and food preferences. Cuckoos forage in dense, leafy trees and shrubs, plucking caterpillars; flight is smooth and flowing like kingbirds; calls are guttural cooing. Anis are found in weedy or brushy areas, feeding on insects and some fruit; usually very inconspicuous, they perch prominently at times; flight is weak and flopping with sailing glides; calls are squeaky whistles. Greater Roadrunner is found in open desert, brushland, and open pine forests, feeding on lizards, snakes, large insects, and other animal prey; flight is mainly low glides; runs smoothly and rapidly, using tail for balance. Nest of all species is a sloppy or flimsy platform of twigs in bush or low tree. Adults are shown.

Genus *Coccyzus*

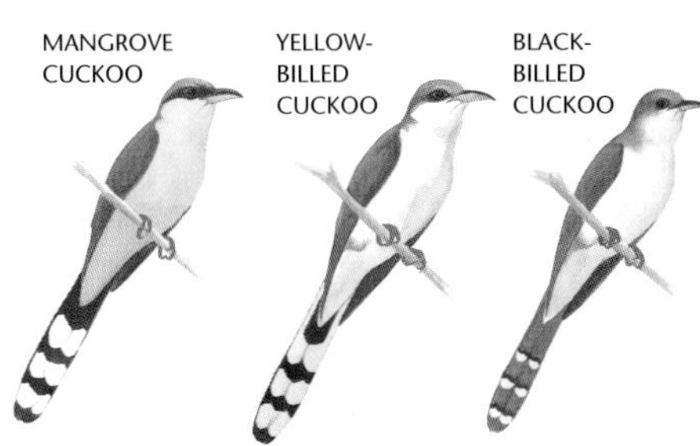
MANGROVE CUCKOO
YELLOW-BILLED CUCKOO
BLACK-BILLED CUCKOO

Genus *Crotophaga*

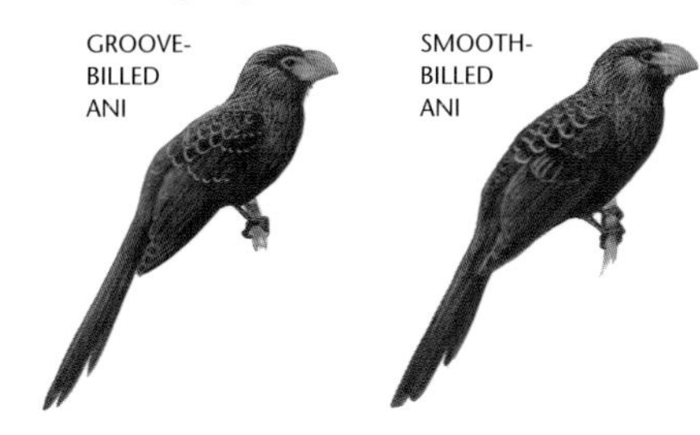
GROOVE-BILLED ANI
SMOOTH-BILLED ANI

Genus *Geococcyx*

GREATER ROADRUNNER

Mangrove Cuckoo

Coccyzus minor

L 12" WS 17" WT 2.3 oz (65 g)

Stouter-billed than other cuckoos, with buffy belly. Combination of large white tail spots and plain brown primaries distinctive.

Adult

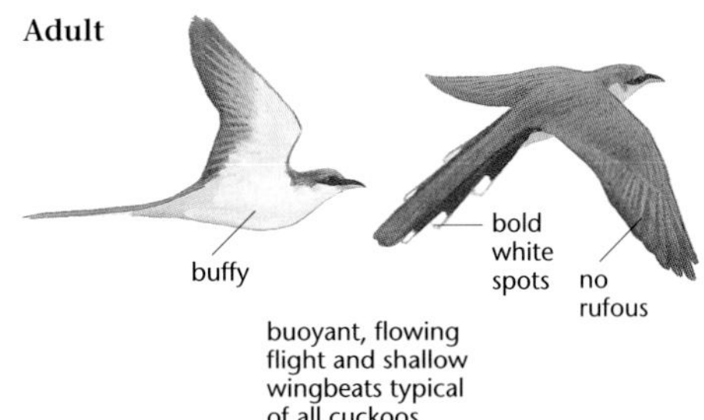
buffy
bold white spots
no rufous
buoyant, flowing flight and shallow wingbeats typical of all cuckoos

Juvenile (Jun–Nov)

Adult

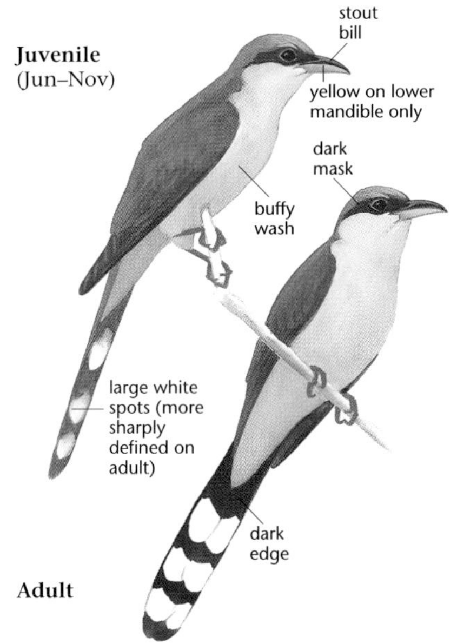
stout bill
yellow on lower mandible only
dark mask
buffy wash
large white spots (more sharply defined on adult)
dark edge

Voice: Very nasal, unmusical *aan aan aan aan aan aan aan urmm urmm,* slightly accelerating; last two notes lower and longer.

All three cuckoos are slender, long-tailed, and inconspicuous; they move furtively through dense foliage of bushes and trees in search of caterpillars.

Yellow-billed Cuckoo

Coccyzus americanus

L 12" WS 18" WT 2.3 oz (65 g)

Larger and stronger-billed than Black-billed, but less so than Mangrove. Clean white underparts, large white tail spots, and bright rufous primaries distinctive.

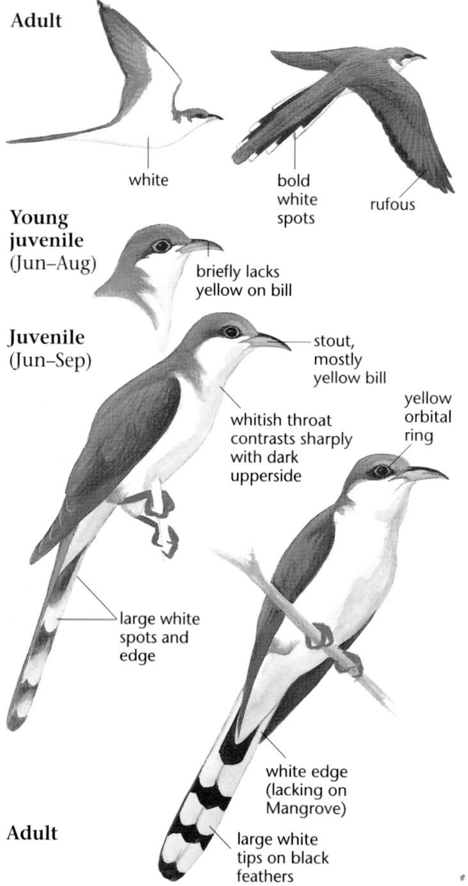
Adult
white
bold
white
spots
rufous
Young
juvenile
(Jun–Aug)
briefly lacks
yellow on bill
Juvenile
(Jun–Sep)
stout,
mostly
yellow bill
whitish throat
contrasts sharply
with dark
upperside
yellow
orbital
ring
large white
spots and
edge
white edge
(lacking on
Mangrove)
Adult
large white
tips on black
feathers

Voice: Song a guttural, hard, knocking series *ku-ku-ku-ku-ku-ku-kddowl-kddowl* . . . ; sometimes single *kddowl* notes. Also deep, swallowed, dovelike cooing *cloom* repeated with long pauses; a slow cooing series descending and weakening *too too too too to to to*; a fairly rapid series of single, hard *tok* notes on one pitch *tok tok tok tok*. . . .

Black-billed Cuckoo

Coccyzus erythropthalmus

L 12" WS 17.5" WT 1.8 oz (52 g)

More slender than other cuckoos, with weaker bill. Much smaller, with less contrasting tail spots.

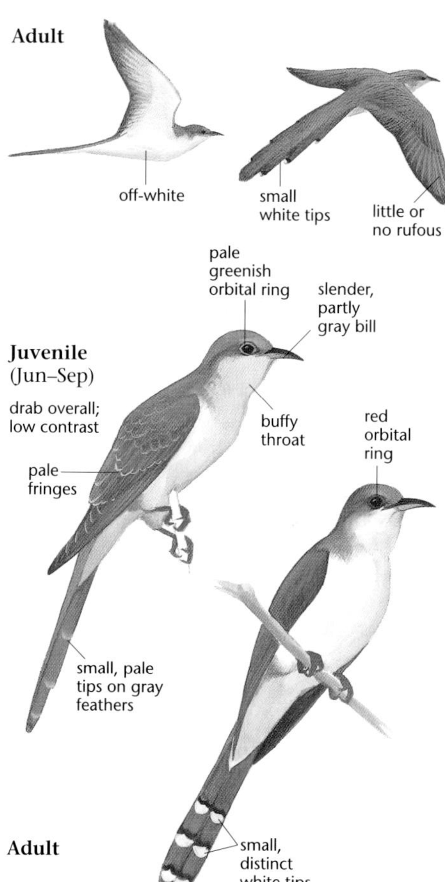
Adult
off-white
small
white tips
little or
no rufous
pale
greenish
orbital ring
slender,
partly
gray bill
Juvenile
(Jun–Sep)
drab overall;
low contrast
buffy
throat
red
orbital
ring
pale
fringes
small, pale
tips on gray
feathers
Adult
small,
distinct
white tips

Voice: Song a hollow, whistled *po po po* repeated; sometimes a long, rapid series gradually falling into triplet pattern (see Least Bittern). A rolling call of *kddow* notes higher-pitched, quicker, and not as guttural as Yellow-billed; beginning rapidly and ending with decelerating *cloo* notes. Also a rapid, hard, descending *k-k-k-k* or two-part, descending *kru-dru*.

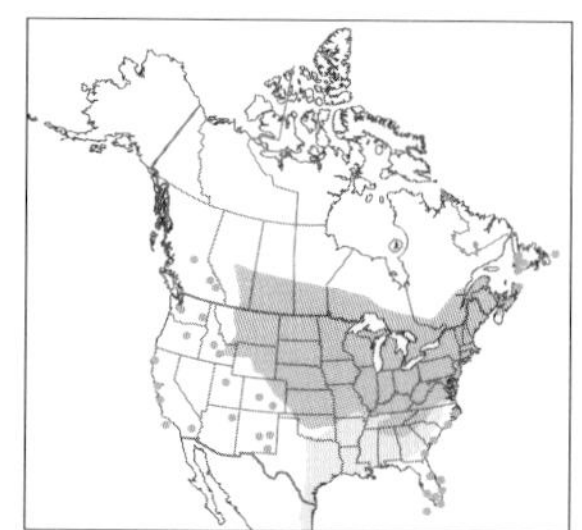

ANIS

Rather retiring in brushy or weedy fields, anis often look disheveled, with wings drooping and tails spread. The two species are very similar and are best distinguished by voice.

Groove-billed Ani

Crotophaga sulcirostris

L 13.5" WS 17" WT 3 oz (85 g) ♂>♀

Averages slightly smaller and relatively longer-tailed than Smooth-billed but much overlap; smaller than Smooth-billed with smaller bulge at base of culmen but some overlap.

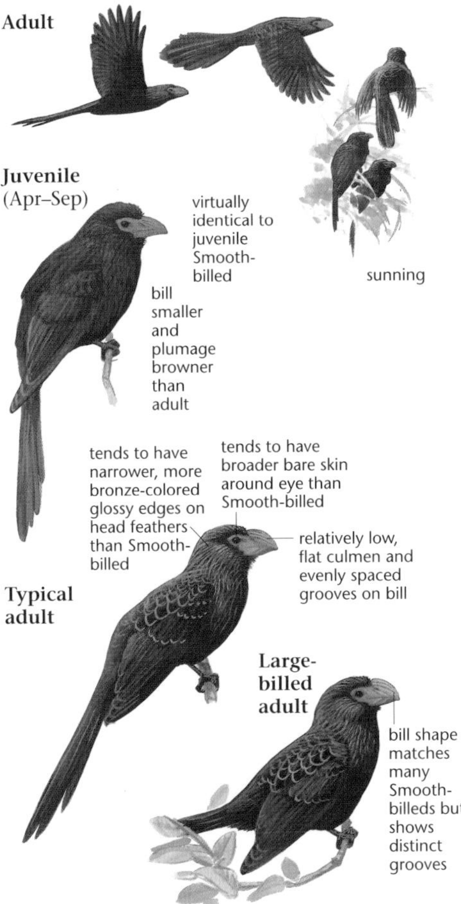

Adult
sunning
Juvenile
(Apr–Sep)
virtually identical to juvenile Smooth-billed
bill smaller and plumage browner than adult
tends to have narrower, more bronze-colored glossy edges on head feathers than Smooth-billed
tends to have broader bare skin around eye than Smooth-billed
relatively low, flat culmen and evenly spaced grooves on bill
Typical adult
Large-billed adult
bill shape matches many Smooth-billeds but shows distinct grooves

Voice: Common call a sharp, high whistle with slurred, whining ending *PEET-uaay* or *PEE-ho.* Often simply a sharp, inhaled *PEEt;* also a sharp, hollow *pep, pep . . .* or low, grating *krr krr. . . .*

Smooth-billed Ani

Crotophaga ani

L 14.5" WS 18.5" WT 3.7 oz (105 g) ♂>♀

Structure very similar to Groove-billed; both anis distinguished from grackles by deep bill, shaggy plumage, very different flight and habits.

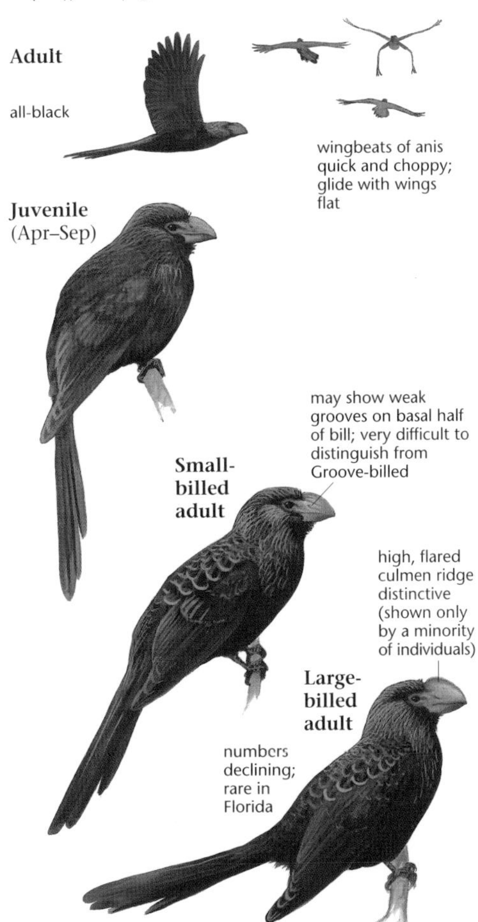

Adult
all-black
wingbeats of anis quick and choppy; glide with wings flat
Juvenile
(Apr–Sep)
may show weak grooves on basal half of bill; very difficult to distinguish from Groove-billed
Small-billed adult
high, flared culmen ridge distinctive (shown only by a minority of individuals)
Large-billed adult
numbers declining; rare in Florida

Voice: Common call a whining, metallic, ascending whistle *queee-ik;* also a thin, descending *teeew.* Other whistles and clucks less melodious than Groove-Billed.

Groove-billed **Smooth-billed**

Lower mandible of Smooth-billed much stronger with more pronounced gonydeal angle; this feature may be more reliable for identification than upper mandible characteristics.

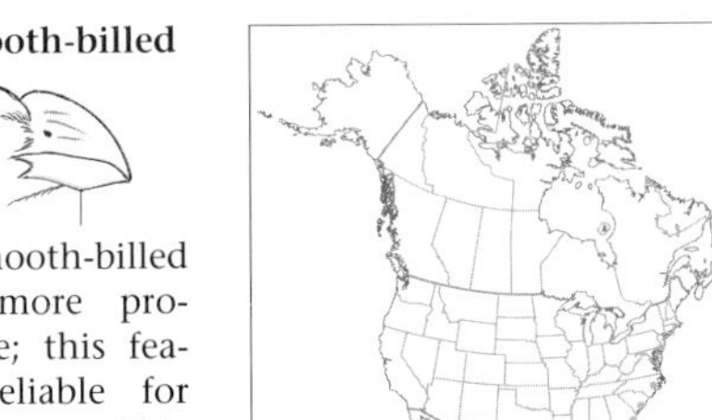

Greater Roadrunner

This well-known bird is found in any dry, open habitat, from rocky desert to grassland; it is often seen perched on fence posts or rocks. It feeds on a variety of small prey, mainly lizards and snakes.

Greater Roadrunner

Geococcyx californianus

L 23" WS 22" WT 13 oz (380 g)

Distinctive; large and long-tailed, with shaggy, streaked appearance; short, ragged crest often raised. Running action smooth and strong, but standing bird adopts a variety of comical poses.

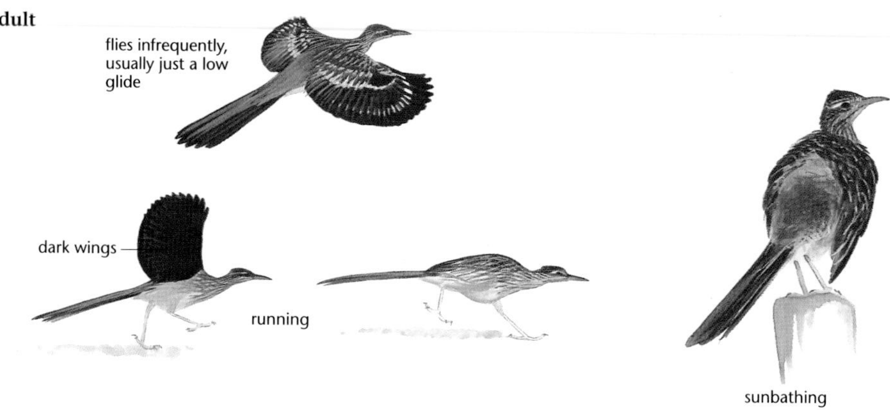
Adult
flies infrequently, usually just a low glide
dark wings
running
sunbathing

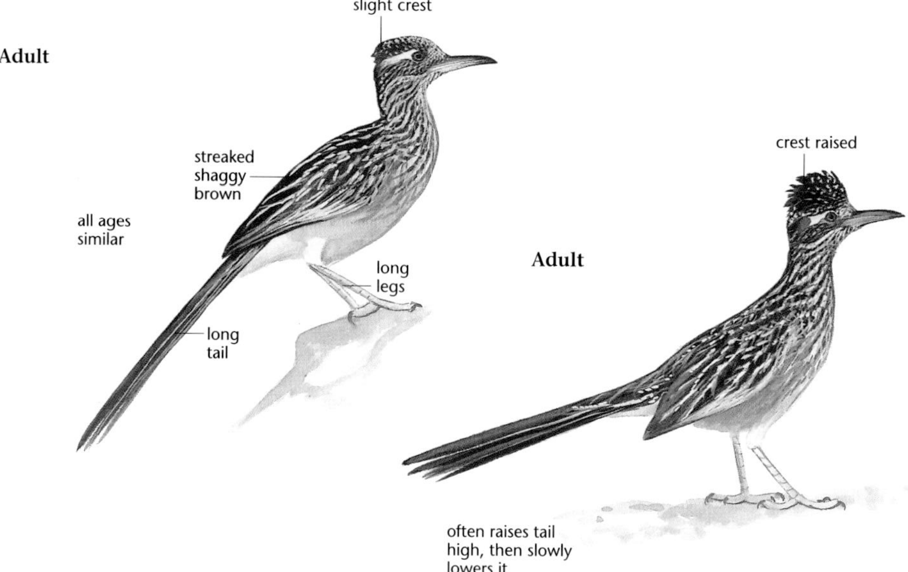
slight crest
Adult
streaked shaggy brown
all ages similar
long legs
long tail
crest raised
Adult
often raises tail high, then slowly lowers it

Voice: Song a slow, descending series of about six resonant, low-pitched coos: *cooo cooo cooo cooo coo coo;* weaker at end. Also a low, hollow, wooden clatter or rattle *trrrt* produced by bill.

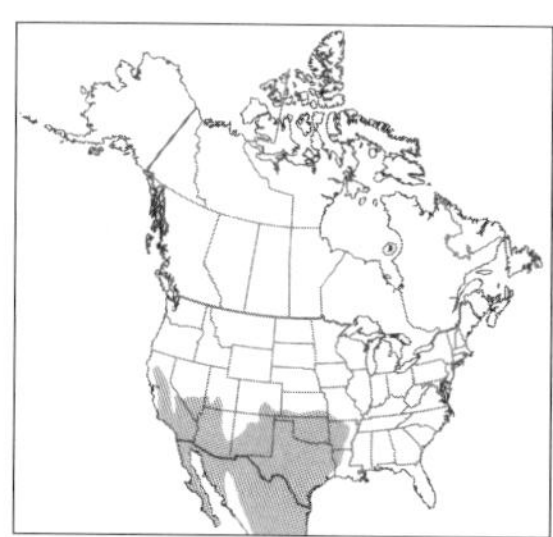

Owls

Families: Strigidae, Tytonidae

19 species in 11 genera; all in family Strigidae, except Barn Owl in Tytonidae. Owls are mainly nocturnal predators, with hooked bills and needle-sharp talons; their large eyes and facial discs are distinctive (compare hawks, especially Northern Harrier). Voice is a hooting, screeching, or whistling (compare cooing calls of doves). All forage mainly by perching and watching for prey. Different species specialize in different prey: many smaller species are insectivores; larger species eat mainly rodents and other small mammals. Most species nest in cavities (natural, man-made, or old tree cavities of other species); some usurp old tree nests from raptors or crows; Burrowing Owl nests and roosts in burrows. Adults are shown.

Genus *Tyto*

BARN OWL

Genus *Asio*

LONG-EARED OWL

SHORT-EARED OWL Northern

Genus *Bubo*

GREAT HORNED OWL Pacific

Genus *Nyctea*

SNOWY OWL

Genus *Strix*

SPOTTED OWL Interior West (Mexican)

BARRED OWL

GREAT GRAY OWL

Genus *Aegolius*

BOREAL OWL

NORTHERN SAW-WHET OWL

Genus *Athene*

BURROWING OWL Western

Genus *Otus*

FLAMMULATED OWL

WHISKERED SCREECH-OWL

WESTERN SCREECH-OWL Pacific

EASTERN SCREECH-OWL

Genus *Micrathene*

ELF OWL

Genus *Glaucidium*

NORTHERN PYGMY-OWL Pacific

FERRUGINOUS PYGMY-OWL

Genus *Surnia*

NORTHERN HAWK OWL

Medium-size Owls

These two species hunt mainly on the wing at night, patrolling open areas in search of rodents. Barn Owl is distinctive; Long-eared superficially resembles the much larger Great Horned.

Barn Owl

Tyto alba

L 16" WS 42" WT 1 lb (460 g) ♀>♂

Broad but fairly pointed wings, large head, long legs; pale tawny and white plumage and heart-shaped face distinctive.

Adult ♀
Adult ♂
very pale, ghostly
Fledgling
(any month)
Adult ♀
Adult ♂
heart-shaped face; dark eyes
pale tawny
white
long legs

Voice: Common call year-round simply a long hissing shriek *cssssssshhH.* Female call averages softer than male and juvenile averages less hoarse, but overall little variation.

Long-eared Owl

Asio otus

L 15" WS 36" WT 9 oz (260 g) ♀>♂

Fairly long-winged and slender; wings shorter and broader than Short-eared.

flying away

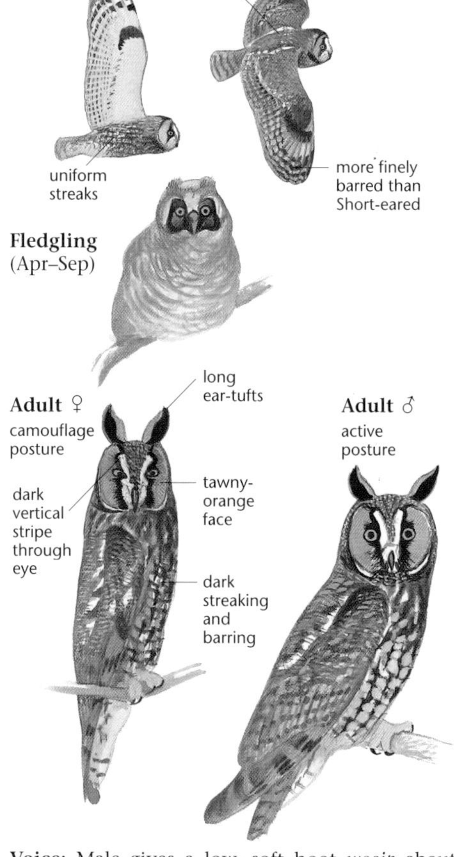
Adult
plain gray above
uniform streaks
more finely barred than Short-eared
Fledgling
(Apr–Sep)
long ear-tufts
Adult ♀
camouflage posture
dark vertical stripe through eye
tawny-orange face
dark streaking and barring
Adult ♂
active posture

Voice: Male gives a low, soft hoot *wooip* about every three seconds. Female call higher and softer *sheoof.* Alarm (both sexes) variable soft, nasal barks *bwah bwah bwah;* also a quiet moan and squealing or mewing calls. Juvenile gives a high, squeaky *wee-ee* like rusty hinge.

Both sexes of Long-eared Owl wing-clap during display flight, producing a sound like cracking whip given singly at irregular intervals. Compare wing-clapping display of Short-eared Owl.

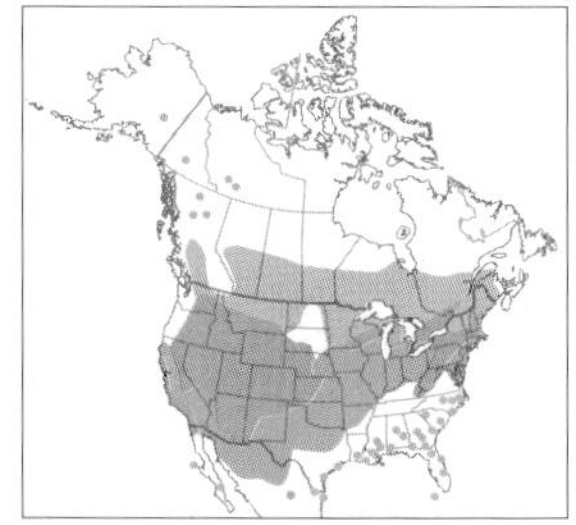

Medium-size Owls (continued)

Short-eared Owl—our most aerial owl—can be confused with Northern Harrier. It is found in any open expanse (marshes, fields, prairie, tundra), coursing in search of rodents, often in daylight.

Short-eared Owl

Asio flammeus

L 15" WS 38" WT 12 oz (350 g) ♀>♂

Long, narrow wings; easy, floating flight; wingbeats stiffer than Northern Harrier, with usually bowed wings. Also note plumage and large head.

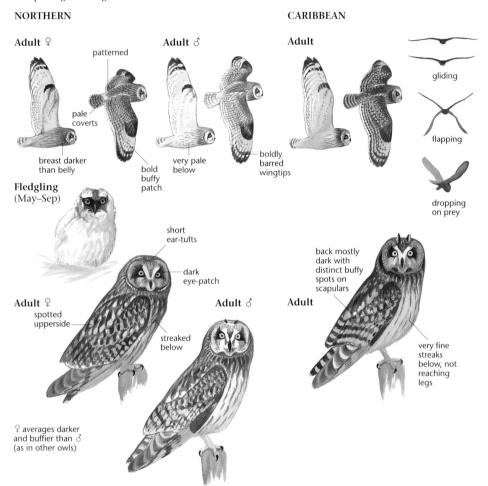

NORTHERN

CARIBBEAN

Adult ♀

patterned

pale coverts

breast darker than belly

bold buffy patch

Adult ♂

very pale below

boldly barred wingtips

Adult

gliding

flapping

dropping on prey

Fledgling
(May–Sep)

short ear-tufts

dark eye-patch

Adult ♀

spotted upperside

streaked below

Adult ♂

♀ averages darker and buffier than ♂ (as in other owls)

Adult

back mostly dark with distinct buffy spots on scapulars

very fine streaks below, not reaching legs

Voice: Silent except in nesting season. Male gives muffled *poo poo poo . . .* (5–6/sec in series 2 sec long). Alarm (both sexes) high, nasal barks and wheezy notes *cheef cheef* and *cheewaaay.* Wing-clapping sounds like cracking whip, given in rapid, rattling series. Voice of Caribbean birds not known to differ from Northern.

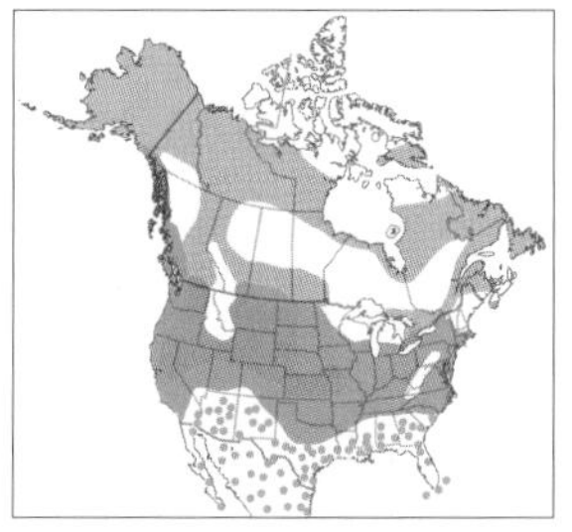

Caribbean Short-eared Owl is a rare visitor from the West Indies to Florida, mainly Apr–Jul. Most records are from the Florida Keys, where Northern subspecies is very rare or unrecorded. Averages smaller than Northern. Both sexes resemble female Northern but are even darker, with streaks on the belly reduced to very fine lines not reaching the legs. Caribbean also has a bolder frame of dark feathers around the face, and the mantle and scapulars are dark with bold buffy spots, rather than the more patterned upperside of Northern. Check also for dark uppertail coverts (usually conspicuously pale on Northern); it is also possible that remiges average more neatly barred, though this may be age-related.

Great Horned Owl

Our most widespread owl, Great Horned is found in many wooded habitats and is often seen on prominent perches at dusk. It hunts mammals (up to rabbit-size) from a perch.

Great Horned Owl

Bubo virginianus

L 22" WS 44" WT 3.1 lb (1,400 g) ♀>♂

Large (like Red-tailed Hawk) and bulky, with broad body and large head; stout ear-tufts create catlike head shape.

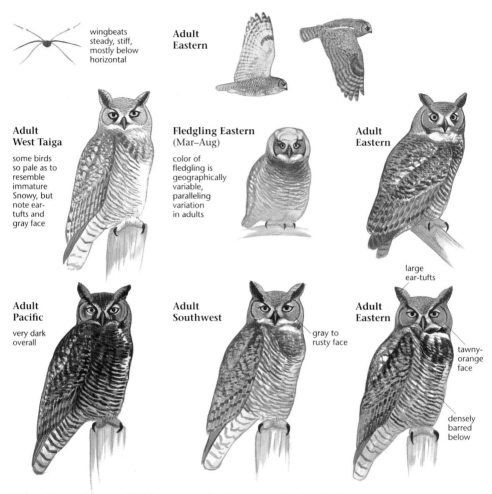

wingbeats steady, stiff, mostly below horizontal

Adult Eastern

Adult West Taiga

some birds so pale as to resemble immature Snowy, but note ear-tufts and gray face

Fledgling Eastern (Mar–Aug)

color of fledgling is geographically variable, paralleling variation in adults

Adult Eastern

Adult Pacific

very dark overall

Adult Southwest

gray to rusty face

Adult Eastern

large ear-tufts

tawny-orange face

densely barred below

Voice: Song a deep, muffled hooting in rhythmic series *hoo hoodoo hoooo hoo* or longer *ho hoo hoo hoododo hooooo hoo;* only slightly deeper than Mourning Dove. Female voice higher-pitched than male; courting female answers male with low, nasal, barking *guwaay*. Juvenile begs with high, wheezy, scratchy, or hoarse bark *reeeek* or *sheew* or *cheeoip*; variable, usually shorter and less rasping than Barn Owl but some very similar.

Variation is clinal, with many intermediate subspecies and intergrades between subspecies, but within a given region typical individuals of different subspecies are identifiable. As in other owls, females average browner and more heavily marked than males. Eastern birds are richly colored. Birds in the western interior region are generally pale and grayish in tone, varying clinally from the darker Southwest population to the very pale West Taiga. Pacific populations are very dark; this same darkness is approached by populations in Labrador.

LARGE NORTHERN OWLS

Snowy, our heaviest owl, perches prominently in open areas; more agile in flight than other owls, it often catches birds. Great Gray, our longest owl, is found in woods near open meadows.

Snowy Owl

Nyctea scandiaca

L 23" WS 52" WT 4 lb (1,830 g) ♀>♂

Very large and sleeker than other owls, with relatively small head, smooth plumage.

1st year ♀

Adult ♂

all-white

relatively narrow, pointed wings; wingbeats stiff

Fledgling (Jul–Sep)

gray with white face

face always white

dense, dark bars on white

1st year ♀

Adult ♂

some are nearly pure white

adult ♀ and 1st year ♂ intermediate between plumages shown

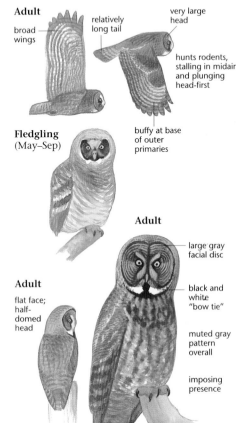

Voice: Common call a high-pitched, drawn-out scream heard in territorial disputes year-round. Song of male a deep, muffled hoot *brooo* repeated. Barking (female) or quacking (male) sounds in alarm; also a slurred whistle.

Great Gray Owl

Strix nebulosa

L 27" WS 52" WT 2.4 lb (1,080 g) ♀>♂

Related to Spotted and Barred Owls. Very large size, disproportionately large head, and rather long tail.

Adult

broad wings

relatively long tail

very large head

hunts rodents, stalling in midair and plunging head-first

buffy at base of outer primaries

Fledgling (May–Sep)

Adult

large gray facial disc

Adult

flat face; half-domed head

black and white "bow tie"

muted gray pattern overall

imposing presence

Voice: Courtship call of male five to ten very deep, muffled, pumping hoots, slightly lower and weaker at end; higher-pitched than Blue Grouse and longer. Female answers with emphatic, mellow whistle *iihWEW;* also a low, hooting *hooaahp*. Juvenile gives muted, trumpetlike *bweek*.

Individuals of both species seen far to the south of normal range are often starved and stressed for food, and thus active in daylight. Healthy birds are mainly nocturnal, like other owls.

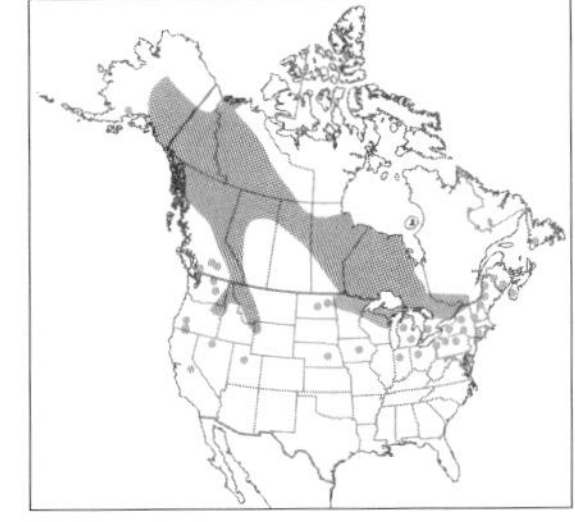

Wood-Owls: Genus *Strix*

These two species are similar in all respects, with brown plumage, dark eyes, and barking calls. Both are found in mixed woods, where they hunt rodents from perches.

Spotted Owl

Strix occidentalis

L 17.5" WS 40" WT 1.3 lb (610 g) ♀>♂

Slightly smaller than Barred Owl but proportions similar; best distinguished by spotted flanks and voice.

Adult
dark brown with whitish spots
dark eyes
narrowly barred
greenish bill
Fledgling (May–Oct)

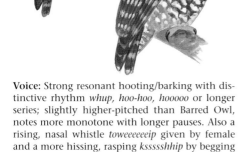

Adult Pacific (Northern)
Adult Interior West (Mexican)
dark eyes

Voice: Strong resonant hooting/barking with distinctive rhythm *whup, hoo-hoo, hooooo* or longer series; slightly higher-pitched than Barred Owl, notes more monotone with longer pauses. Also a rising, nasal whistle *toweeeeeeip* given by female and a more hissing, rasping *kssssshhip* by begging juvenile.

Barred Owl

Strix varia

L 21" WS 42" WT 1.6 lb (720 g) ♀>♂

Stocky, round-headed, broad-winged, and short-tailed.

Adult
flight heavy and direct
coarsely barred
yellowish bill
Fledgling (May–Sep)
Lighter adult
Darker adult
distinguished from Spotted by larger size, streaked belly, orange-yellow bill, paler face; paler overall than Pacific (Northern) Spotted Owl

Voice: Clear-voiced, expressive, hooting/barking *hoo hoo ho-ho, hoo hoo ho-hoooooaw* ("who cooks for you, who cooks for you all") ending with descending and rolling *hoooaaaw* note. In chorus a tremendous variety of barking, cackling, and gurgling notes. Juvenile begs with rising hiss *kssssshhip* like Spotted.

Barred and Spotted Owls hybridize occasionally where ranges overlap. Two populations of Spotted Owl do not overlap in range, differing only in plumage: Pacific (Northern) darker overall than Interior West (Mexican), with rufous-buff wash on vent and smaller white marks on scapulars and flanks; pale bars on flight feathers narrower and brownish.

SMALL OWLS: GENUS *AEGOLIUS*

These two small northern species are found in mixed coniferous-deciduous woods. They roost in cavities or in dense vegetation and hunt rodents from perches.

Boreal Owl

Aegolius funereus

L 10" WS 21" WT 4.7 oz (135 g) ♀>♂

Relatively large-headed, long-winged, and long-tailed.

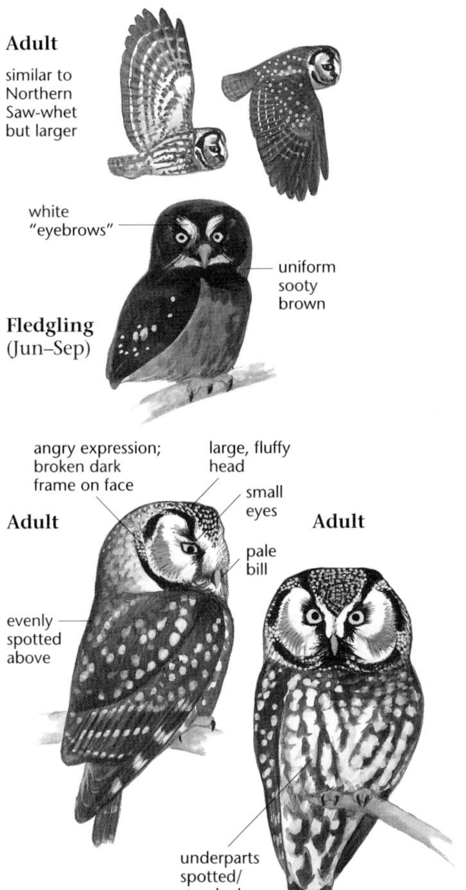
Adult
similar to Northern Saw-whet but larger
white "eyebrows"
uniform sooty brown
Fledgling
(Jun–Sep)
angry expression; broken dark frame on face
large, fluffy head
small eyes
pale bill
Adult
Adult
evenly spotted above
underparts spotted/ streaked

Voice: Song a rapid series of low, whistled toots *po po po po po po po po po,* slightly louder, clearer at end, two seconds long; similar to Common Snipe winnowing but does not fade at end. Also a low, nasal *hoooA* falling at end and a short, sharp *skiew*. Juvenile gives a rather high, clear chirp and occasionally a short chatter.

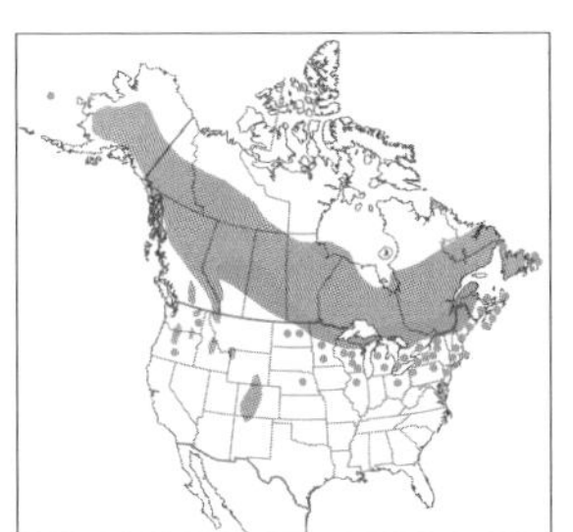

Northern Saw-whet Owl

Aegolius acadicus

L 8" WS 17" WT 2.8 oz (80 g) ♀>♂

Like Boreal but smaller, with slightly shorter tail. Smaller than screech-owls, with longer wings.

Adult

flight generally low and direct; wingbeats quick and entirely below horizontal (reminiscent of American Woodcock)

white triangle on forehead
Fledgling
(May–Sep)
bright buffy underparts

pale buffy facial disc

Adult

Adult

distinct white braces on back

brown streaking below

Voice: Song repeated, low, whistled toots (about 2/sec) *poo poo poo . . .* or *toit toit toit . . .* very similar to Northern Pygmy-Owl but with regular rhythm. Also wheezy, rising, catlike screech *shweeee;* soft, nasal barks *keew* or *pew* very similar to Elf Owl; whining, soft whistle *eeeooi.*

Northern Saw-whet Owl population resident on Queen Charlotte Islands is darker overall than mainland populations, with buffy wash on underparts and face, white only on eyebrows.

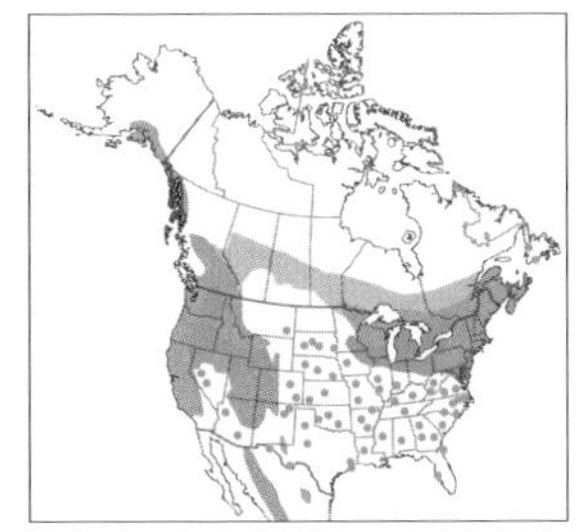

BURROWING OWL

This distinctive species is found in open grassland and similar habitat; it nests and roosts in abandoned animal burrows or other crevices. It is often seen perched on the ground or on fence posts.

Burrowing Owl

Athene cunicularia

L 9.5" WS 21" WT 5 oz (155 g)

Long-legged and short-tailed, with relatively long, narrow wings and flat head. Only small owl likely to be seen perched in the open in daylight.

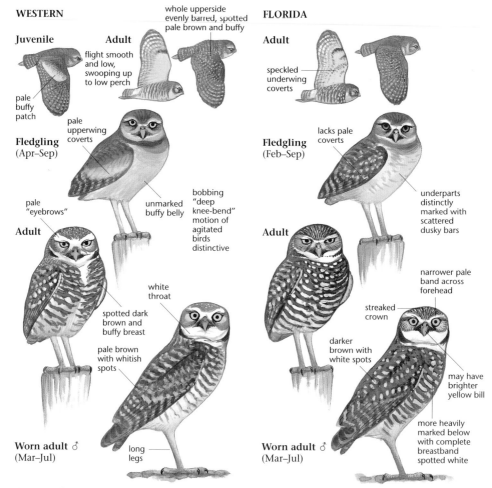

WESTERN

Juvenile

Adult

whole upperside evenly barred, spotted pale brown and buffy

flight smooth and low, swooping up to low perch

pale buffy patch

pale upperwing coverts

Fledgling (Apr–Sep)

unmarked buffy belly

bobbing "deep knee-bend" motion of agitated birds distinctive

pale "eyebrows"

Adult

white throat

spotted dark brown and buffy breast

pale brown with whitish spots

long legs

Worn adult ♂ (Mar–Jul)

FLORIDA

Adult

speckled underwing coverts

lacks pale coverts

Fledgling (Feb–Sep)

underparts distinctly marked with scattered dusky bars

Adult

narrower pale band across forehead

streaked crown

darker brown with white spots

may have brighter yellow bill

more heavily marked below with complete breastband spotted white

Worn adult ♂ (Mar–Jul)

Voice: Male gives high, nasal, trumpeting *coo-cooo* call on one pitch; female answers with short, clear *eeep* or harsher, rasping *ksshh*. Rasping call given by both sexes in alarm. Short, sharp, husky *chuk* or barking series of *chuk* notes, often with a rasping scream *kweee-ch-ch-ch-ch* or *cheee-twikit-twik* heard year-round. Other smacking or warbling calls rarely heard. Juvenile begs with short, harsh, rasping calls. Florida male song may differ from Western: *co-codooo* higher-pitched than Western with very short first note and two-part second note; sounds more hurried than Western.

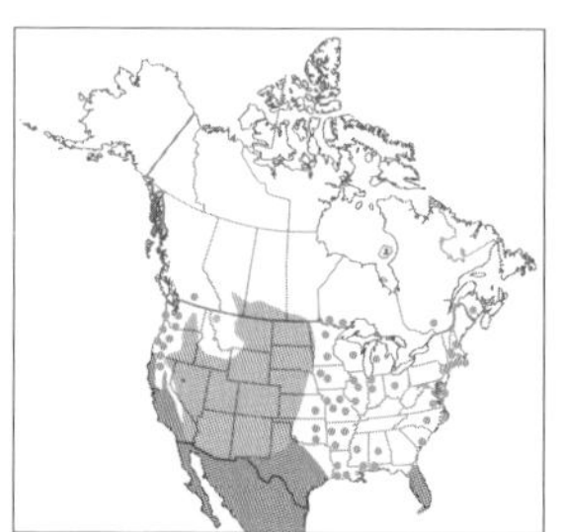

Two populations with no range overlap (except vagrants of both populations along Atlantic coast). Florida adults are darker brown overall; details are shown above. Florida birds have feathering on tarsi reduced to sparse hairlike shafts (Western more feathered but variable and can become worn by spring). Spotted underwing coverts of Florida birds reliable but difficult to see in the field.

Tiny Owls

Our two smallest owls are almost exclusively insectivorous and migrate south in winter. Elf Owl is found in the desert and riparian woods, Flammulated in mountain pine-oak forests.

Elf Owl

Micrathene whitneyi

L 5.75" WS 13" WT 1.4 oz (40 g)

Tiny—our smallest owl—and relatively small-headed. Finely speckled gray overall.

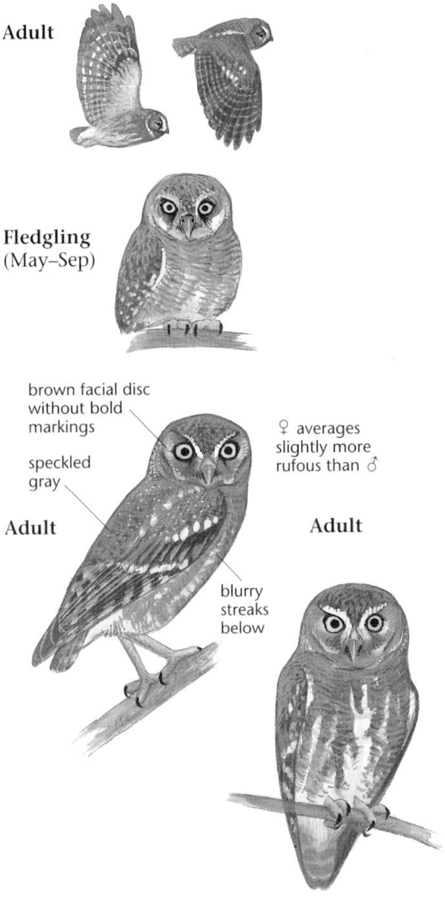

Adult
Fledgling
(May–Sep)
brown facial disc without bold markings
speckled gray
Adult
♀ averages slightly more rufous than ♂
Adult
blurry streaks below

Voice: Common call a fairly sharp, high bark *pew* or *peew;* slightly squeaky series with steady rhythm *pe pe pe pe pe pe pe pe pe* highest in middle. Also soft, high, quiet, whistled *meeeew* descending.

Flammulated Owl

Otus flammeolus

L 6.75" WS 16" WT 2.1 oz (60 g)

In the same genus as screech-owls but smaller, with shorter ear-tufts and relatively longer and pointier wings. Dark eyes distinctive.

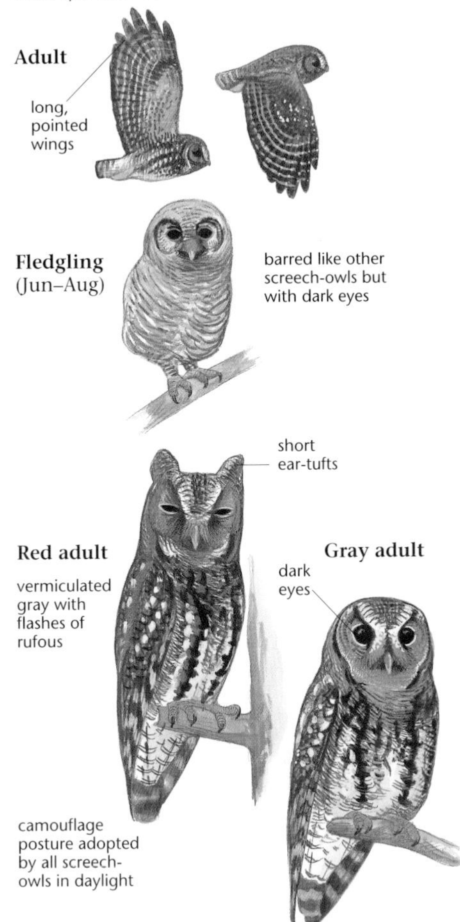

Adult
long, pointed wings
Fledgling
(Jun–Aug)
barred like other screech-owls but with dark eyes
short ear-tufts
Red adult
vermiculated gray with flashes of rufous
Gray adult
dark eyes
camouflage posture adopted by all screech-owls in daylight

Voice: Song a low, soft hoot *poop* or *pooip,* sometimes *podo poot* repeated once every two to three seconds; lower-pitched than other screech-owls. Female call dissimilar; higher-pitched with quavering, whining quality.

Screech-Owls: Genus *Otus*

These small, "eared" owls are found in open woods at forest edges; they hunt rodents and insects from perches. All species have similar plumage and are best identified by voice.

Whiskered Screech-Owl

Otus trichopsis

L 7.25" WS 17.5" WT 3.2 oz (90 g) ♀>♂

Smaller than Western, with small feet.

Adult
found in oaks, usually at higher elevation than Western, but much overlap
Fledgling (May–Aug)
more coarsely barred than other screech-owls; best distinguished from Western by size, foot size, bill color
Adult
only gray morph occurs in North America
more coarsely marked above than Western
Adult
eyes tinged orange
bill color varies from dark gray to yellowish, usually paler than Western
short, thick dark streaks below look somewhat spotted
overlaps with Mexican population of Western
relatively small feet

Voice: Common call a steady series of four to eight evenly spaced notes *po po po po po po* higher in middle, slightly slower at end. Syncopated, rhythmic *pidu po po, pidu po po, pidu po po, po* (pitch same as Western Screech-Owl). Female voice slightly higher than male. Also a descending soft whistle *oooo,* higher than other calls.

Western Screech-Owl

Otus kennicottii

L 8.5" WS 20" WT 5 oz (150 g) ♀>♂

Larger than Whiskered, with larger feet and more streaked plumage pattern (see Eastern).

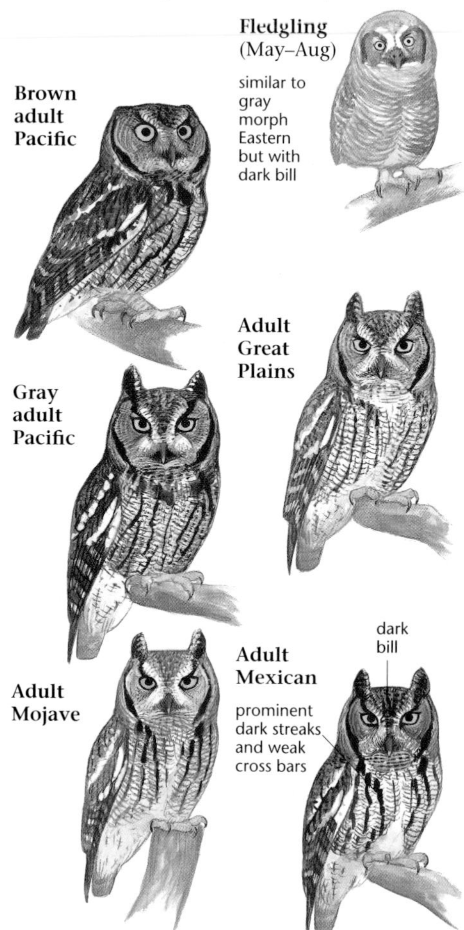

Fledgling (May–Aug)
similar to gray morph Eastern but with dark bill
Brown adult Pacific
Adult Great Plains
Gray adult Pacific

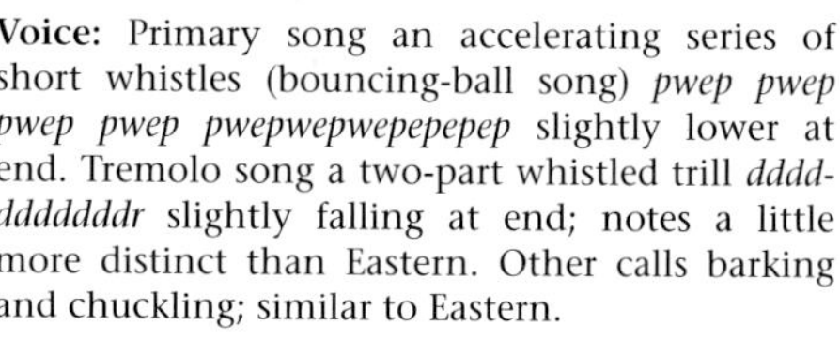

Adult Mojave
Adult Mexican
dark bill
prominent dark streaks and weak cross bars

Voice: Primary song an accelerating series of short whistles (bouncing-ball song) *pwep pwep pwep pwep pwepwepwepepepep* slightly lower at end. Tremolo song a two-part whistled trill *dddd-dddddddr* slightly falling at end; notes a little more distinct than Eastern. Other calls barking and chuckling; similar to Eastern.

Subtle regional variation in size and color of Western Screech-Owl is clinal. Up to 7 percent of Pacific population is brown; the rest are gray; there is no red morph.

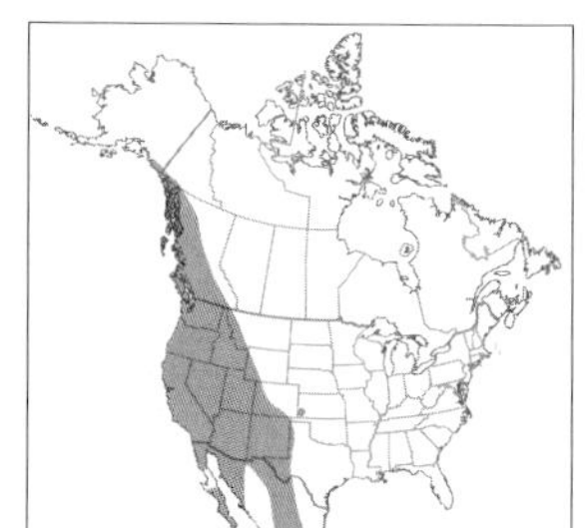

This species is nearly identical to Western Screech-Owl in appearance and habits. Their ranges overlap only slightly, and in those areas birds are reliably identified only by voice.

Eastern Screech-Owl

Otus asio

L 8.5" WS 20" WT 6 oz (180 g) ♀>♂

In general, underparts relatively strongly barred (underparts pattern on Western is of strong, dark streaks with less distinct, fine crossbars); pale greenish bill (Western usually dark gray; both have whitish bill tip).

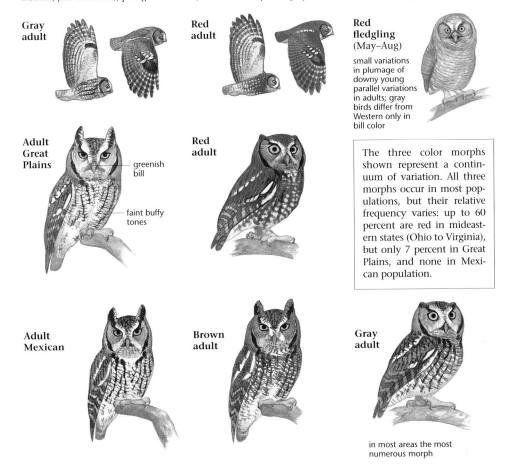

Gray adult

Red adult

Red fledgling (May–Aug)

small variations in plumage of downy young parallel variations in adults; gray birds differ from Western only in bill color

Adult Great Plains

greenish bill

faint buffy tones

Red adult

The three color morphs shown represent a continuum of variation. All three morphs occur in most populations, but their relative frequency varies: up to 60 percent are red in mideastern states (Ohio to Virginia), but only 7 percent in Great Plains, and none in Mexican population.

Adult Mexican

Brown adult

Gray adult

in most areas the most numerous morph

Voice: Primary song a strongly descending whinny with husky falsetto quality reminiscent of whinnying horse. Tremolo song a long, whistled trill on one pitch, up to three seconds long. All calls given by both sexes, but female voice slightly higher-pitched than male. Juvenile begs with short, harsh rasp usually falling in pitch. Other calls infrequently heard include soft bark and short chuckle. MEXICAN: Voice differs slightly from northern populations: whinny call short, weak, and infrequently given; tremolo call more rapid, wooden-sounding, with more distinct notes and uneven tempo.

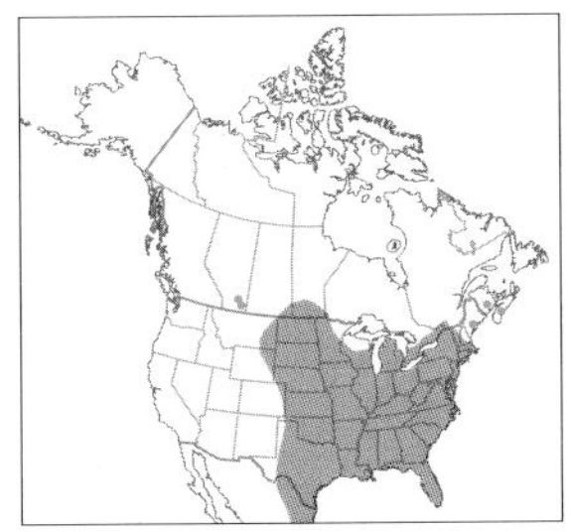

Most Eastern Screech-Owls are much browner than Western, but the two species look nearly identical where their ranges meet (compare Great Plains and Mexican populations of both); hybrids have been recorded, and not all individuals can be safely identified.

Regional variation in Eastern Screech-Owls is fairly striking but clinal, with many intermediate populations. In general, northern birds are larger, paler, and fluffier than southern. Mexican birds are most distinctive, always gray with markings tending toward Western Screech-Owl and slightly different voice.

Pygmy-Owls

Northern and Ferruginous Pygmy-Owls are very aggressive diurnal bird-hunters. Northern is found in oak-conifer woods and has been known to take prey as large as a Mourning Dove.

Northern Pygmy-Owl

Glaucidium gnoma

L 6.75" WS 12" WT 2.5 oz (70 g) ♀>♂

A compact, small owl; relatively long-tailed and short-winged. Usually perched inconspicuously within tree canopy, pygmy-owls can often be located by watching for scolding songbirds.

Adult

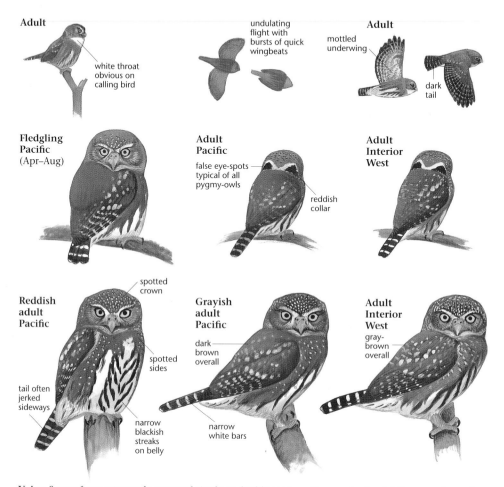

white throat obvious on calling bird

undulating flight with bursts of quick wingbeats

Adult

mottled underwing

dark tail

Fledgling Pacific (Apr–Aug)

Adult Pacific

false eye-spots typical of all pygmy-owls

reddish collar

Adult Interior West

Reddish adult Pacific

spotted crown

spotted sides

tail often jerked sideways

narrow blackish streaks on belly

Grayish adult Pacific

dark brown overall

narrow white bars

Adult Interior West

gray-brown overall

Voice: Song of monotonously repeated single or double toots; pattern and rate of delivery varies regionally (see below). Always lower-pitched and slower than Ferruginous Pygmy-Owl; most populations slower than Northern Saw-whet, but Mexican populations virtually identical. Sometimes begin with a low, descending series of rapid toots followed by normal series *popopopopo, too-too too.* . . . All populations give a very high rattle or trill *tsisisisisisisi.*

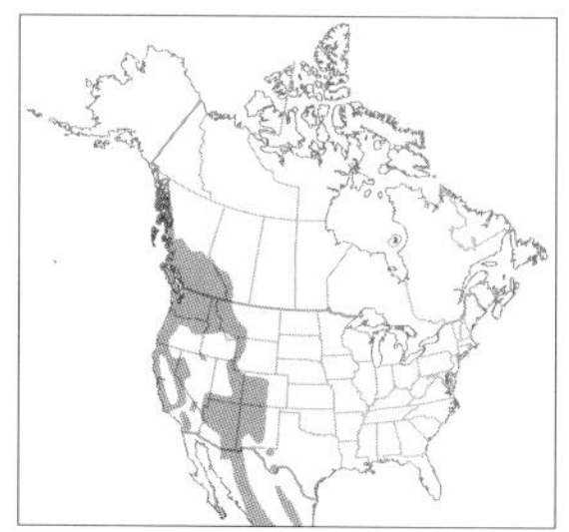

Two or three populations differ in overall color and voice; more study is needed. Pacific birds are darkest and brownest. They give very slow single toots (1 note every 2 or more sec). Interior West birds are grayer overall, and the pale spots on breast and crown are often broadened into short bars. They give mainly single toots with some paired notes, resulting in irregular rhythm *too, too-too, too, too, too-too, too* . . . (about 1 note every 1.4 sec or 1 pair every 2 sec). Mexican population (not shown), found in southeastern Arizona, averages smaller and darker than Interior West birds; Mexican birds give mainly paired notes more rapidly (about 1 pair every sec).

Pygmy-Owls (continued) and Northern Hawk Owl

Ferruginous Pygmy-Owl is found in woods or saguaro deserts. Northern Hawk Owl hunts rodents in daylight from treetops in open spruce or aspen woods and burned areas.

Ferruginous Pygmy-Owl

Glaucidium brasilianum

L 6.75" WS 12" WT 2.5 oz (70 g) ♀>♂

Similar to Northern Pygmy-Owl, but range and habitat normally do not overlap; found adjacent to grayest population of Northern Pygmy-Owl.

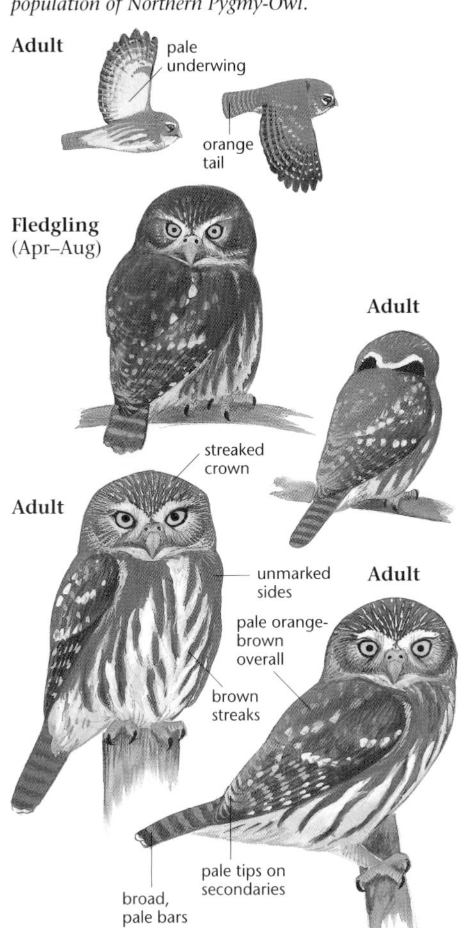
Adult
pale underwing
orange tail
Fledgling
(Apr–Aug)
Adult
streaked crown
Adult
unmarked sides
Adult
pale orange-brown overall
brown streaks
pale tips on secondaries
broad, pale bars

Voice: Song rapidly repeated whistled notes (about 3/sec), each note slightly rising *pwip pwip pwip* . . . ; often a few higher, weaker notes at beginning; usually higher-pitched than Northern Pygmy-Owl but variable in pitch and quality. When agitated may give a sharper, more barking whistle.

A much brighter rufous morph of Ferruginous Pygmy-Owl is found in Mexico and could occur in North America.

Northern Hawk Owl

Surnia ulula

L 16" WS 28" WT 11 oz (320 g) ♀>♂

Very distinctive shape with long, pointed tail.

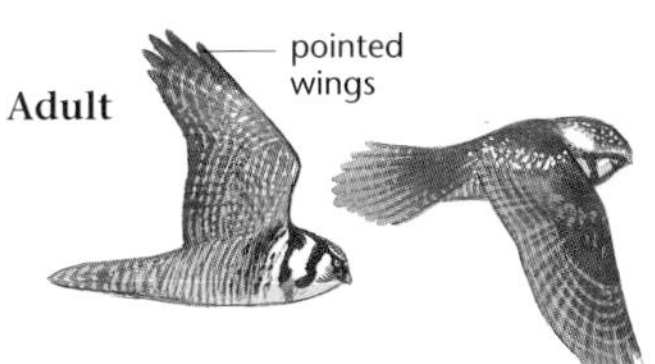
Adult
pointed wings
flight accipiter-like: low and fast with quick, stiff wingbeats; swoops up to perch; often hovers

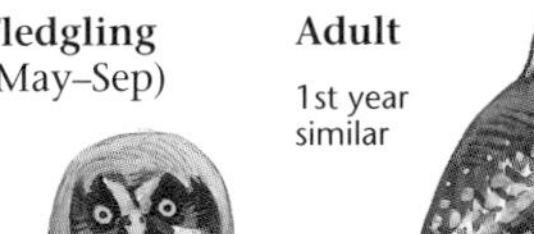
black frame on whitish face
Fledgling
(May–Sep)
Adult
1st year similar
finely barred belly

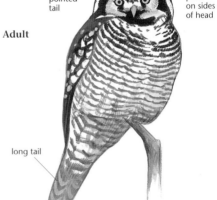

thin, pointed tail
dark pattern on sides of head
Adult
long tail

Voice: Courtship call (heard mainly at night) a series of popping whistles up to six seconds long *popopopopo* . . . ; reminiscent of Boreal Owl but higher, sharper, and longer. Female and juvenile give weak, screeching *tshooolP*. Also a thin, rising whistle *feeeee*. Alarm a shrill, chirping *quiquiquiqui*.

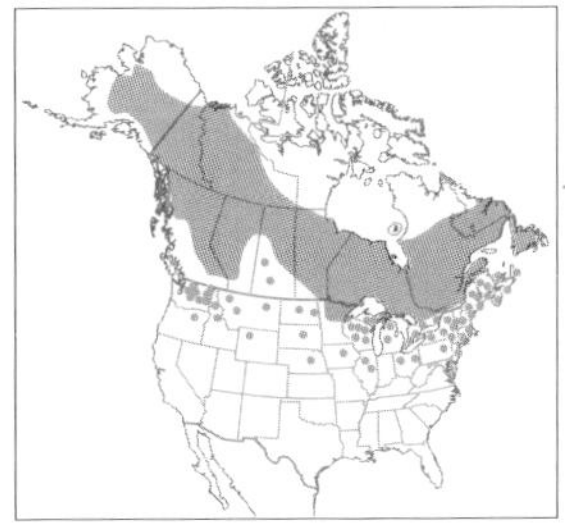

Goatsuckers and Swifts

Families: Caprimulgidae, Apodidae

GOATSUCKERS 8 species in 4 genera; all in family Caprimulgidae. Nightjars and nighthawks are both very cryptically colored. Nightjars have a relatively large head and rounded wings; they forage exclusively at night by perching and watching for flying insects in woodland clearings and open desert. Nighthawks have long, pointed wings and are sometimes seen in daylight flying over open areas to catch insects in flight. All species roost on the ground or on low branches within woods. Most are active primarily at night. Nest is a simple scrape on leafy or gravelly ground. Nestlings are capable of flight at just 10 days old, when much smaller than adults. Adults are shown.

Nightjars

Genus *Nyctidromus*

COMMON PAURAQUE

Genus *Phalaenoptilus*

COMMON POORWILL

Genus *Caprimulgus*

BUFF-COLLARED NIGHTJAR

WHIP-POOR-WILL Eastern

CHUCK-WILL'S-WIDOW

Nighthawks

Genus *Chordeiles*

COMMON NIGHTHAWK

ANTILLEAN NIGHTHAWK

LESSER NIGHTHAWK

SWIFTS 4 species in 3 genera; all in family Apodidae. Swifts are related to hummingbirds, with similar wing structure but obvious differences in bill shape, habits, and flight style. Entirely aerial insectivores, they are seen only in flight, never perched. All species roost and nest on concealed vertical walls inside chimneys, hollow trees, or cliff crevices; Black Swift on cliff ledges behind waterfalls. During inclement weather swifts are often seen at low elevation with swallows but forage at very high altitude in fair weather. They are superficially similar to swallows but have different wing shape with short "arm" and shorter tails; their wingbeats are much stiffer and flight is fast and direct, without the buoyant floating action of swallows. Adults are shown (except juvenile Black).

Genus *Chaetura*

swifts not to scale with goatsuckers

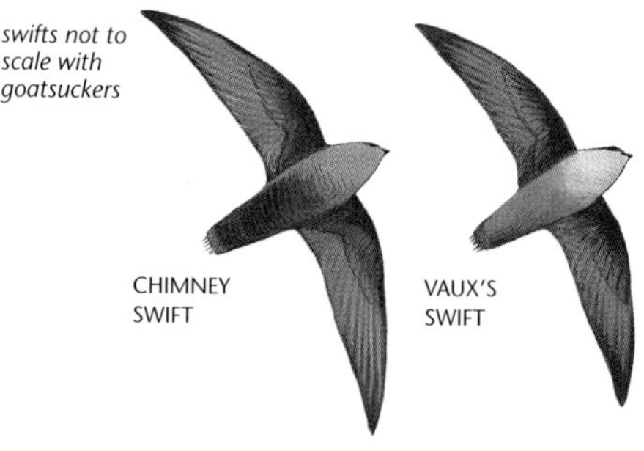

CHIMNEY SWIFT

VAUX'S SWIFT

Genus *Cypseloides*

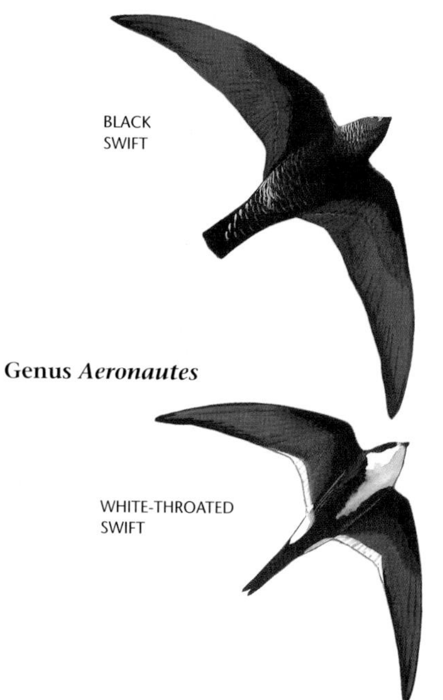

BLACK SWIFT

Genus *Aeronautes*

WHITE-THROATED SWIFT

Distinctive Nightjars

Common Pauraque is found in dense, brushy cover within woods. Common Poorwill is found in open, arid habitat with scattered bushes and trees and is known to hibernate in winter.

Common Pauraque

Nyctidromus albicollis

L 11" WS 24" WT 1.8 oz (52 g)

Long, rounded tail and wings.

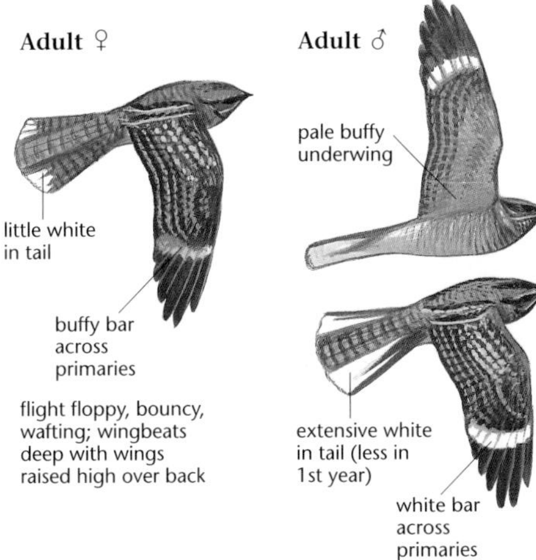

Adult ♀
Adult ♂
pale buffy underwing
little white in tail
buffy bar across primaries
flight floppy, bouncy, wafting; wingbeats deep with wings raised high over back
extensive white in tail (less in 1st year)
white bar across primaries

Rufous adult
rare or absent in North America

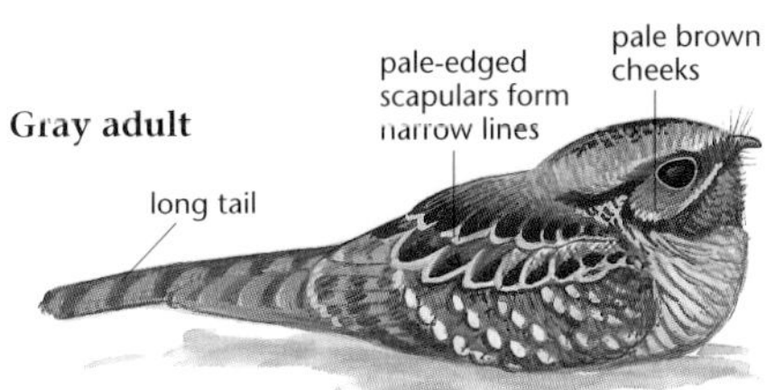

pale-edged scapulars form narrow lines
pale brown cheeks
Gray adult
long tail

Voice: Song a sharp, wild, buzzy whistle *poWIz-heeeeeer;* year-round call more slurred, builds slowly to crescendo *po po po po . . . po pup purrEEy-eeeeeeeerrrr.* Also a simple, husky, buzzy *urrREEErrr.* When flushed gives a low, soft, liquid *quup.*

Common Poorwill

Phalaenoptilus nuttallii

L 7.75" WS 17" WT 1.8 oz (50 g)

Short wings and tail; very large head.

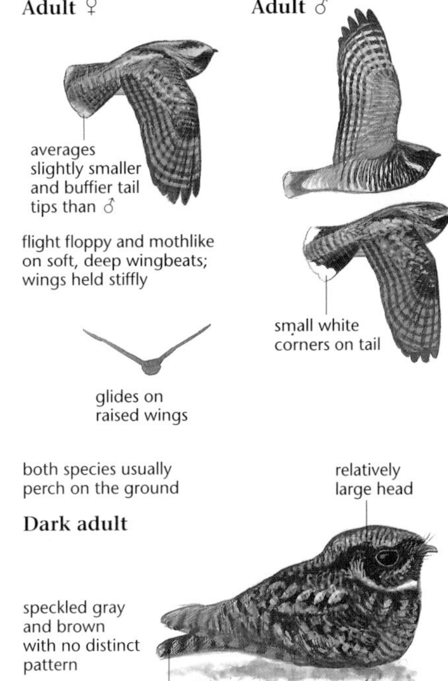

Adult ♀
Adult ♂
averages slightly smaller and buffier tail tips than ♂
flight floppy and mothlike on soft, deep wingbeats; wings held stiffly
glides on raised wings
small white corners on tail
both species usually perch on the ground
relatively large head
Dark adult
speckled gray and brown with no distinct pattern
short tail

Light adult

Voice: Song a gentle, low whistle *poowJEEwup;* from distance sounds like simple, soft whistle "poor will." Also a rough, low *wep* or *gwep* slightly rising, lower than any part of normal call, and soft clucks.

Color of Common Poorwill varies regionally, but light and dark individuals are found in all populations: darkest and brownest birds in Pacific; palest in Mojave region.

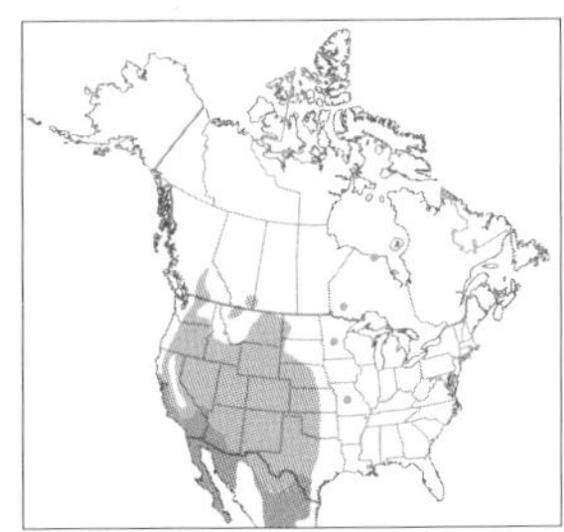

NIGHTJARS: GENUS *CAPRIMULGUS*

Buff-collared Nightjar is found in brushy, desert canyons, overlapping with Common Poorwill. Chuck-will's-widow, our largest nightjar, is found in mixed woods and usually roosts in trees.

Buff-collared Nightjar

Caprimulgus ridgwayi

L 8.75" WS 18" WT 1.7 oz (48 g)

Slightly smaller than Whip-poor-will with slightly shorter tail and more rounded wings; larger and longer-tailed than Common Poorwill.

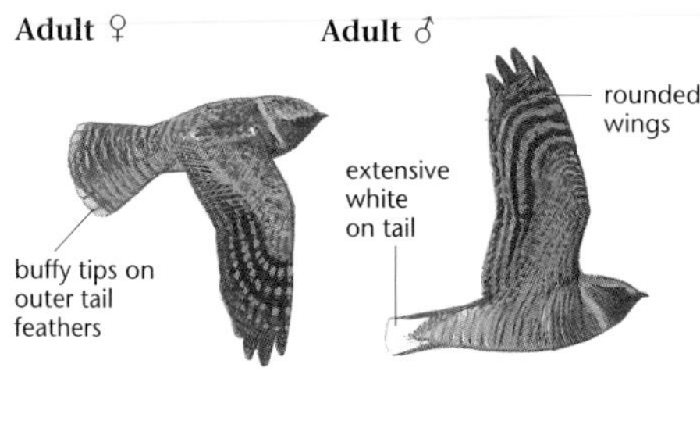

Adult ♀
Adult ♂
rounded wings
extensive white on tail
buffy tips on outer tail feathers

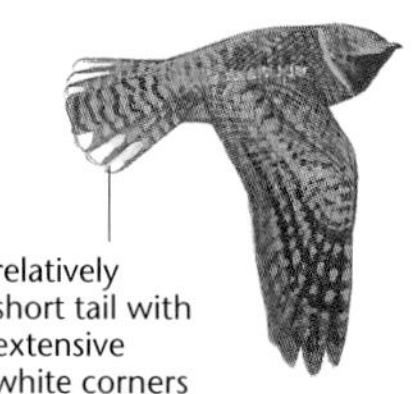

often hunts from perch at top of small bush
1st year ♂ shows white only on outer two tail feathers
relatively short tail with extensive white corners

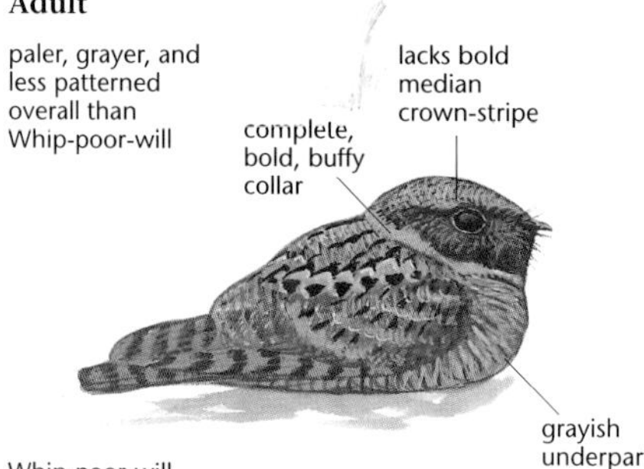

Adult
paler, grayer, and less patterned overall than Whip-poor-will
complete, bold, buffy collar
lacks bold median crown-stripe
grayish underparts
Whip-poor-will shows a faint, buffy collar

Voice: Song of rapid, sharp, dry chips in crescendoing series *tup to to tu tu ti ti trridip* accelerating and rising to flourish at end; pattern similar to song of Cassin's Kingbird but notes sharper and drier. Also rapid, dry, clicking notes.

Chuck-will's-widow

Caprimulgus carolinensis

L 12" WS 26" WT 4.2 oz (120 g)

Much larger than Whip-poor-will, with longer and pointier wings. Many are more rufous overall than Whip-poor-will.

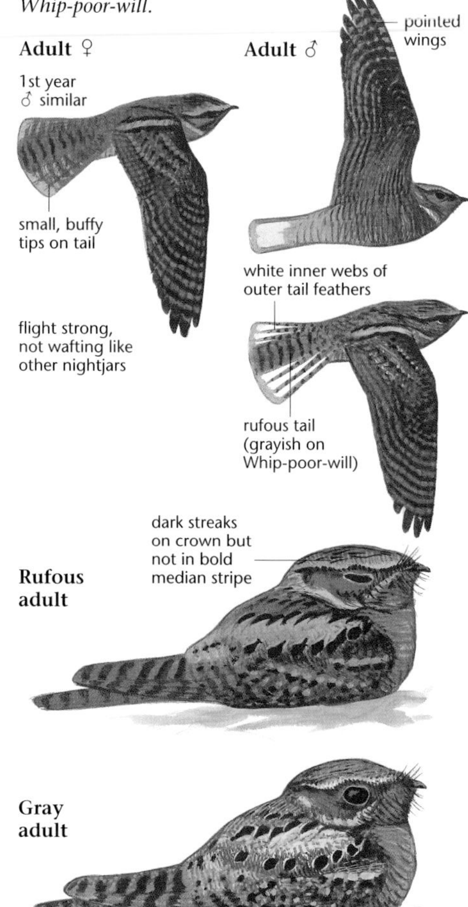

pointed wings
Adult ♀
Adult ♂
1st year ♂ similar
small, buffy tips on tail
white inner webs of outer tail feathers
flight strong, not wafting like other nightjars
rufous tail (grayish on Whip-poor-will)
dark streaks on crown but not in bold median stripe
Rufous adult
Gray adult

Voice: Song a loud, repeated, emphatic whistle *CHIP wido WIDO;* also low, nasal, froglike croaking or growling *wukrr wukrr-wukrr . . .* and hard, tongue-clicking cluck. When flushed often gives several muffled, low, gruff barks *grof, grof, grof.*

Goatsuckers often rest in the open on quiet roads just after sunset and just before sunrise. Their eyes reflect light directly back toward the source, so they can be located at a great distance by watching for the telltale points of reflected light (usually orange or red). This is a very useful technique, but beware that all birds' and mammals' eyes (even spiders' eyes) reflect light.

Nightjars: Genus *Caprimulgus* (continued)

Whip-poor-will is found in open, mature woods: hardwood forests in the east and montane pine-oak in the southwest. Like similar species, it perches quietly, flying out to catch passing insects.

Whip-poor-will

Caprimulgus vociferus

L 9.75" WS 19" WT 1.9 oz (54 g)

Smaller than Chuck-will's-widow, with more rounded wings.

MEXICAN

Adult ♂

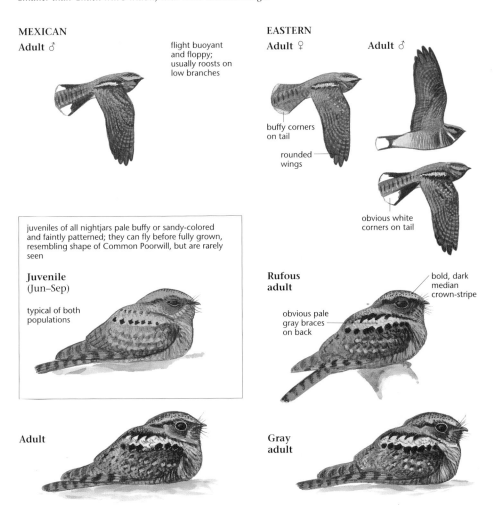

flight buoyant and floppy; usually roosts on low branches

EASTERN

Adult ♀

buffy corners on tail

rounded wings

Adult ♂

obvious white corners on tail

juveniles of all nightjars pale buffy or sandy-colored and faintly patterned; they can fly before fully grown, resembling shape of Common Poorwill, but are rarely seen

Juvenile (Jun–Sep)

typical of both populations

Rufous adult

bold, dark median crown-stripe

obvious pale gray braces on back

Adult

Gray adult

Voice: MEXICAN: Song a rolling, trilled *g-prrip prrEE;* lower, rougher, and with different rhythm than Eastern. When flushed gives rather deep, muffled, rising *gwirp* like start of song. EASTERN: Song a loud, clear, emphatic whistle *WHIP puwiw WEEW* ("whip poor will"); also a single, liquid *pwip* like Swainson's Thrush.

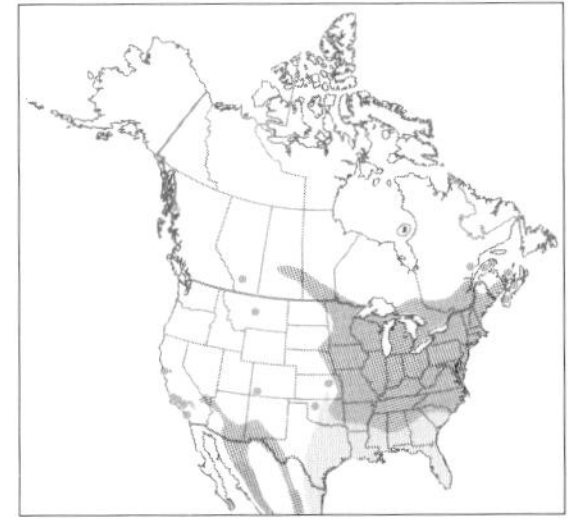

The two populations, which normally do not overlap, are easily distinguished by voice (see above) but are essentially indistinguishable in appearance. Mexican birds average slightly larger and paler, and adult males have less white on tail, but these characteristics overlap and are difficult to judge.

Nighthawks

Nighthawks are often seen in daylight, especially evening, flying over woods, fields, or towns catching insects. Their slender shape and erratic, bounding flight is distinctive.

Common Nighthawk

Chordeiles minor

L 9.5" WS 24" WT 2.2 oz (62 g)

Larger and longer-winged than other nighthawks. Primaries project beyond tail tip at rest. Most are white-bellied, but some are as buffy as other nighthawk species.

Adult ♀

Adult ♂

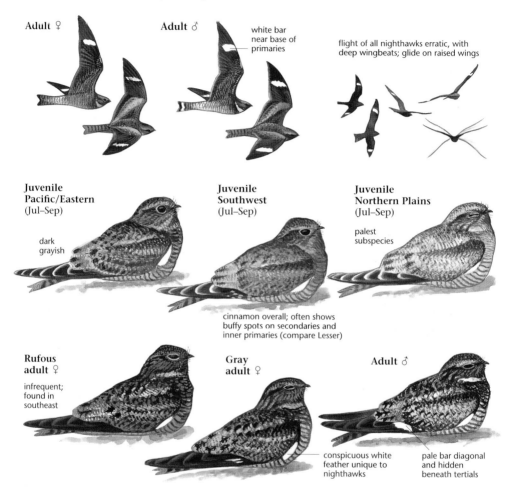

white bar near base of primaries

flight of all nighthawks erratic, with deep wingbeats; glide on raised wings

Juvenile Pacific/Eastern (Jul–Sep)

dark grayish

Juvenile Southwest (Jul–Sep)

cinnamon overall; often shows buffy spots on secondaries and inner primaries (compare Lesser)

Juvenile Northern Plains (Jul–Sep)

palest subspecies

Rufous adult ♀

infrequent; found in southeast

Gray adult ♀

Adult ♂

conspicuous white feather unique to nighthawks

pale bar diagonal and hidden beneath tertials

Voice: Territorial male gives rasping, nasal, descending buzz *BEEErzh;* given in flight with several quick "stutter flaps." Occasionally gives rapid, clucking *quit-quit-quit-quit* in chase; not as staccato as Antillean. At nest site female gives low clucks and purring or hissing growls. Display dive of male produces humming, whooshing *Hoooov* at bottom of dive.

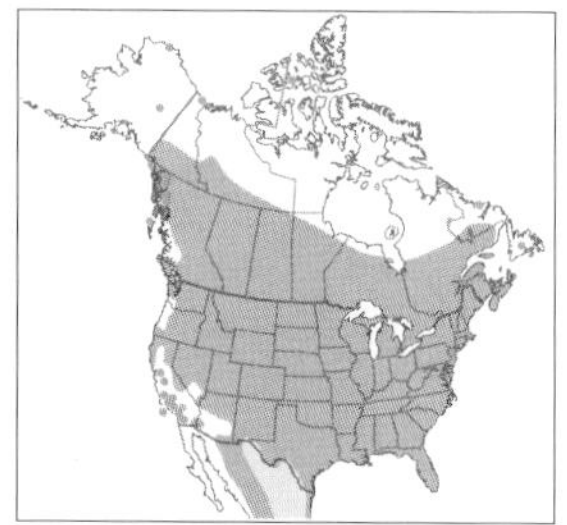

Color of Common Nighthawk varies regionally, but all variation is clinal (most conspicuous in juveniles, as illustrated). Variation overshadows any plumage differences between Common and Antillean Nighthawks. Lesser Nighthawk differs from Common in having the pale primary bar placed about midway along the primaries and tapered to the rear; the bar is small and buffy on Lesser females. On the folded wing the pale bar of Lesser is straight across the primaries and extends beyond the tertial tips. Lesser also has buffy spots on the primaries (shown by some Common Nighthawks).

NIGHTHAWKS (CONTINUED)

Antillean Nighthawk is very closely related to Common and usually distinguishable only by voice. Lesser is more distinctive, but identification still requires careful study of wing pattern.

Antillean Nighthawk

Chordeiles gundlachii

L 8.5" WS 21" WT 1.8 oz (50 g)

Proportions like Common but about 12 percent smaller; primary tips reach tail tip.

Adult ♀

Adult ♂

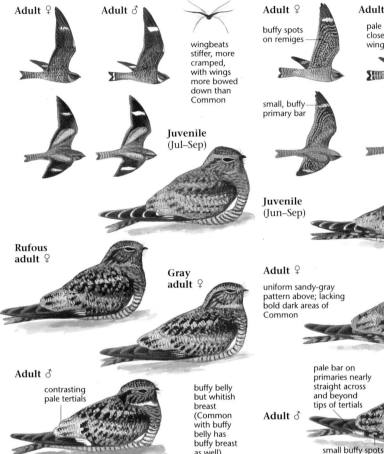

wingbeats stiffer, more cramped, with wings more bowed down than Common

Juvenile (Jul–Sep)

Rufous adult ♀

Gray adult ♀

Adult ♂

contrasting pale tertials

buffy belly but whitish breast (Common with buffy belly has buffy breast as well)

Voice: Male gives two to six very rapid, staccato syllables in descending series *bztbztbzt;* pitch and quality similar to Common but rapid, hard, sputtering. Display dive of male produces humming *whoosh* similar to Common but much quieter, usually inaudible.

Lesser Nighthawk

Chordeiles acutipennis

L 9" WS 22" WT 1.8 oz (50 g)

Relatively longer-tailed than other nighthawks. Wingtips less pointed than Common; broadest at wrist/outer secondaries. Primary tips reach tail tip.

Adult ♀

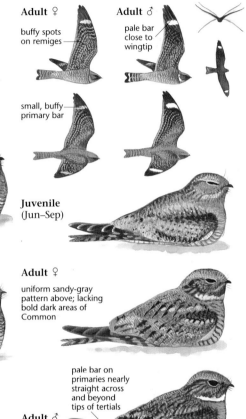

buffy spots on remiges

Adult ♂

pale bar close to wingtip

small, buffy primary bar

Juvenile (Jun–Sep)

Adult ♀

uniform sandy-gray pattern above; lacking bold dark areas of Common

Adult ♂

pale bar on primaries nearly straight across and beyond tips of tertials

small buffy spots on primaries

Voice: Song up to ten seconds long: a low, whistled trill on one pitch like tremolo of Eastern Screech-Owl but longer, notes more distinct. Also a nasal laughing or bleating *mememeng*. Lacks diving display; silent in flight.

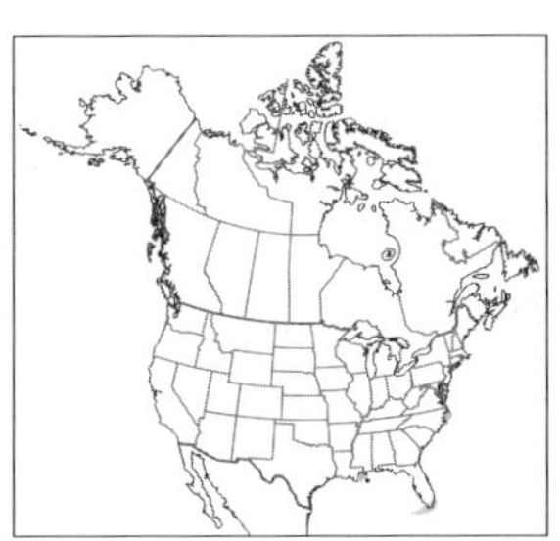

Lesser Nighthawk molts on breeding grounds Jun–Sep; other nighthawks molt flight feathers on wintering grounds Nov–Mar. A nighthawk molting flight feathers in summer is likely to be adult Lesser; a nighthawk with worn flight feathers during fall migration is likely to be adult Common or Antillean.

Swifts

These two species of small, short-tailed swifts are aptly described as "cigars with wings." Both roost and nest in cavities with a vertical entry, such as hollow trees or chimneys.

Vaux's Swift

Chaetura vauxi

L 4.75" WS 12" WT 0.6 oz (17 g)

Slightly smaller than Chimney Swift, with relatively shorter wings and tail, quicker wingbeats. Averages paler on breast and rump, but color overlaps.

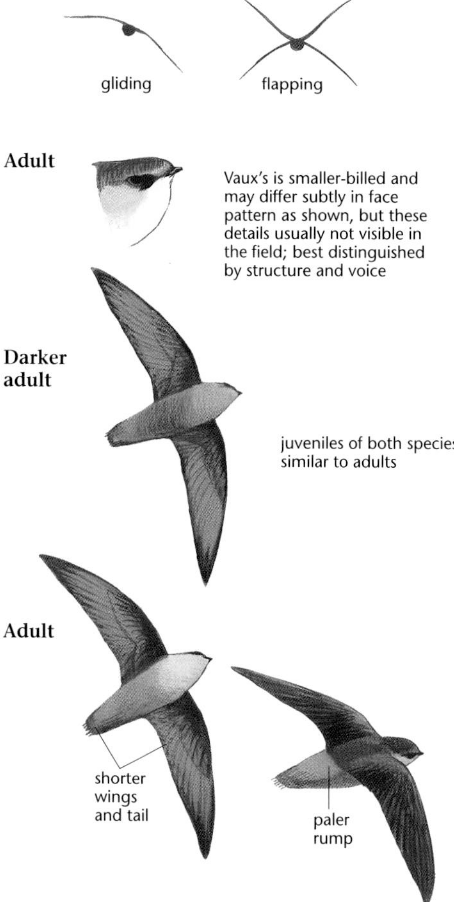

gliding
flapping
Adult
Vaux's is smaller-billed and may differ subtly in face pattern as shown, but these details usually not visible in the field; best distinguished by structure and voice
Darker adult
juveniles of both species similar to adults
Adult
shorter wings and tail
paler rump

Voice: Sharp chips higher than Chimney Swift; full call is several sharp chips followed by buzzy trills *tip tip tip tipto tipto tzeeeerip*. Chipping notes higher and final buzz much higher and finer than Chimney; reminiscent of Eastern Kingbird.

Chimney Swift

Chaetura pelagica

L 5.25" WS 14" WT 0.81 oz (23 g)

Very similar to Vaux's; smaller and shorter-tailed than Black and White-throated. Wings relatively narrow-based.

Adult
Darker adult
Adult
longer wings and tail
darker rump

Voice: Single high, hard chips run together into rapid, uneven, twittering, chattering series: a rolling, descending twitter. Single chips often heard are similar to some warblers.

clinging to wall

Chimney Swift adult

Swifts cannot perch; they cling to vertical surfaces at nest and roost sites.

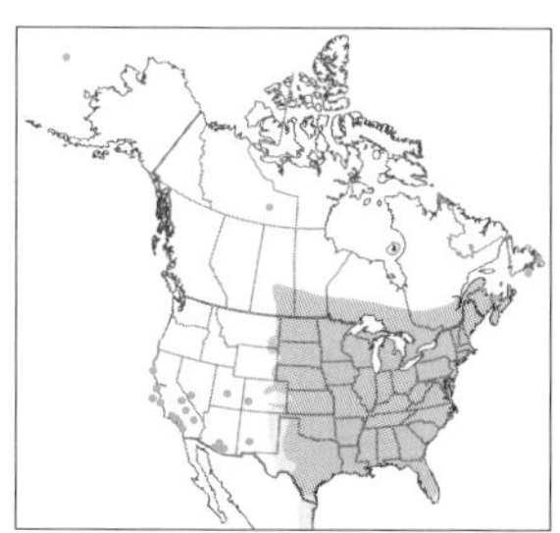

These two large swifts differ from Vaux's and Chimney in having longer square or notched tails and broad-based wings. Both nest in crevices on cliffs, Black Swift near waterfalls.

Black Swift

Cypseloides niger

L 7.25" WS 18" WT 1.6 oz (45 g)

Our largest swift; all-dark. Wings broad-based, long, and curved. Tail broad, often fanned; distinctly notched only on adult male.

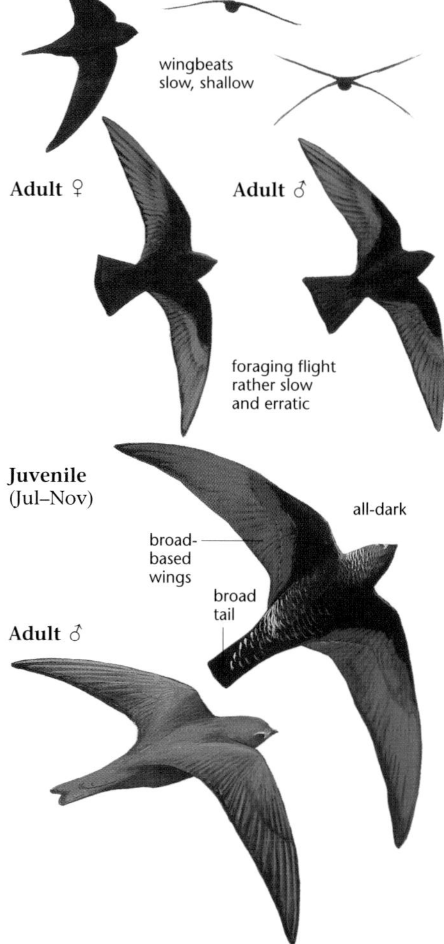
wingbeats
slow, shallow
Adult ♀
Adult ♂
foraging flight
rather slow
and erratic
Juvenile
(Jul–Nov)
all-dark
broad-
based
wings
broad
tail
Adult ♂

Voice: Low, flat, twittering chips, often a rapid series of chips slowing at end; lower-pitched than Chimney Swift. Individual notes reminiscent of higher, clearer notes of Red Crossbill.

White-throated Swift

Aeronautes saxatalis

L 6.5" WS 15" WT 1.1 oz (32 g)

Slender overall, with long, straight wings and narrow tail usually held closed and pointed. White markings distinctive but can be surprisingly difficult to see.

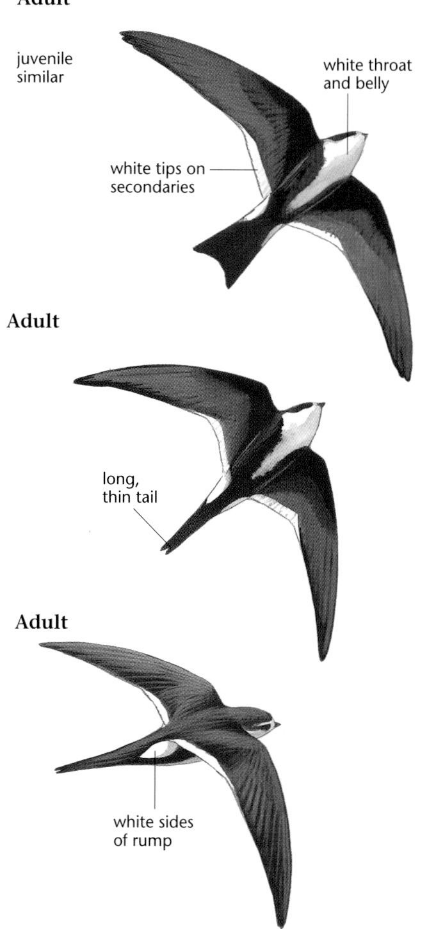
Adult
juvenile
similar
white throat
and belly
white tips on
secondaries
Adult
long,
thin tail
Adult
white sides
of rump

Voice: Common call a long, descending series of scraping notes *ki ki ki kir kir kiir kiir kirsh krrsh, krrsh;* begins high and twittering, ends lower and rasping; often given in chorus by small, wheeling flocks.

White-throated
Swift
full throat
pouch

All swifts carry food for their young in an expandable throat pouch, which can be very conspicuous when full.

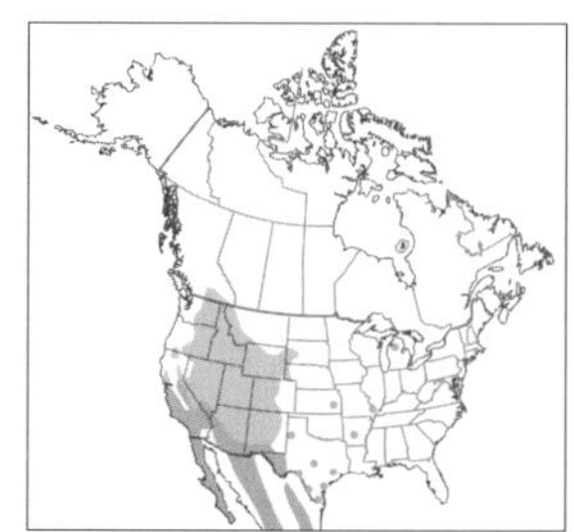

Hummingbirds

Family: Trochilidae

18 species in 12 genera. These unmistakable, small to tiny birds are long-billed and short-tailed, with overdeveloped primaries and hovering flight. Habitat preferences are real but of little use for identification, since all species congregate at feeders or flowering plants. All feed primarily on nectar from flowers but also take many tiny insects, either picking them from vegetation or capturing them in flight. Nest is a small cup built of spiderwebs and usually decorated with lichens, placed on top of a horizontal branch or in a fork. Adult females are shown.

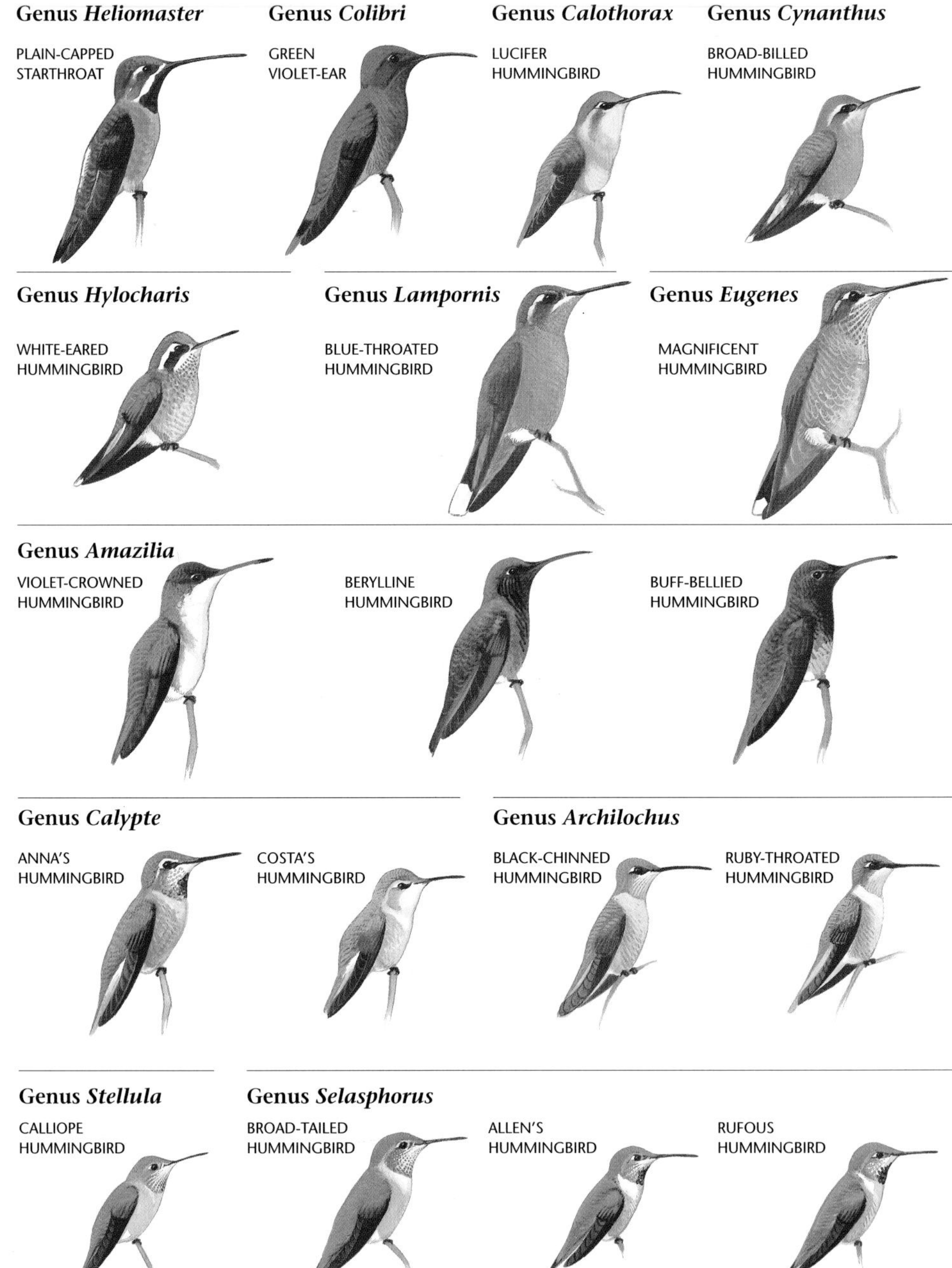

Genus *Heliomaster*
PLAIN-CAPPED STARTHROAT
Genus *Colibri*
GREEN VIOLET-EAR
Genus *Calothorax*
LUCIFER HUMMINGBIRD
Genus *Cynanthus*
BROAD-BILLED HUMMINGBIRD
Genus *Hylocharis*
WHITE-EARED HUMMINGBIRD
Genus *Lampornis*
BLUE-THROATED HUMMINGBIRD
Genus *Eugenes*
MAGNIFICENT HUMMINGBIRD
Genus *Amazilia*
VIOLET-CROWNED HUMMINGBIRD
BERYLLINE HUMMINGBIRD
BUFF-BELLIED HUMMINGBIRD
Genus *Calypte*
ANNA'S HUMMINGBIRD
COSTA'S HUMMINGBIRD
Genus *Archilochus*
BLACK-CHINNED HUMMINGBIRD
RUBY-THROATED HUMMINGBIRD
Genus *Stellula*
CALLIOPE HUMMINGBIRD
Genus *Selasphorus*
BROAD-TAILED HUMMINGBIRD
ALLEN'S HUMMINGBIRD
RUFOUS HUMMINGBIRD

Rare Hummingbirds

These relatively large, distinctive species are rare visitors from Mexico. Plain-capped Starthroat might be confused with Magnificent Hummingbird; note white markings on head and back.

Plain-capped Starthroat

Heliomaster constantii

L 5" WS 7" WT 0.26 oz (7.3 g) ♀>♂

Large and lanky; long-necked, very long-billed.

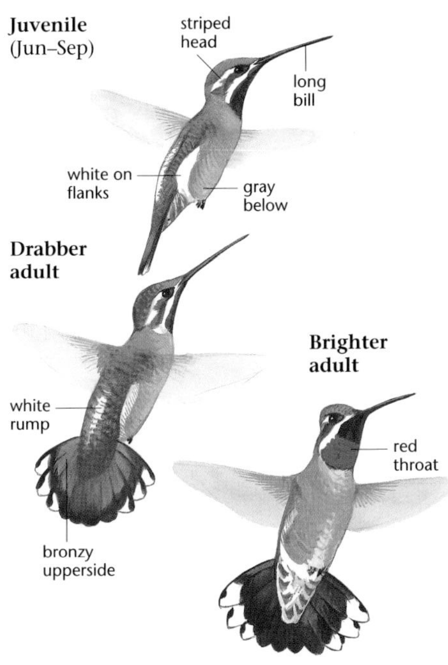
Juvenile
(Jun–Sep)
striped
head
long
bill
white on
flanks
gray
below
Drabber
adult
Brighter
adult
white
rump
red
throat
bronzy
upperside

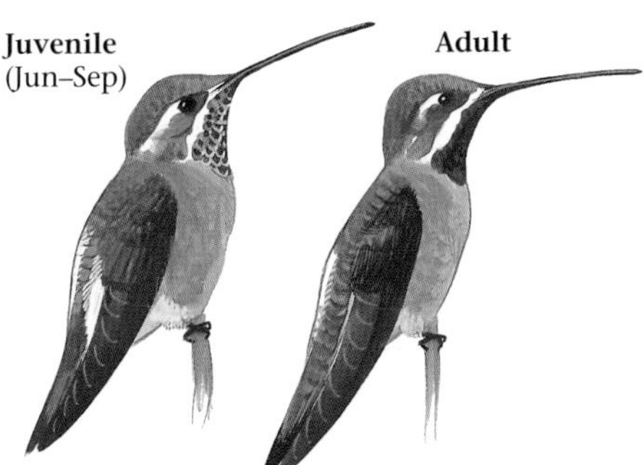
Juvenile
(Jun–Sep)
Adult

Voice: Call strong, sharp chips like Magnificent Hummingbird but huskier. Song a series of sharp chips with occasional two-syllable chips *chip chip chip pichip chip. . . .*

Green Violet-ear

Colibri thalassinus

L 4.75" WS 7" WT 0.21 oz (5.9 g) ♂>♀

Large and fairly stocky; long, broad tail.

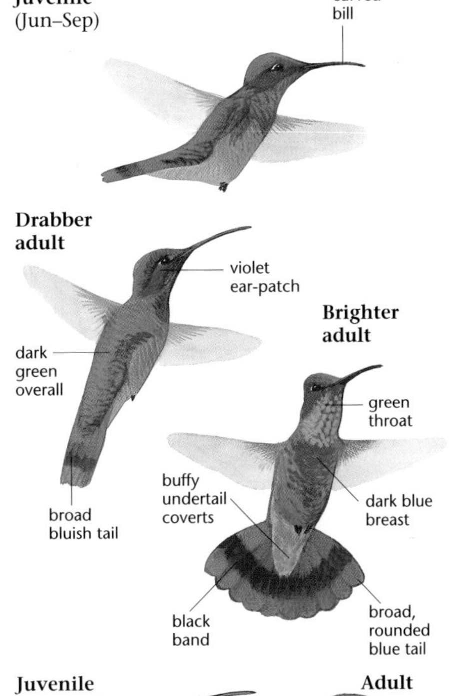
Juvenile
(Jun–Sep)
curved
bill
Drabber
adult
violet
ear-patch
Brighter
adult
dark
green
overall
green
throat
buffy
undertail
coverts
dark blue
breast
broad
bluish tail
black
band
broad,
rounded
blue tail
Juvenile
(Jun–Sep)
Adult

Voice: Call a sharp, dry chip (usually in rapid series of 2–4 notes), quality reminiscent of Violet-crowned Hummingbird. Song a series of dry, metallic chips *chitik-chitik, chitik-chitik . . .* with irregular rhythm.

HUMMINGBIRDS: GENERA *CALOTHORAX* AND *AMAZILIA*

These two distinctive species have patchy distribution and are found regularly in only a few locations. Lucifer is found mainly in desert with agave plants, Violet-crowned in riparian trees.

Lucifer Hummingbird

Calothorax lucifer

L 3.5" WS 4" WT 0.11 oz (3.1 g) ♀>♂

Tiny, relatively large-headed, with distinctly curved bill; female distinguished from similar species by bill shape, head pattern, buffy underparts.

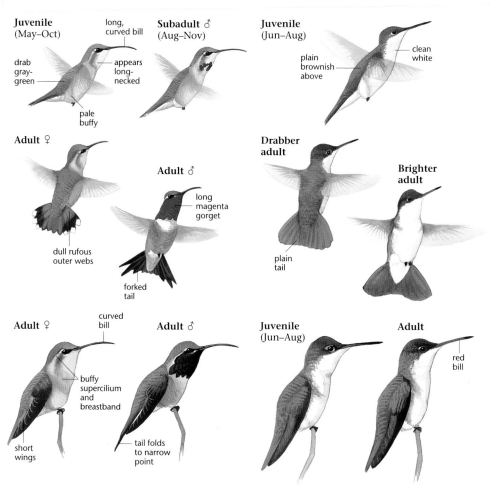

Juvenile (May–Oct)

long, curved bill
drab gray-green
appears long-necked
pale buffy

Subadult ♂ (Aug–Nov)

Adult ♀

dull rufous outer webs

Adult ♂

long magenta gorget
forked tail

Adult ♀

curved bill
buffy supercilium and breastband
short wings

Adult ♂

tail folds to narrow point

Voice: Call a dry, sharp, twittering chip, often doubled. Chase call louder, sharper chips in series. Shuttle display of male produces fluttering rattle like shuffling of a deck of cards; a quieter fluttering sound produced at end of dive display.

Violet-crowned Hummingbird

Amazilia violiceps

L 4.5" WS 6" WT 0.19 oz (5.5 g) ♂>♀

Large and rather long-bodied; our only hummingbird that is plain brownish above and clean white below.

Juvenile (Jun–Aug)

plain brownish above
clean white

Drabber adult

plain tail

Brighter adult

Juvenile (Jun–Aug)

Adult

red bill

Voice: Call a rather dry *tak* or *chap;* sometimes a drier *tek* like Broad-billed. Chase call a squeaky, laughing series *kweesh twik twik twik wik wik*. Song a series of very high, thin, descending notes *seew seew seew seew seew.*

The strongly curved bill of Lucifer Hummingbird is an excellent field mark, but beware that many other species have slightly curved bills, particularly Black-chinned, and that the curvature can be exaggerated at certain angles, such as head-on views.

These two species are quite similar, but their ranges do not overlap. Unlike all other hummingbirds, they are dark green overall with rufous tails. They differ from each other in plumage and voice.

Berylline Hummingbird

Amazilia beryllina

L 4.25" WS 5.75" WT 0.16 oz (4.6 g) ♂>♀

Found in oak woods; distinguished from Buff-bellied by rufous wings, dark uppertail coverts, and gray belly.

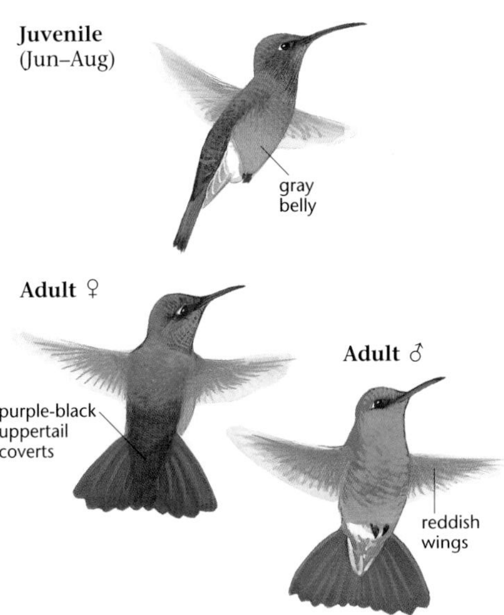
Juvenile
(Jun–Aug)
gray
belly
Adult ♀
Adult ♂
purple-black
uppertail
coverts
reddish
wings

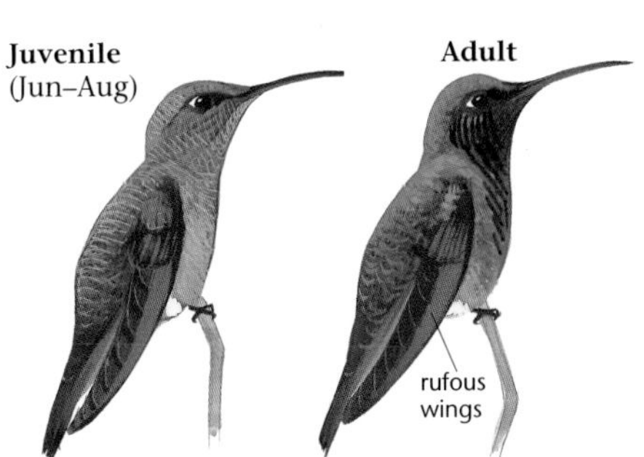
Juvenile
(Jun–Aug)
Adult
rufous
wings

Voice: Call a short, buzzy rattle *trrrk*. Chase call a high, thin *seek* like Blue-throated. Song scratchy and squeaky *urr-toPIKoPIKoPIKo* and variations.

Buff-bellied Hummingbird

Amazilia yucatanensis

L 4.25" WS 5.75" WT 0.13 oz (3.8 g) ♂>♀

Easily distinguished from most other hummingbirds by size, red bill, rufous tail, and overall dark color.

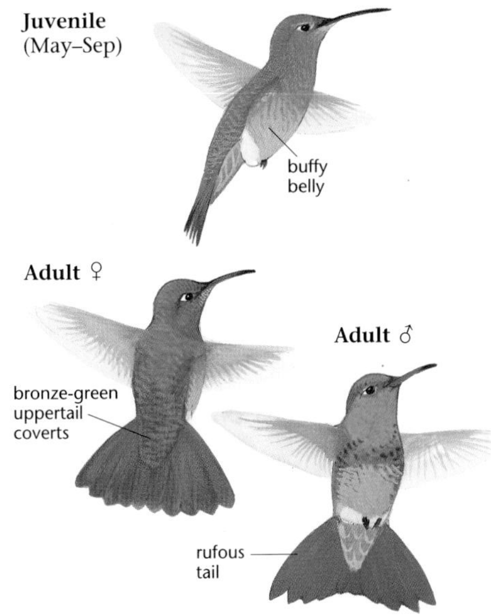
Juvenile
(May–Sep)
buffy
belly
Adult ♀
Adult ♂
bronze-green
uppertail
coverts
rufous
tail

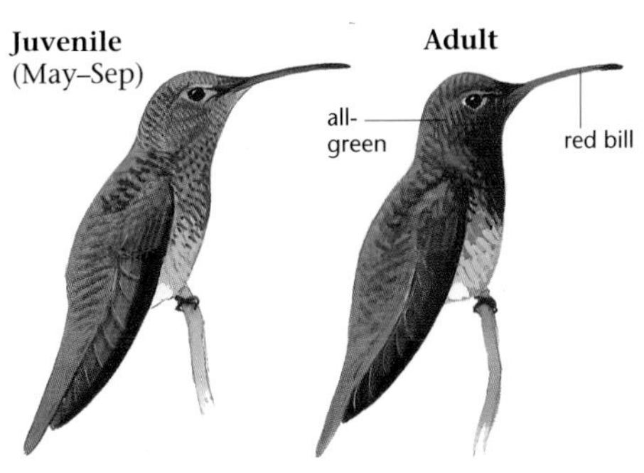
Juvenile
(May–Sep)
Adult
all-
green
red bill

Voice: Call a very high, sharp, metallic smack; nearly always given in short series of two to four notes; weaker single notes when perched. Chase call a dry, sharp buzz *jjjjjj;* a piercing *seek-seek* when chasing predator.

Broad-billed and White-eared Hummingbirds

These species have dark plumage, broad red bills, and broad, dark tails. White-eared prefers higher-elevation pine-oak forests, Broad-billed lower riparian woods, but ranges completely overlap.

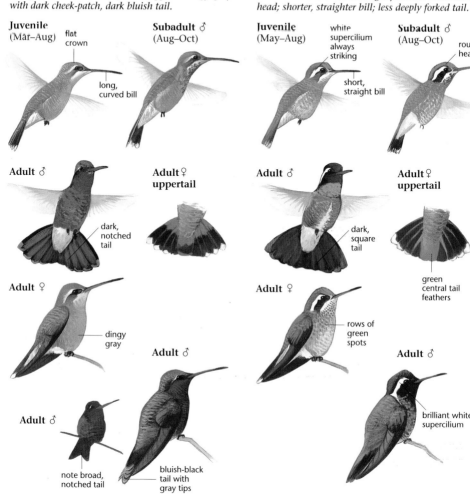

Broad-billed Hummingbird

Cynanthus latirostris

L 4" WS 5.75" WT 0.1 oz (2.9 g)

Stocky and broad-tailed; female appears dingy gray with dark cheek-patch, dark bluish tail.

Juvenile (Mar–Aug)

flat crown

long, curved bill

Subadult ♂ (Aug–Oct)

Adult ♂

dark, notched tail

Adult ♀ uppertail

Adult ♀

dingy gray

Adult ♂

Adult ♂

note broad, notched tail

bluish-black tail with gray tips

Voice: Call a dry *tek* or *tetek* like Ruby-crowned Kinglet but sharper; also high, sharp *seek* and thin *tseeew*. Chase call staccato chips followed by dry laughing: *tsik tsitik tilk-ilk-ilk-ilk*. Song high, tinkling with buzzy end *situ ti ti ti ti ti zreet zreet zreet*. Male dive display produces a high *zing*.

White-eared Hummingbird

Hylocharis leucotis

L 3.75" WS 5.75" WT 0.12 oz (3.3 g)

Similar to Broad-billed but slightly stockier with rounder head; shorter, straighter bill; less deeply forked tail.

Juvenile (May–Aug)

white supercilium always striking

short, straight bill

Subadult ♂ (Aug–Oct)

round head

Adult ♂

dark, square tail

Adult ♀ uppertail

green central tail feathers

Adult ♀

rows of green spots

Adult ♂

brilliant white supercilium

Voice: Call a high, flat chip similar to Magnificent; often doubled or tripled with the series slightly descending (rising in Magnificent). Chase call a very rapid series of about five sharp, high chips. Song a series of high chips alternating with short, staccato rattles.

Large Hummingbirds

These largest hummingbirds dwarf other species when seen together, but size may not be obvious with lone birds. Blue-throated is found in shady wooded canyons, Magnificent in pine-oak forests.

Blue-throated Hummingbird

Lampornis clemenciae

L 5" WS 8" WT 0.27 oz (7.6 g) ♂>♀

Our largest hummingbird. Often fans its very long, broad tail.

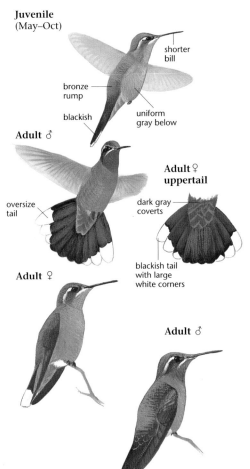

Juvenile
(May–Oct)

shorter bill
bronze rump
blackish
uniform gray below

Adult ♂

oversize tail

Adult ♀ uppertail

dark gray coverts
blackish tail with large white corners

Adult ♀

Adult ♂

Voice: Call a penetrating, high, clear *seek* (given endlessly by perched male). Chase call not well-developed; sometimes a loud, popping chip or *seek krrkr*. Both calls similar to some Magnificent vocalizations. Song a quiet, mechanical rattle with hissing quality *situtee trrrrrrrr* repeated.

Blue-throated has the slowest wingbeats of North American hummingbirds, visibly and audibly slower than Magnificent. Differences in wingbeat rates exist between many smaller species as well and may be detectable with experience and careful observation, or with a measuring device. More study is needed.

Magnificent Hummingbird

Eugenes fulgens

L 5.25" WS 7.5" WT 0.25 oz (7 g) ♂>♀

Large, strikingly long-billed, relatively slender. Hovers with back straight; fans tail less than Blue-throated.

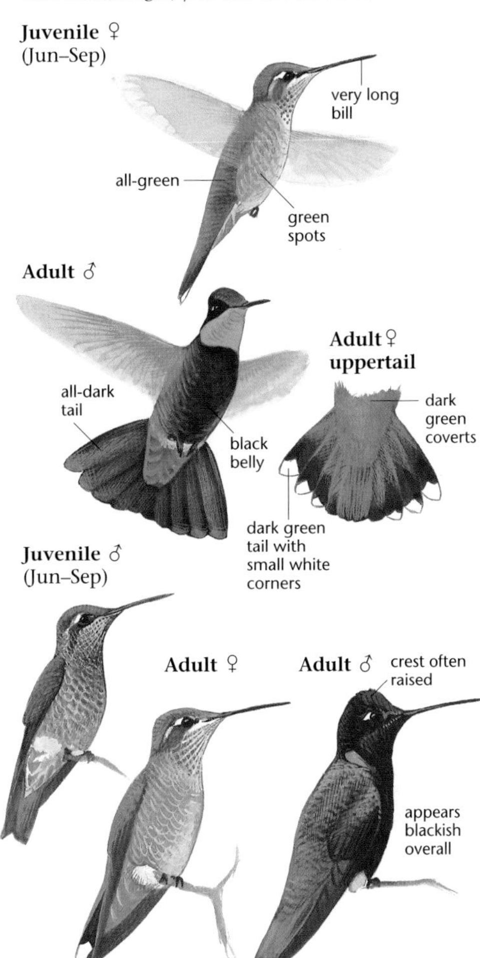

Juvenile ♀
(Jun–Sep)
very long bill
all-green
green spots
Adult ♂
all-dark tail
black belly
Adult ♀ uppertail
dark green coverts
dark green tail with small white corners
Juvenile ♂
(Jun–Sep)
Adult ♀
Adult ♂
crest often raised
appears blackish overall

Voice: Call a sharp chip; varies from high chip like Anna's to low, solid chip or flat, squeaky *tiip*. Chase call variable: a rapid, laughing series *twik twik wik wik wik wik ik ik ikikikikikik* rising; a steady whining *twee kwee kwee kwee kwee kwee;* and a crackling *chip krr krr*.

Males of this genus are distinctive, with elongated gorgets and iridescent crowns. Females are similar to *Archilochus* hummingbirds but distinguished by details of plumage, structure, and voice.

Anna's Hummingbird

Calypte anna

L 4" WS 5.25" WT 0.15 oz (4.3 g)

Large and sturdy-looking; tubular body with tail held stationary and in line with body. Short, straight bill and long, sloping forehead.

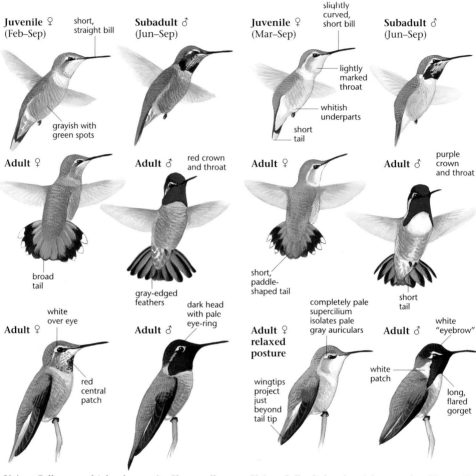

Juvenile ♀ (Feb–Sep)
short, straight bill
grayish with green spots

Subadult ♂ (Jun–Sep)

Adult ♀
broad tail

Adult ♂
red crown and throat
gray-edged feathers

Adult ♀
white over eye
red central patch

Adult ♂
dark head with pale eye-ring

Voice: Call a very high, sharp *stit*. Chase call a rapid, dry chatter *zrrr jika jika jika jika jika*. Song from perch scratchy, thin, and dry *sturee sturee sturee, scrrrr, zveeee, street street*. Male dive display ends with explosive buzz/squeak *tewk* very similar to some Ground Squirrel alarm calls.

Costa's Hummingbird

Calypte costae

L 3.5" WS 4.75" WT 0.11 oz (3.1 g) ♀>♂

Small and dumpy; short-tailed and round-headed with short, thick neck.

Juvenile ♀ (Mar–Sep)
slightly curved, short bill
lightly marked throat
whitish underparts
short tail

Subadult ♂ (Jun–Sep)

Adult ♀
short, paddle-shaped tail

Adult ♂
purple crown and throat
short tail

Adult ♀ relaxed posture
completely pale supercilium isolates pale gray auriculars
wingtips project just beyond tail tip

Adult ♂
white "eyebrow"
white patch
long, flared gorget

Voice: Call a light, dry *tink* somewhat like cardinals. Chase call a very sharp, high twitter *stirrr, stirrr* or rapid series of *tink* notes followed by lower, scratchy squeal. Song an extremely thin, high buzz *szeeeee-eeeeeeeeew* rising then falling. Male dive display produces continuous shrill whistle.

Calypte wing shape

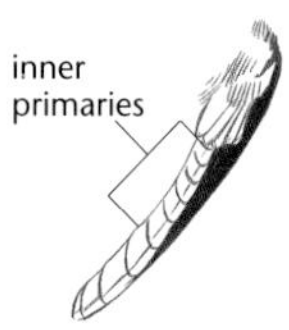
inner primaries

Inner primaries on *Selasphorus* and *Calypte* hummingbirds are not as narrow as on *Archilochus*.

Hummingbirds: Genus *Archilochus*

These species are very similar in all plumages. Males are distinguished by throat color, but identification of females requires very close study, and even then some are unidentifiable.

Black-chinned Hummingbird

Archilochus alexandri

L 3.75" WS 4.75" WT 0.12 oz (3.3 g) ♀>♂

Structure like Ruby-throated: slender, small-headed, and thin-necked. Female distinguished from similar species by overall shape, long bill, flat forehead, drab grayish color.

Juvenile (May–Oct)

grayer crown and auriculars contrast less with throat

long bill

pumps tail frequently when hovering

Subadult ♂ (Sep–Dec)

Adult ♀

Adult ♂

purple band

black chin

Adult ♀ alert posture

usually grayish crown

tail projects slightly beyond wingtips

Adult ♂

looks black-headed

Voice: Call a soft, husky *tiup* or *tiv* or *tipip*. Chase call sharp, sputtering, cascading *spirrr spididddr* and variations. Song a high, weak warble. Male dive display produces soft, stuttering *dididididit*. Adult male's wings produce soft, low whistle in flight.

Black-chinned wing shape

tips broad and curved

Ruby-throated Hummingbird

Archilochus colubris

L 3.75" WS 4.5" WT 0.11 oz (3.2 g) ♀>♂

Nearly identical to Black-chinned; averages shorter billed, longer tailed. Female averages more brightly colored; best distinguished by primary shape, but some individuals are intermediate.

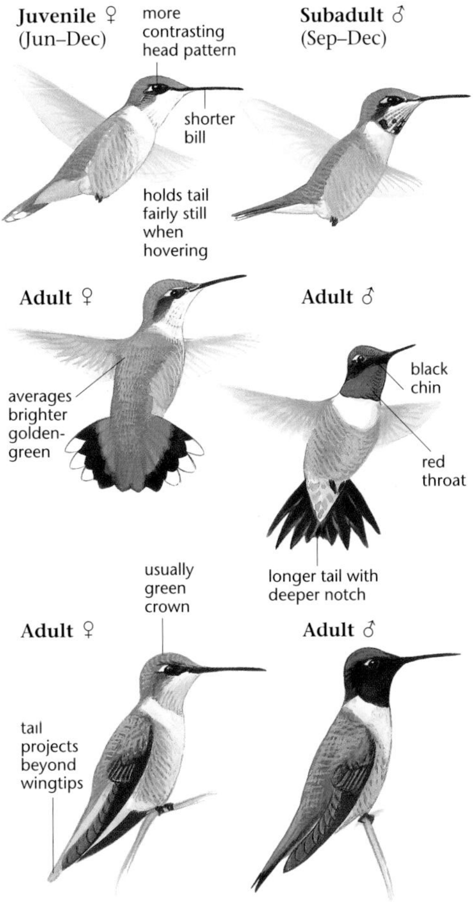

Juvenile ♀ (Jun–Dec)

more contrasting head pattern

shorter bill

holds tail fairly still when hovering

Subadult ♂ (Sep–Dec)

Adult ♀

averages brighter golden-green

Adult ♂

black chin

red throat

longer tail with deeper notch

Adult ♀

usually green crown

tail projects beyond wingtips

Adult ♂

Voice: Call soft and husky like Black-chinned but may average slightly sharper and higher. Chase call sharp, sputtering *zeeek ididididid* like Black-chinned, often repeated. Song from perch faint, high rattling *t t t t*. Adult male's wings produce very faint, high buzz in flight.

Ruby-throated wing shape

tips narrow and straight

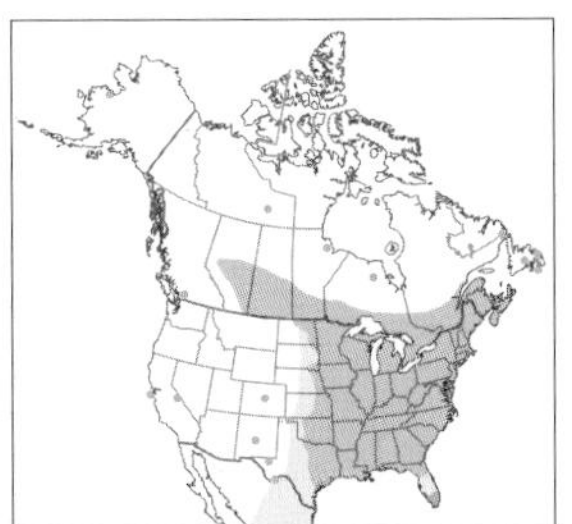

Calliope Hummingbird, our smallest bird, is generally quiet and inconspicuous. Females of both these species can be difficult to distinguish from Rufous and Allen's Hummingbirds.

Calliope Hummingbird

Stellula calliope

L 3.25" WS 4.25" WT 0.1 oz (2.7 g) ♀>♂

Tiny and short-tailed with short, thin bill.

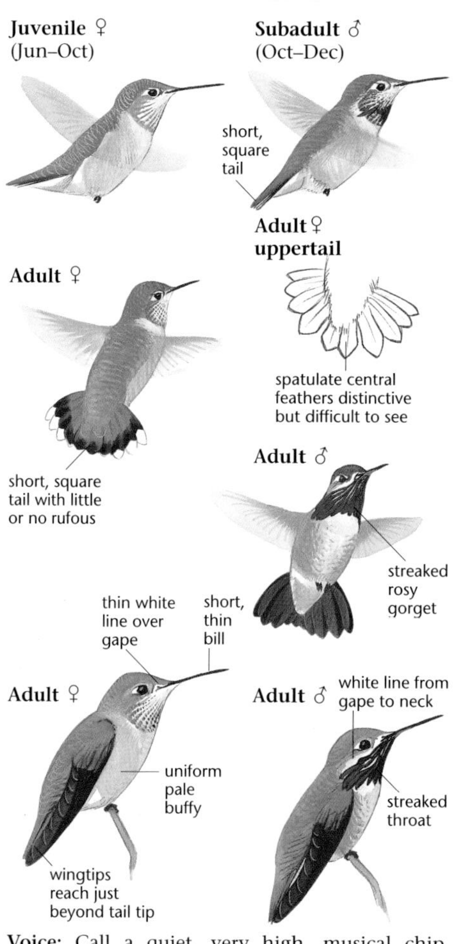

Juvenile ♀
(Jun–Oct)
Subadult ♂
(Oct–Dec)
short, square tail
Adult ♀ uppertail
Adult ♀
spatulate central feathers distinctive but difficult to see
short, square tail with little or no rufous
Adult ♂
streaked rosy gorget
thin white line over gape
short, thin bill
Adult ♀
uniform pale buffy
wingtips reach just beyond tail tip
Adult ♂
white line from gape to neck
streaked throat

Voice: Call a quiet, very high, musical chip. Chase call alternates rattle and buzz *tototo zeee tototo zeeee. . . .* Song a very high, thin whistle *tseeeee-ew*. Male dive display produces short, high, muffled *pvrrr*.

Broad-tailed Hummingbird

Selasphorus platycercus

L 4" WS 5.25" WT 0.13 oz (3.6 g) ♀>♂

Rather long-bodied; long, broad tail conspicuously larger than Rufous and Allen's.

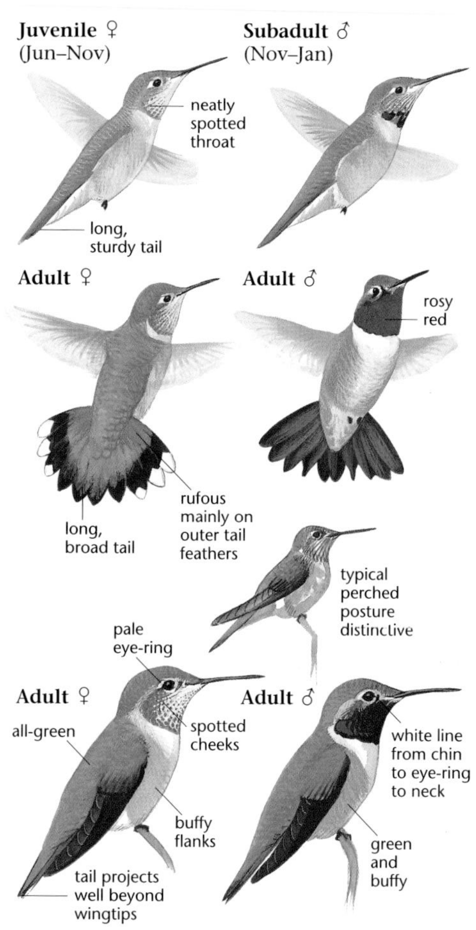

Juvenile ♀
(Jun–Nov)
neatly spotted throat
long, sturdy tail
Subadult ♂
(Nov–Jan)
Adult ♀
long, broad tail
rufous mainly on outer tail feathers
Adult ♂
rosy red
typical perched posture distinctive
pale eye-ring
Adult ♀
all-green
spotted cheeks
buffy flanks
tail projects well beyond wingtips
Adult ♂
white line from chin to eye-ring to neck
green and buffy

Voice: Call a sharp, high, *chip* similar to Rufous but slightly higher. Chase call *tiputi tiputi . . .* like Rufous but lower, variable. Male dive display produces loud wing buzz. Wings of adult male produce high trill in flight like Cedar Waxwing call; lower and more musical than Rufous and Allen's.

Broad-tailed adult ♂ wing shape

Narrow tips of outer primaries produce trill in flight. Trill may be faint or absent if tips are worn (often Nov–Jan).

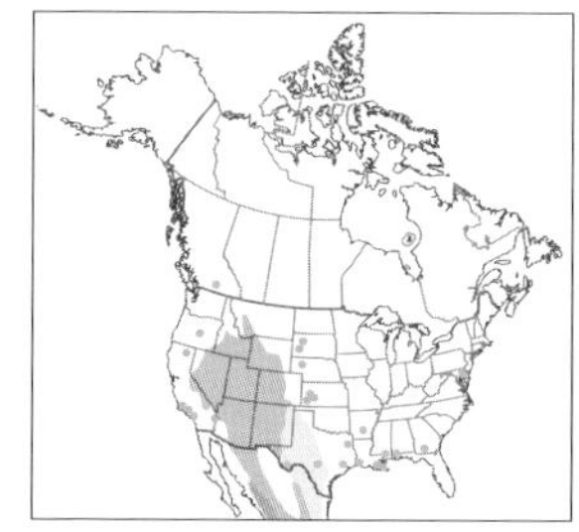

Barely distinguishable from each other, these two small, aggressive species differ from all other hummingbirds in their compact shape, buffy orange flanks, and usually extensively orange tails.

Allen's Hummingbird

Selasphorus sasin

L 3.75" WS 4.25" WT 0.11 oz (3 g) ♀>♂

Nearly identical to Rufous; averages slightly smaller with smaller tail and relatively long bill.

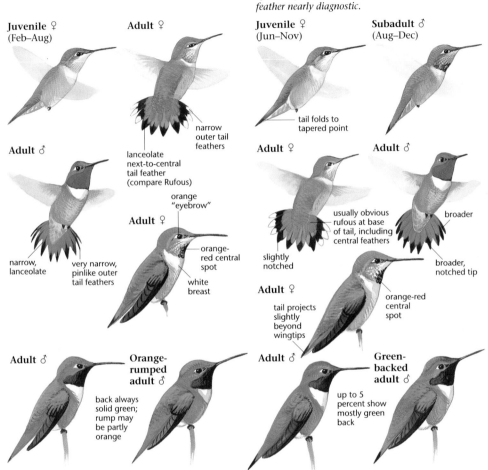

Juvenile ♀ (Feb–Aug)

Adult ♀

narrow outer tail feathers

lanceolate next-to-central tail feather (compare Rufous)

Adult ♂

narrow, lanceolate

very narrow, pinlike outer tail feathers

Adult ♀

orange "eyebrow"

orange-red central spot

white breast

Adult ♂

back always solid green; rump may be partly orange

Orange-rumped adult ♂

Voice: Calls apparently all like Rufous. Male dive display produces high, humming whistle, not stuttering like Rufous. Wings of adult male produce high, buzzy trill, faster and higher than Broad-tailed; like Rufous but may average slightly higher-pitched.

Rufous Hummingbird

Selasphorus rufus

L 3.75" WS 4.5" WT 0.12 oz (3.4 g) ♀>♂

Small and compact; rather short-winged. Outer tail feathers average broader than Allen's (comparing birds of like age and sex); notch near tip of second tail feather nearly diagnostic.

Juvenile ♀ (Jun–Nov)

tail folds to tapered point

Subadult ♂ (Aug–Dec)

Adult ♀

usually obvious rufous at base of tail, including central feathers

slightly notched

Adult ♂

broader

broader, notched tip

Adult ♀

tail projects slightly beyond wingtips

orange-red central spot

Adult ♂

up to 5 percent show mostly green back

Green-backed adult ♂

Voice: Call a high, hard chip *tyuk*. Chase call a sharp buzz followed by three-syllable phrases *tzzew tzupity tzupity tzup*; also *zeee chew chew chew* or *zeelk zeelk*. Male dive display produces stuttering, humming *vi vi vi virrr*. Wings of adult male produce high, buzzy trill like Allen's.

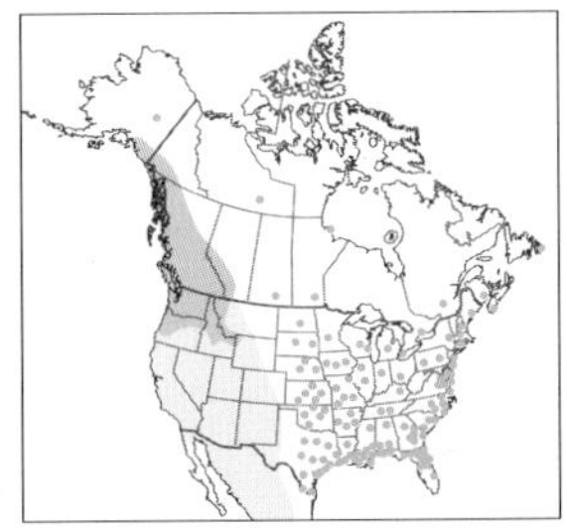

Identification of Hummingbirds

Male hummingbirds of some species perform elaborate swooping or diving aerial displays for females. The paths followed during these display flights differ among species. A distinctive sound is produced at the bottom of the dive (described under voice of individual species). Most species also perform a low, short (2- to 10-foot) back-and-forth movement called a shuttle display, often accompanied by tail-pumping and buzzing sounds. The display paths of a few species are diagrammed here: dotted lines indicate a slow, upward movement; solid lines indicate a rapid descent. In addition to those shown below, Ruby-throated and Black-chinned perform a series of relatively low, shallow, U-shaped arcs; Broad-tailed a simple J-shaped dive; and Lucifer an L-shaped dive with swerving horizontal path at end.

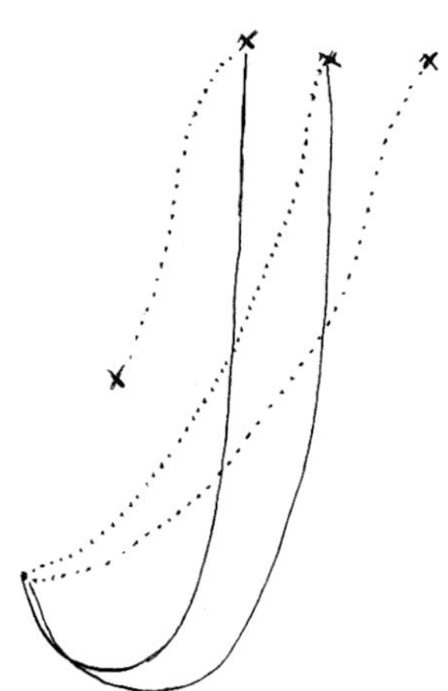

Rufous Hummingbird
series of steep, J-shaped dives; all ending at same point but with starting points progressing around a circle

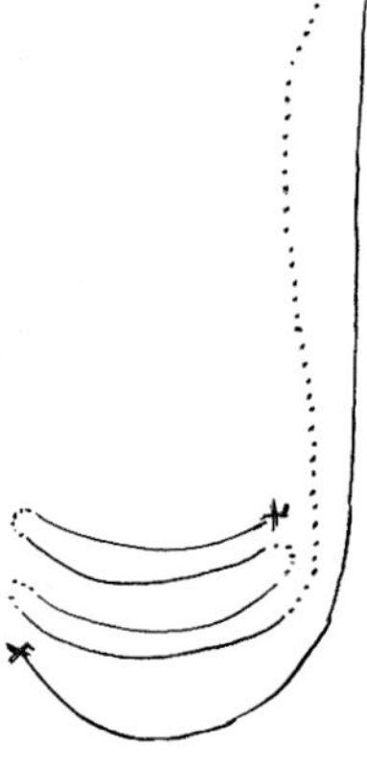

Allen's Hummingbird
dive similar to Rufous but not in series and begins with shuttle display; dive sounds differ

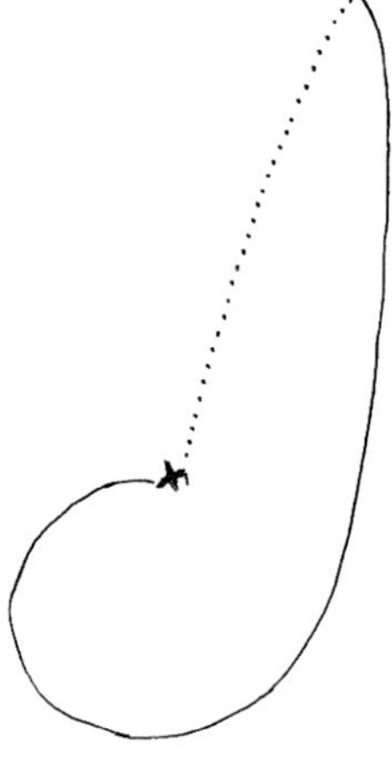

Anna's Hummingbird
steep, J-shaped dive, curling around at the bottom; often repeated on same path

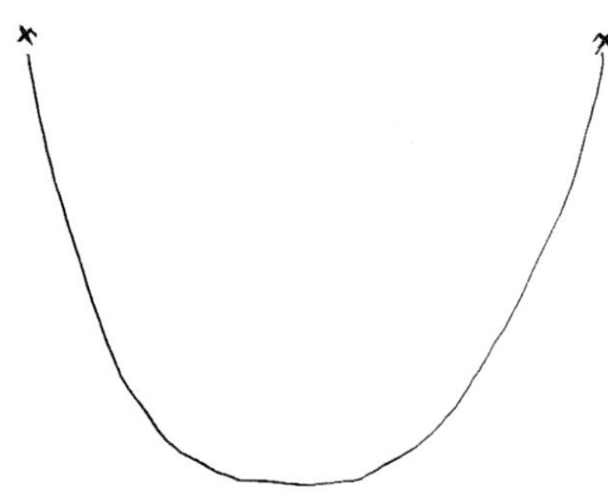

Costa's Hummingbird
single, very broad, U-shaped dive

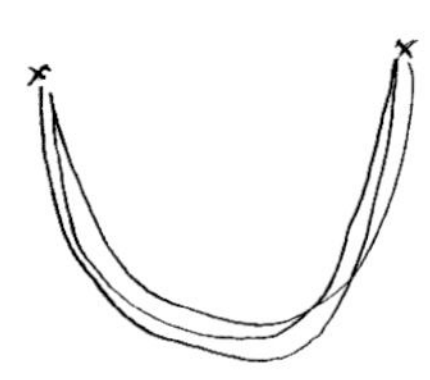

Calliope Hummingbird
series of U-shaped dives

Hummingbirds feeding on flower nectar often become dusted or stained with pollen on their throats and/or foreheads (different species of flowers deposit pollen in different locations). This creates a yellow to orange patch that can be quite conspicuous but should not cause identification problems (beyond momentary surprise) as no hummingbird species is normally yellow on the head.

Anna's Hummingbird juvenile ♂

dusted with pollen

Trogons
Family: Trogonidae

Eared Trogon
Euptilotis neoxenus
L 14" WS 24" WT unknown
Larger than Elegant Trogon and not very closely related, with oddly small head and bill, very broad tail.

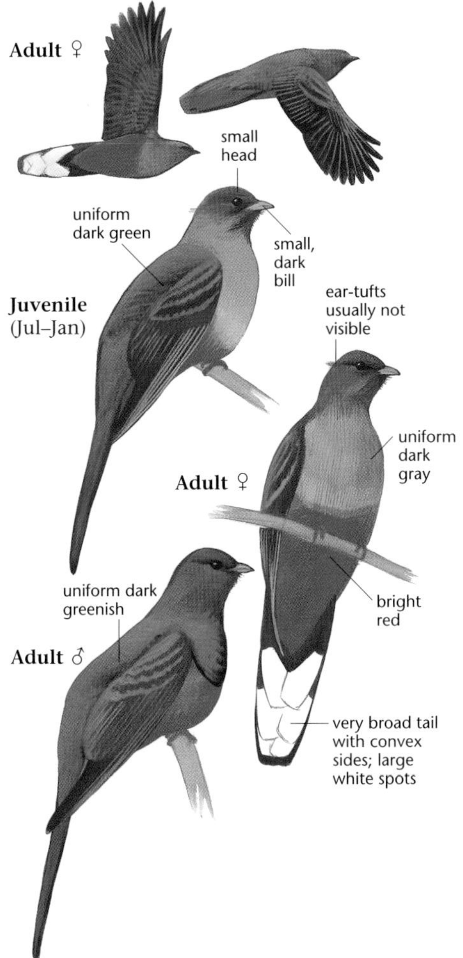

Adult ♀
small head
uniform dark green
small, dark bill
Juvenile (Jul–Jan)
ear-tufts usually not visible
uniform dark gray
Adult ♀
uniform dark greenish
bright red
Adult ♂
very broad tail with convex sides; large white spots

Voice: Call a high, squealing *kweeeeeeee-chk* strongly rising with sharp cluck at end. Series of high whistles rising in pitch and intensity *fwee fwee fwee . . . fwEErk fwEErk.* Toneless descending cackle given in flight *chikikikik* similar to some calls of Steller's Jay but harder.

Elegant Trogon
Trogon elegans
L 12.5" WS 16" WT 2.5 oz (70 g)
Unique; stout-billed with long, square-tipped tail, unusual wing shape.

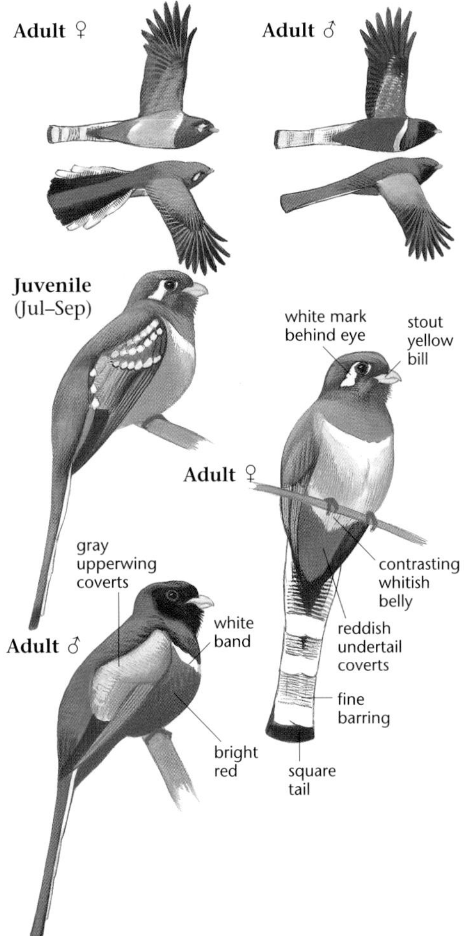

Adult ♀
Adult ♂
Juvenile (Jul–Sep)
white mark behind eye
stout yellow bill
Adult ♀
gray upperwing coverts
contrasting whitish belly
white band
reddish undertail coverts
Adult ♂
fine barring
bright red
square tail

Voice: Common call of both sexes soft, hoarse, croaking *brr brr brr brr . . .* or stronger *bwarr bwarr bwarr . . .*; sometimes a hoarse, spitting *weck weck weck . . .* (in series of 5–15 notes). Alarm call a rapid, hoarse *bekekekekekek.* Also gives low, soft, hooting or clucking notes.

TROGONIDAE
2 species in 2 genera. Trogons are peculiar birds, perching quietly, tilting their heads, and suddenly flying out to pluck fruit or insects. Eared is found in pine-oak forests, Elegant at lower elevations in sycamores. Both trogons perch with rump out and tail straight down and nest in tree cavities.

Kingfishers

Family: Alcedinidae

3 species in 2 genera. North American kingfishers are fish-eating birds found on sheltered waters. They use trees or wires for lookout perches and catch fish by plunge-diving headfirst, often after hovering. Belted and Ringed are large, conspicuous, and loud; they are found on open water, perch prominently, and hover frequently. Green is small, inconspicuous, and quiet; it is found on sheltered creeks and pools, perches low on twigs, flies low over water, and rarely hovers. All species nest in holes excavated in dirt banks. Adult females are shown.

Genus *Ceryle*

BELTED
KINGFISHER
RINGED
KINGFISHER

Genus *Chloroceryle*

GREEN
KINGFISHER

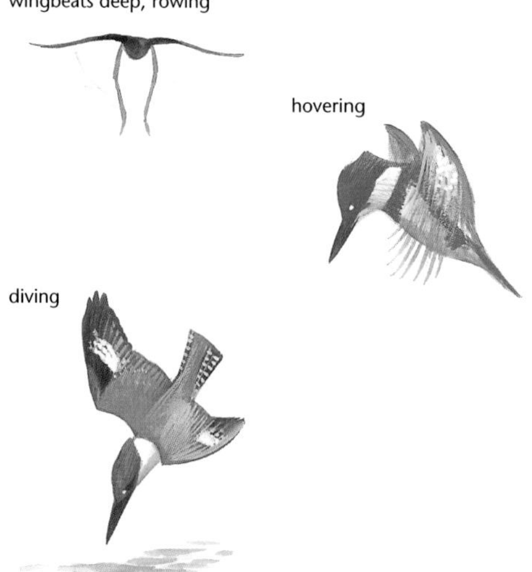

wingbeats deep, rowing
hovering
diving

Belted Kingfisher

Ceryle alcyon

L 13" WS 20" WT 5 oz (150 g)

Familiar and widespread. Like other kingfishers; very large-headed with long, heavy bill and short tail; legs very short.

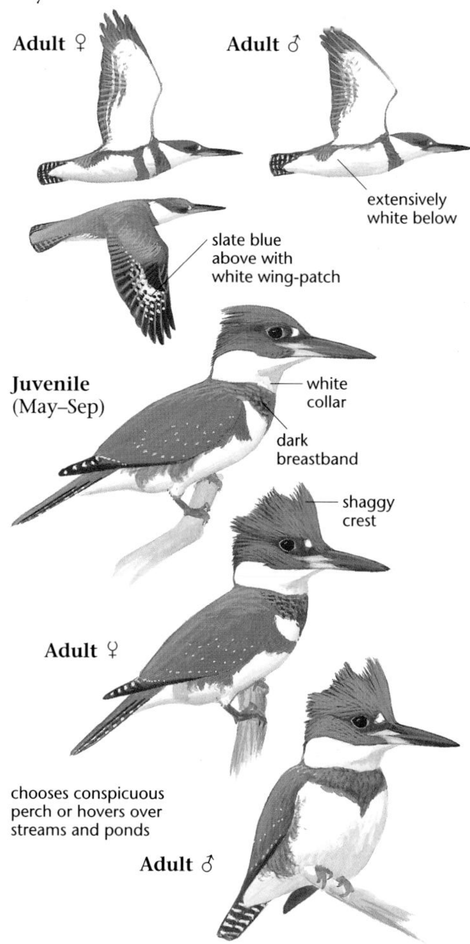

Adult ♀
Adult ♂
extensively
white below
slate blue
above with
white wing-patch
Juvenile
(May–Sep)
white
collar
dark
breastband
shaggy
crest
Adult ♀
chooses conspicuous
perch or hovers over
streams and ponds
Adult ♂

Voice: Common territorial call a long, uneven rattle most similar to Hairy Woodpecker rattle but harsher, unsteady, clattering. Also a higher, shorter, more musical, rapid trill *tirrrrr.*

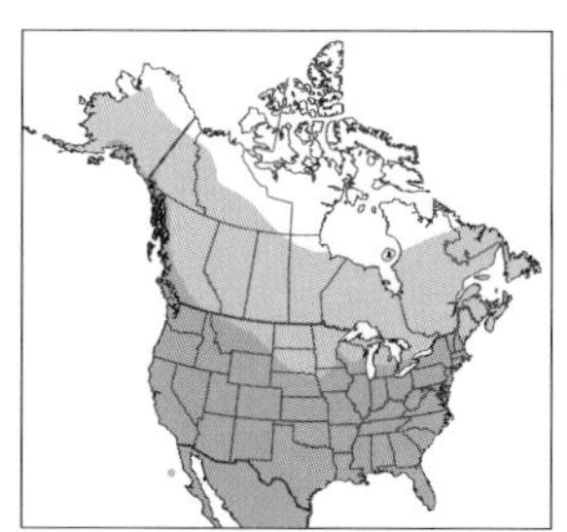

Ringed, our largest kingfisher, is loud and conspicuous like Belted. The much smaller and less conspicuous Green is usually seen perched or flying just above the water's surface.

Ringed Kingfisher

Ceryle torquata

L 16" WS 25" WT 11 oz (315 g)

Huge and commanding; larger than Belted Kingfisher, with rufous belly.

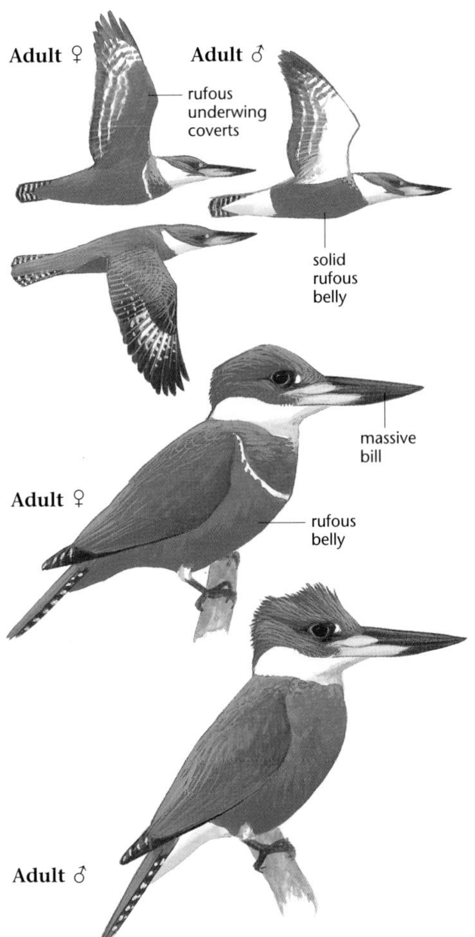
Adult ♀
Adult ♂
rufous underwing coverts
solid rufous belly
massive bill
Adult ♀
rufous belly
Adult ♂

Voice: Common call in flight a loud, double-note *ktok* similar to (but deeper than) some calls of Great-tailed Grackle. Rattle call a loud, very hard "machine-gun" rattle all on one pitch *ke ke ke ke ke ke ke ke . . .* ; much slower and lower-pitched than Belted Kingfisher rattle.

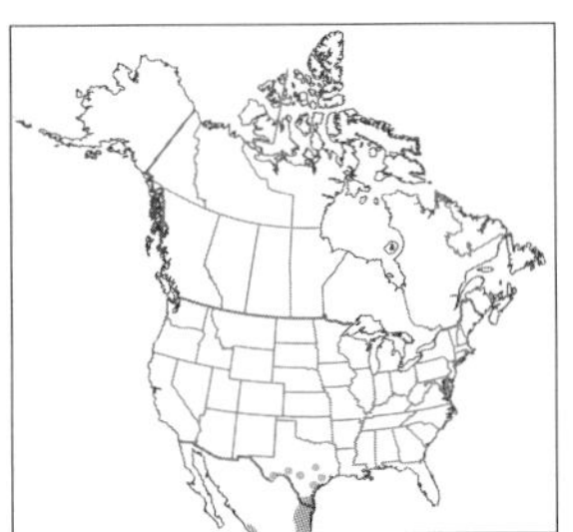

Green Kingfisher

Chloroceryle americana

L 8.75" WS 11" WT 1.3 oz (36 g)

Small and relatively large-billed, with obvious white collar.

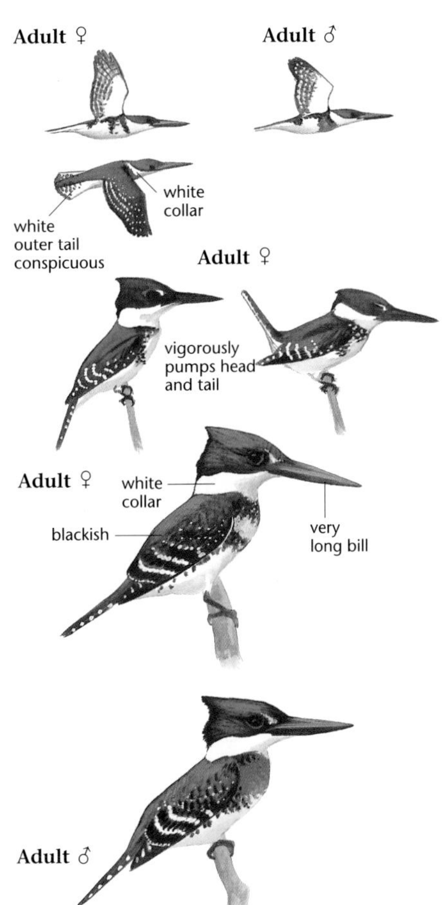
Adult ♀
Adult ♂
white collar
white outer tail conspicuous
Adult ♀
vigorously pumps head and tail
Adult ♀
white collar
blackish
very long bill
Adult ♂

Voice: Common call a dry, quiet, staccato clicking like tapping pebbles together, usually single or double; also a short, mushy, descending buzz *tsheersh*. Other calls during interactions include a high, squealing *tseelp* and grating sounds.

Woodpeckers

Family: Picidae

22 species in 5 genera. All woodpeckers have stiff tails that are used as props while the birds cling to tree bark and stout chisel-like bills that are used to peel bark or excavate wood to uncover insects. Woodpeckers nest in excavated tree cavities; the size and shape of the hole differs slightly among species. These birds are generally found singly in wooded areas. Flight of most species is deeply undulating. Compare Brown Creeper (nuthatches have different feeding motions). Adult females are shown.

Genus *Melanerpes*

ACORN WOODPECKER

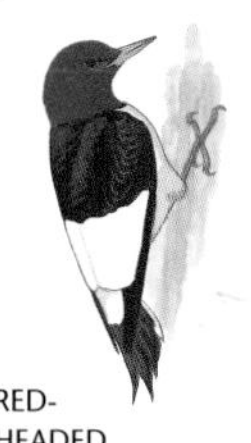
RED-HEADED WOODPECKER

LEWIS'S WOODPECKER

GILA WOODPECKER

GOLDEN-FRONTED WOODPECKER

RED-BELLIED WOODPECKER

Genus *Picoides*

DOWNY WOODPECKER
Eastern

HAIRY WOODPECKER
Eastern

Genus *Sphyrapicus*

WILLIAMSON'S SAPSUCKER

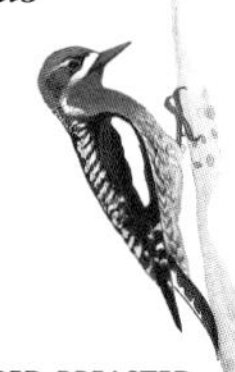
RED-BREASTED SAPSUCKER
Southern

RED-NAPED SAPSUCKER

YELLOW-BELLIED SAPSUCKER

THREE-TOED WOODPECKER
East Taiga

BLACK-BACKED WOODPECKER

Genus *Colaptes*

GILDED FLICKER

NORTHERN FLICKER
Yellow-shafted

Genus *Dryocopus*

PILEATED WOODPECKER

RED-COCKADED WOODPECKER

NUTTALL'S WOODPECKER

LADDER-BACKED WOODPECKER

ARIZONA WOODPECKER

WHITE-HEADED WOODPECKER

DRUMMING SOUNDS

All woodpeckers tap their bills rapidly against wood to proclaim territory and attract mates; this "drumming" replaces the song in most species. Within a region, species can often be identified by their drumming; listen especially for the length and speed of the drumming as well as changes in tempo, frequency, or intensity. Sapsuckers have a distinctive rhythmic pattern; all other species give a continuous burst. Pileated Woodpecker usually sounds "bigger" than Downy and other small woodpeckers, but the quality of the sound depends more on the resonance of the drumming post than on the species doing the drumming, and consequently is not very useful for identification.

These strikingly colored species and Lewis's Woodpecker all fly with rowing, jaylike wingbeats. All store food (especially Acorn Woodpecker), and all will fly out to catch insects in midair.

Acorn Woodpecker

Melanerpes formicivorus

L 9" WS 17.5" WT 2.8 oz (80 g)

Noisy and gregarious with complex social system and distinctive voice; strikingly patterned.

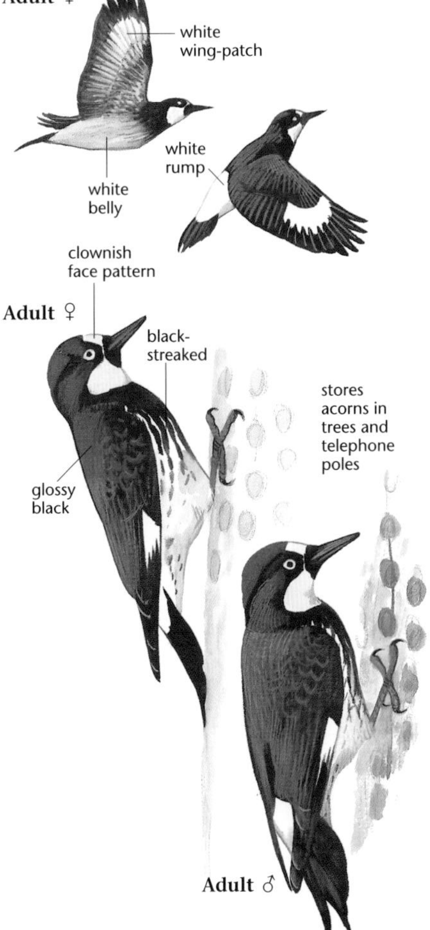
Adult ♀
white wing-patch
white rump
white belly
clownish face pattern
Adult ♀
black-streaked
stores acorns in trees and telephone poles
glossy black
Adult ♂

Voice: Very vocal. Raucous laughing; most common call a nasal *wheka wheka . . .* or *RACK-up RACK-up. . . .* Also nasal, vibrant, trilled *ddddrridrr* or high, burry *ddrreeerr;* nasal *waayk, waaayk* or rising *quaay*. Close contact a high squeaky *Ik a Ik a Ik a*. Drum short, slow, accelerating, variable.

Pacific populations of Acorn Woodpecker average 15 to 20 percent longer-billed than interior populations, with little overlap. They are also less streaked on flanks, but identifying individual birds in the field is difficult.

Red-headed Woodpecker

Melanerpes erythrocephalus

L 9.25" WS 17" WT 2.5 oz (72 g)

Quiet and inconspicuous; striking white rump and secondaries. Flight actions very similar to Blue Jay.

Juvenile
Adult
white
broad white area
Juvenile (Jul–Feb)
brown head
red head
white secondaries
prominent white patch
Adult

Voice: Contact call a wheezy *queeah* or *queerp;* weaker and less vibrant than Red-bellied, variable. In flight a low, harsh *chug* like Red-bellied. Close contact call a gentle, dry rattle *krrrrrr*. Drum short, weak, fairly slow.

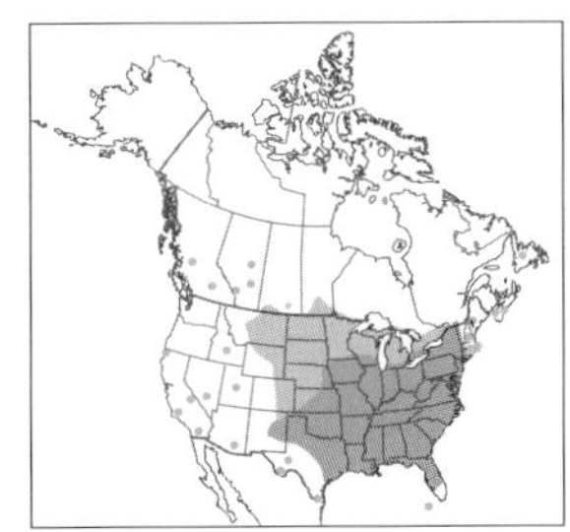

Lewis's Woodpecker, related to Acorn and Red-headed, is often seen on a prominent perch, sallying out to catch flying insects. Gila is related to Golden-fronted and Red-bellied.

Lewis's Woodpecker

Melanerpes lewis

L 10.75" WS 21" WT 4 oz (115 g)

Large, long-winged, and long-tailed, with smooth crowlike wingbeats; usually appears all-dark.

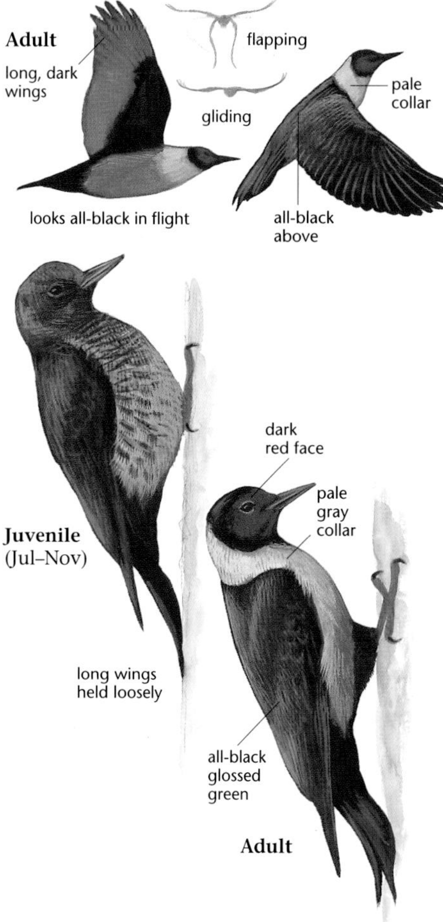
Adult
long, dark wings
flapping
gliding
pale collar
looks all-black in flight
all-black above
dark red face
pale gray collar
Juvenile (Jul–Nov)
long wings held loosely
all-black glossed green
Adult

Voice: Contact call a weak, sneezy *teef* or *kitsif;* also a high, squeaky, descending *rik rik rik*. Dry, rattling chase series reminiscent of European Starling. Song a series of short, harsh *chr* calls. Drum short, weak, medium speed; followed by several individual taps.

Gila Woodpecker

Melanerpes uropygialis

L 9.25" WS 16" WT 2.3 oz (66 g) ♂>♀

Shape and size like Red-bellied; note barred rump, head pattern.

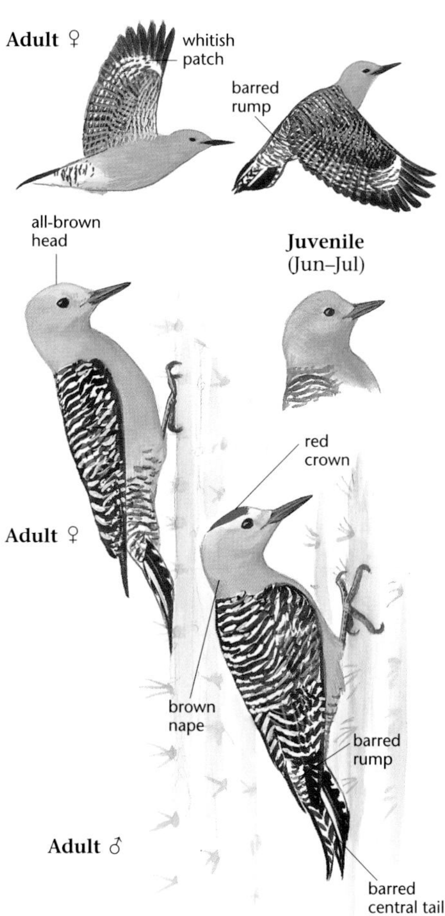
Adult ♀
whitish patch
barred rump
all-brown head
Juvenile (Jun–Jul)
red crown
Adult ♀
brown nape
barred rump
Adult ♂
barred central tail feathers

Voice: Contact call a loud, harsh *quirrr* slightly rising like Red-bellied. Also raucous, laughing, well-spaced *geet geet geet geet geet* and high, nasal, squeaky *kee-u kee-u kee-u . . .* higher and clearer than comparable calls of Red-bellied and Golden-fronted. Drum long and steady.

These two species and Gila are all closely related, with brown bodies, barred backs and wings, deeply undulating flight, and similar voices. They are found in wooded areas.

Golden-fronted Woodpecker

Melanerpes aurifrons

L 9.5" WS 17" WT 2.9 oz (82 g) ♂>♀

Fractionally larger than Red-bellied and Gila. Most are easily identified by head pattern; rump and tail pattern diagnostic.

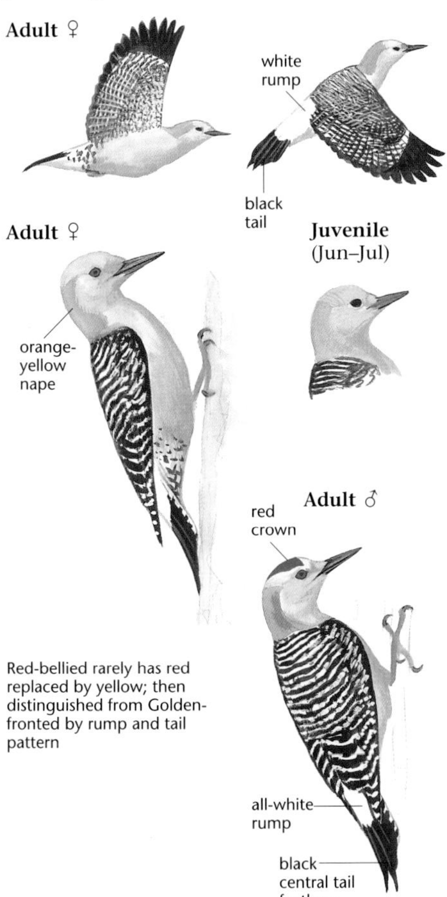

Adult ♀
white rump
black tail
Adult ♀
Juvenile (Jun–Jul)
orange-yellow nape
red crown
Adult ♂
all-white rump
black central tail feathers

Red-bellied rarely has red replaced by yellow; then distinguished from Golden-fronted by rump and tail pattern

Voice: Contact call a loud, harsh, level *kirrr;* all calls harder and harsher than Red-bellied and Gila. Also slow, strained *kih-wrr kih-wrr . . . ; tig tig . . .* calls harder than Red-bellied; a grating *krrr krrr. . . .* Drum medium speed, short, much slower than Ladder-backed.

Red-bellied Woodpecker

Melanerpes carolinus

L 9.25" WS 16" WT 2.2 oz (63 g) ♂>♀

Medium-size; fairly long bill, short wings, and heavy body.

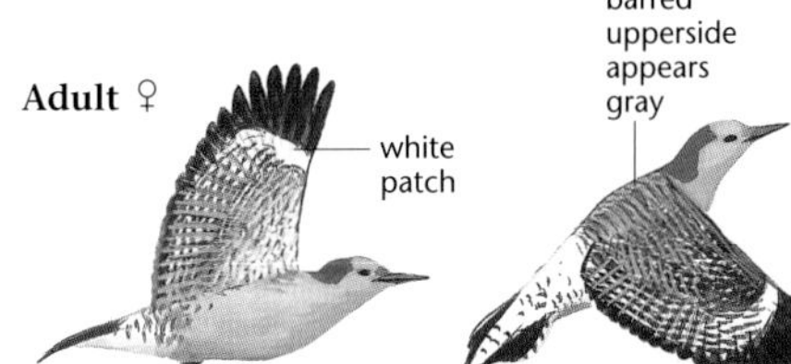

Adult ♀
white patch
barred upperside appears gray

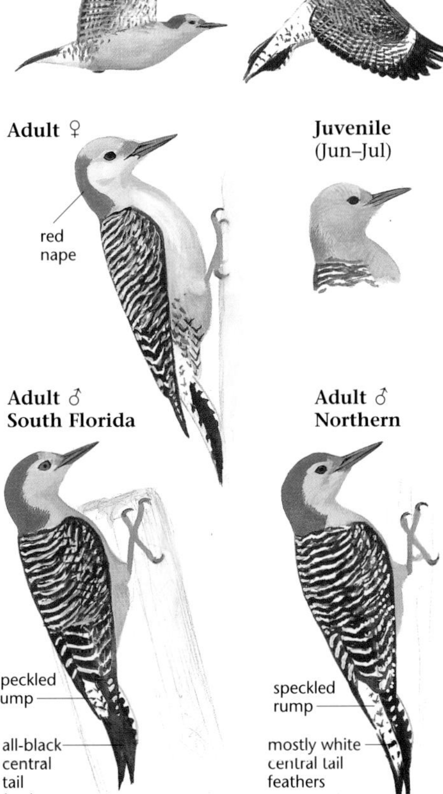

Adult ♀
Juvenile (Jun–Jul)
red nape
Adult ♂ South Florida
Adult ♂ Northern
speckled rump
all-black central tail feathers
speckled rump
mostly white central tail feathers

Voice: Contact call a loud, harsh, but rich *quirrr* slightly rising; in flight a single, low *chug.* Also a harsh *chig-chig,* a series of *chig* notes delivered slowly, or a rapid, chuckling series *chig chigh-chchchchchchch* descending. Drum medium speed and length with steady tempo.

South Florida Red-bellied averages smaller with less white in tail, smaller white wing-patch; males have brown foreheads. Voice may be higher-pitched and laughing call slower than Northern. Plumage differences are clinal and variable.

Red-bellied and Golden-fronted hybridize where ranges overlap in Texas and Oklahoma.

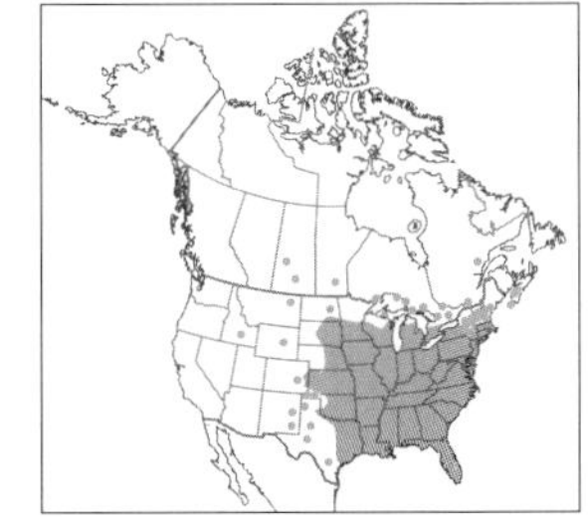

These four species of long-winged, rather delicate woodpeckers are quiet and inconspicuous. They drill rows of shallow holes in tree bark, returning to drink sap and eat insects.

Williamson's Sapsucker

Sphyrapicus thyroideus

L 9" WS 17" WT 1.8 oz (50 g)

The largest sapsucker. Very distinctive plumage; striking difference between male and female.

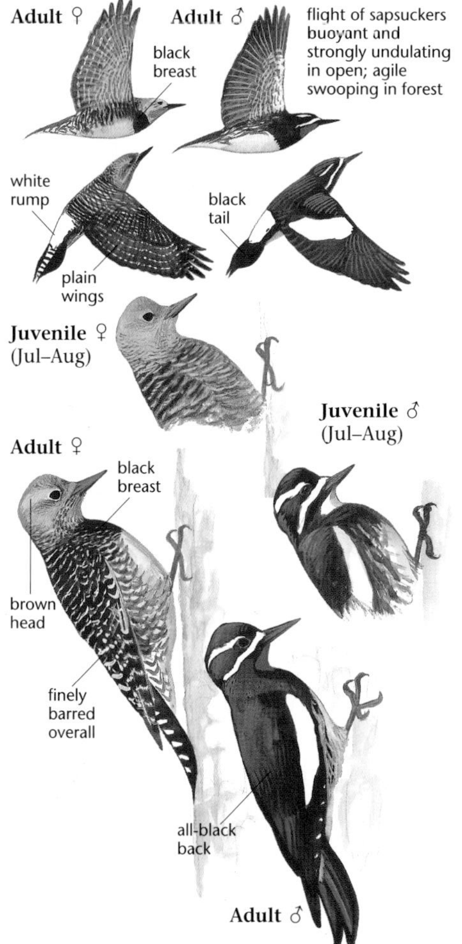
Adult ♀
Adult ♂
black breast
flight of sapsuckers buoyant and strongly undulating in open; agile swooping in forest
white rump
black tail
plain wings
Juvenile ♀ (Jul–Aug)
Juvenile ♂ (Jul–Aug)
Adult ♀
black breast
brown head
finely barred overall
all-black back
Adult ♂

Voice: Contact call a strong, clear *queeah;* less mewing than other sapsuckers. Initial burst of drumming faster than other sapsuckers, followed by loud taps with fading vibration; pauses between these latter bursts longer than other sapsuckers.

Red-breasted Sapsucker

Sphyrapicus ruber

L 8.5" WS 16" WT 1.8 oz (50 g)

Structure identical to Red-naped. Plumage less white and more red.

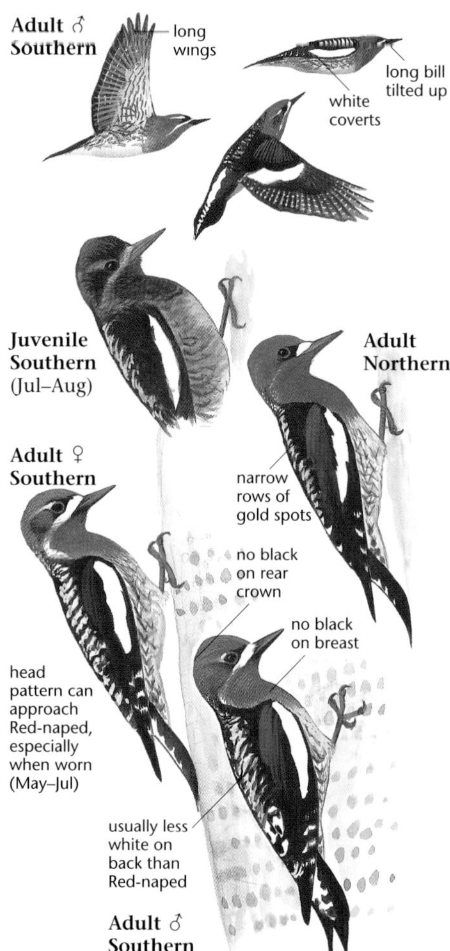
Adult ♂ Southern
long wings
long bill tilted up
white coverts
Juvenile Southern (Jul–Aug)
Adult Northern
narrow rows of gold spots
Adult ♀ Southern
no black on rear crown
no black on breast
head pattern can approach Red-naped, especially when worn (May–Jul)
usually less white on back than Red-naped
Adult ♂ Southern

Voice: All calls and drum similar to Yellow-bellied and Red-naped. Contact call may average lower and hoarser than Yellow-bellied, but variable. All sapsuckers are quiet in winter.

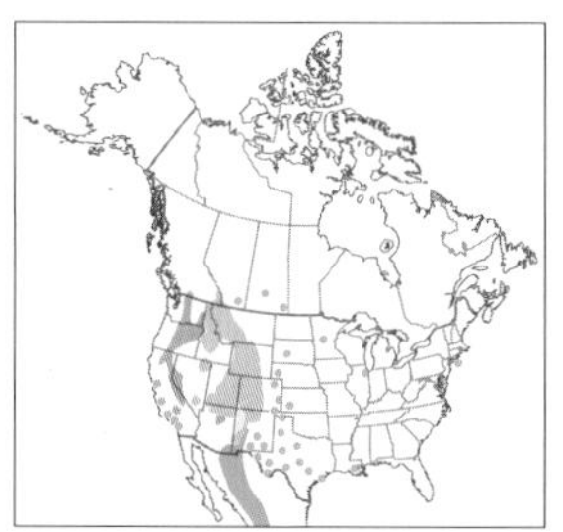

Red-breasted Sapsucker subspecies are divided sharply in southern Oregon. Northern populations are slightly larger, with brighter and more extensive red ending abruptly against yellow belly, little white on head, and narrow rows of yellow spots on back (vs. more white spots); sexes are alike. Juvenile has all-dark back.

Woodpeckers: Sapsuckers (continued)

These two species and the Red-breasted are very closely related. Together they form a cline from more red and less white in the west to less red and more white in the east.

Red-naped Sapsucker

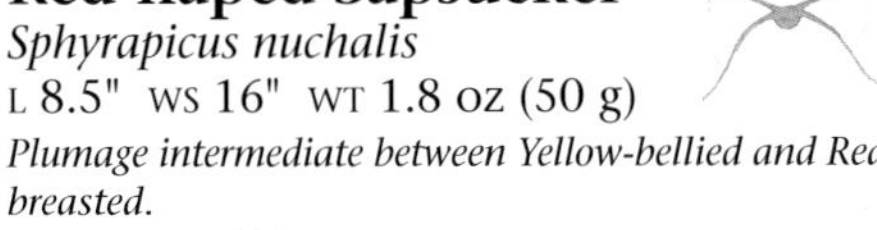

Sphyrapicus nuchalis

L 8.5" WS 16" WT 1.8 oz (50 g)

Plumage intermediate between Yellow-bellied and Red-breasted.

Adult ♂

uniform dark

Juvenile (Jul–Oct)

brown breast often retained until Dec; darker overall than juvenile Yellow-bellied; paler than all juvenile Red-breasted

white chin; sometimes all-red (such birds very similar to ♂ Yellow-bellied)

nape usually red, sometimes white

Adult ♀

extensive red with incomplete black border

white markings on back are most extensive in winter, least extensive when worn in summer; ♂ averages less white than ♀

white markings in two rows

Adult ♂

Yellow-bellied Sapsucker

Sphyrapicus varius

L 8.5" WS 16" WT 1.8 oz (50 g)

Very similar to Red-naped; some overlap in plumage.

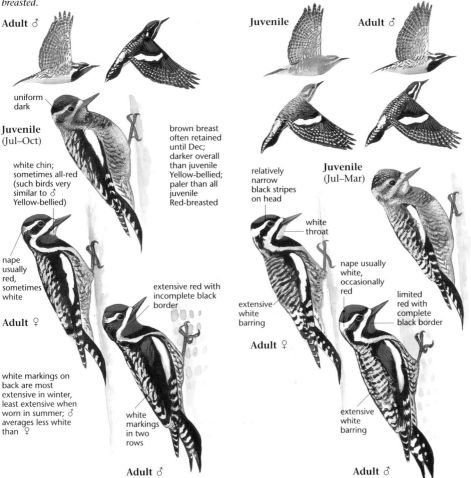

Juvenile

Adult ♂

relatively narrow black stripes on head

Juvenile (Jul–Mar)

white throat

nape usually white, occasionally red

extensive white barring

limited red with complete black border

Adult ♀

extensive white barring

Adult ♂

Voice: Essentially identical in these two species and Red-breasted. Contact call a nasal squealing or mewing *neeah;* on territory an emphatic *QUEEah.* Close contact call *wik-a-wik-a . . .* series, hoarse and uneven. In flight sometimes gives nasal *geert.* Drum a burst of about five rapid taps followed by gradual slowing with occasional double taps.

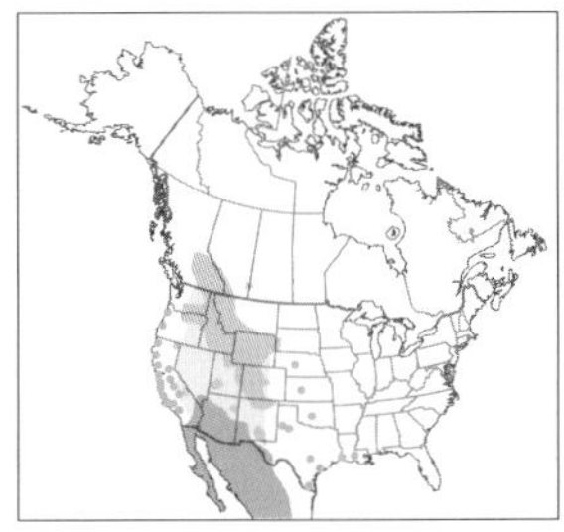

Plumage variation within each of the three closely related sapsuckers—and interbreeding where ranges overlap—produces a small number of individuals not safely identified. Note that any hybrid combination of the three species is possible. All plumage features (and molt on 1st winter birds) should match before an identification is made.

This species is distinguished from all woodpeckers except Hairy by white or whitish back and usually unmarked flanks. Found near or in woods, it often forages along small twigs or weed stalks.

Downy Woodpecker

Picoides pubescens

L 6.75" WS 12" WT 0.95 oz (27 g) ♂>♀

Our smallest woodpecker; dainty with very short bill.

Adult ♀ Eastern

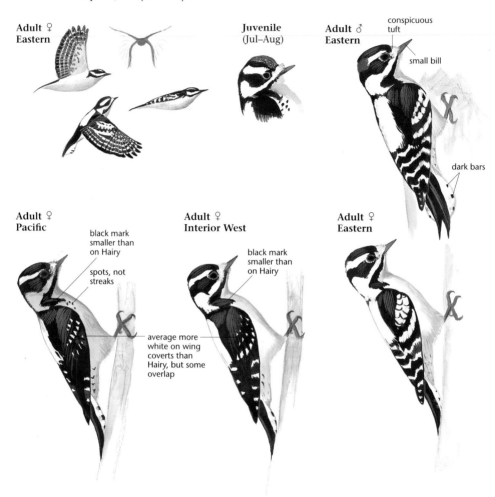

Juvenile (Jul–Aug)

Adult ♂ Eastern

conspicuous tuft

small bill

dark bars

Adult ♀ Pacific

black mark smaller than on Hairy

spots, not streaks

Adult ♀ Interior West

black mark smaller than on Hairy

average more white on wing coverts than Hairy, but some overlap

Adult ♀ Eastern

Voice: Contact call a short, gentle, flat *pik*. Rattle call slow, similar in quality to *pik* note; beginning slow and squeaky, ending lower, faster; varies from *kikikikiki* . . . to slow, squeaky *twi twi twi* . . . ; variable *chik* or *kweek* notes in spring. Rattle call of Pacific and Interior West birds often level or lacks low ending: a shorter, cut-off *kikikikikikikik*. Drum almost slow enough to count, short; usually several drums in fairly rapid sequence (9–16 per minute, only a few seconds pause between drums).

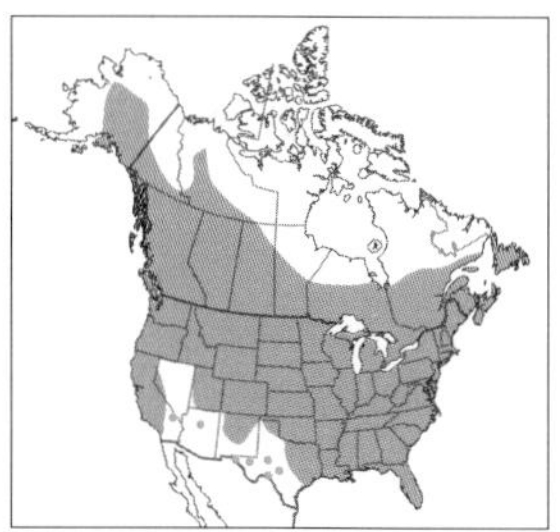

Geographic variation is significant but mostly parallels variation in Hairy Woodpecker. The two species are best separated by Downy's smaller overall size and relatively smaller bill. Bill size is slightly larger in males than females, so male Downy and female Hairy are the most similar. Also note more conspicuous tuft of nasal bristles on Downy. Downy usually has dark bars on outer tail feathers, but these are sometimes lacking and can be shown by Hairy populations in Newfoundland and the northwest. Other regional clues are noted above.

This species is very similar to Downy Woodpecker but larger, with a stronger voice. Hairy Woodpecker favors more mature woods and larger branches; it never forages on weed stalks.

Hairy Woodpecker

Picoides villosus

L 9.25" WS 15" WT 2.3 oz (66 g) ♂>♀

Large and strong, with relatively long and sturdy bill.

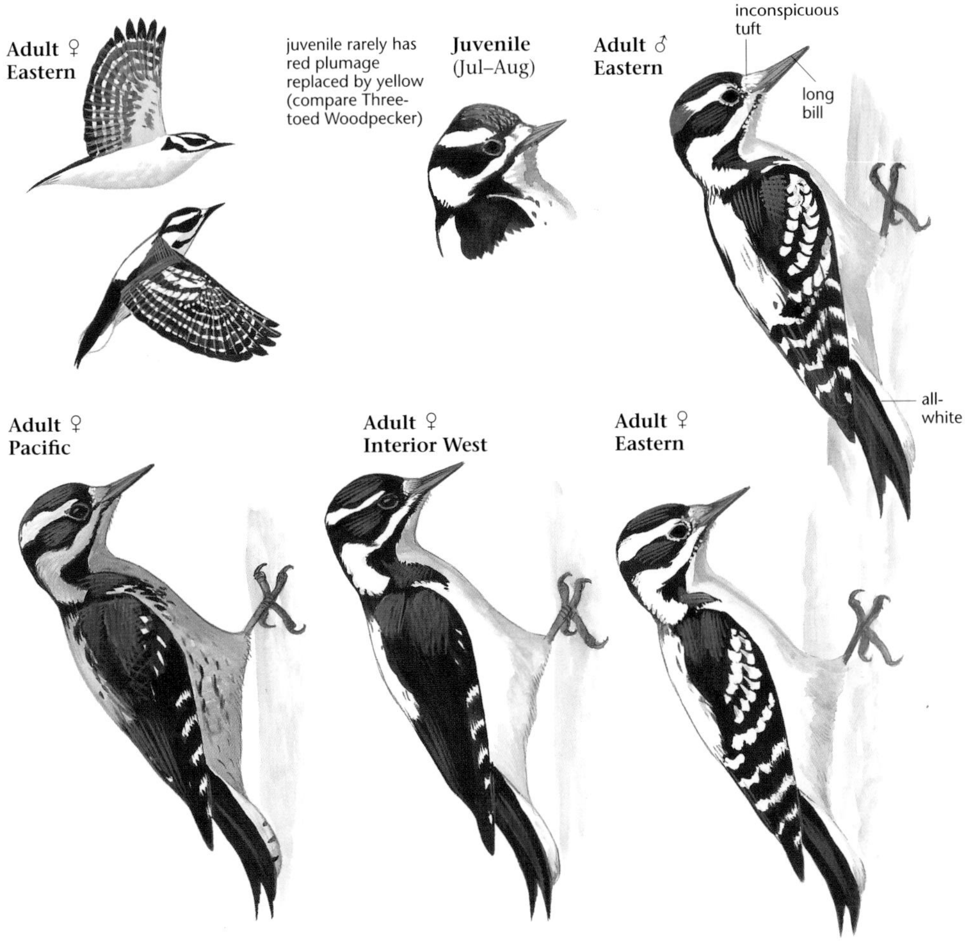

Adult ♀ Eastern

juvenile rarely has red plumage replaced by yellow (compare Three-toed Woodpecker)

Juvenile (Jul–Aug)

Adult ♂ Eastern

inconspicuous tuft

long bill

all-white

Adult ♀ Pacific

Adult ♀ Interior West

Adult ♀ Eastern

Voice: Contact call a sharp, strong *peek* or *peech,* sharper, louder, and higher-pitched than Downy. When agitated a stuttering *peek rr krr.* Rattle call sharp and high like contact call: a rapid series of notes on one pitch; variable high *kweek . . .* notes in spring. Pacific and Interior West calls may be harsher than Eastern. Drum very fast buzzing usually slowing at end; notes indistinguishable, fairly long, usually long pause between drums, four to nine per minute.

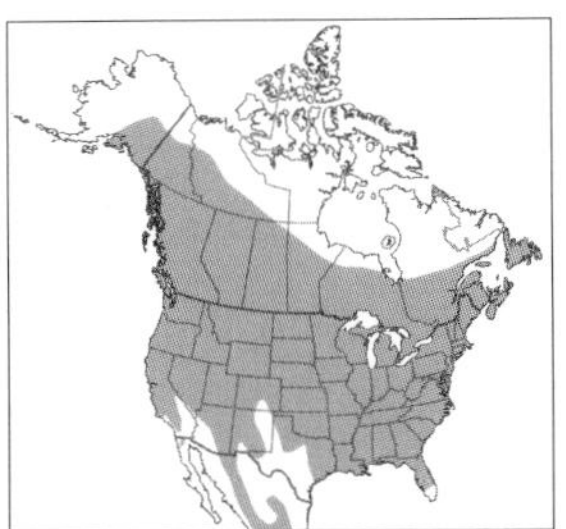

Variation, as in Downy, is marked but clinal. Pacific populations are dark and heavily marked. Interior West populations are whitish below but extensively black above. Most others (Taiga and Eastern) are whitish below with extensive white on back and wing coverts. Newfoundland population is darker, resembling Interior West birds.

Typical Woodpeckers (continued)

Three-toed and Black-backed Woodpeckers lack inner rear toes. They can be found in high density where large numbers of recently dead trees (as from a fire or insect outbreak) provide food.

Three-toed Woodpecker

Picoides tridactylus

L 8.75" WS 15" WT 2.3 oz (65 g)

Size and shape similar to Hairy Woodpecker, but stockier, short-billed, and shorter-tailed. Smaller, shorter-necked, and shorter-billed than Black-backed.

Adult ♀

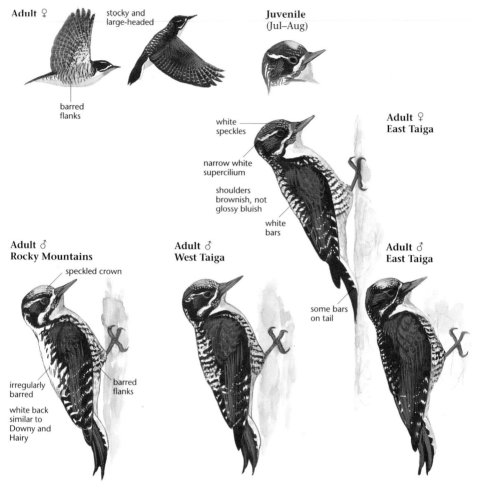

stocky and large-headed

barred flanks

Juvenile
(Jul–Aug)

Adult ♀
East Taiga

white speckles

narrow white supercilium

shoulders brownish, not glossy bluish

white bars

some bars on tail

Adult ♂
Rocky Mountains

speckled crown

irregularly barred

barred flanks

white back similar to Downy and Hairy

Adult ♂
West Taiga

Adult ♂
East Taiga

Voice: Contact call a relatively low, flat *pwik;* similar to Downy but deeper, more hollow or wooden; weaker than Black-backed. Rattle call short, shrill *kli kli kli kli kli;* varied *twiit twiit*, etc. Drum short, slow, speeding up and trailing off at end, two per minute; slower and shorter than Black-backed.

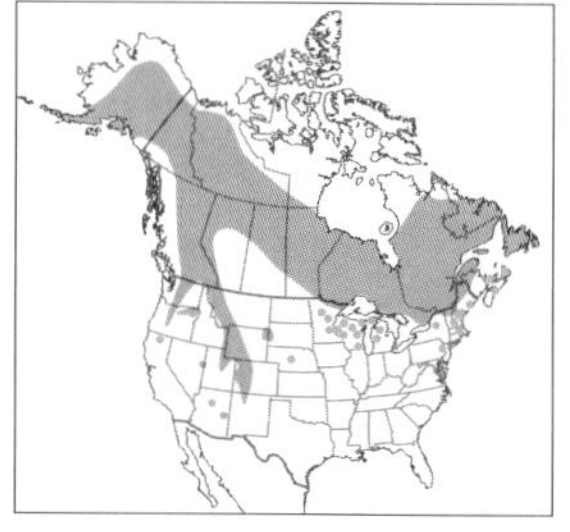

This species and Black-backed flake bark rather than excavating wood. This produces a quiet scraping and tapping sound and results in large patches of flaked bark on favored trees. Hairy Woodpecker uses the same foraging technique at times. Subspecies differ in plumage, but there is extensive variation and many intermediates. East Taiga birds are darkest, with limited white markings on back and forehead (equally dark birds occur in southern British Columbia). West Taiga populations are intermediate, and Rocky Mountain birds average slightly larger and have almost entirely white backs like Hairy Woodpecker.

Black-backed Woodpecker is closely related to Three-toed. The rare and declining Red-cockaded is found only in mature pine forests, where small social groups (clans) nest and forage together.

Black-backed Woodpecker

Picoides arcticus

L 9.5" WS 16" WT 2.5 oz (70 g)

Relatively large and strong; even larger than Hairy Woodpecker; appears large-headed, short-tailed.

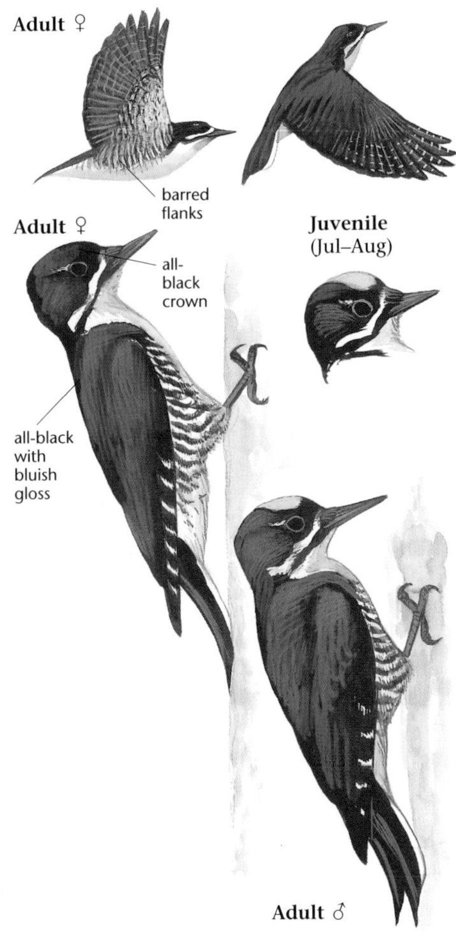
Adult ♀
barred flanks
Adult ♀
all-black crown
Juvenile (Jul–Aug)
all-black with bluish gloss
Adult ♂

Voice: Contact call reminiscent of Hairy but much deeper, hollow, wooden. Rattle call a peculiar grating, clicks, then a rasping snarl. Apparently no *wicka* type notes as in other *Picoides*. Drum fairly long, slow but distinctly accelerating.

Red-cockaded Woodpecker

Picoides borealis

L 8.5" WS 14" WT 1.5 oz (44 g)

Relatively slender, long-tailed, and small-billed.

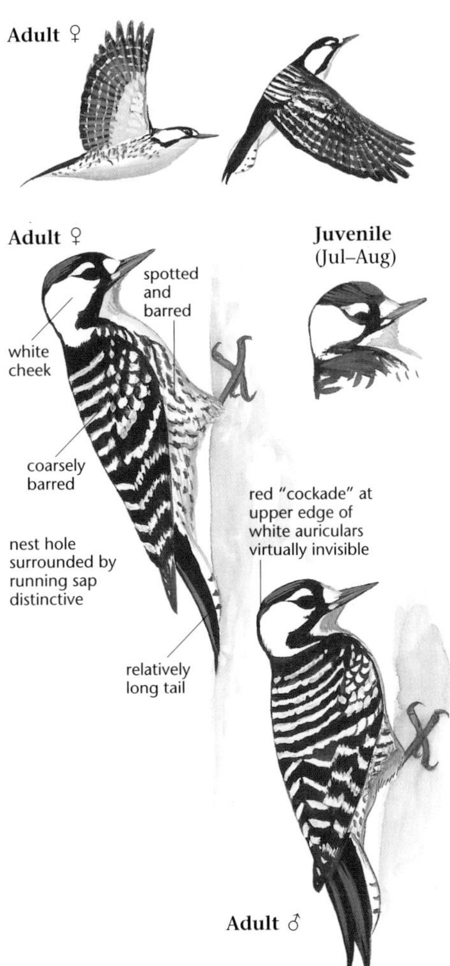
Adult ♀
Adult ♀
spotted and barred
Juvenile (Jul–Aug)
white cheek
coarsely barred
red "cockade" at upper edge of white auriculars virtually invisible
nest hole surrounded by running sap distinctive
relatively long tail
Adult ♂

Voice: Rather vocal in groups. Contact call a unique sharp, nasal, buzzy/squeaky *shirrp* or *shrrit*. Rattle call infrequent *shirrp-chrchrchrchr. . . .* Varied notes low and short to high clear *wica wica. . . .* Drum infrequent and rather quiet.

These two species resemble Downy Woodpecker but have barred backs, spotted underparts, and black enclosing the white "mustache" stripe. Nuttall's is found in oak woods, Ladder-backed in desert.

Nuttall's Woodpecker

Picoides nuttallii

L 7.5" WS 13" WT 1.3 oz (38 g)

Averages slightly larger than Ladder-backed; best distinguished by head and back pattern, voice.

Adult ♀

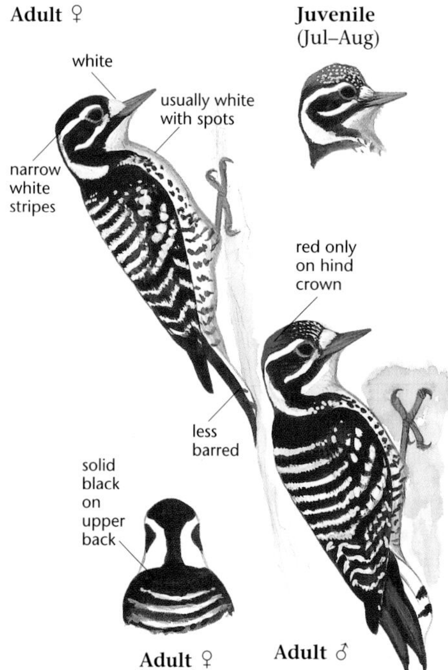
Adult ♀
Juvenile
(Jul–Aug)
white
usually white with spots
narrow white stripes
red only on hind crown
less barred
solid black on upper back
Adult ♀
Adult ♂

Voice: Contact call a sharp, rising, two- or three-note *pitik* (occasionally a single-note *pik*); quality like Hairy. Rattle call level and steady *pitikikik*. . . . Drum steady, medium speed, relatively long; noticeably longer and faster than Downy.

Ladder-backed Woodpecker

Picoides scalaris

L 7.25" WS 13" WT 1.1 oz (30 g)

Averages slightly larger than Downy Woodpecker.

Adult ♀

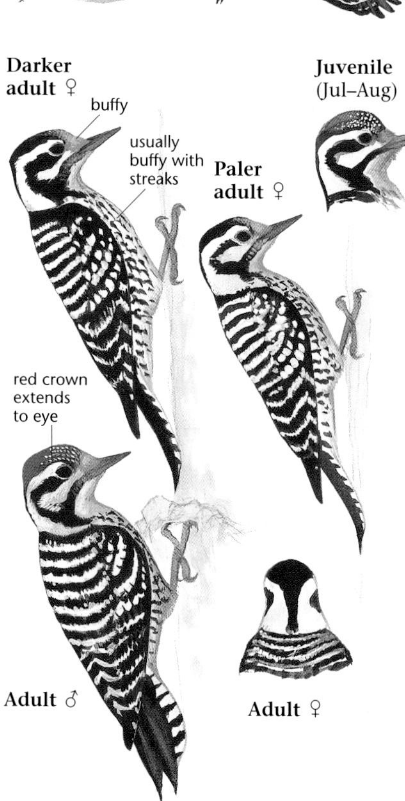
Darker adult ♀
Juvenile
(Jul–Aug)
buffy
usually buffy with streaks
Paler adult ♀
red crown extends to eye
Adult ♂
Adult ♀

Voice: Contact call a sharp *pwik* slightly lower-pitched and more musical than Downy. Rattle call always ends with low, grating notes *kweek-weekweekweekweechrchr*. Drum very rapid buzzing, medium length (about 1 sec long); shorter and faster than Nuttall's.

Nuttall's Woodpecker occasionally hybridizes with Downy and Ladder-backed where ranges overlap.

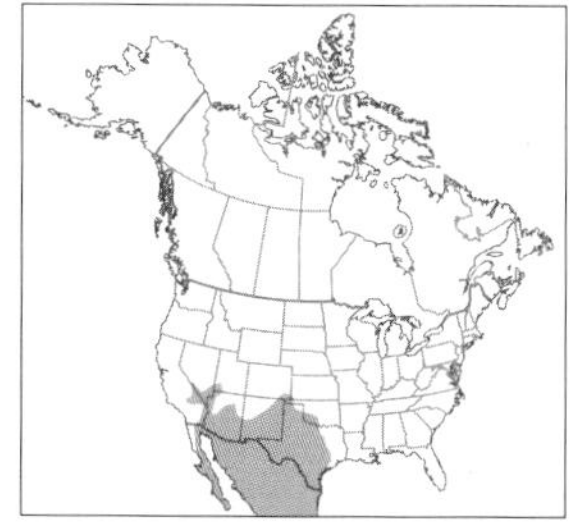

These species both have distinctive plumage, but their habits and voice are typical of the genus *Picoides*. Arizona is found in oak woods, White-headed in mountain conifers.

Arizona Woodpecker

Picoides arizonae

L 7.5" WS 14" WT 1.6 oz (47 g) ♂>♀

Our only brown-backed woodpecker; stocky and dark. Formerly known as Strickland's Woodpecker.

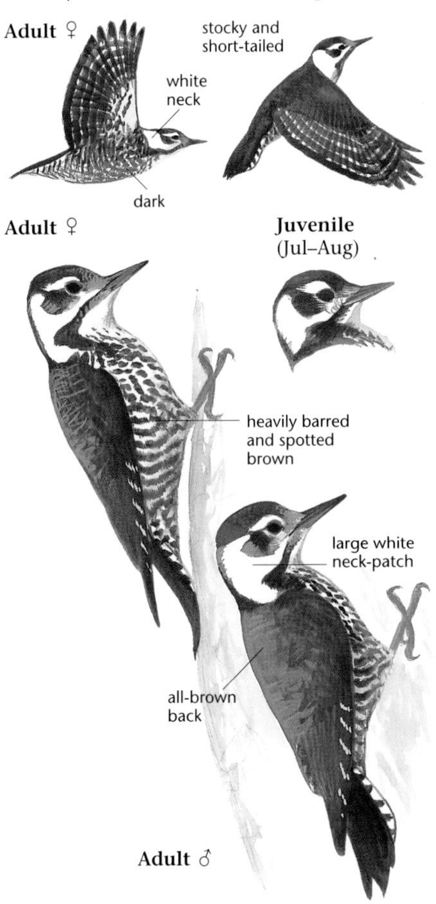
Adult ♀
stocky and short-tailed
white neck
dark
Adult ♀
Juvenile (Jul–Aug)
heavily barred and spotted brown
large white neck-patch
all-brown back
Adult ♂

Voice: Contact call a sharp *keech* similar to Hairy but higher, distinctly long and squeaky. Rattle call of grating notes, descending *keechrchrchrchr.* Drum long, three to four per minute.

White-headed Woodpecker

Picoides albolarvatus

L 9.25" WS 16" WT 2.1 oz (61 g) ♂>♀

Unique plumage; the only North American bird with black body and white head.

Adult ♀
white patch (compare Acorn)

Adult ♀
white head
Juvenile (Jul–Aug)
all-black
Adult ♂

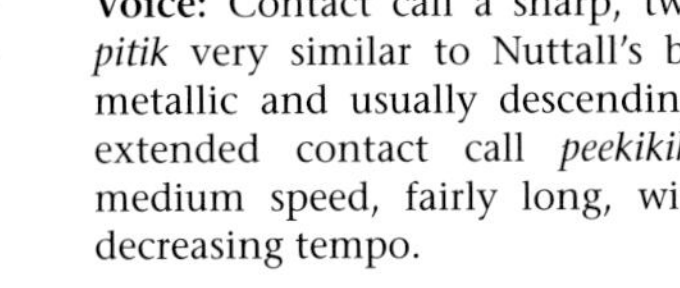

Voice: Contact call a sharp, two- or three-note *pitik* very similar to Nuttall's but higher, more metallic and usually descending. Rattle call an extended contact call *peekikikikikkikik*. Drum medium speed, fairly long, with increasing or decreasing tempo.

Flickers are large, distinctive woodpeckers often seen on the ground in open areas, eating ants. Their bright flight feathers and white rumps are instantly recognizable in flight.

Gilded Flicker

Colaptes chrysoides

L 11" WS 18" WT 3.9 oz (111 g)

Very similar to Northern Flicker but averages smaller and shorter-winged and differs in plumage details.

Adult ♀

yellow

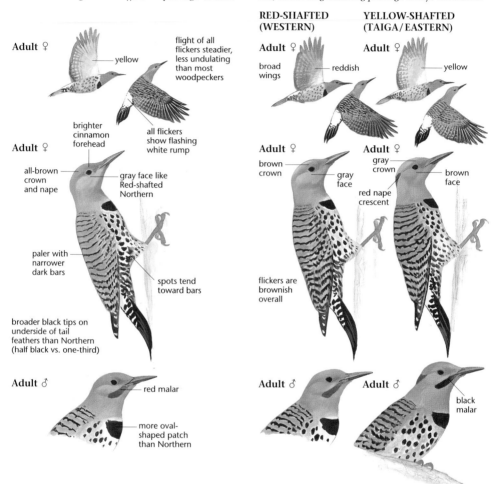

flight of all flickers steadier, less undulating than most woodpeckers

all flickers show flashing white rump

Adult ♀

brighter cinnamon forehead

all-brown crown and nape

gray face like Red-shafted Northern

paler with narrower dark bars
spots tend toward bars
broader black tips on underside of tail feathers than Northern (half black vs. one-third)

Adult ♂

red malar

more oval-shaped patch than Northern

Northern Flicker

Colaptes auratus

L 12.5" WS 20" WT 4.6 oz (130 g)

Large, with long, slightly downcurved bill, fairly long tail, broad wings. Striking plumage always distinctive.

RED-SHAFTED (WESTERN)
YELLOW-SHAFTED (TAIGA/EASTERN)
Adult ♀
broad wings
reddish
Adult ♀
yellow
Adult ♀
brown crown
gray face
Adult ♀
gray crown
brown face
red nape crescent
flickers are brownish overall
Adult ♂
Adult ♂
black malar

Voice: Both species essentially identical but calls of Gilded average higher-pitched. Contact call a high, piercing, clear *keew;* when flushed a soft, muffled *bwirr.* Close contact a soft, lilting *wik-a-wik-a-wik-a. . . .* Song a long, strong, relatively low-pitched series *kwikwikwikwi . . .* continued steadily for up to 15 seconds. Drum averages moderate to fast speed, but variable, overlapping many species.

Hybrids between Red-shafted Northern and Gilded occur regularly in the narrow range overlap. Red-shafted and Yellow-shafted Northern intergrade broadly in the Great Plains and western Canada, with intermediate birds frequent over most of the continent.

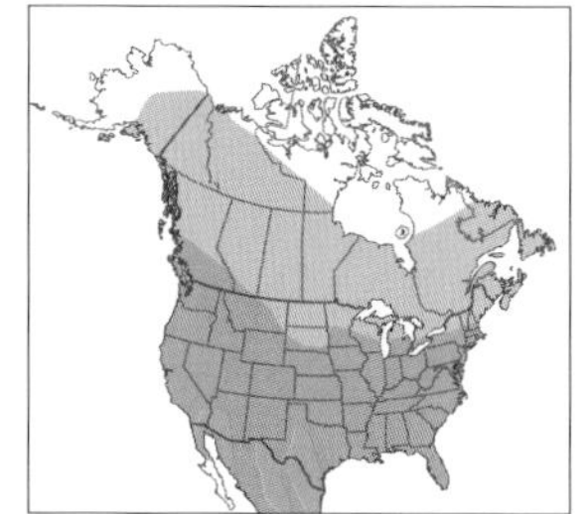

PILEATED WOODPECKER

Our largest woodpecker, this spectacular crow-size species is found in mature forests, where it searches for its favorite food—carpenter ants—by excavating large rectangular holes.

Pileated Woodpecker

Dryocopus pileatus

L 16.5" WS 29" WT 10 oz (290 g) ♂>♀

Long-necked, broad-winged, and long-tailed, with prominent crest. Unmistakable, although crows with white in wings (occasional) may cause momentary confusion in flight.

Adult ♀

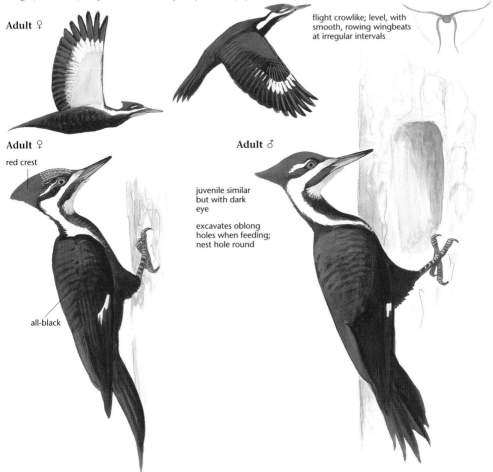

flight crowlike; level, with smooth, rowing wingbeats at irregular intervals

Adult ♀

red crest

all-black

Adult ♂

juvenile similar but with dark eye

excavates oblong holes when feeding; nest hole round

Voice: Contact call single, loud, deep, resonant *wek* or *kuk* notes, often given in flight, with higher-pitched calls on landing; often a slow series of *wek* notes; like flickers but slower, with irregular rhythm and deeper, wilder sound. Main territorial call higher-pitched *kuk kuk keekeekeekeekeekeekeekuk kuk*. Drum slow, powerful, accelerating and trailing off at end; short or up to three seconds long with slight variations in tempo and intensity throughout, only one or two per minute.

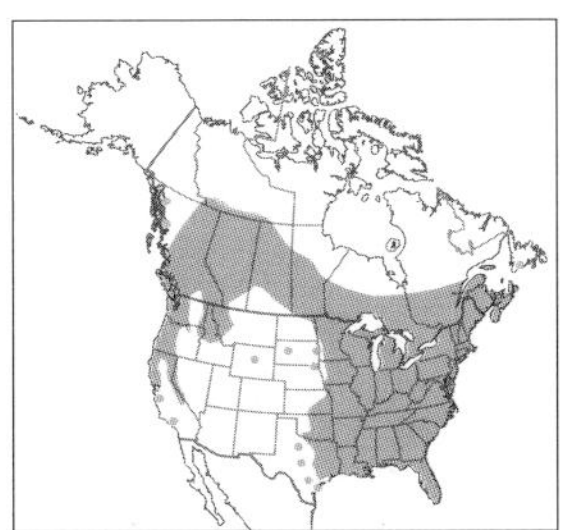

Tyrant Flycatchers

Family: Tyrannidae

37 species in 10 genera. Most have drab plumage and short, rather broad-based, flattened bills. Small species are found mainly in brushy woods. Larger species are more conspicuous and aggressive. All feed mainly on insects captured in flight; flight is strong, buoyant, and agile, with quick turns and abrupt movements as birds pursue insects. Flycatching habits are also employed by warblers, kinglets, gnatcatchers, hummingbirds, and others. Most species sort out into well-defined groups; plumage and structure are so similar within groups that voice is the primary field mark. Nest structure and placement offer useful clues. Adults are shown.

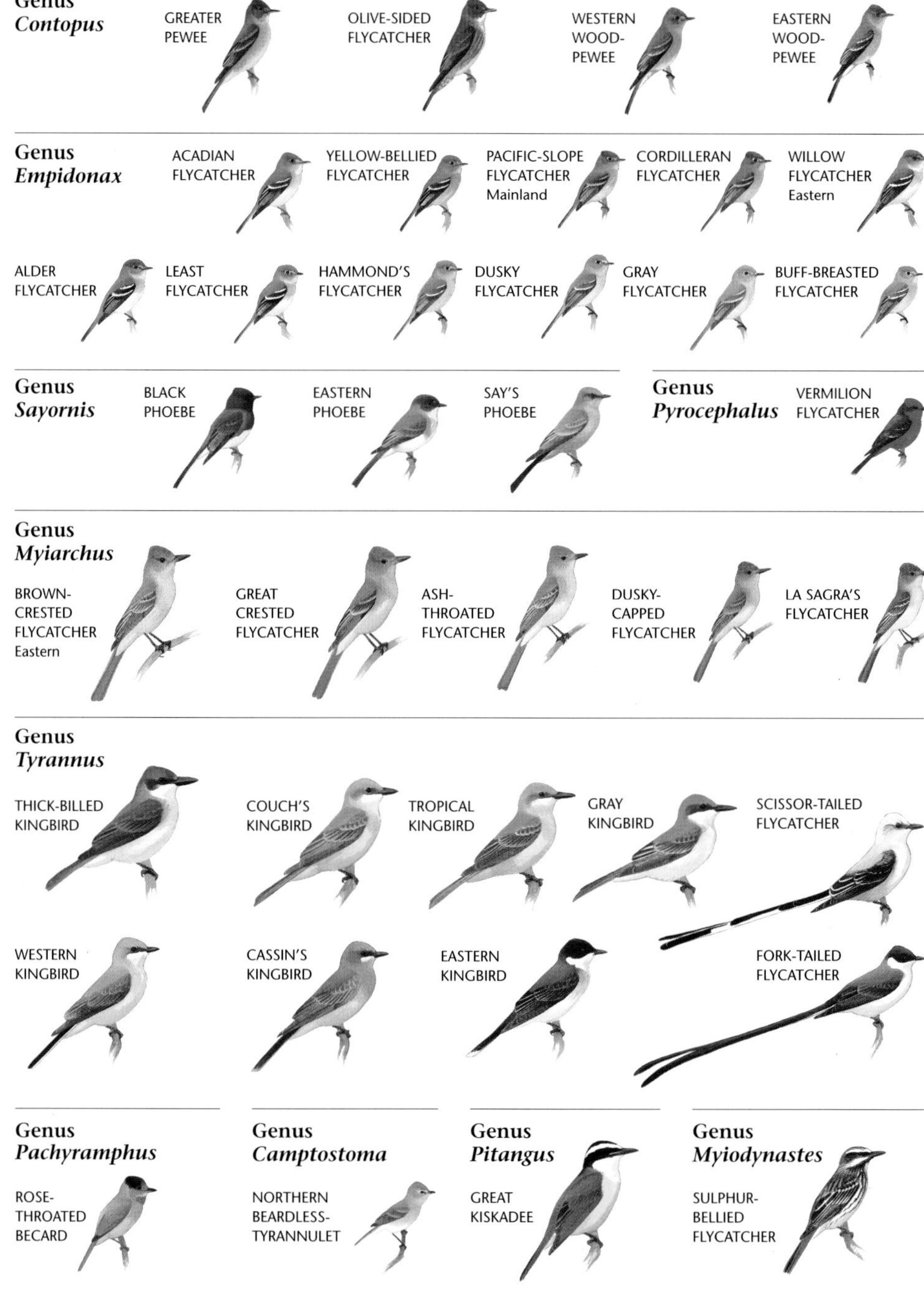

Genus
Contopus
GREATER PEWEE
OLIVE-SIDED FLYCATCHER
WESTERN WOOD-PEWEE
EASTERN WOOD-PEWEE
Genus
Empidonax
ACADIAN FLYCATCHER
YELLOW-BELLIED FLYCATCHER
PACIFIC-SLOPE FLYCATCHER Mainland
CORDILLERAN FLYCATCHER
WILLOW FLYCATCHER Eastern
ALDER FLYCATCHER
LEAST FLYCATCHER
HAMMOND'S FLYCATCHER
DUSKY FLYCATCHER
GRAY FLYCATCHER
BUFF-BREASTED FLYCATCHER
Genus
Sayornis
BLACK PHOEBE
EASTERN PHOEBE
SAY'S PHOEBE
Genus
Pyrocephalus
VERMILION FLYCATCHER
Genus
Myiarchus
BROWN-CRESTED FLYCATCHER Eastern
GREAT CRESTED FLYCATCHER
ASH-THROATED FLYCATCHER
DUSKY-CAPPED FLYCATCHER
LA SAGRA'S FLYCATCHER
Genus
Tyrannus
THICK-BILLED KINGBIRD
COUCH'S KINGBIRD
TROPICAL KINGBIRD
GRAY KINGBIRD
SCISSOR-TAILED FLYCATCHER
WESTERN KINGBIRD
CASSIN'S KINGBIRD
EASTERN KINGBIRD
FORK-TAILED FLYCATCHER
Genus
Pachyramphus
ROSE-THROATED BECARD
Genus
Camptostoma
NORTHERN BEARDLESS-TYRANNULET
Genus
Pitangus
GREAT KISKADEE
Genus
Myiodynastes
SULPHUR-BELLIED FLYCATCHER

Small Tropical Flycatchers

These tropical species are not closely related to other flycatchers or to each other. Rose-throated Becard is found in riparian woods, Beardless-Tyrannulet in dense brush and low trees, usually near water.

Rose-throated Becard

Pachyramphus aglaiae

L 7.25" WS 12" WT 1.1 oz (30 g)

Stocky, stout-billed, and short-tailed.

Juvenile

Adult ♂

short ninth primary

rufous tail

nest large and globular, suspended near tip of long branch

Juvenile (Jun–Aug)

dark cap

rufous

buffy

Adult ♂

all-gray with dark crown

Adult ♀

1st year ♂ similar

Adult ♂

inconspicuous rose throat-patch

gray

Voice: Common call a very high, thin whistle *sweetsoo* or *seeelee*. Also a high, squeaky, nasal chatter often ending with thin, descending note *kit-kiddleit-ti-ti-teew;* a very high, ringing *tzeeeeew*.

Northern Beardless-Tyrannulet

Camptostoma imberbe

L 4.5" WS 7" WT 0.26 oz (7.5 g)

Very small with short, narrow tail; tall, bushy crest; and very short, blunt-tipped bill.

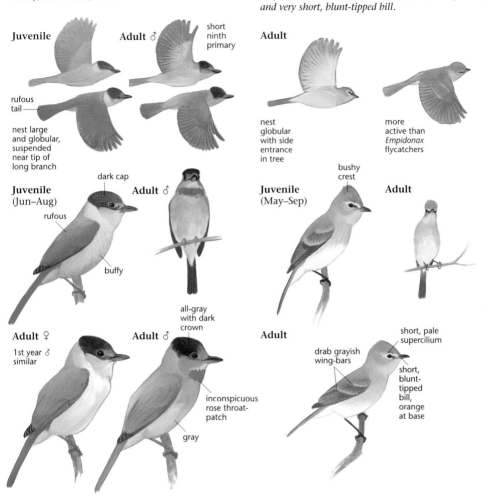

Adult

nest globular with side entrance in tree

more active than *Empidonax* flycatchers

Juvenile (May–Sep)

bushy crest

Adult

Adult

short, pale supercilium

drab grayish wing-bars

short, blunt-tipped bill, orange at base

Voice: Song lazy, clear, piping whistles in descending series usually introduced by short, rising series *piti pi pi PEEE dee dee* or slow series *peeh peeeh peeh peeh peeh peeh peeh peeh* gradually descending. Common call a clear, piping *peeehk;* also a descending *peeewk* and a chuckling *piklkhlk*.

Northern Beardless-Tyrannulet is named for its lack of rictal bristles (around the base of the bill); other flycatchers have rictal bristles.

Large Pewees

These two species are similar to but larger and heavier than wood-pewees. Both nest in coniferous forests and choose a conspicuous treetop perch from which they chase large insects.

Greater Pewee

Contopus pertinax

L 8" WS 13" WT 0.95 oz (27 g)

Differs from Olive-sided by longer tail, rounder wingtips, thinner bill, and pointed crest.

Adult

long, notched tail

rather rounded wings

Adult

plain grayish

Juvenile (Jun–Nov)

thin, pointed crest

pale lores

gray-buff wing-bars

plain grayish underparts

Adult

Voice: Song a lazy, clear whistle *soo saay sooweeoo* ("Jose Maria") usually introduced by several gentle *hoo didip* phrases; phrase often repeated without song. Call a soft, low *pip* or *pip-pip-pip;* higher, softer, and slower than Olive-sided.

Greater Pewee is the only *Contopus* pewee that molts remiges on the breeding grounds (adults only, Jul–Aug). Other species molt entirely on the wintering grounds (Oct–Mar), so fall adults are very worn.

Olive-sided Flycatcher

Contopus cooperi

L 7.5" WS 13" WT 1.1 oz (32 g)

Large and sturdy, with tapered body, large head, pointed wings, short tail, and obvious dark "vest."

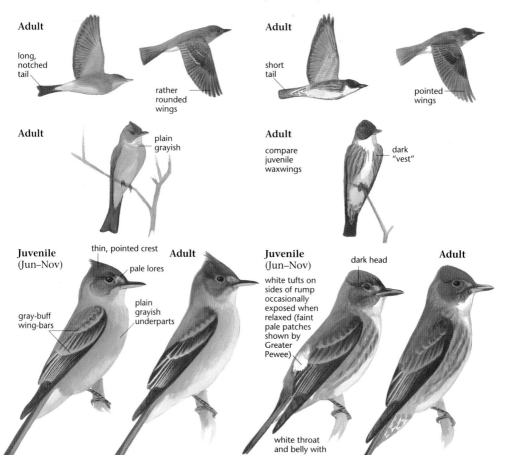

Adult

short tail

pointed wings

Adult

compare juvenile waxwings

dark "vest"

Juvenile (Jun–Nov)

dark head

white tufts on sides of rump occasionally exposed when relaxed (faint pale patches shown by Greater Pewee)

white throat and belly with contrasting dark flanks

Adult

Voice: Song a sharp, penetrating whistle *whip WEEDEEER* or "quick, three beers" (Pacific birds sing subtly different "what peeves yoou" with equal emphasis on all syllables). Call a low, hard *pep pep pep* with variations from soft, rapid *piw-piw-piw* to harder *pew, pew* to single note *pep* or *quip*.

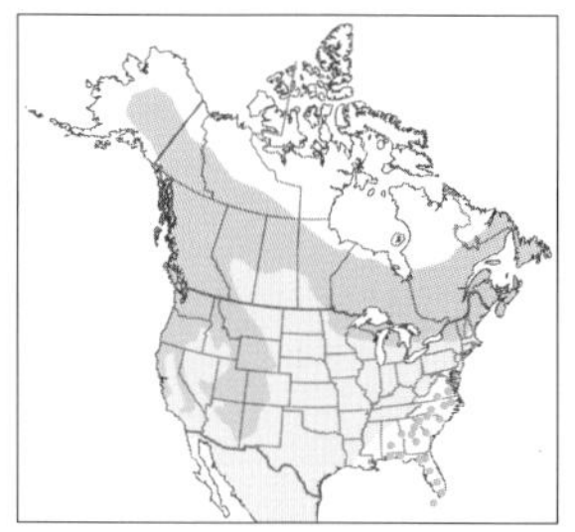

WOOD-PEWEES

These two species are very similar in all respects and are usually distinguishable only by voice. Found in and along edges of woods, they choose fairly high and conspicuous perches.

Western Wood-Pewee

Contopus sordidulus

L 6.25" WS 10.5" WT 0.46 oz (13 g)

Appearance essentially identical to Eastern; averages darker, slightly shorter-tailed, and longer-winged, but differences are subtle and overlapping (see Voice).

Adult

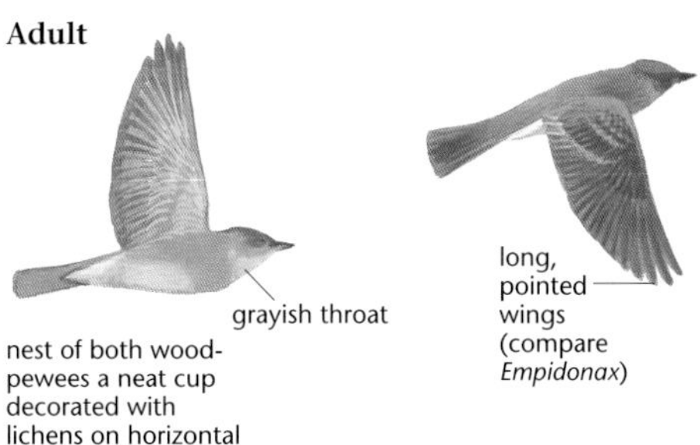
grayish throat
long, pointed wings (compare *Empidonax*)
nest of both wood-pewees a neat cup decorated with lichens on horizontal branch

Juvenile (Jun–Nov)

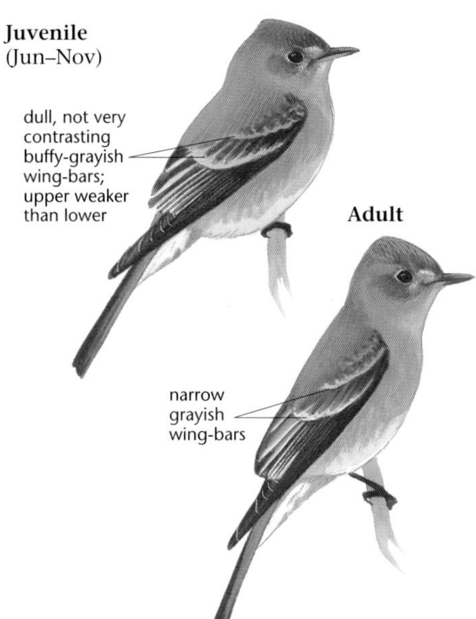
dull, not very contrasting buffy-grayish wing-bars; upper weaker than lower
Adult
narrow grayish wing-bars

Voice: Song a burry, nasal whistle *DREE-yurr* or *breerrr* or *brreeee* with distinctive rough quality. Also gives a variety of clear, whistled phrases virtually identical to Eastern: a thin, clear *peee-didip* or *pee-ee* or *peeaa*. Call a flat, sneezy *brrt* or *dup;* varied sputtering notes in aggression.

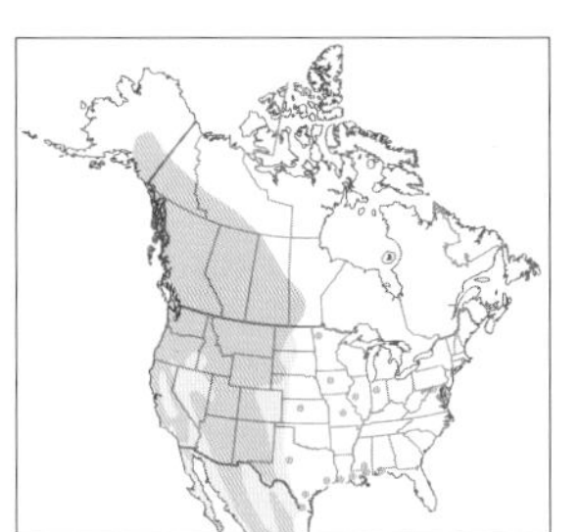

Eastern Wood-Pewee

Contopus virens

L 6.25" WS 10" WT 0.49 oz (14 g)

Like Western; smaller and more slender with longer wings and tail than Greater Pewee and Olive-sided Flycatcher.

Both wood-pewees are distinguished from all *Empidonax* flycatchers by longer wings, long primary projection, and relatively short legs; also by dark face with weak partial eye-ring, dusky "vest," and grayish smudges on undertail coverts. Wood-pewees do not flick their tails when perched; foraging birds choose a prominent, high perch and return to it repeatedly.

Eastern adult

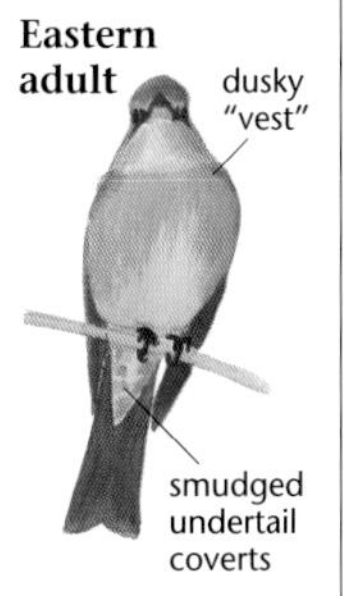
dusky "vest"
smudged undertail coverts

Western virtually identical

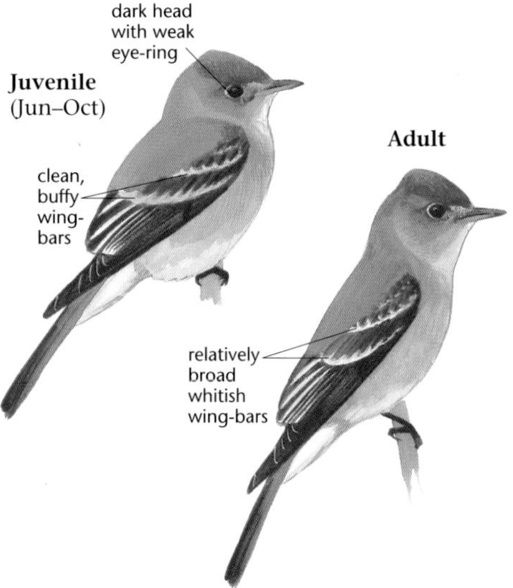
dark head with weak eye-ring
Juvenile (Jun–Oct)
clean, buffy wing-bars
Adult
relatively broad whitish wing-bars

Voice: Song plaintive, slurred, high, clear whistles *PEEaweee* and *peeyoooo;* also short, upslurred *pawee* (given by migrants), downslurred *peeaaa,* and others. Dawn song alternates regular song phrases with *peee-didip*. Call a flat, dry chip *plit;* sputtering notes in aggression.

Wing-bar patterns noted above may be the best way to distinguish these two species visually, but these characteristics overlap and are variable with age and wear. Western averages darker overall, evident in complete grayish breastband, darker centers of undertail coverts, less greenish color on back, and mostly dark lower mandible.

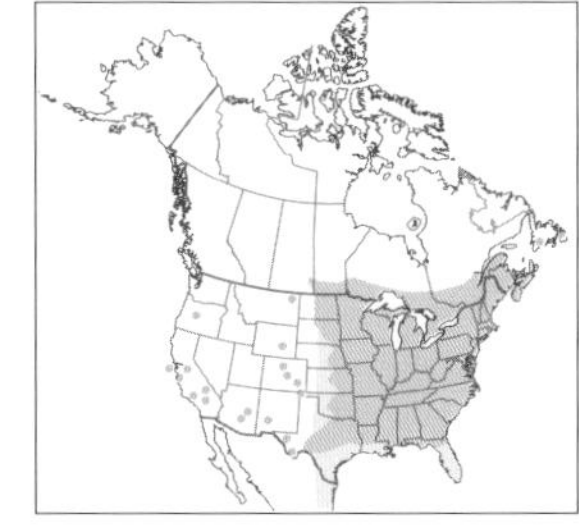

Western Flycatcher, very similar to Yellow-bellied, was recently split into these two species. They are found in shaded forests, often along streams; only males can be identified, by voice only.

Pacific-slope Flycatcher

Empidonax difficilis

L 5.5" WS 8" WT 0.39 oz (11 g)

Averages 5 percent smaller than Cordilleran, with 10 percent shorter bill, slightly more rounded wings, and paler, duller plumage, but nearly complete overlap.

Adult

Identification of *Empidonax* flycatchers is very difficult. Differences in overall color and pattern are subtle and easily misjudged as well as being subject to fading and other variation. Structural differences are subtle and overlapping. Identification should be based on a combination of characteristics including, most important, voice.

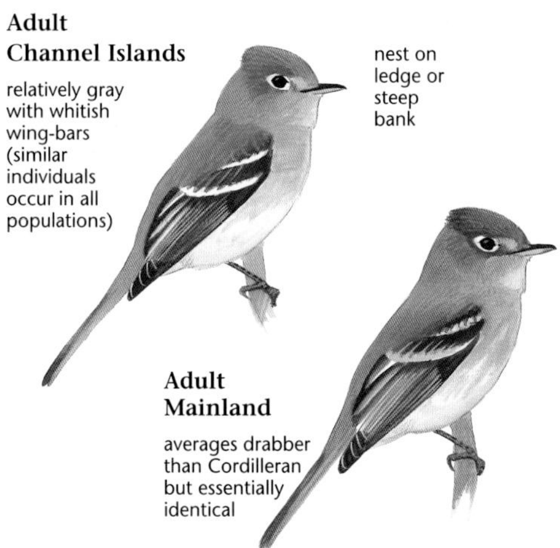
Adult
Channel Islands
relatively gray with whitish wing-bars (similar individuals occur in all populations)
nest on ledge or steep bank
Adult
Mainland
averages drabber than Cordilleran but essentially identical

Voice: Song higher-pitched and thinner than other *Empidonax*. Three phrases repeated in sequence: a high, sharp *tsip;* a thin, high, slurred *klseewii;* and an explosive *ptik*. Female call a very high, short *tseet*. Male position note a very high, thin whistle; Mainland gives a slurred *tseeweep*. Juvenile call a husky squeak *wiveet*.

Pacific-slope Channel Islands population averages drabber than Mainland. Differs also in voice: *tsip* note of song is downward-inflected rather than upward, and entire song is lower in pitch; male position note is a simple, rising *tsweep*.

Cordilleran Flycatcher

Empidonax occidentalis

L 5.5" WS 8" WT 0.39 oz (11 g)

Similar to Pacific-slope. Very similar to Yellow-bellied but less compact; slightly longer-tailed, shorter-winged, longer-billed; crest slightly ragged; browner overall with drabber wing markings.

Adult

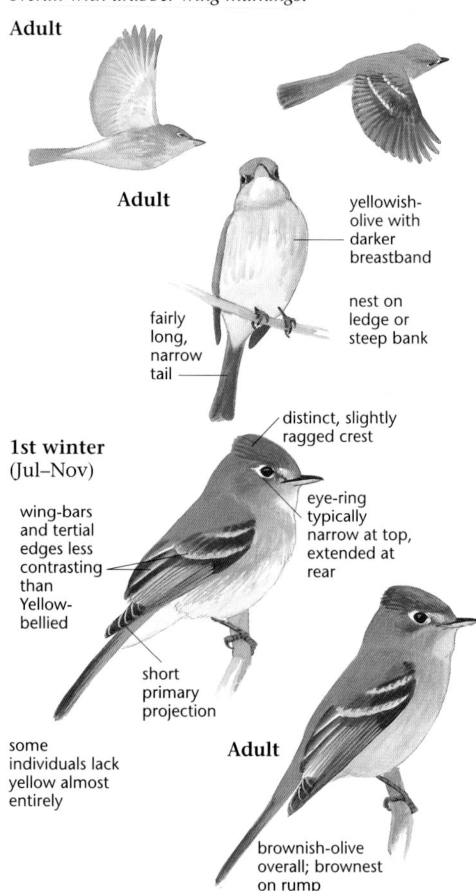
Adult
yellowish-olive with darker breastband
nest on ledge or steep bank
fairly long, narrow tail
distinct, slightly ragged crest
1st winter
(Jul–Nov)
eye-ring typically narrow at top, extended at rear
wing-bars and tertial edges less contrasting than Yellow-bellied
short primary projection
some individuals lack yellow almost entirely
Adult
brownish-olive overall; brownest on rump

Voice: Barely differs from Pacific-slope. In song, *ptik* note has first syllable higher than second (reverse of Pacific-slope). Male position note variable; two-part *tee-seet* distinctive, but other birds give rising *tsweep* like Channel Islands or slurred *tseeweep* like Mainland. Other calls very similar.

Acadian Flycatcher is found in broadleaf trees usually near water or high in trees within forests. Yellow-bellied nests in spruce woods; migrants are often found low within shady woods.

Acadian Flycatcher

Empidonax virescens

L 5.75" WS 9" WT 0.46 oz (13 g)

Large and long-winged. Flat forehead with distinct peak on rear crown and broad bill.

Adult

Adult

broad, pale bill

pale underparts

nest a shaggy cup in fork of horizontal branch

broad, straight-sided tail

1st winter (Jun–Feb)

greenish above

narrow, pale yellow eye-ring

pale malar contrasts little with whitish throat

long primary projection

Adult

often seen in treetops

Voice: Song an explosive, loud, high, rising *spit a KEET;* recalls some phrases of Red-eyed Vireo but always more explosive. Call a loud, flat *peek* and strong, squeaky *pweest;* sharper and higher than other *Empidonax* flycatchers. Common call on nesting grounds a relatively long, low *wheeeew;* also a slow, whistled *pwipwipwipwipwipwipwi.*

Yellow-bellied Flycatcher

Empidonax flaviventris

L 5.5" WS 8" WT 0.4 oz (11.5 g)

Small and compact with relatively long wings, short tail, and rounded head. Bright olive overall with sharply contrasting wing pattern.

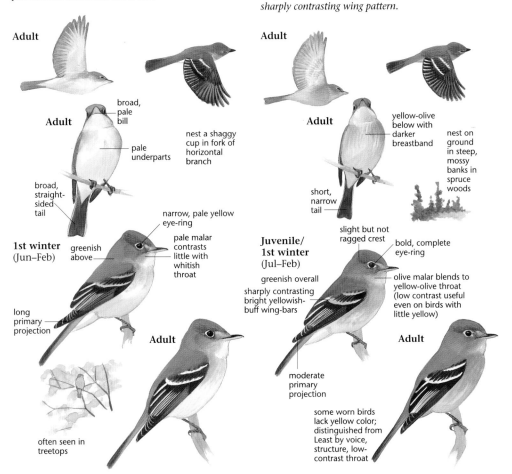

Adult

Adult

yellow-olive below with darker breastband

nest on ground in steep, mossy banks in spruce woods

short, narrow tail

Juvenile/ 1st winter (Jul–Feb)

slight but not ragged crest

bold, complete eye-ring

greenish overall

sharply contrasting bright yellowish-buff wing-bars

olive malar blends to yellow-olive throat (low contrast useful even on birds with little yellow)

moderate primary projection

Adult

some worn birds lack yellow color; distinguished from Least by voice, structure, low-contrast throat

Voice: Song a hoarse *chebunk* or *cheberk* very similar to Least Flycatcher but lower, buzzier, softer, without strong emphasis. Call a short, clear, rising whistle *tuwee* reminiscent of wood-pewees. Also shorter versions *pwee* or *peee;* a sharp, descending *pyew* (given by migrants); somewhat plaintive, long *peehk;* a sharp monotone *wsee.*

Some *Empidonax* flycatchers (Acadian, Hammond's, Buff-breasted, and occasionally Least) molt on the breeding grounds and migrate south in fresh plumage. Any *Empidonax* flycatcher seen molting in North America is likely to be one of these species; any worn adult seen in fall is likely to be one of the other species, which molt on the wintering grounds.

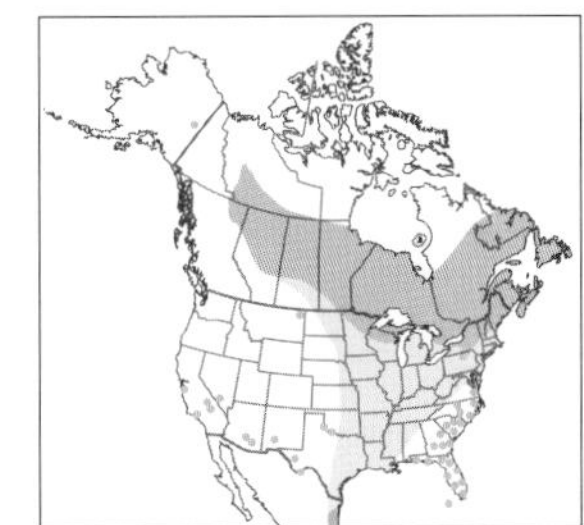

The most peweelike *Empidonax* flycatcher, this species is usually indistinguishable from Alder Flycatcher except by voice. It is found in low, brushy habitats, often near water.

Willow Flycatcher

Empidonax traillii

L 5.75" WS 8.5" WT 0.47 oz (13.5 g)

One of our largest Empidonax, *with relatively flat forehead and distinct peak on rear crown; long, broad bill; moderate primary projection; and broad, straight-sided tail.*

Adult

EASTERN

Adult

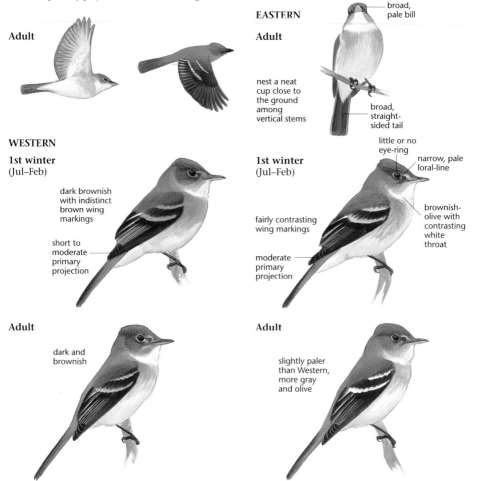

broad, pale bill

nest a neat cup close to the ground among vertical stems

broad, straight-sided tail

WESTERN

1st winter (Jul–Feb)

dark brownish with indistinct brown wing markings

short to moderate primary projection

1st winter (Jul–Feb)

little or no eye-ring

narrow, pale loral-line

fairly contrasting wing markings

brownish-olive with contrasting white throat

moderate primary projection

Adult

dark and brownish

Adult

slightly paler than Western, more gray and olive

Voice: Song a harsh, burry *RITZbew* or *RRRITZbeyew* or *rrrEEP-yew,* often alternating among these variations: sometimes merely a strong *rrrrrIP,* rough and low with emphatic rising ending (similar calls of Alder are not sharply rising); also *zweeoo, churr,* and *churr-weeoo,* suggesting Alder. Call a thick, liquid *whit* unlike Alder; averages lower and fuller-sounding than similar calls of other *Empidonax*.

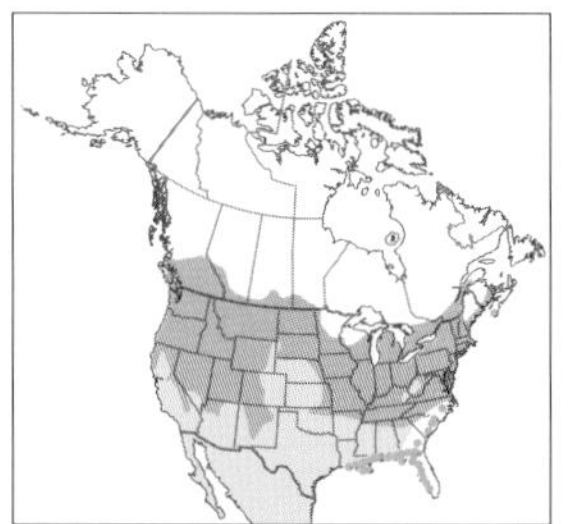

Eastern populations appear similar to Alder but average paler gray on the face, contrasting less with the throat. Western birds are slightly browner overall and most are also darker (but southwestern birds are pale); they have dingy whitish and less contrasting wing-bars and tertial edges, and the dingy eye-ring is less conspicuous than on Eastern birds. Western birds also average slightly shorter and more rounded wings with shorter primary projection than Eastern.

Alder Flycatcher is similar to Willow and is found in the same wet, brushy habitats. Least is found in forest clearings and edges, nesting in mature hardwood trees.

Alder Flycatcher

Empidonax alnorum

L 5.75" WS 8.5" WT 0.47 oz (13.5 g)

Virtually identical to Eastern Willow Flycatcher: fractionally longer-winged and -tailed, slightly shorter-billed, and possibly rounder-headed; averages greener-backed and darker-headed. Identify by voice.

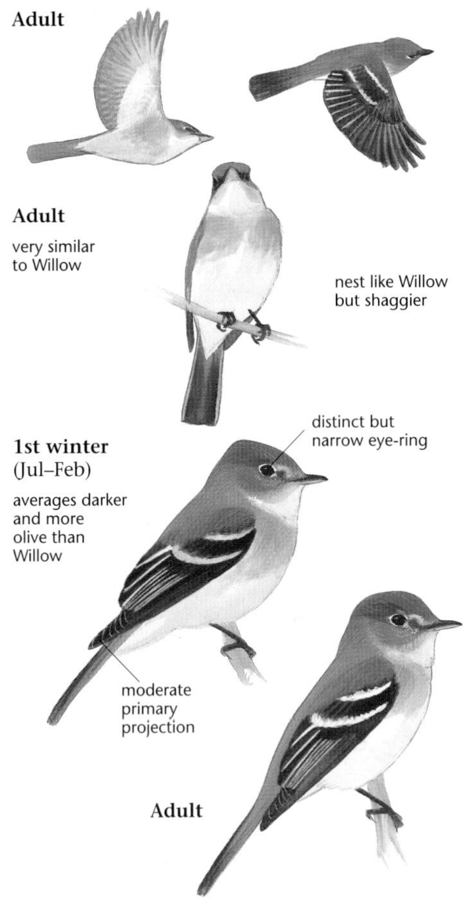
Adult
Adult
very similar to Willow
nest like Willow but shaggier
1st winter (Jul–Feb)
averages darker and more olive than Willow
distinct but narrow eye-ring
moderate primary projection
Adult

Voice: Song a harsh, burry *rreeBEEa;* sometimes merely an ascending *rrreep* or *rrreeea* similar to Willow but not as sharp or rising. Also low, clear, whistled *pew* and *peewi.* Call a flat *pip* reminiscent of single note of Olive-sided, unlike the *whit* of Willow and other *Empidonax.*

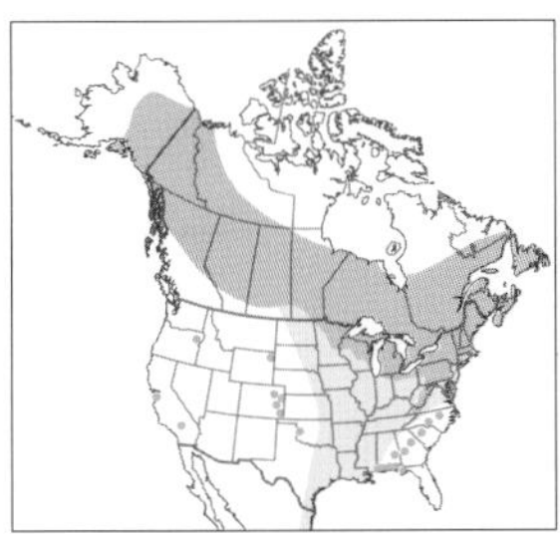

Least Flycatcher

Empidonax minimus

L 5.25" WS 7.75" WT 0.36 oz (10.3 g)

Small and compact, with short wings, relatively large head, short bill, and short, narrow tail.

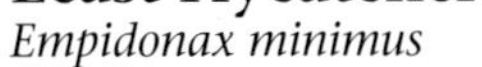

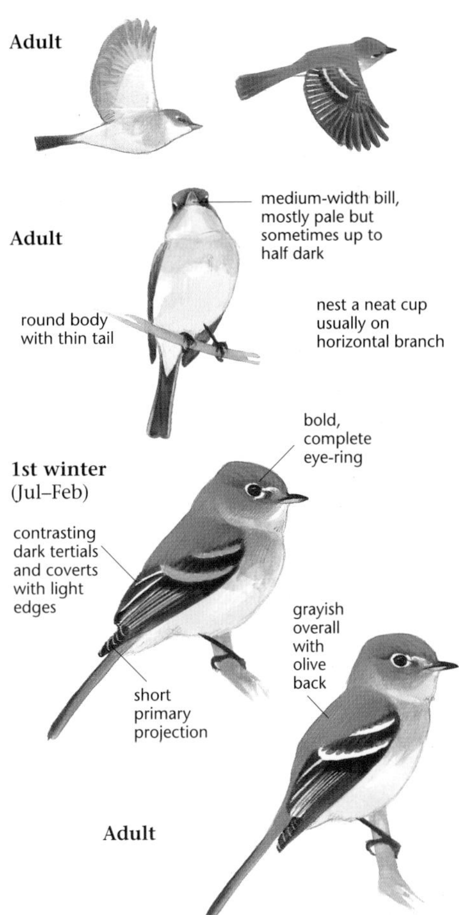
Adult
Adult
medium-width bill, mostly pale but sometimes up to half dark
round body with thin tail
nest a neat cup usually on horizontal branch
1st winter (Jul–Feb)
bold, complete eye-ring
contrasting dark tertials and coverts with light edges
grayish overall with olive back
short primary projection
Adult

Voice: Song an emphatic, dry *CHEbek* or *cheBIK* repeated rapidly. Call a sharp, dry *pwit* or *pit;* shorter, drier, and sharper than Willow. Also gives high *wees wees wees . . .* interspersed with *pit* notes.

Willow and Alder were formerly considered a single species (Traill's Flycatcher), and since few individuals can be identified, that name is still often used by birders.

Some *Empidonax* flycatchers (fewer as one gains experience) seem to show intermediate characteristics and should not be identified beyond the genus.

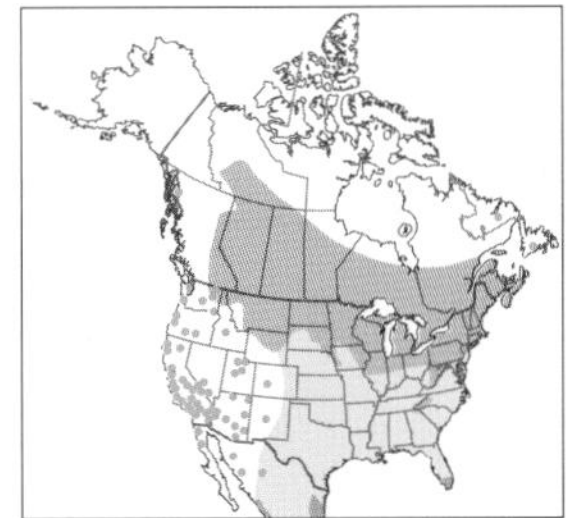

Flycatchers: Genus *Empidonax* (continued)

Although very similar in plumage, these two species differ in habitat, structure, and voice. Hammond's is usually found high in tall conifers, Dusky in low chaparral, brush, and small trees.

Hammond's Flycatcher

Empidonax hammondii

L 5.5" WS 8.75" WT 0.35 oz (10 g)

Small and compact, with short tail and long primary projection; bill very small and dark.

Adult

Adult

short, narrow, mostly dark bill

distinct "vest"

long wings

shorter, narrow tail, always notched

slight crest

nest high on horizontal branch

tiny, dark bill

1st winter (Jul–Feb)

rather dark olive breast and back contrasts with gray head

long primary projection

Adult

Voice: Song of three phrases (usually in this sequence): *tsi-pik* suggesting Least; *swi-vrk* high then scratchy; *grr-vik* lower and rougher than any phrase of Dusky. Phrases more strongly two-syllabled than Dusky; never includes high, clear notes. Call a sharp *peek*; sharper and higher than Alder. Also a low, whistled *weew*.

Dusky Flycatcher

Empidonax oberholseri

L 5.75" WS 8.25" WT 0.36 oz (10.3 g)

Small but not as compact as Hammond's: longer-tailed, shorter-winged, longer-billed; rounded head.

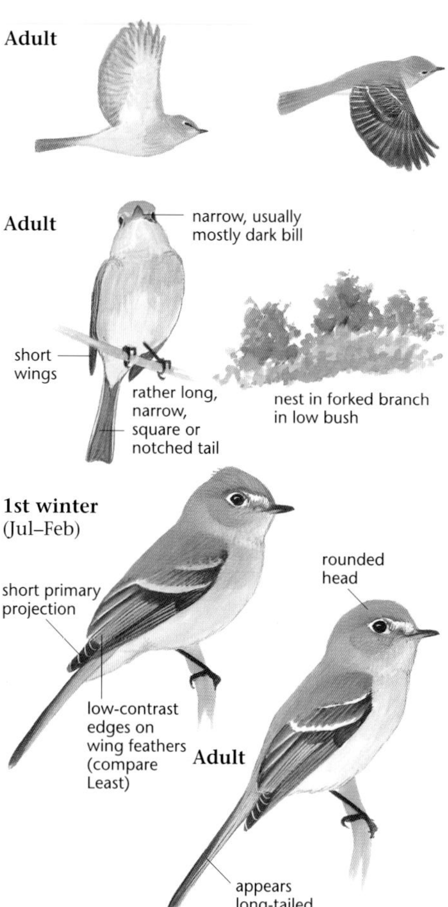
Adult
Adult
narrow, usually mostly dark bill
short wings
rather long, narrow, square or notched tail
nest in forked branch in low bush
1st winter
(Jul–Feb)
short primary projection
rounded head
low-contrast edges on wing feathers (compare Least)
Adult
appears long-tailed

Voice: Song of three phrases (usually in this sequence): a short, high, quick *sibip;* a rough, nasal *quwerrrp;* a clear, high *psuweet* similar to Pacific-slope Flycatcher position note. Call a soft, dry *whit* or fuller *twip* similar to Willow, Least, and Gray. Male call a soft, plaintive whistle *deew* or *dew-hidi* repeated at regular intervals.

These two species are distinguished from Least Flycatcher by their grayer throat, gray head contrasting with greenish breast and back, narrower bill with mostly dark lower mandible, and weak contrast on wing coverts and tertials. Best distinguished by voice.

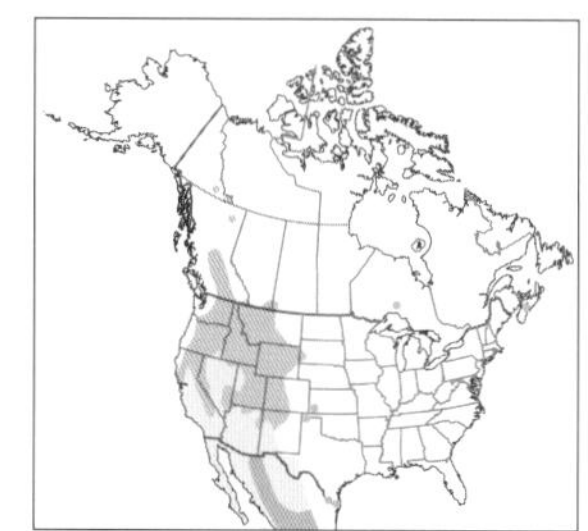

Flycatchers: Genus *Empidonax* (continued)

Gray, our longest *Empidonax,* is found in sagebrush and similar arid, bushy habitats. Buff-breasted, our smallest *Empidonax,* is found in open pine forests with some bushes.

Gray Flycatcher

Empidonax wrightii

L 6" WS 8.75" WT 0.44 oz (12.5 g)

Large, with long, narrow bill and long tail. Pale overall with distinctive tail-dipping action.

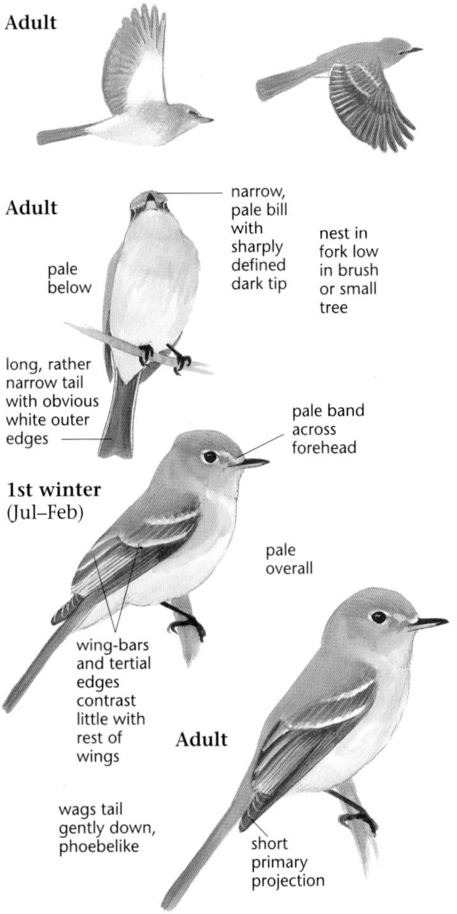

Adult

Adult

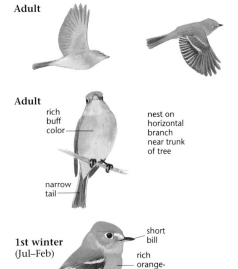

narrow, pale bill with sharply defined dark tip

nest in fork low in brush or small tree

pale below

long, rather narrow tail with obvious white outer edges

pale band across forehead

1st winter (Jul–Feb)

pale overall

wing-bars and tertial edges contrast little with rest of wings

Adult

wags tail gently down, phoebelike

short primary projection

Voice: Song of two phrases: mostly a rough, emphatic *jr-vrip* (or similar rough *jhrrr*) with a high, whistled *tidoo* interspersed; the two phrases are so different they seem unrelated. Also gives abrupt *chivip* and low, whistled *weew.* Common call a sharp, dry *whit* similar to Dusky, Least, and Willow Flycatchers.

The gentle downward tail wag of Gray Flycatcher is unique among *Empidonax* flycatchers. All other species flick their tails quickly upward, although Least occasionally gives a weak downward flick.

Buff-breasted Flycatcher

Empidonax fulvifrons

L 5" WS 7.5" WT 0.28 oz (8 g)

Small and dumpy, with narrow tail and very short bill.

Adult

Adult

rich buff color

nest on horizontal branch near trunk of tree

narrow tail

1st winter (Jul–Feb)

short bill

rich orange-buff on underparts

Adult

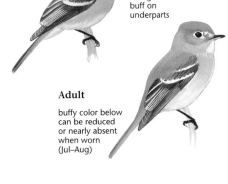

buffy color below can be reduced or nearly absent when worn (Jul–Aug)

Voice: Song of two similar phrases: sharp and musical, often alternating *PIdew, piDEW, PIdew, piDEW . . .*; also gives rolling *prrrew* or *pijrr.* Common call a hard, dry *pit* sharper and higher than the *whit* calls of other *Empidonax.*

Phoebes

These two species are similar in shape, habits, and voice. Both are found in open areas, usually near water; they choose low, conspicuous perches and dip their tails in a characteristic motion.

Black Phoebe

Sayornis nigricans

L 7" WS 11" WT 0.67 oz (19 g)

Averages slightly longer-winged and longer-tailed than Eastern, with peaked head and very different plumage.

Adult

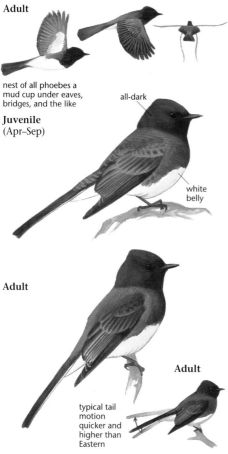

nest of all phoebes a mud cup under eaves, bridges, and the like

Juvenile (Apr–Sep)

all-dark

white belly

Adult
Adult

typical tail motion quicker and higher than Eastern

Voice: Song of two high, thin, whistled phrases usually alternated *sisee, sitsew, sisee, sitsew . . .* ; also gives high, thin, whistled *tseew* year-round. Common call a simple, high, clear chip like Eastern but flatter and more whistled.

Eastern Phoebe

Sayornis phoebe

L 7" WS 10.5" WT 0.7 oz (20 g)

Larger than Empidonax *and wood-pewees; relatively longer-tailed, with dark head and tail, black bill, weak wing-bars.*

Adult

long, dark tail

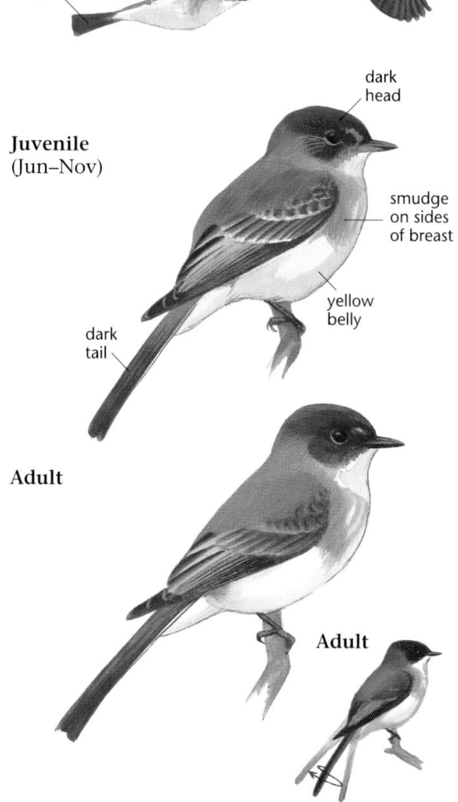

dark head
Juvenile
(Jun–Nov)
smudge on sides of breast
yellow belly
dark tail
Adult
Adult

Voice: Song of two rough, whistled phrases usually alternated *seeeriddip, seebrrr, seeeriddip, seebrrr . . .* ; also gives clear, whistled *weew* or *tiboo* and abrupt *wijik* year-round. Common call a distinctive simple chip: high, clear, and descending (sharper than Black).

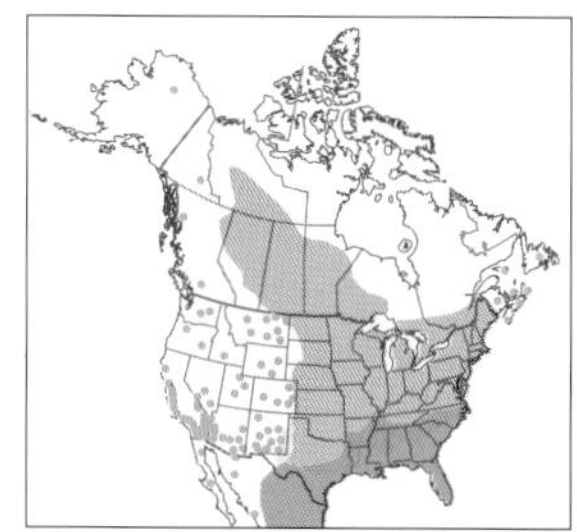

These species are distinctively colored. Say's Phoebe is found in open expanses: tundra, prairie, desert, fields. The smaller Vermilion Flycatcher is found in open bushes and trees near water.

Say's Phoebe

Sayornis saya

L 7.5" WS 13" WT 0.74 oz (21 g)

Slender and relatively small-headed; wings and tail longer than other phoebes.

Vermilion Flycatcher

Pyrocephalus rubinus

L 6" WS 10" WT 0.51 oz (14.5 g)

Small and short-tailed, with small bill; dips and spreads tail like phoebes.

Adult
black tail
very pale, translucent remiges
rounded wings
1st year ♀
Adult ♂
short, dark tail

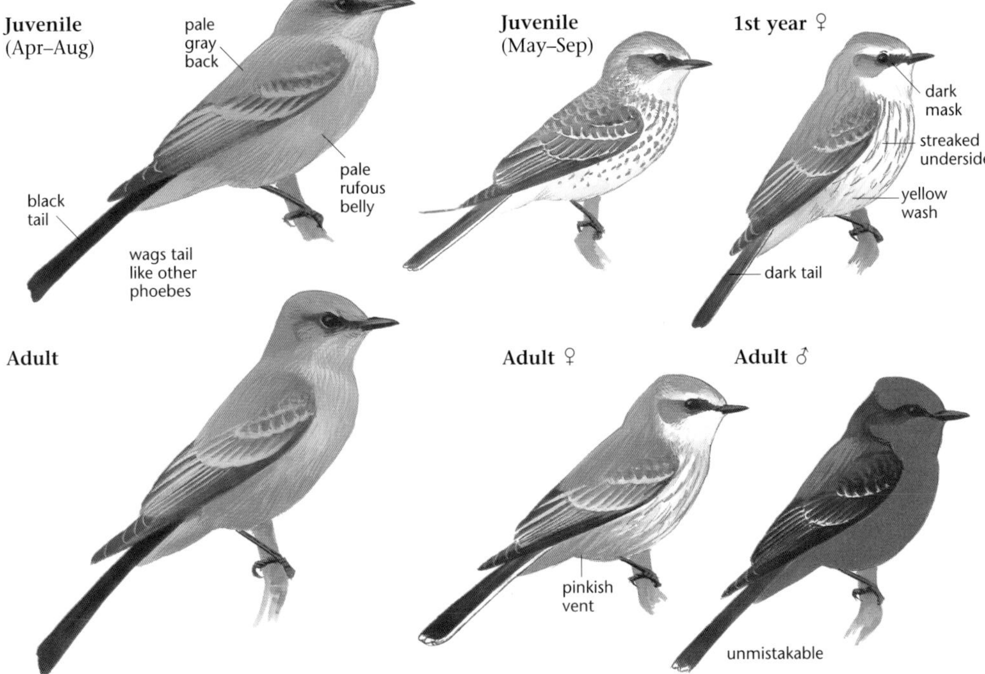
Juvenile (Apr–Aug)
pale gray back
pale rufous belly
black tail
wags tail like other phoebes
Adult
Juvenile (May–Sep)
1st year ♀
dark mask
streaked underside
yellow wash
dark tail
Adult ♀
Adult ♂
pinkish vent
unmistakable

Voice: Song of two relatively low, whistled phrases, usually alternated *pidiweew, pidireep, pidiweew, pidireep. . . .* Common call a low, plaintive, clear whistle *pdeeer* or *tueeee.*

Voice: Song of high, sharp, flat notes and a higher, rolling trill, falling at end *pit pit pit pidddrrrreedrr;* given from prominent perch or in flopping song flight with breast expanded. Common call a high, sharp *pees.*

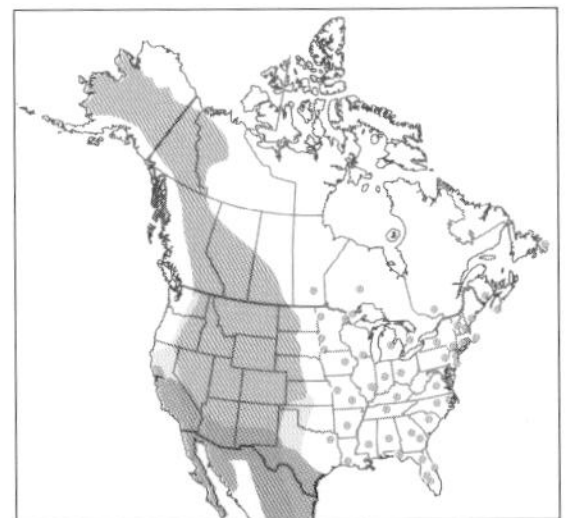

Vermilion Flycatcher
1st year ♂
Variable.

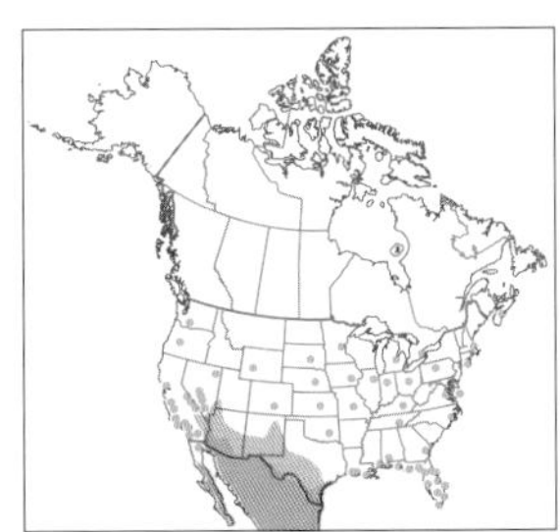

Dusky-capped is found mainly in shady oak woods, Ash-throated often in more open, arid habitats. All *Myiarchus* species nest in cavities, unlike other flycatchers, and are difficult to identify.

Dusky-capped Flycatcher

Myiarchus tuberculifer

L 7.25" WS 10" WT 0.7 oz (20 g)

Smaller than Ash-throated and relatively slender, with thin, straight bill and rounder head. Note brownish head and near lack of rufous in tail.

Adult

similar to some other flycatchers (e.g., Eastern Phoebe) but note lankier shape, reddish primaries

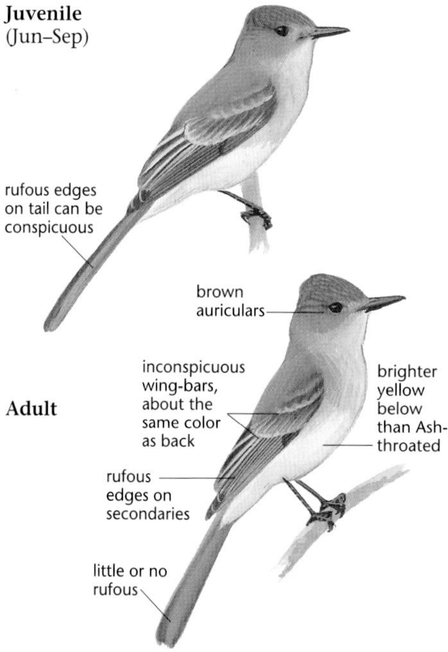
Juvenile
(Jun–Sep)
rufous edges on tail can be conspicuous
brown auriculars
Adult
inconspicuous wing-bars, about the same color as back
brighter yellow below than Ash-throated
rufous edges on secondaries
little or no rufous

Voice: Song *pidi pew pew pedrrrrrrrr* with long trill or an impatient, rhythmic *pididi-peeeeeer* ("I'm over here"); higher-pitched than other *Myiarchus*. Call prolonged, soft whistles: a melancholy *hweeeeeew* or *pwE-Deeeeeeeeew*. Also a sharp *whit* like other *Myiarchus* flycatchers and a rapid, complaining *treedr treerdr teeer teer.*

Ash-throated Flycatcher

Myiarchus cinerascens

L 8.5" WS 12" WT 0.95 oz (27 g)

Just slightly smaller than Great Crested; bill 4 percent shorter and relatively thinner. Distinguished by paler plumage (but beware faded Great Crested).

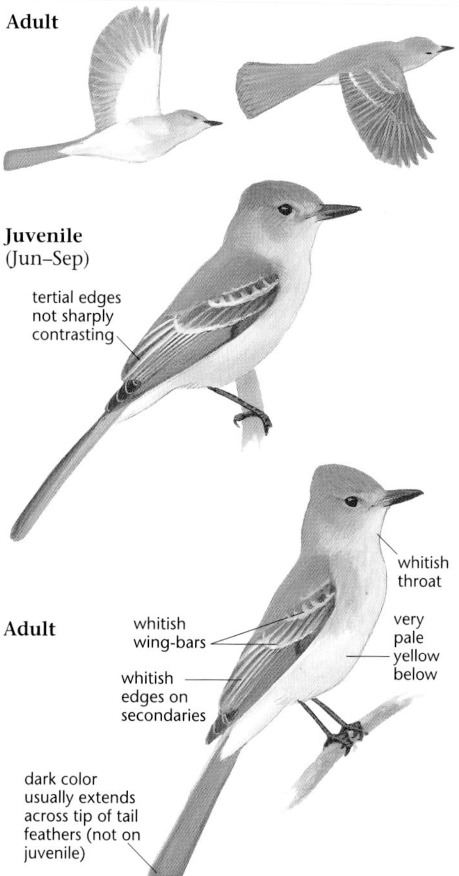
Adult
Juvenile
(Jun–Sep)
tertial edges not sharply contrasting
Adult
whitish throat
whitish wing-bars
very pale yellow below
whitish edges on secondaries
dark color usually extends across tip of tail feathers (not on juvenile)

Voice: Song a series of repeated phrases *kibrr, kibrr . . .*, or short, musical *kaBRIK.* All calls have low, flat quality; mostly short, abrupt, two-syllable phrases; always higher-pitched and lighter than Brown-crested; never raucous level notes. Common call a sharp *bik;* also *ki-brrnk-brr.* In fall and winter simply a soft *prrt.*

Great Crested adult

All *Myiarchus* flycatchers lean forward and bob their heads up and down when agitated.

Brown-crested Flycatcher is found mainly in riparian woods, Great Crested in hardwood forests. These two large species can be difficult to distinguish; note breast color, tertial pattern, and voice.

Brown-crested Flycatcher

Myiarchus tyrannulus

L 8.75" WS 13" WT 1.5 oz (44 g)

Heavier than Great Crested and Ash-throated; relatively short-winged and long-tailed, with very heavy bill and feet. Eyes look small.

Adult

Juvenile Eastern (May–Sep)

drab tertial edges

Adult Eastern

large bill (10 percent longer than Great Crested)

Adult Western

slightly larger, with very large bill (20 percent longer than Great Crested)

fairly extensive rufous

color like Ash-throated but averages slightly brighter yellow below (paler than Great Crested)

Voice: Song of low, rolling, alternating phrases *prEErrr-prdrdrrr, wrrp-didider* . . . lower than Ash-throated; low *trrrp,* strong *kreep* less rough and more nasal than Great Crested. Loud, raucous, descending *keeerp* often in series (e.g., *keeerp keeerp keeerp breeek brit brit bik* . . .). Low, strong, liquid *whip* often followed by a rolling *brrrg.*

Western populations of Brown-crested Flycatcher average 7 percent larger overall with 12 percent larger bill than Eastern. Plumage and voice are identical.

Great Crested Flycatcher

Myiarchus crinitus

L 8.75" WS 13" WT 1.2 oz (34 g)

Large and fairly heavy; just slightly larger and heavier-billed than Ash-throated, with longer wings. Note brighter colors than any other Myiarchus.

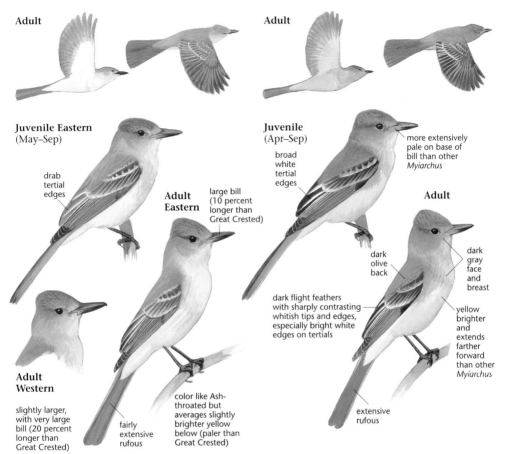

Adult

Juvenile (Apr–Sep)

broad white tertial edges

more extensively pale on base of bill than other *Myiarchus*

Adult

dark olive back

dark gray face and breast

dark flight feathers with sharply contrasting whitish tips and edges, especially bright white edges on tertials

yellow brighter and extends farther forward than other *Myiarchus*

extensive rufous

Voice: Song of alternating phrases *quitta, queeto, quitta.* . . . Distinctive call a strong, clear, rising *wheeeep* or *queEEEEP.* Other calls include a very rough, level *KRREEEP;* lower, softer *krrrriip;* low, sharp, dry *kwip;* all often combined into excited series (e.g., *KRREEEP, KRREEP, kwip-kwip-kwip-kwip-kwip kweep kweep, krrriip*).

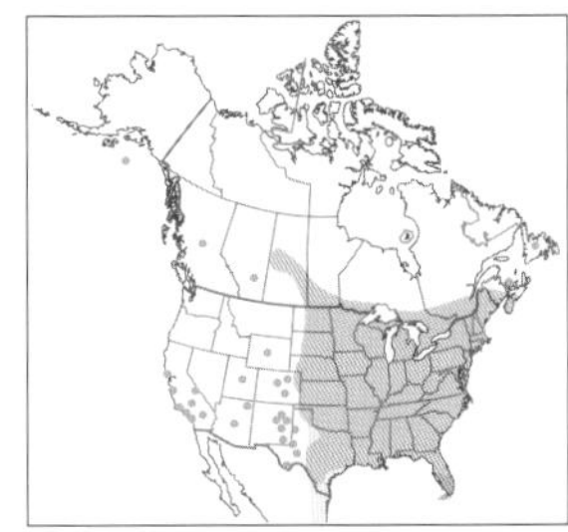

La Sagra's Flycatcher, related to Brown-crested and Great Crested, is found low in woods. Thick-billed Kingbird is found locally in mesquite and cottonwoods near water.

La Sagra's Flycatcher

Myiarchus sagrae

L 7.25" WS 10.5" WT 0.63 oz (18 g)

Most similar in appearance to Ash-throated; note smaller size, relatively larger head and longer bill, shorter wings, whitish underparts, and limited rufous in tail.

Adult

Juvenile
(May–Nov)
contrasting tertial edges
short primary projection
bulky crest on large head
very pale below with little or no yellow
Adult
little rufous on tail

Voice: Call a high, rising, clear, whistle *weeek* or *weeeit* like high-pitched Great Crested; a series becoming lower and rougher *weeek weeep kreeep kreep krip;* a clear *whidip* and sharp, buzzy *keee* or *keew.* Also *weep wida-weer* like Dusky-capped but higher and more rapid.

Thick-billed Kingbird

Tyrannus crassirostris

L 9.5" WS 16" WT 2 oz (56 g)

Thick-necked, with very large bill. Distinct peak on rear crown.

Adult
all-dark, square tail

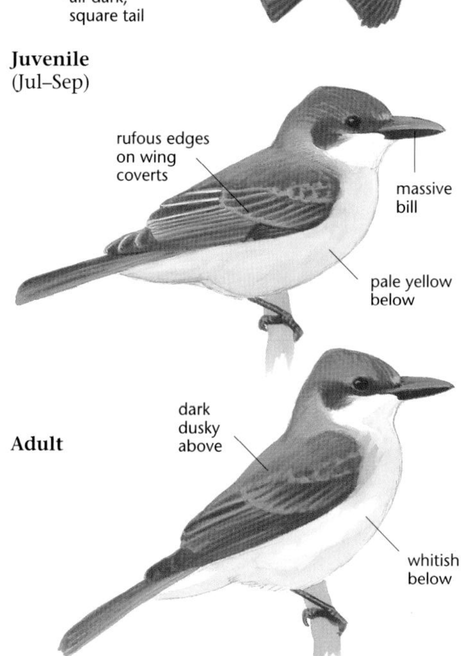
Juvenile
(Jul–Sep)
rufous edges on wing coverts
massive bill
pale yellow below
dark dusky above
Adult
whitish below

Voice: Call a buzzy or dry, metallic *tzwee-eerrr* or *to to to zweeerrr.* Also a dry, clicking *ket ket-ket ket . . .* or a buzzy, nasal *kotoREEEF,* sharply ascending, squealed, burry, with emphatic questioning end.

Each *Tyrannus* species builds a stick nest in the outer branches of a tree.

Like other kingbirds, these two conspicuous gray and white birds are found in open areas with scattered trees and bushes, perching on wires or treetops to watch for flying insects.

Gray Kingbird

Tyrannus dominicensis

L 9" WS 14" WT 1.5 oz (44 g)

Distinguished from Eastern by much larger bill, heavier body, longer tail, and shorter wings.

Adult

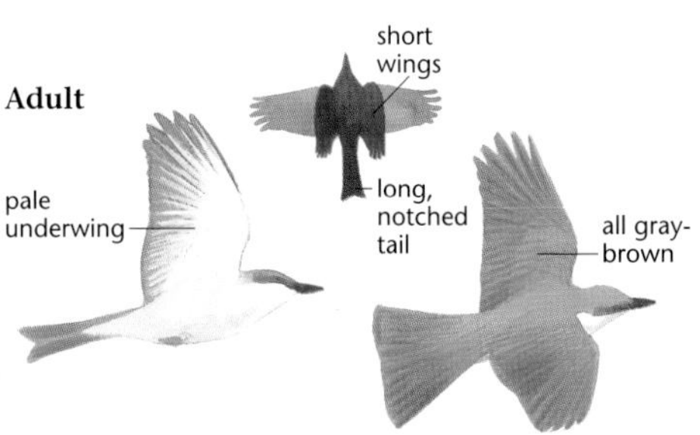
short wings
pale underwing
long, notched tail
all gray-brown

Juvenile (Jun–Nov)

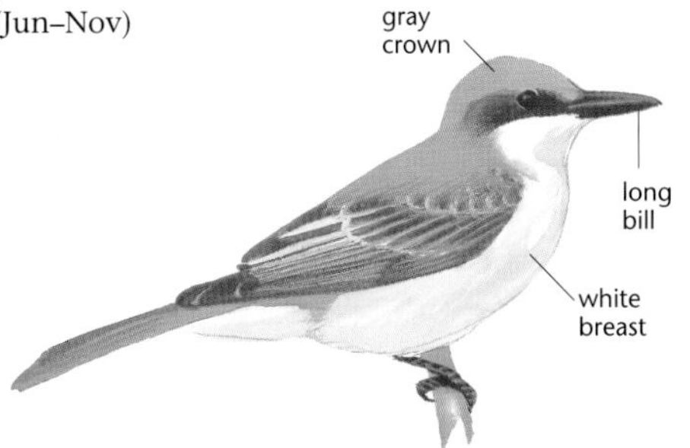
gray crown
long bill
white breast

Adult

paler and colder gray than Eastern

dark mask

Voice: Common call a high, sharp, twittering chatter *tik-teeerr* or *preeerr-krrr;* similar to Tropical Kingbird but fuller and rougher.

Eastern Kingbird

Tyrannus tyrannus

L 8.5" WS 15" WT 1.4 oz (40 g)

Smaller with narrower and more pointed wings than other kingbirds.

Adult

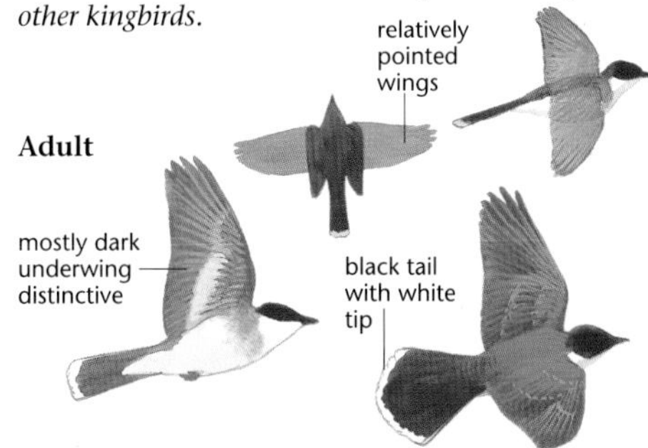
relatively pointed wings
mostly dark underwing distinctive
black tail with white tip

Juvenile (Jul–Oct)

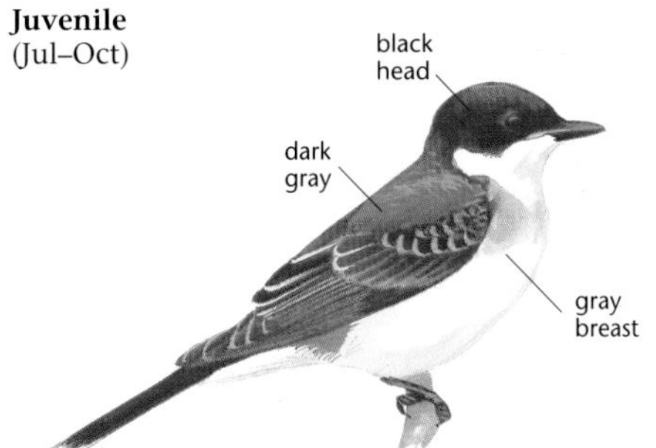
black head
dark gray
gray breast

Adult

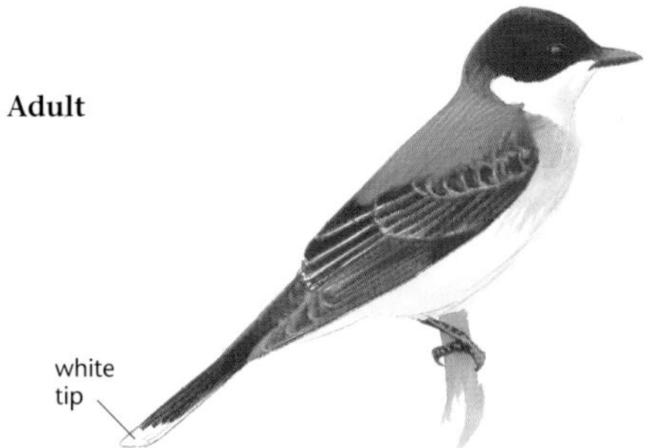
white tip

Voice: Song of sharp, electric, rasping or sputtering notes in series ending with emphatic, descending buzz *kdik kdik kdik PIKa PIKa PIKa kzeeeer;* elements often given separately. Most frequently heard call a sharp, buzzy *kzeer.* Dawn song a high, rapid, electric rattling building to crescendo *kiu kitttttttttttiu ditide.*

All species in the genus *Tyrannus* have an orange or red median crown-stripe usually concealed by the dark crown feathers; the stripe is brightest in adult male and exposed only during displays.

These two species are very closely related and are reliably distinguished only by voice. More brightly colored than other kingbirds, both are found in open areas with trees near water.

Tropical Kingbird

Tyrannus melancholicus

L 9.25" WS 14.5" WT 1.4 oz (40 g)

Compared to other kingbirds has relatively short, rounded wings, long tail with distinct notch, large head, and long bill.

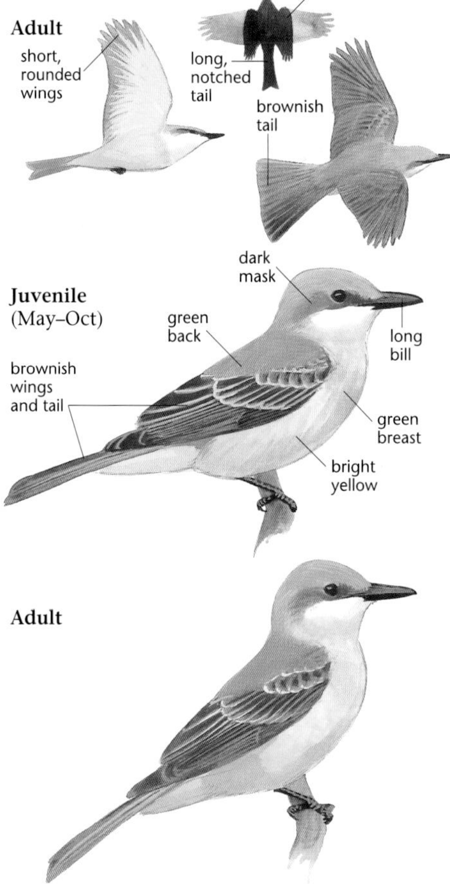
short
wings
Adult
short,
rounded
wings
long,
notched
tail
brownish
tail
dark
mask
Juvenile
(May–Oct)
green
back
long
bill
brownish
wings
and tail
green
breast
bright
yellow
Adult

Voice: Song of Arizona birds has sharp, metallic quality; rapid, rising, tinkling *tr tr twididid twididid twididi*. Song may differ in Texas: shorter (1 sec vs. 2), more varied and complex, beginning with *wit* notes. Common call of all populations a high, sputtering twitter of sharp, metallic notes *twitrrr* or *tzitzitzitzi;* never a single note like Couch's.

Couch's Kingbird

Tyrannus couchii

L 9.25" WS 15.5" WT 1.5 oz (43 g)

Very similar to Tropical, but bill averages shorter and thicker with curved culmen.

Adult
Juvenile
(May–Aug)
shorter,
heavier
bill
Adult
slightly paler brown
wings and tail than
Tropical with less
contrasting buffy
edges; averages
brighter colors
overall

Voice: Song of high, thin, nasal squeals *towi towi toWITItoo* or *gewit gewit geWEETyo*. Dawn song a series of long, slow phrases *pleerrr pleerrr pleerrr plity plity plity plity chew*. Common call a high, sharp *dik* (like Western) and an insectlike, trailing buzz *kweeeerz* or *dik dik dikweeeerz;* also a sharp, dry *ch-eek*.

Note that worn adult Western Kingbird (Aug–Oct) can have brownish-black tail without white sides; compare Tropical and Couch's Kingbirds.

These two widespread, yellow-bellied kingbirds are relatively long-winged and have square dark tails. Both are found in a variety of open habitats; Cassin's prefers areas with scattered trees.

Cassin's Kingbird

Tyrannus vociferans

L 9" WS 16" WT 1.6 oz (46 g)

Similar to Western; darker overall with different tail pattern, slightly heavier bill, more rounded wings, broader and more flared tail.

Adult

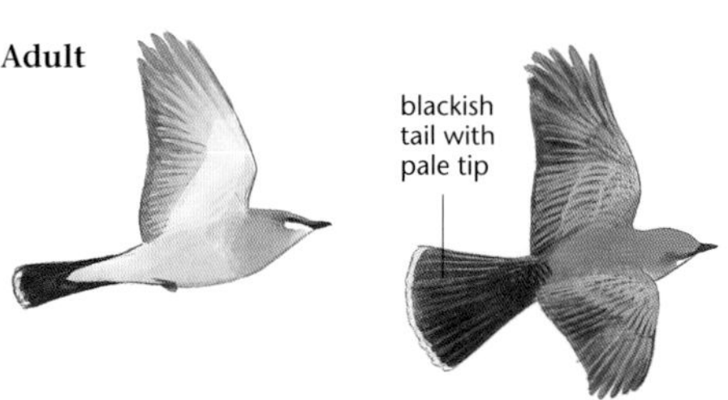
blackish
tail with
pale tip

Juvenile (Jun–Aug)

Adult

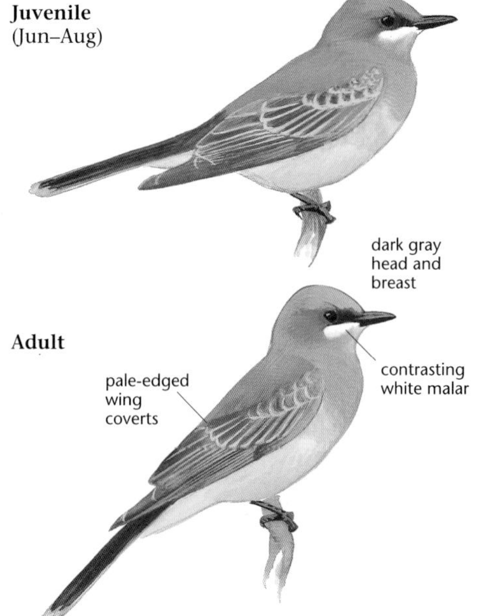
dark gray
head and
breast
pale-edged
wing
coverts
contrasting
white malar

Voice: Song of clear, nasal notes and hoarse *churr* notes rising to crescendo *teew, teew, teew tewdi tidadidew*. Call a husky *CHI-Vrrrr*. Also clearer, nasal *keew* notes in series; rough, burry, descending *ch-queeer;* and nasal *gdeerr-gdeerr . . .* in rapid series of up to ten notes, lower and more nasal than Western.

Western Kingbird

Tyrannus verticalis

L 8.75" WS 15.5" WT 1.4 oz (40 g)

Longer-winged, shorter-tailed, and smaller-billed than Tropical; square tail and pale gray breast.

Adult

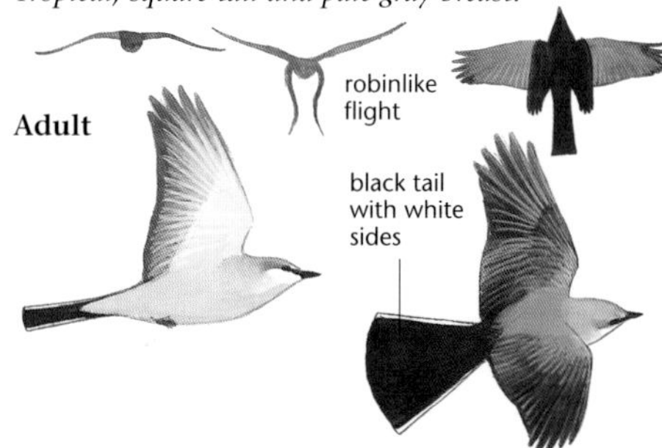
robinlike
flight
black tail
with white
sides

Juvenile (Jun–Oct)

Adult

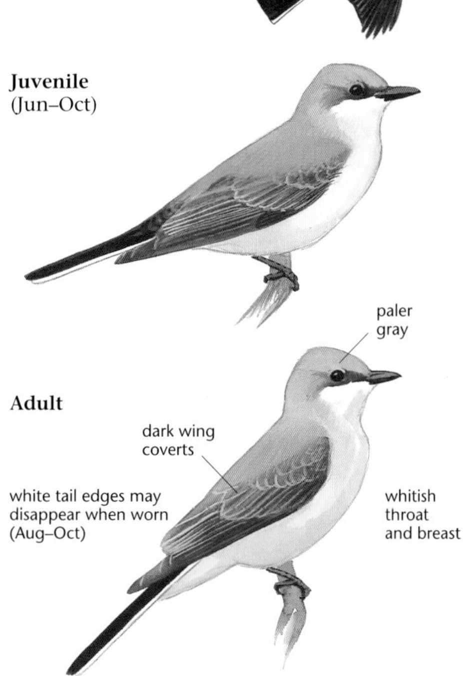
paler
gray
dark wing
coverts
white tail edges may
disappear when worn
(Aug–Oct)
whitish
throat
and breast

Voice: Song high, hard, squeaky *pidik pik pidik PEEKado*. Calls lower-pitched than Eastern; higher and clearer than Cassin's. Calls include a rapid, rising series of shrill, sputtering notes *widik pik widi pik pik pik*; very hard, sharp *kit* often in accelerating rising series or long, sputtering series; also a lower series *kdew kdew kdew kdew*.

Western Kingbird

coasting to
a landing

Long-tailed Flycatchers

These spectacularly long-tailed species are found in open areas with scattered bushes. Both are closely related to kingbirds and have similar habits but forage mainly close to the ground.

Fork-tailed Flycatcher

Tyrannus savana

L 10" (adult ♂ to 16") WS 14" WT 1 oz (29 g)

Smaller than Scissor-tailed and kingbirds; adult male even longer-tailed than Scissor-tailed.

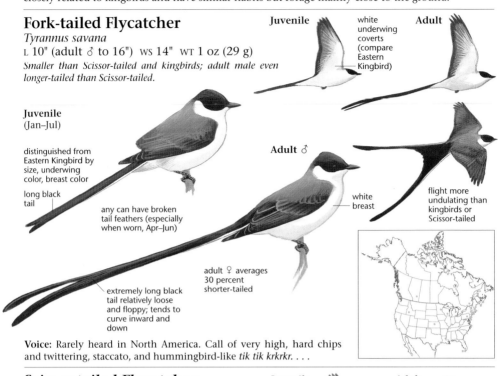

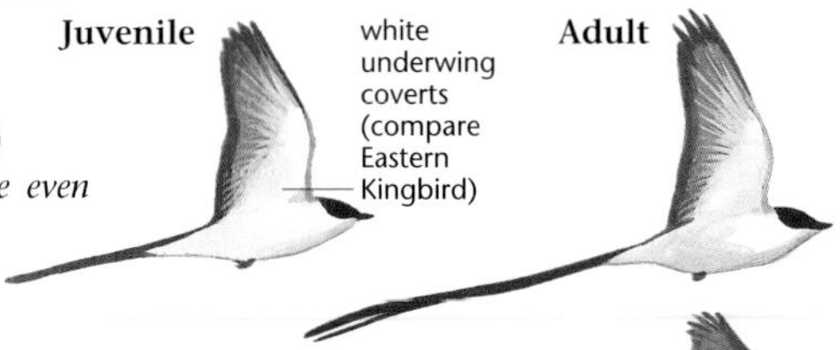

Juvenile

white underwing coverts (compare Eastern Kingbird)

Adult

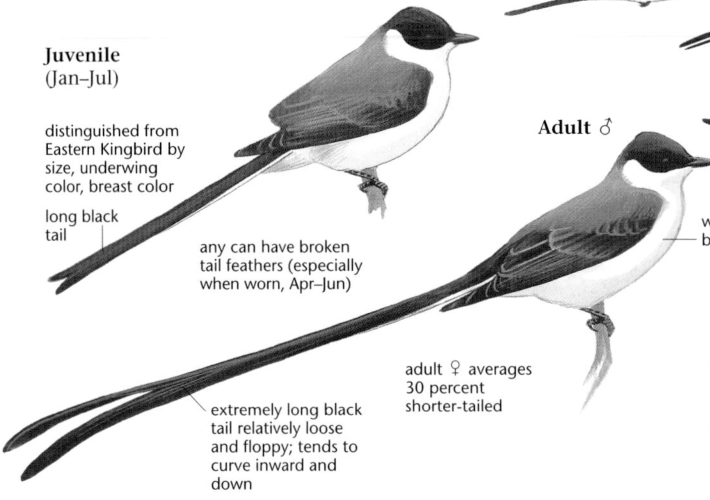

Juvenile (Jan–Jul)

distinguished from Eastern Kingbird by size, underwing color, breast color

long black tail

any can have broken tail feathers (especially when worn, Apr–Jun)

Adult ♂

white breast

flight more undulating than kingbirds or Scissor-tailed

adult ♀ averages 30 percent shorter-tailed

extremely long black tail relatively loose and floppy; tends to curve inward and down

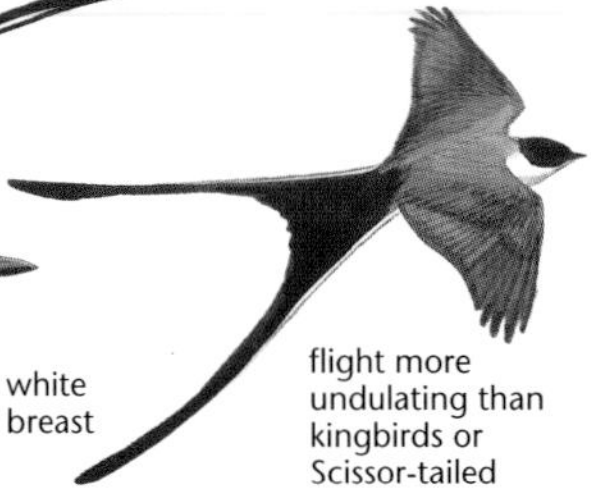

Voice: Rarely heard in North America. Call of very high, hard chips and twittering, staccato, and hummingbird-like *tik tik krkrkr. . . .*

Scissor-tailed Flycatcher

Tyrannus forficatus

L 10" (adult ♂ to 15") WS 15" WT 1.5 oz (43 g)

Size and shape similar to Western Kingbird; adult much longer-tailed. Flight may recall cuckoos.

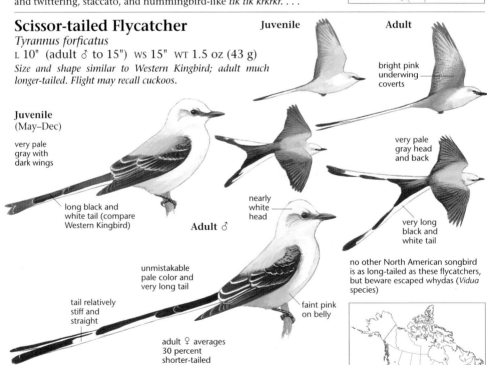

Juvenile

Adult

bright pink underwing coverts

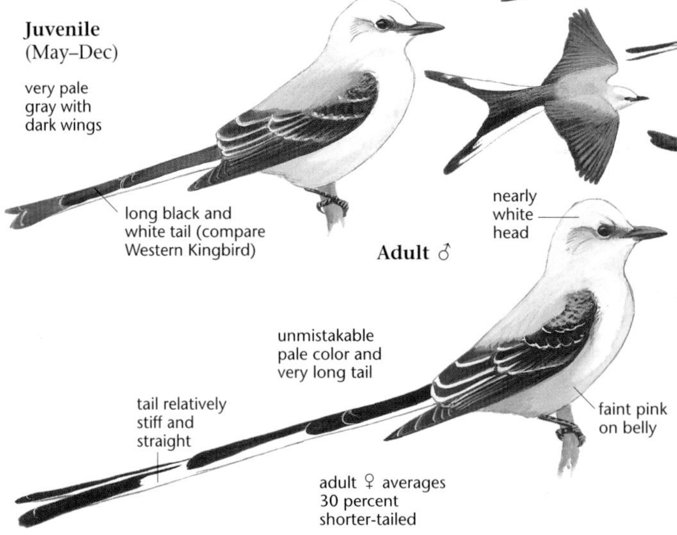

Juvenile (May–Dec)

very pale gray with dark wings

very pale gray head and back

long black and white tail (compare Western Kingbird)

nearly white head

Adult ♂

very long black and white tail

no other North American songbird is as long-tailed as these flycatchers, but beware escaped whydas (*Vidua* species)

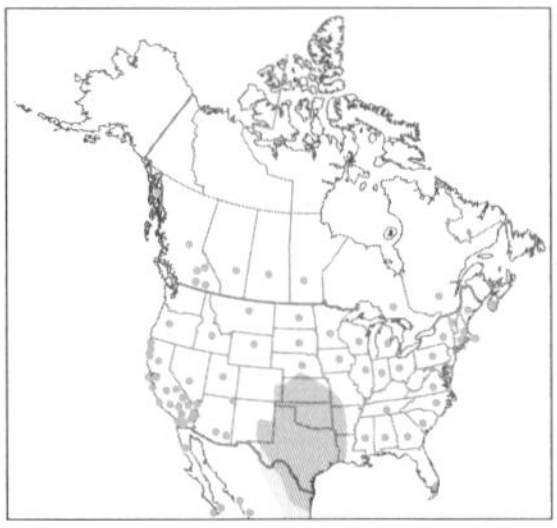

unmistakable pale color and very long tail

tail relatively stiff and straight

faint pink on belly

adult ♀ averages 30 percent shorter-tailed

Voice: Song lower-pitched and flatter than Western Kingbird, with slightly different pattern *pidik pek pik pik pidEEK*. Dawn song *pup pup pup pup pup perek*. Common call a relatively low, flat *pik;* lower than Western Kingbird. Also *pik-prrr* or *kopik* or higher, sharper *kid*.

Large Tropical Flycatchers

These strikingly patterned species are unlike any other of our flycatchers. Sulphur-bellied is found in broadleaf trees along mountain streams, Great Kiskadee in dense, brushy woods near water.

Sulphur-bellied Flycatcher

Myiodynastes luteiventris

L 8.5" WS 14.5" WT 1.6 oz (46 g)

Sturdy, large-headed, and short-tailed.

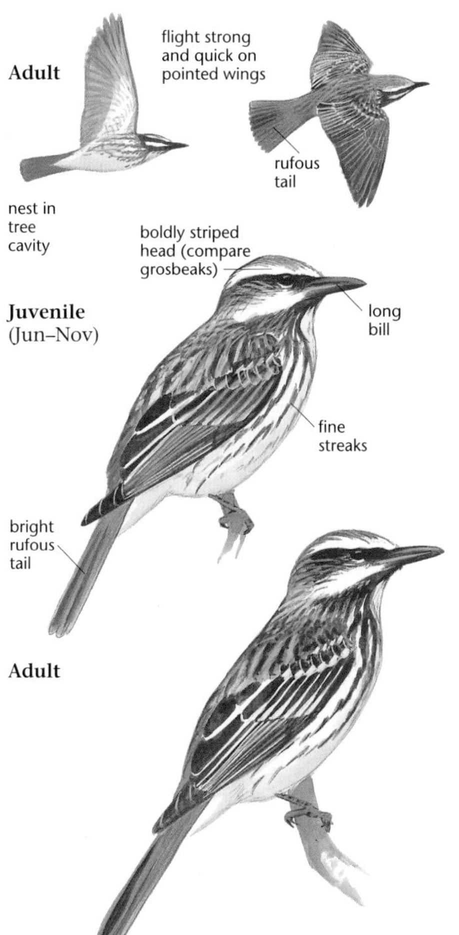

Adult
flight strong and quick on pointed wings
rufous tail
nest in tree cavity
boldly striped head (compare grosbeaks)
long bill
Juvenile (Jun–Nov)
fine streaks
bright rufous tail
Adult

Voice: Common calls high, squeaky, whistled phrases, penetrating squeaks like a child's toy *tooWI drrdip* or *wee-dee-yoo;* a forceful *seedeeyee;* a lower, nasal *kweeda kweeda . . . ;* a rather low, hollow, nasal *ket* often in series, suddenly exploding into loud, high squealing.

Great Kiskadee

Pitangus sulphuratus

L 9.75" WS 15" WT 2.1 oz (60 g)

Stocky, short-tailed, round-winged, and large-headed with heavy bill.

plain rufous above
striped head
Adult
short tail
bright yellow below
short, rounded wings
nest a large ball of twigs and grasses with side entrance in tree
Juvenile (May–Aug)
striped head
reddish-brown above
Adult
white throat
yellow belly

Voice: Song a raucous, high, repeated *KREEtaperr* ("Kiskadee" or "Christopher"); often repeated in chorus with several individuals. All calls loud, clear, raucous, repeated; most common a rather long, level squeal *weee;* also a high, rough *grrt.*

Shrikes and Vireos

Families: Laniidae, Vireonidae

SHRIKES 2 species in 1 genus; all in family Laniidae. Shrikes are found singly in open, brushy fields, hedgerows, and the edges of woods. They are predatory songbirds with strong, hooked bills they use to kill and dismember prey (insects or small vertebrates, including birds, small mammals, and reptiles). The Loggerhead Shrike has been observed attacking prey much larger than itself, although its normal diet is insects. When foraging, both species perch conspicuously on fences, wires, and treetops. Captured prey may be hung on thorns for later consumption. Compare Northern Mockingbird, Blue Jay, and American Kestrel. Adults are shown.

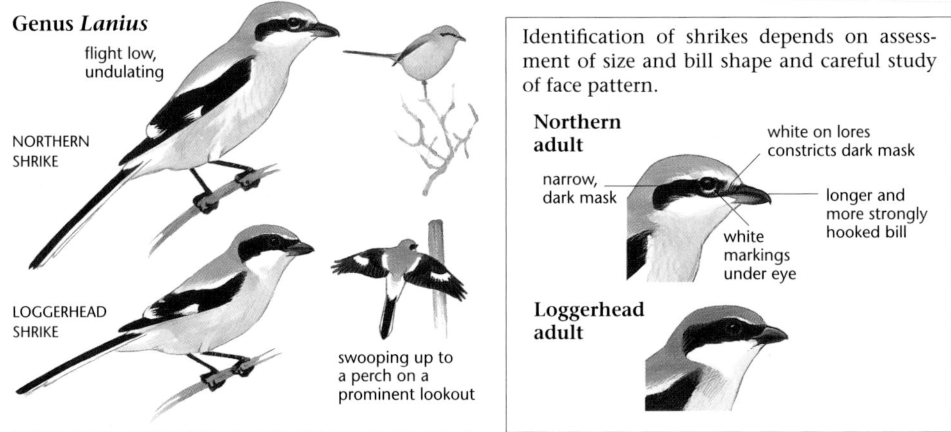
Genus Lanius
flight low, undulating
NORTHERN SHRIKE
LOGGERHEAD SHRIKE
swooping up to a perch on a prominent lookout
Identification of shrikes depends on assessment of size and bill shape and careful study of face pattern.
Northern adult
white on lores constricts dark mask
narrow, dark mask
longer and more strongly hooked bill
white markings under eye
Loggerhead adult

VIREOS 15 species in 1 genus; all in family Vireonidae. Vireos are small, relatively stocky songbirds with large, hooked bills and short, strong legs. Plumage of all species is mostly drab with subtle markings. Found in dense brush and leafy trees, vireos feed on berries and insects and larvae gleaned from leaves. They habitually fly to perch and sit still for a minute or two (warblers move continuously). Nest is a neat, compact cup suspended in a horizontal fork. Songs and calls are remarkably similar among some species. Compare flycatchers, kinglets, and warblers. Adults are shown.

Genus *Vireo*

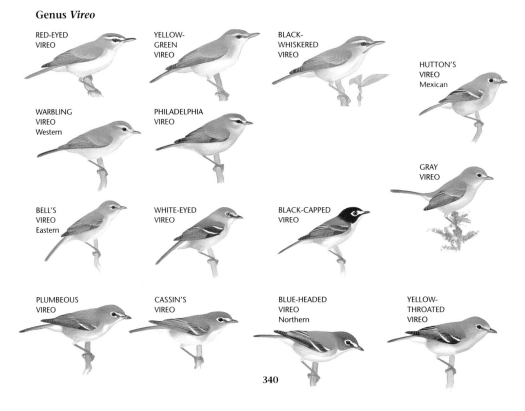

RED-EYED VIREO

YELLOW-GREEN VIREO

BLACK-WHISKERED VIREO

HUTTON'S VIREO
Mexican

WARBLING VIREO
Western

PHILADELPHIA VIREO

GRAY VIREO

BELL'S VIREO
Eastern

WHITE-EYED VIREO

BLACK-CAPPED VIREO

PLUMBEOUS VIREO

CASSIN'S VIREO

BLUE-HEADED VIREO
Northern

YELLOW-THROATED VIREO

Shrikes

The two species of shrikes are quite similar to each other. Their ranges overlap only in winter. Identification is based on details of size, shape, and head pattern.

Northern Shrike

Lanius excubitor

L 10" WS 14.5" WT 2.3 oz (65 g)

Larger than Loggerhead, with relatively longer and more strongly hooked bill, relatively smaller head, and longer wings and tail. Often hovers when hunting.

Juvenile — little white on wings

Adult

Brown 1st winter (Jul–Apr)
brownish overall
pale bill
distinctly scaled

Gray 1st winter (Jul–Apr)
thin, dark mask
white eye-ring

Adult
narrow mask

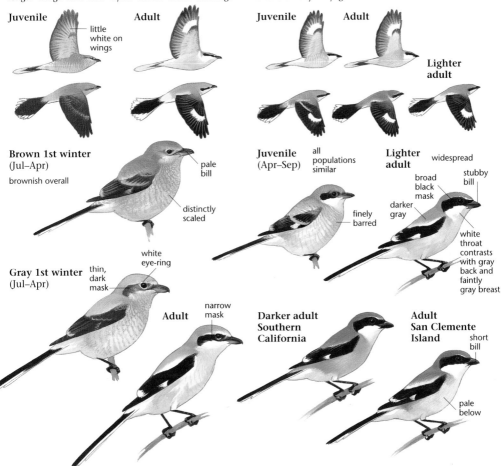

Voice: Song of repeated short phrases like Loggerhead, but lower-pitched with mellower, more liquid quality *kdldi* or *plid-plid.* Can sound soft and thrasherlike. Calls include a very nasal, complaining *fay fay . . .*, a harsher *reed reed reed . . .*, and a very harsh, dry *shraaaa.*

Loggerhead Shrike

Lanius ludovicianus

L 9" WS 12" WT 1.7 oz (48 g)

Large-headed with stout, conical bill; shorter-winged and -tailed than Northern, with quicker wingbeats and less buoyant flight.

Juvenile

Adult

Lighter adult

Juvenile (Apr–Sep)
all populations similar
finely barred

Lighter adult
widespread
broad black mask
stubby bill
darker gray
white throat contrasts with gray back and faintly gray breast

Darker adult Southern California

Adult San Clemente Island
short bill
pale below

Voice: Song generally sharp, precise, mechanical two-syllable phrases *krrDI* or *JEEuk* (etc.) with the phrase often repeated over and over at short intervals. Calls include a harsh, scolding *jaaa,* grating *teeen raad raad raad raad raad,* and other variations similar to song phrases.

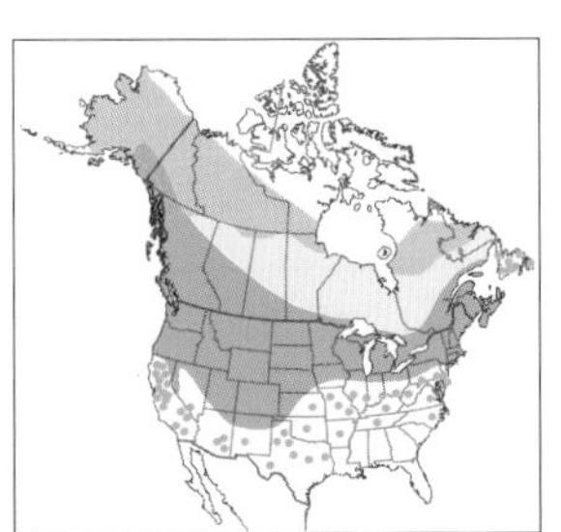

Regional variation in darkness of Loggerhead Shrike plumage is subtle and complex. Dark-rumped birds are found in the southeast and California, variably white-rumped birds elsewhere; darkest overall birds in southern California. Channel Islands populations, including San Clemente Island, have less white in primaries and are darker above and paler below.

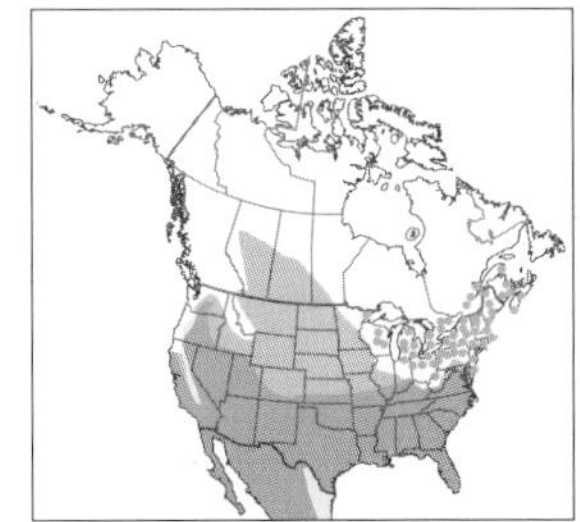

Gray and Red-eyed Vireos

Gray Vireo is found almost exclusively on dry hillsides with scattered junipers. Red-eyed is found in broadleaf forests; it forms a well-defined group with Yellow-green and Black-whiskered.

Gray Vireo

Vireo vicinior

L 5.5" WS 8" WT 0.46 oz (13 g)

Plain gray, long-tailed, and small-billed; superficially similar to Plumbeous but differs in shape, habits, call, and many plumage details.

Adult

long
tail

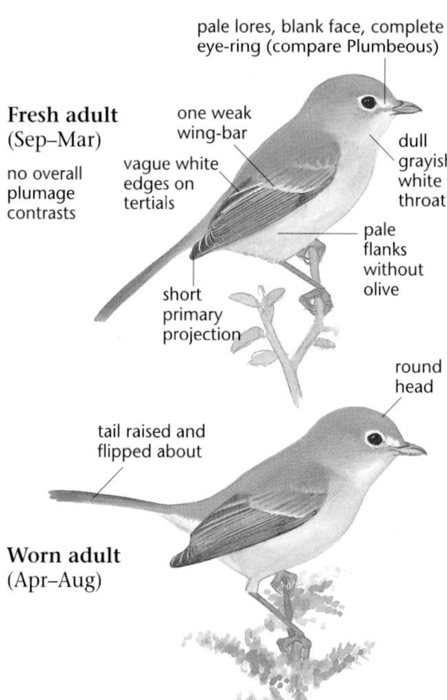
pale lores, blank face, complete eye-ring (compare Plumbeous)
Fresh adult
(Sep–Mar)
no overall plumage contrasts
one weak wing-bar
vague white edges on tertials
dull grayish white throat
pale flanks without olive
short primary projection
round head
tail raised and flipped about
Worn adult
(Apr–Aug)

Voice: Song very similar to Plumbeous but phrases average shorter, simpler, delivered more rapidly (average one phrase every 1.5 sec); less varied *tiree pwideer dew tiree pwideer dew. . . .* Call a low, harsh *charrr* similar to Bewick's Wren; also a short, harsh *chik,* a rapid series of popping whistles, and a harsh descending series.

Red-eyed Vireo

Vireo olivaceus

L 6" WS 10" WT 0.6 oz (17 g)

Fairly large and relatively long-billed; wings unpatterned.

Adult

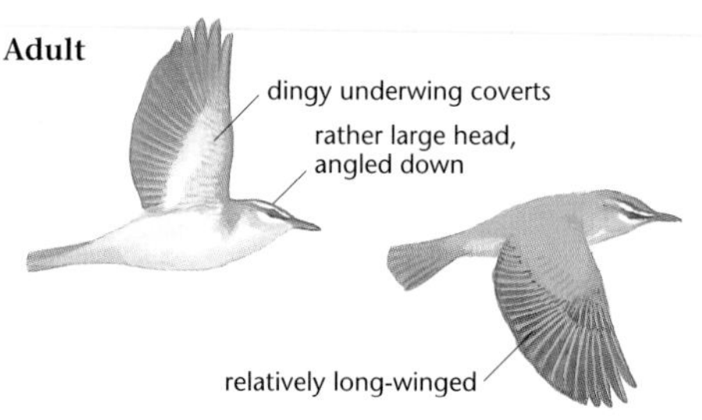
dingy underwing coverts
rather large head, angled down
relatively long-winged

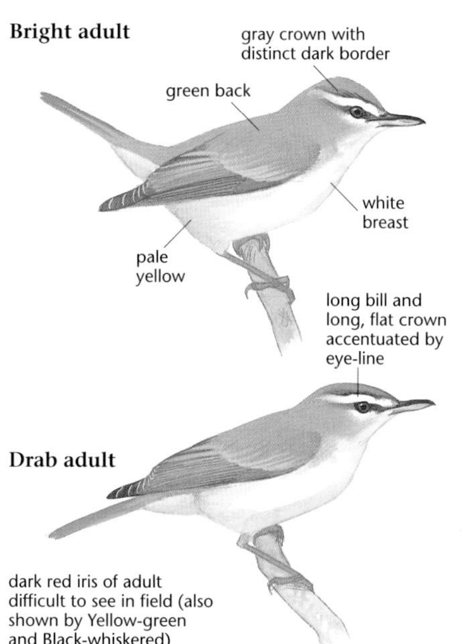
Bright adult
gray crown with distinct dark border
green back
white breast
pale yellow
long bill and long, flat crown accentuated by eye-line
Drab adult
dark red iris of adult difficult to see in field (also shown by Yellow-green and Black-whiskered)

Voice: Song of simple, hurried, whistled phrases *here-I-am, in-the-tree, look-up, at-the-top . . . ;* averages one phrase every two seconds. Call a nasal, fairly soft, mewing *meerf* or *zherr;* a longer, more whining, descending *rreeea* when agitated; also chatter and *gwit* note similar to Black-whiskered but rarely heard.

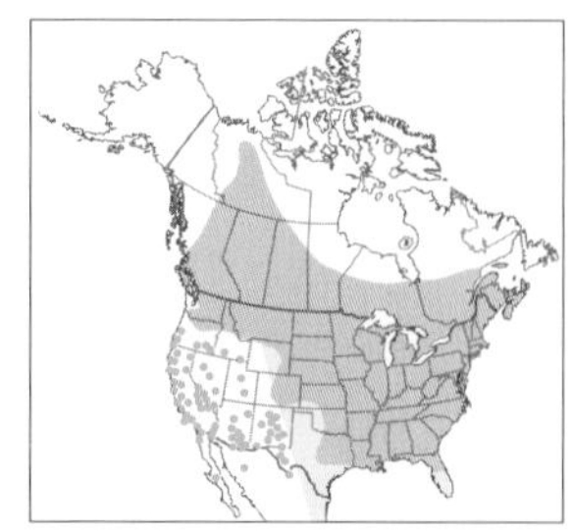

Large Vireos

These closely related species, along with Red-eyed, share long bills, dark eye-lines, and similar voices. Found in broadleaf trees, they are distinguished by details of head pattern and song.

Yellow-green Vireo

Vireo flavoviridis

L 6.25" WS 10" WT 0.63 oz (18 g)

Bill averages heavier and 15 percent longer than Red-eyed; wings more rounded. Plumage suffused with yellow; head pattern drab.

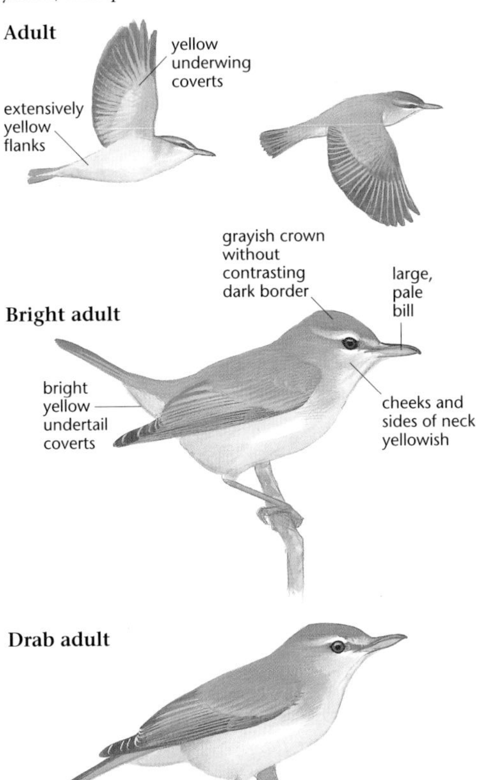

Adult
yellow underwing coverts
extensively yellow flanks
Bright adult
grayish crown without contrasting dark border
large, pale bill
bright yellow undertail coverts
cheeks and sides of neck yellowish
Drab adult

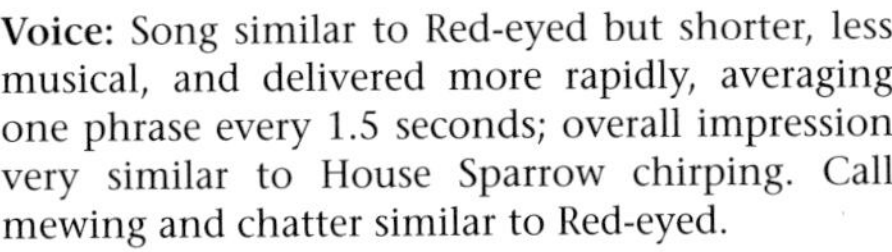

Voice: Song similar to Red-eyed but shorter, less musical, and delivered more rapidly, averaging one phrase every 1.5 seconds; overall impression very similar to House Sparrow chirping. Call mewing and chatter similar to Red-eyed.

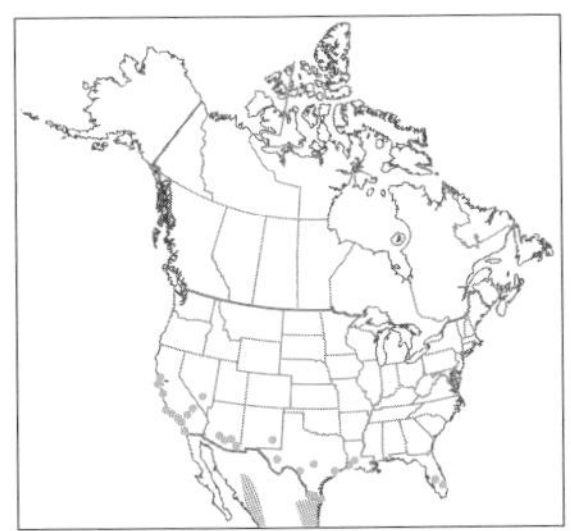

Black-whiskered Vireo

Vireo altiloquus

L 6.25" WS 10" WT 0.63 oz (18 g)

Similar to Yellow-green; larger-billed and browner overall then Red-eyed. Dark "whisker" diagnostic but can be difficult to see.

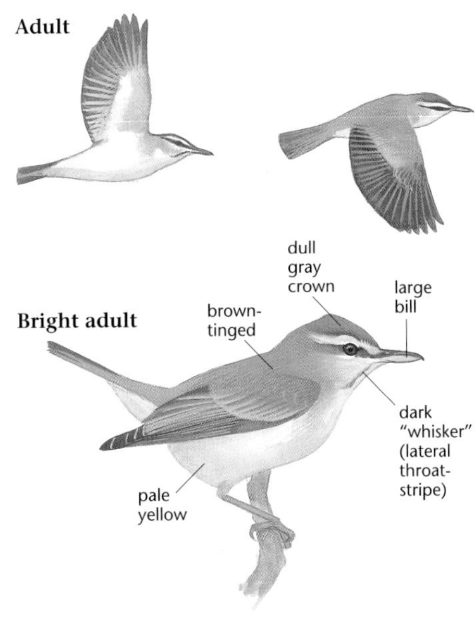

Adult
Bright adult
dull gray crown
brown-tinged
large bill
dark "whisker" (lateral throat-stripe)
pale yellow

Drab adult

Voice: Song of three- or four-syllable phrases *chip john phillip, chiip phillip . . . , chillip phillip;* sharper with more abrupt pitch changes than Red-eyed, averaging one phrase every two seconds. Call varies from nasal mew like Red-eyed to soft, low *vwirr* like Veery; also a rapid, nasal chatter and a short, low *gwit.*

Black-whiskered Vireo Caribbean subspecies (vagrant to Florida and Louisiana, not shown) is 15 percent longer-billed than Florida population and browner overall, with an indistinct supercilium.

Small Plain-winged Vireos

Although similar to large vireos, these species are smaller and stockier, with relatively shorter bills, rounder heads, and subtly different plumages. They are found mainly in broadleaf trees.

Warbling Vireo

Vireo gilvus

L 5.5" WS 8.5" WT 0.42 oz (12 g)

Always paler than Red-eyed; grayish, with plain, pale lores creating a "blank-faced" look.

Adult

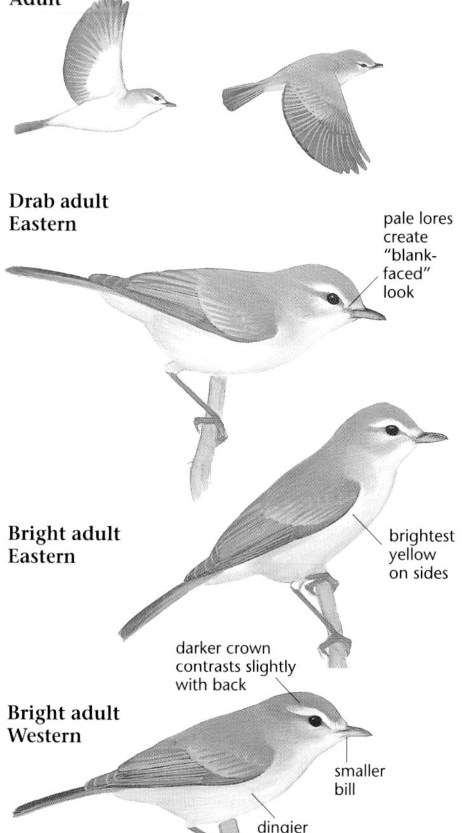

Drab adult
Eastern
pale lores create "blank-faced" look
Bright adult
Eastern
brightest yellow on sides
darker crown contrasts slightly with back
Bright adult
Western
smaller bill
dingier underparts

Voice: Song a rapid, run-on warble *viderveedeev-iderveedeeviderVEET* without pause and with distinctive, husky vireo quality. Call a harsh, nasal mewing *meeerish* (slightly two-syllabled) or a swelling *meeezh;* also a short, dry *git* or *gwit;* a high, slightly nasal chatter rising then falling.

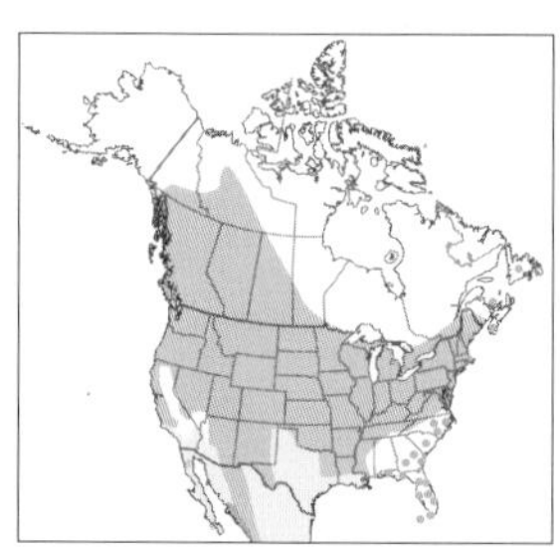

Western population of Warbling differs from Eastern as shown. Song of Western averages slightly higher-pitched, choppier, and buzzier, often ending with a descending buzzy note. Eastern song lower, clearer with singsong rhythm; usually ends with emphatic high note, the highest note of the song. Calls may also differ subtly between populations.

Philadelphia Vireo

Vireo philadelphicus

L 5.25" WS 8" WT 0.42 oz (12 g)

A little smaller, shorter-tailed, and rounder-headed than Warbling; note dark lores and yellow throat.

Adult

Drab adult

can be very similar to Warbling
dark lores
yellow throat, brightest in center
dark remiges
short tail

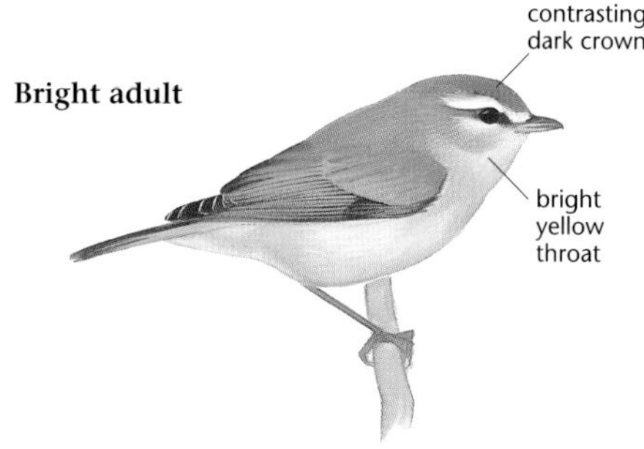

contrasting dark crown
Bright adult
bright yellow throat

Voice: Song very similar to Red-eyed but higher-pitched on average, weaker and choppier, with longer pauses averaging one phrase every three seconds (but Red-eyed can match these characteristics). Call nasal and soft like Red-eyed but three to five short notes in slightly descending series *weeej weeezh weeezh weeezh.*

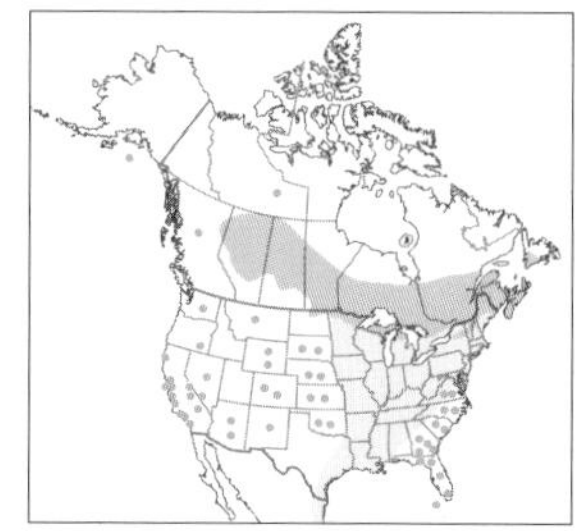

Small Barred-winged Vireos

This small, barred-winged, active species is found in dense, low brush near water (e.g., willows or mesquite). It is distinguished by its faint wing-bars and faintly "spectacled" head pattern.

Bell's Vireo

Vireo bellii

L 4.75" WS 7" WT 0.3 oz (8.5 g)

Very small; flicks and bobs relatively long tail. This and other small vireos are superficially like kinglets or warblers; note stout bill and legs.

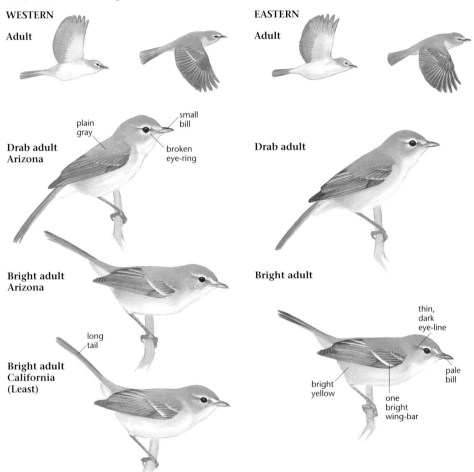

WESTERN

Adult

EASTERN

Adult

Drab adult Arizona

plain gray

small bill

broken eye-ring

Drab adult

Bright adult Arizona

Bright adult

long tail

Bright adult California (Least)

thin, dark eye-line

pale bill

bright yellow

one bright wing-bar

Voice: Song husky, chatty, musical *chewede jechewide cheedle jeeew;* slight emphasis on ending but basically flat; variations in details, but quality distinctive. Call fairly high, soft, nasal *biiv biiv . . .* or *chee chee.* Similar call also given singly: nasal, rising *mreee* repeated.

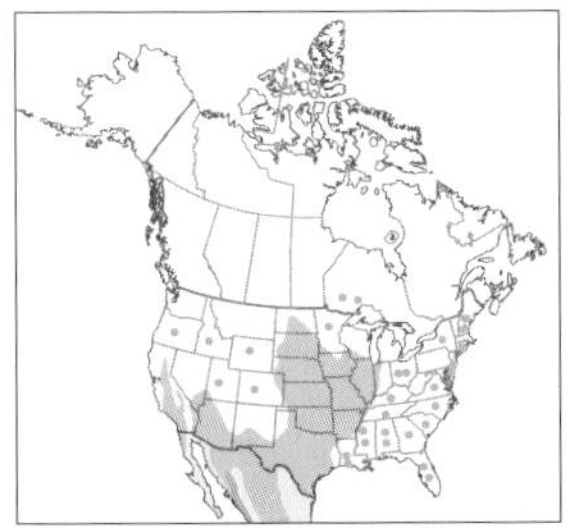

Two populations are normally distinguishable in the field, but intermediate birds are found in west Texas. Eastern population birds are brighter and shorter-tailed than Western. Eastern birds bob tail like Palm Warbler; Western birds flip longer tail up and sideways like gnatcatchers. Eastern may have brighter blue legs than Western. Western population is subdivided into Arizona and California (latter also called Least: smaller with virtually no yellow tones). There is no known difference in voice.

Hutton's is found in oak woods, moving through the trees with flocks of other small birds. Black-capped, related to White-eyed, is found in brushy vegetation in oak-juniper habitats.

Hutton's Vireo

Vireo huttoni

L 5" WS 8" WT 0.39 oz (11 g)

Small, stocky, and active. Strikingly similar to Ruby-crowned Kinglet but stockier (also compare Empidonax *flycatchers).*

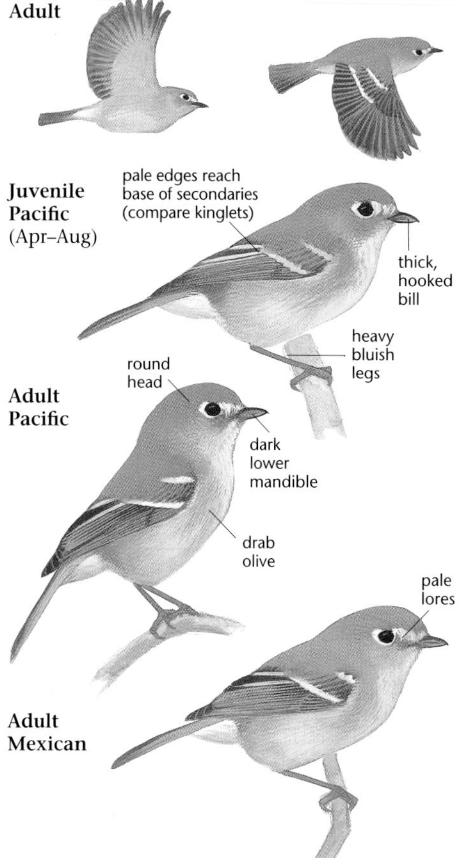
Adult
Juvenile Pacific (Apr–Aug)
pale edges reach base of secondaries (compare kinglets)
thick, hooked bill
heavy bluish legs
round head
Adult Pacific
dark lower mandible
drab olive
pale lores
Adult Mexican

Black-capped Vireo

Vireo atricapillus

L 4.5" WS 7" WT 0.3 oz (8.5 g)

Very small and relatively thin-billed; dark cap and entirely pale lores distinctive.

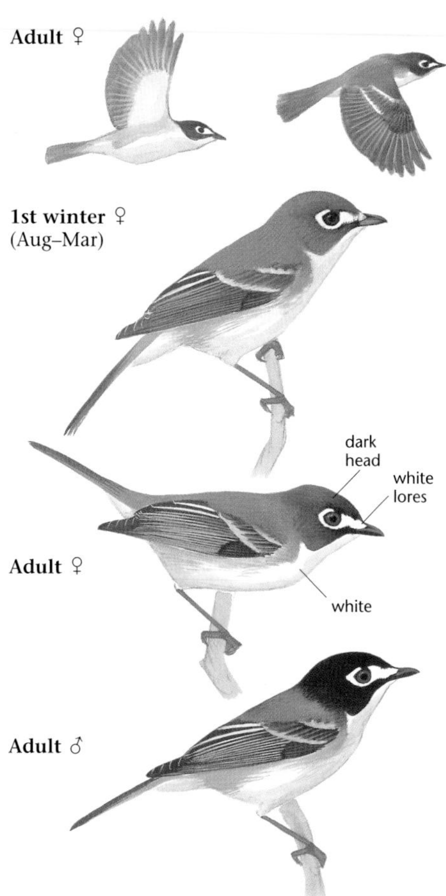
Adult ♀
1st winter ♀ (Aug–Mar)
dark head
white lores
Adult ♀
white
Adult ♂

Voice: Song of simple whistled phrases repeated every one to two seconds, each phrase repeated many times before switching to another phrase *trrweer trrweer trrweer . . . tsuwiif tsuwiif. . . .* Call a nasal, rising *reeee dee de* or laughing *rrrreeeee-dee-dee-dee-dee*. Also a high, harsh mewing *shhhhhrii shhhri shhr shhr* and a dry *pik* like Hermit Thrush.

Voice: Song of well-spaced complex phrases *grrtzeepididid, prididzeegrrt . . . ,* with husky chattering quality. Call a long, harsh, rising *zhreee* similar to Bewick's Wren scold; many variations. Also a short, dry *tidik* like Ruby-crowned Kinglet.

Two populations of Hutton's Vireo—Pacific and Mexican—differ slightly and are perhaps not identifiable. Mexican birds average about 10 percent larger and are grayer with more distinct whitish eye-ring and wingbars, while Pacific birds are washed with yellow-olive. Minor differences in voice need further study.

These two species, similar in all respects, with bold "spectacles" and complex, harsh songs, are related to Black-capped. Somewhat secretive, both are found in dense, brushy tangles within woods.

White-eyed Vireo

Vireo griseus

L 5" WS 7.5" WT 0.4 oz (11.5 g)

Small and stocky; short-necked and short-tailed. White wing-bars and yellow "spectacles" distinctive.

Adult

Worn juvenile (Aug–Sep)

can become very pale and gray (compare Bell's)

dark iris becomes pale during winter (some retain grayish iris through spring; beware confusion with Thick-billed)

1st winter (Jul-Feb)

white iris unique

bright yellow "spectacles"

gray nape

Adult

whitish throat

pale yellow flanks

Voice: Song rapid, nasal, harsh; typically begins and/or ends with sharp *chik* notes and includes at least one long, whining note: *tik-a-purrreeer-chik* or *chik-errrr-topikerreerr-chik;* many variations. Call a harsh *meerr* level or slightly descending; commonly a level series *rikrikrikrik rik rik rik rik;* sometimes a single rising *rik.*

White-eyed Vireo often incorporates imitations of other species' call notes into its song. Commonly used are call notes of Downy Woodpecker, Great Crested Flycatcher, Wood Thrush, Summer Tanager, Eastern Towhee, and others.

Thick-billed Vireo

Vireo crassirostris

L 5" WS 7.25" WT 0.46 oz (13 g)

Slightly thicker-billed than White-eyed; best distinguished by pattern of eye markings and dull yellow throat.

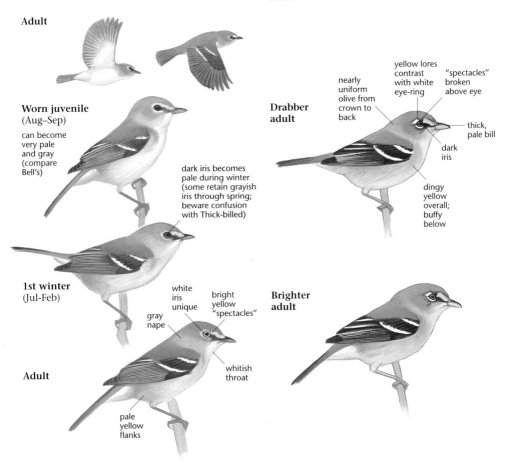

Drabber adult

nearly uniform olive from crown to back

yellow lores contrast with white eye-ring

"spectacles" broken above eye

thick, pale bill

dark iris

dingy yellow overall; buffy below

Brighter adult

Voice: Song very similar to White-eyed; averages harsher (but given variation in White-eyed this is of limited use). Call a slow series of harsh scold notes; notes longer and series slower than White-eyed.

Large Spectacled Vireos

These two species and Cassin's and Blue-headed are closely related, forming a distinctive group with similar shape, plumage, and voice. All forage in trees in mixed woods.

Yellow-throated Vireo

Vireo flavifrons

L 5.5" WS 9.5" WT 0.63 oz (18 g)

Large-headed and heavy-billed, even shorter-tailed than Solitary Vireos; distinctive bright yellow wash over head and breast (compare Pine Warbler).

Adult

yellow "spectacles"

1st fall
(Jul–Mar)

bright yellow throat

whitish belly

Worn adult
(Mar–Aug)

Voice: Song of short two- or three-syllable phrases, most slurred with a burry quality *rrreeyoo, rreeooee, three-eight . . .* ; averages one phrase every three seconds; distinct from all except Plumbeous Vireo. Call of rapid, harsh notes falling or steady *ship shep shep shep shep shep shep shep* very similar to Solitary Vireos.

Plumbeous Vireo

Vireo plumbeus

L 5.75" WS 10" WT 0.63 oz (18 g)

Averages a little larger and larger-billed than Cassin's, has broader white wing-bars, and almost entirely lacks yellow tones.

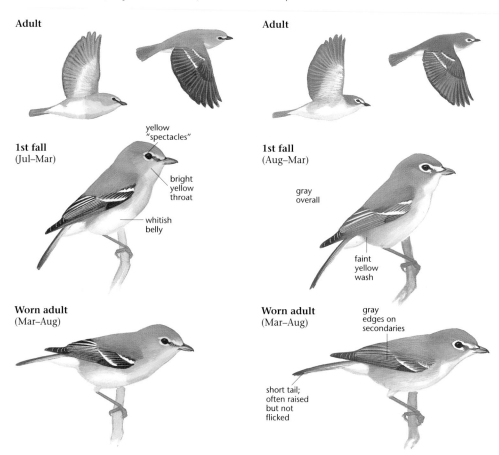

Adult

1st fall
(Aug–Mar)

gray overall

faint yellow wash

Worn adult
(Mar–Aug)

gray edges on secondaries

short tail; often raised but not flicked

Voice: Song of rough, burry phrases similar to Yellow-throated and Gray; lower-pitched, rougher, and with slightly shorter phrases on average than Blue-headed or Cassin's; averages one phrase every three seconds. Call a harsh series like Yellow-throated, often ending with rising *zink* note.

Song in vireos is learned. There are numerous records of Yellow-throated singing like Blue-headed, and vice versa; presumably the same phenomenon occurs with other species as well and should be considered when identifying birds by sound.

Large Spectacled Vireos (continued)

These two species and Plumbeous Vireo were until recently considered a single species, Solitary Vireo. All three are very similar, with bright white "spectacles," stout bills, and short tails.

Cassin's Vireo

Vireo cassinii

L 5.5" WS 9.5" WT 0.56 oz (16 g)

Plumage intermediate between Blue-headed and Plumbeous.

Adult

1st fall (Aug–Mar)

uniform greenish on upperside

weak contrast between throat and auriculars

Bright adult (Aug–Mar)

weak contrast

similar to Blue-headed

Drab adult (Mar–Aug)

similar to Plumbeous

greenish edges on secondaries

Voice: Song similar to Plumbeous but slightly higher-pitched and with more clear phrases, tending toward Blue-headed; distinctly lower-pitched and more burry than Blue-headed (but much overlap). Calls like those of other Solitary Vireos.

Blue-headed Vireo

Vireo solitarius

L 5.5" WS 9.5" WT 0.56 oz (16 g)

Shape identical to Cassin's; plumage usually obviously brighter and more contrasting, but some nearly overlap.

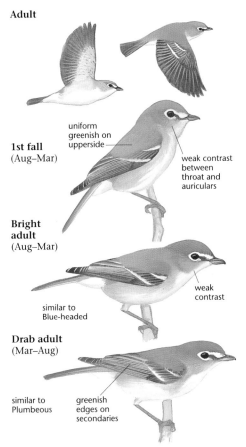

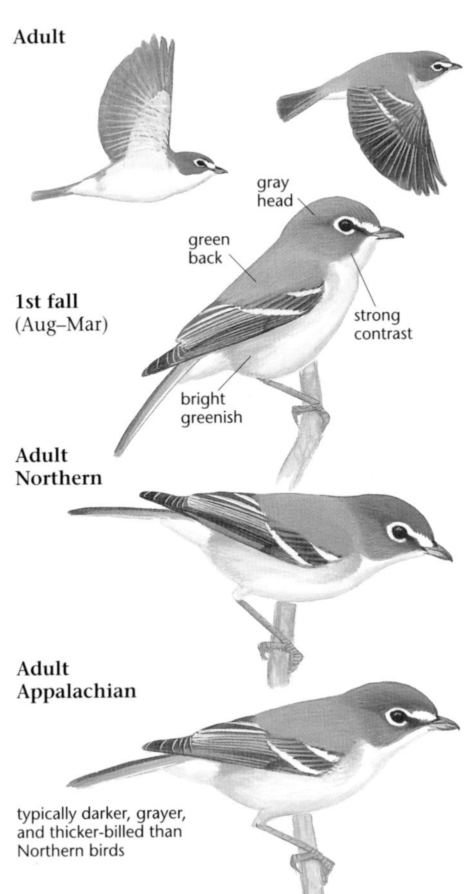
Adult
gray head
green back
1st fall
(Aug–Mar)
strong contrast
bright greenish
Adult Northern
Adult Appalachian
typically darker, grayer, and thicker-billed than Northern birds

Voice: Song of high, clear, sweet phrases with slurred notes *see you, cheerio, be-seein-u, so-long, seeya* . . . ; sometimes gives burry phrases, especially in western portion of range. Averages one phrase every 2.5 seconds, slightly slower than Red-eyed. Call like other Solitary Vireos.

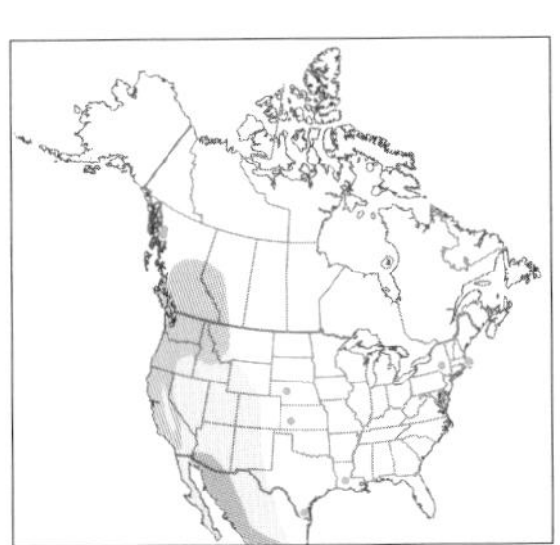

The three species in the Solitary Vireo group are rather poorly differentiated. Variation in song is partly clinal, and individuals can learn the "wrong" song. Intermediate birds (and perhaps hybrids) should be expected, and not every individual will be identifiable.

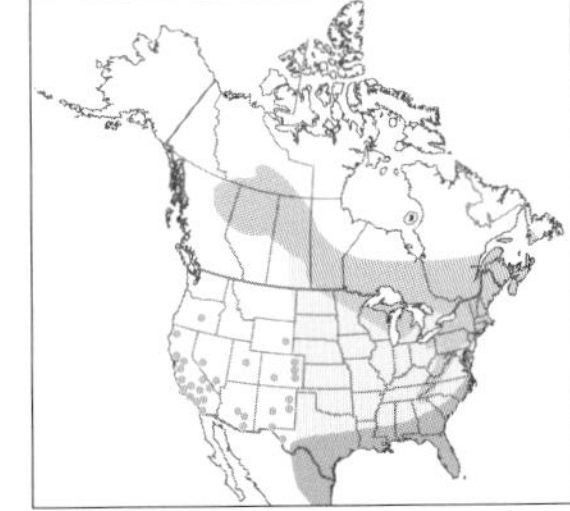

Jays, Crows, and Their Allies
Family: Corvidae

20 species in 8 genera. Jays are long-tailed and most are brightly colored; crows and ravens are all-black. Pinyon Jay, Clark's Nutcracker, and magpies are distinctive. All species are often found in small groups. They are omnivorous but feed mainly on seeds and nuts; some species' diets are very specialized. Flight is generally strong and buoyant with rowing wingbeats. Nest is a bulky cup of sticks in a tree (both magpies build a large conspicuous ball of sticks); ravens usually build their nests on ledges or telephone poles. They are noisy and aggressive birds but are very inconspicuous when nesting. All species mob predators, and owls and hawks can sometimes be found by following agitated jays and crows. Adults are shown.

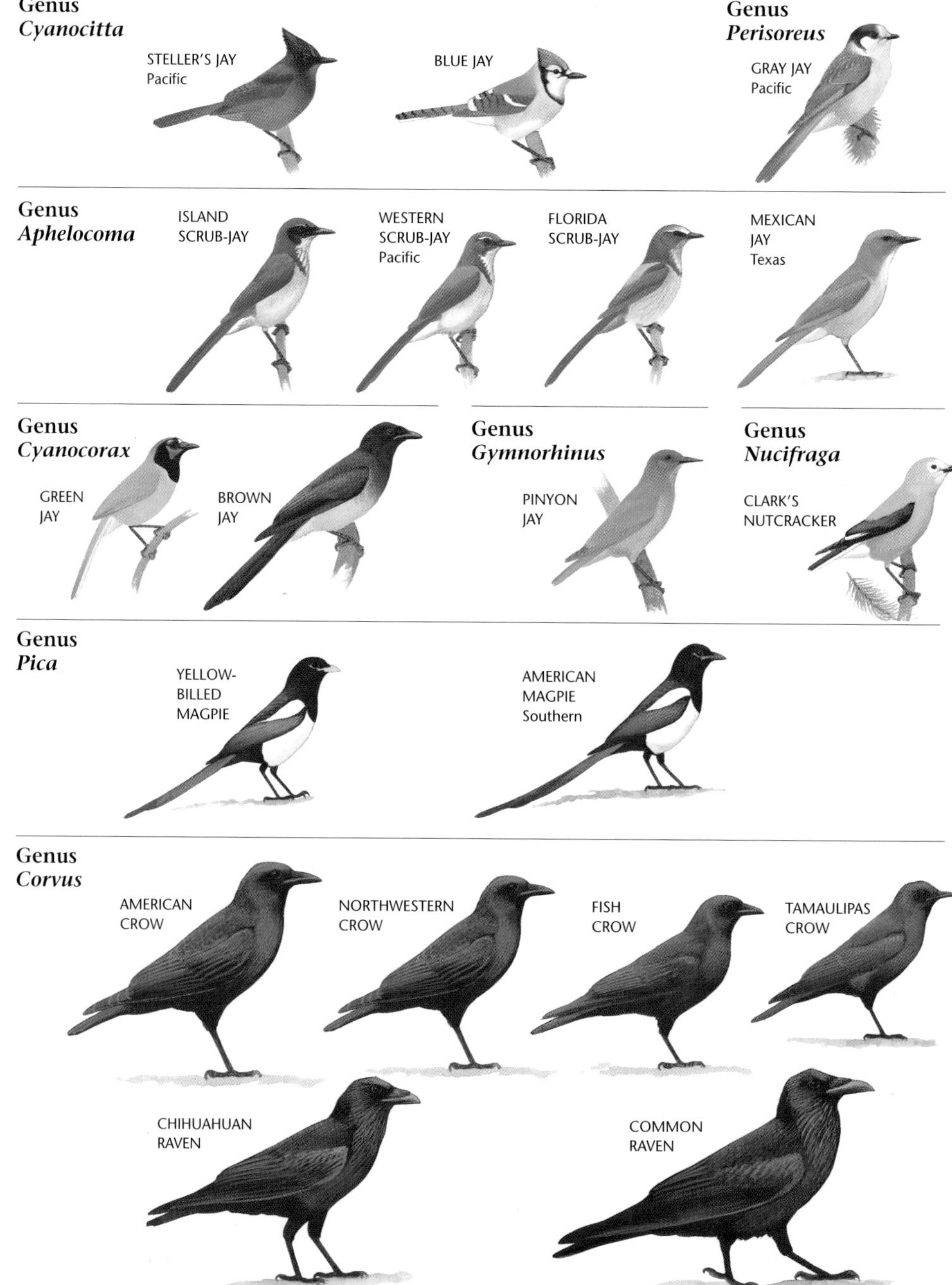

Genus
Cyanocitta
STELLER'S JAY
Pacific
BLUE JAY
Genus
Perisoreus
GRAY JAY
Pacific
Genus
Aphelocoma
ISLAND
SCRUB-JAY
WESTERN
SCRUB-JAY
Pacific
FLORIDA
SCRUB-JAY
MEXICAN
JAY
Texas
Genus
Cyanocorax
GREEN
JAY
BROWN
JAY
Genus
Gymnorhinus
PINYON
JAY
Genus
Nucifraga
CLARK'S
NUTCRACKER
Genus
Pica
YELLOW-
BILLED
MAGPIE
AMERICAN
MAGPIE
Southern
Genus
Corvus
AMERICAN
CROW
NORTHWESTERN
CROW
FISH
CROW
TAMAULIPAS
CROW
CHIHUAHUAN
RAVEN
COMMON
RAVEN

Crested Jays: Genus *Cyanocitta*

These two crested species are broad-winged and relatively short-tailed. Both are noisy and conspicuous residents of woods, often traveling in small groups.

Steller's Jay

Cyanocitta stelleri

L 11.5" WS 19" WT 3.7 oz (105 g)

Overall dark color with paler blue rump distinctive; shorter-tailed than scrub-jays.

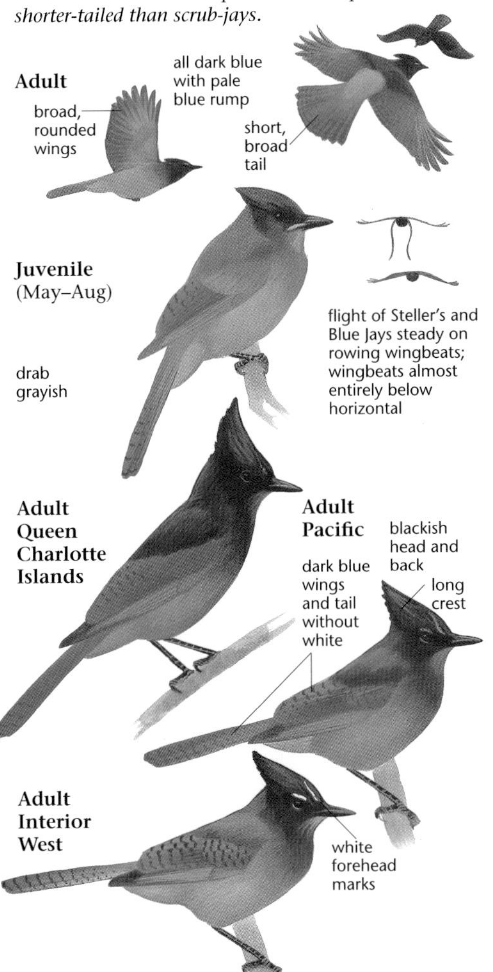

Adult
broad, rounded wings
all dark blue with pale blue rump
short, broad tail
Juvenile (May–Aug)
drab grayish
flight of Steller's and Blue Jays steady on rowing wingbeats; wingbeats almost entirely below horizontal
Adult Queen Charlotte Islands
Adult Pacific
blackish head and back
dark blue wings and tail without white
long crest
Adult Interior West
white forehead marks

Voice: Varied; most common a very harsh, unmusical, descending *shaaaaar;* also a rapid, popping *shek shek shek shek;* generally lower, harsher than scrub-jays. Also a clear, whistled *whidoo* and quiet, thrasherlike song.

Blue Jay

Cyanocitta cristata

L 11" WS 16" WT 3 oz (85 g)

Pale blue upperside with flashing white tail and wing-patches. Our only migratory jay; migrates in loose flocks during day.

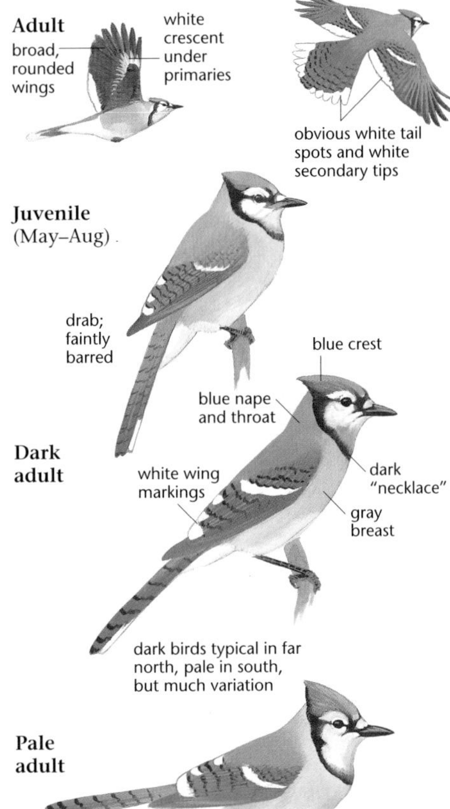

Adult
broad, rounded wings
white crescent under primaries
obvious white tail spots and white secondary tips
Juvenile (May–Aug)
drab; faintly barred
blue crest
blue nape and throat
Dark adult
white wing markings
dark "necklace"
gray breast
dark birds typical in far north, pale in south, but much variation
Pale adult

Voice: Varied; most common a shrill, harsh, descending scream *jaaaay*. Many other calls include clear, whistled phrases *toolili;* quiet, clicking rattle; and rarely a quiet, thrasherlike song. Short, harsh *shkrrr* when attacking predator. Expert mimic, especially of raptors.

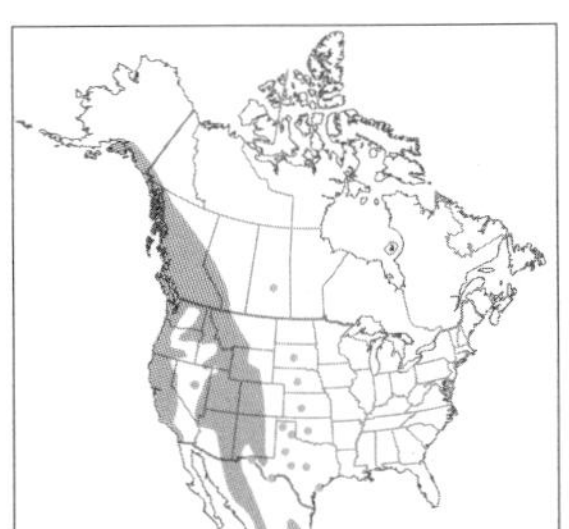

Subspecies of Steller's Jay sort out into two main groups, but variation is clinal with many intermediate populations. Interior West birds are paler overall with white streaks on the forehead; Pacific populations are darker overall, with smaller blue streaks on the forehead; darkest birds occur on Queen Charlotte Islands, off British Columbia.

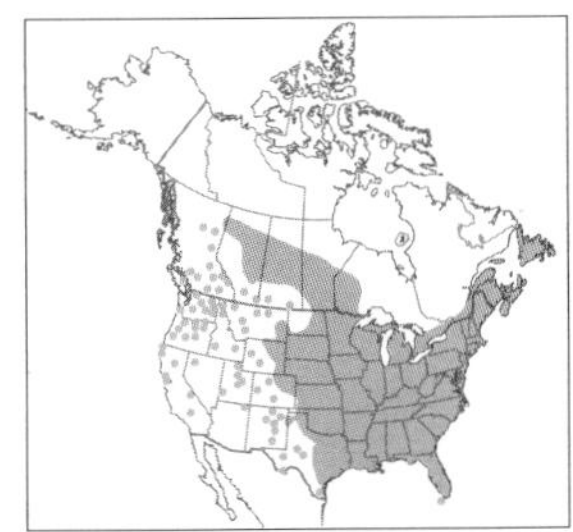

Scrub-Jays: Genus *Aphelocoma*

This species, Island, and Florida Scrub-Jays are very closely related and similar in all respects. All are found in dense, brushy areas among oak or juniper trees.

Western Scrub-Jay

Aphelocoma californica

L 11.5" WS 15.5" WT 3 oz (85 g)

More slender and relatively longer-tailed than Steller's Jay; smaller and more slender than Mexican Jay.

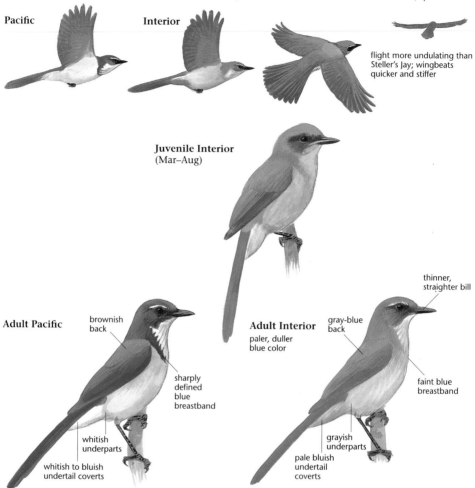

Pacific

Interior

flight more undulating than Steller's Jay; wingbeats quicker and stiffer

Juvenile Interior
(Mar–Aug)

Adult Pacific

brownish back

sharply defined blue breastband

whitish underparts

whitish to bluish undertail coverts

Adult Interior
paler, duller blue color

gray-blue back

thinner, straighter bill

faint blue breastband

grayish underparts

pale bluish undertail coverts

Voice: Generally harsh and angry-sounding. Most common call a harsh, rising *shreeeeenk* with some musical quality; often in rapid series *wenk wenk wenk wenk* or *kkew kkew kkew* . . . ; also a harsh, pounding *sheeyuk sheeyuk* . . . in long series. Other calls include a low clucking *chudduk* or clicking sounds. Interior population averages lower, hoarser, less electric-sounding than Pacific.

Two well-differentiated populations, with almost no range overlap, are distinguishable by plumage; there are few intermediates. Pacific population is thicker-billed and darker overall, with richer colors; distinctive plumage details are noted above. Pacific birds are generally bold and conspicuous; Interior birds are shy and inconspicuous, and seem to be sparsely distributed.

Scrub-Jays: Genus *Aphelocoma* (continued)

Closely related to Western Scrub-Jay but not overlapping in range, these two species have a limited distribution. All scrub-jays were formerly considered a single species, Scrub Jay.

Island Scrub-Jay

Aphelocoma insularis

L 13" WS 17" WT 4.1 oz (116 g)

About 10 percent larger and up to 30 percent longer-billed than Western; the only jay in its limited range (Santa Cruz Island).

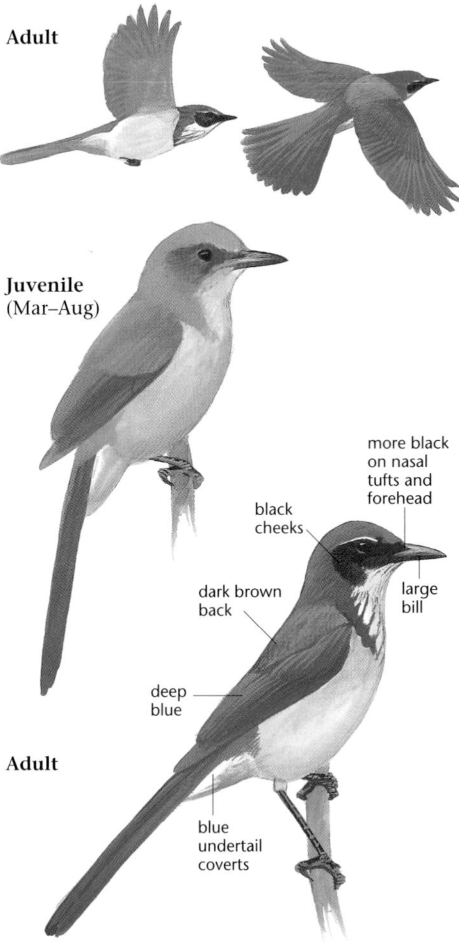
Adult
Juvenile
(Mar–Aug)
more black
on nasal
tufts and
forehead
black
cheeks
large
bill
dark brown
back
deep
blue
Adult
blue
undertail
coverts

Voice: Essentially identical to Pacific population of Western Scrub-Jay.

Florida Scrub-Jay

Aphelocoma coerulescens

L 11" WS 13.5" WT 2.8 oz (80 g)

Slightly smaller and relatively longer-tailed than Blue Jay; uncrested and without white on wings or tail. Smaller and longer-tailed than Western but no range overlap.

Adult

Juvenile
(Mar–Aug)
whitish
forehead
pale gray-
brown back
blue
cheeks
Adult
faintly
streaked
brown
underparts

Voice: Similar to Western Scrub-Jay but distinctly lower, harsher, flatter, less rising *kreesh;* also a low, husky *kereep* and other variations. All calls very unlike higher, more expressive voice of Blue Jay.

Mexican Jay

Closely related to scrub-jays but differing in many ways, this large and social species travels in noisy groups through oak woods.

Mexican Jay

Aphelocoma ultramarina

L 11.5" WS 19.5" WT 4.4 oz (125 g)

Large, long-billed, and short-tailed, with long, broad wings.

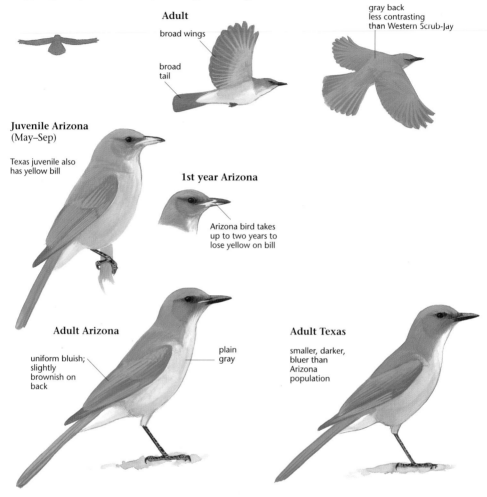

Adult

broad wings

broad tail

gray back less contrasting than Western Scrub-Jay

Juvenile Arizona (May–Sep)

Texas juvenile also has yellow bill

1st year Arizona

Arizona bird takes up to two years to lose yellow on bill

Adult Arizona

uniform bluish; slightly brownish on back

plain gray

Adult Texas

smaller, darker, bluer than Arizona population

Voice: Somewhat less varied than other jays; common call a rather soft, musical, rising *zhenk* or *wink* repeated in series *wink wink wink* . . . ; notes softer and shorter than scrub-jays and with almost finchlike quality. Also gives a soft thrasherlike song. Texas calls shorter, harsher, and less musical than Arizona: *jink jink jink*. . . . Texas birds also give a territorial call: a mechanical rattle; lacking in communal Arizona populations.

Although Texas and Arizona populations differ in plumage, size, voice, and habits, they are apparently the ends of a cline, connected by a series of intermediate populations in Mexico, but more study is needed. Texas birds are 10 percent smaller, darker overall, and brighter blue with a whitish throat (vs. grayish like breast); juvenile acquires black bill just after fledging (Arizona juvenile is yellow-billed for two years); pairs are territorial (vs. cooperative flocks of six to ten birds year-round); eggs are speckled (vs. unmarked).

Tropical Jays: Genus *Cyanocorax*

These two species are usually the only jays in their range and are not easily confused with others. Found mainly within dense, brushy woods, both travel in noisy groups.

Green Jay

Cyanocorax yncas

L 10.5" WS 13.5" WT 3.5 oz (100 g)

Rather small; unmistakable pale green with flashing yellow outer tail feathers and black and blue head.

Adult
flight rather labored, with quick wingbeats and short, stiff glides

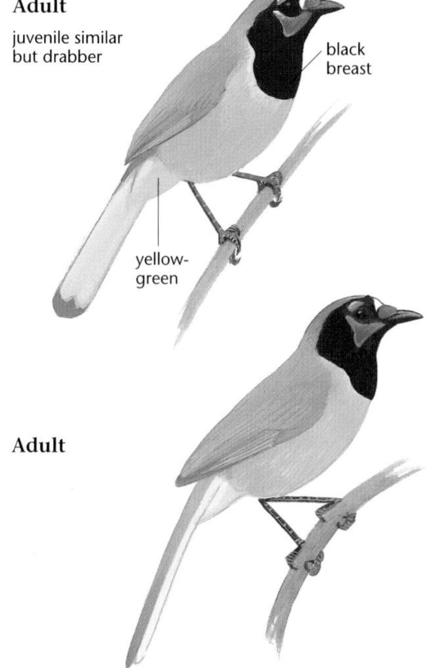

Adult
juvenile similar but drabber
black breast
yellow-green
Adult

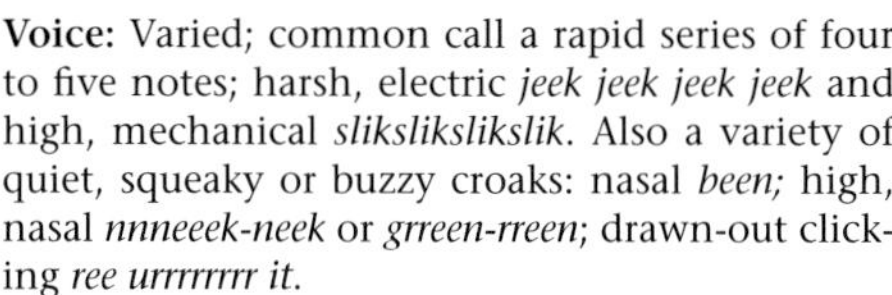

Voice: Varied; common call a rapid series of four to five notes; harsh, electric *jeek jeek jeek jeek* and high, mechanical *sliksliksliksIik*. Also a variety of quiet, squeaky or buzzy croaks: nasal *been;* high, nasal *nnneeek-neek* or *grreen-rreen*; drawn-out clicking *ree urrrrrrr it.*

Brown Jay

Cyanocorax morio

L 16.5" WS 26" WT 7 oz (200 g) ♂>♀

Very large, long-necked, and long-tailed, with large, floppy wings.

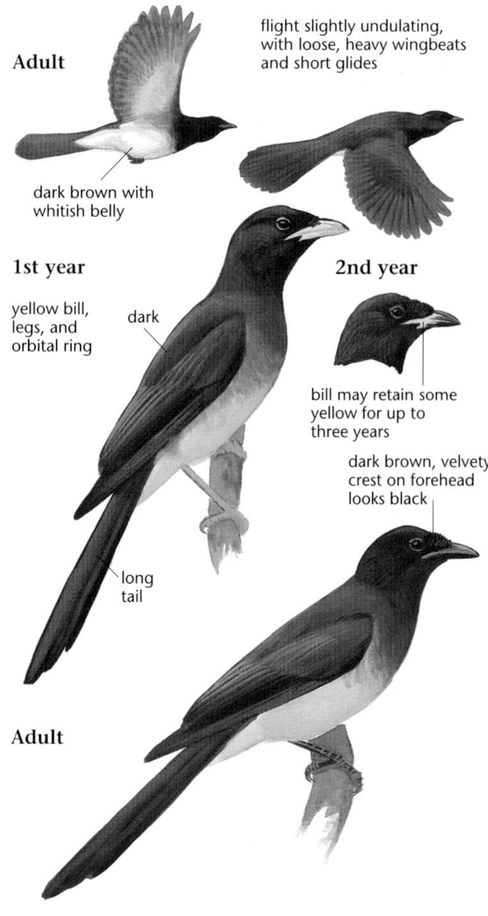

Adult
flight slightly undulating, with loose, heavy wingbeats and short glides
dark brown with whitish belly
1st year
2nd year
yellow bill, legs, and orbital ring
dark
bill may retain some yellow for up to three years
dark brown, velvety crest on forehead looks black
long tail
Adult

Voice: Common call an intense, clear bugling *keerg* or *paow* often repeated in series and given in chorus by flock; much like Red-shouldered Hawk but higher, more raucous, without upslur at beginning. Also gives a popping rattle audible at close range.

GRAY JAY

This rather quiet and fluffy jay of coniferous forests is usually found in small groups. Bold, inquisitive behavior has earned this species many nicknames, including "camp-robber."

Gray Jay

Perisoreus canadensis

L 11.5" WS 18" WT 2.5 oz (70 g)

Distinctive fluffy plumage, long tail, and short bill; resembles an oversize chickadee.

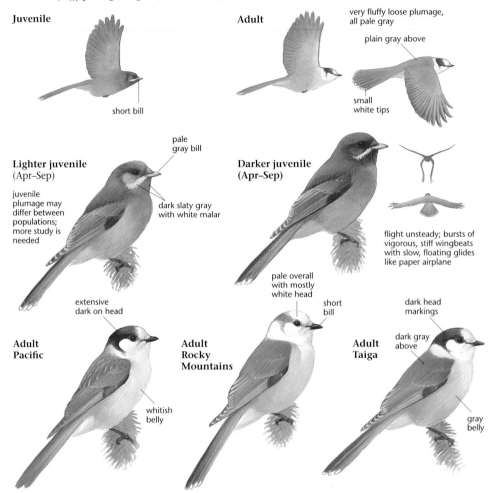

Juvenile

short bill

Adult

very fluffy loose plumage, all pale gray

plain gray above

small white tips

Lighter juvenile (Apr–Sep)

pale gray bill

juvenile plumage may differ between populations; more study is needed

dark slaty gray with white malar

Darker juvenile (Apr–Sep)

flight unsteady; bursts of vigorous, stiff wingbeats with slow, floating glides like paper airplane

Adult Pacific

extensive dark on head

whitish belly

Adult Rocky Mountains

pale overall with mostly white head

short bill

Adult Taiga

dark head markings

dark gray above

gray belly

Voice: Calls generally soft, whistled or husky notes in short series. Vary from clear *weeoo* and *weef weef weef weef* to musical, husky *chuf-chuf-weef* to soft, dry *chef chef chef chef* and very rough, dry *kreh kreh kreh kreh*. Short, whistled *weeoo* and variations also common. Also gives screeching *jaaay* reminiscent of Blue Jay (may mimic). Voice of all populations similar; calls of Pacific birds may average higher and sharper.

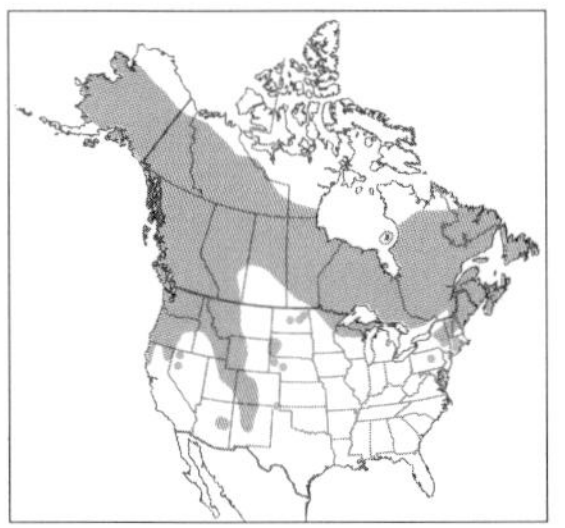

Extensive clinal variation has resulted in three distinguishable populations, but all are connected by intermediate populations. Rocky Mountain birds south of Canada have very limited black on head; Pacific populations are darker overall but with whitish belly, extensively dark head, lack white on tail and secondaries, and have brownish-tinged backs with pale shaft streaks. There may be subtle variations in juvenal plumage and in voice; more study is needed.

Specialized Jays

Pinyon Jay is usually found near pinyon pines in nomadic flocks. Clark's Nutcracker is found in mountain coniferous forests, often seen perching in treetops or flying strongly over head.

Pinyon Jay

Gymnorhinus cyanocephalus

L 10.5" WS 19" WT 3.5 oz (100 g)

Short-tailed and plain-colored.

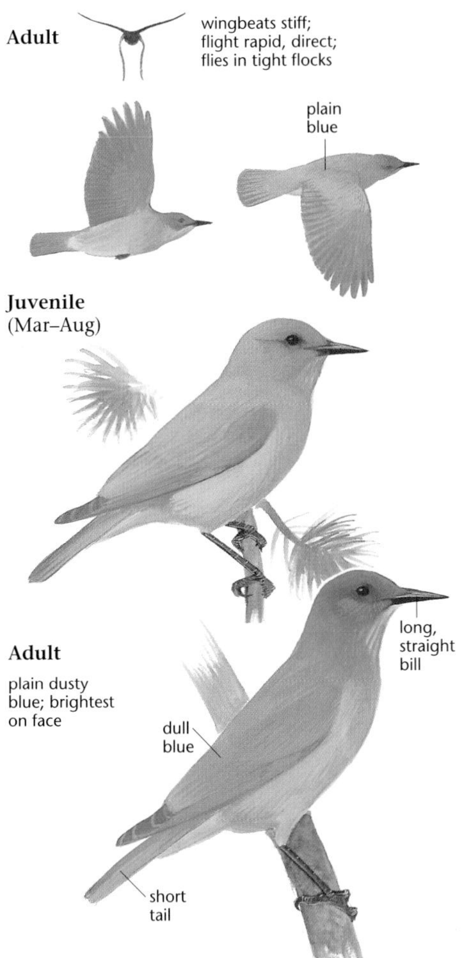

Adult
wingbeats stiff; flight rapid, direct; flies in tight flocks
plain blue
Juvenile (Mar–Aug)
Adult
plain dusty blue; brightest on face
dull blue
long, straight bill
short tail

Voice: Calls rather nasal and soft for a jay; quality reminiscent of California and Gambel's Quail. Calls constantly in flight: a soft, conversational series *hoi hoi hoi* . . . or single *hoya;* also a series of harsher rising notes *kwee kwee kwee* . . . and loud, clear, nasal *waoow.*

Clark's Nutcracker

Nucifraga columbiana

L 12" WS 24" WT 4.6 oz (130 g)

Distinctive plumage; short tail, long wings, and long primaries.

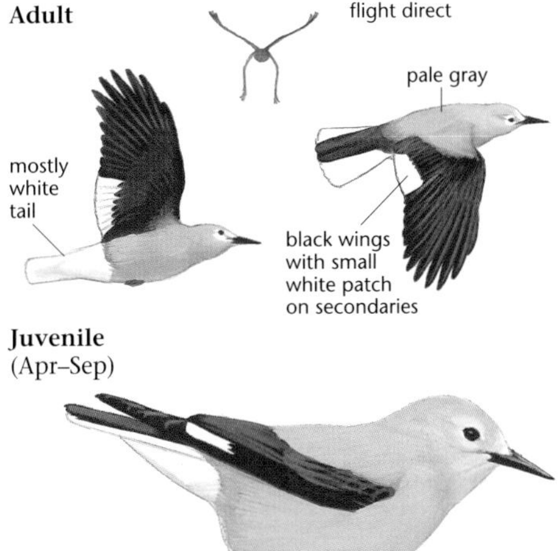

Adult
flight direct
pale gray
mostly white tail
black wings with small white patch on secondaries

Juvenile (Apr–Sep)
Adult
black wings
pale gray with white face
black and white tail

Voice: Varied; common call a long, harsh, slightly rising *shraaaaaaa;* hollow and slightly buzzing. Other calls include a higher, descending *taaar;* a very hard, slow rattle *k-k-k-k-k;* a strong yelping *keeeew;* a clear, nasal *waaat* reminiscent of Pinyon Jay; and a high, clear, electric *deeen.*

In some respects, these two distinctive species are intermediate between jays and crows. They have short tails, straight bills, and direct flight, and they often walk rather than hop (jays always hop).

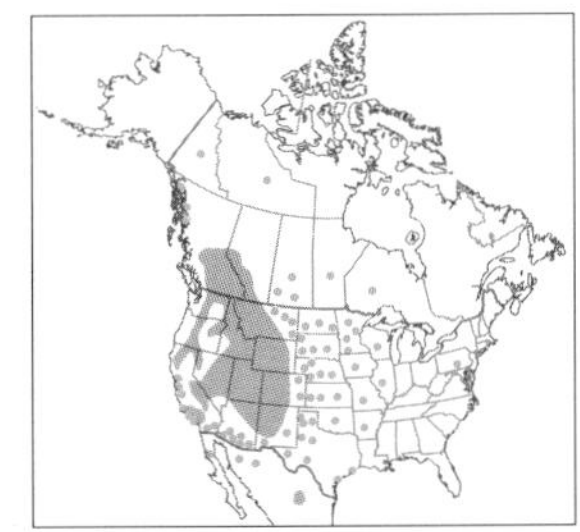

MAGPIES

These two species are found in small groups year-round in open country with scattered trees, often on the ground. They have striking pied plumage and long tails.

American Magpie

Pica hudsonia

L 19" WS 25" WT 6 oz (175 g) ♂>♀

Fairly large and heavy with long tail, stout bill, broad wings. Formerly known as Black-billed Magpie.

Adult

long tail

flashing white wing-patches

Juvenile (Jun–Aug)

white scapulars

white belly

Adult Northern

Adult Southern

Voice: Call a nasal, rising *jeeeek;* harsher, lower *rek rek rek rek* or *weg weg weg weg weg;* rapid *shek shek shek shek,* three to five notes. Also higher, long, nasal *gway gway* or *gwaaaaay;* rather nasal, hard, querulous *ennk.*

Yellow-billed Magpie

Pica nuttalli

L 16.5" WS 24" WT 5 oz (155 g) ♂>♀

Differs from American only in yellow color of bare parts and small size (but overlaps with smallest American); very slight differences in voice.

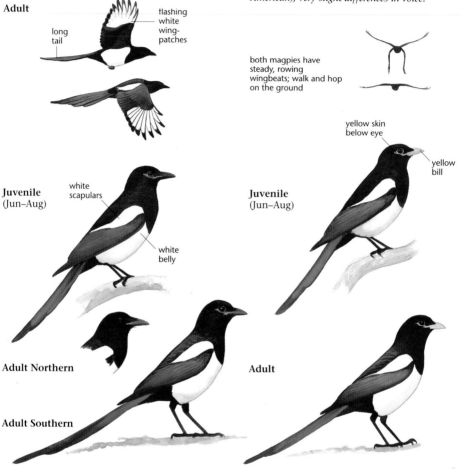

both magpies have steady, rowing wingbeats; walk and hop on the ground

yellow skin below eye

yellow bill

Juvenile (Jun–Aug)

Adult

Voice: Nearly identical to American; chatter call reportedly higher-pitched and clearer than American.

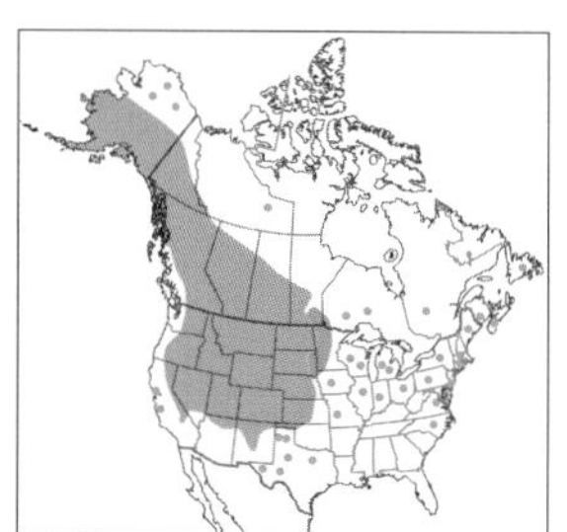

Southern populations of American (adjacent to Yellow-billed) average smaller and smaller-billed than Northern and show some bare blackish skin around the eye, thus approaching Yellow-billed in appearance.

Ravens

Ravens are larger and lankier than crows, with heavier bills and deeper voices. Common is found mainly in mountainous areas, Chihuahuan mainly in flat, arid grassland, but much overlap.

Common Raven

Corvus corax

L 24" WS 53" WT 2.6 lb (1,200 g) ♂>♀

Large, with long, narrow wings; long, wedge-shaped tail; heavy bill.

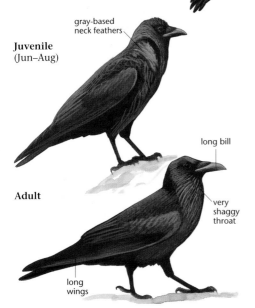

ravens often soar, crows never do
pairs engage in aerial acrobatics
Adult
long head and bill
wedge-shaped tail
gray-based neck feathers
Juvenile (Jun–Aug)
long bill
Adult
very shaggy throat
long wings

Voice: Incredibly varied: from low, deep baritone croaks to high, bell-like and twanging notes. Long, hoarse *kraaah;* lower, hollow *brrronk;* and deep, resonant *prruk* are typical. Some calls like Chihuahuan. Juvenile calls higher, more squawking than adult.

Chihuahuan Raven

Corvus cryptoleucus

L 19.5" WS 44" WT 1.2 lb (530 g) ♂>♀

Intermediate between Common Raven and American Crow; distinctly longer-winged and heavier-billed than crows.

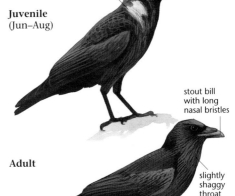

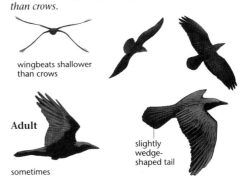

wingbeats shallower than crows

Adult

slightly wedge-shaped tail

sometimes found in very large flocks in winter

white-based neck feathers

Juvenile (Jun–Aug)

stout bill with long nasal bristles

Adult

slightly shaggy throat

Voice: Less varied than Common. Typically fairly high, crowlike croak; usually a slightly rising *graak,* but this can be matched by Common. Apparently also gives *kre* and growling sounds similar to Common.

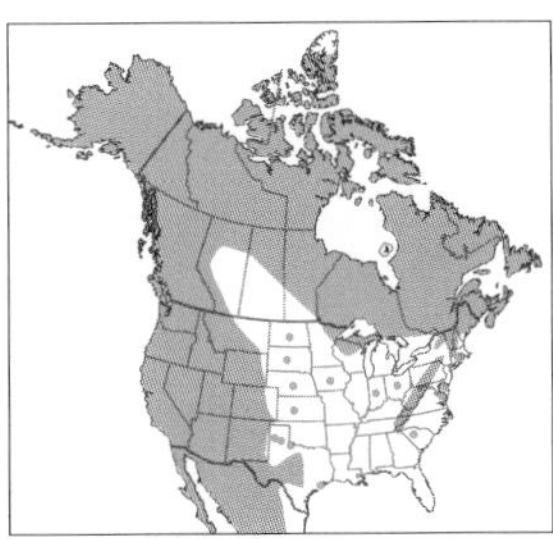

Distinguishing Chihuahuan Raven from small Common individuals can be extremely difficult. Voice is helpful but overlaps. Chihuahuan is subtly more crowlike in shape and relatively thicker-billed, with usually longer nasal bristles. It is best distinguished by the bright white bases of the body feathers, which are often exposed by wind or by preening.

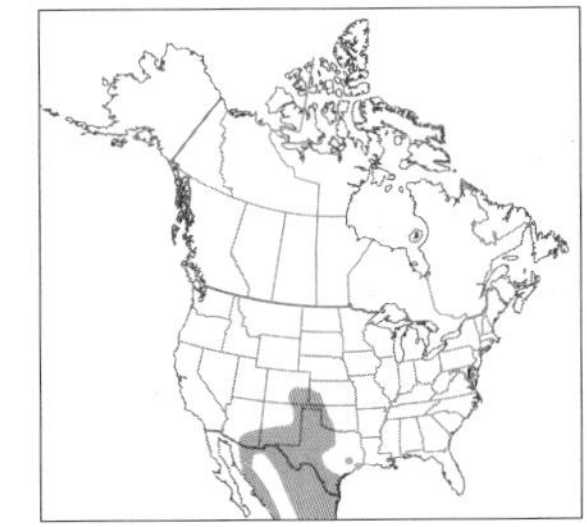

Crows

Familiar and conspicuous, these all-black birds are often seen in small groups, foraging mainly on the ground. Eurasian Jackdaw is distinctive in plumage, but crows are best identified by voice.

American Crow

Corvus brachyrhynchos

L 17.5" WS 39" WT 1 lb (450 g)

Large size, black plumage, short tail, and broad wings distinguish crows from all other birds.

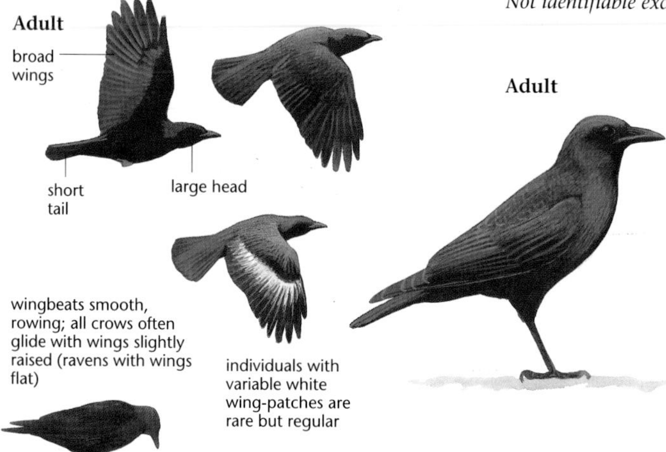

Adult
broad wings
short tail
large head
wingbeats smooth, rowing; all crows often glide with wings slightly raised (ravens with wings flat)
individuals with variable white wing-patches are rare but regular
foraging
Juvenile (Jun–Aug)
Adult

Voice: Call varied; typically the familiar full-voiced hoarse *carrr* or *caaw* with great variety of inflection and pitch. Also a rapid, hollow rattle *tatatato;* sometimes soft call *prrrk* similar to Common Raven. Juvenile gives higher, hoarser, nasal calls; usually also longer calls (e.g., *carrrr*).

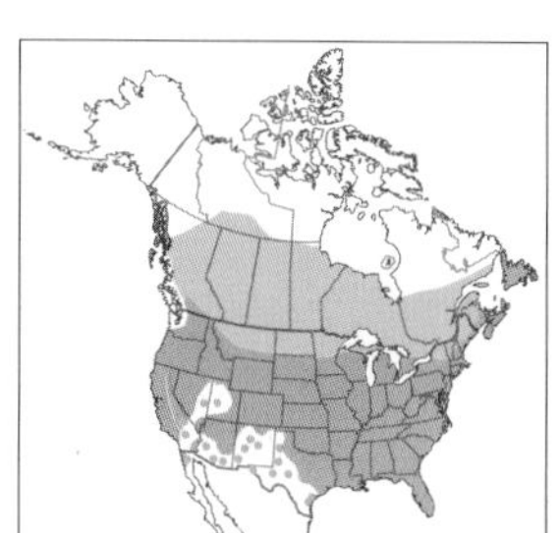

Northwestern Crow

Corvus caurinus

L 16" WS 34" WT 13 oz (380 g)

Averages smaller than American with slightly lower-pitched and hoarser voice, but all variation clinal. Not identifiable except by range.

Adult

Voice: Some calls a little lower, hoarser, and more rapid than adjacent populations of American (note that American Crow from Pacific region sounds distinctly lower and hoarser than eastern birds, thus approaching Northwestern).

Eurasian Jackdaw

Corvus monedula

L 14.5" WS 29" WT 7 oz (200 g)

Small and stocky with pigeonlike gait; wings shorter and pointier than other crows.

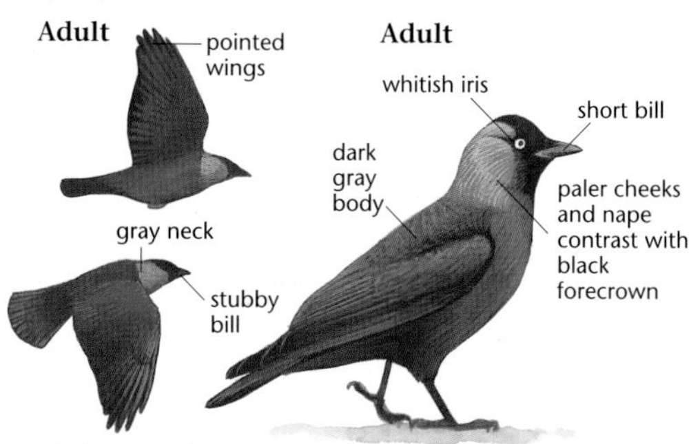

Adult
pointed wings
gray neck
stubby bill
Adult
whitish iris
short bill
dark gray body
paler cheeks and nape contrast with black forecrown

wingbeats quick; flight rapid

Voice: Call a sharp, hard *jeck* reminiscent of *chig* note of Red-bellied Woodpecker.

SMALL CROWS

These two species of small crows have restricted ranges and distinctive voices. Both are found in small groups in open areas, often mixed with other crows.

Fish Crow

Corvus ossifragus

L 15" WS 36" WT 10 oz (280 g)

Averages slightly smaller than American with subtle differences in shape; best distinguished by voice.

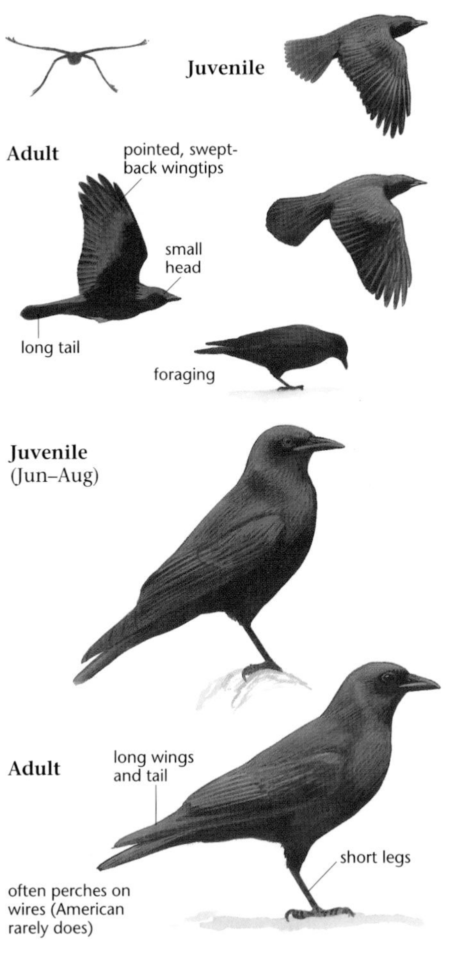

Juvenile
Adult
pointed, swept-back wingtips
small head
long tail
foraging
Juvenile (Jun–Aug)
Adult
long wings and tail
short legs
often perches on wires (American rarely does)

Voice: Call a simple, short, nasal *cah* or *cah-ah;* less often a hoarser *cahrr* like some high-pitched calls of American. Juvenile gives high *keeer* like American but higher, clearer. Throaty rattle *grrrr* higher and more nasal than American.

Tamaulipas Crow

Corvus imparatus

L 14.5" WS 30" WT 8 oz (240 g)

Small and slender. The only other crow within its normal range is the much larger Chihuahuan Raven (compare male Great-tailed Grackle).

Adult
small and sleek with long wings and tail

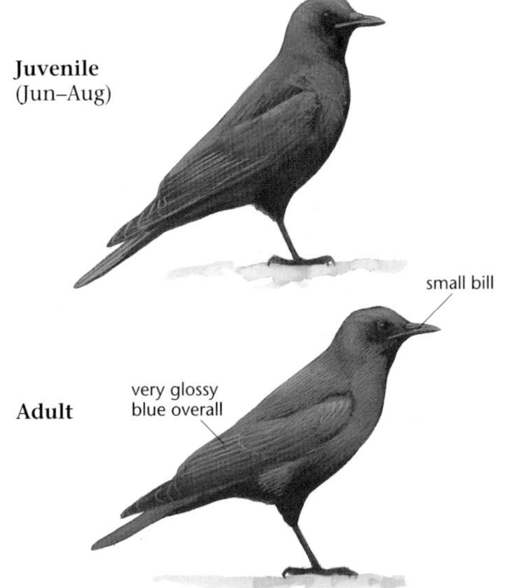

Juvenile (Jun–Aug)
small bill
very glossy blue overall
Adult

Voice: Call a very rough, nasal, flat burp/croak *brraarp* usually in series: *brraap brraap brraap.*

1st year crows and ravens retain juvenile flight feathers one full year; they are slightly shorter, more pointed, and browner than adult feathers (much browner by end of 1st year), contrasting with blackish coverts.

Larks

Family: Alaudidae

2 species in 2 genera. These cryptically colored birds nearly always perch on the ground or on low fence posts in open areas and are found in flocks in nonbreeding season. They run or walk with a shuffling gait. Flight is generally smooth and undulating; both species often fly low over fields. Larks are renowned for the song given by the male in flight. They nest on the ground at the base of a bush or grass tuft. Adult females are shown.

Genus
Alauda
SKY LARK
Genus
Eremophila
HORNED
LARK

OPEN-GROUND BIRDS

Only a few species of small songbirds are normally seen on open ground such as golf courses, plowed fields, and pastures. These include:

Larks: Flocks stay close together, walk with shuffling gait; flight low, flowing, swooping, with chirping or lisping flight calls.

American and Red-throated Pipits: Flocks disperse on the ground, with individuals standing upright and walking randomly in all directions; flight buoyant, rising quickly and undulating; high, squeaky flight calls.

Longspurs and Snow Bunting: Short legs and shuffling motions; flight low but less flowing than larks; individuals can often be picked out of flocks of larks because they stay at the edges of the lark flock, both on the ground and in flight, flying either higher or lower than larks; rattling or whistled flight calls.

Savannah Sparrow (also to some extent Vesper Sparrow, Lark Sparrow, and others, but all sparrows generally seek more cover): Flocks never tightly organized; move by hopping actions and fly in a straight line to another perch, unlike the circling, surveying flight of the species above; high, thin, weak flight calls.

AMERICAN PIPIT
Adult
nonbreeding
LAPLAND
LONGSPUR
1st winter ♀
SAVANNAH
SPARROW
Adult

Sky Lark

Alauda arvensis

L 7.25" WS 13" WT 1.4 oz (40 g)

Slightly larger, stockier, and shorter-tailed than Horned. Small introduced population near Vancouver originated in Britain; records elsewhere are vagrants from Asia.

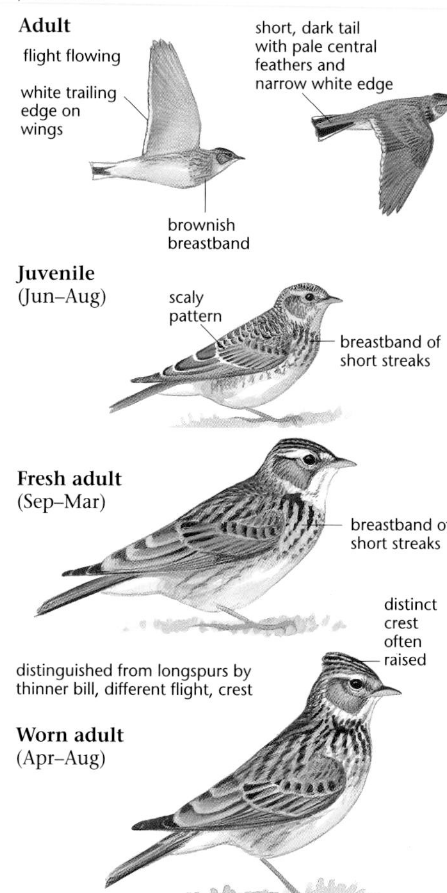
Adult
flight flowing
white trailing edge on wings
short, dark tail with pale central feathers and narrow white edge
brownish breastband
Juvenile
(Jun–Aug)
scaly pattern
breastband of short streaks
Fresh adult
(Sep–Mar)
breastband of short streaks
distinct crest often raised
distinguished from longspurs by thinner bill, different flight, crest
Worn adult
(Apr–Aug)

Voice: Song a spectacular varied warble of high, liquid, rolling notes in long series; often including mimicry of other species; given from high in the air. Flight call a low, rolling chortle *drirdrirk*.

Horned Lark

This species is found on barren ground with short grass or scattered bushes. In winter it may form large flocks, often containing several subspecies and mixed with longspurs and Snow Buntings.

Horned Lark

Eremophila alpestris

L 7.25" WS 12" WT 1.1 oz (32 g)

Fairly slender and long-winged, with short, stout bill and square tail. Note dark mask and dark breastband in all plumages. Flight buoyant and flowing.

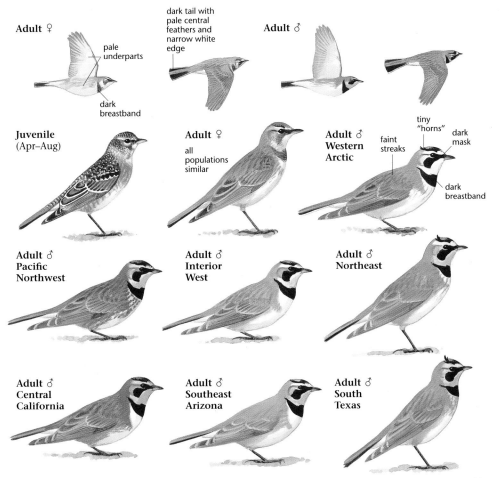

Adult ♀

pale underparts

dark breastband

dark tail with pale central feathers and narrow white edge

Adult ♂

Juvenile (Apr–Aug)

Adult ♀

all populations similar

Adult ♂ Western Arctic

faint streaks

tiny "horns"

dark mask

dark breastband

Adult ♂ Pacific Northwest

Adult ♂ Interior West

Adult ♂ Northeast

Adult ♂ Central California

Adult ♂ Southeast Arizona

Adult ♂ South Texas

Voice: Song rather high and weak: a few weak, lisping chirps followed by a rapid, tinkling, rising warble *reeek trik treet tritilititi treet.* Flight calls high, rather soft, weak, lisping *see-tu* or *see-titi* and other variations; some buzzy notes.

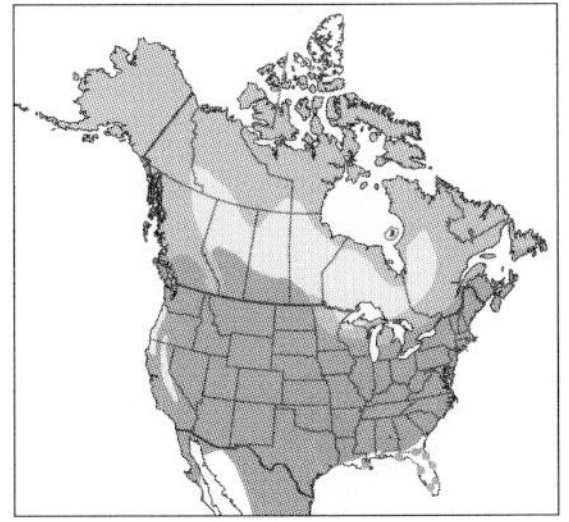

Geographic variation, which is complex and clinal with many intermediates, mostly involves plumage color and is most evident in summer males. Certain patterns of variation are evident. Pacific populations have a dark reddish "shawl," heavy streaking, and bright yellow face. Interior West populations are pale and grayish, less streaked, culminating in the very pale Southeast Arizona birds. Northeast and Arctic populations are darker, with pinkish nape and moderate streaks.

Swallows

Family: Hirundinidae

9 species in 6 genera. These species are often seen lined up on high, open wires by the hundreds or thousands. Aerial, with smooth, flowing flight, all have pointed wings and forked tails. They feed almost exclusively on insects captured in flight (Tree Swallow also eats berries). Nest habits vary by species and between genera. Two genera, *Hirundo* and *Petrochelidon,* build nests out of mud; while gathering mud, Barn Swallow holds its wings still, and Cliff and Cave Swallows flutter their wings over their backs. Compare swifts and European Starling. Adult females are shown.

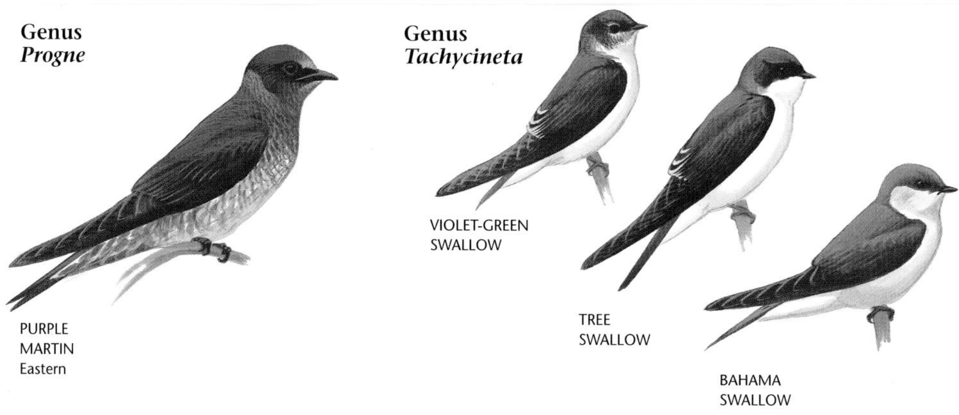

Genus
Progne
PURPLE
MARTIN
Eastern
Genus
Tachycineta
VIOLET-GREEN
SWALLOW
TREE
SWALLOW
BAHAMA
SWALLOW

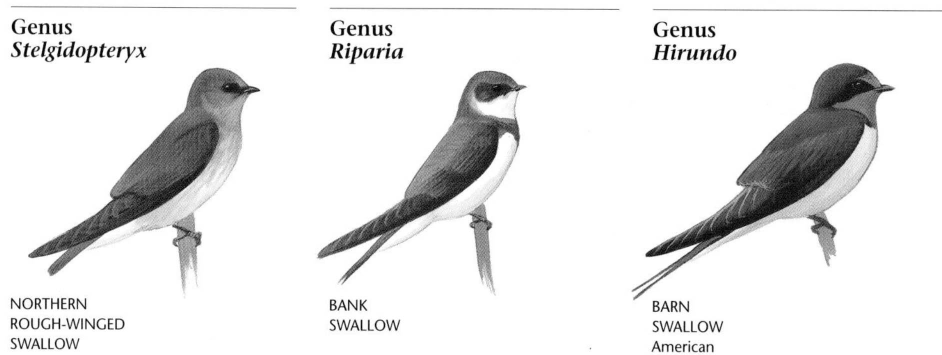

Genus
Stelgidopteryx
NORTHERN
ROUGH-WINGED
SWALLOW
Genus
Riparia
BANK
SWALLOW
Genus
Hirundo
BARN
SWALLOW
American

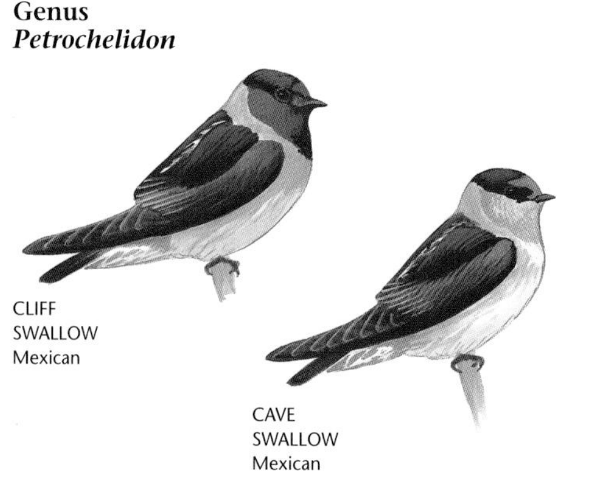

Genus
Petrochelidon
CLIFF
SWALLOW
Mexican
CAVE
SWALLOW
Mexican

MOLT IN SWALLOWS

Tree, Violet-green, Northern Rough-winged, and Cave Swallows molt remiges in late summer and the fall. All other swallows molt exclusively on their wintering grounds outside North America. Thus, any swallow molting remiges in North America is likely to be one of these four species.

Tree Swallow adult

active molt in primaries (old outermost feathers); typical of Sep migrants

PURPLE MARTIN

Our largest swallow, this species nests colonially in holes in trees or (mostly) in man-made martin houses. Males are an unmistakable bluish-black overall; other plumages are also quite dark.

Purple Martin

Progne subis

L 8" WS 18" WT 2 oz (56 g)

Distinctly larger than other swallows. Longer-winged with slower wingbeats (can be confused with European Starling); long-headed and large-billed for a swallow.

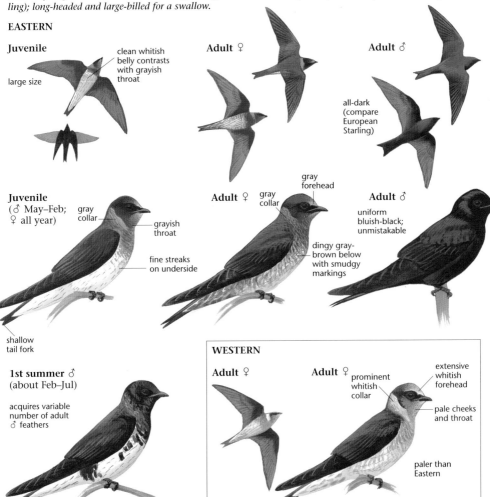

EASTERN

Juvenile

large size

clean whitish belly contrasts with grayish throat

Adult ♀

Adult ♂

all-dark (compare European Starling)

Juvenile (♂ May–Feb; ♀ all year)

gray collar

grayish throat

fine streaks on underside

shallow tail fork

Adult ♀

gray collar

gray forehead

dingy gray-brown below with smudgy markings

Adult ♂

uniform bluish-black; unmistakable

1st summer ♂ (about Feb–Jul)

acquires variable number of adult ♂ feathers

WESTERN

Adult ♀

Adult ♀

prominent whitish collar

extensive whitish forehead

pale cheeks and throat

paler than Eastern

Voice: Male song a low-pitched, rich, liquid gurgling; female song a mixture of chortle calls and downslurred whistles. Calls melodious, rich, low whistles; most common call a rich, descending *cherr;* also a more complex chortle. Variety of other calls include a harsh, buzzy *geerrt* in alarm; a dry, rattling *skrrr* when actually stooping on a predator; and a hard *gip* given by juvenile.

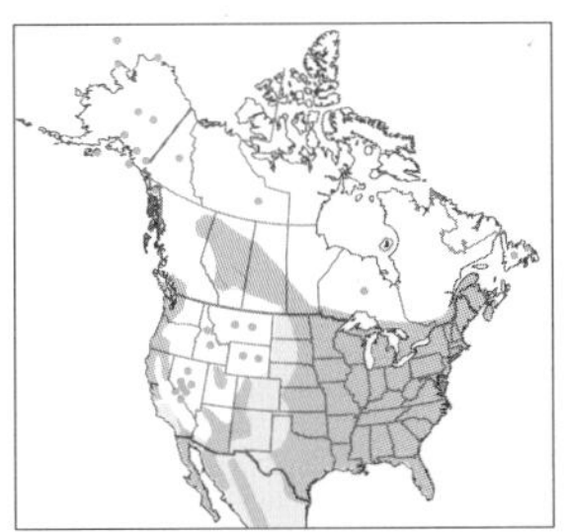

Western birds are similar to Eastern: some populations average smaller; adult males are identical in plumage; all others average paler (details noted above). Voice also differs: *cherr* and chortle calls slightly higher-pitched and often repeated in rapid series; male song longer (2–6 sec vs. 1.5–3 sec) with longer notes and usually at least three grating phrases interspersed (Eastern gives grating phrases only at end, if at all); female song includes more whistles than chortle calls (reverse in Eastern female).

Brown Swallows

These two species share many similarities but differ fundamentally in shape and plumage. Both nest in holes in sandbanks: Northern Rough-winged singly, Bank colonially.

Northern Rough-winged Swallow

Stelgidopteryx serripennis

L 5.5" WS 14" WT 0.56 oz (16 g)

Larger and stockier than Bank, with broader wings; shorter, square tail; bulkier body.

Juvenile
Adult
wingbeats smooth; flight flowing
pale bases of flight feathers translucent
plain drab below with dusky throat
plain brown above
square tail
broad white undertail coverts often visible from above
Juvenile (May–Nov)
buffy throat
bright cinnamon wing-bars
Adult
plain brown with drab, buffy throat
no contrasting markings

Voice: Song simply a steady repetition of rough, rising notes like call *frrip frrip frrip*. . . . Call a low, coarse *prriit* slightly rising; lower and softer than Bank.

Bank Swallow

Riparia riparia

L 5.25" WS 13" WT 0.47 oz (13.5 g)

Our smallest swallow; small-headed and slender with thin wings and rather long, notched tail.

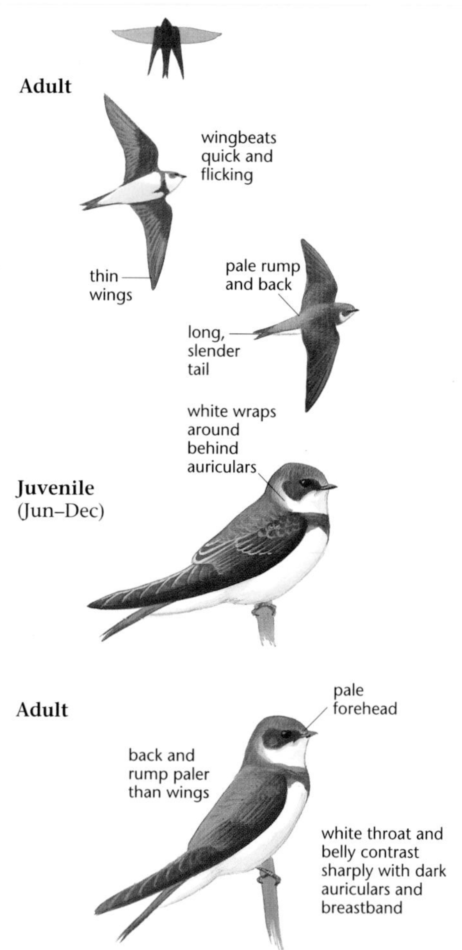

Adult
wingbeats quick and flicking
thin wings
pale rump and back
long, slender tail
white wraps around behind auriculars
Juvenile (Jun–Dec)
Adult
pale forehead
back and rump paler than wings
white throat and belly contrast sharply with dark auriculars and breastband

Voice: Song *wit wit dreee drr drr drr* repeated. Call a short, dry, scratchy *chirr* or *shrrit;* often repeated in rapid, run-on series. Alarm at colony a longer, descending buzz and a thin, mewing *veeew* like Cliff but higher and longer.

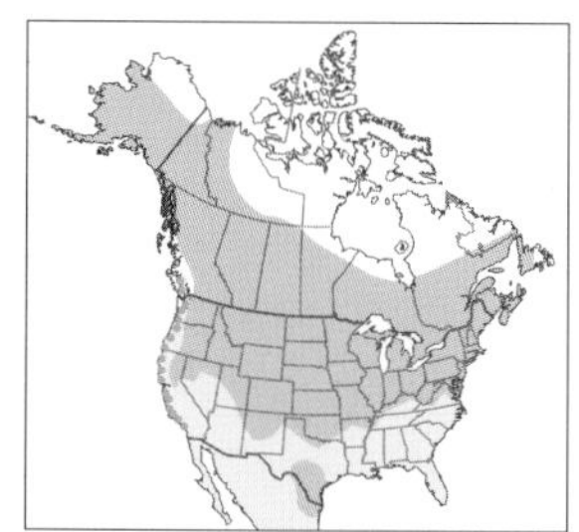

These two species are similar in all respects. Both have similar bicolored plumage and chirping voice; both nest singly in cavities in trees, birdhouses, or cliff crevices.

Violet-green Swallow

Tachycineta thalassina

L 5.25" WS 13.5" WT 0.49 oz (14 g)

Small and very short-tailed; wingtips project well beyond tail tip. Note white sides of rump.

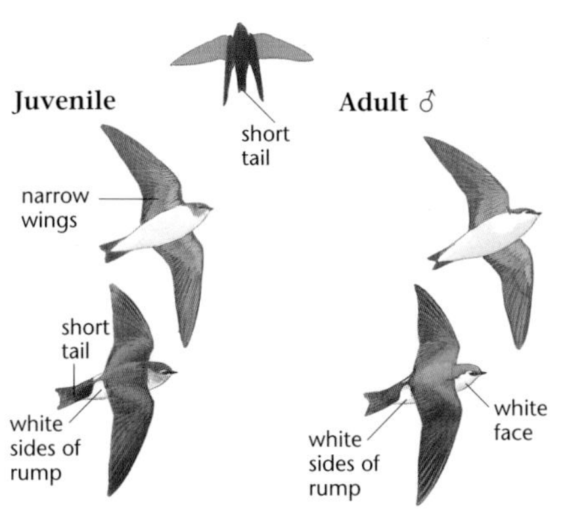
Juvenile
short tail
Adult ♂
narrow wings
short tail
white sides of rump
white sides of rump
white face

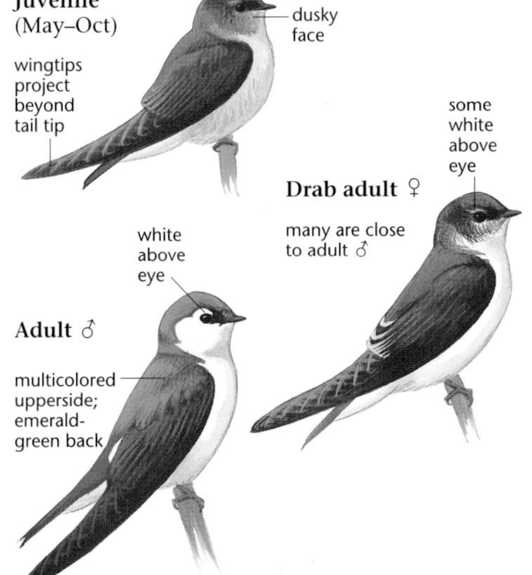
Juvenile (May–Oct)
dusky face
wingtips project beyond tail tip
some white above eye
Drab adult ♀
many are close to adult ♂
white above eye
Adult ♂
multicolored upperside; emerald-green back

Voice: Song a creaking *teer twee, tsip-tsip-tsip. . . .* Call chirping like Tree Swallow but sharper, harder *chilp* or *chip-lip;* almost swiftlike without twittering quality of Tree. Also clear, descending notes in alarm *tseer* or *teewp* repeated.

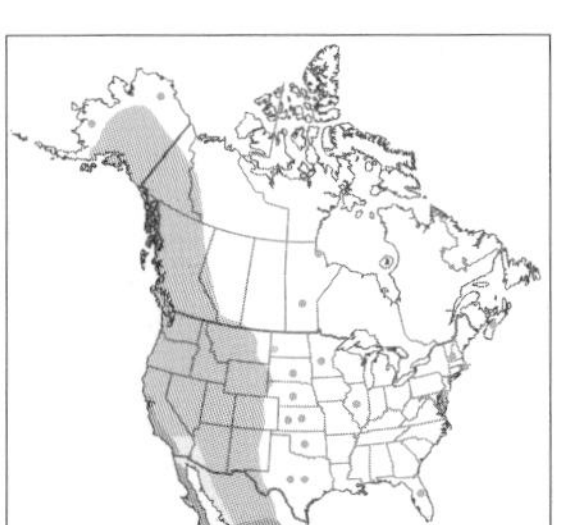

Tree Swallow

Tachycineta bicolor

L 5.75" WS 14.5" WT 0.7 oz (20 g)

Stocky and broad-winged; wingtips reach tail tip.

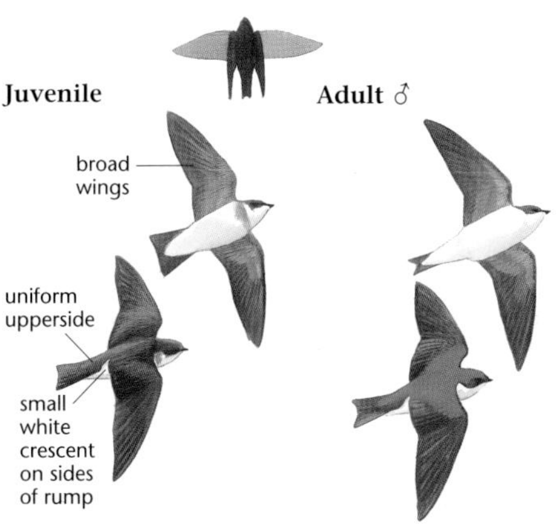
Juvenile
Adult ♂
broad wings
uniform upperside
small white crescent on sides of rump

Juvenile (May–Sep)
uniform gray-brown upperside
sharp contrast on sides of head
pale grayish breastband (compare Bank)
white tips on tertials
Drab adult ♀
many are close to adult ♂
Adult ♂
blue-green back

Voice: Song of clear, sweet whistles *twit-weet twit-weet liliweet twit-weet . . . ;* also a clear *tsuwi tsuw* repeated. Call high, liquid chirping or twittering. Alarm a harsh chatter. Noise from large autumn flocks mainly thin, scratchy *tzeev* notes.

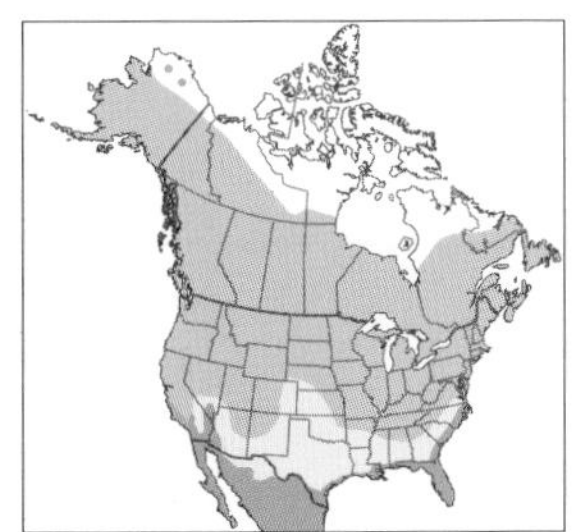

Bahama Swallow is closely related to other *Tachycineta* swallows; it nests in open pine woods. Cliff Swallow nests colonially, building an enclosed jug-shaped mud nest on rocks or buildings.

Bahama Swallow

Tachycineta cyaneoviridis

L 5.75" WS 14" WT 0.6 oz (17 g)

Tail long and deeply forked. Slightly longer-winged and longer-billed than Tree, with striking bicolored underwing.

Juvenile

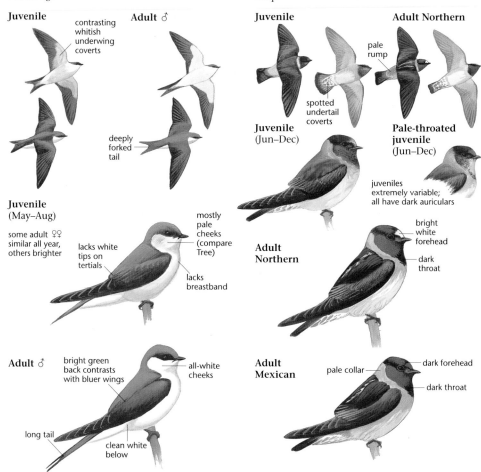

contrasting whitish underwing coverts

Adult ♂

deeply forked tail

Juvenile (May–Aug)

some adult ♀♀ similar all year, others brighter

lacks white tips on tertials

mostly pale cheeks (compare Tree)

lacks breastband

Adult ♂

bright green back contrasts with bluer wings

all-white cheeks

long tail

clean white below

Voice: Song liquid gurgling reminiscent of Tree Swallow but softer; also a high, plaintive *seew-seew-seew-seew* given by pair. Calls *chilpilp* and *killf* softer and chirpier than Tree Swallow.

Cliff Swallow

Petrochelidon pyrrhonota

L 5.5" WS 13.5" WT 0.74 oz (21 g)

Relatively broad, rounded wings and short, square tail; broad, square head. Dark throat and pale buffy rump.

Juvenile

Adult Northern

pale rump

spotted undertail coverts

Juvenile (Jun–Dec)

Pale-throated juvenile (Jun–Dec)

juveniles extremely variable; all have dark auriculars

Adult Northern

bright white forehead

dark throat

Adult Mexican

pale collar

dark forehead

dark throat

Voice: Song thin, strained, with drawn-out creaking and rattling sounds; shorter and simpler than Barn Swallow. Call a low, soft, husky *verr* or lower, drier, rolled *vrrrt*. Alarm at colony a soft, low *veew*.

Mexican populations of Cliff Swallow average 8 percent smaller than Northern; adult has dark rufous forehead (like throat).

Cave Swallow

Similar in all respects, Cave and Cliff Swallows are stocky and pale-rumped. Cave nests colonially, building a partly enclosed half cup of mud in caves or culverts.

Cave Swallow

Petrochelidon fulva

L 5.5" WS 13" WT 0.53 oz (15 g)

Like Cliff but slightly smaller (especially Caribbean birds). Pale throat contrasts with dark cap. Rump always about the same color as throat and forehead; always paler than throat on Cliff Swallow.

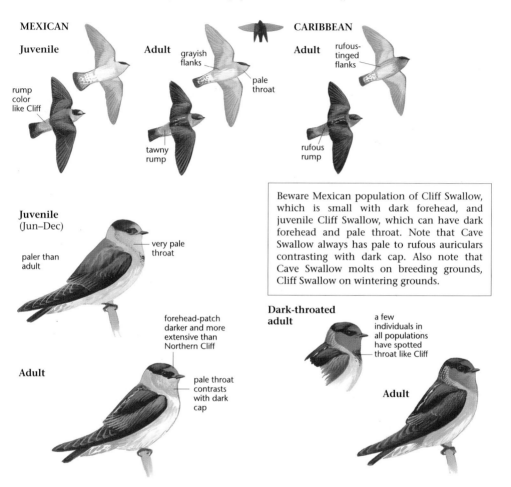

MEXICAN

Juvenile

rump color like Cliff

Adult

grayish flanks

pale throat

tawny rump

CARIBBEAN

Adult

rufous-tinged flanks

rufous rump

Juvenile (Jun–Dec)

paler than adult

very pale throat

Adult

forehead-patch darker and more extensive than Northern Cliff

pale throat contrasts with dark cap

> Beware Mexican population of Cliff Swallow, which is small with dark forehead, and juvenile Cliff Swallow, which can have dark forehead and pale throat. Note that Cave Swallow always has pale to rufous auriculars contrasting with dark cap. Also note that Cave Swallow molts on breeding grounds, Cliff Swallow on wintering grounds.

Dark-throated adult

a few individuals in all populations have spotted throat like Cliff

Adult

Voice: Song a disjointed mix of call notes and nasal buzzes and rattles; quieter, higher, and less musical than Barn Swallow. Common flight call a soft, rising *pwid* like Barn Swallow but softer, clearer. Alarm a sharper, higher *jeewv* higher than Cliff; also a very high, thin *teeer*.

Caribbean populations of Cave Swallow average 10 percent smaller than Mexican, with darker cinnamon-rufous, especially on rump, forehead, throat, and flanks. Juveniles are paler than adults, so juvenile Caribbean is about as dark as adult Mexican, but color varies in both populations with some overlap, which may render field identification impossible. Voice may be softer and less nasal in Mexican birds; more study is needed.

Barn Swallow

Barn Swallow resembles Cliff Swallow in voice and nesting habits, but its shape and plumage are unique. Its nest is a half cup built of mud and hidden under eaves of buildings.

Barn Swallow

Hirundo rustica

L 6.75" WS 15" WT 0.67 oz (19 g)

Very elegant with long, slender, pointed wings and long, deeply forked tail. Flight easier, more flowing than other swallows.

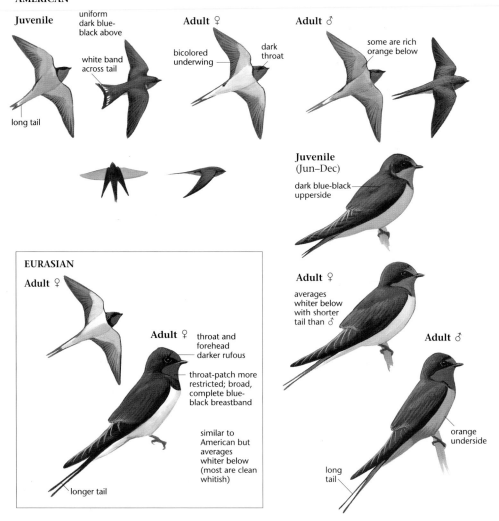

AMERICAN

Juvenile

uniform dark blue-black above

white band across tail

long tail

Adult ♀

bicolored underwing

dark throat

Adult ♂

some are rich orange below

Juvenile (Jun–Dec)

dark blue-black upperside

Adult ♀

averages whiter below with shorter tail than ♂

Adult ♂

orange underside

long tail

EURASIAN

Adult ♀

Adult ♀

throat and forehead darker rufous

throat-patch more restricted; broad, complete blue-black breastband

similar to American but averages whiter below (most are clean whitish)

longer tail

Voice: Song lilting with husky, squeaky quality like call notes; regularly interrupted by dry, creaking rattles. Call a short, husky *vit* or *vit-vit;* alarm a stronger and sharper *vit-VEET* or *si-VLIT.*

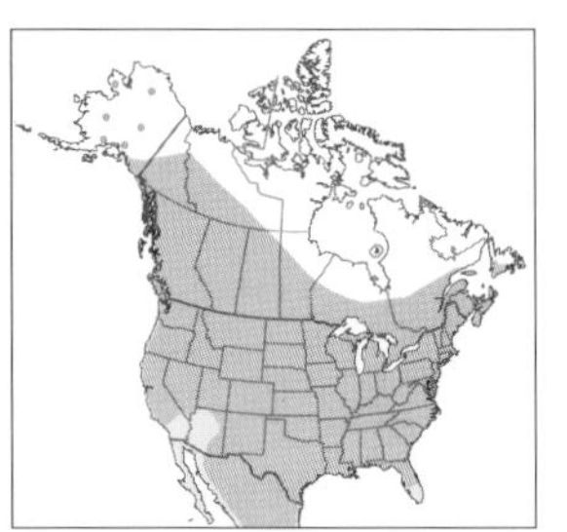

Eurasian birds have been recorded regularly in western Alaska, several times south to Washington. Although best distinguished by throat pattern, suspects might be picked out by whitish belly and long tail. Note that shortest-tailed Eurasian juveniles are similar to adult female American; adult female Eurasian has tail length like adult male American; and adult male Eurasian is longer-tailed than any American.

Chickadees and Their Allies

Families: Aegithalidae, Paridae, Remizidae

13 species in 4 genera; titmice and chickadees in family Paridae, Verdin in Remizidae, Bushtit in Aegithalidae. These small, drab (but often contrastingly patterned) birds have strong legs and short, strong bills. Found in small flocks, all species are fairly social and inquisitive. They feed on insects and seeds gleaned from bark and twigs. Flight is rather hesitant and undulating. Chickadees and titmice nest in tree cavities or birdhouses. Verdin's nest is a spherical ball of twigs; Bushtit's nest is a pendulous, hanging basket. Adults are shown.

Genus *Baeolophus*

JUNIPER TITMOUSE
OAK TITMOUSE
BRIDLED TITMOUSE
TUFTED TITMOUSE Northern

Genus *Poecile*

BLACK-CAPPED CHICKADEE Eastern
MOUNTAIN CHICKADEE Rocky Mountains
CAROLINA CHICKADEE
CHESTNUT-BACKED CHICKADEE Central California Coast
MEXICAN CHICKADEE
GRAY-HEADED CHICKADEE
BOREAL CHICKADEE

Genus *Auriparus*

VERDIN

Genus *Psaltriparus*

BUSHTIT Pacific

Bridled Titmouse

Baeolophus wollweberi

L 5.25" WS 8" WT 0.37 oz (10.5 g)

Distinctive; smaller than other titmice, with unique face pattern. Found mainly in oak woods.

Adult

Adult

juvenile similar

Adult

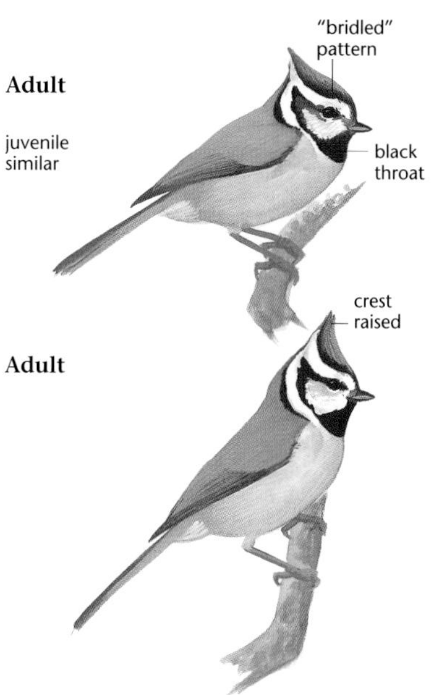
"bridled" pattern
black throat
crest raised

Voice: Song a rapid series of six to eight low, clear, whistled phrases with popping quality: *pidi pidi pidi pidi pidi* or *pipipipi. . . .* Call simply a rapid series of low, harsh notes in chickadee-like chatter *ji ji ji ji ji* or *jedededededed;* sometimes preceded by high, clear notes *tsi tsi tsi jedededededed.*

Until recently considered a single species—the aptly named Plain Titmouse—these two very drab species are best distinguished by range and voice. Both are found in open, dry woods.

Oak Titmouse

Baeolophus inornatus

L 5.75" WS 9" WT 0.6 oz (17 g)

Smaller and relatively shorter-tailed than Tufted; marginally smaller and smaller-billed than Juniper.

Adult

Adult

juvenile similar

short crest
plain face
plain, drab
brown-tinged overall

Adult

Voice: Song of strong, whistled, repeated phrases *tjiboo* . . . or paired *tuwituwi* . . . and other variations. Also a rapid, popping trill. Call a few high, thin notes followed by a single harsh scold *si si si chrr;* the same pattern often given in clear, whistled notes *pi pi pi peeew.*

Juniper Titmouse

Baeolophus ridgwayi

L 5.75" WS 9" WT 0.6 oz (17 g)

Essentially identical to Oak in appearance; usually easily identified by range. In summer and east of range beware juvenile Black-crested Tufted.

Adult

Adult

juvenile similar

faint or no brown tinge

Adult

Voice: Song averages lower-pitched and more rapid than Oak with less whistled quality; phrases often in groups of three, resulting in a pulsing rattle on one pitch *jijiji jijiji jijiji.* . . . Also gives a rapid, popping trill faster than Oak. Call a rapid *sisisi-ch-ch-ch-ch* or *si-ch-ch-ch* and other variations.

Neither of these species is restricted to its namesake tree; some local populations are found in the "wrong" habitat. Range overlaps only on the Modoc Plateau of northeastern California.

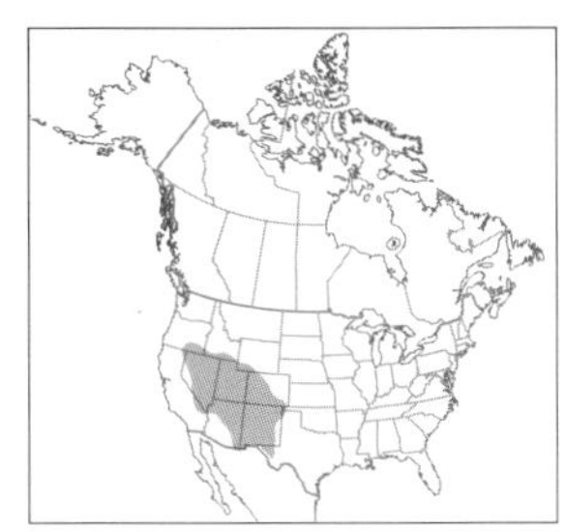

Our largest titmouse, this species is found in broadleaf trees (e.g., oaks). The two populations were previously considered separate species.

Tufted Titmouse

Baeolophus bicolor

L 6.5" WS 9.75" WT 0.75 oz (21.5 g)

Larger than other titmice; larger and stockier than chickadees. Plain head, short crest, and relatively short, broad tail.

BLACK-CRESTED (MEXICAN)

Adult

Juvenile
(May–Aug)

Adult

two populations easily distinguished by head pattern; Black-crested averages slightly smaller

black crest often raised higher than Northern

pale forehead

NORTHERN (TUFTED)

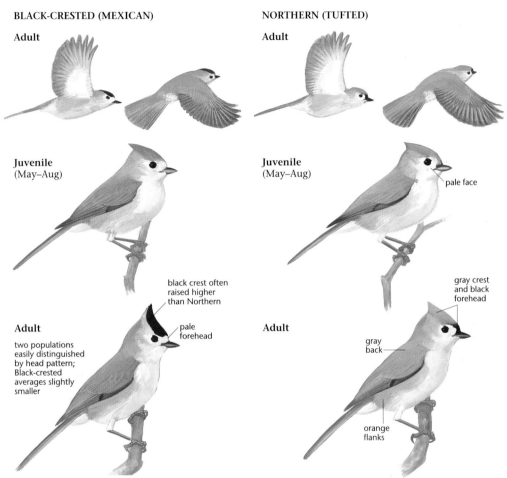

Adult

Juvenile
(May–Aug)

pale face

Adult

gray crest and black forehead

gray back

orange flanks

Voice: Song a low, clear whistle *peter peter peter peter* usually strongly two-syllabled. Call angry, nasal, rising notes often preceded by very high, thin notes *ti ti ti sii sii zhree zhree zhree.* Also simple whistled notes such as *see-toit* and high, sharp *tsip* like Field Sparrow. Calls of Black-crested average higher-pitched with notes delivered more rapidly; song typically consists of five to seven slurred phrases delivered more rapidly *peew peew peew peew peew* rather than three to four slower, two-syllable phrases of Northern.

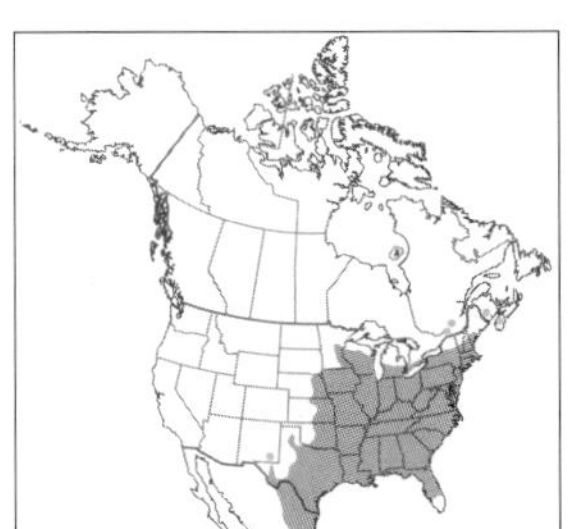

BLACK-CRESTED

Intergrade adult

Intergrades are frequent in a narrow zone where ranges meet in central Texas. Such birds combine characteristics of both populations; they typically have dark gray crest and pale forehead, but a complete range occurs.

This bold and inquisitive species is our most widespread chickadee. Found in a variety of wooded habitats, it is similar in appearance and voice to Carolina and Mountain Chickadees.

Black-capped Chickadee

Poecile atricapilla

L 5.25" WS 8" WT 0.39 oz (11 g)

Relatively longer-tailed than other chickadees; rather large-headed and fluffy.

Adult

Overall, Black-capped is brighter, more colorful, and more contrastingly marked than Carolina; it is larger, fluffier, larger-headed, and longer-tailed, with darker tail and wings that have brighter white edges; its cheek-patch is entirely white (Carolina blends to pale gray at rear), and it has a greenish back and buffy flanks (Carolina is duller grayish); its song is lower-pitched and its call slower. All these features are relative and subject to variation, but in combination they should serve to identify most birds. Hybrids are recorded in the narrow zone of overlap (there is disagreement over the extent of hybridization). Song is learned, so not very helpful for identification, as individual birds can learn the "wrong" song type.

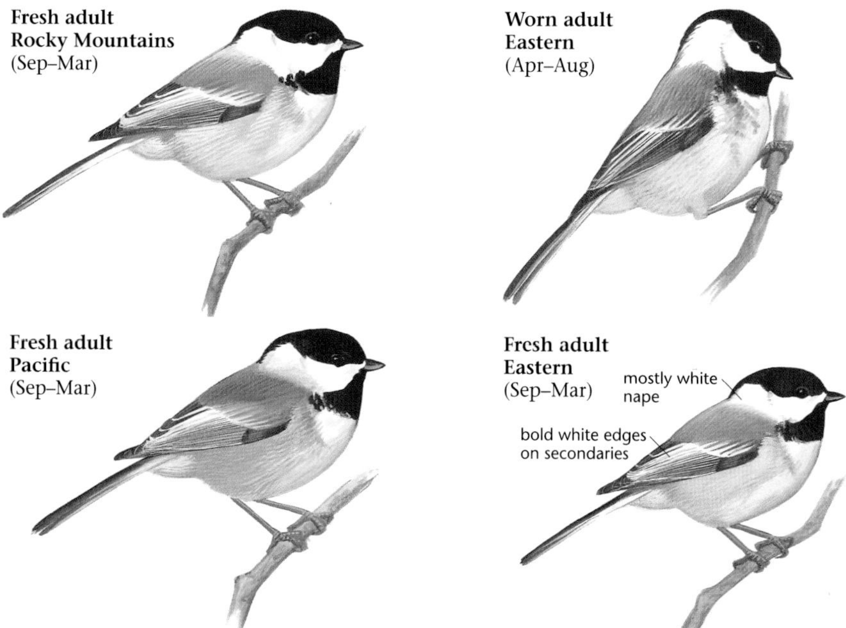
Fresh adult
Rocky Mountains
(Sep–Mar)
Worn adult
Eastern
(Apr–Aug)
Fresh adult
Pacific
(Sep–Mar)
Fresh adult
Eastern
(Sep–Mar)
mostly white nape
bold white edges on secondaries

Voice: Song of most populations a simple, high, pure whistle *feebee,* with second note lower than first and relative pitch of two notes constant; sometimes sounds three-noted, second part broken by slight falter but no real temporal break *fee beeyee*. Common and familiar call *chikadee dee dee dee*. Contact call a sharp *chik* or *tsik* slightly harsh, often leading into *chik-a-dee* call. Gargle call a complex, descending jumble of short notes and alarm a very high, thin series *teeteeteeteetee;* both similar in all chickadees. Voice of Pacific population differs (see below).

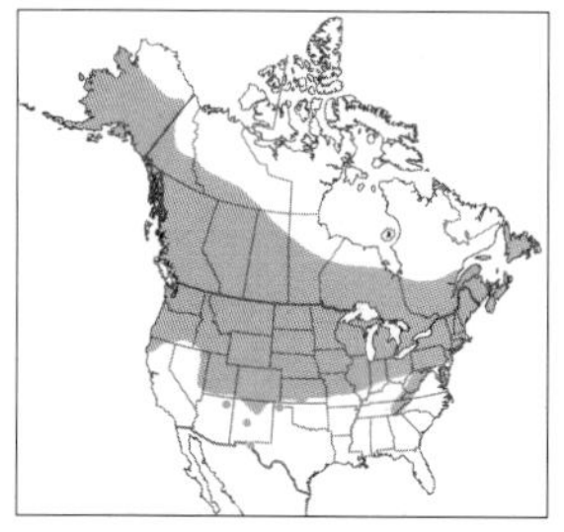

Populations vary subtly in plumage and size; most variation is clinal, with many intermediates. Eastern birds are relatively bright and contrastingly marked; Rocky Mountain populations are larger and paler "frosty" with broad white edges on flight feathers. Pacific populations are most distinctive, being small and dark, with drab grayish-olive edges on flight feathers and different voice. Call is slightly more rapid than other populations; repertoire of several unique calls, including a rapid, whistled, titmouse-like series *peto peto peto*. Song of high, clear whistles like other populations but pattern variable *fee feee feee feee* or *beeyee fee* and others. Variable songs also given by birds on islands off Massachusetts.

CHICKADEES (CONTINUED)

These two species, closely related to one another and to Black-capped, can be difficult to identify. All are found in woods and have similar plumage, calls, and whistled song.

Carolina Chickadee

Poecile carolinensis

L 4.75" WS 7.5" WT 0.37 oz (10.5 g)

Smaller, smaller-headed, and shorter-tailed than Black-capped; drabber overall with slightly different voice.

Adult
Worn adult
(Apr–Aug)
Drabber fresh adult
(Sep–Mar)
much less buffy; found to the west
mostly grayish nape
Brighter fresh adult
(Sep–Mar)
gray edges on secondaries
the brightest population (most like Black-capped) found in Northeast

Voice: Song three to five notes on different pitches *see bee see bay* and other variations; like Black-capped but higher-pitched; all notes clearly separated by pauses. Call *chikadeedeedeedee* higher-pitched and more rapid than Black-capped (5–7 *dee* notes/sec vs. 3–4 in Black-capped).

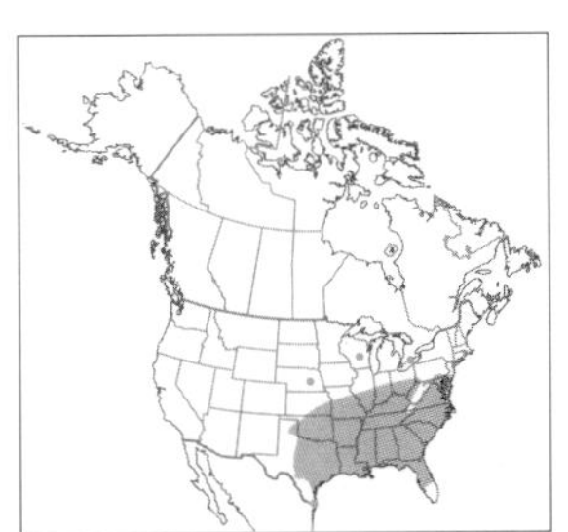

Mountain Chickadee

Poecile gambeli

L 5.25" WS 8.5" WT 0.39 oz (11 g)

Similar to Black-capped but slightly longer-billed and longer-winged, and shorter-tailed; note white supercilium, plain grayish wings.

Adult
white supercilium unique but often indistinct
Worn adult
(Apr–Aug)
relatively plain gray wings
Fresh adult Pacific
(Sep–Mar)
Fresh adult Rocky Mountains
(Sep–Mar)

Voice: Song of clear, high whistles like Black-capped but with three to six syllables; pattern variable with many local dialects. Call *chika dzee dzee* similar to Black-capped but *dzee* notes slightly harsher, slower, and often descending. Other calls like Black-capped.

Mountain Chickadees of the Rocky Mountains average more olive-tinged with broader white supercilium than more westerly birds, but variation is subtle and clinal. Prominence of white supercilium is strongly influenced by wear, and it is sometimes lost Jun–Aug; other species rarely show traces of white supercilium.

Northern Chickadees

These fluffy brownish chickadees of the far north have hoarse, wheezy calls. Gray-headed is found at the treeline in riverside alder and spruce thickets, Boreal in dense coniferous forests.

Gray-headed Chickadee

Poecile cincta

L 5.5" WS 8.5" WT 0.44 oz (12.5 g)

On average our largest and longest-tailed chickadee; very fluffy plumage, grayish crown, and white-edged flight feathers distinctive.

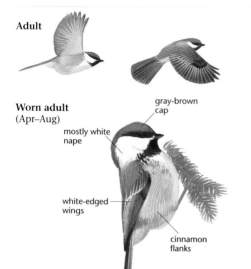

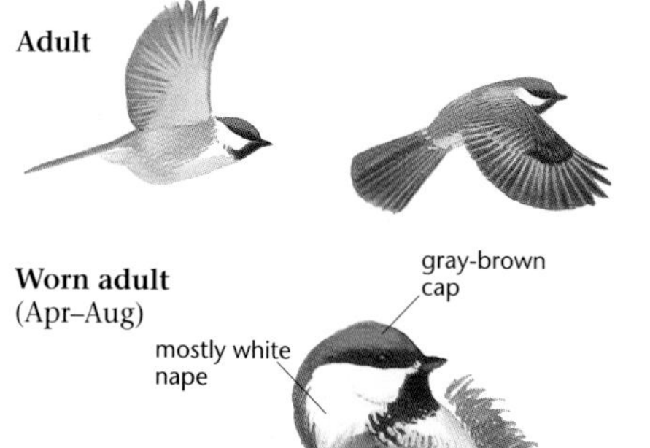
Adult
Worn adult
(Apr–Aug)
gray-brown cap
mostly white nape
white-edged wings
cinnamon flanks
long, white-edged tail

Fresh adult
(Sep–Mar)
limited dark bib

Voice: Song unknown; certain short, high phrases may function as song. Call *tsiti ti ti jeew jeew jeew* or simply *jeew jeew jeew* lower than Boreal.

Boreal Chickadee

Poecile hudsonica

L 5.5" WS 8.25" WT 0.35 oz (10 g)

Size and shape like Black-capped but a little shorter-tailed; dark brownish and gray overall plumage and very wheezy call distinctive.

Adult

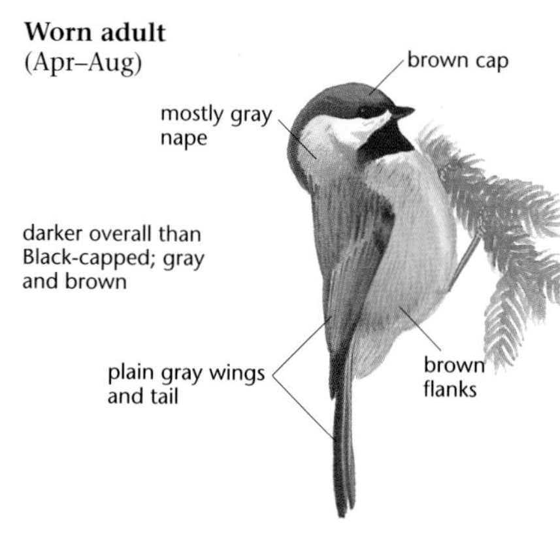
Worn adult
(Apr–Aug)
brown cap
mostly gray nape
darker overall than Black-capped; gray and brown
plain gray wings and tail
brown flanks

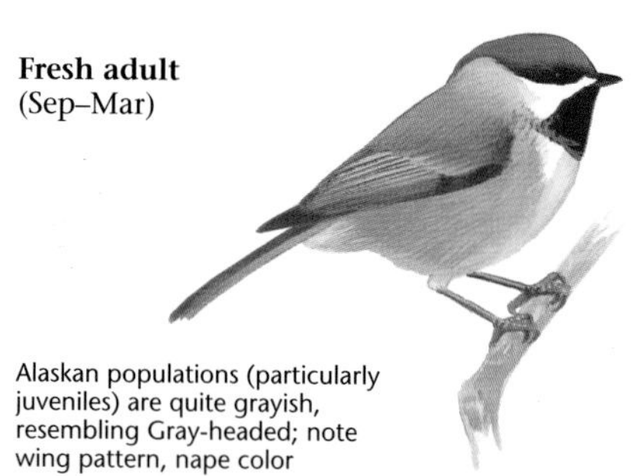
Fresh adult
(Sep–Mar)
Alaskan populations (particularly juveniles) are quite grayish, resembling Gray-headed; note wing pattern, nape color

Voice: Song a simple, clear trill with short introductory note *p-twee-titititititititi.* Call a labored, wheezy, nasal *tsi-jaaaay* or *tsi ti jaaaay jaaay* ("yesterdaaay"); no other species gives single *dee* note; *chit* or *tchidk* call (harsher, more staccato than Black-capped) very common year-round in many variations.

Black-capped Chickadee adult

Strong legs and feet allow chickadees and titmice to hang upside down while foraging, a habit shared by only a few other birds.

Western Chickadees

These two western chickadees are each quite distinctive. Mexican is found in mountain pine forests, Chestnut-backed in coniferous forests and mixed woods.

Mexican Chickadee

Poecile sclateri

L 5" WS 8.25" WT 0.39 oz (11 g)

Extensive black bib and dark gray flanks distinctive.

Adult

Worn adult
(Apr–Aug)

head often looks peaked

white curls up in front of eye

very extensive black bib

gray wings with narrow, indistinct white wing-bar

dark gray flanks

Fresh adult
(Sep–Mar)

beware worn Mountain (Jun–Aug), which may lack white supercilium and have grayish flanks; identify by black bib, range

Voice: Song a series of short, abrupt phrases *peeta peeta peeta;* may recall Oak and Juniper Titmice. Characteristic call note a high, buzzy *sschleeeer* level or slightly descending; also high, buzzy trills preceding slow, hissing notes *tzee tzee tzee shhhh shhhh* and a low, husky trill *didididididi.*

Mexican Chickadee is found only in the Chiricahua Mountains of Arizona and the nearby Animas Mountains of New Mexico, where it is normally the only chickadee present.

Chestnut-backed Chickadee

Poecile rufescens

L 4.75" WS 7.5" WT 0.34 oz (9.7 g)

On average our smallest and shortest-tailed chickadee; dark chestnut back unique.

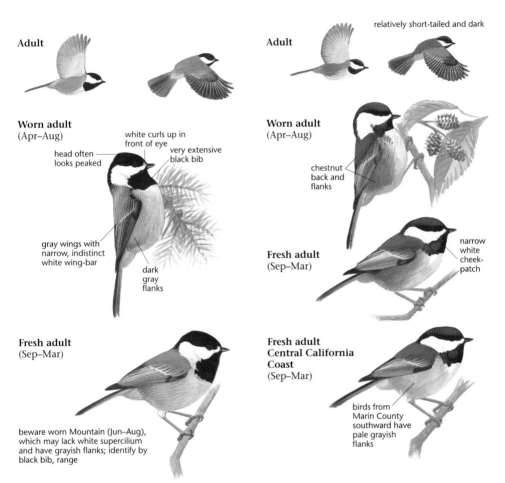

Adult

relatively short-tailed and dark

Worn adult
(Apr–Aug)

chestnut back and flanks

Fresh adult
(Sep–Mar)

narrow white cheek-patch

Fresh adult Central California Coast
(Sep–Mar)

birds from Marin County southward have pale grayish flanks

Voice: Lacks whistled song; an accelerating series of chips may function as song. Calls generally higher than other chickadees. Typical call high, buzzy notes with lower nasal, husky notes: *tsidi-tsidi-tsidi-cheer-cheer* or weaker *tsity ti jee jee.* Some buzzy notes like *Dendroica* warbler flight calls.

Tiny and active, but usually solitary or in pairs, this species is found in arid brush. It forages chickadee-like, gleaning insects from twigs and flowers.

Verdin

Auriparus flaviceps

L 4.5" WS 6.5" WT 0.24 oz (6.8 g)

Tiny, short-tailed, with short and sharply pointed bill; pale grayish plumage.

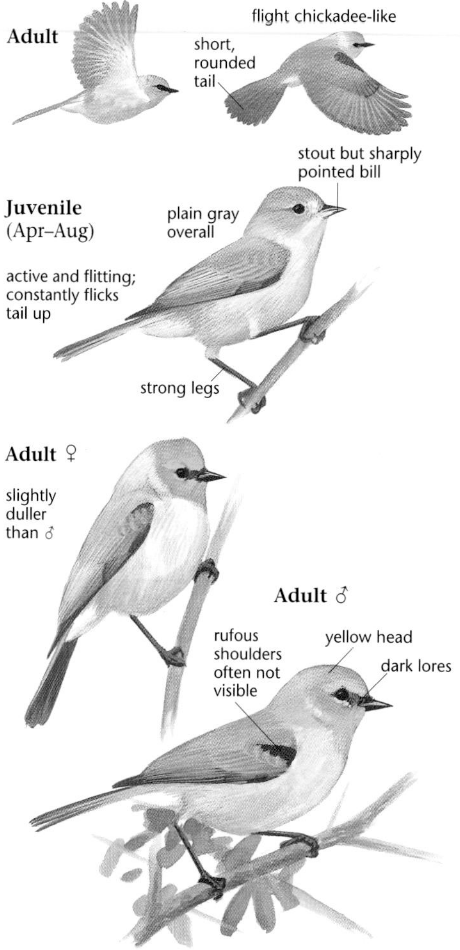
Adult
flight chickadee-like
short, rounded tail
stout but sharply pointed bill
Juvenile (Apr–Aug)
plain gray overall
active and flitting; constantly flicks tail up
strong legs
Adult ♀
slightly duller than ♂
Adult ♂
rufous shoulders often not visible
yellow head
dark lores

Voice: Call a high, piercing *tseewf;* also a lower-pitched, strong whistle *tee too too* or *tee too tee tee.* Contact call a flat, hard *kit* or *tsik* often repeated rapidly, three to four times per second; also high, sharp, slightly nasal *kleeu.*

Drab Gray Birds of the Arid Southwest

The southwestern region is home to a number of small grayish birds. For identification, note shape, habits, and bill shape.

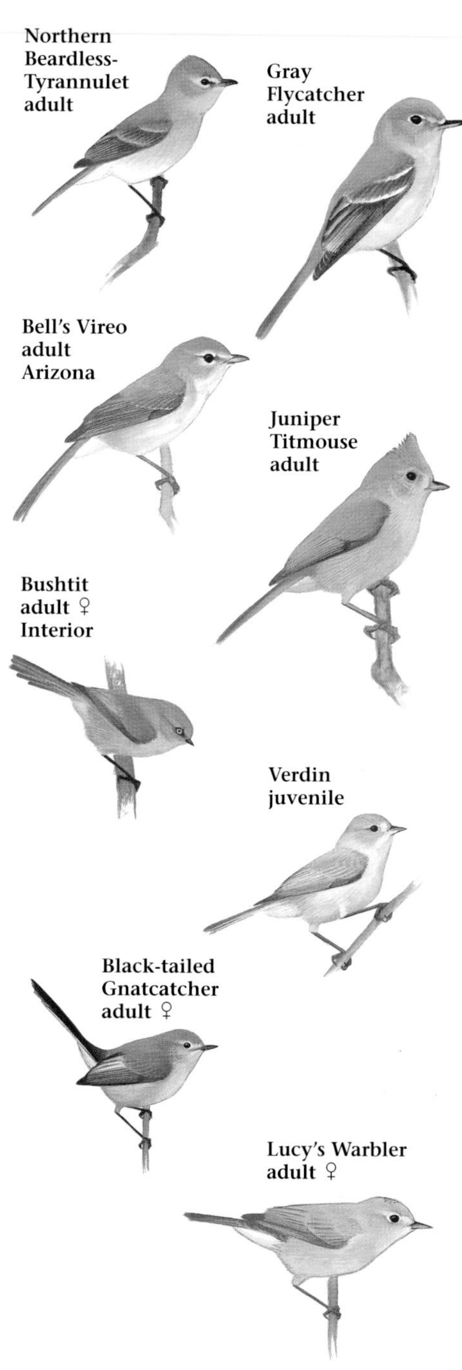
Northern Beardless-Tyrannulet adult
Gray Flycatcher adult
Bell's Vireo adult Arizona
Juniper Titmouse adult
Bushtit adult ♀ Interior
Verdin juvenile
Black-tailed Gnatcatcher adult ♀
Lucy's Warbler adult ♀

Bushtit

This tiny, distinctive species—a disheveled-looking, long-tailed ball of fluff—is seen in lively, chattering flocks except when nesting. It is found in chaparral and in open, low woods.

Bushtit

Psaltriparus minimus

L 4.5" WS 6" WT 0.19 oz (5.3 g)

One of our smallest birds, with long tail, short neck, and short, stubby bill.

Adult ♂

long, thin tail seems to drag in flight

PACIFIC

Adult ♀

juvenile (Apr–Aug) similar but dark-eyed

INTERIOR

Adult ♀

Adult ♂

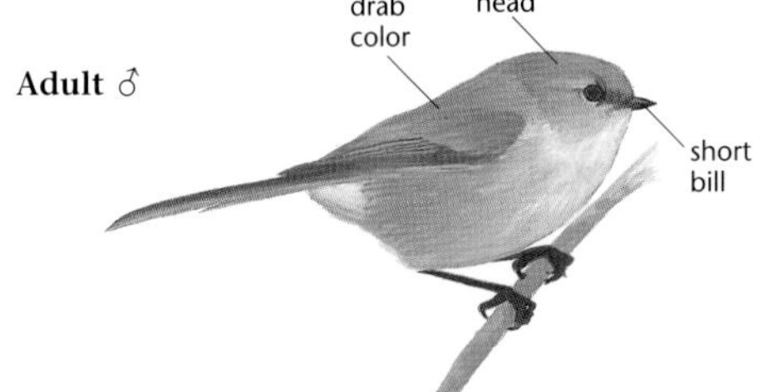
drab color
plain head
short bill

Adult ♂

plain gray

Black-eared form is uncommon in southwestern mountains; seen mainly in Texas but recorded rarely (juveniles only) to Colorado and eastern California. Shown mostly by juvenile male, occasionally by juvenile female or adult male. Fully black-eared adults are rare in North America, common in Mexico.

Partly black-eared adult ♂

Fully black-eared adult ♂

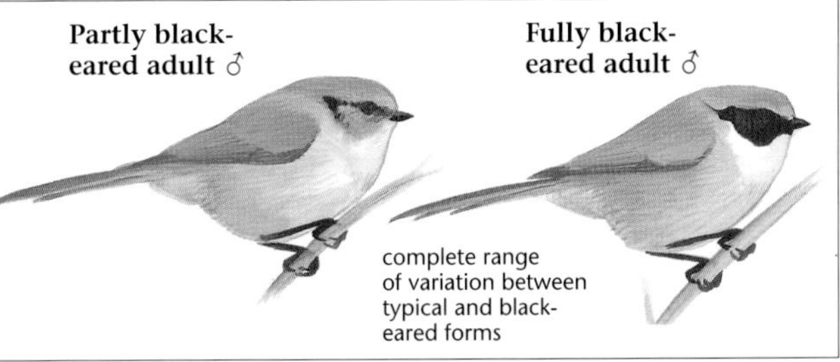

complete range of variation between typical and black-eared forms

Voice: Calls include a sharp, scraping buzz ending with several high, clear chips *skrrti ti ti;* dry *spik* notes like Lazuli Bunting; and high, thin, scraping *tseeez tzee tzee tzee . . .* in long, slightly descending series. All calls given constantly by flock, producing sharp, buzzing, sparkling chatter: a mixture of thin, scratchy notes and high, clear chips. Aerial predator alarm very high, clear, tinkling, descending *tsidididididi;* usually given by several birds at once as flock seeks cover.

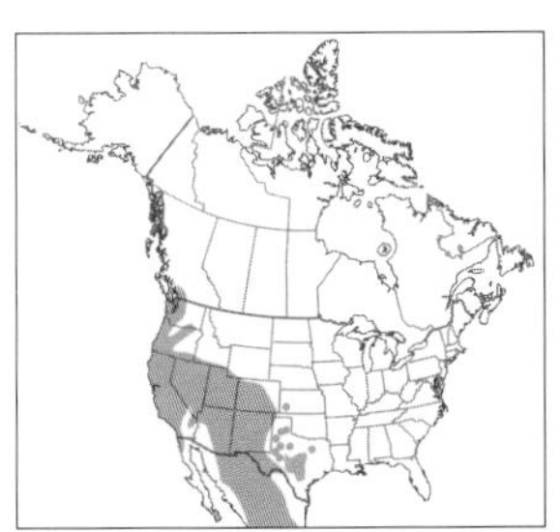

Although similar in all other respects, Interior and Pacific populations differ consistently in plumage; intermediates occur where ranges meet. Interior birds are paler and grayer overall, with gray crown matching back color; Pacific birds are browner overall, with dark brownish crown that contrasts with back. In addition, Pacific birds may have more obvious dark lores (Interior have paler lores). Calls of Interior birds are a little lower-pitched and flatter than Pacific.

Nuthatches and Creepers

Families: Certhiidae, Sittidae

5 species in 2 genera; nuthatches in family Sittidae, Brown Creeper in Certhiidae. Nuthatches are short-tailed and long-billed with a unique tree-climbing method; they often climb head down, feeding on insects gleaned from bark crevices. The cryptically colored Brown Creeper uses its tail as a woodpecker-like prop as it forages. Nuthatches nest in cavities; Brown Creeper nests in a cavity or behind a sheet of loose bark. Flight of all species is undulating, similar to woodpeckers. The smaller species often join flocks of chickadees, warblers, and other small birds during nonbreeding season. Adults are shown.

Genus *Sitta*

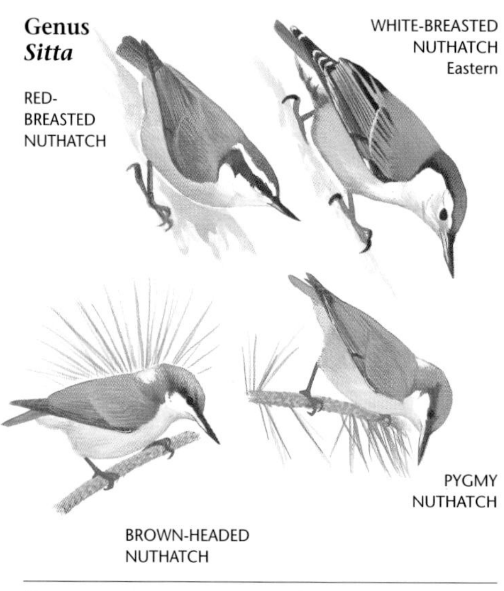
RED-BREASTED NUTHATCH
WHITE-BREASTED NUTHATCH Eastern
BROWN-HEADED NUTHATCH
PYGMY NUTHATCH

Genus *Certhia*

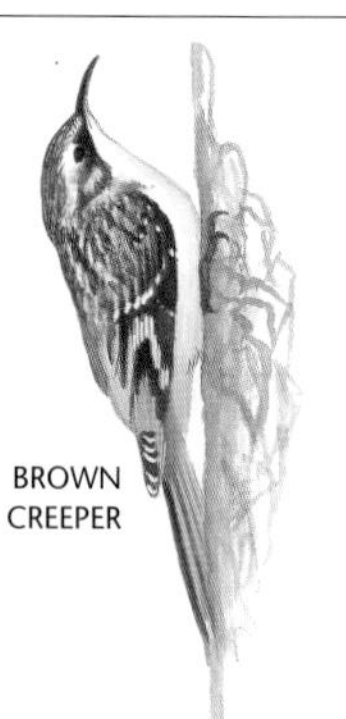
BROWN CREEPER

Nuthatches climb trees using only their strong legs and feet: one foot is placed lower and used as a brace; the other foot is placed higher and grips the bark. A similar climbing method is used by Black-and-white Warbler and, to a lesser extent, Yellow-throated Warbler. In contrast, all woodpeckers and Brown Creeper use their tails as a brace and are incapable of climbing head down.

Red-breasted Nuthatch

Sitta canadensis

L 4.5" WS 8.5" WT 0.35 oz (10 g)

Smaller and stubbier than White-breasted; smaller-headed than Pygmy and Brown-headed.

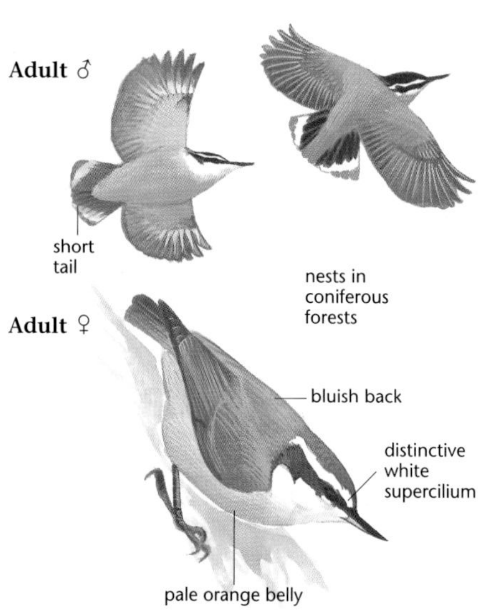
Adult ♂
short tail
nests in coniferous forests
Adult ♀
bluish back
distinctive white supercilium
pale orange belly

Adult ♂

Voice: Song a monotonous series of clear, nasal, rising calls repeated slowly *eeeen eeeen eeeen. . . .* Call a weak, nasal *ink* or *yenk;* when agitated a longer, rising *iiink* and lower, hoarser series *iik iik iik. . . .* Calls generally shorter, more nasal than White-breasted.

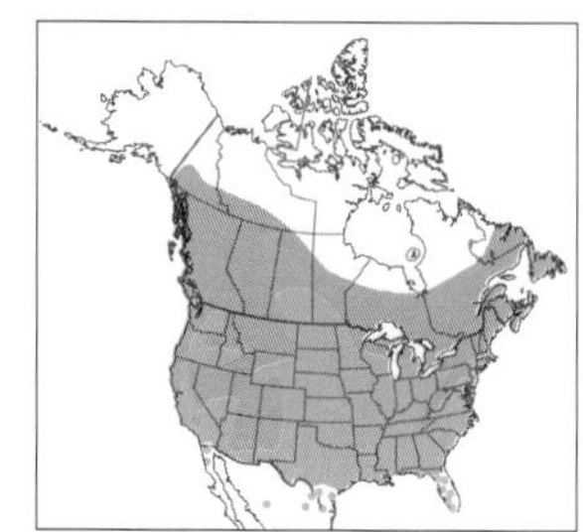

WHITE-BREASTED NUTHATCH

Our largest nuthatch, this species is found in open woods with mature trees, most often oak and pine trees, where its nasal calls are heard frequently.

White-breasted Nuthatch

Sitta carolinensis

L 5.75" WS 11" WT 0.74 oz (21 g)

Large with long, upturned bill. Relatively longer-winged than other nuthatches; short, broad tail.

Adult ♂ Eastern

flight
undulating

PACIFIC **INTERIOR WEST** **EASTERN**

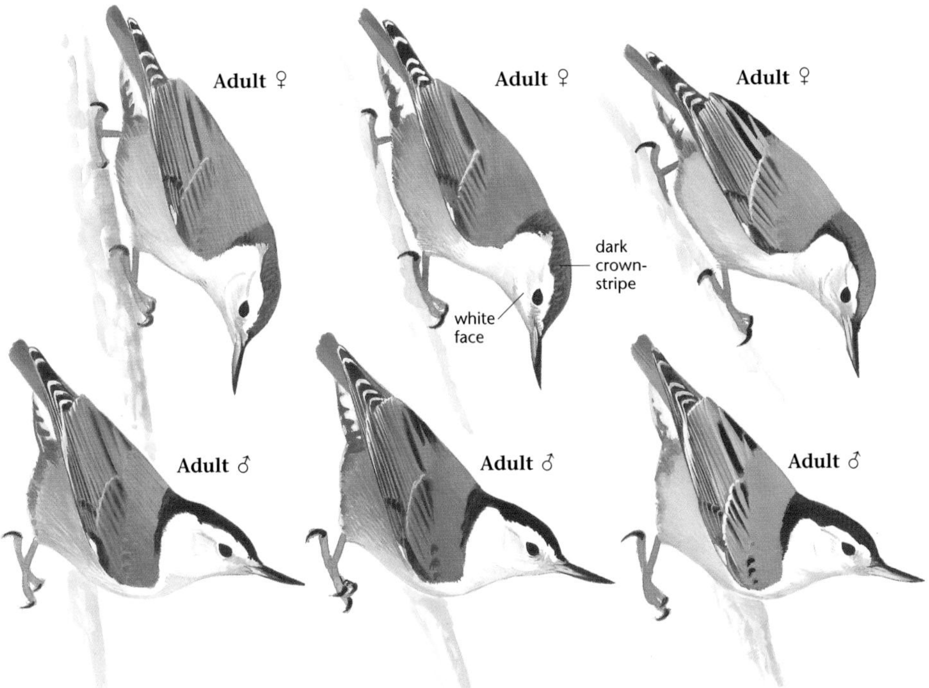

Adult ♀ **Adult ♀** **Adult ♀**

dark crown-stripe

white face

Adult ♂ **Adult ♂** **Adult ♂**

Voice: Songs of all populations a series of soft, slightly nasal, whistled notes on one pitch *whi-whi-whi-whi-whi-whi-whi*. All give short, nasal contact calls and soft, high *ink* notes while foraging. EASTERN: Call a nasal *yenk* or *renk* slightly descending; often slightly trilled or rolling, unlike Red-breasted; lower, coarser when agitated. INTERIOR WEST: Call a short series of rapid, nasal notes *yididididi* often grouped in twos or threes *yidi-yidi-yidi-yidi* or *yididi-yididi-yididi*, all with equal emphasis. PACIFIC: Call a high, nasal yelping *eeern* or *beeerf* distinctly longer, higher, harsher than Eastern; quiet contact notes huskier than Eastern.

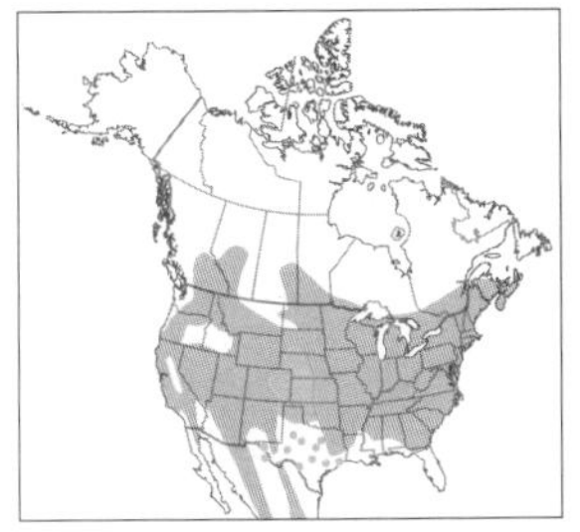

Three populations differ in voice and subtly in plumage and shape. Eastern has thickest bill and palest gray back with sharply contrasting black marks on tertials and coverts. Eastern also has a broader dark crown-stripe than either of the western populations. Pacific and Interior West both have thinner bills, darker gray backs with less contrasting dark marks on tertials and coverts, and narrower dark crown-stripes. Interior West differs from Pacific in darker back and much darker flanks. Voice differs between populations; all should be reliably identified by call. Song differs subtly between populations; more study is needed.

Small Nuthatches

These two species differ mainly in voice. Both are tiny and stocky with disproportionately large bills. They are usually found in pine forests and often join mixed-species flocks in winter.

Pygmy Nuthatch

Sitta pygmaea

L 4.25" WS 7.75" WT 0.37 oz (10.5 g)

Tiny, short-tailed, large-headed, and long-billed. Note plain grayish upperside and dark eye-line.

Adult

Worn adult
(Apr–Aug)

Fresh adult
(Sep–Mar)

Voice: Call high, clear, hard peeping usually given in chorus by flock: amazing variety of loud chips, most frequently *bip-bip-bip* and many higher squeaks and chips; loud *kip* on variable pitch; rather flat, high, strident *peet* or *peeta*. In flight weaker *imp imp*.

Pygmy Nuthatch along the coast ranges of central California has much more rapid vocalizations than all others. It averages smaller, with paler, dusky eye-line and buffier flanks, but plumage differences are subtle and overlapping.

Brown-headed Nuthatch

Sitta pusilla

L 4.5" WS 7.75" WT 0.35 oz (10 g)

Nearly identical to Pygmy, but no range overlap.

Adult

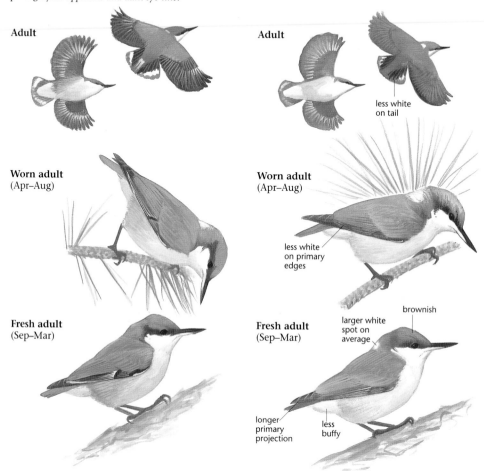

less white on tail

Worn adult
(Apr–Aug)

less white on primary edges

Fresh adult
(Sep–Mar)

larger white spot on average

brownish

longer primary projection

less buffy

Voice: Call a high, sharp, spunky, slightly nasal *KEWde* usually followed by lower, hard, nasal notes *KEWdododo teew;* also a hard *pik*.

BROWN CREEPER

This unique species can be difficult to spot; its cryptic colors and tree-hugging creeping motions blend in with the bark of large trees. It is found in mature woods.

Brown Creeper

Certhia americana

L 5.25" WS 7.75" WT 0.29 oz (8.4 g)

Tiny with long, thin tail and thin, curved bill. Creeping habits, mottled brownish plumage, and high, lisping calls distinctive.

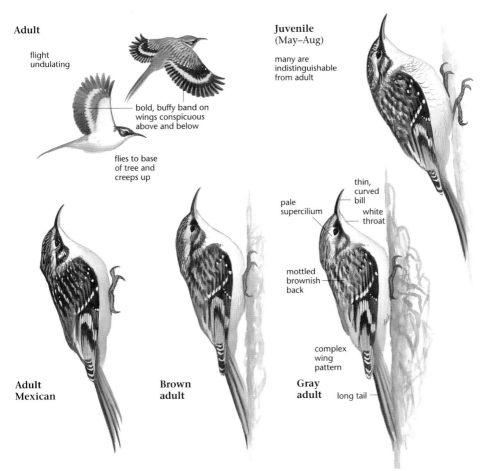

Adult

flight undulating

bold, buffy band on wings conspicuous above and below

flies to base of tree and creeps up

Juvenile (May–Aug)

many are indistinguishable from adult

Adult Mexican

Brown adult

pale supercilium

thin, curved bill

white throat

mottled brownish back

complex wing pattern

long tail

Gray adult

Voice: Song a very high, thin series of accelerating, cascading notes. Eastern begins with two long, high notes followed by irregular jumble ending on a low note *seee sooo sideeda sidio;* western song usually ends on a high note *seee sitsweeda sowit-see* ("trees trees pretty little trees"), overall clearer, simpler, and more rhythmic with less quavering or trilled quality. Eastern call a very high, thin, quavering *seee* or *sreee* similar to Golden-crowned Kinglet but single, with relaxed, liquid quality; weaker than waxwings; western call often buzzier, often doubled *teeesee.* In flight much weaker, extremely high notes *tit, titip,* or *zip* sharper than Golden-crowned Kinglet.

There is much subtle variation in plumage within this species, but regional variation is overshadowed by the presence of reddish, brown, and gray morphs within many populations. In general, western populations are relatively small, dark, and long-billed; eastern populations are slightly larger, paler, buffier, and shorter-billed. Mexican population resident from southeastern Arizona into Mexico is darker, particularly on the gray belly and chestnut rump, and averages shorter- and rounder-winged and shorter-billed than other western birds. Regional differences in voice, some of which are described above, deserve more study.

Wrens

Family: Troglodytidae

9 species in 7 genera. Wrens are mostly small, brown, and active but secretive; they creep through vegetation, foraging for insects and fruit, often with their tails raised above their backs. Their flight is quick and erratic on short, rounded wings. All have narrow heads and long, slender bills, an adaptation for probing deep into crevices. Most nest in cavities, including birdhouses; Cactus, Sedge, and Marsh Wrens build globular nests of sticks or grass. Compare sparrows and Palm Warbler. Adults are shown.

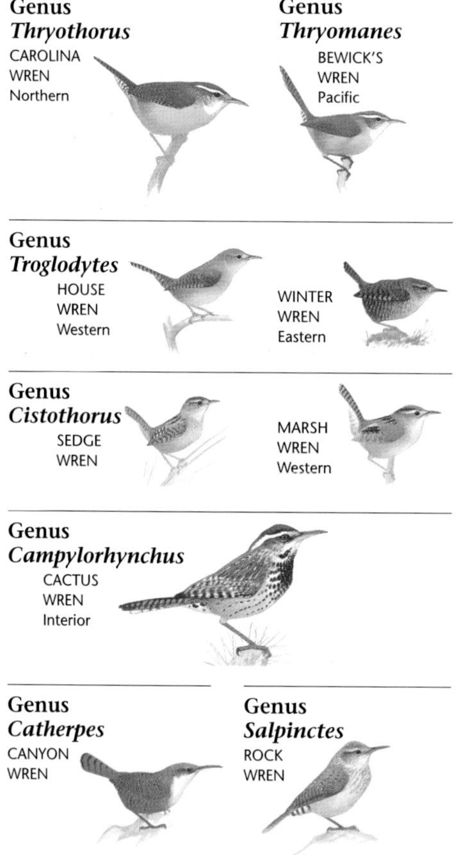

Genus
Thryothorus
CAROLINA
WREN
Northern
Genus
Thryomanes
BEWICK'S
WREN
Pacific
Genus
Troglodytes
HOUSE
WREN
Western
WINTER
WREN
Eastern
Genus
Cistothorus
SEDGE
WREN
MARSH
WREN
Western
Genus
Campylorhynchus
CACTUS
WREN
Interior
Genus
Catherpes
CANYON
WREN
Genus
Salpinctes
ROCK
WREN

SCOLD NOTES

Some wrens (including Carolina, Bewick's, and House) give a tremendous variety of harsh scold notes, varying within each species from soft and nasal to loud and rasping. Other species of birds unrelated to wrens also give similar harsh notes (White-eyed, Bell's, and Gray Vireos; Tufted Titmouse; Black-tailed and California Gnatcatchers). These sounds can be difficult to distinguish from one another, but knowing the limited number of possibilities in your area will aid in the identification of many species.

Carolina Wren

Thryothorus ludovicianus

L 5.5" WS 7.5" WT 0.74 oz (21 g)

Large-headed, short-billed, and stocky overall with bright reddish-brown plumage.

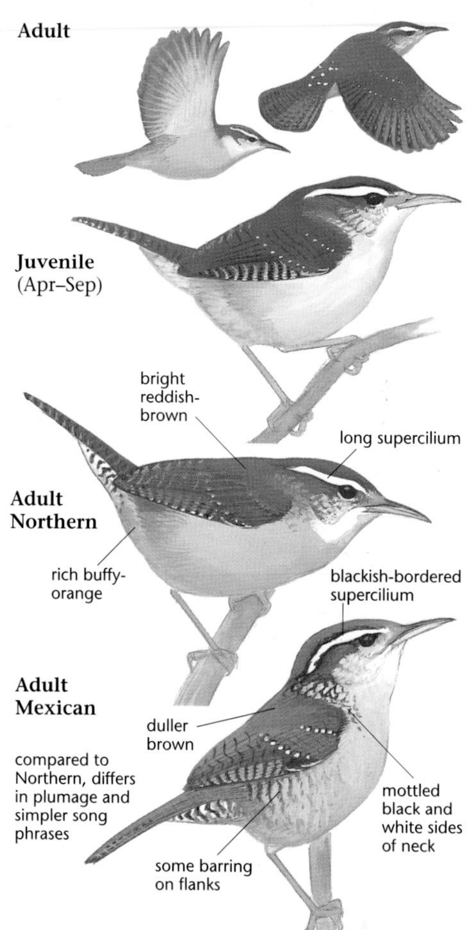

Adult
Juvenile
(Apr–Sep)
bright
reddish-
brown
long supercilium
Adult
Northern
rich buffy-
orange
blackish-bordered
supercilium
Adult
Mexican
duller
brown
compared to
Northern, differs
in plumage and
simpler song
phrases
mottled
black and
white sides
of neck
some barring
on flanks

Voice: Extremely varied. Song a rolling chant of rich phrases *pidaro pidaro pidaro* or *TWEE pudo TWEE pudo TWEEP* and other variations. A long, buzzing chatter sometimes given with song. Calls generally richer than other wrens: a harsh, complaining *zhwee zhwee zhwee . . .* ; a descending, musical trill; a low, solid *dip* or *didip*.

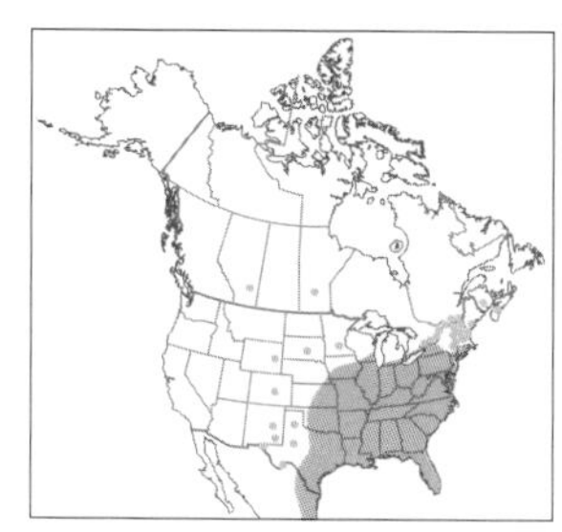

More slender than other wrens, with a long tail flicked expressively up and sideways, this species is found in a variety of dense, brushy habitats. Color and song vary regionally.

Bewick's Wren

Thryomanes bewickii

L 5.25" WS 7" WT 0.35 oz (10 g)

Slender, rather long-necked, and very long-tailed. Relatively clean, unmarked plumage and long white supercilium distinctive.

Adult

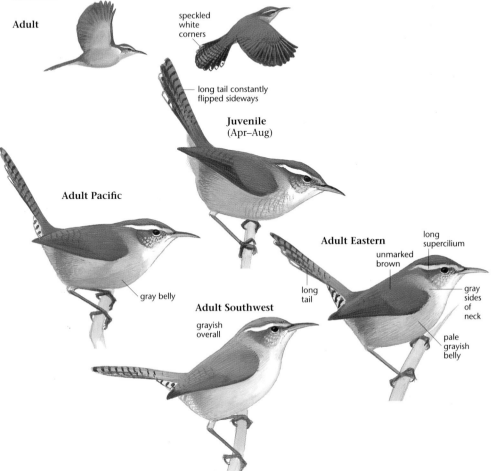

speckled white corners

long tail constantly flipped sideways

Juvenile (Apr–Aug)

Adult Pacific

gray belly

Adult Eastern

long supercilium

unmarked brown

long tail

gray sides of neck

pale grayish belly

Adult Southwest

grayish overall

Voice: Extremely varied. Song varies regionally but always has thin, rising buzzes and slow trills, with distinctive quality and overall descending pitch: Arizona birds simple (e.g., *tuk zweee-drrrrrrr*); Pacific birds more complex (e.g., *t-t zree drr-dree tutututututututu*); Eastern birds most complex, recalling Song Sparrow with high, clear notes and musical trills (e.g., *zrink zrink oozeeee delzeedle-eedle-ooh tsetetetetetete*). Call generally dry, harsh, and unmusical, but also varied soft notes. Scold drawn-out harsh notes *shreeee, zheeeeer* or *jree jree* . . . and other variations; also a soft, dry *chrrr,* harsh *jik,* soft *wijo,* or sharp *spik.* Most distinctive is a high, rising *zrink* with characteristic zippy quality, often incorporated into song.

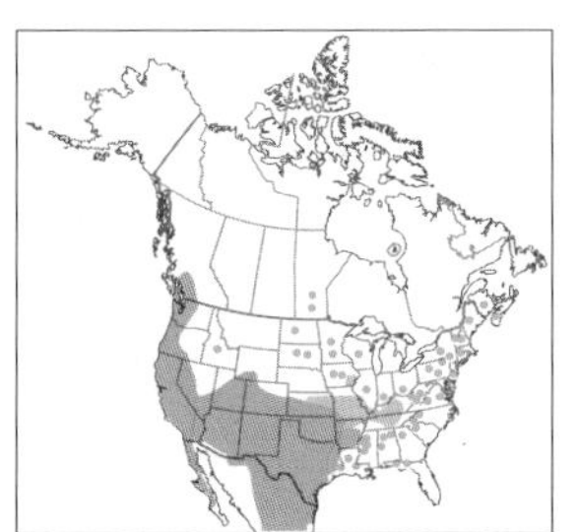

Regional variation in plumage color is subtle and clinal, but the three extremes are quite distinctive, as illustrated. Interestingly, song variation corresponds to plumage variation: simplest songs are given by the grayest birds (Southwest) and much more complex songs are given by the reddest birds (Eastern).

This species is the familiar small grayish-brown wren of gardens, hedgerows, and brushy woods. It is fairly secretive, but its loud, bubbling song is conspicuous in summer.

House Wren

Troglodytes aedon

L 4.75" WS 6" WT 0.39 oz (11 g)

Small and relatively slender; note drab plumage with weakly marked face pattern.

Adult

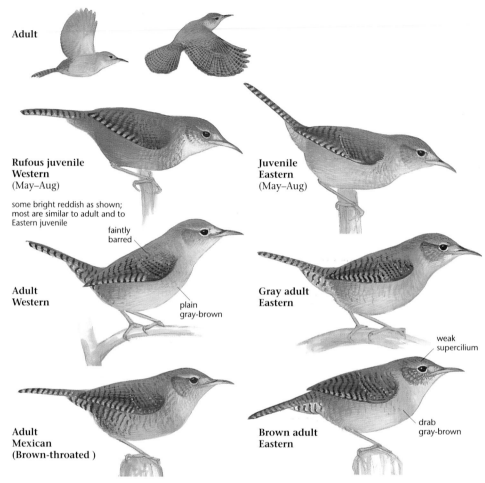

Rufous juvenile Western (May–Aug)

some bright reddish as shown; most are similar to adult and to Eastern juvenile

Juvenile Eastern (May–Aug)

Adult Western

faintly barred

plain gray-brown

Gray adult Eastern

weak supercilium

Adult Mexican (Brown-throated)

Brown adult Eastern

drab gray-brown

Voice: Extremely varied. Song a rapid, rolling series of rattles and trills culminating in a descending series of bubbling liquid trills. Calls generally low, dry, short, often rather soft notes. One call commonly heard in west but never in east: a rolling, trilled, musical *dirrd;* other possible differences overshadowed by variation. Scold a nasal whining or mewing *merrrrr* reminiscent of gnatcatchers or Gray Catbird; also long, harsh rising *sshhhhp;* series of harsh *chrrf* notes generally weaker and more hissing than Bewick's, much softer and drier than Carolina. Also low *ch* or *chek* notes given singly.

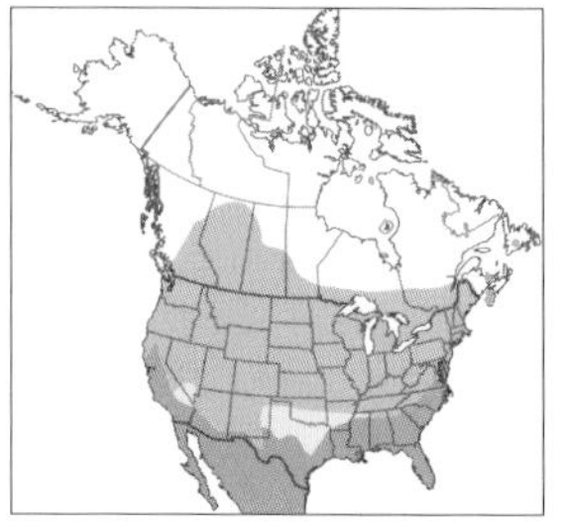

Western birds average grayer than Eastern with more contrasting reddish-brown tail coverts and flanks, but there is extensive overlap. Some Western juveniles are strikingly rufous. One Western call is unique. Brown-throated population of southeastern Arizona (mainly Huachuca and Santa Rita Mountains) averages warmer buff on underparts, with more barring on flanks and more prominent buffy supercilium, but Arizona populations are variable and intermediate between northern birds and the true Brown-throated populations in Mexico. Brown-throated song is slightly sweeter and more complex than Eastern; calls are like other western populations.

Wrens (continued)

Our smallest, darkest wren, this tiny species usually keeps its very short tail cocked up. Found in wet, shady woods and dense brush, it forages along the ground and through dark crevices.

Winter Wren

Troglodytes troglodytes

L 4" WS 5.5" WT 0.32 oz (9 g)

Tiny, short-tailed, and thin-billed. Overall dark brown plumage and short but well-defined supercilium distinctive.

Adult Western

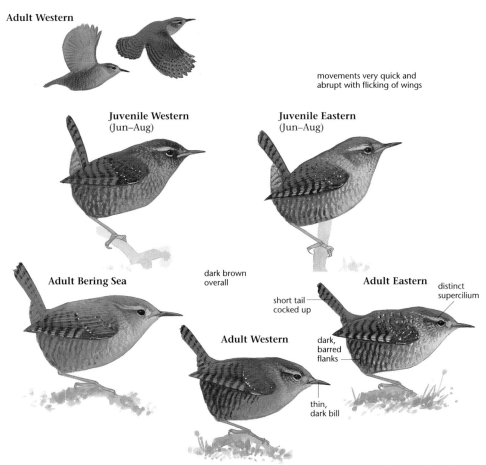

movements very quick and abrupt with flicking of wings

Juvenile Western (Jun–Aug)

Juvenile Eastern (Jun–Aug)

Adult Bering Sea

dark brown overall

short tail cocked up

Adult Eastern

distinct supercilium

Adult Western

dark, barred flanks

thin, dark bill

Voice: Song long and complex: a remarkable continuous series of very high, tinkling trills and thin buzzes. Song of Western birds more rapid (36 notes/sec vs. 16), more mechanical-sounding, buzzy with hard trills; averages longer than Eastern; individual males have 30 or more song patterns each vs. only two of Eastern. Song of Bering Sea birds lower-pitched and harsher than southern birds. Call a short, usually doubled hard note *jip-jip* (Eastern quality close to Song Sparrow but harder) or *chat-chat* (Western higher and sharper than Eastern, more like Wilson's Warbler). Agitated birds give a rapid series of extremely high staccato notes (higher in Western).

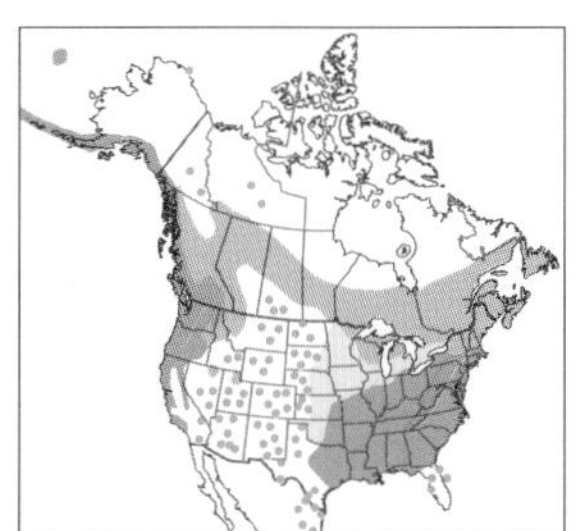

Three populations are distinguished by plumage and especially by voice. Eastern populations are slightly paler than Western overall, especially paler (more whitish, less ruddy) on the throat, with more barring on flanks extending forward to sides of breast and more white spotting on back. Bering Sea birds (resident on Pribilof and Aleutian Islands) are similar to Western but paler and up to 20 percent larger.

Tiny, very secretive, and difficult to see, Sedge Wren is found in damp, tall-grass meadows with scattered bushes. Like other wrens, it is most easily located when singing.

Sedge Wren and Grass Sparrows

Sedge Wren is one of several species of small, secretive birds that spend most of their time hiding in dense, tall grass. Identifying these species is difficult only because they usually flush very close underfoot and fly away quickly before dropping back into cover. Knowing what to expect and being prepared will allow identification of many of these little brown blurs, even if the views are not very satisfying. Pay close attention to tail shape, tail pattern, back and rump pattern, and overall color. Although difficult to do, the best hope of identifying many of these birds is to get a glimpse of the face pattern. Habitat can also provide clues; however, remember that not all can be identified. Note that any species of sparrow can act secretive, flushing out of dense grass and dropping quickly back into cover; the following species do so habitually.

Sedge Wren: Found in damp, dense grass with scattered bushes; the smallest and weakest-flying of the group; short, rounded tail and wings; often gives sharp calls when flushed.

Le Conte's Sparrow: Often shares habitat with Sedge Wren; quite similar in overall appearance but more boldly patterned, with longer tail; more brightly marked than other grass sparrows.

Henslow's Sparrow: Found in more weedy habitat with open ground; often flies to bushes or into woods when flushed; small and dark.

Grasshopper Sparrow: Found in drier habitat but can occur together with Le Conte's; larger and relatively plain gray-buff but very difficult to distinguish from Le Conte's and Baird's in normal flight views.

Baird's Sparrow: Found in dry grassland, often with Grasshopper; very difficult to distinguish from Grasshopper and Savannah.

Nelson's and Saltmarsh Sharp-tailed Sparrows: Normally found in wet, marshy grasses, but migrants can occur in drier habitat; small and dark with bright orange face.

Savannah Sparrow: Relatively longer-winged and shorter-tailed with stronger and more bounding flight than other grass sparrows, but this is difficult to judge; note clean white belly revealed in higher flight.

In southwestern grasslands watch for the heavier and longer-tailed Cassin's and Botteri's Sparrows. The similar Bachman's is found in southeastern pinewoods. Other species that flush out of dense grass include Sprague's Pipit and some longspurs.

Sedge Wren

Cistothorus platensis

L 4.5" WS 5.5" WT 0.32 oz (9 g)

Tiny, short-billed, and fairly short-tailed; smaller and paler than Marsh Wren. Overall color varies from sandy buff to cinnamon.

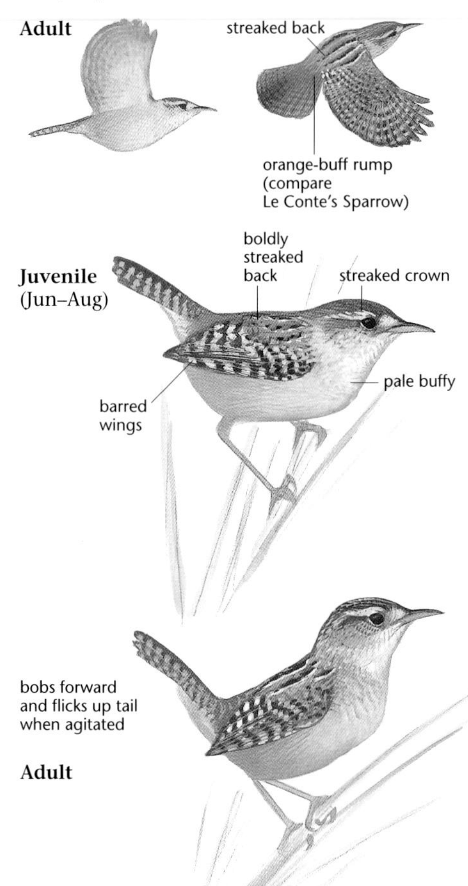
Adult
streaked back
orange-buff rump (compare Le Conte's Sparrow)
Juvenile (Jun–Aug)
boldly streaked back
streaked crown
pale buffy
barred wings
bobs forward and flicks up tail when agitated
Adult

Voice: Song very sharp, staccato chips followed by a more rapid series *chap chap chatatatat* or *chap chap ch jee jee;* compare more rapid staccato rattle of Common Yellowthroat. Common call a very sharp, staccato, bouncing *chadt;* less intense *chep* sometimes in series like House Wren. Scold a quiet, nasal, low, buzz *krrt.*

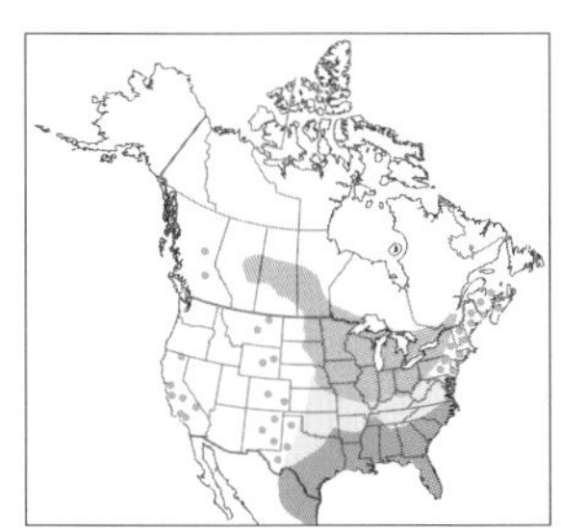

This small wren, found almost exclusively in tall reeds or similar marsh vegetation, is generally secretive and difficult to see. Its gurgling song is heard day and night in the breeding season.

Marsh Wren

Cistothorus palustris

L 5" WS 6" WT 0.39 oz (11 g)

Small and stocky with relatively long bill. Note relatively brightly patterned plumage.

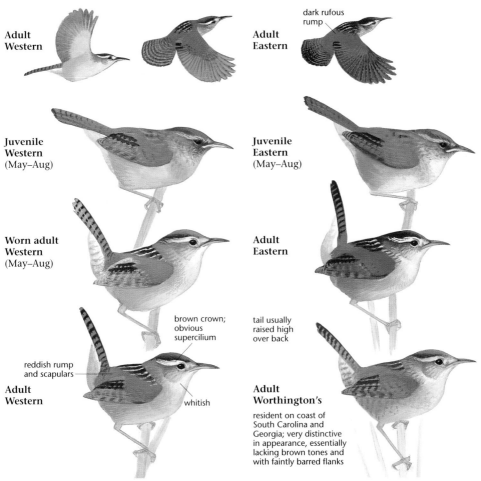

Adult Western

Adult Eastern

dark rufous rump

Juvenile Western (May–Aug)

Juvenile Eastern (May–Aug)

Worn adult Western (May–Aug)

Adult Eastern

brown crown; obvious supercilium

tail usually raised high over back

reddish rump and scapulars

Adult Western

whitish

Adult Worthington's

resident on coast of South Carolina and Georgia; very distinctive in appearance, essentially lacking brown tones and with faintly barred flanks

Voice: Western song a gurgling, rattling trill with distinctive musical and mechanical quality; usually introduced by a few *tek* notes *tik k jijijijijijiji-jrr* or *tuk t jet-t-t-t-t-t-t-t-trr.* Eastern song similar but more musical, less rattling; often introduced by nasal *gran* note. Individual Western males sing more than 100 song types; Eastern males sing only a few song types. Call a low, dry *tek* similar to some hard, quiet flight calls of blackbirds. Scold a harsh, descending *shrrrr;* also a low, rolling rattle *chrddd* similar to House Wren.

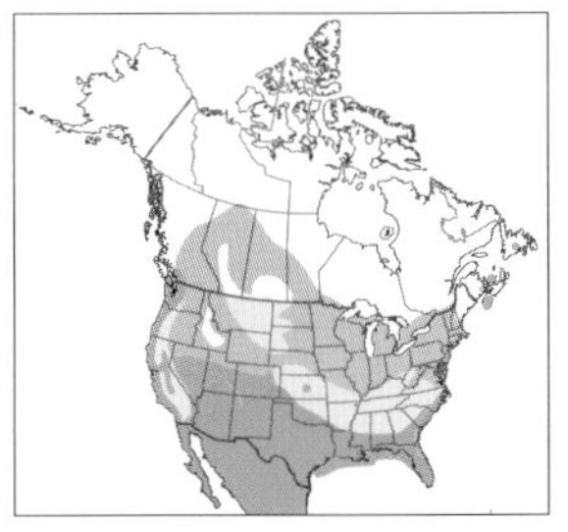

Eastern and Western populations show subtle differences in plumage but have marked differences in song. Comparing mid-continent populations where Eastern and Western meet, Western averages paler and drabber overall, with generally drab reddish-brown scapulars and flanks; mostly brown crown and nape; smudged brownish sides of neck (vs. speckled black and white); duller grayish-white throat; off-white supercilium; dark eye-stripe (not as black as Eastern); paler tail with fewer dark bars; paler primaries and tertials (becoming very pale when worn); and usually barred uppertail coverts. However, individual variation, and the existence of several distinctive local populations along southern coasts, renders sight identification very difficult.

WRENS (CONTINUED)

Our largest wren, Cactus is bold, inquisitive, and distinctively patterned. It is found in open, arid brushland or desert and is more likely to be confused with the smaller thrashers than with wrens.

Cactus Wren

Campylorhynchus brunneicapillus

L 8.5" WS 11" WT 1.4 oz (39 g)

Large and bulky with long, heavy bill and rounded tail. Note bold supercilium and spotted breast.

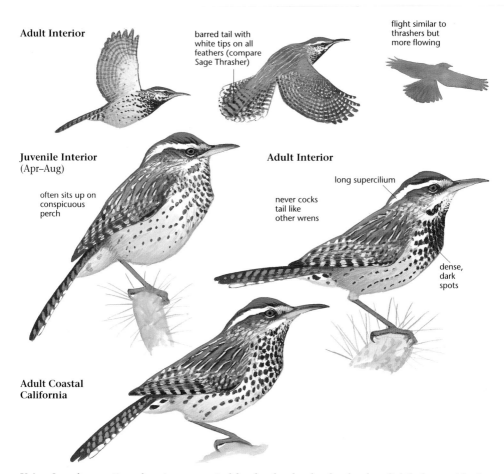

Adult Interior

barred tail with white tips on all feathers (compare Sage Thrasher)

flight similar to thrashers but more flowing

Juvenile Interior
(Apr–Aug)

often sits up on conspicuous perch

Adult Interior

long supercilium

never cocks tail like other wrens

dense, dark spots

Adult Coastal California

Voice: Song low, grating, chugging, unmusical *krrr krrr krrr krrr krrr krrr krrr krrr* slightly lower at beginning but quickly up to speed, with little variation in pitch or tempo. Common call a low, hollow knocking *kot* or *kut* repeated in long series. Also a low, coarse, dry *trrk trrk* . . . or dry, clicking *krrrr;* deep *cheg* notes; series of higher, fairly harsh notes *deeu deeu deeu* . . . or *raap raap raap* . . . like a quacking duck.

Population along the coastal plain of southern California differs slightly but distinctly from Interior populations in having more uniform breast pattern with more widely spaced black spots; paler buffy flanks with larger, rounder black spots; browner back with more continuous white streaks. Juveniles of both populations are similar, less densely spotted than adults. Songs of Coastal California birds are reportedly slower in tempo and lower-pitched, with a raspier quality than Interior birds.

These relatively large and long-billed species prefer rocky habitats. Canyon is found on or near cliffs or steep, rocky slopes; Rock Wren is found around piles of rocks (e.g., talus slopes).

Rock Wren

Salpinctes obsoletus

L 6" WS 9" WT 0.58 oz (16.5 g)

Overall pale grayish, with distinctive pale buffy tips on tail feathers.

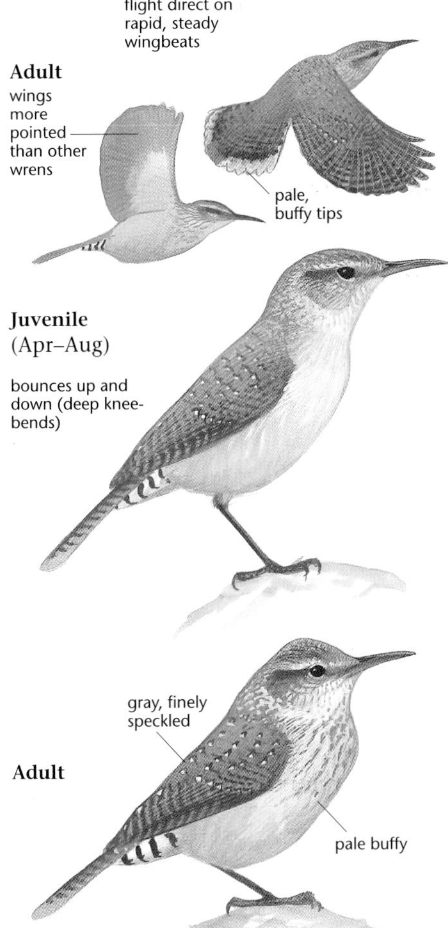
flight direct on rapid, steady wingbeats
Adult
wings more pointed than other wrens
pale, buffy tips
Juvenile
(Apr–Aug)
bounces up and down (deep knee-bends)
gray, finely speckled
Adult
pale buffy

Voice: Song of buzzy, trilled, ringing phrases, each repeated three to six times: *cheer cheer cheer cheer, krjee krjee krjee krjee, preeyerr preeyerr . . . ;* well-spaced in regular rhythm. Call a ringing, buzzy, trill *pdzeeee* audible at great distance; also a fine, buzzy *deee-dee* and *deee der-dr-dr-dr-dr-dr.*

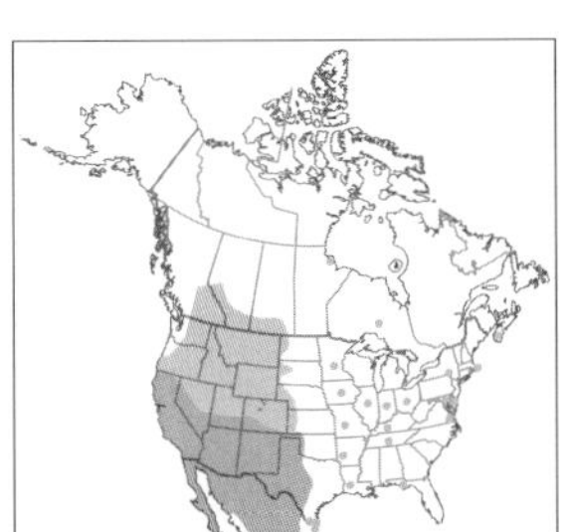

Canyon Wren

Catherpes mexicanus

L 5.75" WS 7.5" WT 0.37 oz (10.5 g)

Distinctive: unique dark rufous belly contrasts with white breast and throat; short, broad, rufous tail; very long bill.

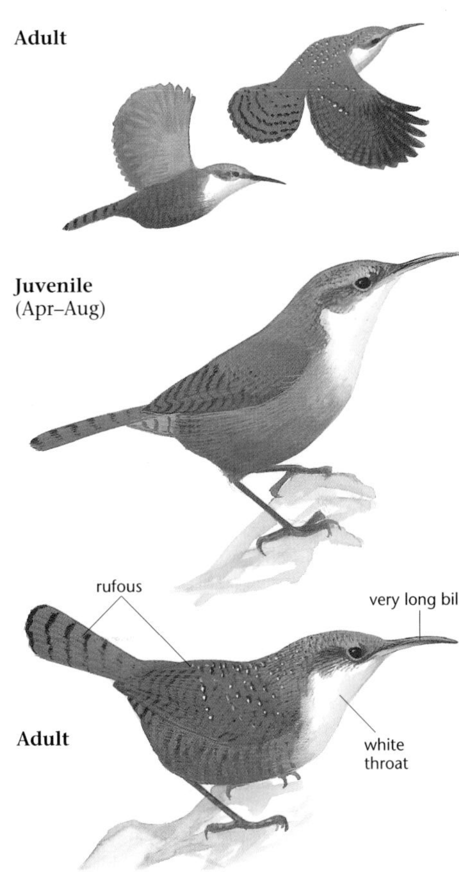
Adult
Juvenile
(Apr–Aug)
rufous
very long bill
Adult
white throat

Voice: Song a cascading series of clear whistles, falling and slowing down, ending with nasal, hissing notes *twi twi twi towi towi towi toowi toowi jeev jeev.* Call a high, ringing buzz *jiink* or *jeeeet* given with a quick bob; higher and simpler than Rock call.

Old World Warblers, Thrushes, and Their Allies

Families: Cinclidae, Regulidae, Sylviidae, Timaliidae, Turdidae

28 species in 14 genera (including typical thrushes, shown on page 402); American Dipper in family Cinclidae, Wrentit in Timaliidae, Old World warblers and gnatcatchers in Sylviidae, kinglets in Regulidae, all thrushes in Turdidae. These diverse species are not all closely related. The unique American Dipper, an aquatic passerine, gleans insects and other prey from rocks under fast-flowing streams; nest is a ball of moss under a bridge or ledge. The secretive Wrentit, found in dense cover, has a short, stout bill; nest is a neat cup. Kinglets are tiny and active and have boldly patterned wings; they feed mainly on tiny insects and often hover at the tips of branches; nest is a small cup high in an evergreen tree. The drab Arctic and Dusky Warblers represent a large and diverse Old World family; similar in habits to wood-warblers, they are generally found gleaning insects from low, dense, brushy vegetation; nest is a neat cup low in a bush. Gnatcatchers are tiny and active insectivores found in brushy vegetation or woods; all raise, flick, and flash their long tails to scare prey, then capture the insects in the air in short, sudden flights; nest is a tiny cup placed on top of a horizontal branch and often decorated, hummingbird-like, with lichens. Thrushes are a diverse group with varying habits; most species have beautiful, fluting songs and give soft, whistled calls; they feed mainly on insects, snails, and fruit; flight is strong, smooth, and buoyant; nest is a neat cup of grass and mud or in a cavity. Adult females are shown.

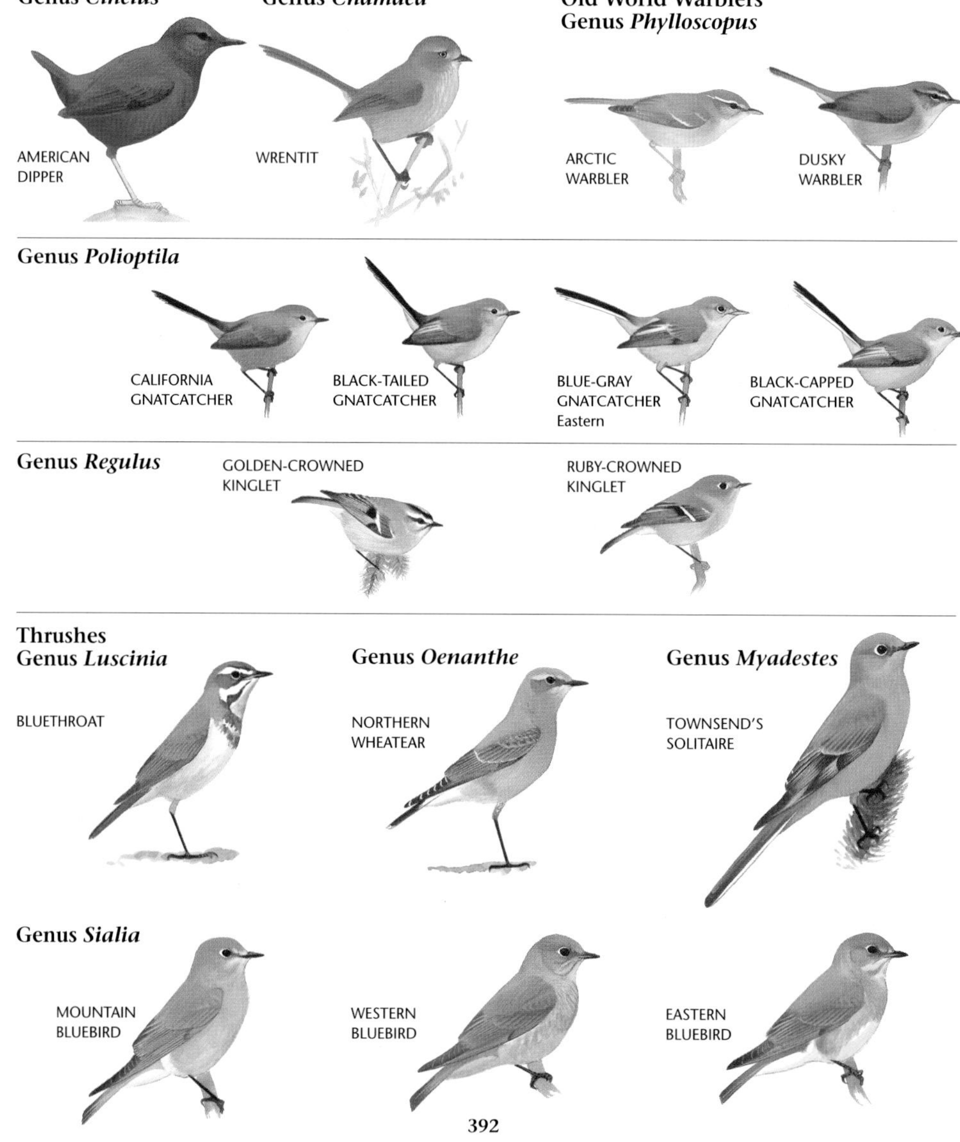

Genus *Cinclus*
AMERICAN DIPPER
Genus *Chamaea*
WRENTIT
Old World Warblers
Genus *Phylloscopus*
ARCTIC WARBLER
DUSKY WARBLER
Genus *Polioptila*
CALIFORNIA GNATCATCHER
BLACK-TAILED GNATCATCHER
BLUE-GRAY GNATCATCHER
Eastern
BLACK-CAPPED GNATCATCHER
Genus *Regulus*
GOLDEN-CROWNED KINGLET
RUBY-CROWNED KINGLET
Thrushes
Genus *Luscinia*
BLUETHROAT
Genus *Oenanthe*
NORTHERN WHEATEAR
Genus *Myadestes*
TOWNSEND'S SOLITAIRE
Genus *Sialia*
MOUNTAIN BLUEBIRD
WESTERN BLUEBIRD
EASTERN BLUEBIRD

American Dipper and Wrentit

Neither of these two distinctive songbirds has any close relatives in North America. American Dipper is found only along fast-flowing, rocky streams, the secretive Wrentit in dense chaparral.

American Dipper

Cinclus mexicanus

L 7.5" WS 11" WT 2 oz (58 g) ♂>♀

Stocky with short tail and long legs. Unique; the only songbird that regularly swims.

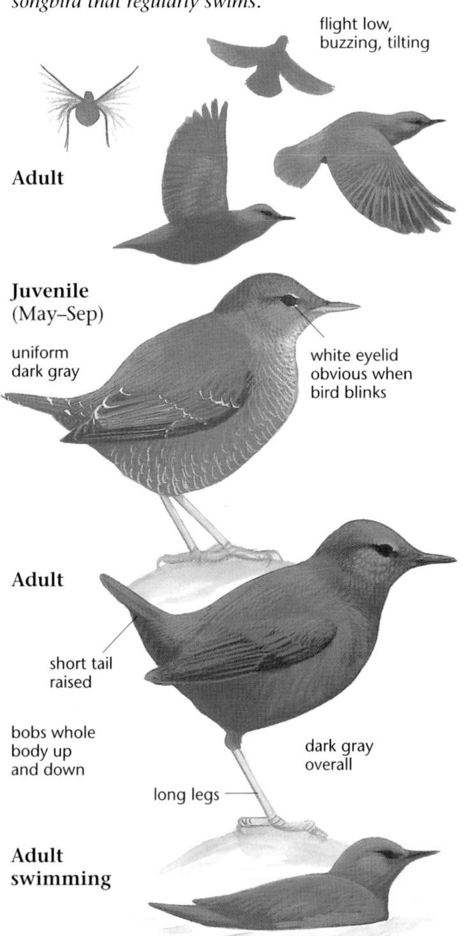

flight low, buzzing, tilting
Adult
Juvenile
(May–Sep)
uniform dark gray
white eyelid obvious when bird blinks
Adult
short tail raised
bobs whole body up and down
dark gray overall
long legs
Adult swimming

Voice: Song of high, whistled or trilled phrases repeated two to four times in thrasherlike pattern *k-tee k-tee wij-ij-ij-ij treeoo treeoo tsebrr tsebrr tsebrr tsebrr . . .*; has steady rhythm and is much higher and clearer than any thrasher. Call a high, buzzy, metallic *dzeet* often doubled or tripled in rapid series *dzik-dzik*.

Wrentit

Chamaea fasciata

L 6.5" WS 7" WT 0.49 oz (14 g)

This aptly named species combines characteristics of wrens and titmice: large head, stout bill, and a long tail often raised. Plain brownish color distinctive.

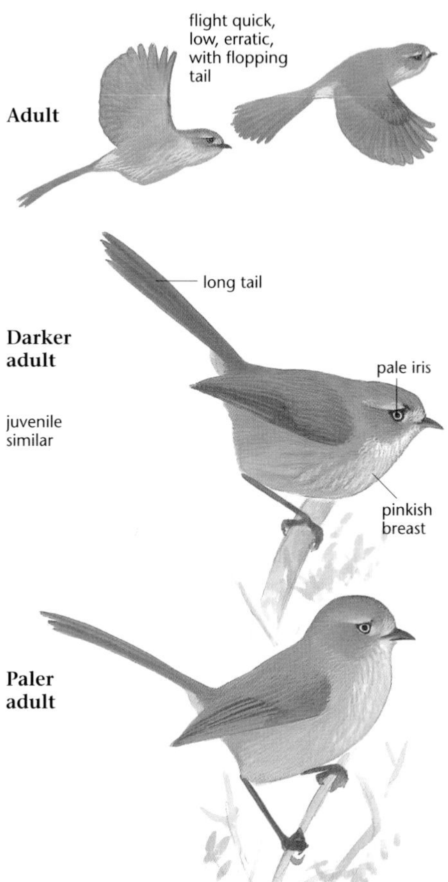

flight quick, low, erratic, with flopping tail
Adult
long tail
Darker adult
pale iris
juvenile similar
pinkish breast
Paler adult

Voice: Song of clear, popping whistles *pwip pwip pwip pwip pwip* or *pwid pwid pwidwidrdrdrdr* in accelerating series apparently given by male; slow, regular, short series by female. Call a dry, ratcheting *trrrk*.

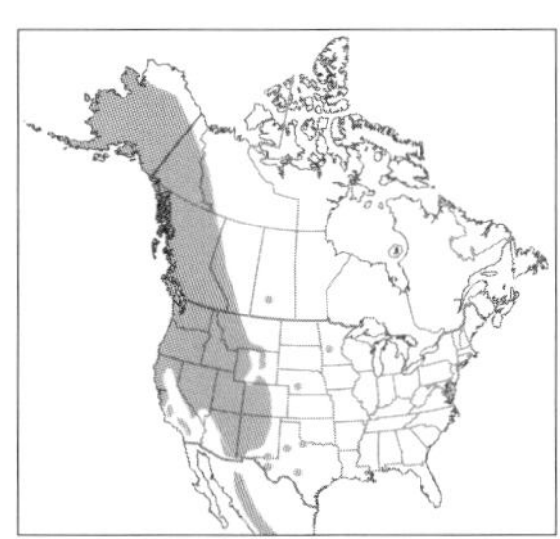

Wrentit variation in color is clinal: darker and redder coastally and northward in wetter climates; paler and grayer inland and southward in drier climates.

Although in the same genus, these two species of tiny insectivores differ in many respects. Both are found in mixed woods; Golden-crowned is particularly fond of conifers year-round.

Golden-crowned Kinglet

Regulus satrapa

L 4" WS 7" WT 0.21 oz (6 g)

Noticeably smaller than Ruby-crowned; flight weaker and more gnatcatcher-like. Often hangs upside down when gleaning (Ruby-crowned rarely does).

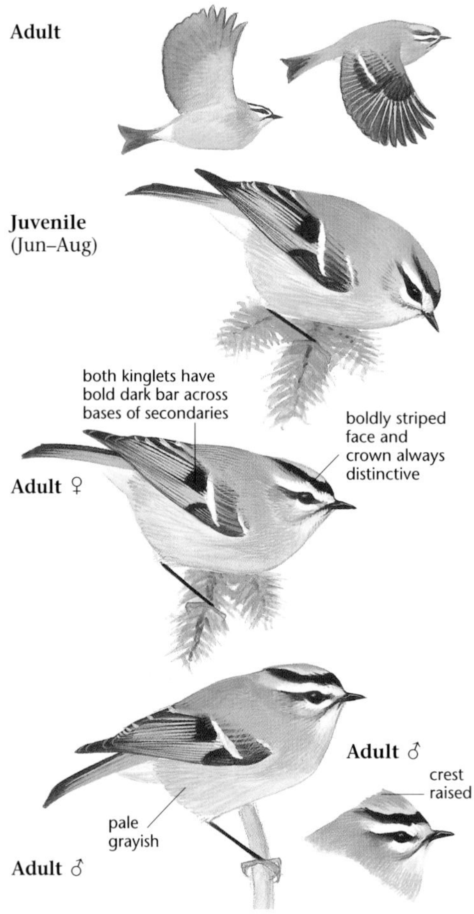
Adult
Juvenile
(Jun–Aug)
both kinglets have bold dark bar across bases of secondaries
boldly striped face and crown always distinctive
Adult ♀
Adult ♂
crest raised
pale grayish
Adult ♂

Voice: Song two-part: a rising series of very high, thin notes followed by a lower, tumbling chickadee-like chatter *see see see si si si tititichichi-chichi*. Typical call a very high, thin, slightly buzzing *zree* or *zee-zee-zee;* also very high, weak *tip* notes. Juvenile begs with sharp, high chips.

Ruby-crowned Kinglet

Regulus calendula

L 4.25" WS 7.5" WT 0.23 oz (6.5 g)

Tiny and drab with small bill; overall a bit larger and more elongated than Golden-crowned (compare Hutton's Vireo and Empidonax *flycatchers).*

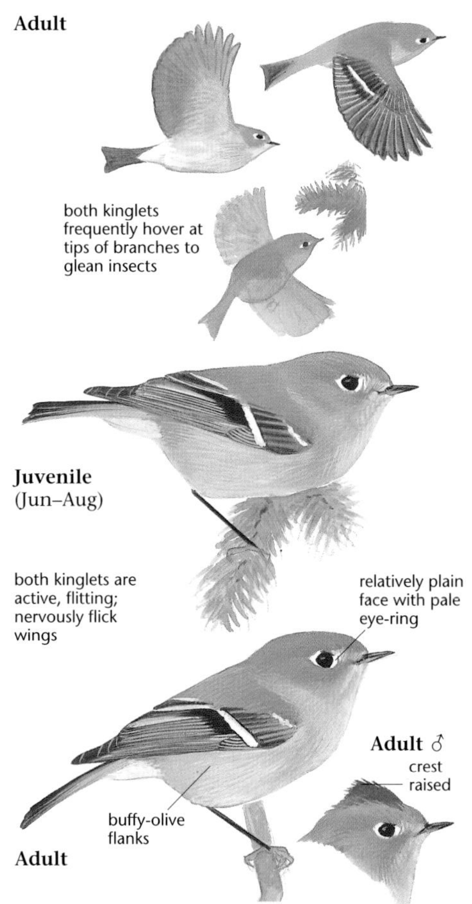
Adult
both kinglets frequently hover at tips of branches to glean insects
Juvenile
(Jun–Aug)
both kinglets are active, flitting; nervously flick wings
relatively plain face with pale eye-ring
Adult ♂
crest raised
buffy-olive flanks
Adult

Voice: Song lively, varied, and loud: begins with high, clear notes and ends with low, whistled chant *sii si sisisi berr berr berr pudi pudi pudi see*. Call a low, husky, dry *jidit;* often a single *jit* or in long series when agitated. Adult in summer gives low, laughing *gido*. Juvenile gives very high, trilled *sreeet*.

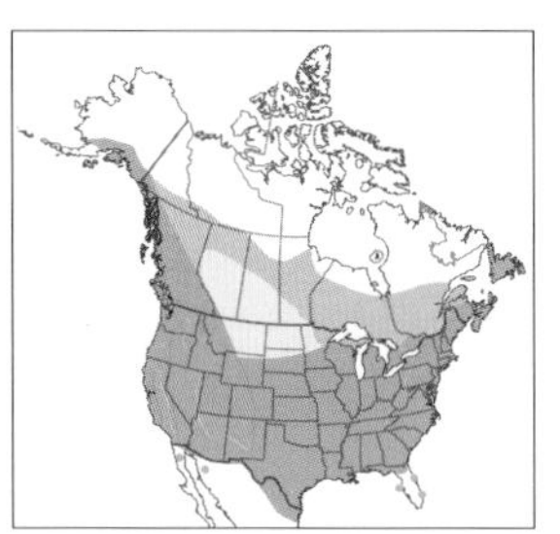

Western populations of Golden-crowned differ on average from birds in the east: slightly smaller overall but longer-billed; brighter green above; longer white supercilium reaches nape; narrower and drabber wing-bars. Voice similar, but song of birds in the west may have more emphatic ending and calls may be buzzier on average.

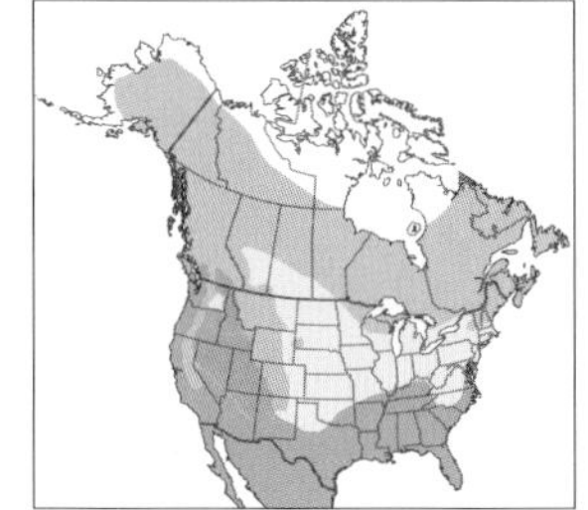

Old World Warblers

Representing a diverse Eurasian group, these two species barely reach North America. Both are rather skulking and active and found in dense, low vegetation (Arctic usually in willows).

Arctic Warbler

Phylloscopus borealis

L 5" WS 8" WT 0.32 oz (9 g)

Small and active; resembles Tennessee Warbler. Relatively large-headed, short-tailed, long-winged, with long supercilium.

Adult

flight low
and dashing

Bright adult

Drab adult

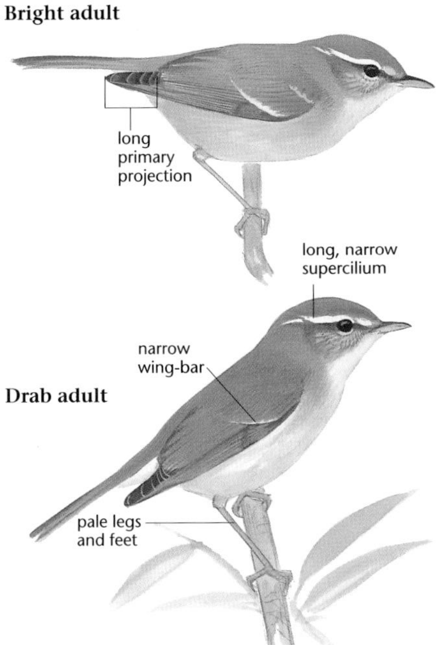
long
primary
projection
long, narrow
supercilium
narrow
wing-bar
pale legs
and feet

Voice: Song fast, mechanical, and rhythmic: a hammering trill *chrchrchrchrchrchrchr-chrchr* or *chingingingingingng* with no change in pitch or rhythm; reminiscent of redpoll trill. Call a short, penetrating, buzzy *jeet* or *dzrk* with little musical quality; reminiscent of American Dipper.

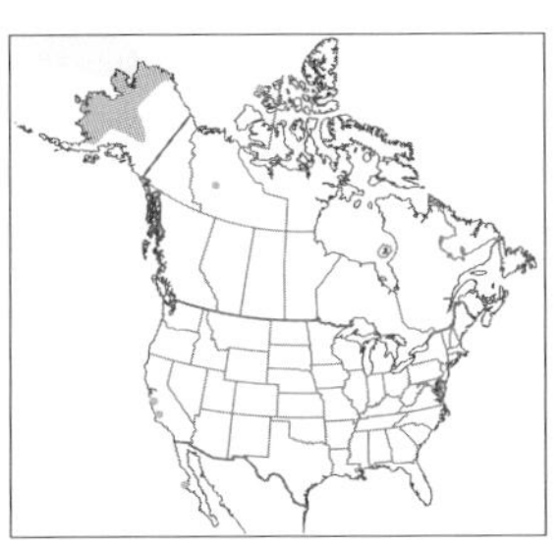

These two species are superficially similar to wood-warblers (especially Tennessee Warbler) but are unrelated, having ten primaries rather than nine and other anatomical distinctions. In the field, look for their less pointed bill with yellowish lower mandible, pale legs, longer supercilium, voice, and more skulking habits.

Dusky Warbler

Phylloscopus fuscatus

L 5.25" WS 7.5" WT 0.31 oz (8.8 g)

Averages shorter-winged and longer-tailed than Arctic; best distinguished by overall color, wing color, and call.

Adult

Adult

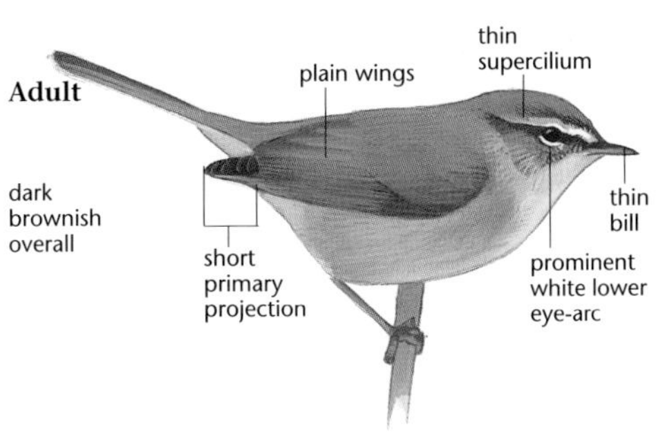
plain wings
thin
supercilium
dark
brownish
overall
thin
bill
short
primary
projection
prominent
white lower
eye-arc

Voice: Song a varied, short series of high, slow trills. Call a sharp, hard *stak* like Lincoln's Sparrow but drier; repeated in rapid rattle when agitated.

GNATCATCHERS

These are our smallest gnatcatchers, with little white on their tails. Found low in dry, desert brush or coastal chaparral, they are usually seen in pairs year-round.

California Gnatcatcher

Polioptila californica

L 4.5" WS 5.5" WT 0.18 oz (5 g)

Structure differs subtly from Blue-gray: small and compact with thin, short bill, shorter tail, rounded wings.

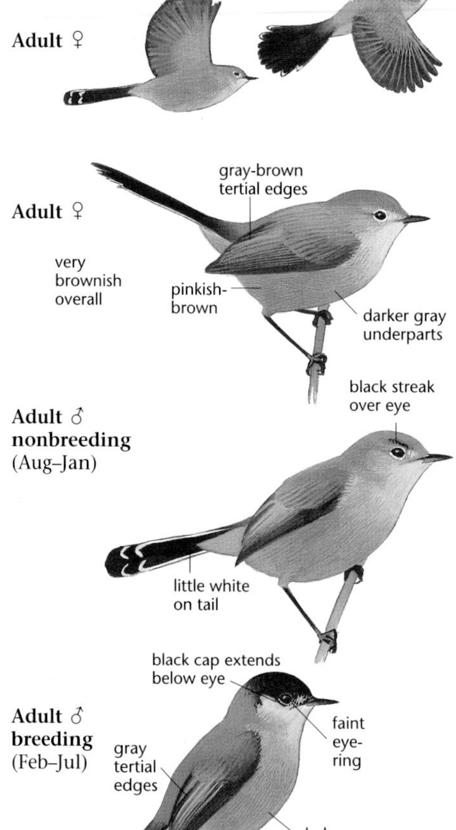

Adult ♀
Adult ♀
gray-brown tertial edges
very brownish overall
pinkish-brown
darker gray underparts
Adult ♂ nonbreeding (Aug–Jan)
black streak over eye
little white on tail
Adult ♂ breeding (Feb–Jul)
black cap extends below eye
faint eye-ring
gray tertial edges
dark gray

Voice: Common call a nasal, mewing *mee-eeew* or *vwee-eeew;* kittenlike when relaxed, harsher when agitated; always with distinctive rising then falling pattern. Other calls include a soft *dear dear dear . . . ;* a harsh *tssshh;* and *jew jew jew jew* similar to Black-tailed.

Black-tailed Gnatcatcher

Polioptila melanura

L 4.5" WS 5.5" WT 0.18 oz (5 g)

Size and shape like California, but paler overall, with more white on tail, different voice.

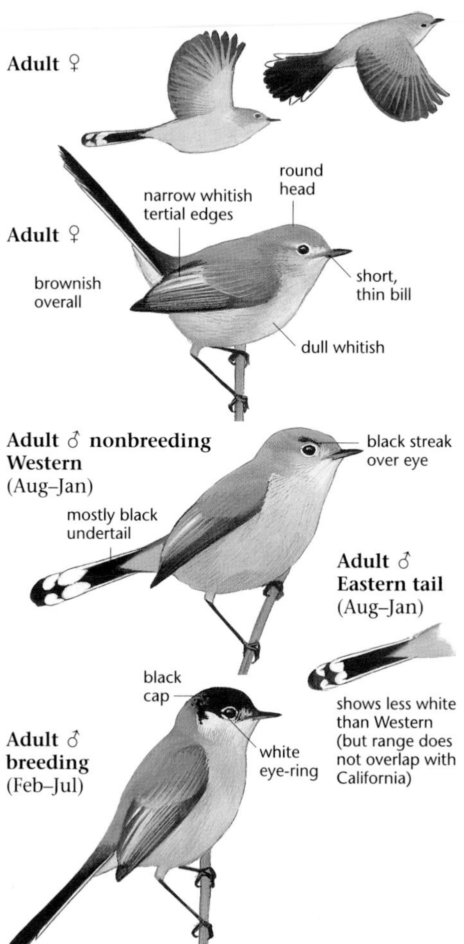

Adult ♀
Adult ♀
round head
narrow whitish tertial edges
brownish overall
short, thin bill
dull whitish
Adult ♂ nonbreeding Western (Aug–Jan)
black streak over eye
mostly black undertail
Adult ♂ Eastern tail (Aug–Jan)
shows less white than Western (but range does not overlap with California)
Adult ♂ breeding (Feb–Jul)
black cap
white eye-ring

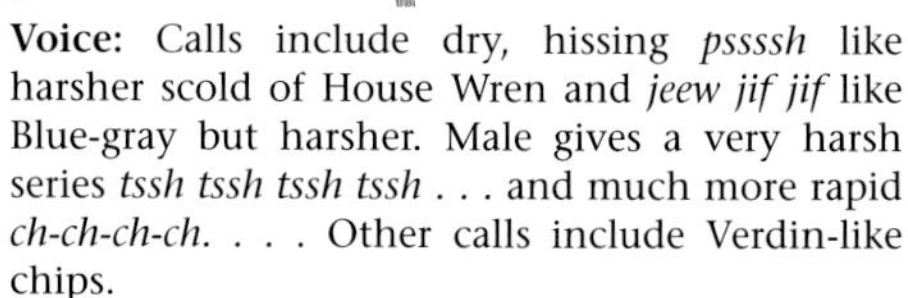

Voice: Calls include dry, hissing *pssssh* like harsher scold of House Wren and *jeew jif jif* like Blue-gray but harsher. Male gives a very harsh series *tssh tssh tssh tssh . . .* and much more rapid *ch-ch-ch-ch. . . .* Other calls include Verdin-like chips.

In these two species the series of short, harsh notes described above seems to function as song. Both have a true song more like other gnatcatchers—a complex jumble of high chips and warbled notes—but it is rarely heard.

Gnatcatchers (continued)

Blue-gray is our most widespread gnatcatcher. It has extensive white on its tail, bright white tertial edges, and a relatively bright, clean color. It is often found high in trees or taller brush.

Blue-gray Gnatcatcher

Polioptila caerulea

L 4.5" WS 6" WT 0.21 oz (6 g)

Tiny and long-tailed, with fairly long, pale bill and more pointed wings than other gnatcatchers.

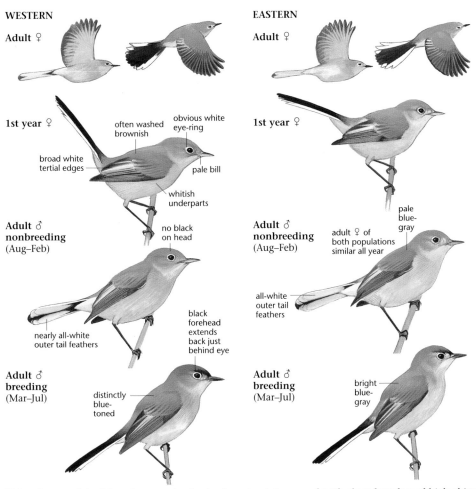

WESTERN

Adult ♀

1st year ♀

obvious white eye-ring

often washed brownish

broad white tertial edges

pale bill

whitish underparts

Adult ♂ nonbreeding (Aug–Feb)

no black on head

nearly all-white outer tail feathers

Adult ♂ breeding (Mar–Jul)

black forehead extends back just behind eye

distinctly blue-toned

EASTERN

Adult ♀

1st year ♀

Adult ♂ nonbreeding (Aug–Feb)

pale blue-gray

adult ♀ of both populations similar all year

all-white outer tail feathers

Adult ♂ breeding (Mar–Jul)

bright blue-gray

Voice: Song mainly thin, wheezy notes in steady series, interspersed with short bunches of high chips and slurs *zeee zeet zeet zill zill zwee zwee. . . .* Western song significantly different: lower, harsher, less varied *jeew jeew bidi bilf. . . .* Common call a very thin, nasal, variable buzz *speee, szeeewv,* or *zeeewv zeef zeef.* Western birds average lower and harsher calls than Eastern; shorter and more strongly descending *jeewf* (vs. *szeeee* of Eastern); more similar to House Wren and all other gnatcatchers.

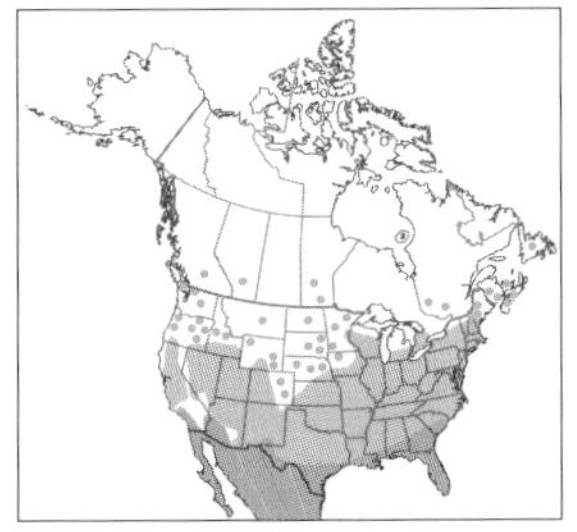

Western populations average less white on tail than Eastern, with black usually visible on the base of the outer tail feathers and only small white tips on the next-to-outermost feathers; drabber overall, males have gray back with dark bluish crown and broader, shorter black forehead mark; females are often distinctly brownish above (Eastern females are always gray); voice is harsher overall. Habitat choice of breeding birds is also quite different: Eastern birds nest in swampy woods; Western nest in arid, dense brush, pinyon-juniper, or open woods.

This rare visitor from Mexico has nested in Arizona in low hackberry thickets along desert streams. Identification requires careful study of tail and face pattern, bill shape, and voice.

Black-capped Gnatcatcher

Polioptila nigriceps

L 4.25" WS 6" WT 0.2 oz (5.6 g)

Female similar to Blue-gray but with longer bill, more graduated tail, more rounded wings; voice also differs.

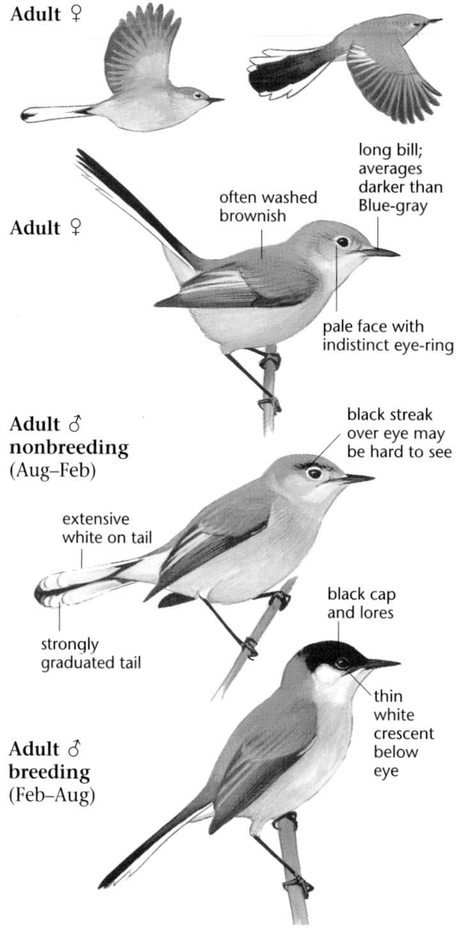
Adult ♀
Adult ♀
often washed brownish
long bill; averages darker than Blue-gray
pale face with indistinct eye-ring
Adult ♂ nonbreeding (Aug–Feb)
black streak over eye may be hard to see
extensive white on tail
strongly graduated tail
black cap and lores
thin white crescent below eye
Adult ♂ breeding (Feb–Aug)

Voice: Song often heard: slow, low-pitched, and varied; includes hard *che che che* or *trk trk,* husky *jip* like Wilson's Warbler, and high, sharp *tip*. Common call rather harsh with rising then falling inflection like California *je-eew;* a variety of other notes given, including a soft *dear-dear-dear . . .* series like California.

Identification of Gnatcatchers

Distinguishing a gnatcatcher from any other bird is normally a simple task, but separating gnatcatcher species from one another can be difficult.

Assessing tail pattern is critical in identifying gnatcatchers. Keep in mind that when the tail is folded closed, the outer tail feathers are visible only from below.

Gnatcatchers molt their tail feathers just once a year Jul–Aug. During that time it is not unusual to see a gnatcatcher with missing tail feathers. A Blue-gray Gnatcatcher with the mostly white outermost tail feathers missing will show the mostly black next-to-outer feathers and easily could be mistaken for a Black-tailed Gnatcatcher. Also note that in the summer months before molt begins, the outer tail feathers can be very worn or broken, again creating the appearance of a mostly black tail.

Black-capped Gnatcatcher has a more graduated tail than Blue-gray; the distance from the tip of the outer (shortest) tail feather to the tip of the central (longest) tail feather averages 50 percent greater in Black-capped. Under exceptional conditions this may be visible in the field.

California Gnatcatcher
little white on tail

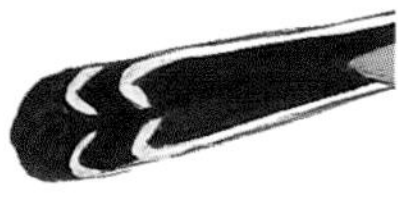

Western Black-tailed Gnatcatcher
mostly black undertail

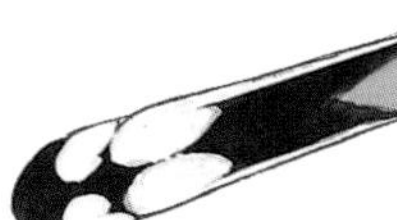

Eastern Black-tailed Gnatcatcher
shows less white than Western

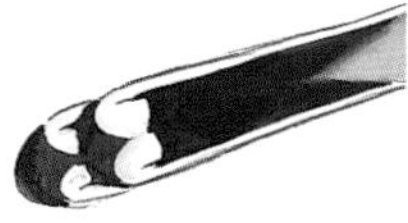

Western Blue-gray Gnatcatcher
nearly all-white outer tail feathers

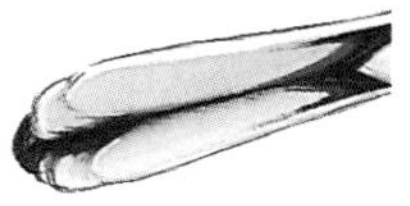

Eastern Blue-gray Gnatcatcher
all-white outer tail feathers

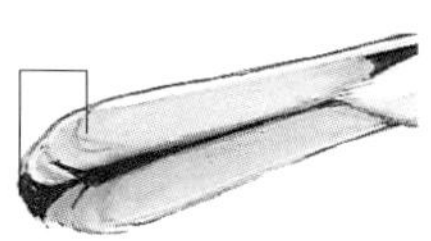

Black-capped Gnatcatcher
extensive white on tail; more graduated tail shape

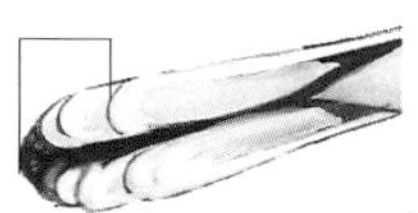

Bluethroat and Northern Wheatear

These two Eurasian species barely enter North America. The secretive Bluethroat is found in dense, low vegetation. Northern Wheatear is found on the ground in open habitats: tundra, fields, beaches.

Bluethroat

Luscinia svecica

L 5.75" WS 9" WT 0.74 oz (21 g)

Small and short-tailed with stubby, rounded wings.

1st winter

Adult

flight low and fast; dives into cover

rufous base of tail obvious in flight as tail is flicked open

Juvenile (Jul–Aug)

1st winter ♀ (Aug–Mar)

whitish supercilium

plain brown upperside

white throat with "necklace" of dark spots

Adult ♀

Adult ♂

blue and rufous throat unmistakable

Voice: Song begins with a slowly accelerating series of high, short whistles, then a series of trilled or buzzy notes; includes imitations of other species and distinctive, bell-like notes. Call a sharp, dry *chak* and high, whistled *heet* like Northern Wheatear.

Northern Wheatear

Oenanthe oenanthe

L 5.75" WS 12" WT 0.81 oz (23 g)

Relatively long-winged, short-tailed, and long-legged.

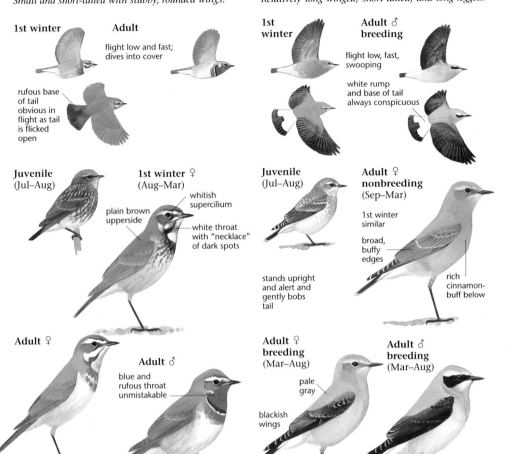

1st winter

Adult ♂ breeding

flight low, fast, swooping

white rump and base of tail always conspicuous

Juvenile (Jul–Aug)

Adult ♀ nonbreeding (Sep–Mar)

1st winter similar

broad, buffy edges

stands upright and alert and gently bobs tail

rich cinnamon-buff below

Adult ♀ breeding (Mar–Aug)

pale gray

blackish wings

Adult ♂ breeding (Mar–Aug)

Voice: Song an unpatterned, level, rapid warbling; overall longspurlike; combines husky, sliding whistles with dry, crackling, toneless phrases. Call a weak, high whistle *heet* and dry, clicking *tek*.

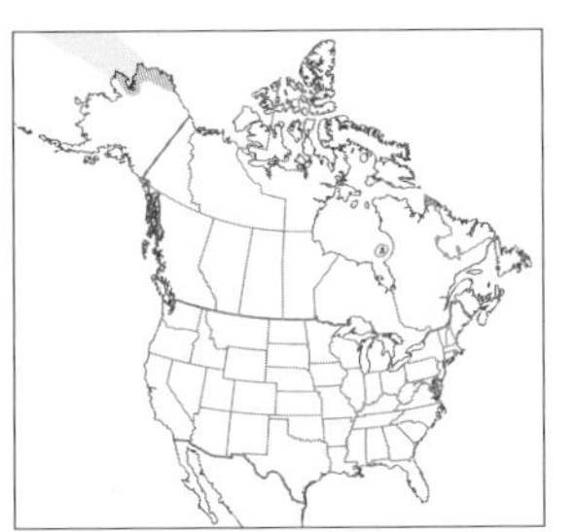

Northern Wheatears found in eastern North America nest in eastern Canada and Greenland; on average, they are 10 percent larger, longer-legged, and more richly colored than birds in Alaska but are not safely distinguished in the field.

Townsend's Solitaire and Mountain Bluebird

Townsend's Solitaire nests in montane coniferous forests; some move to lower elevations in winter. Mountain Bluebird is found in open areas with scattered trees, often in flocks in winter.

Townsend's Solitaire

Myadestes townsendi

L 8.5" WS 14.5" WT 1.2 oz (34 g)

Long-tailed like mockingbirds; short-billed and small-headed. Tail tapered when closed; posture upright.

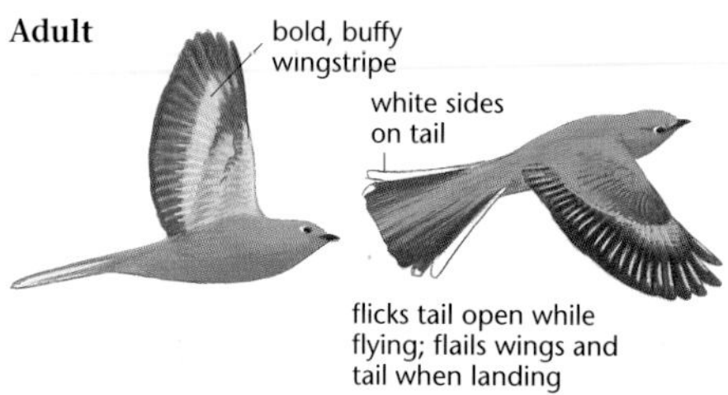
Adult
bold, buffy wingstripe
white sides on tail
flicks tail open while flying; flails wings and tail when landing

Juvenile (Jun–Sep)
dark and scaly with buffy spots
Drab-winged adult
Bright-winged adult
white eye-ring
intricate wing pattern
plain gray overall

Voice: Song a continuous, disjointed, finchlike warble; clear, whistled notes with low, husky notes interspersed but no distinct pattern. Call a clear, soft whistle *heeh,* reminiscent of a single toot of Northern Pygmy-Owl.

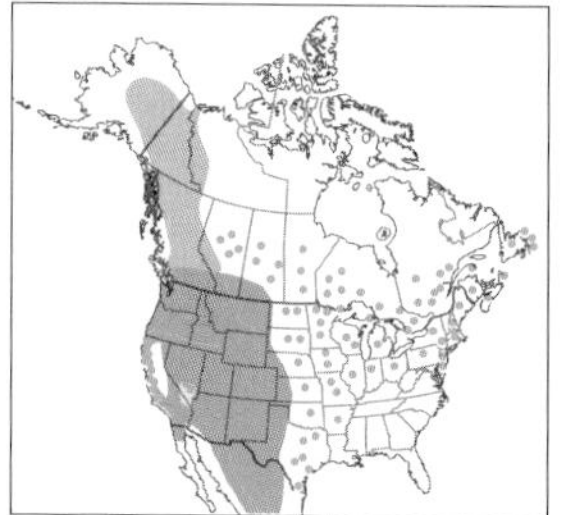

Mountain Bluebird

Sialia currucoides

L 7.25" WS 14" WT 1 oz (29 g)

Slimmer than other bluebirds; especially longer-winged and -tailed, thinner-billed.

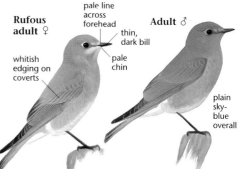

Adult ♀
Adult ♂
long wings and tail
often hovers when foraging
Juvenile (May–Aug)
unspotted back
Gray Adult ♀
pale blue remiges
plain ashy-gray overall
pale blue tail
gray-brown flanks
Rufous adult ♀
pale line across forehead
thin, dark bill
pale chin
whitish edging on coverts
Adult ♂
plain sky-blue overall

Voice: Song a series of low, burry whistles like call *jerrf jerrf jewr jipo jerrf.* Call a soft whistle similar to other bluebirds but thinner and clearer: *feeer* or a mellow, muffled *perf,* always descending; also a short, harsh *chik* or *chak.*

Many Mountain Bluebirds (even adult males) show a trace of rufous on throat and breast. Some females with rufous wash on breast are very similar to other bluebirds; note long wings and tail, thin bill with little or no yellow at base, and plumage characteristics noted above. Eastern and Mountain Bluebirds hybridize occasionally.

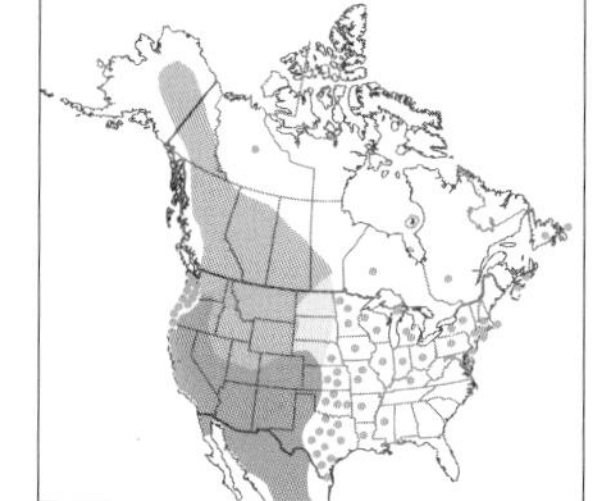

Western and Eastern Bluebirds

These two closely related species are found in small groups in fields or open woods, often perched on wires or fences. Both constantly give musical calls in flight.

Western Bluebird

Sialia mexicana

L 7" WS 13.5" WT 1 oz (29 g)

Stocky with rather short tail and wings, stout bill, large head (compare Mountain).

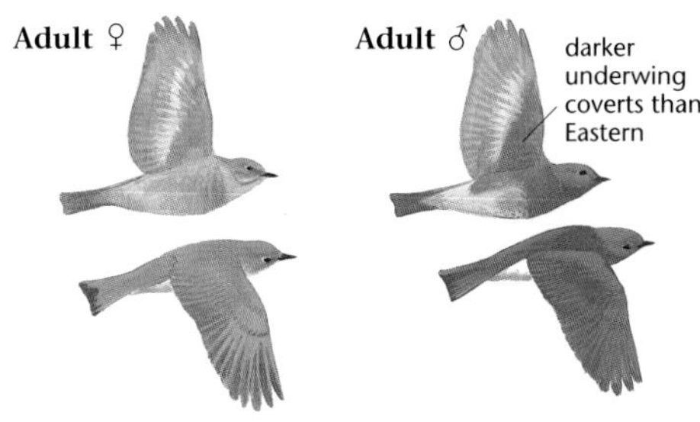
Adult ♀
Adult ♂
darker underwing coverts than Eastern

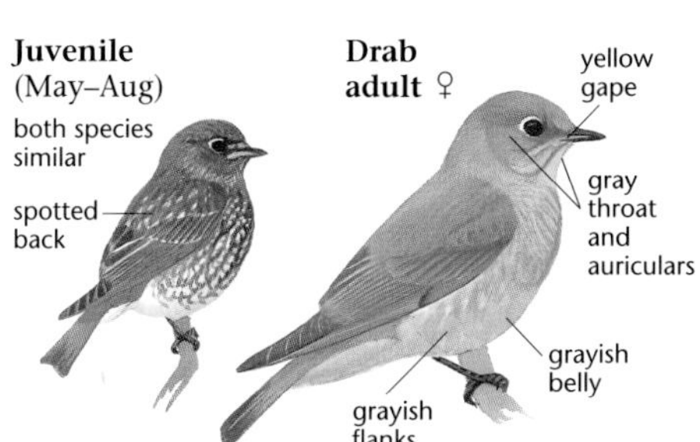
Juvenile (May–Aug)
both species similar
spotted back
Drab adult ♀
yellow gape
gray throat and auriculars
grayish belly
grayish flanks

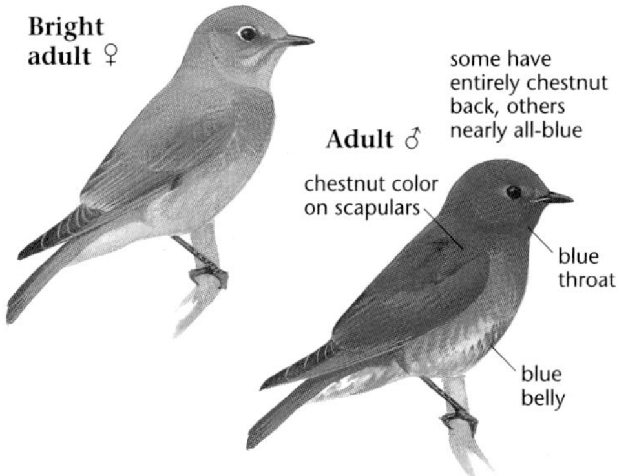
Bright adult ♀
some have entirely chestnut back, others nearly all-blue
Adult ♂
chestnut color on scapulars
blue throat
blue belly

Voice: Song heard infrequently, mainly at dawn; simply a series of call notes. Call a fairly hard, low whistle *jewf* or *pew pew pew* shorter and lower than Eastern; also a short, dry chatter.

Eastern Bluebird

Sialia sialis

L 7" WS 13" WT 1.1 oz (31 g)

Like Western but smaller overall and slightly thicker-billed.

Adult ♀
Adult ♂

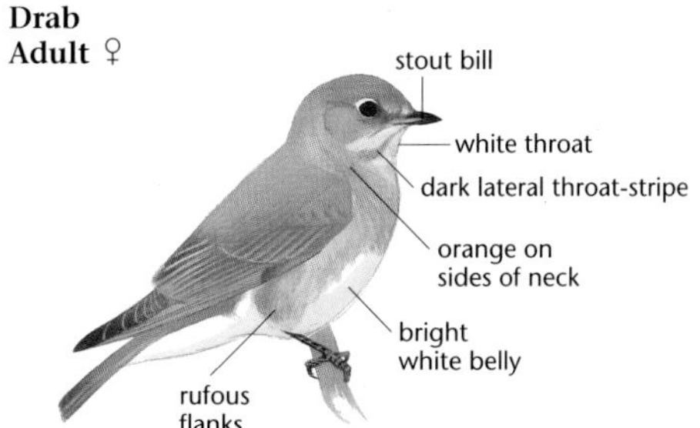
Drab Adult ♀
stout bill
white throat
dark lateral throat-stripe
orange on sides of neck
bright white belly
rufous flanks

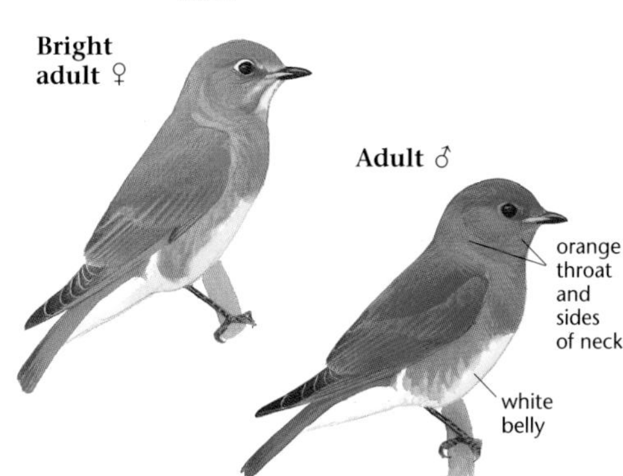
Bright adult ♀
Adult ♂
orange throat and sides of neck
white belly

Voice: Song a pleasing soft phrase of mellow whistles *chiti WEEW wewidoo* and variations. Call of similar pleasant musical quality: a soft, husky whistle *jeew* or *jeew wiwi;* also a short, dry chatter.

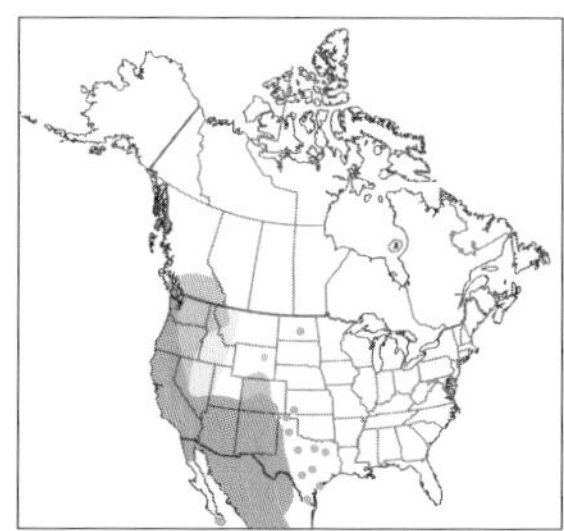

Eastern Bluebirds resident in southeastern Arizona mountains average slightly larger and distinctly paler than birds to the east (which are shown above); males in fresh plumage often have cinnamon fringes on scapulars.

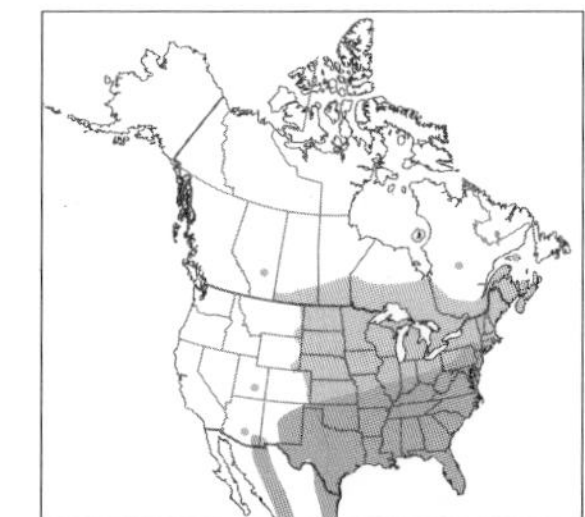

VARIED THRUSH

Varied Thrush is closely associated with the damp, shaded coniferous forests of the Pacific Northwest. Often found in flocks in winter, it is similar in habits to American Robin but more secretive.

Typical Thrushes

Robins are large, boldly colored thrushes; they are often found in flocks on grassy lawns, etc., or seen in high flight. Species in the spotted thrushes group are medium-size and brown with spotted breasts; they are found singly within shaded woods. Spotted thrushes are identified by face and breast pattern and flank and overall color. Adult or 1st year females are shown.

Robins
Genus *Turdus*

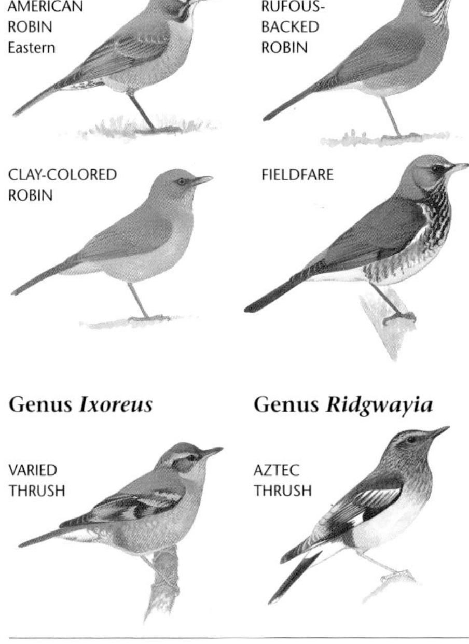
AMERICAN ROBIN Eastern
RUFOUS-BACKED ROBIN
CLAY-COLORED ROBIN
FIELDFARE
Genus Ixoreus
Genus Ridgwayia
VARIED THRUSH
AZTEC THRUSH

Spotted Thrushes
Genus *Hylocichla*

WOOD THRUSH

Genus *Catharus*

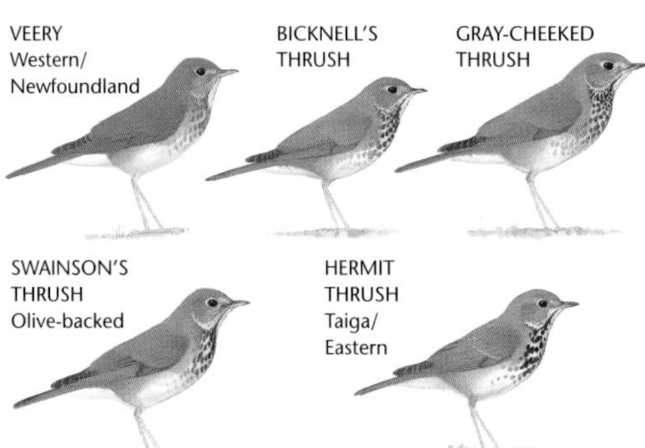
VEERY Western/ Newfoundland
BICKNELL'S THRUSH
GRAY-CHEEKED THRUSH
SWAINSON'S THRUSH Olive-backed
HERMIT THRUSH Taiga/ Eastern

Varied Thrush

Ixoreus naevius

L 9.5" WS 16" WT 2.7 oz (78 g)

Potbellied, long-necked, and short-tailed, with intricate wing pattern and bold supercilium; can be confused only with American Robin.

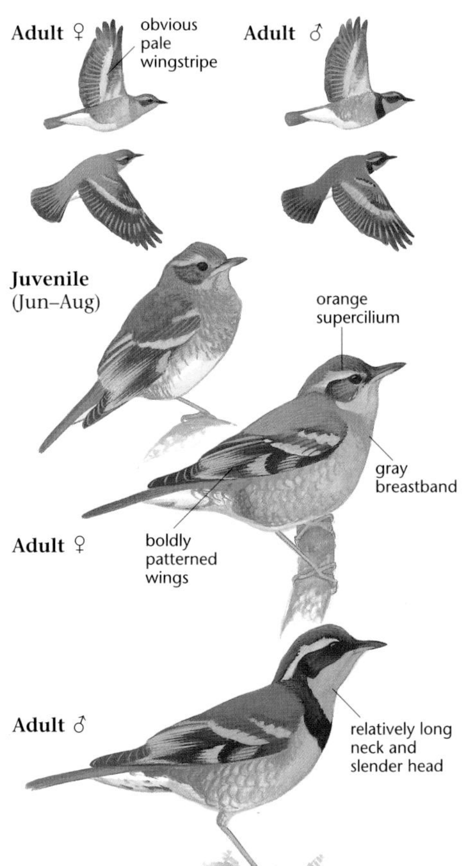
Adult ♀
obvious pale wingstripe
Adult ♂
Juvenile (Jun–Aug)
orange supercilium
gray breastband
Adult ♀
boldly patterned wings
Adult ♂
relatively long neck and slender head

Voice: Song a single, long whistle on one pitch: one and a half seconds long and repeated about every ten seconds; each whistle on a different pitch; some notes trilled or buzzy. Call a short, low, dry *chup* very similar to Hermit Thrush but harder; also a hard, high *gipf* and a soft, short *tiup*. Flight call a short, humming whistle.

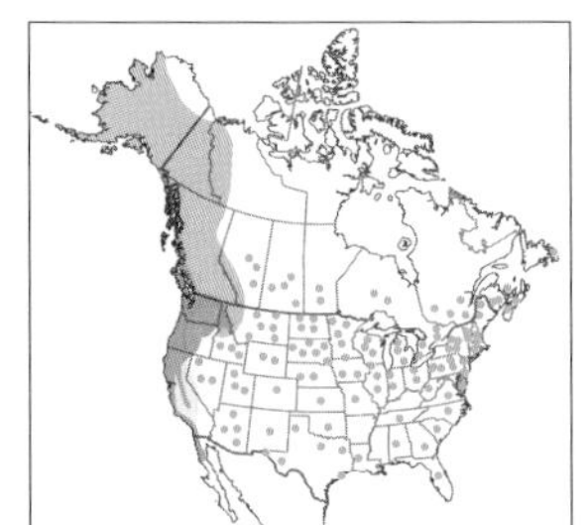

Large and conspicuous, this species is one of our most familiar birds. It is commonly seen on grassy lawns but is found in many habitats from tundra to forests, often in large flocks in winter.

American Robin

Turdus migratorius

L 10" WS 17" WT 2.7 oz (77 g)

Large and sturdy, with long legs and fairly long tail; plain orange breast and grayish back distinctive in all plumages.

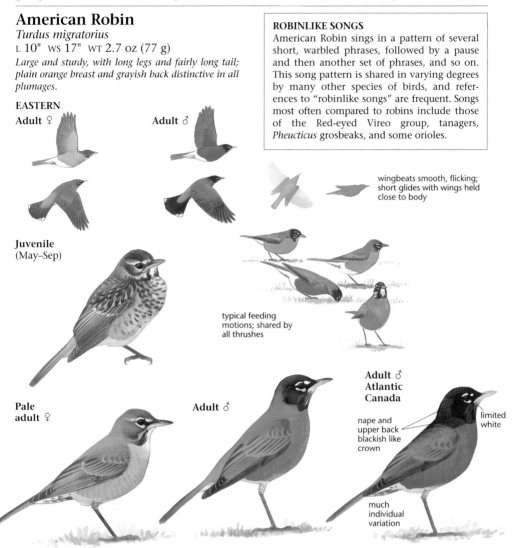

ROBINLIKE SONGS

American Robin sings in a pattern of several short, warbled phrases, followed by a pause and then another set of phrases, and so on. This song pattern is shared in varying degrees by many other species of birds, and references to "robinlike songs" are frequent. Songs most often compared to robins include those of the Red-eyed Vireo group, tanagers, *Pheucticus* grosbeaks, and some orioles.

EASTERN

Adult ♀

Adult ♂

wingbeats smooth, flicking; short glides with wings held close to body

Juvenile (May–Sep)

typical feeding motions; shared by all thrushes

Pale adult ♀

Adult ♂

Adult ♂ Atlantic Canada

nape and upper back blackish like crown

limited white

much individual variation

Voice: Song a series of low, whistled phrases with liquid quality typical of thrushes; each phrase delivered rather quickly but with long pauses between phrases; often two or three phrases alternately repeated over and over *plurrri, kliwi, plurrri, kliwi. . . .* Call varies from a low, mellow *pup* or a sharp, clucking, often doubled *piik* to a sharper, rapid, urgent series *kli quiquiquiqui koo;* also a lower, softer *puk puk puk* and a harsh, high, descending *shheerr.* Flight call a very high, trilled, descending *srreel;* often combined with other calls such as *srreel puk puk puk.* Alarm like other thrushes: a very high, thin *tseeew* or shorter *seew.*

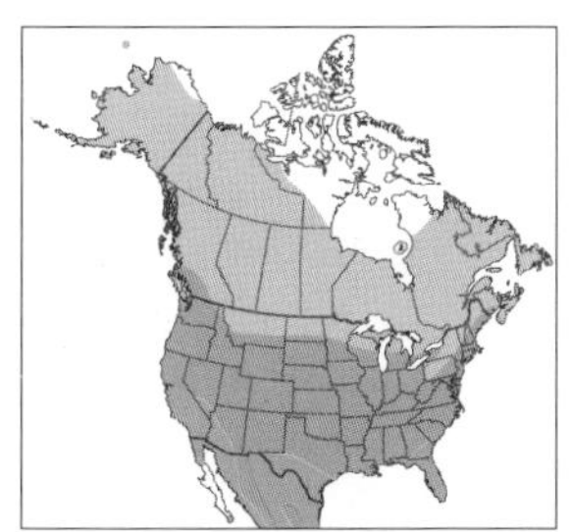

Geographic variation is limited and clinal. Most Western populations average paler and drabber than Eastern and nearly lack white corners on tail. Breeders of Atlantic Canada are richly colored with extensive black on nape and mantle.

Adult ♀ Western

Western birds have very limited white tail corners

Rare Thrushes

Aztec Thrush, related to Varied, is found in montane pine-oak forests. Rufous-backed Robin, closely related to American, is found in riparian woods.

Aztec Thrush

Ridgwayia pinicola

L 9.25" WS 16" WT 2.7 oz (78 g)

Distinctive but very inconspicuous; long-necked and short-tailed, with boldly patterned plumage (compare juvenile Spotted Towhee).

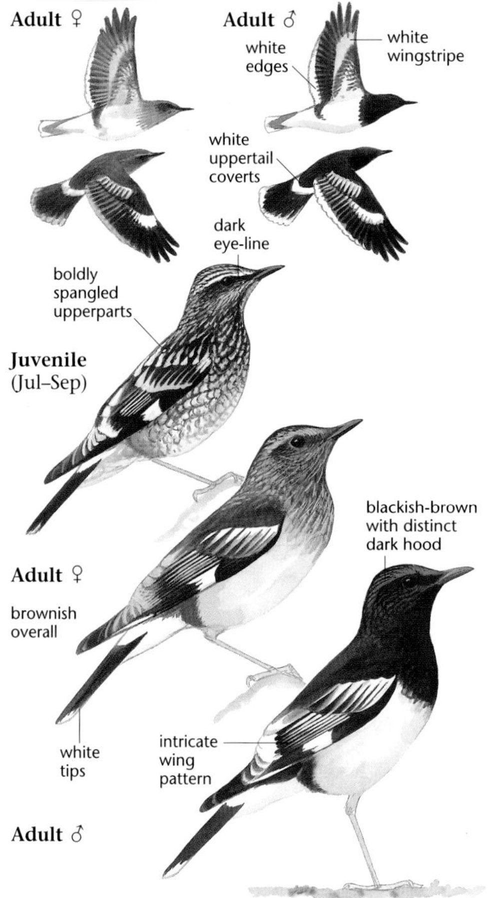
Adult ♀
Adult ♂
white edges
white wingstripe
white uppertail coverts
dark eye-line
boldly spangled upperparts
Juvenile (Jul–Sep)
blackish-brown with distinct dark hood
Adult ♀
brownish overall
white tips
intricate wing pattern
Adult ♂

Voice: Generally silent. Song unknown (possibly simply a louder, repeated version of call note). Call a rather harsh, buzzy or whining *prreep* or *wheeerr;* also a soft, upslurred *seeep*.

Rufous-backed Robin

Turdus rufopalliatus

L 9.25" WS 16" WT 2.7 oz (77 g)

More secretive than American Robin; wings slightly shorter and more rounded. Note dark face and rufous back.

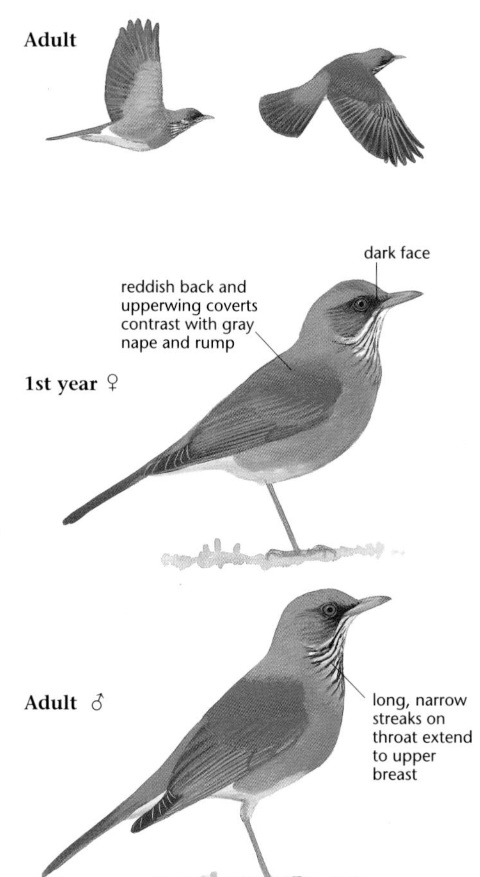
Adult
dark face
reddish back and upperwing coverts contrast with gray nape and rump
1st year ♀
Adult ♂
long, narrow streaks on throat extend to upper breast

Voice: Song low-pitched, slow, warbling *weedele loo loo freerlii . . .* with simple, repeated pattern. Call a short, descending *cherrp* and a rapid series *che che che che* analogous to American. Alarm a long, mellow, descending whistle. Flight call a high, short, rising *zeep,* thinner than American.

Both these species are closely related to American Robin. Clay-colored is found in dense woods. Fieldfare prefers woodland edges and is usually found with flocks of American Robin.

Clay-colored Robin

Turdus grayi

L 9" WS 15.5" WT 2.6 oz (74 g)

More secretive than American Robin; stockier with shorter, more rounded wings.

Adult

underwing
coverts brighter
than flanks

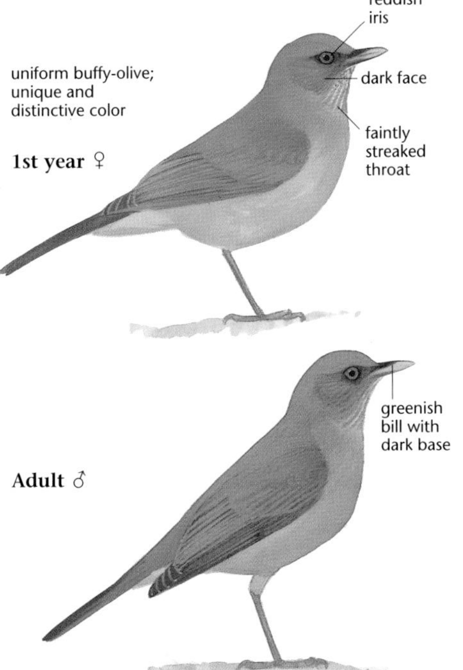
reddish
iris
uniform buffy-olive;
unique and
distinctive color
dark face
faintly
streaked
throat
1st year ♀
greenish
bill with
dark base
Adult ♂

Voice: Song a slow, low-pitched warbling with steady, monotonous tempo and repeated phrases such as mellow, slurred *tooowiip tooowip.* Call a long, husky, sliding whistle with nasal, mewing quality *teeweeooip;* similar to call given frequently by Long-billed Thrasher. Flight call weaker and buzzier than American Robin.

Fieldfare

Turdus pilaris

L 10" WS 18" WT 3.5 oz (99 g)

Larger and lankier than American Robin but slightly shorter-billed; plumage distinctive.

Adult

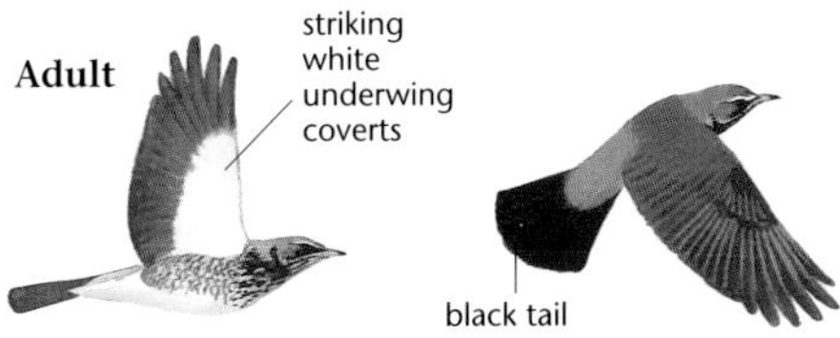
striking
white
underwing
coverts
black tail

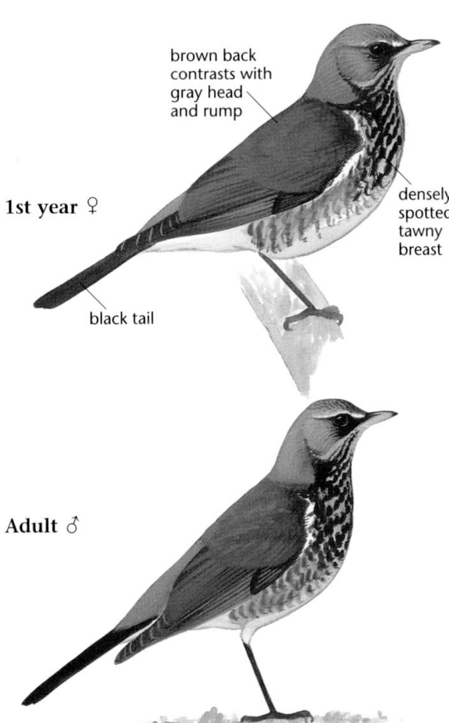
brown back
contrasts with
gray head
and rump
1st year ♀
densely
spotted
tawny
breast
black tail
Adult ♂

Voice: Song an unmusical, squeaky chatter delivered without pauses. Call a loud, harsh *chr-chr-chr-chr* in descending series like scold of Blue-headed Vireo *feee feee chr-chr-chr-chr;* often given in flight. Also a dry rattle reminiscent of Gray Catbird. Flight call a thin, nasal, rising *zreep.*

Wood Thrush is distinctive in shape and plumage; Veery is similar to other *Catharus* thrushes. Both are found in shady woods with leafy understory, foraging mainly on the ground.

Wood Thrush

Hylocichla mustelina

L 7.75" WS 13" WT 1.6 oz (47 g)

The largest of the spotted thrushes, with distinctive shape: potbelly, relatively large bill, and short tail.

Adult

1st year

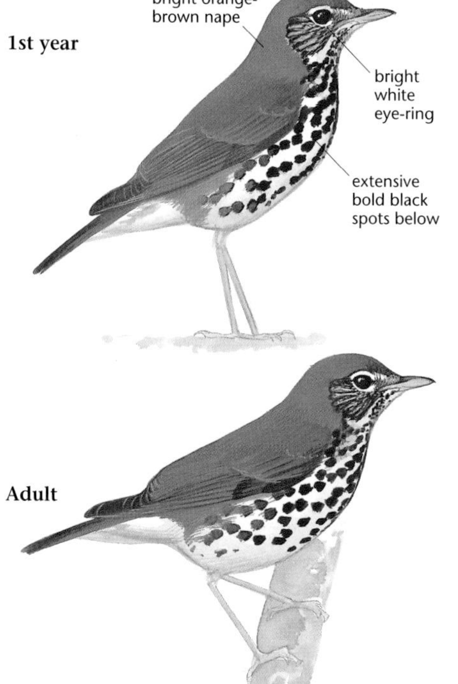
bright orange-brown nape
bright white eye-ring
extensive bold black spots below

Adult

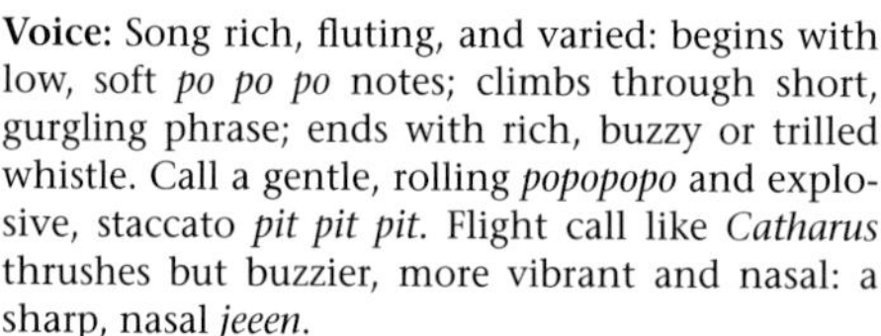

Voice: Song rich, fluting, and varied: begins with low, soft *po po po* notes; climbs through short, gurgling phrase; ends with rich, buzzy or trilled whistle. Call a gentle, rolling *popopopo* and explosive, staccato *pit pit pit.* Flight call like *Catharus* thrushes but buzzier, more vibrant and nasal: a sharp, nasal *jeeen.*

Veery

Catharus fuscescens

L 7" WS 12" WT 1.1 oz (31 g)

Generally reddish above and weakly spotted on breast.

Adult

1st year Eastern

Adult Western/ Newfoundland

Adult Eastern

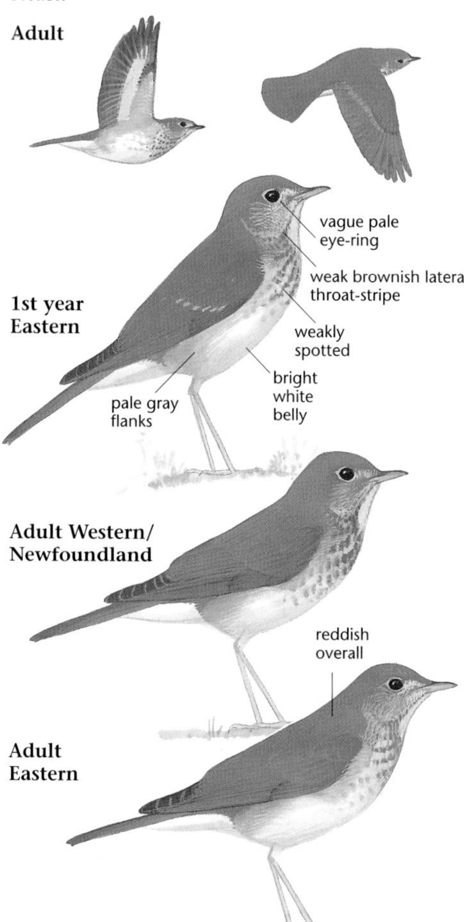
vague pale eye-ring
weak brownish lateral throat-stripe
weakly spotted
bright white belly
pale gray flanks
reddish overall

Voice: Song smooth, rolling, somewhat nasal, fluting *vrdi vrreed vreed vreer vreer* descending in two stages. Call a nasal, rough, braying *jerrr* and calls resembling flight call; also a very rapid, harsh chuckle *ho-ch-ch-ch-ch.* Flight call *veer, veerre,* or *veeyer;* relatively gentle and low-pitched; more variable from the ground.

Western and Newfoundland populations of Veery average darker, duller brown above and are more heavily spotted on breast than Eastern birds, but differences are subtle. Song of Western birds may be longer and more "stuttering" than Eastern.

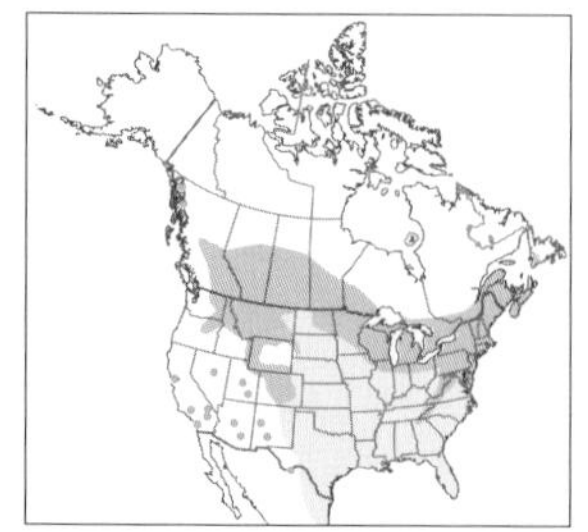

Similar to other *Catharus* thrushes, Swainson's is found in dense, shady woods; it nests in mixed coniferous woods. Olive-backed has bolder "spectacles"; Russet-backed is more similar to Veery.

Swainson's Thrush

Catharus ustulatus

L 7" WS 12" WT 1.1 oz (31 g)

Very similar to other Catharus *thrushes; note pale buffy "spectacles."*

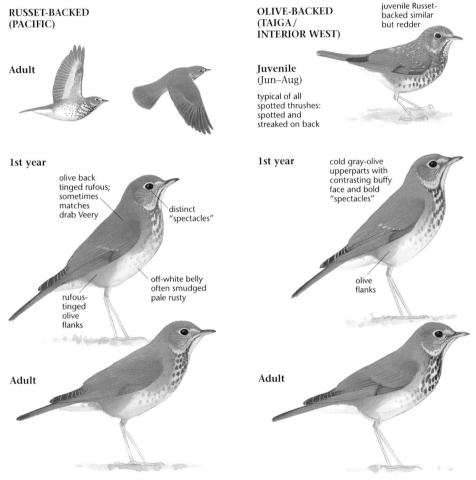

RUSSET-BACKED (PACIFIC)

Adult

1st year

olive back tinged rufous; sometimes matches drab Veery

distinct "spectacles"

off-white belly often smudged pale rusty

rufous-tinged olive flanks

Adult

OLIVE-BACKED (TAIGA/ INTERIOR WEST)

juvenile Russet-backed similar but redder

Juvenile
(Jun–Aug)

typical of all spotted thrushes: spotted and streaked on back

1st year

cold gray-olive upperparts with contrasting buffy face and bold "spectacles"

olive flanks

Adult

Voice: Song fluting, smooth, and rolling like Veery but rising. Russet-backed song (at least in California) more nasal, longer, and more complex than Olive-backed birds: *po po tu tu tu tureel tureel tiree tree tree.* Olive-backed usually gives one introductory note (sometimes none) followed by single-syllable slurred phrases *po rer reer reeer re-e-e-e-e-e.* Call a low, liquid *pwip* or *quip;* also rough, nasal, braying or chatter usually introduced by call note *qui-brrrrr.* Flight call a mostly clear, level, emphatic *heep* or *queev* reminiscent of Spring Peeper (treefrog) call.

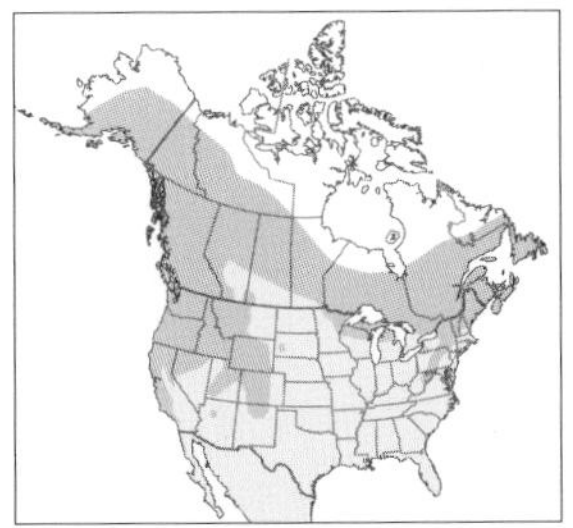

Russet-backed birds are found in the Pacific region, wintering in Mexico. Olive-backed birds occupy the remainder of the range and winter in South America. Russet-backed is warmer reddish-brown overall, with less bold "spectacles" and less distinct spotting on breast, all tending toward Veery. Song differences are described above. Calls are similar, but Russet-backed calls may be slightly flatter and longer (less liquid) than Olive-backed; also sometimes gives a burry, descending *vreew* like Veery, which is not heard from Olive-backed.

Spotted Thrushes (continued)

Both formerly known as Gray-cheeked Thrush, these two species have only recently been split; both nest in low spruce woods. As all characteristics overlap, they are best distinguished by voice.

Gray-cheeked Thrush

Catharus minimus

L 7.25" WS 13" WT 1.1 oz (32 g)

Averages slightly larger and longer-winged than other Catharus *thrushes; note plain grayish face.*

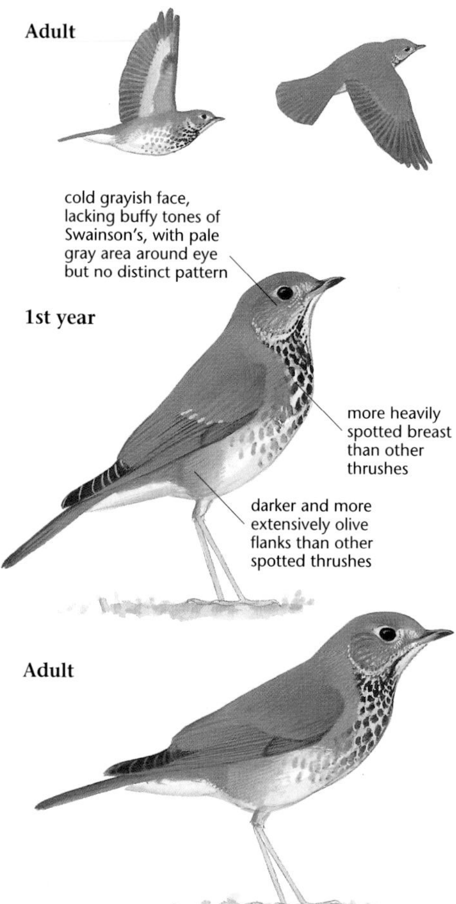
Adult
cold grayish face, lacking buffy tones of Swainson's, with pale gray area around eye but no distinct pattern
1st year
more heavily spotted breast than other thrushes
darker and more extensively olive flanks than other spotted thrushes
Adult

Voice: Song a descending spiral like Veery but higher, thinner, and nasal with stuttering pauses *ch-ch zreeew zi-zi-zreeee zi-zreeew;* middle phrase rising. Flight call a high, penetrating, nasal *jee-er* or *queer;* many other variations given by perched birds; generally higher and more nasal than Veery.

Bicknell's Thrush

Catharus bicknelli

L 6.75" WS 11.5" WT 1.1 oz (30 g)

Averages about 10 percent smaller than Gray-cheeked, with shorter and more rounded wings. May appear more chunky in the field, but all measurements overlap. Overall warmer brown color and distinctly reddish tail, sometimes obvious but overlap; extremely difficult to judge under field conditions.

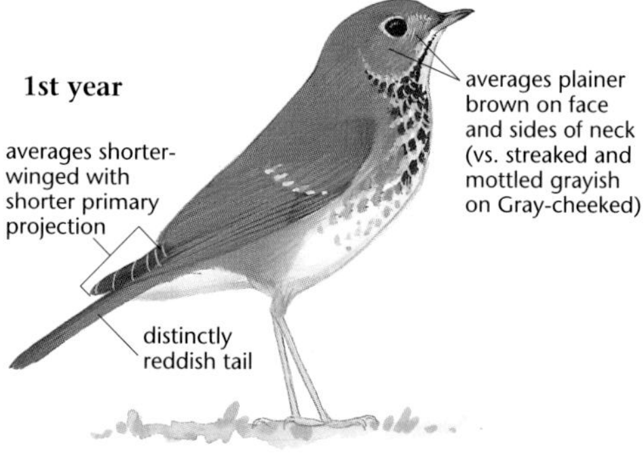
size and reddish tail recall Hermit Thrush, but note vague grayish eye-ring (not distinct whitish), olive flanks, voice
1st year
averages plainer brown on face and sides of neck (vs. streaked and mottled grayish on Gray-cheeked)
averages shorter-winged with shorter primary projection
distinctly reddish tail

Adult

Voice: Song similar to Gray-cheeked but higher-pitched, even more nasal and wiry; middle phrase descending and last phrase often rising *ch-ch zreee p-zreeew p-p-zreee.* Flight call a sharp, buzzy, descending *peeez* similar to Gray-cheeked but higher and less slurred; many other variations given by perched birds.

Some birds intermediate between Bicknell's and Gray-cheeked occur. Newfoundland population of Gray-cheeked (not shown) averages smaller and redder than other populations, approaching Bicknell's.

This widespread and variable species is the only spotted thrush likely to be encountered in North America Nov–Mar, often in more open, brushier habitat than other thrushes.

Hermit Thrush

Catharus guttatus

L 6.75" WS 11.5" WT 1.1 oz (31 g)

Relatively stocky, shorter-winged, and less elongated than other thrushes; always shows reddish tail and complete white eye-ring.

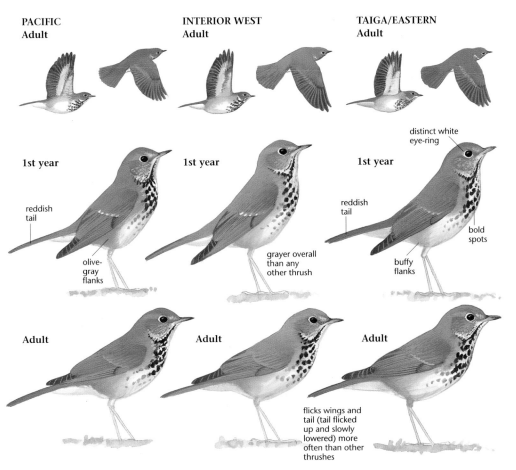

PACIFIC
Adult

INTERIOR WEST
Adult

TAIGA/EASTERN
Adult

1st year

reddish tail

olive-gray flanks

1st year

grayer overall than any other thrush

1st year

distinct white eye-ring

reddish tail

bold spots

buffy flanks

Adult

Adult

flicks wings and tail (tail flicked up and slowly lowered) more often than other thrushes

Adult

Voice: Song ethereal, fluting, without clear rising or falling trend; begins with a long whistle followed by two or three higher twirling phrases fading at end; successive songs differ. Taiga/Eastern and Interior West birds sing liquid pure tones *seeeeeee freediila fridla-fridla*. Pacific song a little higher, harsher, more mechanical-sounding *zreeeeew cheedila chli-chli-chli;* introductory note often downslurred and buzzy. Call a low, soft, dry *chup* reminiscent of muffled blackbird call; slightly higher and sharper by Pacific and Interior West birds; also a whining, rising *zhweeee*. Flight call a clear, plaintive whistle *peew* without husky or buzzy quality of other thrushes.

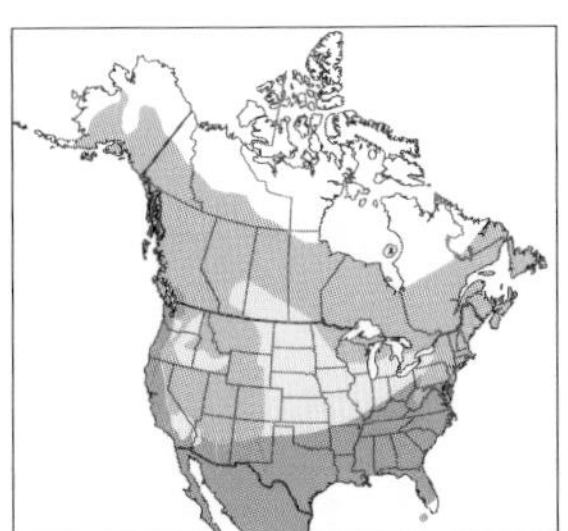

Populations sort into three main groups, but there is extensive intergradation. Pacific birds are small, slender, and thin-billed; they are dingy brown with olive-gray flanks, white undertail coverts, and more spotted throat than Taiga/Eastern. Interior West birds are larger, longer-winged, and thin-billed; they are pale and grayish overall with gray flanks and limited reddish wash on flight feathers. Taiga/Eastern birds are medium-size, stocky, and thick-billed; they are clean and brightly colored overall with buffy flanks and undertail coverts and have pale buffy tips on the greater coverts at all ages.

Mimids
Family: Mimidae

11 species in 4 genera. These medium-size, long-tailed songbirds are generally solitary. They forage mainly on the ground, using their long, sturdy bills to toss leaves and sticks, raking the dirt in search of food. Most species frequently run on the ground with their tails raised; they will often run to escape danger rather than flying. Flight is generally low and rapid. Nest is a bulky stick cup in a bush. Adults are shown.

Genus *Mimus*

NORTHERN
MOCKINGBIRD
BAHAMA
MOCKINGBIRD
Genus Dumetella
Genus Oreoscoptes
GRAY
CATBIRD
SAGE
THRASHER

Genus *Toxostoma*

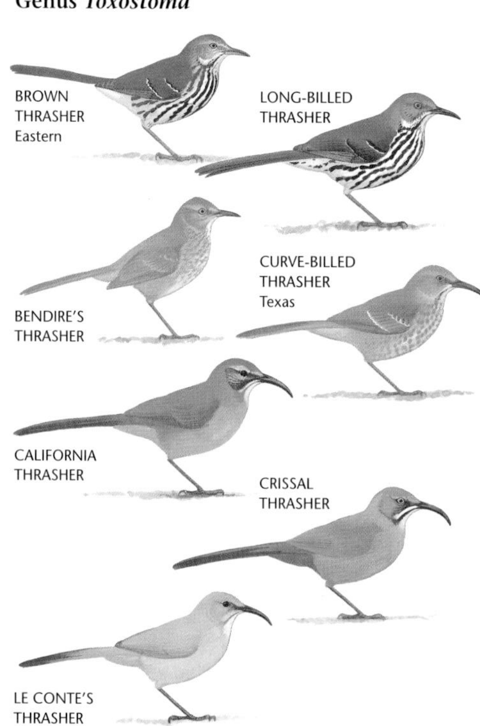
BROWN
THRASHER
Eastern
LONG-BILLED
THRASHER
BENDIRE'S
THRASHER
CURVE-BILLED
THRASHER
Texas
CALIFORNIA
THRASHER
CRISSAL
THRASHER
LE CONTE'S
THRASHER

Gray Catbird
Dumetella carolinensis

L 8.5" WS 11" WT 1.3 oz (37 g)

Distinctive; no other species is uniform slaty gray. Found in dense thickets.

Adult

black tail

Adult

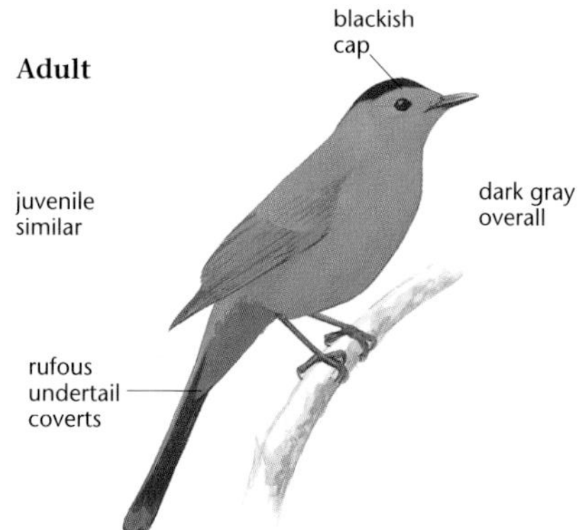
blackish
cap
juvenile
similar
dark gray
overall
rufous
undertail
coverts

Adult

Voice: Song a rambling, halting warble with slow tempo; distinctive mewing quality of low, hoarse notes with high, sharp chips and squeaks interspersed; little repetition and little mimicry. Call a hoarse, catlike mewing *mwee* or *meeurr;* also a loud crackling *kedekekek* when startled and a low *whurf* deeper and softer than Hermit Thrush.

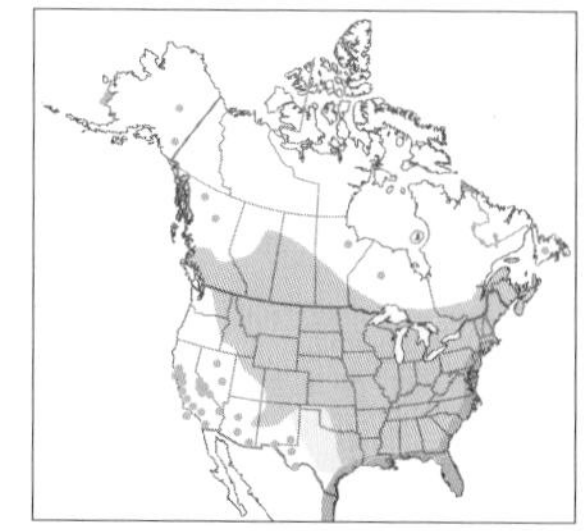

Mockingbirds

These two long-tailed, short-billed species are found in open areas near dense bushes, often in suburban neighborhoods. Northern is aggressive and conspicuous; Bahama is more secretive.

Northern Mockingbird

Mimus polyglottos

L 10" WS 14" WT 1.7 oz (49 g)

Slender-bodied with long tail and legs; flashing white wing and tail pattern distinctive (compare shrikes).

Adult

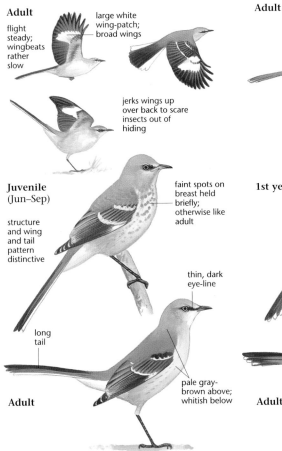

flight steady; wingbeats rather slow

large white wing-patch; broad wings

jerks wings up over back to scare insects out of hiding

Juvenile (Jun–Sep)

structure and wing and tail pattern distinctive

faint spots on breast held briefly; otherwise like adult

thin, dark eye-line

long tail

pale gray-brown above; whitish below

Adult

Voice: Song of varied phrases in regimented series: each phrase repeated two to six times, then an obvious pause followed by a different series *krrDEE-krrDEE-krrDEE, jeurrrdi jeurrrdi jeurrrdi . . .* ; most phrases musical; many imitations of other species. Call a harsh, dry *chak;* harsher and longer than blackbirds; aggressive call a high, wheezy *skeeeh.*

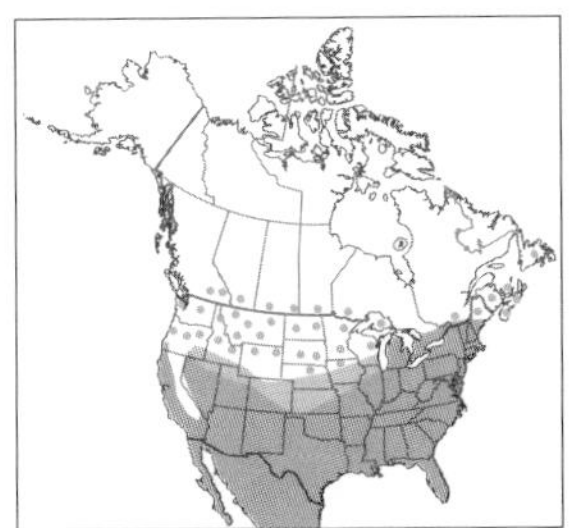

Bahama Mockingbird

Mimus gundlachii

L 11" WS 14.5" WT 2.3 oz (67 g)

Larger and heavier than Northern; more secretive with more thrasherlike actions and very different plumage.

Adult

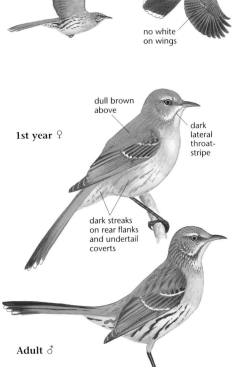

white tips on most tail feathers

no white on wings

dull brown above

1st year ♀

dark lateral throat-stripe

dark streaks on rear flanks and undertail coverts

Adult ♂

Voice: Song similar to Northern but less regimented in structure and with less varied phrases; overall more thrasherlike. Phrases nearly all two-syllabled; average lower and harsher than Northern with shorter pauses and little mimicry. Call a loud *czaak* slightly longer and rougher than Northern.

THRASHERS: GENUS *TOXOSTOMA*

Rufous above and streaked below, these two species are very similar. Both are found in dense, tangled thickets; they forage on the ground, turning over leaves and debris.

Brown Thrasher

Toxostoma rufum

L 11.5" WS 13" WT 2.4 oz (69 g)

Long-tailed but relatively short-billed, with more pointed wings and longer primary projection than Long-billed.

Adult

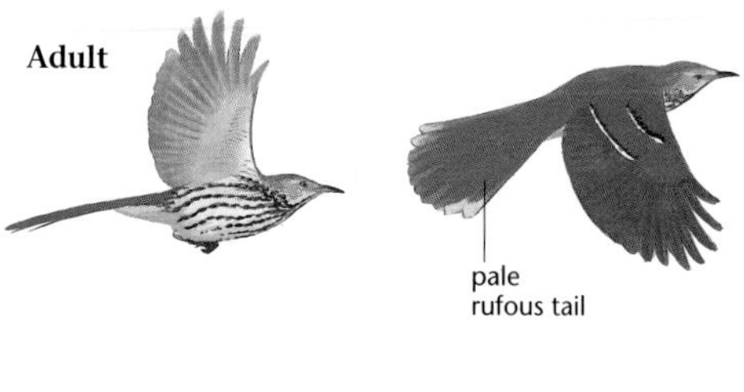
pale
rufous tail

Adult Western

bright
rufous
buffy
ground
color of
underparts
thin, dark
streaks

Adult Eastern

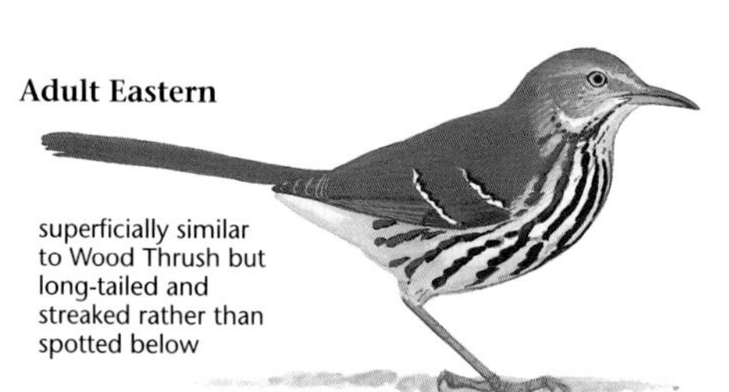
superficially similar
to Wood Thrush but
long-tailed and
streaked rather than
spotted below

Voice: Song of rich, musical phrases, each repeated two or three times with pause between each set; no other species has such clearly paired rhythm; often gives partial phrase such as *whichoo-which.* Calls include a loud, sharp *chak* like Fox Sparrow; a low, toneless growl *chhhr;* a sharp *tsssuk;* a rich, low whistle *peeooori* or *breeeew.*

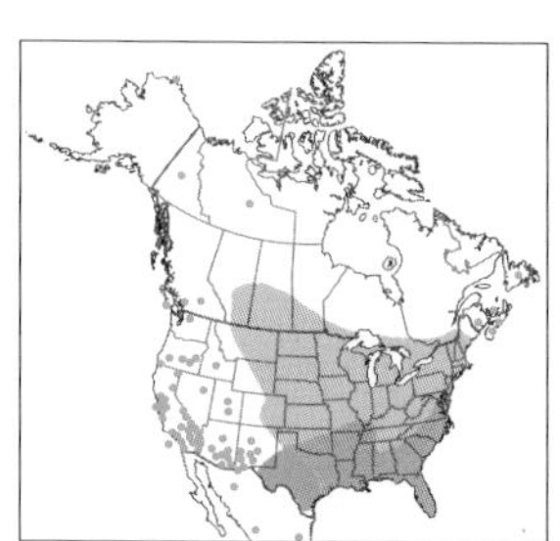

Western populations of Brown Thrasher are noticeably larger and paler than Eastern populations and have sparser streaking below.

Long-billed Thrasher

Toxostoma longirostre

L 11.5" WS 12" WT 2.5 oz (70 g)

Structure like Brown but averages slightly heavier with longer bill.

Adult

Adult

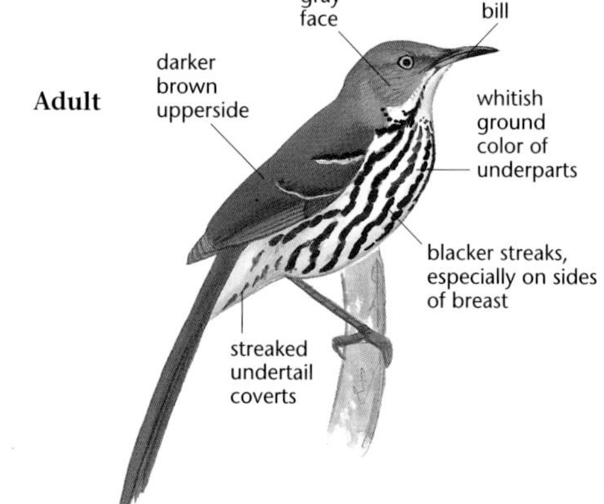
gray
face
all-blackish
bill
darker
brown
upperside
whitish
ground
color of
underparts
blacker streaks,
especially on sides
of breast
streaked
undertail
coverts

Adult

Voice: Song of rather rich, musical phrases; harsher and more rambling than Brown with less clearly paired phrases; distinguished from Curve-billed by slower rhythm, more musical overall. Calls similar to Brown: a loud, sharp *chak;* a mellow, whistled *tweeooip* or *oooeh*; also a very rapid, sharp rattle *chtttr.*

Thrashers: Genus *Toxostoma* (continued)

These two species are similar in all plumages but differ in structure and voice. Both are found in a variety of desert habitats: Bendire's prefers grassland; Curve-billed prefers thorny brush.

Bendire's Thrasher

Toxostoma bendirei

L 9.75" WS 13" WT 2.2 oz (62 g)

Similar to Curve-billed but smaller; bill shorter with straight lower mandible. Slight peak on rear crown; often appears smaller-headed.

Adult

Juvenile (Apr–Aug)

Adult

shorter, straighter bill, usually pale at base

paler yellow iris on average

buffier malar

small triangular spots on breast

tail often raised

buffy-brown flanks

Voice: Song a rapid, husky warble building from a few short, high whistles to a rapid, jumbled warble with many husky, whining slurred notes; most phrases repeated but difficult to discern individual phrases; husky quality and slurred delivery with no pauses distinctive. Call a low, husky *chuk*.

Curve-billed Thrasher

Toxostoma curvirostre

L 11" WS 13.5" WT 2.8 oz (79 g)

Bulky and large-headed, with thick, curved bill. Juvenile has shorter bill and fine spots on breast, resembling Bendire's. Note bill color, voice.

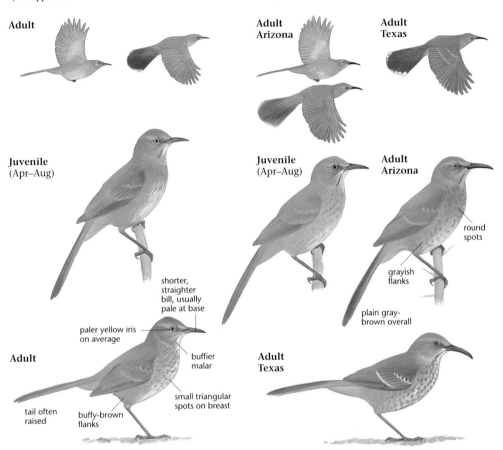

Adult Arizona

Adult Texas

Juvenile (Apr–Aug)

Adult Arizona

round spots

grayish flanks

plain gray-brown overall

Adult Texas

Voice: Song rather harsh, crisp, and hurried with many short, sharp notes such as *quit-quit* and *weet*; more rattling or trilled phrases than other thrashers (e.g., *kitkitkitkitkit*). Call a very distinctive sharp, liquid whistle *wit-WEET-wit;* also a sharp, dry *pitpitpitpit* and a low, harsh *chuck*.

Populations of Curve-billed are quite distinctive in plumage but intergrade where ranges meet in southeastern Arizona. Birds to the east of Arizona are 15 percent shorter-tailed with distinct white wing-bars and tail spots; spots on the underparts contrast distinctly with paler ground color.

These two species are similar in shape and habits; they are also similar to Le Conte's Thrasher. Preferring dense brush and foraging on the ground, they are difficult to find except when singing.

California Thrasher

Toxostoma redivivum

L 12" WS 12.5" WT 2.9 oz (84 g)

Size and shape like Crissal but thicker-billed, browner, with more patterned face and paler undertail coverts.

Adult

Adult

dark iris
strong, dark eye-line
buffy underparts; darker on breast
orange undertail coverts

Adult

Voice: Song of rather low, harsh notes repeated two to three times but not strongly patterned; overall quality husky, slightly scratchy; often incorporates very high, thin notes like Cedar Waxwing. Call a musical *dlulit* sometimes doubled; also a hard, somewhat musical *djik* or *djik-djik*.

Crissal Thrasher

Toxostoma crissale

L 11.5" WS 12.5" WT 2.2 oz (62 g)

Grayer overall than California. Larger and grayer than Curve-billed.

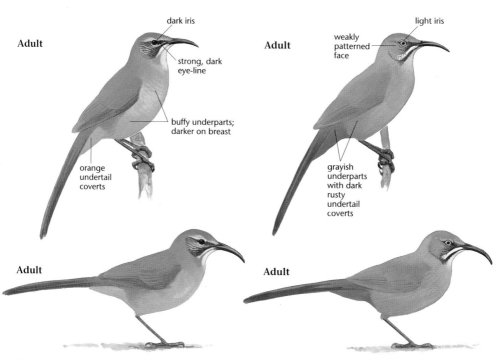

Adult

Adult

light iris
weakly patterned face
grayish underparts with dark rusty undertail coverts

Adult

Voice: Song relatively soft and musical with a few *quit* type notes interspersed; not as harsh as California or Curve-billed. Call a rather soft, rolling, rising *pjurrre-durrre*.

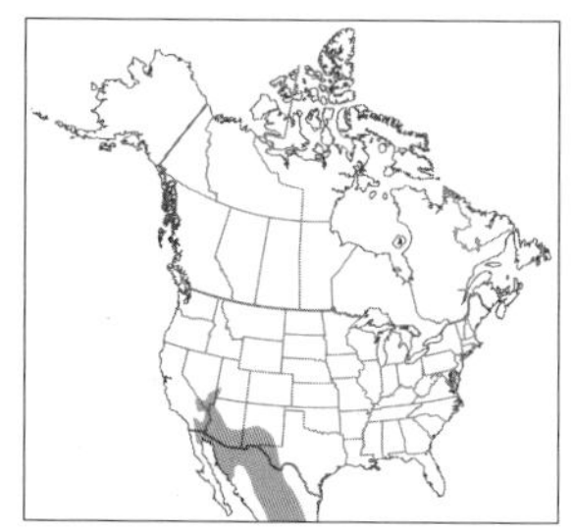

Le Conte's is closely related to California and Crissal, but it is found in extremely barren desert with scattered vegetation. The aptly named distinctive Sage Thrasher is found in sagebrush.

Le Conte's Thrasher

Toxostoma lecontei

L 11" WS 12" WT 2.2 oz (62 g)

Slightly smaller, shorter-tailed, and much paler overall than California and Crissal; more slender and longer-tailed than Curve-billed.

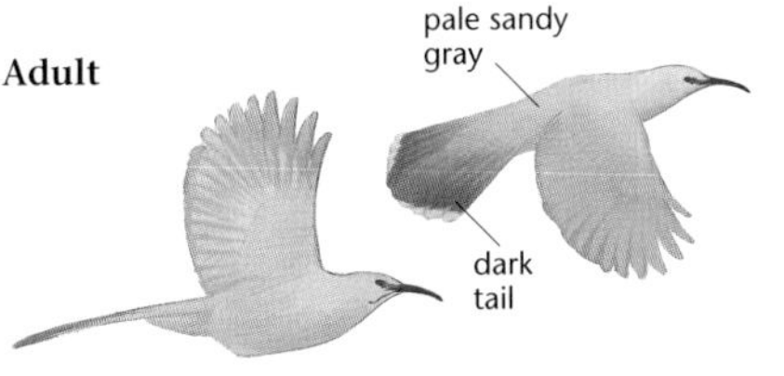
Adult
pale sandy gray
dark tail

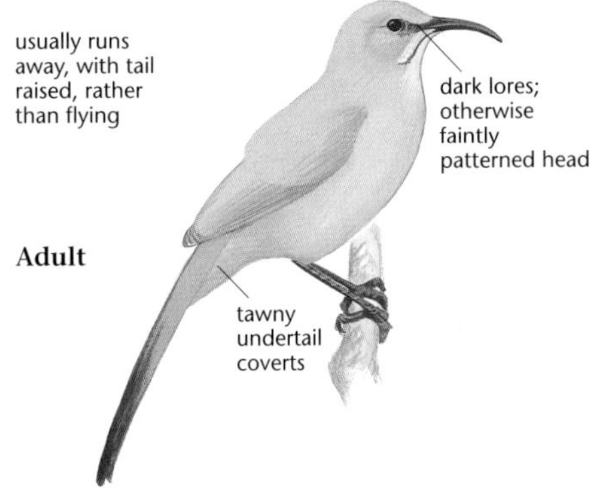
usually runs away, with tail raised, rather than flying
dark lores; otherwise faintly patterned head
Adult
tawny undertail coverts

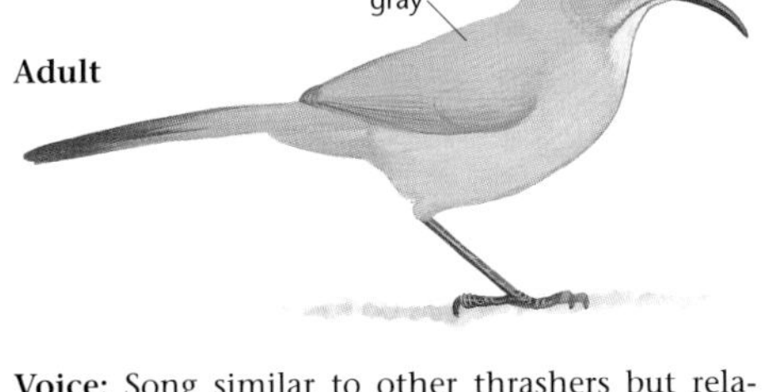
sandy gray
Adult

Voice: Song similar to other thrashers but relatively soft and husky; fairly high-pitched, long, slurred notes distinctive; distinguished from Crissal by more relaxed, smooth rhythm and husky, slurred notes. Call a simple, questioning *weeip* or a quick, husky *kooi-dwid,* like Crissal but simpler.

Sage Thrasher

Oreoscoptes montanus

L 8.5" WS 12" WT 1.5 oz (43 g)

Small and short-billed; longer-winged than other thrashers.

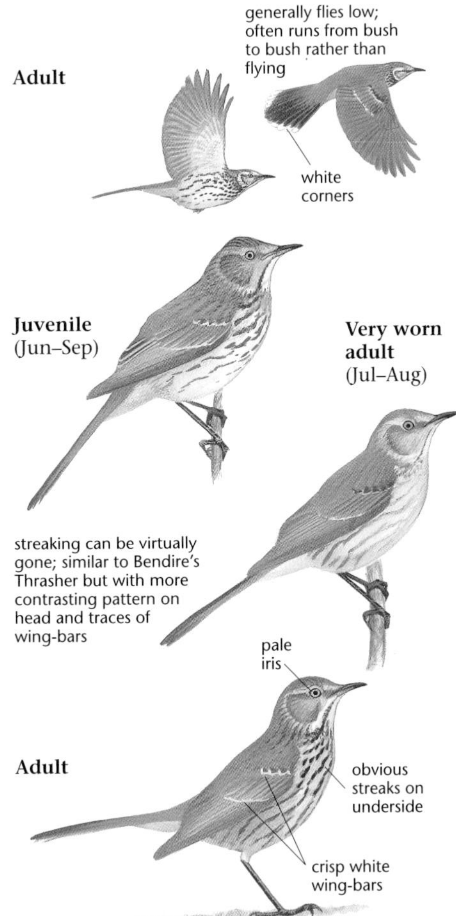
generally flies low; often runs from bush to bush rather than flying
Adult
white corners
Juvenile (Jun–Sep)
Very worn adult (Jul–Aug)
streaking can be virtually gone; similar to Bendire's Thrasher but with more contrasting pattern on head and traces of wing-bars
pale iris
Adult
obvious streaks on underside
crisp white wing-bars

Voice: Song a run-on warble of mellow, rolling or churring whistles with changeable tempo but very little pitch change; one accented phrase may be interspersed repeatedly; distinguished from Bendire's by clearer, less husky quality. Often gives a sweet, high *wheeurr*. Call a low *chup* like Hermit Thrush but harder.

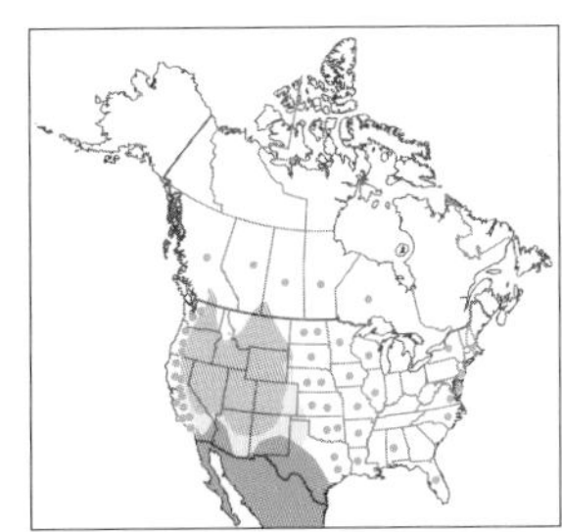

Starlings and Mynas

Family: Sturnidae

European Starling

Sturnus vulgaris

L 8.5" WS 16" WT 2.9 oz (82 g) ♂>♀

Short, square tail; pointed, triangular wings; straight, pointed bill. In flight can be confused with waxwings, meadowlarks, or Purple Martin.

Juvenile

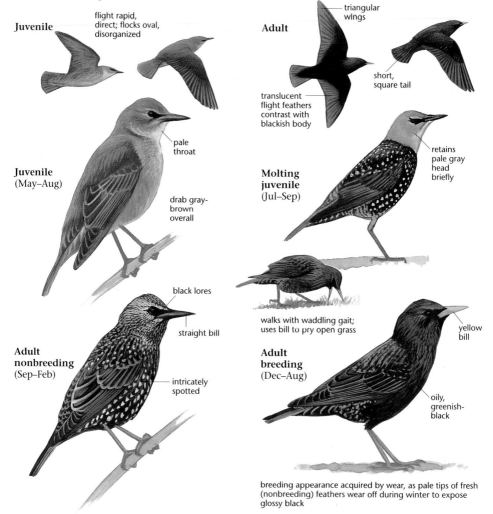

flight rapid, direct; flocks oval, disorganized

Adult

triangular wings

short, square tail

translucent flight feathers contrast with blackish body

Juvenile (May–Aug)

pale throat

drab gray-brown overall

Molting juvenile (Jul–Sep)

retains pale gray head briefly

walks with waddling gait; uses bill to pry open grass

black lores

straight bill

Adult nonbreeding (Sep–Feb)

intricately spotted

Adult breeding (Dec–Aug)

yellow bill

oily, greenish-black

breeding appearance acquired by wear, as pale tips of fresh (nonbreeding) feathers wear off during winter to expose glossy black

Voice: Song mainly quiet, harsh rattling with some high, thin, slurred whistles; overall a mushy, gurgling, hissing chatter with high, sliding whistles. Often includes imitations of other birds' calls. Common call a harsh chatter *che-che-che-che.* Flight call a muffled, dry, buzzing *wrrsh.*

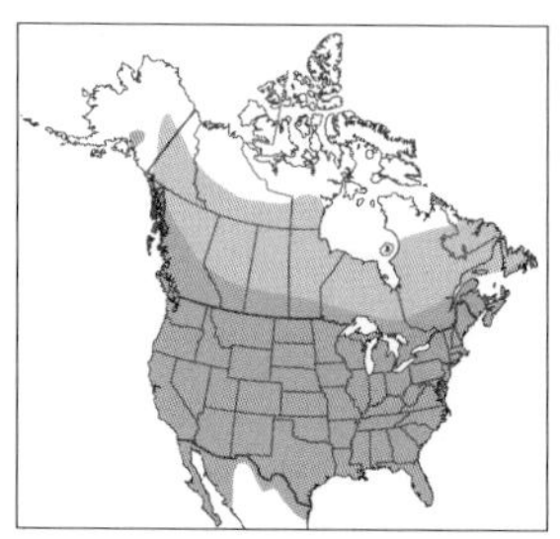

STURNIDAE

4 species in 3 genera. European Starling, introduced from Europe, is now found in virtually all human-modified habitats, often feeding and roosting in huge flocks. When disturbed by a raptor, flocks form a very tight, cohesive ball, visible at a great distance and a good clue as to the presence of a hawk. European Starling nests in any cavity, often in man-made structures, and competes aggressively with woodpeckers, bluebirds, etc., for nest sites. It feeds mainly on berries and insects. Mynas, introduced from Asia, are found in suburban habitats. Other similar species of mynas could also escape.

Mynas

These three species were introduced from Asia and are marginally established. Found in suburban habitats, they have long yellow legs and white wing-patches and give varied calls.

Hill Myna

Gracula religiosa

L 10.5" WS 20" WT 7 oz (205 g)

Small numbers in Florida and California may be augmented by frequent escapes.

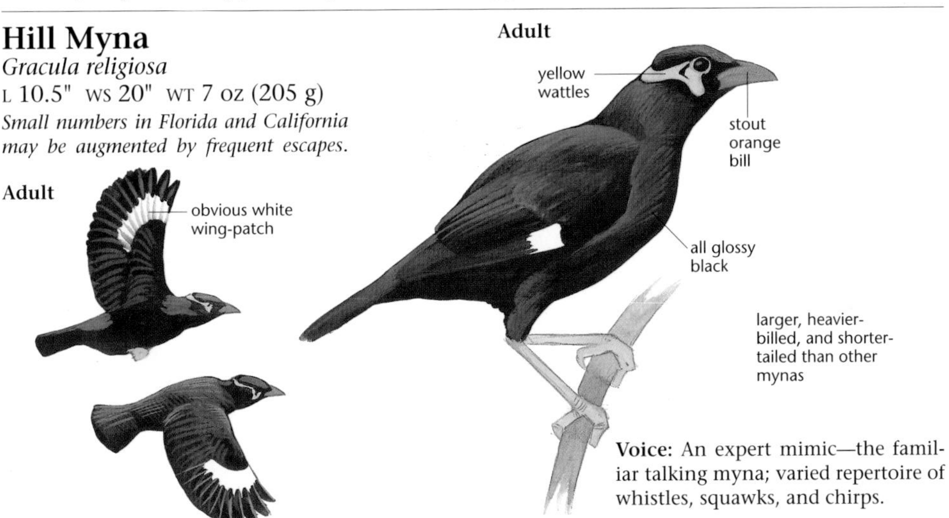
Adult
obvious white wing-patch
Adult
yellow wattles
stout orange bill
all glossy black
larger, heavier-billed, and shorter-tailed than other mynas

Voice: An expert mimic—the familiar talking myna; varied repertoire of whistles, squawks, and chirps.

Common Myna

Acridotheres tristis

L 9.75" WS 18" WT 3.7 oz (106 g)

Rapidly increasing population in southern Florida.

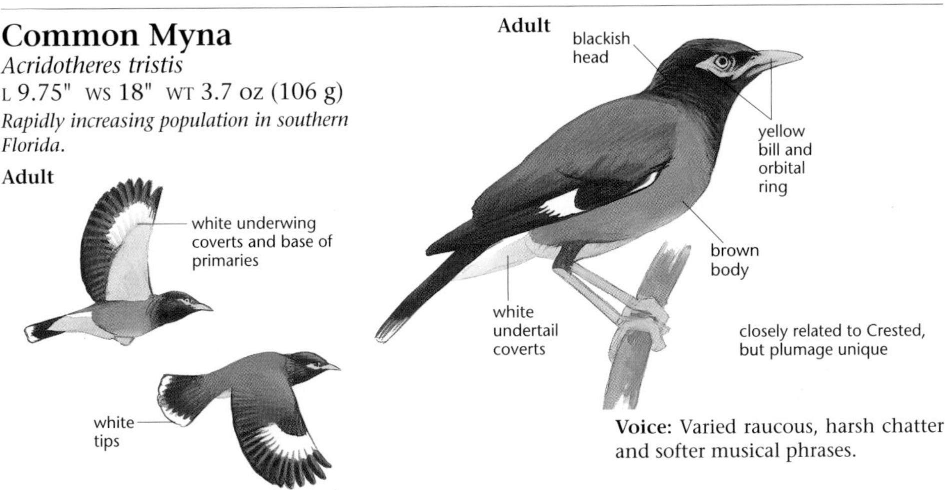
Adult
white underwing coverts and base of primaries
white tips
Adult
blackish head
yellow bill and orbital ring
brown body
white undertail coverts
closely related to Crested, but plumage unique

Voice: Varied raucous, harsh chatter and softer musical phrases.

Crested Myna

Acridotheres cristatellus

L 9.75" WS 18" WT 4 oz (113 g)

Small and declining population around Vancouver, British Columbia.

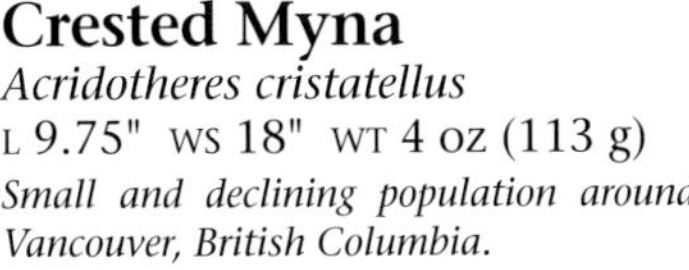

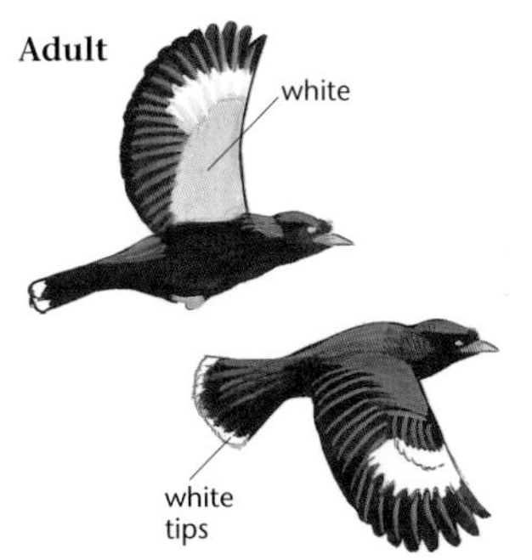
Adult
white
white tips

Adult
staring, pale eye
short, bushy crest
juvenile dark brown, without crest or white tail tip
all-black

Voice: Similar to Common; varied harsh chattering and musical phrases.

Wagtails and Pipits

Family: Motacillidae

6 species in 2 genera. These rather slender and long-billed birds walk with dainty steps and bob their heads pigeonlike. They are ground-dwelling, feeding on insects and small seeds; nest is a neat cup on the ground. Flight is strong but undulating; their sharp flight calls are distinctive. Wagtails are generally solitary and found on open ground, often in wetlands. The cryptically colored pipits are often found on dry ground or in grassy areas; Sprague's Pipit is solitary, but the other two species are flocking. Compare longspurs, larks, and sparrows (see Open-Ground Birds, page 362). 1st winter female wagtails and 1st winter pipits are shown.

Genus *Motacilla*

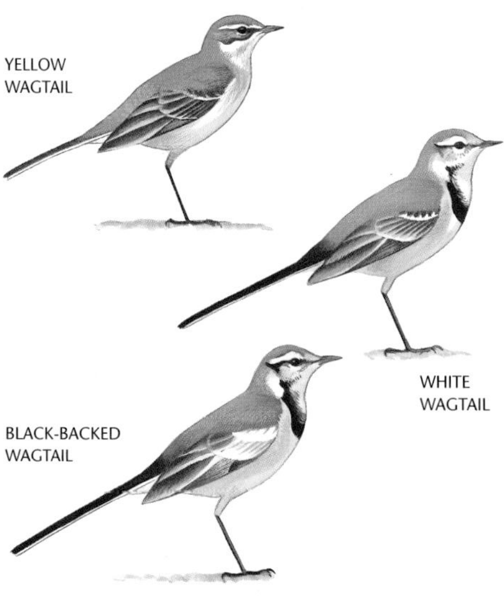
YELLOW WAGTAIL
WHITE WAGTAIL
BLACK-BACKED WAGTAIL

Genus *Anthus*

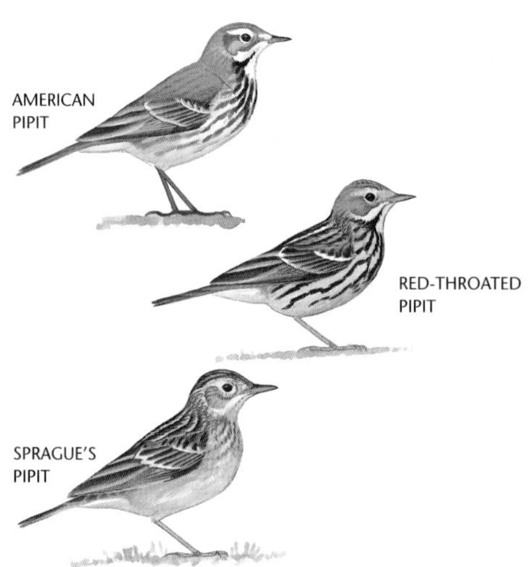
AMERICAN PIPIT
RED-THROATED PIPIT
SPRAGUE'S PIPIT

Yellow Wagtail

Motacilla flava

L 6.5" WS 9.5" WT 0.56 oz (16 g)

Much shorter-tailed than other wagtails, but longer-tailed than pipits.

1st winter

shorter tail than other wagtails

Adult ♂ breeding

yellow

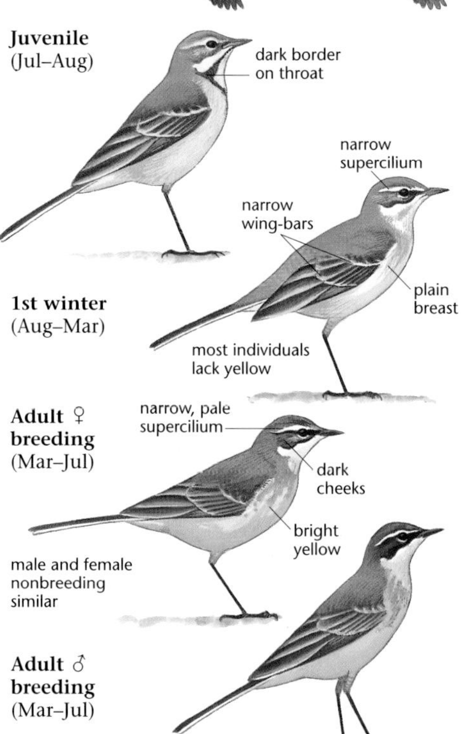
Juvenile (Jul–Aug)
dark border on throat
narrow supercilium
narrow wing-bars
plain breast
1st winter (Aug–Mar)
most individuals lack yellow
Adult ♀ breeding (Mar–Jul)
narrow, pale supercilium
dark cheeks
bright yellow
male and female nonbreeding similar
Adult ♂ breeding (Mar–Jul)

Voice: Song repetitious phrases resembling calls *tzeeu tzeeu tzeek. . . .* Flight call an explosive, vibrant, buzzy *tzeer;* occasionally a higher, clear *tsewee;* also a clear, ringing *tzeen tzeen tzeen.*

Wagtails

These very similar species are found singly on open expanses, usually near water. Although distinctive as a pair, separating the two requires careful study; hybrids and intermediates may not be identifiable.

Black-backed Wagtail

Motacilla lugens

L 7.25" WS 10.5" WT 0.67 oz (19 g)

Averages slightly larger than White with heavier bill; best distinguished by wing pattern details.

1st winter ♀

Adult ♂ breeding

black back

mostly white remiges

1st winter ♀ (Aug–Mar)

all wagtails vigorously pump tail while standing

dark rump

all-white median coverts

pale base of primaries may be evident

usually darker-backed

white chin

1st summer ♀ (Mar–Jul)

all-white median coverts

Adult ♀ nonbreeding (Aug–Mar)

some black on scapulars

1st winter ♂ similar

more black

bold white wing covert panel shown by most ages and both sexes (only by adult ♂ in White)

black back

white chin

Adult ♂ breeding (Mar–Jul)

White Wagtail

Motacilla alba

L 7.25" WS 10.5" WT 0.63 oz (18 g)

Larger and longer-tailed than Yellow Wagtail; median coverts of female and 1st year show dark bases.

1st winter ♀

long, tapered tail typical of all wagtails

Adult ♂ breeding

all-dark remiges

Juvenile (Jul–Aug)

gray head

1st winter ♀ (Aug–Mar)

two narrow wing-bars (not a panel)

pale gray upper rump

dark bases visible on median coverts

1st summer ♀ (Mar–Jul)

Adult ♀ nonbreeding (Aug–Mar)

1st winter ♂ similar

Adult ♂ breeding (Mar–Jul)

Voice: Both species apparently identical. Song a regular series of high, thin, finchlike phrases of two or three syllables, each phrase short and clear with little pitch change. Flight call a staccato, harsh *jijik*. Call a musical, finchlike phrase *didleer*.

Adult Black-backed is distinctive, with white-based remiges year-round (female has less white than male). 1st winter White has distinct narrow wing-bars unlike any Black-backed. On 1st year Black-backed vs. adult White, look for all-white median coverts (vs. dark-based), darker rump, sometimes dark scapulars, and pale base of primaries.

Sprague's is distinctive, solitary, and secretive and found in short grass with open patches. Red-throated is a little more secretive than American but is often found with American on open fields.

Sprague's Pipit

Anthus spragueii

L 6.5" WS 10" WT 0.88 oz (25 g)

Relatively stocky, short-tailed, and stout-billed. Often confused with juvenile Horned Lark; note structure, tail pattern, voice.

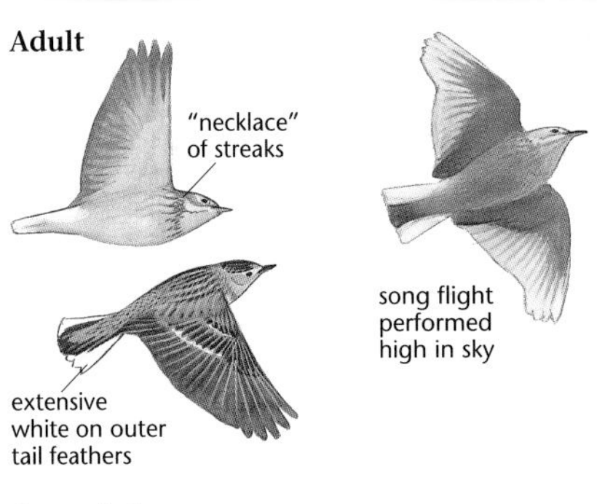
Adult
"necklace" of streaks
song flight performed high in sky
extensive white on outer tail feathers

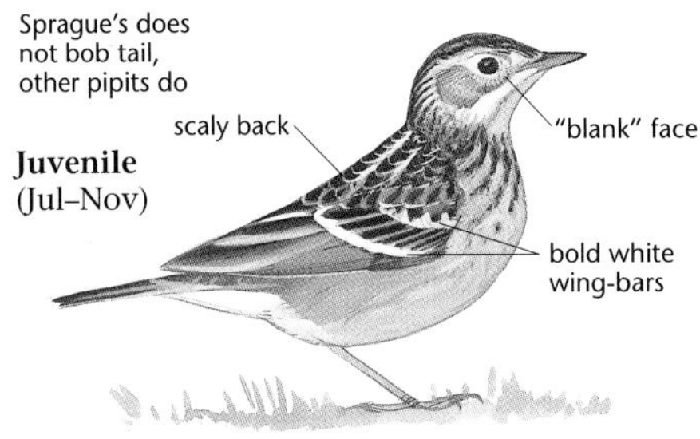
Sprague's does not bob tail, other pipits do
scaly back
"blank" face
Juvenile (Jul–Nov)
bold white wing-bars

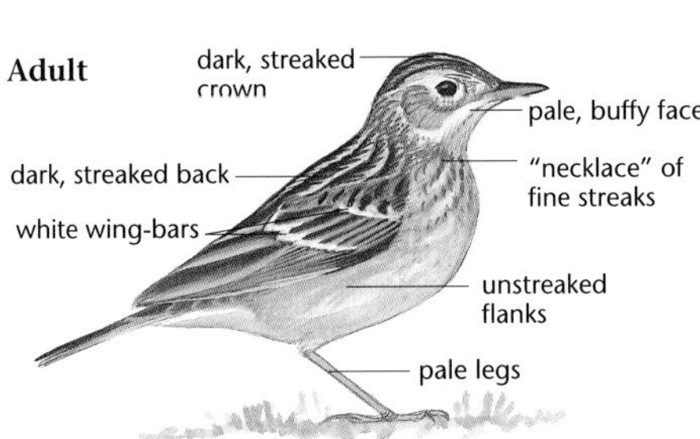
Adult
dark, streaked crown
pale, buffy face
dark, streaked back
"necklace" of fine streaks
white wing-bars
unstreaked flanks
pale legs

Voice: Song given in flight from high altitude a rolling, jingling cascade of high, dry whistles *shirl shirl shirrl. . . .* Flight call a high, sharp, slightly nasal *squeet* often repeated; reminiscent of sharper calls of Barn Swallow.

Sprague's Pipit is difficult to see on the ground. It flushes close, flies high, and has a distinctive habit of simply folding its wings and plummeting downward, breaking its fall with wings spread just a few feet above the ground, then dropping into dense grass.

Red-throated Pipit

Anthus cervinus

L 6.25" WS 10.5" WT 0.74 oz (21 g)

Structure like American but slightly shorter-tailed and -billed; bold streaks above and below distinctive.

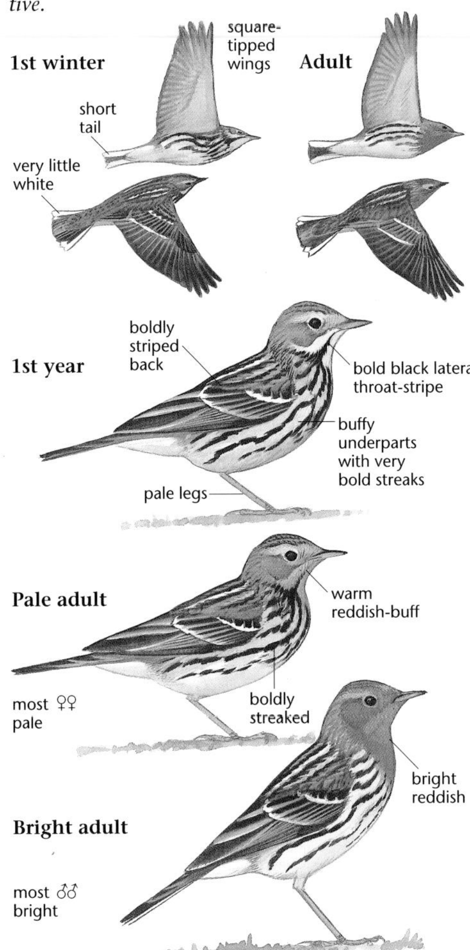
1st winter
square-tipped wings
Adult
short tail
very little white
1st year
boldly striped back
bold black lateral throat-stripe
buffy underparts with very bold streaks
pale legs
Pale adult
warm reddish-buff
most ♀♀ pale
boldly streaked
bright reddish
Bright adult
most ♂♂ bright

Voice: Song a long series of jingling phrases, all about the same pitch and rhythm, each one repeated about five times *jrr jrr jrr jrr jrr jrr tree tree tree tree tree tseew tseew tseew*. Flight call a very high, thin, drawn-out *psssss* reminiscent of Yellow Wagtail but thinner, not buzzy.

This slender species is found on open ground (tundra, beaches, fields), often in flocks. Its slender bill, long legs, upright walking, and tail bobbing distinguish it from longspurs and larks.

American Pipit

Anthus rubescens

L 6.5" WS 10.5" WT 0.74 oz (21 g)

Longer-tailed than other pipits; faintly streaked back and dark legs distinctive.

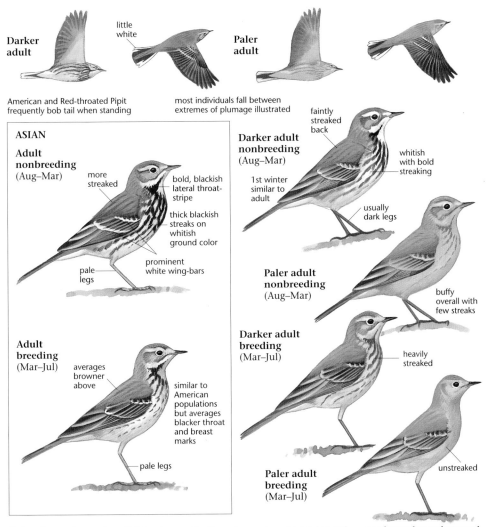

Darker adult

little white

Paler adult

American and Red-throated Pipit frequently bob tail when standing

most individuals fall between extremes of plumage illustrated

ASIAN

Adult nonbreeding (Aug–Mar)

more streaked

bold, blackish lateral throat-stripe

thick blackish streaks on whitish ground color

prominent white wing-bars

pale legs

Adult breeding (Mar–Jul)

averages browner above

similar to American populations but averages blacker throat and breast marks

pale legs

Darker adult nonbreeding (Aug–Mar)

faintly streaked back

whitish with bold streaking

1st winter similar to adult

usually dark legs

Paler adult nonbreeding (Aug–Mar)

buffy overall with few streaks

Darker adult breeding (Mar–Jul)

heavily streaked

Paler adult breeding (Mar–Jul)

unstreaked

Voice: Song a low series of high, clear or jingling phrases *tseewl-tseewl-tseewl* . . . or *pleetrr-pleetrr-pleetrr* and other variations; given in flight for up to 15 seconds. All populations similar. Flight call a high, squeaky chirp *slip* or *slip-ip;* when flushed a higher *tseep* or *tsitiip*. Alarm call near nest a much lower, rising *pwisp*.

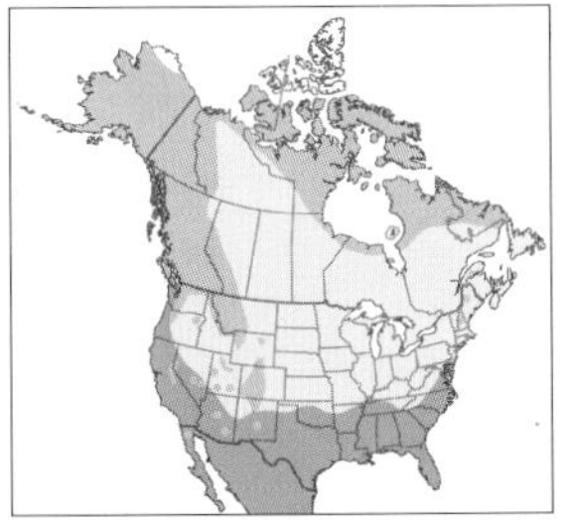

The pale birds illustrated are typical of populations nesting in the Rocky Mountain region; most Arctic breeders are darker and more heavily streaked. Asian birds (seen regularly on Bering Sea islands, with a few records father south on Pacific coast) have pale legs and plumage differences as noted above; they are most distinctive in nonbreeding plumage.

Phainopepla
Phainopepla nitens
L 7.75" WS 11" WT 0.84 oz (24 g)
Sleek, long-tailed, and round-winged.

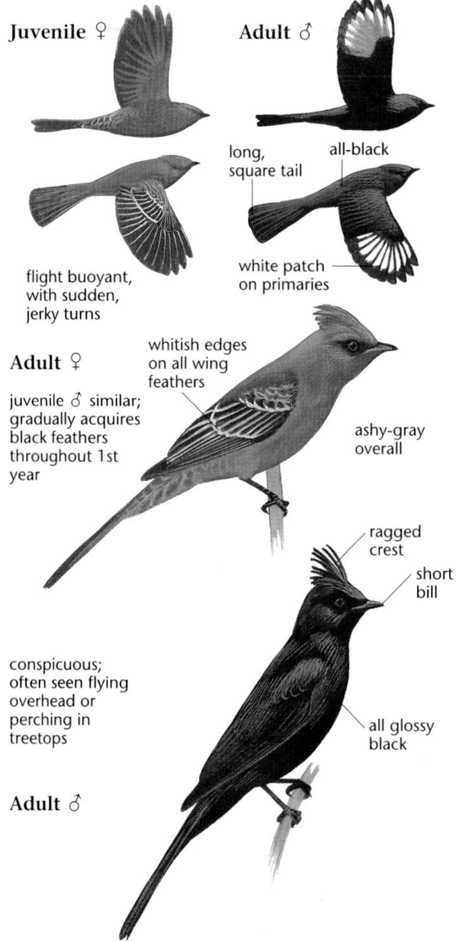

Juvenile ♀
Adult ♂
long, square tail
all-black
flight buoyant, with sudden, jerky turns
white patch on primaries
Adult ♀
whitish edges on all wing feathers
juvenile ♂ similar; gradually acquires black feathers throughout 1st year
ashy-gray overall
ragged crest
short bill
conspicuous; often seen flying overhead or perching in treetops
all glossy black
Adult ♂

Voice: Song a series of short phrases with long pauses between; phrases rather low, liquid, grating (e.g., *krrtiiilwa*); also mimics other species; often accompanied by somersaulting flight display. Call a distinctive, soft, rising whistle *hoi,* low and questioning.

Red-whiskered Bulbul
Pycnonotus jocosus
L 7" WS 11" WT 1 oz (29 g)
Rounded wings; rather long, square tail and tall, pointed crest.

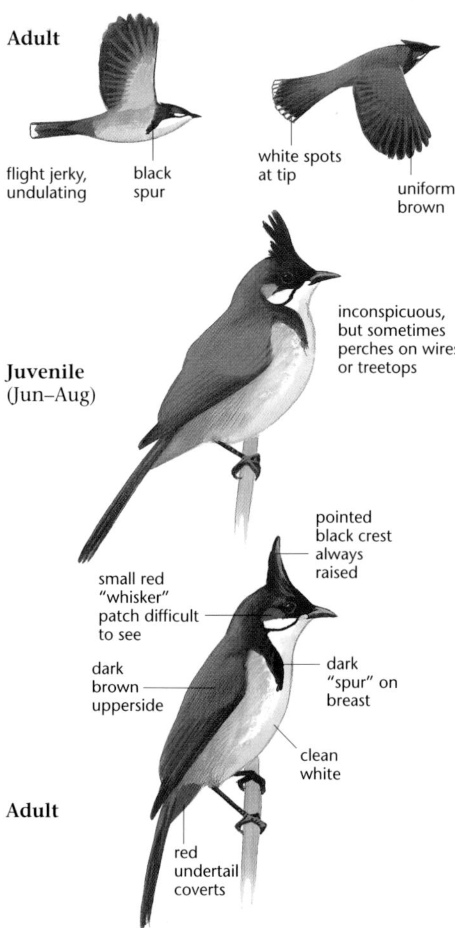

Adult
flight jerky, undulating
black spur
white spots at tip
uniform brown
inconspicuous, but sometimes perches on wires or treetops
Juvenile (Jun–Aug)
pointed black crest always raised
small red "whisker" patch difficult to see
dark brown upperside
dark "spur" on breast
clean white
Adult
red undertail coverts

Voice: Song a chattering and musical scolding. Call a staccato *kink-a-jou.*

PTILOGONATIDAE and PYCNONOTIDAE
2 species in unrelated families; Phainopepla in Ptilogonatidae, Bulbul in Pycnonotidae. Each occurs in small flocks and forages mainly on berries. Phainopepla is found in open woods or scattered trees, Red-whiskered Bulbul (introduced from India) in suburban neighborhoods with lush vegetation.

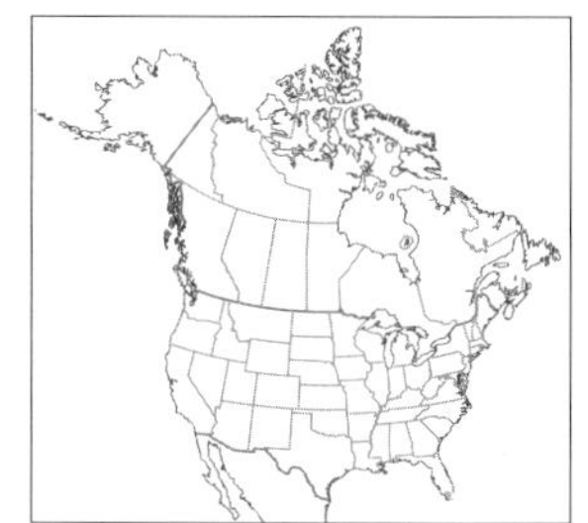

WAXWINGS

Family: Bombycillidae

Bohemian Waxwing

Bombycilla garrulus

L 8.25" WS 14.5" WT 2 oz (56 g)

Larger and slightly shorter-tailed than Cedar; appears small-headed and round-bodied.

Juvenile
Adult
dark
undertail
coverts
compare
European
Starling
dark gray
belly
Juvenile
(Jul–Jan)
white wing
markings
1st year ♀
little or no
white on
forehead
rufous-
tinged
face
white tips
on wing
feathers
grayish
belly
rufous
undertail
coverts
Adult

Voice: Similar to Cedar but calls lower-pitched and more clearly trilled; trill slower, more like a rattle.

Cedar Waxwing

Bombycilla cedrorum

L 7.25" WS 12" WT 1.1 oz (32 g)

Smooth, sleek; distinguished from other passerines by short tail, pointed wings, stubby bill, crest.

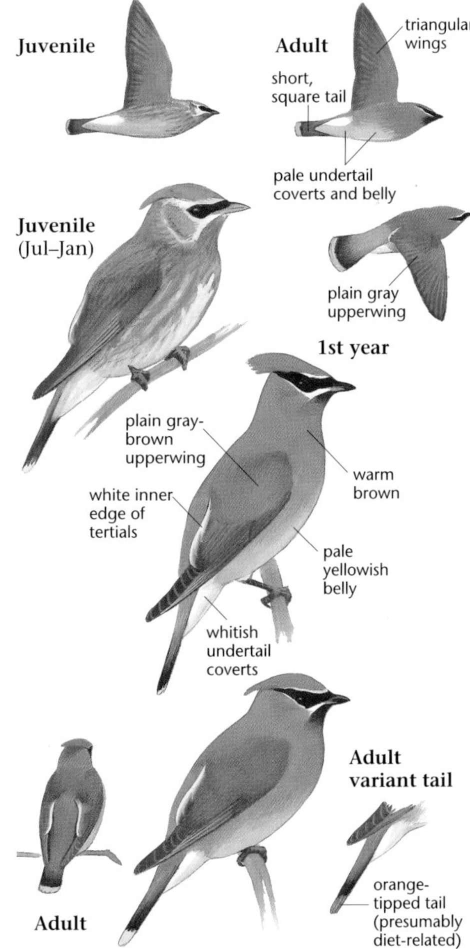

Juvenile
Adult
triangular
wings
short,
square tail
pale undertail
coverts and belly
Juvenile
(Jul–Jan)
plain gray
upperwing
1st year
plain gray-
brown
upperwing
warm
brown
white inner
edge of
tertials
pale
yellowish
belly
whitish
undertail
coverts
Adult
variant tail
orange-
tipped tail
(presumably
diet-related)
Adult

Voice: Song simply a series of high *sreee* notes in irregular rhythm. Call a very high, thin, clear or slightly trilled *sreee*. Aerial predator alarm a piercing *seeeew* similar to thrushes.

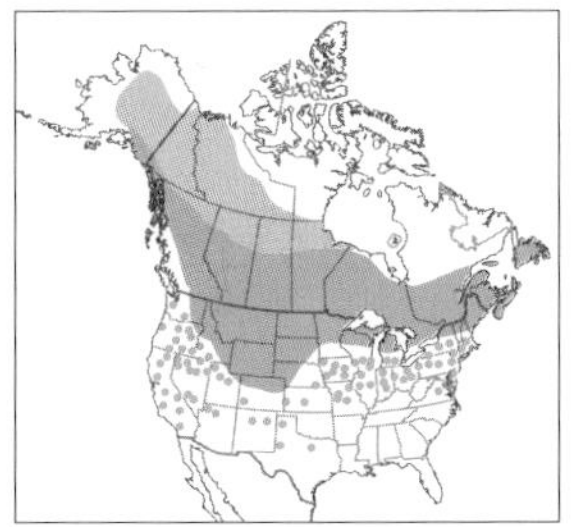

BOMBYCILLIDAE

2 species in 1 genus. Unique, with sleek plumage, crests, pointed wings, and short, yellow-tipped tails. Except when nesting, waxwings are found in flocks, feeding on berries; they are easily detected by their constant, high-pitched calls. Compare European Starling in flight. The two species differ mainly in size and plumage.

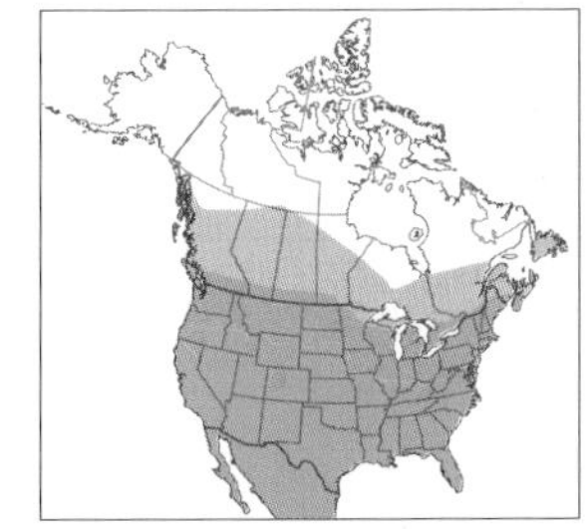

Wood-Warblers

Families: Parulidae, Peucedramidae

54 species in 17 genera; all in family Parulidae, except Olive Warbler in Peucedramidae. Wood-warblers are small and active birds with short, pointed bills. Plumage is varied; in general, treetop species are brightly colored and ground-dwelling species are drab. Flight of all is generally strong and slightly undulating. Nest is a cup built on the ground or in a bush or tree; Lucy's and Prothonotary nest in cavities. Compare vireos, kinglets, orioles, and tanagers. 1st winter females are shown.

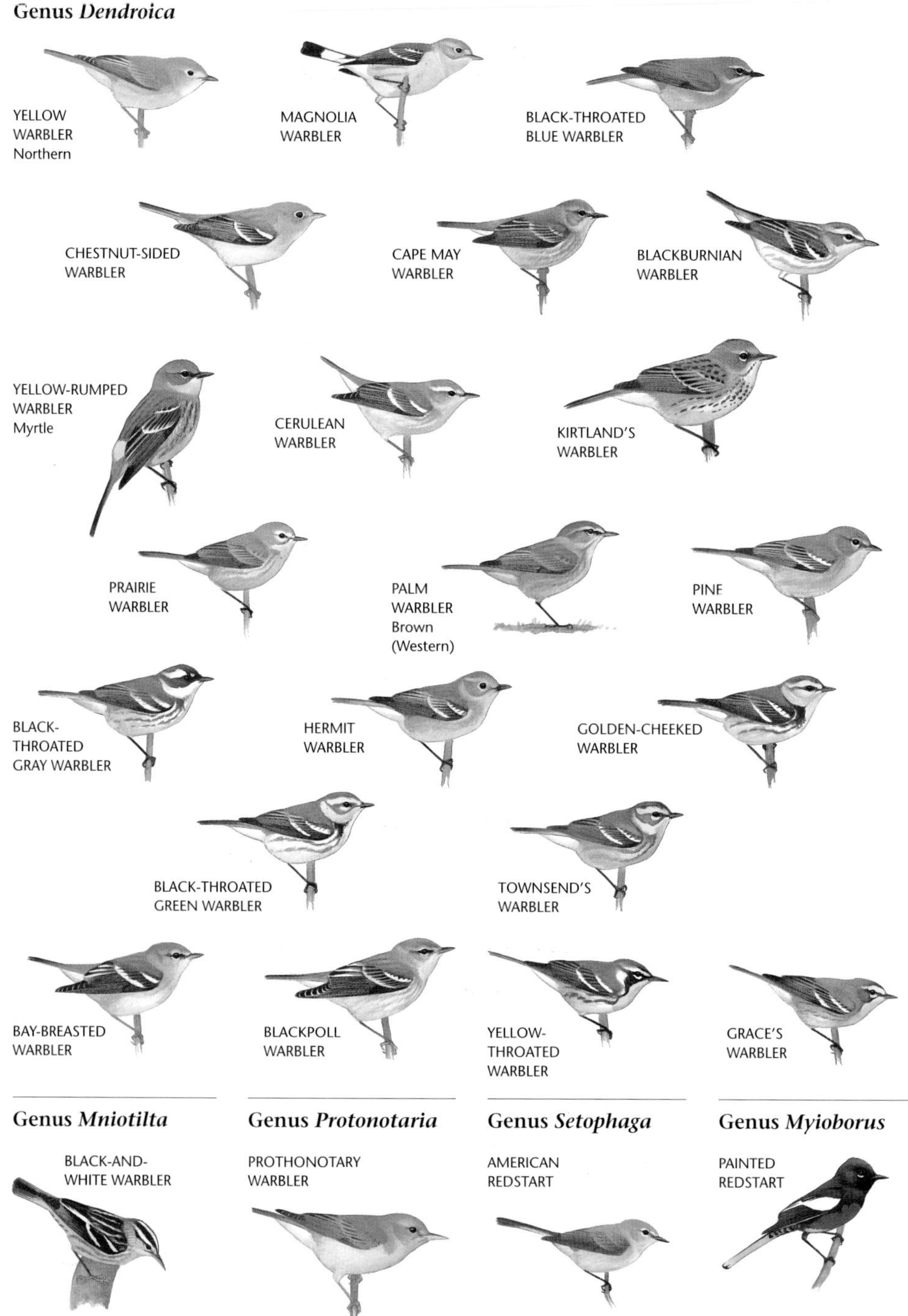

Genus *Dendroica*
YELLOW WARBLER Northern
MAGNOLIA WARBLER
BLACK-THROATED BLUE WARBLER
CHESTNUT-SIDED WARBLER
CAPE MAY WARBLER
BLACKBURNIAN WARBLER
YELLOW-RUMPED WARBLER Myrtle
CERULEAN WARBLER
KIRTLAND'S WARBLER
PRAIRIE WARBLER
PALM WARBLER Brown (Western)
PINE WARBLER
BLACK-THROATED GRAY WARBLER
HERMIT WARBLER
GOLDEN-CHEEKED WARBLER
BLACK-THROATED GREEN WARBLER
TOWNSEND'S WARBLER
BAY-BREASTED WARBLER
BLACKPOLL WARBLER
YELLOW-THROATED WARBLER
GRACE'S WARBLER
Genus *Mniotilta*
BLACK-AND-WHITE WARBLER
Genus *Protonotaria*
PROTHONOTARY WARBLER
Genus *Setophaga*
AMERICAN REDSTART
Genus *Myioborus*
PAINTED REDSTART

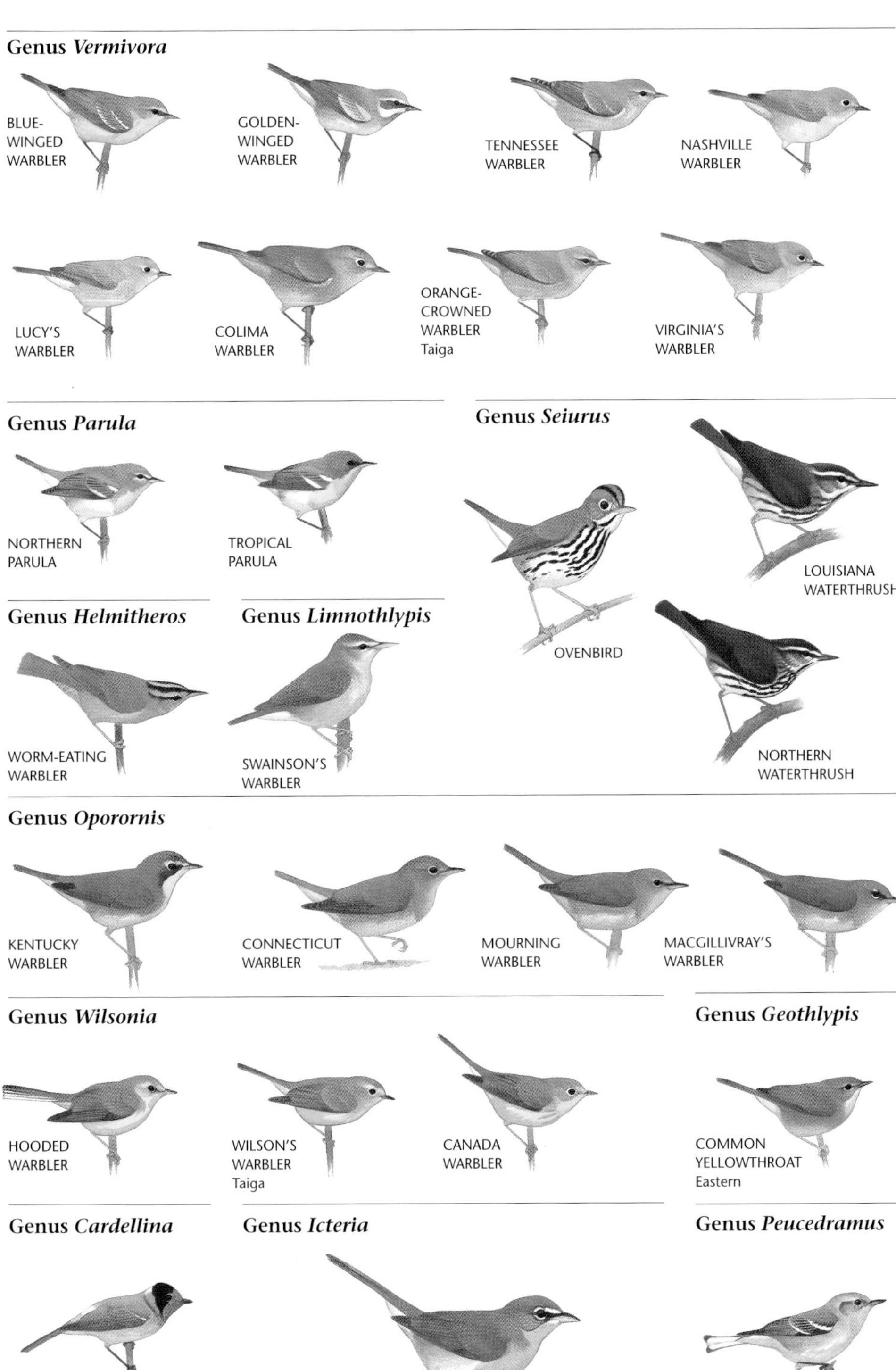
Genus Vermivora
BLUE-WINGED WARBLER
GOLDEN-WINGED WARBLER
TENNESSEE WARBLER
NASHVILLE WARBLER
LUCY'S WARBLER
COLIMA WARBLER
ORANGE-CROWNED WARBLER
Taiga
VIRGINIA'S WARBLER
Genus Parula
NORTHERN PARULA
TROPICAL PARULA
Genus Seiurus
LOUISIANA WATERTHRUSH
OVENBIRD
NORTHERN WATERTHRUSH
Genus Helmitheros
WORM-EATING WARBLER
Genus Limnothlypis
SWAINSON'S WARBLER
Genus Oporornis
KENTUCKY WARBLER
CONNECTICUT WARBLER
MOURNING WARBLER
MACGILLIVRAY'S WARBLER
Genus Wilsonia
HOODED WARBLER
WILSON'S WARBLER
Taiga
CANADA WARBLER
Genus Geothlypis
COMMON YELLOWTHROAT
Eastern
Genus Cardellina
RED-FACED WARBLER
Genus Icteria
YELLOW-BREASTED CHAT
Eastern
Genus Peucedramus
OLIVE WARBLER

Wood-Warblers: Parulas

These two very small warblers are found in woods, usually near water. Their bluish upperparts, bold wing-bars, yellow throat and lower mandible, and buzzy crescendo songs are distinctive.

Tropical Parula

Parula pitiayumi

L 4.5" WS 6.25" WT 0.25 oz (7 g)

Structure like Northern but a little smaller with slightly shorter primary projection; note more extensive yellow throat and breast, dark face.

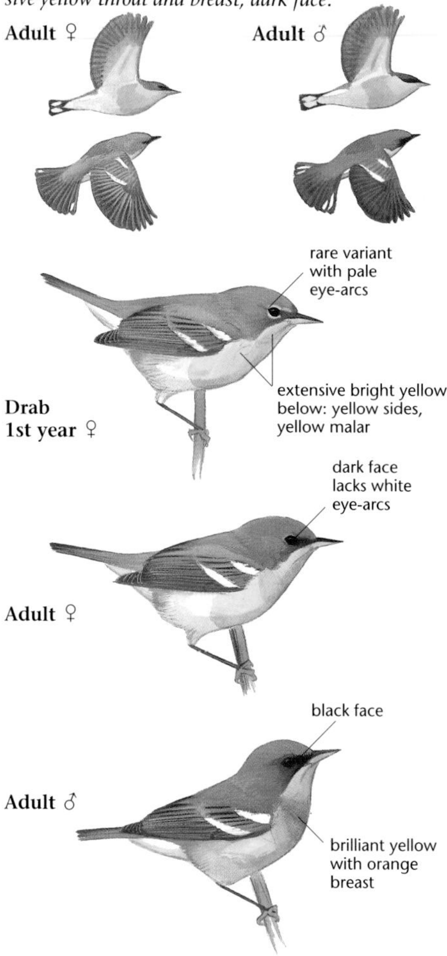

Adult ♀
Adult ♂
rare variant
with pale
eye-arcs
extensive bright yellow
below: yellow sides,
yellow malar
Drab
1st year ♀
dark face
lacks white
eye-arcs
Adult ♀
black face
Adult ♂
brilliant yellow
with orange
breast

Voice: Song like Northern but final note usually buzzy (unlike eastern populations of Northern but similar to western birds); may be slightly higher, more insectlike overall. Call and flight call similar to Northern.

Northern Parula

Parula americana

L 4.5" WS 7" WT 0.3 oz (8.6 g)

Small, dumpy, and short-necked, with sharply pointed bill and fairly short tail.

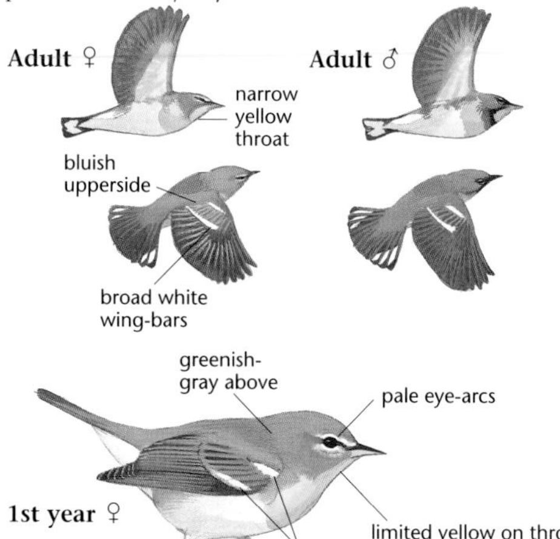

Adult ♀
Adult ♂
narrow
yellow
throat
bluish
upperside
broad white
wing-bars

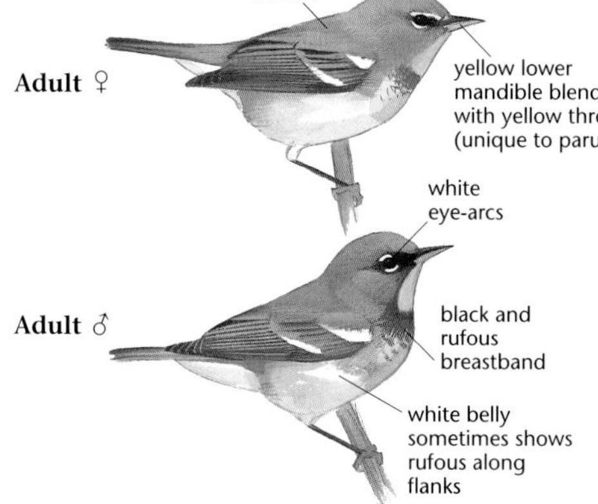

greenish-
gray above
pale eye-arcs
1st year ♀
limited yellow on throat
and breast; gray malar
short
wing-bars
green
mantle
blue-gray
above
Adult ♀
yellow lower
mandible blends
with yellow throat
(unique to parulas)
white
eye-arcs
Adult ♂
black and
rufous
breastband
white belly
sometimes shows
rufous along
flanks

Voice: Song a rather unmusical, rising buzz with distinctive, sharp final note *zeeeeeeeeeeee-tsup* or *zid zid zid zeeeeee tsup* (final note often lacking); compare Cerulean and Black-throated Blue Warblers. Call a surprisingly strong, clear chip. Flight call a high, clear, descending, frequently repeated *tsif* or *tsiip*.

Populations of Northern Parula nesting west of the Mississippi River barely differ in appearance (average smaller and brighter) but end song with longer, buzzier *tzzew* unlike the sharp *tsup* of eastern birds.

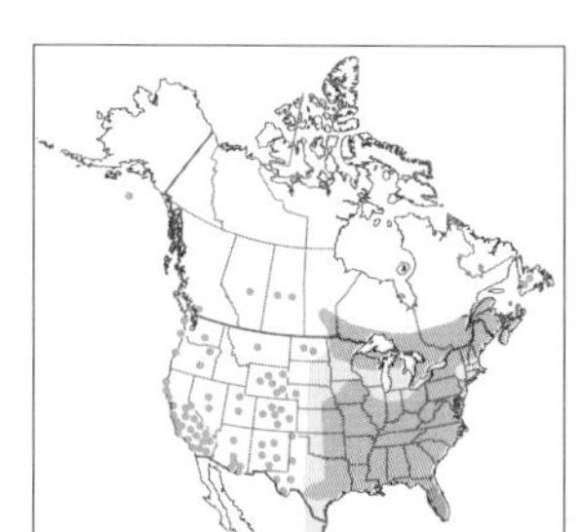

This small, drab species is found at edges of low trees and in weedy habitat. Its drab plumage causes confusion with many other species; the orange crown-patch is rarely seen in the field.

Orange-crowned Warbler

Vermivora celata

L 5" WS 7.25" WT 0.32 oz (9 g)

Small with sharply pointed bill. Relatively longer-tailed than most other Vermivora *warblers; shorter primary projection than Tennessee. Note yellow undertail coverts and short, dark eye-line in all plumages.*

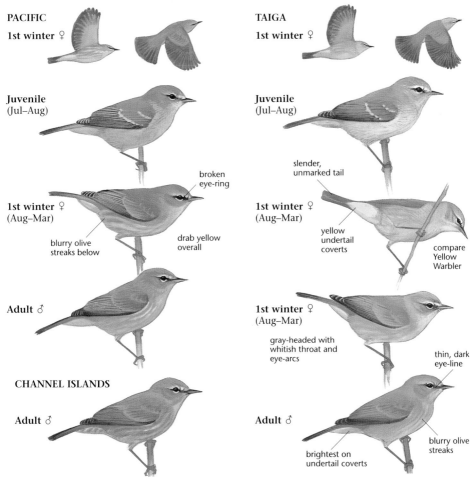

PACIFIC

1st winter ♀

Juvenile (Jul–Aug)

1st winter ♀ (Aug–Mar)

broken eye-ring

blurry olive streaks below

drab yellow overall

Adult ♂

CHANNEL ISLANDS

Adult ♂

TAIGA

1st winter ♀

Juvenile (Jul–Aug)

slender, unmarked tail

1st winter ♀ (Aug–Mar)

yellow undertail coverts

compare Yellow Warbler

1st winter ♀ (Aug–Mar)

gray-headed with whitish throat and eye-arcs

thin, dark eye-line

Adult ♂

brightest on undertail coverts

blurry olive streaks

Voice: Song a fast trill of fairly flat notes; individual notes not very distinct, last few notes on lower pitch *titititititititititututu;* notes generally downslurred but so sharp this is hard to hear. Taiga song trill soft and slow (averages 11 notes/sec); Pacific song trill fast and hard (averages 17 notes/sec); Channel Islands song trill slower and lower-pitched than Pacific. Call distinctive: a simple, clear, high, sharp chip very similar to Field Sparrow but a little richer. Flight call a short, high, clear or slightly husky, rising *seet.*

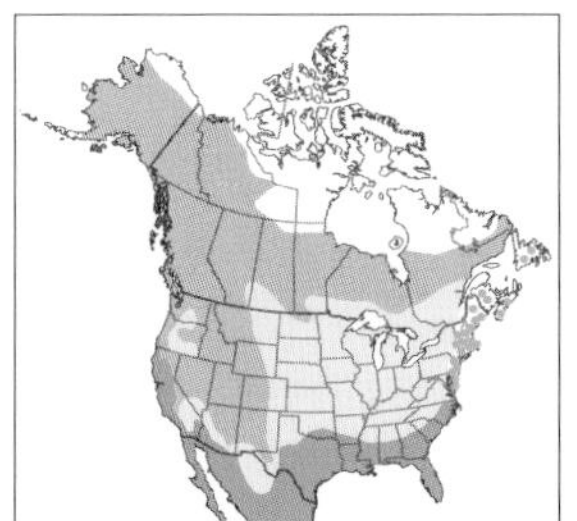

Four populations differ slightly in plumage and song. Pacific is brightest overall and yellow in all plumages. Channel Islands is bright but larger and darker and more heavily streaked olive below. Taiga is drabbest. Interior West (not shown) is intermediate between Pacific and Taiga, so few can be safely identified in the field. Song differs slightly (see above).

Tennessee Warbler nests in boggy spruce woods; in winter and spring it is found mainly in flowering trees, where it uses its sharp bill to probe flowers for insects and nectar.

Tennessee Warbler

Vermivora peregrina

L 4.75" WS 7.75" WT 0.35 oz (10 g)

Small, sharp-billed, short-tailed, and long-winged, with long primary projection. Note lack of streaking, short but prominent supercilium, and whitish undertail coverts.

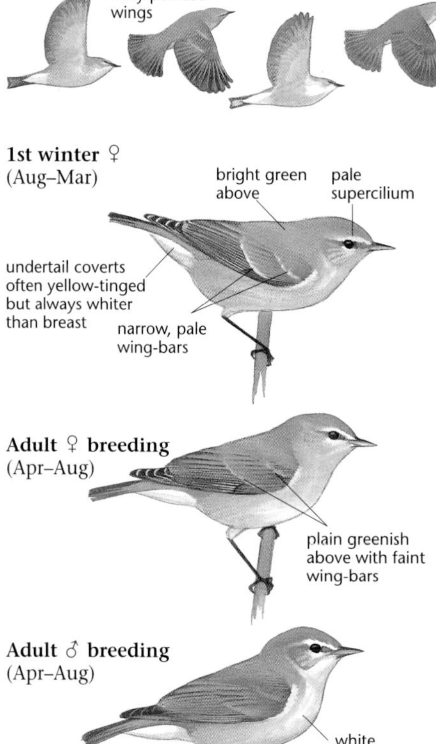
1st winter ♀
Adult ♂ breeding
fairly pointed wings
1st winter ♀
(Aug–Mar)
bright green above
pale supercilium
undertail coverts often yellow-tinged but always whiter than breast
narrow, pale wing-bars
Adult ♀ breeding
(Apr–Aug)
plain greenish above with faint wing-bars
Adult ♂ breeding
(Apr–Aug)
white below

Voice: Song a trill of sharp, spitting, high chips, usually in three parts with each slightly different in pitch and tempo *tip tip tip tip teepit teepit teepit teepit ti ti ti ti ti ti ti,* the last series generally faster. Call a sharp, high, smacking *stik.* Flight call a slightly husky *tseet.*

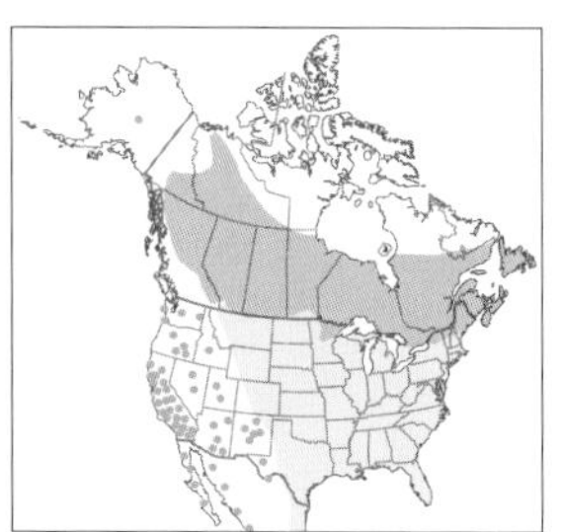

Blue-winged × Golden-winged Hybrids

These two species hybridize regularly. All 1st generation hybrids (offspring of pure parents, originally named as a separate species: Brewster's Warbler) show dominant traits of black eye-line and whitish underparts. Hybrids paired with either species produce a variety of backcrosses (including the form named Lawrence's Warbler). Other backcrosses show a continuum of variation between the two parent species. Song of hybrids may be like either parent or, more often, an abnormal song combining characteristics of both species.

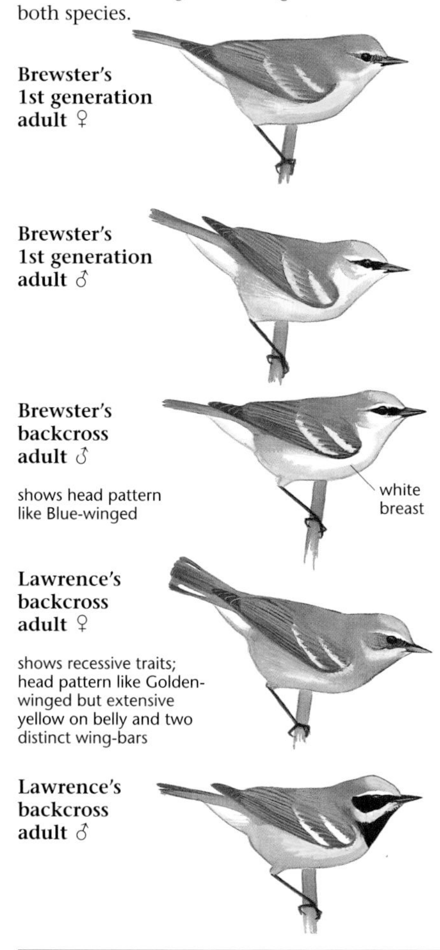
Brewster's 1st generation adult ♀
Brewster's 1st generation adult ♂
Brewster's backcross adult ♂
shows head pattern like Blue-winged
white breast
Lawrence's backcross adult ♀
shows recessive traits; head pattern like Golden-winged but extensive yellow on belly and two distinct wing-bars
Lawrence's backcross adult ♂

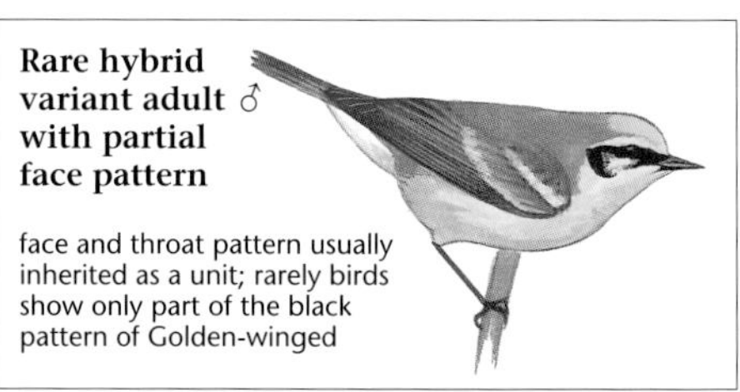
Rare hybrid variant adult ♂ with partial face pattern
face and throat pattern usually inherited as a unit; rarely birds show only part of the black pattern of Golden-winged

Wood-Warblers: Genus *Vermivora* (continued)

Despite striking plumage differences, these two species are very closely related and often hybridize where ranges overlap (see opposite). They are found in brushy, second-growth and open woods.

Blue-winged Warbler

Vermivora pinus

L 4.75" WS 7.5" WT 0.3 oz (8.5 g)

Small and bright yellow; sharp-billed, short-tailed.

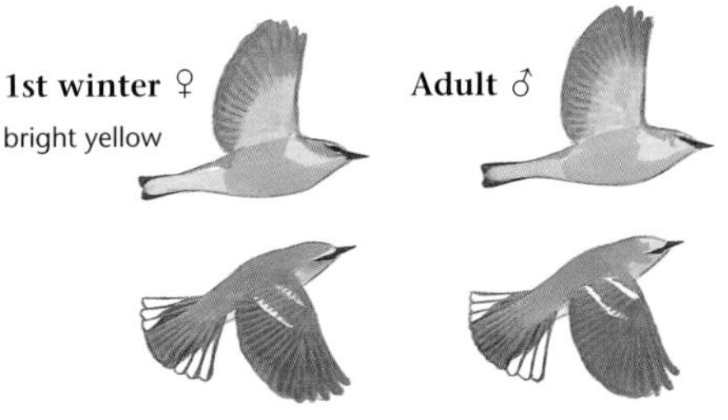
1st winter ♀
bright yellow
Adult ♂

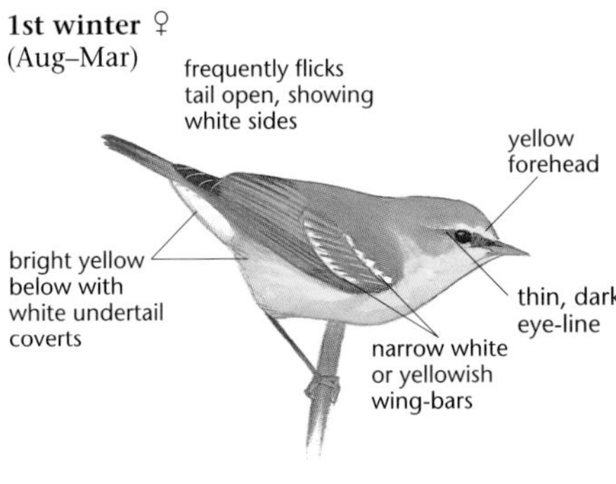
1st winter ♀
(Aug–Mar)
frequently flicks tail open, showing white sides
yellow forehead
bright yellow below with white undertail coverts
thin, dark eye-line
narrow white or yellowish wing-bars

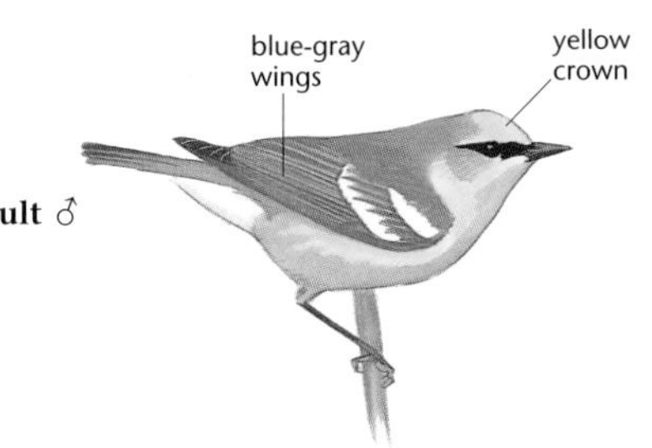
blue-gray wings
yellow crown
Adult ♂

Voice: Song a rather harsh, buzzy *beeee-BZZZZZ* like a deep sigh; first part high and thin, second part low and rough. Also a long, high buzz with stuttering notes at beginning and end *tsi tsi tsi tsi tsi zweeeeeee zt zt zt zt*. Call a sharp, dry *snik* or *chik*. Flight call a short, high, slightly buzzy *dzit* or *zzip*.

Golden-winged Warbler

Vermivora chrysoptera

L 4.75" WS 7.5" WT 0.31 oz (8.8 g)

Like Blue-winged but slightly more elongated, with bold head pattern, yellow wing coverts.

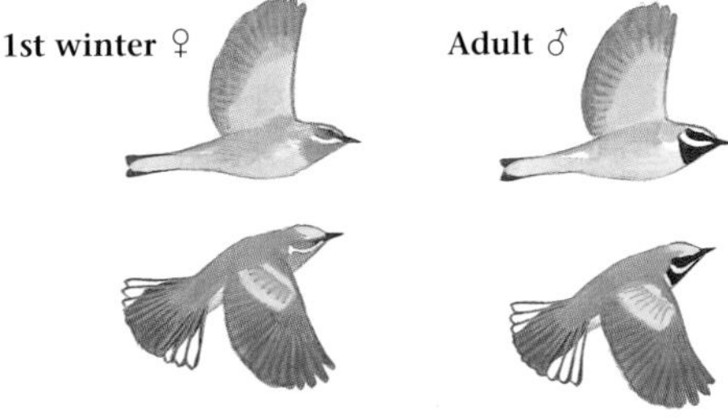
1st winter ♀
Adult ♂

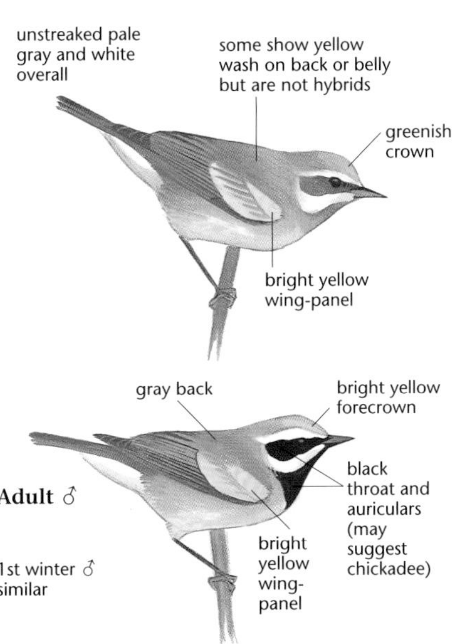
Adult ♀
unstreaked pale gray and white overall
some show yellow wash on back or belly but are not hybrids
greenish crown
bright yellow wing-panel
gray back
bright yellow forecrown
black throat and auriculars (may suggest chickadee)
Adult ♂
bright yellow wing-panel
1st winter ♂ similar

Voice: Song a very fine, high buzz *zeee zaa-zaa-zaa* with first note higher than following; all higher and finer than Blue-winged. Also a longer, varied song like Blue-winged. Calls like Blue-winged.

These two species are very closely related. Gray and yellow with a complete white eye-ring, they differ slightly in plumage and voice. They are found in brushy areas and low woods, often in oaks.

Virginia's Warbler

Vermivora virginiae

L 4.75" WS 7.5" WT 0.27 oz (7.8 g)

Slightly longer-tailed than Nashville; best distinguished by overall gray color, including remiges and wing coverts.

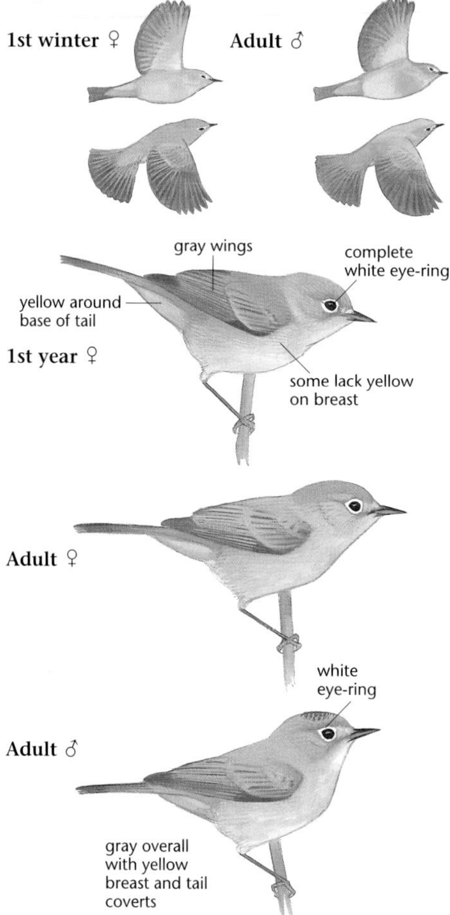
1st winter ♀
Adult ♂
gray wings
complete white eye-ring
yellow around base of tail
1st year ♀
some lack yellow on breast
Adult ♀
white eye-ring
Adult ♂
gray overall with yellow breast and tail coverts

Voice: Song a fairly weak, clear warble; unaccented, not crisply delivered, usually two-part; resembles some songs of Western Nashville but lower and less structured; some also resemble some songs of Yellow. Often a three-part *seedi seedi seedi seedi silp silp suwi suwi*. Calls like Western Nashville.

Nashville Warbler

Vermivora ruficapilla

L 4.75" WS 7.5" WT 0.3 oz (8.7 g)

Small, stubby, and active with short tail, round head, and sharp bill; distinguished from Oporornis *warblers by smaller size, sharp bill, dark legs.*

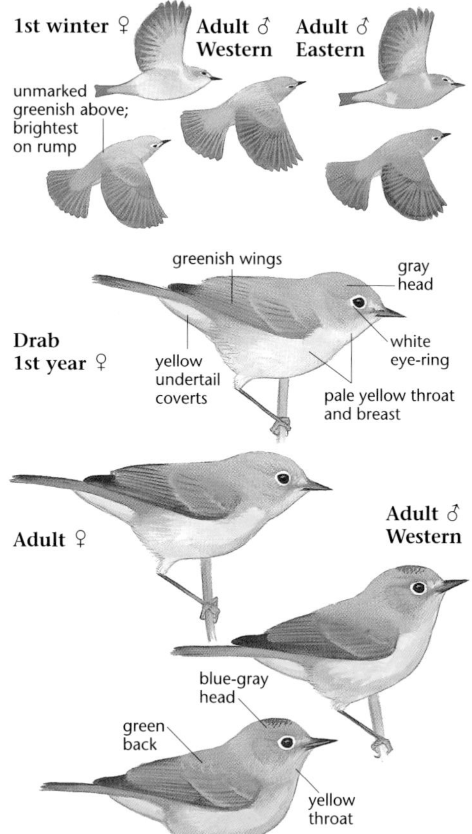
1st winter ♀
Adult ♂ Western
Adult ♂ Eastern
unmarked greenish above; brightest on rump
greenish wings
gray head
Drab 1st year ♀
yellow undertail coverts
white eye-ring
pale yellow throat and breast
Adult ♀
Adult ♂ Western
blue-gray head
green back
yellow throat
Adult ♂ Eastern

Voice: Song of Eastern a fairly slow, simple, two-part, musical trill *seeta seeta seeta seeta pli pli pli pli* softer than Tennessee. Alternate song a series of single or double notes irregularly descending in pitch *tee tee tee tee tay tay tay tay tati toti toti to*. Call a sharp, rattling, metallic *spink* like a small Northern Waterthrush. Flight call a high, clear *swit*.

Western Nashville Warbler averages grayer on the back and brighter on the rump than Eastern. The slightly longer tail is pumped constantly (only occasionally by Eastern). Song is lower and richer than Eastern with less structured ending rather than a simple trill; call is slightly sharper and more metallic.

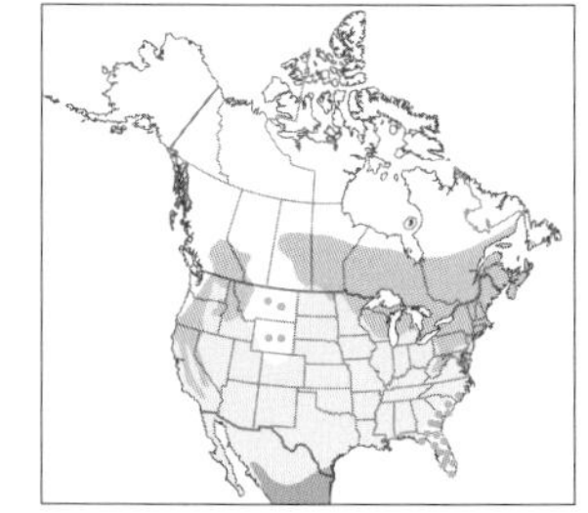

These two species are related to Virginia's and Nashville. Lucy's is found in mesquite and brushy woods, often near water. Colima is found only in oak woods in its limited range.

Lucy's Warbler

Vermivora luciae

L 4.25" WS 7" WT 0.23 oz (6.6 g)

Our smallest wood-warbler; tiny, slender, very pale, and entirely lacking yellow (compare gnatcatchers).

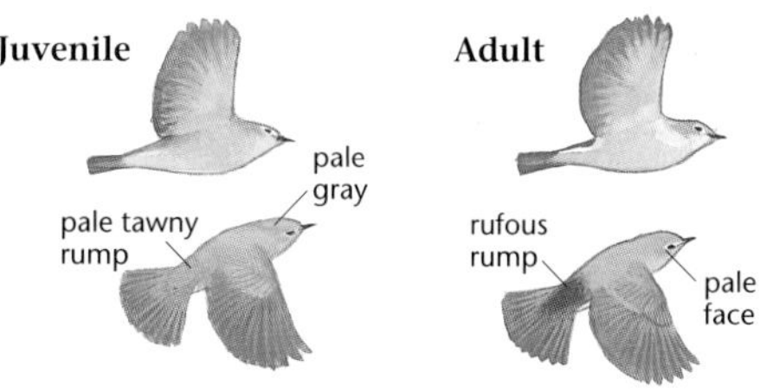
Juvenile
Adult
pale gray
pale tawny rump
rufous rump
pale face

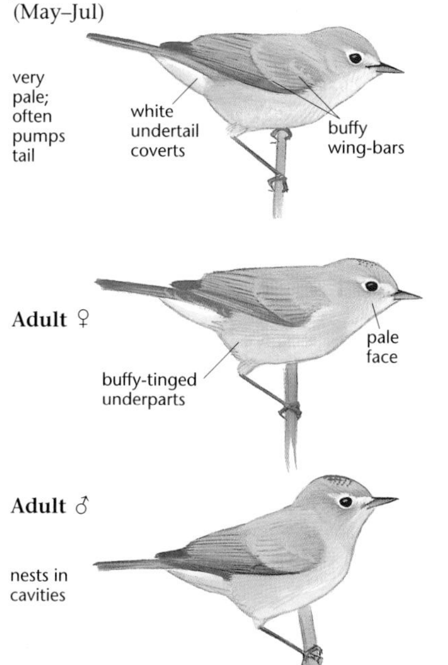
Juvenile
(May–Jul)
very pale; often pumps tail
white undertail coverts
buffy wing-bars
Adult ♀
pale face
buffy-tinged underparts
Adult ♂
nests in cavities

Voice: Song a simple trill with several pitch changes; higher-pitched than Virginia's with simpler, sharper notes. More complex songs of clear, high whistles *sweeo sweeo sweeo seet seet seet seet sit it it it it,* like unaccented songs of Yellow but usually simpler, more rapid. Call a slightly husky, rattling *vink*. Flight call a high, clear, weak *tsiit.*

Colima Warbler

Vermivora crissalis

L 5.75" WS 7.75" WT 0.34 oz (9.7 g)

Larger, sturdier, and relatively longer-tailed than Virginia's.

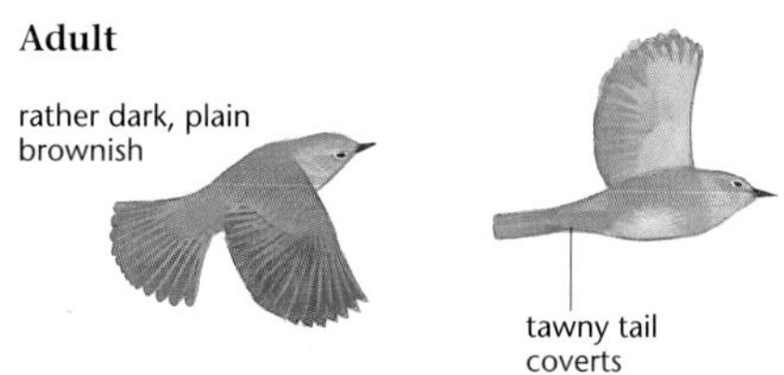
Adult
rather dark, plain brownish
tawny tail coverts

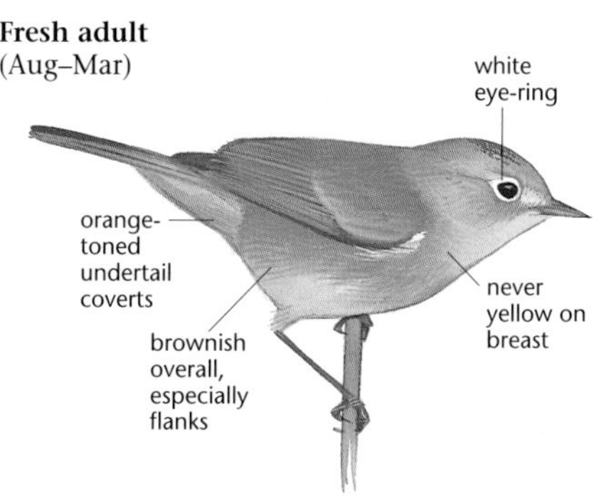
Fresh adult
(Aug–Mar)
white eye-ring
orange-toned undertail coverts
never yellow on breast
brownish overall, especially flanks

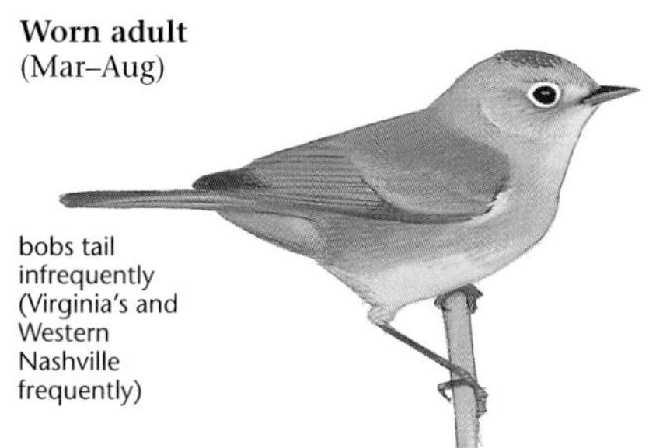
Worn adult
(Mar–Aug)
bobs tail infrequently (Virginia's and Western Nashville frequently)

Voice: Song a hard, chattering, wavering trill, sometimes with high, clear *tew* note at end; notes clearly upslurred, unlike Orange-crowned and most other similar species. Song usually rises slightly near end then drops *tetetetetetetetetititi-tew*. Call similar to close relatives (Virginia's, Nashville, Lucy's) but may be huskier. Flight call unknown.

This common and widespread species is found in low trees and woodland edges, especially willows in wet areas. Note bright yellow plumage, plain pale face, and short tail with yellow spots.

Yellow Warbler

Dendroica petechia

L 5" WS 8" WT 0.33 oz (9.5 g)

Fairly stout but long-bodied; relatively short-tailed and stout-billed with smooth contours.

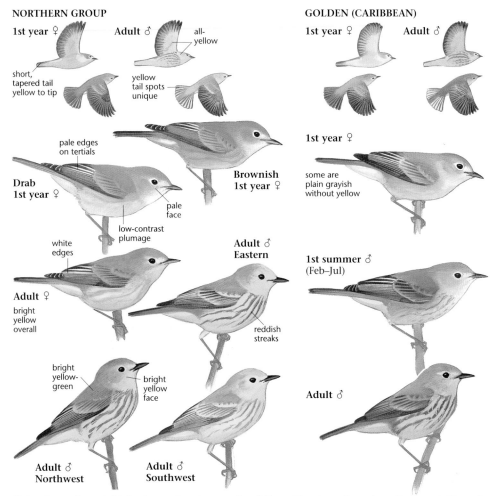

NORTHERN GROUP

1st year ♀

short, tapered tail yellow to tip

Adult ♂

all-yellow

yellow tail spots unique

pale edges on tertials

Drab 1st year ♀

pale face

low-contrast plumage

Brownish 1st year ♀

white edges

Adult ♀

bright yellow overall

Adult ♂ Eastern

reddish streaks

bright yellow-green

bright yellow face

Adult ♂ Northwest

Adult ♂ Southwest

GOLDEN (CARIBBEAN)

1st year ♀

Adult ♂

1st year ♀

some are plain grayish without yellow

1st summer ♂ (Feb–Jul)

Adult ♂

Voice: Song of sweet, high, clear notes: sharp upslurs followed by sharp downslurs, then emphatic ending *sweet sweet sweet ti ti ti to soo* or *swee swee swee ti ti ti swee;* variable in details of phrasing. Alternate song longer and less structured without emphatic ending *seedl seedl seedl seedl sitew sitew sitew;* variable, resembles Chestnut-sided. Call a clear, loud chip; varies from high and sweet to staccato to low and dull. Flight call a high, clear trill *tzip;* varies from rough to fine, ascending to descending.

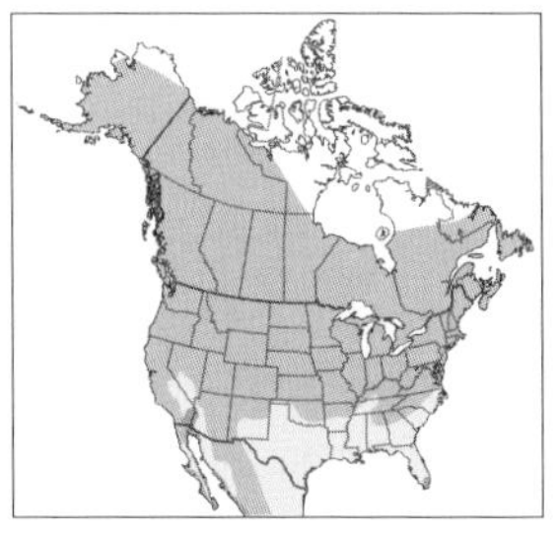

Geographic variation within the Northern group is fairly weak and clinal, with drabber plumage to the north and west and paler to the southwest. The disjunct Golden population (resident in the Florida Keys) has rounder wings and shorter primary projection; bill averages thinner with slight decurve. Male is relatively rich golden yellow with broader red streaks on underparts but darker olive crown; some 1st winter birds are nearly plain gray, lacking yellow, and 1st summer males can have distinctive pattern of gray head and yellow body.

These two species are distinctive. Chestnut-sided is closely related to Yellow despite plumage differences. It nests in second-growth deciduous woods, Magnolia in mixed coniferous woods.

Chestnut-sided Warbler

Dendroica pensylvanica

L 5" WS 7.75" WT 0.34 oz (9.6 g)

Slightly longer-tailed and stouter-billed than Yellow; very different in plumage. Nearly always holds tail cocked up above wingtips.

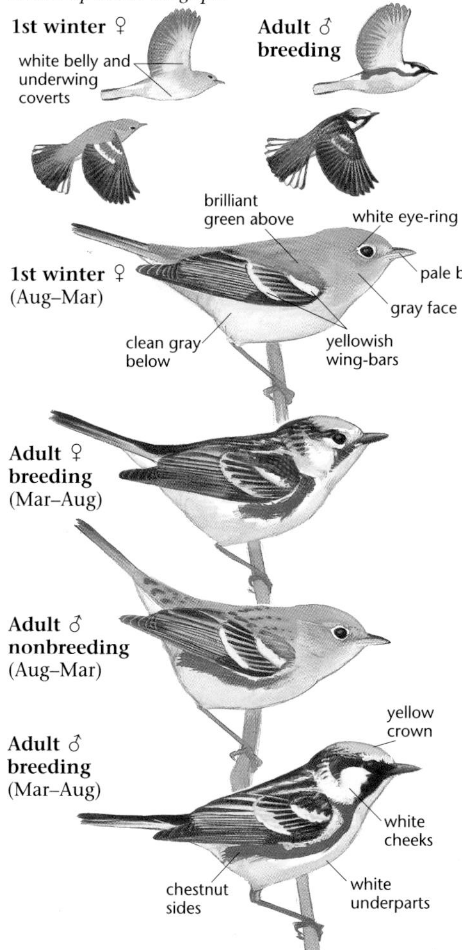
1st winter ♀
white belly and underwing coverts
Adult ♂ breeding
brilliant green above
white eye-ring
1st winter ♀ (Aug–Mar)
pale bill
gray face
clean gray below
yellowish wing-bars
Adult ♀ breeding (Mar–Aug)
Adult ♂ nonbreeding (Aug–Mar)
yellow crown
Adult ♂ breeding (Mar–Aug)
white cheeks
chestnut sides
white underparts

Voice: Song clear, musical with emphatic ending *witew witew witew WEECHEW* (compare Hooded). Alternate song longer, rambling like Yellow. Both song types average lower-pitched than Yellow; can be matched by some Yellow. Call a low, flat *chidp*. Flight call a rather low, buzzy, nasal *jrrt*.

Magnolia Warbler

Dendroica magnolia

L 5" WS 7.5" WT 0.3 oz (8.7 g)

Round-headed, small-billed, and long-tailed; white band and black tip of tail pattern unique.

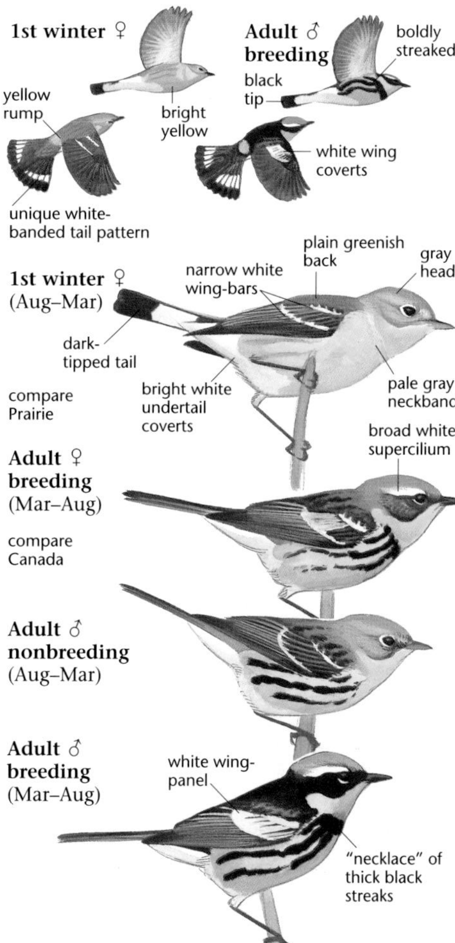
1st winter ♀
Adult ♂ breeding
boldly streaked
black tip
yellow rump
bright yellow
white wing coverts
unique white-banded tail pattern
plain greenish back
gray head
1st winter ♀ (Aug–Mar)
narrow white wing-bars
dark-tipped tail
bright white undertail coverts
pale gray neckband
compare Prairie
broad white supercilium
Adult ♀ breeding (Mar–Aug)
compare Canada
Adult ♂ nonbreeding (Aug–Mar)
Adult ♂ breeding (Mar–Aug)
white wing-panel
"necklace" of thick black streaks

Voice: Song short, musical but rather weak and simple *sweeter sweeter SWEETEST*; variable; most similar to Redstart but much less emphatic. Call a unique, tinny, hoarse *vint* or *chuif*. Flight call a very high, weak, lightly trilled, rather soft *zzip*.

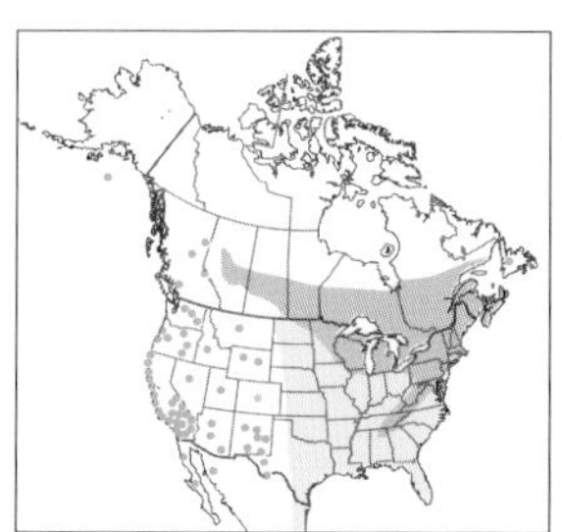

Other warblers that habitually cock their tails like Chestnut-sided include Blackburnian and Cerulean Warblers and Common Yellowthroat.

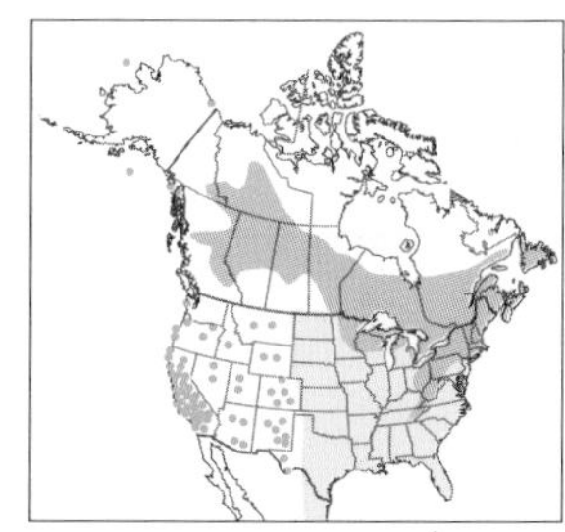

These two species are distinctive. Cape May favors short-needled conifers or flowering trees; Black-throated Blue is usually found in dark, shaded understory within forests.

Cape May Warbler

Dendroica tigrina

L 5" WS 8.25" WT 0.39 oz (11 g)

Sharp, slightly decurved bill always dark; short tail. Very drab 1st winter female can be distinctive.

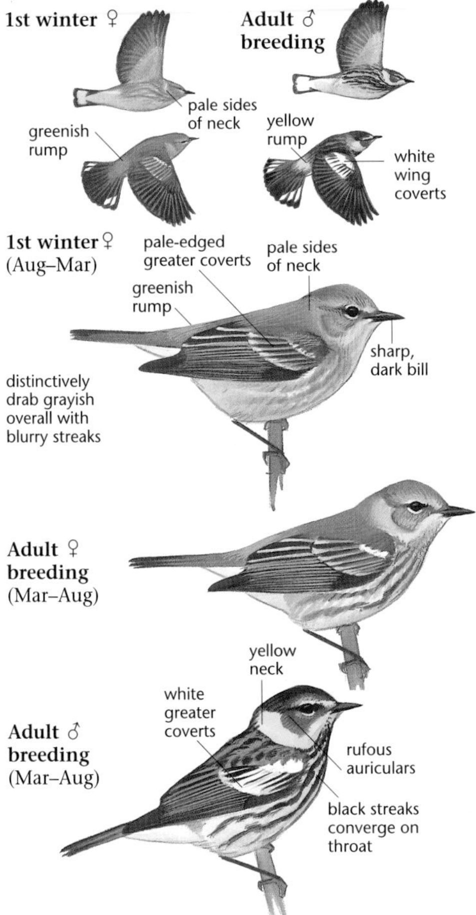
1st winter ♀
Adult ♂ breeding
pale sides of neck
greenish rump
yellow rump
white wing coverts
1st winter ♀ (Aug–Mar)
pale-edged greater coverts
pale sides of neck
greenish rump
sharp, dark bill
distinctively drab grayish overall with blurry streaks
Adult ♀ breeding (Mar–Aug)
yellow neck
white greater coverts
Adult ♂ breeding (Mar–Aug)
rufous auriculars
black streaks converge on throat

Voice: Song very high and thin; may sound slightly buzzy; four to seven unslurred notes (5/sec) *seet seet seet seet seet* or slightly lower-pitched, faster, more complex *seeo seeo seeo seeo seeo* or *witse witse witse wit.* Call a very high, hard, short *ti.* Flight call a very high, slightly buzzy *tzew* or *tzee* slightly descending.

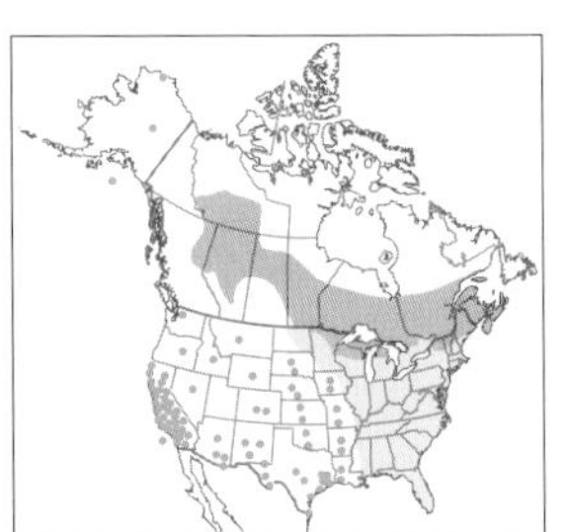

Black-throated Blue Warbler

Dendroica caerulescens

L 5.25" WS 7.75" WT 0.36 oz (10.2 g)

Rather stocky and short-necked. Female has distinctive drab olive color and face pattern.

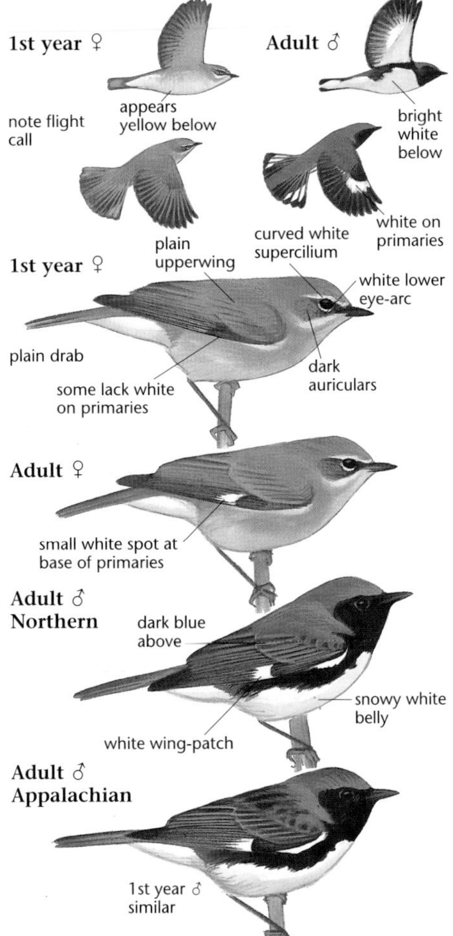
1st year ♀
Adult ♂
note flight call
appears yellow below
bright white below
white on primaries
curved white supercilium
plain upperwing
1st year ♀
white lower eye-arc
plain drab
some lack white on primaries
dark auriculars
Adult ♀
small white spot at base of primaries
Adult ♂ Northern
dark blue above
snowy white belly
white wing-patch
Adult ♂ Appalachian
1st year ♂ similar

Voice: Song a husky but musical buzz, lazy and drawling; several introductory notes followed by rather harsh, slow, rising buzz *zheew zheew zheeeeeee* or *zo zo zo zo zo zo zo zeeeeeee.* Call a very high, sharp smack *stip* like juncos. Flight call a sharp, dry *tik* or *twik* reminiscent of soft, sharp notes of cardinals; given frequently.

Male Black-throated Blue Warblers of the Appalachian population have variable black streaks on the mantle; also shown by occasional Northern birds.

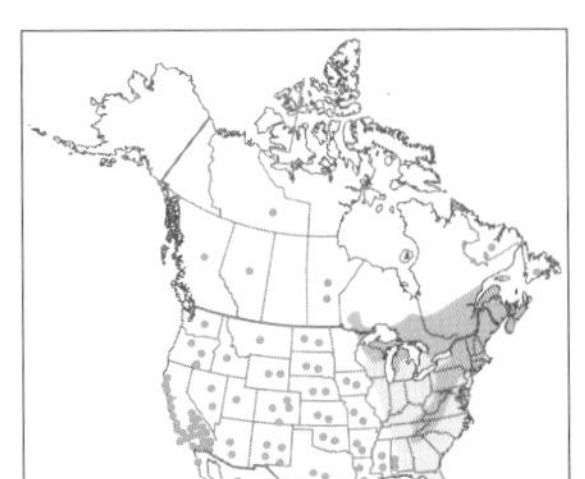

These two birds are strikingly colored. Cerulean nests in tall broadleaf trees near water (e.g., along rivers), Blackburnian in mature mixed coniferous woods, often singing from the highest treetops.

Cerulean Warbler

Dendroica cerulea

L 4.75" WS 7.75" WT 0.33 oz (9.3 g)

Very short-tailed; short-legged and stout-billed, with very pointed wings. Blue or blue-green upperparts always distinctive.

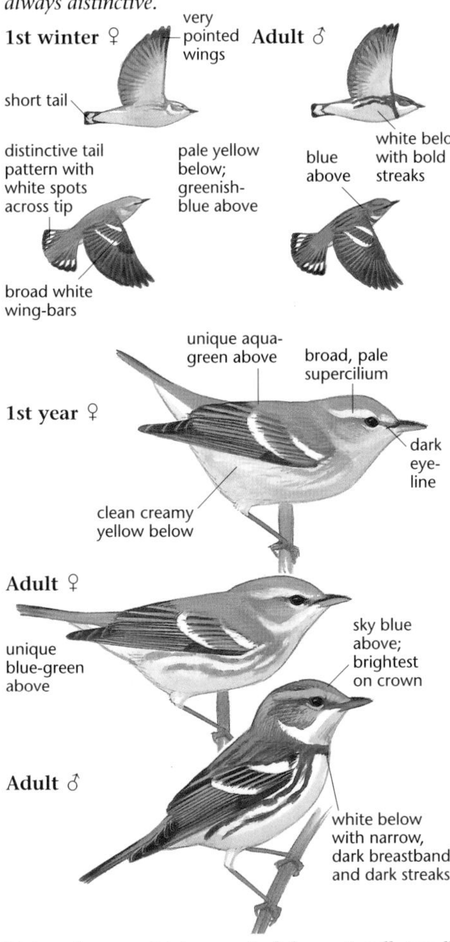

1st winter ♀
very pointed wings
Adult ♂
short tail
distinctive tail pattern with white spots across tip
pale yellow below; greenish-blue above
blue above
white below with bold streaks
broad white wing-bars
unique aqua-green above
broad, pale supercilium
1st year ♀
dark eye-line
clean creamy yellow below
Adult ♀
sky blue above; brightest on crown
unique blue-green above
Adult ♂
white below with narrow, dark breastband and dark streaks

Voice: Song a high, musical buzz *tzeedl tzeedl tzeedl ti ti ti tzeeeeee;* generally three-part, each part higher than the preceding one; more musical than parulas with no slurred notes; pattern very similar to Blackburnian but with buzzy quality. Call a clear chip. Flight call a short buzz *dzzt.*

Blackburnian Warbler

Dendroica fusca

L 5" WS 8.5" WT 0.34 oz (9.8 g)

Relatively long, streamlined body, with pointed wings and longer tail than Cerulean. Dark auriculars with pale outline distinctive.

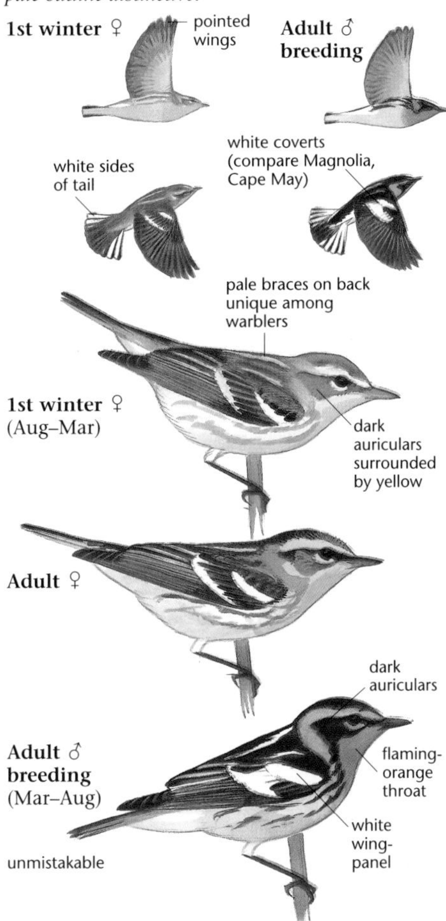

1st winter ♀
pointed wings
Adult ♂ breeding
white sides of tail
white coverts (compare Magnolia, Cape May)
pale braces on back unique among warblers
1st winter ♀ (Aug–Mar)
dark auriculars surrounded by yellow
Adult ♀
dark auriculars
Adult ♂ breeding (Mar–Aug)
flaming-orange throat
white wing-panel
unmistakable

Voice: Song has sharp, dry quality and usually includes some incredibly high notes *tsi tsi tsi tsi tsi ti ti ti ti ti seeeeee* ending extremely high and thin. Alternate song very high, slow, rising series with rattling quality *tseekut tseekut tseekut tsee;* compare Golden-crowned Kinglet. Call a sharp *tsick.* Flight call a high, thin buzz.

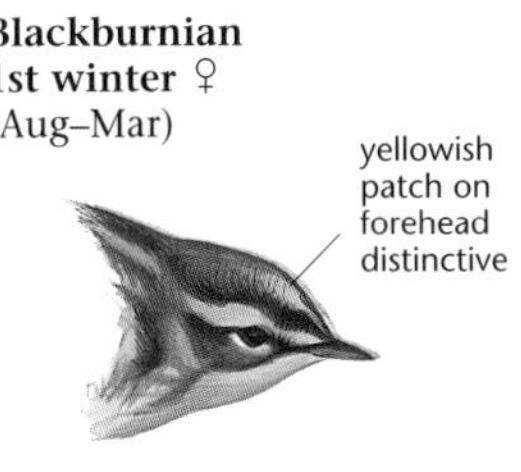

Blackburnian 1st winter ♀ (Aug–Mar)
yellowish patch on forehead distinctive

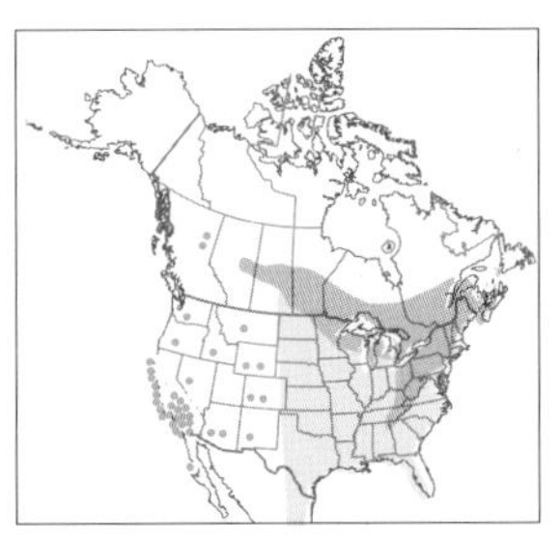

Our most visible warbler, found in open woods and brushy areas, this species often perches upright on prominent twigs with its yellow rump exposed, flitting up to catch flying insects.

Yellow-rumped Warbler

Dendroica coronata

L 5.5" WS 9.25" WT 0.43 oz (12.3 g)

Rather large; long tail flared at tip; round head and stout black bill. Adult male grayish, but all other plumages washed with brown.

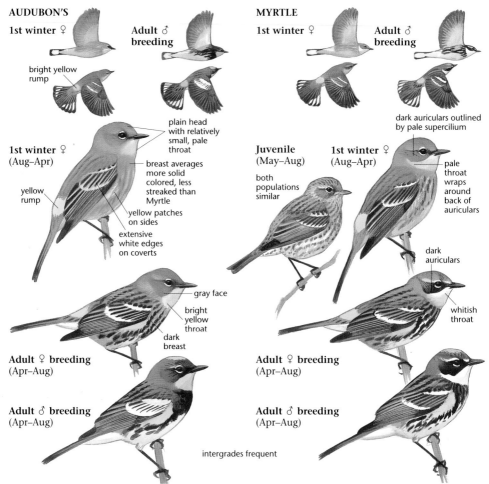

AUDUBON'S

1st winter ♀

Adult ♂ breeding

bright yellow rump

1st winter ♀ (Aug–Apr)

plain head with relatively small, pale throat

breast averages more solid colored, less streaked than Myrtle

yellow rump

yellow patches on sides

extensive white edges on coverts

gray face

bright yellow throat

dark breast

Adult ♀ breeding (Apr–Aug)

Adult ♂ breeding (Apr–Aug)

MYRTLE

1st winter ♀

Adult ♂ breeding

dark auriculars outlined by pale supercilium

Juvenile (May–Aug)

both populations similar

1st winter ♀ (Aug–Apr)

pale throat wraps around back of auriculars

dark auriculars

whitish throat

Adult ♀ breeding (Apr–Aug)

Adult ♂ breeding (Apr–Aug)

intergrades frequent

Voice: AUDUBON'S: Song a clear warble, soft and rather flat, usually two-part with last few phrases lower or higher in pitch *sidl sidl sidl sidl sidl seedl seedl seedl seedl* with little variation, usually fading at end; another version stronger, mainly two-syllable phrases usually rising slightly in pitch. Call a dry, husky *chwit* with slightly rising inflection. Flight call a clear, rising *svit* or *ssit*. MYRTLE: Song like Audubon's but slightly higher-pitched with shorter phrases; tends to sound faster, more hurried, less musical. Call a low, flat *chep* or flat, hard *tep;* lower and harder than Audubon's without rising inflection. Flight call like Audubon's.

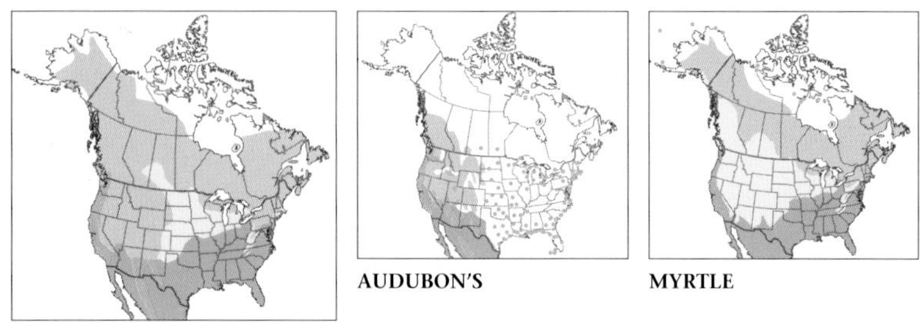
AUDUBON'S
MYRTLE

Black-throated Wood-Warblers: Genus *Dendroica*

The neatly marked Black-throated Gray, found in dry oak and juniper woods, is closely related to the following black-throated warblers. All are similar in basic appearance and voice.

Warbler Plumages

Many species of warblers have strikingly different male and female, breeding and nonbreeding plumages. In all cases, the adult male is the brightest, most colorful, and most contrastingly patterned, while the 1st year female is the drabbest and least contrastingly patterned. The adult female and 1st year male are intermediate between these two extremes and are similar to each other during the nonbreeding season, but 1st year males become nearly identical to adult males in the breeding season. This simple rule of thumb holds true nearly all the time, but there is great variation in each species and much overlap among ages and sexes. Field observers should not attempt to label individual birds without experience and reference to the detailed literature on determining the age and sex of birds.

Myrtle × Audubon's Yellow-rumped intergrade

Adult ♂
breeding

Intergrades show intermediate characteristics or a mosaic combination; they are frequent where breeding ranges overlap in the Canadian Rockies but rarely identified south of there.

Hermit × Townsend's hybrids

1st winter ♀
Adult ♂

Hermit and Townsend's Warblers hybridize regularly where ranges overlap in Washington and Oregon, but hybrids are rarely identified elsewhere. Typical hybrids are shown; many other variations occur. Hybrids generally have face and head pattern like Hermit, breast and flanks like Townsend's. Female and 1st winter male hybrids can resemble Black-throated Green, but note white vent, yellow breast, pale forehead, and streaked back.

Black-throated Gray Warbler

Dendroica nigrescens

L 5" WS 7.75" WT 0.29 oz (8.4 g)

Structure typical of black-throated warblers: stout bill; rather long, straight-edged tail entirely white from below; bold wing-bars; black throat.

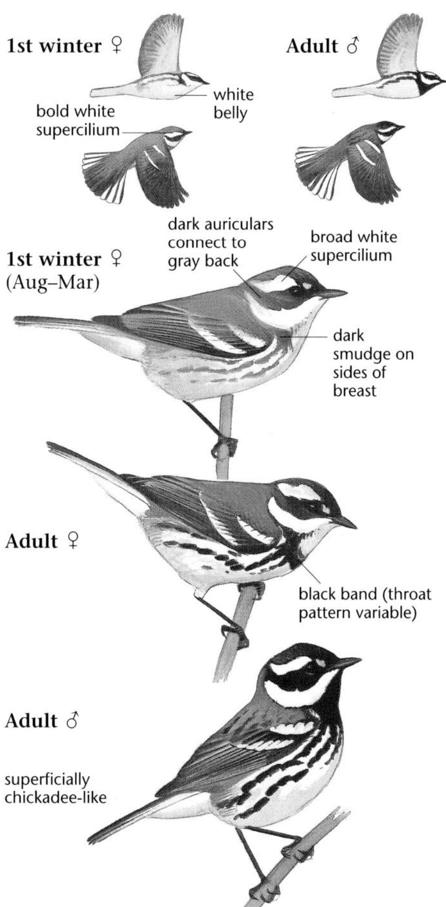
1st winter ♀
Adult ♂
white belly
bold white supercilium
1st winter ♀ (Aug–Mar)
dark auriculars connect to gray back
broad white supercilium
dark smudge on sides of breast
Adult ♀
black band (throat pattern variable)
Adult ♂
superficially chickadee-like

Voice: Song of mostly musical, buzzy notes with fast tempo and emphatic ending *zeea zeea zeea ZEEE zaa zoo* or simple, repeated, buzzy phrases *zidza zidza zidza zidza*. Call a low, dull *tip* or *tep* similar to Myrtle Yellow-rumped; lower than other black-throated warblers. Flight call like Black-throated Green.

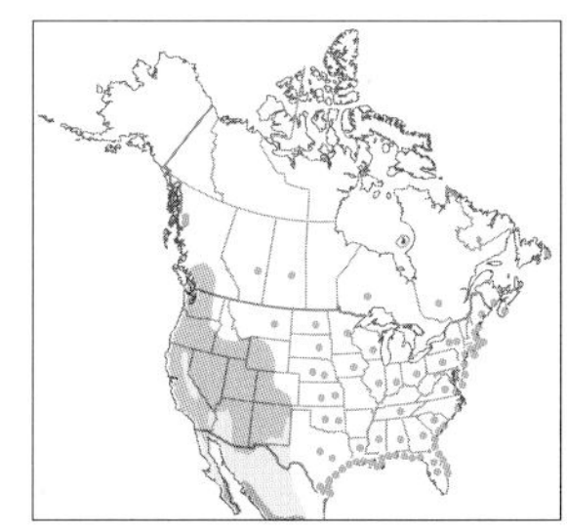

These two species are found in coniferous forests and often hybridize where their ranges overlap. Their structure and voices are typical of the black-throated group.

Townsend's Warbler

Dendroica townsendi

L 5" WS 8" WT 0.31 oz (8.8 g)

Structure like Black-throated Green; yellow breast and contrasting dark auricular-patch distinctive.

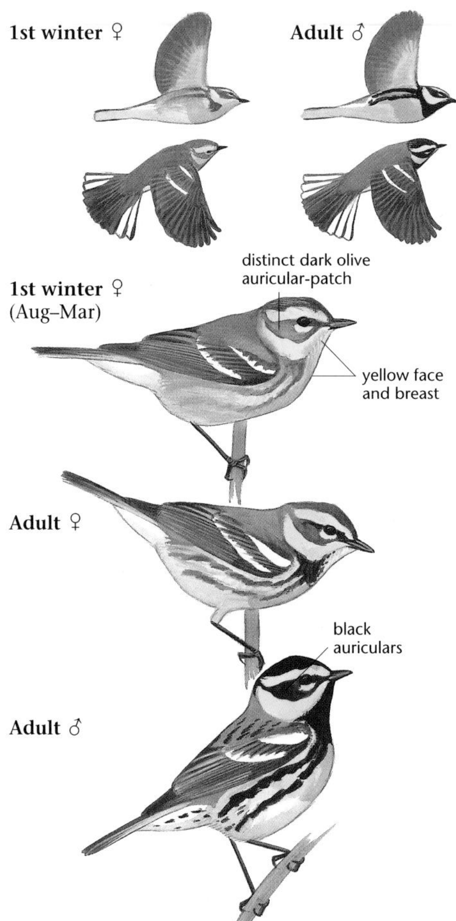
1st winter ♀
Adult ♂
1st winter ♀
(Aug–Mar)
distinct dark olive auricular-patch
yellow face and breast
Adult ♀
black auriculars
Adult ♂

Voice: Song a rapid series of mainly buzzy notes; variable in pattern but often rising; higher and thinner than Black-throated Gray: *zoo zoo zoo zeeee skeea skeea* or *zi zi zi zi zi zeedl zeedl* or *weezy weezy weezy dzeee*. Call averages slightly sharper than other black-throated warblers. Flight call like Hermit.

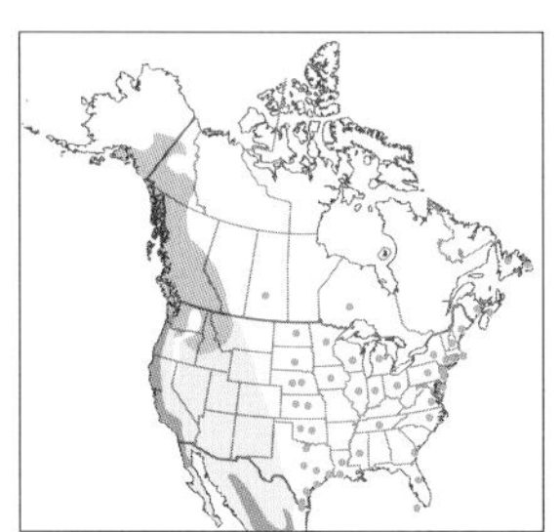

Hermit Warbler

Dendroica occidentalis

L 5" WS 8" WT 0.32 oz (9.2 g)

Plain yellow face and virtually unstreaked flanks distinctive.

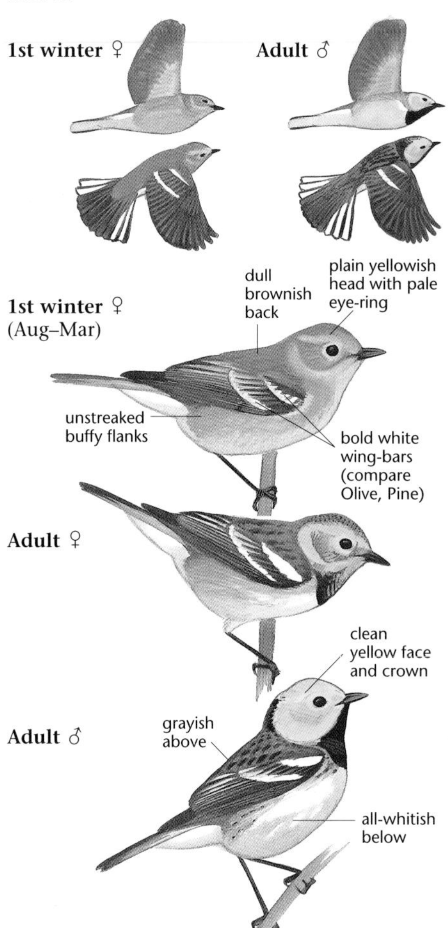
1st winter ♀
Adult ♂
1st winter ♀
(Aug–Mar)
dull brownish back
plain yellowish head with pale eye-ring
unstreaked buffy flanks
bold white wing-bars (compare Olive, Pine)
Adult ♀
clean yellow face and crown
grayish above
Adult ♂
all-whitish below

Voice: Song variable: a rapid series of high, buzzy phrases, typically accelerating and ending with abruptly higher or lower notes *ze ze ze ze ze ze zee sitew;* some songs similar to Townsend's but generally softer and clearer; other songs long and repetitive *ze ze ze zeea zeea zeea zeea ZEEA ZEEA tleep*. Calls like Black-throated Green.

Both these species are similar to other black-throated warblers. Black-throated Green nests in coniferous woods; Golden-cheeked is found in mixed woods with mature junipers.

Black-throated Green Warbler

Dendroica virens

L 5" WS 7.75" WT 0.31 oz (8.8 g)

Olive auriculars, bright green back, and yellow wash across vent distinctive.

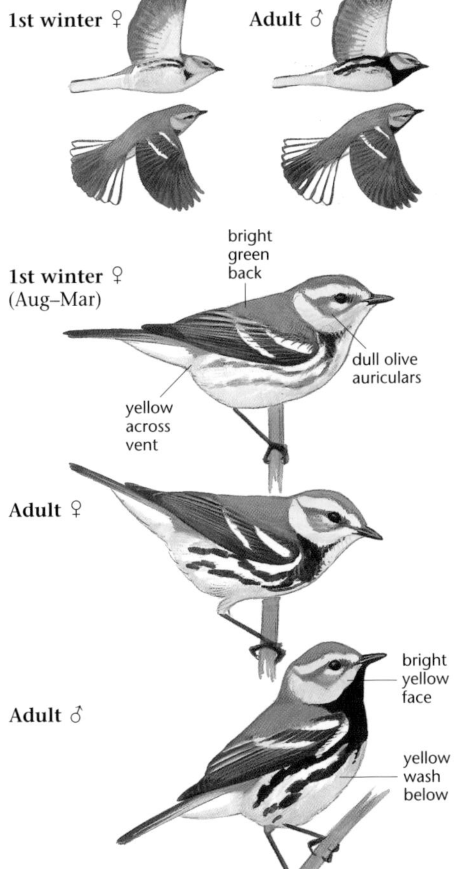

1st winter ♀
Adult ♂
bright green back
1st winter ♀ (Aug–Mar)
dull olive auriculars
yellow across vent
Adult ♀
bright yellow face
Adult ♂
yellow wash below

Voice: Song a series of short, level buzzes; two commonly heard patterns: a rather fast *zee zee zee zee zo zeet* and a more relaxed *zoooo zeee zo zo zeet;* some Townsend's songs similar. Call a sharp *tsik* or *tek* like Hermit; sharper and higher than Myrtle Yellow-rumped. Flight call a clear, high, rising *swit;* shorter than Yellow-rumped.

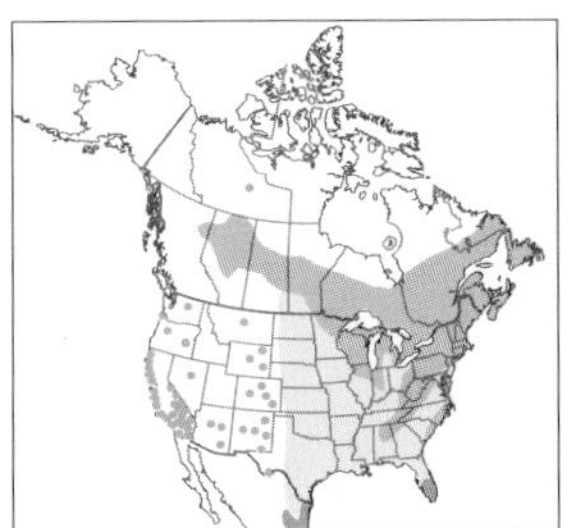

Golden-cheeked Warbler

Dendroica chrysoparia

L 5" WS 7.75" WT 0.34 oz (9.8 g)

Yellow auriculars, strong, dark eye-line, and clean white underparts distinctive.

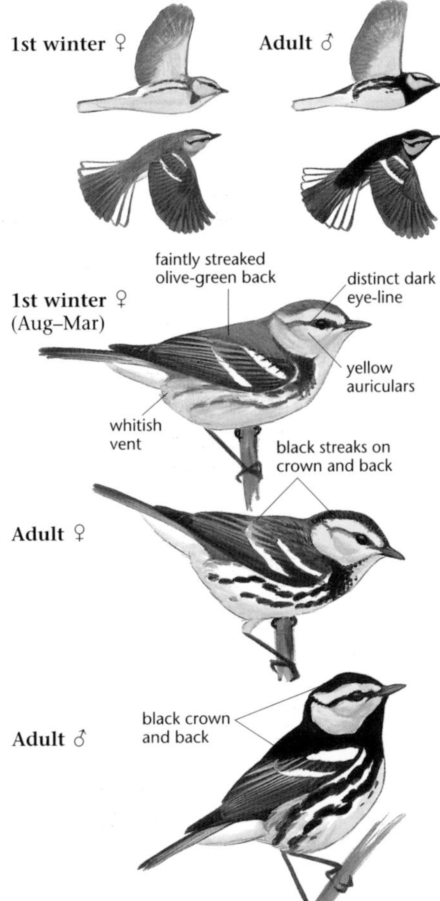

1st winter ♀
Adult ♂
faintly streaked olive-green back
distinct dark eye-line
1st winter ♀ (Aug–Mar)
yellow auriculars
whitish vent
black streaks on crown and back
Adult ♀
black crown and back
Adult ♂

Voice: Song buzzy like other black-throated warblers; slightly harsher than Black-throated Green; relatively low-pitched, slow, lazy *zrr zooo zeedl zeeee twip* or *brrr zweee seezle zeeeee titip* or *zeedl zeedl zeedl zeedl zweeee tsip.* Calls like Black-throated Green and its other close relatives.

Kirtland's, one of our rarest birds, is found very locally in sparse, young jack-pine forests. Prairie is found in low, brushy areas, second-growth woods, and mangroves.

Kirtland's Warbler

Dendroica kirtlandii

L 5.75" WS 8.75" WT 0.48 oz (13.8 g)

Rather large and stocky; large-billed, fairly long tail. Plain grayish above and pale yellow below distinctive.

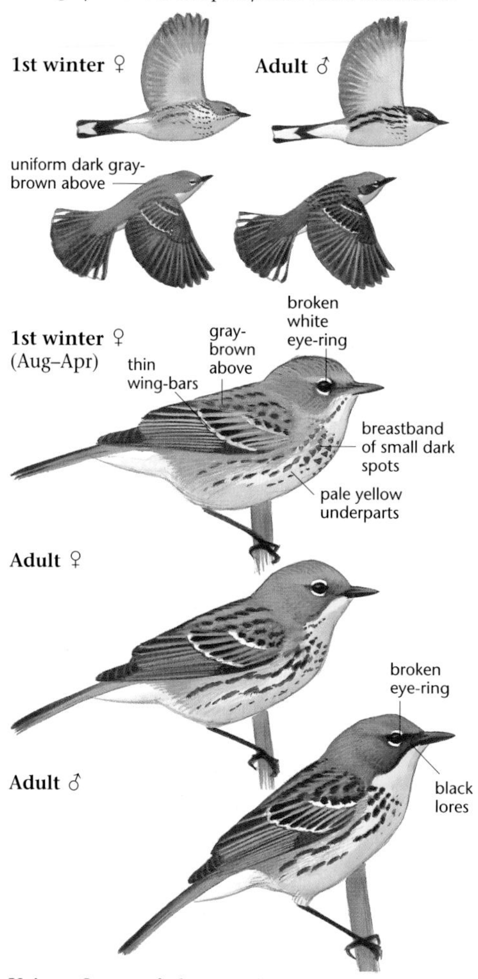
1st winter ♀
Adult ♂
uniform dark gray-brown above
1st winter ♀ (Aug–Apr)
thin wing-bars
gray-brown above
broken white eye-ring
breastband of small dark spots
pale yellow underparts
Adult ♀
broken eye-ring
black lores
Adult ♂

Voice: Song of low, rich notes; loud and emphatic, rising in pitch and intensity *flip lip lip-lip-tip-tip-CHIDIP.* Alternate song a short chatter reminiscent of House Wren. Call a strong, clear, descending chip like Ovenbird. Flight call a short, high buzz.

Prairie Warbler

Dendroica discolor

L 4.75" WS 7" WT 0.27 oz (7.7 g)

Small, round-headed; long, narrow tail. Bright yellow underparts and dark semicircle under eye distinctive.

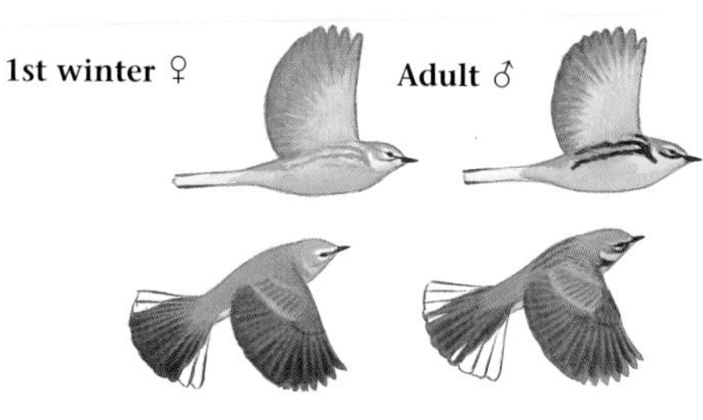
1st winter ♀
Adult ♂

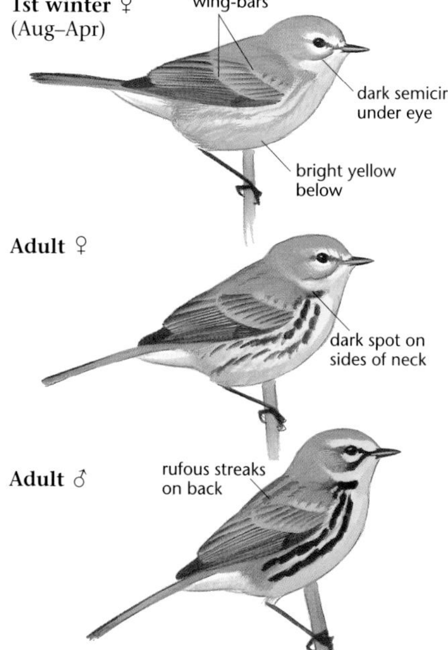
1st winter ♀ (Aug–Apr)
yellowish wing-bars
dark semicircle under eye
bright yellow below
Adult ♀
dark spot on sides of neck
Adult ♂
rufous streaks on back

Voice: Song a series of high, fine, musical buzzes nearly always steadily rising in pitch; may be fast or slow; also series with first few notes level and later notes rising *zooo zoo zo zozozozoZEEEET.* Call a musical chip with a hint of the huskiness of Palm. Flight call a high, slightly husky, level *tss.*

These two species and Palm persistently pump their tails. This habit can be useful in identification, but note that other warblers also pump their tails (Nashville, Virginia's, Lucy's, Blackpoll, Bay-breasted), although they do so either less often or less conspicuously. Other species may occasionally pump their tails.

This species nests in spruce bogs, but at other times it is found in small groups on grassy or weedy open ground, searching for insects and constantly pumping its tail.

Palm Warbler

Dendroica palmarum

L 5.5" WS 8" WT 0.36 oz (10.3 g)

Relatively long-tailed, round-winged, and flat-headed; head shape accentuated by striped pattern. Yellow tail coverts also distinctive.

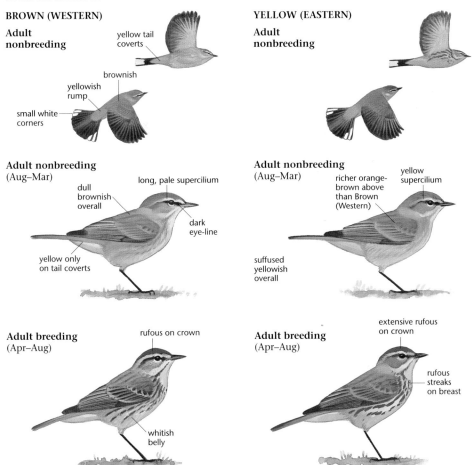

BROWN (WESTERN)

Adult nonbreeding

yellow tail coverts

brownish

yellowish rump

small white corners

Adult nonbreeding (Aug–Mar)

long, pale supercilium

dull brownish overall

dark eye-line

yellow only on tail coverts

Adult breeding (Apr–Aug)

rufous on crown

whitish belly

YELLOW (EASTERN)

Adult nonbreeding

Adult nonbreeding (Aug–Mar)

richer orange-brown above than Brown (Western)

yellow supercilium

suffused yellowish overall

Adult breeding (Apr–Aug)

extensive rufous on crown

rufous streaks on breast

Voice: Song a rather dull, uneven, buzzy trill *zzizzizzizzizzizzi* slightly changing in pitch and volume but overall steady; rather weak and infrequently heard. Further study may reveal differences between songs of two populations. Call a sharp, husky, distinctive *chik;* closest to Prairie but stronger, deeper. Flight call a husky *sink*. Yellow (Eastern) population may average slightly sharper calls than Brown (Western).

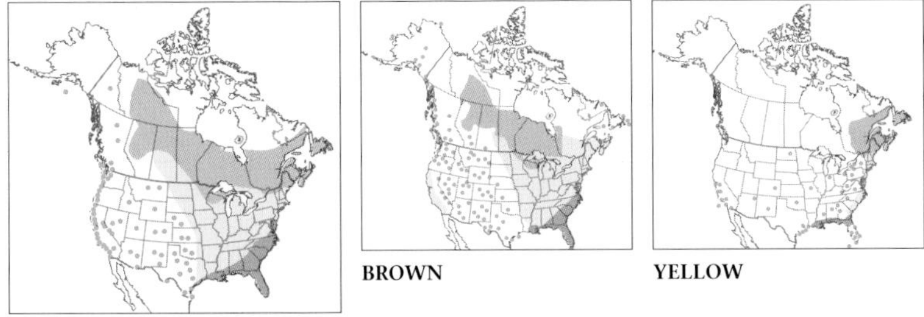
BROWN
YELLOW

The aptly named Pine Warbler is found mainly in pine forests. Superficially similar to Bay-breasted and Blackpoll, it differs in many features of structure, head pattern, and wing pattern.

Identification of Fall Warblers

Identification of wood-warblers can be daunting Aug–Mar when most species show drab nonbreeding plumage. 1st year female Pine Warblers are particularly confusing to inexperienced birders simply because of their drabness, but it is important to realize that the drabness itself is distinctive and is matched by only the drabbest individuals of a few species; compare Orange-crowned, Yellow, Cape May, Yellow-rumped, and Olive Warblers. Other species that are only slightly brighter include Tennessee, Hermit, Blackburnian, Bay-breasted, and Blackpoll Warblers.

Distinguishing 1st winter Bay-breasted and Blackpoll Warblers can be tricky, but given good views all birds should be readily identifiable. Bay-breasted is brighter greenish above and warmer buffy yellow below, the buffy color extending to the undertail coverts (vs. lemon-yellow breast contrasting with whitish belly and undertail coverts on Blackpoll); bright green sides of neck (vs. gray); a suggestion of pale "spectacles" that may recall Yellow-throated Vireo (Blackpoll has a thin, dark eye-line reminiscent of Tennessee Warbler); unstreaked breast; broader wing-bars, but fainter pale edges on greater coverts; thicker and paler bill; unstreaked back and crown; always gray legs (vs. dark legs with yellowish toes or yellow legs on adults); grayer rump.

Tail pattern is a very useful clue for identifying wood-warblers. A good view of the spread tail in flight or the underside of the tail on a perched bird can greatly narrow the choices. On Pine Warbler, Prairie Warbler, and others the mostly white outer tail feathers create white sides on the spread tail from above and a mostly white surface on the closed tail from below. Conversely, the smaller white spots on the outer tail feathers of Bay-breasted and Blackpoll and others create white corners on the spread tail, with dark color visible at the base of the closed tail from below.

Pine Warbler adult ♂

white sides

Blackpoll Warbler 1st winter ♀

white corners

Pine Warbler

Dendroica pinus

L 5.5" WS 8.75" WT 0.42 oz (12 g)

Long-tailed with long tail projection (short undertail coverts), stout bill, round head, short primary projection. Pale neck-patch and dark cheeks distinctive.

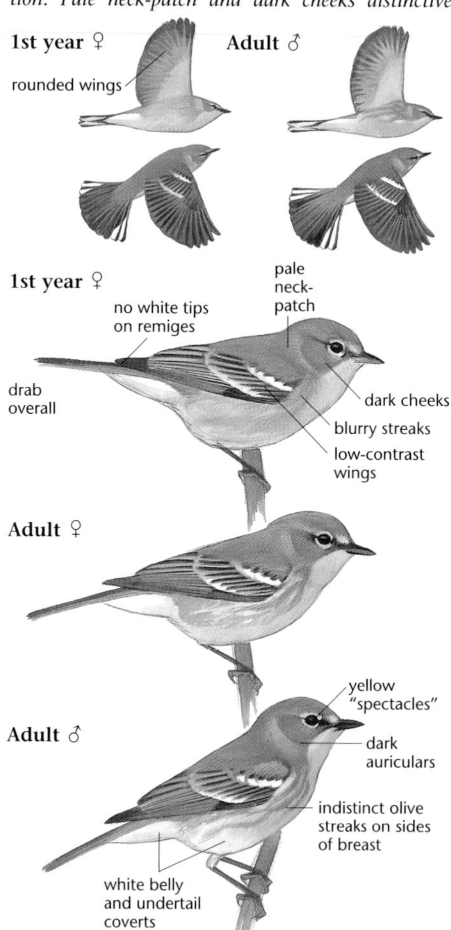
1st year ♀
rounded wings
Adult ♂
1st year ♀
no white tips on remiges
pale neck-patch
drab overall
dark cheeks
blurry streaks
low-contrast wings
Adult ♀
yellow "spectacles"
Adult ♂
dark auriculars
indistinct olive streaks on sides of breast
white belly and undertail coverts

Voice: Song a rapid trill of simple upslurred notes (similar to but more musical than Chipping Sparrow). Also a slower trill of two-syllable, more musical whistles; whole trill slightly varying in pitch. Call a high, flat chip. Flight call a high, clear, descending *seet.*

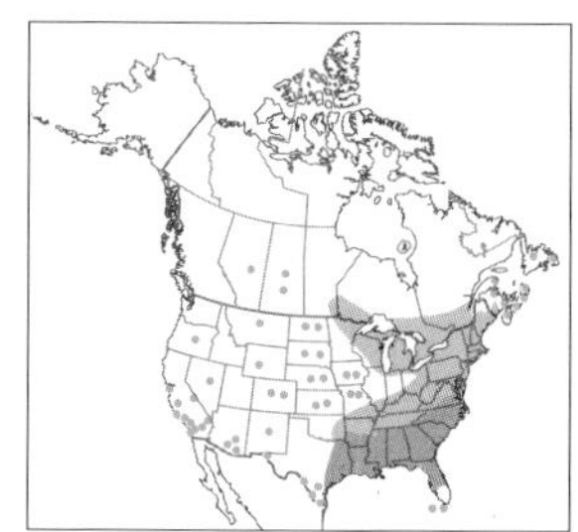

These two relatively large and long-winged species are similar in size and shape but show very distinctive plumage most of the year. Both nest in spruce woods; migrants are found in any woods.

Bay-breasted Warbler

Dendroica castanea

L 5.5" WS 9" WT 0.44 oz (12.5 g)

Large and sturdy; slightly thicker-billed and rounder-winged than Blackpoll.

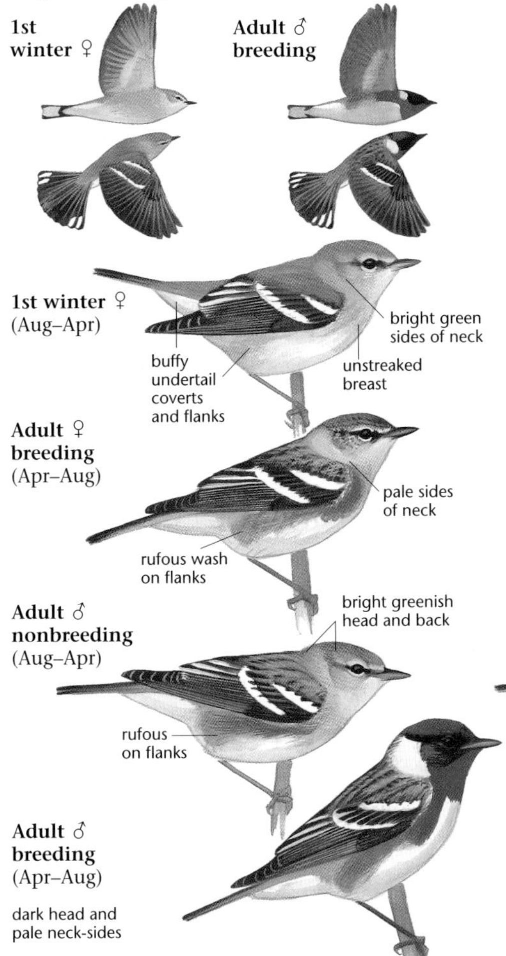
1st winter ♀
Adult ♂ breeding
1st winter ♀ (Aug–Apr)
bright green sides of neck
buffy undertail coverts and flanks
unstreaked breast
Adult ♀ breeding (Apr–Aug)
pale sides of neck
rufous wash on flanks
Adult ♂ nonbreeding (Aug–Apr)
bright greenish head and back
rufous on flanks
Adult ♂ breeding (Apr–Aug)
dark head and pale neck-sides

Voice: Song high and thin but musical like Black-and-white; usually short with poorly defined syllables all on one pitch or slightly rising overall *se-seew se-seew se-seew* or *teete teete teete tee tee tee*. Call a clear chip. Flight call a short buzz like other *Dendroica* warblers.

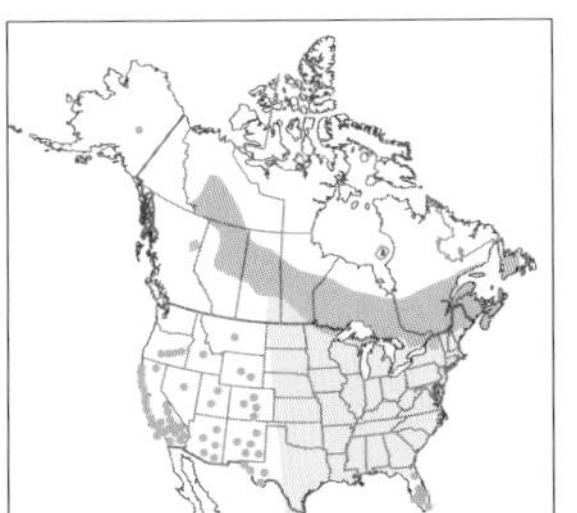

Blackpoll Warbler

Dendroica striata

L 5.5" WS 9" WT 0.46 oz (13 g)

Large and streamlined with long undertail coverts, short tail, and long, pointed wings.

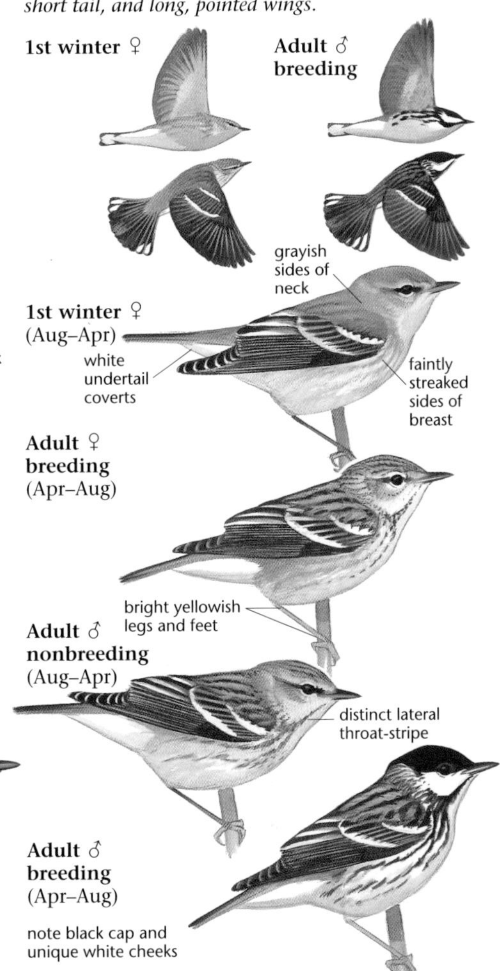
1st winter ♀
Adult ♂ breeding
grayish sides of neck
1st winter ♀ (Aug–Apr)
white undertail coverts
faintly streaked sides of breast
Adult ♀ breeding (Apr–Aug)
bright yellowish legs and feet
Adult ♂ nonbreeding (Aug–Apr)
distinct lateral throat-stripe
Adult ♂ breeding (Apr–Aug)
note black cap and unique white cheeks

Voice: Song a very high, rapid series of short notes all on one pitch, strongest in middle *sisisisisiSISISISISIsisisisisis*. Some give a very rapid, insect-like trill *tttttTTTTTTTttttt*. Call a sharp, clear chip. Flight call a high, sharp buzz *tzzz* similar to other *Dendroica* warblers.

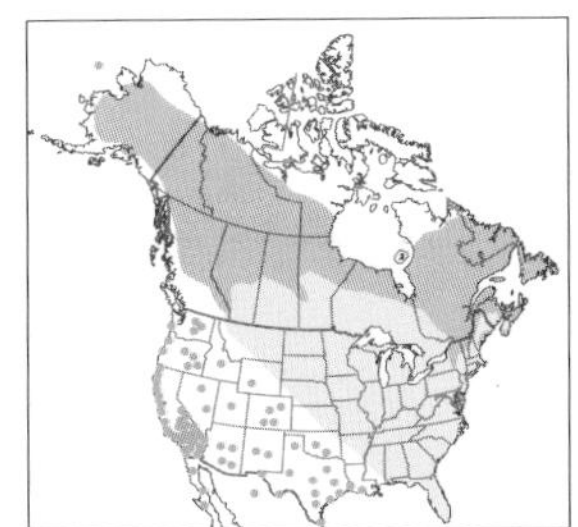

Wood-Warblers: Genus *Dendroica* (continued)

These two species both have gray upperparts, streaked flanks, and yellow throats. Yellow-throated is found in mixed pine and broadleaf woods near water, Grace's in pine trees in the mountains.

Yellow-throated Warbler

Dendroica dominica

L 5.5" WS 8" WT 0.33 oz (9.4 g)

Long with long bill and head; white neck spot distinctive.

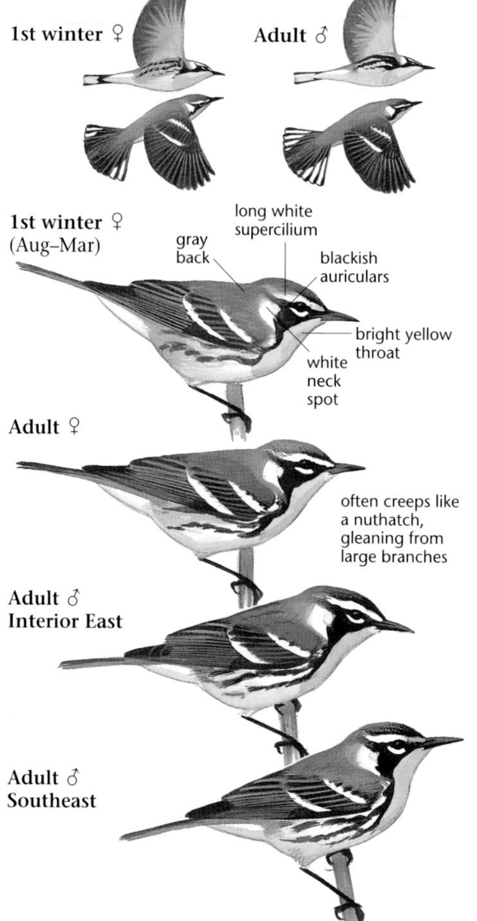
1st winter ♀
Adult ♂
1st winter ♀
(Aug–Mar)
long white supercilium
gray back
blackish auriculars
bright yellow throat
white neck spot
Adult ♀
often creeps like a nuthatch, gleaning from large branches
Adult ♂
Interior East
Adult ♂
Southeast

Voice: Song a simple and rather gentle series of sweet, clear whistles *teedl teedl teedl teedl teedl teedl teedl tew tew twee* steadily descending with a couple of rising notes at end; may suggest Louisiana Waterthrush or Yellow Warbler. Call a soft, clear, descending chip reminiscent of Eastern Phoebe. Flight call a high, clear *seet*.

Southeast populations (coastal plain from New Jersey to Alabama) of Yellow-throated average longer-billed than Interior East (Texas to New Jersey) and usually have yellow lores and chin (usually white on Interior birds). Song may differ slightly.

Grace's Warbler

Dendroica graciae

L 5" WS 8" WT 0.28 oz (8.1 g)

Small with small bill; round-headed but long-bodied. Broad yellow supraloral creates distinctive face pattern.

1st winter ♀
Adult ♂

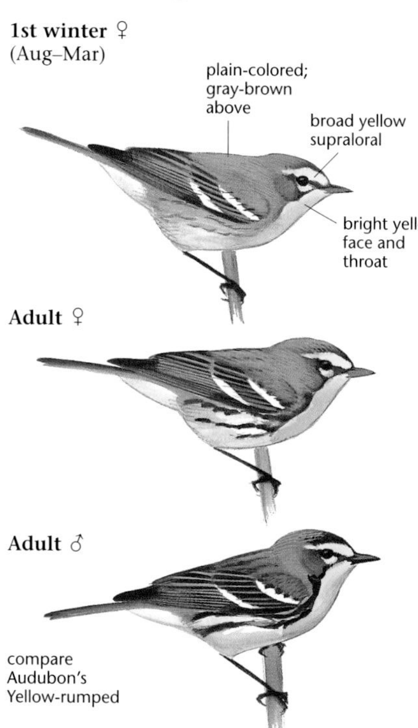
1st winter ♀
(Aug–Mar)
plain-colored; gray-brown above
broad yellow supraloral
bright yellow face and throat
Adult ♀
Adult ♂
compare Audubon's Yellow-rumped

Voice: Song a slow, choppy trill: usually higher and faster at end, two- or three-part, downslurred *tew tew tew tew tew tee tee tee tee;* resembles some variations of Audubon's Yellow-rumped and Virginia's Warblers as well as Dark-eyed Junco. Call a soft chip. Flight call a very high, thin, short *fss*.

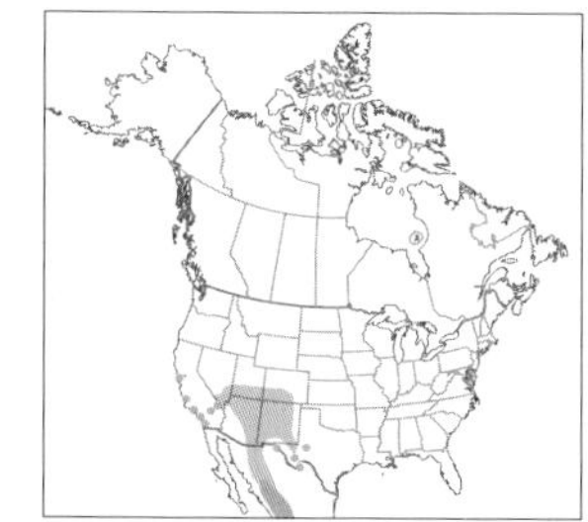

These two distinctive, relatively large species have long bills and short, broad tails. Worm-eating is found in woods in dense, low and mid-level vegetation; Prothonotary is found in wooded swamps.

Worm-eating Warbler

Helmitheros vermivora

L 5.25" WS 8.5" WT 0.46 oz (13 g)

Stocky; short, broad tail; large bill; flat head. Buffy-olive color and striped head distinctive.

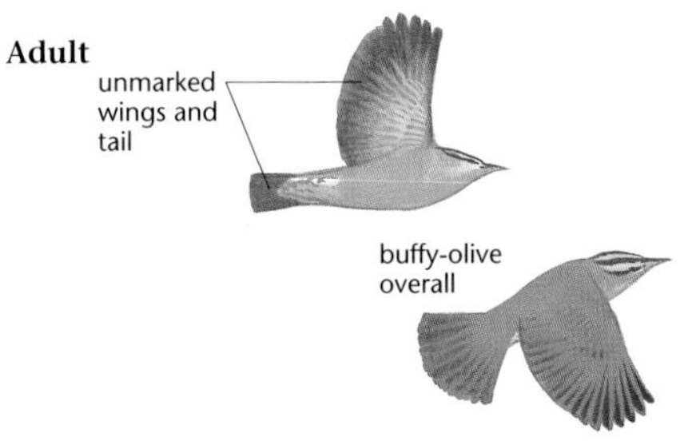
Adult
unmarked wings and tail
buffy-olive overall

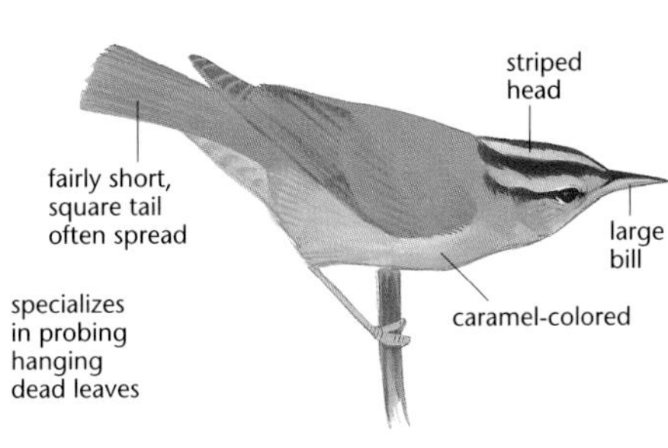
Adult
striped head
fairly short, square tail often spread
large bill
specializes in probing hanging dead leaves
caramel-colored

Adult
all plumages similar

Voice: Song a rapid, flat buzz (like Chipping Sparrow but usually faster and more insectlike); usually begins softly and builds up, often introduced by chips. Call a loud, clear chip. Flight call a very short, sharp, high buzz *dzt;* repeated rapidly in series of two or three.

Prothonotary Warbler

Protonotaria citrea

L 5.5" WS 8.75" WT 0.56 oz (16 g)

Large-headed; short-legged; short, broad tail; large bill. Brilliant golden-yellow color with white undertail.

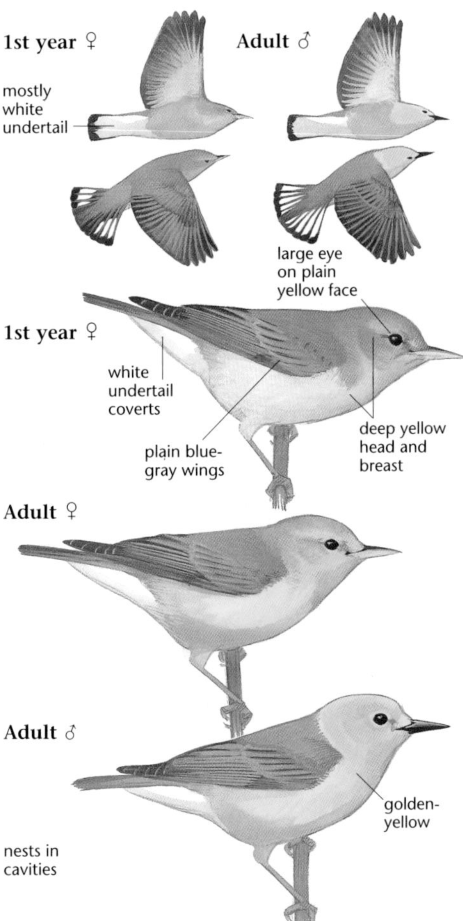
1st year ♀
Adult ♂
mostly white undertail
large eye on plain yellow face
1st year ♀
white undertail coverts
plain blue-gray wings
deep yellow head and breast
Adult ♀
Adult ♂
golden-yellow
nests in cavities

Voice: Song high, clear, and metallic with emphatic rising notes *tsweet tsweet tsweet tsweet tsweet;* little variation. Call a clear, metallic squeak *tsiip*. Flight call a loud, clear, high *swiit;* rising like American Redstart but less squeaky.

Bill and leg color of warblers are worth noting, as they often differ among species. Note that bill color changes seasonally on many species, including Prothonotary: blackish in breeding season (Mar–Jul), paler in nonbreeding (Aug–Feb).

Two of our most distinctive warblers with distinctive foraging actions, these species are related to *Dendroica* warblers. Both are found in a variety of broadleaf or mixed forest habitats.

Black-and-white Warbler

Mniotilta varia

L 5.25" WS 8.25" WT 0.37 oz (10.7 g)

Long, decurved bill and long toes; fairly short, square tail; always black and white striped.

1st winter ♀

Adult ♂ breeding

streaked back looks surprisingly bluish at times

1st winter ♀ (Aug–Mar)

white tertial-stripe connects to wing-bars

black-spotted undertail coverts

streaked black and white

striped head

pale auriculars

Adult ♂ breeding

creeps like a nuthatch

Adult ♀

black auriculars

Adult ♂ breeding (Mar–Aug)

boldly streaked overall

uneven black throat

Voice: Song a high, thin, simple series of two-syllable phrases with five to ten repetitions *weesa weesa weesa weesa weesa weesa weesa;* may be two- or three-part *weesa weesa weetee weetee weetee weetee weet weet weet.* Call a sharp, rattling *stick.* Flight call a high, hissing, rising *fsss.*

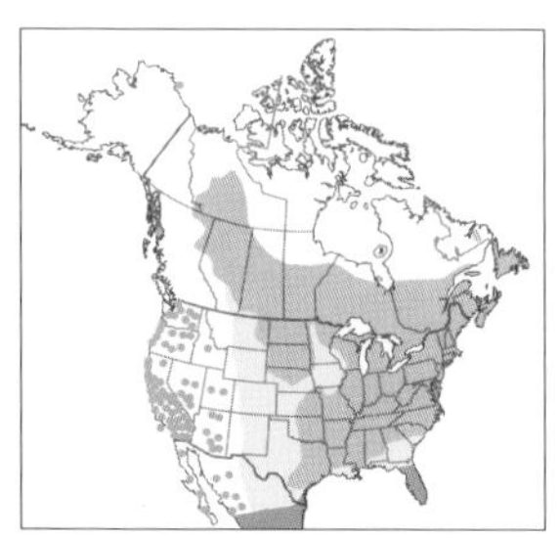

American Redstart

Setophaga ruticilla

L 5.25" WS 7.75" WT 0.29 oz (8.3 g)

Long tail; short, broad bill; rounded wings.

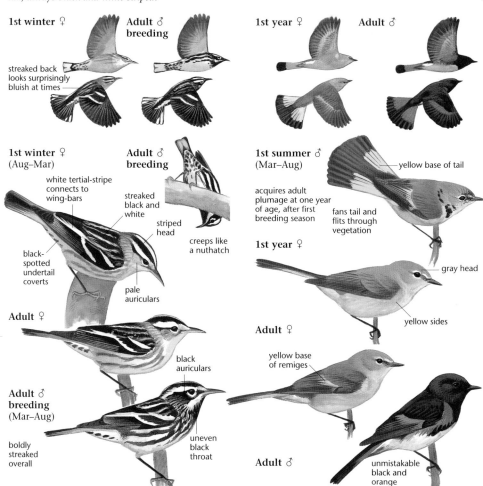

1st year ♀

Adult ♂

1st summer ♂ (Mar–Aug)

yellow base of tail

acquires adult plumage at one year of age, after first breeding season

fans tail and flits through vegetation

1st year ♀

gray head

yellow sides

Adult ♀

yellow base of remiges

Adult ♂

unmistakable black and orange

Voice: Song of high and rather sharp notes: one distinctive pattern with emphatic buzzy, down-slurred ending *tsee tsee tsee tsee tzirr;* also a softer, lower *tseeta tseeta tseeta tseet* and many variations. Call a clear, high, squeaky chip. Flight call a high, squeaky, rising *tsweet.*

American Redstart, unlike most other wood-warblers, usually alternates between two different songs during bouts of singing. Other species generally sing the same song repeatedly.

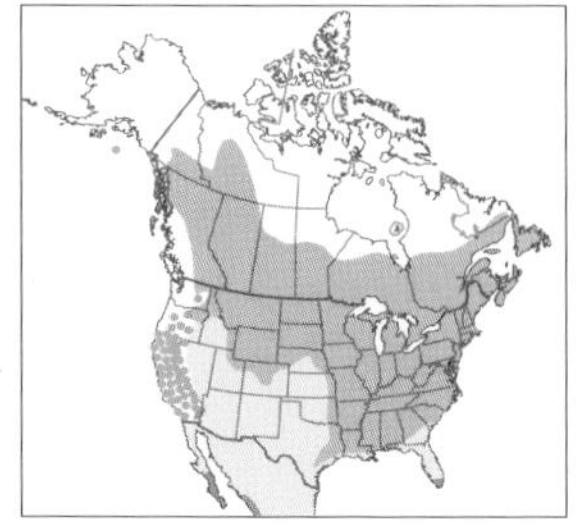

This flashing black, white, and red species is found in open pine-oak or oak woods. Very active and acrobatic, it constantly spreads and flicks its wings and tail.

Identifying Songs

Songs are a very important identification clue for wood-warblers Mar–Jul, when most species are more easily heard than seen. Most songs are distinctive and easily identified with practice. Identifying species in particular groups of similar song types can be more challenging. Compare pattern, rhythm, and pitch and listen for accented endings or other changes within the song; even so, some songs will be indistinguishable.

One of the greatest challenges is provided by the following widespread species that sing simple trilled songs (Colima and Grace's Warblers also give such songs). In every case the song is a rapid series of short notes on the same pitch or with small changes in pitch. Listening for details of the individual notes that make up the trill is the best hope of identifying these species, but hearing such details is a challenging and somewhat subjective exercise.

Orange-crowned Warbler: Trill of sharp, downslurred chips; last notes lower-pitched.

Pine Warbler: Trill of simple, upslurred, musical notes, or slower, two-syllable notes; pitch and volume unsteady.

Worm-eating Warbler: Trill of sharp, high notes; very rapid, buzzy; strongest in middle, weaker at ends.

Wilson's Warbler: Slow trill of sharp, downslurred notes with chattering quality; last notes lower and faster.

Chipping Sparrow: Usually rapid trill of sharp, mechanical notes; ends abruptly; averages longer than Dark-eyed Junco.

Swamp Sparrow: Trill of two-syllable notes, sounds like two slow trills superimposed *ts-wi-ts-wi-ts-wi . . . ;* usually slow, but some faster like Chipping Sparrow; fades slightly at end.

Dark-eyed Junco: Rather soft, musical trill of complex *tli* or *tidl* phrases; slower than most Chipping Sparrows; ends abruptly.

Another challenging group of species sings very high-pitched songs with a simple repetitive pattern: Magnolia Warbler, Cape May Warbler, Blackburnian Warbler, Bay-breasted Warbler, Blackpoll Warbler, Black-and-white Warbler, and American Redstart.

To aid in the process of identifying singing birds, try making lists of other groups of similar-sounding species in your area.

Painted Redstart

Myioborus pictus

L 5.75" WS 8.75" WT 0.28 oz (8 g)

Relatively long tail, slightly crested head, small bill. Plumage and actions unique.

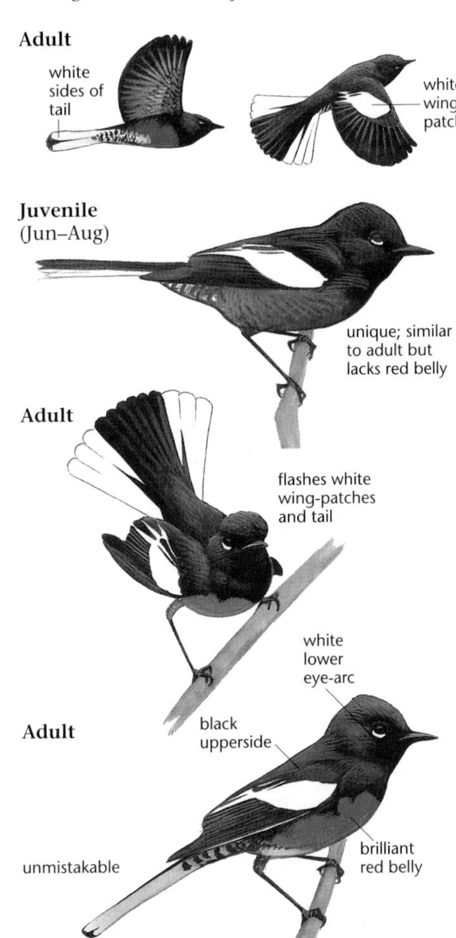
Adult
white sides of tail
white wing-patch
Juvenile (Jun–Aug)
unique; similar to adult but lacks red belly
Adult
flashes white wing-patches and tail
white lower eye-arc
Adult
black upperside
unmistakable
brilliant red belly

Voice: Song a relatively low, soft, musical warble *che-wee che-wee weeta weeta witi wi;* phrases given in pairs but in run-on tempo and with little difference between phrases. Call a loud, relatively low *chidi-ew* or *bdeeyu* reminiscent of Pine Siskin; very dissimilar to other warblers. Juvenile gives very high, thin, weak, slightly descending *tsee.*

WOOD-WARBLERS: GENERA *LIMNOTHLYPIS* AND *SEIURUS*

These species of large brownish warblers forage almost entirely on the ground within shaded, wooded areas. Swainson's is usually found in damp woods, turning over dead leaves with its bill.

Swainson's Warbler

Limnothlypis swainsonii

L 5.5" WS 9" WT 0.67 oz (19 g)

Plain brownish overall with rufous-tinged crown; massive, straight bill; short, broad tail.

Adult
plain brown
short, broad tail
long bill
Adult
all plumages similar
unstreaked
compare Carolina Wren

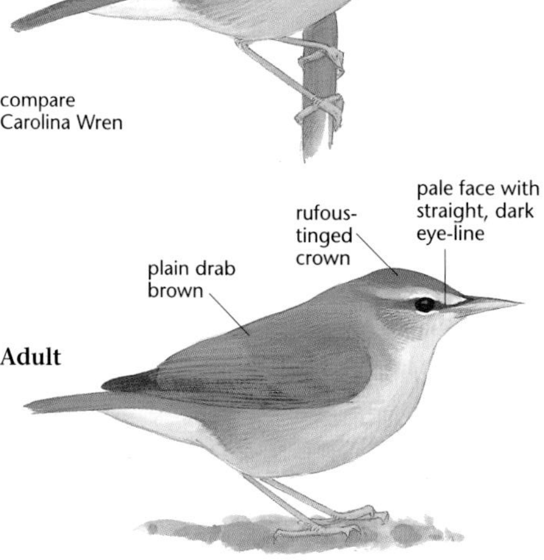
Adult
plain drab brown
rufous-tinged crown
pale face with straight, dark eye-line

Voice: Song of strong, clear, slurred notes *seew seew seee SISTerville;* downslurred notes at beginning with emphatic ending (compare Louisiana Waterthrush, Hooded Warbler). Call varies from squeaky *teep* like Hooded to strong, descending chip like Louisiana Waterthrush. Flight call a very high, thin *sees* often repeated.

Ovenbird

Seiurus aurocapillus

L 6" WS 9.5" WT 0.68 oz (19.5 g)

Large-eyed and short-tailed. Thrushlike but smaller, with different actions.

Adult

plain olive above

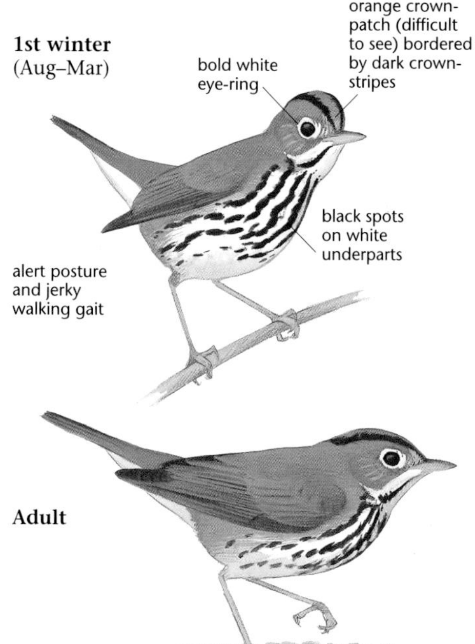
1st winter (Aug–Mar)
bold white eye-ring
orange crown-patch (difficult to see) bordered by dark crown-stripes
black spots on white underparts
alert posture and jerky walking gait
Adult

Voice: Song of explosive two-syllable phrases increasing in volume *chertee chertee cherTEE CHERTEE CHERTEE CHERTEE;* sometimes simpler *chreet chreet CHREET CHREET CHREET.* Call a rather hard and unmusical chip: varies from high, hard *chap* to low, flat *chup* or *dik* when agitated. Flight call a short, high, piercing, rising *seek.*

Ovenbird has a complex flight song that is often heard at night over wooded areas. It consists of a jumbled series of chirps and whistles with a short series of strong *teecher* phrases inserted. Most other warblers also have flight songs, given infrequently.

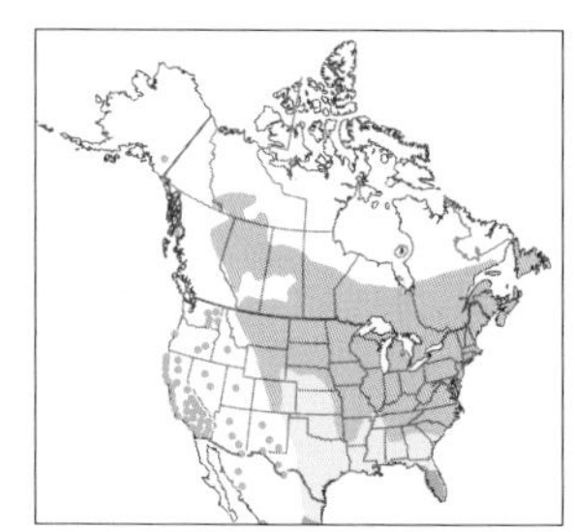

These two species of large brownish warblers are similar in all respects. Found along wooded streams and pond edges, they walk along the water's edge, bobbing their tails rhythmically.

Northern Waterthrush

Seiurus noveboracensis

L 6" WS 9.5" WT 0.63 oz (18 g)

Both waterthrushes are rather long-bodied, with narrow heads, short tails, and long legs.

Adult

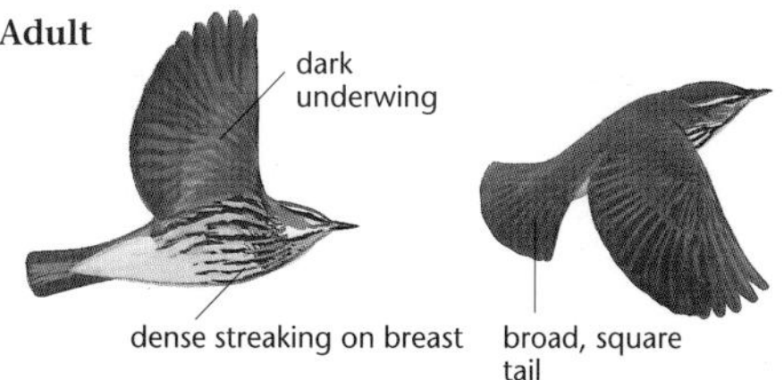
dark
underwing
dense streaking on breast
broad, square
tail

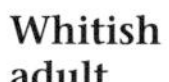

Whitish adult

Yellow adult

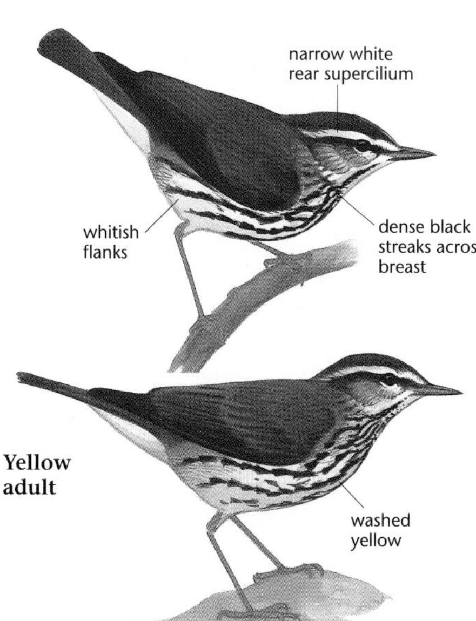
narrow white
rear supercilium
whitish
flanks
dense black
streaks across
breast
washed
yellow

Voice: Song of loud, emphatic, clear chirping notes generally falling in pitch and accelerating; loosely paired or tripled, with little variation. Call a loud, hard *spwik* rising with strong *k* sound. Flight call a buzzy, high, slightly rising *zzip*.

Louisiana Waterthrush

Seiurus motacilla

L 6" WS 10" WT 0.72 oz (20.5 g)

Bulkier than Northern, with longer bill and heavier body; broader white supercilium and sparser streaking below.

Adult

Adult

Adult

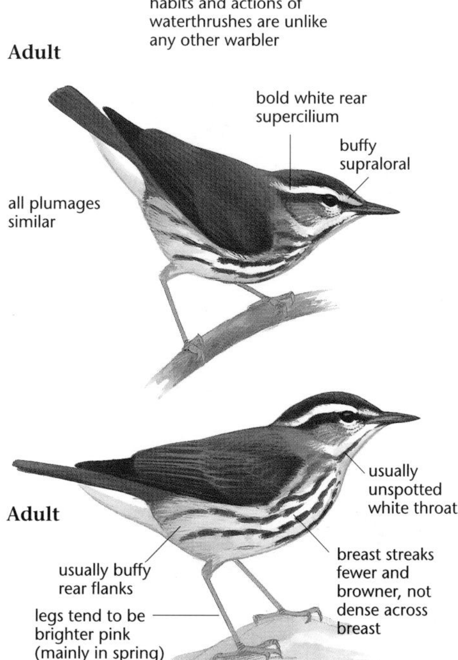
habits and actions of
waterthrushes are unlike
any other warbler
bold white rear
supercilium
buffy
supraloral
all plumages
similar
usually
unspotted
white throat
breast streaks
fewer and
browner, not
dense across
breast
usually buffy
rear flanks
legs tend to be
brighter pink
(mainly in spring)

Voice: Song musical, clear, and sweet: beginning with three or four high, clear, slurred whistles, then a series of jumbled, descending chips and chirps. Alternate song similar but much longer and rambling. Call a loud, strong *spich* not as hard as Northern. Flight call like Northern.

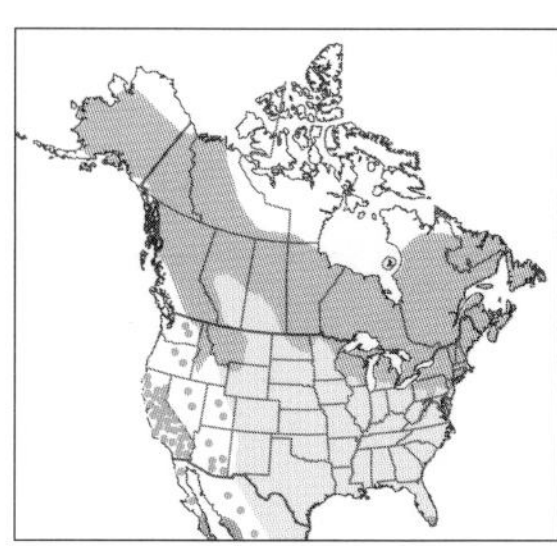

Very whitish Northern Waterthrush individuals can cause confusion because they resemble Louisiana Waterthrush; characteristics noted above are useful. More subtle clues include smaller size and smaller bill, narrower and darker eye-line, darker leg color, and different call note and habits (e.g., Louisiana bobs tail more slowly and in semicircular pattern).

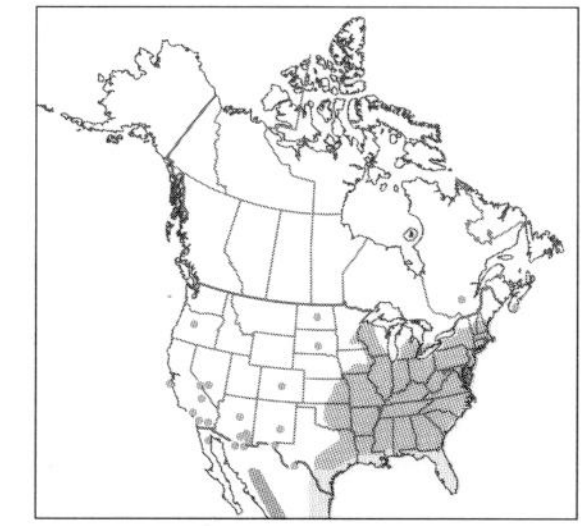

WOOD-WARBLERS: GENUS *OPORORNIS*

The genus *Oporornis* includes four species of rather heavy, secretive warblers with rich, chanting songs. All are found on or near the ground in dense, brushy vegetation.

Kentucky Warbler

Oporornis formosus

L 5.25" WS 8.5" WT 0.49 oz (14 g)

Heavy and short-tailed. Dark mask with yellow "spectacles" distinctive.

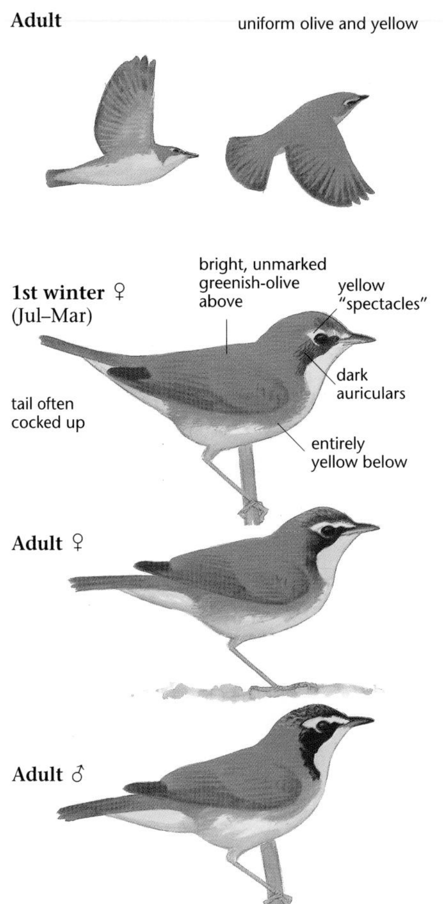

Adult
uniform olive and yellow
1st winter ♀
(Jul–Mar)
bright, unmarked greenish-olive above
yellow "spectacles"
dark auriculars
tail often cocked up
entirely yellow below
Adult ♀
Adult ♂

Voice: Song a rolling series of vaguely two-syllable phrases *prr-reet prr-reet prr-reet prr-reet prr-reet prr-reet* similar to Carolina Wren or Ovenbird; distinguished by rich quality, steady rolling tempo, and lack of clearly defined syllables. Call a low, hollow *chok* to higher, sharper *chuk* when agitated. Flight call a short, rough buzz *drrt.*

Connecticut Warbler

Oporornis agilis

L 5.75" WS 9" WT 0.53 oz (15 g)

Sturdy, sleek, and thrushlike; long-billed, short-tailed, and long-legged.

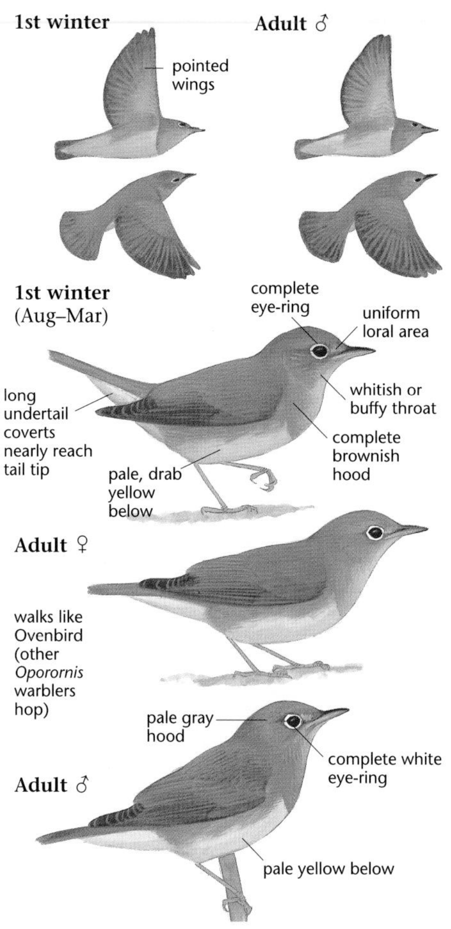

1st winter
Adult ♂
pointed wings
1st winter
(Aug–Mar)
complete eye-ring
uniform loral area
whitish or buffy throat
long undertail coverts nearly reach tail tip
complete brownish hood
pale, drab yellow below
Adult ♀
walks like Ovenbird (other Oporornis warblers hop)
pale gray hood
complete white eye-ring
Adult ♂
pale yellow below

Voice: Song a series of four-syllable phrases with strong, clear, chirping quality like Northern Waterthrush *tup-a-teepo tup-a-teepo tupateepo-tupateepo;* accelerating tempo unlike all similar species. Call rarely heard; a rather soft *pwik.* Flight call a rough buzz like many *Dendroica* warblers.

Connecticut, Mourning, and MacGillivray's Warblers are generally sought-after species wherever they occur. Eager observers can be misled by other faintly hooded species with eye-rings, especially Nashville, Orange-crowned, and Yellow Warblers and Common Yellowthroat. Note structure and habits and bill and leg color.

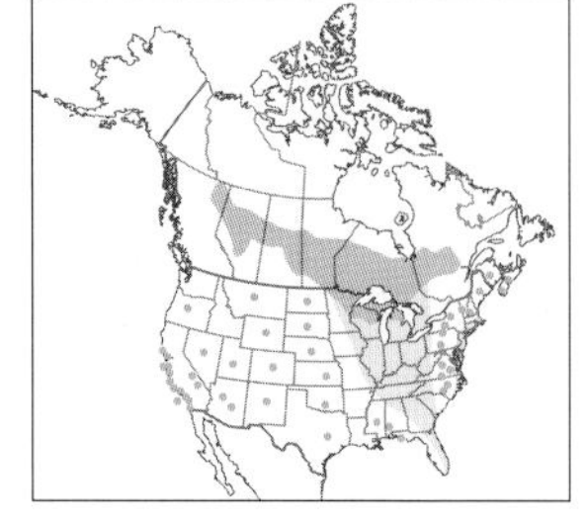

Wood-Warblers: Genus *Oporornis* (continued)

These two species, very similar to each other, are both smaller than Connecticut Warbler, with longer tails and shorter undertail coverts, less pointed wings, broken eye-rings, and different voices.

Mourning Warbler

Oporornis philadelphia

L 5.25" WS 7.5" WT 0.44 oz (12.5 g)

Sturdy, flat-headed, rather short-tailed, long-bodied; intermediate between Connecticut and MacGillivray's.

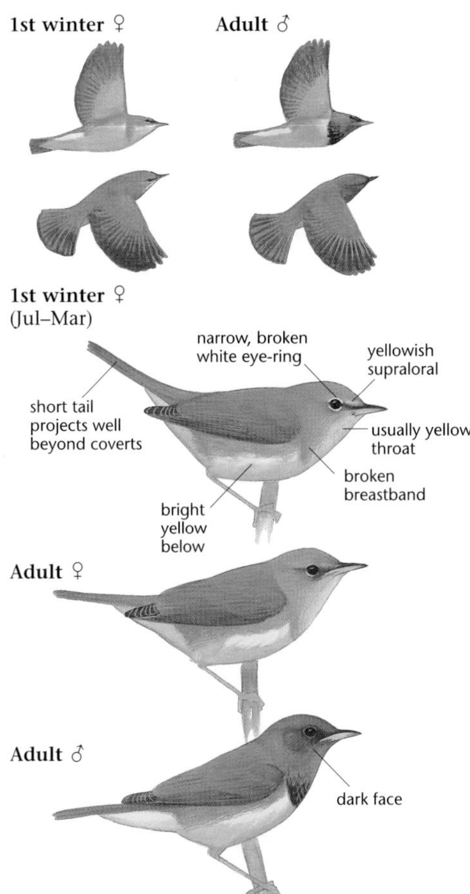

1st winter ♀
Adult ♂
1st winter ♀
(Jul–Mar)
narrow, broken white eye-ring
yellowish supraloral
short tail projects well beyond coverts
usually yellow throat
broken breastband
bright yellow below
Adult ♀
Adult ♂
dark face

Voice: Song short and rhythmic with rich, churring quality *churree churree churree turi turi;* last phrases lower, weaker, shorter. Song less variable than MacGillivray's: usually two-part in eastern birds and one-part in western. Call a dry, flat, husky *pwich.* Flight call a clear, high *svit.*

MacGillivray's Warbler

Oporornis tolmiei

L 5.25" WS 7.5" WT 0.37 oz (10.5 g)

Averages slightly longer-tailed and rounder-headed than Mourning; smaller and shorter-winged. Broad, short white eye-arcs distinctive in all plumages.

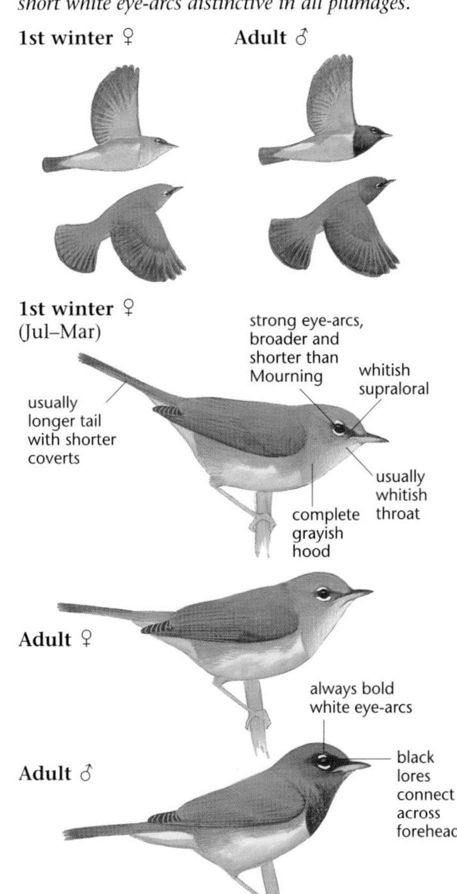

1st winter ♀
Adult ♂
1st winter ♀
(Jul–Mar)
strong eye-arcs, broader and shorter than Mourning
whitish supraloral
usually longer tail with shorter coverts
usually whitish throat
complete grayish hood
Adult ♀
always bold white eye-arcs
Adult ♂
black lores connect across forehead

Voice: Song a short, rhythmic series like Mourning but averages higher-pitched and less rich in quality, more buzzy and less rolling; final phrases usually buzzy and not lower than rest of song. Some songs can be very similar. Call a hard, dry *chik* or *twik* sharper than Mourning; similar to Common Yellowthroat. Flight call like Mourning.

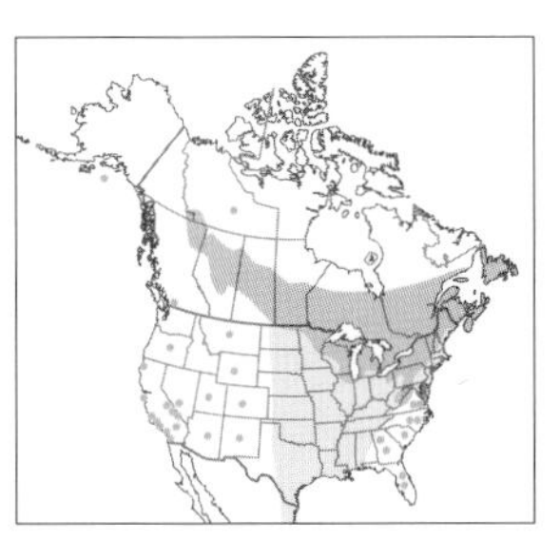

Mourning Warbler adult ♂ variant

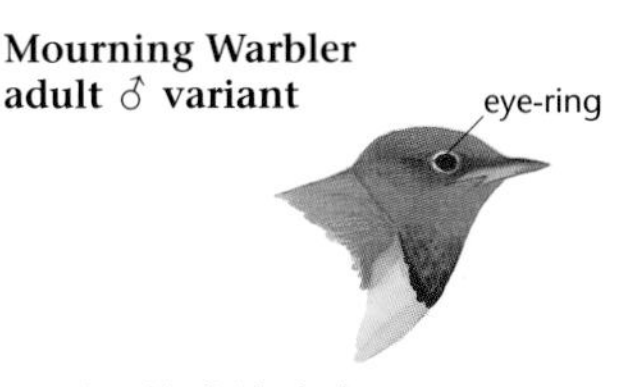

eye-ring

occasional individuals show narrow partial eye-ring, never broad eye-arcs like MacGillivray's

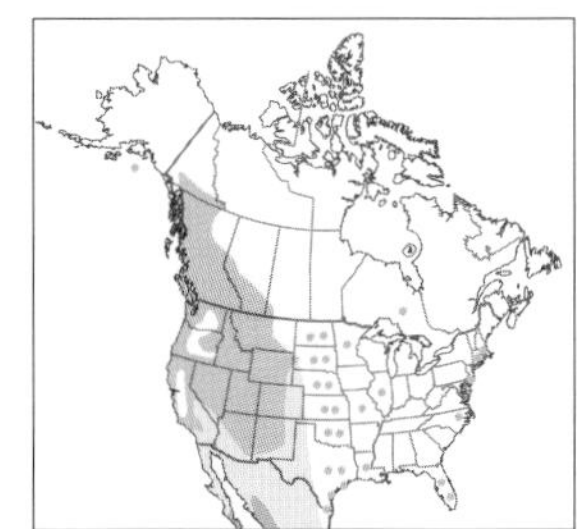

Wood-Warblers: Genus *Geothlypis*

This ubiquitous, rather secretive denizen of marshy or brushy vegetation near water is closely related to *Oporornis* warblers but is smaller and stockier and usually lacks yellow on its belly.

Common Yellowthroat

Geothlypis trichas

L 5" WS 6.75" WT 0.35 oz (10 g)

Small and dumpy; short neck, small bill, round wings, rounded tail. Always shows contrast between dark malar and pale throat.

1st year ♀

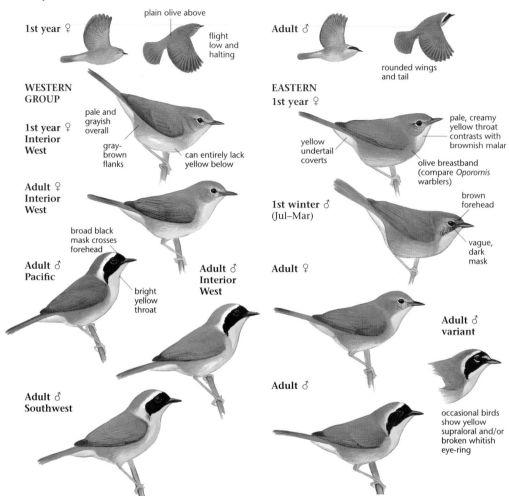

plain olive above

flight low and halting

Adult ♂

rounded wings and tail

WESTERN GROUP

1st year ♀ Interior West

pale and grayish overall

gray-brown flanks

can entirely lack yellow below

Adult ♀ Interior West

broad black mask crosses forehead

Adult ♂ Pacific

bright yellow throat

Adult ♂ Interior West

Adult ♂ Southwest

EASTERN

1st year ♀

yellow undertail coverts

pale, creamy yellow throat contrasts with brownish malar

olive breastband (compare *Oporornis* warblers)

1st winter ♂ (Jul–Mar)

brown forehead

vague, dark mask

Adult ♀

Adult ♂ variant

occasional birds show yellow supraloral and/or broken whitish eye-ring

Adult ♂

Voice: Song a gentle, musical whistle in repeated phrases of three to five syllables *wichety wichety wichety;* many variations in pattern but pitch, quality, and rhythmic pattern distinctive. Eastern population has softer, less forceful song and averages more syllables per phrase than all birds to the west (4–5 vs. 2–3 in west). Staccato rattle on one pitch often heard in breeding season (compare Sedge Wren). Call a dry *chedp;* variable from sharp *pik* to softer, longer, descending *jierrk*. Flight call a short, nasal, electric buzz *dzik*.

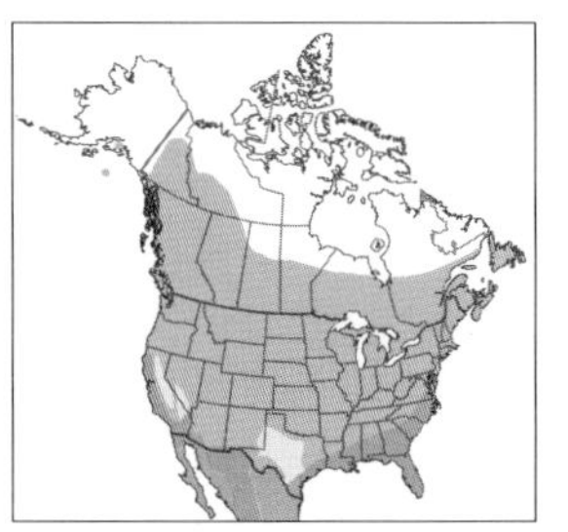

The four varieties of adult males shown differ in the following ways. Eastern: Fairly dark brownish with medium extent of yellow; grayish frontal band. Interior West: Paler and grayer with limited yellow on throat; whitish frontal band. Pacific: Small and dark brown with whitish frontal band and extensive yellow below. Southwest: Relatively large and bright olive; can be entirely yellow below; black mask may be reduced behind auriculars with yellow throat wrapping around rear auriculars; frontal band white with yellow tinge.

WOOD-WARBLERS: GENERA *GEOTHLYPIS* AND *CARDELLINA*

Gray-crowned Yellowthroat, closely related to Common, is found in grassy and weedy vegetation. Red-faced Warbler, related to *Wilsonia* warblers, is found in mountain canyons among maples and firs.

Gray-crowned Yellowthroat

Geothlypis poliocephala

L 5.5" WS 8" WT 0.51 oz (14.6 g)

Larger, relatively longer-tailed, and much thicker-billed than Common; curved culmen; more graduated tail.

Adult

1st year ♀

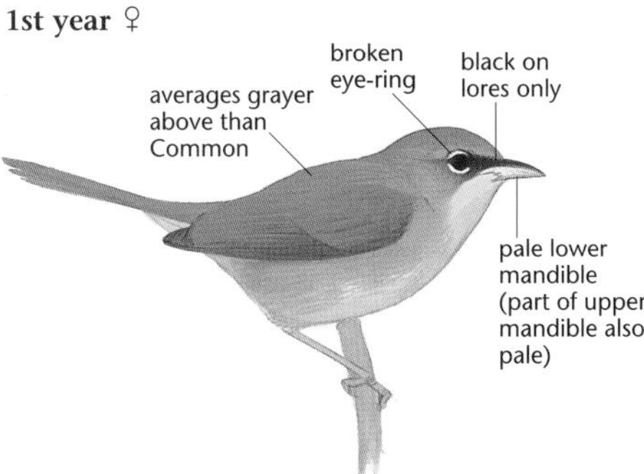
broken eye-ring
black on lores only
averages grayer above than Common
pale lower mandible (part of upper mandible also pale)

Adult ♂

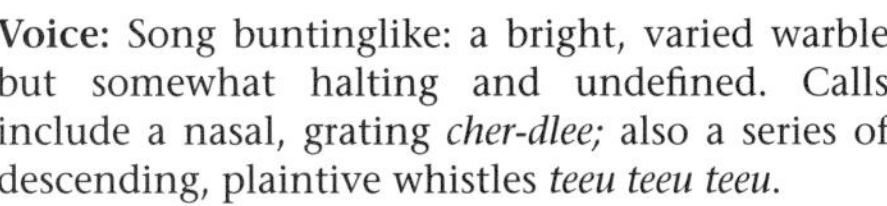

Voice: Song buntinglike: a bright, varied warble but somewhat halting and undefined. Calls include a nasal, grating *cher-dlee;* also a series of descending, plaintive whistles *teeu teeu teeu.*

Gray-crowned Yellowthroat is reported annually in southern Texas, but only two records have been confirmed since 1950. Most reports presumably refer to Common Yellowthroat; at least one well-studied individual was apparently a hybrid Gray-crowned × Common Yellowthroat. Identification should be made with extreme care.

Red-faced Warbler

Cardellina rubrifrons

L 5.5" WS 8.5" WT 0.34 oz (9.8 g)

Rather long and slender; long-tailed; short, thick bill. Shares several characteristics with Wilsonia *warblers.*

Adult

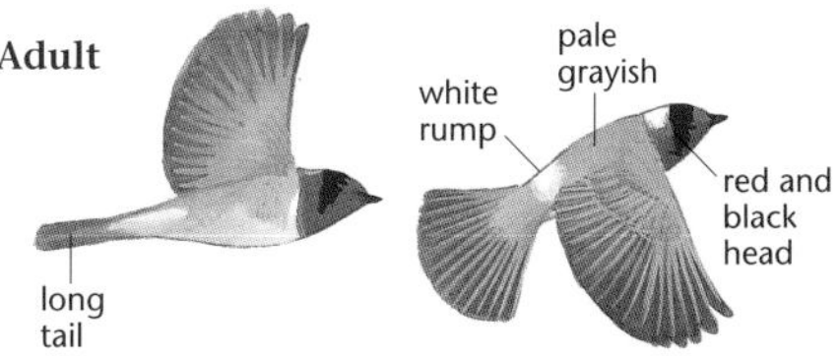
pale grayish
white rump
red and black head
long tail

1st year ♀

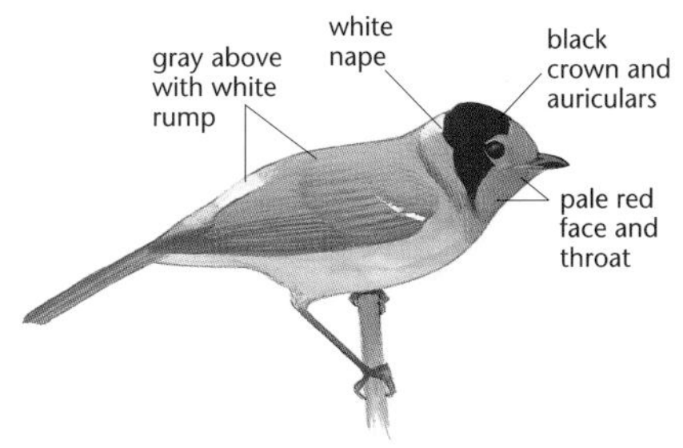
white nape
gray above with white rump
black crown and auriculars
pale red face and throat

Adult ♂

long tail freely flipped (like *Wilsonia* warblers)

Voice: Song high, thin, sweet *towee towee towee tsew tsew wetoo weeeeew* with overall descending trend. Call a sharp *tuk* like Canada. Flight call unknown.

Wood-Warblers: Genus *Wilsonia*

This very small, active species is found in dense, brushy vegetation near water, especially willow thickets. Its size, yellow plumage, and unmarked wings and tail are distinctive.

Wilson's Warbler

Wilsonia pusilla

L 4.75" WS 7" WT 0.27 oz (7.7 g)

Small and small-billed; long, thin tail; rounded wings. Large dark eye on plain yellow face; always bright yellow overall.

PACIFIC

1st year ♀

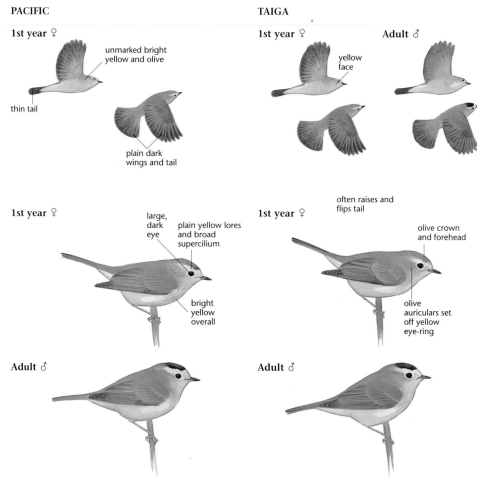

unmarked bright yellow and olive

thin tail

plain dark wings and tail

1st year ♀

large, dark eye

plain yellow lores and broad supercilium

bright yellow overall

Adult ♂

TAIGA

1st year ♀

yellow face

Adult ♂

1st year ♀

often raises and flips tail

olive crown and forehead

olive auriculars set off yellow eye-ring

Adult ♂

Voice: Song a rapid series of 10 to 15 short, whistled notes *chchchchchchchch* with sharp, chattery quality; last few notes usually lower and faster, generally downslurred, sometimes two-syllable. Trill slower than Orange-crowned, notes sharp and clear. Song of Pacific averages higher and sharper notes than Taiga. Call a husky, sharp *jimp* or *jip* like Western Winter Wren. Flight call a clear, abrupt *tilk*.

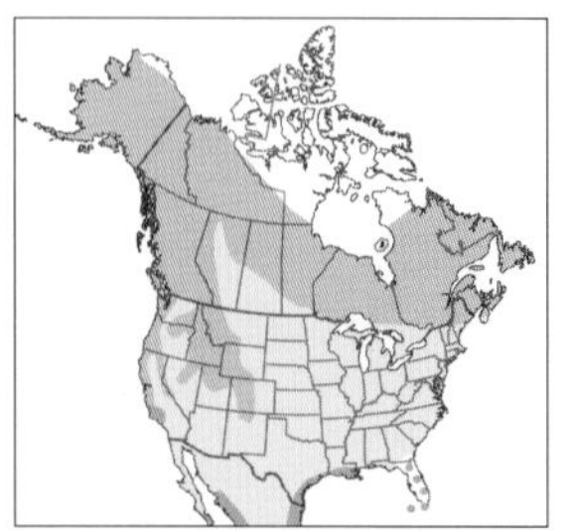

These two populations are distinctive, but the Interior West population (not shown) is intermediate in plumage, and therefore few are identifiable in the field. Pacific has brighter golden-yellow on its face and breast and always bright yellow on its forehead and auriculars. Taiga is paler lemon-yellow overall with darker olive auriculars and forehead; 1st year female can be very drab-faced.

WOOD-WARBLERS: GENUS *WILSONIA* (CONTINUED)

These two distinctive species are found low in dense, shady, leafy understory, often near water. Both are relatively long-tailed and flip their tails conspicuously when foraging.

Canada Warbler

Wilsonia canadensis

L 5.25" WS 8" WT 0.36 oz (10.3 g)

Round head; long, thin tail. Plain grayish upperside and clean, simple pattern distinctive.

1st year ♀

Adult ♂

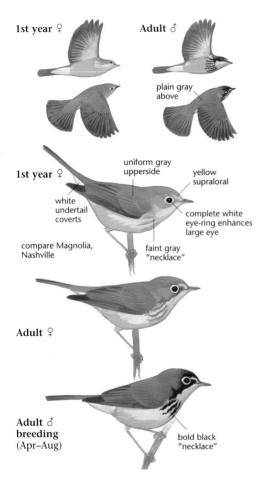

plain gray above

1st year ♀

uniform gray upperside

yellow supraloral

white undertail coverts

complete white eye-ring enhances large eye

compare Magnolia, Nashville

faint gray "necklace"

Adult ♀

Adult ♂ breeding (Apr–Aug)

bold black "necklace"

Voice: Song of high, clear, liquid notes; varied: sputtery, descending, and ending loudly; all notes different; tempo sometimes suggests Common Yellowthroat but erratic with scattered, sharp chips inserted. Call a sharp, dry, slightly squeaky *tyup*. Flight call a relatively low, liquid *plik*.

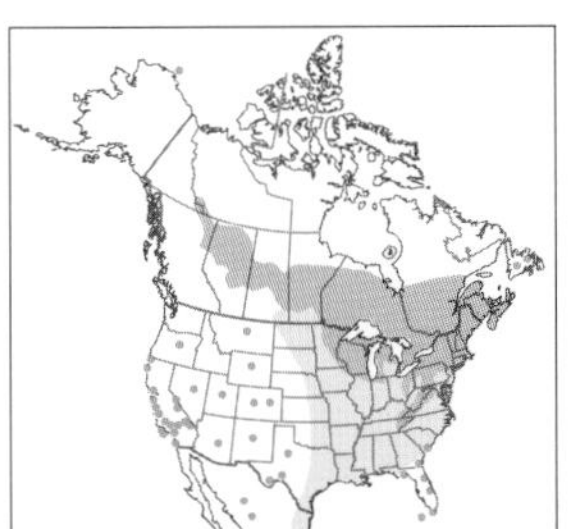

Hooded Warbler

Wilsonia citrina

L 5.25" WS 7" WT 0.37 oz (10.5 g)

Plain olive and yellow plumage with bright yellow face distinctive.

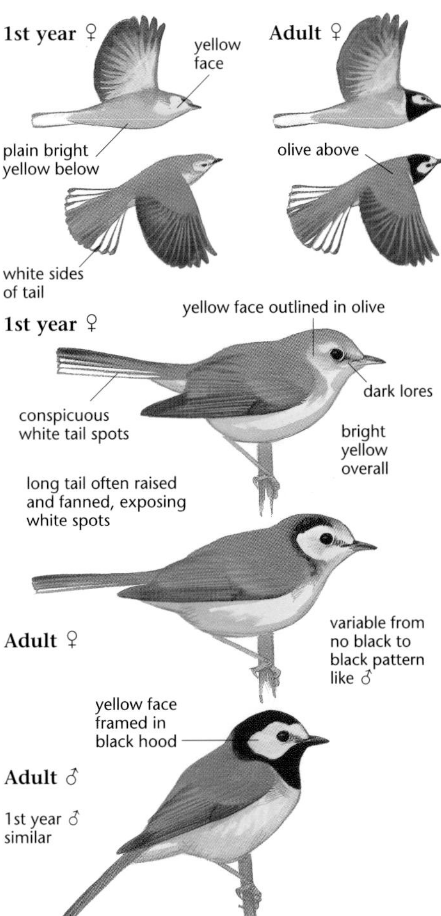
1st year ♀
yellow face
Adult ♀
plain bright yellow below
olive above
white sides of tail
yellow face outlined in olive
1st year ♀
dark lores
conspicuous white tail spots
bright yellow overall
long tail often raised and fanned, exposing white spots
Adult ♀
variable from no black to black pattern like ♂
yellow face framed in black hood
Adult ♂
1st year ♂ similar

Voice: Song loud, clear, and musical, without sharp notes: a short series of slurred notes with emphatic end *tawee tawee tawee-teeoo* or *tew tew tew teew teo twee tweee teew*. Song most like Chestnut-sided, Magnolia, and Swainson's. Call a flat, squeaky *tiip*. Flight call a clear, rising *tsiip* like American Redstart.

Wood-Warblers: Genus *Basileuterus*

Rufous-capped is found in scrubby or brushy habitats in or near oak woods; Golden-crowned is found in dense understory within woods. Both are often found near water.

Rufous-capped Warbler

Basileuterus rufifrons

L 5.25" WS 7" WT 0.39 oz (11 g)

Short, stout bill; long legs; long, rounded, slender tail with unique spindly tail feathers; rounded wings.

Adult

Drab adult

tail always raised and flicked sideways

all plumages similar

Bright adult

white supercilium

rufous crown and auriculars

plain olive above

white malar

bright yellow throat and breast

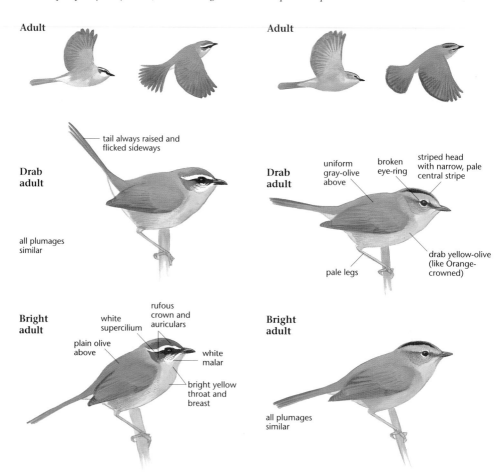

Voice: Song a rapid series of chips with jumbled tempo, often accelerating; reminiscent of Rufous-crowned Sparrow. Call a hard *chik* often in series; also a high *tsik.*

Golden-crowned Warbler

Basileuterus culicivorus

L 5" WS 7.5" WT 0.37 oz (10.5 g)

Heavy and fairly long-tailed. Plain drab plumage and striped head pattern distinctive.

Adult

Drab adult

uniform gray-olive above

broken eye-ring

striped head with narrow, pale central stripe

drab yellow-olive (like Orange-crowned)

pale legs

Bright adult

all plumages similar

Voice: Song of clear, slurred whistles reminiscent of Hooded but not quite as emphatic. Call a hard, dry *tek,* much like Ruby-crowned Kinglet but more musical; also a long, loose rattle.

Rufous-capped Warblers in the east average longer-tailed than in the west, with slightly paler colors overall and less extensive rufous on crown, but differences are subtle and overlapping.

Arguably our most distinctive wood-warbler, Yellow-breasted Chat is superficially tanagerlike in appearance, with a somewhat thrasherlike song. It is found skulking in dense but sunny brush.

Yellow-breasted Chat

Icteria virens

L 7.5" WS 9.75" WT 0.88 oz (25 g)

Larger than any other wood-warbler; thick bill; long, rounded tail; rounded wings. Plain olive upperside, white "spectacles," and intensely yellow throat distinctive.

Adult

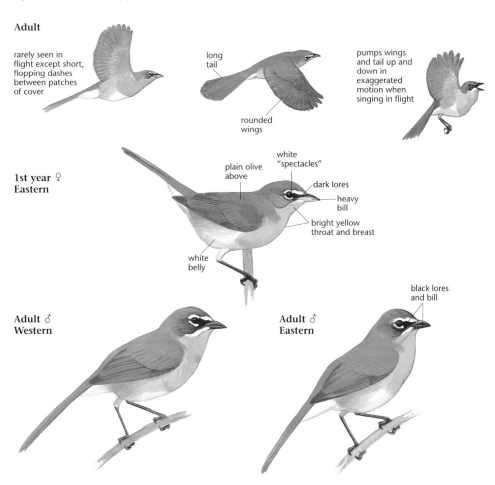

rarely seen in flight except short, flopping dashes between patches of cover

long tail

rounded wings

pumps wings and tail up and down in exaggerated motion when singing in flight

1st year ♀ Eastern

plain olive above

white "spectacles"

dark lores

heavy bill

bright yellow throat and breast

white belly

Adult ♂ Western

Adult ♂ Eastern

black lores and bill

Voice: Song extremely varied: mostly simple notes repeated in slow, decelerating series or given singly but with long pause between each utterance; distinctive low, liquid whistled or harsh, rasping quality *toop-toop-toop-toop toop toop toop; chook; terp; jedek; chrrr chrrr chrrr chrrr chrrr* . . . ; slow series and long pauses distinctive. Often includes mimicry of other species and even mechanical sounds such as woodpecker drumming. Song of Western higher-pitched with more rapid rattle than Eastern (most rapid trill 20 notes/sec vs. 10 notes/sec for Eastern). Call a harsh, nasal *cheewb;* also a low, soft, unmusical *tuk* or *ka.*

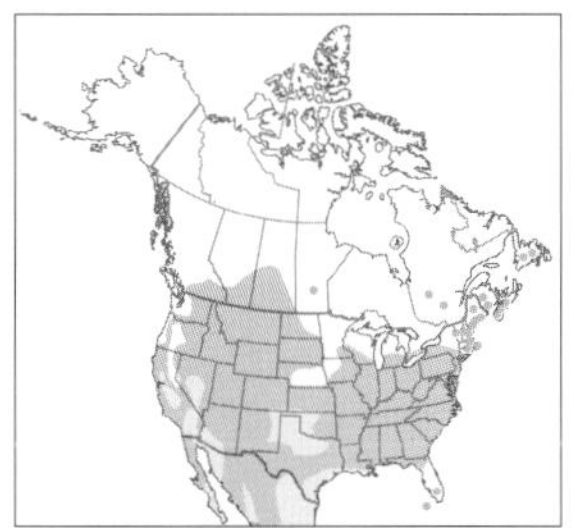

Western populations differ slightly in appearance and song, but many birds are intermediate. Western averages slightly longer-tailed than Eastern and slightly grayer above, with mostly white malar (vs. mostly yellow). Western birds also average deeper yellow-orange on the throat and breast, but some individuals of all populations acquire partly or completely orange throat (presumably diet-related as in Cedar Waxwing variant with orange-tipped tail).

Olive Warbler

This species, superficially similar to wood-warblers but different in voice, bill and tail shape, and other details, is now placed in its own family: Peucedramidae. It is found in montane conifer forests.

Olive Warbler

Peucedramus taeniatus

L 5.25" WS 9.25" WT 0.39 oz (11 g)

Relatively long, slender bill; long wings; strongly flared and notched tail.

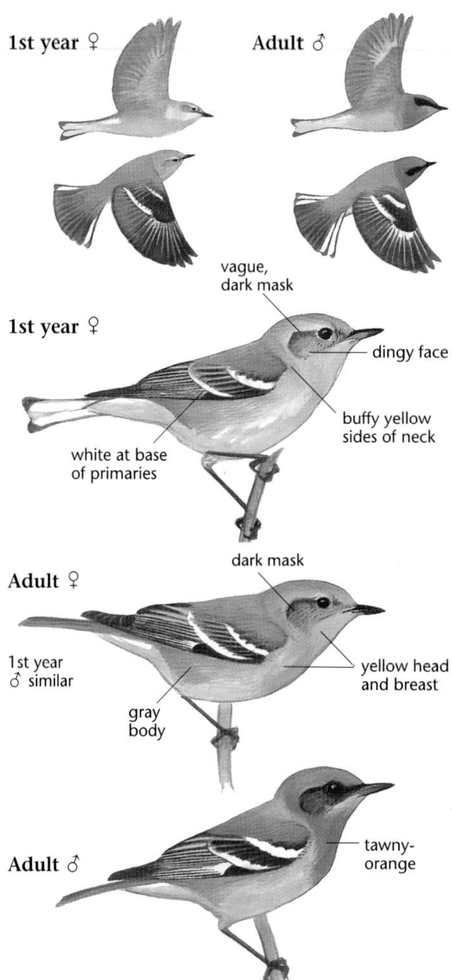

1st year ♀
Adult ♂
vague, dark mask
1st year ♀
dingy face
buffy yellow sides of neck
white at base of primaries
dark mask
Adult ♀
1st year ♂ similar
yellow head and breast
gray body
tawny-orange
Adult ♂

Voice: Song of simple, whistled, rapidly repeated phrases *hirrJI hirrJI hirrJI* or *plida plida plida plida;* often a two-part *plida plida plida chir chir;* clear, rich whistle like titmice. Call a soft, clear whistle *teew* or *tewp;* also a hard *pit.*

Aberrant Passerines

Olive Warbler has long been considered part of the wood-warbler family, although some experts have pointed out similarities to the Old World warblers. Recent DNA studies suggest that Olive Warbler is a unique species deserving its own family, an early offshoot of the entire warblers/sparrows/icterids branch. As such, its proper placement in the list is just before the wood-warblers. (The sequence of species in a linear list is somewhat arbitrary, as the actual relationships form a branching tree, and it is impossible to show that complexity on a linear list sequence.)

Recent DNA studies augment traditional morphological and behavioral evidence, and our understanding of the relationships of different bird families is constantly being refined. In the 1980s, all species of wood-warblers, tanagers, cardinalids, sparrows, and icterids were combined into a single family: the Emberizidae. In 1998, that decision was reversed, and the very large family was divided again into a number of smaller families. This decision was made with the caveat that all of these families are closely related and that certain genera show intermediate characteristics and cannot be placed easily. For example:

- —Dickcissel: Status uncertain; may be an icterid or an aberrant cardinalid.
- —White-collared Seedeater (and related tropical species): Currently placed in the family Emberizidae but also shows characteristics of cardinalids and tanagers.
- —Yellow-breasted Chat: Clearly an aberrant species; its placement within the wood-warblers is often questioned, but most evidence supports that relationship.
- —Bananaquit: Currently in its own family (Coerebidae), but how that family is related to others is unclear.

As ornithologists continue to study and debate every level of the classification of birds, we can expect to see many future changes in the structure and sequence of the official list. It is an exciting time for taxonomy, and birders are well advised to pay attention to changes in family arrangements, as these indicate fundamental similarities that can be useful in field identification. The most recent genetic research suggests that the whole Cardinalidae-Thraupidae complex should be revised, with many genera currently in Thraupidae being moved to Cardinalidae and vice versa.

Tanagers, Cardinals, and Their Allies

Families: Cardinalidae, Coerebidae, Emberizidae, Thraupidae

21 species in 11 genera; all in family Cardinalidae, except tanagers in Thraupidae, Bananaquit in Coerebidae, White-collared Seedeater in Emberizidae. Generally small and often brightly colored, these songbirds are found in brushy or wooded habitats. Bananaquit has a sharply pointed bill and feeds mainly on nectar and insects from flowering trees. Tanagers have distinctive stout, pointed bills and feed on insects and fruit in trees. Cardinals, grosbeaks, and buntings have thick, conical bills (like sparrows and finches) and feed on seeds, fruit, and insects in weedy or brushy habitats. White-collared Seedeater is no longer placed in family Cardinalidae, but it shares many features with cardinalids. All species build cup-shaped nests, except Bananaquit, which builds a globular nest. 1st winter females are shown.

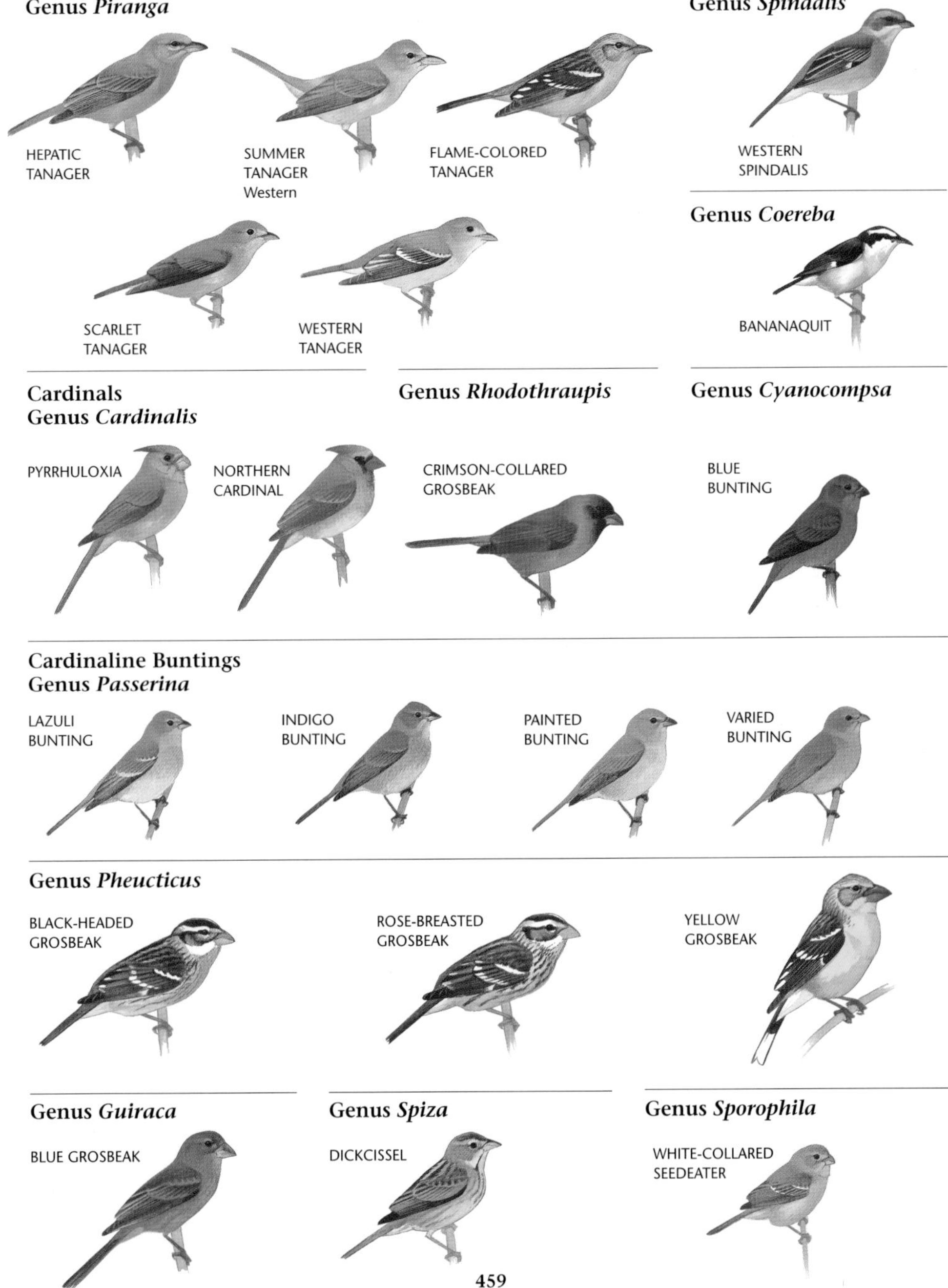
Genus *Piranga*
HEPATIC TANAGER
SUMMER TANAGER Western
FLAME-COLORED TANAGER
SCARLET TANAGER
WESTERN TANAGER
Genus *Spindalis*
WESTERN SPINDALIS
Genus *Coereba*
BANANAQUIT
Cardinals Genus *Cardinalis*
PYRRHULOXIA
NORTHERN CARDINAL
Genus *Rhodothraupis*
CRIMSON-COLLARED GROSBEAK
Genus *Cyanocompsa*
BLUE BUNTING
Cardinaline Buntings Genus *Passerina*
LAZULI BUNTING
INDIGO BUNTING
PAINTED BUNTING
VARIED BUNTING
Genus *Pheucticus*
BLACK-HEADED GROSBEAK
ROSE-BREASTED GROSBEAK
YELLOW GROSBEAK
Genus *Guiraca*
BLUE GROSBEAK
Genus *Spiza*
DICKCISSEL
Genus *Sporophila*
WHITE-COLLARED SEEDEATER

These two distinctive species are rare visitors to Florida from the Bahamas. Both are found in open or brushy woods, often at fruiting or flowering trees in suburban neighborhoods.

Bananaquit

Coereba flaveola

L 4.5" WS 7.75" WT 0.33 oz (9.5 g)

Short-tailed with decurved, pointed bill. Note plain pale underside, dark upperside.

Adult

small yellow rump

short, square tail

Juvenile (Apr–Aug)

compare Black-throated Blue Warbler ♀

Adult

broad, arched white supercilium

short, decurved bill

white at base of primaries

white throat

pale yellow belly

Voice: Song of high, hissing squeaks and buzzes that sound as if they are squeezed out with great effort *ezeereezee eyteer eyteer sizit zet;* ends with dry, insectlike crackling. Call quite warblerlike: a slightly rising, metallic *ssint.*

Western Spindalis

Spindalis zena

L 6.75" WS 9.5" WT 0.74 oz (21 g)

Our smallest tanager; relatively long-tailed and small-billed, with very distinctive plumage.

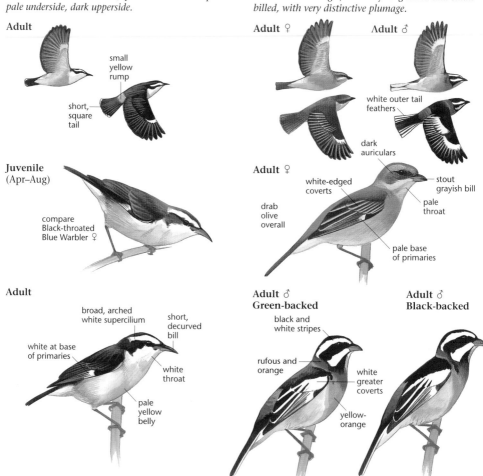

Adult ♀ **Adult ♂**

white outer tail feathers

dark auriculars

Adult ♀

white-edged coverts

stout grayish bill

pale throat

drab olive overall

pale base of primaries

Adult ♂ Green-backed **Adult ♂ Black-backed**

black and white stripes

rufous and orange

white greater coverts

yellow-orange

Voice: Song a series of high, thin notes beginning like Black-and-white Warbler but changing to buzzier phrases. Calls varied but all very high and thin: a series of descending notes *see see see see see;* a rather strong *seeee;* rapid, high twittering; very high, sharp *tit.*

Both Green-backed and Black-backed Western Spindalis males have been recorded in Florida; Green-backed individuals come from the northern Bahamas and Black-backed from the southern. There is much overlap, however, and many intermediate individuals occur. This species is one of several that were formerly known as Stripe-headed Tanager.

This species is a rare visitor to pine-oak forests in the southwestern mountains. It is distinguished from other tanagers by its wing and face pattern, streaked back, and bill size and color.

Flame-colored Tanager

Piranga bidentata

L 7.75" WS 12" WT 1.2 oz (35 g)

Averages larger than Western, with longer tail and larger bill.

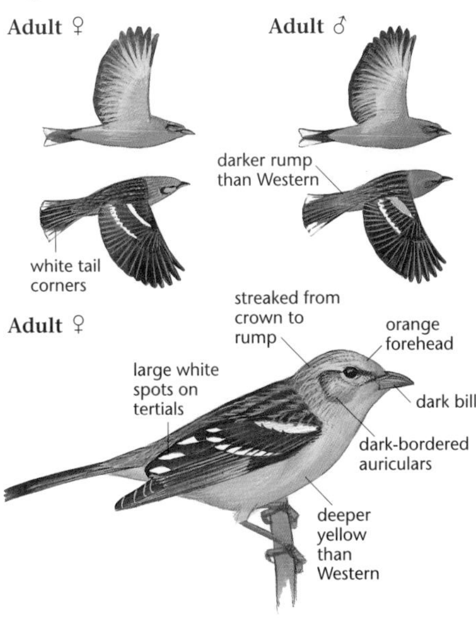
Adult ♀
Adult ♂
darker rump than Western
white tail corners
Adult ♀
streaked from crown to rump
orange forehead
large white spots on tertials
dark bill
dark-bordered auriculars
deeper yellow than Western

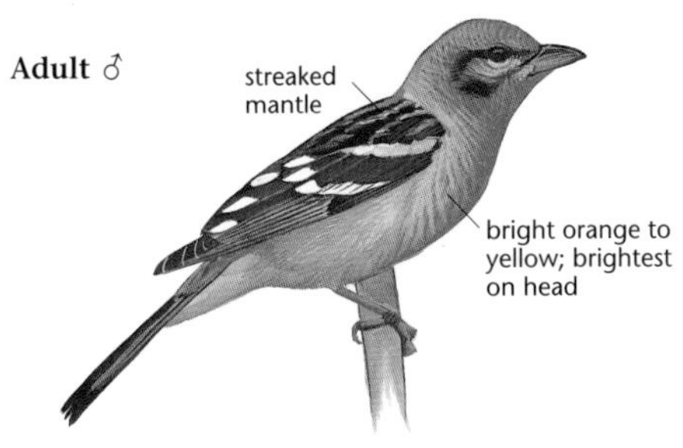
Adult ♂
streaked mantle
bright orange to yellow; brightest on head

Voice: Song similar to Western but slower, rougher, with longer pauses between phrases and little pitch change *zheer, zheeree, zhrree, zherri.* All calls apparently very similar to Western.

Identification of Tanagers

Overall plumage color of female tanagers is variable, complicating identification. Summer is most variable, from grayish to orange-red. Western varies from grayish to bright yellow. Scarlet is less variable, usually greenish-yellow, but a rare orange morph does occur. Hepatic is less well known but may vary from greenish to brighter orange-yellow.

Juvenal plumage of all tanagers is streaked dusky overall; this plumage is held very briefly and may be seen Jun–Aug.

Tanager songs all follow a basic robinlike pattern of three to five short, warbled phrases strung together with short pauses. All tanagers, however, use at least a few hoarse or burry phrases and lack the liquid, thrushlike, gurgling quality of robins. Species of tanagers are distinguished by subtle differences in rhythm and in the overall quality of the song (hoarse or clear). Western and Scarlet both sing mainly hoarse phrases delivered with almost imperceptible pauses, while Summer and especially Hepatic sing mainly clear, musical (less hoarse) phrases with distinct pauses between each phrase. Also compare *Pheucticus* grosbeaks, which sing a similar pattern but with a soft, airy quality to the phrases.

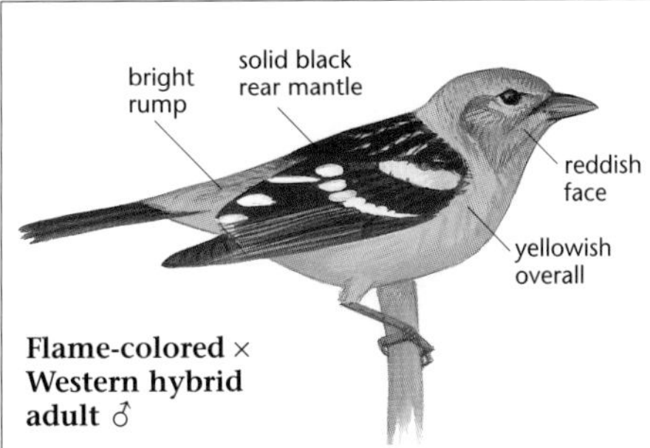
bright rump
solid black rear mantle
reddish face
yellowish overall

Flame-colored × Western hybrid adult ♂

Several of the North American records of Flame-colored Tanager involve birds paired with Western Tanager, and at least one adult hybrid has been seen. Hybrids have proven difficult to identify, however, as they closely resemble variations of pure Flame-colored. The characteristics noted above should be looked for when identifying a suspected Flame-colored or hybrid. Female hybrids might be unidentifiable in the field.

These two large tanagers have reddish or greenish flight feathers (grayish on other tanagers). Hepatic is found in mountain pine-oak forests, Summer in mixed woods, often near water.

Hepatic Tanager

Piranga flava

L 8" WS 12.5" WT 1.3 oz (38 g)

Large, with stout gray bill; dark lores and dusky auriculars distinctive.

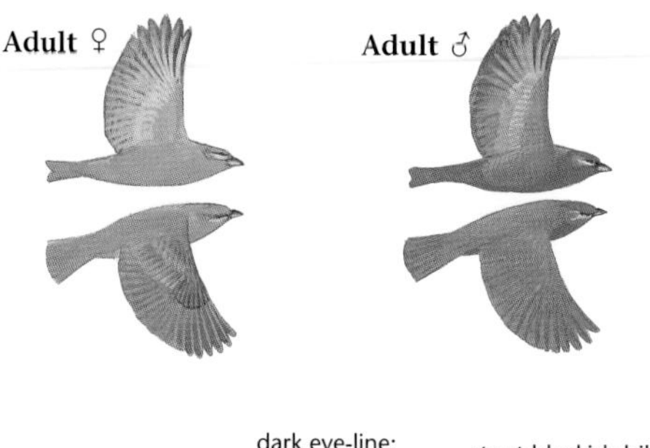
Adult ♀
Adult ♂

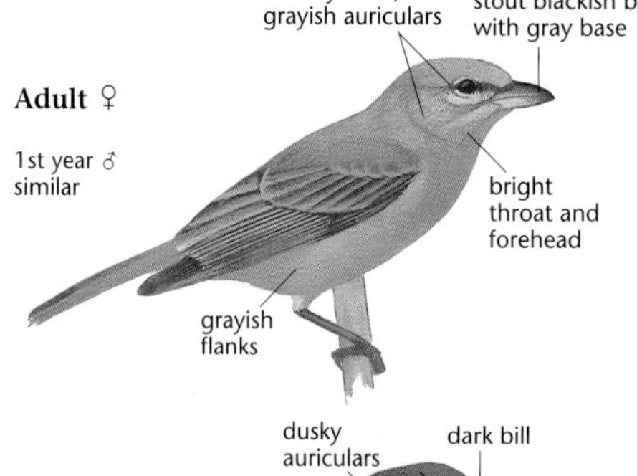
Adult ♀
1st year ♂ similar
dark eye-line; grayish auriculars
stout blackish bill with gray base
bright throat and forehead
grayish flanks

Adult ♂
dusky auriculars
dark bill
red-orange brightest on crown and throat

Voice: Song clearer than other tanagers; more like Black-headed Grosbeak; delivered slowly with distinct pauses; softer and less metallic than Black-headed Grosbeak, with a few hoarse notes. Call a low, dry *chup* like Hermit Thrush. Flight call a husky, rising *weet.*

Summer Tanager

Piranga rubra

L 7.75" WS 12" WT 1 oz (29 g)

Large, with relatively long, heavy bill; often appears crested.

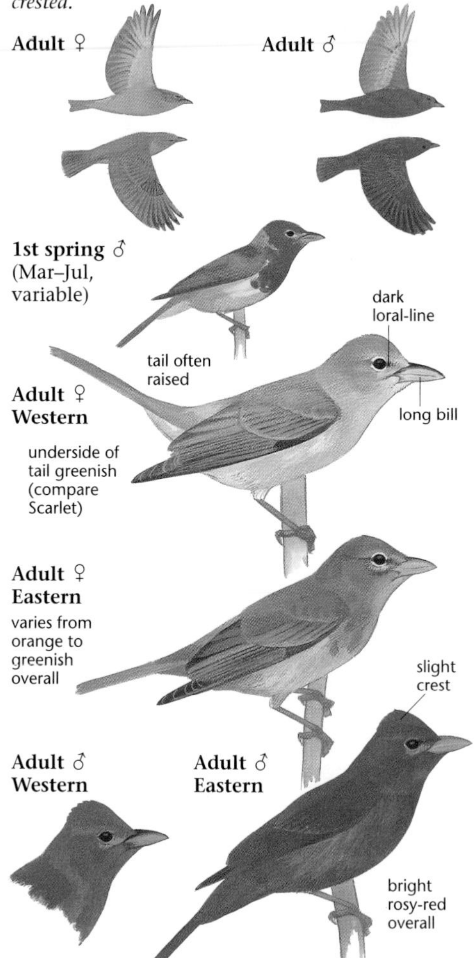
Adult ♀
Adult ♂
1st spring ♂ (Mar–Jul, variable)
dark loral-line
tail often raised
Adult ♀ Western
long bill
underside of tail greenish (compare Scarlet)
Adult ♀ Eastern
varies from orange to greenish overall
slight crest
Adult ♂ Western
Adult ♂ Eastern
bright rosy-red overall

Voice: Song of five to ten robinlike, musical, three-syllable phrases; some hoarse with brief but distinct pauses between phrases. Call a descending series of hard, unmusical notes *pituk* to *pikitukituk;* also a more rapid, descending rattle *kddddrrrddi.* Flight call a soft, wheezy *veedrr* or *verree.*

Western populations of Summer average slightly larger overall and are 15 percent longer-billed and longer-tailed than Eastern. Western are paler in all plumages, and their pale rump and nape may contrast more with their back. Females of both populations vary from greenish to orange overall; dark orange plumage may be more frequent on Eastern birds.

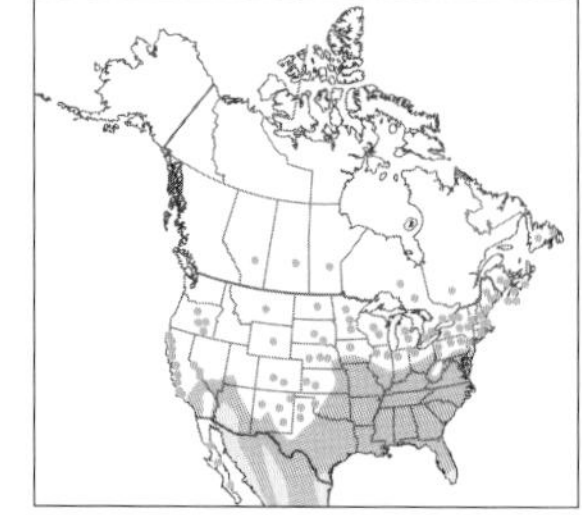

These two species of small tanagers are closely related but are usually easily distinguished by plumage and voice. Both are found in a variety of wooded habitats.

Western Tanager

Piranga ludoviciana

L 7.25" WS 11.5" WT 0.98 oz (28 g)

Small and relatively short-tailed, with small bill and long, pointed wings.

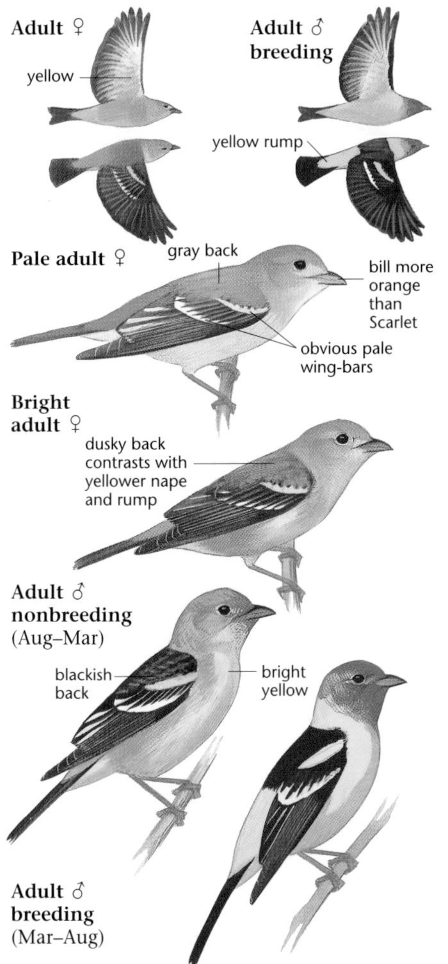

Adult ♀
yellow
Adult ♂ breeding
yellow rump
Pale adult ♀
gray back
bill more orange than Scarlet
obvious pale wing-bars
Bright adult ♀
dusky back contrasts with yellower nape and rump
Adult ♂ nonbreeding (Aug–Mar)
blackish back
bright yellow
Adult ♂ breeding (Mar–Aug)

Voice: Song similar to Scarlet. Call a quick, soft, rising rattle *prididit*. Flight call a soft whistle *howee* or *weet*.

Scarlet Tanager

Piranga olivacea

L 7" WS 11.5" WT 0.98 oz (28 g)

Slightly shorter-tailed than Western; uniform green upperside unlike Western and Summer.

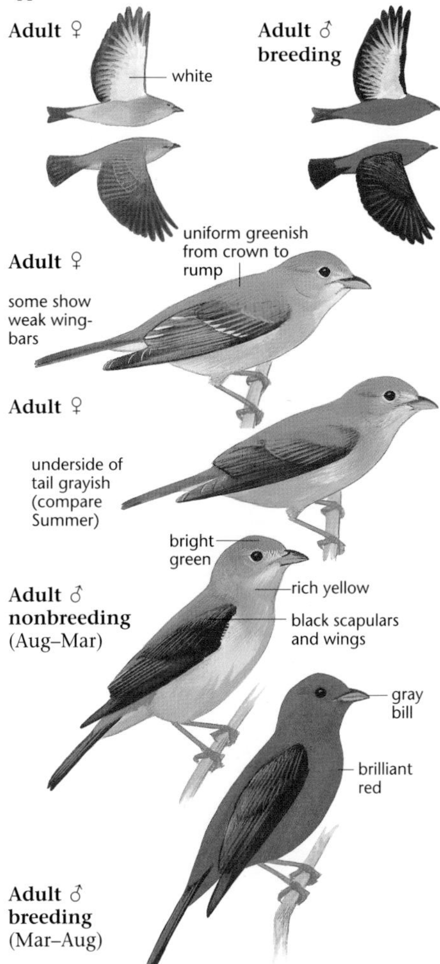

Adult ♀
white
Adult ♂ breeding
uniform greenish from crown to rump
Adult ♀
some show weak wing-bars
Adult ♀
underside of tail grayish (compare Summer)
bright green
rich yellow
Adult ♂ nonbreeding (Aug–Mar)
black scapulars and wings
gray bill
brilliant red
Adult ♂ breeding (Mar–Aug)

Voice: Song of about five phrases in fairly rapid, continuous series; pattern reminiscent of American Robin but phrases hoarse, notes more slurred. Call a hard *chik-brrr;* may give single or double *chik* note without *brr*. Flight call a clear whistle *puwi*.

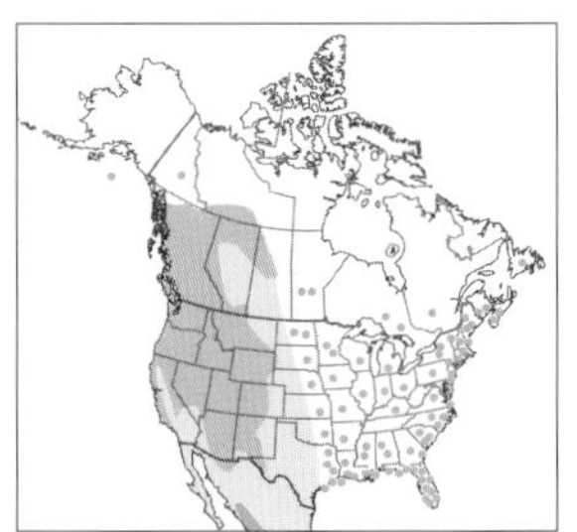

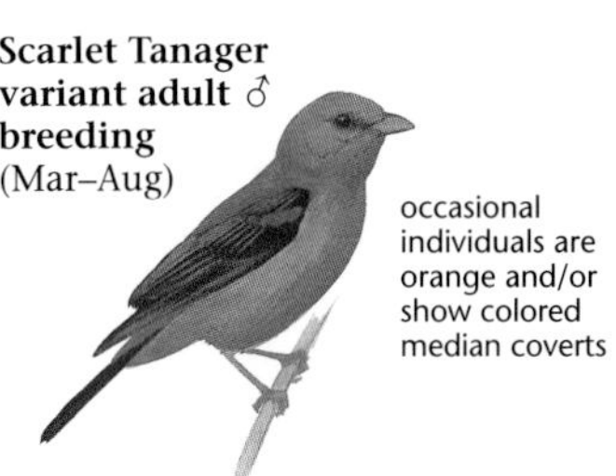

Scarlet Tanager variant adult ♂ breeding (Mar–Aug)
occasional individuals are orange and/or show colored median coverts

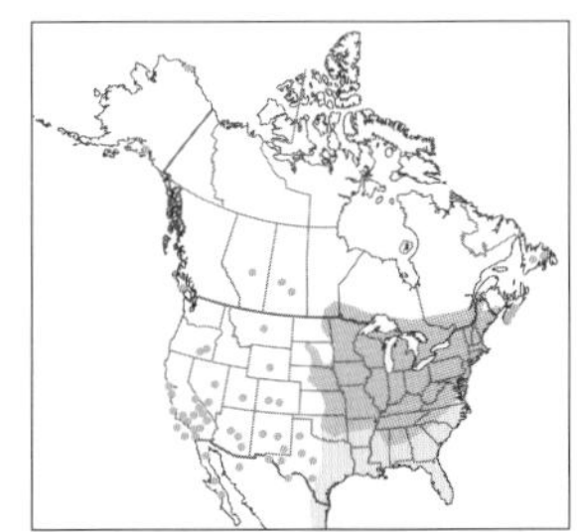

Cardinals

These crested, long-tailed, stout-billed species have similar habits and voice, but differ in color and bill shape. Both are found in brushy habitats with open areas, often in small groups.

Pyrrhuloxia

Cardinalis sinuatus

L 8.75" WS 12" WT 1.3 oz (36 g)

Unique, strongly curved, stubby bill. Slimmer overall, longer-crested, and grayer than Northern Cardinal.

Adult ♀

pink

Adult ♂

Juvenile (May–Sep)

grayish overall

rounded bill

Adult ♀

long, pointed crest

rounded gray-yellow bill

Adult ♂

clean gray

rosy-red

bill is yellow in summer, dusky in winter

Voice: Song a series of clear, sharp whistles like Northern Cardinal but slightly sharper, higher-pitched. Call notes a little longer and squeakier than Northern Cardinal: a low, flat *spik;* also *tik tikikikikikit* series lower, less musical than Northern Cardinal.

Northern Cardinal

Cardinalis cardinalis

L 8.75" WS 12" WT 1.6 oz (45 g)

Large, triangular bill always red or orange on adults.

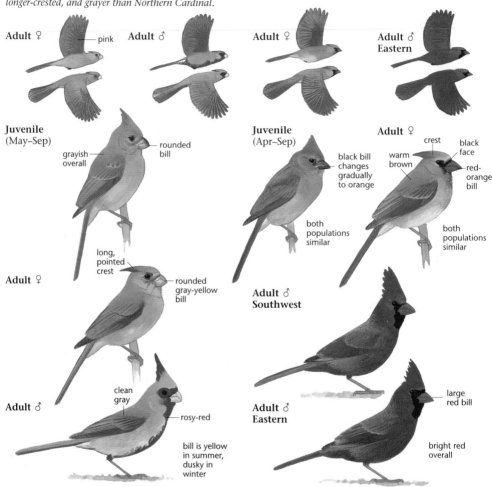

Adult ♀

Adult ♂ Eastern

Juvenile (Apr–Sep)

black bill changes gradually to orange

both populations similar

Adult ♀

crest

black face

warm brown

red-orange bill

both populations similar

Adult ♂ Southwest

Adult ♂ Eastern

large red bill

bright red overall

Voice: Song a series of high, clear, sharp, mostly slurred whistles *woit woit woit chew chew chew chew chew* or *pichew pichew tiw tiw tiw tiw tiw tiw;* many variations. Call a high, hard *tik;* also a softer, rising *twik*.

Southwest populations of Northern Cardinal (mainly Arizona) have a larger bill with slightly decurved culmen and a longer and bushier crest than Eastern. Southwest males are paler overall with less black on the face, particularly across the forehead; females are more variable and more difficult to distinguish.

RARE GROSBEAKS

The dark, often secretive Crimson-collared Grosbeak is found in dense, brushy woods. Yellow Grosbeak, a member of genus *Pheucticus,* is found in oak or riparian woods. Both are rare visitors.

Crimson-collared Grosbeak

Rhodothraupis celaeno

L 8.75" WS 13" WT unknown

Relatively long tail and short, rounded wings; thick bill with distinctly curved culmen.

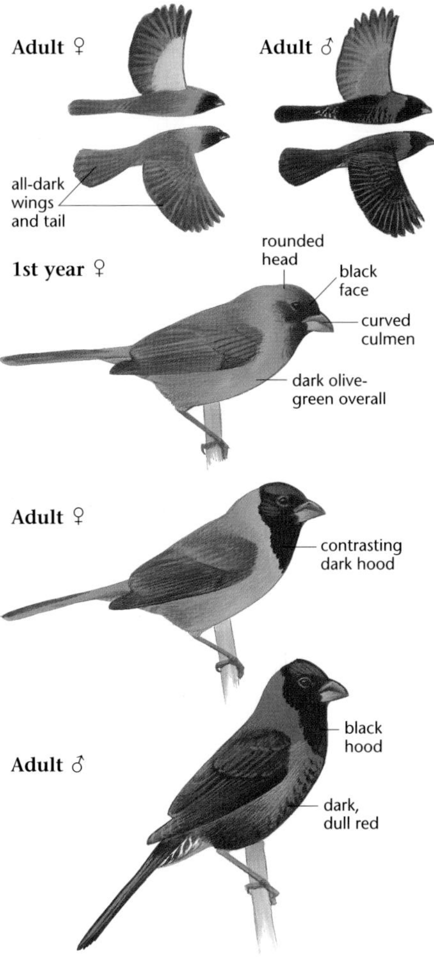

Adult ♀
Adult ♂
all-dark wings and tail
rounded head
1st year ♀
black face
curved culmen
dark olive-green overall
Adult ♀
contrasting dark hood
Adult ♂
black hood
dark, dull red

Voice: Song a varied, low, husky warble with quality like Black-headed but more varied with accelerating tempo; ending with bouncy phrases, dry rattle, and upslurred *weeee*. Call a strong, clear, piercing *pweees* or *seeeuw*.

Yellow Grosbeak

Pheucticus chrysopeplus

L 9.25" WS 14.5" WT 2.2 oz (62 g)

Much larger than other Pheucticus *grosbeaks, with massive head and bill. Yellow underparts and white-spotted wings unique.*

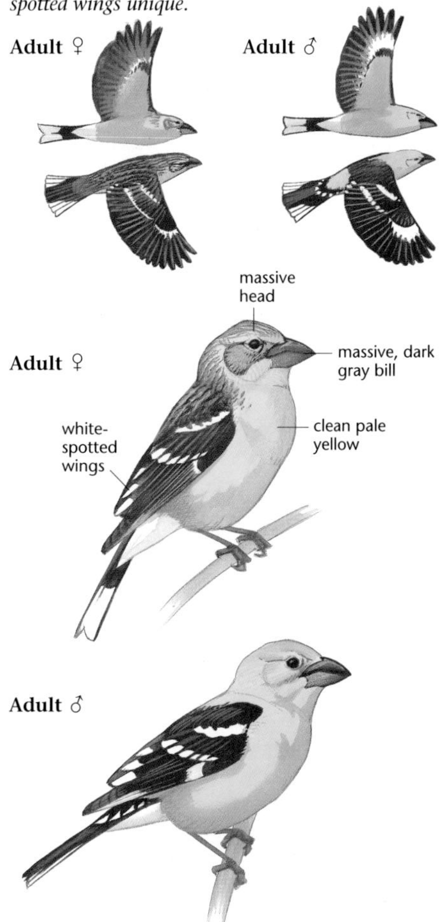

Adult ♀
Adult ♂
massive head
massive, dark gray bill
Adult ♀
white-spotted wings
clean pale yellow
Adult ♂

Voice: Song of rich, clear whistles resembling Black-headed but lower, slower, simpler, with halting rhythm: oriole-like *toodi todi toweeoo*. Call a sharp, metallic *piik* intermediate between other *Pheucticus* grosbeaks. Flight call a soft, whistled *hoee*.

There are few confirmed records of Yellow Grosbeak from Arizona, despite many reports. As always when reporting such a rare bird, take extra care in the identification and be sure to eliminate all similar species, in this case especially Western Tanager and Scott's Oriole.

GROSBEAKS: GENUS *PHEUCTICUS*

These two species, found in hardwood forests, are very closely related and similar in all respects except adult male plumage. The bold head pattern of females recalls the smaller Purple Finch.

Black-headed Grosbeak

Pheucticus melanocephalus

L 8.25" WS 12.5" WT 1.6 oz (45 g)

Stocky, with large head and very large bill; breast usually finely streaked, and underwing coverts always pale or lemon yellow.

Adult ♀

lemon-yellow

Adult ♂

1st winter ♂
(Aug–Mar)

Adult ♀ nonbreeding
(Aug–Mar)

buffy nape and supercilium

fine streaks weak or absent on center of buffy breast

Adult ♀ breeding
(Mar–Aug)

bicolored bill

breast may become whitish; fine streaks also disappear

Adult ♂ breeding
(Mar–Aug)

Voice: Song a whistled warble, faster, higher, and choppier than Rose-breasted. Call a high, sharp *pik;* more wooden and less squeaky than Rose-breasted; recalls Downy Woodpecker. Flight call like Rose-breasted. Juvenile begs with plaintive, low whistle *weeoo* with wide pitch change.

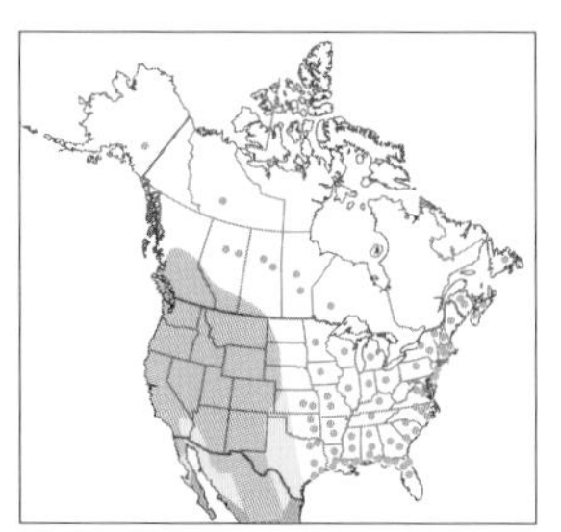

Rose-breasted Grosbeak

Pheucticus ludovicianus

L 8" WS 12.5" WT 1.6 oz (45 g)

Structure identical to Black-headed; breast often coarsely streaked, and underwing coverts buffy yellow or pink.

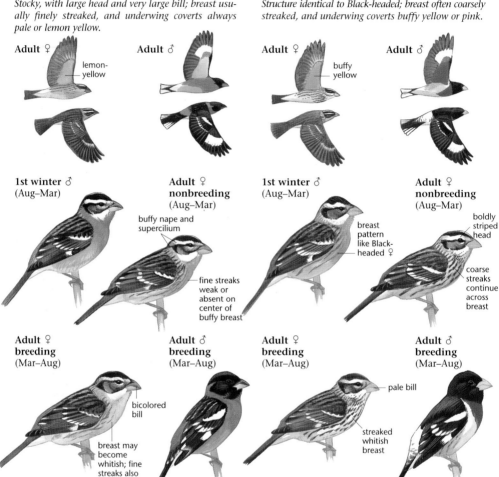

Adult ♀

buffy yellow

Adult ♂

1st winter ♂
(Aug–Mar)

breast pattern like Black-headed ♀

Adult ♀ nonbreeding
(Aug–Mar)

boldly striped head

coarse streaks continue across breast

Adult ♀ breeding
(Mar–Aug)

pale bill

streaked whitish breast

Adult ♂ breeding
(Mar–Aug)

Voice: Song a slow, whistled warble, robinlike but slightly husky in quality, without gurgling notes; pace steady, slow. Call a sharp, squeaky *iik* like sneakers on a gym floor. Flight call a soft, wheezy *wheek;* thrushlike, with airy quality (unlike husky trumpet sound of Baltimore Oriole).

Black-headed × Rose-breasted hybrid adult ♂ breeding
(Mar–Aug)

1st summer ♂ Rose-breasted can be similar

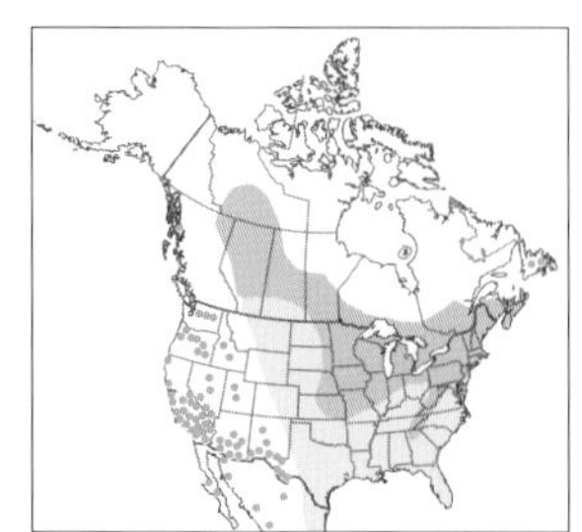

This species shares similar calls and tail-flicking habit with *Passerina* buntings, but it is larger, with a relatively heavier bill and longer tail. It is found in brushy or weedy areas with scattered trees.

Identification of Grosbeaks

The plumage sequence of Black-headed Grosbeak is illustrated below. Molts and plumages of this species follow the pattern typical of most passerines.

Juvenile ♂
(Jul–Aug)

body molt to 1st winter

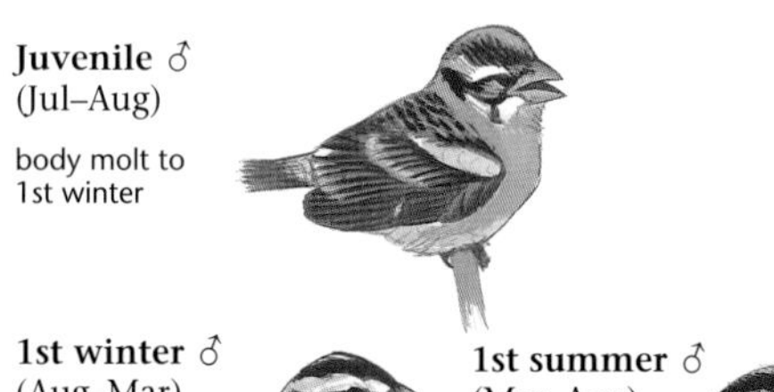

1st winter ♂
(Aug–Mar)

body molt to 1st summer

1st summer ♂
(Mar–Aug)

retains worn juvenile flight feathers, complete molt to adult nonbreeding

Adult ♂ nonbreeding
(Aug–Mar)

Adult ♂ breeding
(Mar–Aug)

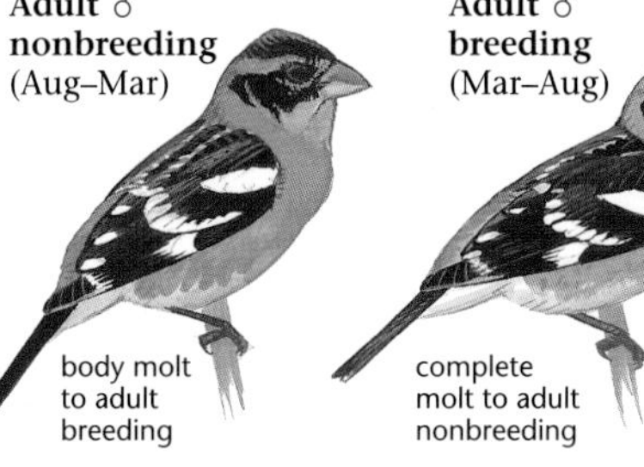

body molt to adult breeding

complete molt to adult nonbreeding

> **IDENTIFYING BLACK-HEADED AND ROSE-BREASTED GROSBEAKS**
>
> Breast color and streaking separates most female birds of these two species, but there is variation, and not all individuals are identifiable. Also beware of hybrids, which are seen regularly in the small area of range overlap but only occasionally elsewhere. Confusion is created by some worn Black-headed females (May–Aug) with whitish breasts, but these will have also lost most breast streaking through wear. A more common source of confusion is some 1st winter Rose-breasted males (Aug–Mar) with finely streaked buffy breasts like Black-headed. These birds have pink underwing coverts, however, and usually some pinkish on the breast. Also beware that 1st summer males of both species are quite variable and that Rose-breasted can be extensively buffy on underparts. Determining age and sex can be a useful step toward identification (see above).

Blue Grosbeak

Guiraca caerulea

L 6.75" WS 11" WT 0.98 oz (28 g)

Similar to Indigo Bunting in all plumages but larger; relatively large-headed, with heavy bill and long, rounded tail.

Adult ♀

Adult ♂

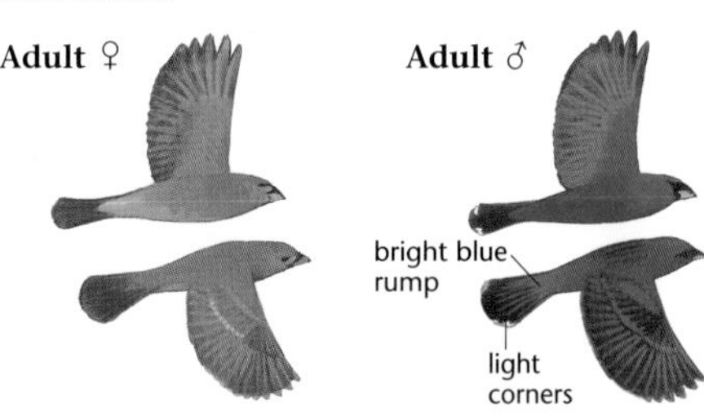
bright blue rump
light corners

1st winter
(Aug–Mar)

♀ and ♂ similar

unstreaked, warm rufous-brown overall

1st summer ♂
(Mar–Sep)

variable

Adult ♀

Adult ♂

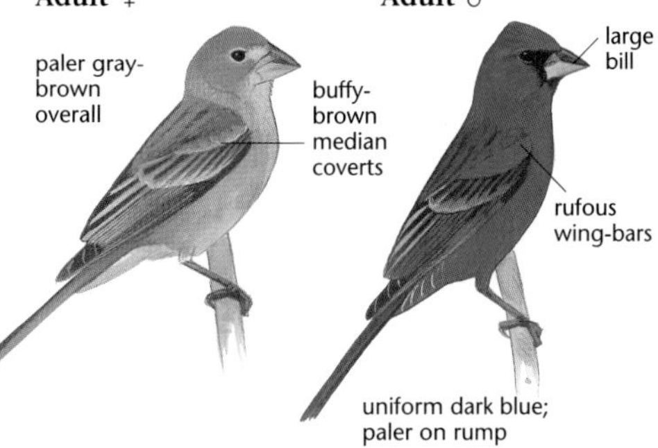
paler gray-brown overall
buffy-brown median coverts
large bill
rufous wing-bars
uniform dark blue; paler on rump

Voice: Song a rich, husky warble with distinctive unbroken tempo and mumbled quality; steady tempo recalls Warbling Vireo and Painted Bunting. Call a very metallic, hard *tink* or *chink*. Flight call a harsh buzz like buntings but stronger, rougher, lower.

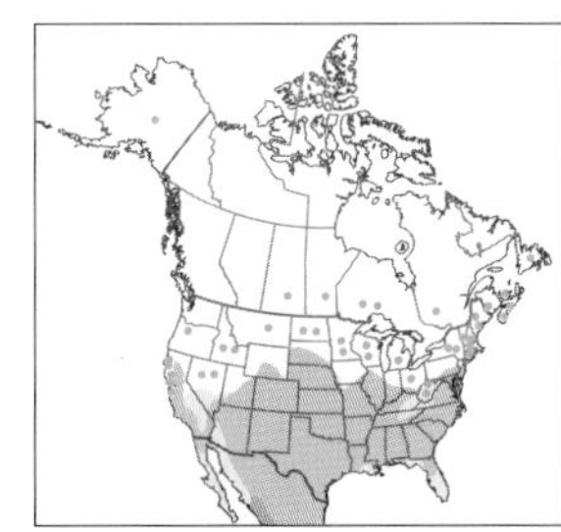

BUNTINGS: GENUS *PASSERINA*

These two species are very closely related, sharing similar habits, plumage, and voice. Both are found in grassy or weedy, open areas near brush or trees and may form small flocks when not breeding.

Lazuli Bunting

Passerina amoena

L 5.5" WS 8.75" WT 0.54 oz (15.5 g)

Structure like Indigo; female best distinguished by wing-bars, unstreaked buffy breast, and drab grayish throat.

Adult ♀

Adult ♂

Adult ♀ nonbreeding (Sep–Apr)

1st winter ♀ similar

grayish throat

buffy wing-bars

unstreaked, warm buffy

slightly paler and grayer rump

Adult ♀ breeding (Apr–Sep)

drab grayish-brown

narrow whitish wing-bars

Adult ♂ nonbreeding (Sep–Apr)

1st winter ♂ similar

Adult ♂ breeding (Apr–Sep)

Voice: Song a high, sharp warble; averages slightly longer, higher, faster, and perhaps less repetitive than Indigo. Call a dry *pik;* may average slightly higher and harder than Indigo. Flight call averages higher and clearer than Indigo.

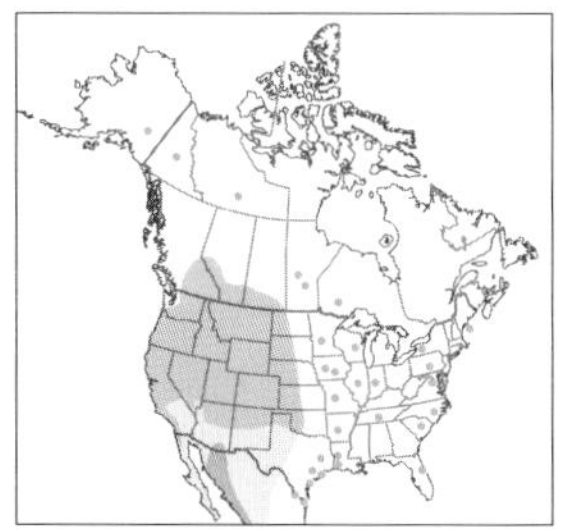

Indigo Bunting

Passerina cyanea

L 5.5" WS 8" WT 0.51 oz (14.5 g)

Rather stocky, short-tailed, and small-billed like Lazuli (compare Blue Grosbeak); female best distinguished by streaked breast and whitish throat.

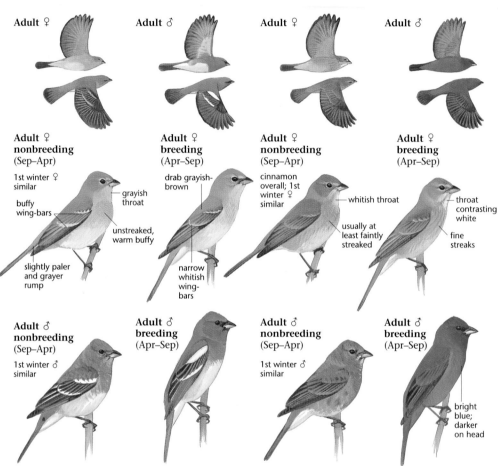

Adult ♀

Adult ♂

Adult ♀ nonbreeding (Sep–Apr)

cinnamon overall; 1st winter ♀ similar

whitish throat

usually at least faintly streaked

Adult ♀ breeding (Apr–Sep)

throat contrasting white

fine streaks

Adult ♂ nonbreeding (Sep–Apr)

1st winter ♂ similar

Adult ♂ breeding (Apr–Sep)

bright blue; darker on head

Voice: Song a high, sharp warble with most phrases repeated; quality musical and metallic *ti ti whee whee zerre zerre* ("fire fire where where here here"); similar to other buntings and American Goldfinch. Call a dry, sharp *spik*. Flight call a relatively long, shrill buzz.

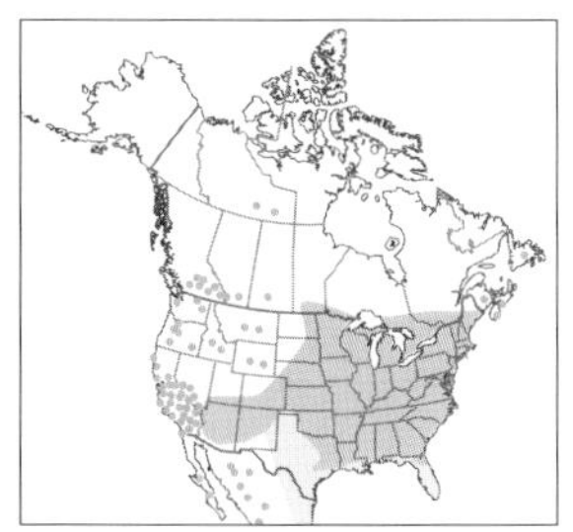

These species are very similar in habits, voice, and structure to each other and to Lazuli and Indigo. Females are slightly more distinctive in plumage but still require care in identification.

Varied Bunting

Passerina versicolor

L 5.5" WS 7.75" WT 0.42 oz (12 g)

Similar to other buntings, but culmen decurved and wings slightly more rounded (shorter primary projection); female more uniform brownish overall than Lazuli and Indigo.

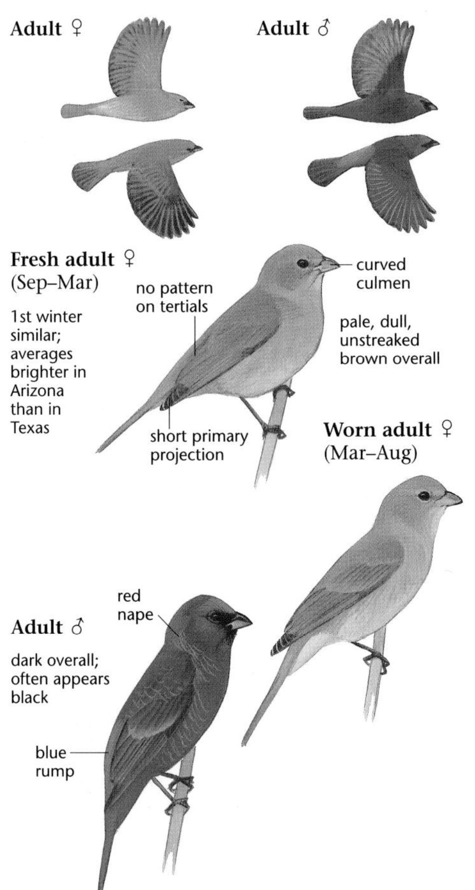
Adult ♀
Adult ♂
Fresh adult ♀
(Sep–Mar)
no pattern on tertials
curved culmen
1st winter similar; averages brighter in Arizona than in Texas
pale, dull, unstreaked brown overall
short primary projection
Worn adult ♀
(Mar–Aug)
red nape
Adult ♂
dark overall; often appears black
blue rump

Voice: Song lower-pitched and slightly harsher than other buntings, without repeated phrases; often includes hoarse, descending *veer;* rhythm intermediate between choppy (like Lazuli) and smooth (like Painted). Call a dry *spik* and flight call a long buzz, both like other buntings.

Painted Bunting

Passerina ciris

L 5.5" WS 8.75" WT 0.54 oz (15.5 g)

Structure like other buntings, but bill slightly longer with curved culmen; plain greenish plumage of female distinctive.

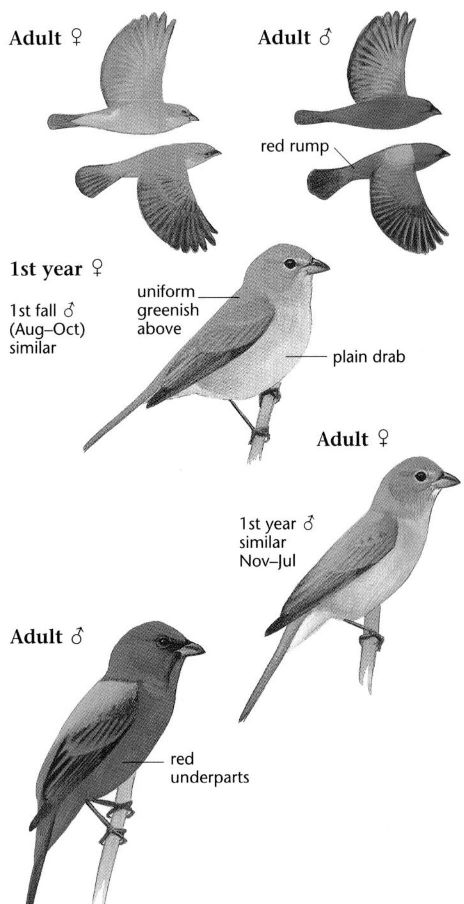
Adult ♀
Adult ♂
red rump
1st year ♀
1st fall ♂ (Aug–Oct) similar
uniform greenish above
plain drab
Adult ♀
1st year ♂ similar Nov–Jul
Adult ♂
red underparts

Voice: Song a sweet, continuous warble; quality like Indigo but with unbroken singsong rhythm like Blue Grosbeak. Call *pwich* averages lower and softer than Indigo, with rising inflection. Flight call a buzzing, slightly rising *vvvit;* not as strong or musical as other buntings.

It has been suggested that the isolated eastern and western populations of Painted Bunting represent two species, based on differences in size, molt timing, and migration routes, but individuals are not distinguishable in the field.

Blue Bunting

Although similar to buntings of the genus *Passerina,* this species differs in overall shape, voice, and habits. Found in dense, brushy woods, it is quite secretive and difficult to see.

Identification of Cardinaline Buntings

Indigo Bunting adult ♂ breeding (Apr–Sep)

twitching, sideways tail-wag characteristic of *Passerina* buntings and Blue Grosbeak

Separation of female and 1st winter male Indigo and Lazuli Buntings can be very difficult because of the variation in plumage of each species. Lazuli averages 4 percent larger overall, but size is rarely useful in the field. Overall color of Indigo is variable, from grayish-brown to cinnamon. Lazuli averages grayer overall, with a contrastingly bright buffy breast, but color overlaps. Indigo usually has at least faint streaking on the breast (vs. unstreaked on all Lazulis except juveniles); a more contrasting whitish throat and dark lateral throat-stripe (vs. duller grayish and less contrasting); uniform brown upperside from crown to rump (vs. grayish or bluish on the rump); and usually narrower, less contrasting, and cinnamon to whitish pale tips of the wing coverts (vs. broader, more distinct, and whitish). Voice also differs slightly. Despite these differences, however, some individuals (perhaps hybrids) are not identifiable.

Indigo and Lazuli Buntings hybridize frequently in broad area of range overlap, producing a variety of intermediate plumages. Male hybrids are fairly easy to recognize; female hybrids are very difficult to distinguish.

Indigo × Lazuli hybrid adult ♂ breeding (Apr–Sep)

Blue Bunting

Cyanocompsa parellina

L 5.5" WS 8.5" WT 0.53 oz (15 g)

Similar in size to Indigo but stockier, with relatively large bill; female plain reddish-brown overall.

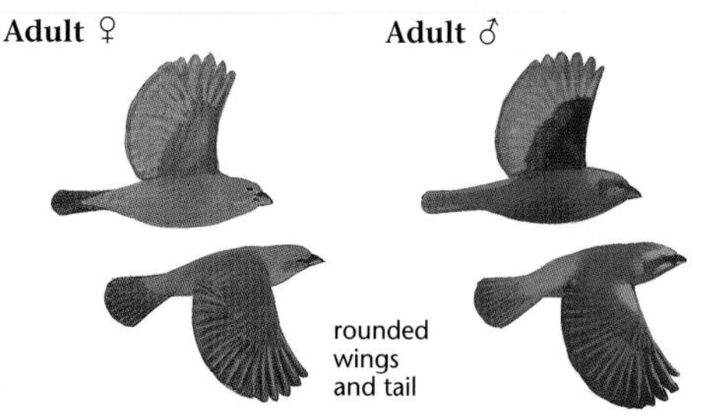
Adult ♀
Adult ♂
rounded wings and tail

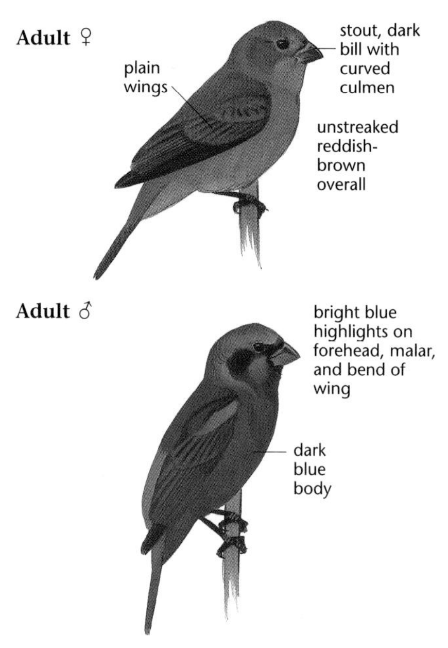
Adult ♀
plain wings
stout, dark bill with curved culmen
unstreaked reddish-brown overall
Adult ♂
bright blue highlights on forehead, malar, and bend of wing
dark blue body

Voice: Song a high, sweet, tinkling warble of clear phrases: beginning with a couple of separate notes; rhythm jumbled without pauses; fading at end. Call a clear, simple, metallic chip reminiscent of Eastern Phoebe or Hooded Warbler, unlike other buntings.

Dickcissel and White-collared Seedeater

Dickcissel is found in grassy or weedy fields or in nearby brush; vagrants are often with House Sparrows. White-collared Seedeater is found locally in dense grass near patches of tall cane.

Dickcissel

Spiza americana

L 6.25" WS 9.75" WT 0.95 oz (27 g) ♂>♀

Stocky and short-tailed like House Sparrow but sleeker, with relatively longer bill and more pointed wings. Plumage cleaner and more contrasting.

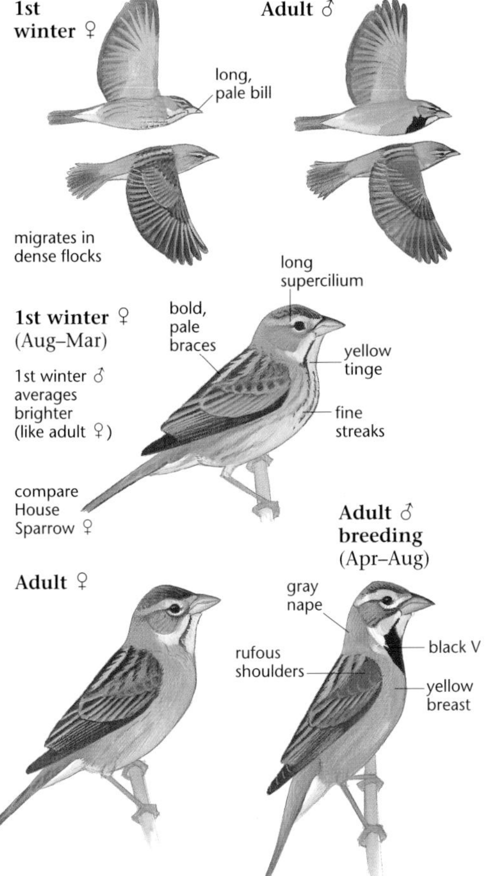

1st winter ♀
Adult ♂
long, pale bill
migrates in dense flocks
long supercilium
1st winter ♀ (Aug–Mar)
bold, pale braces
yellow tinge
fine streaks
1st winter ♂ averages brighter (like adult ♀)
compare House Sparrow ♀
Adult ♂ breeding (Apr–Aug)
Adult ♀
gray nape
rufous shoulders
black V
yellow breast

Voice: Song a series of short notes with dry, insectlike quality *skee-dlees chis chis chis* ("dick dick ciss ciss ciss"); quality reminiscent of song of Henslow's Sparrow. Call a dry, husky *chek* or *pwik.* Flight call a very distinctive, low, electric buzz *fpppt.*

White-collared Seedeater

Sporophila torqueola

L 4.5" WS 6.25" WT 0.32 oz (9 g)

Very small; short, rounded tail, rounded wings, and very stubby bill.

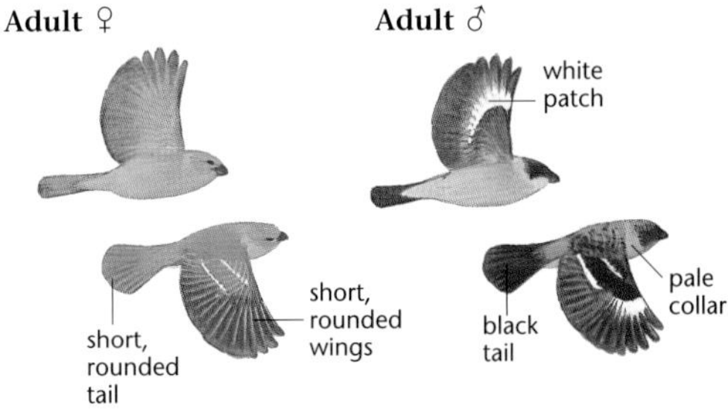

Adult ♀
Adult ♂
white patch
short, rounded wings
short, rounded tail
black tail
pale collar

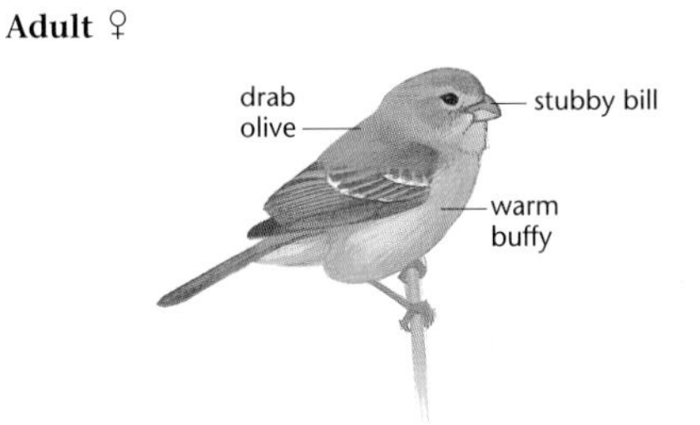

Adult ♀
drab olive
stubby bill
warm buffy

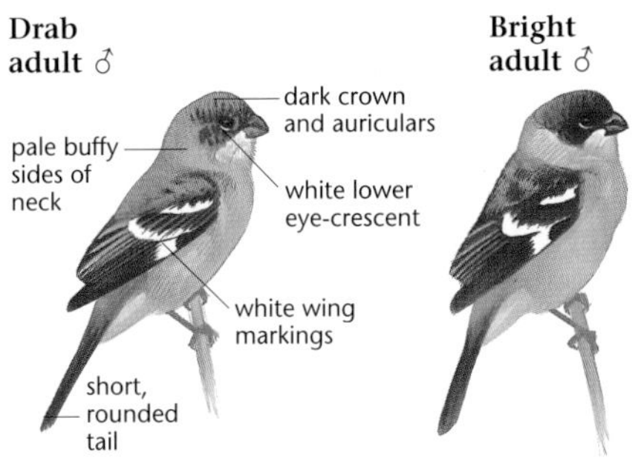

Drab adult ♂
Bright adult ♂
dark crown and auriculars
pale buffy sides of neck
white lower eye-crescent
white wing markings
short, rounded tail

Voice: Song of high, clear, sweet whistles in series *sweet sweet tew tew tew tew sit sit;* reminiscent of Yellow Warbler but simpler, thinner, with jingling quality. Common call a husky, rising *quit* or *quitl* or hard, rising *dwink* like Bewick's Wren; also a high, clear, descending whistle *cheew.*

Affinities of these two species are unclear. Dickcissel may belong in the family Icteridae or here in Cardinalidae, but it is not clearly related to either. White-collared Seedeater (now in the family Emberizidae) is superficially like goldfinches but may be most closely related to tanagers or to cardinalids.

EMBERIZINE SPARROWS AND THEIR ALLIES

Family: Emberizidae

49 species in 17 genera. These ground-dwelling, often secretive birds are generally drab brownish and mostly streaked, with short, conical bills. All feed on seeds in winter and mainly insects in summer. Many species use both feet simultaneously (a hop-scratch) to kick leaves back and uncover food. Nest is a cup in a low bush or on the ground. Some species form large mixed flocks in grassy or weedy areas in winter; other species have very specific habitat preferences and do not flock. Compare cardinalids and finches. 1st winter females are shown.

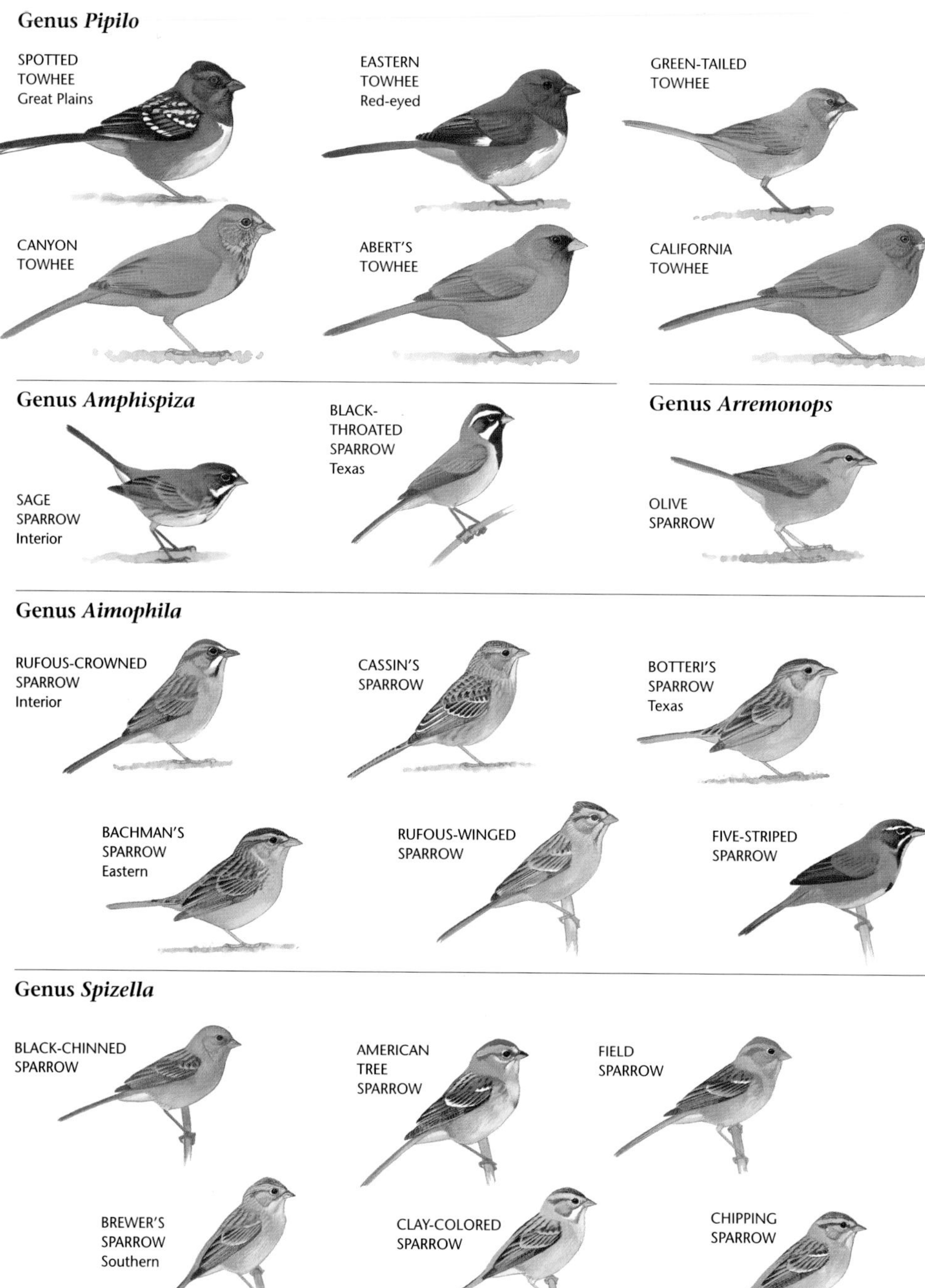

Genus *Pipilo*
SPOTTED TOWHEE Great Plains
EASTERN TOWHEE Red-eyed
GREEN-TAILED TOWHEE
CANYON TOWHEE
ABERT'S TOWHEE
CALIFORNIA TOWHEE
Genus *Amphispiza*
BLACK-THROATED SPARROW Texas
SAGE SPARROW Interior
Genus *Arremonops*
OLIVE SPARROW
Genus *Aimophila*
RUFOUS-CROWNED SPARROW Interior
CASSIN'S SPARROW
BOTTERI'S SPARROW Texas
BACHMAN'S SPARROW Eastern
RUFOUS-WINGED SPARROW
FIVE-STRIPED SPARROW
Genus *Spizella*
BLACK-CHINNED SPARROW
AMERICAN TREE SPARROW
FIELD SPARROW
BREWER'S SPARROW Southern
CLAY-COLORED SPARROW
CHIPPING SPARROW

Genus *Ammodramus*

Genus *Passerculus*

Genus *Pooecetes*

Genus *Chondestes*

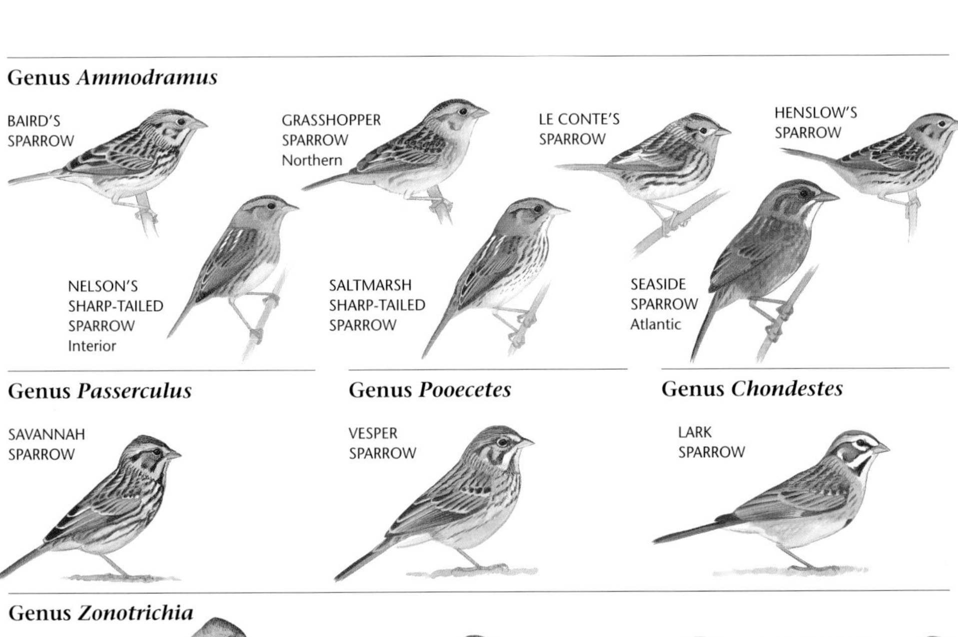
BAIRD'S SPARROW
GRASSHOPPER SPARROW Northern
LE CONTE'S SPARROW
HENSLOW'S SPARROW
NELSON'S SHARP-TAILED SPARROW Interior
SALTMARSH SHARP-TAILED SPARROW
SEASIDE SPARROW Atlantic
SAVANNAH SPARROW
VESPER SPARROW
LARK SPARROW

Genus *Zonotrichia*

HARRIS'S SPARROW
GOLDEN-CROWNED SPARROW
WHITE-THROATED SPARROW
WHITE-CROWNED SPARROW West Taiga

Genus *Junco*

Genus *Passerella*

DARK-EYED JUNCO Oregon
YELLOW-EYED JUNCO
FOX SPARROW Red (Taiga)

Genus *Melospiza*

SWAMP SPARROW
LINCOLN'S SPARROW
SONG SPARROW Eastern

Emberizine Buntings

Genus *Calamospiza*

Genus *Emberiza*

Genus *Plectrophenax*

LARK BUNTING
RUSTIC BUNTING
SNOW BUNTING
MCKAY'S BUNTING

Genus *Calcarius*

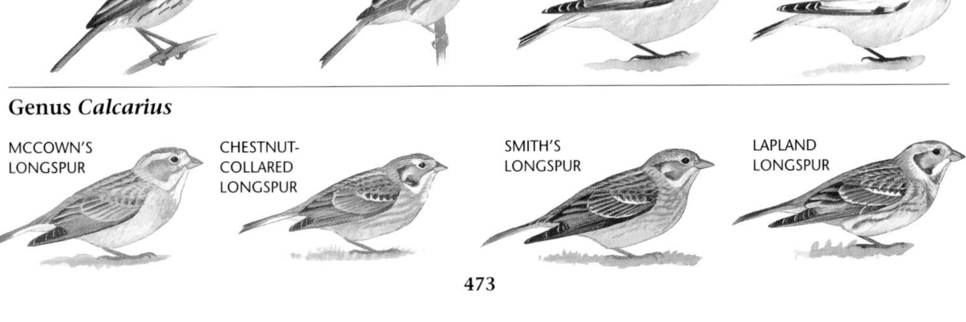
MCCOWN'S LONGSPUR
CHESTNUT-COLLARED LONGSPUR
SMITH'S LONGSPUR
LAPLAND LONGSPUR

This species is very closely related to Eastern Towhee; both are found in dense brush, where they scratch noisily through dead leaves but are often difficult to see.

Spotted Towhee

Pipilo maculatus

L 8.5" WS 10.5" WT 1.4 oz (40 g)

Stocky and long-tailed; dark head and rufous flanks always distinctive. Structure very similar to Eastern Towhee, but often looks slightly crested.

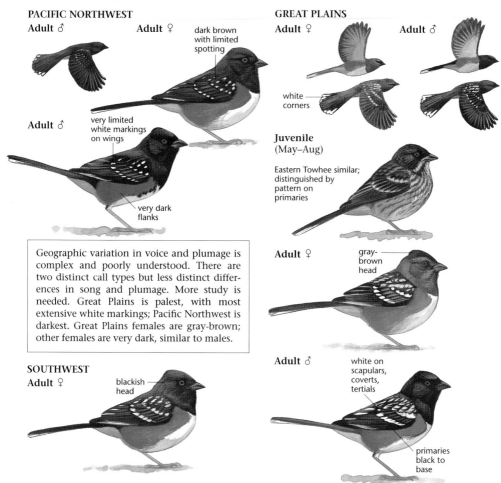

PACIFIC NORTHWEST

Adult ♂

Adult ♀

dark brown with limited spotting

Adult ♂

very limited white markings on wings

very dark flanks

GREAT PLAINS

Adult ♀

Adult ♂

white corners

Juvenile (May–Aug)

Eastern Towhee similar; distinguished by pattern on primaries

Adult ♀

gray-brown head

Adult ♂

white on scapulars, coverts, tertials

primaries black to base

Geographic variation in voice and plumage is complex and poorly understood. There are two distinct call types but less distinct differences in song and plumage. More study is needed. Great Plains is palest, with most extensive white markings; Pacific Northwest is darkest. Great Plains females are gray-brown; other females are very dark, similar to males.

SOUTHWEST

Adult ♀

blackish head

Voice: Song varies geographically; zero to eight identical introductory notes followed by a harsh or buzzy, rapid trill; buzzier and less varied than Eastern; Pacific Northwest gives a simple buzzy trill *che zheeeee* or *chzchzchzchzchz;* Great Plains one to eight quick notes followed by a buzzy trill *che che che che zheeee;* Southwest similar to Great Plains but averages fewer introductory notes followed by slower trill. Calls of two distinct types: Pacific Northwest and Great Plains give a harsh, rising, growling *zhreeee;* Southwest a harsher, descending *grreeer*. Flight call a high, thin buzz *zeeeeweee* like Eastern.

Spotted × Eastern hybrid adult ♂

Hybrids occur regularly in limited area of range overlap. Note that it is also possible for apparently pure Eastern birds to show white spots on scapulars and for Spotted to show limited white at base of primaries.

Eastern Towhee is very closely related to Spotted; until recently they were considered one species, Rufous-sided Towhee. Green-tailed, distinctive but definitely towheelike, is found in dense brush.

Eastern Towhee

Pipilo erythrophthalmus

L 8.5" WS 10.5" WT 1.4 oz (40 g)

The only towhee over most of its range; larger and stockier than sparrows, with long tail.

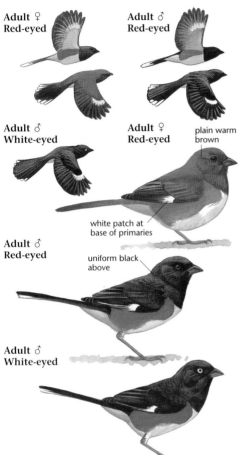

Adult ♀ Red-eyed

Adult ♂ Red-eyed

Adult ♂ White-eyed

Adult ♀ Red-eyed

plain warm brown

white patch at base of primaries

Adult ♂ Red-eyed

uniform black above

Adult ♂ White-eyed

Voice: Song typically one to three short, husky introductory notes followed by slow, musical trill *jink denk te-e-e-e-e-e-e* ("drink your teeeee"); much variation in details. Call typically a strongly rising *chewink* or *zhwink* with husky, nasal quality. Flight call a long, thin buzz *zeeeeweee.*

White-eyed Eastern Towhee is found in the southeast, with a clinal transition to Red-eyed in the north. It averages less white in the tail and gives a simpler upslurred *zwink* call and more variable song than Red-eyed. Also note that some individuals on the outer banks of North Carolina give a hoarse *merrre* call like Southwest Spotted Towhee.

Green-tailed Towhee

Pipilo chlorurus

L 7.25" WS 9.75" WT 1 oz (29 g)

Smaller and shorter-tailed than other towhees, but still larger than sparrows. Greenish flight feathers and rufous crown distinctive.

Adult
Juvenile
(Jun–Aug)
1st winter
(Aug–Mar)
rufous
crown
Adult
bright greenish-
yellow edging on
wings and tail
bright
white
throat
dark
gray

Voice: Song typically several short introductory notes followed by two or more trills *tip seeo see tweeeee chchchch* or *tlip tseetseetsee tlitlitli chrrrr.* Call a mewing, nasal *meewe.* Flight call a long, thin buzz *zeereesh;* rougher and more level than other towhees.

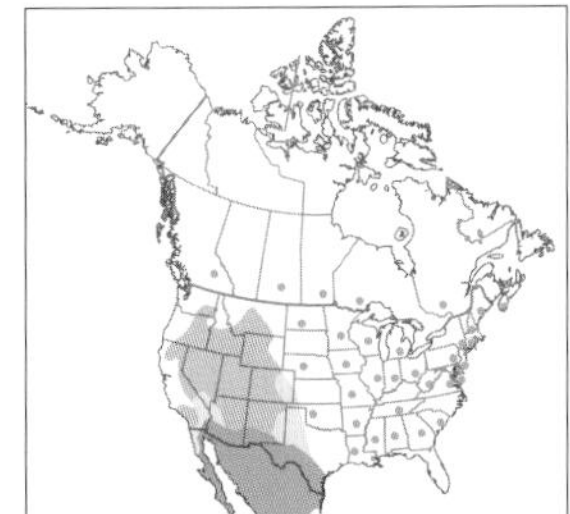

Towhees (continued)

These two species of stocky, drab, ground-dwellers live in dense brush but are often seen foraging on open ground nearby. Until recently they were considered a single species, Brown Towhee.

California Towhee

Pipilo crissalis

L 9" WS 11.5" WT 1.5 oz (44 g)

Stocky, rather sluggish; distinguished from Canyon by voice, range, and head and breast pattern.

Adult

Adult

lacks dark central spot

dusky belly

Browner adult

Grayer adult

gray-brown overall

cinnamon lores

faint streaks

Voice: Song an accelerating series of high, flat *teek* notes, sometimes with lower notes near end: *teek teek teek eek eekeekeekeek t-t-t-t-teek.* Call a high, hard, flat *teek.* Flight call a high, buzzy *zeeeee.*

Canyon Towhee

Pipilo fuscus

L 9" WS 11.5" WT 1.9 oz (53 g)

Tends to be more slender than California; slightly crested and shorter-tailed.

Adult

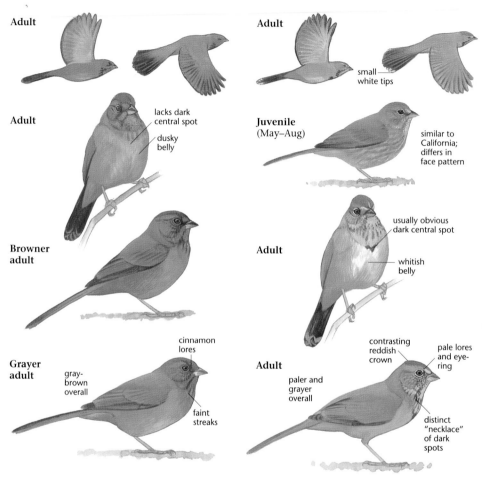

small white tips

Juvenile (May–Aug)

similar to California; differs in face pattern

Adult

usually obvious dark central spot

whitish belly

Adult

paler and grayer overall

contrasting reddish crown

pale lores and eye-ring

distinct "necklace" of dark spots

Voice: Song a simple, methodical, slow trill of short, whistled notes introduced by call note *kild ti ti ti ti ti ti ti kil* or *kild tiwi tiwi tiwi tiwi tiwi;* lower than California and Abert's. Call a nasal, dry *kidl* or loud, tinny *kilt;* also a dry, clicking *ch-ch-ch-ch.* Flight call a high, buzzy *zeeeee.*

Geographic variation in both these species is subtle and clinal, with paler and grayer populations in more arid regions, darker and browner in more humid regions. Thus the palest, grayest California Towhees are found in southeastern California, but range does not overlap with the still paler and grayer Canyon.

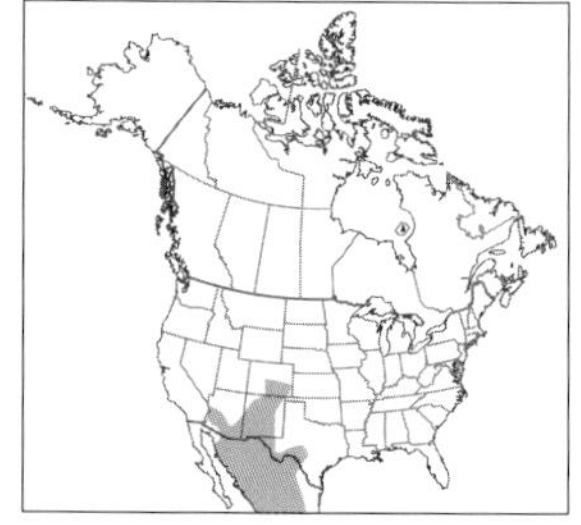

Abert's Towhee, closely related to California and Canyon, is found in dense brush near water. Olive Sparrow is secretive and found in woods with dense patches of grass and brush.

Abert's Towhee

Pipilo aberti

L 9.5" WS 11" WT 1.6 oz (46 g)

Structure nearly identical to Canyon, but appears stocky and averages slightly longer-tailed. Easily identified by face pattern and voice.

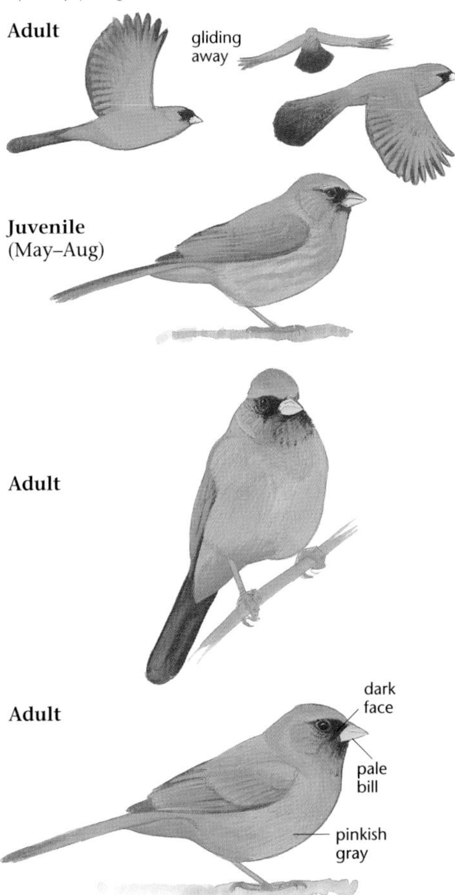
Adult
gliding
away
Juvenile
(May–Aug)
Adult
Adult
dark
face
pale
bill
pinkish
gray

Voice: Song of high, flat notes followed by an accelerating jumble of stuttering, harsh notes *tuk teek teek teek chi-chi-chi-chi-kll.* Call a high, flat *teek* lower than California; also a very high, clear *seeeep.* Flight call a high buzz *zeeoeeet.*

Olive Sparrow

Arremonops rufivirgatus

L 6.25" WS 7.75" WT 0.84 oz (24 g)

Heavy, short-winged, and long-billed. Relatively plain plumage and brown crown-stripes distinctive.

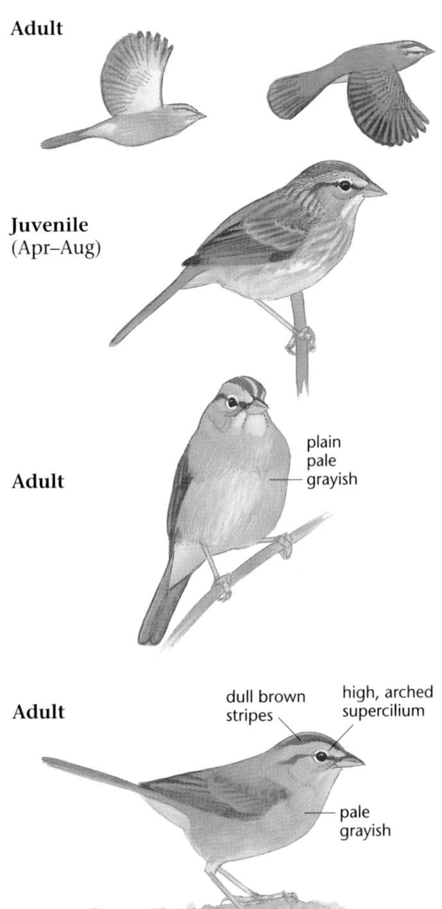
Adult
Juvenile
(Apr–Aug)
Adult
plain
pale
grayish
Adult
dull brown
stripes
high, arched
supercilium
pale
grayish

Voice: Song an accelerating series of sharp, hard chips ending with fading trill *tsip tsip tsiptsiptsip-tiptiptptptptp* (see Botteri's Sparrow). Call a very high, sharp, clicking *stip.* Flight call a high, thin buzz *seere;* towheelike but plainer and thinner.

Rufous-crowned is found in brush and grass on rocky hillsides, often in pairs. Cassin's, found singly in dense, tall grass with scattered bushes, is secretive except when singing.

Rufous-crowned Sparrow

Aimophila ruficeps

L 6" WS 7.75" WT 0.65 oz (18.5 g)

Heavy and stocky with fairly long tail. Note plain gray breast, rufous crown, distinct pale malar.

Adult
rufous crown
Juvenile (May–Aug)
Adult Pacific
rufous crown
white eye-ring
Adult Interior
dark lateral throat-stripe
plain gray breast

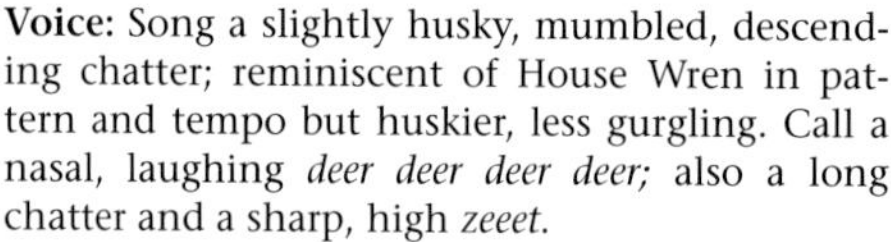
Adult Interior
compare Canyon Towhee
pale malar

Voice: Song a slightly husky, mumbled, descending chatter; reminiscent of House Wren in pattern and tempo but huskier, less gurgling. Call a nasal, laughing *deer deer deer deer;* also a long chatter and a sharp, high *zeeet.*

Cassin's Sparrow

Aimophila cassinii

L 6" WS 7.75" WT 0.67 oz (19 g)

Round-headed; smaller-billed than Botteri's and Bachman's. Dark subterminal bars on all upperpart feathers create distinctive spotted pattern.

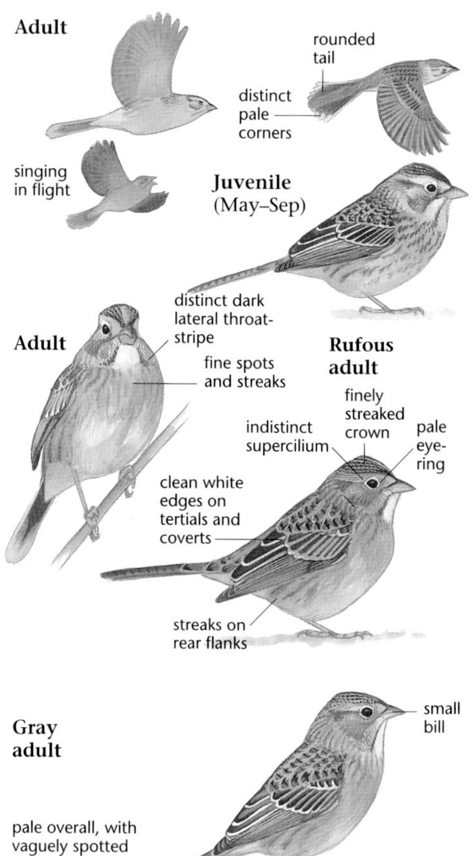
Adult
rounded tail
distinct pale corners
singing in flight
Juvenile (May–Sep)
Adult
distinct dark lateral throat-stripe
fine spots and streaks
Rufous adult
finely streaked crown
indistinct supercilium
pale eye-ring
clean white edges on tertials and coverts
streaks on rear flanks
Gray adult
small bill
pale overall, with vaguely spotted pattern

Voice: Song given mainly in flight: four plaintive, trilled whistles with long, level second note *tsisi seeeeeeeee ssoot ssiit.* Call a very high, abrupt *teep;* also very high, sharp chips; sometimes a series of squeaks when agitated.

Pacific Rufous-crowned Sparrow averages smaller and is relatively smaller-billed and browner than Interior, with darker streaks on nape and scapulars and washed overall with dingy buff. Interior birds appear cleaner gray and rufous overall with whitish throat, malar, and belly.

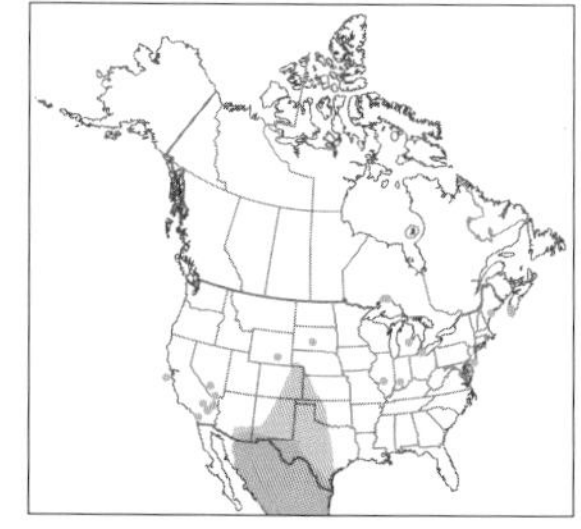

Botteri's is found in open grassland with scattered bushes, often with Cassin's where ranges overlap. Bachman's is found in grassy and brushy patches within open pine woods.

Botteri's Sparrow

Aimophila botterii

L 6" WS 7.75" WT 0.7 oz (20 g)

Flat-headed; averages shorter-tailed and much longer-billed than Cassin's. Note weakly patterned face and strongly streaked back.

Adult

indistinct pale tips

Juvenile (May–Sep)

Adult

unmarked throat and breast

Adult Arizona

poorly defined supercilium

dark crown

plain wing-panel

Adult Texas

strong, dark streaks

long bill

Voice: Song a varied, slow series of sharp, whistled notes ending with accelerating trill *tik tik swidi trrr trik tidik tew tew twitwitititititttttttt;* each note in trill sharp and rising (vs. lower and descending notes of Olive). Call a high, sharp chip or rapid chatter.

Bachman's Sparrow

Aimophila aestivalis

L 6" WS 7.25" WT 0.68 oz (19.5 g)

Structure like Botteri's but no range overlap. More brightly colored overall with whitish belly.

Adult

small, indistinct pale tips

Juvenile (May–Sep)

Adult

small spots on sides

buffy breastband contrasts with whitish belly

Adult Western

well-defined supercilium

bright rufous and gray pattern

rufous-edged tertials

Adult Eastern

strong black streaks

Voice: Song a simple, clear whistle with a musical trill on a different pitch; successive songs differ slightly in pitch and trill: *feeeee-trrrr, sooo-treee. . . .* Call of high *tsip* notes. When flushed may give piercing, sharp *tsees;* when agitated an extremely high-pitched *tsisisisisi.*

Arizona populations of Botteri's Sparrow average redder and usually darker above than the pale grayish Texas population.

Bachman's Sparrows east of the Mississippi River are drabber, with much black streaking above (especially Florida birds), while those west of the Mississippi River are brighter with little or no black above.

These species are found locally in specific habitats: Rufous-winged in small flocks in sparse desert grassland mixed with mesquite, Five-striped in tall, dense brush on rocky hillsides.

Rufous-winged Sparrow

Aimophila carpalis

L 5.75" WS 7.5" WT 0.53 oz (15 g)

Fairly long, rounded tail. Resembles Chipping Sparrow in plumage but is larger with larger bill.

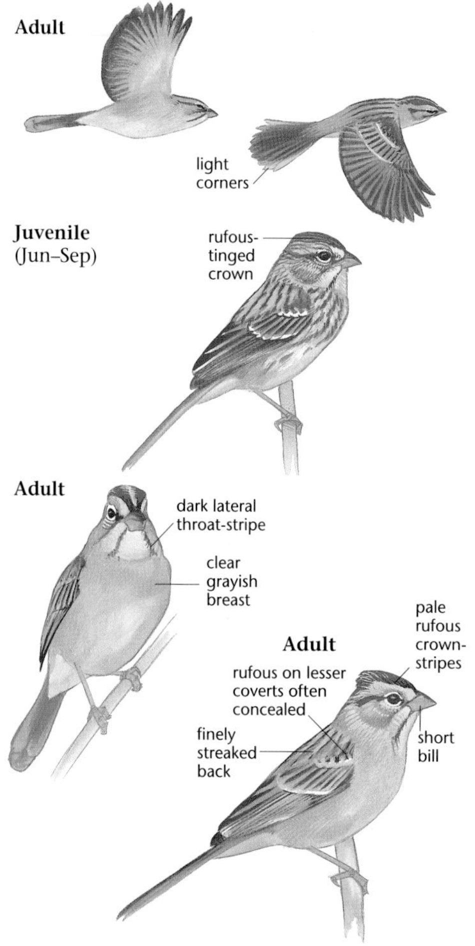
Adult
light corners
Juvenile
(Jun–Sep)
rufous-tinged crown
Adult
dark lateral throat-stripe
clear grayish breast
Adult
pale rufous crown-stripes
rufous on lesser coverts often concealed
finely streaked back
short bill

Voice: Song variable in pattern but always sweet, clear notes; two common patterns: an accelerating series of chips *tip tiptiptptptptp* and a simple *tip tip tee trrrrrrrr*. Alarm call a very high, piercing *tsiddp*.

Five-striped Sparrow

Aimophila quinquestriata

L 6" WS 8" WT 0.7 oz (20 g)

Large, stocky, and long-billed. Overall dark gray and brown with striped face.

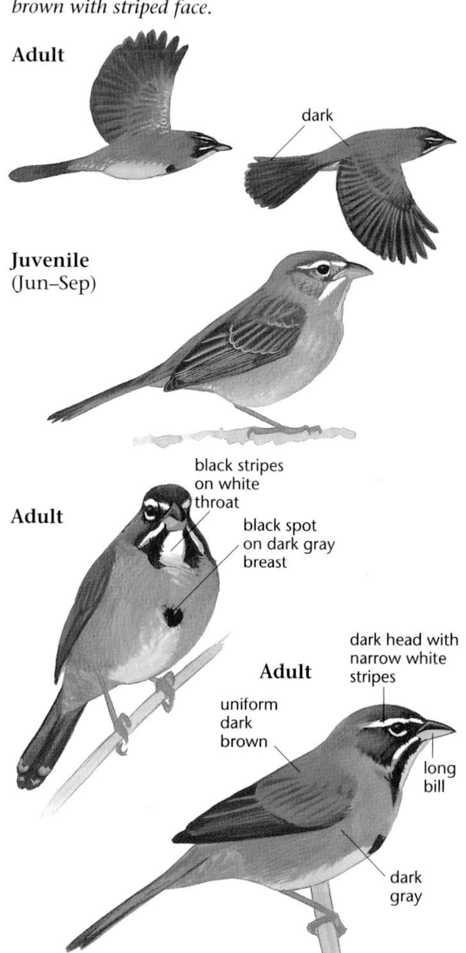
Adult
dark
Juvenile
(Jun–Sep)
Adult
black stripes on white throat
black spot on dark gray breast
Adult
dark head with narrow white stripes
uniform dark brown
long bill
dark gray

Voice: Song of short, high, liquid or tinkling phrases, each repeated two or more times, then a pause and another series *tlik, kleesh kleesh; tlees tlees; chik sedlik sedlik sedlik; kwij kwij kwij. . . .* Call a husky *terp;* occasionally a higher, dry *chik* or very high *tip*.

SPARROWS: GENUS *AMPHISPIZA*

This distinctive species is found singly in barren sagebrush deserts. Pacific populations are found in dense coastal chaparral. This species usually runs on the ground with its tail raised.

Sage Sparrow

Amphispiza belli

L 6" WS 8.25" WT 0.58 oz (16.5 g)

Medium-size, with relatively long tail. Note gray upperside, dark central breast spot, white eye-ring.

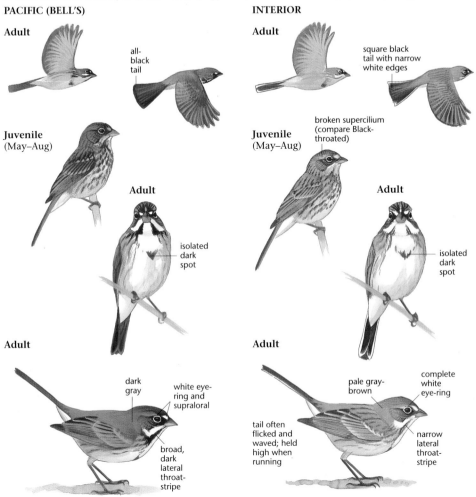

PACIFIC (BELL'S)

Adult

all-
black
tail

Juvenile
(May–Aug)

Adult

isolated
dark
spot

Adult

dark
gray

white eye-
ring and
supraloral

broad,
dark
lateral
throat-
stripe

INTERIOR

Adult

square black
tail with narrow
white edges

Juvenile
(May–Aug)

broken supercilium
(compare Black-
throated)

Adult

isolated
dark
spot

Adult

pale gray-
brown

complete
white
eye-ring

tail often
flicked and
waved; held
high when
running

narrow
lateral
throat-
stripe

Voice: Song rather hoarse or mumbled with little pitch change and no sharp notes or accented phrases *flip flip freeeee flip flip freeo;* mechanical, singsong quality; song of Pacific more rapid, longer; notes run together like Blue Grosbeak, unlike slower, jerkier tempo of Interior. Call an irregular series of high, weak, variable *tip* notes: *tip . . . tip . . . tiptip . . . tip . . . ;* also high, bell-like *tink* notes singly or in series.

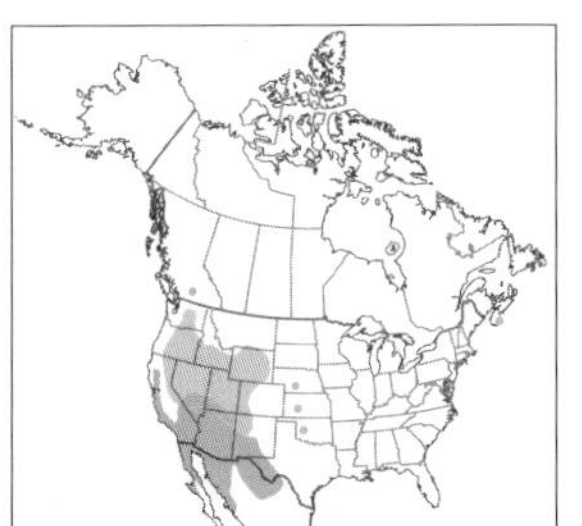

Two distinctive populations, but birds breeding in eastern California are intermediate. Pacific averages 5 percent smaller than Interior; much darker with indistinct streaks on the back (vs. paler with distinct streaks); little contrast between head and back (vs. pale brownish back contrasting with gray head); broad, dark lateral throat-stripe (vs. narrow and incomplete); no white on tail; darker head isolating complete white eye-ring and small white supraloral spot.

Sparrows: Genera *Amphispiza* (continued) and *Spizella*

These two species, in two different genera, are similar only in common name. Black-throated is found in deserts with bare, open ground, Black-chinned in chaparral and brushy habitats.

Black-throated Sparrow

Amphispiza bilineata

L 5.5" WS 7.75" WT 0.47 oz (13.5 g)

Related to Sage but distinctive in plumage and habits. Clean plumage and striking face pattern unique.

Adult Western

Adult Texas

Juvenile (Jun–Oct)

bold white supercilium

faintly streaked grayish

breastband of indistinct small streaks

Adult

striking black throat

Adult Western

Adult Texas

smooth gray back

very bold, clean head pattern

unmarked, pale underparts

Voice: Song a short, simple, mechanical tinkling *swik swik sweeee te-errrr* or *tip tik to tik tik trr tredr-rrrr;* also rapid repetitions of tinkling phrases on different pitches *teeteetee, tototo, tletletle. . . .* Call of high, weak, tinkling notes: a hard, bell-like *tip;* also series of high *tee* notes.

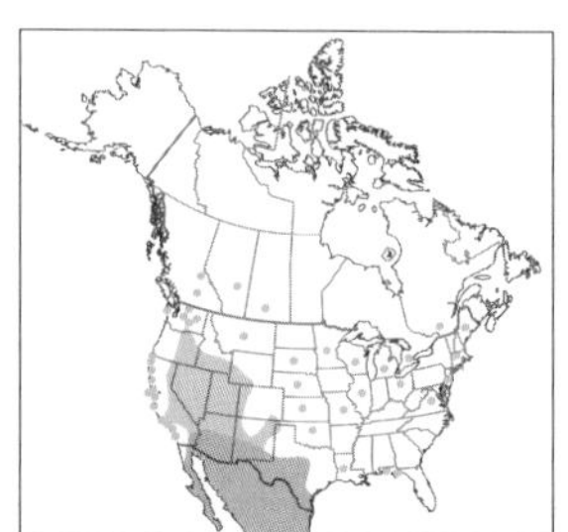

Populations of Black-throated in central and southern Texas average slightly smaller, darker, with larger white spots on the outer tail feathers than Western birds, but differences are subtle and populations in western Texas are intermediate.

Black-chinned Sparrow

Spizella atrogularis

L 5.75" WS 7.75" WT 0.42 oz (12 g)

Slender shape; longer-tailed than other Spizella *sparrows. Dark gray head and body unique.*

Adult

plain gray head

Juvenile (Jun–Aug)

1st winter (Aug–Apr)

adult ♀ and adult ♂ nonbreeding similar

streaked back

small pink bill

gray head and breast

poorly defined whitish belly

Adult ♂ breeding (Apr–Aug)

compare Dark-eyed Junco

black throat

Voice: Song of high, sharp, slurred notes accelerating to rapid trill; higher and more mechanical than Field Sparrow; final trill usually rising. Call a high, weak *stip.* Flight call a soft *ssip* similar to Chipping Sparrow.

Sparrows: Genus *Spizella* (continued)

These two small and long-tailed sparrows are slightly larger than other *Spizella* sparrows. Both winter in small flocks in brushy or weedy areas and nest in brushy habitats.

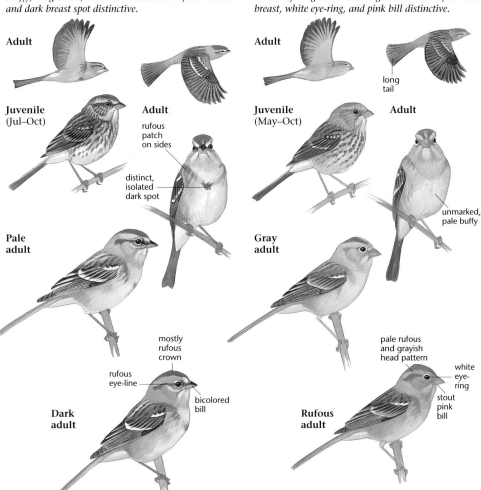

American Tree Sparrow

Spizella arborea

L 6.25" WS 9.5" WT 0.7 oz (20 g)

Fluffy, long-tailed, and round-headed. Rufous crown and dark breast spot distinctive.

Adult

Juvenile (Jul–Oct)

Adult

rufous patch on sides

distinct, isolated dark spot

Pale adult

mostly rufous crown

rufous eye-line

bicolored bill

Dark adult

Voice: Song a very sweet, clear, high warble with descending trend *swee swee ti sidi see zidi zidi zew;* slightly buzzy at end. Call a unique soft, jingling *teedleoo.* Flight call a high, sharp *tsiiw;* similar to Field but usually not descending.

Field Sparrow

Spizella pusilla

L 5.75" WS 8" WT 0.44 oz (12.5 g)

Relatively long-tailed and large-billed. Plain face and breast, white eye-ring, and pink bill distinctive.

Adult

long tail

Juvenile (May–Oct)

Adult

unmarked, pale buffy

Gray adult

pale rufous and grayish head pattern

white eye-ring

stout pink bill

Rufous adult

Voice: Song an accelerating series of soft, sweet whistles *teew teew tew tew tewtewtetetetetititititi.* Call clear and rather strong like Orange-crowned Warbler; stronger than Chipping Sparrow. Flight call a distinctive, descending, clear *tseeew.*

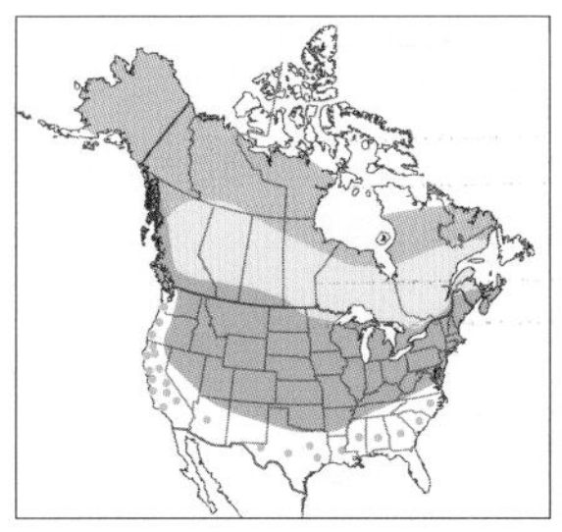

In both these species, western populations average slightly larger, paler, and grayer than eastern, but the color variations illustrated above can be found within each population. Note also that worn and faded birds are paler and grayer than fresh birds.

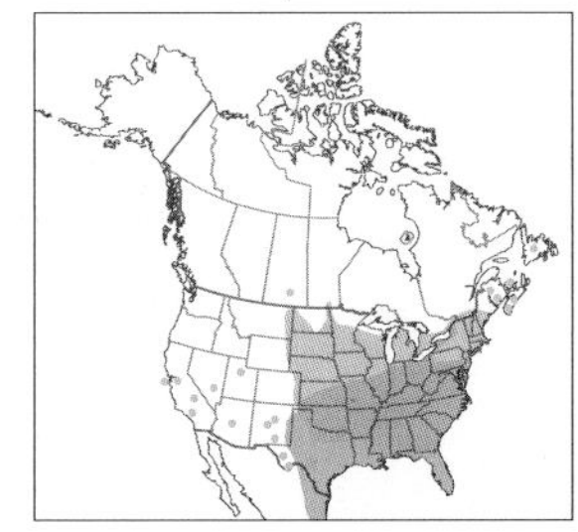

Found in open, brushy habitats such as sagebrush, this species can be difficult to distinguish from Clay-colored and Chipping, especially in fall and winter, when plumage and range can overlap.

Brewer's Sparrow

Spizella breweri

L 5.5" WS 7.5" WT 0.37 oz (10.5 g)

Our smallest sparrow; relatively long-tailed, small-billed, and round-headed compared to other Spizella *sparrows. Plain drab color and complete white eye-ring are best field marks.*

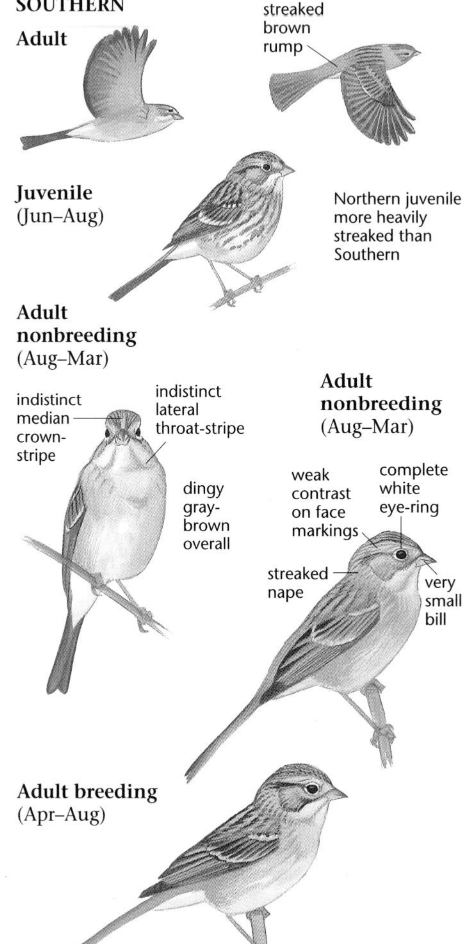
SOUTHERN
Adult
streaked brown rump
Juvenile (Jun–Aug)
Northern juvenile more heavily streaked than Southern
Adult nonbreeding (Aug–Mar)
indistinct median crown-stripe
indistinct lateral throat-stripe
dingy gray-brown overall
Adult nonbreeding (Aug–Mar)
weak contrast on face markings
complete white eye-ring
streaked nape
very small bill
Adult breeding (Apr–Aug)

IDENTIFICATION OF *SPIZELLA* SPARROWS
Brewer's, Clay-colored, and Chipping Sparrows are distinctive in breeding plumage (Apr–Aug), but the patterns and colors of fall and winter birds (particularly immatures) can be very similar. Identification requires careful study of head pattern. Chipping is most distinctive, with a dark loral-stripe, but this may be faint; more useful is the fact that the face pattern is dominated by the dark eye-line (eye-line of other species is about as dark as other facial markings). Clay-colored is usually more colorful and more contrasting than Brewer's, but some drab Clay-coloreds can overlap with bright Brewer's, and rare individuals may be unidentifiable. Concentrate on the cleaner and more colorful face pattern of Clay-colored, with clean buffy supercilium, contrasting light malar, and buffy breast. Brewer's is less contrasting overall, patterned weakly in grayish-brown.

NORTHERN (TIMBERLINE)

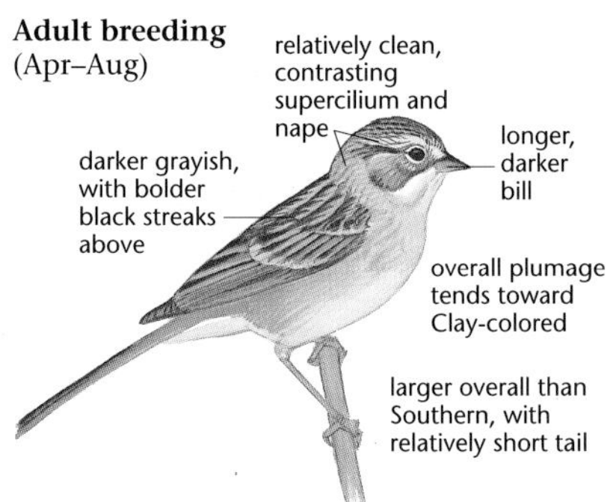
Adult breeding (Apr–Aug)
relatively clean, contrasting supercilium and nape
darker grayish, with bolder black streaks above
longer, darker bill
overall plumage tends toward Clay-colored
larger overall than Southern, with relatively short tail

Voice: Song a long, varied series of trills and buzzes, overall descending: *zerr-zerr-zerr tir-tir-tir-tir cheeeeeeee deee-deee-deee zrr-zrr-zrr-zrr zreeeee . . .* ; some notes are high, clear, and musical, and others are low and rasping like Clay-colored. Call a high, sharp *tsip* like other *Spizella* sparrows. Flight call rising, short, and weak, with abrupt ending: *swit.*

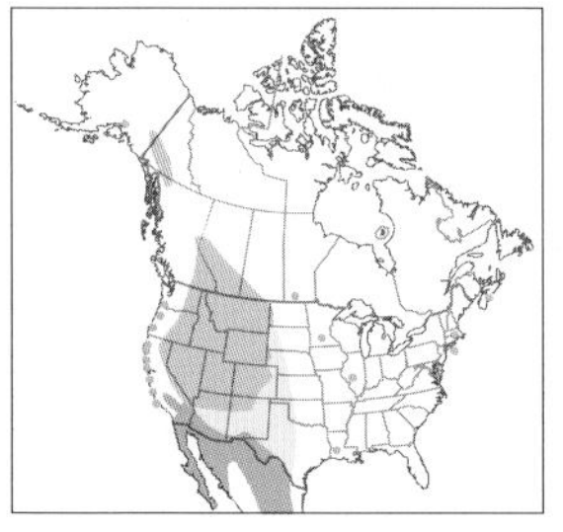

Two populations with separate breeding ranges differ in subtleties of plumage and song but may not be reliably identified in the field. More study is needed. Northern population (breeds in brushy habitat at treeline in mountains of Canada and Alaska and possibly farther south; winter range overlaps with Southern) averages slightly larger and darker overall with broader black streaks on the back and flanks and darker gray breast contrasting slightly with the paler belly; bill may average darker and longer; head pattern is more contrasting, with possibly cleaner gray nape, and may suggest Clay-colored Sparrow. Northern song averages lower, clearer, and less buzzy with slower, more musical trills but lacks slower series of high, clear notes.

Although Chipping prefers open woods and Clay-colored brushy areas away from trees, in winter they are often found together in small flocks and can be difficult to distinguish from each other.

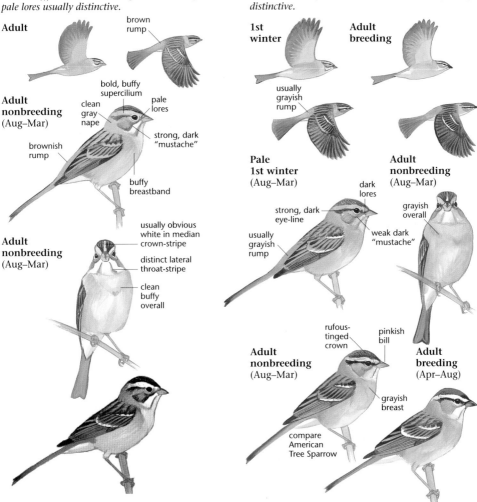

Clay-colored Sparrow

Spizella pallida

L 5.5" WS 7.5" WT 0.42 oz (12 g)

Averages smaller and smaller-billed than Chipping. Clean buffy colors, contrasting head markings, and pale lores usually distinctive.

Adult

brown rump

Adult nonbreeding (Aug–Mar)

bold, buffy supercilium

clean gray nape

pale lores

strong, dark "mustache"

brownish rump

buffy breastband

Adult nonbreeding (Aug–Mar)

usually obvious white in median crown-stripe

distinct lateral throat-stripe

clean buffy overall

Voice: Song a series of two to five rasping buzzes on one pitch *zheee zheee zheee*. Call a high, sharp *tsip* like other *Spizella* sparrows. Flight call a rising, short *swit* similar to Brewer's.

Chipping Sparrow

Spizella passerina

L 5.5" WS 8.5" WT 0.42 oz (12 g)

Averages larger, longer-billed, and relatively shorter-tailed than Clay-colored. Dark lores and gray rump distinctive.

1st winter

Adult breeding

usually grayish rump

Pale 1st winter (Aug–Mar)

dark lores

strong, dark eye-line

usually grayish rump

weak dark "mustache"

Adult nonbreeding (Aug–Mar)

grayish overall

Adult nonbreeding (Aug–Mar)

rufous-tinged crown

pinkish bill

grayish breast

compare American Tree Sparrow

Adult breeding (Apr–Aug)

Voice: Song a simple, usually rather long and mechanical trill. Call a sharp chip like other *Spizella* sparrows. Flight call a high, thin, slightly rising *tsiis*.

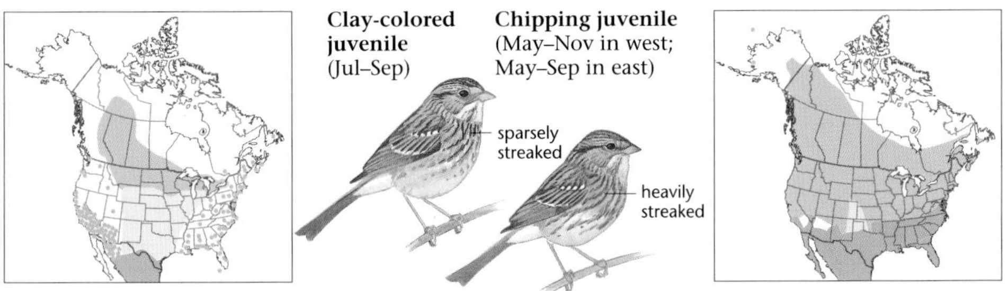
sparsely streaked
heavily streaked

Clay-colored juvenile (Jul–Sep)

Chipping juvenile (May–Nov in west; May–Sep in east)

Sparrows: Genus *Ammodramus*

These two secretive species are found singly in tall, dense grass. Typical of the genus *Ammodramus*, they are short-tailed, large-headed, and intricately patterned.

Baird's Sparrow

Ammodramus bairdii

L 5.5" WS 8.75" WT 0.61 oz (17.5 g)

Relatively large-billed, with longer and squarer tail than other Ammodramus *sparrows. Ochre color on head and dark neck spots distinctive.*

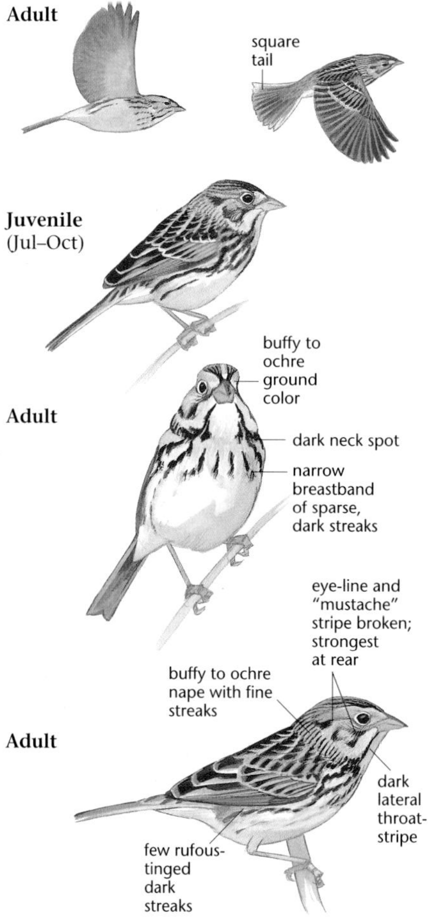
Adult
square tail
Juvenile (Jul–Oct)
buffy to ochre ground color
Adult
dark neck spot
narrow breastband of sparse, dark streaks
eye-line and "mustache" stripe broken; strongest at rear
buffy to ochre nape with fine streaks
Adult
dark lateral throat-stripe
few rufous-tinged dark streaks

Voice: Song high, clear jingling; several high, clear *tink* notes followed by clear, musical trill *tik a tl tleeeeee*. Call a very high, weak *teep*. Flight call a high, thin *tsee;* higher than Grasshopper.

Grasshopper Sparrow

Ammodramus savannarum

L 5" WS 7.75" WT 0.6 oz (17 g)

Relatively long-billed and flat-headed, with short tail and somewhat pointed wings. Compare Orange Bishop.

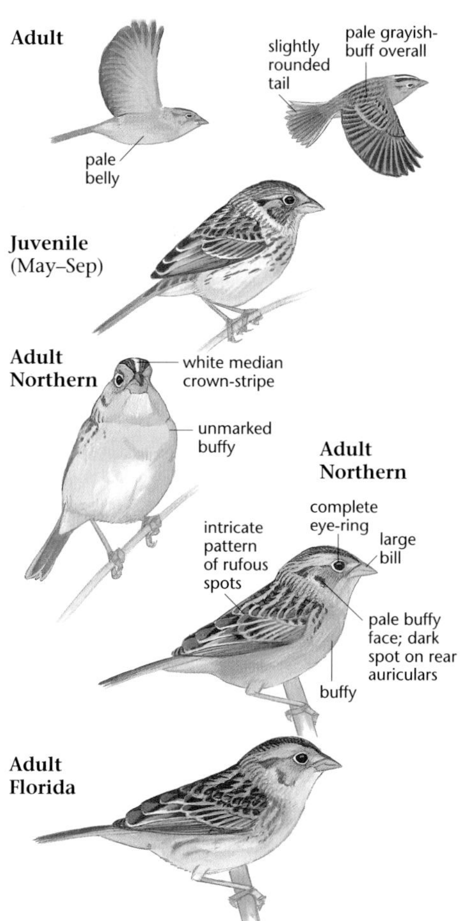
Adult
slightly rounded tail
pale grayish-buff overall
pale belly
Juvenile (May–Sep)
Adult Northern
white median crown-stripe
unmarked buffy
Adult Northern
complete eye-ring
large bill
intricate pattern of rufous spots
pale buffy face; dark spot on rear auriculars
buffy
Adult Florida

Voice: Song a very high, hissing, insectlike buzz preceded by weak *tik* notes *tik tuk tikeeeeeeeeeeez;* also a rolling jumble of high, buzzy, slurred phrases. Call a very high, thin, sharp *tip;* usually rapidly doubled or tripled *titip*. Flight call a sharp, high, rising *tswees*.

Grasshopper Sparrows vary slightly in color over most of their range, but Florida birds are darker above (brown with blackish streaks vs. gray with rufous streaks) and paler below (breast whitish vs. buffy). Song may also differ: a rapid *tzeeeeeeee tze tze tze tze tze* and other variations, unlike Northern birds.

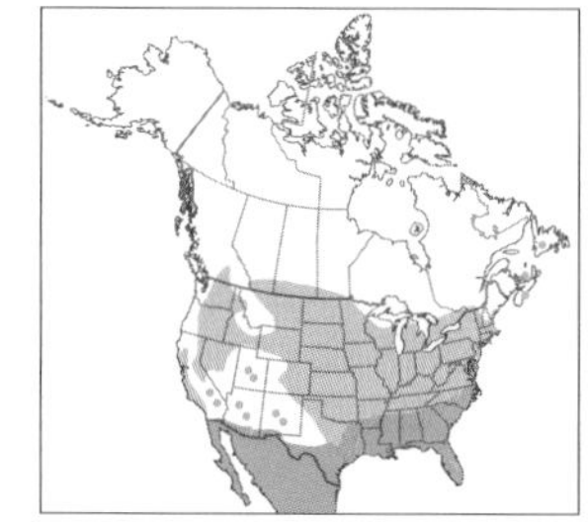

These species, the smallest *Ammodramus* sparrows, have short, spiky tails. Both are very secretive; Le Conte's is found in grassy meadows, Henslow's in patchy, weedy fields.

Le Conte's Sparrow

Ammodramus leconteii

L 5" WS 6.5" WT 0.46 oz (13 g)

Small with small bill. Pale and brightly patterned overall.

Adult

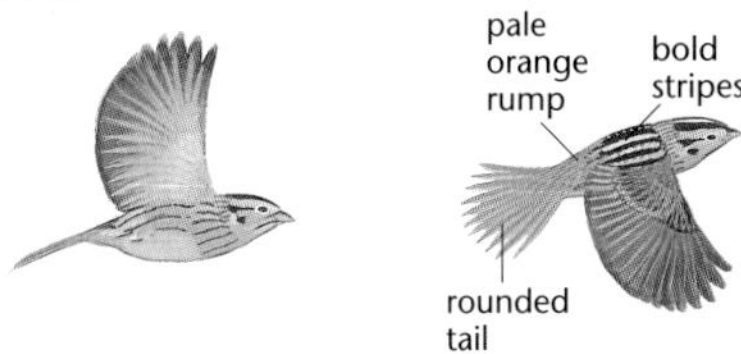
pale orange rump
bold stripes
rounded tail

Juvenile (Jul–Nov)

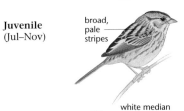

broad, pale stripes

Adult

white median crown-stripe
thin, dark lateral throat-stripe
breastband of fine streaks

Adult

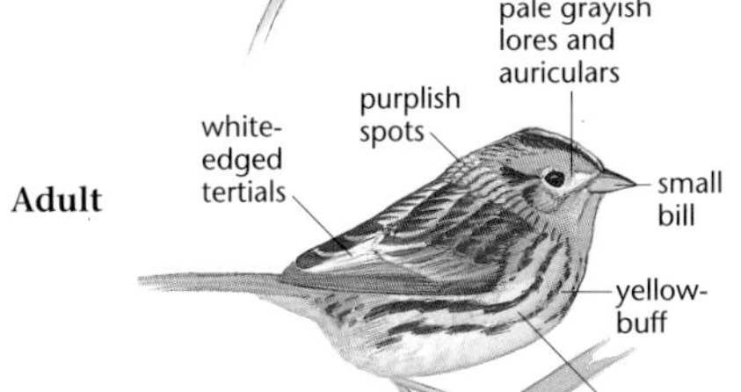
pale grayish lores and auriculars
purplish spots
white-edged tertials
small bill
yellow-buff
crisp, fine black streaks

Voice: Song a fine, hissing, unmusical buzz *tik a t-sshhhhhhhh-t;* softer, higher, more hissing than Grasshopper Sparrow; sharp introductory notes unlike Nelson's Sharp-tailed. Call a high, thin, descending *tseeez.*

Henslow's Sparrow

Ammodramus henslowii

L 5" WS 6.5" WT 0.46 oz (13 g)

Small but relatively large-headed with large, thick bill. Dark overall.

Adult

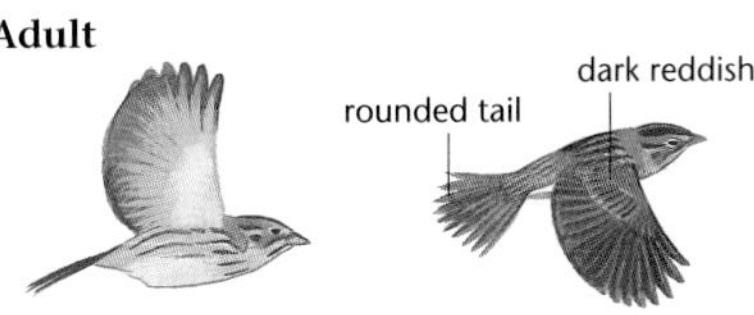
dark reddish
rounded tail

Juvenile (Jun–Aug)

Adult

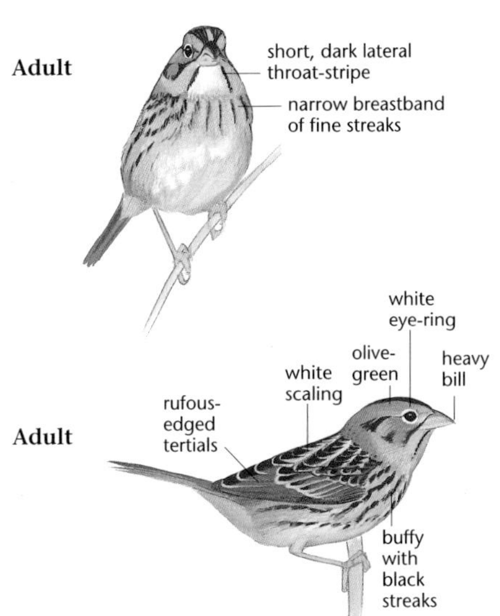
short, dark lateral throat-stripe
narrow breastband of fine streaks
white eye-ring
olive-green
heavy bill
white scaling
rufous-edged tertials
buffy with black streaks

Adult

Voice: Song a dry, insectlike, feeble hiccup *tsezlik* or *tsillik*. Call a high, sharp *tsik*. Flight call a high, almost waxwinglike trill *sreee*.

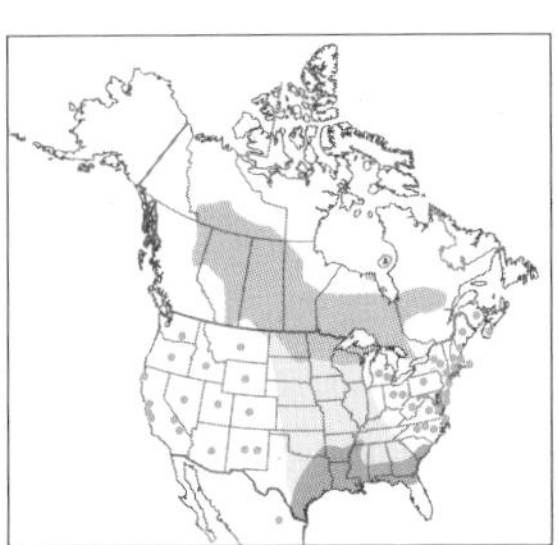

Glimpses of these and other secretive grass sparrows are often only of a small brown bird flying away. With experience, some can be identified by overall color, back pattern, tail shape, and face and breast pattern. Also consider Sedge Wren, Sprague's Pipit, and longspurs, and note that any species of sparrow can be secretive.

These two very closely related species are found almost exclusively in grassy marshes. They were until recently considered a single species, Sharp-tailed Sparrow.

Nelson's Sharp-tailed Sparrow

Ammodramus nelsoni

L 5" WS 7" WT 0.6 oz (17 g)

Averages smaller with rounder head and smaller bill than Saltmarsh. Differs from Saltmarsh in overall color and breast-belly contrast.

Adult Interior **Adult Atlantic**

Juvenile (Jul–Aug)

bright orange-buff with few streaks

gray crown

Adult Interior

well-defined white belly

Adult Atlantic

Adult Interior

bright overall

short bill

bright face and breast

rufous-tinged streaks

Adult Atlantic

drab gray overall

blurry grayish streaks

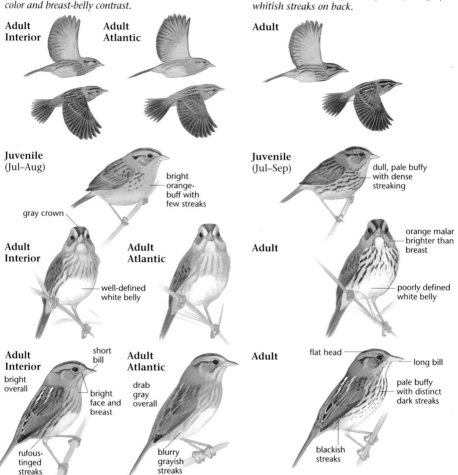

Voice: Song a weak, soft, airy, fading hiss with slightly lower notes at beginning and end *pl-tesh hhhhh-ush* (compare Le Conte's). Call a hard *tek* higher and harder than Seaside. Flight call a high, lisping *ssis*. Flight song a series of sharp chips followed by typical song during higher flight.

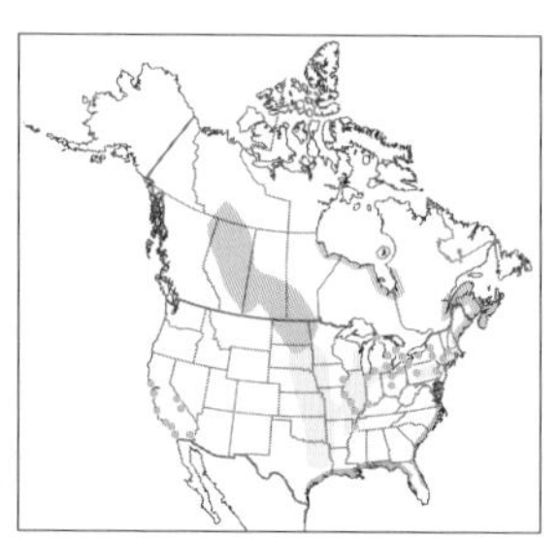

Atlantic population of Nelson's Sharp-tailed (wintering New Jersey to Florida) is distinctive: grayish overall, with weak pattern and blurry grayish streaking below. Interior birds (wintering New Jersey to Texas) average smaller and shorter-billed and are much brighter overall, with orange-buff face and breast and distinct streaking on flanks.

Saltmarsh Sharp-tailed Sparrow

Ammodramus caudacutus

L 5.25" WS 7" WT 0.67 oz (19 g)

Similar to Nelson's but longer-billed. Both species have distinctive orange triangle on face, gray crown, whitish streaks on back.

Adult

Juvenile (Jul–Sep)

dull, pale buffy with dense streaking

Adult

orange malar brighter than breast

poorly defined white belly

Adult

flat head

long bill

pale buffy with distinct dark streaks

blackish streaks

Voice: Song much softer than Nelson's, less frequently heard; includes sweet gurgling notes and lacks final lower note; usually given in rapid sequence. Calls presumably like Nelson's. Flight song a series of weak songs, all different; delivered rapidly during low flight.

Found exclusively in saltmarsh grass, Seaside Sparrow is distinguished from other sparrows by its large size, overall dark gray color, white throat, and long bill.

Seaside Sparrow

Ammodramus maritimus

L 6" WS 7.5" WT 0.81 oz (23 g)

Large and stocky, with round body, short, rounded tail, and very long bill.

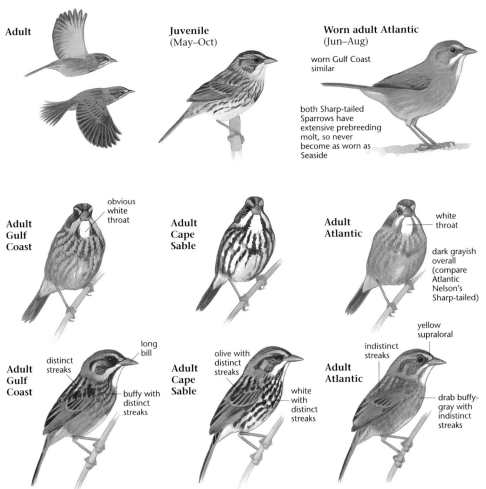

Adult

Juvenile (May–Oct)

Worn adult Atlantic (Jun–Aug)

worn Gulf Coast similar

both Sharp-tailed Sparrows have extensive prebreeding molt, so never become as worn as Seaside

Adult Gulf Coast

obvious white throat

Adult Cape Sable

Adult Atlantic

white throat

dark grayish overall (compare Atlantic Nelson's Sharp-tailed)

Adult Gulf Coast

distinct streaks

long bill

buffy with distinct streaks

Adult Cape Sable

olive with distinct streaks

white with distinct streaks

Adult Atlantic

indistinct streaks

yellow supraloral

drab buffy-gray with indistinct streaks

Voice: Song a rather muffled *tup teetle-zhrrrr;* more complex and fuller-sounding than Sharp-tailed Sparrows; reminiscent of song of distant Red-winged Blackbird. Call a low, husky *tup*. Flight call a long, thin, towheelike buzz *zeeeooee.*

Three populations differ in range and plumage, but some Atlantic birds are similar to some Gulf Coast in appearance. Song varies geographically, with complex local dialects; more study is needed to determine whether voice differs consistently among the three main populations. Atlantic song is described above. Gulf Coast song is similar but may be more complex: three- to four-part, with descending trend. Song of Cape Sable population in southern Florida a simple, long, nasal buzz *tli-zheeeeee*. Flight song may also differ among populations: Atlantic gives a series of high, thin, wispy trills and rattles sometimes followed by normal song; Gulf Coast gives a series of chips usually followed by normal song.

Savannah Sparrow

Related to *Ammodramus* sparrows, this species is found in a variety of grassy habitats, often in small flocks. It is usually not too secretive, perching in bushes when disturbed.

Savannah Sparrow

Passerculus sandwichensis

L 5.5" WS 6.75" WT 0.7 oz (20 g)

Neat and cleanly marked, with small bill, slight crest, pointed wings, and short, notched tail; note crisp streaking and yellow tinge on lores.

Typical adult

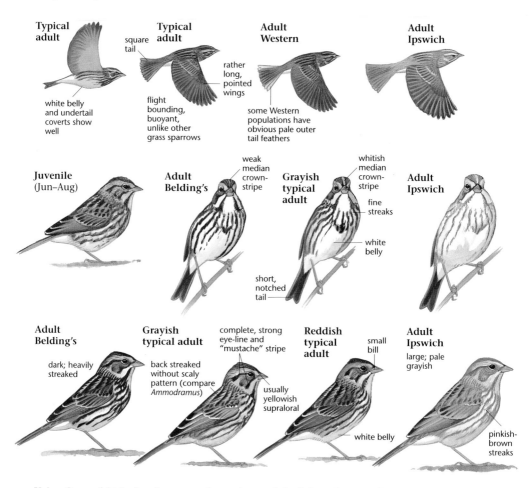

white belly and undertail coverts show well

Typical adult

square tail

flight bounding, buoyant, unlike other grass sparrows

rather long, pointed wings

Adult Western

some Western populations have obvious pale outer tail feathers

Adult Ipswich

Juvenile (Jun–Aug)

Adult Belding's

weak median crown-stripe

Grayish typical adult

whitish median crown-stripe

fine streaks

white belly

short, notched tail

Adult Ipswich

Adult Belding's

dark; heavily streaked

Grayish typical adult

back streaked without scaly pattern (compare *Ammodramus*)

complete, strong eye-line and "mustache" stripe

usually yellowish supraloral

Reddish typical adult

small bill

white belly

Adult Ipswich

large; pale grayish

pinkish-brown streaks

Voice: Song of high, fine buzzes, each one lower-pitched than the preceding *ti ti ti tseeeeeee tisoooo;* harsher and lower than Grasshopper, with final low buzz; often a simpler *t t t tzeeeeeeee tzz.* Call a very high, sharp *stip.* Flight call a high, thin, weak *tsiw* similar to *Spizella* sparrows but descending and fading. Limited geographic variation in song: Ipswich lower, fuller, more musical *tip tip tip tseeeee-laaair.*

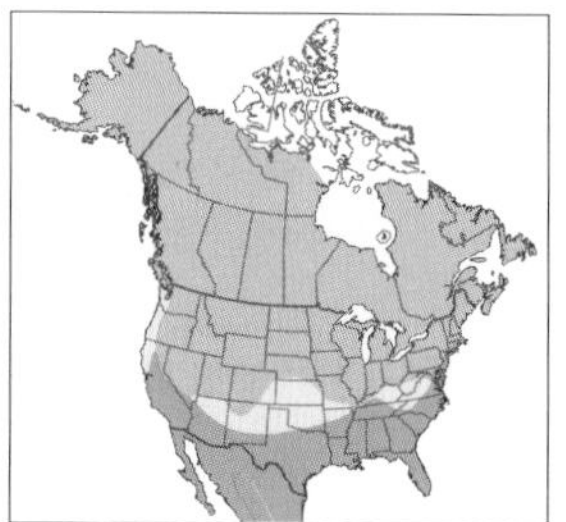

Most geographic variation is subtle, involving size and average color, with clinal transitions from reddish to grayish birds found throughout the range. Belding's (resident in southern California saltmarshes) is dark and heavily streaked; averages 5 percent smaller overall but with 10 percent longer bill than typical birds. Ipswich (nests on Sable Island, Nova Scotia, and winters in coastal dunes south to Florida) is much paler overall; averages 10 percent larger than typical birds. Aleutian breeders (not shown, winter south to California) are as large as Ipswich but colored like typical birds.

Large-billed Savannah Sparrow is a distinctive population of Savannah Sparrow, found on sparsely vegetated ground near water. Vesper is found in open fields and pastures, often near trees.

Savannah Sparrow

Passerculus sandwichensis

LARGE-BILLED

Like typical Savannah Sparrow in size, but stockier, with 30 percent larger bill, curved culmen, faintly streaked crown and back, and different voice.

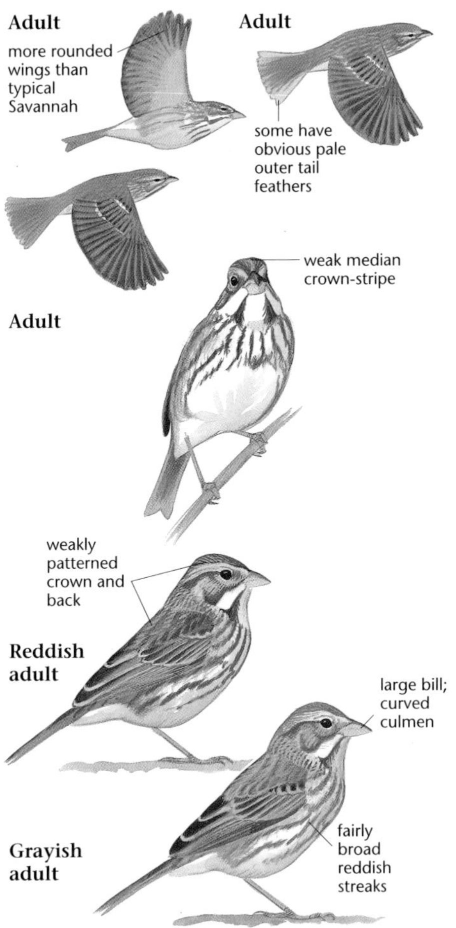
Adult
more rounded wings than typical Savannah
Adult
some have obvious pale outer tail feathers
weak median crown-stripe
Adult
weakly patterned crown and back
Reddish adult
large bill; curved culmen
fairly broad reddish streaks
Grayish adult

Voice: Song three rich buzzes *zaaaaaa zooooooo zeeee* bearing little resemblance to other populations of Savannah Sparrow; other songs closer to typical Savannah in pattern but fuller-sounding. Flight call a little longer and lower-pitched.

Vesper Sparrow

Pooecetes gramineus

L 6.25" WS 10" WT 0.91 oz (26 g)

Relatively large; most similar to Savannah but longer-tailed. Note clean white outer tail feathers and white eye-ring.

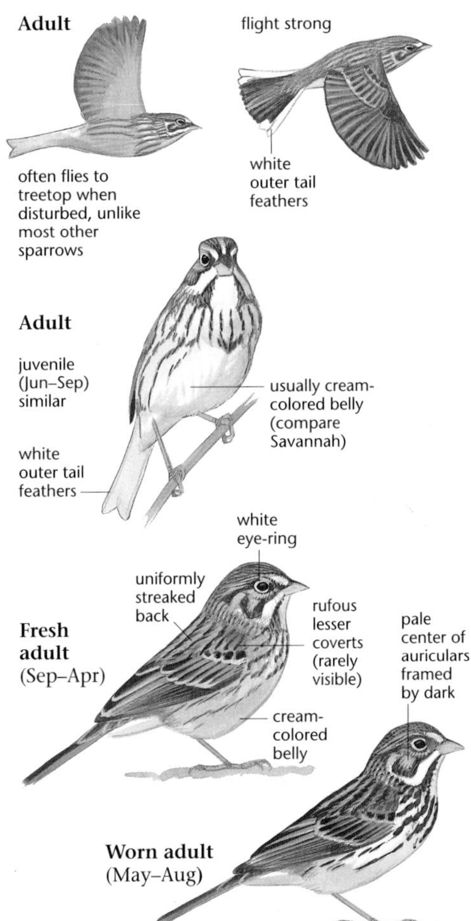
Adult
flight strong
often flies to treetop when disturbed, unlike most other sparrows
white outer tail feathers
Adult
juvenile (Jun–Sep) similar
usually cream-colored belly (compare Savannah)
white outer tail feathers
white eye-ring
uniformly streaked back
Fresh adult (Sep–Apr)
rufous lesser coverts (rarely visible)
pale center of auriculars framed by dark
cream-colored belly
Worn adult (May–Aug)

Voice: Song begins with paired low whistles then slow, musical trills accelerating and descending *too too tee tee chididididi swiswi-swiswiteew;* similar to Song Sparrow. Call a sharp chip, lower and harder than Savannah. Flight call a slightly buzzy, rising, sharp *ssit* or *seeet*.

LARGE-BILLED

Most sparrows molt much of their plumage twice a year (maintaining fresh feathers without significantly changing their appearance). Vesper is one of a few species that molt only once a year, thus becoming dark and quite worn by Aug, just before molting.

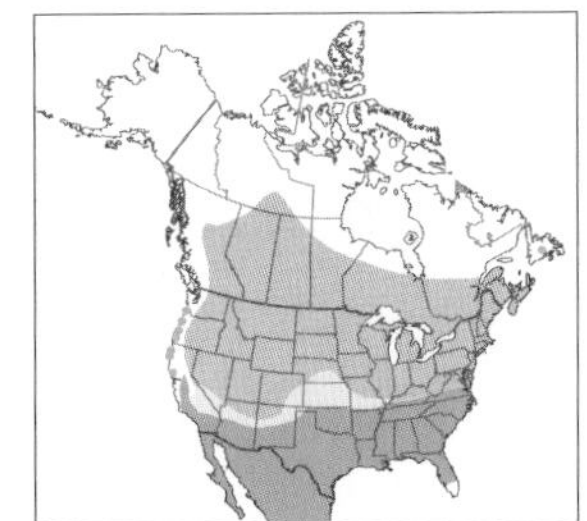

Lark Bunting

This unique species differs from all sparrows in structure, voice, and plumage. It is found in arid, grassy or brushy areas, often in very large flocks in winter.

Sparrowlike Birds

Many more or less unrelated species of small, brownish, streaked birds are frequently mistaken for emberizine sparrows; some are shown below. In particular note habits: many of these species fly high and strongly, perch in treetops, and frequently give calls in flight or when perched, all behaviors that are not typical of emberizine sparrows.

American Pipit (and other pipits): Thin bill; walks on ground; strong flight with squeaky flight calls.

Adult nonbreeding (Aug–Mar)

Indigo Bunting (and other *Passerina* buntings): Rounded tail flicked and wagged; strong flight with buzzy calls.

Adult ♀ breeding (Apr–Sep)

Bobolink: Pointed wings; strong flight with soft calls.

Adult nonbreeding (Aug–Mar)

Red-winged Blackbird: Larger than most sparrows; walks on ground; strong flight with sharp calls.

Adult ♀

Purple Finch (and other finches): Notched tail; strong flight with sharp calls.

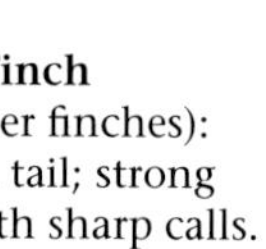

Adult ♀ Pacific

House Sparrow: An Old World sparrow with stocky shape; chirping calls.

Adult ♀

Lark Bunting

Calamospiza melanocorys

L 7" WS 10.5" WT 1.3 oz (38 g)

Large and stocky; broad-headed, large-billed, with short tail and short, rounded wings.

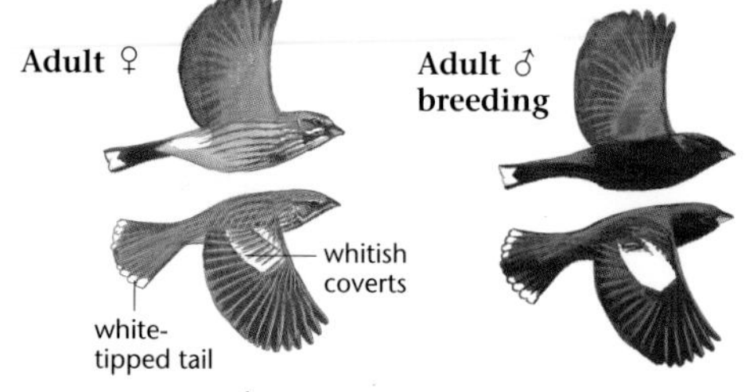

Adult ♀
Adult ♂ breeding
whitish coverts
white-tipped tail

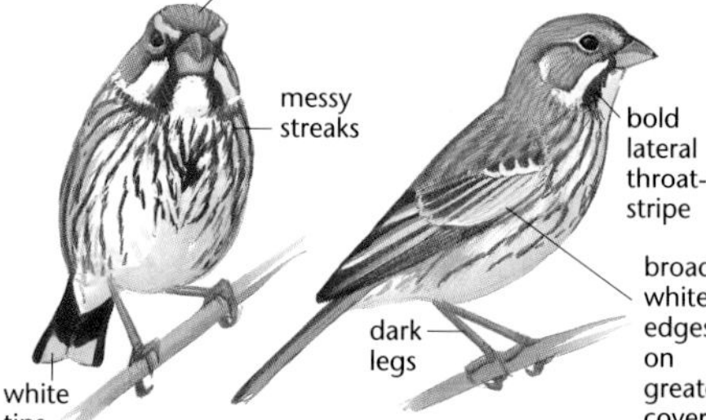

Adult ♀
large head
Adult ♀
messy streaks
bold lateral throat-stripe
broad white edges on greater coverts
dark legs
white tips

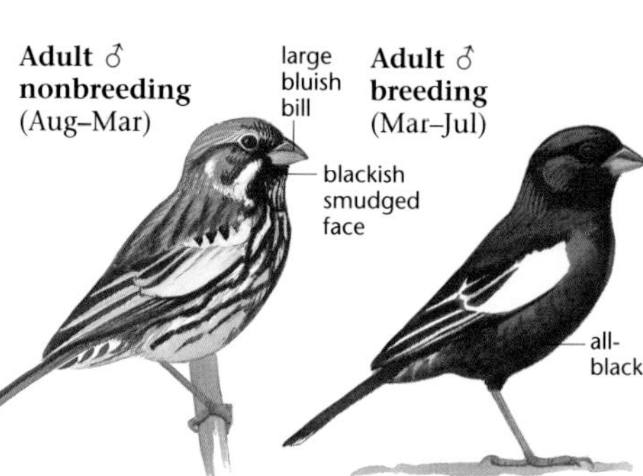

Adult ♂ nonbreeding (Aug–Mar)
large bluish bill
Adult ♂ breeding (Mar–Jul)
blackish smudged face
all-black

Voice: Song of repeated low, liquid, whistled notes *pwid pwid pwid pwid too too too too kree kree kree kree pwido pwido . . .* ; interspersed and overlaid with high, silvery rattles *tt tt tt tt;* entire song rich, complex, and repetitious, with relatively slow tempo. Call a low, soft, whistled *heew* or *howik*.

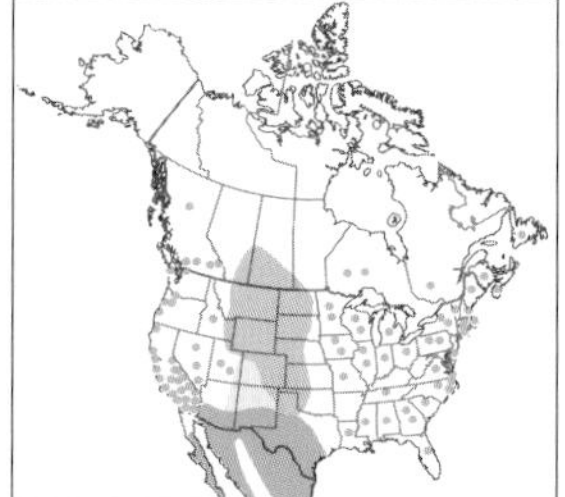

Sparrows: Genera *Chondestes* and *Zonotrichia*

These species are two of our largest sparrows. Lark is found on open ground: lawns, fields, and open woods; Harris's is found in brush with other *Zonotrichia* sparrows.

Lark Sparrow

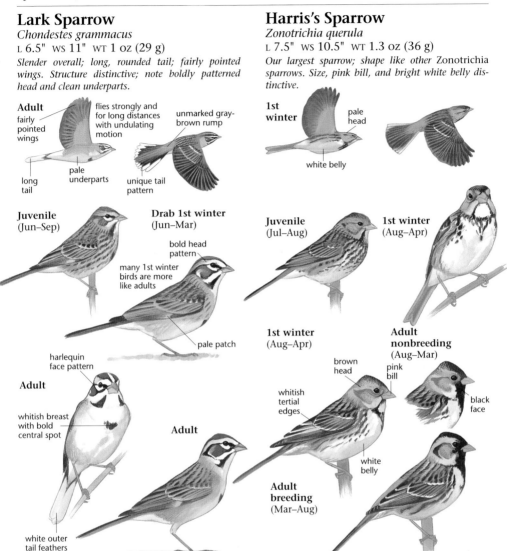

Chondestes grammacus

L 6.5" WS 11" WT 1 oz (29 g)

Slender overall; long, rounded tail; fairly pointed wings. Structure distinctive; note boldly patterned head and clean underparts.

Adult
fairly pointed wings
flies strongly and for long distances with undulating motion
unmarked gray-brown rump
long tail
pale underparts
unique tail pattern
Juvenile (Jun–Sep)
Drab 1st winter (Jun–Mar)
bold head pattern
many 1st winter birds are more like adults
pale patch
harlequin face pattern
Adult
whitish breast with bold central spot
Adult
white outer tail feathers

Voice: Song rather slow-paced and varied with choppy rhythm; phrases generally high, mechanical rattling with some long trills *zeer puk treeeeeee chido chido kreet-kreet-kreet-kreet trrrrrrrrr. . . .* Flight call a high, sharp, metallic *tink*. Alarm a high, piercing *tsewp*.

Harris's Sparrow

Zonotrichia querula

L 7.5" WS 10.5" WT 1.3 oz (36 g)

Our largest sparrow; shape like other Zonotrichia *sparrows. Size, pink bill, and bright white belly distinctive.*

1st winter
pale head
white belly
Juvenile (Jul–Aug)
1st winter (Aug–Apr)
1st winter (Aug–Apr)
Adult nonbreeding (Aug–Mar)
brown head
pink bill
whitish tertial edges
black face
white belly
Adult breeding (Mar–Aug)

Voice: Song of high, clear whistles like White-throated, but typically two or three notes with no pitch change *seeeeeeee seeee seeee;* some White-throated sing identical songs. Call a rather harsh *cheek* like White-throated but less sharp.

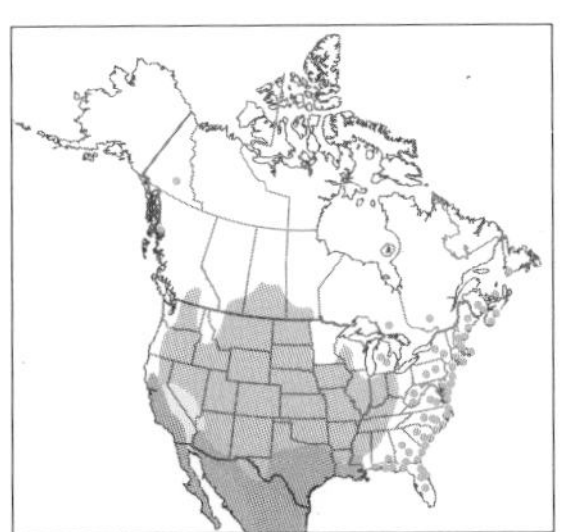

Zonotrichia sparrows sing all winter, unlike other species. A typical chorus of sounds from a winter flock of Harris's Sparrows includes clear or buzzy song phrases and varied call notes *feeee foooooo zeeeee zaaa wheewdi wheewdi djuk djuk djuk djuk zoooo wheewdi. . . .* Flocks of each *Zonotrichia* species produce their own distinctive chorus.

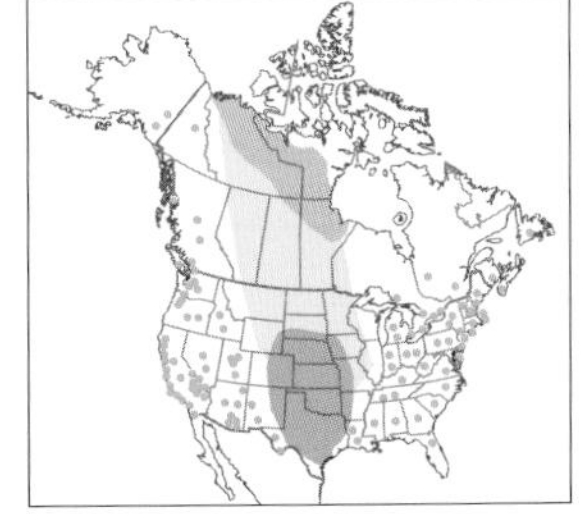

These two species are typical of the genus *Zonotrichia*. Large, heavy-bodied, and long-tailed, they winter in mixed flocks in dense brush, often singing.

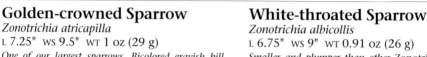

Golden-crowned Sparrow

Zonotrichia atricapilla

L 7.25" WS 9.5" WT 1 oz (29 g)

One of our largest sparrows. Bicolored grayish bill and plain face distinctive.

1st winter

Juvenile (Jul–Aug)

weakly defined, dark crown-stripes

1st winter (Aug–Mar)

1st winter (Aug–Mar)

faint eye-line

yellowish forecrown

gray bill

drab grayish

Adult breeding (Mar–Aug)

black to eye

yellow forecrown

bicolored bill

dull gray

Adult nonbreeding (Aug–Mar)

Voice: Song of high, clear whistles: typically only three notes with one or more notes slurred *seeeea seeeeeew soooo* ("oh deear mee"); birds in Canadian Rockies sing more complex song *seeeoo tooo teeee tetetetetete*. Call a loud, hard, clear, sharp *bink*. Flight call a high, level, rather short *seeep*.

White-throated Sparrow

Zonotrichia albicollis

L 6.75" WS 9" WT 0.91 oz (26 g)

Smaller and plumper than other Zonotrichia *sparrows. Rufous on wings and sharply outlined white throat distinctive.*

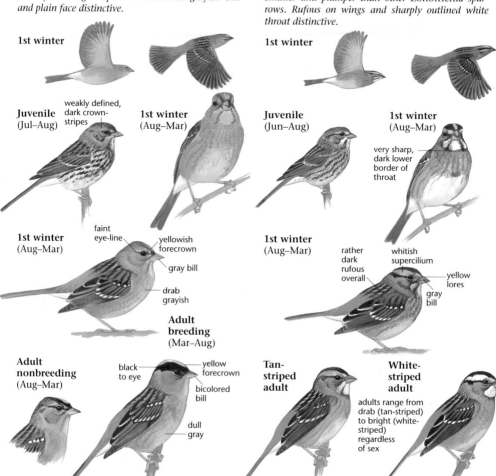

1st winter

Juvenile (Jun–Aug)

1st winter (Aug–Mar)

very sharp, dark lower border of throat

1st winter (Aug–Mar)

rather dark rufous overall

whitish supercilium

yellow lores

gray bill

Tan-striped adult

White-striped adult

adults range from drab (tan-striped) to bright (white-striped) regardless of sex

Voice: Song a high, pure whistle *sooo seeeeeee dididi dididi dididi* ("Old Sam Peabody Peabody Peabody") with little or no pitch change. Call a loud, sharp, metallic *chink*. Flight call a high, level, long *seeeet,* often with slight trill. Flock call a relatively low, laughing *kll kll kll kll. . . .*

White-throated Sparrow × Dark-eyed Junco hybrid adult

This combination is rare.

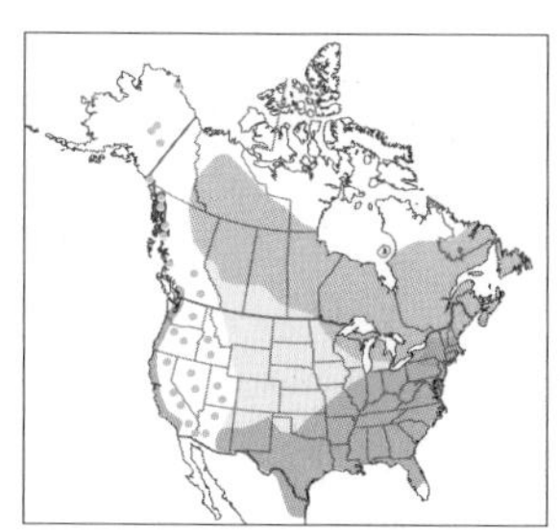

This rather pale, large, and slender species is often found in large flocks in brushy and weedy habitats, generally not in woods (where other *Zonotrichia* sparrows are most numerous).

White-crowned Sparrow

Zonotrichia leucophrys

L 7" WS 9.5" WT 1 oz (29 g)

Slightly more slender than other Zonotrichia; *long-tailed and long-necked; note pale pinkish or yellowish bill. Often raises crown feathers in slight crest.*

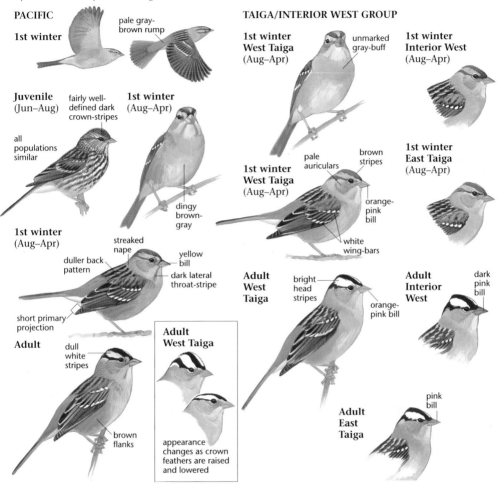

PACIFIC

1st winter

pale gray-brown rump

Juvenile (Jun–Aug)

fairly well-defined dark crown-stripes

all populations similar

1st winter (Aug–Apr)

dingy brown-gray

1st winter (Aug–Apr)

streaked nape

duller back pattern

yellow bill

dark lateral throat-stripe

short primary projection

Adult

dull white stripes

brown flanks

Adult West Taiga

appearance changes as crown feathers are raised and lowered

TAIGA/INTERIOR WEST GROUP

1st winter West Taiga (Aug–Apr)

unmarked gray-buff

1st winter Interior West (Aug–Apr)

1st winter West Taiga (Aug–Apr)

pale auriculars

brown stripes

orange-pink bill

white wing-bars

1st winter East Taiga (Aug–Apr)

Adult West Taiga

bright head stripes

orange-pink bill

Adult Interior West

dark pink bill

Adult East Taiga

pink bill

Voice: Song begins with clear whistles like White-throated then a series of buzzes or trills on different pitches; varies regionally. Taiga breeders sing buzzy, lazy *feeee odi odi zeeeeee zaaaaa zooo* with little variation. Pacific birds sing a clearer, more rapid *seeee sitli-sitli te-te-te-te-te-zrrrr* or *seeee zreee chidli chidli chi-chi-chi teew* with quick, slurred notes, often in pairs; many local dialects. Interior West birds also sing many local variations; usually most like Pacific. Call a sharp *pink* lower and drier than White-throated; varies regionally: flatter in Pacific, harder in Interior West. Flight call a high, thin, rising *seeep*.

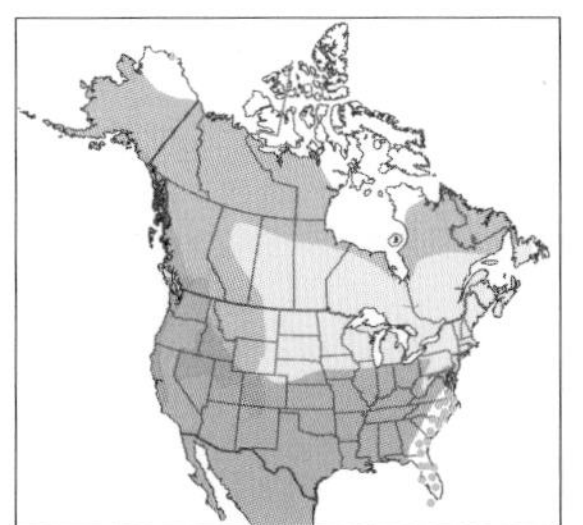

Pacific population differs from Taiga/Interior West group in appearance and voice: stockier and browner overall with yellow bill (details shown above); also note that the bend of the wing is yellow (vs. white) and nests are placed in a low bush (not on the ground). Populations within Taiga/Interior West group are distinguished only by color of bill and lores and song, but they intergrade where ranges meet. Interior West breeders (wintering mostly in Mexico) have extensively dark lores and dark pink bill. Taiga breeders west of the Hudson Bay have pale lores and orange bill; east of the Hudson Bay, they approach Interior West in appearance, with dark lores and pinkish bill.

Fox Sparrow

One of our largest sparrows, this stocky and round-headed species is related to sparrows of genus *Zonotrichia*. The four main populations are sometimes considered separate species.

Fox Sparrow

Passerella iliaca

L 7" WS 10.5" WT 1.1 oz (32 g)

THICK-BILLED (CALIFORNIA)

This population and Slate-colored both relatively long-tailed with plain gray back; note massive bill.

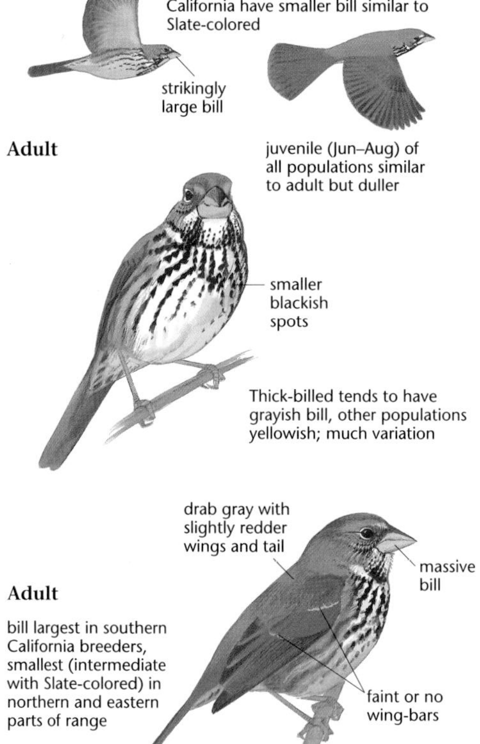

Adult
connected to Slate-colored by intermediates; populations in northern California have smaller bill similar to Slate-colored
strikingly large bill
Adult
juvenile (Jun–Aug) of all populations similar to adult but duller
smaller blackish spots
Thick-billed tends to have grayish bill, other populations yellowish; much variation
drab gray with slightly redder wings and tail
massive bill
Adult
bill largest in southern California breeders, smallest (intermediate with Slate-colored) in northern and eastern parts of range
faint or no wing-bars

Voice: Song variable but basically similar to other forms: one to three syllables with bubbling warble and one to four ending notes; individuals sing multiple songs, usually alternating among different songs; quality may suggest House Finch or Blue Grosbeak. Call a high, flat squeak *teep* like California Towhee.

SLATE-COLORED (INTERIOR WEST)

Plumage like Thick-billed but heavier spotting on underparts.

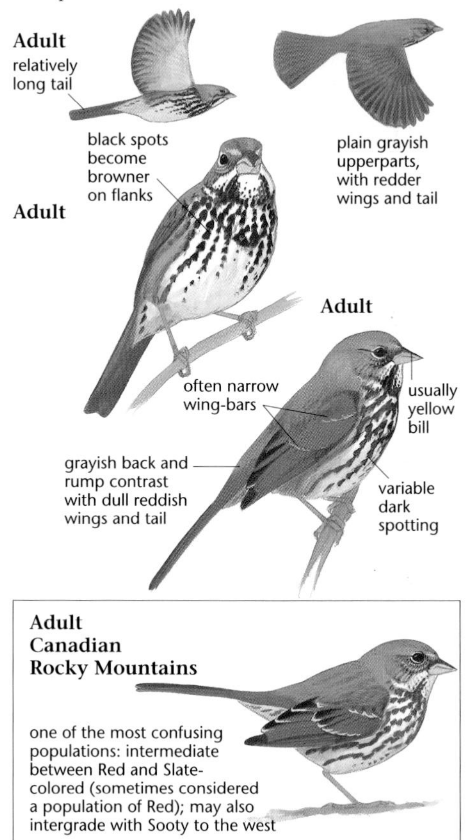

Adult
relatively long tail
black spots become browner on flanks
plain grayish upperparts, with redder wings and tail
Adult
Adult
often narrow wing-bars
usually yellow bill
grayish back and rump contrast with dull reddish wings and tail
variable dark spotting
Adult
Canadian
Rocky Mountains
one of the most confusing populations: intermediate between Red and Slate-colored (sometimes considered a population of Red); may also intergrade with Sooty to the west

Voice: Song clear and ringing; every other note emphasized, some buzzy or trilled; often similar to Green-tailed Towhee; individuals sing two to five different songs, never the same song twice in a row. Call a sharp *smack* like Sooty and Red populations.

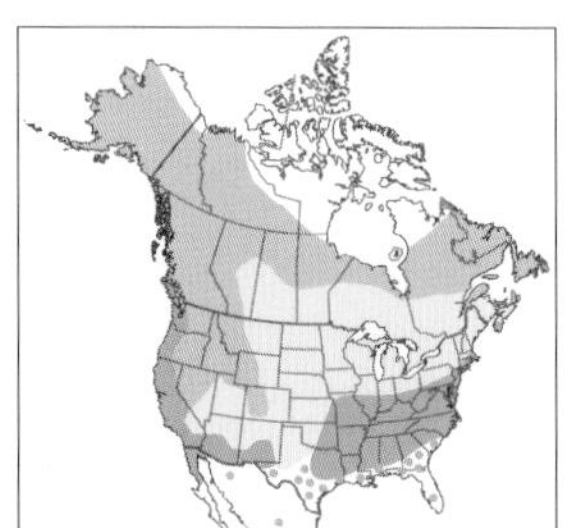

THICK-BILLED

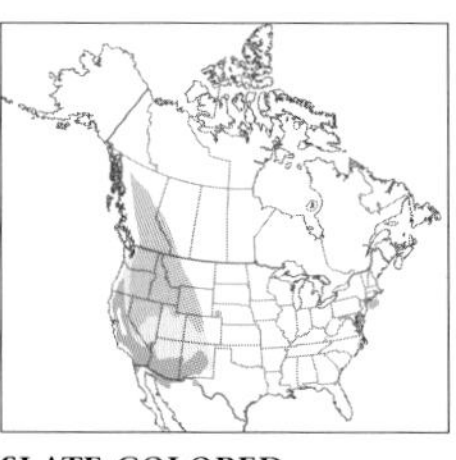

SLATE-COLORED

Fox Sparrow (continued)

These two northern populations intergrade both with each other and with Slate-colored where ranges overlap. They are found in brushy habitats within woods.

Fox Sparrow

Passerella iliaca

SOOTY (PACIFIC)

Shorter-tailed than Thick-billed and Slate-colored; plumage uniform brownish with densely spotted breast.

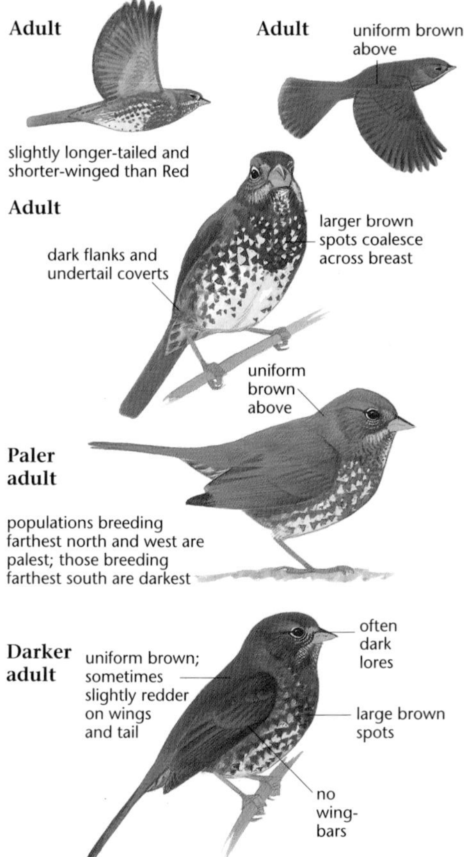
Adult
Adult
uniform brown above
slightly longer-tailed and shorter-winged than Red
Adult
dark flanks and undertail coverts
larger brown spots coalesce across breast
uniform brown above
Paler adult
populations breeding farthest north and west are palest; those breeding farthest south are darkest
Darker adult
uniform brown; sometimes slightly redder on wings and tail
often dark lores
large brown spots
no wing-bars

Voice: Song a long, irregular series with widely separated notes at beginning *wit; tip; swit, wit swit-swit teer zeep-zet-zet-zweeer;* buzzier, thinner, and more staccato than Red; individuals sing same song repeatedly. Calls like Red.

RED (TAIGA)

Slightly shorter-tailed and longer-winged than Sooty; the most brightly marked Fox Sparrow.

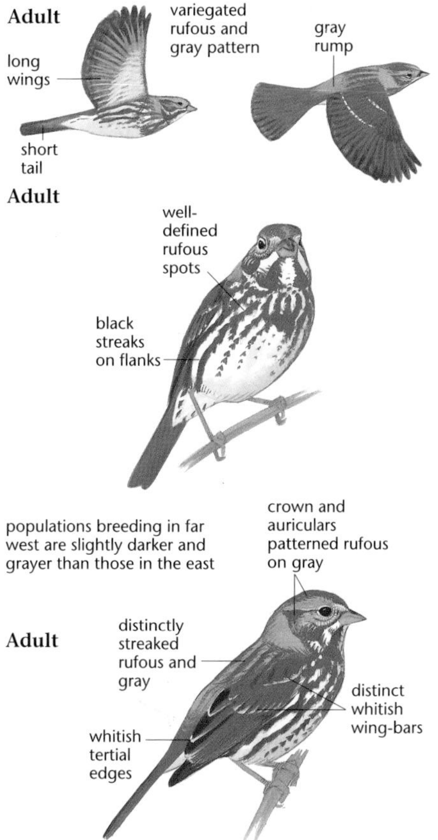
Adult
long wings
short tail
variegated rufous and gray pattern
gray rump
Adult
well-defined rufous spots
black streaks on flanks
populations breeding in far west are slightly darker and grayer than those in the east
crown and auriculars patterned rufous on gray
Adult
distinctly streaked rufous and gray
distinct whitish wing-bars
whitish tertial edges

Voice: Song a somewhat halting, relatively low, rich warble; richest and most melodious of all sparrows; mainly clear whistles, lacking trills or rapidly repeated notes *weet weeto teeoo teeo tzee tzer zezer reep;* individuals sing only one song. Call a very hard, sharp *smack* like Brown Thrasher. Flight call a high, sharp, rising *seeeep.*

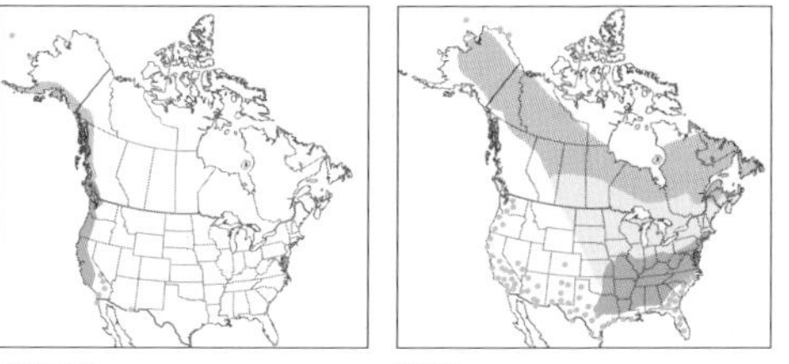

SOOTY

RED

All populations intergrade at the edges of their ranges. Some broad areas are occupied by intermediate populations, and many individuals are not safely identifiable in the field.

Sparrows: Genus *Melospiza*

This rather stocky, coarsely marked sparrow is our most widespread species. Individuals are found in any low, open, weedy or brushy habitat, sometimes in small flocks.

Song Sparrow

Melospiza melodia

L 6.25" WS 8.25" WT 0.7 oz (20 g)

Fairly long-tailed, round-headed, and stout-billed; coarsely streaked, with bold brown lateral throat-stripe and central breast-spot. Soft call note very distinctive.

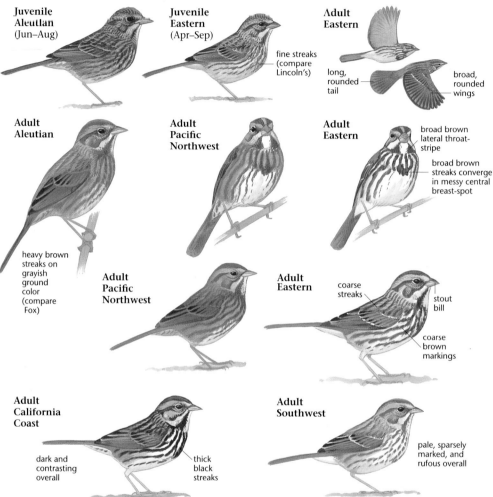

Juvenile Aleutian (Jun–Aug)

Juvenile Eastern (Apr–Sep)

fine streaks (compare Lincoln's)

Adult Eastern

long, rounded tail

broad, rounded wings

Adult Aleutian

heavy brown streaks on grayish ground color (compare Fox)

Adult Pacific Northwest

Adult Eastern

broad brown lateral throat-stripe

broad brown streaks converge in messy central breast-spot

Adult Pacific Northwest

Adult Eastern

coarse streaks

stout bill

coarse brown markings

Adult California Coast

dark and contrasting overall

thick black streaks

Adult Southwest

pale, sparsely marked, and rufous overall

Voice: Song a variable series of trills and clear notes with slightly husky quality and pleasant gentle rhythm; begins with several short, sharp notes, usually one long trill in middle of song *seet seet seet to zeeeeeee tipo zeet zeet.* Call a very distinctive, husky *jimp*. Alarm a very high, hard *tik*. Flight call a high, thin, level *seeet*. Chase call a rapid series of rising then falling sharp call notes.

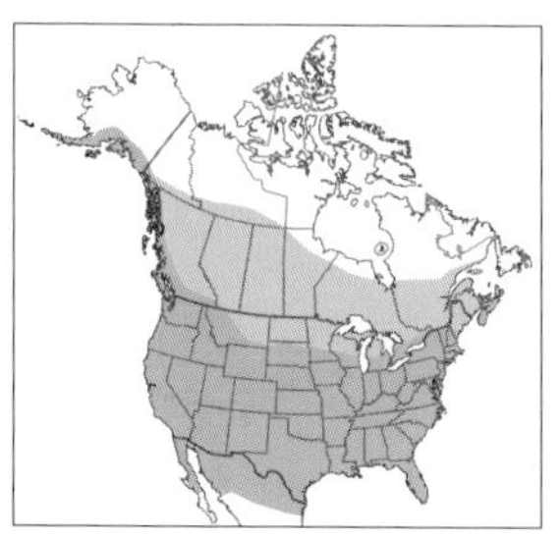

Typical regional variations are shown, but all populations are connected by an unbroken cline of intergrades; many birds seen will be intermediate between those illustrated. Variation is most pronounced in overall color as well as color and thickness of streaking on underparts. Aleutian, Pacific Northwest, and California Coast populations average longer- and thinner-billed than Eastern; Aleutian breeders are 25 percent larger than the general average, while California Coast breeders are 10 percent smaller. There is essentially no variation in voice throughout the range.

Sparrows: Genus *Melospiza* (continued)

These two species are closely related to each other and to Song Sparrow. Both are found in grassy, weedy, and brushy areas, often near water, Swamp Sparrow especially in marshy areas.

Lincoln's Sparrow

Melospiza lincolnii

L 5.75" WS 7.5" WT 0.6 oz (17 g)

Similar to Song Sparrow but smaller, more delicate, and shorter-tailed. Small, pointed bill, crisp streaking overall, and distinctive calls.

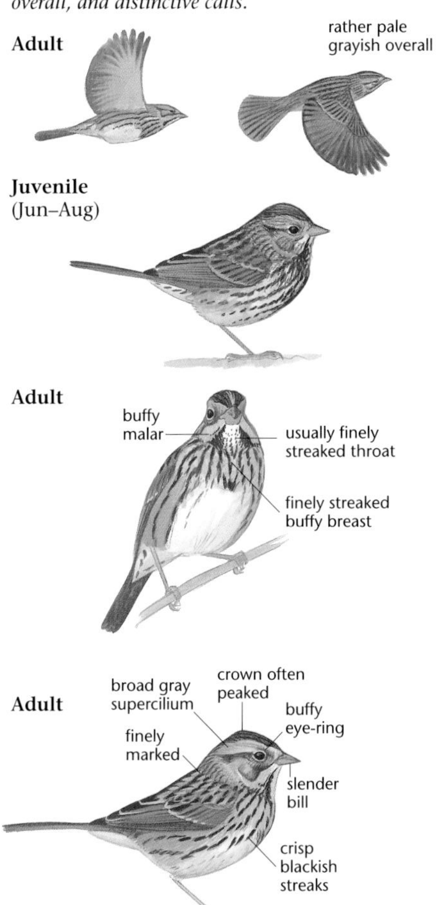
Adult
rather pale grayish overall
Juvenile (Jun–Aug)
Adult
buffy malar
usually finely streaked throat
finely streaked buffy breast
Adult
broad gray supercilium
crown often peaked
buffy eye-ring
finely marked
slender bill
crisp blackish streaks

Voice: Song a continuous jumble of husky, chirping trills with several pitch changes *jew-jew-jew-jew-je-eeeeeeeeee-do-je-e-e-e-to;* bubbling quality and pattern reminiscent of House Wren. Call a sharp, light chip. Flight call a high, buzzy *zeeet* like Swamp but finer and rising.

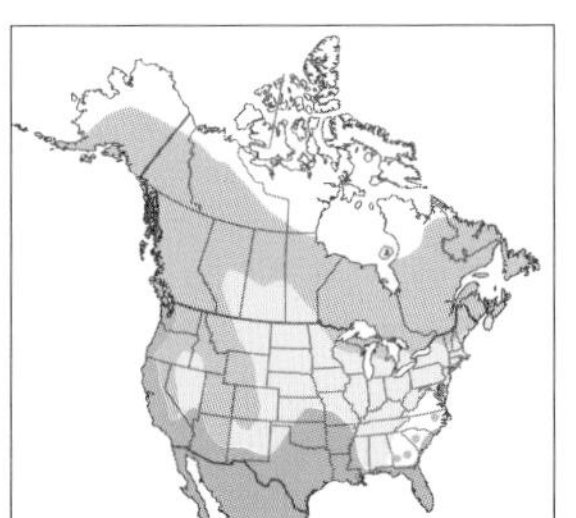

Swamp Sparrow

Melospiza georgiana

L 5.75" WS 7.25" WT 0.6 oz (17 g)

Structure very similar to Lincoln's; differs in overall dark rufous wings, coarsely streaked (or unstreaked) breast and crown, and call.

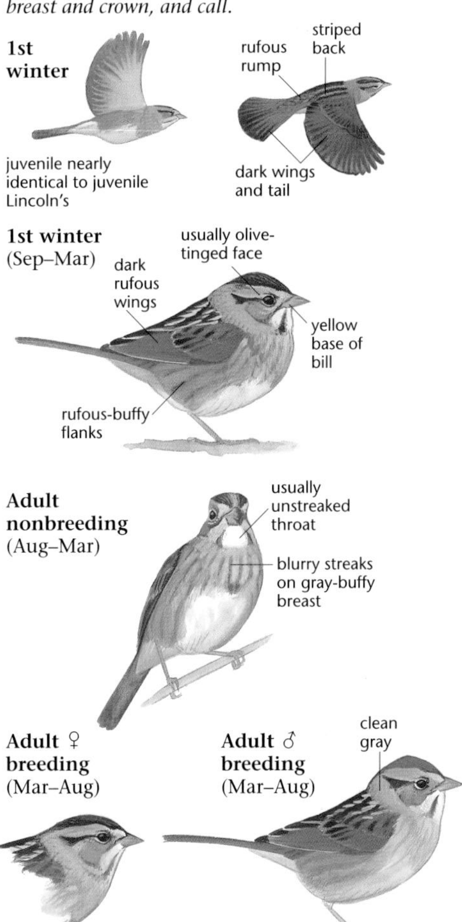
1st winter
rufous rump
striped back
juvenile nearly identical to juvenile Lincoln's
dark wings and tail
1st winter (Sep–Mar)
dark rufous wings
usually olive-tinged face
yellow base of bill
rufous-buffy flanks
Adult nonbreeding (Aug–Mar)
usually unstreaked throat
blurry streaks on gray-buffy breast
Adult ♀ breeding (Mar–Aug)
Adult ♂ breeding (Mar–Aug)
clean gray

Voice: Song a simple, musical trill with slow tempo *chinga chinga chinga* . . . fading at end. Call a loud, hard chip; not as metallic as White-throated. Flight call a high, buzzy *zeeet* like Lincoln's but coarser and level.

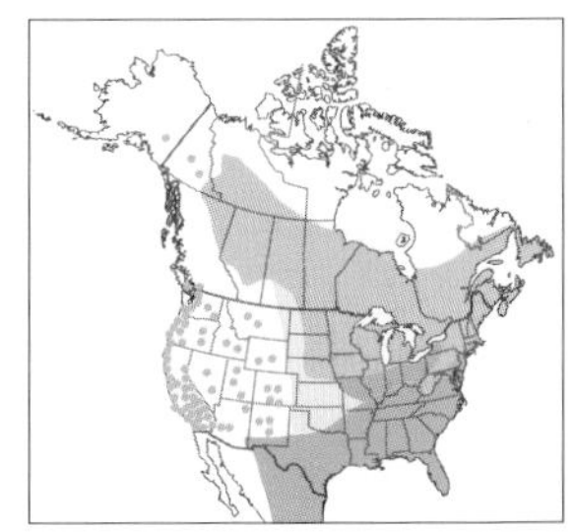

DARK-EYED JUNCO

This species currently includes at least six recognizable populations. Similar in shape and habits, all nest in coniferous woods and in winter flock together in open woods and brushy clearings.

Dark-eyed Junco

Junco hyemalis

L 6.25" WS 9.25" WT 0.67 oz (19 g)

OREGON

Marginally the smallest junco. Dark, dull-gray hood contrasts sharply with brown back and flanks.

Adult ♀

1st year ♀

brownish sides

Adult ♀

dark, sooty hood

reddish back

pinkish-brown flanks

Pale adult ♂

Dark adult ♂

PINK-SIDED

Averages 5 percent larger than Oregon. Clean blue-gray hood (palest on throat) contrasts with blackish lores and extensive pinkish flanks.

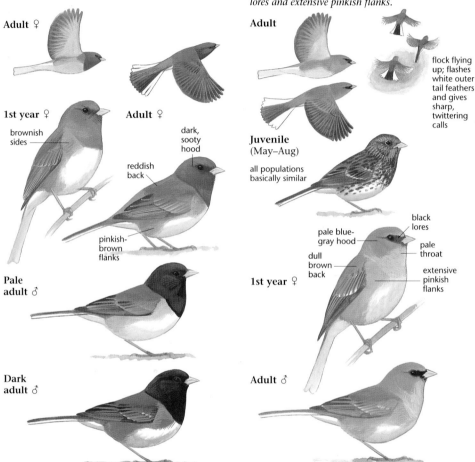

Adult

flock flying up; flashes white outer tail feathers and gives sharp, twittering calls

Juvenile (May–Aug)

all populations basically similar

black lores

pale blue-gray hood

pale throat

dull brown back

extensive pinkish flanks

1st year ♀

Adult ♂

Voice: Songs of most populations indistinguishable: a short trill averaging slower and more musical than Chipping Sparrow; Slate-colored may average longer song with more rapid tempo and smaller repertoire than Oregon; all populations sing quiet, varied warbling phrases in early spring. Call a very high, hard, smacking *stip*. Flight call a sharp, buzzy *tzeet;* also high, tinkling chips when flushed *tsititit tit*. Chase call a series of high, clear *keew* notes.

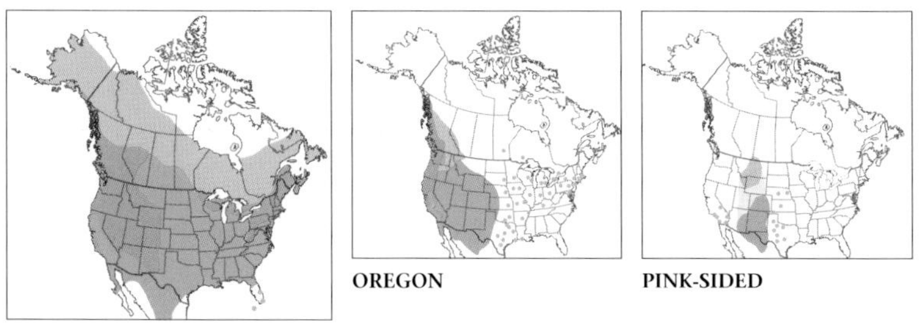

OREGON

PINK-SIDED

All juncos are small, slender, cleanly marked sparrows with striking white outer tail feathers. They differ mainly in the color and contrast of head and body plumage.

Dark-eyed Junco

Junco hyemalis

WHITE-WINGED

The largest junco; averages 12 percent larger than Slate-colored, with relatively larger bill. Rather pale gray overall (palest on throat), with weak wing-bars and extensive white on tail.

SLATE-COLORED

Size and shape like Oregon. Overall color varies from pale brown to dark gray; little or no contrast between head and body.

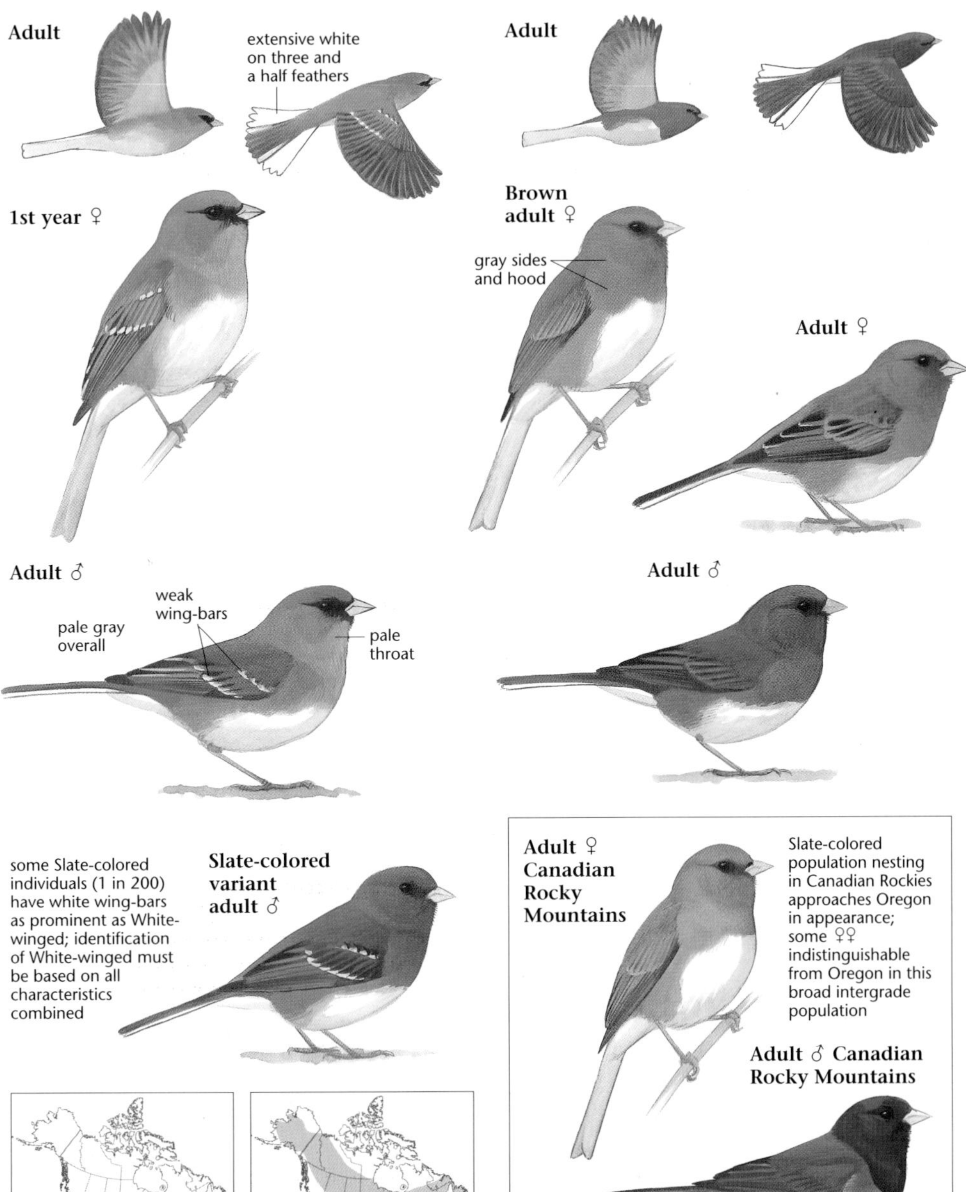
Adult
extensive white on three and a half feathers
1st year ♀
Adult ♂
weak wing-bars
pale gray overall
pale throat
some Slate-colored individuals (1 in 200) have white wing-bars as prominent as White-winged; identification of White-winged must be based on all characteristics combined
Slate-colored variant adult ♂
Adult
Brown adult ♀
gray sides and hood
Adult ♀
Adult ♂
Adult ♀ Canadian Rocky Mountains
Slate-colored population nesting in Canadian Rockies approaches Oregon in appearance; some ♀♀ indistinguishable from Oregon in this broad intergrade population
Adult ♂ Canadian Rocky Mountains

WHITE-WINGED

SLATE-COLORED

Gray-headed and Red-backed are two forms of Dark-eyed Junco. The similar Yellow-eyed Junco is found in open coniferous and mixed woods and differs in plumage, habits, and voice.

Dark-eyed Junco

Junco hyemalis

Both of these populations average 5 percent larger than Oregon. Note low-contrast gray plumage with dark rufous mantle.

Adult

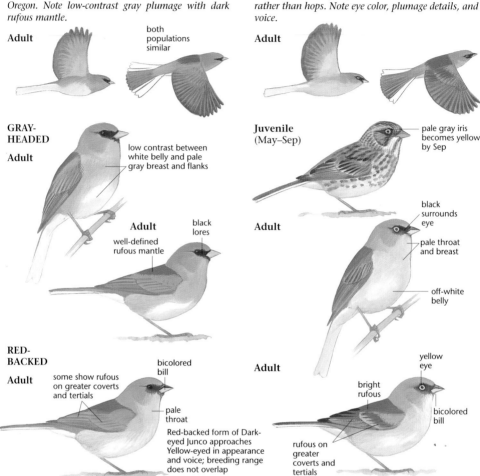

both populations similar

GRAY-HEADED

Adult

low contrast between white belly and pale gray breast and flanks

Adult

black lores

well-defined rufous mantle

RED-BACKED

Adult

some show rufous on greater coverts and tertials

bicolored bill

pale throat

Red-backed form of Dark-eyed Junco approaches Yellow-eyed in appearance and voice; breeding range does not overlap

Voice: GRAY-HEADED: Song and calls identical to Oregon and other Dark-eyed Juncos; a few sing complex song *tu-tu-tu-tu-tu-zeeeeeeee-tip* or *tititititititititototototo*. RED-BACKED: Song often three-part, approaching Yellow-eyed. Call more like Yellow-eyed.

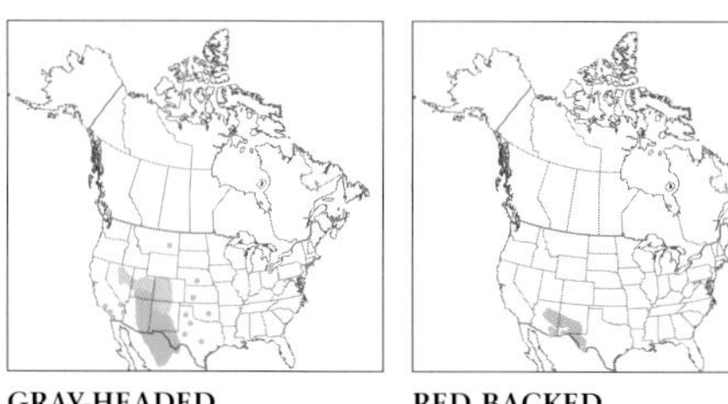

GRAY-HEADED RED-BACKED

Yellow-eyed Junco

Junco phaeonotus

L 6.25" WS 10" WT 0.74 oz (21 g)

Similar to Dark-eyed Junco but walks on the ground rather than hops. Note eye color, plumage details, and voice.

Adult

Juvenile (May–Sep)

pale gray iris becomes yellow by Sep

Adult

black surrounds eye

pale throat and breast

off-white belly

Adult

yellow eye

bright rufous

bicolored bill

rufous on greater coverts and tertials

Voice: Song a high, whistled *tzew tzew titititititi tsidip* or *shidle shidle shidle shidle titititititi;* first part slurred and bouncy, trill short and rattling (but may be left out). Song unlike Dark-eyed (except Red-backed form), but compare Bewick's Wren and Spotted Towhee. Call slightly lower and fuller than Dark-eyed.

Rustic Bunting

This species is the only bunting of the Old World genus *Emberiza* recorded regularly in North America. It is found in weedy or brushy areas, foraging on the ground with other sparrows.

Rustic Bunting

Emberiza rustica

L 6" WS 9.5" WT 0.67 oz (19 g)

Relatively long, notched tail and long wings; distinct crest. Differs from sparrows in pattern of tail, tertials, breast, and head.

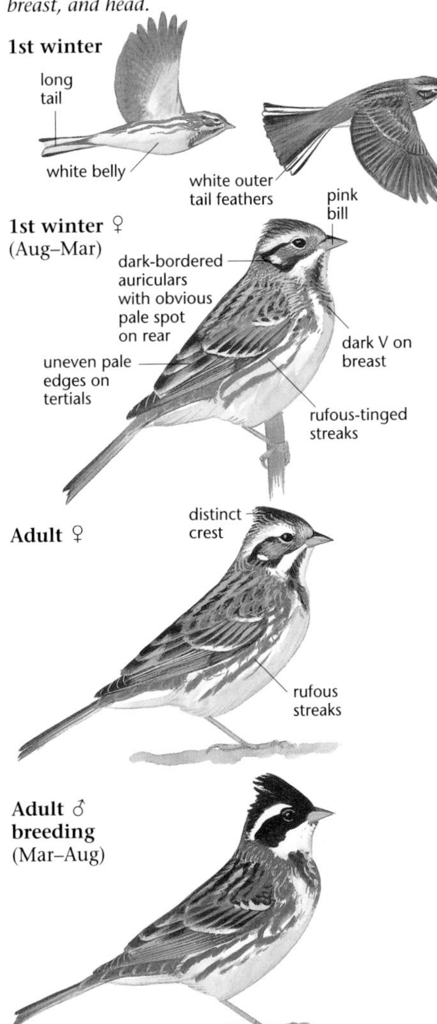

1st winter
long tail
white belly
white outer tail feathers
pink bill
1st winter ♀
(Aug–Mar)
dark-bordered auriculars with obvious pale spot on rear
uneven pale edges on tertials
dark V on breast
rufous-tinged streaks
Adult ♀
distinct crest
rufous streaks
Adult ♂ breeding
(Mar–Aug)

Voice: Song a fairly short, mellow warble reminiscent of Lapland Longspur. Call a short, hard *tick.*

Identification of Emberizine Buntings

Like some other common names (e.g., robin, flycatcher, warbler), the name "bunting" has been borrowed from British usage and applied to unrelated North American species. The original buntings were species in the Old World genus *Emberiza* (represented here by Rustic Bunting) and related genera, including longspurs (in Britain, Lapland Longspur is known as Lapland Bunting) and Snow and McKay's Buntings. Early ornithologists in North America named many species "buntings," and in a few cases the names have persisted. Thus we have Lark Bunting, which is distinctive but may be closely related to Snow Bunting, and the colorful buntings of the genera *Passerina* and *Cyanocompsa,* in the family Cardinalidae, which have little in common with the emberizine buntings.

Snow and McKay's differ only in extent of black in plumage; virtually all McKay's Buntings are significantly whiter than Snow, but female McKay's can resemble male Snow. The primary problem is that female McKay's Bunting in breeding plumage resembles adult male breeding Snow Bunting or hybrid. Female McKay's differs in having brownish primaries with a less sharply contrasting white base; close views should reveal dusky speckling on forehead and dull streaked pattern on back. Adult males of both species have sharply contrasting black and white primaries and a clean white head; male Snow has a black back. Hybrids and backcrosses, regularly seen on the Bering Sea islands, show intermediate extent of black on wings and tail and white streaks on back. Female hybrids may be undetectable.

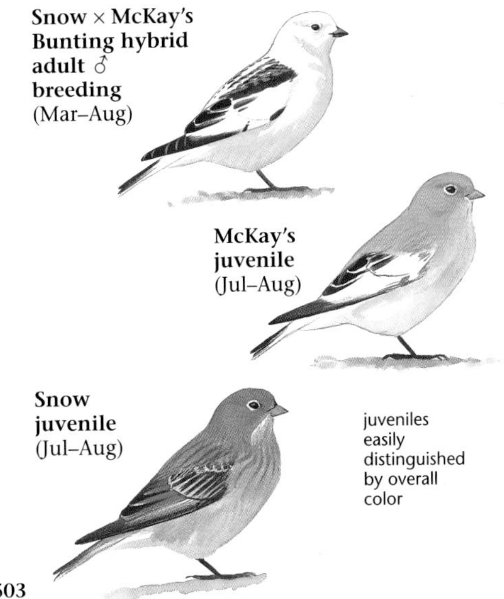

Snow × McKay's Bunting hybrid adult ♂ breeding
(Mar–Aug)
McKay's juvenile
(Jul–Aug)
Snow juvenile
(Jul–Aug)
juveniles easily distinguished by overall color

Longspurs

These prairie longspurs are stocky and fairly short-tailed. Chestnut-collared is found in dense grass; McCown's is found on barren, open ground such as dry lakebeds and overgrazed pastures.

McCown's Longspur

Calcarius mccownii

L 6" WS 11" WT 0.81 oz (23 g)

Heavy, stocky, short-tailed, and large-billed, appearing large-headed. Palest overall of all longspurs; distinctively plain-faced (recalls female House Sparrow).

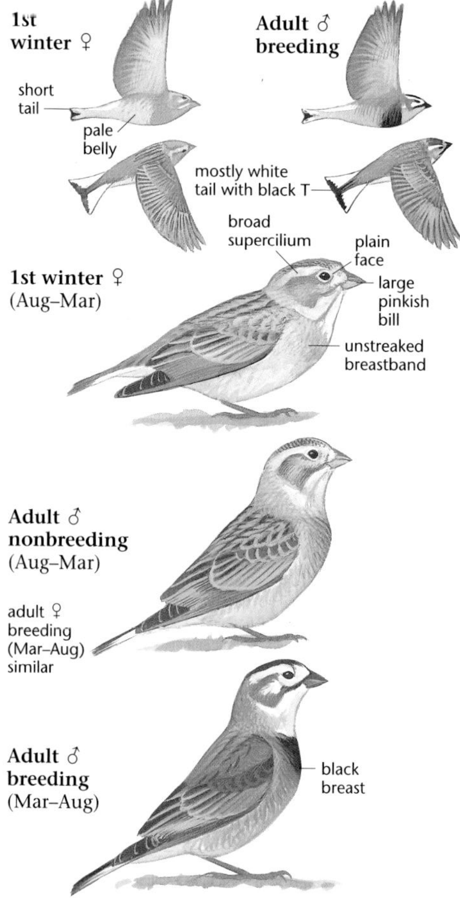

1st winter ♀
short tail
pale belly
Adult ♂ breeding
mostly white tail with black T
broad supercilium
plain face
1st winter ♀ (Aug–Mar)
large pinkish bill
unstreaked breastband
Adult ♂ nonbreeding (Aug–Mar)
adult ♀ breeding (Mar–Aug) similar
Adult ♂ breeding (Mar–Aug)
black breast

Voice: Song a formless, soft, liquid warble of short, rapid phrases with halting pauses *flideli fledeli fleedlili freew;* lower than other longspurs and with different rhythm. Call a liquid, musical rattle like Lapland but softer and shorter, often shortened to *kittip;* also a single or double *poik,* a metallic *pink,* and a sharp, whistled *teep.*

Chestnut-collared Longspur

Calcarius ornatus

L 6" WS 10.5" WT 0.67 oz (19 g)

Our smallest longspur, with short, rounded wings, short tail, relatively small bill. Female drab gray-brown overall.

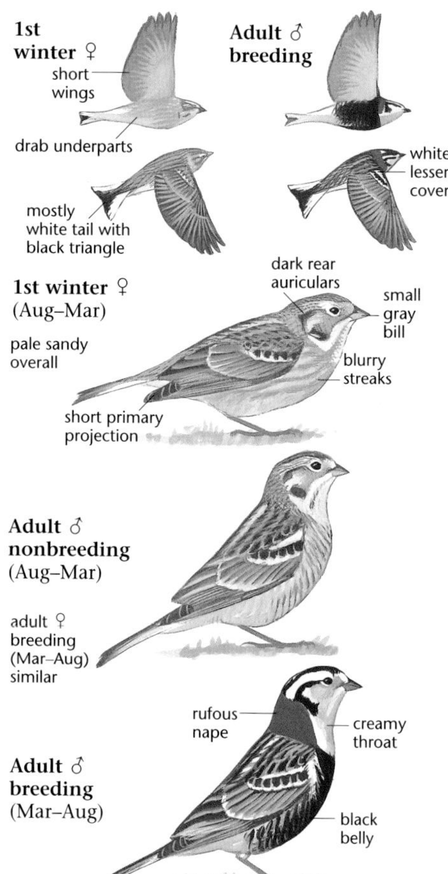

1st winter ♀
short wings
drab underparts
Adult ♂ breeding
white lesser coverts
mostly white tail with black triangle
dark rear auriculars
1st winter ♀ (Aug–Mar)
small gray bill
pale sandy overall
blurry streaks
short primary projection
Adult ♂ nonbreeding (Aug–Mar)
adult ♀ breeding (Mar–Aug) similar
rufous nape
creamy throat
Adult ♂ breeding (Mar–Aug)
black belly

Voice: Song a sweet warble *seet sidee tidee zeek zeerdi* beginning high and clear, ending lower and buzzy; pattern of gurgling pitch changes and falling trend reminiscent of Western Meadowlark but much higher-pitched. Flight call a soft, husky, two- or three-note *kiddle* or *kidedel;* also a buzz and a soft rattle.

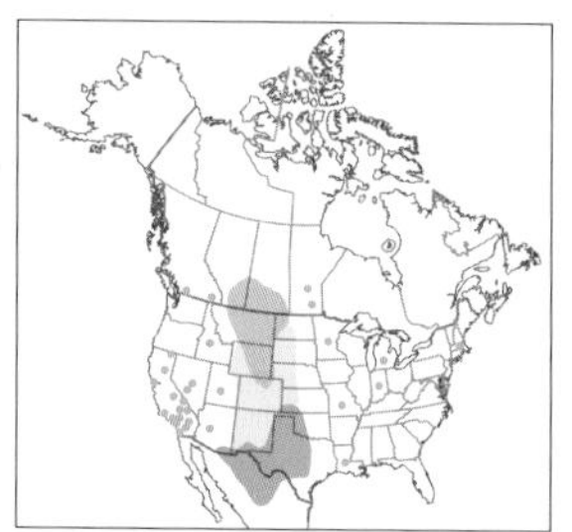

McCown's Longspur

Chestnut-collared Longspur

Primary projections of Longspurs. Note length of projection and spacing of primary tips.

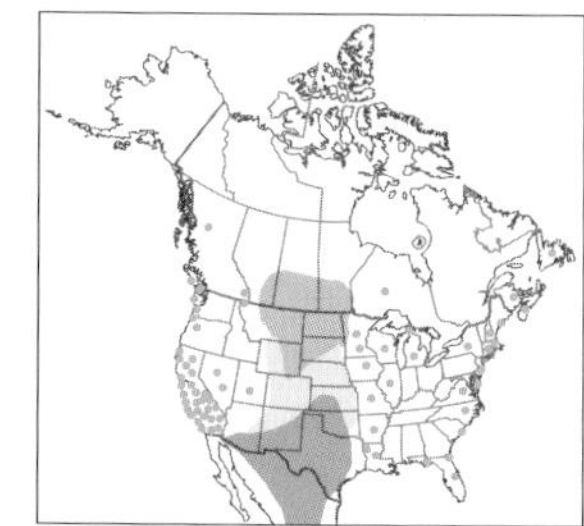

These two tundra-breeding longspurs are slender with long, pointed wings and fairly long tails. Smith's is found in short, dry grass, Lapland on open ground such as fields, beaches, pastures.

Smith's Longspur

Calcarius pictus

L 6.25" WS 11.25" WT 0.91 oz (26 g)

Structure similar to Lapland but slightly longer-tailed and thinner-billed. Female finely streaked with buffy belly.

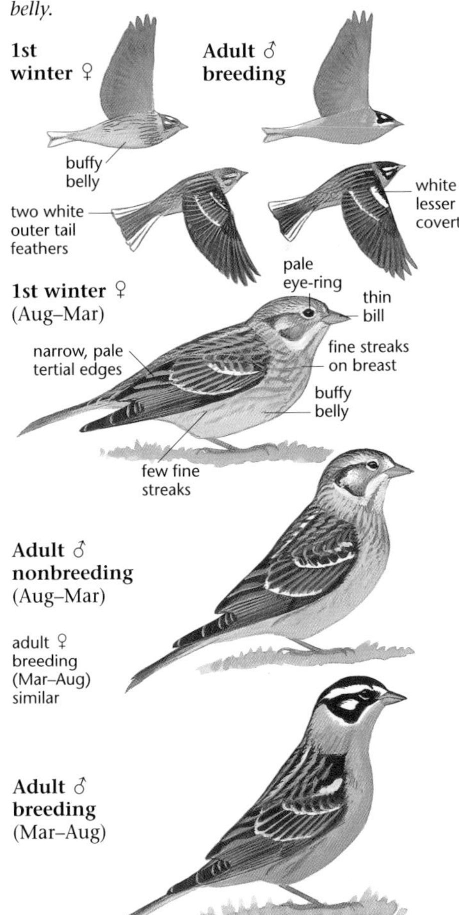
1st winter ♀
Adult ♂ breeding
buffy belly
two white outer tail feathers
white lesser coverts
pale eye-ring
thin bill
1st winter ♀ (Aug–Mar)
narrow, pale tertial edges
fine streaks on breast
buffy belly
few fine streaks
Adult ♂ nonbreeding (Aug–Mar)
adult ♀ breeding (Mar–Aug) similar
Adult ♂ breeding (Mar–Aug)

Voice: Song a high, sweet warble *seet seet seeo see zeet zidi zeet zeet zeeo;* similar to American Tree Sparrow but with rising trend. Call on breeding grounds a nasal, buzzy *goeet.* Flight call a staccato rattle similar to Lapland but sharp clicks more widely spaced and falling slightly at end; whole pattern reminiscent of rattle of cowbirds.

Lapland Longspur

Calcarius lapponicus

L 6.25" WS 11.5" WT 0.95 oz (27 g)

Long-winged and stout-billed. Female has bold auricular frame, rufous on coverts and tertials, distinct streaks on flanks.

1st winter ♀
Adult ♂ breeding
one white outer tail feather
bold supercilium
1st winter ♀ (Aug–Mar)
rufous-edged greater coverts
dark frame on auriculars
buffy breast
white belly
broad rufous tertial edges
broad streaks
Adult ♂ nonbreeding (Aug–Mar)
dark breastband
adult ♀ breeding (Mar–Aug) similar
yellow bill
Adult ♂ breeding (Mar–Aug)

Voice: Song a gentle, jingling warble *freew didi freer di fridi fideew* with rich, husky quality. Common call a husky, whistled *tleew* similar to Snow Bunting; common calls in summer include sharp, dry, whistled *chich* and *chi-kewoo.* Flight call a dry, mechanical rattle similar to Smith's and McCown's and to Snow Bunting.

Smith's Longspur

Lapland Longspur

Primary projections of Longspurs. Note length of projection and spacing of primary tips.

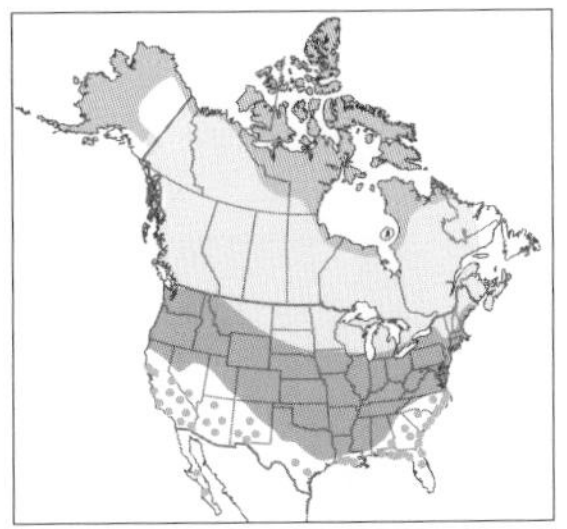

McKay's and Snow Buntings

These species are very closely related (perhaps conspecific) but distinctive as a pair. Both are found in flocks on barren, open ground—beaches, fields, tundra—often with larks and longspurs.

McKay's Bunting

Plectrophenax hyperboreus

L 6.75" WS 14" WT 1.9 oz (54 g)

Identical to Snow Bunting but with more white and less black, particularly on wings and tail.

1st winter ♀

Adult ♂

wing pattern like Snow ♂ but browner

mostly white tail

nearly all-white

1st winter ♀ (Aug–Mar)

Adult ♀ breeding (Mar–Aug)

speckled forehead

dull, streaked back

some resemble Snow ♂ or hybrid

Adult ♂ nonbreeding (Aug–Mar)

Adult ♂ breeding (Mar–Aug)

white back

in all plumages shows mostly white wing coverts

Snow Bunting

Plectrophenax nivalis

L 6.75" WS 14" WT 1.5 oz (42 g)

Larger than longspurs and Horned Larks with fluffy plumage, shuffling gait, and flashing white wing-patches.

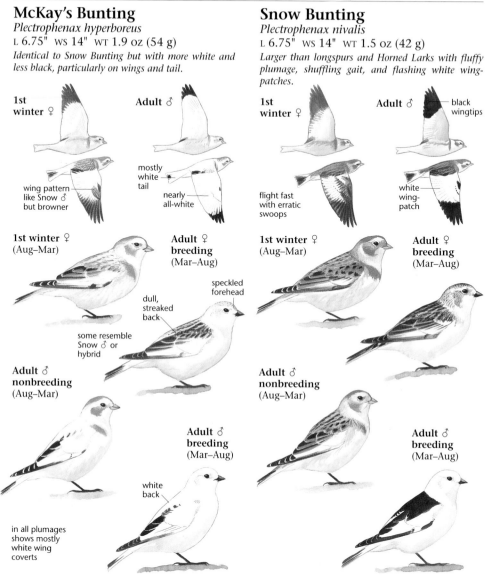

1st winter ♀

Adult ♂

black wingtips

flight fast with erratic swoops

white wing-patch

1st winter ♀ (Aug–Mar)

Adult ♀ breeding (Mar–Aug)

Adult ♂ nonbreeding (Aug–Mar)

Adult ♂ breeding (Mar–Aug)

Voice: Both species apparently identical. Song a rather low, husky warbling with repeated pattern *hudidi feet feet feew hudidi feet feet feew hudidi;* similar to Lapland Longspur but a bit lower-pitched and less flowing; repetition distinctive. Calls include a soft, husky rattle *didididi* softer than Lapland Longspur, and a clear, descending whistle *cheew* clearer and sweeter than Lapland Longspur; when in flock also gives a short, nasal buzz *zrrt.*

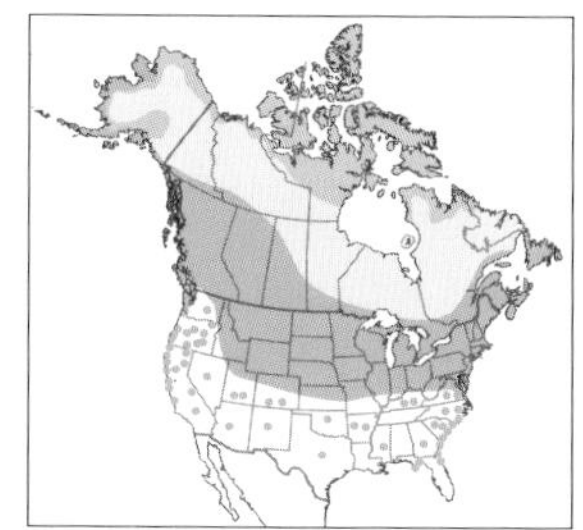

Icterids

Family: Icteridae

23 species in 8 genera. All icterids have rather slender, pointed bills; otherwise their structure is difficult to generalize. Meadowlarks are starlinglike in shape and are found in grassy areas and build domed nests on the ground. Bobolink is unique. Cowbirds, blackbirds, and grackles are all found in large mixed flocks in open fields and woods in nonbreeding season; they feed on grain and insects, and most nest and roost colonially (cowbirds are brood parasites). Orioles are brightly colored (resembling tanagers and wood-warblers) with rich, fluting songs; they are found singly in open woods and feed on insects, fruit, and nectar; nest is a pendulous cup in a tree (nests of Altamira and Streak-backed are up to two feet long). Adult females are shown.

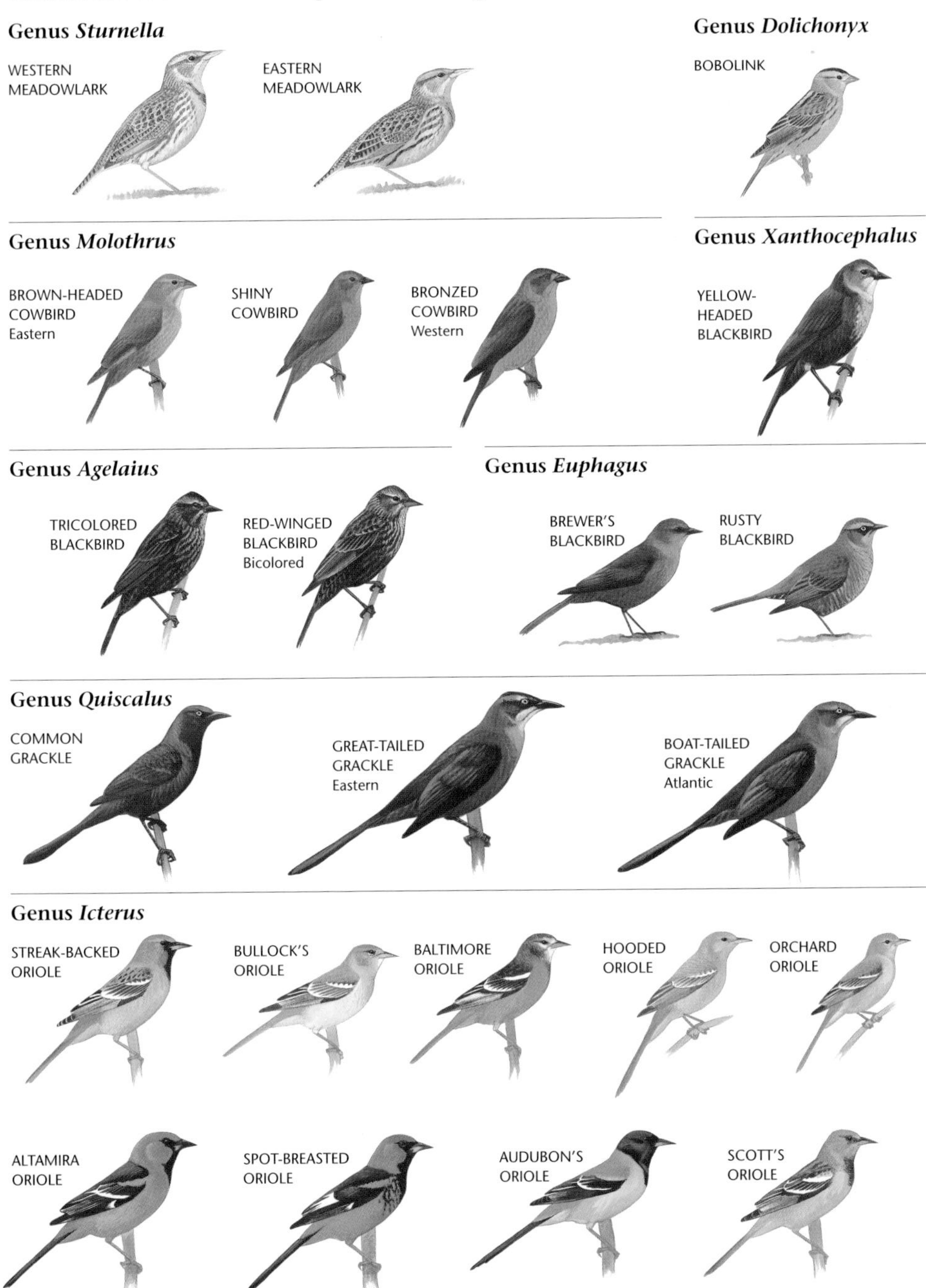

Genus *Sturnella*
WESTERN MEADOWLARK
EASTERN MEADOWLARK
Genus *Dolichonyx*
BOBOLINK
Genus *Molothrus*
BROWN-HEADED COWBIRD Eastern
SHINY COWBIRD
BRONZED COWBIRD Western
Genus *Xanthocephalus*
YELLOW-HEADED BLACKBIRD
Genus *Agelaius*
TRICOLORED BLACKBIRD
RED-WINGED BLACKBIRD Bicolored
Genus *Euphagus*
BREWER'S BLACKBIRD
RUSTY BLACKBIRD
Genus *Quiscalus*
COMMON GRACKLE
GREAT-TAILED GRACKLE Eastern
BOAT-TAILED GRACKLE Atlantic
Genus *Icterus*
STREAK-BACKED ORIOLE
BULLOCK'S ORIOLE
BALTIMORE ORIOLE
HOODED ORIOLE
ORCHARD ORIOLE
ALTAMIRA ORIOLE
SPOT-BREASTED ORIOLE
AUDUBON'S ORIOLE
SCOTT'S ORIOLE

Meadowlarks

These two species are distinctive as a pair but are barely distinguishable from each other. Both are found in open, grassy habitats, often perching on fences or bushes in small, loose flocks.

Western Meadowlark

Sturnella neglecta

L 9.5" WS 14.5" WT 3.4 oz (97 g) ♂>♀

Both meadowlarks are heavy-bodied, short-tailed, and long-billed. Obvious white outer tail feathers.

Adult

flight weak, fluttering

limited white

Adult nonbreeding (Sep–Jan)

low-contrast head pattern

pale gray-brown overall

whitish flanks

Adult breeding (Feb–Aug)

yellow malar

Voice: Song a rich, low, descending warble *sleep loo lidi lidijuvi;* begins with well-spaced, clear, short whistles and ends with rapid gurgle. Common call a low, bell-like *pluk;* blackbirdlike but more musical; also a slow, dull rattle *vidididididi-didi*. Flight call slightly lower than Eastern.

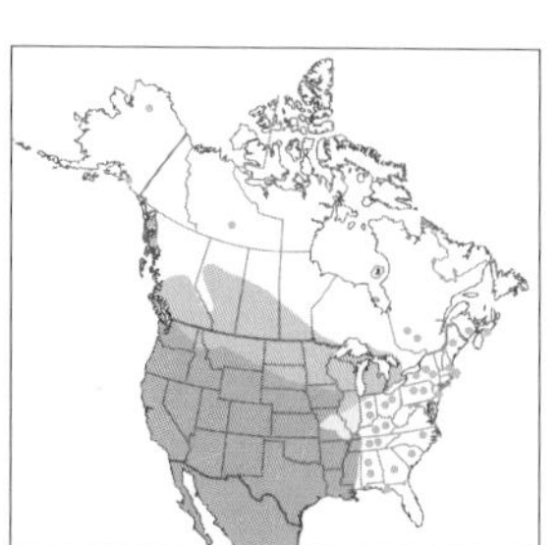

Eastern Meadowlark

Sturnella magna

L 9.5" WS 14" WT 3.2 oz (90 g) ♂>♀

Virtually identical to Western; best identified by voice. Plumage characteristics very subtle.

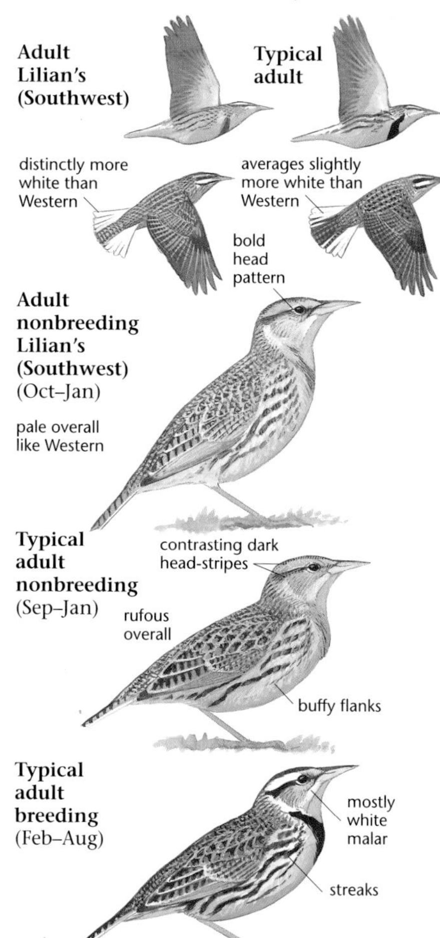

Adult Lilian's (Southwest)
Typical adult
distinctly more white than Western
averages slightly more white than Western
bold head pattern
Adult nonbreeding Lilian's (Southwest) (Oct–Jan)
pale overall like Western
Typical adult nonbreeding (Sep–Jan)
contrasting dark head-stripes
rufous overall
buffy flanks
Typical adult breeding (Feb–Aug)
mostly white malar
streaks

Voice: Song of simple, clear, slurred whistles *seeeooaaa seeeeadoo* with many variations; higher and clearer than Western with no complex gurgling phrases. Call a sharp, electric *dziit* or *jerZIK* and hard, mechanical rattle *ztttttttttt*. Flight call a thin, rising *veeet* or *rrink*.

Breeding plumage of meadowlarks is acquired by wear; some individuals (probably adult males) have breeding appearance year-round, while others (probably females) have pale brownish feather tips completely veiling the yellow and black underparts Aug–Mar. Females average drabber than males.

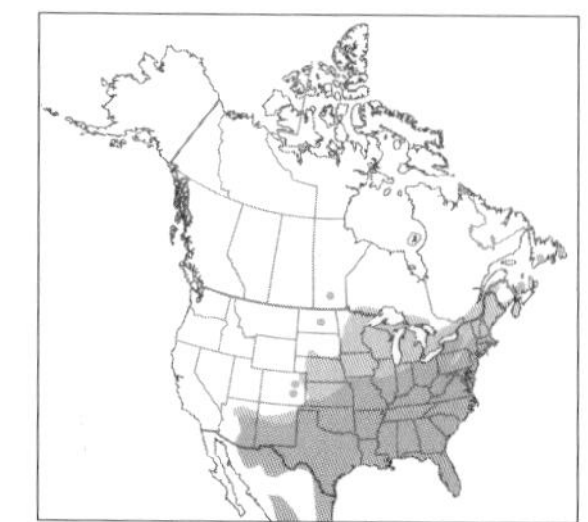

Identification of Meadowlarks

Voice may be the most reliable clue in identifying meadowlarks, but individual birds can learn the "wrong" song. Listen for details of pitch and for repertoire size (Eastern male sings 50–100 songs, Western fewer than 10). A bird usually gives the same song several times before switching to another one, so extended listening is required to assess a bird's repertoire size. Imitated songs are generally intermediate in pitch, not perfect imitations, and intermediate songs make up only part of a bird's repertoire, so extended listening should reveal typical songs of the species, which can then be identified with confidence. Calls can also be learned or inherited by hybrids, but intermediate or "wrong" calls are apparently rare.

Southwest populations of Eastern (Lilian's Meadowlark) may represent a separate species; more study is needed. Lilian's song is similar to typical Eastern populations but averages lower-pitched, with some songs close to Western; all calls are identical to typical Eastern. Western averages slightly smaller and shorter-legged but longer-winged than typical Eastern; Lilian's is smallest overall but relatively long-winged like Western. All shape differences, however, are too subtle to be useful in the field.

Lilian's Eastern is usually distinguished from Western Meadowlark by extensive white in tail (no overlap) and more contrasting head pattern with pale auriculars and bold, dark eye-line (Western has brownish auriculars and paler, less contrasting eye-line). Typical Eastern populations are similar to Western Meadowlark, but many can be distinguished by the following average differences: overall color more rufous-tinged, especially on secondaries, greater coverts, and scapulars; flanks buffy with continuous streaks (Western has whitish flanks, often with broken streaks); head pattern more contrasting as on Lilian's (most apparent on males); tail with slightly more extensive white; malar whitish (usually partly yellow on Western but often veiled by buffy feather tips on both species); dark crossbars on upperpart feathers run together along the feather shaft (Western has discrete crossbars without dark shaft streak).

In the southwest, Western Meadowlark prefers wetter and more open short-grass habitats, such as lawns and agricultural land, while Lilian's Eastern prefers desert grasslands. Farther east, Western prefers drier and sandier habitat than Eastern, but there is much overlap.

There may be other subtle differences. Eastern takes off with more explosive, quail-like burst of wingbeats, Western with slower and gentler wingbeats.

Bobolink

Dolichonyx oryzivorus

L 7" WS 11.5" WT 1.5 oz (43 g) ♂>♀

Female and nonbreeding birds most like sparrows but larger, with plain nape, pale lores, and pointed wings.

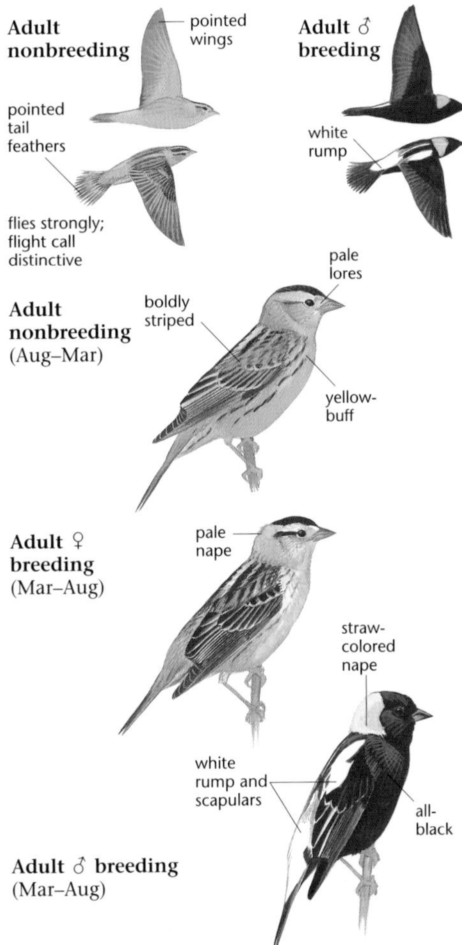
Adult nonbreeding
pointed wings
Adult ♂ breeding
pointed tail feathers
white rump
flies strongly; flight call distinctive
pale lores
Adult nonbreeding (Aug–Mar)
boldly striped
yellow-buff
Adult ♀ breeding (Mar–Aug)
pale nape
straw-colored nape
white rump and scapulars
all-black
Adult ♂ breeding (Mar–Aug)

Voice: Song given in flight a cheerful, bubbling, jangling warble with short notes on widely different pitches; ending faster, fuller, higher. Call a soft, low *chuk* similar to blackbirds. Flight call a soft, musical *bink* or *bwink* similar to some short notes of House Finch.

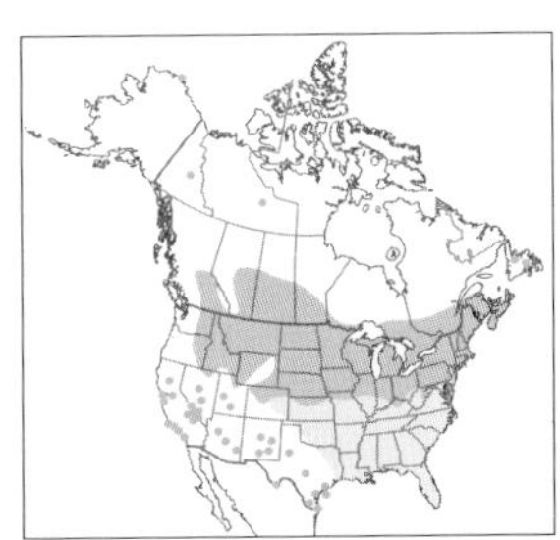

Cowbirds

These two species are closely related. Found in woods, edges, and open fields, both are smaller and more slender than Bronzed Cowbird; note bill shape and overall color.

Brown-headed Cowbird

Molothrus ater

L 7.5" WS 12" WT 1.5 oz (44 g) ♂>♀

Stout bill, short tail, and pointed wings.

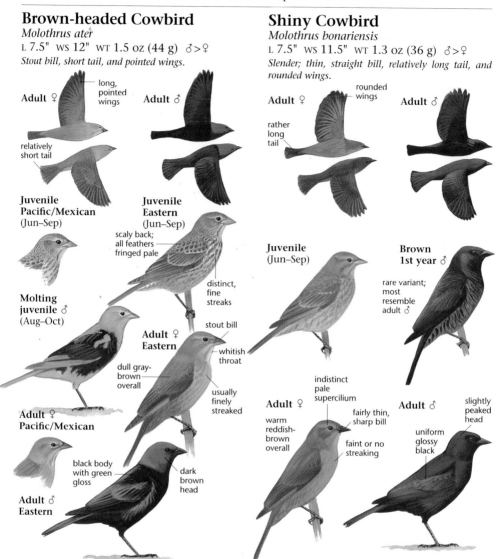

Adult ♀ long, pointed wings; relatively short tail

Adult ♂

Juvenile Pacific/Mexican (Jun–Sep)

Juvenile Eastern (Jun–Sep) scaly back; all feathers fringed pale; distinct, fine streaks

Molting juvenile ♂ (Aug–Oct)

Adult ♀ Eastern stout bill; whitish throat; dull gray-brown overall; usually finely streaked

Adult ♀ Pacific/Mexican

Adult ♂ Eastern black body with green gloss; dark brown head

Voice: Song low, gurgling notes followed by thin, slurred whistles. Flight whistle of Eastern male high, thin whistles *tseeeee-teeea* or *seeeeeetiti;* flight whistle of Pacific/Mexican more varied, with many local dialects. Call a flat, hard, rising rattle *kkkkkk*. No other flight calls.

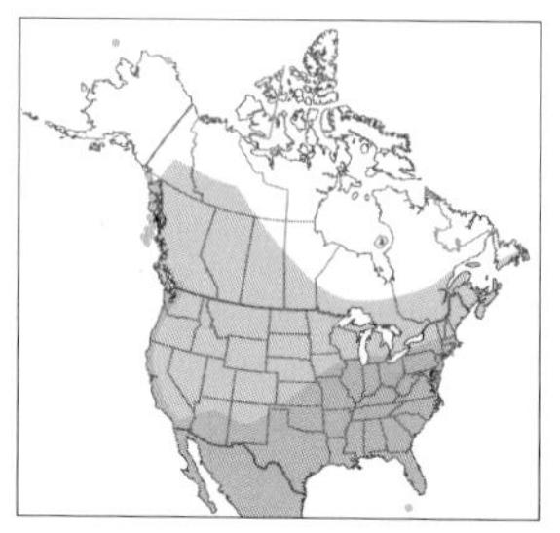

Pacific/Mexican Brown-headed Cowbirds are small, with thin bill and straight culmen; female plumage pale; juvenile's gape yellowish (vs. whitish); juvenile begging call a long, scratchy *cheep* (Eastern a sharp, dry *chip*). Eastern are larger and darker with curved culmen; Interior West birds (not shown) are intermediate; voice differs subtly.

Shiny Cowbird

Molothrus bonariensis

L 7.5" WS 11.5" WT 1.3 oz (36 g) ♂>♀

Slender; thin, straight bill, relatively long tail, and rounded wings.

Adult ♀ rounded wings; rather long tail

Adult ♂

Juvenile (Jun–Sep)

Brown 1st year ♂ rare variant; most resemble adult ♂

Adult ♀ indistinct pale supercilium; fairly thin, sharp bill; warm reddish-brown overall; faint or no streaking

Adult ♂ slightly peaked head; uniform glossy black

Voice: Song a high, squeaky, clear, liquid series of notes; more varied, not gurgling like Brown-headed; slightly accelerating and descending; ends with one to three liquid *quit* notes. Call a rolling rattle like Brown-headed but slower and more metallic. No other flight call.

COWBIRDS (CONTINUED)

Similar in shape and habits to Brown-headed and Shiny Cowbirds, this species is stockier and shorter-tailed, with a unique thick ruff of feathers making it look thick-necked.

Bronzed Cowbird

Molothrus aeneus

L 8.75" WS 14" WT 2.2 oz (62 g) ♂>♀

Stocky with long, heavy bill; relatively short tail; rounded wings. Ruff on neck most prominent on male. Red eye of adult distinctive.

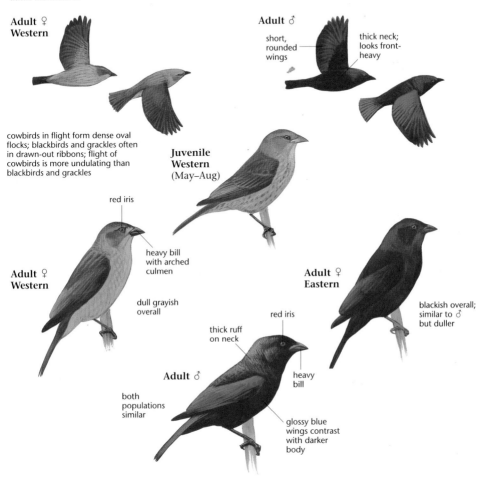

Adult ♀ Western

Adult ♂

short, rounded wings

thick neck; looks front-heavy

cowbirds in flight form dense oval flocks; blackbirds and grackles often in drawn-out ribbons; flight of cowbirds is more undulating than blackbirds and grackles

Juvenile Western (May–Aug)

red iris

heavy bill with arched culmen

Adult ♀ Western

dull grayish overall

Adult ♀ Eastern

blackish overall; similar to ♂ but duller

red iris

thick ruff on neck

Adult ♂

heavy bill

both populations similar

glossy blue wings contrast with darker body

Voice: Song a soft, tinny, rising whistle with quiet gurgling or rustling noise at beginning and end *kweee-lk;* often repeated on slightly different pitches. Whistle call of male 6–10 seconds long and infrequently heard, a series of tinny or wheezy whistles and grating trills; several regional dialects (see below). Rattle call of female similar to Brown-headed but slower and sharper. Chorus of roosting flock may suggest European Starling.

Two distinctive populations differ primarily in female and juvenile plumage; ranges meet in western Texas. Eastern female and juvenile are dark blackish-brown overall, similar to male; Western female and juvenile are pale gray-brown, similar to female Brown-headed. At least three regional dialects in male whistle call are most easily distinguished by the introductory note. Eastern birds give a clear, level whistle about one second long *pseeeeeee.* Western birds in west Texas give a slow, slightly rising trill up to one second long *brrrrreet.* Birds from there west through Arizona give a short upslurred whistle *wink,* and a fourth dialect may exist in western Arizona.

Blackbirds: Genera *Xanthocephalus* and *Agelaius*

The distinctive Yellow-headed is related to meadowlarks; Tricolored is very closely related to Red-winged. Both nest in reedy marshes, wintering in flocks often mixed with other blackbirds.

Yellow-headed Blackbird

Xanthocephalus xanthocephalus

L 9.5" WS 15" WT 2.3 oz (65 g) ♂>♀

Large; heavy-billed, broad-winged, and relatively short-tailed. Note uniform dark body and yellow breast.

Adult ♀

Adult ♂

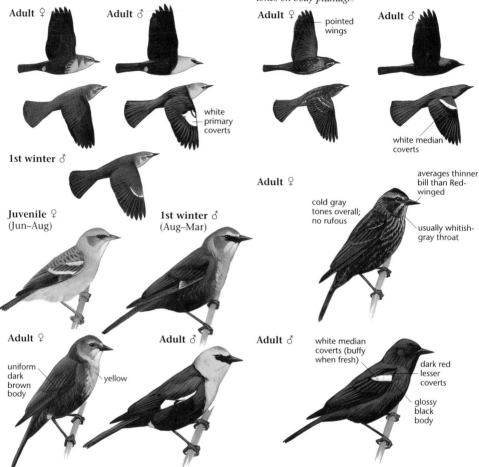

white primary coverts

1st winter ♂

Juvenile ♀ (Jun–Aug)

1st winter ♂ (Aug–Mar)

Adult ♀

uniform dark brown body

yellow

Adult ♂

Voice: Song extremely harsh, unmusical; a few hard, clacking notes on different pitches followed by wavering raucous wail like chainsaw. Varied calls in colony include a slow, raucous *rad rad rad rad*, a rasping rattle, and a descending, whistled trill. Flight call a low, dry *kuduk* or *kek*.

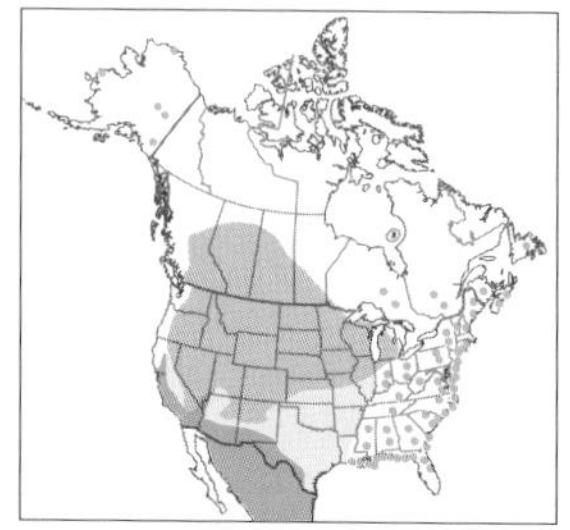

Tricolored Blackbird

Agelaius tricolor

L 8.75" WS 14" WT 2.1 oz (59 g) ♂>♀

Very similar to Red-winged: wingtips distinctly more pointed, bill averages thinner; always lacks rufous tones on body plumage.

Adult ♀

pointed wings

Adult ♂

white median coverts

Adult ♀

averages thinner bill than Red-winged

cold gray tones overall; no rufous

usually whitish-gray throat

Adult ♂

white median coverts (buffy when fresh)

dark red lesser coverts

glossy black body

Voice: Song a harsh, nasal, descending *oo-grreee drdodrp;* lower-pitched, more nasal, and less musical than Red-winged; flock in song sounds like cats fighting. All calls lower-pitched and some more nasal than analogous calls of Red-winged. Descending, whistled alarm call absent.

This widespread species nests in virtually every wet, brushy or marshy area within its wide range; it forms large winter flocks with other blackbirds in farmland and suburbs.

Red-winged Blackbird

Agelaius phoeniceus

L 8.75" WS 13" WT 1.8 oz (52 g) ♂>♀

Rather stocky; rounded wings, fairly short tail, and moderately thick bill.

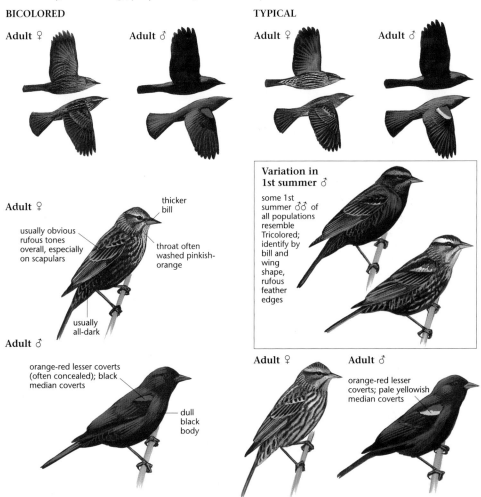

BICOLORED

TYPICAL

Adult ♀

Adult ♂

Adult ♀

Adult ♂

Variation in 1st summer ♂

some 1st summer ♂♂ of all populations resemble Tricolored; identify by bill and wing shape, rufous feather edges

Adult ♀

thicker bill

usually obvious rufous tones overall, especially on scapulars

throat often washed pinkish-orange

usually all-dark

Adult ♂

orange-red lesser coverts (often concealed); black median coverts

dull black body

Adult ♀

Adult ♂

orange-red lesser coverts; pale yellowish median coverts

Voice: Song of several liquid introductory notes followed by variable, harsh, gurgling trill *kon-ka-reeeee;* many western birds (including Bicolored population) sing a less musical *ooPREEEEEom;* female song an explosive, harsh rattle (rarely heard from Bicolored). Flight call a low, dry *kek* or *chek*. Alarm call a high, clear, descending *teeeew* or buzzy *zeeer* given by male. Variety of other calls heard mainly from male in nesting season.

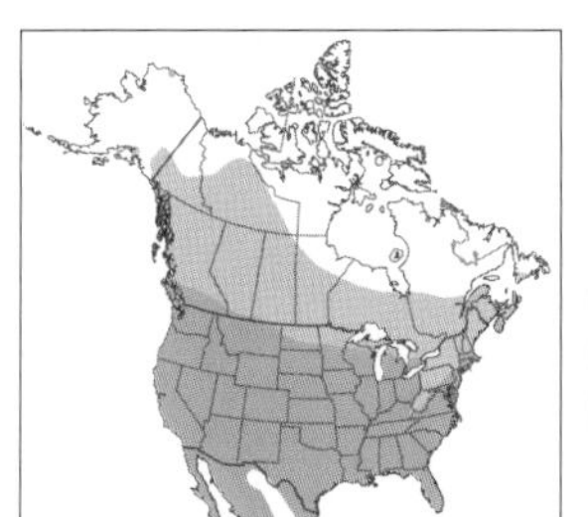

BICOLORED

Male and female Bicolored are distinctive but intergrade at edges of range with typical Red-winged. Voice of Bicolored differs slightly: *chek* call is lower and softer, and some other calls differ slightly; song is similar to other western populations of typical Red-winged.

Blackbirds: Genus *Euphagus*

These two species are closely related to grackles, but they are smaller, more slender, and square-tailed. Brewer's prefers open agricultural land or suburbs; Rusty prefers wooded swamps.

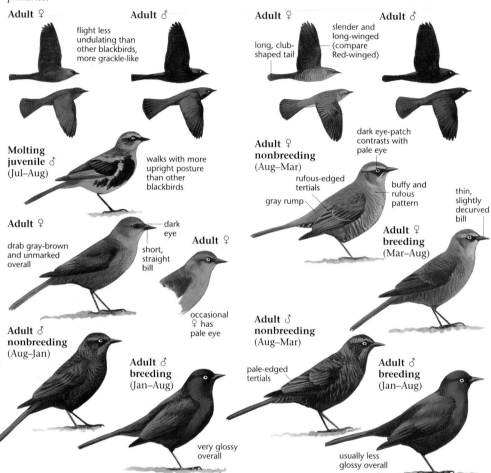

Brewer's Blackbird

Euphagus cyanocephalus

L 9" WS 15.5" WT 2.2 oz (63 g) ♂>♀

Slender and long-tailed. Distinguished from cowbirds by thinner bill, long tail, long legs, and dark-edged primaries.

Adult ♀

Adult ♂

flight less undulating than other blackbirds, more grackle-like

Molting juvenile ♂ (Jul–Aug)

walks with more upright posture than other blackbirds

Adult ♀

dark eye

drab gray-brown and unmarked overall

short, straight bill

Adult ♀

occasional ♀ has pale eye

Adult ♂ nonbreeding (Aug–Jan)

Adult ♂ breeding (Jan–Aug)

very glossy overall

Voice: Song a short, high, crackling *t-kzzzz* or *t-zherr;* usually buzzy (never so in Rusty). Flight call a dry *ket;* averages higher, harder, and more nasal than other blackbirds.

Rusty Blackbird

Euphagus carolinus

L 9" WS 14" WT 2.1 oz (60 g) ♂>♀

Averages shorter-tailed, thinner-billed, and shorter-legged than Brewer's.

Adult ♀

Adult ♂

long, club-shaped tail

slender and long-winged (compare Red-winged)

Adult ♀ nonbreeding (Aug–Mar)

dark eye-patch contrasts with pale eye

rufous-edged tertials

gray rump

buffy and rufous pattern

thin, slightly decurved bill

Adult ♀ breeding (Mar–Aug)

Adult ♂ nonbreeding (Aug–Mar)

pale-edged tertials

Adult ♂ breeding (Jan–Aug)

usually less glossy overall

Voice: Song a soft gurgle followed by high, thin whistle *ktlr-teee;* often alternated with a soft, rustling or gurgling, descending *chrtldltlr;* similar to Brewer's but softer, more gurgling. Flight call a low *tyuk;* lower, longer, more descending than Red-winged; not as sharp as Brewer's.

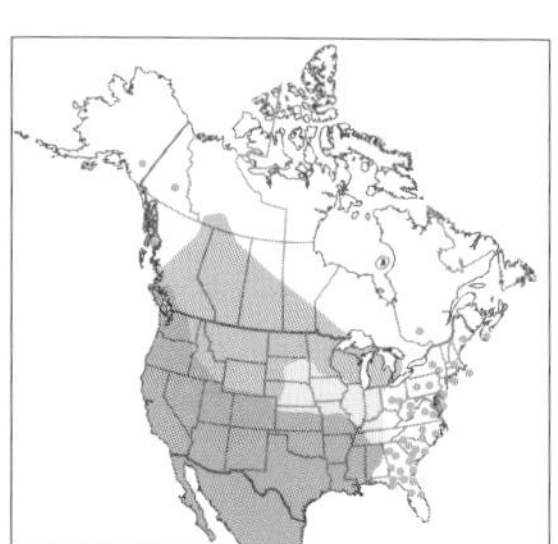

Brewer's Blackbirds foraging

All blackbirds often hold body inclined and/or tail raised while feeding.

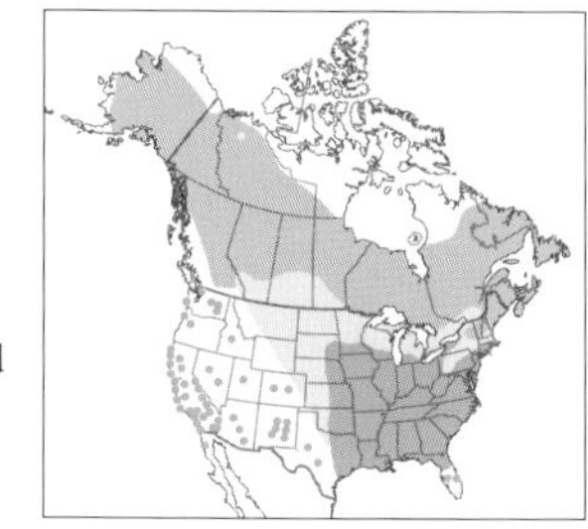

Grackles

Common Grackle is distinguished from blackbirds by its long, heavy bill, heavy structure, keeled tail, and voice. It is found in open woods and fields, often in large flocks with blackbirds.

Common Grackle

Quiscalus quiscula

L 12.5" WS 17" WT 4 oz (115 g) ♂>♀

Our smallest grackle, but larger and heavier than blackbirds, with relatively long, keeled tail and heavy bill. All adults glossy blackish with pale eyes.

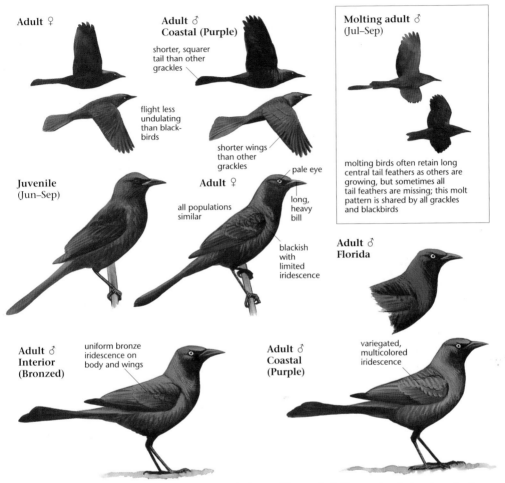

Adult ♀

flight less undulating than blackbirds

Adult ♂ Coastal (Purple)

shorter, squarer tail than other grackles

shorter wings than other grackles

Molting adult ♂ (Jul–Sep)

molting birds often retain long central tail feathers as others are growing, but sometimes all tail feathers are missing; this molt pattern is shared by all grackles and blackbirds

Juvenile (Jun–Sep)

Adult ♀

all populations similar

pale eye

long, heavy bill

blackish with limited iridescence

Adult ♂ Florida

Adult ♂ Interior (Bronzed)

uniform bronze iridescence on body and wings

Adult ♂ Coastal (Purple)

variegated, multicolored iridescence

Voice: Song an unmusical, harsh, metallic hiss *kh-sheee* or *khr-reezzh*. Call a very harsh, toneless, dry *karrz* or *kerrrr* or *karrrg*. Male call a thin, wheezy, toneless *zweeesh* and nasal, hoarse *krrrjk*. Flight call a low, dry *kek;* deeper than all blackbirds, with distinctive harsh quality. Song may differ slightly between populations.

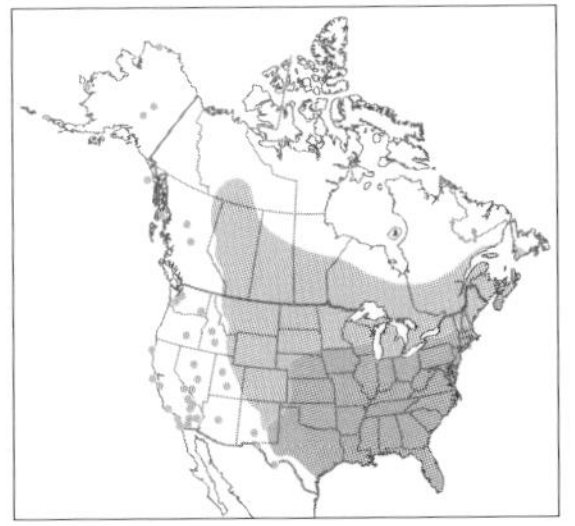

Florida birds average 5 percent smaller with bill 10 percent longer and slightly thinner than Interior (Bronzed), but Coastal (Purple) is intermediate and differences are broadly clinal. Three populations differ in male plumage (female resembles respective male but is less distinctive): widespread Interior (Bronzed) uniform bronze on body and wings with bluish or blue-green head; Florida glossy blue-violet on head and underparts with greenish back; intermediate Coastal (Purple) variable, mainly bluish and purplish, with multicolored iridescence on body and wing coverts ranging from violet to blue, bronze, green, and golden (found on coastal plain from Louisiana to New York).

GRACKLES (CONTINUED)

Boat-tailed is similar to Great-tailed; some may be indistinguishable. It is found in or near coastal saltmarshes and adjacent open areas, generally not flocking with other species.

Boat-tailed Grackle

Quiscalus major

♂ L 16.5" WS 23" WT 8 oz (215 g)
♀ L 14.5" WS 17.5" WT 4.2 oz (120 g)

Very similar to Great-tailed; averages shorter-tailed and rounder-headed, with relatively long legs; long, slender bill; and distinctive voice. Eye color differs where range overlaps.

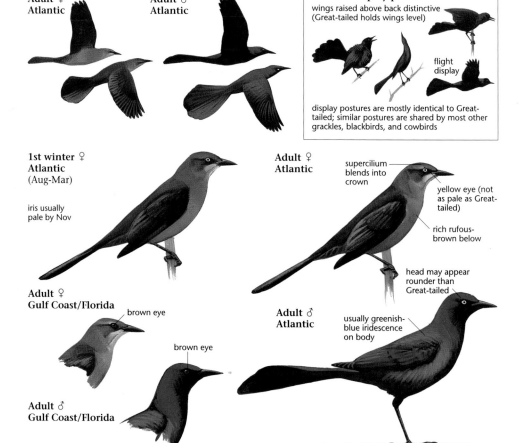

Adult ♀ Atlantic

Adult ♂ Atlantic

Adult ♂ display postures

wings raised above back distinctive (Great-tailed holds wings level)

flight display

display postures are mostly identical to Great-tailed; similar postures are shared by most other grackles, blackbirds, and cowbirds

1st winter ♀ Atlantic (Aug-Mar)

iris usually pale by Nov

Adult ♀ Atlantic

supercilium blends into crown

yellow eye (not as pale as Great-tailed)

rich rufous-brown below

Adult ♀ Gulf Coast/Florida

brown eye

Adult ♂ Atlantic

head may appear rounder than Great-tailed

usually greenish-blue iridescence on body

Adult ♂ Gulf Coast/Florida

brown eye

Voice: Song a varied series of mostly high, ringing notes *kent kent* . . . or *teer teer* . . . or *shreet shreet shreet shreet KEET;* most distinctive a ringing *kreen kreen*. . . . Also a lower, harsher series mixed with dry, rustling sounds; a very loud, clear whistle *teewp;* a harsh, trilling *kjaaaaar;* and a throaty, rattling *kluklukl k*. Call of male a deep *chuk;* female call a rather soft, low *chenk* or *chuup,* may average softer than Great-tailed female. Songs of Atlantic and Gulf Coast/Florida populations may differ.

Populations differ in structure (Gulf Coast and Florida longer-tailed, Atlantic shorter-tailed) and eye color. Gulf Coast and Florida birds are dark-eyed (except in coastal Alabama and Mississippi, where they have dirty-yellow eyes); Atlantic birds north of Florida are pale-eyed.

Grackles (continued)

Great-tailed, our largest grackle, was formerly considered a subspecies of Boat-tailed. It is found in various open upland habitats, from farmland to city parks.

Great-tailed Grackle

Quiscalus mexicanus

♂ L 18" WS 23" WT 7 oz (190 g)
♀ L 15" WS 19" WT 3.7 oz (105 g)

Large and lanky. Male has exceptionally long tail; female is much smaller, approaching Common Grackle in size and shape.

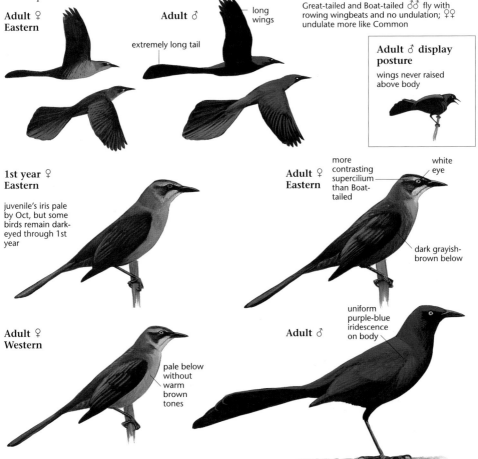

Adult ♀ Eastern

Adult ♂

long wings

extremely long tail

Great-tailed and Boat-tailed ♂♂ fly with rowing wingbeats and no undulation; ♀♀ undulate more like Common

Adult ♂ display posture

wings never raised above body

1st year ♀ Eastern

juvenile's iris pale by Oct, but some birds remain dark-eyed through 1st year

Adult ♀ Eastern

more contrasting supercilium than Boat-tailed

white eye

dark grayish-brown below

Adult ♀ Western

pale below without warm brown tones

Adult ♂

uniform purple-blue iridescence on body

Voice: Song a series of loud, rather unpleasant noises: mechanical rattles *kikikiki* or *ke ke ke ke ke teep;* sliding, tinny whistles *whoit whoit . . . ;* harsh, rustling sounds like thrashing branches or flushing toilet; loud, hard *keek keek . . .* or *kidi kidi. . . .* Common call of male a low, hard *chuk* or *kuk;* female call a softer, husky *whidik* or *whid.*

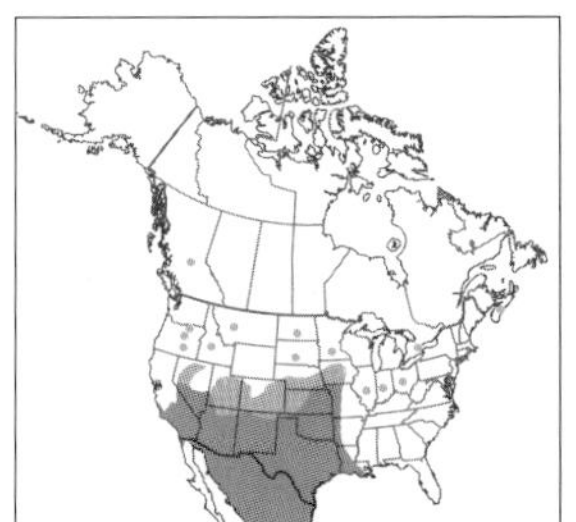

Female is generally grayer than Boat-tailed, with darker belly, more contrasting dark crown and pale supercilium, and usually bright white iris, but some individuals overlap. Eastern and Western populations differ in size and female plumage color. Far Western birds average 15 percent smaller, with relatively short tail and long bill; some females are very pale grayish. From central Arizona eastward all are larger, with Western birds (Arizona to west Texas) averaging grayer than Eastern. Song differs geographically; more study is needed.

STREAK-BACKED ORIOLE

This rare visitor from Mexico is usually found in riparian vegetation or exotic plantings. It is most similar to Hooded but is larger with heavier structure, a shorter tail, and a different back pattern.

Streak-backed Oriole

Icterus pustulatus

L 8.25" WS 12.5" WT 1.3 oz (37 g)

Fairly large with distinctly streaked back. Slightly longer-tailed than Bullock's; shorter-tailed than Hooded.

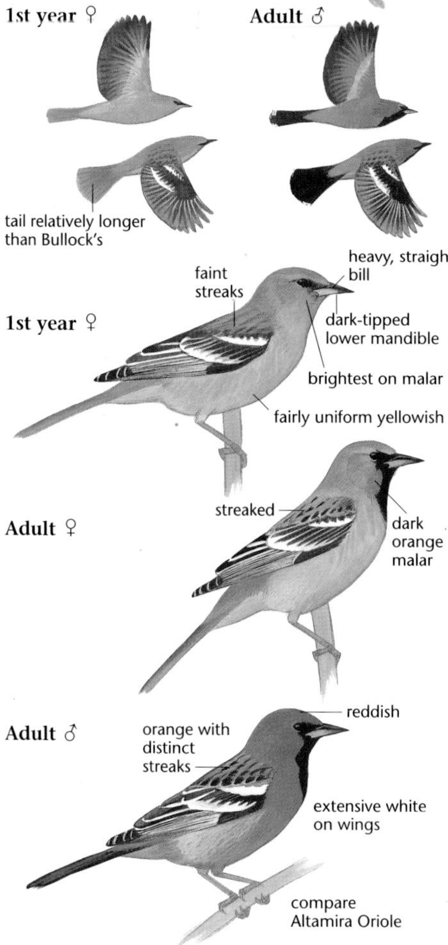
1st year ♀
Adult ♂
tail relatively longer than Bullock's
faint streaks
heavy, straight bill
1st year ♀
dark-tipped lower mandible
brightest on malar
fairly uniform yellowish
streaked
Adult ♀
dark orange malar
reddish
Adult ♂
orange with distinct streaks
extensive white on wings
compare Altamira Oriole

Voice: Song a rather thin and simple whistled *to do, teweeep, yoo teewi;* quality like Bullock's but with short pauses and halting rhythm. Call a dry rattle like Baltimore; faster than Bullock's. Flight call a rising *wheet;* a little higher than Bullock's and slightly rising; lower and hoarser than Hooded.

Identification of Orioles

Bullock's and Baltimore are usually easily distinguished by plumage. 1st year male Bullock's develops a black throat by Oct and is subsequently easily identified. Female Bullock's varies little from the gray-bodied/yellow-ended pattern shown, but female Baltimore is extremely variable. The drabbest pale female Baltimore is most confusing, as it closely resembles Bullock's female. Careful study of head pattern reveals that on Baltimore the brightest color is on the breast (usually tinged orange, unlike the paler yellow of Bullock's), while on Bullock's the brightest color is on the malar; Baltimore has dusky-brown auriculars washed with orange-yellow about the same color as the crown, while Bullock's has cleaner and brighter yellow auriculars and supercilium contrasting with a dark eye-line and crown. Bullock's tends to have broader whitish edges on the greater coverts, mirroring the panel of adult males, and pointed dark centers on the median coverts, creating a jagged border; Baltimore has a straight border. Many Bullock's Orioles have grayish undertail coverts, unlike all Baltimores.

Note also that molt timing differs: Bullock's molts later, during or after fall migration (Sep–Nov); Baltimore molts on the breeding grounds before migration (Jul–Aug).

Hybrids and backcrosses are fairly common where ranges overlap, creating a confusing array of intermediate plumages. Only male hybrids are identifiable.

Bullock's × Baltimore Oriole hybrid adult ♂

intermediate pattern on head, wing coverts, and tail; backcrosses produce complete range of variation between parent species

Northern Orioles

These two species are very closely related and are sometimes merged as a single species, Northern Oriole. Both are found in open broadleaf woods, foraging among leaves in trees.

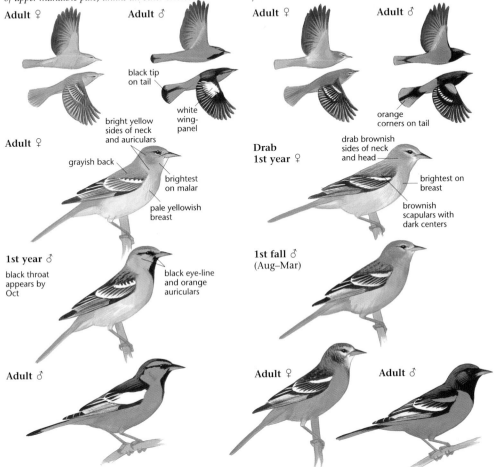

Bullock's Oriole

Icterus bullockii

L 9" WS 12" WT 1.3 oz (36 g)

Like Baltimore: medium-size with rather short, square tail and straight bill. Entire lower mandible and edge of upper mandible pale, unlike all other orioles.

Adult ♀

Adult ♂

black tip on tail

white wing-panel

bright yellow sides of neck and auriculars

Adult ♀

grayish back

brightest on malar

pale yellowish breast

1st year ♂

black throat appears by Oct

black eye-line and orange auriculars

Adult ♂

Voice: Song whistled like Baltimore but less rich, more nasal and barking, with shorter notes and sharper pitch changes *goo gidoo goo peeka peeka*. Simple whistled calls less frequent than Baltimore; a dry, husky chatter or slow, muffled *cheg cheg . . .* slower than Baltimore. Flight call like Baltimore.

Baltimore Oriole

Icterus galbula

L 8.75" WS 11.5" WT 1.2 oz (33 g)

Shape like Bullock's, but averages slightly smaller. Some very drab females are difficult to distinguish from Bullock's.

Adult ♀

Adult ♂

orange corners on tail

Drab 1st year ♀

drab brownish sides of neck and head

brightest on breast

brownish scapulars with dark centers

1st fall ♂ (Aug–Mar)

Adult ♀

Adult ♂

Voice: Song a short series of rich, clear, whistled notes *pidoo tewdi tewdi yewdi tew tidew;* variable in pattern, with pauses between each phrase; often gives simple two-note whistle *hulee* and variations. Call a dry, harsh, uneven rattle. Flight call a husky, tinny, trumpeting *veeet.*

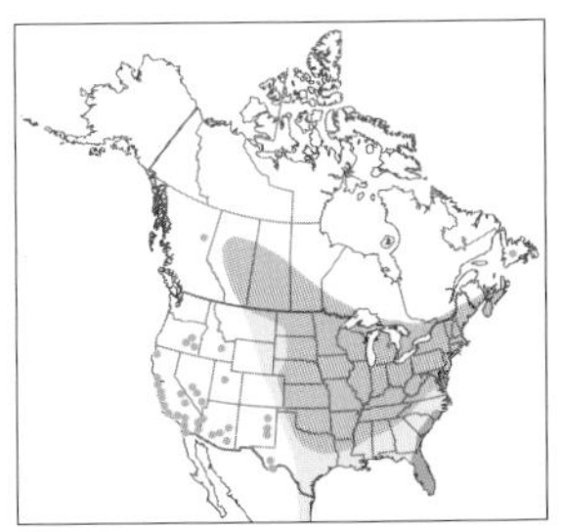

Small Orioles

These two small and slender orioles are similar in female and 1st year plumages. Both are found in scrubby or open woods; Hooded is often associated with fan palms in suburban settings.

Hooded Oriole

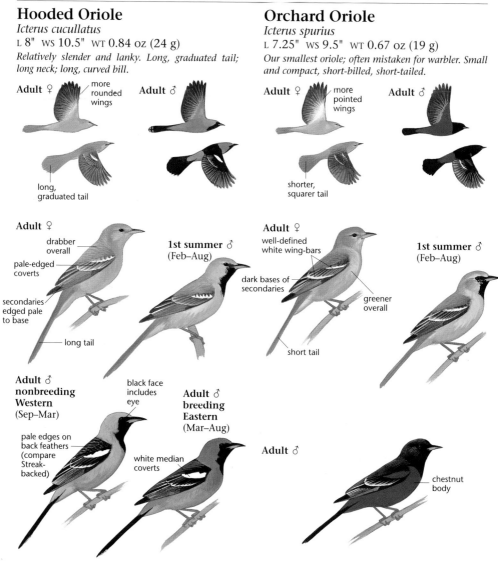

Icterus cucullatus

L 8" WS 10.5" WT 0.84 oz (24 g)

Relatively slender and lanky. Long, graduated tail; long neck; long, curved bill.

Adult ♀
more rounded wings
Adult ♂
long, graduated tail

Adult ♀
drabber overall
pale-edged coverts
secondaries edged pale to base
long tail

1st summer ♂ (Feb–Aug)

Adult ♂ nonbreeding Western (Sep–Mar)
black face includes eye
pale edges on back feathers (compare Streak-backed)

Adult ♂ breeding Eastern (Mar–Aug)
white median coverts

Voice: Song rapid, varied, choppy; combining short, slurred whistles, call notes, and imitations of other species. Call a high, hard *chet* and high, rapid chatter; also a very hard, descending *chairr.* Flight call a sharp, rising, metallic *veek* reminiscent of meadowlarks.

Western populations of Hooded Oriole (California to New Mexico) average 10 percent longer-billed than Eastern with little overlap and also average slightly longer-winged and shorter-tailed. Males are paler yellowish, and females are drabber overall, without the orange tones of Eastern birds.

Orchard Oriole

Icterus spurius

L 7.25" WS 9.5" WT 0.67 oz (19 g)

Our smallest oriole; often mistaken for warbler. Small and compact, short-billed, short-tailed.

Adult ♀
more pointed wings
Adult ♂
shorter, squarer tail

Adult ♀
well-defined white wing-bars
dark bases of secondaries
greener overall
short tail

1st summer ♂ (Feb–Aug)

Adult ♂
chestnut body

Voice: Song a rich, lively warbling with wide pitch range; higher than other orioles; distinctive ending a ringing *pli titi zheeeer.* Common call of male a clear, whistled *tweeo.* Call a low, soft *chut* sometimes in slow chatter; also a rasping scold *jarrsh.* Flight call a relatively low, soft, level *yeeep.*

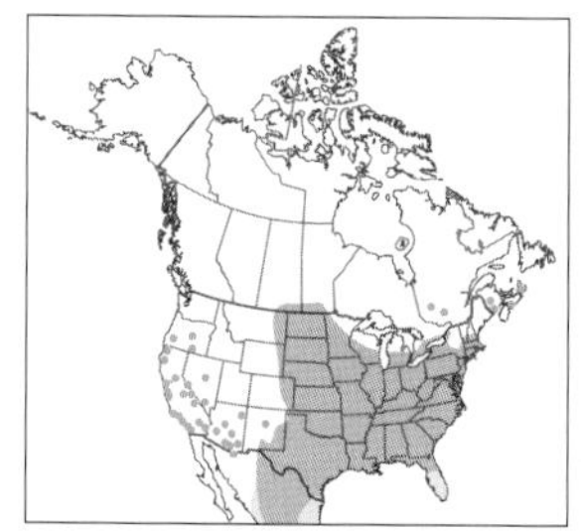

Altamira and Spot-breasted Orioles

Males and females of these two large tropical species are similar in plumage. Both are found in woods: Altamira in scrubby habitats, Spot-breasted in mature trees in suburban neighborhoods.

Altamira Oriole

Icterus gularis

L 10" WS 14" WT 2 oz (58 g)

Our largest oriole. Large-headed, with very thick bill and short tail.

1st year
Adult

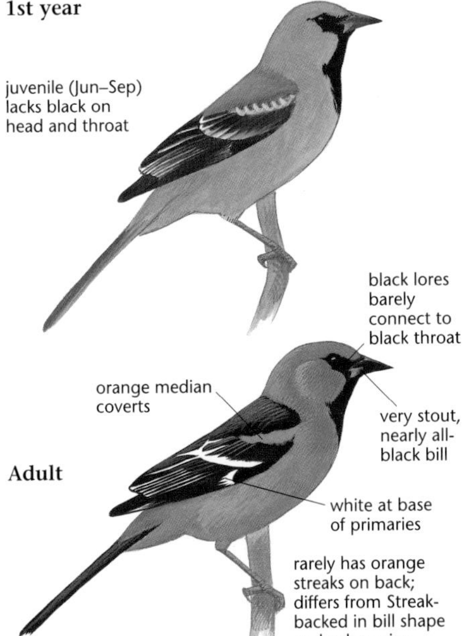
1st year
juvenile (Jun–Sep) lacks black on head and throat
black lores barely connect to black throat
orange median coverts
very stout, nearly all-black bill
Adult
white at base of primaries
rarely has orange streaks on back; differs from Streak-backed in bill shape and color, wing pattern

Voice: Song of low, clear, short, well-spaced one-syllable whistled notes; slow and deliberate with very simple pattern *tooo tooo tooo teeeo tow tow.* Common call a short, whistled note like a single syllable from song *TIHoo* or *teeu* and variations. Flight call a hoarse, nasal, rising *griink* repeated.

Spot-breasted Oriole

Icterus pectoralis

L 9.5" WS 13" WT 1.5 oz (42 g)

Introduced from Central America. Larger than Baltimore; longer-tailed, with slender, decurved bill.

1st year
Adult

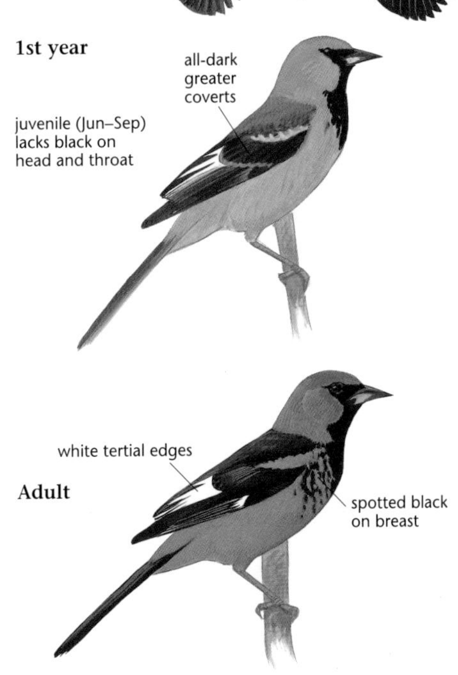
1st year
all-dark greater coverts
juvenile (Jun–Sep) lacks black on head and throat
white tertial edges
Adult
spotted black on breast

Voice: Song a rich, melodious whistle; rather long, relaxed, and repetitive; doubling of some phrases conspicuous and distinctive. Calls include a nasal *jaaa,* a sharp *whip,* and a chattering *ptcheck.*

Scott's and Audubon's Orioles

These two yellow species are superficially similar but do not overlap in range. Scott's is found on open, dry hillsides where yucca and oaks meet, Audubon's in live-oak and riparian woods.

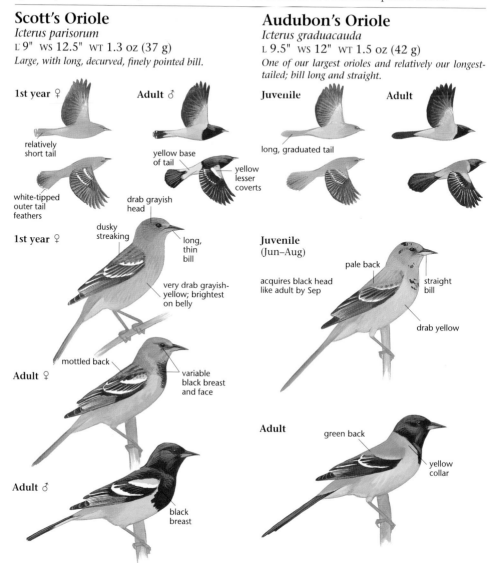

Scott's Oriole

Icterus parisorum

L 9" WS 12.5" WT 1.3 oz (37 g)

Large, with long, decurved, finely pointed bill.

1st year ♀

relatively short tail

white-tipped outer tail feathers

Adult ♂

yellow base of tail

yellow lesser coverts

drab grayish head

1st year ♀

dusky streaking

long, thin bill

very drab grayish-yellow; brightest on belly

mottled back

Adult ♀

variable black breast and face

Adult ♂

black breast

Voice: Song of low, clear whistles with slightly gurgling quality; reminiscent of Western Meadowlark but pitch level or slightly rising overall. Call a harsh, relatively low-pitched *cherk* or *jug*. Flight call a husky, low *zhet*.

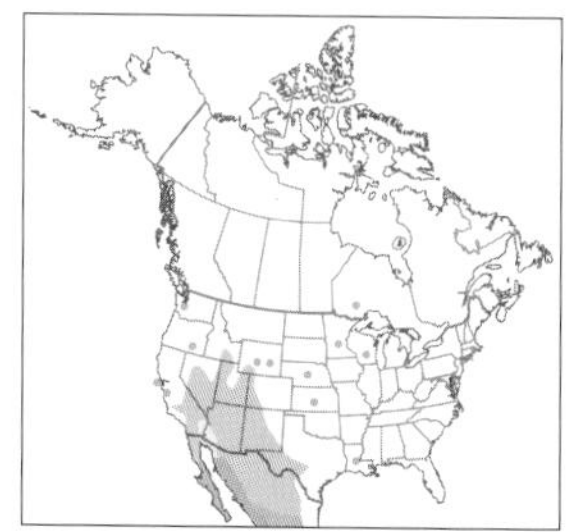

Audubon's Oriole

Icterus graduacauda

L 9.5" WS 12" WT 1.5 oz (42 g)

One of our largest orioles and relatively our longest-tailed; bill long and straight.

Juvenile

long, graduated tail

Adult

Juvenile (Jun–Aug)

pale back

acquires black head like adult by Sep

straight bill

drab yellow

Adult

green back

yellow collar

Voice: Song of very low, slow, melancholy, slurred whistles *hooooo, heeeowee, heeew, heweee;* like a person just learning to whistle. Call an unenthusiastic whistle *tooo* or *oooeh;* also a wrenlike series of harsh, husky, rising notes *jeeek jeeek. . . .*

Finches and Old World Sparrows

Families: Fringillidae, Passeridae

19 species in 8 genera; all in family Fringillidae, except Old World Sparrows in Passeridae (plus 6 exotic finches in 4 families, each in a separate genus, shown on page 537). Finches are small to medium-size birds with relatively pointed wings; they have conical, sparrowlike bills and short, notched tails. They constantly give distinctive calls in high, strong, and undulating flight and often perch in treetops. Nest is a cup in a tree or shrub. Both Old World sparrows are introduced. Similar to emberizine sparrows, they are usually found in small flocks, often hover while landing, and give chirping calls. Nest is a bulky mass of grasses concealed in a cavity (house, streetlamp, etc.). Compare emberizine sparrows and cardinalids. 1st year females are shown.

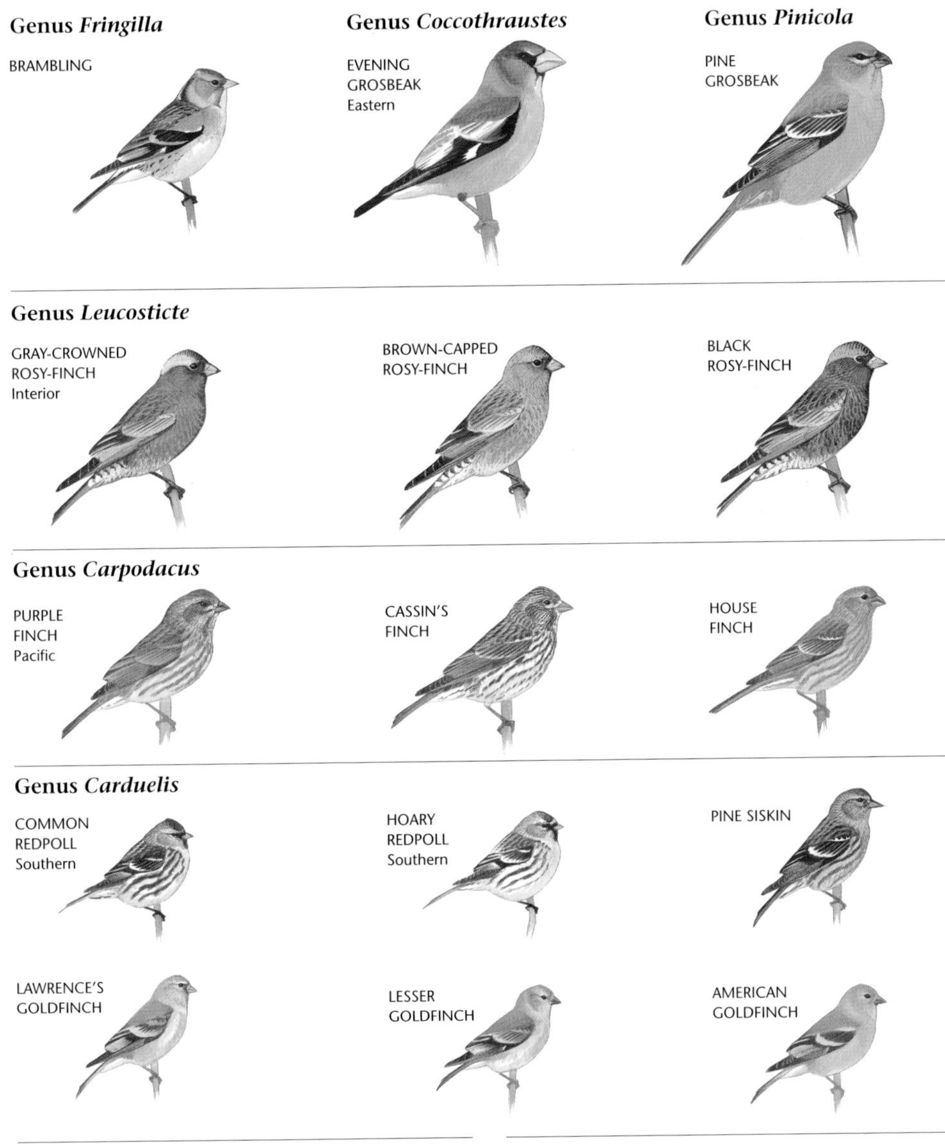

Genus *Fringilla*
BRAMBLING
Genus *Coccothraustes*
EVENING GROSBEAK Eastern
Genus *Pinicola*
PINE GROSBEAK
Genus *Leucosticte*
GRAY-CROWNED ROSY-FINCH Interior
BROWN-CAPPED ROSY-FINCH
BLACK ROSY-FINCH
Genus *Carpodacus*
PURPLE FINCH Pacific
CASSIN'S FINCH
HOUSE FINCH
Genus *Carduelis*
COMMON REDPOLL Southern
HOARY REDPOLL Southern
PINE SISKIN
LAWRENCE'S GOLDFINCH
LESSER GOLDFINCH
AMERICAN GOLDFINCH
Genus *Loxia*
RED CROSSBILL
WHITE-WINGED CROSSBILL
Old World Sparrows Genus *Passer*
HOUSE SPARROW
EURASIAN TREE SPARROW

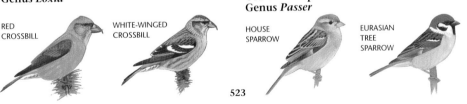

Brambling and Evening Grosbeak

These two species are distinctive. Brambling is found in open woods and fields, often with sparrows. Evening Grosbeak is usually seen in noisy flocks in treetops or at bird feeders.

Brambling

Fringilla montifringilla

L 6.25" WS 11" WT 0.74 oz (21 g)

Relatively long-winged with long, notched tail. Note whitish rump, orange breast and scapulars.

Adult ♀ nonbreeding

long wings
fairly long tail
white rump
orange lesser coverts
pale wingstripe

Adult ♂ breeding

gray head

Adult ♀ nonbreeding (Aug–Mar)

yellow bill
orange breast

Adult ♂ nonbreeding (Aug–Mar)

Adult ♂ breeding (Mar–Aug)

black head
orange breast and shoulder

Voice: Song a simple, wheezy or rattling, nasal trill *dzhreeeeee*. Call a distinctive, harsh, rising *jaaaek* reminiscent of Gray Catbird. Flight call a short, low, hard, often doubled *tup*.

Evening Grosbeak

Coccothraustes vespertinus

L 8" WS 14" WT 2.1 oz (60 g)

Massive head and bill, short tail, relatively short but pointed wings. White wing-patches always conspicuous.

Adult ♀

white oval at base of primaries
short tail
large head and bill

Adult ♂

white secondaries

Juvenile ♂ (Jun–Sep)

Adult ♀ Eastern

massive olive-gray bill

yellow supercilium

Adult ♂ Western

Adult ♂ Eastern

white secondaries
bright yellow

Voice: Song apparently a regular repetition of call notes. Call a high, sharp, ringing trill *kleerr* reminiscent of House Sparrow; in flocks a low, dry rattle or buzz *thirrr*. Song and call of Western birds similar to Eastern, but flight call a high, clear, whistled *teew* not ringing or trilled.

Western Evening Grosbeak averages 15 percent longer-billed than Eastern and has a narrower yellow band across the forehead. Flight call is distinctly different (see above); more study is needed.

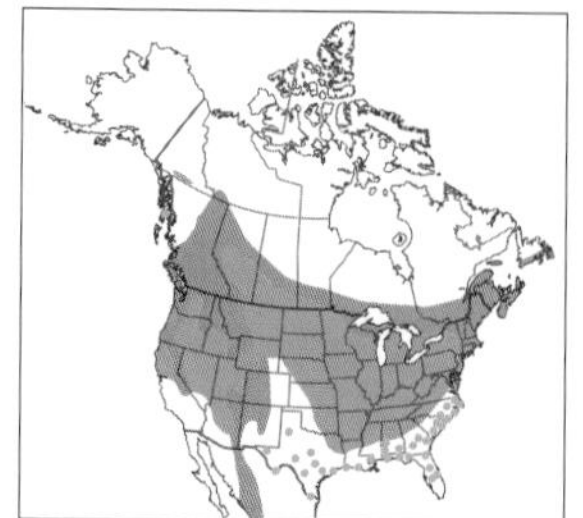

PINE GROSBEAK

This large, fluffy, long-tailed species is sedate and inconspicuous and gives soft call notes. Often seen in small groups in spruce and fir forests, it feeds on berries in winter.

Pine Grosbeak

Pinicola enucleator

L 9" WS 14.5" WT 2 oz (56 g)

Large, long-tailed, and round-headed with short, rounded bill. Subtle colors and grayish overall plumage distinctive.

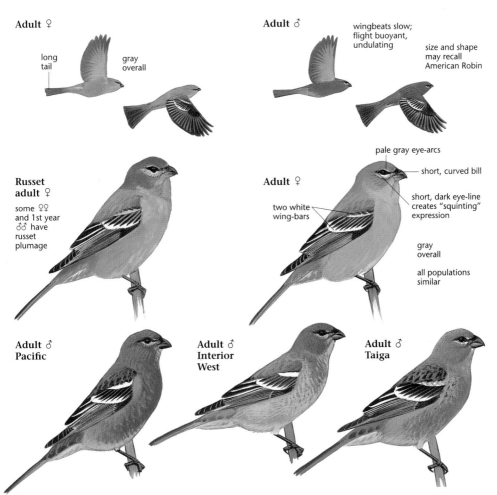

Adult ♀

long tail

gray overall

Adult ♂

wingbeats slow; flight buoyant, undulating

size and shape may recall American Robin

Russet adult ♀

some ♀♀ and 1st year ♂♂ have russet plumage

Adult ♀

pale gray eye-arcs

short, curved bill

short, dark eye-line creates "squinting" expression

two white wing-bars

gray overall

all populations similar

Adult ♂ Pacific

Adult ♂ Interior West

Adult ♂ Taiga

Voice: Song a relatively low, lazy, unaccented warble of soft, whistled notes *fillip illy dilly didalidoo* usually with descending trend; metallic quality reminiscent of *Pheucticus* grosbeaks. Quieter "whisper song" often includes imitations of other species. Flight call varies geographically. Taiga gives rather lethargic, soft, whistled notes *peew* or *po peew peew;* vaguely reminiscent of Greater Yellowlegs. Pacific and Interior West give more complex, harder, husky notes *quid quid quid* or *quidip quidip* generally rising in pitch; reminiscent of Western Tanager. All populations also give quiet, low calls such as *pidididid* or *ip ip.*

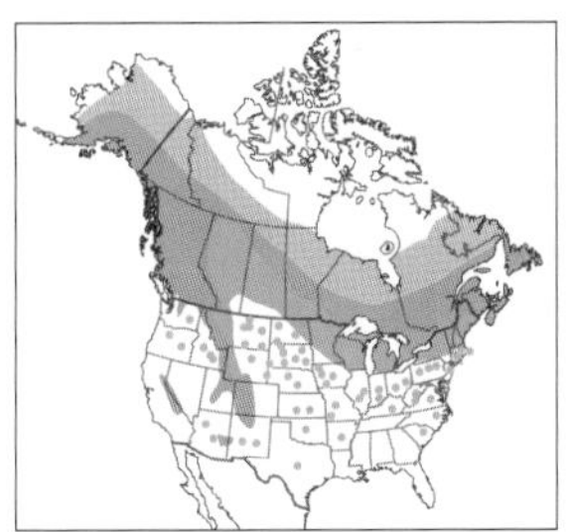

Subtle regional variation in size and male plumage is partly overshadowed by variation. Regional variation in flight calls and song (see above) combined with plumage may allow identification of populations, but more study is needed. Pacific male has dark and extensive red on underparts; Interior West male has duller red, with much gray mottling on the breast and entirely gray flanks, as well as little or no dark spotting on the back; Taiga male has pinkish-red of intermediate extent.

Rosy-Finches

This species is very closely related to the other rosy-finches. All are found on open ground, usually tundra, where small flocks forage on or near snow patches. All always hop on the ground.

Gray-crowned Rosy-Finch

Leucosticte tephrocotis

L 6.25" WS 13" WT 0.91 oz (26 g)

Medium to large; slender with long wings and tail, short legs. Note plain brownish body with black forehead and gray crown, hints of pink on belly and wing coverts.

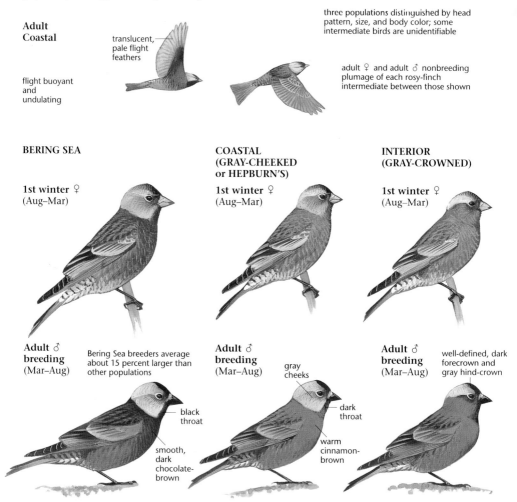

Adult Coastal

translucent, pale flight feathers

three populations distinguished by head pattern, size, and body color; some intermediate birds are unidentifiable

adult ♀ and adult ♂ nonbreeding plumage of each rosy-finch intermediate between those shown

flight buoyant and undulating

BERING SEA

1st winter ♀ (Aug–Mar)

Adult ♂ breeding (Mar–Aug)

Bering Sea breeders average about 15 percent larger than other populations

black throat

smooth, dark chocolate-brown

COASTAL (GRAY-CHEEKED or HEPBURN'S)

1st winter ♀ (Aug–Mar)

Adult ♂ breeding (Mar–Aug)

gray cheeks

dark throat

warm cinnamon-brown

INTERIOR (GRAY-CROWNED)

1st winter ♀ (Aug–Mar)

Adult ♂ breeding (Mar–Aug)

well-defined, dark forecrown and gray hind-crown

Voice: Song heard infrequently; a slow, descending series of husky, whistled notes *jeew jeew jeew . . .*; a more varied Purple Finch–like song has also been described. Flight call a rather soft, husky chirp *jeewf* or *cheew* or a buzzy *jeerf;* may recall House Sparrow or Evening Grosbeak but softer. Many variations on this call create a chorus from winter flocks.

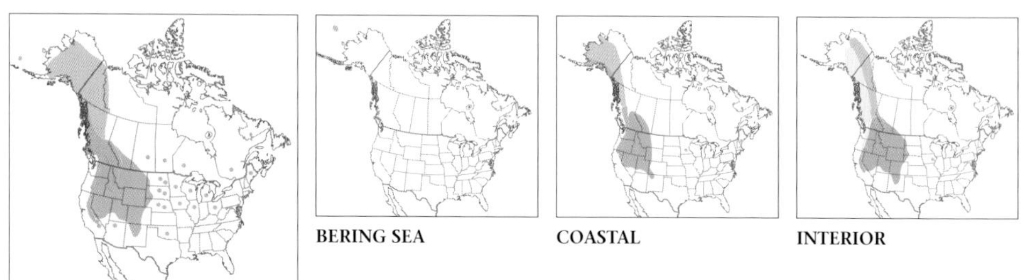
BERING SEA
COASTAL
INTERIOR

These two species have more variable plumage than Gray-crowned; females are distinctly drabber than males. All rosy-finches are sometimes considered a single species, Rosy Finch.

Brown-capped Rosy-Finch

Leucosticte australis

L 6.25" WS 13" WT 0.91 oz (26 g)

Averages slightly smaller-billed than other rosy-finches. More pink on underparts and little or no gray on crown.

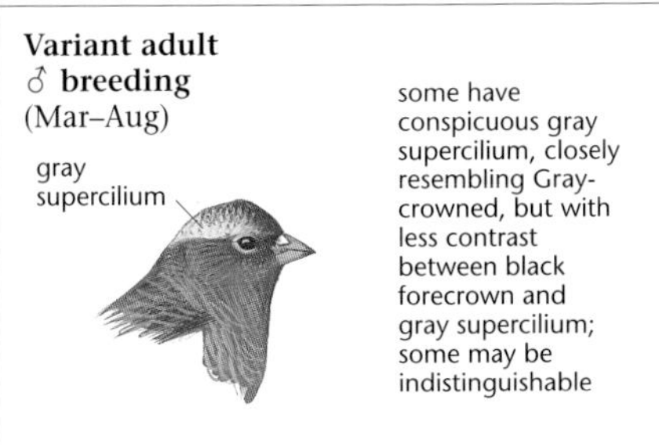

Variant adult ♂ breeding
(Mar–Aug)
gray supercilium
some have conspicuous gray supercilium, closely resembling Gray-crowned, but with less contrast between black forecrown and gray supercilium; some may be indistinguishable

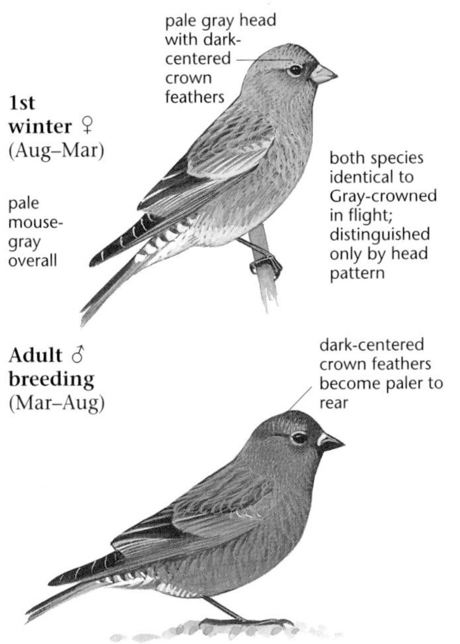

1st winter ♀
(Aug–Mar)
pale gray head with dark-centered crown feathers
pale mouse-gray overall
both species identical to Gray-crowned in flight; distinguished only by head pattern
Adult ♂ breeding
(Mar–Aug)
dark-centered crown feathers become paler to rear

Voice: Similar to Gray-crowned.

Black Rosy-Finch

Leucosticte atrata

L 6.25" WS 13" WT 0.91 oz (26 g)

Distinctly colder grayish body color than other rosy-finches. Very limited pink color on underparts.

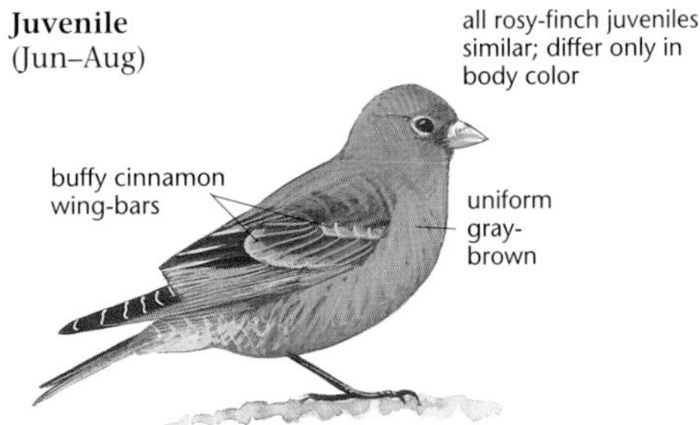

Juvenile
(Jun–Aug)
all rosy-finch juveniles similar; differ only in body color
buffy cinnamon wing-bars
uniform gray-brown

1st winter ♀
(Aug–Mar)
grayish overall

Adult ♂ breeding
(Mar–Aug)

blackish

averages less rosy on belly than other rosy-finches

Voice: Similar to Gray-crowned.

These two species hybridize where ranges overlap, complicating especially the identification of Brown-capped breeding males. Black also hybridizes with Gray-crowned, but extent of hybridization is unknown.

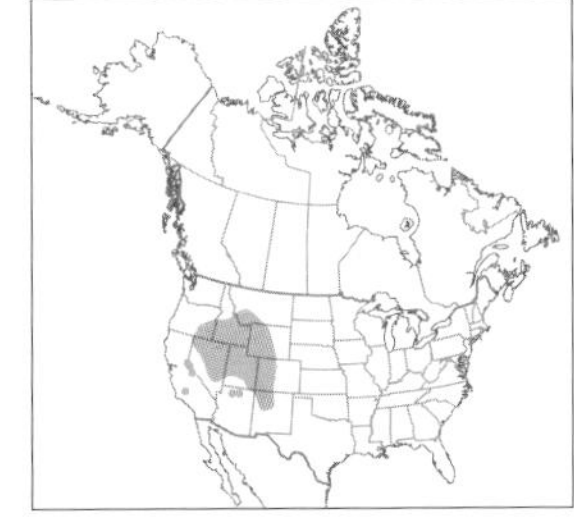

Finches: Genus *Carpodacus*

This species is similar to other *Carpodacus* finches. Found in small flocks in open woods and shrubs, it is most often detected in flight giving its distinctive flight call.

Purple Finch

Carpodacus purpureus

L 6" WS 10" WT 0.88 oz (25 g)

Stockier than other Carpodacus *finches, with short tail, medium-length wings, stout bill; often looks large-headed. Female has boldly patterned face and underparts.*

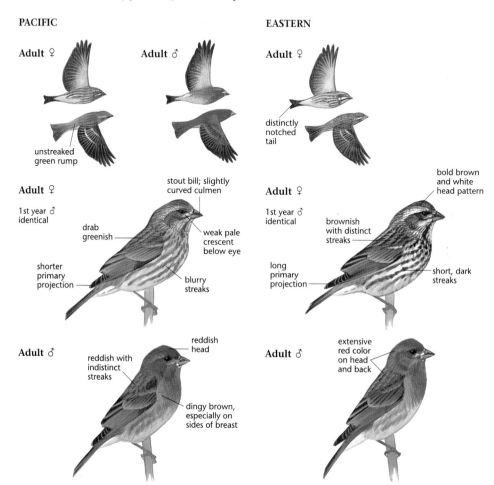

PACIFIC

Adult ♀

Adult ♂

unstreaked green rump

Adult ♀

1st year ♂ identical

stout bill; slightly curved culmen

drab greenish

weak pale crescent below eye

shorter primary projection

blurry streaks

Adult ♂

reddish head

reddish with indistinct streaks

dingy brown, especially on sides of breast

EASTERN

Adult ♀

distinctly notched tail

Adult ♀

1st year ♂ identical

bold brown and white head pattern

brownish with distinct streaks

long primary projection

short, dark streaks

Adult ♂

extensive red color on head and back

Voice: Pacific: Song a mumbled, low, unstructured *fridi ferdi frididifri fridi frrr;* more rapid than House Finch. Call a husky, muffled whistle *wheeoo* or *fwidowip;* quality like song, unlike the clearer, vireolike calls of Eastern. Flight call a *bik* slightly lower than Eastern with hard overtones like Brewer's Blackbird. Eastern: Song a slightly hoarse, warbled *plidi tididi preete plidi tititi preeer;* bright, lively, and clearly structured with accented ending; generally ends with strongly descending trill *cheeeer;* overall trend rising. Call a short, whistled phrase like vireo song *tweeyoo.* Flight call a light, hard *pik* with musical overtones.

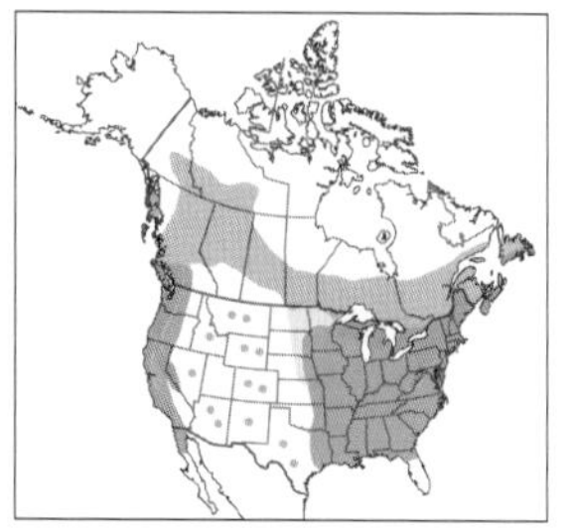

Pacific and Eastern populations are moderately distinctive. Pacific birds average slightly rounder-winged with shorter primary projection and are longer-tailed with more curved culmen than Eastern (tending toward House Finch in shape). Pacific females are greenish above, have indistinct streaks, and are washed yellowish below with longer, paler, more blurry streaks (Eastern are brownish above and white below with shorter, darker streaks). Underparts of Pacific males are washed dull brown and rump is dark red (Eastern males have cleaner, brighter colors overall). See differences in voice above.

Cassin's Finch is found in montane pine forests, House Finch in open woods and suburbs. Both are similar to Purple Finch and can be difficult to identify; note distinctive flight calls.

Cassin's Finch

Carpodacus cassinii

L 6.25" WS 11.5" WT 0.91 oz (26 g)

Larger than Purple with longer wings and tail; bill averages longer with straighter culmen. Female pale and very crisply streaked.

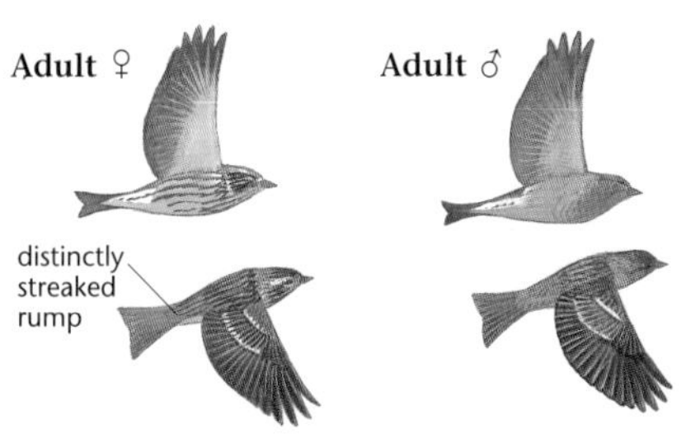
Adult ♀
Adult ♂
distinctly streaked rump

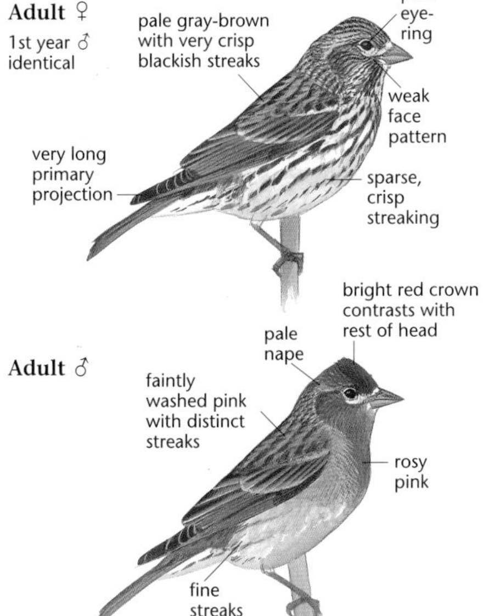
Adult ♀
1st year ♂ identical
pale gray-brown with very crisp blackish streaks
pale eye-ring
weak face pattern
very long primary projection
sparse, crisp streaking
Adult ♂
bright red crown contrasts with rest of head
pale nape
faintly washed pink with distinct streaks
rosy pink
fine streaks

Voice: Song a brighter and higher warble than Pacific Purple; higher and more rapid than House with descending trend slightly rising at end. Call similar to Purple but drier *tedeyo* or *widee-ooli*. Flight call a distinctive, high, dry warble *krdlii* or *chidilip*.

House Finch

Carpodacus mexicanus

L 6" WS 9.5" WT 0.74 oz (21 g)

Structure distinctive: smaller body but longer tail than other Carpodacus *finches, slightly notched tail, shorter and more rounded wings, rounded head, and short bill with distinctly curved culmen. Female has drab blurry streaks, weak face pattern.*

Adult ♀
Adult ♂
relatively long, slightly notched tail

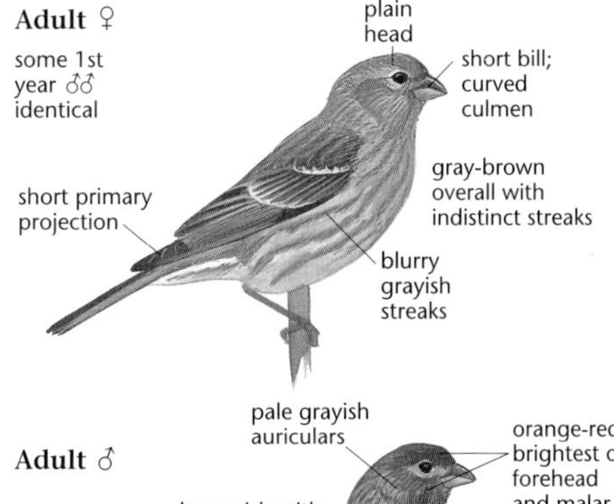
Adult ♀
some 1st year ♂♂ identical
plain head
short bill; curved culmen
gray-brown overall with indistinct streaks
short primary projection
blurry grayish streaks
Adult ♂
pale grayish auriculars
orange-red brightest on forehead and malar
brownish with indistinct streaks
streaked flanks

Voice: Song a varied warble; generally begins with husky, whistled notes and ends with slightly lower, burry notes; often a long *veeerrr* note; steady tempo with distinct downward trend. Call a soft, mellow *fillp* or *fiidlp*. Flight call a soft, husky *vweet* like softer notes of House Sparrow.

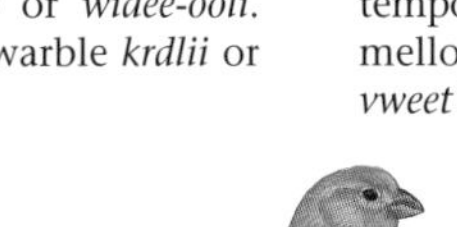

House Finch yellow variant adult ♂

Occasional; most frequent in the southwest. Yellow variant is extremely rare in Purple and Cassin's.

CROSSBILLS

Crossbills are found in single-species flocks year-round, wandering erratically in search of food, mainly the cones of pines, spruces, and firs. Seeds are pried out using the unique crossed bill tip.

Red Crossbill

Loxia curvirostra

L 6.25" WS 11" WT 1.3 oz (36 g)

Relatively large-headed and short-tailed, with long, pointed wings; bill varies in size but generally large. Clambers parrotlike over pinecones, using short legs and stout bill.

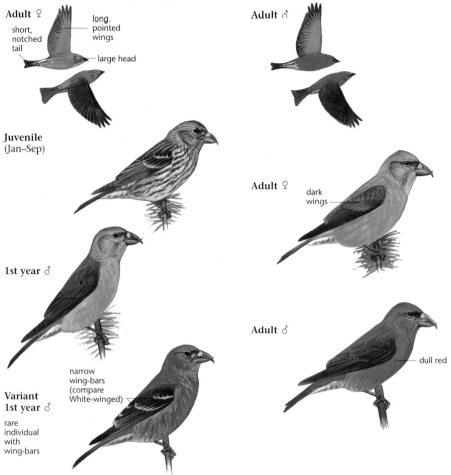

Adult ♀
short, notched tail
long, pointed wings
large head

Adult ♂

Juvenile
(Jan–Sep)

Adult ♀
dark wings

1st year ♂

Adult ♂
dull red

narrow wing-bars (compare White-winged)

Variant 1st year ♂
rare individual with wing-bars

Voice: Song a series of short, hard or clicking phrases, some buzzy, with many call notes interspersed: *tikuti ti chupity chupity chupity tokit kyip kyip kyip jree-jree-jree. . . .* Flight calls are fundamentally similar in all types: very hard, sharp *gyp* or *kip* notes usually repeated in short series *gyp-gyp-gyp*.

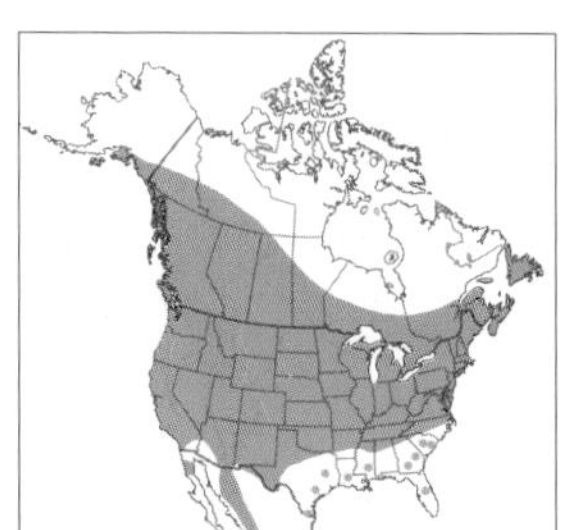

RED CROSSBILL TYPES

Recent research shows that there are at least nine discrete populations, or types, of Red Crossbill, possibly representing nine separate species. Each type wanders erratically in search of its preferred food, often co-occurring with other types. Most are not reliably distinguished in the field and should be identified only by careful analysis of tape-recorded flight calls. Note that intermediate calls do occur and rare individuals give calls of two different types; some are simply unidentifiable. Average differences in size, range, and food preferences also provide clues that may be useful for identification.

Crossbills (continued)

The smaller-billed White-winged Crossbill prefers smaller cones than Red, mainly larch, hemlock, and spruce. It is somewhat less nomadic than Red, yet has not evolved multiple populations.

Identification of Red Crossbills

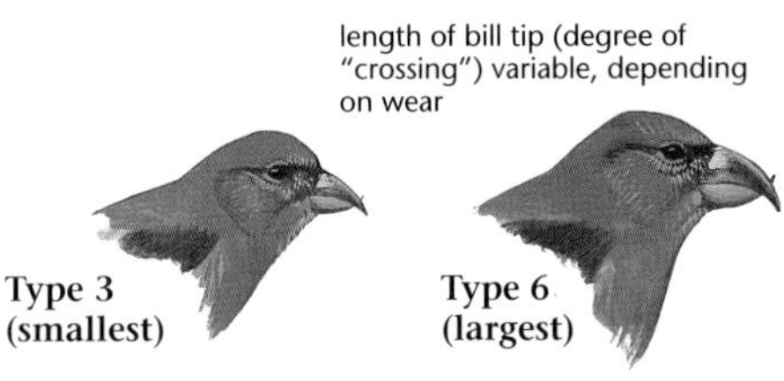
length of bill tip (degree of "crossing") variable, depending on wear
Type 3 (smallest)
Type 6 (largest)

The bill of type 6 can be as much as twice as long as type 3. The other types all have intermediate bill size overlapping little with types 3 and 6. Among the medium-size types there are subtle variations in bill proportions: types 1, 2, and 4 are relatively slender-billed; types 8 and 9 are relatively stout-billed.

millimeters *(enlarged)*
12 13 14 15 16 17
3 1 4 7 8 9 5 2 6
White-winged

Mean bill length of each of the nine types of Red Crossbill, as well as White-winged Crossbill.

Bill structure of each type is optimized for extracting seeds from a particular type of cone. In general the larger- and stouter-billed types forage most efficiently on larger and harder cones (pines), while the smaller-billed types forage most efficiently on smaller and softer cones (spruce, fir, hemlock). These preferences may provide clues to identification, but there is overlap, especially for wandering flocks where the choice of cones may be very limited.

Distribution of each type is still being studied: types 1 through 4 are known to occur continent-wide, types 5 and 7 are recorded only from the west, type 6 only from the extreme southwest, type 8 only from Newfoundland (now rare), and type 9 only from southern Idaho. All types may wander widely to find food, and more types may await discovery.

Flight calls provide the best means of identification, but differences are subtle, and written descriptions offer a poor representation of the calls. Consult the technical literature for more details.

Type 1: *kiip* like 3, 5, and 9, but level
Type 2: *kewp* distinctive, clear, descending
Type 3: *kyip* like 1, 5, and 9, descending
Type 4: *kwit* distinctive, upslurred
Type 5: *kyip* like 1, 3, and 9, descending
Type 6: *chep* like 7, low, descending
Type 7: *chip* like 6, but level
Type 8: *kwip* like 4, but lower
Type 9: *kyip* like 1, 3, and 5

White-winged Crossbill

Loxia leucoptera

L 6.5" WS 10.5" WT 0.91 oz (26 g)

Longer-tailed and smaller-headed with thinner bill than Red; bold white wing markings distinctive.

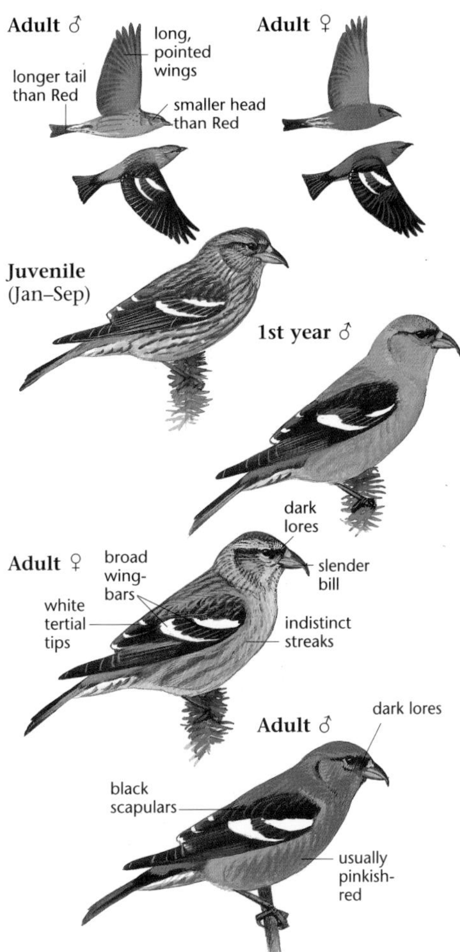
Adult ♂
long, pointed wings
longer tail than Red
smaller head than Red
Adult ♀
Juvenile (Jan–Sep)
1st year ♂
dark lores
Adult ♀
broad wing-bars
white tertial tips
slender bill
indistinct streaks
Adult ♂
dark lores
black scapulars
usually pinkish-red

Voice: Song a series of nervous, rattling, mechanical trills on different pitches *jrrr jrrr jrrr treeeeeee kerrrrrr treeeeeee krrr.* Call *tyik-tyik* weaker and thinner than Red; a rising *veeeht* singly or in series unlike Red; also a redpoll-like *chut-chu.* Flock produces a dry, rattling chorus.

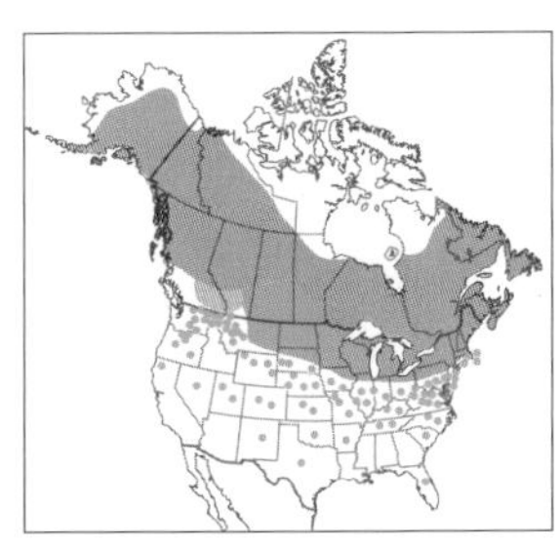

Redpolls

Redpolls are fluffy, small, brown-streaked finches with tiny yellow bills, dark lores, and red forecrowns. Both Common and Hoary are found in open willow and birch thickets and weedy fields.

Common Redpoll

Carduelis flammea

L 5.25" WS 9" WT 0.46 oz (13 g)

Smaller-billed and longer-tailed than goldfinches and Pine Siskin. Dark face, yellow bill, and streaked flanks distinctive.

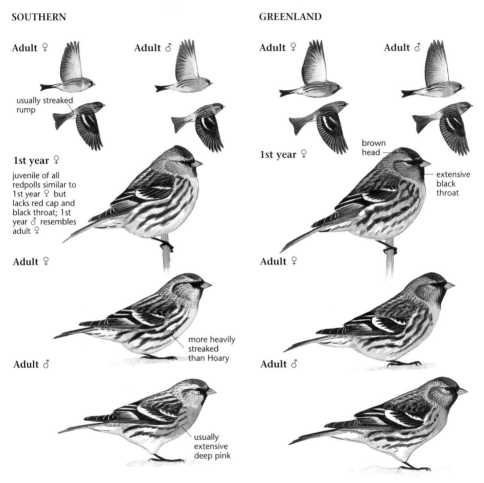

SOUTHERN

Adult ♀

Adult ♂

usually streaked rump

1st year ♀

juvenile of all redpolls similar to 1st year ♀ but lacks red cap and black throat; 1st year ♂ resembles adult ♀

Adult ♀

more heavily streaked than Hoary

Adult ♂

usually extensive deep pink

GREENLAND

Adult ♀

Adult ♂

1st year ♀

brown head

extensive black throat

Adult ♀

Adult ♂

Voice: Song a series of short, repeated notes; mainly call notes and short trills *chit chit chit twirrrrrr toweeowee-owee chrrr chit chit chit tiree tiree . . .* ; in flight a long, rattling buzz *chrrrrrr*. Call a husky, wiry, rising *tweweee* and a soft, rising *vweeii*. Feeding flock gives constant soft *tip* notes; harder than American Goldfinch. Flight call a hard, rapid, bouncy *chid chid chid* or *tjip tjip* varying from soft to hard and dry (higher, more ringing versions on breeding grounds) or a rapid rattle *jijijiji;* also a strong, nasal, husky *tew* or *kewp*.

Greenland population is scarce southward in winter; averages 10 percent larger than Southern and is heavier-billed, darker with heavier streaking overall, more extensive black on throat, and darker buffy-brown wash on head; adult male has limited red on breast. Intergrades occur where range meets Southern, and many individuals are not identifiable.

Very similar to Common Redpoll and often mixed with it in flocks, this species averages paler overall. Some females can be nearly identical, but males are more easily identified.

Hoary Redpoll

Carduelis hornemanni

L 5.5" WS 9" WT 0.46 OZ (13 g)

Averages slightly shorter- and deeper-billed than Common with straighter culmen; also averages longer-tailed and may appear fluffier and thicker-necked; overall paler, especially on rear scapulars, flanks, and undertail coverts.

SOUTHERN

Adult ♀

usually unstreaked rump

Adult ♂

1st year ♀

pale rear scapulars

short-billed appearance emphasized by fluffy nasal feathering

Adult ♀

pale "frosty" overall

averages more white on secondaries and coverts than Common

stubby bill with straight culmen

fine streaking

Adult ♂

faintly streaked

limited pale pink on breast

GREENLAND (HORNEMANN'S)

Adult ♀

Adult ♂

1st year ♀

Adult ♀

Adult ♂

whitish overall

very little pale pink

Greenland population scarce southward in winter; averages 12 percent larger and overall paler than Southern

Voice: Essentially identical to Common. Call a wiry *juwee;* may be lower and simpler than Common. Flight call a *chif chif chif;* each note slightly descending; may average lower and softer than Common, at least in spring.

Pattern of streaks on undertail coverts are often useful for identifying redpolls. Common averages more streaks (from A to C), Hoary fewer (from C and D to entirely unstreaked). In both species males average fewer streaks than females.

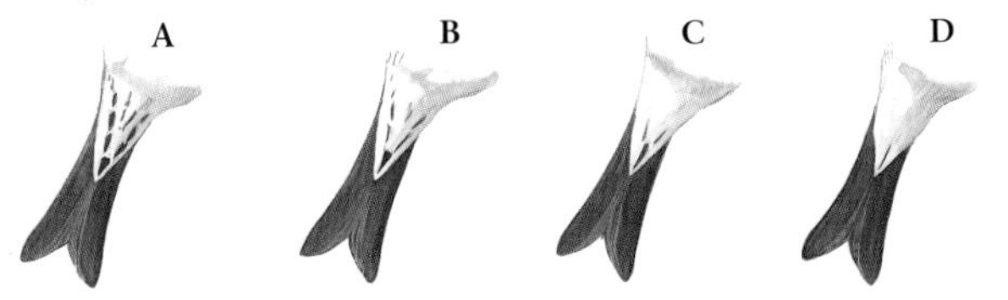
A
B
C
D

Pine Siskin and Lawrence's Goldfinch

These small, active birds are similar in shape and habits to other *Carduelis* species. Pine Siskin is found mainly in open coniferous forest, Lawrence's Goldfinch in weeds among oak savanna.

Pine Siskin

Carduelis pinus

L 5" WS 9" WT 0.53 oz (15 g)

Small and short-tailed, with rather long, pointed wings and long, slender bill.

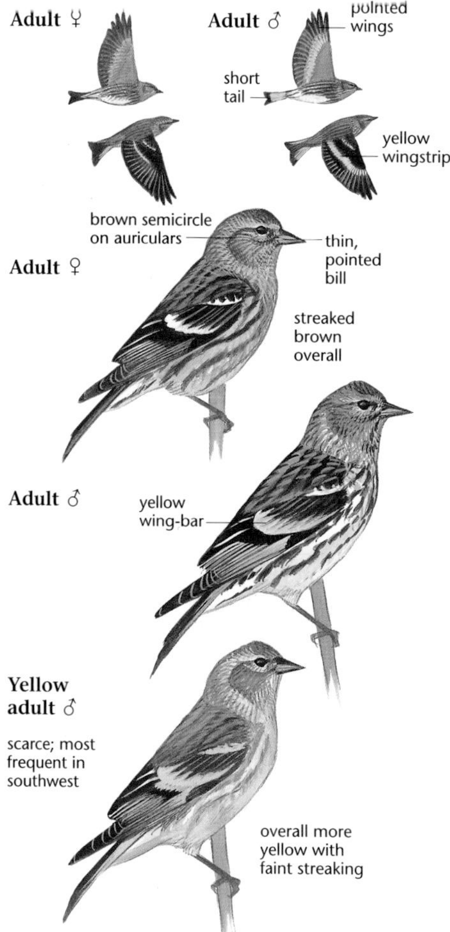

Adult ♀
Adult ♂
pointed wings
short tail
yellow wingstripe
brown semicircle on auriculars
thin, pointed bill
Adult ♀
streaked brown overall
Adult ♂
yellow wing-bar
Yellow adult ♂
scarce; most frequent in southwest
overall more yellow with faint streaking

Voice: Song a rapid, run-on jumble of fairly low, husky notes; generally a string of call notes like goldfinches but husky and harsh. Common call a rough, rising buzz *zhreeeeee.* Flight call a high, sharp *kdeew* and a dull *bid bid* or *ji ji ji.*

Lawrence's Goldfinch

Carduelis lawrencei

L 4.75" WS 8.25" WT 0.4 oz (11.5 g)

Medium-size goldfinch, with small, stubby bill and fairly long tail.

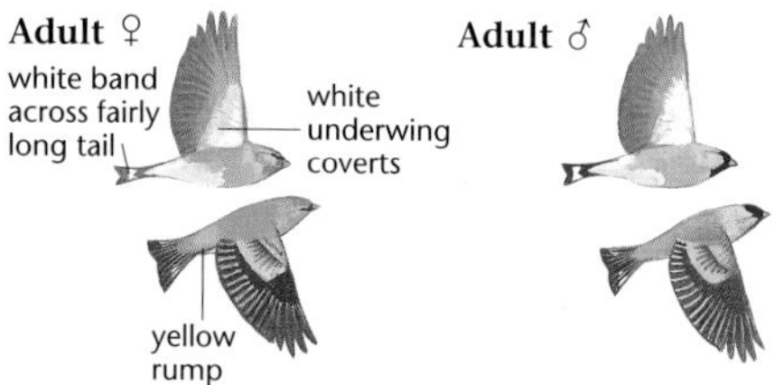

Adult ♀
white band across fairly long tail
white underwing coverts
Adult ♂
yellow rump

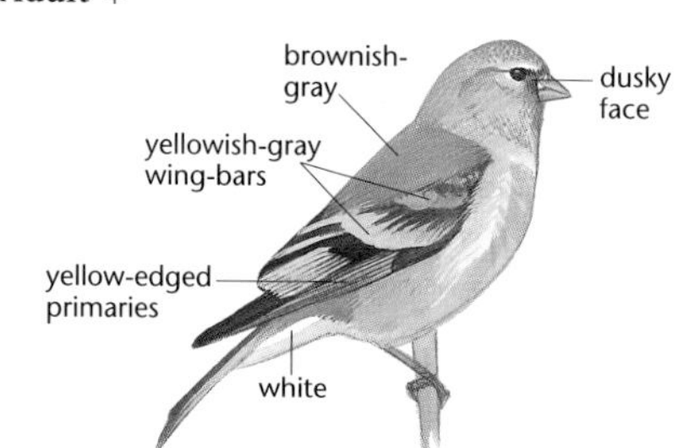

Adult ♀
brownish-gray
dusky face
yellowish-gray wing-bars
yellow-edged primaries
white

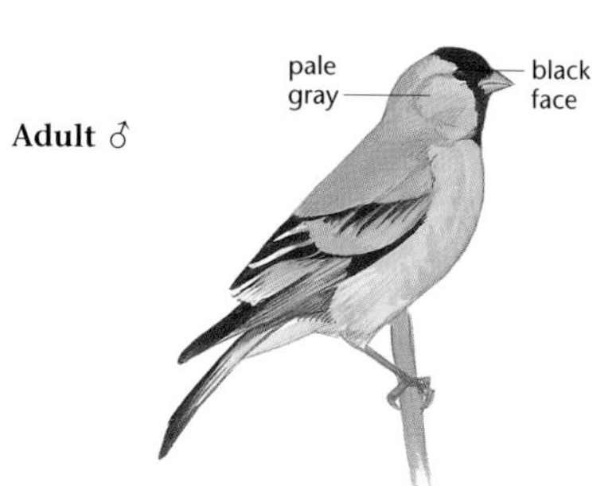

Adult ♂
pale gray
black face

Voice: Song a high, extended, tinkling warble; rapid and varied without repeated phrases; composed almost entirely of imitations of call notes of other species. Call a nasal *too-err;* also a sharp, high *PIti* and *Itititi*. Flight call a high, clear *ti-too.*

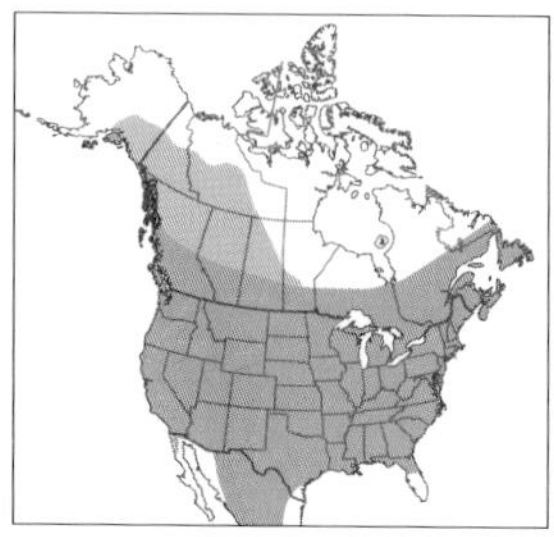

All species in the genus *Carduelis* are known to incorporate imitations of other species' calls into their song. Lawrence's and Lesser Goldfinches use many imitations, Pine Siskin fewer, and American Goldfinch and redpolls the fewest.

Lesser and American Goldfinches

Like other *Carduelis* finches, these species are active and acrobatic when foraging for weed seeds and tree buds. They are usually seen in flocks, with bounding flight and distinctive flight calls.

Lesser Goldfinch

Carduelis psaltria

L 4.5" WS 8" WT 0.33 oz (9.5 g)

Our smallest goldfinch; tiny, stocky, and short-tailed, with short, rounded wings and large bill.

Adult ♀
all-dark upperside
little or no white
Adult ♂
obvious white patch
dark underwing
short tail
large white patches
Pale adult ♀
narrow whitish wing-bars
olive
usually yellowish
Bright adult ♀
green back
stout, dark gray bill
white at base of primaries
yellow
Adult ♂ Western
black cap
Adult ♂ Texas

Voice: Song slower, hoarser, and more disjointed than American; little repetition of notes; includes many imitations of call notes of other species. Call a distinctive, very high, clear, wiry *tleeee, teeeeyEE,* and *tseee-eeeew* and variations. Flight call a hoarse, grating *chig chig chig.*

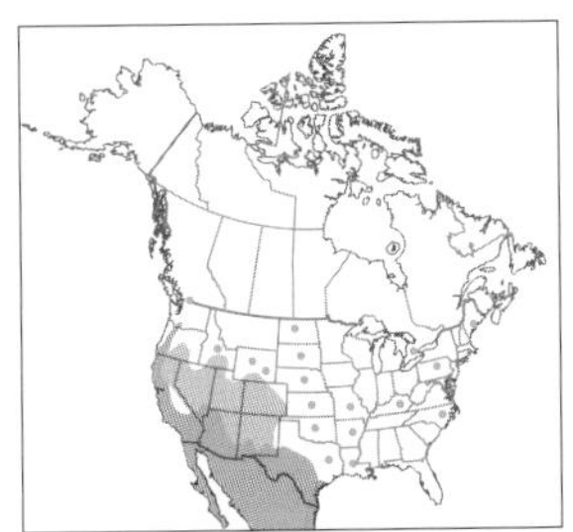

Back color of Lesser Goldfinch varies geographically. 1st year males throughout the range are green-backed. Virtually all adult males in southern Texas are black-backed, and virtually all west of Colorado and New Mexico are green-backed. Between Colorado and Texas the average amount of black increases clinally to the south and east.

American Goldfinch

Carduelis tristis

L 5" WS 9" WT 0.46 oz (13 g)

Our largest goldfinch (but still a very small bird); stocky. Note whitish undertail coverts and well-defined wing-bars.

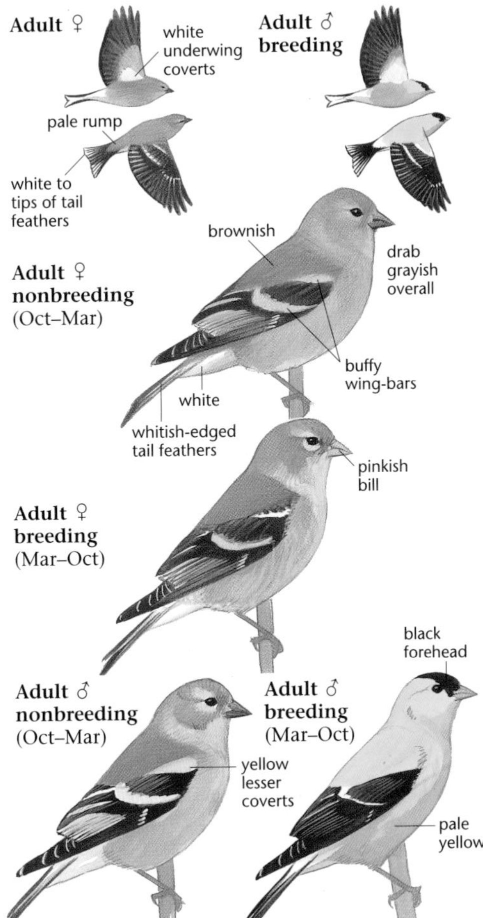

Adult ♀
white underwing coverts
Adult ♂ breeding
pale rump
white to tips of tail feathers
brownish
drab grayish overall
Adult ♀ nonbreeding (Oct–Mar)
buffy wing-bars
white
whitish-edged tail feathers
pinkish bill
Adult ♀ breeding (Mar–Oct)
black forehead
Adult ♂ nonbreeding (Oct–Mar)
Adult ♂ breeding (Mar–Oct)
yellow lesser coverts
pale yellow

Voice: Song high, musical, rapidly repeated phrases *toWEE toWEE toWEEto tweer tweer tweer ti ti ti ti;* may suggest buntings but less stereotyped; fading at end. Call a thin, wiry *toweeeowee* or *tweeee;* also a soft *tihoo* and variations. Flight call a soft, whistled, descending series *ti di di di.*

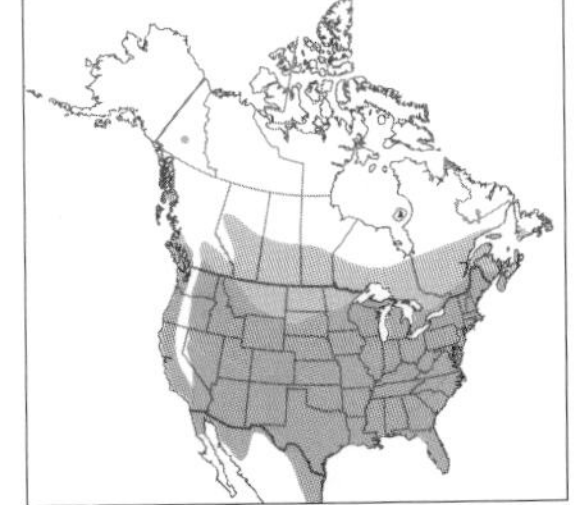

Old World Sparrows

These two introduced species are usually seen in small flocks near human habitation and are the only sparrows in most urban habitats. They nest in all types of natural and man-made cavities.

House Sparrow

Passer domesticus

L 6.25" WS 9.5" WT 0.98 oz (28 g)

Relatively large-headed and short-tailed, with stout, blunt-tipped bill and short wings. Note plain face and dingy gray-brown plumage (compare female Dickcissel).

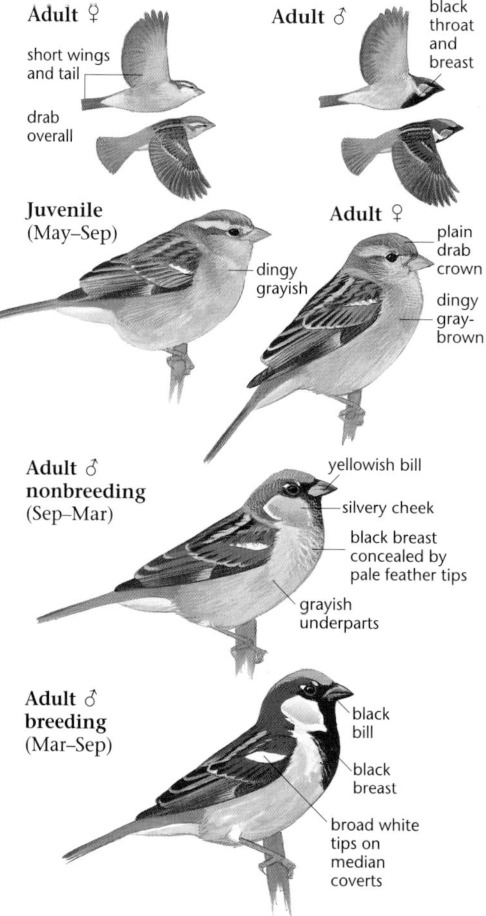
Adult ♀
short wings and tail
drab overall
Adult ♂
black throat and breast
Juvenile (May–Sep)
dingy grayish
Adult ♀
plain drab crown
dingy gray-brown
Adult ♂ nonbreeding (Sep–Mar)
yellowish bill
silvery cheek
black breast concealed by pale feather tips
grayish underparts
Adult ♂ breeding (Mar–Sep)
black bill
black breast
broad white tips on median coverts

Voice: Song a monotonous series of nearly identical chirps. Call a husky *fillip;* a low, rattling series in excitement; and constant chatter from flocks. Flight call a soft, husky *pido* and high *pirv.*

Eurasian Tree Sparrow

Passer montanus

L 6" WS 8.75" WT 0.77 oz (22 g)

Averages 10 percent smaller than House, with relatively small bill. All plumages show distinctive rufous crown and whitish collar.

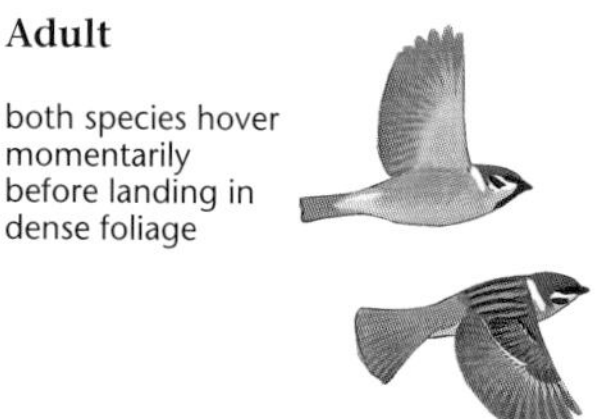
Adult
both species hover momentarily before landing in dense foliage

Juvenile (Jun–Aug)
dark spot on whitish cheek

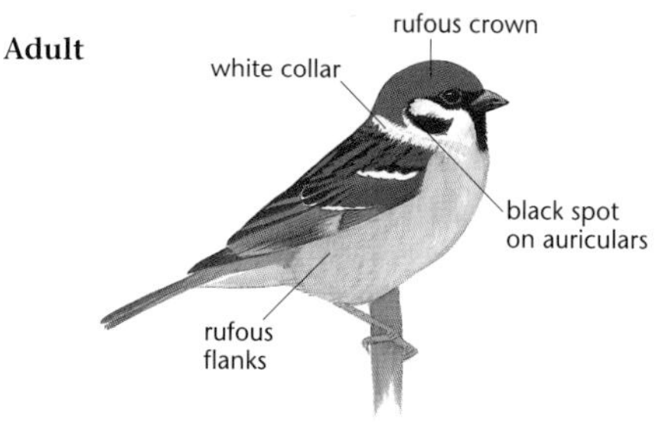
Adult
rufous crown
white collar
black spot on auriculars
rufous flanks

Voice: Similar to House, but all calls harder and clearer. Flight call a hard *pik, pik, pik.*

House Sparrow was introduced to New York in 1850 and spread to California by 1910. Geographic variation has developed in response to widely differing environmental conditions. Populations in the north average larger than in the south, and arid southwestern populations are paler than Pacific and eastern.

Exotic Finches

Of these six species (in four families), Orange Bishop and Nutmeg Mannikin have established feral populations in North America. Many other species occasionally escape from captivity.

FAMILY EMBERIZIDAE
RED-CRESTED CARDINAL
Paroaria coronata

L 7" WS 11"

Escapes regularly occur in Florida and California.

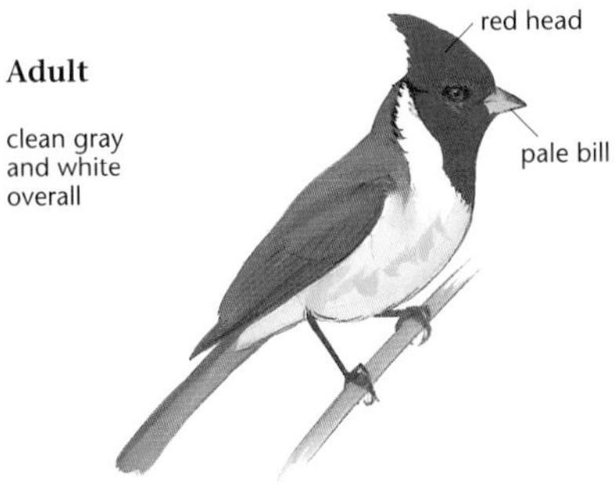
Adult
red head
clean gray and white overall
pale bill

FAMILY PLOCEIDAE
ORANGE BISHOP
Euplectes franciscanus

L 4.5" WS 6.5" ♂>♀

Small population established in California.

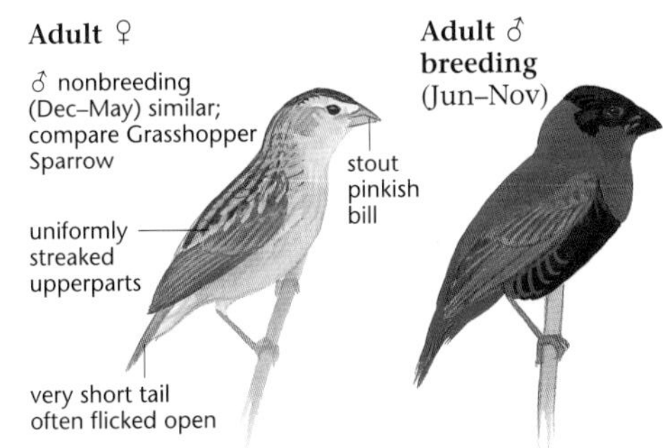
Adult ♀
♂ nonbreeding (Dec–May) similar; compare Grasshopper Sparrow
uniformly streaked upperparts
stout pinkish bill
very short tail often flicked open
Adult ♂ breeding (Jun–Nov)

FAMILY FRINGILLIDAE
EUROPEAN GOLDFINCH
Carduelis carduelis

L 5.5" WS 10"

Many attempts at introduction around North America have failed; occasionally escapes from captivity.

Adult
whitish band across face
yellow band on wings

FAMILY FRINGILLIDAE
YELLOW-FRONTED CANARY
Serinus mozambicus

L 4.75" WS 8.5"

*An ancestral canary type, this species and Common Canary (*S. canaria*) occasionally escape from captivity. Captives often have partly or entirely white or yellow plumage. Also known as Green Singing Finch.*

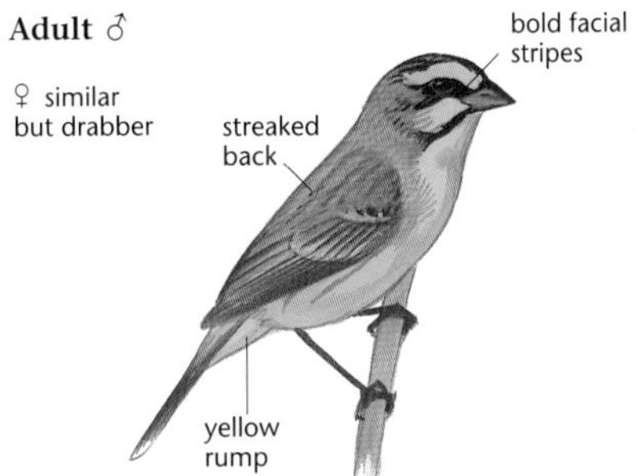
Adult ♂
♀ similar but drabber
streaked back
bold facial stripes
yellow rump

FAMILY ESTRILDIDAE
JAVA SPARROW
Padda oryzivora

L 6" WS 8.5"

Escapes mainly occur in Florida and California.

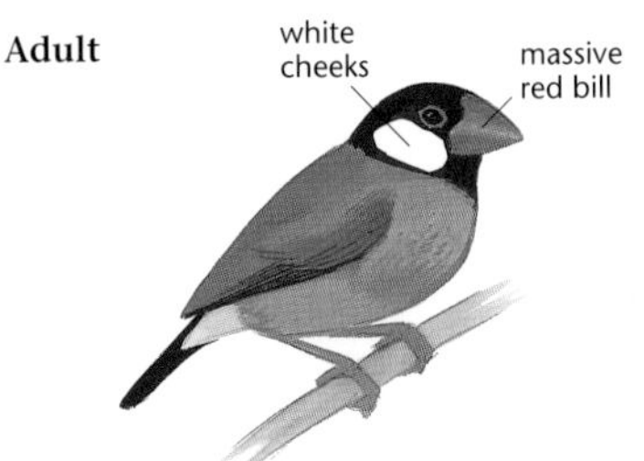
Adult
white cheeks
massive red bill

FAMILY ESTRILDIDAE
NUTMEG MANNIKIN
Lonchura punctulata

L 4" WS 7"

Small populations established in California and southeast Florida (since 1980s). Also known as Spice Finch or Spotted Munia.

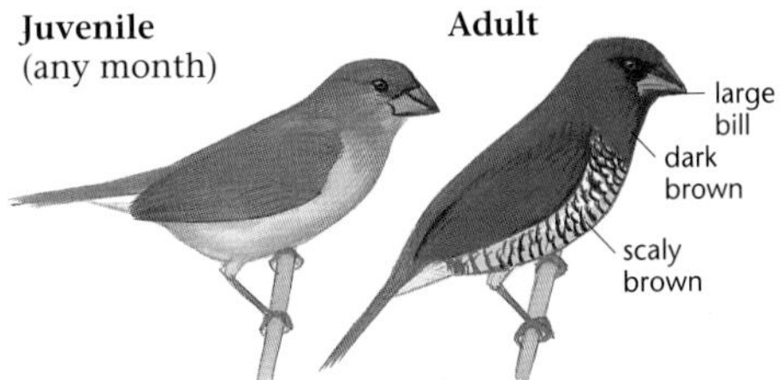
Juvenile (any month)
Adult
large bill
dark brown
scaly brown

Index

D

E

ARCTIC OCEAN
Saint Lawrence Island
Seward Peninsula
Brooks Range
Beaufort Sea
Banks Island
Amundsen Gulf
Nunivak Island
PRIBILOF ISLANDS
Bering Sea
Yukon River
ALASKA (U.S.)
ALEUTIAN ISLANDS
Alaska Range
Wrangell Mts.
YUKON TERRITORY
Mackenzie River
Mackenzie Mts.
Great Bear Lake
Kodiak Island
Gulf of Alaska
NORTHWEST TERRITORIES
Coast Mountains
Peace R.
QUEEN CHARLOTTE ISLANDS
BRITISH COLUMBIA
ALBERTA
ROCKY
Vancouver Island
PACIFIC OCEAN
WASHINGTON
Coast Ranges
Cascade Range
Columbia R.
MONTANA
OREGON
IDAHO
WYOMING
NEVADA
Sierra Nevada
CENTRAL VALLEY
GREAT BASIN
Great Salt Lake
UTAH
CALIFORNIA
Colorado River
COLORADO PLATEAU
MOJAVE DESERT
GRAND CANYON
ARIZONA
CHANNEL ISLANDS
SONORAN DESERT